CRIMINAL PROCESS

Part Two—Prosecution

SECOND EDITION

by

LLOYD L. WEINREB
Dane Professor of Law, Harvard University

Reprinted from Weinreb's Criminal Process (Sixth Edition)

NEW YORK, NEW YORK
FOUNDATION PRESS
1998

Reprinted from

Weinreb's

Criminal Process
Cases, Comment, Questions
(Sixth Edition)

Pages 525–1283

*PRINTED ON 10% POST
CONSUMER RECYCLED PAPER*

PREFACE

This book is a complete, unchanged reprint of Part Two of Weinreb, Criminal Process—Cases, Comment, Questions (sixth edition, 1998). It provides a close examination of criminal prosecution, including adjudication and post-adjudication proceedings. All the important constitutional decisions are included. They are studied from the perspective of criminal prosecution, however, and not, at least in the first instance, as matters of constitutional law. Accordingly, discussion in the opinions of issues like federalism, jurisdiction, and precedent, which do not have anything directly to do with criminal prosecution, are usually omitted. The Federal Rules of Criminal Procedure provide a model of such rules generally.

In order to bring rules and procedures down to earth, I have included descriptions of a large number of concrete factual situations, drawn from actual cases. Although citations to the cases are always given, students should not ordinarily need to refer to the opinions; it is the facts of the cases and how the rules and procedures in question ought to be applied in various contexts that are of principal concern, rather than the particular answer that the court gave. Forms used at various stages of a federal criminal prosecution are included in the appropriate place.

Notes are numbered consecutively through the book from 285 to 641. Footnotes are numbered consecutively in each chapter. I have generally omitted footnotes in reproduced materials. Those which appear are renumbered but are in the original materials unless the footnote number is enclosed in brackets. In Supreme Court cases, separate opinions of Justices that are not reproduced are indicated in a footnote at the end, along with the votes of Justices who did not join one of the reproduced opinions. I have corrected obvious typographical and similar errors and have made a few other small changes in reproduced materials not affecting their sense.

Cross-references to pages in Part One of Criminal Process, which covers criminal investigation, can generally be disregarded. If there is special reason to look up the reference in some instances, they can be found in that book or in a separate publication, Criminal Process—Investigation, which is a companion volume to this one and contains only Part One.

I am grateful to the American Bar Association for permission to reproduce the extract from the Model Code of Professional Responsibility (1981) that appears on pp. 1029–30; the extract from the Model Rules of Professional Conduct (1996) that appears on pp. 1050–52; and the extracts from the ABA Standards for Criminal Justice, Pleas of Guilty (2d ed. Supp. 1986), Prosecution Function and Defense Function (3d ed. 1993), The Function of the Trial Judge (2d ed. 1978), and The Prosecution Function (1971), which appear, in the order cited, on pp. 759–60, 1028, 1039, 1042, 1054, and 730. Copies of these publications are available from Order Fulfillment, American Bar Association, P.O. Box 10892, Chicago, Illinois, 60610–0892.

Benjamin Gruenstein, while a student at Harvard Law School gave me substantial research and editorial assistance for this edition. Melinda

Eakin was responsible for preparation of the manuscript and did extensive copy-editing. Her help was invaluable. As in the past, I am grateful to Raymond S. Andrews ("Sherwood"), who did the illustrations.

LLOYD L. WEINREB

August 1998

SUMMARY OF CONTENTS

PART TWO. PROSECUTION

TABLE OF CONTENTS

TABLE OF CASES

Principal cases are in bold type. Non-principal cases are in roman type. References are to Pages.

XV

PART TWO

PROSECUTION

When the investigation of a crime is completed and the investigating officials have concluded firmly that an identified person is guilty, what should happen next? The person may or may not have participated in the investigation; if he was arrested, once the investigative functions of the arrest have been accomplished, what should be done to terminate the arrest? If the investigation does not point firmly to his guilt, so far as criminal process is concerned, he should, of course, be released.

One answer to the question of what to do next is that, the government's agencies having concluded in good faith after thorough investigation that Smith is guilty, nothing remains to be done but decide whether and, if so, how much to punish Smith; then, to punish him. Constitutional requirements aside, how would such a process be lacking? What more needs to be done to complete satisfactorily the process leading to the imposition of punishment for crime? How should it be done? According to what schedule?

Rule 58.

PROCEDURE FOR MISDEMEANORS AND OTHER PETTY OFFENSES

(a) Scope.

(1) In General.   This rule governs the procedure and practice for the conduct of proceedings involving misdemeanors and other petty offenses, and for appeals to judges of the district courts in such cases tried by United States magistrate judges.

(2) Applicability of Other Federal Rules of Criminal Procedure.   In proceedings concerning petty offenses for which no sentence of imprisonment will be imposed the court may follow such provisions of these rules as it deems appropriate, to the extent not inconsistent with this rule. In all other proceedings the other rules govern except as specifically provided in this rule.

(3) Definition.   The term "petty offenses for which no sentence of imprisonment will be imposed" as used in this rule, means any petty offenses as defined in 18 U.S.C. § 19 as to which the court determines, that, in the event of conviction, no sentence of imprisonment will actually be imposed.

(b) Pretrial Procedures.

(1) Trial Document.   The trial of a misdemeanor may proceed on an indictment, information, or complaint or, in the case of a petty offense, on a citation or violation notice.

(2) Initial Appearance.   At the defendant's initial appearance on a misdemeanor or other petty offense charge, the court shall inform the defendant of:

(A) the charge, and the maximum possible penalties provided by law, including payment of a special assessment under 18 U.S.C. § 3013, and restitution under 18 U.S.C. § 3663;

(B) the right to retain counsel;

(C) unless the charge is a petty offense for which appointment of counsel is not required, the right to request the assignment of counsel if the defendant is unable to obtain counsel;

(D) the right to remain silent and that any statement made by the defendant may be used against the defendant;

(E) the right to trial, judgment, and sentencing before a judge of the district court, unless the defendant consents to trial, judgment, and sentencing before a magistrate judge;

(F) unless the charge is a petty offense, the right to trial by jury before either a United States magistrate judge or a judge of the district court; and

(G) if the defendant is held in custody and charged with a misdemeanor other than a petty offense, the right to a preliminary examination in accordance with 18 U.S.C. § 3060, and the general circumstances under which the defendant may secure pretrial release.

(3) Consent and Arraignment.

(A) Trial Before a United States Magistrate Judge. If the defendant signs a written consent to be tried before the magistrate judge which specifically waives trial before a judge of the district court, the magistrate judge shall take the defendant's plea. The defendant may plead not guilty, guilty, or with the consent of the magistrate judge, nolo contendere.

(B) Failure to Consent. If the defendant does not consent to trial before the magistrate judge, the defendant shall be ordered to appear before a judge of the district court for further proceedings on notice.

(c) Additional Procedures Applicable Only to Petty Offenses for Which No Sentence of Imprisonment Will be Imposed. With respect to petty offenses for which no sentence of imprisonment will be imposed, the following additional procedures are applicable:

(1) Plea of Guilty or Nolo Contendere. No plea of guilty or nolo contendere shall be accepted unless the court is satisfied that the defendant understands the nature of the charge and the maximum possible penalties provided by law.

(2) Waiver of Venue for Plea and Sentence. A defendant who is arrested, held, or present in a district other than that in which the indictment, information, complaint, citation or violation notice is pending against that defendant may state in writing a wish to plead guilty or nolo contendere, to waive venue and trial in the district in which the proceeding is pending, and to consent to disposition of the case in the district in which that defendant was arrested, is held, or is present. Unless the defendant thereafter pleads not guilty, the prosecution shall be had as if venue were in such district, and notice of the same shall be given to the magistrate judge in the district where the proceeding was originally commenced. The defendant's statement of a desire to plead guilty or nolo contendere is not admissible against the defendant.

(3) Sentence. The court shall afford the defendant an opportunity to be heard in mitigation. The court shall then immediately proceed to sentence the defendant, except that in the discretion of the court, sentencing may be continued to allow an investigation by the probation service or submission of additional information by either party.

(4) Notification of Right to Appeal. After imposing sentence in a case which has gone to trial on a plea of not guilty, the court shall advise the defendant of the defendant's right to appeal including any right to appeal the sentence. There shall be no duty on the court to advise the defendant of any right of appeal after sentence is imposed following a plea of guilty or nolo contendere, except that the court shall advise the defendant of any right to appeal the sentence.

(d) Securing the Defendant's Appearance; Payment in Lieu of Appearance.

(1) Forfeiture of Collateral. When authorized by local rules of the district court, payment of a fixed sum may be accepted in suitable cases in lieu of appearance and as authorizing the termination of the proceedings. Local

rules may make provision for increases in fixed sums not to exceed the maximum fine which could be imposed.

(2) Notice to Appear.   If a defendant fails to pay a fixed sum, request a hearing, or appear in response to a citation or violation notice, the clerk or a magistrate judge may issue a notice for the defendant to appear before the court on a date certain. The notice may also afford the defendant an additional opportunity to pay a fixed sum in lieu of appearance, and shall be served upon the defendant by mailing a copy to the defendant's last known address.

(3) Summons or Warrant.   Upon an indictment or a showing by one of the other documents specified in subdivision (b)(1) of probable cause to believe that an offense has been committed and that the defendant has committed it, the court may issue an arrest warrant or, if no warrant is requested by the attorney for the prosecution, a summons. The showing of probable cause shall be made in writing upon oath or under penalty for perjury, but the affiant need not appear before the court. If the defendant fails to appear before the court in response to a summons, the court may summarily issue a warrant for the defendant's immediate arrest and appearance before the court.

(e) Record.   Proceedings under this rule shall be taken down by a reporter or recorded by suitable sound equipment.

(f) New Trial.   The provisions of Rule 33 shall apply.

(g) Appeal.

(1) Decision, Order, Judgment or Sentence by a District Judge.   An appeal from a decision, order, judgment or conviction or sentence by a judge of the district court shall be taken in accordance with the Federal Rules of Appellate Procedure.

(2) Decision, Order, Judgment or Sentence by a United States Magistrate Judge.

(A) Interlocutory Appeal.   A decision or order by a magistrate judge which, if made by a judge of the district court, could be appealed by the government or defendant under any provision of law, shall be subject to an appeal to a judge of the district court provided such appeal is taken within 10 days of the entry of the decision or order. An appeal shall be taken by filing with the clerk of court a statement specifying the decision or order from which an appeal is taken and by serving a copy of the statement upon the adverse party, personally or by mail, and by filing a copy with the magistrate judge.

(B) Appeal From Conviction or Sentence.   An appeal from a judgment of conviction or sentence by a magistrate judge to a judge of the district court shall be taken within 10 days after entry of the judgment. An appeal shall be taken by filing with the clerk of court a statement specifying the judgment from which an appeal is taken, and by serving a copy of the statement upon the United States Attorney, personally or by mail, and by filing a copy with the magistrate judge.

(C) Record.   The record shall consist of the original papers and exhibits in the case together with any transcript, tape, or other recording of the proceedings and a certified copy of the docket entries which shall be transmitted promptly to the clerk of court. For purposes of the appeal, a copy of the record of such proceedings shall be made available at the expense of the United States to a person who establishes by affidavit the inability to pay or give security therefor, and the expense of such copy shall be paid by the Director of the Administrative Office of the United States Courts.

(D) Scope of Appeal.   The defendant shall not be entitled to a trial de novo by a judge of the district court. The scope of the appeal shall be the same as an appeal from a judgment of a district court to a court of appeals.

(3) Stay of Execution; Release Pending Appeal.   The provisions of Rule 38 relating to stay of execution shall be applicable to a judgment of conviction or sentence. The defendant may be released pending appeal in accordance with the provisions of law relating to release pending appeal from a judgment of a district court to a court of appeals.

AO 86A (Rev. 4/91) Consent to Proceed—Misdemeanor ⊕

United States District Court

_____ DISTRICT OF _____

UNITED STATES OF AMERICA
V.

**CONSENT TO PROCEED BEFORE
UNITED STATES MAGISTRATE JUDGE
IN A MISDEMEANOR CASE**

CASE NUMBER:

    The United States magistrate judge has explained to me the nature of the offense(s) with which I am charged and the maximum possible penalties which might be imposed if I am found guilty. The magistrate judge has informed me of my right to the assistance of legal counsel. The magistrate judge has informed me of my right to trial, judgment, and sentencing before a United States district judge or a United States magistrate judge.

    I HEREBY: Waive (give up) my right to trial, judgment, and sentencing before a United States district judge, and I consent to trial, judgment and sentencing before a United States magistrate judge.

             X _____,
                                              Defendant

....

WAIVER OF RIGHT TO TRIAL BY JURY

    The magistrate judge has advised me of my right to trial by jury.

    I HEREBY: Waive (give up) my right to trial by jury. _____
                                                       Defendant

                     Consented to by United States _____
                                                 Signature

                                              _____
                                            Name and Title

....

WAIVER OF RIGHT TO HAVE THIRTY DAYS TO PREPARE FOR TRIAL

    The magistrate judge has also advised me of my right to have at least thirty days to prepare for trial before the magistrate judge.

    I HEREBY: Waive (give up) my right to have at least thirty days to prepare for trial.

             X _____,
                                                Defendant

....

_____
Defendant's Attorney (if any)

Approved By: _____
                                U.S. Magistrate Judge

                                  _____
                                               Date

AO 245H (3/96) Judgment in a Criminal Case for a Petty Offense (Short Form)
        Sheet 1

UNITED STATES DISTRICT COURT

———————————District of———————————

UNITED STATES OF AMERICA	**JUDGMENT IN A CRIMINAL CASE**
V.	**(For a Petty Offense)** – Short Form
	CASE NUMBER:

THE DEFENDANT: Defendant's Attorney

☐ pleaded guilty to count(s)_____

Title & Section	**Nature of Offense**	**Date Offense Concluded**	**Count Number(s)**

☐ Count(s) _____ (is)(are) dismissed on the motion of the United States.

CRIMINAL MONETARY PENALTIES

All criminal monetary penalty payments are to be made as directed by the court, the probation officer, or the United States attorney.

	Assessment	**Fine**
Totals:	$	$

Defendant's Soc. Sec. No.:_____

Defendant's Date of Birth.: _____   Date of Imposition of Judgment

Defendant's USM No.: _____

Defendant's Residence Address: Signature of Judicial Officer

_____

_____

_____   Name and Title of Judicial Officer

Defendant's Mailing Address:

_____

_____   Date

_____

_____

CHAPTER 7

PRELIMINARY EXAMINATION

Gerstein v. Pugh

420 U.S. 103, 95 S.Ct. 854, 43 L.Ed.2d 54 (1975).

■ MR. JUSTICE POWELL delivered the opinion of the Court.

The issue in this case is whether a person arrested and held for trial under a prosecutor's information is constitutionally entitled to a judicial determination of probable cause for pretrial restraint of liberty.

I

In March 1971 respondents Pugh and Henderson were arrested in Dade County, Fla. Each was charged with several offenses under a prosecutor's information. Pugh was denied bail because one of the charges against him carried a potential life sentence, and Henderson remained in custody because he was unable to post a $4,500 bond.

In Florida, indictments are required only for prosecution of capital offenses. Prosecutors may charge all other crimes by information, without a prior preliminary hearing and without obtaining leave of court. . . . At the time respondents were arrested, a Florida rule seemed to authorize adversary preliminary hearings to test probable cause for detention in all cases. . . . But the Florida courts had held that the filing of an information foreclosed the suspect's right to a preliminary hearing. . . . They had also held that habeas corpus could not be used, except perhaps in exceptional circumstances, to test the probable cause for detention under an information. . . . The only possible methods for obtaining a judicial determination of probable cause were a special statute allowing a preliminary hearing after 30 days . . . and arraignment, which the District Court found was often delayed a month or more after arrest. . . . As a result, a person charged by information could be detained for a substantial period solely on the decision of a prosecutor.

Respondents Pugh and Henderson filed a class action against Dade County officials in the Federal District Court, claiming a constitutional right to a judicial hearing on the issue of probable cause and requesting declaratory and injunctive relief. Respondents Turner and Faulk, also in custody under informations, subsequently intervened. Petitioner Gerstein, the State Attorney for Dade County, was one of several defendants.

[T]he District Court granted the relief sought. . . . The court . . . held that the Fourth and Fourteenth Amendments give all arrested persons charged by information a right to a judicial hearing on the question of probable cause. The District Court ordered the Dade County defendants to give the named plaintiffs an immediate preliminary hearing to determine probable cause for further detention. It also ordered them to submit a plan providing preliminary hearings in all cases instituted by information.

. . .

II

As framed by the proceedings below, this case presents two issues: whether a person arrested and held for trial on an information is entitled to a judicial determination of probable cause for detention, and if so, whether the adversary hearing ordered by the District Court and approved by the Court of Appeals is required by the Constitution.

A

Both the standards and procedures for arrest and detention have been derived from the Fourth Amendment and its common-law antecedents. . . . The standard for arrest is probable cause, defined in terms of facts and circumstances "sufficient to warrant a prudent man in believing that the [suspect] had committed or was committing an offense." Beck v. Ohio, 379 U.S. 89, 91 (1964). . . . This standard, like those for searches and seizures, represents a necessary accommodation between the individual's right to liberty and the State's duty to control crime. . . .

To implement the Fourth Amendment's protection against unfounded invasions of liberty and privacy, the Court has required that the existence of probable cause be decided by a neutral and detached magistrate whenever possible. . . .

Maximum protection of individual rights could be assured by requiring a magistrate's review of the factual justification prior to any arrest, but such a requirement would constitute an intolerable handicap for legitimate law enforcement. Thus, while the Court has expressed a preference for the use of arrest warrants when feasible, . . . it has never invalidated an arrest supported by probable cause solely because the officers failed to secure a warrant. . . .

Under this practical compromise, a policeman's on-the-scene assessment of probable cause provides legal justification for arresting a person suspected of crime, and for a brief period of detention to take the administrative steps incident to arrest. Once the suspect is in custody, however, the reasons that justify dispensing with the magistrate's neutral judgment evaporate. There no longer is any danger that the suspect will escape or commit further crimes while the police submit their evidence to a magistrate. And, while the State's reasons for taking summary action subside, the suspect's need for a neutral determination of probable cause increases significantly. The consequences of prolonged detention may be more serious than the interference occasioned by arrest. Pretrial confinement may imperil the suspect's job, interrupt his source of income, and impair his family relationships. . . . Even pretrial release may be accompanied by burdensome conditions that effect a significant restraint of liberty. . . . When the stakes are this high, the detached judgment of a neutral magistrate is essential if the Fourth Amendment is to furnish meaningful protection from unfounded interference with liberty. Accordingly, we hold that the Fourth Amendment requires a judicial determination of probable cause as a prerequisite to extended restraint of liberty following arrest.

This result has historical support in the common law that has guided interpretation of the Fourth Amendment. . . . At common law it was customary, if not obligatory, for an arrested person to be brought before a justice of the peace shortly after arrest. . . . The justice of the peace would "examine" the prisoner and the witnesses to determine whether there was reason to believe the prisoner had committed a crime. If there was, the suspect would be committed to jail or bailed pending trial. If not, he would be discharged from custody. . . . The initial determination of probable cause also could be reviewed by higher courts on a writ of habeas corpus. . . . This practice furnished the model for criminal procedure in America immediately following the adoption of the Fourth Amendment . . . and there are indications that the Framers of the Bill of Rights regarded it as a model for a "reasonable" seizure. . . .

B

Under the Florida procedures challenged here, a person arrested without a warrant and charged by information may be jailed or subjected to other restraints pending trial without any opportunity for a probable cause determination. Petitioner defends this practice on the ground that the prosecutor's decision to file an information is itself a determination of probable cause that furnishes sufficient reason to detain a defendant pending trial. Although a conscientious decision that the evidence warrants prosecution affords a measure of protection against unfounded detention, we do not think prosecutorial judgment standing alone meets the requirements of the Fourth Amendment. Indeed, we think the Court's previous decisions compel disapproval of the Florida procedure. In Albrecht v. United States, 273 U.S. 1, 5 (1927), the Court held that an arrest warrant issued solely upon a United States Attorney's information was invalid because the accompanying affidavits were defective. Although the Court's opinion did not explicitly state that the prosecutor's official oath could not furnish probable cause, that conclusion was implicit in the judgment that the arrest was illegal under the Fourth Amendment. More recently, in Coolidge v. New Hampshire, 403 U.S. 443, 449–453 (1971), the Court held that a prosecutor's responsibility to law enforcement is inconsistent with the constitutional role of a neutral and detached magistrate. We reaffirmed that principle in Shadwick v. City of Tampa, 407 U.S. 345 (1972), and held that probable cause for the issuance of an arrest warrant must be determined by someone independent of police and prosecution. . . . The reason for this separation of functions was expressed by Mr. Justice Frankfurter in a similar context:

"A democratic society, in which respect for the dignity of all men is central, naturally guards against the misuse of the law enforcement process. Zeal in tracking down crime is not in itself an assurance of soberness of judgment. Disinterestedness in law enforcement does not alone prevent disregard of cherished liberties. Experience has therefore counseled that safeguards must be provided against the dangers of the overzealous as well as the despotic. The awful instruments of the criminal law cannot be entrusted to a single functionary. The complicated process of criminal justice is therefore divided into different parts, responsibility for which is separately vested in the various participants upon whom the criminal law relies for its vindication." McNabb v. United States, 318 U.S. 332, 343 (1943).

In holding that the prosecutor's assessment of probable cause is not sufficient alone to justify restraint of liberty pending trial, we do not imply that the accused is entitled to judicial oversight or review of the decision to prosecute. Instead, we adhere to the Court's prior holding that a judicial hearing is not prerequisite to prosecution by information. . . . Nor do we retreat from the established rule that illegal arrest or detention does not void a subsequent conviction. . . . Thus, as the Court of Appeals noted below, although a suspect who is presently detained may challenge the probable cause for that confinement, a conviction will not be vacated on the ground that the defendant was detained pending trial without a determination of probable cause. . . .

III

Both the District Court and the Court of Appeals held that the determination of probable cause must be accompanied by the full panoply of adversary safeguards—counsel, confrontation, cross-examination, and compulsory process for witnesses. A full preliminary hearing of this sort is modeled after the procedure used in many States to determine whether the evidence justifies going to trial under an information or presenting the case to a grand jury. . . . The standard of proof required of the prosecution is usually referred to as "probable cause," but in some jurisdictions it may approach a prima facie case of guilt. . . . When the hearing takes this form, adversary procedures are customarily employed. The importance of the issue to both the State and the accused justifies the presentation of witnesses and full exploration of their testimony on cross-examination. This kind of hearing also requires appointment of counsel for indigent defendants. . . . And, as the hearing assumes increased importance and the procedures become more complex, the likelihood that it can be held promptly after arrest diminishes. . . .

These adversary safeguards are not essential for the probable cause determination required by the Fourth Amendment. The sole issue is whether there is probable cause for detaining the arrested person pending further proceedings. This issue can be determined reliably without an adversary hearing. The standard is the same as that for arrest. That standard—probable cause to believe the suspect has committed a crime—traditionally has been decided by a magistrate in a nonadversary proceeding on hearsay and written testimony, and the Court has approved these informal modes of proof. . . .

The use of an informal procedure is justified not only by the lesser consequences of a probable cause determination but also by the nature of the determination itself. It does not require the fine resolution of conflicting evidence that a reasonable-doubt or even a preponderance standard demands, and credibility determinations are seldom crucial in deciding whether the evidence supports a reasonable belief in guilt. . . . This is not to say that confrontation and cross-examination might not enhance the reliability of probable cause determinations in some cases. In most cases, however, their value would be too slight to justify holding, as a matter of constitutional principle, that these formalities and safeguards designed for trial must also be employed in making the Fourth Amendment determination of probable cause.

Because of its limited function and its nonadversary character, the probable cause determination is not a "critical stage" in the prosecution that would require appointed counsel. The Court has identified as "critical stages" those pretrial procedures that would impair defense on the merits if the accused is required to proceed without counsel. Coleman v. Alabama, 399 U.S. 1 (1970); United States v. Wade, 388 U.S. 218, 226–227 (1967). In Coleman v. Alabama, where the Court held that a preliminary hearing was a critical stage of an Alabama prosecution, the majority and concurring opinions identified two critical factors that distinguish the Alabama preliminary hearing from the probable cause determination required by the Fourth Amendment. First, under Alabama law the function of the preliminary hearing was to determine whether the evidence justified charging the suspect with an offense. A finding of no probable cause could mean that he would not be tried at all. The Fourth Amendment probable cause determination is addressed only to pretrial custody. To be sure, pretrial custody may affect to some extent the defendant's ability to assist in preparation of his defense, but this does not present the high probability of substantial harm identified as controlling in *Wade* and *Coleman*. Second, Alabama allowed the suspect to confront and cross-examine prosecution witnesses at the preliminary hearing. The Court noted that the suspect's defense on the merits could be compromised if he had no legal assistance for exploring or preserving the witnesses' testimony. This consideration does not apply when the prosecution is not required to produce witnesses for cross-examination.

Although we conclude that the Constitution does not require an adversary determination of probable cause, we recognize that state systems of criminal procedure vary widely. There is no single preferred pretrial procedure, and the nature of the probable cause determination usually will be shaped to accord with a State's pretrial procedure viewed as a whole. While we limit our holding to the precise requirement of the Fourth Amendment, we recognize the desirability of flexibility and experimentation by the States. It may be found desirable, for example, to make the probable cause determination at the suspect's first appearance before a judicial officer, . . . or the determination may be incorporated into the procedure for setting bail or fixing other conditions of pretrial release. In some States, existing procedures may satisfy the requirement of the Fourth Amendment. Others may require only minor adjustment, such as acceleration of existing preliminary hearings. Current proposals for criminal procedure reform suggest other ways of testing probable cause for detention. Whatever procedure a State may adopt, it must provide a fair and reliable determination of probable cause as a condition for any significant pretrial restraint of liberty,[1] and this determination must be made by a judicial officer either before or promptly after arrest.

IV

We agree with the Court of Appeals that the Fourth Amendment requires a timely judicial determination of probable cause as a prerequisite to detention, and we accordingly affirm that much of the judgment. As we do not agree that the Fourth Amendment requires the adversary hearing outlined in the District Court's decree, we reverse in part and remand to the Court of Appeals for further proceedings consistent with this opinion.

. . .[2]

County of Riverside v. McLaughlin

500 U.S. 44, 111 S.Ct. 1661, 114 L.Ed.2d 49 (1991)

■ JUSTICE O'CONNOR delivered the opinion of the Court.

In Gerstein v. Pugh, 420 U.S. 103 (1975), this Court held that the Fourth Amendment requires a prompt judicial determination of probable cause as a prerequisite to an extended pretrial detention following a warrantless arrest. This case requires us to define what is "prompt" under *Gerstein*.

I

This is a class action brought under 42 U.S.C. § 1983 challenging the manner in which the county of Riverside, California (County), provides probable cause determinations to persons arrested without a warrant. At

---

1. Because the probable cause determination is not a constitutional prerequisite to the charging decision, it is required only for those suspects who suffer restraints on liberty other than the condition that they appear for trial. There are many kinds of pretrial release and many degrees of conditional liberty. . . . We cannot define specifically those that would require a prior probable cause determination, but the key factor is significant restraint on liberty.

[2] Justice Stewart wrote a concurring opinion, which Justice Douglas, justice Brennan, and Justice Marshall joined.

issue is the County's policy of combining probable cause determinations with its arraignment procedures. Under County policy . . . arraignments must be conducted without unnecessary delay and, in any event, within two days of arrest. This two-day requirement excludes from computation weekends and holidays. Thus, an individual arrested without a warrant late in the week may in some cases be held for as long as five days before receiving a probable cause determination. Over the Thanksgiving holiday, a 7-day delay is possible.

. . .

In August 1987, Donald Lee McLaughlin filed a complaint in the United States District Court for the Central District of California, seeking injunctive and declaratory relief on behalf of himself and " 'all others similarly situated.' " The complaint alleged that McLaughlin was then currently incarcerated in the Riverside County Jail and had not received a probable cause determination. He requested " 'an order and judgment requiring that the defendants and the County of Riverside provide in-custody arrestees, arrested without warrants, prompt probable cause, bail and arraignment hearings.' " Pet. for Cert. 6. . . .

. . .

The second amended complaint named three additional plaintiffs—Johnny E. James, Diana Ray Simon, and Michael Scott Hyde—individually and as class representatives. The amended complaint alleged that each of the named plaintiffs had been arrested without a warrant, had received neither prompt probable cause nor bail hearings, and was still in custody. . . . In November 1988, the District Court certified a class comprising "all present and future prisoners in the Riverside County Jail including those pretrial detainees arrested without warrants and held in the Riverside County Jail from August 1, 1987 to the present, and all such future detainees who have been or may be denied prompt probable cause, bail or arraignment hearings." 1 App. 7.

In March 1989, plaintiffs asked the District Court to issue a preliminary injunction requiring the County to provide all persons arrested without a warrant a judicial determination of probable cause within 36 hours of arrest. . . . The District Court issued the injunction, holding that the County's existing practice violated this Court's decision in *Gerstein*. Without discussion, the District Court adopted a rule that the County provide probable cause determinations within 36 hours of arrest, except in exigent circumstances. The court "retained jurisdiction indefinitely" to ensure that the County established new procedures that complied with the injunction. 2 App. 333–334.

. . .

On November 8, 1989, the Court of Appeals affirmed the order granting the preliminary injunction against Riverside County. . . .

The Court of Appeals . . . determined that the County's policy of providing probable cause determinations at arraignment within 48 hours was "not in accord with *Gerstein*'s requirement of a determination 'promptly after arrest'" because no more than 36 hours were needed "to complete the administrative steps incident to arrest." [888 F.2d], at 1278.

The Ninth Circuit thus joined the Fourth and Seventh Circuits in interpreting *Gerstein* as requiring a probable cause determination immediately following completion of the administrative procedures incident to arrest. . . . By contrast, the Second Circuit understands *Gerstein* to "stres[s] the need for flexibility" and to permit States to combine probable cause determinations with other pretrial proceedings. . . . We granted certiorari to resolve this conflict among the Circuits as to what constitutes a "prompt" probable cause determination under *Gerstein*.

. . .

III

A

. . .

. . . Our purpose in *Gerstein* was to make clear that the Fourth Amendment requires every State to provide prompt determinations of probable cause, but that the Constitution does not impose on the States a rigid procedural framework. Rather, individual States may choose to comply in different ways.

Inherent in *Gerstein*'s invitation to the States to experiment and adapt was the recognition that the Fourth Amendment does not compel an immediate determination of probable cause upon completing the administrative steps incident to arrest. Plainly, if a probable cause hearing is constitutionally compelled the moment a suspect is finished being "booked," there is no room whatsoever for "flexibility and experimentation by the States." [420 U.S., at 123.] Incorporating probable cause determinations "into the procedure for setting bail or fixing other conditions of pretrial release"—which *Gerstein* explicitly contemplated, id., at 124—would be impossible. Waiting even a few hours so that a bail hearing or arraignment could take place at the same time as the probable cause determination would amount to a constitutional violation. Clearly, *Gerstein* is not that inflexible.

. . . As we have explained, *Gerstein* struck a balance between competing interests; a proper understanding of the decision is possible only if one takes into account both sides of the equation.

. . .

B

Given that *Gerstein* permits jurisdictions to incorporate probable cause determinations into other pretrial procedures, some delays are inevitable. For example, where, as in Riverside County, the probable cause determination is combined with arraignment, there will be delays caused by paperwork and logistical problems. Records will have to be reviewed, charging documents drafted, appearance of counsel arranged, and appropriate bail determined. On weekends, when the number of arrests is often higher and available resources tend to be limited, arraignments may get pushed back even further. In our view, the Fourth Amendment permits a reasonable postponement of a probable cause determination while the police cope with the everyday problems of processing suspects through an overly burdened criminal justice system.

But flexibility has its limits; *Gerstein* is not a blank check. A State has no legitimate interest in detaining for extended periods individuals who have been arrested without probable cause. The Court recognized in *Gerstein* that a person arrested without a warrant is entitled to a fair and reliable determination of probable cause and that this determination must be made promptly.

Unfortunately, as lower court decisions applying *Gerstein* have demonstrated, it is not enough to say that probable cause determinations must be "prompt." This vague standard simply has not provided sufficient guidance. Instead, it has led to a flurry of systemic challenges to city and county practices, putting federal judges in the role of making legislative judgments and overseeing local jailhouse operations. . . .

Our task in this case is to articulate more clearly the boundaries of what is permissible under the Fourth Amendment. Although we hesitate to announce that the Constitution compels a specific time limit, it is important to provide some degree of certainty so that States and counties may establish procedures with confidence that they fall within constitutional bounds. Taking into account the competing interests articulated in *Gerstein*, we believe that a jurisdiction that provides judicial determinations of probable cause within 48 hours of arrest will, as a general matter, comply with the promptness requirement of *Gerstein*. For this reason, such jurisdictions will be immune from systemic challenges.

This is not to say that the probable cause determination in a particular case passes constitutional muster simply because it is provided within 48 hours. Such a hearing may nonetheless violate *Gerstein* if the arrested individual can prove that his or her probable cause determination was delayed unreasonably. Examples of unreasonable delay are delays for the purpose of gathering additional evidence to justify the arrest, a delay motivated by ill will against the arrested individual, or delay for delay's sake. In evaluating whether the delay in a particular case is unreasonable, however, courts must allow a substantial degree of flexibility. Courts cannot ignore the often unavoidable delays in transporting arrested persons from one facility to another, handling late-night bookings where no magistrate is readily available, obtaining the presence of an arresting officer who may be busy processing other suspects or securing the premises of an arrest, and other practical realities.

Where an arrested individual does not receive a probable cause determination within 48 hours, the calculus changes. In such a case, the arrested individual does not bear the burden of proving an unreasonable delay. Rather, the burden shifts to the government to demonstrate the existence of a bona fide emergency or other extraordinary circumstance. The fact that in a particular case it may take longer than 48 hours to consolidate pretrial proceedings does not qualify as an extraordinary circumstance. Nor, for that matter, do intervening weekends. A jurisdiction that chooses to offer combined proceedings must do so as soon as is reasonably feasible, but in no event later than 48 hours after arrest.

. . .

Everyone agrees that the police should make every attempt to minimize the time a presumptively innocent individual spends in jail. One way to do so is to provide a judicial determination of probable cause immediately upon completing the administrative steps incident to arrest—i.e., as soon as the suspect has been booked, photographed, and fingerprinted. . . . [S]everal States, laudably, have adopted this approach. The Constitution does not compel so rigid a schedule, however. Under *Gerstein*, jurisdictions may choose to combine probable cause determinations with other pretrial proceedings, so long as they do so promptly. This necessarily means that only certain proceedings are candidates for combination. Only those proceedings that arise very early in the pretrial process—such as bail hearings and arraignments—may be chosen. Even then, every effort must be made to expedite the combined proceedings. . . .

IV

For the reasons we have articulated, we conclude that Riverside County is entitled to combine probable cause determinations with arraignments. The record indicates, however, that the County's current policy and practice do not comport fully with the principles we have outlined. The County's current policy is to offer combined proceedings within two days, exclusive of Saturdays, Sundays, or holidays. As a result, persons arrested on Thursdays may have to wait until the following Monday before they receive a probable cause determination. The delay is even longer if there is an intervening holiday. Thus, the County's regular practice exceeds the 48-hour period we deem constitutionally permissible, meaning that the County is not immune from systemic challenges, such as this class action.

As to arrests that occur early in the week, the County's practice is that "arraignment[s] usually tak[e] place on the last day" possible. 1 App. 82. There may well be legitimate reasons for this practice; alternatively, this may constitute delay for delay's sake. We leave it to the Court of Appeals and the District Court, on remand, to make this determination.

The judgment of the Court of Appeals is vacated and the case is remanded for further proceedings consistent with this opinion.

. . . [3]

---

[3] Justice Marshall wrote a dissenting opinion which Justice Blackmun and Justice Stevens joined. Justice Scalia also wrote a dissenting opinion.

285. Before the adoption of the federal rules, leave of court had to be obtained in order to initiate a prosecution by information; the court, moreover, was required to make a determination that there was probable cause for the prosecution.[4] Albrecht v. United States, 273 U.S. 1, 5 (1927). See Gerstein v. Pugh, above. The requirement of leave of court was explicitly eliminated by Rule 7(a), without explanation in the Notes of the Advisory Committee. Rule 9(a), however, which provides for the issuance of a warrant or summons based on an indictment or information, allows a warrant to issue on an information only if it is "supported by a showing of probable cause under oath as is required by Rule 4(a)."

FEDERAL RULES OF CRIMINAL PROCEDURE

Rule 5.

INITIAL APPEARANCE BEFORE THE MAGISTRATE

(a) In General. Except as otherwise provided in this rule, an officer making an arrest under a warrant issued upon a complaint or any person making an arrest without a warrant shall take the arrested person without unnecessary delay before the nearest available federal magistrate judge or, if a federal magistrate is not reasonably available, before a state or local judicial officer authorized by 18 U.S.C. § 3041. If a person arrested without a warrant is brought before a magistrate judge, a complaint satisfying the probable cause requirements of Rule 4(a), shall be promptly filed. When a person, arrested with or without a warrant or given a summons, appears initially before the magistrate judge, the magistrate judge shall proceed in accordance with the applicable subdivisions of this rule. An officer making an arrest under a warrant issued upon a complaint charging solely the violation of 18 U.S.C. § 1073 need not comply with this rule if the person arrested is transferred without unnecessary delay to the custody of appropriate state or local authorities in the district of arrest and an attorney for the government moves promptly, in the district in which the warrant was issued, to dismiss the complaint.

(b) Misdemeanors and Other Petty Offenses. If the charge against the defendant is a misdemeanor or other petty offense triable by a United States magistrate judge under 18 U.S.C. § 3401, the magistrate judge shall proceed in accordance with Rule 58.

---

4. An information is a formal charge against the defendant. It is like an indictment in content but is filed by the prosecutor independently, without action by the grand jury. See Fed.R.Crim.P. 7, p. 680 below.

(c) Offenses Not Triable by the United States Magistrate Judge. If the charge against the defendant is not triable by the United States magistrate judge, the defendant shall not be called upon to plead. The magistrate judge shall inform the defendant of the complaint against the defendant and of any affidavit filed therewith, of the defendant's right to retain counsel or to request the assignment of counsel if the defendant is unable to obtain counsel, and of the general circumstances under which the defendant may secure pretrial release. The magistrate judge shall inform the defendant that the defendant is not required to make a statement and that any statement made by the defendant may be used against the defendant. The magistrate judge shall also inform the defendant of the right to a preliminary examination. The magistrate judge shall allow the defendant reasonable time and opportunity to consult counsel and shall detain or conditionally release the defendant as provided by statute or in these rules.

A defendant is entitled to a preliminary examination, unless waived, when charged with any offense, other than a petty offense, which is to be tried by a judge of the district court. If the defendant waives preliminary examination, the magistrate judge shall forthwith hold the defendant to answer in the district court. If the defendant does not waive the preliminary examination, the magistrate judge shall schedule a preliminary examination. Such examination shall be held within a reasonable time but in any event not later than 10 days following the initial appearance if the defendant is in custody and no later than 20 days if the defendant is not in custody, provided, however, that the preliminary examination shall not be held if the defendant is indicted or if an information against the defendant is filed in district court before the date set for the preliminary examination. With the consent of the defendant and upon a showing of good cause, taking into account the public interest in the prompt disposition of criminal cases, time limits specified in this subdivision may be extended one or more times by a federal magistrate judge. In the absence of such consent by the defendant, time limits may be extended by a judge of the United States only upon a showing that extraordinary circumstances exist and that delay is indispensable to the interests of justice.

Rule 5.1

PRELIMINARY EXAMINATION

(a) Probable Cause Finding. If from the evidence it appears that there is probable cause to believe that an offense has been committed and that the defendant committed it, the federal magistrate judge shall forthwith hold the defendant to answer in district court. The finding of probable cause may be based upon hearsay evidence in whole or in part. The defendant may cross-examine adverse witnesses and may introduce evidence. Objections to evidence on the ground that it was acquired by unlawful means are not properly made at the preliminary examination. Motions to suppress must be made to the trial court as provided in Rule 12.

(b) Discharge of Defendant. If from the evidence it appears that there is no probable cause to believe that an offense has been committed or that the defendant committed it, the federal magistrate judge shall dismiss the complaint and discharge the defendant. The discharge of the defendant shall not preclude the government from instituting a subsequent prosecution for the same offense.

(c) Records. After concluding the proceeding the federal magistrate judge shall transmit forthwith to the clerk of the district court all papers in the proceeding. The magistrate judge shall promptly make or cause to be made a record or summary of such proceeding.

(1) On timely application to a federal magistrate, the attorney for a defendant in a criminal case may be given the opportunity to have the recording of the hearing on preliminary examination made available to that attorney in connection with any further hearing or preparation for trial. The court may, by local rule, appoint the place for and define the conditions under which such opportunity may be afforded counsel.

(2) On application of a defendant addressed to the court or any judge thereof, an order may issue that the federal magistrate judge make available a copy of the transcript, or of a portion thereof, to defense counsel. Such order shall provide for prepayment of costs of such transcript by the defendant unless the defendant makes a sufficient affidavit that the defendant is unable to pay or to give security therefor, in which case the expense shall be paid by the Director of the Administrative Office of the United States Courts from available appropriated funds. Counsel for the government may move also that a copy of the transcript, in whole or in part, be made available to it, for good cause shown, and an order may be entered granting such motion in whole or in part, on appropriate terms, except that the government need not prepay costs nor furnish security therefor.

(d) Production of Statements.

(1) In General. Rule 26.2(a)–(d) and (f) applies at any hearing under this rule, unless the court, for good cause shown, rules otherwise in a particular case.

(2) Sanctions for Failure to Produce Statement. If a party elects not to comply with an order under Rule 26.2(a) to deliver a statement to the moving party, the court may not consider the testimony of a witness whose statement is withheld.

———

286. With respect to the requirement of Rule 5(a) that a complaint filed after an arrest show probable cause, see United States v. Fernandez-Guzman, 577 F.2d 1093, 1099 (7th Cir.1978): "[W]hen the facts known to the officers at the time of arrest are such as to make the arrest constitutional when it occurred, the omission of some of those facts from later-filed 5(a) complaints cannot make the arrest retroactively unconstitutional."

287. Rule 5(c) evidently does not contemplate a role for counsel at the initial appearance. In United States v. Melanson, 691 F.2d 579 (1st Cir.1981), the court noted that the need for a prompt hearing might conflict with an arrested person's interest in having the advice of counsel, when the magistrate questions him preliminarily with respect to appointment of counsel and bail. Rejecting a general rule that uncounseled statements are inadmissible against the defendant later, the court said that there are "formidable conditions which must be satisfied before any uncounseled admissions 'blurted out' in the course of such a hearing are to be allowed in at the latter trial." Id. at 584. In the latter connection, the court referred to Massiah v. United States, p. 411 above.

288. The provision of Rule 5(c) that there shall be no preliminary examination if the defendant has been indicted or an information has been filed reflects settled law. "A post-indictment preliminary examination would be an empty ritual, as the government's burden of showing probable cause would be met merely by offering the indictment. Even if the commissioner disagreed with the grand jury, he could not undermine the authority of its finding." Sciortino v. Zampano, 385 F.2d 132, 133 (2d Cir.1967). "Should the judicial officer determine that for the purpose of the detention hearing no probable cause exists that the defendant committed the crime for which he was indicted, presumably the defendant would still be brought to trial upon the same indictment." United States v. Contreras, 776 F.2d 51, 55 (2d Cir.1985).

"It reasonably cannot be doubted that, in the court to which the indictment is returned, the finding of an indictment, fair upon its face, by a properly constituted grand jury, conclusively determines the existence of probable cause for the purpose of holding the accused to answer." Ex parte United States, 287 U.S. 241, 250 (1932). See Costello v. United States, 350 U.S. 359, 363 (1956), p. 694 below.

The Court has said repeatedly that there is no constitutional objection to a prosecution by information without any prior judicial determination of probable cause (provided that the defendant's liberty is not restrained). E.g., Beck v. Washington, 369 U.S. 541, 545 (1962). In Gerstein v. Pugh, p. 532 above, the Court said that it did not depart from its "prior holding that a judicial hearing is not prerequisite to prosecution by information." Is that holding consistent with the Court's holdings involving the requirement of a judicial determination of probable cause when a person's rights under the Fourth Amendment are involved, e.g., in Gerstein v. Pugh itself? If so, on what basis?

The Supreme Court of California held that a defendant who is indicted by a grand jury in a state criminal case is entitled to a post-indictment preliminary examination like that available to a defendant charged by information. The court said that the difference in procedural rights available to defendants by the two methods of accusation was substantial and insufficiently justified, and constituted a denial of equal protection of the laws. Hawkins v. Superior Court, 586 P.2d 916 (Cal.1978). Thereafter, the post-indictment preliminary examination was eliminated by ballot initiative enacting a new constitutional provision. Bowens v. Superior Court, 820 P.2d 600 (Cal.1991).

In State v. Mitchell, 512 A.2d 140 (Conn.1986), the court discussed a recently enacted provision of the state constitution that a person shall not be prosecuted for a crime punishable by death or life imprisonment "unless upon probable cause shown at a hearing in accordance with procedures prescribed by law." The court said that the provision "guarantees that no one will be forced to stand trial for a serious crime unless a court has first made a finding of probable cause at an open hearing in which the accused is provided with a full panoply of adversarial rights." Id. at 144–45. In order to give effect to the provision, the court said, an opportunity for appellate review of the determination of probable cause was required.

United States Ex Rel. Wheeler v. Flood

269 F.Supp. 194 (E.D.N.Y.1967).

■ WEINSTEIN, DISTRICT JUDGE.

Petitioners—as yet unindicted though in federal custody—seek a writ of habeas corpus in order to compel a United States Commissioner to hold a preliminary examination pursuant to subdivision (c) of Rule 5 of the Rules of Criminal Procedure. For the reasons set out below, if such a hearing is not granted forthwith, petitioners are entitled to be released.

Petitioner Susan Wheeler has been in custody since her arrest on May 12, 1967, pursuant to a warrant issued upon a detailed sworn complaint. She was charged with conspiring to illegally import narcotic drugs. 21 U.S.C. § 174 (illegal importation of narcotic drug into United States); 26 U.S.C. § 4704(a) (sale of untaxed narcotic). She was brought before a Commissioner that day. Represented by counsel she demanded an immediate preliminary examination. Charged with the same conspiracy, petitioner Robert Wyler has been in custody since May 17, 1967; he appeared before a Commissioner on May 18, 1967, when his counsel also sought such an examination.

At the request of the United States, the Commissioner set June 5, 1967, in both cases for preliminary examination—some three and one-half weeks after Wheeler's arrest and two and one-half weeks from Wyler's arrest. The adjournment was sought, in the words of the Assistant United States Attorney prosecuting the two cases, "to allow me sufficient time to gather up my evidence in a presentable form." Bail was set for $25,000 for each petitioner but they have remained in custody.

On May 22, 1967, petitioners obtained an order to show cause, returnable May 24th, why a writ of habeas corpus should not issue in view of the failure to provide a preliminary examination. The next day, May 23rd, the United States Attorney began presenting evidence in the matter to the Grand Jury.

Defendants' position is that subdivision (c) of Rule 5 requires a preliminary examination "within a reasonable time" after an accused is brought before the Commissioner; and that, having been in jail for more than a week unable to raise bail, more than a "reasonable time" has elapsed. . . .

The Assistant United States Attorney argues that in good faith he sought an adjournment of the preliminary examination until June 5 and that subsequent events permitted him to proceed earlier before the Grand Jury. He declares that inasmuch as the "hearing date had been fixed by the United States Commissioners," he had "not the right to advance the date" nor did he have an obligation to let the defendant know that the United States was in fact prepared to present evidence to the Commissioner. He also points out that he "freely" offered the defendant the right to appear before the Grand Jury and that an immediate hearing before the Commissioner would place "a burden upon me which is unfair." In his view the evidence already presented to the Grand Jury "would be more than sufficient to warrant the return of an indictment even as of this moment" and it was sufficient to require the Commissioner to find probable cause. In addition, he states, "if these people are released, I fear for the safety of several people."

While the argument was not made on behalf of the United States, it might have been added that in this case the government was following a widespread practice "of delaying preliminary hearing until an indictment can be obtained." 8 Moore's Federal Practice, ¶ 5.04[3]. . . . Most courts have felt compelled to deny relief on the ground that the issue of delay was mooted by indictment. . . .

Part of the prosecution's attitude undoubtedly stems from its view that both preliminary examinations and Grand Jury indictments serve equally to assure that an accused is being held on probable cause—a main purpose of our criminal pretrial machinery. But from the defendant's vantage point—looking forward to a possible trial at which he will have to defend himself—these devices operate quite differently.

Rule 5 preliminary hearings require the government to produce evidence—although it is not clear whether it must be admissible at a trial . . .—before a Commissioner, who in this district is an experienced lawyer. The defendant is entitled to have counsel present even if he cannot afford to pay an attorney; the government's witnesses are subject to cross-examination; the defendant has the right to present evidence and to subpoena witnesses. . . . He may obtain a transcript whether or not he has funds to pay for it. . . .

At least since the opinion in United States v. Costello, 350 U.S. 359, 363 . . . (1956), evidence introduced before the Grand Jury need not be admissible at a trial. The defendant cannot be present while evidence against him is received. If he appears, he is not permitted to have counsel with him. He has no opportunity to cross-examine witnesses and the Grand Jury minutes are generally not available to him.

Although the primary purpose served by the federal preliminary examination is to insure that there is "probable cause to believe that an offense has been committed" (Crump v. Anderson, 122 U.S.App.D.C. 173, 352 F.2d 649, 652 (1965), . . . in practice this hearing may provide the defense with the most valuable discovery technique available to him. . . . Nevertheless, many defense counsel prefer to waive preliminary hearings since they may harden and preserve the government's case. . . .

Under the Federal Rules the choice of waiver is the defendant's, not the government's. Upon a defendant's demand, a hearing is required within a "reasonable time." While some delay is envisaged . . . the hearing cannot, as in this case, be put off for weeks. It is significant that the Task Force on Administration of Justice of the President's Commission on Law Enforcement and Administration of Justice recently declared: "If the defendant is jailed, the preliminary hearing should be held within 72 hours." p. 85 (1967). The Task Force suggested a maximum of seven days delay where the defendant is not in custody. Ibid. The New York system—which, in many respects seems more protective of defendant's rights prior to trial than does the federal system—limits adjournments of the preliminary examination to 48 hours. N.Y. Code of Criminal Procedure, § 191.

It was unreasonable in this case to delay a preliminary hearing for incarcerated accuseds beyond the time the United States was prepared to present the matter to the Grand Jury. Should the United States Attorney ask for an adjournment of the preliminary examination on the ground that he is not prepared to proceed with the hearing, he should assume the obligation to inform defense counsel when he is ready. He should then cooperate in arranging for the examination as promptly as possible.

At the insistence of the defendant, the preliminary hearing of a defendant brought before a Commissioner prior to indictment should take place before, or simultaneously with, presentment to the Grand Jury unless, of course, the Grand Jury is operating independently of the United States Attorney—a circumstance most rare. . . . Inconvenience to the prosecutor is never an excuse for denying the preliminary examination. Inconvenience to witnesses can be minimized. "Where the preliminary hearing serves as a discovery device, presentment of the case to the grand jury on the same day as the preliminary hearing would avoid bringing the witnesses to the

PRELIMINARY EXAMINATION 549

courthouse twice." Task Force on Administration of Justice, The President's Commission on Law Enforcement and Administration of Justice, 85 (1967).

Accordingly, Susan Wheeler and Robert Wyler are ordered released from custody unless a hearing is held today, May 24, 1967, pursuant to subdivision (c) of Rule 5 of the Rules of Criminal Procedure for the United States District Court.

. . .

―――――

289. The rule that a preliminary hearing need not be held once the defendant has been indicted is applied even if the hearing has been continued at the request of the government, so long as no prejudice to the defendant is shown. E.g., United States v. Mulligan, 520 F.2d 1327 (6th Cir.1975).

In United States v. Gurary, 793 F.2d 468 (2d Cir.1986), however, the court questioned an order of the district court extending the time for return of an indictment by sixty days (under 18 U.S.C. § 3161(h)(8)(A), see p. 833 below) and simultaneously extending the time for a preliminary hearing to the same later date, under Rule 5(c). The court observed that although there might be special circumstances in which extensions of both the indictment and the preliminary hearing would coincide, in this case the apparent purpose of the extension of the hearing was to enable the government to avoid it by the return of an indictment. "Rule 5 contemplates that a preliminary hearing will be held promptly after arrest so that the existence of probable cause may be tested by the defendant before a neutral magistrate. Only in the event that the Government initiates a prosecution by an indictment or obtains the return of an indictment prior to the scheduled date of the preliminary hearing may the hearing be obviated. The grand jury's decision to indict is thought to be an adequate determination of the existence of probable cause. . . . However, the provision of Rule 5 that dispenses with a preliminary hearing when an indictment is returned before the hearing date is not a license to the Government or to the District Court to postpone a preliminary hearing for whatever length of time may be justified to secure the return of an indictment. Indeed, the time limits in Rule 5(c) and the strict 'extraordinary circumstances' standard for granting continuances were added to the Rule in 1972 to prohibit the practice in some districts of routinely granting a continuance to allow the Government to satisfy the probable cause requirement by filing an indictment. . . . Rule 5 recognizes the Government's opportunity to accelerate the grand jury investigation so that an indictment is returned prior to the scheduled date for the preliminary injunction; it does not allow the hearing date to be retarded to accommodate the pace of the grand jury investigation.

AO 468 (1/86) Waiver of Preliminary Examination or Hearing

United States District Court

DISTRICT OF

UNITED STATES OF AMERICA

V.

**WAIVER OF PRELIMINARY
EXAMINATION OR HEARING
(Rule 5 or 32.1, Fed. R. Crim. P.)**

Case Number:

I, _____ , charged in a (complaint) (petition)

pending in this District with_____

in violation of Title _____ , U.S.C., _____ ,

and having appeared before this Court and been advised of my rights as required by Rule 5 or Rule 32.1, Fed. R.

Crim. P., including my right to have a preliminary (examination) (hearing), do hereby waive (give up) my right to a

preliminary (examination) (hearing).

_____
Defendant

_____
Date

_____
Counsel for Defendant

"The scheme of the Speedy Trial Act and the Rules of Criminal Procedure also make it evident that preliminary hearings are not to be routinely continued for the period necessary for return of an indictment. Initially, the time period for a preliminary hearing, ten days for an incarcerated defendant and twenty days for a defendant on pretrial release, is shorter than the time period for return of an indictment, thirty days where a grand jury is in session and sixty days where one is not in session. Furthermore, continuance of the time to indict is governed by the somewhat flexible 'ends of justice' standard of section 3161(h)(8)(A), whereas continuance of the time for a preliminary hearing, over a defendant's objection, is subject to the far more rigorous criteria of Rule 5(c) that 'extraordinary circumstances' exist and that delay is 'indispensable' to the interests of justice. Not only are the standards different, but, of greater significance, the purposes of the continuances differ. Extension of the time to indict permits the grand jury to complete its investigation of the defendant and to determine the appropriate charges on which trial should be held; extension of the time for a preliminary hearing is justified only to permit the prosecution to ready its presentation of probable cause to support the arrest on charges already made in the complaint." Id. at 472–73.

290. The government can properly prosecute by indictment following dismissal of a complaint for lack of probable cause at a preliminary examination. United States v. Kysar, 459 F.2d 422 (10th Cir.1972); United States v. Coley, 441 F.2d 1299 (5th Cir.1971). To the same effect, see People v. Noline, 917 P.2d 1256 (1996). In similar circumstances, if it were otherwise permissible, could the government prosecute by information?

———

United States v. Quinn

357 F.Supp. 1348 (N.D.Ga.1973).

■ EDENFIELD, DISTRICT JUDGE.

Defendant seeks to quash the indictment returned against him on January 24, 1973, charging a violation of the Hobbs Act, 18 U.S.C. § 1951. In the alternative defendant moves that the preliminary examination which was begun before a United States Magistrate as provided in Rule 5(c), Fed.R.Crim.P., and which was cancelled subsequent to the return of an indictment, be reopened, presumably for the purpose of allowing defendant's counsel to complete cross-examination of a government witness. The facts alleged are as follows.

Defendant was arrested on January 6, 1973, and brought before a federal magistrate who set January 12, 1973 as the date for the preliminary examination. At the examination, an FBI agent testified for the government on the only issue to be determined in that proceeding, viz., whether or not there was probable cause to bind defendant over to the grand jury. During the course of his testimony the agent referred to written "field notes" which on cross-examination defendant's counsel demanded to inspect. The government objected to revealing the contents of the agent's notes, and the magistrate continued the examination until January 26, 1973, apparently for the purpose of allowing the agent to remove from his notes any material which was unrelated to the subject matter of defense counsel's cross-examination. Before the proceedings could be recommended, a federal grand jury returned an indictment on January 24, 1973, and the preliminary examination was cancelled.

Defendant claims that the indictment should be quashed because "[o]nce the preliminary examination has begun, the United States Magistrate has jurisdiction over the matter and the action of the grand jury must defer to that jurisdiction." In support of his position, defendant cites 18 U.S.C. § 3060, which in relevant part states: "(e) No preliminary examination in compliance with subsection (a) of this section shall be required to be accorded an arrested person . . . if at any time subsequent to the initial appearance of such persons before a judge or magistrate and *prior to the date fixed for the preliminary examination pursuant to subsections (b) and (c) an indictment is returned. . . ."* (Emphasis added.) Defendant argues that since the indictment was returned after the preliminary hearing had begun, by the terms of the statute, and under the substantially similar language of Rule 5(c), defendant was entitled to have the preliminary examination proceed.

In addition, defendant cites three cases from the District of Columbia Circuit which hold generally that the denial of a timely requested preliminary examination, or defects in a preliminary examination, are not excused by an intervening grand jury indictment. . . . Particularly noted is United States v. Pollard [335 F.Supp. 868 (D.D.C.1971)], where as a condition to the government's conduct of a lineup, the examining magistrate required the government to provide defense counsel with any prior descriptions given to the police or to the government by each witness who would be present at the lineup. Not wishing to comply with a ruling which it considered an undesirable precedent, the government immediately entered a *nolle prosequi* and obtained a grand jury indictment of defendant some two months later. The court found in the face of allegations that the government deliberately misled defense counsel into believing that the case was not being presented to the grand jury, that an "already scheduled preliminary hearing should not be barred where, as here, the indictment does not intervene in the normal course of events, but rather is the result of unilateral action of the Government, solely for its own benefit, and accompanied by indicia of vexatiousness." 335 F.Supp. at 870.

Without passing on whether the government's conduct in the present case was "vexatious", the court is in sympathy with the notion that the government ought not to be allowed to freely abandon its prosecution in a preliminary examination the moment that an unfavorable ruling is made or an adverse result seems imminent. Such a practice does nothing to encourage respect for law, creating as it does a feeling that the search for probable cause in a preliminary examination amounts to no more than a game in which the government can never lose, regardless of what the evidence reveals. Nevertheless, while this court may object to how the game is played, in the present case no substantive rights of the defendant have been lost, and consistent with the strong weight of authority, contrary to the cited cases in the District of Columbia Circuit, defendant's motions must be denied.

In United States v. Coley, 441 F.2d 1299 (5th Cir.1971), defendant Coley cited as error the district court's denial of his motion to quash the indictment. The reviewing court found that at Coley's preliminary examination, prior to indictment, a government witness refused to answer questions propounded by defendant's counsel. "Though advised by the United States Commissioner [precursor to the present position of United States Magistrate] that he must reply or risk dismissal of the case, the witness continued to refuse. The commissioner then dismissed the charges against Coley. Subsequently, however, a grand jury indicted Coley for the same offense." Similar to the present defendant, Coley maintained that "he had a substantial right to cross-examine witnesses at the preliminary hearing and that the commissioner's failure to enforce this right denied him due process." 441 F.2d at 1300. The Court of Appeals, in affirming the district court, replied to this argument that "the primary function of a preliminary hearing is not to expedite discovery. The purpose of such a hearing is to ascertain whether or not there is probable cause to warrant detention of the accused pending a grand jury hearing." There is no constitutional right to a preliminary hearing, and "[i]n the instant case, the distinction between an aborted preliminary hearing and no hearing is one without a difference." 441 F.2d at 1301.

In Coley the court had before it the relevant provisions of 18 U.S.C. § 3060(e). In Coley, not only was the defendant denied the right to cross-examine the government witness at the preliminary examination, but after the magistrate had dismissed the charges against him, he was subsequently and lawfully indicted by a grand jury. From this decision it seems clear that the magistrate in the present case had no power to compel the FBI agent to disclose his notes to defendant's counsel, as long as the government was willing to accept a dismissal of the charges against defendant. The magistrate had no power to compel disclosure on January 26th and he has no such power now. A finding of probable cause in this case was returned by the grand jury indictment on January 24th. Therefore, under the court's decision in Coley, which controls the case at bar, both defendant's motions to quash the indictment and to reopen the preliminary examination must be denied. . . .

Before concluding, two things should perhaps be noted to dispel at least somewhat the atmosphere of unfairness left when an intervening indictment cuts short a preliminary examination. First, a defendant's opportunity for discovery is not denied, by the abridgement of a preliminary examination, it is merely delayed. Rule 16, Fed.R.Crim.P., and the disclosure requirements of Brady v. Maryland, 373 U.S. 83 . . . (1963), as applied in Giglio v. United States, 405 U.S. 150 . . . (1972), and in Williams v. Dutton, 400 F.2d 797 (5th Cir.1968), afford ample opportunity for discovery after an indictment has been returned. If it is argued to the contrary that additional discovery is necessary then, as stated by Professor Wright, it should be provided by "carefully considered amendment of the rules, rather than by a novel construction of the existing rule." 1 C. Wright, Federal Practice and Procedure, Criminal: § 80 at 139–140 (1969 ed.).

Second, the preliminary examination does serve an important, substantive purpose, although at times the proceedings must appear to the defendant as little more than a legal charade. Even though the grand jury indictment, not the preliminary examination, is dispositive of determining probable cause, the magistrate's examination stands as a safeguard to ensure that the defendant will not be held in custody without probable cause while the government waits to present its evidence to the grand jury. A cogent statement of the preliminary hearing's place in our system of justice is provided by Professor A. Kenneth Pye's testimony in support of the predecessor "commissioner's hearing", before the Subcommittee on Improvements in Judicial Machinery of the Senate Judiciary Committee: "One of the most important purposes is to provide protection against arrests for investigation. It is not only a determination of probable cause but a determination of probable cause shortly after the arrest which is significant. The requirement that the defendant be brought before the Commissioner without unnecessary delay and the right of the defendant to have a hearing to determine whether there is probable cause combine to discourage law enforcement officers from arresting on suspicion and then investigating the case at their leisure to determine whether there is probable cause. The elimination of the Commissioner's hearing is an open invitation to arrests for investigation. If a subsequent investigation develops no probable cause, or establishes the defendant's innocence, the grand jury can be requested to return an ignoramus. During the interval, the defendant will have been deprived of his liberty in violation of the Constitution, but will be without redress. The present hearing provision is one of the best devices which we have found to implement the Fourth Amendment's requirement of arrest on probable cause." Hearings on the United States Commissioner System, before the Subcommittee on Improvements in Judicial Machinery of the Senate Committee on the Judiciary, 89th Cong., 1st Sess., pt. 2, at 270 (1965).

In certain cases the government's ability to opt out of an unfavorable proceeding may undermine belief in and respect for the fair administration of justice. Such conduct is not to be applauded. Nevertheless, in those cases where the government abandons prosecution rather than suffer the consequences, the principal overriding value of the preliminary examination is vindicated and remains undisturbed. In the present case no substantive rights of defendant have been lost and for the reasons stated above, defendant's motions are denied.

---

291. In some parts of the discussion in *Quinn*, above, the court evidently did not distinguish between the purpose of the initial appearance, as explained in Gerstein v. Pugh, p. 532 above, and the preliminary examination, discussed in Coleman v. Alabama, below. If there were found to be probable cause at the initial appearance and subsequently, at the preliminary examination, it were found that there was not probable cause, presumably the magistrate judge would order that the defendant be released pending an indictment. Once an indictment were returned, however, the defendant would again be subject to custody. In practice, once a magistrate judge has determined at the initial appearance that there is probable cause, it is highly unlikely that the same magistrate judge or a different magistrate judge would thereafter conclude otherwise, even though the defendant would have a greater opportunity to challenge the government's evidence of probable cause at the preliminary examination. For practical purposes, the issue of probable cause is ordinarily resolved at the initial appearance (or by the issuance of an arrest warrant). The function of the preliminary examination, aside from its collateral benefits to the defense, is problematic. Often enough, the defense waives a preliminary examination despite the potential benefits of discovery or fixing prosecution witnesses' testimony. One reason for such waiver is simply that defense counsel has not yet received payment of an agreed fee "up front." See note 296 p. 564 below.

Coleman v. Alabama

399 U.S. 1, 90 S.Ct. 1999, 26 L.Ed.2d 387 (1970).

■ MR. JUSTICE BRENNAN announced the judgment of the Court and delivered the following opinion.

Petitioners were convicted in an Alabama Circuit Court of assault with intent to murder in the shooting of one Reynolds after he and his wife parked their car on an Alabama highway to change a flat tire. The Alabama Court of Appeals affirmed . . . and the Alabama Supreme Court denied review . . . . We granted certiorari . . . . We vacate and remand.

Petitioners . . . argue that the preliminary hearing prior to their indictment was a "critical stage" of the prosecution and that Alabama's failure to provide them with appointed counsel at the hearing therefore unconstitutionally denied them the assistance of counsel.

. . .

II

This Court has held that a person accused of crime "requires the guiding hand of counsel at every step in the proceedings against him," Powell v.

Alabama, 287 U.S. 45, 69 (1932), and that that constitutional principle is not limited to the presence of counsel at trial. "It is central to that principle that in addition to counsel's presence at trial, the accused is guaranteed that he need not stand alone against the State at any stage of the prosecution, formal or informal, in court or out, where counsel's absence might derogate from the accused's right to a fair trial." United States v. Wade, [388 U.S. 218 (1967)] at 226. Accordingly, "the principle of Powell v. Alabama and succeeding cases requires that we scrutinize *any* pretrial confrontation of the accused to determine whether the presence of his counsel is necessary to preserve the defendant's basic right to a fair trial as affected by his right meaningfully to cross-examination the witnesses against him and to have effective assistance of counsel at the trial itself. It calls upon us to analyze whether potential substantial prejudice to defendant's rights inheres in the particular confrontation and the ability of counsel to help avoid that prejudice." Id., at 227. . . .

The preliminary hearing is not a required step in an Alabama prosecution. The prosecutor may seek an indictment directly from the grand jury without a preliminary hearing. . . . The opinion of the Alabama Court of Appeals in this case instructs us that under Alabama law the sole purposes of a preliminary hearing are to determine whether there is sufficient evidence against the accused to warrant presenting his case to the grand jury, and if so to fix bail if the offense is bailable. . . . The court continued:

> "At the preliminary hearing . . . the accused is not required to advance any defenses, and failure to do so does not preclude him from availing himself of every defense he may have upon the trial of the case. Also Pointer v. State of Texas [380 U.S. 400 (1965)] bars the admission of testimony given at a pretrial proceeding where the accused did not have the benefit of cross-examination by and through counsel. Thus, nothing occurring at the preliminary hearing in absence of counsel can substantially prejudice the rights of the accused on trial." 44 Ala.App., at 433, 211 So.2d, at 921.

This Court is of course bound by this construction of the governing Alabama law. . . . However, from the fact that in cases where the accused has no lawyer at the hearing the Alabama courts prohibit the State's use at trial of anything that occurred at the hearing, it does not follow that the Alabama preliminary hearing is not a "critical stage" of the State's criminal process. The determination whether the hearing is a "critical stage" requiring the provision of counsel depends, as noted, upon an analysis "whether potential substantial prejudice to defendant's rights inheres in the . . . confrontation and the ability of counsel to help avoid that prejudice." United States v. Wade, supra, at 227. Plainly the guiding hand of counsel at the preliminary hearing is essential to protect the indigent accused against an erroneous or improper prosecution. First, the lawyer's skilled examination and cross-examination of witnesses may expose fatal weaknesses in the State's case that may lead the magistrate to refuse to bind the accused over. Second, in any event, the skilled interrogation of witnesses by an experienced lawyer can fashion a vital impeachment tool for use in cross-examination of the State's witnesses at the trial, or preserve testimony favorable to the accused of a witness who does not appear at the trial. Third, trained counsel can more effectively discover the case the State has against his client and make possible the preparation of a proper defense to meet that case at the trial. Fourth, counsel can also be influential at the preliminary hearing in making effective arguments for the accused on such matters as the necessity for an early psychiatric examination or bail.

The inability of the indigent accused on his own to realize these advantages of a lawyer's assistance compels the conclusion that the Alabama preliminary hearing is a "critical stage" of the State's criminal process at which the accused is "as much entitled to such aid [of counsel] . . . as at the trial itself." Powell v. Alabama, supra, at 57.

. . .

[The Court remanded the case for a determination whether the failure to provide counsel at the preliminary hearing was harmless error.][5]

FEDERAL RULES OF CRIMINAL PROCEDURE

Rule 44.

RIGHT TO AND ASSIGNMENT OF COUNSEL

(a) Right to Assigned Counsel. Every defendant who is unable to obtain counsel shall be entitled to have counsel assigned to represent that defendant at every stage of the proceedings from initial appearance before the federal magistrate or the court through appeal, unless that defendant waives such appointment.

(b) Assignment Procedure. The procedures for implementing the right set out in subdivision (a) shall be those provided by law and by local rules of court established pursuant thereto.

(c) Joint Representation. Whenever two or more defendants have been jointly charged pursuant to Rule 8(b) or have been joined for trial pursuant to Rule 13, and are represented by the same retained or assigned counsel or by retained or assigned counsel who are associated in the practice of law, the court shall promptly inquire with respect to such joint representation

---

[5] Justice Black and Justice White wrote concurring opinions. Justice Douglas, who joined Justice Brennan's opinion, also wrote a separate opinion. Justice Harlan wrote an opinion concurring in part and dissenting in part. Chief Justice Burger wrote a dissenting opinion. Justice Stewart wrote a dissenting opinion, which Chief Justice Burger joined.

and shall personally advise each defendant of the right to the effective assistance of counsel, including separate representation. Unless it appears that there is good cause to believe no conflict of interest is likely to arise, the court shall take such measures as may be appropriate to protect each defendant's right to counsel.

———

292. In Gideon v. Wainwright, 372 U.S. 335 (1963), the Court held that the Sixth Amendment right to the assistance of counsel requires the appointment of counsel for indigent defendants in state courts as it had previously been required in federal courts. Gideon was accused of a felony. Nine years later, *Gideon* was extended to a defendant accused of a misdemeanor for which a sentence of imprisonment was authorized, in Argersinger v. Hamlin, 407 U.S. 25 (1972). The Court held that "absent a knowing and intelligent waiver, no person may be imprisoned for any offense, whether classified as petty, misdemeanor, or felony, unless he was represented by counsel at his trial." Id. at 37. In Scott v. Illinois, 440 U.S. 367 (1979) (5–4), the Court held that an indigent defendant who is charged with a crime for which a sentence of imprisonment is authorized but who, if he is convicted, is sentenced only to pay a fine is not constitutionally entitled to appointed counsel. "[T]he Sixth and Fourteenth Amendments to the United States Constitution require only that no indigent criminal defendant be sentenced to a term of imprisonment unless the State has afforded him the right to assistance of appointed counsel in his defense." Id. at 373–74. The Court said that such a line had been drawn in *Argersinger*, but that even if it had not, "the central premise of *Argersinger*—that actual imprisonment is a penalty different in kind from fines or the mere threat of imprisonment—is eminently sound and warrants adoption of actual imprisonment as the line defining the constitutional right to appointment of counsel." Id. at 373.

In a dissenting opinion in *Scott*, Justice Brennan urged that the proper constitutional standard "would require the appointment of counsel for indigents accused of any offense for which imprisonment for any time is authorized." Id. at 382. He pointed out that the defendant, who was convicted of theft the authorized penalty for which was up to a year in prison, would have been entitled to appointed counsel under the law of at least thirty-three states.

The right of an indigent to be assigned counsel does not require a court to honor a request for the assignment of a particular lawyer, even if that lawyer is willing to accept the appointment. United States v. Davis, 604 F.2d 474 (7th Cir.1979). See People v. Perez, 594 P.2d 1 (Cal.1979), in which the court upheld the representation of indigent defendants, with their consent, by "certified" law students acting under the supervision of a regular attorney.

AO 458 (Rev. 5/85)   Appearance

United States District Court

_____ DISTRICT OF _____

APPEARANCE

CASE NUMBER:

To the Clerk of this court and all parties of record:

Enter my appearance as counsel in this case for

_____   _____
Date   _Signature_

                                  _____
                                  Print Name

                                  _____
                                  Address

                                  _____
                                  City   _State_   _Zip Code_

                                  _____
                                  Phone Number

In Fuller v. Oregon, 417 U.S. 40 (1974), the Supreme Court upheld a state scheme which provided counsel for indigent defendants but required that a defendant who was convicted repay the cost of his defense if he later became financially able to do so.

293. Title 18 U.S.C. § 3006A(a) provides for the appointment of counsel "for any person financially unable to obtain adequate representation." In Wood v. United States, 389 U.S. 20, 21 (1967), the Supreme Court vacated the defendant's conviction and remanded the case for consideration of the question whether the defendant's request for appointment of counsel pursuant to § 3006A was improperly denied in light of "the relevant criteria" of the act. The statute itself contains no criteria for determination whether a defendant is entitled to appointment of counsel other than the phrase "financially unable" (or "financially able"). The legislative history indicates that appointment was not to be limited to "destitute" persons. H.R.Rep. No. 864, 88th Cong., 2d Sess. 7 (1964) (letter of the Attorney General).

Section 3006A(e)(1) provides that "counsel for a person who is financially unable to obtain investigative, expert, or other services necessary for an adequate defense may request them in an ex parte application. Holding that the defendant was entitled to appointment of a fingerprint expert, the court in United States v. Patterson, 724 F.2d 1128, 1130 (5th Cir.1984), said, "[W]here the government's case rests heavily on a theory most completely addressed to expert testimony, an indigent defendant must be afforded the opportunity to prepare and present his defense to such a theory with the assistance of his own expert pursuant to section 3006A(e)." See Ake v. Oklahoma, 470 U.S. 68, 74 (1985) (8–1), holding that "when a defendant has made a preliminary showing that his sanity at the time of the offense is likely to be a significant factor at trial, the Constitution requires that a State provide access to a psychiatrist's assistance on this issue, if the defendant cannot otherwise afford one."

294. Federal statutory provisions authorizing forfeiture to the government of the proceeds of illegal drug activities and collateral provisions authorizing pretrial restraint against transfer of assets potentially forfeitable under the statute, 21 U.S.C. § 853, contain no exemption for assets that the defendant intends to use to pay attorney's fees in the criminal case. Application of the provisions to prevent a defendant from transferring assets to an attorney for his defense does not violate the Sixth Amendment right to counsel or the Due Process Clause. United States v. Monsanto, 491 U.S. 600 (1989) (5–4); Caplin & Drysdale v. United States, 491 U.S. 617 (1989) (5–4).

On the nature of the hearing required to authorize pretrial restraint of a transfer of assets needed to retain counsel of choice, see United States v. Monsanto, 924 F.2d 1186 (2d Cir.1991).

CJA 20 (Rev. 11/90) **APPOINTMENT OF AND AUTHORITY TO PAY COURT APPOINTED COUNSEL**

1. JURISDICTION 3 ☐ APPEALS 1 ☐ MAG. 2 ☐ DIST. 4 ☐ OTHER _____	2. MAG. DOCKET NO.	3. DIST. CT. DOCKET NO.	VOUCHER NK

4. APPEALS DOCKET NO.	5. FOR (DISTRICT/CIRCUIT)	6. LOC. CODE	7. CHARGE/OFFENSE (U.S. or other code citation)	7A. CASE CODE

8. IN THE CASE OF VS	9. PERSON REPRESENTED (FULL NAME)	9A. NO. REPRES.

10. PERSON REPRESENTED (STATUS) 1 ☐ DEFENDANT—ADULT 3 ☐ APPELLANT 5 ☐ OTHER 2 ☐ DEFENDANT—JUVENILE 4 ☐ APPELLEE _____	11. PROCEEDINGS (Describe briefly)

12. PAYMENT CATEGORY
A ☐ FELONY   C ☐ PETTY OFFENSE   E ☐ OTHER _____
B ☐ MISDEMEANOR   D ☐ APPEAL

13. COURT ORDER O ☐ Appointing Counsel F ☐ Subs. for FD C ☐ Co-Counsel R ☐ Subs. for Retained Atty. P ☐ Subs. for Panel Atty. _____ Name of prior panel attorney Appt. Date _____ Voucher No. _____ Because the above-named "person represented" has testified under oath or has otherwise satisfied this court that he or she (1) is financially unable to employ counsel and (2) does not wish to waive counsel, and because the interests of justice so require, the attorney whose name appears in item 14 is appointed to represent this person in this case. ▶ _____ Sig. of Presiding Judicial Officer or By Order of Court (Clerk/Deputy) ▶ _____ ▶ _____ Date of Order Nunc Pro Tunc Date	14. FULL NAME OF ATTORNEY/PAYEE (First Name, M.I., Last Name, Including Suffix) AND MAILING ADDRESS

14. FULL NAME OF ATTORNEY/PAYEE (First Name, M.I., Last Name, Including Suffix) AND MAILING ADDRESS

15. WORK PHONE	16A. Does the attorney have the preexisting agreement (see Instructions) with a corporation, including a professional corporation? ☐ Yes ☐ No

16B. SOCIAL SECURITY NO. (Only provide per instructions)	16C. EMPLOYER I.D. NO. (Only provide per instructions)

16D. NAME AND MAILING ADDRESS OF LAW FIRM (Only provide per instructions)

CLAIM FOR SERVICES OR EXPENSES

	SERVICE	HOURS	DATES	Multiply rate per hour times total hours to obtain "In Court" compensation. Enter total below.
17 IN COURT	a. Arraignment and/or Plea			
	b. Bail and Detention Hearings			
	c. Motions Hearings			
	d. Trial			17A. TOTAL IN COURT COMP.
	e. Sentence Hearings			
	f. Revocation Hearings			
	g. Appeals Court			
	h. Other (Specify on additional sheets)			
	(Rate per hour = _____) TOTAL HOURS =			$
18 OUT OF COURT	a. Interviews and conferences			Multiply rate per hour times total hours. Enter total "out of court" compensation below.
	b. Obtaining and reviewing records			
	c. Legal research and brief writing			
	d. Travel time (Specify on additional sheets)			18A. TOTAL OUT OF COURT COMP.
	e. Investigative and other work (Specify on additional sheets)			
	(Rate per hour = _____) TOTAL HOURS =			$

19 EXPENSES	TRAVEL, LODGING, MEALS ETC.	AMOUNT	OTHER EXPENSES	AMOUNT	19A. TOTAL TRAVEL EXP. $
					19B. TOTAL OTHER EXP. $
					20. GRAND TOTAL CLAIMED $

21. CERTIFICATION OF ATTORNEY/PAYEE FOR PERIOD _____ TO _____

F ☐ Final Payment I ☐ Interim Payment No. _____ Has compensation and/or reimbursement for work in this case previously been applied for? ☐ YES ☐ NO
If yes, were you paid? ☐ YES ☐ NO If yes, by whom were you paid? _____ How much? _____ Has the person represented paid any
money to you, or to your knowledge to anyone else, in connection with the matter for which you were appointed to provide representation? ☐ YES ☐ No
If yes, give details on additional sheets. _____
I swear or affirm the truth or correctness of the above statements ▶ _____   ▶ _____

SIGNATURE OF ATTORNEY/PAYEE _____ DATE _____

22. IN COURT COMP. $	23. OUT OF COURT COMP. $	24. TRAVEL EXPENSE $	25. OTHER EXPENSES $	26. TOTAL AMT. APPROVED/CERT. $
27. SIGNATURE OF PRESIDING JUDICIAL OFFICER		DATE		27A. JUDGE/MAG. CODE
28. SIGNATURE OF CHIEF JUDGE, CT. OF APPEALS (OR DELEGATE)		DATE		29. TOTAL AMT. APPROVED $

(left margin for rows 22-29: APPROVED FOR PAYMENT)

ORIGINAL MAILED TO ADMINISTRATIVE OFFICE AFTER ENTRY OF PAYMENT DATA

295. Title 18 U.S.C. § 3006A provides for compensation to be paid to appointed counsel. The maximum hourly rate of compensation is determined by the Judicial Conference "for each circuit . . . with variations by district, where appropriate, taking into account such factors as the minimum range of the prevailing hourly rates for qualified attorneys in the district in which the representation is provided and the recommendations of the judicial councils of the circuit." §3006(A)(d)(1). Although the Judicial Conference has approved an hourly rate of $75 for in-court and out-of-court work in all districts (except the District of Rhode Island, where the rates are $65 and $45), the actual rates in most districts in early 1998 were $65 and $45, due to the unavailability of funds. The maximum amount payable for representation of a defendant charged with a felony before the magistrate judge or in the district court is $3,500, and for a defendant charged with a misdemeanor, $1,000. §3006(A)(2)(d). The maximum amount for other services for the defense is $1,000. The maximums may be exceeded if "necessary to provide fair compensation." §3006(A)(d)(3).

———

United States v. Gipson

517 F.Supp. 230 (W.D.Mich.1981).

■ ENSLEN, DISTRICT JUDGE.

This matter is before the Court on Defendant, Thomas P. Gipson's (hereinafter Defendant) Motion for Court Appointed Counsel. Presently, Defendant is represented by retained counsel, who in the Court's estimation has heretofore provided Defendant with exemplary services.[6] The Court notes that on May 26, 1981 the Defendant pled guilty to one count of the Indictment and inquiry discloses that, nevertheless, counsel for the Defendant desires to proceed with the Motion. The sole issue is whether that representation should continue through the appointment of counsel. For the reasons discussed below, the Court is of the opinion that such appointment is inappropriate.

The Criminal Justice Act of 1964 provides that the court, "if satisfied after appropriate inquiry that the defendant is financially unable to obtain counsel, shall appoint counsel to represent him." 18 U.S.C. § 3006A(b). Financial inability as considered for the purposes of the Act does not mean indigency. The Defendant does not have to be destitute to be eligible for an

---

6. The Motion in no way implies that the Defendant is dissatisfied with the legal services rendered by his counsel of record to date. Indeed, the Defendant desires that in the event his Motion is granted that his current counsel be appointed by the Court to continue his defense.

appointment of counsel. The Court need only be satisfied that the representation essential to an adequate defense is beyond the means of the Defendant. . . .

In the case at bar, the Defendant has submitted as indicia of indigency a financial affidavit, which after careful consideration by this Court, does not reveal a Defendant without adequate means of obtaining legal representation. The Affidavit discloses that Defendant has approximately $42,850 of assets and a monthly income of $600, being the salary of his wife. Defendant is currently on indefinite lay-off from the Niles Township Police force. In addition, the Affidavit reflects a total indebtedness of $27,785, and total monthly bills of approximately $530.40. Thus far, according to Defendant's allegation in his brief in support, he has expended approximately $2,500 in the furtherance of his defense. Since the Defendant has already pled guilty to one count of the Indictment filed against him in return for the dismissal of the other counts in the Indictment and his cooperation at the trial of co-defendants in this matter, and because that trial is expected to be expeditiously resolved, the Court is of the opinion that the Defendant has sufficient resources to marshall his remaining defenses. I cannot say, based upon his Affidavit as submitted, that the Defendant cannot afford legal counsel of his own choosing.

Moreover, even if the Defendant in the case sub judice were unable to afford counsel at this juncture, his present attorney of record, is under a continuing duty to represent him in a punctilious and zealous manner. Lawyers, as guardians of the law, play a vital role in the preservation of our society. As such, it is not only the right but the duty of the legal profession as a whole to utilize such methods as may be developed to bring the services of its members to those who need them, so long as this can be done ethically and with dignity. ABA Opinion 250 (1965). . . .

As President Theodore Roosevelt aptly put it, "Every man owes some of his time to the upbuilding of the profession to which he belongs." The soundness and the necessity of President Roosevelt's admonition insofar as it relates to the legal profession cannot be doubted. . . . These enlightening principles are embodied in the Code of Professional Responsibility. There, it is stated:

> The legal profession cannot remain a viable force in fulfilling its role in our society unless its members receive adequate compensation for services rendered, and reasonable fees should be charged in appropriate cases to clients able to pay them. Nevertheless, persons unable to pay all or a portion of a reasonable fee should be able to obtain necessary legal services, and lawyers should support and participate in ethical activities designed to achieve that objective. EC 2–16.

In the instant case, counsel for the Defendant should be guided by the exhortations of the aforementioned ethical consideration. See also EC 2–17 and 2–18. Additionally, the Court directs counsel for the Defendant to EC 6–4 where it is stated in part: "Having undertaken representation, a lawyer should use proper care to safeguard the interest of his client." See for example, DR 2–110, which provides that a lawyer must take reasonable steps to avoid foreseeable prejudice to the rights of his client if the lawyer moves to withdraw his or her services from the case. It appears to the Court that if the spirit and letter of the Code of Professional Responsibility are to be followed in this case, then the Defendant, who has already employed legal counsel is entitled to that particular counsel's best representation regardless of intervening financial difficulties. Counsel's obligation to represent a criminal Defendant is not so slight or so transitory as to obviate the need for undaunted protection from the impending onslaught of the prosecution in the criminal justice system.

Defendant's Motion is therefore denied.

———

296.

(i)

The defendant is charged with a draft violation. He earns $500 per week as a truck driver. He has no dependents, and no property. He asks that counsel be appointed to defend him.

Should the magistrate appoint counsel? See Samuel v. United States, 420 F.2d 371 (5th Cir.1969).

Assume that the magistrate declines to appoint counsel on the ground that the defendant is not "financially unable to obtain an adequate defense." The defendant then states that the charges against him are unfounded, that in his own judgment he cannot afford to retain counsel, and that he does not intend to do so. What should the magistrate do?

(ii)

The defendant is charged with a serious narcotics offense. He is a graduate student at a large private university. He receives a tuition scholarship from the university and occasionally does odd jobs from which he earns about $150 per week; he has no other income. He is not physically or otherwise unable to maintain regular employment but does not choose to do so. He has completed all coursework for his graduate program and has no present obligation other than to write a dissertation. He asks that counsel be appointed to defend him.

Should the magistrate appoint counsel? See March v. Municipal Court, 498 P.2d 437, 442 (Cal.1972), in which, applying the indigency standard to students, the court said: "The relevant consideration in determining indigency is whether the petitioner's *current financial status* affords him equal access to the legal process. Such a determination cannot include an evaluation of the appellant's future earning potential or even his present potential had he chosen to employ himself in a more financially rewarding manner."

———

FINANCIAL AFFIDAVIT

CJA 23

IN SUPPORT OF REQUEST FOR ATTORNEY, EXPERT OR OTHER COURT SERVICES WITHOUT PAYMENT OF FEE   REV. 1/90

IN UNITED STATES	☐ MAGISTRATE ☐ DISTRICT ☐ APPEALS COURT or ☐ OTHER PANEL (Specify below)		LOCATION NUMBER
IN THE CASE OF		FOR	
_____ VS. _____		AT	

PERSON REPRESENTED (Show your full name)		DOCKET NUMBERS

1 ☐ Defendant—Adult
2 ☐ Defendant—Juvenile
3 ☐ Appellant
4 ☐ Probation Violator
5 ☐ Parole Violator
6 ☐ Habeas Petitioner
7 ☐ 2255 Petitioner
8 ☐ Material Witness
9 ☐ Other (Specify)_____

Magistrate

District Court

Court of Appeals

CHARGE/OFFENSE (describe if applicable & check box →)   ☐ Felony   ☐ Misdemeanor

ASSETS

EMPLOYMENT

Are you now employed? ☐ Yes ☐ No ☐ Am Self Employed

Name and address of employer:_____

IF YES, how much do you earn per month? $_____

IF NO, give month and year of last employment
How much did you earn per month $_____

If married is your Spouse employed?   ☐ Yes   ☐ No

IF YES, how much does your Spouse earn per month $_____

If a minor under age 21, what is your Parents or Guardian's approximate monthly income $_____

OTHER INCOME

Have you received within the past 12 months any income from a business, profession or other form of self-employment, or in the form of rent payments, interest, dividends, retirement or annuity payments, or other sources? ☐ Yes ☐ No

IF YES, GIVE THE AMOUNT RECEIVED & IDENTIFY THE SOURCES $

RECEIVED | SOURCES

CASH

Have you any cash on hand or money in savings or checking account ☐ Yes ☐ No   **IF YES,** state total amount $_____

PROPERTY

Do you own any real estate, stocks, bonds, notes, automobiles, or other valuable property (excluding ordinary household furnishings and clothing)? ☐ Yes ☐ No

IF YES, GIVE VALUE AND DESCRIBE IT $

VALUE | DESCRIPTION

OBLIGATIONS & DEBTS

DEPENDENTS

MARITAL STATUS
☐ SINGLE
☐ MARRIED
☐ WIDOWED
☐ SEPARATED OR DIVORCED

Total No. of Dependents

List persons you actually support and your relationship to them

DEBTS & MONTHLY BILLS

(LIST ALL CREDITORS, INCLUDING BANKS, LOAN COMPANIES, CHARGE ACCOUNTS, ETC.)

APARTMENT OR HOME:	Creditors	Total Debt	Monthly Payt.
		$_____	$_____
		$_____	$_____
		$_____	$_____
		$_____	$_____

I certify the above to be correct.

SIGNATURE OF DEFENDANT
(OR PERSON REPRESENTED)

Coleman v. Burnett

477 F.2d 1187 (D.C.Cir.1973).

■ SPOTTSWOOD W. ROBINSON, III, CIRCUIT JUDGE.

This appeal tenders for resolution questions as to the examinatorial entitlements of the criminally accused at federal preliminary hearings. Appellants, Lawrence D. Coleman, Jorge D. Dancis and Ronald Shepard, were arrested and charged with the commission of unrelated crimes within the District of Columbia. Following arrest, each was brought before a judicial officer for the proceedings prescribed by then Rule 5 of the Federal Rules of Criminal Procedure. Coleman and Dancis each sought, and each was denied, a subpoena requiring the attendance at his preliminary hearing of the only apparent eyewitness to his alleged offenses. Shepard, during his preliminary hearing, was restricted in cross-examination of the complainant and a corroborating Government witness, and in the presentation of evidence of his own.

Subsequent to the preliminary hearings, the three appellants joined in a class-action complaint in the District Court. They sought declaratory judgments that the preliminary hearings were defective, writs of mandamus reopening them, and an injunction restraining, pendente lite, presentation of their cases for grand jury consideration. The District Court denied a preliminary injunction and dismissed the action, and this appeal ensued. For reasons which follow, we reverse the District Court's judgment to the extent that it denied a declaration that Dancis' preliminary hearing was faulty and remand the case in order that the declaration may be made. In all other respects we affirm, but without prejudice to rectification in the criminal proceeding pending against Dancis of the error committed at his preliminary hearing.

Some of the questions advanced on appeal are common to the cases of two or more of the three appellants. Each appeal, however, also tenders an issue not present in either of the others. We therefore treat the three cases separately.

I. COLEMAN'S APPEAL

After joining in this appeal, Coleman was indicted in two bills for multiple violations of the federal narcotic laws. Two days before oral argument on the appeal, he entered a plea of guilty to two counts, one in each of the two indictments. He insists that his preliminary hearing, at which the charges laid in one of the indictments were aired, was fatally infirm and that we should now direct that it be reopened. He further argues, as he must, that the plea does not stand in the way of the appeal brought here for that purpose. We do not agree.

. . .

[The court held that Coleman's appeal was barred by the plea of guilty.]

II. SHEPARD'S APPEAL

Appellant Shepard was charged with assaulting a Deputy United States Marshal while a prisoner in the cellblock of the District of Columbia

Court of General Sessions. A judge of that court, sitting as a committing magistrate, presided over his preliminary hearing. The complaining witness, Deputy Marshal John H. Lonien, testified that while he was on duty in the cellblock, Shepard committed an unprovoked attack upon him, striking him above the right eye with a fist. Another Government witness, Herbert Rutherford, employed as a guard in the cellblock, corroborated Marshal Lonien's testimony.

Shepard's counsel was permitted considerable latitude in cross-examination of these witnesses as to matters they had testified to on direct examination. The judge, however, sustained the Government's objections to a number of inquiries directed to them on other topics. The specific complaint Shepard refers to us runs to the judge's rulings on eleven questions propounded to Marshal Lonien and four to Guard Rutherford. Those questions, in the main, solicited testimony as to disparaging remarks assertedly directed to cellblock personnel by prisoners other than Shepard, and to the nature and extent of any injuries inflicted by Shepard on Marshal Lonien and of injuries allegedly sustained by Shepard himself. The judge also ruled out Shepard's proffer of photographs purporting to show his post-altercation physical condition, and inquiry of a defense witness as to whether cellblock personnel had tried to confiscate the photographs.

The more common basis of the Government's objections to defense counsel's cross-examinatorial approach was that he was venturing beyond the boundaries of a hearing designed to explore probable cause and embarking on a quest for discovery of elements of the Government's case. After some amount of prior ambivalence on the subject, Shepard now disclaims any attempt at discovery, as distinguished from refutation of probable cause. He further argues that the questions addressed to Marshal Lonien and Guard Rutherford bore a substantial relationship to the existence or nonexistence of probable cause.

. . .

A. *Discovery at Preliminary Hearings*

Former Rule 5(c) granted the accused, and its present counterpart continues to confer, the right to "cross-examine witnesses against him" at a preliminary hearing. The true dimension of that right is bound to depend in considerable measure upon the degree to which discovery by the defense may be a purpose the preliminary hearing is designed to serve. That, in turn, is a topic upon which the judges of this court have expressed views which, to say the least, have not been entirely harmonious. One view has been that the sole objective of a preliminary hearing is to determine whether there is probable cause to believe that the accused has committed an offense, and that the accused may lay claim to the benefit of only so much discovery as may become incidental to a properly conducted inquiry into probable cause. That view has now been incorporated into federal jurisprudence by the Federal Magistrates Act.

This Act provides mandatorily, with exceptions later to be considered, for "a preliminary [hearing] . . . to determine whether there is probable cause to believe that an offense has been committed and that the arrested person has committed it." The reason the Act indulges the preliminary hearing no independent discovery role is evident from its legislative history. During hearings before the Senate Committee on the Judiciary, witnesses urged "that preliminary examination afforded a necessary and useful medium for defense counsel to obtain discovery of the prosecution's evidence."[7] The Committee, however, was "of the opinion that the problem of discovery should be treated separately from that of the preliminary hearing."[8] Although the need for expanded pretrial discovery procedures was recognized, the Committee felt that

> The preliminary hearing does not present an ideal opportunity for discovery. It is designed for another purpose; namely, that of determining whether there is probable cause to justify further proceedings against an arrested person. Thus, the degree of discovery obtained in a preliminary hearing will vary depending upon how much evidence the presiding judicial officer thinks is necessary to establish probable cause in a particular case. This may be quite a bit, or it may be very little, but in either event it need not be all the evidence within the possession of the Government that should be subject to discovery.[9]

The Committee accordingly concluded "that discovery procedure should remain separate and distinct from the preliminary examination. . . ."[10]

That settles the matter, of course, for Shepard and others whose hearings took place after the effective date of the Act. The mission of the hearing is an investigation into probable cause for further proceedings against the accused. It does not include discovery for the sake of discovery. To be sure, the evidence the Government offers to establish probable cause is by nature also discovery for the accused. So also is information adduced on cross-examination of Government witnesses on the aspects of direct-examination testimony tending to build up probable cause. In those senses, some discovery becomes a by-product of the process of demonstrating probable cause. But in no sense is discovery a legitimate end unto itself.

B. *Cross-Examination at Preliminary Hearings*

To say merely that discovery is not a primary function of federal preliminary hearings is to respond only incompletely to the issue Shepard poses. As we have said, former Rule 5(c) conferred upon the accused the right to "cross-examine witnesses against him," and that right he continues to enjoy. Moreover, in Coleman v. Alabama,[11] the Supreme Court, in holding that a preliminary hearing to ascertain probable cause to bind an accused for additional proceedings is a critical stage of the criminal process at which the Sixth Amendment right to counsel obtains, pointed out as one of the considerations supporting its holding that "the lawyer's skilled examination and cross-examination of witnesses may expose fatal weaknesses in the [prosecution's] case that may lead the magistrate to refuse to bind the

---

7. S.Rep. No. 371, 90th Cong., 1st Sess. 34 (1967).

8. Id.

9. Id.

10. Id. at 35.

11. 399 U.S. 1 . . . (1970).

accused over."[12] Since the right to counsel is the right to effective assistance of counsel, *Coleman* requires us to evaluate Shepard's challenge with the increased solicitude appropriate when constitutional rights are at stake. This we have done, and we are led to the conclusion that the District Court's disposition of Shepard's grievance should not be disturbed.

According to Shepard's brief on appeal, the purpose of his counsel's questions on cross-examination of the two Government witnesses was to show that "(a) there were no physical injuries to the Marshals; (b) there were severe injuries to Mr. Shepard rendering him unconscious; (c) the assault charge was brought as a subterfuge for the Marshals' own conduct; (d) the Marshals were provoked by disparaging remarks by prisoners other than Mr. Shepard; (e) there was mass confusion in the cellblock seriously impeding the perception of the Marshals; and (f) there was evidence that Mr. Shepard acted in self-defense, if he acted at all." The first difficulty we have encountered is that the handling of the cross-examination made this understanding all too difficult to come by. Cross-examination at a preliminary hearing, like the hearing itself, is confined by the principle that a probe into probable cause is the end and aim of the proceeding, and the line between refutation of probable cause and discovery into the prosecution's case ofttimes is thin. Here counsel's purpose in propounding the questions which the presiding judge excluded was unquestionably blurred by the fact that counsel frequently appeared to be off on an impermissible quest for discovery. At no time prior to the rulings complained of did counsel delineate for the judge's edification the factual thesis he was seeking to promote. Only as the hearing neared its close, and after the rulings had been made, did counsel broach anything remotely similar to the defensive theory now explained on appeal. Our reading of the hearing record leaves us with the conviction that the presiding judge, when ruling on counsel's questions, could hardly divine what counsel had in mind. Therefore, we cannot say that he committed error in barring responses to inquiries that seemed unrelated to the task of evaluating probable cause.

Moreover, cross-examination is properly to be limited at preliminary hearing, as at trial, to the scope of the witness' direct examination. To the extent that it is not—and here it was not—cross-examination ostensibly, even if undesignedly, becomes an effort at some sort of discovery. We do not suggest that magistrates may not indulge variations from the usual order of offering evidence, and during presentation of the Government's case permit the defense to get in elements of its own. But when cross-examination exceeds the range of direct examination unaccompanied by an elucidation of its connection with probable cause, it is small wonder that discovery is taken to be the examiner's goal.

An even more important consideration stems from the difference between the objective of the preliminary hearing and that of the trial. While, of course, conviction necessitates proof at trial of all elements of a crime beyond a reasonable doubt, it suffices for purposes of a binding over for trial that the evidence show "probable cause to believe that an offense

12. . . . 399 U.S. at 9 . . . .

has been committed and that the defendant has committed it." The preliminary hearing is not a minitrial of the issue of guilt, but is rather an investigation into the reasonableness of the bases for the charge, and examination of witnesses thereat does not enjoy the breadth it commands at trial. "A preliminary hearing," the Supreme Court has said, "is ordinarily a much less searching exploration into the merits of a case than a trial, simply because its function is the more limited one of determining whether probable cause exists to hold the accused for trial."[13]

It is the contrast of probable cause and proof beyond a reasonable doubt that inevitably makes for examinatorial differences between the preliminary hearing and the trial. Probable cause signifies evidence sufficient to cause a person of ordinary prudence and caution to conscientiously entertain a reasonable belief of the accused's guilt. Proof beyond a reasonable doubt, on the other hand, connotes evidence strong enough to create an abiding conviction of guilt to a moral certainty. The gap between these two concepts is broad. A magistrate may become satisfied about probable cause on much less than he would need to be convinced. Since he does not sit to pass on guilt or innocence, he could legitimately find probable cause while personally entertaining some reservations. By the same token, a showing of probable cause may stop considerably short of proof beyond a reasonable doubt, and evidence that leaves some doubt may yet demonstrate probable cause. In the instance before us, the testimony of two witnesses on direct examination furnished more than an ample foundation for a finding of probable cause which the cross-examination allowed did not impair. By our appraisal the convoluted defensive theory Shepard now says he wanted to develop was not likely to change the result. Whatever its potency as a basis for a reasonable doubt at trial, its capability to dissolve enough of the Government's showing to negate probable cause strikes us as highly improbable. We speak not only of the cross-examination which was banned but also of the items of similar purport which on Shepard's presentation were excluded. In any event, the situation is far too cloudy to warrant a grant of the extraordinary relief which Shepard seeks.

Magistrates presiding over preliminary hearings, no less than judges presiding over trials, are endowed with broad powers to supervise examination of witnesses. Beyond that, they should be indulged some leeway in their resolution of probable cause issues. Courts should not upset these judgmatic exercises unless a supervisory excess or a decisional error is clearly shown, and we do not perceive either here. Shepard's counsel was permitted to cross-examine each Government witness closely as to the elements of his direct testimony and, for the reasons stated, we cannot say that disallowance of the questions ruled out was improper. For similar reasons, we are unable to say that the photographs and the questions as to the defense witness possessed such a tendency to dissolve probable cause that their exclusion was erroneous. A writ of mandamus lies only to enforce a plain, positive duty; it is not available to exact a response to a dubious

13. Barber v. Page, 390 U.S. 719, 725, 88 S.Ct. 1318, 1322, 20 L.Ed.2d 255 (1968).

claim. At best, any obligation to reverse the rulings on the excluded evidence is entirely too unclear. We accordingly affirm as to Shepard.

III. DANCIS' APPEAL

Dancis, our third appellant, was charged with two violations of the Marijuana Tax Act. The charges came on for ventilation at a preliminary hearing over which a United States Magistrate presided. The magistrate denied his counsel's request for a subpoena requiring the attendance of an unnamed undercover agent, who apparently was the sole available eyewitness to the two marijuana transactions attributed to Dancis. The Government's only witness at the hearing was the agent's supervisor, whose testimony as to the alleged transactions was necessarily hearsay, and as to the transactor's identity was simply that the agent had identified Dancis from a six-year old photograph. The magistrate, on a finding of probable cause, held Dancis for grand jury action, and the District Court, in the case under review, held that the hearing was legally sufficient.

Dancis argues that each of two flaws vitiated his preliminary hearing. One is that the magistrate's refusal to allow him access to the undercover agent's testimony was prejudicial error. The other is that the Confrontation Clause outlaws the magistrate's finding of probable cause solely upon the hearsay testimony of the agent's supervisor. We deem it unnecessary to reach the constitutional issue posed by Dancis' second contention because we agree that he is on sound ground in advancing the first.

A. *Defensive Evidence at Preliminary Hearings*

Former Rule 5(c) confirmed the right of an accused to "introduce evidence in his own behalf" at his preliminary hearing. It also imposed the requirement that an affirmative decision on probable cause be reached "on the evidence." The specifications of present Rule 5.1(a) are identical. Thus a federal preliminary hearing is not only the occasion upon which the Government must justify continued detention by a showing of probable cause, but also an opportunity for the accused to rebut that showing. Rule 5(c) made it clear that it is as much the arrestee's prerogative to endeavor to minimize probable cause as it is the Government's to undertake to maximize it, and that both sides must be indulged reasonably in their respective efforts. And the Government's demonstration on probable cause must surmount not only difficulties of its own but also any attack the accused may be able to mount against it.[14]

14. While the standard of probable cause which the Government must meet at preliminary hearings is roughly equivalent to the standard required for issuance of an arrest warrant or for an arrest without a warrant . . . the procedure at preliminary hearings differs from that upon the issuance of a warrant or a warrantless arrest in at least one very important respect. That difference is the presence of the accused at the preliminary hearing and his right to cross-examine prosecution witnesses and introduce evidence in his own behalf. Arrest warrants, on the other hand, are issued upon the Government's ex parte presentation to a magistrate, and warrantless arrests are made on information communicated ex parte to arresting officers. The traditional function of the preliminary hearing is a second determination on probable cause, this time after according the accused a reasonable opportunity to rebut it. Unless the accused is indulged in that respect, the preliminary hearing is little more than a duplication of the probable cause decisions that foreran his arrest.

In sum, "the evidence" which alone must guide resolution of the probable cause issue is the whole evidence—for the defense as well as the prosecution. The magistrate must "listen to . . . [the] versions [of all witnesses] and observe their demeanor and provide an opportunity to defense counsel to explore their account on cross-examination."[15] The magistrate "sits as a judicial officer to sift all the evidence before resolving the probable cause issue. . . ."[16] He "cannot decline to issue subpoenas on the ground that only the Government's evidence is probative."[17]

These provisions of the Rules and our interpretations of them are now reinforced by the holding in Coleman v. Alabama that the Sixth Amendment secures for the accused the assistance of counsel at a preliminary hearing having for its purpose a determination on probable cause to hold him for further proceedings. Among counsel's potential contributions, the Court stated, is "skilled examination . . . of witnesses [which] may expose fatal weaknesses in the [prosecution's] case that may lead the magistrate to refuse to bind the accused over." It cannot be gainsaid that what the Sixth Amendment mandated for Alabama's preliminary hearing it exacts equally for the federal preliminary hearing which, we repeat, is exclusively an exploration into probable cause to hold the accused to answer the prosecution further. Nor can it be doubted that *Coleman* demands more than the mere presence of counsel at the hearing. The right to counsel which *Coleman* declared would amount to no more than a pious overture unless it is a right to counsel able to function efficaciously in his client's behalf. The Sixth Amendment's guaranty of counsel is a pledge of effective assistance by counsel, and *Coleman* makes it clear that federal preliminary hearings, as critical stages of criminal prosecutions, require no less. If the accused's counsel is reduced to a state of impotence in the discharge of this responsibility, it is evident that the accused is deprived of the very benefit which the Sixth Amendment's boon of counsel was designed to confer.

So, an accused is normally entitled to subpoenas compelling the attendance at his preliminary hearing of witnesses whose testimony promises appreciable assistance on the issue of probable cause. The test, our past utterances on the subject have indicated, couples the witness's materiality with an absence of good cause for not requiring his presence, and its operation does not depend upon which side might have been expected to call the witness. Certainly an accused will not in every instance qualify for a subpoena for the production of a Government witness at his preliminary hearing, but where he succeeds in a plausible showing that that witness could contribute significantly to the accuracy of the probable cause determination, the request for the subpoena should be granted. "This," we have said, "is consistent with the principal purpose of the preliminary hearing as a mechanism to determine whether the evidence is adequate to establish probable cause."[18]

15. Ross v. Sirica, 127 U.S.App.D.C. [10 (1967)] at 18, 380 F.2d [557] at 565 (statement of Judges McGowan and Leventhal).

16. Id. at 12, 380 F.2d at 559.

17. Id.

18. Ross v. Sirica, supra note 15, 127 U.S.App.D.C. at 13, 380 F.2d at 560.

We think the testimony of the undercover agent Dancis desired at his preliminary hearing met the standard of materiality. From aught that appears, he was the only available person who could testify to the two charged marijuana transfers from personal observation, and by the same token the only one who could directly identify the party responsible for them. Since probable cause to bind Dancis over for further prosecution depended on the caliber of the Government's showing that he was that party and that what he did on the two occasions under scrutiny was illegal, it seems clear that the witness he requested could have given testimony bearing critically upon those matters. In Washington v. Clemmer[19] it was the complainant in a rape case who was sought, and in Ross v. Sirica the only three eyewitnesses to a murder. In both cases we held that denial of the accused's access to them was error, and it appears to us that the sole eyewitness to the transgressions laid to Dancis was equally material.

As we admonished in *Ross*, "[w]hatever the full reach of the accused's subpoena rights at a preliminary hearing, . . . he is entitled to compel the attendance of eyewitnesses unless, of course, 'because of physical or psychological disability in a particular case' such witnesses cannot attend."[20] That seems the more so when the nature of the Government's presentation at Dancis' preliminary hearing is taken fully into account. The Government offered but one witness, and he could testify on the vital issues of offenses and identity only from hearsay, and it is evident that that weakened the showing. To the extent that hearsay is employed, the effort to establish probable cause becomes more prone to attack since the reliability of the absent hearsay declarant always becomes an added factor to be reckoned with. In *Ross*, where, similarly to Dancis' case the Government's one witness at a preliminary hearing on a murder charge was a police officer who could merely relay what three eyewitnesses had told him about the crime, two judges of this court aptly observed, without dispute from the rest, that

> A judicial officer engaged in a judicial determination of probable cause can hardly rest easy solely with the hearsay account of the policeman of what these eyewitnesses told him if the eyewitnesses can be available, so that he can listen to their versions and observe their demeanor, and provide an opportunity to defense counsel to explore their account on cross-examination. The presence of those witnesses impresses us as falling within the orbit of the rights conferred upon the accused by the fourth sentence of Rule 5(c). . . .[21]

Indeed, the problem addressed in *Ross* is compounded in the situation before us now. The Government's evidence at Dancis' preliminary hearing was not only hearsay but also hearsay without any apparent means of refutation whatever. The undercover agent was not only absent from the hear-

---

19. . . .[339 F.2d 715, 725 (D.C.Cir.1964)].

20. Ross v. Sirica, supra note 15, 127 U.S.App.D.C. at 13, 380 F.2d at 560, quoting Washington v. Clemmer [330 F.2d 715 (D.C.Cir.1964)] at 718 n.11.

21. Ross v. Sirica, supra note 15, 127 U.S.App.D.C. at 18, 380 F.2d at 565 (statement of Judges McGowan and Leventhal) (footnote omitted). See also Washington v. Clemmer [330 F.2d 715 (D.C.Cir.1964)] at 728.

ing but at the time was also totally unidentified. He did not sign the complaint against Dancis, nor was he named in it, and the testimony at the hearing referred to him simply by his code name "John P." Defense counsel's inquiries on cross-examination as to his real name, and even as to generic characteristics, drew objections from the Government which the magistrate sustained. There was little or nothing in the Government's presentation to lend credit to the reliability of either the agent or the observations purportedly incriminating and identifying Dancis. It is difficult to imagine a case wherein the accused was more helpless to defend against a hearsay attribution of probable cause.

To say, as we do, that the testimony of the absent witness was material does not mean necessarily that the refusal of the subpoena was error vitiating the preliminary hearing. A refusal may be justified, and if it is a finding of probable cause climaxing the hearing must stand. The record before us, however, is singularly devoid of any such justification. There is no hint that the undercover officer was physically unamenable to a subpoena or in any way disabled from responding to it. There is no suggestion that his information about the episodes under exploration was to any extent privileged from compulsory disclosure. Nor is there a basis for attributing the denial of the subpoena to the exigencies of any undercover operation. The magistrate did not predicate the denial upon any of these grounds, nor did the Government even urge any of them. And to the extent that the record may furnish indications that the magistrate was satisfied on probable cause without hearing from the undercover agent, it suffices to repeat that the issue thereon cannot properly be resolved without accommodating reasonable demands of the prosecution and the defense for the production of evidence capable of shaping the outcome.

. . . [22]

---

297. See United States v. King, 482 F.2d 768 (D.C.Cir.1973), in which, relying on *Coleman*, above, the court held that in the absence of reasons why the complainant was unavailable, a defendant charged with rape was entitled to a subpoena for her attendance as a witness. "It was, of course, possible—perhaps probable—that her testimony would have been unhelpful or even damaging to appellant, but it cannot be gainsaid that it also could have weakened or destroyed probable cause. With that capability, it was for appellant, not the judge, to say whether the try was to be made." Id. at 775.

[22] The court remanded the case to the district court for an appropriate remedy consistent with the fact that Dancis had already been indicted; among the possible remedies, the court said, were disclosure of the agent's testimony before the grand jury, a deposition of the agent by written interrogatories, and so forth.

298. Review. In what circumstances, by what procedure, can a magistrate's determination that there is probable cause to believe that a person has committed a crime be challenged? See DiCesare v. Chernenko, 303 F.2d 423 (4th Cir.1962); United States v. Vassall, 282 F.Supp. 928 (E.D.Pa.1968); United States v. Florida, 165 F.Supp. 328 (E.D.Ark.1958); United States v. Zerbst, 111 F.Supp. 807 (E.D.S.C.1953).

The preliminary examination in federal procedure is evidently something of a hybrid. Ostensibly intended to determine whether there is a basis for holding the defendant for trial, it rarely serves that function explicitly because the matter of bail is resolved before the examination takes place. A determination that there is not probable cause is rare and, in any case, would affect the defendant's situation only if the prosecutor did not obtain an indictment and proceeded by information. On the other hand, although the preliminary examination is not intended to be a pretrial proceedings, it may serve a number of pretrial functions for the defense, as the courts recognized in Coleman v. Alabama and Coleman v. Burnett, pp. 555, 566 above. In view of these conflicting considerations, how should the magistrate proceed? Would it be desirable to assign to the preliminary examination functions expressly related not only to the defendant's present detention or binding over but also to the subsequent prosecution? If so, how could that be accomplished without converting the preliminary examination into a mini-trial? If it were intended expressly to serve pretrial functions like discovery and fixing testimony, how ought its procedures be modified?

CHAPTER 8

BAIL

"[The] tendency to rely on only polar alternatives is at its worst in our law of conditional release pending trial. American practice almost universally utilizes only two extremes: release upon purchase of a bond without any formal police or other supervision during what may be a prolonged pretrial period, or total imprisonment under the most deplorable conditions to be found in American penological practice today. The one extreme subjects society to unjustifiable risks, the other severely penalizes the unconvicted detainee." Foote, "Introduction: The Comparative Study of Conditional Release," 108 U.Pa.L.Rev. 290, 299–300 (1960).

---

299. U.S. Constitution amend. VIII: "Excessive bail shall not be required...."

"We take for granted that, contrary to earlier cases . . . the prohibition in the Eighth Amendment against requiring excessive bail must now be regarded as applying to the States, under the Fourteenth Amendment." Pilkinton v. Circuit Court of Howell County, 324 F.2d 45, 46 (8th Cir.1963).

"The right to release before trial is conditioned upon the accused's giving adequate assurance that he will stand trial and submit to sentence if found guilty. . . . Like the ancient practice of securing the oaths of responsible persons to stand as sureties for the accused, the modern practice of requiring a bail bond or the deposit of a sum of money subject to forfeiture serves as additional assurance of the presence of an accused. Bail set at a figure higher than an amount reasonably calculated to fulfill this purpose is 'excessive' under the Eighth Amendment." Stack v. Boyle, 342 U.S. 1, 4–5 (1951).

Upholding the denial of bail to certain aliens taken into custody pending a determination of deportability, the Court said in Carlson v. Landon, 342 U.S. 524, 545–46 (1952): "The bail clause was lifted with slight changes from the English Bill of Rights Act. In England that clause has never been thought to accord a right to bail in all cases, but merely to provide that bail shall not be excessive in those cases where it is proper to grant bail. When this clause was carried over into our Bill of Rights, nothing was said that indicated any different concept. The Eighth Amendment has not prevented Congress from defining the classes of cases in which bail shall be allowed in this country. Thus in criminal cases bail is not compulsory where the punishment may be death. Indeed, the very language of the Amendment fails to say all arrests must be bailable." Dissenting, Justice Black observed that "when scrutinized with a hostile eye" the "literal language of the framers" of the Eighth Amendment might lend itself to the Court's interpretation, but it was nonetheless a "weird, devitalizing interpretation." Id. at 556.

See Hunt v. Roth, 648 F.2d 1148 (8th Cir.1981), vacated as moot sub nom. Murphy v. Hunt, 455 U.S. 478 (1982), holding that a provision of the Nebraska Constitution denying bail to persons accused of specified noncapital sexual offenses is a violation of the Eighth Amendment. The subject of bail in capital cases is discussed at length in State v. Menillo, 268 A.2d 667 (Conn.1970). See White v. United States, 412 F.2d 145 (D.C.Cir.1968) (defendant in capital case released on personal recognizance with conditions).

A court has inherent power to order that a defendant be detained before trial, in order to protect witnesses. United States v. Payden, 768 F.2d 487 (2d Cir.1985) (defendant attempted to contract for murder of witness; detention order upheld).

In United States v. Dohm, 618 F.2d 1169 (5th Cir.1980), the court rejected the defendant's claim that incriminating statements at the initial appearance, made in order to secure reasonable bail, should not be admitted at trial, lest a defendant be forced to choose between his constitutional right to bail and the privilege against compulsory self-incrimination; provided proper warnings are given, the statements are admissible. But see United States v. Perry, 788 F.2d 100 (3d Cir.1986), holding that the presumption of dangerousness under the federal bail statute, see p. 580 below, requires that the defendant's testimony have use immunity to avoid unconstitutionality.

300. It is well-established that bail is not excessive in the constitutional sense merely because the defendant is unable to pay it. E.g., Hodgdon v. United States, 365 F.2d 679 (8th Cir.1966). In United States v. McConnell, 842 F.2d 105 (5th Cir.1988), the court held that that rule is not contradicted by the provision of 18 U.S.C. § 3142(c)(2), p. 580 below, which provides that bail may not include "a financial condition that results in the pretrial detention of the person." The court said that although that provision precludes the automatic setting of high bail in order to detain, bail can be set as high as necessary to assure the person's appearance, even if such amount is more than the person can pay and results in his detention.

The problem of money bail for indigents is discussed extensively in Pugh v. Rainwater, 572 F.2d 1053 (5th Cir.1978). The court concluded that it is not a denial of equal protection to permit the setting of money bail for an indigent defendant without a presumption that other forms of bail are to

AO 470 (8/85) Order of Temporary Detention

United States District Court

DISTRICT OF —

UNITED STATES OF AMERICA

V.

ORDER OF TEMPORARY DETENTION
PENDING HEARING PURSUANT TO
BAIL REFORM ACT

_____
Defendant

Case Number:

Upon motion of the _____ , it is ORDERED that a

detention hearing is set for _____ at _____
Date   Time

before _____
Name of Judicial Officer

_____
Location of Judicial Officer

Pending this hearing, the defendant shall be held in custody by (the United States marshal) (_____

_____) and produced for the hearing.
Other Custodial Official

_____   _____
Date   Judicial Officer

---

*If not held immediately upon defendant's first appearance, the hearing may be continued for up to three days upon motion of the Government, or up to five days upon motion of the defendant. 18 U.S.C. §3142(f)(2).

    A hearing is required whenever the conditions set forth in 18 U.S.C. §3142(f) are present. Subsection (1) sets forth the grounds that may be asserted only by the attorney for the Government; subsection (2) states that a hearing is mandated upon the motion of the attorney for the Government or upon the judicial officer's own motion if there is a serious risk that the defendant (a) will flee or (b) will obstruct or attempt to obstruct justice, or threaten, injure, or intimidate, or attempt to threaten, injure, or intimidate a prospective witness or juror.

be used when practicable. See also Schilb v. Kuebel, 404 U.S. 357 (1971), in which the Court upheld, against the argument that it violated the Equal Protection Clause, the Illinois 10%-deposit practice, pursuant to which 10% of the deposit (1% of the amount of bail) is retained by the clerk of court as "costs"; the amount retained is used to meet the cost of administering the bail system.

"We are faced with the familiar argument that appellant claims to be an indigent and cannot put up a bond of this size and consequently he should be released on his personal recognizance and upon compliance with non-financial conditions. When this argument is carried to its logical conclusion, every indigent person would always be released on non-financial conditions and the requirement for reasonable bail would be meaningless as it would be turned into a requirement for release of all indigents without bail and solely on non-financial conditions in every instance. In our opinion, the requirement for reasonable bail is a direction that bail be imposed that is reasonable when consideration is given to all circumstances of the case: the nature of the crime, its enormity, the character of the defendant, his ties to the community and similar items." United States v. Cook, 442 F.2d 723, 724 (D.C.Cir.1970). See United States v. James, 674 F.2d 886 (11th Cir.1982); United States v. Beaman, 631 F.2d 85 (6th Cir.1980).

Section 3142(c) of the federal bail statute provides: "The judicial officer may not impose a financial condition that results in the pretrial detention of the person," p. 580 below. The provision is an explicit rejection of the practice familiar in the past (and the present practice in many state courts) of setting bail high enough to ensure the defendant's detention rather than as a condition of release. The practice was a way of avoiding doubts, addressed explicitly in the federal statute, about pretrial detention of someone on the ground that his release was dangerous to the community.

Bail of $1,000,000 cash is upheld pursuant to § 3142(c), in United States v. Szott, 768 F.2d 159 (7th Cir.1985). The court said: "The statute does not require that a defendant be able to post the bail 'readily.' The purpose of bail is not served unless losing the sum would be a deeply-felt hurt to the defendant and his family; the hurt must be so severe that defendant will return for trial rather than flee. This implies that a court must be able to induce a defendant to go to great lengths to raise the funds without violating the condition in § 3142(c) that bail may not be used to deny release altogether." Id. at 160.

The court went further in United States v. McConnell, 842 F.2d 105 (5th Cir.1988). It said that if no other condition will assure the defendant's appearance at trial, bail may be set at an amount higher than that the defendant is able to meet, without violating § 3142(c). The court relied on legislative history of the Bail Reform Act, which indicated that a court may fix bail in an amount high enough to assure the defendant's appearance, without regard to the defendant's ability to meet the amount.

BAIL REFORM ACT OF 1984

18 U.S.C. §§ 3141–3150

§ 3141. Release and detention authority generally

(a) Pending trial. A judicial officer authorized to order the arrest of a person under section 3041 of this title before whom an arrested person is brought shall order that such person be released or detained, pending judicial proceedings, under this chapter.

(b) Pending sentence or appeal. A judicial officer of a court of original jurisdiction over an offense, or a judicial officer of a Federal appellate court, shall order that, pending imposition or execution of sentence, or pending appeal of conviction or sentence, a person be released or detained under this chapter.

§ 3142. Release or detention of a defendant pending trial

(a) In general. Upon the appearance before a judicial officer of a person charged with an offense, the judicial officer shall issue an order that, pending trial, the person be—

(1) released on his personal recognizance or upon execution of an unsecured appearance bond, under subsection (b) of this section;

(2) released on a condition or combination of conditions under subsection (c) of this section;

(3) temporarily detained to permit revocation of conditional release, deportation, or exclusion under subsection (d) of this section; or

(4) detained under subsection (e) of this section.

(b) Release on personal recognizance or unsecured appearance bond. The judicial officer shall order the pretrial release of the person on personal recognizance, or upon execution of an unsecured appearance bond in an amount specified by the court, subject to the condition that the person not commit a Federal, State, or local crime during the period of release, unless the judicial officer determines that such release will not reasonably assure the appearance of the person as required or will endanger the safety of any other person or the community.

(c) Release on conditions. (1) If the judicial officer determines that the release described in subsection (b) of this section will not reasonably assure the appearance of the person as required or will endanger the safety of any other person or the community, such judicial officer shall order the pretrial release of the person—

(A) subject to the condition that the person not commit a Federal, State, or local crime during the period of release; and

(B) subject to the least restrictive further condition, or combination of conditions, that such judicial officer determines will reasonably assure the appearance of the person as required and the safety of any other person and the community, which may include the condition that the person—

(i) remain in the custody of a designated person, who agrees to assume supervision and to report any violation of a release condition to the court, if the designated person is able reasonably to assure the judicial officer that the person will appear as required and will not pose a danger to the safety of any other person or the community;

(ii) maintain employment, or, if unemployed, actively seek employment;

(iii) maintain or commence an educational program;

(iv) abide by specified restrictions on personal associations, place of abode, or travel;

(v) avoid all contact with an alleged victim of the crime and with a potential witness who may testify concerning the offense;

(vi) report on a regular basis to a designated law enforcement agency, pretrial services agency, or other agency;

(vii) comply with a specified curfew;

(viii) refrain from possessing a firearm, destructive device, or other dangerous weapon;

(ix) refrain from excessive use of alcohol, or any use of a narcotic drug or other controlled substance, as defined in section 102 of the Controlled Substances Act (21 U.S.C. 802), without a prescription by a licensed medical practitioner;

(x) undergo available medical, psychological, or psychiatric treatment, including treatment for drug or alcohol dependency, and remain in a specified institution if required for that purpose;

(xi) execute an agreement to forfeit upon failing to appear as required, property of a sufficient unencumbered value, including money, as is reasonably necessary to assure the appearance of the person as required, and shall provide the court with proof of ownership and the value of the property along with information regarding existing encumbrances as the judicial office may require;

(xii) execute a bail bond with solvent sureties; who will execute an agreement to forfeit in such amount as is reasonably necessary to assure appearance of the person as required and shall provide the court with information regarding the value of the assets and liabilities of the surety if other than an approved surety and the nature and extent of encumbrances against the surety's property; such surety shall have a net worth which shall have sufficient unencumbered value to pay the amount of the bail bond;

(xiii) return to custody for specified hours following release for employment, schooling, or other limited purposes; and

(xiv) satisfy any other condition that is reasonably necessary to assure the appearance of the person as required and to assure the safety of any other person and the community.

(2) The judicial officer may not impose a financial condition that results in the pretrial detention of the person.

(3) The judicial officer may at any time amend the order to impose additional or different conditions of release.

(d) Temporary detention to permit revocation of conditional release, deportation, or exclusion. If the judicial officer determines that—

(1) such person—

(A) is, and was at the time the offense was committed, on—

(i) release pending trial for a felony under Federal, State, or local law;

(ii) release pending imposition or execution of sentence, appeal of sentence or conviction, or completion of sentence, for any offense under Federal, State or local law; or

(iii) probation or parole for any offense under Federal, State, or local law; or

(B) is not a citizen of the United States or lawfully admitted for permanent residence, as defined in section 101(a)(20) of the Immigration and Nationality Act (8 U.S.C. 1101(a)(20)); and

(2) the person may flee or pose a danger to any other person or the community;

such judicial officer shall order the detention of the person, for a period of not more than ten days, excluding Saturdays, Sundays, and holidays, and direct the attorney for the Government to notify the appropriate court, probation or parole official, or State or local law enforcement official, or the appropriate official of the Immigration and Naturalization Service. If the official fails or declines to take the person into custody during that period, the person shall be treated in accordance with the other provisions of this section, notwithstanding the applicability of other provisions of law governing release pending trial or deportation or exclusion proceedings. If temporary detention is sought under paragraph (1)(B) of this subsection, the person has the burden of proving to the court such person's United States citizenship or lawful admission for permanent residence.

(e) Detention. If, after a hearing pursuant to the provisions of subsection (f) of this section, the judicial officer finds that no condition or combination of conditions will reasonably assure the appearance of the person as required and the safety of any other person and the community, such judicial officer shall order the detention of the person before trial. In a case described in subsection (f)(1) of this section, a rebuttable presumption arises that no condition or combination of conditions will reasonably assure the safety of any other person and the community if such judicial officer finds that—

(1) the person has been convicted of a Federal offense that is described in subsection (f)(1) of this section, or of a State or local offense that would have been an offense described in subsection (f)(1) of this section if a circumstance giving rise to Federal jurisdiction had existed;

(2) the offense described in paragraph (1) of this subsection was committed while the person was on release pending trial for a Federal, State, or local offense; and

(3) a period of not more than five years has elapsed since the date of conviction, or the release of the person from imprisonment, for the offense described in paragraph (1) of this subsection, whichever is later.

Subject to rebuttal by the person, it shall be presumed that no condition or combination of conditions will reasonably assure the appearance of the person as required and the safety of the community if the judicial officer finds that there is probable cause to believe that the person committed an offense for which a maximum term of imprisonment of ten years or more is prescribed in the Controlled Substances Act (21 U.S.C. 801 et seq.), the Controlled Substances Import and Export Act (21 U.S.C. 951 et seq.), the Maritime Drug Law Enforcement Act (46 U.S.C.App. 1901 et seq.), or an offense under section 924(c) of title 18 of the United States Code.

(f) Detention hearing. The judicial officer shall hold a hearing to determine whether any condition or combination of conditions set forth in subsection (c) of this section will reasonably assure the appearance of the person as required and the safety of any other person and the community—

(1) upon motion of the attorney for the Government, in a case that involves—

(A) a crime of violence;

(B) an offense for which the maximum sentence is life imprisonment or death;

(C) an offense for which a maximum term of imprisonment of ten years or more is prescribed in the Controlled Substances Act (21 U.S.C. 801 et seq.), the Controlled Substances Import and Export Act (21 U.S.C. 951 et seq.), or the Maritime Drug Law Enforcement Act (46 U.S.C.App. 1901 et seq.); or

(D) any felony if the person has been convicted of two or more offenses described in subparagraphs (A) through (C) of this paragraph, or two or more State or local offenses that would have been offenses described in subparagraphs (A) through (C) of this paragraph if a circumstance giving rise to Federal jurisdiction had existed, or a combination of such offenses; or

(2) upon motion of the attorney for the Government or upon the judicial officer's own motion, in a case that involves—

(A) a serious risk that the person will flee; or

(B) a serious risk that the person will obstruct or attempt to obstruct justice, or threaten, injure, or intimidate, or attempt to threaten, injure, or intimidate, a prospective witness or juror.

The hearing shall be held immediately upon the person's first appearance before the judicial officer unless that person, or the attorney for the Government, seeks a continuance. Except for good cause, a continuance on motion of the person may not exceed five days, and a continuance on motion of the attorney for the Government may not exceed three days. During a continuance, the person shall be detained, and the judicial officer, on motion of the attorney for the Government or sua sponte, may order that, while in custody, a person who appears to be a narcotics addict receive a medical examination to determine whether such person is an addict. At the hearing, such person has the right to be represented by counsel, and, if financially unable to obtain adequate representation, to have counsel appointed. The person shall be afforded an opportunity to testify, to present witnesses, to cross-examine witnesses who appear at the hearing, and to present information by proffer or otherwise. The rules concerning admissibility of evidence in criminal trials do not apply to the presentation and consideration of information at the hearing. The facts the judicial officer uses to support a finding pursuant to subsection (e) that no condition or combination of conditions will reasonably assure the safety of any other person and the community shall be supported by clear and convincing evidence. The person may be detained pending completion of the hearing. The hearing may be reopened before or after a determination by the judicial officer, at any time before trial if the judicial officer finds that information exists that was not known to the movant at the time of the hearing and that has a material bearing on the issue whether there are conditions of release that will reasonably assure the appearance of the person as required and the safety of any other person and the community.

(g) Factors to be considered. The judicial officer shall, in determining whether there are conditions of release that will reasonably assure the appearance of the person as required and the safety of any other person and the community, take into account the available information concerning—

(1) the nature and circumstances of the offense charged, including whether the offense is a crime of violence or involves a narcotic drug;

(2) the weight of the evidence against the person;

(3) the history and characteristics of the person, including—

(A) the person's character, physical and mental condition, family ties, employment, financial resources, length of residence in the community, community ties, past conduct, history relating to drug or alcohol abuse, criminal history, and record concerning appearance at court proceedings; and

(B) whether, at the time of the current offense or arrest, the person was on probation, on parole, or on other release pending trial, sentencing, appeal, or completion of sentence for an offense under Federal, State, or local law; and

(4) the nature and seriousness of the danger to any person or the community that would be posed by the person's release. In considering the conditions of release described in subsection (c)(1)(B)(xi) or (c)(1)(B)(xii) of this section, the judicial officer may upon his own motion, or shall upon the motion of the Government, conduct an inquiry

into the source of the property to be designated for potential forfeiture or offered as collateral to secure a bond, and shall decline to accept the designation, or the use as collateral, of property that, because of its source, will not reasonably assure the appearance of the person as required.

(h) Contents of release order. In a release order issued under subsection (b) or (c) of this section, the judicial officer shall—

(1) include a written statement that sets forth all the conditions to which the release is subject, in a manner sufficiently clear and specific to serve as a guide for the person's conduct; and

(2) advise the person of—

(A) the penalties for violating a condition of release, including the penalties for committing an offense while on pretrial release;

(B) the consequences of violating a condition of release, including the immediate issuance of a warrant for the person's arrest; and

(C) sections 1503 of this title (relating to intimidation of witnesses, jurors, and officers of the court), 1510 (relating to obstruction of criminal investigations), 1512 (tampering with a witness, victim, or an informant), and 1513 (retaliating against a witness, victim, or an informant).

(i) Contents of detention order. In a detention order issued under subsection (e) of this section, the judicial officer shall—

(1) include written findings of fact and a written statement of the reasons for the detention;

(2) direct that the person be committed to the custody of the Attorney General for confinement in a corrections facility separate, to the extent practicable, from persons awaiting or serving sentences or being held in custody pending appeal;

(3) direct that the person be afforded reasonable opportunity for private consultation with counsel; and

(4) direct that, on order of a court of the United States or on request of an attorney for the Government, the person in charge of the corrections facility in which the person is confined deliver the person to a United States marshal for the purpose of an appearance in connection with a court proceeding.

The judicial officer may, by subsequent order, permit the temporary release of the person, in the custody of a United States marshal or another appropriate person, to the extent that the judicial officer determines such release to be necessary for preparation of the person's defense or for another compelling reason.

(j) Presumption of innocence. Nothing in this section shall be construed as modifying or limiting the presumption of innocence.

§ 3143. Release or detention of a defendant pending sentence or appeal

(a) Release or detention pending sentence. (1) Except as provided in paragraph (2), the judicial officer shall order that a person who has been found guilty of an offense and who is awaiting imposition or execution of sentence, other than a person for whom the applicable guideline promulgated pursuant to 28 U.S.C. 994 does not recommend a term of imprisonment, be detained, unless the judicial officer finds by clear and convincing evidence that the person is not likely to flee or pose a danger to the safety of any other person or the community if released under section 3142(b) or (c). If the judicial officer makes such a finding, such judicial officer shall order the release of the person in accordance with section 3142(b) or (c).

(2) The judicial officer shall order that a person who has been found guilty of an offense in a case described in subparagraph (A), (B), or (C) of subsection (f)(1) of section 3142 and is awaiting imposition or execution of sentence be detained unless—

(A)(i) the judicial officer finds there is a substantial likelihood that a motion for acquittal or new trial will be granted; or

(ii) an attorney for the Government has recommended that no sentence of imprisonment be imposed on the person; and

(B) the judicial officer finds by clear and convincing evidence that the person is not likely to flee or pose a danger to any other person or the community.

(b) Release or detention pending appeal by the defendant. (1) Except as provided in paragraph (2), the judicial officer shall order that a person who has been found guilty of an offense and sentenced to a term of imprisonment, and who has filed an appeal or a petition for a writ of certiorari, be detained, unless the judicial officer finds—

(A) by clear and convincing evidence that the person is not likely to flee or pose a danger to the safety of any other person or the community if released under section 3142(b) or (c) of this title; and

(B) that the appeal is not for the purpose of delay and raises a substantial question of law or fact likely to result in—

(i) reversal,

(ii) an order for a new trial,

(iii) a sentence that does not include a term of imprisonment, or

(iv) a reduced sentence to a term of imprisonment less than the total of the time already served plus the expected duration of the appeal process.

If the judicial officer makes such findings, such judicial officer shall order the release of the person in accordance with section 3142(b) or (c) of this title, except that in the circumstance described in subparagraph (B)(iv) of this paragraph, the judicial officer shall order the detention terminated at the expiration of the likely reduced sentence.

(2) The judicial officer shall order that a person who has been found guilty of an offense in a case described in subparagraph (A), (B), or (C) of subsection (f)(1) of section 3142 and sentenced to a term of imprisonment, and who has filed an appeal or a petition for a writ of certiorari, be detained.

(c) Release or detention pending appeal by the government. The judicial officer shall treat a defendant in a case in which an appeal has been taken by the United States under section 3731 of this title, in accordance with section 3142 of this title, unless the defendant is otherwise subject to a release or detention order.

Except as provided in subsection (b) of this section, the judicial officer, in a case in which an appeal has been taken by the United States under section 3742, shall—

(1) if the person has been sentenced to a term of imprisonment, order that person detained; and

(2) in any other circumstance, release or detain the person under section 3142.

§ 3144. Release or detention of a material witness

. . . [note 488 p. 985 below]

§ 3145. Review and appeal of a release or detention order

(a) Review of a release order. If a person is ordered released by a magistrate, or by a person other than a judge of a court having original jurisdiction over the offense and other than a Federal appellate court—

(1) the attorney for the Government may file, with the court having original jurisdiction over the offense, a motion for revocation of the order or amendment of the conditions of release; and

(2) the person may file, with the court having original jurisdiction over the offense, a motion for amendment of the conditions of release.

The motion shall be determined promptly.

(b) Review of a detention order. If a person is ordered detained by a magistrate, or by a person other than a judge of a court having original jurisdiction over the offense and other than a Federal appellate court, the person may file, with the court having original jurisdiction over the offense, a motion for revocation or amendment of the order. The motion shall be determined promptly.

(c) Appeal from a release or detention order. An appeal from a release or detention order, or from a decision denying revocation or amendment of such an order, is governed by the provisions of section 1291 of title 28 and section 3731 of this title.[1] The appeal shall be determined promptly. A per-

---

1. Section 1291 of title 28 provides the general statutory basis for appeals from judgments of the federal district courts. Section 3731 of title 18, so far as pertinent to bail, provides: "An appeal by the United States shall lie to a court of appeals from a decision or order, entered by a district court of the United States, granting the release of a person charged with or convicted of an offense, or denying a motion for revocation of, or modification of the conditions of, a decision or order granting release."

son subject to detention pursuant to section 3143(a)(2) or (b)(2), and who meets the conditions of release set forth in section 3143(a)(1) or (b)(1), may be ordered released, under appropriate conditions, by the judicial officer, if it is clearly shown that there are exceptional reasons why such person's detention would not be appropriate.

§ 3146. Penalty for failure to appear

(a) Offense. Whoever, having been released under this chapter knowingly—

(1) fails to appear before a court as required by the conditions of release; or

(2) fails to surrender for service of sentence pursuant to a court order;

shall be punished as provided in subsection (b) of this section.

(b) Punishment. (1) The punishment for an offense under this section is—

(A) if the person was released in connection with a charge of, or while awaiting sentence, surrender for service of sentence, or appeal or certiorari after conviction for—

(i) an offense punishable by death, life imprisonment, or imprisonment for a term of 15 years or more, a fine under this title or imprisonment for not more than ten years, or both;

(ii) an offense punishable by imprisonment for a term of five years or more, a fine under this title or imprisonment for not more than five years, or both;

(iii) any other felony, a fine under this title or imprisonment for not more than two years, or both; or

(iv) a misdemeanor, a fine under this chapter or imprisonment for not more than one year, or both; and

(B) if the person was released for appearance as a material witness, a fine under this chapter or imprisonment for not more than one year, or both.

(2) A term of imprisonment imposed under this section shall be consecutive to the sentence of imprisonment for any other offense.

(c) Affirmative defense. It is an affirmative defense to a prosecution under this section that uncontrollable circumstances prevented the person from appearing or surrendering, and that the person did not contribute to the creation of such circumstances in reckless disregard of the requirement to appear or surrender, and that the person appeared or surrendered as soon as such circumstances ceased to exist.

(d) Declaration of forfeiture. If a person fails to appear before a court as required, and the person executed an appearance bond pursuant to section 3142(b) of this title or is subject to the release condition set forth in clause (xi) or (xii) of section 3142(c)(1)(B) of this title, the judicial officer may, regardless of whether the person has been charged with an offense under this section, declare any property designated pursuant to that section to be forfeited to the United States.

§ 3147. Penalty for an offense committed while on release

A person convicted of an offense committed while released under this chapter shall be sentenced, in addition to the sentence prescribed for the offense to—

(1) a term of imprisonment of not more than ten years if the offense is a felony; or

(2) a term of imprisonment of not more than one year if the offense is a misdemeanor.

A term of imprisonment imposed under this section shall be consecutive to any other sentence of imprisonment.

§ 3148. Sanctions for violation of a release condition

(a) Available sanctions. A person who has been released under section 3142 of this title, and who has violated a condition of his release, is subject to a revocation of release, an order of detention, and a prosecution for contempt of court.

(b) Revocation of release. The attorney for the Government may initiate a proceeding for revocation of an order of release by filing a motion with the district court. A judicial officer may issue a warrant for the arrest of a person charged with violating a condition of release, and the person shall be brought before a judicial officer in the district in which such person's arrest was ordered for a proceeding in accordance with this section. To the extent practicable, a person charged with violating the condition of release that such person not commit a Federal, State, or local crime during the period of release, shall be brought before the judicial officer who ordered the release and whose order is alleged to have been violated. The judicial officer shall enter an order of revocation and detention if, after a hearing, the judicial officer—

(1) finds that there is—

(A) probable cause to believe that the person has committed a Federal, State, or local crime while on release; or

(B) clear and convincing evidence that the person has violated any other condition of release; and

(2) finds that—

(A) based on the factors set forth in section 3142(g) of this title, there is no condition or combination of conditions of release that will assure that the person will not flee or pose a danger to the safety of any other person or the community; or

(B) the person is unlikely to abide by any condition or combination of conditions of release.

If there is probable cause to believe that, while on release, the person committed a Federal, State, or local felony, a rebuttable presumption arises that no condition or combination of conditions will assure that the person will not pose a danger to the safety of any other person or the community. If the judicial officer finds that there are conditions of release that will assure that the person will not flee or pose a danger to the safety of any other person or the community, and that the person will abide by such conditions, the judicial officer shall treat the person in accordance with the provisions of section 3142 of this title and may amend the conditions of release accordingly.

(c) Prosecution for contempt. The judicial officer may commence a prosecution for contempt, under section 401 of this title, if the person has violated a condition of release.

§ 3149. Surrender of an offender by a surety

A person charged with an offense, who is released upon the execution of an appearance bond with a surety, may be arrested by the surety, and if so arrested, shall be delivered promptly to a United States marshal and brought before a judicial officer. The judicial officer shall determine in accordance with the provisions of section 3148(b) whether to revoke the release of the person, and may absolve the surety of responsibility to pay all or part of the bond in accordance with the provisions of Rule 46 of the Federal Rules of Criminal Procedure. The person so committed shall be held in official detention until released pursuant to this chapter or another provision of law.

§ 3150. Applicability to a case removed from a State court

The provisions of this chapter apply to a criminal case removed to a Federal court from a State court.

---

301. In United States v. Salerno, 481 U.S. 739 (1987) (6–3), the Court upheld the Bail Reform Act against the challenge that its provision for the detention of a defendant before trial on the ground of dangerousness violated due process and the Eighth Amendment's bail clause.

With respect to due process, the Court said:

"Respondents first argue that the Act violates substantive due process because the pretrial detention it authorizes constitutes impermissible punishment before trial. . . . The Government, however, has never argued that pretrial detention could be upheld if it were 'punishment.' The Court of Appeals assumed that pretrial detention under the Bail Reform Act is regulatory, not penal, and we agree that it is.

"As an initial matter, the mere fact that a person is detained does not inexorably lead to the conclusion that the government has imposed punishment. . . . To determine whether a restriction on liberty constitutes impermissible punishment or permissible regulation, we first look to legislative intent. . . . Unless Congress expressly intended to impose punitive restrictions, the punitive-regulatory distinction turns on " 'whether an alternative purpose to which [the restriction] may rationally be connected is assignable for it, and whether it appears excessive in relation to the alternative purpose assigned [to it].' " [Schall v. Martin, 467 U.S. 253 (1954)], quoting Kennedy v. Mendoza-Martinez, 372 U.S. 144, 168–169 (1963).

"We conclude that the detention imposed by the Act falls on the regulatory side of the dichotomy. The legislative history of the Bail Reform Act clearly indicates that Congress did not formulate the pretrial detention provisions as punishment for dangerous individuals. . . . Congress instead perceived pretrial detention as a potential solution to a pressing societal problem. . . . There is no doubt that preventing danger to the community is a legitimate regulatory goal. . . .

"Nor are the incidents of pretrial detention excessive in relation to the regulatory goal Congress sought to achieve. The Bail Reform Act carefully limits the circumstances under which detention may be sought to the most serious of crimes. . . . The arrestee is entitled to a prompt detention hearing . . . and the maximum length of pretrial detention is limited by the stringent time limitations of the Speedy Trial Act. . . . Moreover, as in *Schall* v. *Martin*, the conditions of confinement envisioned by the Act 'appear to reflect the regulatory purposes relied upon by the' Government. 467 U.S., at 270. As in *Schall*, the statute at issue here requires that detainees be housed in a 'facility separate, to the extent practicable, from persons awaiting or serving sentences or being held in custody pending appeal.' 18 U.S.C. § 3142(i)(2). We conclude, therefore, that the pretrial detention contemplated by the Bail Reform Act is regulatory in nature, and does not constitute punishment before trial in violation of the Due Process Clause." Id. at 746–48.

Also under the Due Process Clause, the respondents argued that even as a regulatory measure, pretrial detention because of dangerousness is impermissible, without regard to the duration of detention. The Court said:

"We do not think the Clause lays down any such categorical imperative. We have repeatedly held that the Government's regulatory interest in community safety can, in appropriate circumstances, outweigh an individual's liberty interest. For example, in times of war or insurrection, when society's interest is at its peak, the Government may detain individuals whom the Government believes to be dangerous. . . . Even outside the exigencies of war, we have found that sufficiently compelling governmental interests can justify detention of dangerous persons. Thus, we have found no absolute constitutional barrier to detention of potentially dangerous resident aliens pending deportation proceedings. . . . We have also held that the government may detain mentally unstable individuals who present a danger to the public . . . and dangerous defendants who become incompetent to stand trial . . . . We have approved of postarrest regulatory detention of juveniles when they present a continuing danger to the community. . . . Even competent adults may face substantial liberty restrictions as a result of the operation of our criminal justice system. If the police suspect an individual of a crime, they may arrest and hold him until a neutral magistrate determines whether probable cause exists. . . . Finally, respondents concede and the Court of Appeals noted that an arrestee may be incarcerated until trial if he presents a risk of flight . . . or a danger to witnesses.

"Respondents characterize all of these cases as exceptions to the 'general rule' of substantive due process that the government may not detain a person prior to a judgment of guilt in a criminal trial. Such a 'general rule' may freely be conceded, but we think that these cases show a sufficient number of exceptions to the rule that the congressional action challenged here can hardly be characterized as totally novel. Given the well-established authority of the government, in special circumstances, to restrain individuals' liberty prior to or even without criminal trial and conviction, we think that the present statute providing for pretrial detention on the basis of dangerousness must be evaluated in precisely the same manner that we evaluated the laws in the cases discussed above.

. . .

"On the other side of the scale, of course, is the individual's strong interest in liberty. We do not minimize the importance and fundamental nature of this right. But, as our cases hold, this right may, in circumstances where the government's interest is sufficiently weighty, be subordinated to the greater needs of society. We think that Congress' careful delineation of the circumstances under which detention will be permitted satisfies this standard. When the Government proves by clear and convincing evidence that an arrestee presents an identified and articulable threat to an individual or the community, we believe that, consistent with the Due Process Clause, a court may disable the arrestee from executing that threat. Under these circumstances, we cannot categorically state that pretrial detention 'offends some principle of justice so rooted in the traditions and conscience of our people as to be ranked as fundamental.' Snyder v. Massachusetts, 291 U.S. 97, 105 (1934)." Id. at 748–51.

With respect to the Eighth Amendment claim, the Court said:

"Respondents . . . contend that this Clause grants them a right to bail calculated solely upon considerations of flight. They rely on Stack v. Boyle, 342 U.S. 1, 5 (1951), in which the Court stated that '[b]ail set at a figure higher than an amount reasonably calculated [to ensure the defendant's presence at trial] is "excessive" under the Eighth Amendment.' . . . Respondents concede that the right to bail they have discovered in the Eighth Amendment is not absolute. A court may, for example, refuse bail in capital cases. And . . . a court may refuse bail when the defendant presents a threat to the judicial process by intimidating witnesses. . . . Respondents characterize these exceptions as consistent with what they claim to be the sole purpose of bail—to ensure integrity of the judicial process.

"While we agree that a primary function of bail is to safeguard the courts' role in adjudicating the guilt or innocence of defendants, we reject the proposition that the Eighth Amendment categorically prohibits the government from pursuing other admittedly compelling interests through regulation of pretrial release. The above-quoted *dictum* in Stack v. Boyle is far too slender a reed on which to rest this argument. The Court in *Stack* had no occasion to consider whether the Excessive Bail Clause requires courts to admit all defendants to bail, because the statute before the Court in that case in fact allowed the defendants to be bailed. Thus, the Court had to determine only whether bail, admittedly available in that case, was excessive if set at a sum greater than that necessary to ensure the arrestees' presence at trial.

"The holding of *Stack* is illuminated by the Court's holding just four months later in Carlson v. Landon, 342 U.S. 524 (1952). In that case, remarkably similar to the present action, the detainees had been arrested and held without bail pending a determination of deportability. The Attorney General refused to release the individuals, 'on the ground that there was reasonable cause to believe that [their] release would be prejudicial to the public interest and *would endanger the welfare and safety of the United States.*' Id., at 529 (emphasis added). The detainees brought the same challenge that respondents bring to us today: the Eighth Amendment required them to be admitted to bail. The Court squarely rejected this proposition . . . .

"Carlson v. Landon was a civil case, and we need not decide today whether the Excessive Bail Clause speaks at all to Congress' power to define the classes of criminal arrestees who shall be admitted to bail. For even if we were to conclude that the Eighth Amendment imposes some substantive limitations on the National Legislature's powers in this area, we would still hold that the Bail Reform Act is valid. Nothing in the text of the Bail Clause limits permissible government considerations solely to questions of flight. The only arguable substantive limitation of the Bail Clause is that the government's proposed conditions of release or detention not be 'excessive' in light of the perceived evil. Of course, to determine whether the government's response is excessive, we must compare that response against the interest the government seeks to protect by means of that response. Thus, when the government has admitted that its only interest is in preventing flight, bail must be set by a court at a sum designed to ensure that goal, and no more. . . . We believe that when Congress has mandated detention on the basis of a compelling interest other than prevention of flight, as it has here, the Eighth Amendment does not require release on bail." Id. at 752–55.

The most substantial arguments against the constitutionality of the Bail Reform Act are found in Justice Marshall's dissenting opinion in *Salerno*, id. at 755, and Judge Newman's opinion for the court of appeals in United States v. Melendez-Carrion, 790 F.2d 984 (2d Cir.1986).

In a footnote in *Salerno*, the Court suggested that there was a "point at which detention in a particular case might become excessively prolonged, and therefore punitive, in relation to Congress' regulatory goal." 481 U.S. at 747 n.4. In United States v. Hare, 873 F.2d 796 (5th Cir.1989), the court said that a hearing was required to determine whether that point had been

AO 199A (Rev. 3/87) Order Setting Conditions of Release   Page 1 of _____ Pages

United States District Court

_____ DISTRICT OF _____

UNITED STATES OF AMERICA

v.

**ORDER SETTING CONDITIONS
OF RELEASE**

Case Number: _____

_____
Defendant

IT IS ORDERED that the release of the defendant is subject to the following conditions:

   (1) The defendant shall not commit any offense in violation of federal, state or local law while on release in this case.

   (2) The defendant shall immediately advise the court, defense counsel and the U.S. attorney in writing of any change in address and telephone number.

   (3) The defendant shall appear at all proceedings as required and shall surrender for service of any sentence imposed as directed. The defendant shall next appear at (if blank, to be notified)_____
                                                                Place

_____ on _____
                                               Date and Time

Release on Personal Recognizance or Unsecured Bond

IT IS FURTHER ORDERED that the defendant be released provided that:

(✓) (4) The defendant promises to appear at all proceedings as required and to surrender for service of any sentence imposed.

(   ) (5) The defendant executes an unsecured bond binding the defendant to pay the United States the sum of
_____ dollars ($_____)
in the event of a failure to appear as required or to surrender as directed for service of any sentence imposed.

WHITE COPY - COURT   YELLOW - DEFENDANT   BLUE - U.S. ATTORNEY   PINK - U.S. MARSHAL   GREEN - PRETRIAL SERVICES

AO 199B (Rev. 3/87) Additional Conditions of Release   Page_____ of _____ Pages

Additional Conditions of Release

Upon finding that release by one of the above methods will not by itself reasonably assure the appearance of the defendant and the safety of other persons and the community, it is FURTHER ORDERED that the release of the defendant is subject to the conditions marked below:

(   ) (6) The defendant is placed in the custody of:
  (Name of person or organization) _____
  (Address)_____
  (City and State)_____ (Tel. No.) _____
who agrees (a) to supervise the defendant in accordance with all conditions of release, (b) to use every effort to assure the appearance of the defendant at all scheduled court proceedings, and (c) to notify the court immediately in the event the defendant violates any conditions of release or disappears.

       Signed: _____
             Custodian or Proxy

(   ) (7) The defendant shall:
  ( ) (a) maintain or actively seek employment.
  ( ) (b) maintain or commence an educational program.
  ( ) (c) abide by the following restrictions on his personal associations, place of abode, or travel:
    _____
    _____

  ( ) (d) avoid all contact with the following named persons, who are considered either alleged victims or potential witnesses:
    _____

  ( ) (e) report on a regular basis to the following agency:
    _____

  ( ) (f) comply with the following curfew: _____

  ( ) (g) refrain from possessing a firearm, destructive device, or other dangerous weapon.
  ( ) (h) refrain from excessive use of alcohol, and any use or unlawful possession of a narcotic drug and other controlled substances defined in 21 U.S.C. §802 unless prescribed by a licensed medical practitioner.
  ( ) (i) undergo medical or psychiatric treatment and/or remain in an institution, as follows:_____
    _____

  ( ) (j) execute a bond or an agreement to forfeit upon failing to appear as required, the following sum of money or designated property: _____
    _____

  ( ) (k) post with the court the following indicia of ownership of the above-described property, or the following amount or percentage of the above-described money: _____
    _____

  ( ) (l) execute a bail bond with solvent sureties in the amount of $ _____
  ( ) (m) return to custody each (week)day as of _____o'clock after being released each (week)day as of _____
    o'clock for employment, schooling, or the following limited purpose(s): _____

  ( ) (n) surrender any passport to _____
  ( ) (o) obtain no passport.
  ( ) (p) _____
    _____

WHITE COPY - COURT YELLOW - DEFENDANT BLUE - U.S. ATTORNEY PINK - U.S. MARSHAL GREEN - PRETRIAL SERVICES

AO 199C (Rev. 4/91) Advice of Penalties . . .   Page _____ of _____ Pages

Advice of Penalties and Sanctions

TO THE DEFENDANT:

YOU ARE ADVISED OF THE FOLLOWING PENALTIES AND SANCTIONS:

A violation of any of the foregoing conditions of release may result in the immediate issuance of a warrant for your arrest, a revocation of release, an order of detention, and a prosecution for contempt of court and could result in a term of imprisonment, a fine, or both.

The commission of any crime while on pre-trial release may result in an additional sentence to a term of imprisonment of not more than ten years, if the offense is a felony; or a term of imprisonment of not more than one year, if the offense is a misdemeanor. This sentence shall be in addition to any other sentence.

Federal law makes it a crime punishable by up to five years of imprisonment, and a $250,000 fine or both to intimidate or attempt to intimidate a witness, victim, juror, informant or officer of the court, or to obstruct a criminal investigation. It is also a crime punishable by up to ten years of imprisonment, a $250,000 fine or both, to tamper with a witness, victim or informant, or to retaliate against a witness, victim or informant, or to threaten or attempt to do so.

If after release, you knowingly fail to appear as required by the conditions of release, or to surrender for the service of sentence, you may be prosecuted for failing to appear or surrender and additional punishment may be imposed. If you are convicted of:

    (1) an offense punishable by death, life imprisonment, or imprisonment for a term of fifteen years or more, you shall be fined not more than $250,000 or imprisoned for not more than ten years, or both;

    (2) an offense punishable by imprisonment for a term of five years or more, but less than fifteen years, you shall be fined not more than $250,000 or imprisoned for not more than five years, or both;

    (3) any other felony, you shall be fined not more than $250,000 or imprisoned not more than two years, or both;

    (4) a misdemeanor, you shall be fined not more than $100,000 or imprisoned not more than one year, or both.

A term of imprisonment imposed for failure to appear or surrender shall be in addition to the sentence for any other offense. In addition, a failure to appear may result in the forfeiture of any bond posted.

Acknowledgement of Defendant

I acknowledge that I am the defendant in this case and that I am aware of the conditions of release. I promise to obey all conditions of release, to appear as directed, and to surrender for service of any sentence imposed. I am aware of the penalties and sanctions set forth above.

_____
Signature of Defendant

_____
Address

_____
City and State   Telephone

Directions to United States Marshal

(   ) The defendant is ORDERED released after processing.

(   ) The United States marshal is ORDERED to keep the defendant in custody until notified by the clerk or judicial officer that the defendant has posted bond and/or complied with all other conditions for release. The defendant shall be produced before the appropriate judicial officer at the time and place specified, if still in custody.

Date: _____   _____
                                                 Signature of Judicial Officer

_____
Name and Title of Judicial Officer

WHITE COPY - COURT   YELLOW - DEFENDANT   BLUE - U.S. ATTORNEY   PINK - U.S. MARSHAL   GREEN - PRETRIAL SERVICES

AO 472 (Rev. 3/86) Order of Detention Pending Trial

United States District Court

_____ DISTRICT OF _____

UNITED STATES OF AMERICA
V.

ORDER OF DETENTION PENDING TRIAL

_____
Defendant

Case Number: _____

In accordance with the Bail Reform Act, 18 U.S.C. §3142(f), a detention hearing has been held. I conclude that the following facts require the detention of the defendant pending trial in this case.

Part I — Findings of Fact

☐ (1) The defendant is charged with an offense described in 18 U.S.C. §3142(f)(1) and has been convicted of a (federal offense) (state or local offense that would have been a federal offense if a circumstance giving rise to federal jurisdiction had existed) that is
  ☐ a crime of violence as defined in 18 U.S.C. §3156(a)(4).
  ☐ an offense for which the maximum sentence is life imprisonment or death.
  ☐ an offense for which a maximum term of imprisonment of ten years or more is prescribed in _____
  _____.*
  ☐ a felony that was committed after the defendant had been convicted of two or more prior federal offenses described in 18 U.S.C. §3142(f)(1)(A)-(C), or comparable state or local offenses.

☐ (2) The offense described in finding (1) was committed while the defendant was on release pending trial for a federal, state or local offense.

☐ (3) A period of not more than five years has elapsed since the (date of conviction) (release of the defendant from imprisonment) for the offense described in finding (1).

☐ (4) Findings Nos. (1), (2) and (3) establish a rebuttable presumption that no condition or combination of conditions will reasonably assure the safety of (an)other person(s) and the community. I further find that the defendant has not rebutted this presumption.

Alternative Findings (A)

☐ (1) There is probable cause to believe that the defendant has committed an offense
  ☐ for which a maximum term of imprisonment of ten years or more is prescribed in _____.
  ☐ under 18 U.S.C. §924(c).

☐ (2) The defendant has not rebutted the presumption established by finding 1 that no condition or combination of conditions will reasonably assure the appearance of the defendant as required and the safety of the community.

Alternative Findings (B)

☐ (1) There is a serious risk that the defendant will not appear.

☐ (2) There is a serious risk that the defendant will endanger the safety of another person or the community.

_____
_____
_____
_____
_____
_____

Part II - Written Statement of Reasons for Detention

I find that the credible testimony and information submitted at the hearing establishes by (clear and convincing evidence) (a preponderance of the evidence) that

_____
_____
_____
_____
_____
_____
_____

Part III - Directions Regarding Detention

The defendant is committed to the custody of the Attorney General or his designated representative for confinement in a corrections facility separate, to the extent practicable, from persons awaiting or serving sentences or being held in custody pending appeal. The defendant shall be afforded a reasonable opportunity for private consultation with defense counsel. On order of a court of the United States or on request of an attorney for the Government, the person in charge of the corrections facility shall deliver the defendant to the United States marshal for the purpose of an appearance in connection with a court proceeding.

Dated: _____

_____
Signature of Judicial Officer

_____
Name and Title of Judicial Officer

_____
*Insert as applicable: (a) Controlled Substances Act (21 U.S.C. §801 et seq.); (b) Controlled Substances Import and Export Act (21 U.S.C. §951 et seq.); or (c) Section 1 of Act of Sept. 15, 1980 (21 U.S.C. §955a).

reached. The defendant had been detained for over ten months, and trial was not scheduled to begin for another five months. See United States v. Millan, 4 F.3d 1038 (2d Cir.1993) (30 months detention not violative of due process); United States v. Gelfuso, 838 F.2d 358 (9th Cir.1988) (ten months detention not violative of due process).

————

United States v. Ramey

602 F.Supp. 821 (E.D.N.C.1985).

ORDER

■ BRITT, CHIEF JUDGE.

Defendant stands indicted in two indictments for (1) two counts of conspiracy to violate the drug laws of the United States, (2) two counts of possession of controlled substances with intent to distribute, and (3) two counts of interstate travel with the intent to carry on an unlawful activity related to controlled substances.

After defendant's arrest, and upon motion of the government pursuant to Section 3142(f) of the Bail Reform Act of 1984, a detention hearing was held before Magistrate Charles K. McCotter, Jr., on 12 February 1985. 18 U.S.C. § 3142(f) (Supp.1984). Finding that ". . . no conditions of release will reasonably assure the appearance of defendant as required and the safety of the community" Magistrate McCotter ordered the defendant to be detained. See id.

Defendant moved the court for a review of the Detention Order of Magistrate McCotter. . . . Consistent with the requirement of 18 U.S.C. § 3145(b) that the motion be determined promptly, a hearing was held before the undersigned district judge at 2 p.m. on 15 February 1985.

Upon motion of a detainee to a district judge for review of a Detention Order of a magistrate it is the duty of the district court to conduct a *de novo* hearing. . . . As the hearing before Magistrate McCotter was tape recorded, the court advised the parties at the beginning of the review hearing that it would rely on the tapes for a review of the evidence presented before Magistrate McCotter and would entertain such additional evidence and argument of counsel as they might desire.

. . .

From the evidence presented at the hearing before Magistrate McCotter and reviewed by the undersigned, the record in the case and the stipulations of the parties, the court makes the following

FINDINGS OF FACT

1. In late 1984, indictment No. 84–49–02–CR–5 was returned against the defendant by the grand jury for the Eastern District of North Carolina. That indictment charged him with (a) conspiracy to violate the drug laws of the United States, an offense punishable by imprisonment up to fifteen years; (b) possession with intent to distribute marijuana, an offense punishable by imprisonment up to fifteen years; and, (c) two counts of unlawful travel in interstate commerce with intent to promote an unlawful business activity involving narcotics and controlled substances, offenses punishable by imprisonment up to five years on each count.

2. In January 1985, indictment No. 85–10–02–CR–5 was returned against the defendant by the grand jury for the Eastern District of North Carolina which charged him with (a) conspiracy to violate the drug laws of the United States, an offense punishable by imprisonment up to fifteen years; and (b) possession with intent to distribute cocaine, an offense punishable by imprisonment up to fifteen years.

3. Defendant was aware that he was a target of an investigation by the grand jury. He employed counsel, Herman Gaskins, Esq., who advised the office of the United States Attorney of his representation sometime during calendar year 1984.

4. The indictments in both of these cases were sealed by a United States magistrate upon motion of the government.

5. Warrants for the arrest of defendant were issued on 30 January 1985. A check by law enforcement officers at his residence and other places normally frequented by him proved to be fruitless as defendant could not be located. Members of his family professed to be unaware of his whereabouts.

6. Defendant voluntarily surrendered to the United States Marshal on 8 February 1985.

7. Defendant is a lifelong resident of Franklin County, North Carolina, and has lived in the same home for the past 23 years. He is married and the father of two adult children, both of whom live in fairly close proximity to defendant. For approximately 24 years defendant operated a Gulf service station in Franklinton, North Carolina.

8. Defendant is the owner of, or financially interested in, two western wear stores in Durham and Raleigh, North Carolina, Big Dukes Western Wear, one of which is operated by his daughter.

9. Defendant's son operates a tire business in Youngsville, North Carolina, a short distance from Franklinton.

10. Defendant has two sisters living in Franklinton, North Carolina.

11. Defendant is a veteran of the United States Army, having served in Korea during the hostilities there. He was honorably discharged upon completion of his tour of duty.

12. Defendant has no criminal record and has no prior arrests.

13. Defendant is in good physical condition except for having high blood pressure, a condition for which he takes medication.

14. Defendant's financial condition is not apparent to the court. Although he has several deeds of trust on his residence he is financially interested in the two western wear stores. His sisters are the owners of some real estate which they are willing to pledge as security for his release on bail.

15. The co-defendant, Douglas Freeman Ross, who has not yet been apprehended, is the reputed leader of an organization which has been dealing in controlled substances for many years, at least as far back as 1978. Since that time defendant has been a close associate of Ross. He is reputed to be second in command. During a period of time when co-defendant Ross was in prison in Florida the defendant was in charge of the local drug organization.

16. Defendant has been observed by at least three witnesses dealing in large quantities of controlled substances, including up to 2 kilos of cocaine, hundreds of pounds of marijuana and hundreds of thousands of quaalude tablets. He has a reputation in the drug community as the man to see if you are interested in transferring drugs.

17. Defendant is, himself, a drug user.

18. The investigation of defendant Ross and others was well known in Franklin County, North Carolina, and surrounding areas. On at least one occasion a witness who had been subpoenaed to testify before the grand jury was confronted by defendant who inquired of the witness what he was going to testify to. The witness was further advised by defendant that he would check back with the witness after his testimony. That witness was not again contacted by defendant. He was, however, contacted by telephone by the co-defendant Ross who threatened to kill the witness.

19. Co-defendant Ross employed a private investigator to interview grand jury witnesses, some of whom were interviewed on the premises of Big Dukes Western Wear.

20. Threats to the safety of one witness who testified before the grand jury were sufficiently serious that the United States Marshal's service approved the witness for the witness protection program.

21. During the process of the investigation some witnesses have been told that if they cooperated with the government they, or members of their families, would be harmed.

Based on the foregoing findings of fact and in accordance with the legal principles discussed above, the court makes the following

CONCLUSIONS OF LAW

A. There is probable cause to believe that defendant has committed offenses under the Controlled Substances Act for which a maximum term of imprisonment of ten years or more is prescribed.

B. A rebuttable presumption has arisen that no condition or combination of conditions will reasonably assure defendant's appearance as required and the safety of the community.

C. Defendant has failed to offer sufficient evidence to rebut the presumption.

D. There is clear and convincing evidence that no condition or combination of conditions will reasonably assure the appearance of defendant as required and the safety of other persons and the community. Although defendant has never been arrested or convicted of any other offense, the statutory presumption is bolstered by evidence from the government, from which the findings of fact were made, that defendant has longstanding ties with the leader of the drug organization, is himself a user of controlled substances and has participated in harassment and intimidation of grand jury witnesses.

E. The detention of defendant prior to trial is required.

IT IS, THEREUPON, ORDERED that defendant remain committed to the custody of the Attorney General, subject to the following provisions:

a. he shall be confined in a corrections facility separate, to the extent practicable, from persons awaiting or serving sentences or being held in custody pending appeal;

b. he shall be afforded reasonable opportunity for private consultation with his counsel; and,

c. on order of a court of the United States or on request of an attorney for the government the person in charge of the corrections facility in which he is confined shall deliver him to a United States Marshal for the purpose of an appearance in connection with a court proceeding.

———

302. Section 3142(f) of the Bail Reform Act provides for a detention hearing at the defendant's first appearance unless the defendant or the attorney for the government seeks a continuance, which "except for good cause" may not be for more than five days if requested by the defendant or three days if requested by the government.

Failure to comply with the prompt hearing provision does not require that the person be released. In United States v. Montalvo-Murillo, 495 U.S. 711 (1990) (6–3), the detention hearing was held 13 days after the defendant's arrest; there had been no request for a waiver of the time limit, no finding of good cause for a continuance, and no objection to the continuance. The Court said that even assuming that the government was responsible for the delay,

AO 98 (Rev. 8/85) Appearance Bond

United States District Court

DISTRICT OF ───────────

UNITED STATES OF AMERICA

V.

APPEARANCE BOND

_____
Defendant

CASE NUMBER:

Non–surety: I, the undersigned defendant acknowledge that I and my . . .
Surety: We, the undersigned, jointly and severally acknowledge that we and our . . .
personal representatives, jointly and severally, are bound to pay to the United States of America the sum of
$_____, and there has been deposited in the Registry of the Court the sum of
$_____ in cash or _____ (describe other security.)

The conditions of this bond are that the defendant _____.
                                                                                    (name)
is to appear before this court and at such other places as the defendant may be required to appear, in accordance with
any and all orders and directions relating to the defendant's appearance in this case, including appearance for violation
of a condition of defendant's release as may be ordered or notified by this court or any other United States district court
to which the defendant may be held to answer or the cause transferred. The defendant is to abide by any judgment
entered in such a matter by surrendering to serve any sentence imposed and obeying any order or direction in
connection with such judgment.

It is agreed and understood that this is a continuing bond (including any proceeding on appeal or review)
which shall continue until such time as the undersigned are exonerated.

If the defendant appears as ordered or notified and otherwise obeys and performs the foregoing conditions of this
bond, then this bond is to be void, but if the defendant fails to obey or perform any of these conditions, payment of the
amount of this bond shall be due forthwith. Forfeiture of this bond for any breach of its conditions may be declared by any
United States district court having cognizance of the above entitled matter at the time of such breach and if the bond if
forfeited and if the forfeiture is not set aside or remitted, judgment may be entered upon motion in such United States
district court against each debtor jointly and severally for the amount above stated, together with interest and costs, and
execution may be issued and payment secured as provided by the Federal Rules of Criminal Procedure and any other
laws of the United States.

This bond is signed on _____ at _____.
                                          Date   Place
Defendant. _____   Address. _____

Surety. _____   Address. _____

Surety. _____   Address. _____

Signed and acknowledged before me on _____
                                                                        Date

_____
                                                        Judicial Officer/Clerk

Approved: _____
                          Judicial Officer

AO 98 (Rev. 8/85)

JUSTIFICATION OF SURETIES

I, the undersigned surety, say that I reside at _____

_____ ; and that my net worth is the sum of

_____ dollars ($ _____).

I further state that

_____
                                              Surety

Sworn to before me and subscribed in my presence on _____
                                                                Date

at _____
                                    Place

_____   _____
       Name and Title   **Signature of Judicial Officer/Clerk**

I, the undersigned surety, state that I reside at _____

_____ ; and that my net worth is the sum of

_____ dollars ($ _____).

I further state that

_____
                                              Surety

Sworn to before me and subscribed in my presence on _____
                                                                Date

at _____
                                    Place

_____   _____
       Name and Title   **Signature of Judicial Officer/Clerk**

Justification Approved: _____
                              Judicial Officer

it was not barred from seeking a detention order. "It is inevitable that, despite the most diligent efforts of the Government and the courts, some errors in the application of the time requirements of § 3142(f) will occur. Detention proceedings take place during the disordered period following arrest. . . . [C]ircumstances such as the involvement of more than one district, doubts about whether the defendant was subject to temporary detention under § 3142(d), and ambiguity in requests for continuances may contribute to a missed deadline for which no real blame can be fixed. In these situations, there is no reason to bestow upon the defendant a windfall and to visit upon the Government and the citizens a severe penalty by mandating release of possibly dangerous defendants every time some deviation from the strictures of § 3142(f) occurs." Id. at 720. "Whatever other remedies may exist for detention without a timely hearing or for conduct that is aggravated or intentional . . . we hold that once the Government discovers that the time limits have expired, it may ask for a prompt detention hearing and make its case to detain based upon the requirements set forth in the statute." Id. at 721.

In United States v. Dominguez, 783 F.2d 702 (7th Cir.1986) the court held that "first appearance" means first appearance in the charging district rather than in the district where the defendant is arrested. It observed: "In some cases, of course, circumstances may make it appropriate to request detention in the arresting district. Nevertheless, we believe that the most informed decisions will almost always be made in the charging district by prosecutors that have supervised the investigations and by courts that will supervise the remaining proceedings. Those officials should always have the option of seeking detention within the statute's limits and according to its procedures." Id. at 705. Were the rule otherwise, the court said, prosecutors in the district where the defendant is arrested would be obliged routinely to request continuances of the detention hearing until information could be obtained from the prosecutor in the charging district.

Section 3142(f) provides that a finding that a person's release would be dangerous to another person or the community "shall be supported by clear and convincing evidence." See, e.g., United States v. Portes, 786 F.2d 758 (7th Cir.1985) (narcotics offenses, threats of reprisals, possession of dangerous weapons, sufficient to support finding); United States v. Delker, 757 F.2d 1390 (3d Cir.1985) (racketeering and extortion offenses, prior convictions for assault, threats of witnesses, sufficient to support finding). Pretrial detention was upheld in United States v. Tortora, 922 F.2d. 880 (1st Cir.1990), over the "mind-boggling" argument that the defendant, a reputed member of an organized crime ring, could pursue his criminal activities from jail and was, therefore, no *more* dangerous if he were released than if he were detained. Id. at 889. Section 3142(e) prescribes certain presumptions of dangerousness, which, the courts have said, shift "the burden of production but not the burden of persuasion to the defendants." United States v. Portes, above, 786 F.2d at 764. The presumptions are "of the so-called 'middle ground' variety; that is, they do not disappear when rebutted, like a 'bursting bubble' presumption, nor do they actually shift the burden of persuasion to the defendant. They are 'rebutted' when the defendant meets a 'burden of production' by coming forward with some evidence that he will not flee or endanger the community if released. Once this burden of production is met, the presumption is 'rebutted'. . . . [T]he rebutted presumption is not erased. Instead it remains in the case as an evidentiary finding militating against release, to be weighed along with other evidence relevant to factors listed in § 3142(g). . . . The burden of persuasion remains with the government once the burden of production is met." *Dominguez*, above, 783 F.2d at 707. See United States v. Perry, 788 F.2d 100 (3d Cir.1986).

In United States v. Carbone, 793 F.2d 559 (3d Cir.1986), construing § 3142(g), the court said that the fact that friends of the defendant had posted a million dollars in property as surety for his appearance was significant evidence to rebut the presumption that he posed a danger to the community. "Although posting a property bond normally goes to the question of defendant's appearance at trial, where the surety takes the form of residential property posted by community members the act of placing the surety is a strong indication that the private sureties are also vouching for defendant's character." Id. at 561. Judge Garth, dissenting, observed that the friends' action indicated their loyalty to the defendant and confidence that he would appear but had no bearing on the question whether there was a danger that he would continue to engage in large-scale drug sales.

The statute does not specify the standard of proof for a finding that a person may not appear as required. The courts have concluded that the standard should be a preponderance of the evidence, as under the prior law. E.g., United States v. Portes, above; United States v. Fortna, 769 F.2d 243 (5th Cir.1985) (sophisticated international narcotics enterprise, vast sums of money, sufficient to support finding); United States v. Motamedi, 767 F.2d 1403 (9th Cir.1985) (finding not supported; bond of $750,000 and other conditions of release imposed).

On various procedural aspects of the detention hearing, see United States v. Perry, above; United States v. Fortna, above; United States v. Delker, above.

When a district court reviews a magistrate's order for release or for detention under § 3145, the court may refer to and rely on evidence presented at the detention hearing. It may, however, conduct a further hearing. The determination of the district court is *de novo*. United States v. Delker, above; see United States v. Portes, above; United States v. Fortna, above. In United States v. Maull, 773 F.2d 1479 (8th Cir.1985), the court held that upon a request by the defendant for review of conditions of release under 18 U.S.C. § 3145(a)(2), the reviewing court may initiate a pretrial detention proceeding in the manner of § 3142(f), on its own motion.

———

On appeal from a release or detention order under § 3145(c), the courts of appeals have applied different standards of review. The largest number

AO 471 (8/85) Order of Temporary Detention

United States District Court

_____ DISTRICT OF _____

UNITED STATES OF AMERICA

V.

ORDER OF TEMPORARY DETENTION TO
PERMIT REVOCATION OF CONDITIONAL
RELEASE, DEPORTATION OR EXCLUSION

_____
Defendant

Case Number:

I find that the defendant

☐ is, and was at the time the alleged offense was committed:

    ☐ on release pending trial for a felony under federal, state, or local law.

    ☐ on release pending imposition or execution of sentence, appeal of sentence or conviction, or completion of sentence, for an offense under federal, state, or local law.

    ☐ on probation or parole for an offense under federal, state, or local law; or

☐ is not a citizen of the United States or lawfully admitted for permanent residence as defined at (8 U.S.C. §1101(a)(20)).

    and I further find that the defendant may

☐ flee, or ☐ pose a danger to another person or the community.

    I accordingly ORDER the detention of the defendant without bail to and including _____,
which is not more than ten days from the date of this Order, excluding Saturdays, Sundays and holidays.

    I further direct the attorney for the Government to notify the appropriate court, probation or parole official, or state or local law enforcement official, or the appropriate official of the Immigration and Naturalization Service so that the custody of the defendant can be transferred and a detainer placed in connection with this case.

    If custody is not transferred by the above date, I direct the production of the defendant before me on that date so that further proceedings may be considered in accordance with the provisions of 18 U.S.C. § 3142.

Date: _____   _____

                                        Judicial Officer

have concluded that the court should accept the factual findings of the court below if they are not plainly erroneous, but should make an "independent determination" of ultimate facts. E.g., United States v. Perry, above; United States v. Portes, above. Other courts have concluded that the determination below should be accepted if not "clearly erroneous," or if "supported by the proceedings below." Cases are collected in *Portes*, above, 786 F.2d at 762.

303. Section 3149 provides that "a person charged with an offense . . . may be arrested by the surety." The only express qualification on the authority to arrest is that the person "shall be delivered promptly to a United States marshal." On the surety's authority to arrest generally, see Kear v. Hilton, 699 F.2d 181 (4th Cir.1983). Kear, a professional bondsman arrested a bail jumper in Canada and brought him back to the United States to face trial in Florida. The surety for whom Kear worked had given a bond in the amount of $137,500 to assure the person's appearance. Canada sought Kear's extradition to Canada on a charge of kidnapping. The court observed: "Professional bondsmen in the United States enjoy extraordinary powers to capture and use force to compel peremptory return of a bail jumper. They may do so not only in the state where the bail was granted, but in other states as well, without resort to public authorities, either the police to effect the arrest or the appropriate state officials to bring about extradition." Id. at 182. Concluding that these powers extend only within the United States, the court held that Kear should be extradited to Canada. See also United States v. Trunko, 189 F.Supp. 559 (E.D.Ark.1960).

———

United States v. Penn

Crim.No. 1434–67 (D.C.Ct.Gen.Sess., Jan. 30, 1968).

■ HALLECK, J.

The Court has before it an application for review of conditions of release pursuant to 18 U.S.C. § 3146(d).2 The defendant has been indicted for robbery in the United States District Court. However, the application has been filed in this Court because the defendant has been committed to jail in default of $5,000 bond first set by this Court on October 23, 1967. When the defendant was arrested, bond was set and the case was continued for two days. On the continued date, another Judge held the preliminary hearing, found probable cause, and held Penn for the action of the Grand Jury.

---

2. The statutory provisions discussed in the opinion preceded enactment of the Bail Reform Act of 1984.

Thereafter, Penn was indicted on November 15, 1967, and from that point the case has been in the U.S. District Court. The Daily Washington Law Reporter, Vol. 96, No. 15, at p. 121, indicates that the case is now on the ready calendar. . . .

The defendant's three month delay in seeking review of conditions of release is unexplained. Nevertheless, this Court must consider it now. . . .

The Metropolitan Police Department Statement of Facts (P.D. Form 163) initially was considered by the Court in setting bond. Therein, it appears that this defendant, and another, were observed by two policemen in the act of committing a yoke robbery, and were promptly apprehended. Property of the victim was recovered from the defendant. The victim identified this defendant at the scene of the offense. Although this defendant is presumed to be innocent of this charge, it is clear that the case against him is very strong, indeed.

At the time bail was set the Court was presented with the usual completed form prepared by the District of Columbia Bail Agency. That Agency was created by an Act of Congress in 1966. See D.C.Code § 23–901 et seq. It is assigned, by statute, a very limited function. It

". . . shall secure pertinent data and provide for any judicial officer in the District of Columbia reports containing verified information concerning any individual with respect to whom a bail determination is to be made." D.C.Code § 23–901.

The Agency is required by § 23–903 to interview any person charged with an offense in the District of Columbia, and thereafter, it

". . . shall seek independent verification of information obtained during the interview, shall secure any such person's prior criminal record which shall be made available by the Metropolitan Police Department, and shall prepare a written report of such information for submission to the appropriate judicial officer."

In addition, the Agency is to provide a copy of such report to the prosecutor and to counsel for the person concerning whom the report is made. At this point the Agency's task is completed, and by law it has no further obligation or responsibility in the matter.

The Report of the President's Commission on Law Enforcement and Administration of Justice, published in February, 1967, examines the problem of pre-trial release in Chapter Five, and concludes that money bail should be imposed only when reasonable alternatives are not available. The report goes on to say such a release procedure presupposes an information-gathering technique that can promptly provide a magistrate with an array of facts about a defendant's history, circumstances, problems and way of life.

The Bail Bond Reform Act of 1966 deals with pre-trial release criteria in Section 3146(b). The judge

". . . shall, on the basis of available information, take into account the nature and circumstances of the offense charged, the weight of the evidence against the accused, the accused's family ties, employment, financial resources, character and mental condition, the length of his residence in the community, his record of convictions, and his record of appearance at court proceedings or of flight to avoid prosecution or failure to appear at court proceedings."

Initially, it should be observed that the District of Columbia Bail Agency is primarily staffed by bright, young, law students who have little or no practical experience. In preparing reports containing verified information for the Court, these young men do very little more than call the home address given by the defendant and speak to someone there in order to determine if the defendant lives there; and thereafter call his employer to determine if the defendant is employed. Verification is, in the vast majority of cases, made either by placing a telephone call or speaking with some person in Court who identifies himself or herself as a relative or a friend of the defendant. For the most part, the reports prepared by the District of Columbia Bail Agency reflect little more than a defendant's current address, the length of time he has lived in the District of Columbia and a brief notation of the name of his employer and the length of time he has been employed. The extent to which the information is, or is not, verified is frequently never disclosed. The information itself is usually of the sketchiest sort. In fact, it has been this Court's experience that in several cases information put in the supposedly verified reports subsequently turns out to be in error. The shortage of personnel, the lack of experience, and the press of time makes the so-called verified report a mere shadow of the report apparently envisaged by the Crime Commission Report. The judge sitting in the Assignment Branch of the Court of General Sessions frequently has over one hundred cases to deal with each day. He must, of necessity, rely upon the Bail Agency, the prosecutor, and defense counsel for information. By and large, very little is forthcoming from those sources. Yet,

> "A determination by the judicial officer is to be made on the basis of 'available information'. The Act does not indicate how the information is to be gathered, but the report suggests that in most instances the information will be supplied by the accused or his attorney. It is imperative that no coercion be brought to bear on the accused when he is requested to supply information." [Analysis of The Bail Reform Act of 1966, Criminal Division, Department of Justice, at p. 15.]

It would seem that the Act contemplates lengthy and extensive investigation of a defendant, possibly coupled with a full hearing where testimony may be elicited. Such investigation takes time—often several days.

> "Since it is the duty of the judicial officer to make a determination concerning the appropriate release condition to be applied to an accused, it would seem that some affirmative effort on the part of such officers is required to insure that necessary information is available at the bail hearing. Therefore, the judicial officer probably has a duty to question the defendant, if there is no available information, in order to obtain the necessary facts. The duty to make a determination should also include an attempt to collect information from the appropriate

Government officials concerning the past criminal history of the defendant. If such request has been made and the information is not immediately available or the defendant is unwilling to give any information, the officer should proceed with his determination on the basis of the available facts." [Id. p. 16]

"The emphasis of the Bail Reform Act is on the careful study of the individual in order to tailor properly release conditions to him. In the first instance a factual inquiry must be made to develop a profile of the accused." [Id. p. 19]

The Bail Agency report in the present case is typically sparse, but better than most. The opening sentence states

"The following VERIFIED INFORMATION is submitted pursuant to PL–519 for use in determining conditions of release under the Bail Reform Act of 1966 (PL 89–456)."

However, the final sentence in the report discloses that the Bail Agency is unable to recommend personal recognizance or other nonfinancial condition of release *because they are unable to verify any of the information.* The report is, therefore, a non-sequitur. The "unverified" verified information discloses an address for the defendant where he supposedly lives with his brother, who is listed as the only family tie in the area. The report states that the defendant has resided in the District of Columbia area for five years, and with his brother for two years. The defendant is listed as unemployed. His method of support is listed as unascertained. Under a heading "prior convictions" there is listed a 1967 charge of assault and 1967 charges of robbery and carrying a dangerous weapon which are "pending in Va". Also listed is a 1967 assault on a police officer and carrying a gun charge. The Metropolitan Police Department criminal record of this defendant does not appear anywhere in the Court papers. Of course, the local police department would have no record of any convictions of a defendant in any other jurisdiction; nor information regarding his status on parole or probation; nor any other pertinent information from other jurisdictions which could be furnished by the F.B.I. but not by the Metropolitan Police Department. The Bail Agency's "unverified" verified report concludes by pointing out the interview was difficult and that the defendant became belligerent during the interview. Although the Report Form provides a place for the signature of the person submitting the report, it is typically unsigned.

The Bail Bond Reform Act of 1966 creates a presumption in favor of release on personal recognizance. It appears that Congress intended that every accused shall be released when at all possible. In the Report submitted by the Committee on the Judiciary of the United States Senate, accompanying the Act, the release provision was summarized.

"In summary, section 3146(a) is intended to require that every person accused of a noncapital offense, as defined in section 3152(2), is presumed entitled to be released pending trial on his own recognizance or upon the execution of an unsecured appearance bond.

Only if factors appear which reasonably suggest that such a procedure will not adequately assure the appearance of the accused may the judicial officer impose one or more of the additional conditions of release enumerated in the bill or utilize 'any other condition deemed reasonably necessary to assure appearance as required.' "
[Senate Report 750, 89th Congrees, 1st session, page 11]

In most cases the Court is placed in an untenable situation. On the one hand the defendant is now presumed to be entitled to release on personal bond, unless factors appear which reasonably suggest that such a procedure would not assure the appearance of the accused at trial. On the other hand, the burden is placed on the Court to justify any condition other than personal bond. In order to do this, the Court must point to reasons why it acts, but because of the totally inadequate information-gathering technique provided for by the statutory scheme the Court is usually without sufficient information to make any informed decision, or to point to reasons for denying personal bond. The less the Judge knows about a defendant, the higher the risk in placing him on personal bond. Yet, the less the Judge knows, the more difficult it is to justify any condition other than personal bond.

The Bail Bond Reform Act also requires, that in the event the Court does not release a defendant on personal bond, it must then consider the alternative conditions seriatim, and find adequate reasons to reject each one, before money bond may be set. The first alternative is to place a prisoner in the custody of an individual or an organization agreeing to supervise him. It is the Court's experience that very few capable persons or qualified organizations are available to supervise defendants. Supervising a defendant requires the exercise of some degree of active control over him, and a regulating of his comings or goings. As soon as the Court explains to a friend, lawyer, family member, minister, or some organization or group that a definite responsibility is involved, more often than not it develops that such persons or groups are unwilling to assume those responsibilities. The typical example is the mother who is willing to sign for custody of her defendant son, but frequently states that she has no control over him. This is usually obvious by reference to his record and indicated work habits, as well as his proclivity for late hours and bad company.

Rejecting third party custody or supervision, the Court must next consider placing restrictions on travel, association, or place of abode of the defendant during his period of release. The greatest difficulty with these provisions is that no practical way exists to assure that the conditions are being complied with. The Bail Agency is charged solely with the duty of interviewing arrested defendants, verifying information and presenting it to the Court to assist in setting bond. The Bail Agency is not required to supervise anybody when they are out on personal bond awaiting trial. In fact, even mailing post cards to defendants reminding them of trial dates is beyond their authority and represents an unauthorized gratuitous act. The probation department is so overworked now it cannot properly supervise its probationers. The police certainly cannot be expected to be baby-sitters in blue for the defendants they have apprehended.

More importantly, there are no penalties provided for failure to comply with conditions of release, nor are there any sanctions that may be applied to any person assuming the task of supervising a defendant if that task is not performed. The Court is, at most, limited to imposing a penalty of thirty days for contempt of court. Contempt power must be used sparingly, and only against deliberate or wilful contemptuous conduct toward the Court. Third party custodians under The Bail Reform Act hardly fit into such a category.

Section 3146(c) requires that upon releasing a defendant pursuant to the Act the judicial officer who authorizes the release "shall inform such person of the penalties applicable to violations of the conditions of his release and shall advise him that a warrant for his arrest will be issued immediately upon any such violation." As a practical matter, the warnings are hollow threats. Penalties are limited or non-existent, and General Sessions rarely issues warrants, and when they are issued practically no one is assigned to serve them. In order for the Judge to advise a defendant of the penalties, reference must be made to § 3150, "Penalties for Failure to Appear." The penalties provided for in that Section apply only to a defendant who "wilfully fails to appear before any court or judicial officer as required." *There is no penalty for anything other than failure to appear before a Court or Judicial Officer.* Therefore, the Court cannot advise a defendant of penalties for violating "conditions of release" since there are no penalties for such violations. Violations of any conditions of release, which may be established by the Court, cannot be punished except by the Court's contempt powers, which are minimal in terms of the problem. Several examples will illustrate the problem. A frequent condition of release is that a defendant be home by a certain hour every evening. Aside from the fact that no one ever reports to the Court when the defendant is late coming home, the Act provides no penalties for such failure. Another frequently used condition is that a defendant report to a police precinct at stated intervals. Police precincts maintain a notebook on the counter for such defendants to sign, indicating the date and time. Persons signing these books are rarely, if ever, required to identify themselves, so that it is possible for any person to sign on behalf of the defendant. Furthermore, the police department does not supervise the persons who are required to sign in, nor indeed do the police ascertain if these persons actually did sign in as frequently as required. Finally, no penalties exist if the defendant does not report regularly. In short, while the act contemplates that Judges will go to great lengths to establish a variety of conditions of release other than money bail, the act provides no method of enforcement and no penalty for violation of such conditions of release. The only penalties provided for are the penalties for wilful failure to appear before any Court or Judicial Officer *as required.*

Added to the above difficulties are the high rate of failures to appear by persons on personal bond, coupled with the number of offenses committed by persons out on personal bond. No one has accurate figures on these two groups, although some estimates run into the thousands. All of these things must necessarily be considered by this Court when it is called upon to review a money bond previously set and to consider release of the defendant on personal bond. Of course, danger to the community cannot be considered at all. If a professional criminal of demonstrated dangerousness has family ties, a job, and a good record of appearing for trial, he must be let out on personal bond to continue to prey upon innocent citizens while the courts take longer than a year to bring him to trial. When the Bail Reform Act was being considered, Congress recognized this serious problem . . . .

This defendant was caught in the act of a yoke robbery. The "presumption of innocence" cannot wipe out this simple fact when the Court comes to considering the problem of bail. This Court knows full well that if a professional bondsman stands to lose $5,000 in the event this defendant disappears, the likelihood of his disappearing for any period of time is remote. The bondsman will do a better job of keeping track of his investment than will all of the other overworked and understaffed agencies operating under The Bail Reform Act who have no personal or financial interest in the outcome of the matter.

The Court set a money bond initially because the defendant does not appear to have adequate family ties in the community, nor a stable work record. His reported criminal record makes him appear to be untrustworthy, or to put it another way, his "character" appears to be poor. Most importantly, anything short of money bond would be at best impractical and nonenforceable. No reliable person or organization has indicated a willingness to supervise him. The delay in seeking a review of conditions of release has rendered obsolete the little unverified information which was originally presented by the Bail Agency. None of the information presented in his application for review of conditions of release bespeaks a modification of the terms of bond. The defendant has presented nothing new or of value in seeking release on personal bond. Although the drafters of The Bail Reform Act would seem to want everyone out on personal bond, the decision is still one addressed to judicial discretion. A court owes an obligation to society, to its own processes, and to the practical integrity of the judicial system, as well as to defendants.

For the foregoing reasons the Court declines to alter the conditions of release previously imposed.[3]

---

304. "A trial judge indisputably has broad powers to ensure the orderly and expeditious progress of a trial. For this purpose, he has the power to revoke bail and to remit the defendant to custody. But this power must be

[3] It was subsequently ordered that Penn be permitted to deposit 10% of the amount of bail instead of posting bond with sureties. The deposit was not made. On May 28, 1968, Penn pleaded guilty and was sentenced to imprisonment for one to three years.

exercised with circumspection. It may be invoked only when and to the extent justified by danger which the defendant's conduct presents or by danger of significant interference with the progress or order of the trial." Bitter v. United States, 389 U.S. 15, 16 (1967). The Court concluded that an order committing the defendant because of "a single, brief incident of tardiness" was unjustified. Id. at 17. See United States v. Bentvena, 288 F.2d 442 (2d Cir.1961), in which the court of appeals upheld an order of the district court revoking the defendants' bail and remanding them to custody until the termination of their trial. The court observed that "the dangers of releasing a defendant on bail during the course of a trial are substantially greater than those existing before trial," and said that "under all the circumstances of the case, especially a succession of misadventures which have already caused numerous delays and adjournments in the presentation of the evidence, the order of the trial judge was a proper exercise of discretion for the purpose of ensuring the orderly completion of the trial." Id. at 444, 445. The defendants' subsequent application for bail to Justice Harlan was similarly denied. Fernandez v. United States, 81 S.Ct. 642 (1961).

For cases in which the defendant contended unsuccessfully that his detention before trial interfered with the preparation of his defense, see Hodgdon v. United States, 365 F.2d 679, 686–87 (8th Cir.1966); United States ex rel. Hyde v. McMann, 263 F.2d 940 (2d Cir.1959).

Even though a defendant may not be able to show special prejudice from detention before or during trial, there is considerable evidence that in general defendants who are released on bail fare better at trial (and, if convicted, at sentencing) than those who are detained. Among the explanations are the detained defendant's inability to contribute money and labor to investigations for his defense; his inability to locate witnesses and evidence peculiarly accessible to him; difficulties of contact with counsel, who must visit him in inadequate jail facilities during specified hours; and the impact on judge and jury of "prison pallor" and the demeanor that a period of detention in jail may produce. See, e.g., D. Freed & P. Wald, Bail in the United States: 1964, pp. 45–48; Foote, "The Coming Constitutional Crisis in Bail: II," 113 U.Pa.L.Rev. 1125, 1137–51 (1965); Wald, "Pretrial Detention and Ultimate Freedom: A Statistical Study, Foreword" 39 N.Y.U.L.Rev. 631 (1964).

———

Bell v. Wolfish

441 U.S. 520, 99 S.Ct. 1861, 60 L.Ed.2d 447 (1979).

■ MR. JUSTICE REHNQUIST delivered the opinion of the Court.

Over the past five Terms, this Court has in several decisions considered constitutional challenges to prison conditions or practices by convicted prisoners. This case requires us to examine the constitutional rights of pretrial detainees—those persons who have been charged with a crime but who have not yet been tried on the charge. The parties concede that to ensure their presence at trial, these persons legitimately may be incarcerated by the Government prior to a determination of their guilt or innocence . . . and it is the scope of their rights during this period of confinement prior to trial that is the primary focus of this case.

This lawsuit was brought as a class action in the United States District Court for the Southern District of New York to challenge numerous conditions of confinement and practices at the Metropolitan Correctional Center (MCC), a federally operated short-term custodial facility in New York City designed primarily to house pretrial detainees. The District Court, in the words of the Court of Appeals for the Second Circuit, "intervened broadly into almost every facet of the institution" and enjoined no fewer than 20 MCC practices on constitutional and statutory grounds. The Court of Appeals largely affirmed the District Court's constitutional rulings and in the process held that under the Due Process Clause of the Fifth Amendment, pretrial detainees may "be subjected to only those 'restrictions and privations' which 'inhere in their confinement itself or which are justified by compelling necessities of jail administration.'" Wolfish v. Levi, 573 F.2d 118, 124 (1978), quoting Rhem v. Malcolm, 507 F.2d 333, 336 (CA2 1974). We granted certiorari to consider the important constitutional questions raised by these decisions and to resolve an apparent conflict among the Circuits. . . . We now reverse.

I

The MCC was constructed in 1975 to replace the converted waterfront garage on West Street that had served as New York City's federal jail since 1928. It is located adjacent to the Foley Square federal courthouse and has as its primary objective the housing of persons who are being detained in custody prior to trial for federal criminal offenses in the United States District Courts for the Southern and Eastern Districts of New York and for the District of New Jersey. Under the Bail Reform Act, 18 U.S.C. § 3146, a person in the federal system is committed to a detention facility only because no other less drastic means can reasonably ensure his presence at trial. In addition to pretrial detainees, the MCC also houses some convicted inmates who are awaiting sentencing or transportation to federal prison or who are serving generally relatively short sentences in a service capacity at the MCC, convicted prisoners who have been lodged at the facility under writs of habeas corpus *ad prosequendum* or *ad testificandum* issued to ensure their presence at upcoming trials, witnesses in protective custody, and persons incarcerated for contempt.[4]

---

4. This group of nondetainees may comprise, on a daily basis, between 40% and 60% of the MCC population. . . . Prior to the District Court's order, 50% of all MCC inmates spent less than 30 days at the facility and 73% less than 60 days. . . . However, of the unsentenced detainees, over half spent less than 10 days at the MCC, three-quarters were released within a month and more than 85% were released within 60 days . . . .

The MCC differs markedly from the familiar image of a jail; there are no barred cells, dank, colorless corridors, or clanging steel gates. It was intended to include the most advanced and innovative features of modern design of detention facilities. As the Court of Appeals stated: "[I]t represented the architectural embodiment of the best and most progressive penological planning." 573 F.2d, at 121. The key design element of the 12-story structure is the "modular" or "unit" concept, whereby each floor designed to house inmates has one or two largely self-contained residential units that replace the traditional cellblock jail construction. Each unit in turn has several clusters or corridors of private rooms or dormitories radiating from a central 2-story "multipurpose" or common room, to which each inmate has free access approximately 16 hours a day. Because our analysis does not turn on the particulars of the MCC concept or design, we need not discuss them further.

When the MCC opened in August 1975, the planned capacity was 449 inmates, an increase of 50% over the former West Street facility. . . . Despite some dormitory accommodations, the MCC was designed primarily to house these inmates in 389 rooms, which originally were intended for single occupancy. While the MCC was under construction, however, the number of persons committed to pretrial detention began to rise at an "unprecedented" rate. . . . The Bureau of Prisons took several steps to accommodate this unexpected flow of persons assigned to the facility, but despite these efforts, the inmate population at the MCC rose above its planned capacity within a short time after its opening. To provide sleeping space for this increased population, the MCC replaced the single bunks in many of the individual rooms and dormitories with double bunks. Also, each week some newly arrived inmates had to sleep on cots in the common areas until they could be transferred to residential rooms as space became available. . . .

On November 28, 1975, less than four months after the MCC had opened, the named respondents initiated this action by filing in the District Court a petition for a writ of habeas corpus. The District Court certified the case as a class action on behalf of all persons confined at the MCC, pretrial detainees and sentenced prisoners alike. The petition served up a veritable potpourri of complaints that implicated virtually every facet of the institution's conditions and practices. Respondents charged, *inter alia*, that they had been deprived of their statutory and constitutional rights because of overcrowded conditions, undue length of confinement, improper searches, inadequate recreational, educational, and employment opportunities, insufficient staff, and objectionable restrictions on the purchase and receipt of personal items and books.

In two opinions and a series of orders, the District Court enjoined numerous MCC practices and conditions. With respect to pretrial detainees, the court held that because they are "presumed to be innocent and held only to ensure their presence at trial, 'any deprivation or restriction of . . . rights beyond those which are necessary for confinement alone, must be justified by a compelling necessity.'" United States ex rel. Wolfish v. Levi, 439 F.Supp. 114, 124 (1977), quoting Detainees of Brooklyn House of Detention v.

Malcolm, 520 F.2d 392, 397 (CA2 1975). And while acknowledging that the rights of sentenced inmates are to be measured by the different standard of the Eighth Amendment, the court declared that to house "an inferior minority of persons . . . in ways found unconstitutional for the rest" would amount to cruel and unusual punishment. United States ex rel. Wolfish v. United States, 428 F.Supp. 333, 339 (1977).

Applying these standards on cross-motions for partial summary judgment, the District Court enjoined the practice of housing two inmates in the individual rooms and prohibited enforcement of the so-called "publisher-only" rule, which at the time of the court's ruling prohibited the receipt of all books and magazines mailed from outside the MCC except those sent directly from a publisher or a book club. After a trial on the remaining issues, the District Court enjoined, *inter alia*, the doubling of capacity in the dormitory areas, the use of the common rooms to provide temporary sleeping accommodations, the prohibition against inmates' receipt of packages containing food and items of personal property, and the practice of requiring inmates to expose their body cavities for visual inspection following contact visits. The court also granted relief in favor of pretrial detainees, but not convicted inmates, with respect to the requirement that detainees remain outside their rooms during routine inspections by MCC officials.

The Court of Appeals largely affirmed the District Court's rulings, although it rejected that court's Eighth Amendment analysis of conditions of confinement for convicted prisoners because the "parameters of judicial intervention into . . . conditions . . . for sentenced prisoners are more restrictive than in the case of pretrial detainees." 573 F.2d, at 125. Accordingly, the court remanded the matter to the District Court for it to determine whether the housing for sentenced inmates at the MCC was constitutionally "adequate." But the Court of Appeals approved the due process standard employed by the District Court in enjoining the conditions of pretrial confinement. It therefore held that the MCC had failed to make a showing of "compelling necessity" sufficient to justify housing two pretrial detainees in the individual rooms. Id., at 126–127. And for purposes of our review (since petitioners challenge only some of the Court of Appeals' rulings), the court affirmed the District Court's granting of relief against the "publisher-only" rule, the practice of conducting body-cavity searches after contact visits, the prohibition against receipt of packages of food and personal items from outside the institution, and the requirement that detainees remain outside their rooms during routine searches of the rooms by MCC officials. . . .

II

As a first step in our decision, we shall address "double-bunking" as it is referred to by the parties, since it is a condition of confinement that is alleged only to deprive pretrial detainees of their liberty without due process of law in contravention of the Fifth Amendment. We will treat in order the Court of Appeals' standard of review, the analysis which we believe the Court of Appeals should have employed, and the conclusions to which our analysis leads us in the case of "double-bunking."

A

The Court of Appeals did not dispute that the Government may permissibly incarcerate a person charged with a crime but not yet convicted to ensure his presence at trial. However, reasoning from the "premise that an individual is to be treated as innocent until proven guilty," the court concluded that pretrial detainees retain the "rights afforded unincarcerated individuals," and that therefore it is not sufficient that the conditions of confinement for pretrial detainees "merely comport with contemporary standards of decency prescribed by the cruel and unusual punishment clause of the eighth amendment." 573 F.2d, at 124. Rather, the court held, the Due Process Clause requires that pretrial detainees "be subjected to only those 'restrictions and privations' which 'inhere in their confinement itself or which are justified by compelling necessities of jail administration.' " Ibid., quoting Rhem v. Malcolm, 507 F.2d, at 336. Under the Court of Appeals' "compelling necessity" standard, "deprivation of the rights of detainees cannot be justified by the cries of fiscal necessity, . . . administrative convenience, . . . or by the cold comfort that conditions in other jails are worse." 573 F.2d, at 124. The court acknowledged, however, that it could not "ignore" our admonition in Procunier v. Martinez, 416 U.S. 396, 405 (1974), that "courts are ill equipped to deal with the increasingly urgent problems of prison administration," and concluded that it would "not [be] wise for [it] to second-guess the expert administrators on matters on which they are better informed." 573 F.2d, at 124.

Our fundamental disagreement with the Court of Appeals is that we fail to find a source in the Constitution for its compelling-necessity standard. Both the Court of Appeals and the District Court seem to have relied on the "presumption of innocence" as the source of the detainee's substantive right to be free from conditions of confinement that are not justified by compelling necessity. . . . But the presumption of innocence provides no support for such a rule.

The presumption of innocence is a doctrine that allocates the burden of proof in criminal trials; it also may serve as an admonishment to the jury to judge an accused's guilt or innocence solely on the evidence adduced at trial and not on the basis of suspicions that may arise from the fact of his arrest, indictment, or custody, or from other matters not introduced as proof at trial. It is "an inaccurate, shorthand description of the right of the accused to 'remain inactive and secure, until the prosecution has taken up its burden and produced evidence and effected persuasion; . . .' an 'assumption' that is indulged in the absence of contrary evidence." Taylor v. Kentucky, [436 U.S. 478 (1978)], at 484 n. 12. Without question, the presumption of innocence plays an important role in our criminal justice system. . . . But it has no application to a determination of the rights of a pretrial detainee during confinement before his trial has even begun.

The Court of Appeals also relied on what it termed the "indisputable rudiments of due process" in fashioning its compelling-necessity test. We do not doubt that the Due Process Clause protects a detainee from certain conditions and restrictions of pretrial detainment. . . . Nonetheless, that Clause provides no basis for application of a compelling-necessity standard to conditions of pretrial confinement that are not alleged to infringe any other, more specific guarantee of the Constitution.

It is important to focus on what is at issue here. We are not concerned with the initial decision to detain an accused and the curtailment of liberty that such a decision necessarily entails. . . . Neither respondents nor the courts below question that the Government may permissibly detain a person suspected of committing a crime prior to a formal adjudication of guilt. . . . Nor do they doubt that the Government has a substantial interest in ensuring that persons accused of crimes are available for trials and, ultimately, for service of their sentences, or that confinement of such persons pending trial is a legitimate means of furthering that interest. . . . Instead, what *is* at issue when an aspect of pretrial detention that is not alleged to violate any express guarantee of the Constitution is challenged, is the detainee's right to be free from punishment . . . and his understandable desire to be as comfortable as possible during his confinement, both of which may conceivably coalesce at some point. It seems clear that the Court of Appeals did not rely on the detainee's right to be free from punishment, but even if it had that right does not warrant adoption of that court's compelling-necessity test. . . . And to the extent the court relied on the detainee's desire to be free from discomfort, it suffices to say that this desire simply does not rise to the level of those fundamental liberty interests delineated in [other] cases . . . .

B

In evaluating the constitutionality of conditions or restrictions of pretrial detention that implicate only the protection against deprivation of liberty without due process of law, we think that the proper inquiry is whether those conditions amount to punishment of the detainee. For under the Due Process Clause, a detainee may not be punished prior to an adjudication of guilt in accordance with due process of law. . . .

Not every disability imposed during pretrial detention amounts to "punishment" in the constitutional sense, however. Once the Government has exercised its conceded authority to detain a person pending trial, it obviously is entitled to employ devices that are calculated to effectuate this detention. Traditionally, this has meant confinement in a facility which, no matter how modern or how antiquated, results in restricting the movement of a detainee in a manner in which he would not be restricted if he simply were free to walk the streets pending trial. Whether it be called a jail, a prison, or a custodial center, the purpose of the facility is to detain. Loss of freedom of choice and privacy are inherent incidents of confinement in such a facility. And the fact that such detention interferes with the detainee's understandable desire to live as comfortably as possible and with as little restraint as possible during confinement does not convert the conditions or restrictions of detention into "punishment."

This Court has recognized a distinction between punitive measures that may not constitutionally be imposed prior to a determination of guilt and regulatory restraints that may. . . . In Kennedy v. Mendoza-Martinez, [372 U.S. 144 (1963)], the Court examined the automatic forfeiture-of-citizenship provisions of the immigration laws to determine whether that sanction amounted to punishment or a mere regulatory restraint. While it is all but impossible to compress the distinction into a sentence or a paragraph, the Court there described the tests traditionally applied to determine whether a governmental act is punitive in nature:

> "Whether the sanction involves an affirmative disability or restraint, whether it has historically been regarded as a punishment, whether it comes into play only on a finding of scienter, whether its operation will promote the traditional aims of punishment—retribution and deterrence, whether the behavior to which it applies is already a crime, whether an alternative purpose to which it may rationally be connected is assignable for it, and whether it appears excessive in relation to the alternative purpose assigned are all relevant to the inquiry, and may often point in differing directions." 372 U.S., at 168–169 (footnotes omitted).

Because forfeiture of citizenship traditionally had been considered punishment and the legislative history of the forfeiture provisions "conclusively" showed that the measure was intended to be punitive, the Court held that forfeiture of citizenship in such circumstances constituted punishment that could not constitutionally be imposed without due process of law. Id., at 167–170, 186.

The factors identified in *Mendoza-Martinez* provide useful guideposts in determining whether particular restrictions and conditions accompanying pretrial detention amount to punishment in the constitutional sense of that word. A court must decide whether the disability is imposed for the purpose of punishment or whether it is but an incident of some other legitimate governmental purpose. . . . Absent a showing of an expressed intent to punish on the part of detention facility officials, that determination generally will turn on "whether an alternative purpose to which [the restriction] may rationally be connected is assignable for it, and whether it appears excessive in relation to the alternative purpose assigned [to it]." *Kennedy v. Mendoza-Martinez*, supra, at 168–169 . . . . Thus, if a particular condition or restriction of pretrial detention is reasonably related to a legitimate governmental objective, it does not, without more, amount to "punishment."[5] Conversely, if a restriction or condition is not reasonably related

---

5. This is not to say that the officials of a detention facility can justify punishment. They cannot. It is simply to say that in the absence of a showing of intent to punish, a court must look to see if a particular restriction or condition, which may on its face appear to be punishment, is instead but an incident of a legitimate nonpunitive governmental objective. . . . Retribution and deterrence are not legitimate nonpunitive governmental objectives. . . . Conversely, loading a detainee with chains and shackles and throwing him in a dungeon may ensure his presence at trial and preserve the security of the institution. But it would be difficult to conceive of a situation where conditions so harsh, employed to achieve objectives that could be accomplished in so many alternative and less harsh methods, would not support a conclusion that the purpose for which they were imposed was to punish.

to a legitimate goal—if it is arbitrary or purposeless—a court permissibly may infer that the purpose of the governmental action is punishment that may not constitutionally be inflicted upon detainees *qua* detainees. . . . Courts must be mindful that these inquiries spring from constitutional requirements and that judicial answers to them must reflect that fact rather than a court's idea of how best to operate a detention facility. . . .

One further point requires discussion. The petitioners assert, and respondents concede, that the "essential objective of pretrial confinement is to insure the detainees' presence at trial." Brief for Petitioners 43; see Brief for Respondents 33. While this interest undoubtedly justifies the original decision to confine an individual in some manner, we do not accept respondents' argument that the Government's interest in ensuring a detainee's presence at trial is the *only* objective that may justify restraints and conditions once the decision is lawfully made to confine a person. . . . The Government also has legitimate interests that stem from its need to manage the facility in which the individual is detained. These legitimate operational concerns may require administrative measures that go beyond those that are, strictly speaking, necessary to ensure that the detainee shows up at trial. For example, the Government must be able to take steps to maintain security and order at the institution and make certain no weapons or illicit drugs reach detainees. Restraints that are reasonably related to the institution's interest in maintaining jail security do not, without more, constitute unconstitutional punishment, even if they are discomforting and are restrictions that the detainee would not have experienced had he been released while awaiting trial. We need not here attempt to detail the precise extent of the legitimate governmental interests that may justify conditions or restrictions of pretrial detention. It is enough simply to recognize that in addition to ensuring the detainees' presence at trial, the effective management of the detention facility once the individual is confined is a valid objective that may justify imposition of conditions and restrictions of pretrial detention and dispel any inference that such restrictions are intended as punishment.[6]

C

Judged by this analysis, respondents' claim that "double-bunking" violated their due process rights fails. Neither the District Court nor the Court of Appeals intimated that it considered "double-bunking" to constitute punishment; instead, they found that it contravened the compelling-necessity test, which today we reject. On this record, we are convinced as a matter of law that "double-bunking" as practiced at the MCC did not amount to pun-

---

6. In determining whether restrictions or conditions are reasonably related to the Government's interest in maintaining security and order and operating the institution in a manageable fashion, courts must heed our warning that "[s]uch considerations are peculiarly within the province and profes- sional expertise of corrections officials, and, in the absence of substantial evidence in the record to indicate that the officials have exaggerated their response to these considerations, courts should ordinarily defer to their expert judgment in such matters." Pell v. Procunier, 417 U.S. [817 (1974)], at 827.

ishment and did not, therefore, violate respondents' rights under the Due Process Clause of the Fifth Amendment.

Each of the rooms at the MCC that house pretrial detainees has a total floor space of approximately 75 square feet. Each of them designated for "double-bunking," ... contains a double bunkbed, certain other items of furniture, a wash basin, and an uncovered toilet. Inmates generally are locked into their rooms from 11 p.m. to 6:30 a.m. and for brief periods during the afternoon and evening head counts. During the rest of the day, they may move about freely between their rooms and the common areas.

Based on affidavits and a personal visit to the facility, the District Court concluded that the practice of "double-bunking" was unconstitutional. The court relied on two factors for its conclusion: (1) the fact that the rooms were designed to house only one inmate ... ; and (2) its judgment that confining two persons in one room or cell of this size constituted a "fundamental denia[l] of decency, privacy, personal security, and, simply, civilized humanity. . . ." Id., at 339. The Court of Appeals agreed with the District Court. In response to petitioners' arguments that the rooms at the MCC were larger and more pleasant than the cells involved in the cases relied on by the District Court, the Court of Appeals stated:

> "[W]e find the lack of privacy inherent in double-celling in rooms intended for one individual a far more compelling consideration than a comparison of square footage or the substitution of doors for bars, carpet for concrete, or windows for walls. The government has simply failed to show any substantial justification for double-celling." 573 F.2d, at 127.

We disagree with both the District Court and the Court of Appeals that there is some sort of "one man, one cell" principle lurking in the Due Process Clause of the Fifth Amendment. While confining a given number of people in a given amount of space in such a manner as to cause them to endure genuine privations and hardship over an extended period of time might raise serious questions under the Due Process Clause as to whether those conditions amounted to punishment, nothing even approaching such hardship is shown by this record.[7]

Detainees are required to spend only seven or eight hours each day in their rooms, during most or all of which they presumably are sleeping. The rooms provide more than adequate space for sleeping. During the remainder of the time, the detainees are free to move between their rooms and the

---

7. Respondents seem to argue that "double-bunking" was unreasonable because petitioners were able to comply with the District Court's order forbidding "double-bunking" and still accommodate the increased numbers of detainees simply by transferring all but a handful of sentenced inmates who had been assigned to the MCC for the purpose of performing certain services and by committing those tasks to detainees.

... That petitioners were able to comply with the District Court's order in this fashion does not mean that petitioners' chosen method of coping with the increased inmate population—"double-bunking"—was unreasonable. Governmental action does not have to be the only alternative or even the best alternative for it to be reasonable, to say nothing of constitutional. . . .

common area. While "double-bunking" may have taxed some of the equipment or particular facilities in certain of the common areas . . . this does not mean that the conditions at the MCC failed to meet the standards required by the Constitution. Our conclusion in this regard is further buttressed by the detainees' length of stay at the MCC. . . . Nearly all of the detainees are released within 60 days. . . . We simply do not believe that requiring a detainee to share toilet facilities and this admittedly rather small sleeping place with another person for generally a maximum period of 60 days violates the Constitution.

III

Respondents also challenged certain MCC restrictions and practices that were designed to promote security and order at the facility on the ground that these restrictions violated the Due Process Clause of the Fifth Amendment, and certain other constitutional guarantees, such as the First and Fourth Amendments. The Court of Appeals seemed to approach the challenges to security restrictions in a fashion different from the other contested conditions and restrictions. It stated that "once it has been determined that the mere fact of confinement of the detainee justifies the restrictions, the institution must be permitted to use reasonable means to insure that its legitimate interests in security are safeguarded." 573 F.2d, at 124. The court might disagree with the choice of means to effectuate those interests, but it should not "second-guess the expert administrators on matters on which they are better informed. . . . Concern with minutiae of prison administration can only distract the court from detached consideration of the one overriding question presented to it: does the practice or condition violate the Constitution?" Id., at 124–125. Nonetheless, the court affirmed the District Court's injunction against several security restrictions. The court rejected the arguments of petitioners that these practices served the MCC's interest in security and order and held that the practices were unjustified interferences with the retained constitutional rights of *both* detainees and convicted inmates. . . . In our view, the Court of Appeals failed to heed its own admonition not to "second-guess" prison administrators.

Our cases have established several general principles that inform our evaluation of the constitutionality of the restrictions at issue. First, we have held that convicted prisoners do not forfeit all constitutional protections by reason of their conviction and confinement in prison. . . . *A fortiori*, pretrial detainees, who have not been convicted of any crimes, retain at least those constitutional rights that we have held are enjoyed by convicted prisoners.

But our cases also have insisted on a second proposition: simply because prison inmates retain certain constitutional rights does not mean that these rights are not subject to restrictions and limitations. . . . This principle applies equally to pretrial detainees and convicted prisoners. A detainee simply does not possess the full range of freedoms of an unincarcerated individual.

Third, maintaining institutional security and preserving internal order and discipline are essential goals that may require limitation or retraction of the retained constitutional rights of both convicted prisoners and pretrial detainees. . . . Prison officials must be free to take appropriate action to ensure the safety of inmates and corrections personnel and to prevent escape or unauthorized entry. Accordingly, we have held that even when an institutional restriction infringes a specific constitutional guarantee, such as the First Amendment, the practice must be evaluated in the light of the central objective of prison administration, safeguarding institutional security. . . .

Finally, as the Court of Appeals correctly acknowledged, the problems that arise in the day-to-day operation of a corrections facility are not susceptible of easy solutions. Prison administrators therefore should be accorded wide-ranging deference in the adoption and execution of policies and practices that in their judgment are needed to preserve internal order and discipline and to maintain institutional security. . . . "Such considerations are peculiarly within the province and professional expertise of corrections officials, and, in the absence of substantial evidence in the record to indicate that the officials have exaggerated their response to these considerations, courts should ordinarily defer to their expert judgment in such matters." Pell v. Procunier, 417 U.S., at 827. We further observe that, on occasion, prison administrators may be "experts" only by Act of Congress or of a state legislature. But judicial deference is accorded not merely because the administrator ordinarily will, as a matter of fact in a particular case, have a better grasp of his domain than the reviewing judge, but also because the operation of our correctional facilities is peculiarly the province of the Legislative and Executive Branches of our Government, not the Judicial. . . . With these teachings of our cases in mind, we turn to an examination of the MCC security practices that are alleged to violate the Constitution.

A

At the time of the lower courts' decisions, the Bureau of Prisons' "publisher-only" rule, which applies to all Bureau facilities, permitted inmates to receive books and magazines from outside the institution only if the materials were mailed directly from the publisher or a book club. . . . The warden of the MCC stated in an affidavit that "serious" security and administrative problems were caused when bound items were received by inmates from unidentified sources outside the facility. App. 24. He noted that in order to make a "proper and thorough" inspection of such items, prison officials would have to remove the covers of hardback books and to leaf through every page of all books and magazines to ensure that drugs, money, weapons, or other contraband were not secreted in the material. "This search process would take a substantial and inordinate amount of available staff time." Ibid. However, "there is relatively little risk that material received directly from a publisher or book club would contain contraband, and therefore, the security problems are significantly reduced without a drastic drain on staff resources." Ibid.

The Court of Appeals rejected these security and administrative justifications and affirmed the District Court's order enjoining enforcement of the "publisher-only" rule at the MCC. The Court of Appeals held that the rule "severely and impermissibly restricts the reading material available to inmates" and therefore violates their First Amendment and due process rights. 573 F.2d, at 130.

It is desirable at this point to place in focus the precise question that now is before this Court. Subsequent to the decision of the Court of Appeals, the Bureau of Prisons amended its "publisher-only" rule to permit the receipt of books and magazines from bookstores as well as publishers and book clubs. . . . In addition, petitioners have informed the Court that the Bureau proposes to amend the rule further to allow receipt of paperback books, magazines, and other soft-covered materials from any source. . . . The Bureau regards hardback books as the "more dangerous source of risk to institutional security," however, and intends to retain the prohibition against receipt of hardback books unless they are mailed directly from publishers, book clubs, or bookstores. . . . Accordingly, petitioners request this Court to review the District Court's injunction only to the extent it enjoins petitioners from prohibiting receipt of hard-cover books that are not mailed directly from publishers, book clubs, or bookstores. . . .

We conclude that a prohibition against receipt of hardback books unless mailed directly from publishers, book clubs, or bookstores does not violate the First Amendment rights of MCC inmates. That limited restriction is a rational response by prison officials to an obvious security problem. It hardly needs to be emphasized that hardback books are especially serviceable for smuggling contraband into an institution; money, drugs, and weapons easily may be secreted in the bindings. . . . They also are difficult to search effectively. There is simply no evidence in the record to indicate that MCC officials have exaggerated their response to this security problem and to the administrative difficulties posed by the necessity of carefully inspecting each book mailed from unidentified sources. Therefore, the considered judgment of these experts must control in the absence of prohibitions far more sweeping than those involved here. . . .

Our conclusion that this limited restriction on receipt of hardback books does not infringe the First Amendment rights of MCC inmates is influenced by several other factors. The rule operates in a neutral fashion, without regard to the content of the expression. . . . And there are alternative means of obtaining reading material that have not been shown to be burdensome or insufficient. . . . The restriction, as it is now before us, allows soft-bound books and magazines to be received from any source and hardback books to be received from publishers, bookstores, and book clubs. In addition, the MCC has a "relatively large" library for use by inmates. . . . To the limited extent the rule might possibly increase the cost of obtaining published materials, this Court has held that where "other avenues" remain available for the receipt of materials by inmates, the loss of "cost advantages does not fundamentally implicate *free speech* values." See Jones v. North Carolina Prisoners' Labor Union, [433 U.S. 119 (1977)] at 130–131. We are also influenced in our decision by the fact that the rule's impact on pretrial detainees is limited to a maximum period of approximately 60 days.

. . . In sum, considering all the circumstances, we view the rule, as we now find it, to be a "reasonable 'time, place and manner' regulatio[n that is] necessary to further significant governmental interests. . . ." Grayned v. City of Rockford, 408 U.S. 104, 115 (1972) . . .

B

Inmates at the MCC were not permitted to receive packages from outside the facility containing items of food or personal property, except for one package of food at Christmas. This rule was justified by MCC officials on three grounds. First, officials testified to "serious" security problems that arise from the introduction of such packages into the institution, the "traditional file in the cake kind of situation" as well as the concealment of drugs "in heels of shoes [and] seams of clothing." App. 80; see id., at 24, 84–85. As in the case of the "publisher-only" rule, the warden testified that if such packages were allowed, the inspection process necessary to ensure the security of the institution would require a "substantial and inordinate amount of available staff time." Id., at 24. Second, officials were concerned that the introduction of personal property into the facility would increase the risk of thefts, gambling, and inmate conflicts, the "age-old problem of you have it and I don't." Id., at 80; see id., at 85. Finally, they noted storage and sanitary problems that would result from inmates' receipt of food packages. . . . Inmates are permitted, however, to purchase certain items of food and personal property from the MCC commissary.

The District Court dismissed these justifications as "dire predictions." It was unconvinced by the asserted security problems because other institutions allow greater ownership of personal property and receipt of packages than does the MCC. And because the MCC permitted inmates to purchase items in the commissary, the court could not accept official fears of increased theft, gambling, or conflicts if packages were allowed. Finally, it believed that sanitation could be assured by proper housekeeping regulations. Accordingly, it ordered the MCC to promulgate regulations to permit receipt of at least items of the kind that are available in the commissary. . . . The Court of Appeals accepted the District Court's analysis and affirmed, although it noted that the MCC could place a ceiling on the permissible dollar value of goods received and restrict the number of packages.

Neither the District Court nor the Court of Appeals identified which provision of the Constitution was violated by this MCC restriction. We assume, for present purposes, that their decisions were based on the Due Process Clause of the Fifth Amendment, which provides protection for convicted prisoners and pretrial detainees alike against the deprivation of their property without due process of law. . . . But as we have stated, these due process rights of prisoners and pretrial detainees are not absolute; they are subject to reasonable limitation or retraction in light of the legitimate security concerns of the institution.

We think that the District Court and the Court of Appeals have trenched too cavalierly into areas that are properly the concern of MCC officials. It is plain from their opinions that the lower courts simply disagreed with the judgment of MCC officials about the extent of the security interests affected and the means required to further those interests. But our decisions have time and again emphasized that this sort of unguided substitution of judicial judgment for that of the expert prison administrators on matters such as this is inappropriate. . . . We do not doubt that the rule devised by the District Court and modified by the Court of Appeals may be a reasonable way of coping with the problems of security, order, and sanitation. It simply is not, however, the only constitutionally permissible approach to these problems. Certainly, the Due Process Clause does not mandate a "lowest common denominator" security standard, whereby a practice permitted at one penal institution must be permitted at all institutions.

Corrections officials concluded that permitting the introduction of packages of personal property and food would increase the risks of gambling, theft, and inmate fights over that which the institution already experienced by permitting certain items to be purchased from its commissary. "It is enough to say that they have not been conclusively shown to be wrong in this view." Jones v. North Carolina Prisoners' Labor Union, 433 U.S., at 132. It is also all too obvious that such packages are handy devices for the smuggling of contraband. There simply is no basis in this record for concluding that MCC officials have exaggerated their response to these serious problems or that this restriction is irrational. It does not therefore deprive the convicted inmates or pretrial detainees of the MCC of their property without due process of law in contravention of the Fifth Amendment.

C

The MCC staff conducts unannounced searches of inmate living areas at irregular intervals. These searches generally are formal unit "shakedowns" during which all inmates are cleared of the residential units, and a team of guards searches each room. Prior to the District Court's order, inmates were not permitted to watch the searches. Officials testified that permitting inmates to observe room inspections would lead to friction between the inmates and security guards and would allow the inmates to attempt to frustrate the search by distracting personnel and moving contraband from one room to another ahead of the search team.

The District Court held that this procedure could not stand as applied to pretrial detainees because MCC officials had not shown that the restriction was justified by "compelling necessity." The court stated that "[a]t least until or unless [petitioners] can show a pattern of violence or other disruptions taxing the powers of control—a kind of showing not remotely approached by the Warden's expressions—the security argument for banishing inmates while their rooms are searched must be rejected." 439 F.Supp., at 149. It also noted that in many instances inmates suspected guards of thievery. . . . The Court of Appeals agreed with the District Court. It saw "no reason whatsoever not to permit a detainee to observe the search of his room and belongings from a reasonable distance," although the court permitted the removal of any detainee who became "obstructive." 573 F.2d, at 132.

The Court of Appeals did not identify the constitutional provision on which it relied in invalidating the room-search rule. The District Court stated that the rule infringed the detainee's interest in privacy and indicated that this interest in privacy was founded on the Fourth Amendment. ... It may well be argued that a person confined in a detention facility has no reasonable expectation of privacy with respect to his room or cell and that therefore the Fourth Amendment provides no protection for such a person. ... In any case, given the realities of institutional confinement, any reasonable expectation of privacy that a detainee retained necessarily would be of a diminished scope. ... Assuming, *arguendo*, that a pretrial detainee retains such a diminished expectation of privacy after commitment to a custodial facility, we nonetheless find that the room-search rule does not violate the Fourth Amendment.

It is difficult to see how the detainee's interest in privacy is infringed by the room-search rule. No one can rationally doubt that room searches represent an appropriate security measure and neither the District Court nor the Court of Appeals prohibited such searches. And even the most zealous advocate of prisoners' rights would not suggest that a warrant is required to conduct such a search. Detainees' drawers, beds, and personal items may be searched, even after the lower courts' rulings. Permitting detainees to observe the searches does not lessen the invasion of their privacy; its only conceivable beneficial effect would be to prevent theft or misuse by those conducting the search. The room-search rule simply facilitates the safe and effective performance of the search which all concede may be conducted. The rule itself, then, does not render the searches "unreasonable" within the meaning of the Fourth Amendment.

D

Inmates at all Bureau of Prisons facilities, including the MCC, are required to expose their body cavities for visual inspection as a part of a strip search conducted after every contact visit with a person from outside the institution. Corrections officials testified that visual cavity searches were necessary not only to discover but also to deter the smuggling of weapons, drugs, and other contraband into the institution. ... The District Court upheld the strip-search procedure but prohibited the body-cavity searches, absent probable cause to believe that the inmate is concealing contraband. ... Because petitioners proved only one instance in the MCC's short history where contraband was found during a body-cavity search, the Court of Appeals affirmed. In its view, the "gross violation of personal privacy inherent in such a search cannot be outweighed by the government's security interest in maintaining a practice of so little actual utility." 573 F.2d, at 131.

Admittedly, this practice instinctively gives us the most pause. However, assuming for present purposes that inmates, both convicted prisoners and pretrial detainees, retain some Fourth Amendment rights upon commitment to a corrections facility . . . we nonetheless conclude that these searches do not violate that Amendment. The Fourth Amendment prohibits only unreasonable searches . . . and under the circumstances, we do not believe that these searches are unreasonable.

The test of reasonableness under the Fourth Amendment is not capable of precise definition or mechanical application. In each case it requires a balancing of the need for the particular search against the invasion of personal rights that the search entails. Courts must consider the scope of the particular intrusion, the manner in which it is conducted, the justification for initiating it, and the place in which it is conducted. . . . A detention facility is a unique place fraught with serious security dangers. Smuggling of money, drugs, weapons, and other contraband is all too common an occurrence. And inmate attempts to secrete these items into the facility by concealing them in body cavities are documented in this record . . . and in other cases. . . . That there has been only one instance where an MCC inmate was discovered attempting to smuggle contraband into the institution on his person may be more a testament to the effectiveness of this search technique as a deterrent than to any lack of interest on the part of the inmates to secrete and import such items when the opportunity arises.

We do not underestimate the degree to which these searches may invade the personal privacy of inmates. Nor do we doubt, as the District Court noted, that on occasion a security guard may conduct the search in an abusive fashion. . . . Such abuse cannot be condoned. The searches must be conducted in a reasonable manner. . . . But we deal here with the question whether visual body-cavity inspections as contemplated by the MCC rules can *ever* be conducted on less than probable cause. Balancing the significant and legitimate security interests of the institution against the privacy interests of the inmates, we conclude that they can.

IV

Nor do we think that the four MCC security restrictions and practices described in Part III, supra, constitute "punishment" in violation of the rights of pretrial detainees under the Due Process Clause of the Fifth Amendment. Neither the District Court nor the Court of Appeals suggested that these restrictions and practices were employed by MCC officials with an intent to punish the pretrial detainees housed there. Respondents do not even make such a suggestion; they simply argue that the restrictions were greater than necessary to satisfy petitioners' legitimate interest in maintaining security. . . . Therefore, the determination whether these restrictions and practices constitute punishment in the constitutional sense depends on whether they are rationally related to a legitimate nonpunitive governmental purpose and whether they appear excessive in relation to that purpose. . . . Ensuring security and order at the institution is a permissible nonpunitive objective, whether the facility houses pretrial detainees, convicted inmates, or both. . . . For the reasons set forth in Part

III, supra, we think that these particular restrictions and practices were reasonable responses by MCC officials to legitimate security concerns. Respondents simply have not met their heavy burden of showing that these officials have exaggerated their response to the genuine security considerations that actuated these restrictions and practices. . . . And as might be expected of restrictions applicable to pretrial detainees, these restrictions were of only limited duration so far as the MCC pretrial detainees were concerned. . . .

V

There was a time not too long ago when the federal judiciary took a completely "hands-off" approach to the problem of prison administration. In recent years, however, these courts largely have discarded this "hands-off" attitude and have waded into this complex arena. The deplorable conditions and Draconian restrictions of some of our Nation's prisons are too well known to require recounting here, and the federal courts rightly have condemned these sordid aspects of our prison systems. But many of these same courts have, in the name of the Constitution, become increasingly enmeshed in the minutiae of prison operations. Judges, after all, are human. They, no less than others in our society, have a natural tendency to believe that their individual solutions to often intractable problems are better and more workable than those of the persons who are actually charged with and trained in the running of the particular institution under examination. But under the Constitution, the first question to be answered is not whose plan is best, but in what branch of the Government is lodged the authority to initially devise the plan. This does not mean that constitutional rights are not to be scrupulously observed. It does mean, however, that the inquiry of federal courts into prison management must be limited to the issue of whether a particular system violates any prohibition of the Constitution or, in the case of a federal prison, a statute. The wide range of "judgment calls" that meet constitutional and statutory requirements are confided to officials outside of the Judicial Branch of Government.

The judgment of the Court of Appeals is, accordingly, reversed, and the case is remanded for proceedings consistent with this opinion.

. . .[8]

———

[8] Justice Powell wrote a brief opinion concurring in part and dissenting in part. Justice Marshall wrote a dissenting opinion. Justice Stevens wrote a dissenting opinion, which Justice Brennan joined.

305. Relying on Bell v. Wolfish, in Block v. Rutherford, 468 U.S. 576 (1984) the Court held that pretrial detainees do not have a constitutional right to contact visits with members of their families or others. "[T]he Constitution does not require that detainees be allowed contact visits when responsible, experienced administrators have determined, in their sound discretion, that such visits will jeopardize the security of the facility." Id. at 589. In the same case, the Court reaffirmed its holding in *Bell* that detainees do not have a constitutional right to watch "shakedown" searches of their cells. On the general question of detainees' right to privacy under the Fourth Amendment, to which the Court adverts in *Bell*, see Hudson v. Palmer, 468 U.S. 517, (1984), note 159 p. 303 above, holding that "the Fourth Amendment has no applicability to a prison cell," id. at 536.

A much more protective attitude toward pretrial detainees' rights was evident in a Second Circuit case decided before the Court decided *Bell*. Marcera v. Chinlund, 595 F.2d 1231 (2d Cir.), vacated and remanded, 442 U.S. 915 (1979). The majority opinion and opinion dissenting in part in Campbell v. McGruder, 580 F.2d 521 (D.C.Cir.1978), also contain lengthy discussions of the problem of pretrial detention and jail conditions in the District of Columbia.

306. Bail pending appeal. In McKane v. Durston, 153 U.S. 684 (1894), the Court held that there is no constitutional right to bail pending appeal from a conviction: "A review by an appellate court of the final judgment in a criminal case, however grave the offence of which the accused is convicted, was not at common law and is not now a necessary element of due process of law. It is wholly within the discretion of the state to allow or not to allow such a review. . . .

"It is, therefore, clear that the right of appeal may be accorded by the state to the accused upon such terms as in its wisdom may be deemed proper." Id. at 687–88. See the provisions of 18 U.S.C. § 3143(b), p. 586 above.

Section 3143(b)(2) was construed in United States v. Powell, 761 F.2d 1227 (8th Cir.1985). The court concluded: "We hold that a defendant who wishes to be released on bail after the imposition of a sentence including a term of imprisonment must first show that the question presented by the appeal is substantial, in the sense that it is a close question or one that could go either way. It is not sufficient to show simply that reasonable judges could differ (presumably every judge who writes a dissenting opinion is still 'reasonable') or that the issue is fairly debatable or not frivolous. On the other hand, the defendant does not have to show that it is likely or probable that he or she will prevail on the issue on appeal. If this part of the test is satisfied, the defendant must then show that the substantial question he or she seeks to present is so integral to the merits of the conviction that it is more probable than not that reversal or a new trial will occur if the question is decided on the defendant's favor. In deciding whether this part of the burden has been satisfied, the court or judge to whom application for bail is made must assume that the substantial question presented will go the other way on appeal and then assess the impact of such assumed error on the conviction. This standard will, we think, carry out the manifest purpose of Congress to reduce substantially the numbers of convicted persons released on bail pending appeal, without eliminating such release entirely or limiting it to a negligible number of appellants." Id. at 1233–34.

In some other circuits, a somewhat less restrictive standard of what counts as a substantial question has been adopted. See, generally in accord with *Powell*, United States v. Perholtz, 836 F.2d 554 (D.C.Cir.1987); United States v. Bayko, 774 F.2d 516 (1st Cir.1985) (reviewing cases in other courts of appeals). See also United States v. Smith, 793 F.2d 85 (3d Cir.1986). Finetti v. Harris, 609 F.2d 594 (2d Cir.1979), discusses federal review on habeas corpus of a state court's denial of bail pending appeal. Sections 3143(b)(2) and §3145(c) (appeal from a detention order) are construed in United States v. Koon, 6 F.3d 561 (9th Cir.1993).

A district court determining whether a state prisoner whose conviction has been overturned on habeas corpus should be released or detained while the latter decision is under review, or a court of appeals reviewing such determination, see Fed.R.App.P. 23(c)–(d), is not restricted to considering the risk that the prisoner will flee. It may also consider the risk that the prisoner, if released, will pose a danger to the community and the state's interest in continuing custody and rehabilitation pending a final determination of the habeas corpus proceeding. The likelihood that the state will succeed on appeal and the strength of the state's case on the merits are also relevant factors. Hilton v. Braunskill, 481 U.S. 770 (1987) (6–3).

307. Forfeiture. Fed.R.Crim.P. 46(e)(1)–(2):

"(e) Forfeiture.

> "(1) Declaration. If there is a breach of condition of a bond, the district court shall declare a forfeiture of the bail.

> "(2) Setting Aside. The court may direct that a forfeiture be set aside in whole or in part, upon such conditions as the court may impose, if a person released upon execution of an appearance bond with a surety is subsequently surrendered by the surety into custody or if it otherwise appears that justice does not require the forfeiture."

Observing that remission of a forfeited bond is not granted while the defendant remains at large, the court of appeals said that in order to show that "justice necessitates remission" one must show that "the bond forfeiture bears no reasonable relation to several factors: 1) the cost and inconvenience to the government in regaining custody of the defendant, 2) the amount of delay caused by the defendant's default and the stage of the proceedings at the time of his disappearance, 3) the willfulness of the defendant's breach of conditions and the prejudice suffered by the government, and 4) the public interest and necessity of effectuating the appearance of the defendant." United States v. Diaz, 811 F.2d 1412, 1415 (11th Cir.1987). See United States v. Bass, 573 F.2d 258 (5th Cir.1978); United States v. Kirkman, 426 F.2d 747 (4th Cir.1970); United States v. Foster, 417 F.2d 1254 (7th Cir.1969).

CHAPTER 9

THE DECISION TO PROSECUTE

308. "Few subjects are less adapted to judicial review than the exercise by the Executive of his discretion in deciding when and whether to institute criminal proceedings, or what precise charge shall be made, or whether to dismiss a proceeding once brought.

"The United States Attorney, under the direction and control of the Attorney General, is the attorney for the Executive, charged with faithful execution of the laws, protection of the interests of the United States, and prosecution of offenses against the United States. As such he must have broad discretion. . . .

. . .

"An attorney for the United States, as any other attorney, however, appears in a dual role. He is at once an officer of the court and the agent and attorney for a client; in the first capacity he is responsible to the Court for the manner of his conduct of a case, i.e., his demeanor, deportment and ethical conduct; but in his second capacity, as agent and attorney for the Executive, he is responsible to his principal and the courts have no power over the exercise of his discretion or his motives as they relate to the execution of his duty within the framework of his professional employment. . . .

"To say that the United States Attorney must literally treat every offense and every offender alike is to delegate him an impossible task; of course this concept would negate discretion. Myriad factors can enter into the prosecutor's decision. Two persons may have committed what is precisely the same legal offense but the prosecutor is not compelled by law, duty or tradition to treat them the same as to charges. On the contrary, he is expected to exercise discretion and common sense to the end that if, for example, one is a young first offender and the other older, with a criminal record, or one played a lesser and the other a dominant role, one the instigator and the other a follower, the prosecutor can and should take such factors into account; no court has any jurisdiction to inquire into or review his decision.

"It is assumed that the United States Attorney will perform his duties and exercise his powers consistent with his oaths; and while this discretion is subject to abuse or misuse just as is judicial discretion, deviations from his duty as an agent of the Executive are to be dealt with by his superiors.

"The remedy lies ultimately within the establishment where power and discretion reside. The President has abundant supervisory and disciplinary powers—including summary dismissal—to deal with misconduct of his subordinates; it is not the function of the judiciary to review the exercise of executive discretion whether it be that of the President himself or those to whom he has delegated certain of his powers." Newman v. United States, 382 F.2d 479, 480–82 (D.C.Cir.1967).

See also United States v. Gainey, 440 F.2d 290 (D.C.Cir.1971) (district judge may not dismiss charges to reduce court congestion, over prosecutor's objection); United States v. Cox, 342 F.2d 167 (5th Cir.1965), note 342 p. 704 below.

––––––––

Yick Wo v. Hopkins

118 U.S. 356, 6 S.Ct. 1064, 30 L.Ed. 220 (1886).

■ MR. JUSTICE MATTHEWS delivered the opinion of the court.

. . .

[The appellants were found guilty of violating ordinances of the board of supervisors of San Francisco County which prohibited anyone from operating a laundry without the consent of the board except in a building of brick or stone.]

We are . . . constrained, at the outset, to differ from the Supreme Court of California upon the real meaning of the ordinances in question. That court considered these ordinances as vesting in the board of supervisors a not unusual discretion in granting or withholding their assent to the use of wooden buildings as laundries, to be exercised in reference to the circumstances of each case, with a view to the protection of the public against the dangers of fire. We are not able to concur in that interpretation of the power conferred upon the supervisors. There is nothing in the ordinances which points to such a regulation of the business of keeping and conducting laundries. They seem intended to confer, and actually do confer, not a discretion to be exercised upon a consideration of the circumstances of each case, but a naked and arbitrary power to give or withhold consent, not only as to places, but as to persons. So that, if an applicant for such consent, being in every way a competent and qualified person, and having complied with every reasonable condition demanded by any public interest, should, failing to obtain the requisite consent of the supervisors to the prosecution of his business, apply for redress by the judicial process of *mandamus*, to require the supervisors to consider and act upon his case, it would be a sufficient answer for them to say that the law had conferred upon them authority to withhold their assent, without reason and without responsibility. The power given to them is not confided to their discretion in the legal sense of that term, but is granted to their mere will. It is purely arbitrary, and acknowledges neither guidance nor restraint.

. . .

It is contended on the part of the petitioners that the ordinances for violations of which they are severally sentenced to imprisonment, are void on their face, as being within the prohibitions of the Fourteenth Amendment; and, in the alternative, if not so, that they are void by reason of their administration, operating unequally, so as to punish in the present petitioners what is permitted to others as lawful, without any distinction of circumstances—an unjust and illegal discrimination, it is claimed, which, though not made expressly by the ordinances is made possible by them.

When we consider the nature and the theory of our institutions of government, the principles upon which they are supposed to rest, and review the history of their development, we are constrained to conclude that they do not mean to leave room for the play and action of purely personal and arbitrary power. Sovereignty itself is, of course, not subject to law, for it is the author and source of law; but in our system, while sovereign powers are delegated to the agencies of government, sovereignty itself remains with the people, by whom and for whom all government exists and acts. And the law is the definition and limitation of power. It is, indeed, quite true, that there must always be lodged somewhere, and in some person or body, the authority of final decision; and in many cases of mere administration the responsibility is purely political, no appeal lying except to the ultimate tribunal of the public judgment, exercised either in the pressure of opinion or by means of the suffrage. But the fundamental rights to life, liberty, and the pursuit of happiness, considered as individual possessions, are secured by those maxims of constitutional law which are the monuments showing the victorious progress of the race in securing to men the blessings of civilization under the reign of just and equal laws, so that, in the famous language of the Massachusetts Bill of Rights, the government of the commonwealth "may be a government of laws and not of men." For, the very idea that one man may be compelled to hold his life, or the means of living, or any material right essential to the enjoyment of life, at the mere will of another, seems to be intolerable in any country where freedom prevails, as being the essence of slavery itself.

. . .

. . . In the present cases we are not obliged to reason from the probable to the actual, and pass upon the validity of the ordinances complained of, as tried merely by the opportunities which their terms afford, of unequal and unjust discrimination in their administration. For the cases present the ordinances in actual operation, and the facts shown establish an administration directed so exclusively against a particular class of persons as to warrant and require the conclusion, that, whatever may have been the intent of the ordinances as adopted, they are applied by the public authorities charged with their administration, and thus representing the State itself, with a mind so unequal and oppressive as to amount to a practical denial by the State of that equal protection of the laws, which is secured to the petitioners, as to all other persons, by the broad and benign provisions of the Fourteenth Amendment to the Constitution of the United States. Though the law itself be fair on its face and impartial in appearance, yet, if it is applied and administered by public authority with an evil eye and an unequal hand, so as practically to make unjust and illegal discriminations between persons in similar circumstances, material to their rights, the denial of equal justice is still within the prohibition of the Constitution. . . .

The present cases, as shown by the facts disclosed in the record, are within this class. It appears that both petitioners have complied with every requisite, deemed by the law or by the public officers charged with its administration, necessary for the protection of neighboring property from fire, or as a precaution against injury to the public health. No reason whatever, except the will of the supervisors, is assigned why they should not be permitted to carry on, in the accustomed manner, their harmless and useful occupation, on which they depend for a livelihood. And while this consent of the supervisors is withheld from them and from two hundred others who have also petitioned, all of whom happen to be Chinese subjects, eighty others, not Chinese subjects, are permitted to carry on the same business under similar conditions. The fact of this discrimination is admitted. No reason for it is shown, and the conclusion cannot be resisted, that no reason for it exists except hostility to the race and nationality to which the petitioners belong, and which in the eye of the law is not justified. The discrimination is, therefore, illegal, and the public administration which enforces it is a denial of the equal protection of the laws and a violation of the Fourteenth Amendment of the Constitution. The imprisonment of the petitioners is, therefore, illegal, and they must be discharged. . . .

Wayte v. United States

470 U.S. 598, 105 S.Ct. 1524, 84 L.Ed.2d 547 (1985).

■ JUSTICE POWELL delivered the opinion of the Court.

The question presented is whether a passive enforcement policy under which the Government prosecutes only those who report themselves as having violated the law, or who are reported by others, violates the First and Fifth Amendments.

I

On July 2, 1980, pursuant to his authority under § 3 of the Military Selective Service Act, 62 Stat. 605, as amended, 50 U.S.C.App. § 453, the

President issued Presidential Proclamation No. 4771, 3 CFR 82 (1981). This proclamation directed male citizens and certain male residents born during 1960 to register with the Selective Service System during the week of July 21, 1980. Petitioner fell within that class but did not register. Instead, he wrote several letters to Government officials, including the President, stating that he had not registered and did not intend to do so.

Petitioner's letters were added to a Selective Service file of young men who advised that they had failed to register or who were reported by others as having failed to register. For reasons we discuss, infra . . . Selective Service adopted a policy of passive enforcement under which it would investigate and prosecute only the cases of nonregistration contained in this file. In furtherance of this policy, Selective Service sent a letter on June 17, 1981, to each reported violator who had not registered and for whom it had an address. The letter explained the duty to register, stated that Selective Service had information that the person was required to register but had not done so, requested that he either comply with the law by filling out an enclosed registration card or explain why he was not subject to registration, and warned that a violation could result in criminal prosecution and specified penalties. Petitioner received a copy of this letter but did not respond.

On July 20, 1981, Selective Service transmitted to the Department of Justice, for investigation and potential prosecution, the names of petitioner and 133 other young men identified under its passive enforcement system—all of whom had not registered in response to the Service's June letter. At two later dates, it referred the names of 152 more young men similarly identified. After screening out the names of those who appeared not to be in the class required to register, the Department of Justice referred the remaining names to the Federal Bureau of Investigation for additional inquiry and to the United States Attorneys for the districts in which the nonregistrants resided. Petitioner's name was one of those referred.

Pursuant to Department of Justice policy, those referred were not immediately prosecuted. Instead, the appropriate United States Attorney was required to notify identified nonregistrants by registered mail that, unless they registered within a specified time, prosecution would be considered. In addition, an FBI agent was usually sent to interview the nonregistrant before prosecution was instituted. This effort to persuade nonregistrants to change their minds became known as the "beg" policy. Under it, young men who registered late were not prosecuted, while those who never registered were investigated further by the Government. Pursuant to the "beg" policy, the United States Attorney for the Central District of California sent petitioner a letter on October 15, 1981, urging him to register or face possible prosecution. Again petitioner failed to respond.

On December 9, 1981, the Department of Justice instructed all United States Attorneys not to begin seeking indictments against nonregistrants until further notice. On January 7, 1982, the President announced a grace period to afford nonregistrants a further opportunity to register without penalty. This grace period extended until February 28, 1982. Petitioner still did not register.

Over the next few months, the Department decided to begin prosecuting those young men who, despite the grace period and "beg" policy, continued to refuse to register. It recognized that under the passive enforcement system those prosecuted were "liable to be vocal proponents of nonregistration" or persons "with religious or moral objections." Memorandum of March 17, 1982 from Lawrence Lippe, Chief General Litigation and Legal Advice Section, Criminal Division, Department of Justice, to D. Lowell Jensen, Assistant Attorney General, Criminal Division, App. 301. It also recognized that prosecutions would "undoubtedly result in allegations that the [case was] brought in retribution for the nonregistrant's exercise of his first amendment rights." Ibid. The Department was advised, however, that Selective Service could not develop a more "active" enforcement system for quite some time. . . . Because of this, the Department decided to begin seeking indictments under the passive system without further delay. On May 21, 1982, United States Attorneys were notified to begin prosecution of nonregistrants. On June 28, 1982, FBI agents interviewed petitioner and he continued to refuse to register. Accordingly, on July 22, 1982, an indictment was returned against him for knowingly and willfully failing to register with the Selective Service in violation of sections 3 and 12(a) of the Military Selective Service Act. . . . This was the first indictment returned against any individual under the passive policy.

II

Petitioner moved to dismiss the indictment on the ground of selective prosecution. He contended that he and the other indicted nonregistrants were "vocal" opponents of the registration program who had been impermissibly targeted (out of an estimated 674,000 nonregistrants) for prosecution on the basis of their exercise of First Amendment rights. . . .

[T]he District Court dismissed the indictment on the ground that the Government had failed to rebut petitioner's prima facie case of selective prosecution. . . .

The Court of Appeals reversed. . . .

Recognizing both the importance of the question presented and a division in the Circuits, we granted certiorari on the question of selective prosecution. . . . We now affirm.

III

In our criminal justice system, the Government retains "broad discretion" as to whom to prosecute. . . . "[S]o long as the prosecutor has probable cause to believe that the accused committed an offense defined by statute, the decision whether or not to prosecute, and what charge to file or bring before a grand jury, generally rests entirely in his discretion." Bordenkircher v. Hayes, 434 U.S. 357, 364 (1978). This broad discretion rests largely on the recognition that the decision to prosecute is particularly ill-suited to judicial review. Such factors as the strength of the case, the prosecution's general deterrence value, the Government's enforcement priorities, and the case's relationship to the Government's overall enforcement plan are not readily susceptible to the kind of analysis the courts are competent to undertake. Judicial supervision in this area, moreover, entails systemic costs of particular concern. Examining the basis of a prosecution delays the criminal proceeding, threatens to chill law enforcement by subjecting the prosecutor's motives and decisionmaking to outside inquiry, and may undermine prosecutorial effectiveness by revealing the Government's enforcement policy. All these are substantial concerns that make the courts properly hesitant to examine the decision whether to prosecute.

As we have noted in a slightly different context, however, although prosecutorial discretion is broad, it is not " 'unfettered.' Selectivity in the enforcement of criminal laws is . . . subject to constitutional constraints." United States v. Batchelder, 442 U.S. 114, 125 (1979) (footnote omitted). In particular, the decision to prosecute may not be " 'deliberately based upon an unjustifiable standard such as race, religion, or other arbitrary classification,' " Bordenkircher v. Hayes, supra, at 364, quoting Oyler v. Boles, 368 U.S. 448, 456 (1962), including the exercise of protected statutory and constitutional rights . . . .

It is appropriate to judge selective prosecution claims according to ordinary equal protection standards. . . . Under our prior cases, these standards require petitioner to show both that the passive enforcement system had a discriminatory effect and that it was motivated by a discriminatory purpose. . . . All petitioner has shown here is that those eventually prosecuted, along with many not prosecuted, reported themselves as having violated the law. He has not shown that the enforcement policy selected nonregistrants for prosecution on the basis of their speech. Indeed, he could not have done so given the way the "beg" policy was carried out. The Government did not prosecute those who reported themselves but later registered. Nor did it prosecute those who protested registration but did not report themselves or were not reported by others. In fact, the Government did not even investigate those who wrote letters to Selective Service criticizing registration unless their letters stated affirmatively that they had refused to comply with the law. . . . The Government, on the other hand, did prosecute people who reported themselves or were reported by others but who did not publicly protest. These facts demonstrate that the Government treated all reported nonregistrants similarly. It did not subject vocal nonregistrants to any special burden. Indeed, those prosecuted in effect selected themselves for prosecution by refusing to register after being reported and warned by the Government.

Even if the passive policy had a discriminatory effect, petitioner has not shown that the Government intended such a result. The evidence he presented demonstrated only that the Government was aware that the passive enforcement policy would result in prosecution of vocal objectors and that they would probably make selective prosecution claims. As we have noted, however, " '[d]iscriminatory purpose' . . . implies more than . . . intent as awareness of consequences. It implies that the decision-maker . . . selected or reaffirmed a particular course of action at least in part 'because of,' not merely 'in spite of,' its adverse effects upon an identifiable group." Personnel Administrator of Mass. v. Feeney, [442 U.S. 256 (1979)], at 279 (footnotes and citations omitted). In the present case, petitioner has not shown that the Government prosecuted him because of his protest activities. Absent such a showing, his claim of selective prosecution fails.

IV

Petitioner also challenges the passive enforcement policy directly on First Amendment grounds. . . .

. . .

We conclude that the Government's passive enforcement system together with its "beg" policy violated neither the First nor Fifth Amendments. Accordingly, we affirm the judgment of the Court of Appeals.

It is so ordered.[1]

———

309. "To support a defense of selective or discriminatory prosecution, a defendant bears the heavy burden of establishing, at least *prima facie*, (1) that, while others similarly situated have not generally been proceeded against because of conduct of the type forming the basis of the charge against him, he had been singled out for prosecution, and (2) that the government's discriminatory selection of him for prosecution has been invidious or in bad faith, i.e., based upon such impermissible considerations as race, religion, or the desire to prevent his exercise of constitutional rights." United States v. Berrios, 501 F.2d 1207, 1211 (2d Cir.1974). See United States v. Ross, 719 F.2d 615 (2d Cir.1983) (allegation of selective prosecution because defendant refused to act as informer or agent for investigators; prosecution held not improper); United States v. Bourque, 541 F.2d 290 (1st Cir.1976) (allegation that personal vindictiveness motivated tax prosecution was insufficient without further allegation that prosecutions were not normally instituted for offenses charged).

———

[1] Justice Marshall wrote a dissenting opinion, which Justice Brennan joined.

People v. Utica Daw's Drug Co.

16 A.D.2d 12, 225 N.Y.S.2d 128 (1962).

■ Halpern, Justice.

This case presents the question of the proper way in which to deal with a claim by a defendant in a criminal case that the law has been enforced in a discriminatory manner against him in violation of the equal protection clauses of the State and Federal Constitutions.

The defendant maintains a drug store in the City of Utica, New York, which operates under a policy of selling at reduced prices, generally characteristic of stores known as "cut-rate" stores or discount houses. The drug store is open on Sunday as all drug stores are permitted to be under the Sunday statute (Penal Law, § 2147). However, the items which drug stores are permitted to sell on Sunday are limited by the statute. The defendant was indicted for violation of the Sunday statute, it being charged that defendant on Sunday, December 18, 1960, "unlawfully did publicly sell and expose for sale certain property, to wit, a pair of gloves, a doll, a brown belt and a drinking cup" in violation of section 2147 of the Penal Law.

The defendant did not contest the charge that the enumerated items had been sold and offered for sale in its store but contended that similar items had been sold and offered for sale on Sunday throughout the City of Utica and County of Oneida by all other drug stores and that other items, the sale of which on Sunday was prohibited by section 2147 of the Penal Law, had been regularly offered for sale and sold in other types of stores, without any attempt on the part of the public authorities to interfere with the sale or to prosecute the vendors. Only the defendant and one other company (not a drug store) also engaged in a discount operation were prosecuted. The defendant maintained that the prosecution was part of a discriminatory design aimed at the defendant and others engaged in the same type of "cut-rate" operation. It maintained that the public authorities intentionally discriminated against that class and allowed others outside the class to continue to sell the forbidden items in violation of the Sunday law without molestation.

The trial court, with the acquiescence of the District Attorney, held that the defendant's contention, if established, would constitute a good defense to the criminal charge and it submitted the case to the jury accordingly. It left it to the jury to decide as a question of fact whether the defendant's proof established "a clear and intentional discrimination against this defendant and against those in the same class." At the request of the defendant, the court charged in language taken from Yick Wo v. Hopkins, 118 U.S. 356, 373–374, 6 S.Ct. 1064, 30 L.Ed. 220: "Though the law itself be fair on its face, and impartial in appearance, yet, if it is applied and administered by public authority with an evil eye and an unequal hand, so as practically to make unjust and illegal discriminations between persons in similar circumstances, material to their rights, the denial of equal justice is still within the prohibition of the Constitution." The jury found the defendant guilty and this appeal followed.

Under the theory upon which the case was tried and submitted, the judgment of conviction cannot be permitted to stand. While the court accurately stated the principle of Yick Wo v. Hopkins and the cases which have followed it, it did not consistently apply the principle during the course of the trial. The defendant attempted to prove that 21 other drug stores in the City of Utica had engaged in offering for sale and in selling forbidden items on Sunday, December 18, 1960, and on other Sundays but the court sustained objections to most of the questions designed to elicit this proof. While the court allowed the defendant to prove that the stores had been open on Sunday, it sustained objections to questions as to the items which they had offered for sale on Sunday. The court also sustained objection to a question designed to show that a witness who was in the business of selling flags and decorations, advertised that his business was open on Sunday and that in fact he had sold flags and decorations on Sunday. Similar objections were sustained with regard to proof of sales on Sunday by various other types of stores.

It also appeared upon the trial that, after the defendant's arrest on December 18, the defendant engaged a private detective, formerly a member of the police department, to make an investigation on its behalf. On the following Sunday, December 25, he found that throughout the City of Utica in various drug stores which he listed by name and address, he was able to purchase and did purchase items forbidden for sale on Sunday under the statute. He also made purchases of forbidden items at smoke shops, news stores and grocery stores. The private detective then, at the request of the defendant's counsel, went to the Clerk of the City Court and offered to sign and swear to depositions with respect to each of the purchases made by him but the secretary of the City Court Judge who handled the matter declined to accept the depositions. Proof of these facts was admitted upon the trial. However, the court refused to allow the defendant's counsel to prove that he had subsequently written a letter to the Chief of Police of the city, a copy of which was marked for identification, advising of the purchases made by the investigator and offering to have the investigator sign and swear to depositions with respect thereto and requesting the Chief of Police to have officers in his department execute the necessary informations and obtain warrants of arrest. Objection to the admission of the letter into evidence was sustained and the Chief of Police was not allowed to testify with respect to its receipt and his failure to take action thereon.

It is thus apparent that while the court recognized the validity of the defense put forward by the defendant, it prevented the defendant from introducing material evidence which would have tended to support the defense. The court held that the evidence was irrelevant, upon the authority of . . . cases holding that nonenforcement of itself is not sufficient to establish discrimination. In so ruling, the court misconstrued the cases upon which it relied. While it is true that they held that mere nonenforcement is insufficient of itself to establish discrimination, they did not hold that proof of nonenforcement is not admissible in evidence, in a case in which the defendant asserts that there had been intentional discrimination.

It is true that in order to find a violation of the constitutional guarantee, the trier of the facts must be satisfied that there was intentional discrimination, and not mere laxity in enforcement, but in the effort to persuade the trier of the facts of the truth of its ultimate contention, the defendant is entitled to introduce evidence of nonenforcement as relevant evidence bearing upon that contention. . . .

We have therefore concluded that, upon the basis upon which the case was tried and submitted, the judgment of conviction must be reversed because of errors in the exclusion of evidence.

However, we believe that the entire approach to the problem, adopted by the trial court with the approval or acquiescence of the counsel on both sides, was erroneous and that a different approach should be followed, upon the remand of the case. The claim of discriminatory enforcement should not be treated as a defense to the criminal charge, to be tried before the jury and submitted to it for decision, but should be treated as an application to the court for a dismissal or quashing of the prosecution upon constitutional grounds. Insofar as a question of fact may be involved, the court should take the evidence in the absence of the jury and should decide the question itself. If the court finds that there was an intentional and purposeful discrimination, the court should quash the prosecution, not because the defendant is not guilty of the crime charged, but because the court, as an agency of government, should not lend itself to a prosecution the maintenance of which would violate the constitutional rights of the defendant.

. . .

. . . The claim of discriminatory enforcement does not go to the question of the guilt or innocence of the defendant, which is within the province of the jury. The question is rather whether in a community in which there is general disregard of a particular law with the acquiescence of the public authorities, the authorities should be allowed sporadically to select a single defendant or a single class of defendants for prosecution because of personal animosity or some other illegitimate reason. The wrong sought to be prevented is a wrong by the public authorities. To allow such arbitrary and discriminatory enforcement of a generally disregarded law is to place in the hands of the police and the prosecutor a power of the type frequently invoked in countries ruled by a dictator but wholly out of harmony with the principle of equal justice under law prevailing in democratic societies. The court is asked to stop the prosecution at the threshold, not because the defendant is innocent but because the public authorities are guilty of a wrong in engaging in a course of conduct designed to discriminate unconstitutionally against the defendant. Clearly, a contention of this kind is addressed to the court and should be passed upon by the court and not left to the jury.

. . .

Of course, we express no opinion as to whether the prosecution in the present case should be held to be a discriminatory one or not. That is for the trial court to decide after hearing all the evidence, including the evidence which was erroneously excluded upon the first trial and including any countervailing evidence which may be offered by the District Attorney. A heavy burden rests on the defendant to establish conscious, intentional discrimination, but if it succeeds in sustaining that burden, the defendant will be entitled to a dismissal of the prosecution as a matter of law. We believe this to be the necessary consequence of the principle of equal protection of the laws proclaimed in both the Federal and State Constitutions. . . .

. . .

The courts in some States have indicated a reluctance to enjoin a criminal prosecution on the ground of unconstitutional discrimination, for fear that guilty persons would thereby escape prosecution and the flouting of the law would be encouraged. . . . This fear, in our opinion, is an unfounded one. As has been pointed out, the burden resting upon the defendant is a heavy one and, even if the defendant succeeds in sustaining it, he will not be immune from a new prosecution, when and if the public authorities undertake a generalized enforcement of the law. Furthermore, even if the enforcement of a particular law is selective, it does not necessarily follow that it is unconstitutionally discriminatory. Selective enforcement may be justified when the meaning or constitutionality of the law is in doubt and a test case is needed to clarify the law or to establish its validity. Selective enforcement may also be justified when a striking example or a few examples are sought in order to deter other violators, as part of a bona fide rational pattern of general enforcement, in the expectation that general compliance will follow and that further prosecutions will be unnecessary. It is only when the selective enforcement is designed to discriminate against the persons prosecuted, without any intention to follow it up by general enforcement against others, that a constitutional violation may be found. . . .

. . .

310. The courts have agreed that it is not an unconstitutional discrimination to prosecute, as part of a general pattern of prosecution, persons who will furnish a "striking example" because of their public prominence. In United States v. Peskin, 527 F.2d 71, 86 (7th Cir.1975), for example, the court said: "It makes good sense to prosecute those who will receive the media's attention. Publication of the proceedings may enhance the deterrent effect of the prosecution and maintain public faith in the precept that public officials are not above the law." In United States v. Ojala, 544 F.2d 940 (8th Cir.1976), the defendant claimed that he was selected for prosecution for a violation of the tax laws because of his public refusal to pay his taxes as a protest against the government's policies. The court concluded that even if his claim were correct, there had been no violation of his rights.

"The government lacks the means to investigate and prosecute every suspected violation of the tax laws. Selection based in part upon the potential deterrent effect on others serves a legitimate interest in promoting more general compliance with the tax laws, which depend substantially upon a system of voluntary disclosure and reporting. It is difficult to conceive of a more legitimate object of prosecution than one who exploits his own public office and reputation to urge a political position by announcing publicly that he had gone on strike against the tax laws of the nation." Id. at 945. See, to the same effect, United States v. Amon, 669 F.2d 1351 (10th Cir.1981); United States v. Catlett, 584 F.2d 864 (8th Cir.1978).

311. Is it a permissible policy of state officials not to prosecute for violations of Sunday closing laws except when a private person or agency makes a complaint? Suppose that for economic reasons a group of merchants regularly makes complaints against competing merchants who violate the laws but not against noncompeting merchants who violate the laws. Suppose the merchants are motivated not by economic reasons but by the moral dilemma posed for them when competing stores remain open on Sunday in violation of the law. Is there any difference? See People v. Paine Drug Co., 241 N.Y.S.2d 946 (Monroe County Ct.1963), rev'd, 254 N.Y.S.2d 492 (App.Div.1964), aff'd, 208 N.E.2d 176 (N.Y.1965).

Suppose the defendant in a Sunday closing case proves that the mayor's office and police followed a deliberate policy of not prosecuting or interfering with the work on Sunday of workmen on a city job site. See Village of Fairlawn v. Fuller, 221 N.E.2d 851 (Ohio Mun.Ct.1966).

People v. Walker

14 N.Y.2d 901, 200 N.E.2d 779 (1964).

[The defendant was convicted of violations of the Multiple Dwelling Law and the Administrative Code of the City of New York, in that, as president and controlling stockholder of the corporate owner of a house in the City of New York, she failed to obtain a rooming house permit, made unlawful alterations to said premises and failed to repair or replace a broken wheel on the sprinkler valve on said premises.]

MEMORANDUM. The judgment of conviction should be reversed and a new trial ordered. The prosecution of defendant for violations of the Multiple Dwelling Law, Consol.Laws, c. 61–A, came closely in sequence upon the exposure by her of corrupt practices in the Department of

Buildings. She contends that the prosecution was the result of an intentional discrimination which deprived her of the constitutional right to equal protection of the laws. She was unduly restricted on the trial in her attempts to prove this contention. Latitude should be allowed in this complex area of proof. We do not hold that defendant has demonstrated intentional discrimination in her prosecution. We rule, merely, that she should have a fair opportunity to establish it on her trial.

DESMOND, CHIEF JUDGE (dissenting). I protest what appears to be the introduction into our criminal law of a novel and mischievous defense. Is a person guilty of crimes to go free because local officials were actuated by corrupt or vengeful motives in prosecuting? There is no precedent for such a holding. It will certainly worsen the current crisis in criminal law enforcement if we let the culprit go free because the police officer or inspector has not proceeded against every other guilty person. The gambler and the narcotics peddler (even the speeder) will have a new kind of license to violate the law. None of the earlier decisions go so far. From Yick Wo v. Hopkins, 118 U.S. 356 . . . to People v. Utica Daw's Drug Co., 16 A.D.2d 12, 225 N.Y.S.2d 128, the cited cases all refer to a "pattern of discrimination" (see People v. Friedman, 302 N.Y. 75, 81, 96 N.E.2d 184, 186) meaning a situation where the statute itself contemplates or leads to discrimination or where a generally unenforced law is dug up to harass a particular defendant or group. What has all this to do with the State Multiple Dwelling Law and the New York City Administrative Code sections which, as our own records show, are enforced against building owners in thousands of cases?

. . .

BURKE, JUDGE (dissenting). If the constitutional defense of unequal protection of the laws were maintainable solely upon a showing of bad motive on the part of those responsible for the placing of the violations of which appellant is admittedly guilty, then I would concur for reversal. This, however, is not the law; nor does the court say it is. Since the legislation under which appellant has been convicted is itself valid, and since appellant is admittedly guilty of the violations, the defense of unequal protection is established only upon a showing of both bad motive in the subject case and nonenforcement as to others similarly situated. . . . The element of uneven enforcement is of the very essence and substance of the constitutional claim. The violations are not hypertechnical nor have they fallen into a sort of desuetude. The violations, among which are the creation of an additional room by a partition, an additional class B room out of a vestibule, and the maintenance of a defective sprinkler valve, are, in my experience, commonly enforced in New York City. In any event they should not be assumed to be dead letters in the total absence of evidence to that effect.

The fact that the trial court was apparently prepared to exclude any evidence other than that bearing directly on guilt or innocence does not excuse appellant from offering to prove all of the elements of her defense.

Concededly, all her offers of proof went solely to the point of bad motive in her individual case. Sympathetic as we may be toward appellant's unfortunate position as the result of what she alleges were numerous bribe solicitations by Building Department officials, we have no license to play fast and lose with the elements of so volatile a doctrine as equal protection of the laws. If the statutory requirements to which appellant was held were generally enforced, then there was no infringement of her constitutional right when she was prosecuted for their violation—no matter how contemptible may have been the motives of those who enforced the law. Were the law otherwise all enforcement proceedings could be turned into subjective expeditions into motive without the stabilizing, objectively verifiable, element of an unequal pattern of enforcement. No one has a constitutional right to random enforcement of the law. No one has a constitutional right to sincere enforcement of the law. The right is to equal enforcement of the law. All of the cases dealing with this question have required such a showing. . . . Appellant, after all, has the burden of proof of all the elements of this defense and if in fact the violation of which she is guilty were not enforced against others similarly situated it would not be difficult to so prove. Building Department records are amenable to subpoena and the Building Department officials who testified could have been questioned as to the pattern of enforcement of the relevant regulations. None of this was done. According to the respondent, this omission was calculated because it would have shown that the rigorous inspection to which appellant's building was subjected was the result of an established policy of reinspecting all buildings previously inspected by an official under suspicion of misconduct—as was the case with appellant's building. Whether this is true or not is a question essential to appellant's defense and one which she ought to have pursued at the trial in order to now make her constitutional argument. Not having done so, she is without remedy in this court. . . .

On remand, the defendant was convicted of a violation of the Administrative Code of the City of New York, and appealed. The appellate court reversed the conviction and directed that the complaint be dismissed. It said:

"The defendant demonstrated, by a clear preponderance of evidence, that she was singled out for criminal prosecution by an intentional, purposeful and unusual selection process. The manner of prosecution was not the same as that used in the case of other property owners similarly situated and was in sharp contrast to the then existing pattern of enforcement of housing laws in New York City. The time allowed to defendant for correction of alleged housing violations was so unreasonably short as to make correction an impossibility and criminal conviction a certainty. The evidence leads irresistably to the conclusion that this intentional discrimination and prosecution was in retaliation for defendant's public exposure of corruption in the Department of Buildings and was in no wise aimed at securing compliance with the housing laws." People v. Walker, 271 N.Y.S.2d 447, 448 (Sup.Ct.1966).

———

312. In United States v. Armstrong, 517 U.S. 456 (1996) (8–1), the Court considered what threshold showing a defendant was required to make in order to obtain discovery of prosecutorial records pertinent to a claim of discriminatory prosecution. The defendants were prosecuted for conspiracy to possess and to distribute crack cocaine. In their motion for disovery, they alleged that they were selected for prosecution because they were black. Accompanying the motion was an affidavit of a person in the public defender's office, which stated that all of the 24 persons prosecuted for those offenses during the preceeding year were black. The district court issued an order directing the United States Attorney's office to provide information from its files, with which the office refused to comply. The court dismissed the indictment.

The Court held that the affidavit supporting the motion for discovery was insufficient. It said: "If discovery is ordered, the Government must assemble from its own files documents which might corroborate or refute the defendant's claim. Discovery thus imposes many of the costs present when the Government must respond to a prima facie case of selective prosecution. It will divert prosecutors' resources and may disclose the Government's prosecutorial strategy. The justifications for a rigorous standard for the elements of a selective-prosecution claim thus require a correspondingly rigorous standard for discovery in aid of such a claim." Id. at 468. In order to make the necessary threshold showing of racially discriminatory prosecution, the Court said the defendant was required to "produce some evidence that similarly situated defendants of other races could have been prosecuted, but were not." Id. at 469. The fact that all those who were prosecuted were black was an insufficient basis for an inference of discriminatory prosecution without "a credible showing of different treatment of similarly situated persons." Id. at 470.

"Certainly, the prospect of government prosecutors being called to the stand by every criminal defendant for cross-examination as to their motives in seeking an indictment is to be avoided. That does not mean that a criminal defendant is never to be afforded an opportunity to prove that the prosecution stems from an improper prosecutorial design or that he may never question a prosecutor under oath. The presumption is always that a prosecution for violation of a criminal law is undertaken in good faith and in nondiscriminatory fashion for the purpose of fulfilling a duty to bring violators to justice. However, when a defendant alleges intentional purposeful discrimination and presents facts sufficient to raise a reasonable doubt about the prosecutor's purpose, we think a different question is raised." United States v. Falk, 479 F.2d 616, 620–21 (7th Cir.1973). The court concluded that the defendant had made a *prima facie* case of discriminatory enforcement of the draft laws and that the government had the burden of going forward with proof to the contrary. In a dissenting opinion, Judge Cummings observed: "I have been unable to find a single case where a United States Attorney or his superiors in the Department of Justice were required to explain their motives for seeking an indictment at a defendant's behest and as a part of his case under any circumstances, and the majority has cited none." Id. at 631. For another case preceding *Armstrong*, in which the court discussed what showing is required to support a hearing on a claim of discriminatory prosecution, see United States v. Bourgeois, 964 F.2d 935 (9th Cir.1992) (other cases cited).

MacDonald v. Musick

425 F.2d 373 (9th Cir.1970).

■ DUNIWAY, CIRCUIT JUDGE.

Habeas corpus. The District Court denied the writ. We reverse. MacDonald has exhausted his state remedies.

On January 9, 1965, MacDonald was driving his car in Newport Beach, California. He was stopped by the local police and ultimately arrested and taken to the police station. There he was booked as violating section 23102(a) of the Vehicle Code of California, which makes it a misdemeanor for "any person who is under the influence of intoxicating liquor . . . to drive a vehicle upon any highway." On January 11, 1965, a complaint was filed in the Municipal Court of the Newport Beach Judicial District charging him with that offense. On January 14, 1965, MacDonald pled not guilty and demanded a jury trial, which was set for January 26.

On January 26, the prosecutor moved to dismiss the charge. The court asked if MacDonald would stipulate that there was probable cause for his arrest. MacDonald declined, and the prosecutor withdrew the motion. In California, only the court may dismiss a criminal action. . . . Had the action been dismissed, the dismissal would have been a bar to further prosecution for the offense charged. . . . Trial was set for February 2.

On February 2, the prosecutor moved . . . for leave to file an amended complaint, adding a second count charging MacDonald with resisting arrest

. . . also a misdemeanor. The motion was opposed, and was fully argued on February 3. The court granted the motion. MacDonald was then rearraigned and pled not guilty to both charges. Trial before a jury was had, beginning February 9, and on February 11, the jury acquitted MacDonald on the drunk driving charge and found him guilty of resisting arrest.

There was considerable conflict in the evidence as to the events leading to MacDonald's arrest, and particularly as to whether there was probable cause for the arrest, as well as about what happened thereafter. We need not analyze the evidence, however, because of the ground upon which we decide the case. Nor need we consider MacDonald's claim that he was convicted under a statute that makes it illegal to resist an unlawful arrest . . . and that such a conviction violates his federal constitutional rights.

The reason for the prosecutor's withdrawing his motion to dismiss the drunk driving charge and for then seeking to file an amendment to add the resisting arrest charge, is made clear by the record in the state case. At the hearing on the motion for leave to file an amended complaint, on February 3, there were a number of stipulations. MacDonald proposed to call as witnesses six deputies in the District Attorney's office. The prosecutor stipulated:

"It is so stipulated that all these Deputies indicated either displeasure with the case or that it was a weak case or that they would not care to prosecute it."

It was further stipulated that one deputy said:

" 'It appears that the police department has a hard on against this defendant and are out to get him.' or words to that effect, close quote."

It was also stipulated that a police lieutenant said:

"that he would stipulate that they did in fact delete the second charge of resisting arrest from their record, did in fact reduce the bail, and would stipulate that a police official, I think it was a policewoman, did state to the defendant's witness, 'You will be happy to know that the resisting arrest charge has been dropped.' "

In support of the motion for leave to amend, the prosecutor said:

"Normally a defendant will stipulate to probable cause, and there is only one reason, let's face it, for that stipulation, so that the defendant cannot sue the police department. This particular defendant would not stipulate to probable cause, which made it obvious, at least, there was an inference drawn, that perhaps here is a defendant that does have in mind suing the police department.

. . .

"It seems to me that it is the duty of the Deputy District Attorney, in addition to prosecuting criminals, to protect the police officers, and in so protecting the police officers, it seems to me, after evaluating the facts, any Deputy District Attorney worth his salt would have at that point included any offense, obviously, in the report on which the defendant could have been convicted."

We strongly disagree. It is no part of the proper duty of a prosecutor to use a criminal prosecution to forestall a civil proceeding by the defendant against policemen, even where the civil case arises from the events that are also the basis for the criminal charge. We do not mean that the prosecutor cannot present such a criminal charge. What he cannot do is condition a voluntary dismissal of a charge upon a stipulation by the defendant that is designed to forestall the latter's civil case. The situation is made no better by the fact that here the record indicates that it was the court that asked MacDonald whether he would stipulate. Rather, it makes it worse. It brings the court to the aid of the prosecutor in coercing the defendant into agreeing to what amounts to a forfeiture of his civil rights. Nor can the prosecutor, because of failure to obtain the demanded stipulation, then introduce another charge in the hope of defeating the possible civil action of the defendant.

The impropriety of the prosecutor's conduct requires little exposition. In California, extortion is defined as "the obtaining of property from another, . . . induced by a wrongful use of . . . fear, or under color of official right." (Cal.Pen.C. § 518.) There is no doubt that a cause of action for personal injuries is property. . . . Section 519 of the same code defines "fear" as "induced by a threat . . . 2. To accuse the individual threatened . . . of any crime. . . ." . . .

The Canons of Ethics have long prohibited misuse of the criminal process by an attorney to gain advantage for his client in a civil case. . . . In this respect, we can see no difference between public prosecutors and other lawyers. . . .

   . . .

In this case, MacDonald asserts that his arrest was unlawful, that he had a right to resist, and that as a result of his doing so he was badly beaten by the police. We express no views as to the merits of these claims. But MacDonald, in addition to whatever rights he had under the law of California, had a claim to a federal right under the Civil Rights Act, 42 U.S.C. § 1983. . . . Thus in this case, the attempt, by imposing the stipulation as a condition to the dismissal of the drunk driving charge, was to hamper MacDonald in asserting, by civil action, both state and federal civil rights. And the revival of the resisting arrest charge was the bludgeon behind the attempt.

The order appealed from is reversed and the matter is remanded with directions to grant the writ of habeas corpus.

KILKENNY, CIRCUIT JUDGE (dissenting):

I believe the approach of the majority is wholly unrealistic. On many occasions, in the criminal field, the prosecutor must make a decision on whether he will go forward with the prosecution on the original charge or add another count. On some occasions, he may feel that the overall evidence is somewhat weak, even though he believes there is probable cause for the arrest. If, under these circumstances, the charge is dismissed, some person, including the arresting officer, might well be faced with a civil action, even though there was probable cause for the arrest. Of course, this was true long before the passage of the Civil Rights Act. The latter merely gives to the plaintiff, in some instances, a choice of forums.

The civil rights actions, under state law, include among others, those for false arrest and false imprisonment. It is my firm belief that those in charge of prosecution of criminal actions have a duty to protect, if probable cause exists, arresting officers from both state or federal civil actions. We are not here concerned with a coerced plea of guilty. Appellant had his day in court and was found guilty of resisting arrest. The fact that he was acquitted on the original charge does not signify that there was no probable cause for the arrest. It merely means that the state failed to prove guilt beyond a reasonable doubt.

My thinking processes do not shudder at the portrait of the state judge asking appellant if he would agree to probable cause for the arrest. Many, many exceptionally able trial judges use this procedure to determine the appropriate action to take on the motion to dismiss. If appellant had so stipulated, the judge might well have denied the motion to dismiss. Beyond question, he would have inquired, in depth, of the prosecutor as to the appropriateness of a dismissal under these circumstances. The prosecutor, when appellant refused to agree to probable cause, was well within his rights in asking for a withdrawal of the motion to dismiss. In my view, there is nothing constitutionally objectionable in the district attorney's statement that it was his duty to include in the complaint any offense of which the appellant might be convicted. I am persuaded that the majority has erroneously raised a simple procedural act of the prosecutor to the dignity of constitutional dimensions.

. . .

---

313. Rumery was arrested for "tampering with a witness" in violation of state law. The charges grew out of telephone calls that he made to a woman who was the alleged victim and principal witness in a prosecution for aggravated sexual assault against his former hunting companion. The woman was a social and business acquaintance of Rumery. According to the police chief, Rumery made statements suggesting that the woman might be hurt if she testified. Rumery said that he made no threats. The county attorney learned that the woman did not want to testify against Rumery; there was no corroborating evidence of the telephone conversations. He discussed with Rumery's lawyer the possibility of dropping the charges against Rumery if he signed a covenant not to sue the persons connected with his arrest. The lawyer drafted the covenant, which Rumery signed, before a probable cause hearing was to take place. The charges against him were dropped. A little less than a year later, Rumery filed a complaint under 42 U.S.C. § 1983 alleging a violation of his civil rights arising out of the arrest. Town officials pleaded the covenant as an affirmative defense. Rumery was an experienced businessman. The town was a small New England town. Rumery v. Town of Newton, 778 F.2d 66 (1st Cir.1985).

The court of appeals held that the covenant not to sue was void as against public policy. It said: "The need closely to scrutinize contracts or agreements in the criminal law context is particularly important because of the special relationship between a criminal prosecution and the public interest. . . . Since the object of a criminal prosecution is to vindicate the public, not a private individual, an agreement not to prosecute should be upheld only where the *public* interest is served. It is difficult to envision how release agreements, negotiated in exchange for a decision not to prosecute, serve the public interest. Enforcement of such covenants would tempt prosecutors to trump up charges in reaction to a defendant's civil rights claim, suppress evidence of police misconduct, and leave unremedied deprivations of constitutional rights. We agree with those courts which have found that such releases have the effect of injuring the public interest." Id. at 69.

The Court reversed. Town of Newton v. Rumery, 480 U.S. 386 (1987) (5–4). The Court said that although a defendant's promise not to sue in return for dismissal of the charges against him might be unenforceable, because it was not informed and voluntary or because it was contrary to the public interest, there should not be a *per se* rule against the validity of such agreements. It compared such agreements with plea bargains, in which the defendant may give up constitutional rights; and it noted that prosecutors often have legitimate reasons for an agreement, such as avoiding the burden of defending against an insubstantial lawsuit. Examining the facts of this case, the Court concluded that the agreement was enforceable.

314. With MacDonald v. Musick, p. 650 above, and Rumery v. Town of Newton, note 313 above, compare cases in which a defendant moves for dismissal on the ground that the prosecution is due to prosecutorial vindictiveness. In United States v. Andrews, 633 F.2d 449 (6th Cir.1980), for example, the defendants were indicted for narcotics and firearms offenses. The government opposed their release on bail. The magistrate denied bail, and the defendants appealed. The district judge overturned the magistrate's decision, and the defendants were released on bail. Two days later, the Assistant United States Attorney obtained a superseding indictment adding a count of conspiracy. In those circumstances, the court of appeals discussed the issue of prosecutorial vindictiveness. A majority of the court concluded that the test of prosecutorial vindictiveness, which if found would bar the added charge, is "whether, in the particular factual situation presented, there existed a 'realistic likelihood of vindictiveness' for the prosecutor's augmentation of the charges." Id. at 453. See United States v. Groves, 571 F.2d 450 (9th Cir.1978) (indictment for related charge, returned after defendant moved for dismissal of another charge under Speedy Trial Act, dismissed as vindictive). Cf. United States v. Adams, 870 F.2d 1140 (6th Cir.1989) (defendants, allegedly prosecuted for tax offense in retaliation for lawsuit against EEOC, entitled to discovery of basis for prosecution). See generally the discussions of Bordenkircher v. Hayes, 434 U.S. 357 (1978), note 362 p. 738 below, and North Carolina v. Pearce, 395 U.S. 711 (1969), note 585 p. 1169 below.

Denial of a pretrial motion to dismiss an indictment on the ground of prosecutorial vindictiveness is not a final decision immediately appealable under 28 U.S.C. § 1291. United States v. Hollywood Motor Car Co., 458 U.S. 263 (1982) (6–3).

315. "On June 6, appellant was stopped by two police officers for alleged traffic violations [failing to obey the instructions of a police officer, and stopping a vehicle in a manner that obstructed the orderly flow of traffic]. He was neither charged nor ticketed at that time. Two days later, appellant delivered a written complaint to the police department concerning the conduct of the officers who had stopped him. At this point appellant and the Corporation Counsel's office apparently entered into a tacit agreement: appellant would not proceed further with his complaint and the Government would not prosecute the traffic charges.

"On September 1, 1965, however, appellant filed a formal complaint with the District of Columbia Commission's Council on Human Relations. After some 'hearings' at the Corporation Counsel's office, appellant refused to withdraw the complaint. As a result he was charged with the two traffic offenses. As the then Chief of the Law Enforcement Division of the Corporation Counsel explained: We had discussed it back when it originally occurred and, at the time, everybody was happy to forget the whole thing. . . . But three months later he comes in and makes a formal complaint. So we said 'If you are going to play ball like that why shouldn't we proceed with our case?' . . . I had no reason to file until he changed back on his understanding of what we had all agreed on. This is done in many cases." Dixon v. District of Columbia, 394 F.2d 966, 968 (D.C.Cir.1968). Should the prosecution be dismissed?

316. Unenforced statutes. Is it proper for a prosecutor to prosecute under a statute which has been disregarded for many years? Or to refuse to enforce such a statute? Does anything depend on the reasons why the statute has been disregarded by the public, or the police, or the prosecutor? Does anything depend on the reasons why the statute has not been repealed by the legislature? Should any of such questions of fact be subject to proof at trial? Can a judge take judicial notice of facts bearing on any of these questions?

In Poe v. Ullman, 367 U.S. 497 (1961), the Court declined to hear appeals from judgments dismissing actions for a declaratory judgment that the Connecticut statute outlawing the use of contraceptives was unconstitutional. Speaking also for three other Justices, Justice Frankfurter said: "The undeviating policy of nullification by Connecticut of its anti-contraceptive laws throughout all the long years that they have been on the statute books bespeaks more than prosecutorial paralysis. What was said in another context is relevant here. 'Deeply embedded traditional ways of carrying out state policy . . .'—or not carrying it out—'are often tougher and truer law than the dead words of the written text.' Nashville, C. & St. L.R. Co. v. Browning, 310 U.S. 362, 369." 367 U.S. at 502.[2]

With Poe v. Ullman, compare District of Columbia v. John R. Thompson Co., 346 U.S. 100 (1953), in which the Court upheld the validity of a criminal prosecution under acts of the Legislative Assembly of the District of Columbia enacted in 1872 and 1873. The information charged the defendant with refusing to serve persons at a restaurant within the District of Columbia solely on account of race and color, in violation of the acts. The Legislative Assembly was established in 1871 as part of a scheme of local government for the District of Columbia. It ceased to exist in 1874, by act of Congress. The opinion of the Court mentions no prior prosecutions under the acts, and notes that licenses had for 75 years been issued to restaurants in the District without regard to the requirements of the acts. The Court said, "The repeal of laws is as much a legislative function as their enactment." Id. at 114. "Cases of hardship are put where criminal laws so long in disuse as to be no longer known to exist are enforced against innocent parties. But that condition does not bear on the continuing validity of the law; it is only an ameliorating factor in enforcement." Id. at 117.

Should the government be estopped from prosecuting for a violation of the antitrust laws on the ground that over a period of ten years it knew about and acquiesced in the bidding system that was the basis of the alleged violation? See United States v. New Orleans Chapter, Associated General Contractors of America, 238 F.Supp. 273, 279–83 (E.D.La.1964), rev'd per curiam, 382 U.S. 17 (1965).

United States v. Bufalino

285 F.2d 408 (2d Cir.1960).

■ LUMBARD, CHIEF JUDGE.

Russell Bufalino and nineteen co-defendants appeal from judgments of conviction in the Southern District of New York for conspiring to obstruct

2. Four years later, the Court did consider and determine the constitutionality of the Connecticut statute, in Griswold v. Connecticut, 381 U.S. 479 (1965).

justice and commit perjury (18 U.S.C. §§ 371, 1503, 1621) by giving, before federal grand juries, false and evasive testimony regarding a gathering attended by them and at least 39 others at the home of Joseph Barbara, Sr., in Apalachin, New York, on November 14, 1957. Named as members of the conspiracy were seven other co-defendants and 36 co-conspirators. The appellants were all sentenced to prison terms running from three to five years, and in addition thirteen of them were each fined $10,000.

The indictment . . . alleged a conspiracy from November 14, 1957, the date of the Apalachin gathering, to the filing of the indictment on May 13, 1959. The 29 overt acts of the indictment which the court submitted to the jury charged that pursuant to the conspiracy various conspirators made statements and gave testimony under oath at different stated places and times from November 14, 1957 to May 11, 1959, including testimony on eleven occasions before federal grand juries in the Southern District of New York.

The indictment did not allege what the November 14, 1957 gathering at Apalachin was about, and the government stated at the beginning of the trial that it could present no evidence of its purpose. There is nothing in the record of the trial to show that any violation of federal or state law took place or was planned at the gathering, although federal grand juries in the Southern and Western Districts of New York on twenty occasions over the following year and one-half, and a variety of other federal and state officials on numerous other occasions, questioned many of those present about the Apalachin gathering and the surrounding circumstances.

. . .

[The court found that the evidence was insufficient to prove the crime charged.]

The administration of our system of criminal justice and our basic concepts of fair dealing are centered on the requirement that in each case we reach a result based solely on the charges made in the particular indictment and on the evidence which appears on the record with regard to those charges. Doubtless many of Barbara's visitors are bad people, and it is surely a matter of public concern that more is not known of their activities. But bad as many of these alleged conspirators may be, their conviction for a crime which the government could not prove, on inferences no more valid than others equally supported by reason and experience, and on evidence which a jury could not properly assess, cannot be permitted to stand.

Reversed and remanded with directions to dismiss the conspiracy count of the indictment.

CLARK, CIRCUIT JUDGE (concurring). I agree with the decision and opinion herein, but believe it desirable to point out what seems to me an even more basic failure of proof than the two so fully delineated by Chief Judge Lumbard. Perhaps the most curious feature of this strange case is the fact that after all these years there is not a shred of legal evidence that the Apalachin gathering was illegal or even improper in either purpose or fact. For thirteen years prior to the meeting as a modern Inspector Javert State Trooper Croswell pursued Barbara, Sr., in all ways possible (including tapping of his telephone) and got no evidence of illegality, although he did get wind of the meeting if not of its purpose. After it occurred on November 14, 1957, there were no less than 133 examinations of those present (as the government reports in its brief) by various state and federal officials, including 27 instances before federal grand juries and 29 by the FBI. The results were fruitless, as is highlighted by the government's frank admission at the outset of the trial that it would not be able to show what was going on at the meeting. The only suggestion, outside of an innuendo not here provable that the defendants were evil, is the bizarre nature of the gathering itself. But that gets us nowhere; common experience does not suggest that plotting to commit crime is done in convention assembled, or even the converse, also suggested here, namely, plotting to desist from crime. It must be taken, therefore, that for aught we can know the gathering was innocent.

. . .

From its inception this case was given unusual and disturbing publicity in newspapers, journals, and magazines; and this unfortunate feature has persisted up to this date, with even the prosecutors indulging in highly colored accounts while the case has been pending on appeal. Much of this has been in terms of a crisis in law administration seemingly demonstrated by an unexplained gathering of arch criminals and of a general satisfaction that somehow they have now met their just deserts of long imprisonment. This is vastly unfortunate; not only does it go beyond the judicial record necessary for its support, but it suggests that the administration of the criminal law is in such dire straits that crash methods have become a necessity. But it seems we should have known better, and a prosecution framed on such a doubtful basis should never have been initiated or allowed to proceed so far. For in America we still respect the dignity of the individual, and even an unsavory character is not to be imprisoned except on definite proof of specific crime. And nothing in present criminal law administration suggests or justifies sharp relaxation of traditional standards.

. . .

———

317. Is it proper for the government to select for intensive tax investigations those whom it believes, on the basis of evidence that is reliable but inadmissible or otherwise unavailable for use at a trial, to be leaders of organized crime or otherwise dangerous criminals? The Boston Globe reported on June 1, 1966, p. 3, that "at the height of the gangland murders," the Attorney General of Massachusetts had requested a "massive check" on the tax status of 287 persons, including "a number of Boston's big names in organized and even freelance crime"; the Internal Revenue Service apparently granted the request, "in a concerted state-Federal drive against Boston's hoodlum element." The New York Times reported on July 30, 1971, p. 1, that: "Pornography pushers, pimps, prostitutes and others allied with these businesses will be hit with charges of everything from tax evasion to littering under plans discussed yesterday by Mayor Lindsay's cabinet-level task force established to drive prostitution and pornography out of mid-Manhattan." See United States v. Accardo, 298 F.2d 133 (7th Cir.1962), involving the tax prosecution of a defendant who was characterized by one newspaper as "Chicago's jet-age Capone."

The defendants, certified public accountants, were prosecuted for tax offenses. They offered evidence to show that their prosecutions were part of "Project ACE," an Internal Revenue Service program that gave "special priorities" to the prosecution of attorneys, certified public accountants, and enrolled practitioners because of their "special obligation and responsibility to the tax laws." United States v. Swanson, 509 F.2d 1205, 1208 (8th Cir.1975). Is Project ACE proper?

318. Suppose a state's attorney general concludes that the greatest threat to the public order in his state is a vast network of intertwined criminal and lawful activities, over which a small syndicate presides. The criminal activities are "business" enterprises: gambling operations, narcotics distribution, prostitution, extortion, etc. The lawful activities are such things as laundry and motel ownership. Because of the great resources available to the syndicate and the apparent willingness of its members to carry out threats of extreme violence, no investigation or prosecution against any participants in the organization except those at its lowest level has been successful.

Is it proper or desirable for the attorney general to seek the assignment of a special corps of investigators to the investigation of the activities of the syndicate and the assignment of a special group of prosecutors to the preparation of cases against its members? Compare the measures taken by the FBI detailed in Giancana v. Johnson, 335 F.2d 366 (7th Cir.1964), note 189 p. 355 above, apparently not only for investigative purposes but also for harassment.

319. A college student who is employed as a temporary mail carrier during the Christmas holidays is found to have stolen about $50 from several letters given to him for delivery. He is contrite and anxious to make restitution. He is not in great need of money and has no explanation for the thefts. The post office, which has a continuing problem of theft by mail carriers, expends substantial resources to uncover such cases. There are presently pending several other cases of theft, some involving temporary workers including students and some involving regular employees. The postal authorities propose that the student be prosecuted for theft from the mails, a felony which carries a maximum sentence of imprisonment for five years and a fine, 18 U.S.C. § 1709. The cour (not)? If

not, what disposition should the United States attorney's office make of the case?

320. On the same morning three shoplifters are apprehended by a store detective for a large department store and brought to the office of the district attorney for the filing of a complaint:

(i) A college sophomore, who was observed slipping a sweater worth $30 into her purse. She is well-dressed and comes from a comfortable home. She is embarrassed and contrite. She explains that on the previous night she had a quarrel with her boyfriend and was unable to sleep. She had gone to the department store rather than go to classes in order to forget about the quarrel. The sweater is not of a kind that she would ordinarily wear. She states that she has not previously been in trouble with the law. Final examinations will be held at the college during the following week. She is accompanied by a lawyer.

(ii) A woman of 19, who was observed slipping a pocketbook worth $35 into a shopping bag. She is married and has a child. She works part time behind the counter in a luncheonette and receives welfare payments. Her husband does not live with her and contributes little to her or her child's support. She did not complete high school education. She offers no explanation for her act. So far as anyone knows, she has not previously been in trouble with the law.

(iii) A woman of 60, who was observed taking a bead necklace worth $5 into the ladies' washroom; the necklace was found in her pocketbook by the store detective as the woman was about to walk out of the store. The detective states that she had seen the woman do the same thing with other items of small value on many previous occasions and, despite the store's general policy of ignoring occasional acts of this kind by well-to-do patrons, had decided to arrest the woman if she did it again. The woman is wealthy and an "established" member of the community. She indignantly denies any intention to steal; she states that she had gone into the washroom to look at the necklace in a mirror and had absent-mindedly put it in her pocketbook. She threatens to sue the store for false arrest. She states that she has not previously been in trouble with the law. She is accompanied by a lawyer.

How should the assistant district attorney who is in charge of the complaint desk respond to the three cases?

United States Attorneys' Manual

9.27. Principles of Federal Prosecution

. . .

9–27.200 Initiating and Declining Prosecution

. . .

9–27.220 *Grounds for Commencing or Declining Prosecution*

A. The attorney for the government should commence or recommend federal prosecution if he/she believes that the person's conduct constitutes a federal offense and that the admissible evidence will probably be sufficient to obtain and sustain a conviction, unless, in his/her judgment, prosecution should be declined because:

> 1. No substantial federal interest would be served by prosecution;

> 2. The person is subject to effective prosecution in another jurisdiction; or

> 3. There exists an adequate non-criminal alternative to prosecution.

B. Comment

. . .

The potential that—despite the law and the facts that create a sound, prosecutable case—the fact-finder is likely to acquit the defendant because of the unpopularity of some factor involved in the prosecution or because of the overwhelming popularity of the defendant or his/her cause, is not a factor prohibiting prosecution. For example, in a civil rights case or a case involving an extremely popular political figure, it might be clear that the evidence of guilt—viewed objectively by an unbiased fact-finder—would be sufficient to obtain and sustain a conviction, yet the prosecutor might reasonably doubt whether the jury would convict. In such a case, despite his/her negative assessment of the likelihood of a guilty verdict (based on factors extraneous to an objective view of the law and the facts), the prosecutor may properly conclude that it is necessary and desirable to commence or recommend prosecution and allow the criminal process to operate in accordance with its principles.

Merely because the attorney for the government believes that a person's conduct constitutes a federal offense and that the admissible evidence will be sufficient to obtain and sustain a conviction, does not mean that he/she necessarily should initiate or recommend prosecution: USAM 9–27.220 notes three situations in which the prosecutor may properly decline to take action nonetheless: when no substantial federal interest would be served by prosecution; when the person is subject to effective prosecution in another jurisdiction; and when there exists an adequate non-criminal alternative to prosecution. It is left to the judgment of the attorney for the government whether such a situation exists. In exercising that judgment, the attorney for the government should consult USAM 9–27.230, 9–27.240, or 9–27.250, infra, as appropriate.

9–27.230 *Substantial Federal Interest*

A. In determining whether prosecution should be declined because no substantial federal interest would be served by prosecution, the attorney for the government should weigh all relevant considerations, including:

    1. Federal law enforcement priorities;

    2. The nature and seriousness of the offense;

    3. The deterrent effect of prosecution;

    4. The person's culpability in connection with the offense;

    5. The person's history with respect to criminal activity;

    6. The person's willingness to cooperate in the investigation or prosecution of others; and

    7. The probable sentence or other consequences if the person is convicted.

B. Comment

    . . .

    1. Federal Law Enforcement Priorities

Federal law enforcement resources and federal judicial resources are not sufficient to permit prosecution of every alleged offense over which federal jurisdiction exists. Accordingly, in the interest of allocating its limited resources as to achieve an effective nationwide law enforcement program, from time to time the Department establishes national investigative and prosecutorial priorities. These priorities are designed to focus federal law enforcement efforts on those matters within the federal jurisdiction that are most deserving of federal attention and are most likely to be handled effectively at the federal level. In addition, individual U.S. Attorneys may establish their own priorities, within the national priorities, in order to concentrate their resources on problems of particular local or regional significance. In weighing the federal interest in a particular prosecution, the attorney for the government should give careful consideration to the extent to which prosecution would accord with established priorities.

    2. Nature and Seriousness of Offense

It is important that limited federal resources not be wasted in prosecuting inconsequential cases or cases in which the violation is only technical. Thus, in determining whether a substantial federal interest exists that requires prosecution, the attorney for the government should consider the nature and seriousness of the offense involved. A number of factors may be relevant. One factor that is obviously of primary importance is the actual or potential impact of the offense on the community and on the victim.

The impact of an offense on the community in which it is committed can be measured in several ways: in terms of economic harm done to community interests; in terms of physical danger to the citizens or damage to public property; and in terms of erosion of the inhabitants' peace of mind and sense of security. In assessing the seriousness of the offense in these terms, the prosecutor may properly weigh such questions as whether the violation is technical or relatively inconsequential in nature, and what the public attitude is toward prosecution under the circumstances of the case. The public may be indifferent, or even opposed, to enforcement of the controlling statute, whether on substantive grounds, or because of a history of non-enforcement, or because the offense involves essentially a minor matter of private concern and the victim is disinterested in having it pursued. On the other hand, the nature and circumstances of the offense, the identity of the offender or the victim, or the attendant publicity, may be such as to create strong public sentiment in favor of prosecution. While public interest, or lack thereof, deserves the prosecutor's careful attention, it should not be used to justify a decision to prosecute, or to take other action, that cannot be supported on other grounds. Public and professional responsibility sometimes will require the choosing of a particularly unpopular course.

Economic, physical, and psychological considerations are also important in assessing the impact of the offense on the victim. In this connection, it is appropriate for the prosecutor to take into account such matters as the victim's age or health, and whether full or partial restitution has been made. Care should be taken in weighing the matter of restitution, however, to ensure against contributing to an impression that an offender can escape prosecution merely by returning the spoils of his/her crime.

3. Deterrent Effect of Prosecution

Deterrence of criminal conduct, whether it be criminal activity generally or a specific type of criminal conduct, is one of the primary goals of the criminal law. This purpose should be kept in mind, particularly when deciding whether a prosecution is warranted for an offense that appears to be relatively minor; some offenses, although seemingly not of great importance by themselves, if commonly committed would have a substantial cumulative impact on the community.

4. The Person's Culpability

Although the prosecutor has sufficient evidence of guilt, it is nevertheless appropriate for him/her to give consideration to the degree of the person's culpability in connection with the offense, both in the abstract and in comparison with any others involved in the offense. If, for example, the person was a relatively minor participant in a criminal enterprise conducted by others, or his/her motive was worthy, and no other circumstances require prosecution, the prosecutor might reasonably conclude that some course other than prosecution would be appropriate.

5. The Person's Criminal History

If a person is known to have a prior conviction or is reasonably believed to have engaged in criminal activity at an earlier time, this should be considered in determining whether to initiate or recommend federal prosecution. In this connection, particular attention should be given to the nature of the person's prior criminal involvement, when it occurred, its relationship if any to the present offense, and whether he/she previously avoided prosecution as a result of an agreement not to prosecute in return for cooperation or as a result of an order compelling his/her testimony. By the same token, a person's lack of prior criminal involvement or his/her previous cooperation with the law enforcement officials should be given due consideration in appropriate cases.

6. The Person's Willingness to Cooperate

A person's willingness to cooperate in the investigation or prosecution of others is another appropriate consideration in the determination whether a federal prosecution should be undertaken. Generally speaking, a willingness to cooperate should not, by itself, relieve a person of criminal liability. There may be some cases, however, in which the value of a person's cooperation clearly outweighs the federal interest in prosecuting him/her. These matters are discussed more fully . . . in connection with plea agreements and non-prosecution agreements in return for cooperation.

7. The Person's Personal Circumstances

In some cases, the personal circumstances of an accused may be relevant in determining whether to prosecute or to take other action. Some circumstances peculiar to the accused, such as extreme youth, advanced age, or mental or physical impairment, may suggest that prosecution is not the most appropriate response to his/her offense; other circumstances, such as the fact that the accused occupied a position of trust or responsibility which he/she violated in committing the offense, might weigh in favor of prosecution.

8. The Probable Sentence

In assessing the strength of the federal interest in prosecution, the attorney for the government should consider the sentence, or other consequence, that is likely to be imposed if prosecution is successful, and whether such a sentence or other consequence would justify the time and effort of prosecution. If the offender is already subject to a substantial sentence, or is already incarcerated, as a result of a conviction for another offense, the prosecutor should weigh the likelihood that another conviction will result in a meaningful addition to his/her sentence, might otherwise have a deterrent effect, or is necessary to ensure that the offender's record accurately reflects the extent of his/her criminal conduct. For example, it might be desirable to commence a bail-jumping prosecution against a person who already has been convicted of another offense so that law enforcement personnel and judicial officers who encounter him/her in the future will be aware of the risk of releasing him/her on bail. On the other hand, if the person is on probation or parole as a result of an earlier conviction, the prosecutor should consider whether the public interest might better be served by instituting a proceeding for violation of probation or revocation of parole, than by commencing a new prosecution. The prosecutor should also be alert to the desirability of instituting prosecution to prevent the running of the statute of limitations and to preserve the availability of a basis for an adequate sentence if there appears to be a chance that an offender's prior conviction may be reversed on appeal or collateral attack. Finally, if a person previously has been prosecuted in another jurisdiction for the same offense or a closely related offense, the attorney for the government should consult existing departmental policy statements on the subject of "successive prosecution" or "dual prosecution," depending on whether the earlier prosecution was federal or non-federal. . . .

Just as there are factors that it is appropriate to consider in determining whether a substantial federal interest would be served by prosecution in a particular case, there are considerations that deserve no weight and should not influence the decision. These include the time and resources expended in federal investigation of the case. No amount of investigative effort warrants commencing a federal prosecution that is not fully justified on other grounds.

9–27.240 *Prosecution in Another Jurisdiction*

. . .

9–27.250 *Non-Criminal Alternatives to Prosecution*

A. In determining whether prosecution should be declined because there exists an adequate non-criminal alternative to prosecution, the attorney for the government should consider all relevant factors, including:

1. The sanctions available under the alternative means of disposition;

2. The likelihood that an appropriate sanction will be imposed; and

3. The effect of non-criminal disposition on federal law enforcement interests.

B. Comment

When a person has committed a federal offense, it is important that the law respond promptly, fairly, and effectively. This does not mean, however, that a criminal prosecution must be initiated. In recognition of the fact that resort to the criminal process is not necessarily the only appropriate response to serious forms of antisocial activity, Congress and state legislatures have provided civil and administrative remedies for many types of conduct that may also be subject to criminal sanction. Examples of such non-criminal approaches include civil tax proceedings; civil actions under the securities, customs, antitrust, or other regulatory laws; and reference of complaints to licensing authorities or to professional organizations such as bar associations. Another potentially useful alternative to prosecution in some cases is pre-trial diversion . . . .

. . .

9–27.260 *Impermissible Considerations*

A. In determining whether to commence or recommend prosecution or take other action, the attorney for the government should not be influenced by:

1. The person's race; religion; sex; national origin; or political association, activities, or beliefs;

2. His/her own personal feelings concerning the person, the person's associates, or the victim; or

3. The possible effect of his/her decision on his/her own professional or personal circumstances.

. . .

9–27.300 SELECTING CHARGES

9–27.310 *Charging Most Serious Offenses*

A. Except as hereafter provided, once the decision to prosecute has been made, the attorney for the government should charge, or should recommend that the grand jury charge, the most serious offense that is consistent with the nature of the defendant's conduct, and that is likely to result in a sustainable conviction. The "most serious" offense is generally that which yields the highest range under the sentencing guidelines. If mandatory minimum sentences are also involved, their effect must be considered, keeping in mind the fact that a mandatory minimum is statutory and generally overrules a guideline.

B. Comment

Once it has been determined to initiate prosecution, either by filing a complaint or an information, or by seeking an indictment from the grand jury, the attorney for the government must determine what charges to file or recommend. When the conduct in question consists of a single criminal act, or when there is only one applicable statute, this is not a difficult task. Typically, however, a defendant will have committed more than one criminal act and his/her conduct may be prosecuted under more than one statute. Moreover, selection of charges may be complicated further by the fact that different statutes have different proof requirements and provide substantially different penalties. In such cases, considerable care is required to ensure selection of the proper charge or charges. In addition to reviewing the concerns that prompted the decision to prosecute in the first instance, particular attention should be given to the need to ensure that the prosecution will be both fair and effective.

At the outset, the attorney for the government should bear in mind that at trial he/she will have to produce admissible evidence sufficient to obtain and sustain a conviction or else the government will suffer a dismissal. For this reason, he/she should not include in an information or recommend in an indictment charges that he/she cannot reasonably expect to prove beyond a reasonable doubt by legally sufficient evidence at trial.

. . .

As stated, a federal prosecutor should initially charge the most serious, readily provable offense or offenses consistent with the defendant's conduct. Charges should not be filed simply to exert leverage to induce a plea, nor should charges be abandoned in an effort to arrive at a bargain that fails to reflect the seriousness of the defendant's conduct.

USAM 9–27.310 expresses the principle that the defendant should be charged with the most serious offense that is encompassed by his/her conduct and that is readily provable. Ordinarily . . . this will be the offense for which the most severe penalty is provided by law and the guidelines. Where two crimes have the same stautory maximum and the same guideline range, but only one contains a mandatory minimum penalty, the one with the mandatory minimum is more serious. This principle provides the framwork for ensuring equal justice in the prosecution of federal criminal offenders. It guarantees that every defendant will start from the same position, charged with the most serious criminal act he/she commits. . . .

. . .

9–27.320 *Additional Charges*

A. Except as hereafter provided, the attorney for the government should also charge, or recommend that the grand jury charge, other offenses only when, in his/her judgment, additional charges:

    1. Are necessary to ensure that the information or indictment:

        a. Adequately reflects the nature and extent of the criminal conduct involved; and

        b. Provides the basis for an appropriate sentence under all the circumstances of the case; or

    2. Will significantly enhance the strength of the government's case against the defendant or a codefendant.

. . .

---

321. In Berra v. United States, 351 U.S. 131 (1956) (7–2), the defendant was prosecuted for wilfully attempting to evade federal income taxes, a felony punishable by imprisonment for not more than five years and a fine. A different section of the code made it a misdemeanor punishable by imprisonment for not more than one year and a fine to deliver to the Collector a false statement with intent to avoid a tax. The Court held that since in the context of the case the two statutes "covered precisely the same ground" and the facts necessary to prove guilt of the two crimes were "identical," id. at 134, the defendant was not entitled to a jury instruction on the lesser offense.[3] The jury's role, the Court said, was to determine the issues of fact. "When the jury resolved those issues against petitioner, its function was exhausted, since there is here no statutory provision giving to the jury the right to determine the punishment to be imposed after the determination of guilt." Id. at 135.

Justice Black dissented:

"The Government admits here and the Court assumes that filing a false and fraudulent income tax return is both a misdemeanor . . . and a felony. . . . The Government argues that the action of the trial judge must be upheld because 'the government may choose to invoke either applicable law,' and 'the prosecution may be for a felony even though the Government could have elected to prosecute for a misdemeanor.' Election by the Government of course means election by a prosecuting attorney or the Attorney General. I object to any such interpretation of . . . [the statute]. I think we should construe these sections so as not to place control over the liberty of citizens in the unreviewable discretion of one individual—a result which seems to me to be wholly incompatible with our system of justice. Since Congress has specifically made the conduct charged in the indictment a misdemeanor, I would not permit prosecution for a felony . . . . Criminal statutes, which forfeit life, liberty or property, should be construed narrowly, not broadly.

. . .

"A basic principle of our criminal law is that the Government only prosecutes people for crimes under statutes passed by Congress which fairly and clearly define the conduct made criminal and the punishment which can be administered. This basic principle is flouted if either of these statutes can be selected as the controlling law at the whim of the prosecuting attorney or the Attorney General. . . .

"A congressional delegation of such vast power to the prosecuting department would raise serious constitutional questions. Of course it is true that under our system Congress may vest the judge and jury with broad power to say how much punishment shall be imposed for a particular offense. But it is quite different to vest such powers in a prosecuting attorney. A judge and jury act under procedural rules carefully prescribed to protect the liberty of the individual. Their judgments and verdicts are reached after a public trial in which a defendant has the right to be represented by an attorney. No such protections are thrown around decisions by a prosecuting attorney. Substitution of the prosecutor's caprice for the adjudicatory process is an action I am not willing to attribute to Congress in the absence of clear command. Our system of justice rests on the conception of impersonality in the criminal law. This great protection to freedom is lost if the Government is right in its contention here. . . .

---

3. See note 548 p. 1111 below.

"The Government's contention here also challenges our concept that all people must be treated alike under the law. This principle means that no different or higher punishment should be imposed upon one than upon another if the offense and the circumstances are the same. It is true that there may be differences due to different appraisals given the circumstances of different cases by different judges and juries. But in these cases the discretion in regard to conviction and punishment for crime is exercised by the judge and jury in their constitutional capacities in the administration of justice.

"I would reverse this case or at least remand for resentencing under the misdemeanor statute . . . ." Id. at 138–40.

See the opinion of Judge Bazelon, dissenting from denial of a petition for rehearing by the whole court in Lloyd v. United States, 343 F.2d 242, 243 (D.C.Cir.1964). Compare Hutcherson v. United States, 345 F.2d 964 (D.C.Cir.1965) (same offenses under federal and D.C. statutes).

The decision not to prosecute

322. The plaintiff, a spectator at a baseball game at Fenway Park, was struck in the head by a baseball thrown from the visiting team's bullpen. He obtained a complaint from the Municipal Court charging the pitcher who had thrown the ball with assault and battery with a dangerous weapon. At a probable cause hearing, the court dismissed the charge. The district attorney's office declined to pursue the complaint further. Upholding the decisions below, the Supreme Judicial Court said: "The victim of an alleged crime has no right to challenge a judicial determination which forecloses further prosecution of that alleged crime. Although a victim may seek a complaint against the alleged criminal . . ., the prosecution of any complaint, once issued, is conducted in the interests of the Commonwealth and not on behalf of the alleged victim." Manning v. Municipal Court, 361 N.E.2d 1274, 1276 (Mass.1977). See generally Linda R.S. v. Richard D., 410 U.S. 614, 619 (1973): "The Court's prior decisions consistently hold that a citizen lacks standing to contest the policies of the prosecuting authority when he himself is neither prosecuted nor threatened with prosecution. . . . [I]n American jurisprudence at least, a private citizen lacks a judicially cognizable interest in the prosecution or nonprosecution of another."

A robbery of the First Federal Savings and Loan Association in Evansville, Indiana, occurred on October 8, 1962. A witness identified Del Monico as a suspect when his photograph appeared in a local newspaper on May 3, 1963. Thereafter, a group of eyewitnesses to the robbery picked Del Monico's photograph from a group of nine photographs and identified him in person. Every witness, without dissent, identified Del Monico's photograph and Del Monico.

The bank robbery aroused great interest in Evansville. Del Monico's identification as the robber and his subsequent indictment were well-known facts in the community.

UNITED STATES DISTRICT COURT SOUTHERN DISTRICT OF
INDIANA EVANSVILLE DIVISION

UNITED STATES OF AMERICA	)	
V.	)	NO. EV 64–CR–17
CHARLES DEL MONICO	)	

MOTION FOR LEAVE TO DISMISS THE INDICTMENT

Richard P. Stein, United States Attorney for the Southern District of Indiana, by direction of Nicholas Katzenbach, Attorney General of the United States, moves for leave of this Court, under and pursuant to the provisions of Rule 48(a), Federal Rules of Criminal Procedure, to dismiss without prejudice the indictment heretofore returned in the captioned cause on June 15, 1964.

In support of this motion, the United States respectfully shows to the Court as follows:

On May 4, 1964, the defendant's counsel submitted to the United States a copy of a report setting forth the results of a polygraph examination which the defendant had undergone on April 27–28, 1964. The examiner, an established expert in his field, concluded that the defendant was truthful in his denial of involvement in the subject bank robbery.

On June 15, 1964, the United States received from the defendant's counsel the names of witnesses who would testify that the defendant was in Miami Beach, Florida on October 8, 1962, the date of the alleged bank robbery. These witnesses were subsequently made available for interview by agents of the Federal Bureau of Investigation and by the attorneys for the United States. No substantial basis for discrediting the crucial portions of their testimony has yet been uncovered.

On January 22–24, 1965, the defendant submitted to narcoanalysis at Sibley Hospital in Washington, D.C., by Dr. Leon Salzman, Professor of Clinical Psychiatry at the Washington School of Psychiatry. Based upon his examinations, Dr. Salzman concluded that the defendant had no knowledge of the alleged bank robbery.

On January 25–26, 1965, the defendant submitted to a second polygraph examination by John Reid and Associates, Chicago, Illinois, the foremost experts in this field. The examiners again concluded that the defendant was truthful in his denial of knowledge or implication in the subject bank robbery.

On January 29, 1965, the defendant submitted to narcoanalysis a second time by an expert chosen by the United States. The results of this examination, which were made available to the Attorney General and the attorneys for the United States on January 30, 1965, again reflect no findings justifying the conclusion that the defendant was involved in the subject bank robbery.

While the great weight of judicial authority holds that the results of these tests would not be admissible in evidence in the trial of this case, nevertheless, in the light of all the circumstances, they must be accorded some weight in determining whether or not prosecution should be continued at this time.

The evidence of the United States consists entirely of the testimony of eyewitnesses to the robbery, who first identified the defendant as the robber on or about May 3, 1963, seven months after the robbery. Despite intensive investigation by the Federal Bureau of Investigation for many months, no evidence of any kind has been uncovered that would corroborate the testimony of the eyewitnesses or even establish that the defendant was ever in Evansville.

Because of the inherent danger of a miscarriage of justice grounded upon the possibility of honest but mistaken eyewitness identification, the Attorney General has concluded that the proper administration of justice requires that the present indictment be dismissed without prejudice pending further investigation.

WHEREFORE, the United States respectfully prays that the Court grant leave to dismiss the indictment.

Richard P. Stein
United States

Do you agree that the indictment should be dismissed? How much weight should a prosecutor give to the fact that a grand jury has returned an indictment? How much weight should a prosecutor give to the fact that evidence of a defendant's innocence which is presented to him will be inadmissible at trial? How much weight should he give to inadmissible evidence of the defendant's guilt?

323. Should the judge before whom a motion to dismiss an indictment is made exercise independent discretion in deciding whether or not to grant the motion? Fed.R.Crim.P. 48(a) requires "leave of court" for the dismissal of an indictment, information or complaint, and the consent of the defendant for dismissal during trial. In United States v. Cowan, 524 F.2d 504, 512–13 (5th Cir.1975), the court said that the rule "should and can be construed to preserve the essential judicial function of protecting the public interest in the evenhanded administration of criminal justice without encroaching on the primary duty of the Executive to take care that the laws are faithfully executed." Accordingly, the prosecutor was "the first and presumptively the best judge of whether a pending prosecution should be terminated," and his judgment "should not be judicially disturbed unless clearly contrary to manifest public interest." Other cases are cited id. at 511. See generally United States v. Ammidown, 497 F.2d 615 (D.C.Cir.1973), note 373 p. 754 below.

See Rinaldi v. United States, 434 U.S. 22 (1977) (6–3), in which the government moved to dismiss the indictment under Rule 48(a) following the defendant's trial and conviction. The government made the motion because the conviction violated the "Petite" policy against federal and state prosecutions for the same act, see note 625 p. 1251 below. The district court denied the motion because it was not made until the trial was completed and because the prosecutor had acted in bad faith earlier when he advised the court that the prosecution was proper notwithstanding the defendant's state prosecution for the same offense. (The government had pursued the federal prosecution because it had feared a reversal of the state conviction.) The Court held that the motion to dismiss not being "clearly contrary to manifest public interest" (citing *Cowan,* above), it was an abuse of discretion to deny the motion. Id. at 30. It noted also that the "principal object" of requiring leave of court in Rule 48(a) "is apparently to protect a defendant against prosecutorial harassment, e.g., charging, dismissing and recharging, when the Government moves to dismiss an indictment over the defendant's objection." Id. at 29 n. 15. See United States v. Smith, 55 F.3d 157 (4th Cir.1995) (*Renaldi* applied).

In United States v. Moller-Butcher, 723 F.2d 189, 190 (1st Cir.1983), the court observed that "absent extraordinary circumstances, a defendant has no standing to appeal the dismissal of an indictment." See United States v. Palomares, 119 F.3d 556 (7th Cir.1997) (dismissal of indictment upheld); United States v. Salinas, 693 F.2d 348 (5th Cir.1982) (order granting government's motion to dismiss was improper, because motion was not made in good faith); United States v. Hamm, 659 F.2d 624 (5th Cir.1981) (order denying government's motion to dismiss following plea of guilty reversed); United States v. Hastings, 447 F.Supp. 534 (E.D.Ark.1977) (government's motion to dismiss because of improper conduct of investigation granted).

CHAPTER 10

INDICTMENT

——

324. "No person shall be held to answer for a capital, or otherwise infamous crime, unless on a presentment or indictment of a grand jury, except in cases arising in the land or naval forces, or in the militia, when in actual service in time of war or public danger. . . ." U.S. Constitution amend. V.[1]

The states are not required by the Due Process Clause of the Fourteenth Amendment to prosecute by indictment in any case. Hurtado v. California, 110 U.S. 516 (1884). Many states now prosecute entirely by information. The grand jury has been abolished in England, where it originated. Administration of Justice Act, 1933, 23 & 24 Geo. 5, ch. 36.

In Rose v. Mitchell, 443 U.S. 545 (1979) (7–2), the defendants, who were black, appealed from a state conviction of murder on the ground that their pretrial motion to dismiss the indictment was wrongly denied; their motion alleged that the grand jury array and the foreman of the grand jury had been selected in a racially discriminatory fashion. The convictions were affirmed. The defendants then filed a petition for habeas corpus in the federal district court. In the Supreme Court, only the selection of the foreman was in issue. The Court concluded that the defendants had not established that there was racial discrimination. It reaffirmed, however, that discrimination in the selection of the grand jury is ground for setting aside a conviction. "Because discrimination on the basis of race in the selection of members of a grand jury . . . strikes at the fundamental values of our judicial system and our society as a whole, the Court has recognized that a criminal defendant's right to equal protection of the laws has been denied when he is indicted by a grand jury from which members of a racial group

---

1. "The question is whether the crime is one for which the statutes authorize the court to award an infamous punishment, not whether the punishment ultimately awarded is an infamous one. When the accused is in danger of being subjected to an infamous punishment if convicted, he has the right to insist that he shall not be put upon his trial, except on the accusation of a grand jury.

. . .

"What punishments shall be considered as infamous may be affected by the changes of public opinion from one age to another." Ex parte Wilson, 114 U.S. 417, 426–27 (1885). See Duke v. United States, 301 U.S. 492 (1937).

purposefully have been excluded. . . . For this same reason, the Court also has reversed the conviction and ordered the indictment quashed in such cases without inquiry into whether the defendant was prejudiced in fact by the discrimination at the grand jury stage." Id. at 556.

In an opinion concurring only in the judgment, Justice Stewart argued that a grand jury proceeding is "merely one to decide whether there is a prima-facie case" against the defendant. "Any possible prejudice to the defendant resulting from an indictment returned by an invalid grand jury thus disappears when a constitutionally valid trial jury later finds him guilty beyond a reasonable doubt. In short, a convicted defendant who alleges that he was indicted by a discriminatorily selected grand jury is complaining of an antecedent constitutional violation that could have had no conceivable impact on the fairness of the trial that resulted in his conviction." Id. at 575–76. Justice Stewart observed that other means were available to vindicate the "compelling constitutional interest" in eliminating racial discrimination. Id. at 578. Rose v. Mitchell was followed in Vasquez v. Hillery, 474 U.S. 254 (1986) (6–3).

Discrimination in the selection of the foreman of a federal grand jury, which caused black persons and women not to be selected but did not cause them to be under-represented on the grand jury, does not require dismissal of an indictment against a defendant who is a white male. Hobby v. United States, 468 U.S. 339 (1984) (6–3). The Court observed that the position of foreman is ministerial; and the responsibilities attached to the office are essentially clerical. Accordingly, "the role of the foreman of a federal grand jury is not so significant to the administration of justice that discrimination in the appointment of that office impugns the fundamental fairness of the process itself so as to undermine the integrity of the indictment." Nor does discrimination invade the defendant's distinct interests under the Due Process Clause. 468 U.S. at 345. In Rose v. Mitchell, the Court had assumed that discrimination in the selection of the foreman of a state grand jury would require dismissal of an indictment. In *Hobby*, the court distinguished Rose v. Mitchell on the grounds that the defendants in the latter case, as members of the disfavored race, had a claim under the Equal Protection Clause, and further, that in the state system in question the foreman was an additional grand juror, whose selection affected the composition of the jury as a whole, and who played a much more significant role than is played by a federal foreman.

Hobby was distinguished in Campbell v. Louisiana, ____ U.S. ____, 118 S.Ct. 1419 (1998), in which the Court held that the defendant, who was white, had standing to challenge an indictment (by motion to quash), on the ground that the selection of the foreman of the grand jury was racially discriminatory, systematically excluding black persons. Referring to Rose v. Mitchell, the Court noted that, unlike *Hobby*, selection as foreman in *Campbell* was also the basis for inclusion of the person selected as a member of the grand jury, and, therefore, the selection process affected the composition of the grand jury itself. The court relied on Peters v. Kiff, 407 U.S. 493 (1972, note 442 p. 921 below, and Powers v. Ohio, 499 U.S. 400 (1991) (7–2), note 449 p. 931 below, for its conclusion that the defendant had standing to raise the issue.

325. "Prosecution of infamous crimes solely by indictment or presentment by a grand jury was provided for almost universally in American constitutions in our formative period. Informations ex officio by the attorney general were the basis of political prosecutions in England in the seventeenth and eighteenth centuries and the odium which attached to those prosecutions was attributed to the mode by which they were instituted. It was supposed that the requirement of indictment was a guarantee against oppressive prosecutions. But the grand jury had its real justification in the system of private prosecutions which never obtained in the United States. Although in historical origin it had another function, it came to be a check on private prosecutions, insuring that privately instituted proceedings should not go forward unless a representative body of men of the neighborhood found there was probable cause therefor. There was no need of such a check in a régime of public prosecutions. Under such a régime the grand jury merely adds one more to the long series of mitigating devices and opportunities for escape in which our prosecuting system abounds. In effect, as things are today, there are usually three preliminary examinations: One extralegal, conducted by the prosecuting attorney, one before a magistrate to bind accused over to the grand jury, and one before the grand jury.

"[T]here has been ample experience of the workings of a system of prosecution by information. . . . [I]t appears abundantly that prosecution by information has uniformly proved most satisfactory in practice and that none of the bad results feared by those who would retain the old system have been realized.

"It is important, in view of the continually increasing demands upon the public purse, that the expense of administering justice be not augmented unnecessarily by inherited institutions which serve no useful purpose. That the grand-jury system is expensive is obvious. But it involves more than expenditure of money. In large cities grand juries must often sit continuously, or almost continuously, throughout the year. If there are to be good juries, excessive drain is made on the time of busy men who can ill afford to devote to public service the time which such a system, appropriate to the rural communities of the past, demands of them. There is economic waste also in requiring witnesses to attend two preliminary hearings, one before a magistrate and one before the grand jury. Moreover, this requirement of repeated attendance of witnesses, under conditions which obtain in large and busy cities, discourages witnesses and not infrequently leads to no prosecution where one ought to go forward. Again the extra step of indictment by a grand jury contributes to slowing up the already overburdened machinery of prosecution. It offers an additional opportunity of escape where there are now too many, and allows responsibility for failure to prosecute to fall down between the prosecutor and the grand jury. Thus the system wastes money, time, and energy, and diffuses responsibility in a field where responsibility ought to be concentrated.

"Protection of the citizen against hasty and unfounded prosecutions, the advantage claimed for the requirement of an indictment in case of all infamous crimes, is more theoretical than real in the urban community of today. With the enormous lists of arrests in our large cities there is no guaranty against hasty or oppressive prosecutions in a body which can give but little time to the general run of cases and must depend on the prosecuting attorney for its information as to facts. Under such circumstances it must be a very weak case which can not be presented so as to procure an indictment. Where the number of prosecutions is large, it is hard for the grand jury in any ordinary case to get at other facts than those presented to them, or even to know that it is authorized to get at them. It is unusual for grand juries to go into a thorough, independent investigation of any ordinary case unless the prosecutor is willing. If the work of sifting were done as it should be by proper criminal investigation at the outset and by the prosecuting attorney, the grand jury could be given a basis for doing its work thoroughly and well. But the loose methods of investigation and sifting, which prevail generally in large cities, cause that work to be mechanical and perfunctory, except in a small number of sensational or unusual cases.

"It should be added that the requirement of indictment by a grand jury in all prosecutions for infamous crimes involves a number of needless procedural difficulties which do not obtain in a régime of prosecution by information. Thus an indictment can not be amended, while an information may be. There are statutory requirements as to the drawing and composition of grand juries which frequently give rise to dilatory objections to the indictment. There are necessary rules as to the procedure of grand juries, and in particular as to who may be present during their inquiries and deliberations, which likewise offer opportunities for dilatory objections. To-day the grand jury is useful only as a general investigating body for inquiring into the conduct of public officers and in case of large conspiracies. It should be retained as an occasional instrument for such purposes, and the requirement of it as a necessary basis of all prosecutions for infamous crimes should be done away with." National Commission on Law Observance and Enforcement (Wickersham Commission), Report on Prosecution 34–37 (1931).

326. The authority of the grand jury to issue "reports" without indicting anyone or to name persons as "unindicted coconspirators" or otherwise accuse them of crimes without formally indicting them is discussed extensively in United States v. Briggs, 514 F.2d 794 (5th Cir.1975). The court concluded that the grand jury lacks authority to accuse named persons of crimes without indicting them and that for it to do so is a denial of due process. See United States v. International Harvester Co., 720 F.2d 418 (5th Cir.1983) (person named but not charged in indictment not entitled to expungement, because he was indicted in related case in which government would be put to proof).

See generally Ealy v. Littlejohn, 569 F.2d 219 (5th Cir.1978), in which the court held that a grand jury inquiry into the organization and activities of a private association, as a result of public statements made in the name of the association and without any showing of a legitimate investigative purpose, was a violation of First Amendment rights.

FEDERAL RULES OF CRIMINAL PROCEDURE

Rule 6.

THE GRAND JURY

(a) Summoning Grand Juries.

(1) Generally. The court shall order one or more grand juries to be summoned at such time as the public interest requires. The grand jury shall consist of not less than 16 nor more than 23 members. The court shall direct that a sufficient number of legally qualified persons be summoned to meet this requirement.

(2) Alternate Jurors. The court may direct that alternate jurors may be designated at the time a grand jury is selected. Alternate jurors in the order in which they were designated may thereafter be impanelled as provided in subdivision (g) of this rule. Alternate jurors shall be drawn in the same manner and shall have the same qualifications as the regular jurors, and if impanelled shall be subject to the same challenges, shall take the same oath and shall have the same functions, powers, facilities and privileges as the regular jurors.

(b) Objections to Grand Jury and to Grand Jurors.

(1) Challenges. The attorney for the government or a defendant who has been held to answer in the district court may challenge the array of jurors on the ground that the grand jury was not selected, drawn or summoned in accordance with law, and may challenge an individual juror on the ground that the juror is not legally qualified. Challenges shall be made before the administration of the oath to the jurors and shall be tried by the court.

(2) Motion to Dismiss. A motion to dismiss the indictment may be based on objections to the array or on the lack of legal qualification of an individual juror, if not previously determined upon challenge. It shall be made in the manner prescribed in 28 U.S.C. § 1867(e)[2] and shall be granted under the conditions prescribed in that statute. An indictment shall not be dismissed on the ground that one or more members of the grand jury were not legally qualified if it appears from the record kept pursuant to subdivision (c) of this rule that 12 or more jurors, after deducting the number not legally qualified, concurred in finding the indictment.

(c) Foreperson and Deputy Foreperson. The court shall appoint one of the jurors to be foreperson and another to be deputy foreperson. The foreperson shall have power to administer oaths and affirmations and shall sign all indictments. The foreperson or another juror designated by the foreperson shall keep a record of the number of jurors concurring in the finding of every indictment and shall file the record with the clerk of the

---

[2] Enacted as part of the Jury Selection and Service Act of 1968 and containing provisions for challenging the method of selection of grand or petit jurors.

court, but the record shall not be made public except on order of the court. During the absence of the foreperson, the deputy foreperson shall act as foreperson.

(d) Who May Be Present. Attorneys for the government, the witness under examination, interpreters when needed and, for the purpose of taking the evidence, a stenographer or operator of a recording device may be present while the grand jury is in session, but no person other than the jurors may be present while the grand jury is deliberating or voting.

(e) Recording and Disclosure of Proceedings.

(1) Recording of Proceedings. All proceedings, except when the grand jury is deliberating or voting, shall be recorded stenographically or by an electronic recording device. An unintentional failure of any recording to reproduce all or any portion of a proceeding shall not affect the validity of the prosecution. The recording or reporter's notes or any transcript prepared therefrom shall remain in the custody or control of the attorney for the government unless otherwise ordered by the court in a particular case.

(2) General Rule of Secrecy. A grand juror, an interpreter, a stenographer, an operator of a recording device, a typist who transcribes recorded testimony, an attorney for the government, or any person to whom disclosure is made under paragraph (3)(A)(ii) of this subdivision shall not disclose matters occurring before the grand jury, except as otherwise provided for in these rules. No obligation of secrecy may be imposed on any person except in accordance with this rule. A knowing violation of Rule 6 may be punished as a contempt of court.

(3) Exceptions.

(A) Disclosure otherwise prohibited by this rule of matters occurring before the grand jury, other than its deliberations and the vote of any grand juror, may be made to—

(i) an attorney for the government for use in the performance of such attorney's duty; and

(ii) such government personnel (including personnel of a state or subdivision of a state) as are deemed necessary by an attorney for the government to assist an attorney for the government in the performance of such attorney's duty to enforce federal criminal law.

(B) Any person to whom matters are disclosed under subparagraph (A)(ii) of this paragraph shall not utilize that grand jury material for any purpose other than assisting the attorney for the government in the performance of such attorney's duty to enforce federal criminal law. An attorney for the government shall promptly provide the district court, before which was impaneled the grand jury whose material has been so disclosed, with the names of the persons to whom such disclosure has been made, and shall certify that the attorney has advised such persons of their obligation of secrecy under this rule.

(C) Disclosure otherwise prohibited by this rule of matters occurring before the grand jury may also be made—

    (i) when so directed by a court preliminarily to or in connection with a judicial proceeding;

    (ii) when permitted by a court at the request of the defendant, upon a showing that grounds may exist for a motion to dismiss the indictment because of matters occurring before the grand jury;

    (iii) when the disclosure is made by an attorney for the government to another federal grand jury; or

    (iv) when permitted by a court at the request of an attorney for the government, upon a showing that such matters may disclose a violation of state criminal law, to an appropriate official of a state or subdivision of a state for the purpose of enforcing such law.

If the court orders disclosure of matters occurring before the grand jury, the disclosure shall be made in such manner, at such time, and under such conditions as the court may direct.

    (D) A petition for disclosure pursuant to subdivision (e)(3)(C)(i) shall be filed in the district where the grand jury convened. Unless the hearing is ex parte, which it may be when the petitioner is the government, the petitioner shall serve written notice of the petition upon (i) the attorney for the government, (ii) the parties to the judicial proceeding if disclosure is sought in connection with such a proceeding, and (iii) such other persons as the court may direct. The court shall afford those persons a reasonable opportunity to appear and be heard.

    (E) If the judicial proceeding giving rise to the petition is in a federal district court in another district, the court shall transfer the matter to that court unless it can reasonably obtain sufficient knowledge of the proceeding to determine whether disclosure is proper. The court shall order transmitted to the court to which the matter is transferred the material sought to be disclosed, if feasible, and a written evaluation of the need for continued grand jury secrecy. The court to which the matter is transferred shall afford the aforementioned persons a reasonable opportunity to appear and be heard.

    (4) Sealed Indictments. The federal magistrate judge to whom an indictment is returned may direct that the indictment be kept secret until the defendant is in custody or has been released pending trial. Thereupon the clerk shall seal the indictment and no person shall disclose the return of the indictment except when necessary for the issuance and execution of a warrant or summons.

    (5) Closed Hearing. Subject to any right to an open hearing in contempt proceedings, the court shall order a hearing on matters affecting a grand jury proceeding to be closed to the extent necessary to prevent disclosure of matters occurring before a grand jury.

    (6) Sealed Records. Records, orders and subpoenas relating to grand jury proceedings shall be kept under seal to the extent and for such time as is necessary to prevent disclosure of matters occurring before a grand jury.

(f) Finding and Return of Indictment. An indictment may be found only upon the concurrence of 12 or more jurors. The indictment shall be returned by the grand jury to a federal magistrate judge in open court. If a complaint or information is pending against the defendant and 12 jurors do not concur in finding an indictment, the foreperson shall so report to a federal magistrate judge in writing forthwith.

(g) Discharge and Excuse. A grand jury shall serve until discharged by the court, but no grand jury may serve more than 18 months unless the court extends the service of the grand jury for a period of six months or less upon a determination that such extension is in the public interest. At any time for cause shown the court may excuse a juror either temporarily or permanently, and in the latter event the court may impanel another person in place of the juror excused.

Rule 7.

THE INDICTMENT AND THE INFORMATION

(a) Use of Indictment or Information. An offense which may be punished by death shall be prosecuted by indictment. An offense which may be punished by imprisonment for a term exceeding one year or at hard labor shall be prosecuted by indictment or, if indictment is waived, it may be prosecuted by information. Any other offense may be prosecuted by indictment or by information. An information may be filed without leave of court.

(b) Waiver of Indictment. An offense which may be punished by imprisonment for a term exceeding one year or at hard labor may be prosecuted by information if the defendant, after having been advised of the nature of the charge and of the rights of the defendant, waives in open court prosecution by indictment.

(c) Nature and Contents.

(1) In General. The indictment or the information shall be a plain, concise and definite written statement of the essential facts constituting the offense charged. It shall be signed by the attorney for the government. It need not contain a formal commencement, a formal conclusion or any other matter not necessary to such statement. Allegations made in one count may be incorporated by reference in another count. It may be alleged in a single count that the means by which the defendant committed the offense are unknown or that the defendant committed it by one or more specified means. The indictment or information shall state for each count the official or customary citation of the statute, rule, regulation or other provision of law which the defendant is alleged therein to have violated.

(2) Criminal Forfeiture. No judgment of forfeiture may be entered in a criminal proceeding unless the indictment or the information shall allege the extent of the interest or property subject to forfeiture.

(3) Harmless Error. Error in the citation or its omission shall not be ground for dismissal of the indictment or information or for reversal of a

conviction if the error or omission did not mislead the defendant to the defendant's prejudice.

(d) Surplusage. The court on motion of the defendant may strike surplusage from the indictment or information.

(e) Amendment of Information. The court may permit an information to be amended at any time before verdict or finding if no additional or different offense is charged and if substantial rights of the defendant are not prejudiced.

(f) Bill of Particulars. The court may direct the filing of a bill of particulars. A motion for a bill of particulars may be made before arraignment or within ten days after arraignment or at such later time as the court may permit. A bill of particulars may be amended at any time subject to such conditions as justice requires.

Rule 48.

DISMISSAL

(a) By Attorney for Government. The Attorney General or the United States attorney may by leave of court file a dismissal of an indictment, information or complaint and the prosecution shall thereupon terminate. Such a dismissal may not be filed during the trial without the consent of the defendant.

(b) By Court. If there is unnecessary delay in presenting the charge to a grand jury or in filing an information against a defendant who has been held to answer to the district court, or if there is unnecessary delay in bringing a defendant to trial, the court may dismiss the indictment, information or complaint.

---

327. Waiver. Rule 7(a) does not permit waiver of indictment in capital cases. See generally Smith v. United States, 360 U.S. 1 (1959). On withdrawal of a waiver of indictment, see Bartlett v. United States, 354 F.2d 745 (8th Cir.1966), in which the court upheld a ruling that the defendant could withdraw his plea of guilty but not a waiver of indictment.

328. Rule 6(e)(2) provides that the proceedings of the grand jury shall generally remain secret, in conformity with the general rule. In Butterworth v. Smith, 494 U.S. 624 (1990), however, the Court held that a state statute that prohibited *witnesses* before a grand jury from disclosing

AO 455 (Rev. 5/85) Waiver of Indictment

United States District Court

————————————— DISTRICT OF —————————————

UNITED STATES OF AMERICA

V.

WAIVER OF INDICTMENT

CASE NUMBER:

I, _____ , the above named defendant, who is accused of

being advised of the nature of the charge(s), the proposed information, and of my rights, hereby waive in open court on

_____ prosecution by indictment and consent that the proceeding may be by information
　　　　　　　Date
rather than by indictment.

_____
Defendant

_____
Counsel for Defendant

Before _____
　　　　　　　Judicial Officer

their testimony is unconstitutional, insofar as it prohibits a witness from disclosing his own testimony after the term of the grand jury has ended. Such a prohibition, the Court said, violates the First Amendment.

United States v. Mechanik
475 U.S. 66, 106 S.Ct. 938, 89 L.Ed.2d 50 (1986).

■ JUSTICE REHNQUIST delivered the opinion of the Court.

Federal Rule of Criminal Procedure 6(d) states that only specified persons including "the witness under examination" may be present at a grand jury proceeding. In this case, two Government witnesses testified in tandem before the grand jury, which indicted respondents and cross-petitioners (hereafter defendants) Mechanik and Lill for various drug-related offenses and conspiracy to commit such offenses. The Court of Appeals for the Fourth Circuit held that the simultaneous presence of these two witnesses violated Rule 6(d), and that even though the petit jury subsequently returned a verdict of guilty against defendants, the verdict must be set aside on any count that corresponds to a "tainted" portion of the indictment. We believe that the petit jury's verdict of guilty beyond a reasonable doubt demonstrates *a fortiori* that there was probable cause to charge the defendants with the offenses for which they were convicted. Therefore, the convictions must stand despite the rule violation.

A fairly detailed summary of the District Court proceedings will help to illustrate the nature and extent of our holding. A grand jury returned an indictment charging defendants with drug-related offenses and conspiracy. This indictment was concededly free from any claim of error. The grand jury then returned a superseding indictment in which the conspiracy charge was expanded. In support of this superseding indictment, the United States Attorney presented the testimony of two law enforcement agents who were sworn together and questioned in tandem before the grand jury.

The defendants did not learn about this joint testimony until after trial began. Before trial, they filed an omnibus motion requesting, *inter alia*, the names of all the people who appeared before the grand jury. The Government responded that there were no unauthorized persons appearing before the grand jury, and the District Court denied the motion. Trial began in February 1980, and concluded in early July of the same year. During the second week of trial, one Jerry Rinehart, an agent of the Drug Enforcement Administration, testified as a Government witness. At the time of his testimony, the Government furnished the defendants with a portion of the transcript of his grand jury testimony as required by the Jencks Act, 18 U.S.C.

§ 3500. The transcript disclosed that Rinehart and his fellow agent, Randolph James, had testified in tandem before the grand jury.

The defendants moved for dismissal of the indictment on the ground that the simultaneous presence of the two agents had violated Federal Rule of Criminal Procedure 6(d). . . . Judge Copenhaver took the motion under advisement until the conclusion of trial.

In August 1980, after the jury had returned its guilty verdict, Judge Copenhaver ruled upon and denied the defendants' motion for dismissal of the indictment. 511 F.Supp. 50 (S.D.W.Va.1980). He first decided . . . that the joint testimony of Agents Rinehart and James *did* constitute a violation of Rule 6(d). . . . But he declined to set aside the defendants' indictment and convictions because, on the basis of a comparison between the two indictments and the evidence on which the indictments rested, the violation of Rule 6(d) had not harmed the defendants. . . . He justified this conclusion with respect to the substantive counts on the ground that they were materially unchanged from the valid initial indictment to the superseding indictment. . . . With respect to the conspiracy count, which had been expanded by the superseding indictment, he justified his conclusion on the ground that the grand jury "had before it ample independent evidence [apart from the joint testimony] to support a probable cause finding of the charges." Id., at 61. In light of these conclusions, Judge Copenhaver determined that a post-trial dismissal of the indictment would simply confer a windfall benefit on the defendants "who stand convicted after a three-month trial conducted at enormous expense to the United States and the defendants." Ibid. The judge nevertheless undertook to ensure future compliance with the one-witness rule by directing the Government to keep the court advised concerning compliance with Rule 6(d) in future criminal cases. . . .

A divided Court of Appeals reversed the conspiracy convictions, affirmed the others, and dismissed the conspiracy portion of the indictment. 735 F.2d 136 (1984). It reasoned that the language of Rule 6(d) is so "plain and unequivocal in limiting who may appear before a grand jury," id., at 139, that its transgression requires automatic reversal of any subsequent conviction regardless of the lack of prejudice. . . . But the court reversed only the conspiracy convictions because it found that the violation of Rule 6(d) tainted only the portion of the superseding indictment that related to them. . . . A divided en banc decision agreed. . . .

We assume for the sake of argument that the simultaneous presence and testimony of the two Government witnesses before the grand jury violated Rule 6(d), and that the District Court would have been justified in dismissing portions of the indictment on that basis had there been actual prejudice and had the matter been called to its attention before the commencement of the trial. But although the defendants appear to have been reasonably diligent in attempting to discover any error at the grand jury proceeding, they did not acquire the transcript showing that the two agents had appeared jointly in the grand jury proceeding until the second week of trial. Nor is there any suggestion that the Government designedly withheld the information. . . . Although we do not believe that the defendants can be faulted for any lack of diligence, we nonetheless hold that the supervening jury verdict made reversal of the conviction and dismissal of the indictment inappropriate.

Both the District Court and the Court of Appeals observed that Rule 6(d) was designed, in part, "to ensure that grand jurors, sitting without the direct supervision of a judge, are not subject to undue influence that may come with the presence of an unauthorized person." 735 F.2d, at 139. The Rule protects against the danger that a defendant will be required to defend against a charge for which there is no probable cause to believe him guilty. The error involving Rule 6(d) in these cases had the theoretical potential to affect the grand jury's determination whether to indict these particular defendants for the offenses with which they were charged. But the petit jury's subsequent guilty verdict not only means that there was probable cause to believe that the defendants were guilty as charged, but that they are in fact guilty as charged beyond a reasonable doubt. Measured by the petit jury's verdict, then, any error in the grand jury proceeding connected with the charging decision was harmless beyond a reasonable doubt.

It might be argued in some literal sense that because the Rule was designed to protect against an erroneous charging decision by the *grand jury*, the indictment should not be compared to the evidence produced by the Government at *trial*, but to the evidence produced before the *grand jury*. But even if this argument were accepted, there is no simple way after the verdict to restore the defendant to the position in which he would have been had the indictment been dismissed before trial. He will already have suffered whatever inconvenience, expense, and opprobrium that a proper indictment may have spared him. In courtroom proceedings as elsewhere, "the moving finger writes, and having writ moves on." Thus reversal of a conviction after a trial free from reversible error cannot restore to the defendant whatever benefit might have accrued to him from a trial on an indictment returned in conformity with Rule 6(d).

We cannot accept the Court of Appeals' view that a violation of Rule 6(d) requires automatic reversal of a subsequent conviction regardless of the lack of prejudice. Federal Rule of Criminal Procedure 52(a) provides that errors not affecting substantial rights shall be disregarded. We see no reason not to apply this provision to "errors, defects, irregularities or variances" occurring before a grand jury just as we have applied it to such error occurring in the criminal trial itself. . . .

The reversal of a conviction entails substantial social costs: it forces jurors, witnesses, courts, the prosecution, and the defendants to expend further time, energy, and other resources to repeat a trial that has already once taken place; victims may be asked to relive their disturbing experiences. . . . The "[p]assage of time, erosion of memory, and dispersion of witnesses may render retrial difficult, even impossible." Engle v. Isaac, 456 U.S. 107, 127–128 (1982). Thus, while reversal "may, in theory, entitle the defendant only to retrial, in practice it may reward the accused with complete freedom from prosecution," id., at 128, and thereby "cost society the right to punish admitted offenders." Id., at 127. Even if a defendant is convicted in a second trial, the intervening delay may compromise society's "interest in the prompt administration of justice," United States v. Hasting [461 U.S. 499 (1983)], at 509, and impede accomplishment of the objectives of deterrence and rehabilitation. These societal costs of reversal and retrial are an acceptable and often necessary consequence when an error in the first proceeding has deprived a defendant of a fair determination of the issue of guilt or innocence. But the balance of interest tips decidedly the other way when an error has had no effect on the outcome of the trial.

We express no opinion as to what remedy may be appropriate for a violation of Rule 6(d) that has affected the grand jury's charging decision and is brought to the attention of the trial court before the commencement of trial. We hold only that however diligent the defendants may have been in seeking to discover the basis for the claimed violation of Rule 6(d), the petit jury's verdict rendered harmless any conceivable error in the charging decision that might have flowed from the violation. In such a case, the societal costs of retrial after a jury verdict of guilty are far too substantial to justify setting aside the verdict simply because of an error in the earlier grand jury proceedings. The judgment of the Court of Appeals is therefore reversed to the extent it set aside the conspiracy convictions and dismissed the indictment, but is otherwise affirmed.

It is so ordered.[3]

---

329. Declaring that "a federal court may not invoke supervisory power to circumvent the harmless-error inquiry prescribed by Federal Rule of Criminal Procedure 52(a)," the Court held that a district court may not dismiss an indictment for errors in grand jury proceedings unless the errors caused prejudice to the defendants. "[A]t least where dismissal is sought for nonconstitutional error," such prejudice is not shown unless it is established that the error "substantially influenced" the grand jury's decision to indict or there is "grave doubt" that the decision to indict was free from such influence. Bank of Nova Scotia v. United States, 487 U.S. 250, 254, 256 (1988)

---

[3] Justice O'Connor argued in an opinion concurring in the judgment, which Justice Brennan and Justice Blackmun joined, that the Court's analysis rendered the rules governing grand jury proceedings "a dead letter," because it shifted the focus of harmless error from the effect of a violation on the indictment to its effect on the verdict. Even though a verdict has been returned, she argued, "the focus of the court's inquiry should remain on the grand jury's charging decision." 475 U.S. at 73, 76. In a dissenting opinion, Justice Marshall agreed and added that a clear violation of Rule 6 should require dismissal of the indictment even after verdict without a case-by-case analysis to see whether the error was harmless.

(8–1). The Court concluded that the errors in question, multiple violations of the requirements of Rule 6(d) and (e), were harmless.

Mechanik notwithstanding, an order denying the defendant's motion to dismiss an indictment for an alleged violation of Rule 6(e)(2), prohibiting public disclosure of matters occurring before the grand jury, is not appealable as an interlocutory appeal, before final judgment. Midland Asphalt Corp. v. United States, 489 U.S. 794 (1989). The Court declined to decide whether *Mechanik* applies to violations of Rule 6(e). It said that if such violations can be a basis for reversal of a conviction on appeal, then there was no reason to allow an interlocutory appeal. And if a violation cannot be the basis for reversal, it would be because the alleged violation did not involve a fundamental issue completely separable from the merits of the action, again making an interlocutory appeal unavailable.

United States v. Miller

471 U.S. 130, 105 S.Ct. 1811, 85 L.Ed.2d 99 (1985).

■ JUSTICE MARSHALL delivered the opinion of the Court.

The issue presented is whether the Fifth Amendment's grand jury guarantee is violated when a defendant is tried under an indictment that alleges a certain fraudulent scheme but is convicted based on trial proof that supports only a significantly narrower and more limited, though included, fraudulent scheme.

A grand jury in the Northern District of California returned an indictment charging respondent Miller with three counts of mail fraud in violation of 18 U.S.C. § 1341. After the Government moved to dismiss the third count, Miller was tried before a jury and convicted of the remaining two. He appealed asserting that there had been a fatal variance between the "scheme and artifice" to defraud charged in the indictment and that which the Government proved at trial. The Court of Appeals for the Ninth Circuit agreed and vacated the judgment of conviction. . . . We granted certiorari . . . and reverse.

I

A

The indictment had charged Miller with various fraudulent acts in connection with a burglary at his business. Miller allegedly had defrauded his insurer both by consenting to the burglary in advance and by lying to the insurer about the value of his loss. The trial proof, however, concerned only the latter allegation, focusing on whether, prior to the burglary, Miller actually had possessed all the property that he later claimed was taken. This proof was clearly sufficient to support a jury finding that Miller's claim to his insurer had grossly inflated the value of any actual loss.

The Government moved to strike the part of the indictment that alleged prior knowledge of the burglary, and it correctly argued that even without that allegation the indictment still made out a violation of § 1341. Respondent's counsel opposed the change, and at his urging the entire indictment was sent to the jury. The jury found Miller guilty, and respondent appealed on the basis that the trial proof had fatally varied from the scheme alleged in the indictment.

Agreeing that Miller's Fifth Amendment right to be tried only on a grand jury indictment had been violated, the Court of Appeals vacated the conviction. . . .

B

Miller's indictment properly alleged violations of 18 U.S.C. § 1341, and it fully and clearly set forth a number of ways in which the acts alleged constituted violations. The facts proved at trial clearly conformed to one of the theories of the offense contained within that indictment, for the indictment gave Miller clear notice that he would have to defend against an allegation that he "well knew that the amount of copper claimed to have been taken during the alleged burglary was grossly inflated for the purpose of fraudulently obtaining $150,000 from Aetna Insurance Company." 715 F.2d, at 1361–1362 (quoting indictment). Competent defense counsel certainly should have been on notice that that offense was charged and would need to be defended against. Accordingly, there can be no showing here that Miller was prejudicially surprised at trial by the absence of proof concerning his alleged complicity in the burglary; nor can there be a showing that the variance prejudiced the fairness of respondent's trial in any other way. . . . The indictment was also sufficient to allow Miller to plead it in the future as a bar to subsequent prosecutions. Therefore, none of these "notice" related concerns—which of course are among the important concerns underlying the requirement that criminal charges be set out in an indictment—would support the result of the Court of Appeals. . . .

The Court of Appeals did not disagree, but instead argued that Miller had been prejudiced in his right to be free from a trial for any offense other than that alleged in the grand jury's indictment. . . . It reasoned that a grand jury's willingness to indict an individual for participation in a broad criminal plan does not establish that the same grand jury would have indicted the individual for participating in a substantially narrower, even if wholly included, criminal plan. . . . Relying on the Fifth Amendment's grand jury guarantee, the Court of Appeals concluded that a conviction could not stand where the trial proof corresponded to a fraudulent scheme much narrower than, though included within, the scheme that the grand jury had alleged. . . .

II

. . . The Court has long recognized that an indictment may charge numerous offenses or the commission of any one offense in several ways. As long as the crime and the elements of the offense that sustain the conviction are fully and clearly set out in the indictment, the right to a grand jury is not normally violated by the fact that the indictment alleges more crimes or other means of committing the same crime. . . . Indeed, a number of long-standing doctrines of criminal procedure are premised on the notion that each offense whose elements are fully set out in an indictment can independently sustain a conviction. . . .

A review of prior cases allowing convictions to stand in the face of variances between the indictment and proof makes the Court of Appeals' error clear. Convictions generally have been sustained as long as the proof upon which they are based corresponds to an offense that was clearly set out in the indictment. A part of the indictment unnecessary to and independent from the allegations of the offense proved may normally be treated as "a useless averment" that "may be ignored." Ford v. United States, 273 U.S. 593, 602 (1927). . . .

This treatment of allegations independent of and unnecessary to the offense on which a conviction ultimately rests has not been confined to allegations that, like those in *Ford*, would have had no legal relevance if proved. In Salinger v. United States, [272 U.S. 542 (1926)], for example, the Court was presented with facts quite similar to the instant case. A grand jury charged Salinger with mail fraud in an indictment containing several counts, "[a]ll relat[ing] to the same scheme to defraud, but each charg[ing] a distinct use of the mail for the purpose of executing the scheme." 272 U.S., at 546. As was the case with Miller, Salinger's "scheme to defraud as set forth in the indictment . . . comprehended several relatively distinct plans for fleecing intended victims." Id., at 548. Because the evidence only sustained the charge as to one of the plans, the trial judge withdrew from the jury those portions of the indictment that related to all other plans. Salinger argued then, just as Miller argues now, that the variance between the broad allegations in the indictment and the narrower proof at trial violated his right to have had a grand jury screen any alleged offenses upon which he might be convicted at trial.

This Court unanimously rejected Salinger's argument on the ground that the offense proved was fully contained within the indictment. Nothing had been added to the indictment which, in the Court's view, "remained just as it was returned by the grand jury." Ibid. "[T]he trial was on the charge preferred in it and not on a modified charge," ibid., and there was thus "not even remotely an infraction of the constitutional provision that 'no person shall be held to answer for a capital or otherwise infamous crime unless on a presentment or indictment of a grand jury.'" Id., at 549. . . .

The result reached by the Court of Appeals thus conflicts with the results reached by this court in such cases as *Salinger* and *Ford*. . . .

III

The Court of Appeals principally relied on this Court's decision in Stirone v. United States, 361 U.S. 212 (1960), to support its conclusion that the Fifth Amendment's grand jury right is violated by a conviction for a criminal plan narrower than, but fully included within, the plan set forth in the indictment. *Stirone*, however, stands for a very different proposition. In *Stirone* the offense proved at trial was *not* fully contained in the indictment, for trial evidence had "amended" the indictment by *broadening* the possible bases for conviction from that which appeared in the indictment. *Stirone* was thus wholly unlike the cases discussed in Part II, *supra*, and unlike respondent's case, all of which involve trial evidence that narrowed the indictment's charges without adding any new offenses. As the *Stirone* Court said, the issue was "whether [Stirone] was convicted of an offense *not charged in the indictment*." 361 U.S., at 213 (emphasis added).

. . .

Miller has shown no deprivation of his "substantial right to be tried only on charges presented in an indictment returned by a grand jury." 361 U.S., at 217. In contrast to Stirone, Miller was tried on an indictment that clearly set out the offense for which he was ultimately convicted. His complaint is not that the indictment failed to charge the offense for which he was convicted, but that the indictment charged more than was necessary.

. . .

V

In light of the foregoing, the proper disposition of this case is clear. The variance complained of added nothing new to the grand jury's indictment and constituted no broadening. As in *Salinger* and *Ford*, what was removed from the case was in no way essential to the offense on which the jury convicted. We therefore disagree with the Court of Appeals on the issue of whether Miller has shown any compromise of his right to be tried only on offenses for which a grand jury has returned an indictment. No such compromise has been shown. The judgment of the Court of Appeals is accordingly reversed.

. . .

---

330. For cases discussing the problem of variance between the indictment and proof, see, e.g., United States v. Tsinhnahijinnie, 112 F.3d 988 (9th Cir.1997) (variance between date of crime alleged in indictment and proof; conviction reversed); United States v. Leichtnam, 948 F.2d 370 (7th

Cir.1991) (variance between indictment and theory of case according to evidence and instructions); United States v. Weissman, 899 F.2d 1111 (11th Cir.1990) (jury instruction constructively amended indictment and created variance between actual indictment and proof); United States v. Santa-Manzano, 842 F.2d 1 (1st Cir.1988) (variance; conviction reversed). See generally Russell v. United States, 369 U.S. 749 (1962).

Cf. Almendarez-Torres, ___ U.S. ___, 118 S.Ct. 1219 (1998) (5–4), in which the Court held that a statutory provision that a person convicted of the crime of unauthorized reentry by a deported alien is subject to a larger sentence of imprisonment if the deportation was subsequent to the alien's conviction of an aggravated felony does not define a separate crime but only provides for sentence enhancement and, therefore, that the prior conviction need not be alleged in the indictment.

In United States v. Goldstein, 502 F.2d 526 (3d Cir.1974), the court held that a material variance between an indictment for a misdemeanor and the proof was fatal to the conviction, even though the government could have proceeded by information. While amendment to an information is permitted, having elected to proceed by indictment, the government was bound by the rules applicable to an indictment. See Watson v. Jago, 558 F.2d 330, 339 (6th Cir.1977), in which the court of appeals concluded that while the grand jury provision of the Fifth Amendment does not apply to the States, "to allow the prosecution to amend the indictment at trial so as to enable the prosecution to seek a conviction on a charge not brought by the grand jury unquestionably constituted a denial of due process by not giving appellant fair notice of criminal charges to be brought against him." To the same effect, see Koontz v. Glossa, 731 F.2d 365 (6th Cir.1984) (indictment charging arson by defendant failed to give notice of accusation that defendant hired another person to commit arson).

331. Counsel. "A witness before a grand jury cannot insist, as a matter of constitutional right, on being represented by his counsel. . . ." In re Groban, 352 U.S. 330, 333 (1957). Federal Rule 6(d), p. 678 above, preserves the practice that a witness summoned before a grand jury may not be accompanied by counsel. In United States v. Capaldo, 402 F.2d 821, 824 (2d Cir.1968), the court observed that a rule that excluded counsel but allowed a witness "to leave the grand jury room at any time to consult with counsel is a reasonable and workable accommodation of the traditional investigatory role of the grand jury, preserved in the Fifth Amendment, and the self-incrimination and right to counsel provisions of the Fifth and Sixth Amendments." But see In re Grand Jury Proceedings (Matter of Lowry), 713 F.2d 616, 617–18 (11th Cir.1983), in which the court observed: "Grand jury witnesses have no right to the presence of counsel in the jury room during questioning. . . . Nor does a witness have a constitutional right to disrupt the grand jury's proceedings by leaving the room to consult with his

AO 110 (Rev. 5/85) Subpoena to Testify Before Grand Jury ●

United States District Court

_____ DISTRICT OF _____

TO:

SUBPOENA TO TESTIFY
BEFORE GRAND JURY

SUBPOENA FOR:
☐ PERSON   ☐ DOCUMENT(S) OR OBJECT(S)

YOU ARE HEREBY COMMANDED to appear and testify before the Grand Jury of the United States District Court at the place, date, and time specified below.

PLACE	COURTROOM
	DATE AND TIME

YOU ARE ALSO COMMANDED to bring with you the following document(s) or object(s):*

☐ _Please see additional information on reverse_

This subpoena shall remain in effect until you are granted leave to depart by the court or by an officer acting on behalf of the court.

CLERK	DATE
(BY) DEPUTY CLERK	

This subpoena is issued on application of the United States of America	NAME, ADDRESS AND PHONE NUMBER OF ASSISTANT U.S. ATTORNEY

*If not applicable, enter "none".

attorney after every question." See generally Anonymous Nos. 6 and 7 v. Baker, 360 U.S. 287 (1959) (5–4).

The practice of allowing a witness before the grand jury to leave the room at any time to consult with an attorney has been restricted in cases of a witness who has been granted immunity from prosecution. See, e.g., United States v. Soto, 574 F.Supp. 986 (D.Conn.1983), in which the witness sought to write down each question as it was asked and to consult with her attorney after each question. The court ruled: "The Court finds that a practical accommodation for all parties concerned shall be as follows: (1) The Grand Jury shall question the witness Soto continuously for twenty (20) minutes and then allow her ten (10) minutes in which to consult privately with her attorney; and (2) Miss Soto shall not delay the proceedings by writing down the questions during the interrogation, nor her answers. The transcribing process impedes the investigation, virtually brings the attorney into the Grand Jury room, and allows for the possibility that the testimony given will be more that of the witness' counsel than that of the witness. This procedure will expedite the Grand Jury investigation while allowing the witness any necessary legal advice." Id. at 993.

In In re Investigation Before Feb., 1977, Lynchburg Grand Jury (United States v. Barker), 563 F.2d 652 (4th Cir.1977), the court upheld an order disqualifying certain lawyers from representing their clients as witnesses before the grand jury, on the ground that their presence would interfere with the grand jury's function. In one case the lawyer himself and in another other clients of the lawyer were targets of the grand jury's investigation. In that circumstance, the court concluded, the right to be represented by counsel of one's choice had to give way. (The witnesses' right to representation before the jury was not questioned.)

332. A subpoena duces tecum issued by a grand jury is not required to meet the standards of relevance, admissibility, and specificity that apply to a subpoena issued for trial (see note 486 p. 983, below). Since the purpose of a grand jury investigation is to determine whether a crime may have been committed, it necessarily is permitted to investigate more broadly than the inquiry at trial. A grand jury's subpoena is presumed to be reasonable and, if it is challenged on the ground of irrelevance, must be upheld unless "there is no reasonable possibility that the category of materials the Government seeks will produce information relevant to the general subject of the grand jury's investigation." United States v. R. Enterprises, Inc., 498 U.S. 292, 301 (1991).

Costello v. United States

350 U.S. 359, 76 S.Ct. 406, 100 L.Ed. 397 (1956).

■ MR. JUSTICE BLACK delivered the opinion of the Court.

We granted certiorari in this case to consider a single question: "May a defendant be required to stand trial and a conviction be sustained where only hearsay evidence was presented to the grand jury which indicted him?" 350 U.S. 819.

Petitioner, Frank Costello, was indicted for wilfully attempting to evade payment of income taxes due the United States for the years 1947, 1948 and 1949. The charge was that petitioner falsely and fraudulently reported less income than he and his wife actually received during the taxable years in question. Petitioner promptly filed a motion for inspection of the minutes of the grand jury and for a dismissal of the indictment. His motion was based on an affidavit stating that he was firmly convinced there could have been no legal or competent evidence before the grand jury which indicted him since he had reported all his income and paid all taxes due. The motion was denied. At the trial which followed the Government offered evidence designed to show increases in Costello's net worth in an attempt to prove that he had received more income during the years in question than he had reported. To establish its case the Government called and examined 144 witnesses and introduced 368 exhibits. All of the testimony and documents related to business transactions and expenditures by petitioner and his wife. The prosecution concluded its case by calling three government agents. Their investigations had produced the evidence used against petitioner at the trial. They were allowed to summarize the vast amount of evidence already heard and to introduce computations showing, if correct, that petitioner and his wife had received far greater income than they had reported. We have held such summarizations admissible in a "net worth" case like this. . . .

Counsel for petitioner asked each government witness at the trial whether he had appeared before the grand jury which returned the indictment. This cross-examination developed the fact that the three investigating officers had been the only witnesses before the grand jury. After the Government concluded its case, petitioner again moved to dismiss the indictment on the ground that the only evidence before the grand jury was "hearsay," since the three officers had no firsthand knowledge of the transactions upon which their computations were based. Nevertheless the trial court again refused to dismiss the indictment, and petitioner was convicted. The Court of Appeals affirmed, holding that the indictment was valid even though the sole evidence before the grand jury was hearsay. Petitioner here urges: (1) that an indictment based solely on hearsay evidence violates that part of the Fifth Amendment providing that "No person shall be held to answer for a capital, or otherwise infamous crime, unless on a presentment or indictment of a Grand Jury. . . ." and (2) that if the Fifth Amendment does not invalidate an indictment based solely on hearsay we should now lay down such a rule for the guidance of federal courts.

. . .

The Fifth Amendment provides that federal prosecutions for capital or otherwise infamous crimes must be instituted by presentments or indictments of grand juries. But neither the Fifth Amendment nor any other constitutional provision prescribes the kind of evidence upon which grand juries must act. . . .

In Holt v. United States, 218 U.S. 245, this Court had to decide whether an indictment should be quashed because supported in part by incompetent evidence. Aside from the incompetent evidence "there was very little evidence against the accused." The Court refused to hold that such an indictment should be quashed, pointing out that "The abuses of criminal practice would be enhanced if indictments could be upset on such a ground." 218 U.S., at 248. The same thing is true where as here all the evidence before the grand jury was in the nature of "hearsay." If indictments were to be held open to challenge on the ground that there was inadequate or incompetent evidence before the grand jury, the resulting delay would be great indeed. The result of such a rule would be that before trial on the merits a defendant could always insist on a kind of preliminary trial to determine the competency and adequacy of the evidence before the grand jury. This is not required by the Fifth Amendment. An indictment returned by a legally constituted and unbiased grand jury, like an information drawn by the prosecutor, if valid on its face, is enough to call for trial of the charge on the merits. The Fifth Amendment requires nothing more.

Petitioner urges that this Court should exercise its power to supervise the administration of justice in federal courts and establish a rule permitting defendants to challenge indictments on the ground that they are not supported by adequate or competent evidence. No persuasive reasons are advanced for establishing such a rule. It would run counter to the whole history of the grand jury institution, in which laymen conduct their inquiries unfettered by technical rules. Neither justice nor the concept of a fair trial requires such a change. In a trial on the merits, defendants are entitled to a strict observance of all the rules designed to bring about a fair verdict. Defendants are not entitled, however, to a rule which would result in interminable delay but add nothing to the assurance of a fair trial.

Affirmed.[4]

---

333. The reasoning of the Court in United States v. Calandra, 414 U.S. 338 (1974), in which the Court held that the exclusionary rule is inapplicable to grand jury proceedings, effectively extends *Costello* to evidence obtained unconstitutionally.

[4] Justice Burton wrote a concurring opinion.

The United States Attorneys' Manual 9–11.231 states: "A prosecutor should not present to the grand jury for use against a person whose constitutional rights clearly have been violated evidence which the prosecutor personally knows was obtained as a direct result of the constitutional violation." This rule is described in the Manual as an "internal policy of self-restraint."

334. In United States v. Basurto, 497 F.2d 781 (9th Cir.1974), the prosecutor learned before trial that a main witness had lied before the grand jury. He told counsel but neither the judge nor the grand jury. In his opening statement at trial, he acknowledged the witness's lie. The court reversed the conviction: "We hold that the Due Process Clause of the Fifth Amendment is violated when a defendant has to stand trial on an indictment which the government knows is based partially on perjured testimony, when the perjured testimony is material, and when jeopardy has not attached. Whenever the prosecutor learns of any perjury committed before the grand jury, he is under a duty to immediately inform the court and opposing counsel—and, if the perjury may be material, also the grand jury—in order that appropriate action may be taken.

"We base our decision on a long line of cases which recognize the existence of a duty of good faith on the part of the prosecutor with respect to the court, the grand jury, and the defendant. While the facts of these cases may not exactly parallel those of the instant case, we hold that their rulings regarding the consequences of a violation or abuse of this prosecutorial duty must be applied where the prosecutor has knowledge that testimony before the grand jury was perjured." Id. at 785–86.

Basurto was not followed in United States v. Udziela, 671 F.2d 995 (7th Cir.1982), in which the prosecutor learned just before trial that a witness before the grand jury had committed perjury. He disclosed the perjury to defense counsel. During the trial, defense counsel moved to dismiss the indictment. The court of appeals held that the motion was properly denied. It said: "[W]here perjured testimony supporting an indictment is discovered before trial the government has the option of either voluntarily withdrawing the tainted indictment and seeking a new one before the grand jury when it reconvenes, unless it is already sitting, or of appearing with defense counsel before the district court for an *in camera* inspection of the grand jury transcripts for a determination whether other, sufficient evidence exists to support the indictment. If other, sufficient evidence is present so that the grand jury may have indicted without giving any weight to the perjured testimony, the indictment cannot be challenged on the basis of the perjury. . . . Our rationale for these rules is simple enough: errors before the grand jury, such as perjured testimony, normally can be corrected at trial, where evidentiary and procedural rules safeguard the accused's constitutional rights. . . . Put differently, grand jury proceedings need not be perfect." Id. at 1001. See Coppedge v. United States, 311 F.2d 128 (D.C.Cir.1962). See also United States v. Adamo, 742 F.2d 927 (6th

Cir.1984), agreeing with *Basurto*'s "basic ethical philosophy," but affirming the prosecutor's independent responsibility to assess the significance of perjured testimony before the grand jury and take appropriate action.

335. "[The grand jury's] power is only to accuse, not to convict. Its indictment does not even create a presumption of guilt; all that it charges must later be proved before the trial jury, and then beyond a reasonable doubt. The grand jury need not be unanimous. It does not hear both sides but only the prosecution's evidence, and does not face the problem of a choice between two adversaries. Its duty is to indict if the prosecution's evidence, unexplained, uncontradicted and unsupplemented, would warrant a conviction. If so, its indictment merely puts the accused to trial. The difference between the function of the trial jury and the function of the grand jury is all the difference between deciding a case and merely deciding that a case should be tried." Cassell v. Texas, 339 U.S. 282, 302 (1950) (Jackson, J., dissenting).

United States v. Williams

504 U.S. 36, 112 S.Ct. 1735, 118 L.Ed.2d 352 (1992).

■ JUSTICE SCALIA delivered the opinion of the Court.

The question presented in this case is whether a district court may dismiss an otherwise valid indictment because the Government failed to disclose to the grand jury "substantial exculpatory evidence" in its possession.

I

On May 4, 1988, respondent John H. Williams, Jr., a Tulsa, Oklahoma investor, was indicted by a federal grand jury on seven counts of "knowingly mak[ing] [a] false statement or report . . . for the purpose of influencing . . . the action [of a federally insured financial institution]," in violation of 18 U.S.C. § 1014 (1988 ed., Supp. II). According to the indictment, between September 1984 and November 1985 Williams supplied four Oklahoma banks with "materially false" statements that variously overstated the value of his current assets and interest income in order to influence the banks' actions on his loan requests.

Williams' misrepresentation was allegedly effected through two financial statements provided to the banks, a "Market Value Balance Sheet" and a "Statement of Projected Income and Expense." The former included as "current assets" approximately $6 million in notes receivable from three venture capital companies. Though it contained a disclaimer that these assets were carried at cost rather than at market value, the Government asserted that listing them as "current assets"—i.e., assets quickly reducible to cash—was misleading, since Williams knew that none of the venture capital companies could afford to satisfy the notes in the short term. The second document—the Statement of Projected Income and Expense—allegedly misrepresented Williams' interest income, since it failed to reflect that the interest payments received on the notes of the venture capital companies were funded entirely by Williams' own loans to those companies. The Statement thus falsely implied, according to the Government, that Williams was deriving interest income from "an independent outside source." Brief for United States 3.

Shortly after arraignment, the District Court granted Williams' motion for disclosure of all exculpatory portions of the grand jury transcripts . . . . Upon reviewing this material, Williams demanded that the District Court dismiss the indictment, alleging that the Government had failed to fulfill its obligation under the Tenth Circuit's prior decision in United States v. Page, 808 F.2d 723, 728 (1987), to present "substantial exculpatory evidence" to the grand jury (emphasis omitted). His contention was that evidence which the Government had chosen not to present to the grand jury—in particular, Williams' general ledgers and tax returns, and Williams' testimony in his contemporaneous Chapter 11 bankruptcy proceeding—disclosed that, for tax purposes and otherwise, he had regularly accounted for the "notes receivable" (and the interest on them) in a manner consistent with the Balance Sheet and the Income Statement. This, he contended, belied an intent to mislead the banks, and thus directly negated an essential element of the charged offense.

The District Court initially denied Williams' motion, but upon reconsideration ordered the indictment dismissed without prejudice. . . . Upon the Government's appeal, the Court of Appeals affirmed the District Court's order. . . . We granted certiorari . . . .

. . .

III

Respondent does not contend that the Fifth Amendment itself obliges the prosecutor to disclose substantial exculpatory evidence in his possession to the grand jury. Instead, building on our statement that the federal courts "may within limits, formulate procedural rules not specifically required by the Constitution or the Congress," United States v. Hasting, 461 U.S. 499, 505 (1983), he argues that imposition of the Tenth Circuit's disclosure rule is supported by the courts' "supervisory power." We think not. *Hasting*, and the cases that rely upon the principle it expresses, deal strictly with the courts' power to control their *own* procedures. That power has been applied not only to improve the truth-finding process of the trial . . . but also to prevent parties from reaping benefit or incurring harm from violations of substantive or procedural rules (imposed by the Constitution or laws) governing matters apart from the trial itself . . . Thus, Bank of Nova Scotia v. United States, 487 U.S. 250 (1988), makes clear that the supervisory power can be used to dismiss an indictment because of misconduct before the grand jury, at least where that misconduct amounts to a violation of one of those "few, clear rules which were carefully drafted and approved by this Court and by Congress to ensure the integrity of the grand jury's functions," United States v. Mechanik, 475 U.S. 66, 74 (1986) (O'Connor, J., concurring in judgment).

We did not hold in *Bank of Nova Scotia*, however, that the courts' supervisory power could be used, not merely as a means of enforcing or vindicating legally compelled standards of prosecutorial conduct before the grand jury, but as a means of *prescribing* those standards of prosecutorial conduct in the first instance—just as it may be used as a means of establishing standards of prosecutorial conduct before the courts themselves. It is this latter exercise that respondent demands. Because the grand jury is an institution separate from the courts, over whose functioning the courts do not preside, we think it clear that, as a general matter at least, no such "supervisory" judicial authority exists, and that the disclosure rule applied here exceeded the Tenth Circuit's authority.

A

[T]he grand jury is mentioned in the Bill of Rights, but not in the body of the Constitution. It has not been textually assigned, therefore, to any of the branches described in the first three Articles. . . . In fact the whole theory of its function is that it belongs to no branch of the institutional Government, serving as a kind of buffer or referee between the Government and the people. . . . Although the grand jury normally operates, of course, in the courthouse and under judicial auspices, its institutional relationship with the Judicial Branch has traditionally been, so to speak, at arm's length. Judges' direct involvement in the functioning of the grand jury has generally been confined to the constitutive one of calling the grand jurors together and administering their oaths of office. . . .

. . .

Given the grand jury's operational separateness from its constituting court, it should come as no surprise that we have been reluctant to invoke the judicial supervisory power as a basis for prescribing modes of grand jury procedure. . . .

[A]ny power federal courts may have to fashion, on their own initiative, rules of grand jury procedure is a very limited one, not remotely comparable to the power they maintain over their own proceedings. . . . It certainly would not permit judicial reshaping of the grand jury institution, substantially altering the traditional relationships between the prosecutor, the constituting court, and the grand jury itself. . . . As we proceed to discuss, that would be the consequence of the proposed rule here.

B

Respondent argues that the Court of Appeals' rule can be justified as a sort of Fifth Amendment "common law," a necessary means of assuring the constitutional right to the judgment "of an independent and informed grand jury," Wood v. Georgia, 370 U.S. 375, 390 (1962). Brief for Respondent 27.

Respondent makes a generalized appeal to functional notions: Judicial supervision of the quantity and quality of the evidence relied upon by the grand jury plainly facilitates, he says, the grand jury's performance of its twin historical responsibilities, i.e., bringing to trial those who may be justly accused and shielding the innocent from unfounded accusation and prosecution. . . . We do not agree. The rule would neither preserve nor enhance the traditional functioning of the institution that the Fifth Amendment demands. To the contrary, requiring the prosecutor to present exculpatory as well as inculpatory evidence would alter the grand jury's historical role, transforming it from an accusatory to an adjudicatory body.

It is axiomatic that the grand jury sits not to determine guilt or innocence, but to assess whether there is adequate basis for bringing a criminal charge. . . . That has always been so; and to make the assessment it has always been thought sufficient to hear only the prosecutor's side. . . . As a consequence, neither in this country nor in England has the suspect under investigation by the grand jury ever been thought to have a right to testify, or to have exculpatory evidence presented. . . .

Imposing upon the prosecutor a legal obligation to present exculpatory evidence in his possession would be incompatible with this system. If a "balanced" assessment of the entire matter is the objective, surely the first thing to be done—rather than requiring the prosecutor to say what he knows in defense of the target of the investigation—is to entitle the target to tender his own defense. To require the former while denying (as we do) the latter would be quite absurd. It would also be quite pointless, since it would merely invite the target to circumnavigate the system by delivering his exculpatory evidence to the prosecutor, whereupon it would *have* to be passed on to the grand jury—unless the prosecutor is willing to take the chance that a court will not deem the evidence important enough to qualify for mandatory disclosure. . . .

Respondent acknowledges (as he must) that the "common law" of the grand jury is not violated if the *grand jury itself* chooses to hear no more evidence than that which suffices to convince it an indictment is proper. . . . Thus, had the Government offered to familiarize the grand jury in this case with the five boxes of financial statements and deposition testimony alleged to contain exculpatory information, and had the grand jury rejected the offer as pointless, respondent would presumably agree that the resulting indictment would have been valid. Respondent insists, however, that courts must require the modern prosecutor to alert the grand jury to the nature and extent of the available exculpatory evidence, because otherwise the grand jury "merely functions as an arm of the prosecution." Brief for Respondent 27. We reject the attempt to convert a nonexistent duty of the grand jury itself into an obligation of the prosecutor. The authority of the prosecutor to seek an indictment has long been understood to be "coterminous with the authority of the grand jury to entertain [the prosecutor's] charges." United States v. Thompson, 251 U.S., at 414. If the grand jury has no obligation to consider all "substantial exculpatory" evidence, we do not understand how the prosecutor can be said to have a binding obligation to present it.

There is yet another respect in which respondent's proposal not only fails to comport with, but positively contradicts, the "common law" of the Fifth Amendment grand jury. Motions to quash indictments based upon the sufficiency of the evidence relied upon by the grand jury were unheard of at common law in England . . . . And the traditional American practice was described by Justice Nelson, riding circuit in 1852, as follows:

> "No case has been cited, nor have we been able to find any, furnishing an authority for looking into and revising the judgment of the grand jury upon the evidence for the purpose of determining whether or not the finding was founded upon sufficient proof, or whether there was a deficiency in respect to any part of the complaint. . . ." United States v. Reed, 27 Fed.Cas. 727, 738 (No. 16,134) (CCNDNY 1852).

We accepted Justice Nelson's description in Costello v. United States, where we held that "it would run counter to the whole history of the grand jury institution" to permit an indictment to be challenged "on the ground that there was incompetent evidence before the grand jury." 350 U.S., at 363–364. And we reaffirmed this principle recently in *Bank of Nova Scotia*, where we held that "the mere fact that evidence itself is unreliable is not sufficient to require a dismissal of the indictment," and that "a challenge to the reliability or competence of the evidence presented to the grand jury" will not be heard. 487 U.S., at 261. It would make little sense, we think, to abstain from reviewing the evidentiary support for the grand jury's judgment while scrutinizing the sufficiency of the prosecutor's presentation. A complaint about the quality or adequacy of the evidence can always be recast as a complaint that the prosecutor's presentation was "incomplete" or "misleading." Our words in *Costello* bear repeating: Review of facially valid indictments on such grounds "would run counter to the whole history of the grand jury institution[,] [and] [n]either justice nor the concept of a fair trial requires [it]." 350 U.S., at 364.

. . .

[R]espondent argues that a rule requiring the prosecutor to disclose exculpatory evidence to the grand jury would, by removing from the docket unjustified prosecutions, save valuable judicial time. That depends, we suppose, upon what the ratio would turn out to be between unjustified prosecutions eliminated and grand jury indictments challenged—for the latter as well as the former consume "valuable judicial time." We need not pursue the matter; if there is an advantage to the proposal, Congress is free to prescribe it. For the reasons set forth above, however, we conclude that courts have no authority to prescribe such a duty pursuant to their inherent supervisory authority over their own proceedings. The judgment of the Court of Appeals is accordingly reversed and the cause remanded for further proceedings consistent with this opinion.

. . . [5]

---

[5] Justice Stevens wrote a dissenting opinion, which Justice Blackmun and Justice O'Connor joined and part of which Justice Thomas joined.

336. On the question whether there is a constitutional right not to be prosecuted unless there is probable cause, see generally Albright v. Oliver, 510 U.S. 266 (1994) (7–2).

337. Before the decision in *Williams*, above, the Court of Appeals for the Second Circuit had taken the lead in requiring the prosecutor to make a reasonably full and objective presentation of the evidence to the grand jury. In United States v. Ciambrone, 601 F.2d 616, 623 (2d Cir.1979) (conviction affirmed), for example, it said that "where a prosecutor is aware of any substantial evidence negating guilt he should, in the interest of justice, make it known to the grand jury, at least where it might reasonably be expected to lead the jury not to indict." And in United States v. Estepa, 471 F.2d 1132 (2d Cir.1972) (convictions reversed and indictment dismissed), it strongly disapproved the needless use of hearsay evidence before the grand jury. See also United States v. Hogan, 712 F.2d 757 (2d Cir.1983) (convictions reversed and indictment dismissed for prosecutorial misconduct before grand jury). Other federal courts had been more cautious about their exercise of supervisory power over the prosecutor. E.g., United States v. McKenzie, 678 F.2d 629, 631 (5th Cir.1982) (even in case of "the most 'egregious prosecutorial misconduct,'" indictment should be dismissed only if defendant's case has been unfairly prejudiced); United States v. Welch, 572 F.2d 1359, 1360 (9th Cir.1978) (indictment dismissed only if prosecutorial discretion is "abused to such an extent as to be arbitrary and capricious and violative of due process"). The Ninth Circuit upheld dismissal of an indictment in United States v. Samango, 607 F.2d 877, 884 (9th Cir.1979), saying that "the manner in which the prosecution obtained the indictment represented a serious threat to the integrity of the judicial process."

Ciambrone is overruled by *Williams*, as, evidently, is *Estepa*. How much of *Basurto*, note 334 p. 696 above, remains is unclear.

338. "Although neither statutory nor case law imposes upon the prosecutor a legal obligation to present exculpatory evidence to the grand jury ... it is the Department's internal policy to do so under many circumstances. For example, when a prosecutor conducting a grand jury inquiry is personally aware of substantial evidence which directly negates the guilt of a subject of the investigation, the prosecutor must present or otherwise disclose such evidence to the grand jury before seeking an indictment against such a person." United States Attorneys' Manual 9–11.233.

Observing that "the adversary system does not extend to grand jury proceedings," the Supreme Court of California has held that when a district attorney is aware of evidence "reasonably tending to negate guilt" he is required to tell the grand jury about it, so that it can exercise its power to have the evidence produced. Johnson v. Superior Court, 539 P.2d 792, 796 (Cal.1975). The reasoning of *Johnson* was disapproved in Buzbee v. Donnelly, 634 P.2d 1244, 1253 (N.M.1981). See State v. Bell, 589 P.2d 517

(Haw.1978), in which the court declined to follow *Johnson* but said that "where evidence is known to the prosecution, such evidence must be presented to the grand jury." Id. at 520. An example of such evidence, the court said, is "a witness whose testimony is not directly contradicted by any other witness and who maintains that the accused was nowhere near the scene of the crime when it occurred." Id. To the same effect, see State v. Hogan, 676 A.2d 533 (N.J. 1996) (prosecutor has duty to disclose only evidence that directly negate[s] guilt and [is] clearly exculpatory"; additional cases cited).

339. Should a potential defendant be given an opportunity to appear before the grand jury before it decides whether or not to indict him? Why (not)? The United States Attorneys' Manual 9–11.152 states: "It is not altogether uncommon for subjects or targets of the grand jury's investigation, particularly in white-collar cases, to request or demand the opportunity to tell the grand jury their side of the story. While the prosecutor has no legal obligation to permit such witnesses to testify . . . a refusal to do so can create the appearance of unfairness. Accordingly, under normal circumstances, where no burden upon the grand jury or delay of its proceedings is involved, reasonable requests by a 'subject' or 'target' of an investigation . . . personally to testify before the grand jury ordinarily should be given favorable consideration, provided that such witness explicitly waives his/her privilege against self-incrimination and is represented by counsel or voluntarily and knowingly appears without counsel and consents to full examination under oath.

"Some such witnesses undoubtedly will wish to supplement their testimony with the testimony of others. The decision whether to accommodate such requests, reject them after listening to the testimony of the target or the subject, or to seek statements from the suggested witnesses is a matter which is left to the sound discretion of the grand jury. When passing on such requests, it must be kept in mind that the grand jury was never intended to be and is not properly either an adversary proceeding or the arbiter of guilt or innocence."

Section 9–11.153 states: "Where a target is not called to testify . . . and does not request to testify on his/her own motion . . . the prosecutor, in appropriate cases, is encouraged to notify such person a reasonable time before seeking an indictment in order to afford him/her an opportunity to testify . . . before the grand jury. Of course, notification would not be appropriate in routine clear cases nor where such action might jeopardize the investigation or prosecution because of the likelihood of flight, destruction or fabrication or evidence, endangerment of other witnesses, undue delay or otherwise would be inconsistent with the ends of justice."

340. "There are few principles of more importance in the administration of criminal justice than the principle announced in Costello v. United States, 350 U.S. 359, 363 (1956): an indictment returned by a legally constituted and unbiased grand jury, if valid on its face, is sufficient to call for trial of the charges on the merits." United States Attorney's Manual 9–11.230.

"The fact that illegally obtained, privileged, or otherwise incompetent evidence was presented to the grand jury is no cause for abating the prosecution under the indictment, or for inquiring into the sufficiency of the competent evidence before the grand jury, even if the defendant may be expected to have the illegally obtained evidence suppressed or incompetent evidence excluded at trial. . . . Despite some argument that the *Costello* rule has been eroded by cases calling for a more limited use of hearsay in grand jury proceedings, it appears that the rule is entitled to its full force today in light of the broad bases for decision in [United States v.] *Calandra*, [414 U.S. 338 (1974)]." United States Attorneys' Manual 9–11.231.

341. In United States v. Klubock, 832 F.2d 649, aff'd by an equally divided court, 832 F.2d 664 (1st Cir.1987), the court upheld the authority of the district court to issue a local rule as follows: "It is unprofessional conduct for a prosecutor to subpoena an attorney to a grand jury without prior judicial approval in circumstances where the prosecutor seeks to compel the attorney-witness to provide evidence concerning a person who is represented by the attorney-witness." A similar rule had been promulgated by the state supreme court (Massachusetts), at the urging of the state bar association. Is the rule consistent with *Williams*, above?

342. On the relationship between the prosecutor and the grand jury, see United States v. Cox, 342 F.2d 167, 170–72 (5th Cir.1965): "The constitutional requirement of an indictment or presentment as a predicate to a prosecution for capital or infamous crimes has for its primary purpose the protection of the individual from jeopardy except on a finding of probable cause by a group of his fellow citizens, and is designed to afford a safeguard against oppressive actions of the prosecutor or a court. The constitutional provision is not to be read as conferring on or preserving to the grand jury, as such, any rights or prerogatives. The constitutional provision is, as has been said, for the benefit of the accused. . . .

. . .

"The judicial power of the United States is vested in the federal courts, and extends to prosecutions for violations of the criminal laws of the United States. The executive power is vested in the President of the United States, who is required to take care that the laws be faithfully executed. The Attorney General is the hand of the President in taking care that the laws of the United States in legal proceedings and in the prosecution of offenses, be faithfully executed. The role of the grand jury is restricted to a finding as to whether or not there is probable cause to believe that an offense has been committed. The discretionary power of the attorney for the United States in determining whether a prosecution shall be commenced or maintained may well depend upon matters of policy wholly apart from any question of probable cause. Although as a member of the bar, the attorney for the United States is an officer of the court, he is nevertheless an executive official of the Government, and it is as an officer of the executive department that he exercises a discretion as to whether or not there shall be a prosecution in a particular case. It follows, as an incident of the constitutional separation of powers, that the courts are not to interfere with the free exercise of the discretionary powers of the attorneys of the United States in their control over criminal prosecutions. The provision of Rule 7, requiring the signing of the indictment by the attorney for the Government, is a recognition of the power of Government counsel to permit or not to permit the bringing of an indictment. If the attorney refuses to sign, as he has the discretionary power of doing, we conclude that there is no valid indictment. . . . [T]he requirement of the signature is for the purpose of evidencing the joinder of the attorney for the United States with the grand jury in instituting a criminal proceeding in the Court. . . ."

Dennis v. United States

384 U.S. 855, 86 S.Ct. 1840, 16 L.Ed.2d 973 (1966).

[The defendants were convicted of a violation of the general conspiracy statute, 18 U.S.C. § 371, the conspiracy having to do with the filing of false affidavits under the National Labor Relations Act.]

■ MR. JUSTICE FORTAS delivered the opinion of the Court.

. . .

We turn now to petitioners' contention that the trial court committed reversible error by denying their motion to require production for petitioners' examination of the grand jury testimony of four government witnesses. Alternatively, petitioners sought *in camera* inspection by the trial judge to be followed by production to petitioners in the event the judge found inconsistencies between trial testimony and that before the grand jury.

The trial judge denied the motions, made at the conclusion of the direct examination of each of the witnesses, on the ground that no "particularized need" had been shown. See Pittsburgh Plate Glass Co. v. United States, 360 U.S. 395, 400. On appeal the Court of Appeals held that the denial of the motions was not reversible error. . . .

[W]e disagree, and we reverse.

This Court has recognized the "long-established policy that maintains the secrecy of the grand jury proceedings in the federal courts." United

States v. Procter & Gamble Co., 356 U.S. 677, 681. And it has ruled that, when disclosure is permitted, it is to be done "discreetly and limitedly." Id., at 683. Accordingly, the Court has refused in a civil case to permit pretrial disclosure of an entire grand jury transcript where the sole basis for discovery was that the transcript had been available to the Government in preparation of its case. *Procter & Gamble*, supra. And, in Pittsburgh Plate Glass Co. v. United States, supra, the Court sustained a trial court's refusal to order disclosure of a witness' grand jury testimony where the defense made no showing of need, but insisted upon production of the minutes as a matter of right, and where there was "overwhelming" proof of the offense charged without reference to the witness' trial testimony.

In general, however, the Court has confirmed the trial court's power under Rule 6(e) of the Federal Rules of Criminal Procedure to direct disclosure of grand jury testimony "preliminarily to or in connection with a judicial proceeding." In United States v. Socony-Vacuum Oil Co., 310 U.S. 150, 234, the Court acknowledged that "after the grand jury's functions are ended, disclosure is wholly proper where the ends of justice require it." In *Procter & Gamble*, supra, the Court stated that "problems concerning the use of the grand jury transcript at the trial to impeach a witness, to refresh his recollection, to test his credibility . . ." are "cases of particularized need where the secrecy of the proceedings is lifted discretely and limitedly." 356 U.S., at 683. And in *Pittsburgh Plate Glass*, supra, where four members of the Court concluded that even on the special facts of that case the witness' grand jury testimony should have been supplied to the defense, the entire Court was agreed that upon a showing of "particularized need" defense counsel might have access to relevant portions of the grand jury testimony of a trial witness, 360 U.S., at 400, 405. In a variety of circumstances, the lower federal courts, too, have made grand jury testimony available to defendants.

These developments are entirely consonant with the growing realization that disclosure, rather than suppression, of relevant materials ordinarily promotes the proper administration of criminal justice. . . .

Certainly in the context of the present case, where the Government concedes that the importance of preserving the secrecy of the grand jury minutes is minimal and also admits the persuasiveness of the arguments advanced in favor of disclosure, it cannot fairly be said that the defense has failed to make out a "particularized need." The showing made by petitioners, both in the trial court and here, goes substantially beyond the minimum required by Rule 6(e) and the prior decisions of his Court. The record shows the following circumstances:

1. The events as to which the testimony in question related occurred between 1948 and 1955. The grand jury testimony was taken in 1956, while these events were relatively fresh. The trial testimony which petitioners seek to compare with the 1956 grand jury testimony was not taken until 1963. Certainly, there was reason to assay the latter testimony, some of which is 15 years after the event, against the much fresher testimony before the grand jury.

2. The motions in question involved the testimony of four of the eight government witnesses. They were key witnesses. The charge could not be proved on the basis of evidence exclusive of that here involved.

3. The testimony of the four witnesses concerned conversations and oral statements made in meetings. It was largely uncorroborated. Where the question of guilt or innocence may turn on exactly what was said, the defense is clearly entitled to all relevant aid which is reasonably available to ascertain the precise substance of the statements.

4. Two of the witnesses were accomplices, one of these being also a paid informer. A third had separated from the union and had reasons for hostility toward petitioners.

5. One witness admitted on cross-examination that he had in earlier statements been mistaken about significant dates.

A conspiracy case carries with it the inevitable risk of wrongful attribution of responsibility to one or more of the multiple defendants. . . . Under these circumstances, it is especially important that the defense, the judge and the jury should have the assurance that the doors that may lead to truth have been unlocked. In our adversary system for determining guilt or innocence, it is rarely justifiable for the prosecution to have exclusive access to a storehouse of relevant fact. Exceptions to this are justifiable only by the clearest and most compelling considerations. For this reason, we cannot accept the view of the Court of Appeals that it is "safe to assume" no inconsistencies would have come to light if the grand jury testimony had been examined. There is no justification for relying upon "assumption."

In *Pittsburgh Plate Glass*, supra, the Court reserved decision on the question whether *in camera* inspection by the trial judge is an appropriate or satisfactory measure when there is a showing of a "particularized need" for disclosure. 360 U.S., at 401. This procedure, followed by production to defense counsel in the event the trial judge finds inconsistencies, has been adopted in some of the Courts of Appeals. In the Second Circuit it is available as a matter of right. While this practice may be useful in enabling the trial court to rule on a defense motion for production to it of grand jury testimony—and we do not disapprove it for that purpose—it by no means disposes of the matter. Trial judges ought not be burdened with the task or the responsibility of examining sometimes voluminous grand jury testimony in order to ascertain inconsistencies with trial testimony. In any event, "it will be extremely difficult for even the most able and experienced trial judge under the pressures of conducting a trial to pick out all of the grand jury testimony that would be useful in impeaching a witness." Pittsburgh Plate Glass, 360 U.S., at 410 (dissenting opinion). Nor is it realistic to assume that the trial court's judgment as to the utility of material for impeachment or other legitimate purposes, however conscientiously made, would exhaust the possibilities. In our adversary system, it is enough for judges to judge. The determination of what may be useful to the defense can properly and effectively be made only by an advocate. The trial judge's function in this respect is limited to deciding whether a case has been made for production, and to supervise the process: for example, to cause the elimination of extraneous matter and to rule upon applications by the Government for protective orders in unusual situations, such as those involving the Nation's security or clearcut dangers to individuals who are identified by the testimony produced. . . .

Because petitioners were entitled to examine the grand jury minutes relating to trial testimony of the four government witnesses, and to do so while those witnesses were available for cross-examination, we reverse the judgment below and remand for a new trial.

It is so ordered.[6]

———

343. The Court in *Dennis* referred to "the reasons traditionally advanced to justify nondisclosure of grand jury minutes," 384 U.S. at 872 n.18, as set forth by Justice Brennan in Pittsburgh Plate Glass Co. v. United States, 360 U.S. 395, 405 (1959) (dissenting opinion): "Essentially four reasons have been advanced as justification for grand jury secrecy. (1) To prevent the accused from escaping before he is indicted and arrested or from tampering with the witnesses against him. (2) To prevent disclosure of derogatory information presented to the grand jury against an accused who has not been indicted. (3) To encourage complainants and witnesses to come before the grand jury and speak freely without fear that their testimony will be made public thereby subjecting them to possible discomfort or retaliation. (4) To encourage the grand jurors to engage in uninhibited investigation and deliberation by barring disclosure of their votes and comments during the proceedings."

In Douglas Oil Co. v. Petrol Stops Northwest, 441 U.S. 211 (1979) (6–3), the Supreme Court reaffirmed that "the proper functioning of our grand jury system depends upon the secrecy of grand jury proceedings." It said that parties seeking disclosure of grand jury transcripts under Federal Rule 6(e) "must show that the material they seek is needed to avoid a possible injustice in another judicial proceeding, that the need for disclosure is greater than the need for continued secrecy, and that their request is structured to cover only material so needed." Id. at 222. The Court added that the need for secrecy is not gone when the grand jury has completed its work; the effects of disclosure on future grand juries have to be considered.

The Court said further that when disclosure is sought under Rule 6(e), the request should be made to the court of the jurisdiction in which the grand jury sat, which should evaluate the need for continued secrecy; but that if the request is for use in a case pending elsewhere, the question

[6] Justice Black wrote an opinion concurring in part and dissenting in part, which   Justice Douglas joined.

whether there is a need for disclosure should, when appropriate, be referred to the court where the case is pending.

See In re Grand Jury Testimony, 832 F.2d 60 (5th Cir.1987) (*Douglas Oil Co.* applied).

344. The Jencks Act, 18 U.S.C. § 3500, was amended in 1970 to give effect to the Court's holding in *Dennis.* The statute (and Fed.R.Crim.P. 26.2) explicitly include among the pretrial statements of government witnesses that shall be disclosed to the defense after the witness has testified on direct examination at trial "a statement, however taken or recorded, or a transcription thereof, if any, made by said witness to a grand jury." See p. 1025 below.

In United States v. Head, 586 F.2d 508 (5th Cir.1978), the prosecutor deliberately avoided recording certain grand jury witnesses' testimony, to avoid the creation of Jencks Act statements. The court held that the prosecutor's action was improper but that in the absence of some showing of prejudice to the defendant it was not required that the witnesses be barred from testifying at trial. The issue is eliminated by amended Rule 6(e)(1), p. 678 above, which provides that proceedings of the grand jury shall be recorded.

Rule 16(a)(1)(A) provides: "Upon request of a defendant the government shall permit the defendant to inspect and copy or photograph . . . recorded testimony of the defendant before a grand jury which relates to the offense charged." Rule 16(a)(3) states that except as otherwise explicitly provided, "these rules do not relate to discovery or inspection of recorded proceedings of a grand jury."

345. Rule 6(e)(3)(A) permits disclosure of grand jury proceedings to "(i) an attorney for the government for use in the performance of such attorney's duty; and (ii) such government personnel (including personnel of a state or subdivision of a state) as are deemed necessary by an attorney for the government to assist an attorney for the government in the performance of such attorney's duty to enforce federal criminal law." Rule 54(c) defines "attorney for the government" to include "the Attorney General, an authorized assistant of the Attorney General, a United States Attorney, [and] an authorized assistant of a United States Attorney."

In United States v. Sells Engineering, Inc., 463 U.S. 418 (1983) (5–4) attorneys in the Justice Department sought disclosure of grand jury materials for use in a civil suit. The Court held that automatic disclosure under Rule 6(e)(3)(A)(i) is limited "to use by those attorneys who conduct the criminal matters to which the materials pertain." Id. at 427. That conclusion, the Court said, was required "by the general purposes and policies of grand jury secrecy, by the limited policy reasons why Government attorneys are granted access to grand jury materials for criminal use, and by the legislative history of Rule 6(e)." Id. Government attorneys may obtain disclosure for other purposes only by court order under Rule 6(e)(3)(C)(1), upon a showing of particularized need as required by Douglas Oil Co. v. Petrol Stops Northwest, note 343 p. 708 above.

In United States v. John Doe, Inc. I, 481 U.S. 102 (1987) (5–3), however, the Court held that a government attorney who is involved in a grand jury proceeding may use information obtained during that proceeding in a subsequent civil proceeding in which he is involved, without a disclosure order under Rule 6(e). It said that the rule prohibits disclosure of information about the grand jury proceeding to persons who are not authorized to have access to it, but not "the continued use of information by attorneys who legitimately obtained access to the information through the grand jury investigation." Id. at 108. The Court also upheld a disclosure order issued for attorneys who had not been involved in the grand jury proceeding. Discussing the requirement of "particularized need," it said generally that "the question that must be asked is whether the public benefits of the disclosure . . . outweigh the dangers created by the limited disclosure requested." Id. at 113.

Construing Rule 6(e) further, in United States v. Baggot, 463 U.S. 476 (1983) (8–1), the Court held that an order for disclosure "preliminary to or in connection with a judicial proceeding," under subdivision (C)(1), could not be issued for use by the IRS to determine a taxpayer's civil tax liability. The primary function of such use, the Court said, was to assess taxes and not to prepare for or conduct litigation.

————

Neither the preliminary examination nor the grand jury proceeding provides effective supervision of the prosecutor's exercise of discretion (although they may have an effect on how he exercises his discretion). Each of them suggests a kind of supervision that might be available. Would it be desirable to require a prosecutor to obtain leave of court before filing formal charges (perhaps only of serious crimes) against a person? If so, what should be the procedure for obtaining leave to prosecute, and what showing should the prosecutor have to make? Alternatively, would it be desirable to make grand jury proceedings an effective exercise of community control over prosecutorial discretion? Would it be desirable to encourage the grand jury—some changing body of private citizens—to reject prosecution when, whatever the law, the "sentiment of the community" is against it?

CHAPTER 11

PLEAS AND PLEA BARGAINING

---

346. Criminal defendants disposed of in United States District Courts, Oct.1, 1996–Sept. 30, 1997[1]:

Total Defendants	Not Convicted				Convicted and Sentenced				
			Acquitted by					Convicted by	
	Total	Dis-missed	Court	Jury	Total	Plea of Guilty	Nolo Con-tendere	Court	Jury
63,148		6,607	400	493	55,648	**51,647**	271	499	3,231

FEDERAL RULES OF CRIMINAL PROCEDURE

Rule 10.

ARRAIGNMENT

Arraignment shall be conducted in open court and shall consist of reading the indictment or information to the defendant or stating to the defendant the substance of the charge and calling on the defendant to plead thereto. The defendant shall be given a copy of the indictment or information before being called upon to plead.

Rule 11.

PLEAS

(a) Alternatives.

(1) In General. A defendant may plead not guilty, guilty, or nolo contendere. If a defendant refuses to plead or if a defendant corporation fails to appear, the court shall enter a plea of not guilty.

1. From Table D–4, Annual Report of the Director of the Administrative Office of the United States Courts, 1997.

(2) Conditional Pleas. With the approval of the court and the consent of the government, a defendant may enter a conditional plea of guilty or nolo contendere, reserving in writing the right, on appeal from the judgment, to review of the adverse determination of any specified pre-trial motion. A defendant who prevails on appeal shall be allowed to withdraw the plea.

(b) Nolo Contendere. A defendant may plead nolo contendere only with the consent of the court. Such a plea shall be accepted by the court only after due consideration of the views of the parties and the interest of the public in the effective administration of justice.

(c) Advice to Defendant. Before accepting a plea of guilty or nolo contendere, the court must address the defendant personally in open court and inform the defendant of, and determine that the defendant understands, the following:

(1) the nature of the charge to which the plea is offered, the mandatory minimum penalty provided by law, if any, and the maximum possible penalty provided by law, including the effect of any special parole or supervised release term, the fact that the court is required to consider any applicable sentencing guidelines but may depart from those guidelines under some circumstances, and, when applicable, that the court may also order the defendant to make restitution to any victim of the offense; and

(2) if the defendant is not represented by an attorney, that the defendant has the right to be represented by an attorney at every stage of the proceeding and, if necessary, one will be appointed to represent the defendant; and

(3) that the defendant has the right to plead not guilty or to persist in that plea if it has already been made, the right to be tried by a jury and at that trial the right to the assistance of counsel, the right to confront and cross-examine adverse witnesses, and the right against compelled self-incrimination; and

(4) that if a plea of guilty or nolo contendere is accepted by the court there will not be a further trial of any kind, so that by pleading guilty or nolo contendere the defendant waives the right to a trial; and

(5) if the court intends to question the defendant under oath, on the record, and in the presence of counsel about the offense to which the defendant has pleaded, that the defendant's answers may later be used against the defendant in a prosecution for perjury or false statement.

(d) Insuring That the Plea is Voluntary. The court shall not accept a plea of guilty or nolo contendere without first, by addressing the defendant personally in open court, determining that the plea is voluntary and not the result of force or threats or of promises apart from a plea agreement. The court shall also inquire as to whether the defendant's willingness to plead guilty or nolo contendere results from prior discussions between the attorney for the government and the defendant or the defendant's attorney.

(e) Plea Agreement Procedure.

(1) In General. The attorney for the government and the attorney for the defendant or the defendant when acting pro se may engage in discussions with a view toward reaching an agreement that, upon the entering of a plea of guilty or nolo contendere to a charged offense or to a lesser or related offense, the attorney for the government will do any of the following:

(A) move for dismissal of other charges; or

(B) make a recommendation, or agree not to oppose the defendant's request, for a particular sentence, with the understanding that such recommendation or request shall not be binding upon the court; or

(C) agree that a specific sentence is the appropriate disposition of the case.

The court shall not participate in any such discussions.

(2) Notice of Such Agreement. If a plea agreement has been reached by the parties, the court shall, on the record, require the disclosure of the agreement in open court or, on a showing of good cause, in camera, at the time the plea is offered. If the agreement is of the type specified in subdivision (e)(1)(A) or (C), the court may accept or reject the agreement, or may defer its decision as to the acceptance or rejection until there has been an opportunity to consider the presentence report. If the agreement is of the type specified in subdivision (e)(1)(B), the court shall advise the defendant that if the court does not accept the recommendation or request the defendant nevertheless has no right to withdraw the plea.

(3) Acceptance of a Plea Agreement. If the court accepts the plea agreement, the court shall inform the defendant that it will embody in the judgment and sentence the disposition provided for in the plea agreement.

(4) Rejection of a Plea Agreement. If the court rejects the plea agreement, the court shall, on the record, inform the parties of this fact, advise the defendant personally in open court or, on a showing of good cause, in camera, that the court is not bound by the plea agreement, afford the defendant the opportunity to then withdraw the plea, and advise the defendant that if the defendant persists in a guilty plea or plea of nolo contendere the disposition of the case may be less favorable to the defendant than that contemplated by the plea agreement.

(5) Time of Plea Agreement Procedure. Except for good cause shown, notification to the court of the existence of a plea agreement shall be given at the arraignment or at such other time, prior to trial, as may be fixed by the court.

(6) Inadmissibility of Pleas, Plea Discussions, and Related Statements. Except as otherwise provided in this paragraph, evidence of the following is not, in any civil or criminal proceeding, admissible against the defendant who made the plea or was a participant in the plea discussions:

(A) a plea of guilty which was later withdrawn;

(B) a plea of nolo contendere;

(C) any statement made in the course of any proceedings under this rule regarding either of the foregoing pleas; or

(D) any statement made in the course of plea discussions with an attorney for the government which do not result in a plea of guilty or which result in a plea of guilty later withdrawn.

However, such a statement is admissible (i) in any proceeding wherein another statement made in the course of the same plea or plea discussions has been introduced and the statement ought in fairness be considered contemporaneously with it, or (ii) in a criminal proceeding for perjury or false statement if the statement was made by the defendant under oath, on the record, and in the presence of counsel.

(f) Determining Accuracy of Plea. Notwithstanding the acceptance of a plea of guilty, the court should not enter a judgment upon such plea without making such inquiry as shall satisfy it that there is a factual basis for the plea.

(g) Record of Proceedings. A verbatim record of the proceedings at which the defendant enters a plea shall be made and, if there is a plea of guilty or nolo contendere, the record shall include, without limitation, the court's advice to the defendant, the inquiry into the voluntariness of the plea including any plea agreement, and the inquiry into the accuracy of a guilty plea.

(h) Harmless Error. Any variance from the procedures required by this rule which does not affect substantial rights shall be disregarded.

––––––

347. The requirement of Rule 11(c) that a defendant be advised that by pleading guilty he waives the right to a jury trial does not apply specifically to the right to a jury determination of the forfeitability of property under Rule 31(e). Libretti v. United States, 516 U.S. 29 (1995) (8–1).

The provision of Rule 11(e)(6) that statements made by a defendant in the course of plea discussions that do not result in a plea of guilty are not admissible in a criminal proceeding against the defendant can be waived. United States v. Mezzanatto, 513 U.S. 196 (1995) (7–2). The dissent noted that many prosecutors now routinely require such a waiver before entering into plea discussions. In this case, the defendant's statements were admitted on cross-examination to impeach his testimony on direct examination. The dissent observed that if a requirement of waiver were extended to the government's case in chief, it would effectively preclude a defendant from going to trial after having engaged in plea discussions.

Three Justices, who concurred in the judgment, noted that allowing a waiver with respect to the government's case in chief was not before the Court and was not decided.

McCarthy v. United States

394 U.S. 459, 89 S.Ct. 1166, 22 L.Ed.2d 418 (1969).

■ MR. CHIEF JUSTICE WARREN delivered the opinion of the Court.

This case involves the procedure that must be followed under Rule 11 of the Federal Rules of Criminal Procedure before a United States District Court may accept a guilty plea and the remedy for a failure to follow that procedure.

On April 1, 1966, petitioner was indicted on three counts in the United States District Court for the Northern District of Illinois for violating § 7201 of the Internal Revenue Code. He was charged with "willfully and knowingly" attempting to evade tax payments of $928.74 for 1959 (count 1), $5,143.70 for 1960 (count 2), and $1,207.12 for 1961 (count 3). At his arraignment two weeks later, petitioner, who was represented by retained counsel, pleaded not guilty to each count. The court scheduled his trial for June 30; but on June 29, it granted the Government's motion to postpone the trial because of petitioner's illness. The trial was rescheduled for July 15.

On that day, after informing the court that he had "advised . . . [petitioner] of the consequences of a plea," defense counsel moved to withdraw petitioner's plea of not guilty to count 2 and to enter a plea of guilty to that count. The district judge asked petitioner if he desired to plead guilty and if he understood that such a plea waived his right to a jury trial and subjected him to imprisonment for as long as five years and to a fine as high as $10,000. Petitioner stated that he understood these consequences and wanted to plead guilty. The Government consented to this plea change and informed the court that if petitioner's plea of guilty to count 2 were accepted, the Government would dismiss counts 1 and 3. Before the plea was accepted, however, the prosecutor asked the judge to inquire whether it had been induced by any threats or promises. In response to the judge's inquiry, petitioner replied that his plea was not the product of either. He stated that it was entered of his "own volition." The court ordered a presentence investigation and continued the case to September 14, 1966.

At the commencement of the sentencing hearing on September 14, petitioner asserted that his failure to pay taxes was "not deliberate" and that they would have been paid if he had not been in poor health. The prosecutor stated that the "prime consideration" for the Government's agreement to dismiss counts 1 and 3 was petitioner's promise to pay all taxes, penalties, and interest. The prosecutor then requested the court to refer expressly to this agreement. After noting that petitioner possessed sufficient attachable assets to meet these obligations, the court imposed a sentence of one year and a fine of $2,500. Petitioner's counsel immediately moved to suspend the sentence. He emphasized that petitioner, who was then 65 years of age, was in poor health and contended that his failure to pay his taxes had resulted from his "neglectful" and "inadvertent" method of bookkeeping during a period when he had been suffering from a very serious drinking problem. Consequently, asserted petitioner's counsel, "there was never any disposition to deprive the United States of its due." The judge, however, after indicating he had examined the presentence report, stated his opinion that "the manner in which [petitioner's] books were kept was not inadvertent." He declined, therefore, to suspend petitioner's sentence.

On appeal to the United States Court of Appeals for the Seventh Circuit, petitioner argued that his plea should be set aside because it had been accepted in violation of Rule 11 of the Federal Rules of Criminal Procedure. Specifically, petitioner contended that the District Court had accepted his plea (1) "without first addressing [him] . . . personally and determining that the plea [was] . . . made voluntarily with understanding of the nature of the charge . . .," and (2) that the court had entered judgment without determining "that there [was] . . . a factual basis for the plea." In affirming petitioner's conviction, the Court of Appeals held that the District Judge had complied with Rule 11. . . .

[W]e granted certiorari. . . . We agree with petitioner that the District Judge did not comply with Rule 11 in this case; and in reversing the Court of Appeals, we hold that a defendant is entitled to plead anew if a United States district court accepts his guilty plea without fully adhering to the procedure provided for in Rule 11. This decision is based solely upon our construction of Rule 11 and is made pursuant to our supervisory power over the lower federal courts; we do not reach any of the constitutional arguments petitioner urges as additional grounds for reversal.

I.

Rule 11 expressly directs the district judge to inquire whether a defendant who pleads guilty understands the nature of the charge against him and whether he is aware of the consequences of his plea. At oral argument, however, counsel for the Government repeatedly conceded that the judge did not personally inquire whether petitioner understood the nature of the charge. At one point, counsel stated quite explicitly: "The subject on which he [the District Judge] did not directly address the defendant, which is raised here, is the question of the defendant's understanding of the charge." Nevertheless, the Government argues that since petitioner stated his desire to plead guilty, and since he was informed of the consequences of his plea, the District Court "could properly *assume* that petitioner was entering that plea with a complete understanding of the charge against him." (Emphasis added.)

We cannot accept this argument, which completely ignores the two purposes of Rule 11 and the reasons for its recent amendment. First, although the procedure embodied in Rule 11 has not been held to be constitutionally mandated, it is designed to assist the district judge in making the constitutionally required determination that a defendant's guilty plea is truly voluntary. Second, the Rule is intended to produce a complete record at the time the plea is entered of the factors relevant to this voluntariness determination. Thus, the more meticulously the Rule is adhered to, the more it tends to discourage, or at least to enable more expeditious disposition of, the numerous and often frivolous post-conviction attacks on the constitutional validity of guilty pleas.

Prior to the 1966 amendment, however, not all district judges personally interrogated defendants before accepting their guilty pleas. With an awareness of the confusion over the Rule's requirements in this respect, the draftsmen amended it to add a provision "expressly requiring the court to address the defendant personally."[2] This clarification of the judge's responsibilities quite obviously furthers both of the Rule's purposes. By personally interrogating the defendant, not only will the judge be better able to ascertain the plea's voluntariness, but he also will develop a more complete record to support his determination in a subsequent post-conviction attack.

These two purposes have their genesis in the nature of a guilty plea. A defendant who enters such a plea simultaneously waives several constitutional rights, including his privilege against compulsory self-incrimination, his right to trial by jury, and his right to confront his accusers. For this waiver to be valid under the Due Process Clause, it must be "an intentional relinquishment or abandonment of a known right or privilege." Johnson v. Zerbst, 304 U.S. 458, 464 (1938). Consequently, if a defendant's guilty plea is not equally voluntary and knowing, it has been obtained in violation of due process and is therefore void. Moreover, because a guilty plea is an admission of all the elements of a formal criminal charge, it cannot be truly voluntary unless the defendant possesses an understanding of the law in relation to the facts.

Thus, in addition to directing the judge to inquire into the defendant's understanding of the nature of the charge and the consequences of his plea, Rule 11 also requires the judge to satisfy himself that there is a factual basis for the plea. The judge must determine "that the conduct which the defendant admits constitutes the offense charged in the indictment or information or an offense included therein to which the defendant has pleaded guilty."[3] Requiring this examination of the relation between the law and the acts the defendant admits having committed is designed to "protect a defendant who is in the position of pleading voluntarily with an understanding of the nature of the charge but without realizing that his conduct does not

2. [Notes of Advisory Committee, U.S.C.A., following Fed.R.Crim.P. 11.]

3. Fed. Rule Crim.Proc. 11, Notes of Advisory Committee on Criminal Rules.

actually fall within the charge."[4]

To the extent that the district judge thus exposes the defendant's state of mind on the record through personal interrogation, he not only facilitates his own determination of a guilty plea's voluntariness, but he also facilitates that determination in any subsequent post-conviction proceeding based upon a claim that the plea was involuntary. Both of these goals are undermined in proportion to the degree the district judge resorts to "assumptions" not based upon recorded responses to his inquiries. For this reason, we reject the Government's contention that Rule 11 can be complied with although the district judge does not personally inquire whether the defendant understood the nature of the charge.[5]

II.

Having decided that the Rule has not been complied with, we must also determine the effect of that non-compliance, an issue that has engendered a sharp difference of opinion among the courts of appeals. In Heiden v. United States, 353 F.2d 53 (1965), the Court of Appeals for the Ninth Circuit held that when the district court does not comply fully with Rule 11 the defendant's guilty plea must be set aside and his case remanded for another hearing at which he may plead anew. Other courts of appeals, however, have consistently rejected this holding, either expressly or tacitly. Instead, they have adopted the approach urged by the Government, which is to place upon the Government the burden of demonstrating from the record of the Rule 11 hearing that the guilty plea was voluntarily entered with an understanding of the charge. . . . In these circuits, if voluntariness cannot be determined from the record, the case is remanded for an evidentiary hearing on that issue. . . .

We are persuaded that the Court of Appeals for the Ninth Circuit has adopted the better rule. From the defendant's perspective, the efficacy of shifting the burden of proof to the Government at a later voluntariness hearing is questionable. In meeting its burden, the Government will undoubtedly rely upon the defendant's statement that he desired to plead guilty and frequently a statement that the plea was not induced by any threats or promises. This prima facie case for voluntariness is likely to be treated as irrebuttable in cases such as this one, where the defendant's reply is limited to his own plaintive allegations that he did not understand

---

4. Ibid.

5. The nature of the inquiry required by Rule 11 must necessarily vary from case to case, and therefore, we do not establish any general guidelines other than those expressed in the Rule itself. As our discussion of the facts in this particular case suggests, however, where the charge encompasses lesser included offenses, personally address-

ing the defendant as to his understanding of the essential elements of the charge to which he pleads guilty would seem a necessary prerequisite to a determination that he understands the meaning of the charge. In all such inquiries, "[m]atters of reality, and not mere ritual, should be controlling." Kennedy v. United States, 397 F.2d 16, 17 (C.A.6th Cir.1968).

the nature of the charge and therefore failed to assert a valid defense or to limit his guilty plea only to a lesser included offense. No matter how true these allegations may be, rarely, if ever, can a defendant corroborate them in a post-plea voluntariness hearing.

Rule 11 is designed to eliminate any need to resort to a later fact-finding proceeding "in this highly subjective area." Heiden v. United States, supra, at 55. The Rule "contemplates that disputes as to the understanding of the defendant and the voluntariness of his action are to be eliminated at the outset. . . ." Ibid. As the Court of Appeals for the Sixth Circuit explained in discussing what it termed the "persuasive rationale" of Heiden: "When the ascertainment is subsequently made, greater uncertainty is bound to exist since in the resolution of disputed contentions problems of credibility and of reliability of memory cannot be avoided. . . ." Waddy v. Herr, 383 F.2d 789, 794 (1967). There is no adequate substitute for demonstrating in the record at the time the plea is entered the defendant's understanding of the nature of the charge against him.

The wisdom of Rule 11's requirements and the difficulty of achieving its purposes through a post-conviction voluntariness hearing are particularly apparent in this case. Petitioner, who was 65 years old and in poor health at the time he entered his plea, had been suffering from a serious drinking problem during the time he allegedly evaded his taxes. He pleaded guilty to a crime that requires a "knowing and willful" attempt to defraud the Government of its tax money; yet, throughout his sentencing hearing, he and his counsel insisted that his acts were merely "neglectful," "inadvertent," and committed without "any disposition of depriving the United States of its due." Remarks of this nature cast considerable doubt on the Government's assertion that petitioner pleaded guilty with "full awareness of the nature of the charge." Nevertheless, confronted with petitioner's statement that he entered his plea of his "own volition," his counsel's statement that he explained the nature of the charges, and evidence that petitioner did owe the Government back taxes, both the District Court and the Court of Appeals concluded that petitioner's guilty plea was voluntary.

Despite petitioner's inability to convince the courts below that he did not fully understand the charge against him, it is certainly conceivable that he may have intended to acknowledge only that he in fact owed the Government the money it claimed without necessarily admitting that he committed the crime charged; for that crime requires the very type of specific intent that he repeatedly disavowed. . . . Moreover, since the elements of the offense were not explained to petitioner, and since the specific acts of tax evasion do not appear of record, it is also possible that if petitioner had been adequately informed he would have concluded that he was actually guilty of one of two closely related lesser included offenses, which are mere misdemeanors.

On the other hand, had the District Court scrupulously complied with Rule 11, there would be no need for such speculation. At the time the plea was entered, petitioner's own replies to the court's inquiries might well have attested to his understanding of the essential elements of the crime charged, including the requirement of specific intent, and to his knowledge of the acts which formed the basis for the charge. Otherwise, it would be apparent to the court that the plea could not be accepted. Similarly, it follows that, if the record had been developed properly, and if it demonstrated that petitioner entered his plea freely and intelligently, his subsequent references to neglect and inadvertence could have been summarily dismissed as nothing more than overzealous supplications for leniency.

We thus conclude that prejudice inheres in a failure to comply with Rule 11, for noncompliance deprives the defendant of the Rule's procedural safeguards, which are designed to facilitate a more accurate determination of the voluntariness of his plea. Our holding that a defendant whose plea has been accepted in violation of Rule 11 should be afforded the opportunity to plead anew not only will insure that every accused is afforded those procedural safeguards, but also will help reduce the great waste of judicial resources required to process the frivolous attacks on guilty plea convictions that are encouraged, and are more difficult to dispose of, when the original record is inadequate. It is, therefore, not too much to require that, before sentencing defendants to years of imprisonment, district judges take the few minutes necessary to inform them of their rights and to determine whether they understand the action they are taking.

We therefore reverse the judgment of the Court of Appeals for the Seventh Circuit and remand the case for proceedings consistent with this opinion.

It is so ordered.[6]

---

348. In Boykin v. Alabama, 395 U.S. 238, 242 (1969), the Court held that in a state proceeding it was constitutional error for the trial judge to accept a plea of guilty "without an affirmative showing that it was intelligent and voluntary," and that such a showing must appear in the record. "What is at stake for an accused facing death or imprisonment demands the utmost solicitude of which courts are capable in canvassing the matter with the accused to make sure he has a full understanding of what the plea connotes and of its consequence." Id. at 243–44.

349. The standard of competence to plead guilty or to waive the right to counsel is the same as the standard of competence to stand trial. Godinez v.

---

[6] Justice Black wrote a brief concurring opinion.

Moran, 509 U.S. 389 (1993) (7–2). The defendant in *Godinez* pleaded guilty to three counts of first-degree murder, for which he was sentenced to death. Subsequently he filed a petition for post-conviction relief, on the ground that he was mentally incompetent to represent himself. The Court noted that before accepting a plea of guilty, in addition to finding that the defendant is competent to plead guilty, a court must find that the plea is knowing and voluntary.

The defendant, who was mentally retarded, was indicted for first-degree murder. He pleaded guilty to second-degree murder. On collateral attack, he claimed that the plea was involuntary because he was not informed by his lawyers or the court, and did not know, that intent to cause death was an element of the offense. Finding that there was nothing in the record that could "substitute for either a finding after trial, or a voluntary admission" that the defendant had the necessary intent, the Court upheld his claim. It said: "Normally the record contains either an explanation of the charge by the trial judge, or at least a representation by defense counsel that the nature of the offense has been explained to the accused.

No person shall be . . . deprived . . .
without due process of law . . .

Moreover, even without such an express representation, it may be appropriate to presume that in most cases defense counsel routinely explain the nature of the offense in sufficient detail to give the accused notice of what he is being asked to admit. This case is unique because the trial judge found as a fact that the element of intent was not explained to respondent. Moreover, respondent's unusually low mental capacity provides a reasonable explanation for counsel's oversight; it also forecloses the conclusion that the error was harmless beyond a reasonable doubt, for it lends at least a modicum of credibility to defense counsel's appraisal of the homicide as a manslaughter rather than a murder." Henderson v. Morgan, 426 U.S. 637, 646, 647 (1976) (7–2).

See DeVille v. Whitley, 21 F.3d 654 (5th Cir.1994) (*Henderson* distinguished); Gaddy v. Linahan, 780 F.2d 935 (11th Cir.1986) ("malice murder"; defendant illiterate and possessing "minimal mental capacity"); Gregory v. Solem, 774 F.2d 309 (8th Cir.1985) (*Henderson* distinguished); Ames v. New York State Division of Parole, 772 F.2d 13 (2d Cir.1985) (distinguishing elements of the offense and affirmative defenses).

In Allard v. Helgemoe, 572 F.2d 1 (1st Cir.1978), the court observed that "there is no indication in . . . [*Henderson*] that the Court ever considered the problem of a fully informed defendant who lacked the capacity to understand some part of the charges against him." Id. at 5. *Henderson*, it said, was concerned with "a constitutional failure that could be easily determined and prevented," id., and was not establishing a test for guilty pleas that required an inquiry into the defendant's actual understanding of the nature of the offense. Provided that a defendant is fully informed and is competent to plead guilty (by the same standard as competence to stand trial), "the objective requirements of due process" ordinarily are satisfied. Id. at 6. See Nelson v. Callahan, 721 F.2d 397 (1st Cir.1983) (*Allard* applied).

350. "The court must not rely on a routine boilerplate question to the defendant designed to elicit an acknowledgement of understanding. . . . Nor should the court rely solely upon statements that it makes to the defendant. In adhering to the rule's mandate that it address the defendant personally, the court should engage in [as] extensive an interchange as necessary to assure itself and any subsequent reader of the transcript that the defendant does indeed fully understand the charges. With respect to some points the court may choose to have the defendant recount his or her understanding of the charges in narrative form and in his or her own language. We do not suggest an arcane definition of the legal concepts, nor a law review exegesis, but enough simple language that a person unlearned, untutored and unschooled could understand the charges." United States v. Coronado, 554 F.2d 166, 173 (5th Cir.1977).

Concluding that not every failure to comply precisely with the requirements of Rule 11 (which, it noted, are now much more complex than they were when *McCarthy* was decided), the court observed, in United States v. Dayton, 604 F.2d 931, 937–38, 943 (5th Cir.1979): "[W]e are unable to state a simple or mechanical rule but offer some general observations that we hope will be helpful. For simple charges . . . a reading of the indictment, followed by an opportunity given the defendant to ask questions about it, will usually suffice. Charges of a more complex nature, incorporating esoteric terms or concepts unfamiliar to the lay mind, may require more explication. In the case of charges of extreme complexity, an explanation of the elements of the offense like that given the jury in its instructions may be required; this, of course, is the outer limit, for if an instruction informs a jury of the nature of the charge sufficiently for it to convict the defendant of it, surely it informs the defendant sufficiently for him to convict himself. We can do no more than commit these matters to the good judgment of the court, to its calculation of the relative difficulty of comprehension of the charges and of the defendant's sophistication and intelligence.

. . .

". . . What is necessary is that the trial court, given the nature of the charges and the character and capacities of the defendant, personally participate in the colloquy mandated by Rule 11 and satisfy himself fully that, within those limits, the defendant understands what he is admitting and what the consequences of that admission may be, as well as that what he is admitting constitutes the crime charged, and that his admission is voluntarily made. If the court does those things, and if the record of that hearing shows a common-sense basis for agreeing that he did so, we will not disturb its actions."

See United States v. Goldberg, 862 F.2d 101 (6th Cir.1988) (failure to ascertain factual basis for plea; remand for new plea); United States v. Punch, 709 F.2d 889 (5th Cir.1983) (failure to inform defendant fully about nature of the charges; *Dayton* applied, plea vacated).

See generally United States v. Johnson, 1 F.3d 296 (5th Cir.1993) (en banc) (applying rule 11(h) harmless error standard).

351. "[I]t is highly doubtful that a uniform mandatory catechism of pleading defendants should be required. . . . The circumstances are too various. There are knowledgeable and criminally experienced defendants and there are those who are lacking in intellect or experience, or both. There are cases where the seriousness of the crime, the competency and experience of counsel, the actual intensive participation by counsel, the nature of the crime as clearly understood by laymen, the rationality of the 'plea bargain,' and the speed or slowness of procedure in the particular criminal court provide ample data as to how far the court should go in questioning defendants before taking a guilty plea. These are all matters best left to the discretion of the court. In some instances even the most rigorous standards thus far suggested, either in the American Bar Association project[7] or by the Federal rule, are hardly adequate; in others the standards become an unnecessary formalism. . . .

7. ABA Standards, Pleas of Guilty (1968).

"The competency of counsel and the degree of actual participation by counsel as well as his opportunity for and the fact of consultation with the pleading defendant, are particularly important. Indeed, if independent and good advice in the interest of the defendant is the goal, it is more important that he consult with competent counsel than that a harried, calendar-conscious Judge be the one to perform the function in displacement of the lawyer. Moreover, there are many reasons why a defendant may not wish to be subjected to an inquisition by officials; it may affect him on his prison or parole status; it may be an added pillory for him to experience that he would eschew. . . .

"Nevertheless, the standards promulgated by the Bar Association committee, albeit tentatively, and those included in the Federal rule, implement principles that may not be ignored. It is not tolerable for the State to punish its members over protestations of innocence if there be doubt as to their guilt, or if they be unaware of their rights, or if they have not had opportunity to make a voluntary and rational decision with proper advice in pleading guilty. . . .

"It is also quite clear that where initial inquiry exposes difficulties or subsequent interpositions by defendant on sentencing raise questions, the court should be quick to offer the defendant an opportunity to withdraw his plea and at the very least conduct a hearing. Such opportunities offered will squelch the faker and protect the truly misguided ones; and, prompt hearings will be better than later ones after direct appeal or collateral postconviction attack. . . .

"The promptness or staleness of complaint with respect to propriety of a guilty plea has already been noted as a significant factor to be considered.

"In cases involving defendants without lawyers, or those ignorant of the language of the court, particular pains must be taken. Of course these days, it is not likely that there will be many uncounselled defendants, but there will still be . . . defendants who say they do not want a lawyer. In such cases inquiry, well beyond the standards thus far propounded, is indicated.

"But overall, it would seem that a sound discretion exercised in cases on an individual basis is best rather than to mandate a uniform procedure which, like as not, would become a purely ritualistic device. Indeed, today, there is reason to suspect that many pleading defendants are prepared to give the categorical answers only because they know that this is the route to eligibility for the lesser plea. A ritualistic form just because it may save the trouble of thinking is likely to eliminate thinking. . . . An oral questionnaire can become just as mechanical as one printed. The taking of the guilty plea should not be made that easy for the defendant or the court or his lawyer. Moreover, there is a weakness in the catechism system, one which some may think can be avoided if legislation were devised to cover the area in question. It should never be enough to undo a plea because of some omission in inquiry at the time of plea without a showing of prejudice. . . . While the essence of justice may be procedure there can be a point at which the administration of justice becomes only procedure and the essence of justice is lost." People v. Nixon, 234 N.E.2d 687, 695–97 (N.Y.1967).

352. See Fontaine v. United States, 411 U.S. 213, 215 (1973), in which the Court observed that while the purpose of Rule 11 is to avoid later invalidation of a guilty plea, "like any procedural mechanism, its exercise is neither always perfect nor uniformly invulnerable to subsequent challenge calling for an opportunity to prove the allegations." In Blackledge v. Allison, 431 U.S. 63 (1977), the Court discussed generally what procedure should be followed on a request for post-conviction collateral relief from a guilty plea that is proper on the record. The Court said that "the federal courts cannot fairly adopt a *per se* rule excluding all possibility that a defendant's representations at the time his guilty plea was accepted were so much the product of such factors as misunderstanding, duress, or misrepresentation by others as to make the guilty plea a constitutionally inadequate basis for imprisonment." Id. at 75. The Court made it clear on the other hand that a full evidentiary hearing was not always warranted; the usual procedures, such as a motion for summary judgment, were available to avoid an unnecessary hearing.

Collateral attack on a conviction is not available when all that is alleged is a failure to comply with the formal requirements of Rule 11. A formal violation of the rule "is neither constitutional nor jurisdictional." United States v. Timmreck, 441 U.S. 780, 783 (1979). The Court observed that it was not deciding whether collateral relief would be available for a violation of the rule if there were "other aggravating circumstances." Id. at 785. *Timmreck* was applied in Lilly v. United States, 792 F.2d 1541 (11th Cir.1986). Compare United States v. Bernal, 861 F.2d 434 (5th Cir.1988) (violation of "core concerns" of Rule 11 requires reversal of conviction).

353. A plea of guilty "is also a waiver of trial—and unless the applicable law otherwise provides, a waiver of the right to contest the admissibility of any evidence the state might have offered against the defendant." McMann v. Richardson, 397 U.S. 759, 766 (1970). In *McMann*, the defendant sought by collateral attack to vacate his plea of guilty on the ground that his plea was prompted by an unlawfully coerced confession. The Court rejected his claim. "In our view a defendant's plea of guilty based on reasonably competent advice is an intelligent plea not open to attack on the grounds that counsel may have misjudged the admissibility of the defendant's confession. Whether a plea of guilty is unintelligent and therefore vulnerable when motivated by a confession erroneously thought admissible in evidence depends as an initial matter not on whether a court would retrospectively consider counsel's advice to be right or wrong, but on whether that advice was within the range of competence demanded of attorneys in criminal cases." Id. at 770–71.

The reasoning of *McMann* was applied to foreclose collateral attack on a conviction following a plea of guilty, the attack being based on a claim that the grand jury was unconstitutionally composed, in Tollett v. Henderson, 411 U.S. 258 (1973). The Court indicated that *McMann* may apply even though the defendant's counsel did not discuss with him the constitutional claim that was foregone by the guilty plea.

"A guilty plea, voluntarily and intelligently entered, may not be vacated because the defendant was not advised of every conceivable constitutional plea in abatement he might have to the charge, no matter how peripheral such a plea might be to the normal focus of counsel's inquiry. And just as it is not sufficient for the criminal defendant seeking to set aside such a plea to show that his counsel in retrospect may not have correctly appraised the constitutional significance of certain historical facts, *McMann*, supra, it is likewise not sufficient that he show that if counsel had pursued a certain factual inquiry such a pursuit would have uncovered a possible constitutional infirmity in the proceedings.

"The principal value of counsel to the accused in a criminal prosecution often lies not in counsel's ability to abstract, nor in his ability, if time permitted, to amass a large quantum of factual data and inform the defendant of it. Counsel's concern is the faithful representation of the interest of his client and such representation frequently involves highly practical considerations as well as specialized knowledge of the law. Often the interests of the accused are not advanced by challenges that would only delay the inevitable date of prosecution . . . or by contesting all guilt. . . . A prospect of plea bargaining, the expectation or hope of a lesser sentence, or the convincing nature of the evidence against the accused are considerations that might well suggest the advisability of a guilty plea without elaborate consideration of whether pleas in abatement, such as unconstitutional grand jury selection procedures, might be factually supported." Id. at 267–68.

The two-part standard for testing a claim of incompetence of counsel announced in Strickland v. Washington, 466 U.S. 668 (1984), p. 1063 below, applies to claims arising out of the entry of a plea of guilty. In particular, a defendant must not only show that his lawyer's representation fell below the standard of competence; he must also show that the lawyer's ineffective performance was prejudicial, meaning "that there is a reasonable probability that, but for counsel's errors, he would not have pleaded guilty and would have insisted on going to trial." Hill v. Lockhart, 474 U.S. 52 (1985). In *Hill*, the defendant's lawyer told him that he would be eligible for parole after serving one-third of his term of imprisonment. The defendant was not eligible until he had served half his term. The Court held that in the circumstances of the case, prejudice was not shown.

See Downs-Morgan v. United States, 765 F.2d 1534 (11th Cir.1985), in which the defendant alleged that he pleaded guilty on the erroneous advice of his counsel that he would not be subject to deportation if convicted. The court said that in view of the especially harsh alleged consequences of deportation (long-term imprisonment and possibly execution) and the defendant's "at least colorable claim of innocence," an evidentiary hearing on the claim of ineffective assistance of counsel was necessary. See also Iaea v. Sunn, 800 F.2d 861 (9th Cir.1986) (ineffective assistance; remand for determination of prejudice); Dufresne v. Moran, 729 F.2d 18 (1st Cir.1984) (ineffective assistance; prejudice not shown).

354. Does a defendant have a constitutional right to be informed of the prosecution's offer of a plea bargain and to make the final decision whether or not to accept it? In Johnson v. Duckworth, 793 F.2d 898, 902 (7th Cir.1986), the court said: "[I]n the ordinary case criminal defense attorneys have a duty to inform their clients of plea agreements proffered by the prosecution, and . . . failure to do so constitutes ineffective assistance of counsel under the sixth and fourteenth amendments. Apart from merely being informed about the proffered agreement . . . a defendant must be involved in the decision-making process regarding the agreement's ultimate acceptance or rejection." However, in the circumstances of the case, which involved a juvenile defendant, the court concluded that defense counsel's decision to reject the bargain, with the concurrence of the defendant's parents, was not ineffective assistance of counsel.

355. A guilty plea does not foreclose collateral attack based on a constitutional claim that bars prosecution altogether. Blackledge v. Perry, 417 U.S. 21 (1974). See Menna v. New York, 423 U.S. 61 (1975), in which the Court held that a claim of double jeopardy was not waived by the defendant's plea of guilty. For a general discussion of which constitutional claims are foreclosed by a guilty plea and which are not, see United States v. Curcio, 712 F.2d 1532 (2d Cir.1983).

In United States v. Broce, 488 U.S. 563 (1989) (6–3), the defendants pleaded guilty to two separate indictments for conspiracy. Later, they filed a motion to vacate the convictions under the second indictment, on the ground that the facts showed only one conspiracy and their conviction on the second violated the Double Jeopardy Clause. The Supreme Court held that their claim of double jeopardy was waived by the plea of guilty. *Blackledge* and *Menna* were distinguishable, the Court said, because in those cases the constitutional barrier to prosecution was apparent on the face of the record and did not require an evidentiary hearing, which would be required here.

In Lefkowitz v. Newsome, 420 U.S. 283 (1975) (5–4), the Court held that a claim (based on denial of a motion to suppress evidence) that would have been waived by a guilty plea in federal court but was not waived according to state law could be raised by a petition for habeas corpus in federal court. The state law, the Court said, guaranteed that review of the defendant's constitutional claims would continue to be available despite his plea of guilty.

The provision for entry of a conditional plea of guilty in Rule 11(a)(2) was added in 1983. The Note of the Advisory Committee on Rules states: "It must be emphasized that the only avenue of review of the specified pretrial ruling permitted under a rule 11(a)(2) conditional plea is an appeal, which must be brought in compliance with Fed.R.App.P. 4(b). Relief via 28 U.S.C. § 2255 is not available for this purpose." The Note states further that the rule "should not be interpreted as either broadening or narrowing the Menna-Blackledge doctrine or as establishing procedures for its application." 18 U.S.C.A., following Fed.R.Crim.P. 11.

356. A district court may not without the consent of the government accept a plea of guilty to a lesser offense necessarily included in the offense charged in the indictment. "[T]he plea contemplated by Rules 10 and 11 is a plea to the offense charged in the indictment or information, and . . . a plea to a lesser included offense may not be tendered, and cannot be accepted by the court, unless the government consents." United States v. Gray, 448 F.2d 164, 168 (9th Cir.1971). See United States v. Linnier, 125 Fed. 83 (C.C.D.Neb.1903), in which the court held that it had authority under the common law to accept such a plea.

"Factual basis for the plea"

357. What constitutes a "factual basis" for a plea of guilty, as required by Rule 11(f)? The Note of the Advisory Committee on Rules states: "The court should satisfy itself, by inquiry of the defendant or the attorney for the government, or by examining the presentence report, or otherwise, that the conduct which the defendant admits constitutes the offense charged in the indictment or information or an offense included therein to which the defendant has pleaded guilty. Such inquiry should, e.g., protect a defendant who is in the position of pleading voluntarily with an understanding of the nature of the charge but without realizing that his conduct does not actually fall within the charge." 18 U.S.C.A., following Fed.R.Crim.P. 11.

In North Carolina v. Alford, 400 U.S. 25 (1970), the defendant was indicted for first-degree murder, a capital offense. He pleaded guilty to second-degree murder. Before accepting the plea, the trial court heard testimony of several witnesses for the state. The defendant told the court that he was innocent and that he was pleading guilty on the advice of counsel to limit his penalty to that provided for second-degree murder. The Supreme Court held that it was not constitutionally improper to accept the plea.

"[W]hile most pleas of guilty consist of both a waiver of trial and an express admission of guilt, the latter element is not a constitutional requisite to the imposition of criminal penalty. An individual accused of crime may voluntarily, knowingly, and understandably consent to the imposition of a prison sentence even if he is unwilling or unable to admit his participation in the acts constituting the crime.

"Nor can we perceive any material difference between a plea which refuses to admit commission of the criminal act and a plea containing a protestation of innocence when, as in the instant case, a defendant intelligently concludes that his interests require entry of a guilty plea and the record before the judge contains strong evidence of actual guilt. . . .

"... The prohibitions against involuntary or unintelligent pleas should not be relaxed, but neither should an exercise in arid logic render those constitutional guarantees counterproductive and put in jeopardy the very human values they were meant to preserve." Id. at 37, 39. The Court emphasized that it was dealing only with constitutional requirements, and that states might prohibit the result reached in this case. Nor does *Alford* require that a guilty plea in comparable circumstances be accepted in the federal courts.

The Court's statement of facts recites that Alford pleaded guilty to the reduced charge eight days after he was indicted. The unusually short period of time is not otherwise mentioned in the opinion.

See United States v. Tunning, 69 F.3d 107 (6th Cir.1995) (factual basis for plea not shown, where defendant failed to admit facts constituting offense); United States v. Cox, 923 F.2d 519 (7th Cir.1991) (*Alford* situation; trial court had discretion to reject plea); United States v. Keiswetter, 860 F.2d 992 (10th Cir.1988), modified, 866 F.2d 1301 (1989) (en banc) (*Alford* situation, factual basis for plea not evident from record; plea vacated).

The requirement of a factual basis for a plea does not apply to part of a plea agreement that stipulates a forfeiture of assets pursuant to 21 U.S.C § 853. Libretti v. United States, 516 U.S. 29 (1995) (8–1).

358. In People v. Foster, 225 N.E.2d 200 (N.Y.1967), the court held that the defendant was properly convicted and sentenced on his plea of guilty to the "logically and legally impossible" crime of attempted manslaughter. (Manslaughter was defined as an unintentional crime; a specific intent to commit the crime attempted was an element of the crime of attempt.) "While there may be question whether a plea to attempted manslaughter is technically and logically consistent, such a plea should be sustained on the ground that it was sought by a defendant and freely taken as part of a bargain which was struck for the defendant's benefit." Id. at 202. *Foster* was distinguished in People v. Hassin, 368 N.Y.S.2d 253 (App.Div.1975), in which the defendant pleaded guilty to two counts of " 'attempted' felony murder." The court said that there is no such crime and dismissed those counts of the indictment. In *Foster*, the court said, the defendant pleaded guilty to a lesser offense included in the crime charged in the indictment; here the impossible crime, to which the defendant pleaded guilty, was actually charged in the indictment.

359. "It has been raised as a problem of ethics whether an attorney may advise the defendant first that the evidence implicating him is so overwhelming that a guilty plea is his best salvation, and second that this plea will not be accepted unless defendant, departing from truth if need be, states facts that show he is guilty. Freedman, Professional Responsibility of the Criminal Defense Lawyer: The Three Hardest Questions, 64 Mich.L.Rev. 1469 (1966).

"We have no hesitation in saying that an attorney, an officer of the court, may not counsel or practice such a deliberate deception." Bruce v. United States, 379 F.2d 113, 119 n.17 (D.C.Cir.1967).

"[T]o this Court it appears utterly unreasonable for counsel to recommend a guilty plea to a defendant without first cautioning him that, no matter what, he should not plead guilty unless he believed himself guilty. Most certainly such a recommendation should not be made when the defendant in the past has maintained his innocence and has stated that he has two witnesses whom counsel has not attempted to interview. It may well have been trial counsel's opinion that even if defendant were innocent he would still be convicted. Such a view is not only cynical but unwarranted. Innocent men in the past have been convicted; but such instances have been so rare and our judicial system has so many safeguards that no lawyer worthy of his profession justifiably may assume that an innocent person will be convicted.

"Guilty pleas play a necessary and valid role in the criminal process. Plea bargaining, despite understandable criticism, also is proper. But guilty pleas and plea bargaining place a heavy responsibility on defense counsel to insure that neither the rights or interests of defendants nor the integrity of the judicial system are thereby jeopardized. This means that defense attorneys, in their roles as counsel and as officers of the Court, must exercise scrupulous care to see to it that an innocent man does not plead guilty." United States v. Rogers, 289 F.Supp. 726, 729–30 (D.Conn.1968).

360. ABA Standards for Criminal Justice, The Prosecution Function (1971) (since deleted): "4.2 Plea disposition when accused maintains innocence. A prosecutor may not properly participate in a disposition by plea of guilty if he is aware that the accused persists in denying guilt or the factual basis for the plea, without disclosure to the court."

ABA Standards for Criminal Justice, The Defense Function (1971) (since deleted): "5.3 Guilty plea when accused denies guilt. If the accused discloses to the lawyer facts which negate guilt and the lawyer's investigation does not reveal a conflict with the facts disclosed but the accused persists in entering a plea of guilty, the lawyer may not properly participate in presenting a guilty plea, without disclosure to the court."

How should the defense lawyer advise his client if he believes that the judge to whom the case is assigned will accept a plea of guilty only if at the time the plea is entered the defendant describes the crime in sufficient detail to establish his guilt?

Plea Bargaining

Brady v. United States

397 U.S. 742, 90 S.Ct. 1463, 25 L.Ed.2d 747 (1970).

■ MR. JUSTICE WHITE delivered the opinion of the Court.

In 1959, petitioner was charged with kidnaping in violation of 18 U.S.C. § 1201(a). Since the indictment charged that the victim of the kidnaping was not liberated unharmed, petitioner faced a maximum penalty of death if the verdict of the jury should so recommend. Petitioner, represented by competent counsel throughout, first elected to plead not guilty. Apparently because the trial judge was unwilling to try the case without a jury, petitioner made no serious attempt to reduce the possibility of a death penalty by waiving a jury trial. Upon learning that his codefendant, who had confessed to the authorities, would plead guilty and be available to testify against him, petitioner changed his plea to guilty. His plea was accepted after the trial judge twice questioned him as to the voluntariness of his plea. Petitioner was sentenced to 50 years' imprisonment, later reduced to 30.

In 1967, petitioner sought relief under 28 U.S.C. § 2255, claiming that his plea of guilty was not voluntarily given because § 1201(a) operated to coerce his plea, because his counsel exerted impermissible pressure upon him, and because his plea was induced by representations with respect to reduction of sentence and clemency. It was also alleged that the trial judge had not fully complied with Rule 11 of the Federal Rules of Criminal Procedure.

After a hearing, the District Court for the District of New Mexico denied relief. According to the District Court's findings, petitioner's counsel did not put impermissible pressure on petitioner to plead guilty and no representations were made with respect to a reduced sentence or clemency. The court held that § 1201(a) was constitutional and found that petitioner decided to plead guilty when he learned that his codefendant was going to plead guilty; petitioner pleaded guilty "by reason of other matters and not by reason of the statute" or because of any acts of the trial judge. The court concluded that "the plea was voluntarily and knowingly made."

The Court of Appeals for the Tenth Circuit affirmed, determining that the District Court's findings were supported by substantial evidence and specifically approving the finding that petitioner's plea of guilty was voluntary. . . . We granted certiorari . . . to consider the claim that the Court of Appeals was in error in not reaching a contrary result on the authority of this Court's decision in United States v. Jackson, 390 U.S. 570 (1968). We affirm.

I

In United States v. Jackson, supra, the defendants were indicted under § 1201(a). The District Court dismissed the § 1201(a) count of the indictment, holding the statute unconstitutional because it permitted imposition of the death sentence only upon a jury's recommendation and thereby made the risk of death the price of a jury trial. This Court held the statute valid, except for the death penalty provision; with respect to the latter, the Court agreed with the trial court "that the death penalty provision . . . imposes an impermissible burden upon the exercise of a constitutional right. . . ." 390 U.S., at 572. The problem was to determine "whether the Constitution permits the establishment of such a death penalty, applicable only to those defendants who assert the right to contest their guilt before a jury." 390 U.S., at 581. The inevitable effect of the provision was said to be to discourage assertion of the Fifth Amendment right not to plead guilty and to deter exercise of the Sixth Amendment right to demand a jury trial. Because the legitimate goal of limiting the death penalty to cases in which a jury recommends it could be achieved without penalizing those defendants who plead not guilty and elect a jury trial, the death penalty provision "needlessly penalize[d] the assertion of a constitutional right," 390 U.S., at 583, and was therefore unconstitutional.

Since the "inevitable effect" of the death penalty provision of § 1201(a) was said by the Court to be the needless encouragement of pleas of guilty and waivers of jury trial, Brady contends that *Jackson* requires the invalidation of every plea of guilty entered under that section, at least when the fear of death is shown to have been a factor in the plea. Petitioner, however, has read far too much into the *Jackson* opinion.

The Court made it clear in *Jackson* that it was not holding § 1201(a) inherently coercive of guilty pleas: "the fact that the Federal Kidnaping Act tends to discourage defendants from insisting upon their innocence and demanding trial by jury hardly implies that every defendant who enters a guilty plea to a charge under the Act does so involuntarily." 390 U.S., at 583. . . .

Moreover, the Court in *Jackson* rejected a suggestion that the death penalty provision of § 1201(a) be saved by prohibiting in capital kidnaping cases all guilty pleas and jury waivers, "however clear [the defendants'] guilt and however strong their desire to acknowledge it in order to spare themselves and their families the spectacle and expense of protracted courtroom proceedings." "[T]hat jury waivers and guilty pleas may occasionally be rejected" was no ground for automatically rejecting all guilty pleas under the statute, for such a rule "would rob the criminal process of much of its flexibility." 390 U.S., at 584.

Plainly, it seems to us, *Jackson* ruled neither that all pleas of guilty encouraged by the fear of a possible death sentence are involuntary pleas nor that such encouraged pleas are invalid whether involuntary or not. *Jackson* prohibits the imposition of the death penalty under § 1201(a), but that decision neither fashioned a new standard for judging the validity of guilty pleas nor mandated a new application of the test theretofore fashioned by courts and since reiterated that guilty pleas are valid if both "voluntary" and "intelligent.". . .

That a guilty plea is a grave and solemn act to be accepted only with care and discernment has long been recognized. Central to the plea and the foundation for entering judgment against the defendant is the defendant's admission in open court that he committed the acts charged in the indictment. He thus stands as a witness against himself and he is shielded by the Fifth Amendment from being compelled to do so—hence the minimum requirement that his plea be the voluntary expression of his own choice. But the plea is more than an admission of past conduct; it is the defendant's consent that judgment of conviction may be entered without a trial—a waiver of his right to trial before a jury or a judge. Waivers of constitutional rights not only must be voluntary but must be knowing, intelligent acts done with sufficient awareness of the relevant circumstances and likely consequences. On neither score was Brady's plea of guilty invalid.

II

The trial judge in 1959 found the plea voluntary before accepting it; the District Court in 1968, after an evidentiary hearing, found that the plea was voluntarily made; the Court of Appeals specifically approved the finding of voluntariness. We see no reason on this record to disturb the judgment of those courts. Petitioner, advised by competent counsel, tendered his plea after his codefendant, who had already given a confession, determined to plead guilty and became available to testify against petitioner. It was this development that the District Court found to have triggered Brady's guilty plea.

The voluntariness of Brady's plea can be determined only by considering all of the relevant circumstances surrounding it. . . . One of these circumstances was the possibility of a heavier sentence following a guilty verdict after a trial. It may be that Brady, faced with a strong case against him and recognizing that his chances for acquittal were slight, preferred to plead guilty and thus limit the penalty to life imprisonment rather than to elect a jury trial which could result in a death penalty. But even if we assume that Brady would not have pleaded guilty except for the death penalty provision of § 1201(a), this assumption merely identifies the penalty provision as a "but for" cause of his plea. That the statute caused the plea in this sense does not necessarily prove that the plea was coerced and invalid as an involuntary act.

The State to some degree encourages pleas of guilty at every important step in the criminal process. For some people, their breach of a State's law is alone sufficient reason for surrendering themselves and accepting punishment. For others, apprehension and charge, both threatening acts by the Government, jar them into admitting their guilt. In still other cases, the post-indictment accumulation of evidence may convince the defendant and his counsel that a trial is not worth the agony and expense to the defendant and his family. All these pleas of guilty are valid in spite of the State's responsibility for some of the factors motivating the pleas; the pleas are no more improperly compelled than is the decision by a defendant at the close of the State's evidence at trial that he must take the stand or face certain conviction.

Of course, the agents of the State may not produce a plea by actual or threatened physical harm or by mental coercion overbearing the will of the defendant. But nothing of the sort is claimed in this case; nor is there evidence that Brady was so gripped by fear of the death penalty or hope of leniency that he did not or could not, with the help of counsel, rationally weigh the advantages of going to trial against the advantages of pleading guilty. Brady's claim is of a different sort: that it violates the Fifth Amendment to influence or encourage a guilty plea by opportunity or promise of leniency and that a guilty plea is coerced and invalid if influenced by the fear of a possibly higher penalty for the crime charged if a conviction is obtained after the State is put to its proof.

Insofar as the voluntariness of his plea is concerned, there is little to differentiate Brady from (1) the defendant, in a jurisdiction where the judge and jury have the same range of sentencing power, who pleads guilty because his lawyer advises him that the judge will very probably be more lenient than the jury; (2) the defendant, in a jurisdiction where the judge alone has sentencing power, who is advised by counsel that the judge is normally more lenient with defendants who plead guilty than with those who go to trial; (3) the defendant who is permitted by prosecutor and judge to plead guilty to a lesser offense included in the offense charged; and (4) the defendant who pleads guilty to certain counts with the understanding that other charges will be dropped. In each of these situations,[8] as in Brady's case, the defendant might never plead guilty absent the possibility or certainty that the plea will result in a lesser penalty than the sentence that could be imposed after a trial and a verdict of guilty. We decline to hold, however, that a guilty plea is compelled and invalid under the Fifth Amendment whenever motivated by the defendant's desire to accept the certainty or probability of a lesser penalty rather than face a wider range of possibilities extending from acquittal to conviction and a higher penalty authorized by law for the crime charged.

The issue we deal with is inherent in the criminal law and its administration because guilty pleas are not constitutionally forbidden, because the criminal law characteristically extends to judge or jury a range of choice in setting the sentence in individual cases, and because both the State and the defendant often find it advantageous to preclude the possibility of the maximum penalty authorized by law. For a defendant who sees slight possibility of acquittal, the advantages of pleading guilty and limiting the probable penalty are obvious—his exposure is reduced, the correctional processes can begin immediately, and the practical burdens of a trial are eliminated. For the State there are also advantages—the more promptly imposed punishment after an admission of guilt may more effectively attain the objectives

8. We here make no reference to the situation where the prosecutor or judge, or both, deliberately employ their charging and sentencing powers to induce a particular defendant to tender a plea of guilty. In Brady's case there is no claim that the prosecutor threatened prosecution on a charge not justified by the evidence or that the trial judge threatened Brady with a harsher sentence if convicted after trial in order to induce him to plead guilty.

of punishment; and with the avoidance of trial, scarce judicial and prosecutorial resources are conserved for those cases in which there is a substantial issue of the defendant's guilt or in which there is substantial doubt that the State can sustain its burden of proof. It is this mutuality of advantage that perhaps explains the fact that at present well over three-fourths of the criminal convictions in this country rest on pleas of guilty, a great many of them no doubt motivated at least in part by the hope or assurance of a lesser penalty than might be imposed if there were a guilty verdict after a trial to judge or jury.

Of course, that the prevalence of guilty pleas is explainable does not necessarily validate those pleas or the system which produces them. But we cannot hold that it is unconstitutional for the State to extend a benefit to a defendant who in turn extends a substantial benefit to the State and who demonstrates by his plea that he is ready and willing to admit his crime and to enter the correctional system in a frame of mind that affords hope for success in rehabilitation over a shorter period of time than might otherwise be necessary.

A contrary holding would require the States and Federal Government to forbid guilty pleas altogether, to provide a single invariable penalty for each crime defined by the statutes, or to place the sentencing function in a separate authority having no knowledge of the manner in which the conviction in each case was obtained. In any event, it would be necessary to forbid prosecutors and judges to accept guilty pleas to selected counts, to lesser included offenses, or to reduced charges. The Fifth Amendment does not reach so far.

. . .

The standard as to the voluntariness of guilty pleas must be essentially that defined by Judge Tuttle of the Court of Appeals for the Fifth Circuit:

" '[A] plea of guilty entered by one fully aware of the direct consequences, including the actual value of any commitments made to him by the court, prosecutor, or his own counsel, must stand unless induced by threats (or promises to discontinue improper harassment), misrepresentation (including unfulfilled or unfulfillable promises), or perhaps by promises that are by their nature improper as having no proper relationship to the prosecutor's business (e.g. bribes).' 242 F.2d at page 115."[9]

Under this standard, a plea of guilty is not invalid merely because entered to avoid the possibility of a death penalty.

III

The record before us also supports the conclusion that Brady's plea was intelligently made. He was advised by competent counsel, he was made

---

9. Shelton v. United States, 246 F.2d 271, 572 n.2 (C.A. 5th Cir.1957) . . . .

aware of the nature of the charge against him, and there was nothing to indicate that he was incompetent or otherwise not in control of his mental faculties; once his confederate had pleaded guilty and became available to testify, he chose to plead guilty, perhaps to ensure that he would face no more than life imprisonment or a term of years. Brady was aware of precisely what he was doing when he admitted that he had kidnaped the victim and had not released her unharmed.

It is true that Brady's counsel advised him that § 1201(a) empowered the jury to impose the death penalty and that nine years later in United States v. Jackson, supra, the Court held that the jury had no such power as long as the judge could impose only a lesser penalty if trial was to the court or there was a plea of guilty. But these facts do not require us to set aside Brady's conviction.

Often the decision to plead guilty is heavily influenced by the defendant's appraisal of the prosecution's case against him and by the apparent likelihood of securing leniency should a guilty plea be offered and accepted. Considerations like these frequently present imponderable questions for which there are no certain answers; judgments may be made that in the light of later events seem improvident, although they were perfectly sensible at the time. The rule that a plea must be intelligently made to be valid does not require that a plea be vulnerable to later attack if the defendant did not correctly assess every relevant factor entering into his decision. A defendant is not entitled to withdraw his plea merely because he discovers long after the plea has been accepted that his calculus misapprehended the quality of the State's case or the likely penalties attached to alternative courses of action. More particularly, absent misrepresentation or other impermissible conduct by state agents . . . a voluntary plea of guilty intelligently made in the light of the then applicable law does not become vulnerable because later judicial decisions indicate that the plea rested on a faulty premise. A plea of guilty triggered by the expectations of a competently counseled defendant that the State will have a strong case against him is not subject to later attack because the defendant's lawyer correctly advised him with respect to the then existing law as to possible penalties but later pronouncements of the courts, as in this case, hold that the maximum penalty for the crime in question was less than was reasonably assumed at the time the plea was entered.

The fact that Brady did not anticipate United States v. Jackson, supra, does not impugn the truth or reliability of his plea. We find no requirement in the Constitution that a defendant must be permitted to disown his solemn admissions in open court that he committed the act with which he is charged simply because it later develops that the State would have had a weaker case than the defendant had thought or that the maximum penalty then assumed applicable has been held inapplicable in subsequent judicial decisions.

This is not to say that guilty plea convictions hold no hazards for the innocent or that the methods of taking guilty pleas presently employed in this country are necessarily valid in all respects. This mode of conviction is no more foolproof than full trials to the court or to the jury. Accordingly, we take great precautions against unsound results, and we should continue to do so, whether conviction is by plea or by trial. We would have serious doubts about this case if the encouragement of guilty pleas by offers of leniency substantially increased the likelihood that defendants, advised by competent counsel, would falsely condemn themselves. But our view is to the contrary and is based on our expectations that courts will satisfy themselves that pleas of guilty are voluntarily and intelligently made by competent defendants with adequate advice of counsel and that there is nothing to question the accuracy and reliability of the defendants' admissions that they committed the crimes with which they are charged. In the case before us, nothing in the record impeaches Brady's plea or suggests that his admissions in open court were anything but the truth.

Although Brady's plea of guilty may well have been motivated in part by a desire to avoid a possible death penalty, we are convinced that his plea was voluntarily and intelligently made and we have no reason to doubt that his solemn admission of guilt was truthful.

. . .[10]

————

361. "The disposition of criminal charges by agreement between the prosecutor and the accused, sometimes loosely called 'plea bargaining,' is an essential component of the administration of justice. Properly administered, it is to be encouraged. If every criminal charge were subjected to a full-scale trial, the States and the Federal Government would need to multiply by many times the number of judges and court facilities.

"Disposition of charges after plea discussions is not only an essential part of the process but a highly desirable part for many reasons. It leads to prompt and largely final disposition of most criminal cases; it avoids much of the corrosive impact of enforced idleness during pre-trial confinement for those who are denied release pending trial; it protects the public from those accused persons who are prone to continue criminal conduct even while on pre-trial release; and by shortening the time between charges and disposition, it enhances whatever may be the rehabilitative prospects of the guilty when they are ultimately imprisoned." Santobello v. New York, 404 U.S. 257, 261 (1971). See also Blackledge v. Allison, 431 U.S. 63, 76 (1977).

[10] Justice Black noted his concurrence in the judgment and "substantially all" of the Court's opinion. Justice Brennan wrote an opinion concurring in the result, which Justice Douglas and Justice Marshall joined.

362. Bordenkircher v. Hayes, 434 U.S. 357 (1978) (5–4). The defendant was indicted on a charge of uttering a forged instrument for $88.30, an offense punishable by imprisonment for two to ten years. After he was arraigned, he and defense counsel met with the prosecutor to discuss a guilty plea. The prosecutor offered to recommend a sentence of five years imprisonment if the defendant pleaded guilty. If the defendant did not accept the offer, the prosecutor said, he would seek to indict the defendant as an habitual criminal, which would subject him to a mandatory sentence of life imprisonment. The defendant did not plead guilty, was indicted and convicted as an habitual criminal and sentenced. On habeas corpus, the Court upheld the conviction. "As a practical matter," it said, "this case would be no different if the grand jury had indicted Hayes as a recidivist from the outset, and the prosecutor had offered to drop that charge as part of the plea bargain." Id. at 360–61. "[T]he course of conduct engaged in by the prosecutor in this case, which no more than openly presented the defendant with the unpleasant alternatives of foregoing trial or facing charges on which he was plainly subject to prosecution, did not violate the Due Process Clause of the Fourteenth Amendment." Id. at 363–65.

In Corbitt v. New Jersey, 439 U.S. 212 (1978) (6–3), the Court upheld a state statute against the claim that it was invalid for the same reasons that were applied to the federal statute in United States v. Jackson, 390 U.S. 570 (1968), discussed in the *Brady* opinion, pp. 731–32 above. The New Jersey statute provided that the mandatory sentence for a defendant convicted at a jury trial (non-jury trials not being permitted in murder cases) of first-degree murder is life imprisonment. A defendant who pleaded *non vult* or *nolo contendere* (a simple guilty plea not being permitted) in a murder case could be sentenced to life imprisonment or a term up to 30 years. The Court distinguished *Jackson* on the grounds that (1) here the death penalty was not involved, and (2) here, unlike *Jackson*, a defendant could not wholly avoid the possibility of the more serious sentence (life imprisonment) by a plea. It observed that "not every burden on the exercise of a constitutional right, and not every pressure or encouragement to waive such a right, is invalid." 439 U.S. at 218. The Court said that the case of the defendant in *Corbitt*, who went to trial and was convicted could not be distinguished constitutionally from that of the defendant in Bordenkircher v. Hayes. "The States and the Federal Government are free to abolish guilty pleas and plea bargaining; but absent such action, as the Constitution has been construed in our cases, it is not forbidden to extend a proper degree of leniency in return for guilty pleas." Id. at 223.

Bordenkircher v. Hayes was followed in United States v. Goodwin, 457 U.S. 368 (1982) (7–2). The Court rejected the defendant's claim that his indictment on a felony charge following his rejection of a guilty plea and demand for a jury trial on misdemeanor charges was invalid on the ground of prosecutorial vindictiveness. The Court distinguished pretrial situations of this kind from cases in which the prosecutor's allegedly vindictive action occurs after trial. See note 585 p. 1169 below.

In Re Ibarra

34 Cal.3d 277, 666 P.2d 980 (1983).

■ BROUSSARD, JUSTICE.

Petitioner seeks a writ of habeas corpus after conviction upon a plea of guilty of robbery (Pen.Code, § 211) while armed (Pen.Code, § 12022, subd. (a)), and assault with a deadly weapon (Pen.Code, § 245, subd. (a)). Petitioner's plea was entered pursuant to a "package-deal" plea bargain in which his two codefendants also pled guilty. He was sentenced in accordance with the bargain to a three-year term for the robbery, a one-year armed enhancement and a consecutive term of one year for assault with a deadly weapon.

Petitioner raises three basic contentions. First, he claims that he was denied effective assistance of counsel because his attorney urged him to accept a coercive plea bargain. Second, he argues that his plea was involuntary because he had not been properly advised of his rights. Finally, he maintains that his plea bargain was per se invalid because a "package-deal" arrangement is inherently coercive.

We have rejected the ineffective assistance of counsel claim because counsel's decision was a tactical one which might be made by competent counsel. We have also decided that, under normal circumstances, the trial court may properly rely on a validly executed waiver form in determining the voluntariness of a guilty plea. Nevertheless, when a defendant pleads guilty pursuant to a "package-deal" arrangement, the trial court has a duty to conduct further inquiry into the voluntariness of the plea: although such a bargain is not per se coercive, it may be so under a totality of the circumstances. Because petitioner has not alleged sufficient facts to support a showing of coercion, however, we are required to deny the petition for writ of habeas corpus without prejudice to his filing a new petition alleging sufficient facts in accordance with this opinion.

Two armed gunmen robbed a store in Downey. Police obtained a description of the getaway car, and began pursuit. The front-seat passenger of the car leaned out of the window and began shooting at the police. An officer observed the petitioner grabbing the assailant's belt buckle. Eventually, the car pulled over. Petitioner's two codefendants, the driver and frontseat passenger, were later identified by witnesses as the armed robbers.

Petitioner claims that, contrary to his plea, he is not guilty of any offense. He instead alleges that he had been intoxicated and asleep in the back seat of the car. To support his allegation, he cites the testimony of an investigative officer at the preliminary hearing that petitioner had been intoxicated and smelled of alcohol at the time of arrest. The officer also testified that an empty rum bottle was found in the back seat of the car. The sole set of fingerprints found on the bottle belonged to petitioner.

In explaining his guilty plea, petitioner sets out the following sequence of occurrences: He met with his appointed counsel about 15 minutes before his court appearance. Counsel advised him of a proffered plea bargain for a five-year term; however, the bargain was only available if all three defendants were to plead guilty. Counsel informed petitioner that he had filed motions to set aside the information, for severance and for discovery, but urged petitioner to accept the plea bargain, as a jury might nevertheless find him guilty. Counsel also warned petitioner that if the bargain was refused, it would be withdrawn as to his codefendants, who would likely be found guilty and face severe sentences. Counsel then asked petitioner to initial a printed waiver form, which enunciated certain constitutional rights, in order to save the court time in taking his plea. Petitioner complied.

The record of the plea proceeding does not reflect any of these allegations; however, it does show that the judge questioned petitioner as to whether he had read the form, understood his rights and discussed them with counsel. Petitioner replied affirmatively. He now claims that he had not read the form, nor discussed its contents with his attorney, but had responded affirmatively because he felt it was required and expected of him.

At sentencing, petitioner was not advised of his limited appeal rights. He alleges that he did not become aware of these rights until after time for appeal had expired. He nevertheless sent a "Notice of Appeal" to the Los Angeles County Superior Court, which was received but not filed. Petitioner then filed a petition for writ of habeas corpus with the Court of Appeal.

The Court of Appeal sent the Attorney General an ex parte communication requesting a response to the petition for habeas corpus. After receiving the response, but before petitioner could file a traverse, the Court of Appeal denied the petition. Petitioner then petitioned this court for a hearing, which we granted, and issued an order to show cause.

. . .

[The Court's discussion of the defendant's first two contentions, (1) that counsel's urging him to accept a "package-deal" plea bargain was per se ineffective assistance of counsel and (2) that he was not properly advised of his rights, is omitted.]

III. A "package-deal" plea bargain is not coercive per se; nevertheless, the court must be persuaded that the plea is given voluntarily under the totality of the circumstances before accepting a guilty plea pursuant to such a bargain.

Petitioner urges us to adopt a rule invalidating the so-called "package-deal" plea bargain in which the prosecutor offers a defendant the opportunity to plead guilty to a lesser charge, and receive a lesser sentence, contingent upon a guilty plea by all codefendants. We decline to do so, but instead hold that such bargains, while not per se coercive, may nevertheless be so upon an examination of the totality of the circumstances. Therefore . . . the trial court must determine whether the plea is being entered into pursuant to a package deal bargain, and, if so, conduct an inquiry into possible coercive forces prior to accepting the guilty plea.

. . .

Single plea bargains, as opposed to "package-deal" ones, although containing some elements of coercion, have nevertheless been upheld as proper. . . . In the normal bargain, a defendant must choose between pleading guilty and receiving a lesser sentence, or taking his chances at a trial (in which he may be convicted and receive a greater sentence). The prosecutor seeks to avoid the time and expense of trial. These are proper considerations by both parties that do not amount to such coercion as to unduly force a defendant to plead guilty. . . .

"Package-deal" plea bargains, however, may approach the line of unreasonableness. Extraneous factors not related to the case or the prosecutor's business may be brought into play. For example, a defendant may fear that his wife will be prosecuted and convicted if he does not plead guilty; or, a defendant may fear, as alleged in this case, that his codefendant will attack him if he does not plead guilty. Because such considerations do not bear any direct relation to whether the defendant himself is guilty, special scrutiny must be employed to ensure a voluntary plea. . . .

As we point out below, certain factors may appear to render a plea pursuant to a "package-deal" bargain coercive, or not coercive, upon close examination. Because we believe that it is possible for such a plea to be entered without undue force, we choose not to invalidate all "package-deal" bargains as coercive per se. Rather, the trial court assumes a duty to conduct an inquiry into the *totality of the circumstances* to determine whether, in fact, a plea has been unduly coerced, or is instead freely and voluntarily given.

The totality of the circumstances test in examining the voluntariness of a guilty plea pursuant to a "package-deal" bargain appears to be the prevailing view. . . . In those jurisdictions, special care is taken to determine the voluntariness of the plea. . . . We go one step further, however, by *requiring* an inquiry into the totality of the circumstances whenever a plea is taken pursuant to a "package-deal" bargain. We are satisfied that this requirement will suffice to discover any unduly coercive forces which might render such a plea involuntary.

Various factors must be considered at the inquiry. First, the court must determine whether the inducement for the plea is proper. The court should be satisfied that the prosecution has not misrepresented facts to the defendant, and that the substance of the inducement is within the proper scope of the prosecutor's business.[11] . . . The prosecutor must also have a reasonable and good faith case against the third parties to whom leniency is promised. . . .

Second, the factual basis for the guilty plea must be considered. If the guilty plea is not supported by the evidence, it is less likely that the plea was the product of the accused's free will. The same would be true if the "bargained-for" sentence were disproportionate to the accused's culpability.

---

11. We recognize that the "package-deal" may be a *valuable tool* to the prosecutor, who has a need for *all* defendants, or none, to plead guilty. The prosecutor may be properly interested in avoiding the time, delay and expense of trial of all the defendants. He is also placed in a difficult position should one defendant plead and another go to trial, because the defendant who pleads may become an adverse witness on behalf of his codefendant, free of jeopardy. Thus, the prosecutor's motivation for proposing a "package-deal" bargain may be strictly legitimate and free of extrinsic forces.

Third, the nature and degree of coerciveness should be carefully examined. Psychological pressures sufficient to indicate an involuntary plea might be present if the third party promised leniency is a close friend or family member whom the defendant feels compelled to help. . . . If the defendant bears no special relationship to the third party promised leniency, he may nevertheless feel compelled to plead guilty due to physical threat. For example, if the third party had made a specific threat against defendant if he refused to plead guilty, the plea is likely to be involuntary. On the other hand, if the defendant merely thought, as in the case at bar, that his codefendant would attack him if he did not plead guilty, sufficient coercive factors may not be at play.

Fourth, a plea is not coerced if the promise of leniency to a third party was an insignificant consideration by a defendant in his choice to plead guilty. For example, if the motivating factor to plead guilty was the realization of the likelihood of conviction at trial, the defendant cannot be said to have been "forced" into pleading guilty, unless the coercive factors present had nevertheless remained a *substantial factor* in his decision. . . .

Our list is by no means exhaustive. Other factors which may be relevant can and should be taken into account at the inquiry. For example, the age of the defendant . . . whether defendant or the prosecutor had initiated the plea negotiations . . . and whether charges have already been pressed against a third party . . . might be important considerations.

. . .

The petition for habeas corpus is denied without prejudice to petitioner filing a new petition in the superior court alleging sufficient facts to establish that his plea to the charges of robbery and assault with a deadly weapon was involuntary.

. . .

---

363. *Ibarra* was approved in State v. Solano, 724 P.2d 17 (Ariz.1986). See also United States v. Carr, 80 F.3d 413 (10th Cir.1996) (package plea bargain upheld); United States v. Gonzalez, 918 F.2d 1129 (3d Cir.1990) (prosecutor's insistence on package-deal and refusal to accept individual defendant's plea not improper). Compare United States v. Washington, 969 F.2d 1073 (D.C.Cir.1992), holding that it was an abuse of discretion for the trial judge to refuse to accept a guilty plea because the defendant refused to incriminate his codefendant.

In Cortez v. United States, 337 F.2d 699 (9th Cir.1964), the defendant and his wife were indicted on narcotics charges, the penalty for which was a minimum sentence of five years with no probation and a maximum sentence of 20 years. He pleaded guilty. His wife, who was seven months pregnant, pleaded guilty to a lesser charge and was sentenced to the minimum term of two years imprisonment. On a motion to vacate the conviction under 28 U.S.C. § 2255, the defendant claimed that he pleaded guilty in exchange for his wife's being allowed to plead to the lesser charge, as part of a deal between the prosecutor and his lawyer. Upholding the conviction, the court observed that other factors might have led the defendant to plead guilty, including the strength of the government's case and the possibility of having a more lenient judge for sentencing. The court said:

"No competent lawyer, discussing a possible guilty plea with a client, could fail to canvass these possible alternatives with him. Nor would he fail to ascertain the willingness of the prosecutor to 'go along.' Moreover, if a co-defendant is involved, and if the client is anxious to help that co-defendant, a competent lawyer would be derelict in his duty if he did not assist in that regard. At the same time, the lawyer is bound to advise his client fully as to his rights, as to the alternatives available to him, and of the fact that neither the lawyer nor the prosecutor nor anyone else can bargain for the court. There is nothing wrong, however, with a lawyer's giving his client the benefit of his judgment as to what the court is likely to do, always making it clear that he is giving advice, not making a promise." Id. at 701.

364. The defendant was indicted for robbery and other crimes committed against Rodriguez. After the prosecutor had announced the case ready for trial, Rodriguez died. Four days after the prosecutor learned of Rodriguez's death, plea negotiations were completed and the defendant entered a plea of guilty. The prosecutor did not tell the defendant or his counsel that Rodriguez, the principal prosecution witness, had died. The Court of Appeals held that, at least in the absence of an assertion of innocence by the defendant, due process did not require disclosure before the plea of guilty was entered. People v. Jones, 375 N.E.2d 41 (N.Y.1978).

Would you, as prosecutor, have disclosed the death of the witness?

See also Fambo v. Smith, 433 F.Supp. 590 (W.D.N.Y.), aff'd, 565 F.2d 233 (2d Cir.1977), in which the district attorney did not disclose conclusive evidence that the defendant was not guilty of the crime charged in the second of two counts of the indictment. He was, however, guilty of the same crime, on another date, as charged in the first count. (The two counts charged possession of dynamite, on different dates. Before the later date, police officers had discovered the tube containing the dynamite, replaced the dynamite with sawdust, and put the tube back where it had been found. The defendant recovered the tube filled with sawdust, possession of which was the subject of the second count.) The defendant pleaded guilty to a lesser included offense on the second count and the first count was dismissed. Should the plea be vacated?

How much difference does it make that evidence undisclosed before a plea bargain bears directly on the defendant's actual guilt, as in *Fambo*, rather than the likelihood of his being convicted, as in *Jones*?

365. "On June 3, 1978, appellant William L. Campbell, III, used his key to enter the apartment of his former wife, Sheila Campbell. Campbell had been living in the apartment with Sheila and their children until about two weeks earlier. In his statement to the police, Campbell said that he went to the apartment to remove some of his personal property, including a .22 caliber automatic pistol and approximately 300 rounds of ammunition. He alleges that he was drunk and fell asleep at the kitchen table after placing the gun and ammunition on a divider between the table and the apartment's front door. Sometime after midnight Sheila Campbell, their children, and a male companion entered the apartment. Campbell told the police that he asked the man who he was, and the man replied, 'Franket.' Campbell further stated that several months earlier a friend had warned him that Ronald Franket had a gun and was 'looking for him.' Campbell claimed that although he saw no gun, he saw Franket reach into his pocket, and Campbell, therefore, shot Ronald Franket five times. He also shot Sheila Campbell three times. Both died.

"Campbell turned himself in the following day and was subsequently indicted by a Columbiana County, Ohio grand jury on two counts of aggravated murder with specifications and one count of aggravated burglary. The specifications alleged that Campbell committed each murder as a part of the killing of two or more persons and that each was committed during the course of an aggravated burglary. Under Ohio law, Campbell could have received the death penalty if convicted of aggravated murder and at least one of the specifications. . . . If convicted of aggravated murder but neither of the specifications, Campbell's maximum possible sentence was life imprisonment for each count. . . . The aggravated burglary count carried a possible sentence of 4 to 25 years. . . .

"As a part of Campbell's plea bargain, the prosecutor moved both to strike the specifications from the aggravated murder portion of the indictment and to enter a nolle prosequi as to the aggravated burglary charge. In return, Campbell entered a plea of guilty to the two aggravated murder counts.

"Before his plea hearing, Campbell was given a document entitled 'Judicial Advice to Defendant.' That document contained a discussion of each of the constitutional rights Campbell would waive by pleading guilty, the elements of the crime to which he intended to plead, and the maximum penalties he could receive. Campbell completed a written 'Defendant's Response to Court' indicating that he had read and understood the information in the 'Judicial Advice to Defendant.' In his 'Response' he also answered specific questions to establish that his guilty plea was knowing, intelligent, and voluntary. At the plea hearing the state court judge determined that Campbell had read and understood these documents. He also questioned Campbell as to his knowledge of the consequences of his guilty plea and discussed some of the rights Campbell was waiving. The court did not specifically inform Campbell in court that the plea would waive his right to be free from self-incrimination, his right of confrontation, and his right to compulsory process, although a discussion of the waiver of each of these rights was included in the 'Judicial Advice to Defendant.' When asked by the court why he shot Ronald Franket and Sheila Campbell, Campbell replied, 'Because he was with my wife,' and 'Because she was with him.' The court accepted Campbell's guilty plea and sentenced him to two consecutive life sentences.

"Before Campbell decided to plead guilty, his counsel made a specific written request for discovery from the prosecution. He requested any evidence material to Campbell's guilt or punishment as well as a list of the tangible objects which the prosecution intended to use at trial. Campbell subsequently learned that the police had found a .25 caliber semi-automatic pistol on Franket's body and had taken that gun into their possession. The palm-sized weapon was found in the left, rear, hip pocket of Franket's pants. Although they were aware of the gun's existence and had the gun in their possession, the prosecution did not disclose the gun to Campbell or his counsel." Campbell v. Marshall, 769 F.2d 314, 315–16 (6th Cir.1985).

Campbell subsequently claimed "that he pleaded guilty only because he had no believable self-defense claim and that he would have gone to a jury with that defense had he known of the gun." Id. at 317. If Campbell's lawyer had not made the discovery request, should the prosecutor have disclosed that the gun had been found on Franket's body before Campbell pleaded guilty? Was the prosecutor obligated to do so? In view of Campbell's statements to the court at the plea hearing, should his conviction on the plea of guilty be vacated because the request for discovery was not met? (Ordinarily, failure to disclose exculpatory material *at trial* may be a denial of due process. See pp. 951–79 below.)

See White v. United States, 858 F.2d 416 (8th Cir.1988).

366. Defendants Smith and Jones have been indicted jointly in a three-count indictment, as follows:

FIRST COUNT: On or about December 10, 1993, within the State of Ames, Sam Smith and John Jones, feloniously did take, use, operate and remove, one certain automobile, property of Theodore Todd, and in the custody of Adam Angle, from a certain street, and did operate and drive said automobile, for their own profit, use, and purpose, without the consent of Theodore Todd, the owner of said automobile, and without the consent of Adam Angle.

SECOND COUNT: On or about December 10, 1993, within the State of Ames, Sam Smith and John Jones entered the yard of L & L, Inc., a body corporate, with intent to steal property of another.

THIRD COUNT: On or about December 10, 1993, within the State of Ames, Sam Smith and John Jones stole property of L & L, Inc., a body corporate, of the value of about $80.00, consisting of one battery of the value of $80.00.

As the prosecuting attorney assigned to the case, you have investigated it, with the following results:

Theodore Todd will testify that he left his car at Queen's Garage for repairs on the afternoon of December 10. He was notified at 10:30 p.m. that night that his car had been stolen and was recovered by the police. He does not know defendants Smith and Jones. There was no damage to his car.

Adam Angle will testify that he is employed as a mechanic at Queen's Garage. He was there when Todd brought his car in for repairs on December 10. The car was parked in the street beside the garage when Angle left work at 9:00 p.m. He learned that it had been stolen the next morning. He does not know the defendants Smith and Jones.

Mack Matthews, the manager of L & L, Inc., will testify that L & L is an automobile sales agency. He was notified by the police at about 10:00 p.m. on December 10, that the defendants Smith and Jones had been arrested on L & L's used car lot. He was told that they had stolen a battery which was recovered and which he later valued at $80.00. He does not know the defendants.

Private Earl Ernest, a member of the municipal police force, will testify that he and a companion officer were staked out at the L & L used car lot on the night of December 10, 1993, because there had been reports of thefts. The lot is open and separated from the sidewalk only by a low chain. At about 9:50 p.m., he and his companion observed a car, subsequently identified as belonging to Todd, pull into the lot. A man, who proved to be Jones, got out and went to a car parked in the lot. Ernest saw him remove a battery from under the hood of the parked car and return with it to Todd's car which Jones had been driving. As Jones was passing the battery to someone seated on the passenger side of the front seat, Ernest emerged from his cover and arrested Jones. A man, later identified as Smith, came out of the car and Ernest arrested him. Before he was arrested, Jones threw a wrench under the car he was driving. Ernest's companion officer will testify to the same effect if needed.

Jones has a lengthy criminal record, including many detentions for investigation and arrests for "drunks" and "disorderlies." He has been arrested but not prosecuted for robbery and grand larceny. He has six convictions for petit larceny, one for assault, one for soliciting prostitution, and one for a narcotics offense. He is 51 years old.

Smith is 29. When he was 21, he was detained for investigation and released without charge. When he was 22, he was arrested for disorderly conduct and elected to forfeit $25.

Smith's lawyer has discussed the case with you. She has informed you that Smith's defense will be that he and Jones were near Queen's Garage on December 10, and Smith decided to visit his wife, from whom he was estranged. Since he was a friend of Angle, he and Jones went to Queen's

Garage, and Smith asked Angle to let them use Todd's car, which was parked on the street. Angle agreed. Smith could not drive and asked Jones to drive. En route to Smith's wife's apartment, Jones said he had to pick up a battery to give a friend a "hot shot" for a stalled car. Smith had been drinking a bit and didn't question Jones; he thought Jones worked at L & L. He wasn't suspicious at the time and could give no explanation for not telling the police this story at the time of his arrest.

Jones is a tough-looking man who has not been released on bail and will not make a good impression on the witness stand. Smith has been released, holds a steady job, and will make a good impression; he and his wife have been reunited since his indictment.

Petit larceny (third count) carries a maximum sentence of imprisonment for one year.

Unauthorized use of a vehicle (first count) carries a maximum sentence of imprisonment for five years.

Housebreaking (second count) carries a maximum sentence of imprisonment for 15 years.

One hour before the trial is to begin, Jones's lawyer comes to your office and offers to have his client plead guilty to the third count of the indictment if you will dismiss the others. Your witnesses have been summoned to court and are waiting in the witness room.

What should you do?

Assume that you reject the offer. Jones's lawyer then offers to have his client plead guilty to the first count of the indictment if you will dismiss the others.

What should you do?

Assume that you have reason to believe that Angle was lying when he talked to you and that Smith's account of how he and Jones got the car is true.

Assume that Angle will (will not) support Smith's story on the witness stand.

367. United States ex rel. Elksnis v. Gilligan, 256 F.Supp. 244 (S.D.N.Y.1966). The defendant was indicted for second-degree murder, punishable by an indeterminate sentence of imprisonment for not less than 20 years to life. He pleaded guilty to first-degree manslaughter, the maximum penalty for which was imprisonment for 20 years, on the sentencing judge's promise to him and his counsel that the sentence would be not more than ten years imprisonment. He was sentenced and imprisoned. He subsequently sought his release on habeas corpus on the ground that his conviction on the plea of guilty denied him due process of law.

". . . A crucial question here is the impact, if any, of the judge's promise upon the defendant. The fact that the promise may not have been deliberately designed or intended to influence or to induce the defendant to plead guilty is not material—the question is did it have that impact.

. . .

"The unequal positions of the judge and the accused, one with the power to commit to prison and the other deeply concerned to avoid prison, at once raise a question of fundamental fairness. When a judge becomes a participant in plea bargaining he brings to bear the full force and majesty of his office. His awesome power to impose a substantially longer or even maximum sentence in excess of that proposed is present whether referred to or not. A defendant needs no reminder that if he rejects the proposal, stands upon his right to trial and is convicted, he faces a significantly longer sentence. One facing a prison term, whether of longer or shorter duration, is easily influenced to accept what appears the more preferable choice. Intentionally or otherwise, and no matter how well motivated the judge may be, the accused is subjected to a subtle but powerful influence. A guilty plea predicated upon a judge's promise of a definite sentence by its very nature does not qualify as a free and voluntary act. The plea is so interlaced with the promise that the one cannot be separated from the other; remove the promise and the basis for the plea falls.

"A judge's prime responsibility is to maintain the integrity of the judicial system; to see that due process of law, equal protection of the laws and the basic safeguards of a fair trial are upheld. The judge stands as the symbol of evenhanded justice, and none can seriously question that if this central figure in the administration of justice promises an accused that upon a plea of guilty a fixed sentence will follow, his commitment has an all-pervasive and compelling influence in inducing the accused to yield his right to trial. A plea entered upon a bargain agreement between a judge and an accused cannot be squared with due process requirements of the Fourteenth Amendment.

. . .

"Finally, a bargain agreement between a judge and a defendant, however free from any calculated purpose to induce a plea, has no place in a system of justice. It impairs the judge's objectivity in passing upon the voluntariness of the plea when offered. As a party to the arrangement upon which the plea is based, he is hardly in a position to discharge his function of deciding the validity of the plea—a function not satisfied by routine inquiry, but only, as the Supreme Court has stressed, by 'a penetrating and comprehensive examination of all the circumstances under which such a plea is tendered.'[12]" Id. at 253–55.

"The line may well be a fine one between a trial judge 'participating' in the plea bargaining process and a judge merely 'ratifying' an agreement already reached between the accused and the prosecutor. But the likelihood that the judge will overawe the defendant or surrender his impartiality is

---

12. Von Moltke v. Gillies, 332 U.S. 708, 724 . . . (1948).

at least sharply reduced if he does not play a role in the negotiations leading to the formation of a bargain." Scott v. United States, 419 F.2d 264, 275 (D.C.Cir.1969).

In United States v. Werker, 535 F.2d 198, 201 (2d Cir.1976), the court said that the provision of Rule 11(e)(1) that a judge shall not participate in plea negotiations, means that "the sentencing judge should take no part whatever in any discussion or communication regarding the sentence to be imposed prior to the entry of a plea of guilty or conviction, or submission to him of a plea agreement." That prohibition applies to the disclosure by a judge of the sentence that he would impose were a plea of guilty entered. The court said:

"It is immaterial whether we consider pre-plea disclosure of sentence to be per se coercive . . . or only one factor to be considered in determining voluntariness . . . . Rule 11 is obviously intended totally to eliminate pressures emanating from judicial involvement in the plea bargaining process, and this necessarily includes any involvement of the court in divulging pre-plea sentence proposals which are equally likely to generate such pressures.

"Rule 11 implicitly recognizes that participation in the plea bargaining process depreciates the image of the trial judge that is necessary to public confidence in the impartial and objective administration of criminal justice. As a result of his participation, the judge is no longer a judicial officer or a neutral arbiter. Rather, he becomes or seems to become an advocate for the resolution he has suggested to the defendant.

"It would be naive to believe that disclosure of a sentence prior to entry of the plea merely supplies the parties with additional information and therefore does not alter the status of the trial judge. The judge's promise to indicate a specific sentence soon becomes the focal point of further discussions. His assurances to the defendant are the ultimate inducement to the plea . . . . The judge's determination is not simply one more fact to be considered by the defendant in deciding upon a course of action. The defendant, as in this case, is unlikely to approach the judge until the parties have exhausted their own abilities to compromise. Thus, the judge's response to the inquiry becomes the essential element in the ensuing discussions. Consequently, the judge's indication of sentence necessarily constitutes 'participat(ion) in such discussions.'

"Furthermore, the indication of sentence inevitably invites alterations and clarifications of the proposed sentence through direct negotiations with the judge. A defense counsel who obtains assurance, initially based solely on the presentence report, of a maximum sentence on charges similar to those involved in this case would probably next inquire if the judge would modify the sentence still further should the defendant cooperate with government, or if the judge would accept a plea to a lesser offense. Once the judge enters the plea process by announcing a proposed sentence, it becomes impossible not to indicate a response to additional relevant inquiries. Rule 11(e)(1) was designed to avert this very situation. The Rule is based on the sound principle that the interests of justice are best served if the judge remains aloof from all discussions preliminary to the determination of guilt or innocence so that his impartiality and objectivity shall not be open to any question or suspicion when it becomes his duty to impose sentence." Id. at 203. See United States v. Casallas, 59 F.3d 1173 (11th Cir.1995) (judge's effort to be sure that defendant's decision not to plead guilty was well informed crossed line into participation in plea negotiations and invalidated plea); Frank v. Blackburn, 646 F.2d 873 (5th Cir.1980), modified, 646 F.2d 902 (1981), note 369 below.

368. If a defendant pleads guilty in reliance on an explicit statement of the court that he cannot or will not be given more than a specific sentence and the defendant is subsequently given a more severe sentence, the plea of guilty is subject to attack. Smith v. United States, 321 F.2d 954 (9th Cir.1963). "Quite apart from any question of inducement, if a court informs a defendant prior to accepting his plea that five years is the maximum sentence, we think this must in fact be the maximum." Workman v. United States, 337 F.2d 226, 227 (1st Cir.1964). See United States v. Amaya, 111 F.3d 386 (5th Cir.1997) (plea in reliance on judge's commitment to ensure that prosecutor moved for downward sentencing departure, which judge was unable to do; conviction vacated).

369. "[I]t has always been the rule in both the federal and state systems that leniency is always extended on pleas of guilty that is not extended when defendants go to trial . . . ." United States ex rel. Starner v. Russell, 378 F.2d 808, 811–12 (3d Cir.1967).

If it is proper for a trial judge to let it be known that he gives consideration to the fact that a defendant pleads guilty, is it proper for him also to let it be known that he is less likely to be lenient toward a defendant who does not plead guilty? Is there a difference between the two propositions?

Consider Frank v. Blackburn, 646 F.2d 873 (5th Cir.1980), modified, 646 F.2d 902 (1981):

"We agree wholeheartedly . . . that a defendant cannot be punished *simply* for exercising his constitutional right to stand trial. . . . We do not agree, however, that the mere imposition of a longer sentence than the defendant would have received had he pleaded guilty automatically constitutes such punishment. The Supreme Court's plea bargaining decisions make it clear that a state is free to encourage guilty pleas by offering substantial benefits to a defendant, or by threatening an accused with more severe punishment should a negotiated plea be refused. . . . It is equally clear that a defendant is free to accept or reject the 'bargain' offered by the state. Once the bargain—whether it be reduced charges, a recommended sentence, or some other concession—is rejected, however, the defendant cannot complain that the denial of the rejected offer constitutes a punishment or is evidence of judicial vindictiveness. To accept such an argument is to ignore completely the underlying philosophy and purposes of the plea bargaining system. If a defendant can successfully demand the same leniency after standing trial that was offered to him prior to trial in exchange for a guilty plea, all the incentives to plea bargain disappear; the defendant has nothing to lose by going to trial."

Id. at 882–83. "Once the defendant elects to go to trial," the court said, "all bets are off." Id. at 887.

In United States v. Derrick, 519 F.2d 1 (6th Cir.1975), the court held that it was improper to increase a defendant's sentence because he had pleaded not guilty and gone to trial. "In holding that it is improper for a trial judge to impose a heavier penalty because a defendant in a given case has availed himself of his constitutional right to a fair trial by jury, we simply reaffirm its availability to all citizens and, therefore, necessarily to the guilty as well as the innocent. . . .

"We do not doubt that in a given case, sentences for the same offense and otherwise same circumstances may differ where one follows a plea and another is after jury conviction. Realistically many factors come into play in the sentencing process. The most obvious factor is that in pleading guilty, a defendant owns up to what he has done. If it is true that confession is good for the soul, it must be acknowledged that a free and honest admission of guilt is perhaps the first and largest step toward ultimate rehabilitation. It is this concept, we suspect, which prompts most pleas of guilty in the first place. Certainly a trial judge is likely to take into account the difference in mental attitude between the defendant who admits his guilt and seeks to reform and the defendant who, although proved guilty beyond a reasonable doubt, gives no indication of his willingness to be rehabilitated.

"Another factor which we see as almost inevitably influencing the decision of a trial judge is that in a plea of guilty, the crime pleaded is understood only as related in somewhat sterile fashion through the plea taking process or through a printed narration in the presentence report. The sentencing following a trial upon the merits, on the other hand, sees the trial judge in possession not only of more of the detailed facts of the offense itself, but of the flavor of the event and the impact upon any victims. It is for that reason a more real and accurate appraisal of the circumstances which brought the defendant to the bar of justice, and almost inevitably this added knowledge will affect the judge's consideration of what penalty appears most appropriate. This can, of course, work to the benefit or the detriment of the defendant according to the degree of culpability shown by the proofs.

"We do not intend to imply such factors as those mentioned do not or should not influence the trial judge's decisions in sentencing. We simply hold that it is improper for a trial judge to impose a heavier sentence as a penalty for the exercise of the right of jury trial, or as an example to deter others from exercising the right. Such motives are objectionable because they are coercive and because they have little if any relevance to the proper objectives of sentencing." Id. at 4–5.

See *Hess v. United States*, 496 F.2d 936, 938 (8th Cir.1974) (citing additional cases); *United States v. Wiley*, 267 F.2d 453 (7th Cir.1959), 278 F.2d 500 (1960), 184 F.Supp. 679 (N.D.Ill.1960). In *Hess*, the court noted that it did *not* say that a trial judge's belief that a defendant had committed perjury during the trial could not be considered at sentencing. Id. at 939. See note 582 p. 1158 below.

If the practice of plea bargaining depends on the assumption that defendants have something to gain by bargaining—i.e., that defendants who plead guilty generally receive lighter sentences than defendants who are convicted after trial—would it be preferable to make this assumption explicit? If not, why not? If so, what form should the explicit statement take?

In view of the general assumption that a defendant who pleads guilty has a good chance to receive a lighter sentence than he would have received had he gone to trial, how realistic is it to assert, as in *Derrick*, above, that "in pleading guilty, a defendant owns up to what he has done"? Is making the best deal you can "perhaps the first and largest step toward ultimate rehabilitation"? In *Derrick*, the court notes the difference between the "somewhat sterile" account of the defendant's crime if he pleads guilty, on one hand, and the more vivid presentation of the facts at a trial, on the other. Might one conclude that if there is any likelihood of "owning up" either way, it is *greater* if there is a trial?

370. "[W]hen a plea rests in any significant degree on a promise or agreement of the prosecutor, so that it can be said to be part of the inducement or consideration, such promise must be fulfilled." *Santobello v. New York*, 404 U.S. 257, 262 (1971). If such a promise is not fulfilled, it is immaterial whether the failure is deliberate or inadvertent. Id. See *United States v. Benchimol*, 471 U.S. 453 (1985) (prosecutor's "less-than-enthusiastic" recommendation to sentencing judge did not violate plea agreement), with which compare *United States v. Grandinetti*, 564 F.2d 723 (5th Cir.1977) (prosecutor's ineffective recommendation was not fulfillment of bargain).

The defendant pleaded guilty pursuant to a plea agreement that his sentence would be 10–40 years imprisonment, and was sentenced accordingly. Four days later, the prosecutor and trial judge sent a letter to the state parole board, as provided in state law, in which the prosecutor described the circumstances of the crime and the prosecutor and judge jointly recommended that the defendant serve the maximum time possible under the sentence. During the plea negotiations, the subject of parole had not been mentioned. The court of appeals held that the letter did not violate the plea agreement and that the plea of guilty and sentence were valid. *United States ex rel. Robinson v. Israel*, 603 F.2d 635 (7th Cir.1979).

A New York state policy of recognizing only plea agreements that are on the record of the plea proceeding is valid and an off-the-record undertaking of the prosecutor is not enforceable. *Siegel v. New York*, 691 F.2d 620 (2d Cir.1982). The court observed that the state policy increased the likelihood that pleas of guilty are accurate, "enhanced the integrity of the plea bargain process," and assured the finality of convictions.

A defendant is not entitled to enforcement of a prosecutor's offer of a proposed plea bargain, which offer the defendant accepted before it was withdrawn by the prosecutor; the defendant later pleaded guilty according to a subsequent offer of the prosecutor that was harsher than the original offer. Since the defendant was fully informed of the nature of the bargain before he pleaded guilty, the plea was valid. Mabry v. Johnson, 467 U.S. 504 (1984).

371. "Mere prediction by counsel of the court's likely attitude on sentence, short of some implication of an agreement or understanding, is not ground for attacking a plea. . . . Nor, generally, is other advice, simply because it turns out poorly." Domenica v. United States, 292 F.2d 483, 485 (1st Cir.1961). See Knight v. United States, 611 F.2d 918 (1st Cir.1979) (*Domenica* followed). "[A] mere disappointed expectation of leniency, as opposed to an understanding with the trial judge, is not sufficient cause to vitiate a plea." United States ex rel. McGrath v. LaVallee, 319 F.2d 308, 314 (2d Cir.1963). To the same effect, see Harris v. United States, 434 F.2d 23 (9th Cir.1970).

Suppose the defendant's expectation is based on his *mis*understanding of the judge's statements to him, see Pilkington v. United States, 315 F.2d 204 (4th Cir.1963), or to his counsel, see United States v. Lias, 173 F.2d 685 (4th Cir.1949). Suppose his expectation is based on a *mis*understanding created by statements of the prosecutor, see United States v. Lester, 247 F.2d 496 (2d Cir.1957), or other government officials, see Aiken v. United States, 282 F.2d 215 (4th Cir.1960) (postal inspectors). Suppose it is based on the incorrect advice of counsel. See United States v. Unger, 665 F.2d 251 (8th Cir.1981) (plea induced by counsel's incorrect representation of fact about what sentence would be is involuntary). For an alternative argument in such cases, based on a claim of ineffective assistance of counsel, see, e.g., Downs-Morgan v. United States, 765 F.2d 1534 (11th Cir.1985), note 353 p. 726 above. Suppose counsel's incorrect advice did not concern the sentence but some collateral consequence of conviction. See Michel v. United States, 507 F.2d 461 (2d Cir.1974) (counsel incorrectly advised defendant that he would not be subject to deportation; additional cases cited). In a case in which the defendant claims that he was unfairly surprised by his sentence, how much weight should be given to the fact that a defendant does not move to withdraw his plea of guilty promptly after sentence is imposed? See Georges v. United States, 262 F.2d 426, 431 (5th Cir.1959). In cases of this kind, how can the government avoid letting the defendant treat his plea of guilty as "a mere trial balloon to test the attitude of the trial judge," United States v. Weese, 145 F.2d 135, 136 (2d Cir.1944)?

372. The defendant was indicted for first-degree robbery. If convicted, he would have been sentenced as a multiple offender within a sentencing range of 15 to 60 years imprisonment. At a pretrial conference in which the trial judge participated, the defendant agreed to plead guilty to second degree robbery, the sentencing range for which was seven-and-a-half to 30 years imprisonment. At the conference the trial judge did not indicate what sentence he would impose, but observed that the defendant would be able to avoid the very heavy sentence on a conviction of first-degree robbery if he pleaded guilty to the lesser offense. The judge sentenced the defendant to 29 to 30 years imprisonment. "Before imposing this punishment, the judge indicated he was influenced by the accused's unsavory criminal record . . . specifically detailed in a probation report very recently made available to him, but not completed and transmitted to him before he accepted the guilty plea. Indeed, the judge expressed regret, at the time of sentencing, that he had accepted the plea to the lesser offense and indicated that appellant's exceptionally bad record called for a prison term not materially below the statutory maximum." United States ex rel. McGrath v. LaVallee, 348 F.2d 373, 375 (2d Cir.1965).

Years after being sentenced, the defendant claimed that, having determined to impose the maximum sentence the judge should have allowed the defendant to reinstate his plea of not guilty. "Fundamental fairness is somehow lacking, we are told, when a trial judge discusses with a defendant and his counsel the acceptance of a proffered plea on the basis of certain necessarily incomplete information and then, in sentencing, takes into account new, allegedly erroneous information which becomes routinely available in assessing the punishment to be imposed." Id. at 378. What result? Why?

373. The prosecutor and defense counsel negotiated a bargain that the defendant would plead guilty to second-degree murder and testify against an accomplice in his trial for murder, and the charge of first-degree murder against the defendant would be dismissed. The trial judge refused to accept the plea because he believed that the defendant should be convicted of first-degree murder. The defendant pleaded guilty and was convicted of first-degree murder. On appeal the court reversed and remanded with directions that the plea of guilty to second-degree murder be accepted.

The court said that a trial judge was not required to accept a defendant's plea of guilty to an offense less than that charged but that his discretion was not unconstrained. "First, the trial judge must provide a reasoned exercise of discretion in order to justify a departure from the course agreed on by the prosecution and defense. This is not a matter of absolute judicial prerogative. The authority has been granted to the judge to assure protection of the public interest, and this in turn involves one or more of the following components: (a) fairness to the defense, such as protection against harassment; (b) fairness to the prosecution interest, as in avoiding a disposition that does not serve due and legitimate prosecutorial interests; (c) protection of the sentencing authority reserved to the judge. The judge's statement or opinion must identify the particular interest that leads him to require an unwilling defendant and prosecution to go to trial.

"We now turn to the content of these components, and begin by passing any discussion of fairness to the defense, since it is not directly involved in the case at bar. . . . As to fairness to the prosecution interest, here we have a matter in which the primary responsibility, obviously, is that of the prosecuting attorney. The District Court cannot disapprove of his action on the ground of incompatibility with prosecutive responsibility unless the judge is in effect ruling that the prosecutor has abused his discretion. The requirement of judicial approval entitles the judge to obtain and evaluate the prosecutor's reasons. . . . The judge may withhold approval if he finds that the prosecutor has failed to give consideration to factors that must be given consideration in the public interest, factors such as the deterrent aspects of the criminal law. However, trial judges are not free to withhold approval of guilty pleas on this basis merely because their conception of the public interest differs from that of the prosecuting attorney. The question is not what the judge would do if he were the prosecuting attorney, but whether he can say that the action of the prosecuting attorney is such a departure from sound prosecutorial principle as to mark it an abuse of prosecutorial discretion.

"In like vein, we note that a judge is free to condemn the prosecutor's agreement as a trespass on judicial authority only in a blatant and extreme case. In ordinary circumstances, the change in grading of an offense presents no question of the kind of action that is reserved for the judiciary." United States v. Ammidown, 497 F.2d 615, 622 (D.C. Cir.1973). See United States v. Torres-Echavarria, 129 F.3d 692 (2d Cir.1997) (refusal to accept plea upheld); United States v. Severino, 800 F.2d 42 (2d Cir.1986) (same); United States v. Escobar Noble, 653 F.2d 34 (1st Cir.1981) (same); cf. United States v. Shepherd, 102 F.3d 558 (D.C. Cir.1996) (refusal to allow one codefendant to plead guilty to the indictment during trial was abuse of discretion).

374. "We think that plea bargaining serves a useful purpose both for society and the prisoner and is a permanent part of the criminal courtroom scene, but we think that it ought to be brought out into the open. We do not suggest that defense counsel and the prosecutor actually conduct their negotiations in open court, but we do urge that in this circuit a full and complete disclosure of such negotiations be announced to the court and made a part of the record. The matter is, after all, public business, and we deplore the hypocrisy of silent pretense that it has not occurred. Here it seems rather obvious that in return for pleading guilty to one count permitting the court ample latitude for adequate punishment (ten years), the prosecutor agreed, quite properly we think, to dismiss the other counts. Why not say so? Such disclosure would enable the trial judge to exercise a proper controlling influence and to reject any such arrangement he deemed unfair either to the defendant or to the public." United States v. Williams, 407 F.2d 940, 948–49 (4th Cir.1969). To the same effect, see The President's Commission on Law Enforcement and Administration of Justice, The Challenge of Crime in a Free Society 135–36 (1967).

Does Rule 11(e)(2), p. 713 above, fully accomplish the objective suggested in *Williams*, above?

The U.S. National Advisory Commission on Criminal Justice Standards and Goals recommended that plea bargaining be prohibited "as soon as possible." Courts 46 (1973). Among the arguments of the commission are the following:

"Not only does the Commission believe that plea negotiation serves no legitimate function in the processing of criminal cases, it also has concluded that it exacts unacceptable costs from all concerned. Perhaps the major cost is that of reduced rationality in the processing of criminal defendants. Whether a defendant is convicted should depend upon the evidence available to convict him, and what disposition is made of a convicted offender should depend upon what action best serves rehabilitative and deterrent needs. The likelihood that these factors will control conviction and disposition is minimized in the inevitable 'horsetrading' atmosphere of plea negotiation. Some defendants suffer from the resulting irrationality.

"But the public's interest in disposition of cases to serve its interest in protection also suffers. The Commission is convinced that rationality cannot be brought into the system by raising the visibility of the plea negotiation process and structuring the making of the administrative decisions in it. Inherent in plea negotiations is the consideration of factors that should be irrelevant to the disposition of the case. This cannot be prevented by any means short of abolishing the process.

"Another major cost involved in plea negotiation is the burden it inevitably places upon the exercise of the rights involved in trial—the rights to jury trial, to confront and cross-examine witnesses, to have the judge or jury convinced of guilt beyond a reasonable doubt, and similar matters. It is inherent in plea negotiation that leniency will be given in return for nonassertion of these rights.

. . .

"It is inevitable that exercising these rights often will involve financial costs to defendants, time commitments, and the emotionally unpleasant experience of litigation. But it is wholly unacceptable to add to this the necessity of forfeiting a discount that could otherwise have been obtained. Probably the major individual victim of today's plea bargaining system is the defendant who exercises his right to trial and suffers a substantially more severe sentence than he would have received had he pleaded guilty.

"By imposing a penalty upon the exercise of procedural rights in those cases in which there is a reasonable likelihood that the rights will be vindicated, the plea negotiation system creates a significant danger to the innocent. Many of the rights it discourages are rights designed to prevent the conviction of innocent defendants. To the extent these rights are rendered nonoperative by the plea negotiation system, innocent defendants are endangered. Plea negotiation not only serves no legitimate function in the processing of criminal defendants, but it also encourages irrationality in the court process, burdens the exercise of individual rights, and endangers the right of innocent defendants to be acquitted." Id. at 48.

In United States v. Griffin, 462 F.Supp. 928 (E.D.Ark.1978), Judge Eisele explained his refusal to consider a plea agreement as provided in Rule 11(e). He said:

"The Court wishes to make clear some of its reasons for refusing to hear plea bargains. It is the Court's opinion, probably a minority opinion, that the process of negotiating pleas has a tendency to demean all participants: the attorneys, the defendant, and even the court.[13] There are 'back-room,' sinister implications (albeit unjustified) which simply cannot be removed. The result: public cynicism and lack of faith in the integrity of the judicial process. In emphasizing expediency, allegedly based on dollar costs, plea bargaining derogates from the attempt of the Court to deal justice and substitutes therefor a concern for a cost efficient method of disposing of cases. Even if one accepts the validity of the cost argument, which this Court does not (in the federal system), it surely constitutes a poor justification for the process.

"Inasmuch as plea bargaining provides leeway for a strong prosecutor to overwhelm a poorly prepared or timid defense counsel, or a strong defense counsel to take advantage of an inept or overworked prosecutor, there is a tendency to emphasize the disparity of counsel, which has less impact when a case is heard in open court, with all the attendant safeguards of a trial. Perhaps only trial judges fully understand the pervasiveness of the 'fear of trial' experienced by even excellent attorneys. Although good lawyers will not permit this fear to rise to the level of a conscious factor in plea negotiations, it must often remain subconsciously at work in the process, encouraging acceptance of a negotiated plea on some basis other than the merits.

---

13. Judges should not shut their eyes to the dynamics of the process, or its effects, upon them personally—consciously or unconsciously. Some judges, like many lawyers, fear, or do not like trials. They would like to avoid them. All judges welcome the settlement of civil cases. Few are unhappy when a defendant, charged with a crime, decides to plead guilty. There certainly is nothing wrong with such feelings or attitudes. Where negotiated pleas are not accepted, these natural attitudes have no effect on the dispensation of justice. But now introduce plea bargaining. Suddenly the decision of the judge to accept or reject a plea bargain may make the difference between a hard six-weeks trial or, possibly, a chance to clean up his motion calendar. This could conceivably influence his decision—even if only on a subconscious level. Additionally, the reputation of the judge becomes a significant factor in the ability of the prosecutor, or the defense counsel, to prevail upon the defendant to agree to a plea bargain. If it can be demonstrated from the record that those who go to trial and lose get the 'book thrown' at them, or that it 'will cost you to see the hole card' (i.e., if one pleads not guilty and goes to trial), chances are that the defendant will seek an agreement. If, on the other hand, the judge has a reputation for being lenient or even fair, defendants and defense attorneys would be less likely to feel the compulsion to agree. So, nationwide, the process would tend to disparity rather than uniformity. And many argue cogently that reasonable uniformity should be a goal of the federal criminal justice system. So, consciously or unconsciously, a judge may act in a way which has an effect one way or the other on the entire plea bargaining process, perhaps entirely unknown to him.

"Another point: when the convicted defendant goes to prison, the opportunity to compare bargains with other inmates and to speculate on what factors may have influenced the various outcomes lends itself to the creation of cynical disdain for a system that proclaims justice as its goal but, arguably, dispenses deals instead. And this Court is of the opinion that it is very important, overall, how the defendants within the system perceive the operation and effect of that system.

"And what about the rights of the public? Assume that a United States Attorney chooses to present cases against a person to the grand jury, and the grand jury chooses to indict that person on the basis of the evidence. Now, assuming the integrity of the prosecutorial decision and the evidentiary basis therefor (and why should this not be assumed?), the rights of the public are immediately implicated. Either the man is guilty or he is not. The unimpeded process will produce the proper (just) result. But, one says, the prosecutor may *know* the defendant is guilty but simply cannot get the necessary evidence, so why not prosecute, get a deal and at least put him away for a while? Prosecutorial integrity? Sound public policy? Query.

"Revealing the existence of plea bargains and their content is, of course, superior to the silent acceptance of *sub rosa* plea agreements. It is obviously preferable to require that the process be spread on the record to maximize protection for the accused and the public. . . . In the opinion of this Court, even plea agreements acknowledged in the record do not serve the cause of justice. It would be better to insist that there be none (except *possibly* in cases involving great national interests, perhaps certified to, as such, by the Attorney General or the President himself.) Rule 11(e) at least allows the Court the option to refuse to hear bargained pleas. This Court exercises its discretion by so refusing, thereby giving no sanction to the practice.

"It has been said that without plea bargaining the wheels of justice would grind to a halt and that efficient administration of the courts requires the use of plea agreements. This Court doubts the factual basis for this argument in the federal court context. It has been able to handle its criminal docket expeditiously, and has not found clear-cut evidence that there is any great disparity in the percentage of its criminal cases which proceed to trial, when compared to courts in other districts which do accept plea agreements. Even if the refusal to accept plea bargains clearly results, overall, in a greater number of trials, what difference should this make? That is what the courts are for. They should not be considered agencies created to preside over settlement negotiations. But what about delay? The simple answer is that there can be no significant delay in the disposition of criminal cases in the federal system based on clogged dockets. If the Constitution were not enough, we have the Speedy Trial Act.

"Further, there must be more than a lingering concern, when a negotiated plea is heard, that an innocent defendant has been prevailed upon, or has chosen to 'play the odds,' rather than to staunchly maintain his innocence. In fact, must it not be accepted by the proponents of plea bargaining that, statistically, a certain number of innocent people will suffer judicial penalties *because of that system*? The potential risk of consequences of much greater penalties may drag from the mouth of an innocent man a guilty plea if it is coupled with the guarantee of a significantly lesser penalty. One can say that, in such situations, the defendant is simply exercising rational choices affecting his self-interest. That is true, and it may not be unreasonable for him to make such a choice. But should the federal criminal justice system give an innocent man that choice? This Court says, 'No.'

"We always get back to it: when is a plea voluntarily made? The plea 'taken to avoid the risk of being convicted of a more serious crime . . . is truly no more voluntary than is the choice of the rock to avoid the whirlpool.'[14]" 462 F.Supp. at 930–33.

Judge Eisele's practice of refusing to consider a plea bargain was upheld as within his authority in In re Yielding, 599 F.2d 251 (8th Cir.1979).

375. "Consideration of plea in final disposition.

"(a) The fact that a defendant has entered a plea of guilty or nolo contendere should not, by itself alone, be considered by the court as a mitigating factor in imposing sentence. It is proper for the court to grant charge and sentence concessions to defendants who enter a plea of guilty or nolo contendere when consistent with the protection of the public, the gravity of the offense, and the needs of the defendant, and when there is substantial evidence to establish that:

(i) the defendant is genuinely contrite and has shown a willingness to assume responsibility for his or her conduct;

(ii) the concessions will make possible alternative correctional measures which are better adapted to achieving protective, deterrent, or other purposes of correctional treatment, or will prevent undue harm to the defendant from the form of conviction;

(iii) the defendant, by making public trial unnecessary, has demonstrated genuine consideration for the victims of his or her criminal activity, by desiring either to make restitution or to prevent unseemly public scrutiny or embarrassment to them; or

(iv) the defendant has given or offered cooperation when such cooperation has resulted or may result in the successful prosecution of other offenders engaged in equally serious or more serious criminal conduct.

(v) that the defendant has given or offered cooperation when such cooperation has resulted or may result in the successful prosecution of other offenders engaged in equally serious or more serious criminal conduct;

(vi) that the defendant by his plea has aided in avoiding delay (including delay due to crowded dockets) in the disposition of other

---

14. Kuh, Book Review, 82 Harv.L.Rev. 497, 500 (1968).

cases and thereby has increased the probability of prompt and certain application of correctional measures to other offenders.

"(b) The court should not impose upon a defendant any sentence in excess of that which would be justified by any of the protective, deterrent or other purposes of the criminal law because the defendant has chosen to require the prosecution to prove his guilt at trial rather than to enter a plea of guilty or nolo contendere." ABA Standards for Criminal Justice, Pleas of Guilty, Standard 14–1.8 (2d ed. Supp.1986).[15]

Is paragraph (a) consistent with paragraph (b)? If the reference in paragraph (b) to "the rehabilitative, protective, deterrent or other purposes of the criminal law" relates to the imposition of punishment on a particular defendant who has chosen to plead not guilty and not to all defendants generally, *can* the two paragraphs be made consistent?

———

Suppose a defendant obtains the prosecutor's agreement to a sentence concession and then, in good faith and before any action is taken, changes his mind and decides to stand trial. If he is tried and convicted, on what basis can the prosecutor or the court impose a sentence in excess of that which would have been imposed had he pleaded guilty? If the lesser sentence would have been sufficient had he pleaded guilty, on what basis con-

15. Compare The President's Commission on Law Enforcement and Administration of Justice, The Challenge of Crime in a Free Society 135 (1967):

"The negotiated guilty plea serves important functions. As a practical matter, many courts could not sustain the burden of having to try all cases coming before them. The quality of justice in all cases would suffer if overloaded courts were faced with a great increase in the number of trials. Tremendous investments of time, talent, and money, all of which are in short supply and can be better used elsewhere, would be necessary if all cases were tried. It would be a serious mistake, however, to assume that the guilty plea is no more than a means of disposing of criminal cases at minimal cost. It relieves both the defendant and the prosecution of the inevitable risks and uncertainties of trial. It imports a degree of certainty and flexibility into a rigid, yet frequently erratic system. The guilty plea is used to mitigate the harsh-

ness of mandatory sentencing provisions and to fix a punishment that more accurately reflects the specific circumstances of the case than otherwise would be possible under inadequate penal codes. It is frequently called upon to serve important law enforcement needs by agreements through which leniency is exchanged for information, assistance, and testimony about other serious offenders.

"At the same time the negotiated plea of guilty can be subject to serious abuses. In hard-pressed courts, where judges and prosecutors are unable to deal effectively with all cases presented to them, dangerous offenders may be able to manipulate the system to obtain unjustifiably lenient treatment. There are also real dangers that excessive rewards will be offered to induce pleas or that prosecutors will threaten to seek a harsh sentence if the defendant does not plead guilty. Such practices place unacceptable burdens on the defendant who legitimately insists upon his right to trial."

sistent with paragraph (b) of the standards set out in note 375 above can a greater sentence be imposed?[16] Is the same question applicable to a person who from the beginning declines to plead guilty? Is the troubling figure in the plea-bargaining process always the person who bargains successfully or may it sometimes be the person who does not bargain, as the President's Commission suggested, p. 760 n.15 above?

Withdrawal of Guilty Plea

FEDERAL RULES OF CRIMINAL PROCEDURE

Rule 32.

SENTENCE AND JUDGMENT

. . .

(e) Plea Withdrawal. If a motion to withdraw a plea of guilty or nolo contendere is made before sentence is imposed, the court may permit the plea to be withdrawn if the defendant shows any fair and just reason. At any later time, a plea may be set aside only on direct appeal or by motion under 28 U.S.C. § 2255.

376. The provision of Rule 32(e) that a plea of guilty may be withdrawn only for a "fair and just reason" applies after the plea has been entered and accepted, even though the trial judge has not yet indicated whether he accepts the plea agreement pursuant to which the plea was entered. United States v. Hyde, ___ U.S. ___, 117 S.Ct. 1630 (1997).

16. A defendant who is tried and convicted and who successfully appeals from the conviction may not be sentenced more severely following conviction at a second trial, unless reasons based on events subsequent to the first trial affirmatively appear on the record. There is no comparable bar to a more severe sentence if the first conviction was pursuant to a guilty plea. Alabama v. Smith, 490 U.S. 794 (1989) (8–1). Among the reasons that the Court gave for this distinction are that if the first conviction was based on a guilty plea, "in the course of the proof at trial the judge may gather a fuller appreciation of the nature and extent of the crime charged," that "the defendant's conduct during trial may give the judge insights into his moral character and suitability for rehabilitation," and that "after trial, the factors that may have indicated leniency as consideration for the guilty plea are no longer present." Id. at 801. See note 585 p. 1169 below.

Everett v. United States

336 F.2d 979 (D.C.Cir.1964).

■ BURGER, CIRCUIT JUDGE.

Appellant entered a guilty plea to Counts 3 and 4 of a six-count indictment; prior to sentence he sought leave to withdraw these pleas and go to trial on these two counts. After an extended colloquy with appellant in the course of the hearing, the District Court permitted withdrawal of the guilty plea as to Count 3 but declined it as to Count 4 because no valid reason or basis for withdrawal had been claimed or shown. On the remaining guilty plea to Count 4 he sentenced appellant to nine years imprisonment under the Youth Corrections Act, 18 U.S.C. § 5010(c) (1958).

The six-count indictment charged three offenses arising out of unrelated robberies and one attempted robbery on a fourth occasion, spanning a period from April 1962 to January 1963.

At arraignment under FED.R.CRIM.P. 10 on February 25, 1963, appellant entered a plea of not guilty as to all six counts and was released on bail. Two months later, with retained counsel, he withdrew the pleas of not guilty to Count 3 (robbery) and Count 4 (assault with intent to commit robbery) and entered pleas of guilty as to both of these counts.[17] Before accepting these guilty pleas, the District Judge, pursuant to FED.R.CRIM.P. 11 and Resolution of the Judges of the U.S. District Court for the District of Columbia promulgated June 24, 1959 thereunder, conducted an extensive interrogation of appellant as to the facts of the alleged crimes and his reasons for pleading guilty thereto. Appellant freely admitted the charges: as to Count 3 he said, "I went in and robbed the place . . . by myself . . . [and took] about $200.00, sir"; as to Count 4 he said, "Well I entered the liquor store and I demanded money, sir; and well I just remember being shot; that's about all." He stated further that he had brandished a gun both times but did not shoot it; that on the later occasion one of the liquor store employees had shot him; and that he had been apprehended the following day when he had gone to the hospital for treatment of the gunshot wound. The District Judge interrogated appellant carefully as to his awareness of the possible sentence; appellant reiterated his guilt and said he was pleading guilty because he was guilty and not because the Government had moved to dismiss four other counts should he plead guilty to Counts 3 and 4.

Three weeks later, appellant, with his retained counsel, filed a motion under FED.R.CRIM.P. 32(d) to withdraw his guilty pleas to Counts 3 and 4.[18] On June 27, 1963, the District Court conducted a hearing on the motion and at this time appellant said he was innocent of the Count 3 robbery charge and had pleaded guilty to that count only because he "was so confused and worried . . . [and] wanted to try to get this over as soon as possible." As to Count 4, however, he stated to the Court: "Well, Your Honor, I

---

17. On the basis of these two guilty pleas, the United States Attorney's Office moved the dismissal of the remaining four counts. Ruling on this motion has been held in abeyance by the District Judge pending disposition of this appeal.

[18]Former Rule 32(d) was substantially equivalent to current Rule 32(e).

am guilty of that charge. I did attempt to rob this place. That's all." The District Judge granted the motion to withdraw the plea as to Count 3 but denied the motion as to Count 4 on which guilt was admitted.

Appellant is now represented by court-appointed counsel who urges that the District Court committed reversible error in refusing to permit withdrawal of the guilty plea to Count 4 in the circumstances shown here.

We disagree emphatically. We have held that withdrawal of a guilty plea, made by a defendant unrepresented by counsel, "should be freely allowed" when he seeks withdrawal *before* sentencing. . . . [I]n Gearhart v. United States, 106 U.S.App.D.C. 270, 273, 272 F.2d 499, 502, (1959), Judge Washington, speaking for a unanimous court, noted that:

"[T]he Supreme Court in broad dictum already had said that 'The court in exercise of its discretion will permit one accused to substitute a plea of not guilty and have a trial if for *any reason* the granting of the privilege seems *fair and just.*' . . .

"This is not to say that the District Court lacks all discretion in dealing with a motion of the present sort. But discretion must be exercised on the basis of sound information, soundly viewed. Where the accused seeks to withdraw his plea of guilty before sentencing, on the ground that he has a defense to the charge, the District Court should not attempt to decide the merits of the proffered defense, thus determining the guilt or innocence of the defendant. In certain situations, where the issue raised by the motion to withdraw is one of tangential nature, resolvable apart from the merits of the case, the District Court may appropriately hold a factual hearing to determine whether the accused has a 'fair and just' reason for asking to withdraw his plea of guilty."

Far from showing a " 'fair and just' reason" for a change of plea to Count 4, appellant demonstrated by his repeated statements that he had no reason other than wanting a trial on a charge of which he admitted his guilt. Unlike Gearhart, appellant offered no defense to the charge, nor did he allege involuntariness or any other factor which would militate against the correctness and truth of his guilty plea to Count 4 which was entered when he was represented by retained counsel. His contention is virtually a claim of an absolute right to withdraw a guilty plea prior to imposition of sentence. No court has ever so held; our use of the language "freely allowed" plainly implies the existence of some circumstances in which a defendant is *not* entitled to withdraw a plea of guilty before sentencing, and negates any absolute right to do so. Overwhelming authority holds, as has this court, that withdrawal of a guilty plea before sentencing is not an absolute right but a decision within the sound discretion of the trial court which will be reversed by an appellate court only for an abuse of that discretion.

A defendant who stands before a court freely admitting his attempted robbery does not remotely meet the standard of offering a "fair and just reason" for withdrawing his plea of guilty prior to sentence. He must give some reason other than a desire to have a trial the basic purpose of which is to determine the very facts the defendant has just volunteered to the court on the record and while attended by his own counsel.

The record reveals a guilty plea, intelligently and voluntarily made with assistance of retained counsel and candid admission of all essential elements of the crime in open court; this is hardly a predicate for an appellate holding that the District Judge abused his discretion in refusing to permit a withdrawal. We are not disposed to encourage accused persons to "play games" with the courts at the expense of already overburdened calendars and the rights of other accused persons awaiting trial, whose cases may lose both their position on the calendar and the Court's time and facilities which are thus diverted for no useful purpose.

Affirmed.

---

377. In United States v. Nagelberg, 323 F.2d 936 (2d Cir.1963), the defendant had pleaded guilty to three counts of an indictment charging narcotics violations. Four months later, before sentencing, he moved to withdraw the plea on the ground that "he had subsequently cooperated with and been of assistance to governmental authorities," id. The government acquiesced in the motion. The trial judge held that he had no power to grant the motion on such grounds, and sentenced the defendant to the statutory minimum of five years imprisonment on each count, the sentences to run concurrently. The court of appeals affirmed, saying that the defendant's "willingness to be of assistance to the government is not a sufficient basis for permitting his plea of guilty to be withdrawn," and noting that the defendant had never denied his guilt or claimed that his plea was improperly induced, id. In the Supreme Court, the government stated that it had acquiesced in the motion to withdraw the plea because it intended to dismiss the indictment and substitute lesser charges. In these circumstances, the Court said, the trial court had discretion to permit the plea to be withdrawn. Nagelberg v. United States, 377 U.S. 266 (1964).

378. The defendant and his wife were indicted for conspiracy to distribute counterfeit money. The defendant pleaded guilty. Sentencing was deferred until after the trial of his wife. Four months later her case was called for trial. After hearing all of the government's case, she pleaded guilty. Before sentence was imposed on him, the defendant made a motion to withdraw his guilty plea; he alleged that he had pleaded guilty in the expectation that other pending charges against him would be dropped or that he would otherwise be treated favorably. There was no indication that he had been misled in this respect by the prosecutor or by his lawyer. The government opposed withdrawal of the plea on the grounds that by waiting until after the trial of his wife the defendant had learned the government's case and that the government's witnesses were reluctant to come to court another time. Should the motion to withdraw the plea be allowed? Why (not)? See United States v. Stayton, 408 F.2d 559 (3d Cir.1969).

See also United States v. Hickok, 907 F.2d 983 (10th Cir.1990) (withdrawal before sentence not allowed); United States v. Spencer, 836 F.2d 236 (6th Cir.1987) (same); United States v. Ellison, 798 F.2d 1102 (7th Cir.1986) (no absolute right to withdraw plea before court accepts or rejects agreement); United States v. Picone, 773 F.2d 224 (8th Cir.1985) (withdrawal before sentence, following acquittal of codefendant on same charge, not allowed); United States v. Usher, 703 F.2d 956 (6th Cir.1983) (withdrawal before sentence not allowed); Nunez Cordero v. United States, 533 F.2d 723 (1st Cir.1976) (withdrawal before sentence not allowed, even though defendant was unaware that conviction meant he would be deported). In United States v. Blauner, 337 F.Supp. 1394 (S.D.N.Y.1971), after the defendant pleaded guilty the indictment against co-defendants was dismissed because of unnecessary delay by the government; the defendant's motion to withdraw the plea of guilty and for dismissal of the indictment against him also was denied.

379. The defendant in Kercheval v. United States, 274 U.S. 220 (1927), pleaded guilty and was later allowed to withdraw his plea and go to trial. Over objection, the prosecutor put in evidence a certified copy of the plea of guilty. The Court held that this was error. "The effect of the court's order permitting the withdrawal was to adjudge that the plea of guilty be held for naught. Its subsequent use as evidence against petitioner was in direct conflict with that determination. When the plea was annulled it ceased to be evidence. By permitting it to be given weight the court reinstated it *pro tanto*. . . . As a practical matter, it could not be received as evidence without putting petitioner in a dilemma utterly inconsistent with the determination of the court awarding him a trial." Id. at 224.

Rule 11(e)(6)(A) embodies the holding of *Kercheval*.

Nolo Contendere

UNITED STATES ATTORNEYS' MANUAL
9.27. Principles of Federal Prosecution

. . .

9–27.500 Opposing Offers To Plead Nolo Contendere

9–27.510 *Opposition Except in Unusual Circumstances*

A. The attorney for the government should oppose the acceptance of a plea of nolo contendere unless the Assistant Attorney General with supervisory responsibility over the subject matter concludes that the circumstances of the case are so unusual that acceptance of such a plea would be in the public interest.

B. Comment

Rule 11(b), Federal Rules of Criminal Procedure, requires the court to consider "the views of the parties and the interest of the public in the effective administration of justice" before it accepts a plea of nolo contendere. Thus, it is clear that a criminal defendant has no absolute right to enter a nolo contendere plea. The Department has long attempted to discourage the disposition of criminal cases by means of nolo pleas. The basic objections to nolo pleas were expressed by Attorney General Herbert Brownell, Jr., in a departmental directive in 1953:

> One of the factors which has tended to breed contempt for federal law enforcement in recent times has been the practice of permitting as a matter of course in many criminal indictments the plea of nolo contendere. While it may serve a legitimate purpose in a few extraordinary situations and where civil litigation is also pending, I can see no justification for it as an everyday practice, particularly where it is used to avoid certain indirect consequences of pleading guilty, such as loss of license or sentencing as a multiple offender. Uncontrolled use of the plea has led to shockingly low sentences and insignificant fines which are no deterrent to crime. As a practical matter it accomplished little that is useful even where the Government has civil litigation pending. Moreover, a person permitted to plead nolo contendere admits his guilt for the purpose of imposing punishment for his acts and yet, for all other purposes, and as far as the public is concerned, persists in his denial of wrongdoing. It is no wonder that the public regards consent to such a plea by the Government as an admission that it has only a technical case at most and that the whole proceeding was just a fiasco.

For these reasons, government attorneys have been instructed for many years not to consent to nolo pleas except in the most unusual circumstances, and to do so then only with departmental approval. Federal prosecutors should oppose the acceptance of a nolo plea, unless the responsible Assistant Attorney General concludes that the circumstances are so unusual that acceptance of the plea would be in the public interest. Such a determination might be made, for example, in an unusually complex antitrust case if the only alternative to a protracted trial is acceptance of a nolo plea.

9–27.520 *Offer of Proof*

A. In any case in which a defendant seeks to enter a plea of nolo contendere, the attorney for the government should make an offer of proof of the facts known to the government to support the conclusion that the defendant has in fact committed the offense charged.

B. Comment

If a defendant seeks to avoid admitting guilt by offering to plead nolo contendere, the attorney for the government should make an offer of proof of the facts known to the government to support the conclusion that the defendant has in fact committed the offense charged. This should be done even in the rare case in which the government does not oppose the entry of a nolo plea. In addition, as is the case with respect to guilty pleas, the attorney for the government should urge the court to require the defendant to admit publicly the facts underlying the criminal charges. These precautions should minimize the effectiveness of any subsequent efforts by the defendant to portray himself/herself as technically liable perhaps, but not seriously culpable.

9–27.530 *Argument in Opposition*

A. If a plea of nolo contendere is offered over the government's objection, the attorney for the government should state for the record why acceptance of the plea would not be in the public interest; and should oppose the dismissal of any charges to which the defendant does not plead nolo contendere.

B. Comment

When a plea of nolo contendere is offered over the government's objection, the prosecutor should take full advantage of Rule 11(b), Federal Rules of Criminal Procedure, to state for the record why acceptance of the plea would not be in the public interest. In addition to reciting the facts that could be proved to show the defendant's guilt, the prosecutor should bring to the court's attention whatever arguments exist for rejecting the plea. At the very least, such a forceful presentation should make it clear to the public that the government is unwilling to condone the entry of a special plea that may help the defendant avoid legitimate consequences of his/her guilt. If the nolo plea is offered to fewer than all charges, the prosecutor should also oppose the dismissal of the remaining charges.

United States v. Hines

507 F.Supp. 139 (W.D.Mo.1981).

■ SACHS, DISTRICT JUDGE.

The question before the Court is whether I should accept a plea of *nolo contendere* offered by the defendant but opposed by the United States Attorney, pursuant to a departmental policy dating back to a 1953 directive, recently restated. . . . Although a guilty plea may be greatly preferred to a *nolo* plea, I . . . will generally accept a *nolo* plea if necessary to disposition of a criminal case without trial. Because . . . [this] position is said to be extraordinary . . . an explanation of my current thinking on the subject is desirable.

Prior to 1966 it could be said that the "only distinguishable feature between a plea of *nolo contendere* and that of guilty is that the former cannot be used against the defendant as an admission in any civil suit for the same act." Bell v. Commissioner of Internal Revenue, 320 F.2d 953, 956 (8th Cir.1963). By the 1966 amendment to Rule 11, Federal Rules of Criminal Procedure, however, the *nolo* plea serves a new purpose in that, as distinguished from a guilty plea, a *nolo* plea may be accepted without the usual prerequisite of fully satisfying the Court that the defendant has in fact committed the crime charged. . . . The *nolo* plea has thus become quite useful, in the Federal system, for dealing with the defendant who denies guilt, or elects to stand mute, while agreeing to entry of an adverse judgment and the imposition of punishment. Compare North Carolina v. Alford, 400 U.S. 25 . . . (1970), sustaining the constitutionality of accepting a state court guilty plea of a defendant who had in fact denied guilt. The Supreme Court observed in *Alford* (l.c. 36, note 8) that the revisers of Rule 11 thought it "desirable to permit defendants to plead *nolo* without making any inquiry into their actual guilt."

The Department of Justice now offers a stereotype that *nolo* pleas are reserved for "affluent white collar defendants," and may result in lenient treatment. Neither of these suppositions fits my experience, and greater use of *nolo* pleas may alter the generalizations.

A *nolo* plea does not affect my sentencing practices, except that I may take into account that a person offering a guilty plea may be more favorably considered because of apparent honesty and contrition. I would generally not consider protestations of innocence, as grounds for lenient sentencing, any more than I would consider such protestations after a jury verdict of guilty.

It has been my practice to accept a *nolo* plea on request, when a defendant resists admitting guilt in open court. It is generally very desirable for a defendant to make a full confession; that is, however, not always obtainable. Inquiry from the government as to the evidentiary basis for the plea is then useful to limit the possibility that the Court has before it an innocent person. The purpose of the distinction in Rule 11 would be defeated, however, by adamant insistence that the defendant in this case should herself provide a statement showing guilt.

The Court of Appeals for the District of Columbia has ruled that a district judge has a duty to accept a guilty plea tendered by a defendant who protests innocence, if there is a factual basis for the plea. . . . While the distinction may be one of word usage, I would treat such a tender as an offer of a *nolo* plea, rather than a "guilty" plea, and would generally accept it.

Trial in such an instance would usually be a wasteful ritual contrary to the effective administration of justice, and is therefore not required. Rule

11(b), Federal Rules of Criminal Procedure. It is not only "protracted litigation" . . . which should be avoided by accepting such pleas. Unnecessary trial of a short case is also wasteful. . . . [I]t may also be considered an unfair ordeal to impose on a defendant who does not wish to contest the government's case.

Based on the above reasons and the particular facts presented to the Court, defendant's plea of *nolo contendere* will be accepted, and a judgment of guilty based on that plea will be entered in the record. So ordered.

United States v. Chin Doong Art

193 F.Supp. 820 (E.D.N.Y.1961).

■ BARTELS, DISTRICT JUDGE.

This is an application by the defendant Chin Doong Art, a/k/a Arthur Lem, to enter a plea of *nolo contendere* to the first count of the indictment, alleging a conspiracy to violate the Criminal Code of the United States with respect to the entry, residence and citizenship of the defendant and others. The case against this defendant and others on the first and several other counts in the indictment was tried last year and the trial extended over a period of eight weeks, resulting in a deadlocked jury.

In support of his application defendant argues that a new trial would involve many additional witnesses on both sides; that the result would depend upon oral testimony mostly in a foreign language involving Chinese family genealogy; that even if an acquittal were obtained, it would not be conclusive because defendant would be subjected to further prosecution under two other counts which had been previously severed from the first count; that he was a prominent and useful citizen and named "Man of the Year" by the Town of Hempstead in 1958; that a plea of guilty would result in a loss of face not only to him but also to the Chinese community of which he has been a prominent figure; that such a plea would be prejudicial to him in a subsequent civil proceeding before the Immigration and Naturalization Service; and that no useful purpose would be served by a plea of guilty, whereas defendant would be spared harsh and unnecessary results by a plea of *nolo contendere*.

The Government opposes acceptance of this plea and argues that the co-defendant Chin Suie Tung has already entered a plea of guilty to count one and is available to the Government as a witness, and that four other alleged co-conspirators (not named as defendants herein) have entered pleas of guilty to charges of perjury before the Grand Jury; that today it is in a better position than ever to retry the case because it has many more witnesses; that since the defendant is an alien he would be subjected only to the administrative proceeding involving the cancellation of his citizenship certificate, with respect to which the proof and procedure would be the same whether or not he pleaded *nolo contendere*; that there are no extraordinary and exceptional circumstances present to justify the acceptance of a plea of *nolo contendere* and that to do so would be against the public interest and would breed contempt for Federal law enforcement.

There can be no question that this Court may, in its discretion, accept or reject the tendered plea. . . . Such principles as there are to guide it in the exercise of its discretion have been enunciated in many cases and need not be repeated here.

In this case a plea of *nolo contendere* would probably be beneficial to the defendant as far as his standing in the community is concerned and perhaps in other respects. This, however, is not the test. The Court must decide whether the circumstances of the case are so exceptional as to appeal to a favorable exercise of its discretion. Against such circumstances it must weigh the public interest which in the final analysis is paramount. As previously indicated, the policy of this Court has not been favorable to the acceptance of a plea of *nolo contendere*, unless the situation is an extraordinary one. Even then the interest of the public cannot be ignored. The presence of moral turpitude in the charge, as in this case, is often a factor in the determination. However, it has never been held that the nature of the proof to be advanced is relevant since such consideration by the Court might involve an investigation into the issues, the materiality of the proof and to some extent, the merits of the case, which are obviously beyond the scope of this application. Further, any difficulty in proof in this case imposes a greater burden upon the United States Attorney, who has the responsibility of deciding the Government's chance of success in determining the advantage to the Government of dispensing with the trial by consenting to the plea. Acting upon the recommendation of the Attorney General, the United States Attorney has most vigorously opposed the acceptance of this plea. Consequently, the defendant's statement that the previous trial resulted in a hung jury and that the case depends upon oral testimony, loses most of its appeal.

The fact that the case is a difficult and protracted one for the defendant does not *per se* present an exceptional circumstance for this plea, because again the burden is upon the Government to prove its case beyond a reasonable doubt. While the fact that the defendant had a good record in the past and is a prominent man who would lose face by a plea of guilty must be considered in his favor, it cannot override more important interests. Some question has been raised about the collateral effect of a plea of guilty as opposed to a plea of *nolo* in this case, but it is very doubtful whether a plea of *nolo* would offer the defendant any advantage in subsequent administrative proceedings involving his citizenship certificate. It is true that although one item alone may not be sufficient, all the circumstances related by a defendant when taken together may present a picture of exceptional hardship, justifying the acceptance of the plea. The Court, however, cannot reach a conclusion without at the same time considering the other factors militating against the acceptance of such a plea. After careful consideration of all the arguments and particulars, the Court is of the opinion that it cannot accept a plea of *nolo* in this case.

The primary purpose of accepting a plea of *nolo* is to promote the administration of justice. This means justice not only for the defendant but also for the public. The Court cannot permit its action with respect to a plea of this type to breed contempt for law enforcement. After acceptance of a plea of guilty from the co-conspirator (who is now available as a witness for the Government) and the pleas of guilty from the other defendants, it would not only be discriminatory and incongruous but would reflect upon law enforcement generally if the Court accepted a plea of *nolo contendere* from the most prominent of the two defendants. Therefore, the application is denied.

CHAPTER 12

PROCEEDINGS BEFORE TRIAL

FEDERAL RULES OF CRIMINAL PROCEDURE

Rule 12.

PLEADINGS AND MOTIONS BEFORE TRIAL; DEFENSES AND OBJECTIONS

(a) Pleadings and Motions. Pleadings in criminal proceedings shall be the indictment and the information, and the pleas of not guilty, guilty and nolo contendere. All other pleas, and demurrers and motions to quash are abolished, and defenses and objections raised before trial which heretofore could have been raised by one or more of them shall be raised only by motion to dismiss or to grant appropriate relief, as provided in these rules.

(b) Pretrial Motions. Any defense, objection, or request which is capable of determination without the trial of the general issue may be raised before trial by motion. Motions may be written or oral at the discretion of the judge. The following must be raised prior to trial:

(1) Defenses and objections based on defects in the institution of the prosecution; or

(2) Defenses and objections based on defects in the indictment or information (other than that it fails to show jurisdiction in the court or to charge an offense which objections shall be noticed by the court at any time during the pendency of the proceedings); or

(3) Motions to suppress evidence; or

(4) Requests for discovery under Rule 16; or

(5) Requests for a severance of charges or defendants under Rule 14.

(c) Motion Date. Unless otherwise provided by local rule, the court may, at the time of the arraignment or as soon thereafter as practicable, set a time for the making of pretrial motions or requests and, if required, a later date of hearing.

(d) Notice by the Government of the Intention to Use Evidence.

(1) At the Discretion of the Government. At the arraignment or as soon thereafter as is practicable, the government may give notice to the defendant of its intention to use specified evidence at trial in order to afford the defendant an opportunity to raise objections to such evidence prior to trial under subdivision (b)(3) of this rule.

(2) At the Request of the Defendant. At the arraignment or as soon thereafter as is practicable the defendant may, in order to afford an opportunity to move to suppress evidence under subdivision (b)(3) of this rule, request notice of the government's intention to use (in its evidence in chief at trial) any evidence which the defendant may be entitled to discover under Rule 16 subject to any relevant limitations prescribed in Rule 16.

(e) Ruling on Motion. A motion made before trial shall be determined before trial unless the court, for good cause, orders that it be deferred for determination at the trial of the general issue or until after verdict, but no such determination shall be deferred if a party's right to appeal is adversely affected. Where factual issues are involved in determining a motion, the court shall state its essential findings on the record.

(f) Effect of Failure to Raise Defenses or Objections. Failure by a party to raise defenses or objections or to make requests which must be made prior to trial, at the time set by the court pursuant to subdivision (c), or prior to any extension thereof made by the court, shall constitute waiver thereof, but the court for cause shown may grant relief from the waiver.

(g) Records. A verbatim record shall be made of all proceedings at the hearing, including such findings of fact and conclusions of law as are made orally.

(h) Effect of Determination. If the court grants a motion based on a defect in the institution of the prosecution or in the indictment or information, it may also order that the defendant be continued in custody or that bail be continued for a specified time pending the filing of a new indictment or information. Nothing in this rule shall be deemed to affect the provisions of any Act of Congress relating to periods of limitations.

(i) Production of Statements at Suppression Hearing. Rule 26.2 applies at a hearing on a motion to suppress evidence under subdivision (b)(3) of this rule. For purposes of this subdivision, a law enforcement officer is deemed a government witness.

---

380. In United States v. Barletta, 644 F.2d 50 (1st Cir.1981), the government sought a pretrial ruling that certain evidence that had been excluded at a prior trial was admissible. The government sought the ruling to protect its opportunity to appeal an adverse ruling under 18 U.S.C.

§ 3731, p. 896 below. The court of appeals held that the trial court may not defer such a ruling to the prejudice of the government's right to appeal under § 3731, if it is "capable of determination without the trial of the general issue" (Rule 12(b)), and the relevant proof is "almost entirely segregable from the evidence to be introduced at trial." Id. at 59.

Davis v. United States

411 U.S. 233, 93 S.Ct. 1577, 36 L.Ed.2d 216 (1973).

■ MR. JUSTICE REHNQUIST delivered the opinion of the Court.

We are called upon to determine the effect of Rule 12(b)(2) of the Federal Rules of Criminal Procedure on a post-conviction motion for relief which raises for the first time a claim of unconstitutional discrimination in the composition of a grand jury. An indictment was returned in the District Court charging petitioner Davis, a Negro, and two white men with entry into a federally insured bank with intent to commit larceny in violation of 18 U.S.C. §§ 2 and 2113(a). Represented by appointed counsel, petitioner entered a not-guilty plea at his arraignment and was given 30 days within which to file pretrial motions. He timely moved to quash his indictment on the ground that it was the result of an illegal arrest, but made no other pretrial motions relating to the indictment.

On the opening day of the trial, following *voir dire* of the jury, the District Judge ruled on petitioner's pretrial motions in chambers and ordered that the motion to quash on the illegal arrest ground be carried with the case. He then asked twice if there were anything else before commencing trial. Petitioner was convicted and sentenced to 14 years' imprisonment. His conviction was affirmed on appeal. . . .

Post-conviction motions were thereafter filed and denied, but none dealt with the issue presented in this case. Almost three years after his conviction, petitioner filed the instant motion to dismiss the indictment, pursuant to 28 U.S.C. § 2255, alleging that the District Court had acquiesced in the systematic exclusion of qualified Negro jurymen by reason of the use of a "key man" system of selection, an asserted violation of the "mandatory requirement of the statute laws set forth . . . in title 28, U.S.C.A. Section 1861, 1863, 1864, and the 5th amendment of the United States Constitution." His challenge only went to the composition of the grand jury and did not include the petit jury which found him guilty. The District Court . . . denied the motion. In its memorandum opinion it relied on Shotwell Mfg. Co. v. United States, 371 U.S. 341 (1963), and concluded that petitioner had waived his right to object to the composition of the grand jury because such a contention is waived under Rule 12(b)(2) unless raised by motion prior to trial. Also, since the "key man" method of selecting grand jurors had been openly followed for many years prior to petitioner's indictment; since the same grand jury that indicted petitioner indicted his two white accomplices; and since the case against petitioner was "a strong one," the court determined that there was nothing in the facts of the case or in the nature of the claim justifying the exercise of the power to grant relief under Rule 12(b)(2) for "cause shown."

The Court of Appeals affirmed on the basis of *Shotwell*, supra, and Rule 12(b)(2). . . . [W]e granted certiorari. . . .

Petitioner contends that because his § 2255 motion alleged deprivation of a fundamental constitutional right, . . . his collateral attack on his conviction may be precluded only after a hearing in which it is established that he "deliberately bypassed" or "understandingly and knowingly" waived his claim of unconstitutional grand jury composition. . . .

I

Rule 12(b)(2) provides in pertinent part that "[d]efenses and objections based on defects in the institution of the prosecution or in the indictment . . . may be raised only by motion before trial," and that failure to present such defenses or objections "constitutes a waiver thereof, but the court for cause shown may grant relief from the waiver." By its terms, it applies to both procedural and constitutional defects in the institution of prosecutions which do not affect the jurisdiction of the trial court. According to the Notes of the Advisory Committee on Rules, the waiver provision was designed to continue existing law, which . . . was, *inter alia*, that defendants who pleaded to an indictment and went to trial without making any nonjurisdictional objection to the grand jury, even one unconstitutionally composed, waived any right of subsequent complaint on account thereof. Not surprisingly, therefore, the Advisory Committee's Notes expressly indicate that claims such as petitioner's are meant to be within the Rule's purview. . . .

This Court had occasion to consider the Rule's application in Shotwell Mfg. Co. v. United States . . . .

Shotwell . . . confirms that Rule 12(b)(2) precludes untimely challenges to grand jury arrays, even when such challenges are on constitutional grounds. Despite the strong analogy between the effect of the Rule as construed in *Shotwell* and petitioner's § 2255 allegations, he nonetheless contends that Kaufman v. United States, supra, establishes that he is not precluded from raising his constitutional challenge in a federal habeas corpus proceeding. . . . We disagree.

. . .

Shotwell held that a claim of unconstitutional grand jury composition raised four years after conviction, but while the appeal proceedings were still alive, was governed by Rule 12(b)(2). Both the reasons for the Rule and the normal rules of statutory construction clearly indicate that no more lenient standard of waiver should apply to a claim raised three years after conviction simply because the claim is asserted by way of collateral attack rather than in the criminal proceeding itself.

The waiver provisions of Rule 12(b)(2) are operative only with respect to claims of defects in the institution of criminal proceedings. If its time limits are followed, inquiry into an alleged defect may be concluded and, if necessary, cured before the court, the witnesses, and the parties have gone to the burden and expense of a trial. If defendants were allowed to flout its time limitations, on the other hand, there would be little incentive to comply with its terms when a successful attack might simply result in a new indictment prior to trial. Strong tactical considerations would militate in favor of delaying the raising of the claim in hopes of an acquittal, with the thought that if those hopes did not materialize, the claim could be used to upset an otherwise valid conviction at a time when reprosecution might well be difficult.

. . .

We think it inconceivable that Congress, having in the criminal proceeding foreclosed the raising of a claim such as this after the commencement of trial in the absence of a showing of "cause" for relief from waiver, nonetheless intended to perversely negate the Rule's purpose by permitting an entirely different but much more liberal requirement of waiver in federal habeas proceedings. We believe that the necessary effect of the congressional adoption of Rule 12(b)(2) is to provide that a claim once waived pursuant to that Rule may not later be resurrected, either in the criminal proceedings or in federal habeas, in the absence of the showing of "cause" which that Rule requires. We therefore hold that the waiver standard expressed in Rule 12(b)(2) governs an untimely claim of grand jury discrimination, not only during the criminal proceeding, but also later on collateral review.

. . .

II

The principles of Rule 12(b)(2), as construed in *Shotwell*, are not difficult to apply to the facts of this case. Petitioner alleged the deprivation of a substantial constitutional right, recognized by this Court as applicable to state criminal proceedings . . . . But he failed to assert the claim until long after his trial, verdict, sentence, and appeal had run their course. In findings challenged only half-heartedly here, the District Court determined that no motion, oral or otherwise, raised the issue of discrimination in the selection of the grand jurors prior to trial. The Court of Appeals affirmed, and on petition for rehearing conducted its own search of the record in a vain effort to see whether the files or docket entries in the case supported petitioner's contention that he had made such a motion. We will not disturb the coordinate findings of these two courts on a question such as this.

The waiver provision of the Rule therefore coming into play, the District Court held that there had been no "cause shown" which would justify relief. It said:

"Petitioner offers no plausible explanation of his failure to timely make his objection to the composition of the grand jury. The method of selecting grand jurors then in use was the same system employed by this court for years. No reason has been suggested why petitioner or his attorney could not have ascertained all of the facts necessary to present the objection to the court prior to trial. The same grand jury that indicted petitioner also indicted his two white accomplices. The case had no racial overtones. The government's case against petitioner was, although largely circumstantial, a strong one. There was certainly sufficient evidence against petitioner to justify a grand jury in determining that he should stand trial for the offense with which he was charged. . . . Petitioner has shown no cause why the court should grant him relief from his waiver of the objection to the composition of the grand jury. . . ."

In denying the relief, the court took into consideration the question of prejudice to petitioner. This approach was approved in *Shotwell* where the Court stated:

"[W]here, as here, objection to the jury selection has not been timely raised under Rule 12(b)(2), it is entirely proper to take absence of prejudice into account in determining whether a sufficient showing has been made to warrant relief from the effect of that Rule." 371 U.S., at 363.

. . .

We hold that the District Court did not abuse its discretion in denying petitioner relief from the application of the waiver provision of Rule 12(b)(2), and that having concluded he was not entitled to such relief, it properly dismissed his application for federal habeas corpus. Accordingly, the judgment of the Court of Appeals is Affirmed.[1]

————

381. The reasoning and result of *Davis* were applied in a comparable state case in which the defendant sought federal habeas corpus. "[C]onsiderations of comity and federalism," the Court said, required that the state policy like the federal policy expressed in Rule 12 be given effect. Francis v. Henderson, 425 U.S. 536, 541 (1976).

————

[1] Justice Marshall wrote a dissenting opinion, which Justice Douglas and Justice Brennan joined.

Bill of particulars

FEDERAL RULES OF CRIMINAL PROCEDURE

Rule 7.

THE INDICTMENT AND THE INFORMATION

. . .

(f) Bill of Particulars. The court may direct the filing of a bill of particulars. A motion for a bill of particulars may be made before arraignment or within ten days after arraignment or at such later time as the court may permit. A bill of particulars may be amended at any time subject to such conditions as justice requires.

———

United States v. Moore

57 F.R.D. 640 (N.D.Ga.1972).

■ EDENFIELD, DISTRICT JUDGE.

Defendant is charged in an indictment whose complete text reads as follows: "That, on or about the 10th day of May, 1972, in the Northern District of Georgia, Andrea Moore knowingly and intentionally did unlawfully distribute about 1.07 grams of heroin hydrochloride, a Schedule I narcotic drug controlled substance in violation of Title 21, United States Code, Section 841(a)(1)." By her present motions defendant asks that the government file a bill of particulars and that she be allowed to inspect and copy certain enumerated items.

The requested bill of particulars asks the government to:

(1) State the location and address of the alleged distribution;

(2) State whether the alleged distribution occurred inside or outside a building, and if inside a building, state the type of building and the name of any residents or owners thereof;

(3) State the exact date and time of day that the alleged distribution occurred;

(4) State the names and addresses of all persons who directly or indirectly took part in the alleged distribution, either prior to, during, or immediately after the alleged occurrence;

(5) State whether any of the above-named persons were in the employ or were present at the insistence of the United States government, or in the employ of any State or local government;

(6) State the name and address of any informer acting in behalf of the United States government during the alleged distribution.

In its response, the government states that the alleged distribution took place "during the early evening hours" on May 10, 1972, at a residence located in an apartment building at 117 Davage Street, Atlanta, Fulton County, Georgia. The court finds that this information satisfies defendant's requests (1), (2) and (3), above, and as to these requests defendant's motion is denied.

The government has refused to disclose the information requested in paragraphs (4), (5) and (6), above, stating that, "It is sufficient for the purposes of Rule 7(c), Federal Rules of Criminal Procedure, that the indictment apprise the defendant of all the essential facts of the offense charged," and that "The indictment in this case closely follows the language contained in Title 21 U.S.C. § 841(a)(1)." The court disagrees with the notion that a statement of facts sufficient to sustain an indictment is a conclusive argument against granting a bill of particulars. As stated in United States v. Smith, 16 F.R.D. 372, 374 (W.D.Mo.1954), "[T]he fact that an indictment or information conforms to the simple form suggested in the rules is no answer or defense to a motion for a bill of particulars under Rule 7(f). Rule 7(f) necessarily presupposes an indictment or information good against a motion to quash or a demurrer." Rather, "[T]he court may exercise its discretion to order the filing of the bill for the purposes of: (1) informing defendant of the facts constituting the offense and the nature of the charge with sufficient particularity to enable the preparation of an adequate defense; (2) avoiding or minimizing the danger of surprise at trial; and (3) perfecting the record so as to bar a subsequent prosecution for the same offense. [Citations omitted.]" United States v. Davis, 330 F.Supp. 899, 901 (N.D.Ga.1971).

Because the motion for a bill of particulars is directed to the discretion of the court, and is addressed to dissimilar fact situations, it is unsurprising that the decided cases differ as to whether a defendant should be apprised of those who allegedly participated in the wrongful conduct charged, and whether or not their identity as government agents should be ordered disclosed. . . . While no definite rules in this area are possible, guidance is provided by the 1966 Amendment to Rule 7(f) and a number of decisions which have contributed to a desirable decline in the "sporting theory" of criminal justice. . . .

The 1966 Amendment to Rule 7(f) of the Federal Rules of Criminal Procedure, in the words of the Advisory Committee, was "designed to encourage a more liberal attitude by the courts toward bills of particulars without taking away the discretion which courts must have in dealing with such motions in individual cases." Especially recommended by the Committee as an illustration of "wise use of this discretion" was the opinion of Justice Whittaker in United States v. Smith, supra, written when he was a district judge for the Western District of Missouri. In *Smith* the information charged that on August 29, 1954, in Kansas City, Missouri, the defendant transferred several grains of heroin hydrochloride and one marijuana cigarette in violation of federal law. On motion of the defendant the court ordered the government to furnish a bill of particulars stating the date, time and location of the offense, along with the name of the person or persons to whom the defendant allegedly sold and transferred the controlled substances, and whether such person or persons were, at the time of the alleged transfer, employed by or acting at the instance of the government. Said the court: "Nor is it any answer to a motion for a bill of particulars for the government to say: 'The defendant knows what he did, and, therefore, has all the information necessary.' This argument could be valid only if the defendant be *presumed to be guilty*. For only if he is presumed guilty could he know the facts and details of the crime. Instead of being presumed guilty, he is presumed to be innocent. Being presumed to be innocent, it must be assumed 'that he is ignorant of the facts on which the pleader founds his charges'. (citations omitted) . . . Without definite specification of the time and place of commission of the overt acts complained of, *and of the identity of the person or persons dealt with* (emphasis supplied), there may well be difficulty in preparing to meet the general charges of the information, and some danger of surprise." At 375 of 16 F.R.D.

A decision which addresses the exact issue presented here, in the context of an almost identical fact situation, and is specifically cited by the Advisory Committee as an example of how Rule 7(f) should be applied, is strong authority for granting the requested relief.

In addition to *Smith* several cases both prior and subsequent to the 1966 Amendment have required the government to disclose the identity of persons either participants in, or victims of the crime allegedly committed.

. . .

The court recognizes that the present indictment makes no mention of the participants in the alleged unlawful distribution of heroin. Any distinction drawn between this case and those cited above, however, on the basis of the government having excluded reference to an easily supplied "John Doe" or to unnamed conspirators, the court finds to be insubstantial relative to the rights of the accused. In this case, as in *Smith* . . . the defendant has a right to know the names and addresses of those persons, known to the government, who directly took part in the alleged illegal act, and whether such persons were agents of the government. To hold otherwise, as stated in *Smith*, would be to charge the defendant with knowledge of an offense to which she is presumed innocent until proven guilty, and would be to deny information favorable to her case as either direct or impeaching evidence. . . . As a matter of technical pleading it may be questioned that the government should be required to disclose, pursuant to a motion for a bill of particulars, which if any participants in an alleged crime were agents of the government. A request for such disclosure, it might be argued, should be made in the form of a motion for discovery. . . . In the present action, however, such a two-step procedure would involve unnecessary delay where the government, required to disclose the identity of participants known to it, has only to indicate which of those participants were in its employ.

Defendant's motion for particulars is not granted as requested. Here . . . the court must rationalize the disclosure timetable of the Jencks Act,

18 U.S.C. § 3500 (1970), by which statements of witnesses to be called by the government need not be disclosed until trial, with that of Brady v. Maryland, 373 U.S. 83 . . . (1963), and its progeny, requiring the production of information helpful to the defense "at the appropriate time requested." Williams v. Dutton, 400 F.2d [797 (5th Cir.1968)] at 800. There exist here competing considerations of the defendant's right to information which will allow preparation of an adequate defense, and "the prosecution's concern that the furnishing of its witness list to an accused might lead to intimidation of the witnesses and might provide an accused with the opportunity to learn the witnesses' testimony in advance of trial and fabricate appropriate alibis." United States v. Houston, 339 F.Supp. [762 (N.D.Ga.1972)] at 765–766. In allowing defendant's request for particulars, therefore, the court requires the government to disclose the identity of only those persons who participated in and were present at the alleged distribution, or distributions if there were more than one, and does not require the disclosure, at this time, of the names and addresses of non-participant witnesses. . . .

. . .

---

382. "When a bill of particulars has been furnished, the government is strictly limited to the particulars which it has specified, i.e., the bill limits the scope of the government's proof at the trial. . . . This is not to say that *any* variance in the proof from the information in the bill of particulars is grounds for reversal. It is well settled that a variance between the proof and the bill of particulars is not grounds for reversal unless the defendant was prejudiced by the variance." United States v. Haskins, 345 F.2d 111, 114 (6th Cir.1965).

383. "It is obviously a matter of degree how far an accused must be advised in advance of the details of the evidence that will be produced against him, and no definite rules are possible. All that can be said is that he must know enough to be able to produce in season whatever evidence he may have in answer, and that the charge must become clear enough at the trial to make the judgment available to him on a future plea of 'former jeopardy.' The general doctrine is that the extent of the particulars granted lies in the discretion of the trial court, and any abuse of that discretion can of course be reviewed upon appeal." United States v. Russo, 260 F.2d 849, 850 (2d Cir.1958). Accord United States v. Davidoff, 845 F.2d 1151 (2d Cir.1988) (RICO prosecution; bill of particulars detailing uncharged racketeering acts required); United States v. Williams, 679 F.2d 504 (5th Cir.1982).

384. The defendant was indicted for perjury before a grand jury. One count of the indictment charged that she had falsely given a negative answer to the question: "Did you ever collect dues for the Communist Party?" Before trial the government filed a bill of particulars stating that the dues in question had been collected from two named persons "[s]ome-time during the day in the months of August, September and October of 1946. Sometime during the day in January, 1948." On the day after the trial started, the government filed a supplemental bill of particulars listing three additional persons from whom dues had been collected in "1945 and 1946." The prosecuting attorney indicated that although he had the information on which the second bill was based at the time the first bill was filed, it had slipped his mind when he filed the first bill due to "the busyness of his office" and he had recalled it to mind for the first time when he filed the supplemental bill; as soon as he recalled the information, he called defense counsel and advised him of it, prior to filing the supplemental bill. Defense counsel moved that the supplemental bill be stricken or that the defense be given a ten-day continuance to prepare to meet the evidence included in the supplemental bill. United States v. Neff, 212 F.2d 297 (3d Cir.1954). What result?

Joinder

FEDERAL RULES OF CRIMINAL PROCEDURE

Rule 8.

JOINDER OF OFFENSES AND OF DEFENDANTS

(a) Joinder of Offenses. Two or more offenses may be charged in the same indictment or information in a separate count for each offense if the offenses charged, whether felonies or misdemeanors or both, are of the same or similar character or are based on the same act or transaction or on two or more acts or transactions connected together or constituting parts of a common scheme or plan.

(b) Joinder of Defendants. Two or more defendants may be charged in the same indictment or information if they are alleged to have participated in the same act or transaction or in the same series of acts or transactions constituting an offense or offenses. Such defendants may be charged in one or more counts together or separately and all of the defendants need not be charged in each count.

Rule 13.

TRIAL TOGETHER OF INDICTMENTS OR INFORMATIONS

The court may order two or more indictments or informations or both to be tried together if the offenses, and the defendants if there is more than one, could have been joined in a single indictment or information. The procedure shall be the same as if the prosecution were under such single indictment or information.

Rule 14.

RELIEF FROM PREJUDICIAL JOINDER

If it appears that a defendant or the government is prejudiced by a joinder of offenses or of defendants in an indictment or information or by such joinder for trial together, the court may order an election or separate trials of counts, grant a severance of defendants or provide whatever other relief justice requires. In ruling on a motion by a defendant for severance the court may order the attorney for the government to deliver to the court for inspection *in camera* any statements or confessions made by the defendants which the government intends to introduce in evidence at the trial.

———

385. "Joint trials play a vital role in the criminal justice system, accounting for almost one third of federal criminal trials in the past five years. . . . Many joint trials—for example, those involving large conspiracies to import and distribute illegal drugs—involve a dozen or more codefendants. Confessions by one or more of the defendants are commonplace—and indeed the probability of confession increases with the number of participants, since each has reduced assurance that he will be protected by his own silence. It would impair both the efficiency and the fairness of the criminal justice system to require, in all these cases of joint crimes where incriminating statements exist, that prosecutors bring separate proceedings, presenting the same evidence again and again, requiring victims and witnesses to repeat the inconvenience (and sometimes trauma) of testifying, and randomly favoring the last-tried defendants who have the advantage of knowing the prosecution's case beforehand. Joint trials generally serve the interests of justice by avoiding inconsistent verdicts and enabling more accurate assessment of relative culpability—advantages which sometimes operate to the defendant's benefit. Even apart from these tactical considerations, joint trials generally serve the interests of justice by avoiding the scandal and inequity of inconsistent verdicts." Richardson v. Marsh, 481 U.S. 200, 209–10 (1987) (6–3).

United States v. Satterfield

548 F.2d 1341 (9th Cir.1977).

■ ANTHONY M. KENNEDY, CIRCUIT JUDGE:

In this case we reverse a robbery conviction, for the appellant was improperly joined with a codefendant for trial.

On October 9, 1974 a ten-count indictment was returned against appellant Satterfield and one Harvey Willard Merriweather. The charges pertained to five Oregon bank robberies committed in the greater Portland area during the summer of 1974. Merriweather and Satterfield were joined in a single indictment charging that Merriweather alone had perpetrated the first, second, and fifth robberies, and that Merriweather and appellant Satterfield together had committed the third and the fourth.

It was never alleged that Satterfield was involved in the first, second, and fifth robberies, whether as a participant in a common plan or in any other manner. The Government conceded as much at trial. The indictment, moreover, did not charge the defendants with conspiracy. A jury found both defendants guilty as charged. We affirm Merriweather's conviction by separate unpublished memorandum. We reverse the judgment against Satterfield and remand for further proceedings.

At various stages of the proceedings below, Satterfield timely moved for a separate trial on the ground that under Fed.R.Crim.P. 8(b), he had been improperly joined in the indictment. He contends that the trial court erred in refusing to grant his motions. We agree.

. . . Rule 8(a) applies only to joinder of offenses against a single defendant. Where more than one defendant is named in an indictment, the provisions of rule 8(b) control. . . .

Nevertheless, in evaluating an allegation of misjoinder of persons under rule 8(b), the controlling standards for such joinder are best understood by contrasting them with the standards for joinder of offenses in a single defendant trial under rule 8(a). While rule 8(a) permits joinder against one defendant of offenses "of the same or similar character," even where those offenses arise out of wholly separate, unconnected transactions . . . rule 8(b) treats joinder of *multiple* defendants differently. In United States v. Roselli, [432 F.2d 879 (9th Cir.1970)] we described the operation of the rule as follows:

Under Rule 8(b), the sole basis for joinder of charges against multiple defendants is that the defendants "are alleged to have participated in the same act or transaction or in the same series of acts or transactions constituting an offense or offenses." It is irrelevant that Rule 8(a) permits charges "of the same or similar character" to be joined against a single defendant, even though they do not arise out of the same or connected transactions. Charges against multiple defendants may not be joined merely because they are similar in character, and even dissimilar charges may be joined against multiple defendants if they arise out of the same series of transactions constituting an offense or offenses.

432 F.2d at 898. (citations omitted).

From the foregoing, it follows that Satterfield was properly joined in the indictment and for trial only if all of the offenses charged in the indictment arose out of the same series of transactions. Joinder under rule 8(b) cannot be based on a finding that the offenses charged were merely of the same or a similar character. In considering what constitutes a "series of transactions" we have stated that the term "transaction" is a word of flexible meaning. . . . Whether or not multiple offenses joined in an indictment constitute a "series of acts or transactions" turns on the degree to which they are related. In the cases under rule 8(b), that relation is most often established by showing that substantially the same facts must be adduced to prove each of the joined offenses. . . . We have thus stated that rule 8(b)'s " 'goal of maximum trial convenience consistent with minimum prejudice' is best served by permitting initial joinder of charges against multiple defendants whenever the common activity constitutes a substantial portion of the proof of the joint charges." United States v. Roselli, 432 F.2d at 899. Other logical relationships might also be sufficient to establish that a group of offenses constitutes a "series of acts or transactions," but a mere showing that the events occurred at about the same time, or that the acts violated the same statutes, is not enough. . . .

Notwithstanding our express policy that rule 8(b) should be construed broadly in favor of initial joinder . . . we are convinced that in the instant case Satterfield was improperly joined with the codefendant, Merriweather.

Most of the testimony at the trial related to the first, second, and fifth robberies, which were committed by Merriweather alone. The evidence against Merriweather was strong. Descriptions of a vehicle leaving the scene of the fifth robbery matched his car. A search of the car pursuant to a warrant revealed $5,000 in currency, and a mask and clothing similar to that worn at one or more of the robberies by a person later identified as Merriweather. Eye witness testimony and bank surveillance films from closed circuit television cameras were also introduced at trial to identify Merriweather as the perpetrator of the first, second, and fifth robberies. The evidence adduced at trial relative to the first, second, and fifth robberies pertained solely to acts undertaken by Merriweather alone. Furthermore, in a separate trial of Satterfield for the third and fourth robberies, evidence pertaining to the first, second, and fifth robberies would have been irrelevant. Thus, this is not a situation where substantially the same facts would have been adduced at separate trials. Since a nexus between each offense charged in the indictment was absent, we cannot say, on these facts, that the five robberies each arose out of the same series of acts or transactions. Joinder of Satterfield cannot be justified merely because the robberies which Merriweather perpetrated alone were somewhat similar in character to the robberies in which both defendants participated.

Relying on our holding in United States v. Patterson, 455 F.2d 264 (9th Cir.1972), the Government nevertheless argues that joinder was proper in this case because one of the defendants named in the indictment was mentioned in every count and because the modus operandi in each bank robbery was similar. It contends that this similarity provides the needed nexus between the joined offenses and establishes that the offenses charged constituted "a series of transactions." In *Patterson*, the indictment charged that the appellant and one Mortillaro had engaged in multiple counts of mail fraud; it was also alleged that Mortillaro and a third defendant, one Aquino, had engaged in offenses with substantially the same modus operandi. In holding that joinder under rule 8(b) was proper, we noted that Mortillaro was a common participant in each count and that the modus operandi in each count was "basically the same." Id. at 266. We concluded that appellant and the others were charged with "the same basic fraudulent scheme which they jointly and individually executed within a six month period." Id.

Patterson is distinguishable from this case on various grounds. First, a mere similarity in the manner in which several offenses are carried out—a similar "modus operandi"—is insufficient by itself to justify joinder under rule 8(b), absent some factual or logical relation among those offenses. In *Patterson*, the indictment charged that each incident of mail fraud had been carried out in an intricate and highly sophisticated manner that suggested a close connection among the offenses charged against the three defendants. Indeed, we found the existence of a "scheme" that had been jointly and individually executed. In this case, as noted above, the Government conceded at trial that the first, second, and fifth robberies were not part of any common scheme or plan in which Satterfield had participated.

As a practical matter, moreover, the five robberies in this case did not reflect a distinct pattern. They were certainly not virtually identical. Although the robbers were disguised during the robberies, the disguises were not the same every time. In any event, use of disguises is so common in bank robberies that resorting to the device on different occasions does not by itself constitute a common pattern. Any similarity between the disguises worn at the several robberies fails to reach the level of similarity present in *Patterson*, where each count charged that the defendants had engaged in complex criminal ventures that had been carried out in virtually the same manner. Given these factors, we reject the Government's claim that a similar modus operandi justified joining Satterfield in an indictment that charged Merriweather with the five robberies.

The Government makes a second argument, related to the "modus operandi" justification discussed above. It claims that evidence as to all the robberies would have been admissible to establish Merriweather's motive, intent, etc., even if he and Satterfield had been tried jointly in a prosecution limited to the third and fourth robberies. Citing our decision in *Roselli*, the Government concludes that because the evidence as to all robberies would have been admissible in a trial limited to the crimes in which both defendants allegedly participated, joinder was proper.

Although superficially appealing, the argument, on closer scrutiny, is unpersuasive. Even assuming that at a joint trial limited to the third and fourth robberies evidence of Merriweather's involvement in the other three offenses would have been admissible against him to show motive, etc., it does not follow that joinder under rule 8(b) was proper. The evidence put forth to prove an offense for which a defendant is tried will generally be more extensive, and thus more damaging, than that which would be adduced to establish a prior crime as proof of such matters as motive or intent. At a joint trial, where one defendant is charged with offenses in which the other defendants did not participate, the detailed evidence introduced to establish guilt of the separate offense may shift the focus of the trial to the crimes of the single defendant. In such cases, codefendants run a high risk of being found guilty merely by association. That risk was present here, where highly probative evidence was introduced to show that Merriweather had committed the first, second, and fifth robberies.

It is also significant that where evidence of prior criminal acts is proffered, the trial court has discretion to limit, or even to exclude, such evidence if its probative value is substantially outweighed by the danger of unfair prejudice, confusion of the issues, or misleading the jury, or by considerations of undue delay, waste of time, or needless presentation of cumulative evidence. . . . Where multiple offenses are charged in an indictment, however, a trial judge must permit the prosecution to establish each of those offenses beyond a reasonable doubt.

The Government's argument, moreover, is conceptually wrong. Where the prosecution introduces evidence of prior crimes to show motive or like matters, the test of admissibility is frequently whether the prior offenses are similar to those charged. As noted above, while such similarity permits joinder under rule 8(a), it is simply not sufficient for joinder under rule 8(b).

Finally, the Government argues that if joinder under rule 8(b) was improper the error was harmless and reversal is not required. The foregoing discussion, however, shows that Satterfield was substantially prejudiced by joinder with Merriweather. To reiterate: The jury first heard evidence on the fifth robbery, proof of which was exceptionally strong against Meriweather. Subsequently the jury heard evidence pertaining to the first and second robberies. This evidence, relating to Merriweather alone, could have had no other effect than to prejudice Satterfield in the precise manner against which rule 8(b) seeks to protect. Furthermore, the case against Merriweather for the three robberies committed by him alone was stronger than the case against Satterfield for the third and fourth robberies. Although the trial court instructed the jury that the evidence relating to the first, second, and fifth robberies concerned Merriweather alone, in our view the substantial proof of Merriweather's involvement in these robberies prejudiced Satterfield.

We recognize that even permissible joinder will often result in some prejudice to a defendant. The purpose of rule 8(b) is to limit joinder to those cases where considerations of trial efficiency clearly outweigh a defendant's interest in a separate trial. . . . In this case, serious prejudice to Satterfield has been demonstrated. Misjoinder under rule 8(b) therefore requires that his conviction be set aside.

. . .

---

386. "The justification for a liberal rule on joinder of offenses appears to be the economy of a single trial. The argument against joinder is that the defendant may be prejudiced for one or more of the following reasons: (1) he may become embarrassed or confounded in presenting separate defenses; (2) the jury may use the evidence of one of the crimes charged to infer a criminal disposition on the part of the defendant from which is found his guilt of the other crime or crimes charged; or (3) the jury may cumulate the evidence of the various crimes charged and find guilt when, if considered separately, it would not so find. A less tangible, but perhaps equally persuasive, element of prejudice may reside in a latent feeling of hostility engendered by the charging of several crimes as distinct from only one. Thus in any given case the court must weigh prejudice to the defendant caused by the joinder against the obviously important considerations of economy and expedition in judicial administration.

. . .

"It is a principle of long standing in our law that evidence of one crime is inadmissible to prove *disposition* to commit crime, from which the jury may infer that the defendant committed the crime charged. Since the likelihood that juries will make such an improper inference is high, courts presume prejudice and exclude evidence of other crimes unless that evidence can be admitted for some substantial, legitimate purpose. The same dangers appear to exist when two crimes are joined for trial, and the same principles of prophylaxis are applicable.

"Evidence of other crimes is admissible when relevant to (1) motive, (2) intent, (3) the absence of mistake or accident, (4) a common scheme or plan embracing the commission of two or more crimes so related to each other that proof of the one tends to establish the other, and (5) the identity of the person charged with the commission of the crime on trial. When the evidence is relevant and important to one of these five issues, it is generally conceded that the prejudicial effect may be outweighed by the probative value.

"If, then, under the rules relating to other crimes, the evidence of each of the crimes on trial would be admissible in a separate trial for the other, the possibility of 'criminal propensity' prejudice would be in no way enlarged by the fact of joinder. When, for example, the two crimes arose out of a continuing transaction or the same set of events, the evidence would be independently admissible in separate trials. Similarly, if the facts surrounding the two or more crimes on trial show that there is a reasonable probability that the same person committed both crimes due to the concurrence of unusual and distinctive facts relating to the manner in which the crimes were committed, the evidence of one would be admissible in the trial of the other to prove identity. In such cases the prejudice that might result from the jury's hearing the evidence of the other crime in a joint trial would be no different from that possible in separate trials.

"The federal courts . . . have, however, found no prejudicial effect from joinder when the evidence of each crime is simple and distinct, even though such evidence might not have been admissible in separate trials under the rules just discussed. This rests upon the assumption that, with a proper charge, the jury can easily keep such evidence separate in their deliberations and, therefore, the danger of the jury's cumulating the evidence is substantially reduced. . . .

. . .

"In summary, then, even where the evidence would not have been admissible in separate trials, if, from the nature of the crimes charged, it appears that the prosecutor might be able to present the evidence in such a manner that the accused is not confounded in his defense and the jury will be able to treat the evidence relevant to each charge separately and distinctly, the trial judge need not order severance or election at the commencement of the trial. If, however, it appears at any later stage in the trial that the defendant will be embarrassed in making his defense or that there is a possibility that the jury will become or has become confused, then, upon proper motion, the trial judge should order severance." Drew v. United States, 331 F.2d 85, 88–92 (D.C.Cir.1964).

There is a helpful discussion of the matter of joinder generally and the relationship among the provisions of Rule 8(a) and (b) and Rule 14 in United States v. Velasquez, 772 F.2d 1348 (7th Cir.1985). With respect to the element of same or similar transactions, see United States v. Grey Bear, 863 F.2d 572 (8th Cir.1988).

387. "Prejudice may develop when an accused wishes to testify on one but not the other of two joined offenses which are clearly distinct in time, place and evidence. His decision whether to testify will reflect a balancing of several factors with respect to each count: the evidence against him, the availability of defense evidence other than his testimony, the plausibility and substantiality of his testimony, the possible effects of demeanor, impeachment, and cross-examination. But if the two charges are joined for trial, it is not possible for him to weigh these factors separately as to each count. If he testifies on one count, he runs the risk that any adverse effects will influence the jury's consideration of the other count. Thus he bears the risk on both counts, although he may benefit on only one. Moreover, a defendant's silence on one count would be damaging in the face of his express denial of the other. Thus he may be coerced into testifying on the count upon which he wished to remain silent." Cross v. United States, 335 F.2d 987, 989 (D.C.Cir.1964).

"[N]o need for a severance exists until the defendant makes a convincing showing that he has both important testimony to give concerning one count and strong need to refrain from testifying on the other. In making such a showing, it is essential that the defendant present enough information—regarding the nature of the testimony he wishes to give on one count and his reasons for not wishing to testify on the other—to satisfy the court that the claim of prejudice is genuine and to enable it intelligently to weigh the considerations of 'economy and expedition in judicial administration' against the defendant's interest in having a free choice with respect to testifying." Baker v. United States, 401 F.2d 958, 977 (D.C.Cir.1968). See United States v. Scivola, 766 F.2d 37 (1st Cir.1985) (*Baker* followed; *Cross* distinguished).

See United States v. Jordan, 112 F.3d 14 (1st Cir.1997) (defendant prejudiced by joinder, which prevented him from presenting exculpatory evidence as to some counts; conviction on those counts reversed); United States v. Daniels, 770 F.2d 1111 (D.C.Cir.1985) (ruling denying severance even though joint trial allowed introduction of proof of defendant's prior felony conviction, which would not have been admissible as to one count had it been tried separately). *Daniels* is distinguished in United States v. Dockery, 955 F.2d 50 (D.C.Cir.1992) (denial of severance was abuse of discretion; conviction reversed).

388. Courts have sometimes held that an acquittal on some counts of an indictment indicates that the jury based its verdict on the evidence material to each count and that the defendant was not prejudiced by the joinder with respect to the counts on which he was found guilty. E.g., Gornick v. United States, 320 F.2d 325, 326 (10th Cir.1963) ("[T]he ordinary rule is that an acquittal on one misjoined count cures the misjoinder."); United States v. Rabin, 316 F.2d 564 (7th Cir.1963). But see *Cross*, note 387 above, 355 F.2d at 991.

389. The courts of appeals have usually declined to reverse a conviction because a motion under Rule 14 for separate trials of defendants was denied. So long as joinder was proper under Rule 8(b), the courts have relied on the rule that severance pursuant to Rule 14 is a matter within the discretion of the trial judge, whose ruling will not be reversed unless it is an abuse of discretion, and on the giving of instructions to the jury intended to prevent prejudice.

Confirming this practice, in Zafiro v. United States, 506 U.S. 534 (1993), the Court held that there is no "bright-line rule" that requires severance when codefendants have conflicting defenses. It said that "[m]utually antagonistic defenses are not prejudicial *per se*," and that even if prejudice is shown, severance is not necessarily required; rather, the appropriate relief, including measures like limiting instructions, is a matter for the "district court's sound discretion." Id. at 538-39. Noting the preference for a joint trial of codefendants indicted together, the Court said: "[W]hen defendants properly have been joined under Rule 8(b), a district court should grant a severance under Rule 14 only if there is a serious risk that a joint trial would compromise a specific trial right of one of the defendants, or prevent the jury from making a reliable judgment about guilt or innocence." Such a situation might exist, it said, when evidence that a jury should not consider with regard to one defendant is admissible with regard to the other or if exculpatory evidence with respect to one defendant would not be admissible at a joint trial. Id. at 539.

On the other hand, if there has been an improper joinder of defendants under Rule 8(b), courts have not hesitated to reverse. Misjoinder of defendants, however, is not reversible error per se, but is subject to harmless-error analysis. United States v. Lane, 474 U.S. 438 (1986) (7–2).

390. Bruton v. United States, 391 U.S. 123 (1968), casts doubt on courts' reliance on jury instructions to prevent prejudice in joint trials. Overruling Delli Paoli v. United States, 352 U.S. 232 (1957), the Court held that it was reversible error to admit a codefendant's confession inculpating the defendant even though the trial judge instructed the jury that the confession was inadmissible hearsay against the defendant and should not be considered in determining his guilt or innocence. Admission of the confession violated the defendant's "right of cross-examination secured by the Confrontation Clause of the Sixth Amendment," 391 U.S. at 126.[2] The Court said: "[In many cases] . . . the jury can and will follow the trial judge's instructions. . . . Nevertheless . . . there are some contexts in which the risk that the jury will not, or cannot, follow instructions is so great, and the consequences of failure so vital to the defendant, that the practical and human limitations of the jury system cannot be ignored. . . . Such a context is presented here, where the powerfully incriminating extrajudicial statements of a codefendant, who stands accused side-by-side with the defendant, are deliberately spread before the jury in a joint trial." Id. at 135–36.

"[W]here a nontestifying codefendant's confession incriminating the defendant is not directly admissible against the defendant . . . the Confrontation Clause bars its admission at their joint trial, even if the jury

---

2. The Court noted that the confession was clearly inadmissible against the defendant "under traditional rules of evidence," and that its conclusion was not an intimation that recognized exceptions to the hearsay rule "necessarily raise questions under the Confrontation Clause." 391 U.S. at 128 n.3.

is instructed not to consider it against the defendant, and even if the defendant's own confession is admitted against him. Of course, the defendant's confession may be considered at trial in assessing whether his codefendant's statements are supported by sufficient 'indicia of reliability' to be directly admissible against him (assuming the 'unavailability' of the codefendant) despite the lack of opportunity for cross-examination . . . and may be considered on appeal in assessing whether any Confrontation Clause violation was harmless. . . ." Cruz v. New York, 481 U.S. 186, 193–94 (1987) (5–4).

In Richardson v. Marsh, 481 U.S. 200 (1987) (6–3), the Court held that Bruton does not require exclusion of a codefendant's confession from which all references to the defendant have been eliminated and which incriminate her only when linked with other evidence introduced at the trial. "[T]he Confrontation Clause is not violated by admission of a nontestifying codefendant's confession with a proper limiting instruction when, as here, the confession is redacted to eliminate not only the defendant's name, but any reference to her existence." Id. at 211. Distinguishing inferential incrimination from direct incrimination in the codefendant's confession itself, the Court observed: "[W]hile it may not always be simple for the members of the jury to obey the instruction that they disregard an incriminating inference, there does not exist the overwhelming probability of their inability to do so that is the foundation of Bruton's exception to the general rule." Id. at 208. Bruton applies, however, if the defendant's name is redacted from the codefendant's confession and replaced by a blank or the word "deleted." Gray v. Maryland, __ U.S. __, 118 S.Ct. 1151 (1998) (5–4). Richardson was distinguished on the basis that there the confession had been redacted to omit any indication that another person had been named. Exclusion of a codefendant's confession is not required if he takes the stand and denies having made the confession. "[W]here a codefendant takes the stand in his own defense, denies making an alleged out-of-court statement implicating the defendant, and proceeds to testify favorably to the defendant concerning the underlying facts, the defendant has been denied no rights protected by the Sixth and Fourteenth Amendments." Nelson v. O'Neil, 402 U.S. 622, 629–30 (1971) (6–3). Cf. Tennessee v. Street, 471 U.S. 409 (1985). In United States v. Hill, 901 F.2d 880 (10th Cir.1990), the court held that, the codefendant not having testified, Bruton was violated even though the codefendant's counsel had stated in the opening statement that the codefendant would testify. The court observed that the defendant should not be penalized for his codefendant's change of strategy.

391. For cases involving possible or actual prejudice from the joint trial of several defendants, see, e.g., United States v. Breinig, 70 F.3d 850 (6th Cir.1995) (otherwise inadmissible prejudicial evidence admitted; conviction reversed); United States v. Romanello, 726 F.2d 173 (5th Cir.1984) (antagonistic defenses; conviction reversed); United States v. Provenzano, 688 F.2d 194 (3d Cir.1982) (inconsistent defenses, inability to call codefendant as witness; convictions affirmed); United States v. Starr, 584 F.2d 235 (8th

Cir.1978) (same); United States v. Crawford, 581 F.2d 489 (5th Cir.1978) (irreconcilable and antagonistic defenses; convictions reversed); United States v. Walton, 552 F.2d 1354 (10th Cir.1977) (codefendant's unexpected testimony incriminated defendant); United States v. Rosenwasser, 550 F.2d 806 (2d Cir.1977) (evidence admitted of similar crimes committed by codefendant, which implicated defendant); United States v. Lipowitz, 407 F.2d 597 (3d Cir.1969) (conflicting requests concerning instruction to jury on defendants' failure to testify); Brown v. United States, 375 F.2d 310 (D.C.Cir.1966) (codefendant asserted alternative defense of insanity); Temple v. United States, 330 F.2d 724 (5th Cir.1964) (defense counsel required to cross-examine witnesses jointly); Baker v. United States, 329 F.2d 786 (10th Cir.1964) (codefendants, husband and wife, of different races); United States v. Micele, 327 F.2d 222 (7th Cir.1964) (cross-examination of prosecution witness by codefendant's counsel incriminated defendant); Slocum v. United States, 325 F.2d 465 (8th Cir.1963) (codefendant pleaded guilty during trial).

United States v. Zafiro, 945 F.2d 881 (7th Cir.1991), aff'd, 506 U.S. 534 (1993), see note 389 p. 791 above, contains a good discussion of the circumstances in which a severance should be granted. The court observed that "mutual antagonism, finger-pointing, and other manifestations or characterizations of the effort of one defendant to shift the blame from himself to a codefendant neither control nor illuminate the question of severance." Id. at 886. See United States v. Novod, 927 F.2d 726, 728 (2d Cir.1991), in which the court said that the defendant must show "compelling prejudice" to invoke "retroactive misjoinder" of counts.

392. The defendants were indicted as follows:

Count One. The two Schaffers and the three Stracuzzas, for transporting stolen goods from New York to Pennsylvania, between May 15, 1953, and July 27, 1953;

Count Two. Marco and the Stracuzzas, for transporting stolen goods from New York to West Virginia, between June 11, 1953, and July 27, 1953;

Count Three. Karp and the Stracuzzas, for transporting stolen goods from New York to Massachusetts from May 21, 1953, to July 27, 1953;

Count Four. All defendants, for conspiracy to commit the substantive offenses charged in the first three counts.

It was conceded that the joinder of the charges in the indictment and the joint trial of the defendants were proper. At the close of the government's case, however, the conspiracy count was dismissed for failure of proof, the evidence having shown three separate operations all involving the Stracuzzas. On that showing, there was no basis for a joint trial of the Schaffers, Marco, and Karp. Schaffer v. United States, 362 U.S. 511 (1960).

Should the trial court grant a severance and a new trial to those defendants, the prosecution of the Stracuzzas having already been terminated by pleas? Suppose all counts had been submitted to the jury and its verdict was that the defendants were guilty respectively of all the offenses charged in the first three counts and they were all not guilty of conspiracy. See id. at 523–24 (Douglas, J., dissenting). See also United States v. Diaz-Munoz, 632 F.2d 1330 (5th Cir.1980) (*Schaffer* situation, in which trial court relied on government representation that proper joinder would be established; conviction reversed); United States v. Lane, 584 F.2d 60 (5th Cir.1978) (*Schaffer* situation; convictions reversed).

Consolidation

United States v. McDaniels

57 F.R.D. 171 (E.D.La.1972).

ALVIN B. RUBIN, District Judge. Twelve cases have been consolidated for the hearing of pre-trial motions. Some of the defendants moved to consolidate six of these cases for trial, into two groups of three each. The combinations sought are:

Criminal Action Nos.	Group I. Defendants
72–330	Deola R. Richardson, Clyde Jacquet, Carolyn S. McDaniels, Thelma L. Jones
72–331	Deola R. Richardson, Clyde Jacquet, Sharon Morgan, Doris Augustine, Gladys Fascio, Althea Oates
72–334	Deola R. Richardson
	Group II.
72–332	Deola R. Richardson, Theresa Robinson
72–333	Deola R. Richardson, Eartha Brown, Eartha St. Ann
72–335	Audrey Lee Delair, Eartha St. Ann, Samaria Justine Lambert, Valencia L. Smith, Brenda Cryer

Each Group would include eight defendants. The Group I trials would involve two conspiracies charged as 30 separate substantive offenses—a total of 24 counts—while the Group II trials would involve three conspiracies charged separately—32 separate substantive offenses totaling 24 counts.

Defendants urge consolidation on the following grounds: the prosecutions involve allegations of "identical related conduct," charged under the same federal statutes; the time span of the conspiracies and substantive acts charged in each case are virtually the same; it is likely that many of the witnesses in each case will be the same and that much of their testimony will be repetitious; the same defenses [as yet undisclosed] will be developed; the court will be called on to make the same rulings; and the instructions to the jury will be the same. Consolidation will enable counsel to concentrate their efforts and provide a more effective defense.

Further, the consolidation would:

A. Reduce the number of trials involving these two groups from six to two.

B. Only one instead of three defendants would face multiple trials.

C. Mrs. Richardson would face two trials instead of five.

Each argument requires separate examination.

Rule 13, F.R.Cr.P., permits the Court to order two or more indictments to be tried together "if the offenses, and the defendants if there is more than one, could have been joined in a single indictment . . . ." Rule 8(b) determines when two or more defendants may be charged in the same indictment: "if they are alleged to have participated in the *same* act or transaction or in the *same* series of acts or transactions constituting an offense or offenses." (Emphasis supplied.)

When, as here, more than one defendant is involved, the only applicable test for joinder is Rule 8(b). . . .

Rule 8(b) speaks of an allegation of joint participation in the acts or transactions constituting the offense or offenses, but it is not necessary to satisfy its terms that the allegation actually be made. it is enough if, on the facts, a single indictment covering all the defendants could properly have been drawn. . . . Separate indictments can be tried together under Rule 13, therefore, not only if they patently satisfy Rule 8(b) but if, given the facts, the charges could have been written in a way that would meet the requirements of Rule 8(b).

Rule 8(b) also permits a conspiracy count against all of the named defendants to be joined with substantive offenses, each against less than all the defendants, if the substantive offenses arose out of the conspiracy. . . .

Moreover, if defendants are charged jointly with a conspiracy and with substantive acts, the joinder is proper even if the jury acquits on the conspiracy count, the trial court dismisses the conspiracy count for lack of evidence, or the conspiracy count is reversed by an appellate court. . . . Thus, the permissibility of joinder depends not on the fact of joint participation in a conspiracy by all of the defendants but on whether such an allegation could reasonably have been made. . . .

Finally, the Court of Appeals for the Fifth Circuit has held that the Rule's joinder provisions "should not be interpreted in a technical or legalistic sense", but rather with a view toward its purpose of avoiding repetitious proof in separate trials. Tillman v. United States, 5 Cir.1969, 406 F.2d 930, 934.

Essentially, it is defendants' contention that the separate conspiracies charged in Nos. 72–330 and 72–331 could have been charged in one conspiracy in a single indictment, together with substantive offenses charged in Nos. 72–330, 72–331 and 72–334, and that the separate conspiracies charged in Nos. 72–332, 72–333 and 72–335 could have been charged in a single conspiracy, together with the substantive counts alleged in those three indictments.

But the defendants who are alleged to have conspired with Mrs. Richardson and Mrs. Jacquet in 72–330 and 72–331 are not alleged to have acted jointly with each other. While it is settled conspiracy law that all of the conspirators need not have contact with or even knowledge of the identity of all the other conspirators, so long as each conspired with common conspirators in a joint plan . . . it is necessary that there be some evidence that there was in fact a joint or common plan before joinder can be effected under 8(b).

The offenses must arise out of the same transaction or be connected. . . . The conduct upon which each of the counts is based must be part of a factually related transaction or series of events in which all the defendants participated, though not all of the defendants need participate in every act constituting the offense or offenses. . . . And even then, the common activity must constitute a substantial portion of the proof of the joined charges or joinder must fail. . . . The fact that the defendants in 72–330 and 72–331 are charged with the same or similar violations of the law based on conduct taking place during the same time span is not a basis in and of itself for a joint trial. . . .

The situation presented here is much the same as if A, B and C were charged with a conspiracy to rob Y Bank during the period September 1–15, 1972, and with the substantive crime of bank robbery on September 15, while, by separate indictment, A, B and D are charged with a conspiracy to rob Y Bank during the period September 1–15, 1972, and with the substantive crime of bank robbery on September 14. The offenses charged would be unconnected, not properly joinable. The government might fail in its burden of proof, and the defendants might be acquitted. Or it might develop at the trial that in fact there was one joint plan by A, B, C and D to commit two bank robberies. In that event, the charges of two separate conspiracies might fail. But the trial of the hypothetical charges would properly be separate and distinct.

The propriety of a joint trial must be determined on the facts presently available. These do not show that the defendants in the separate cases sought to be consolidated are charged with "identical related conduct" but only that they are charged with committing like crimes involving the names of other applicants during the same general span of time. Without additional factual data, the court can neither assume that there was a joint plan nor that the government will try to prove one.

In No. 72–330 and 72–334, Mrs. Richardson and Mrs. Jacquet are charged with conspiring with two other defendants in a scheme to use the United States mails to receive money fraudulently from the Louisiana Department of Welfare in the period October 7, 1970 to March 15, 1972. In No. 72–331, the same two defendants are charged with conspiracy with four other named defendants to accomplish the same crime in the period October 7, 1970 to February 15, 1972. The evidence adduced at the hearing on the motion to require handwriting exemplars tends to indicate that the offenses charged in these two indictments involve different applications for assistance in different names and different alleged forged endorsements.

In 72–334, where Mrs. Richardson is charged alone, there is no conspiracy allegation, but Mrs. Richardson is charged with substantive offenses that appear to have arisen out of the conspiracies separately alleged in 72–330 and 72–331. . . . It may well be that, by agreement, the counts against Mrs. Richardson that relate to one case could be severed from those relating to the other case, and those counts consolidated with the respective cases, but no motion to this effect has been urged, and the court doubts its authority to order such a division.

The defendants contend that the grand jury could easily have charged one conspiracy involving all of the defendants in 72–330 and 72–331, together with the substantive counts charged in the three indictments. Whether or not the evidence would support such a charge is unknown to the court. If a single conspiracy had been charged, it would have been necessary for the prosecution to prove that only one conspiracy existed, and proof of two separate conspiracies involving different parties would have required acquittal. . . . It is not for the court then to say, a priori, that there must have been evidence of one conspiracy.

Nor does this lodge absolute control over the form of trial in the government and the grand jury. The government and the grand jury have charged certain discrete crimes. The defendants may well urge that, whatever they have done, they have not committed the crimes charged.

Like considerations apply to the requested consolidation of Nos. 72–332, 72–333 and 72–335. In Count I of each of these indictments separate conspiracies are charged. The time periods of the conspiracies alleged in 72–332, 72–333 and 72–335 are September 30, 1970 to February 15, 1972; October 6, 1970 to February 15, 1972 and May 6, 1971 to February 15, 1972, respectively. Each alleges conspiracy to use the United States mail to obtain money fraudulently from the Louisiana Department of Welfare. In 72–333, Mrs. Richardson and Mrs. St. Ann are charged as co-conspirators with one other defendant. In 72–332, Mrs. Richardson is charged with conspiracy with another defendant. In 72–335, Mrs. St. Ann is charged with conspiracy with four others. These are each charges of separate conspiracies and separate crimes.

Finally, we deal with some of the arguments of administrative convenience. While the background testimony may be the same in each case, the details must necessarily be different. Each application must be separately considered. Each check must be separately introduced. It will not be necessary (or even permissible) for *all* of the applications and *all* of the checks to be introduced repeatedly. The handwriting experts will testify separately as to each individual and separately with respect to each application. No great time saving in these will result from consolidation.

Whether or not the defenses will be the same as to each defendant in each case, only the defendants' counsel knows and they perhaps cannot be certain at this time. Experienced defense counsel, like good quarterbacks, should, and do, reserve the power to call audibles even after the team is lined up for the play.

That rulings on the same legal issues may be required in various cases creates no problem. Presumably in connection with legal issues that arise at trial, like those considered in these pre-trial motions, the ruling in the first case on any issue will create a precedent in later cases. The same jury instructions may be required in each case, but, once framed, the court will be able to follow its charge in the initial case as a basic outline.

It must be conceded that consolidation would enable defense counsel to concentrate their efforts and perhaps to provide a more effective defense. But the fact that multiple defendants have chosen to employ one set of defense counsel should not alone be reason for consolidation.

The first of the separate trials will be shorter than a single consolidated trial. It is conceivable that the verdict in the first case might affect further proceedings. For example, if the defendants in the first case are acquitted, the United States might decide not to prosecute all or some of the remaining defendants. Or, if there is a conviction, some of the defendants might alter their strategy. Finally, consolidation would in any event result in multiple trials, since it is urged only that six of twelve pending cases be consolidated.

While, on the whole, administrative convenience would likely be better served by consolidation, the jury charges would be more complex because the jury would be considering three separate indictments, and the chances of jury confusion would be greater.

The requirements of 8(b) not having been met, the considerations relating to administrative efficiency are perhaps irrelevant. . . . But if the court has discretion, the efficiency and administrative desirability of consolidated trials do not appear to be so great as to justify consolidation, over the objection of either party. For these reasons, the motion to consolidate is denied.

Venue

———

"The trial of all crimes . . . shall be held in the state where the said crimes shall have been committed; but when not committed within any state, the trial shall be at such place or places as the Congress may by law have directed." U.S. Constitution art. III, § 2.

"In all criminal prosecutions, the accused shall enjoy the right to a speedy and public trial, by an impartial jury of the State and district wherein the crime shall have been committed, which district shall have been previously ascertained by law. . . ." U.S. Constitution amend. VI.

———

393. "Aware of the unfairness and hardship to which trial in an environment alien to the accused exposes him, the Framers wrote into the Constitution that 'The Trial of all Crimes . . . shall be held in the State where the said Crimes shall have been committed . . .' Article III, § 2, cl. 3. As though to underscore the importance of this safeguard, it was reinforced by the provision of the Bill of Rights requiring trial 'by an impartial jury of the State and district wherein the crime shall have been committed.' Sixth Amendment. By utilizing the doctrine of a continuing offense, Congress may, to be sure, provide that the locality of a crime shall extend over the whole area through which force propelled by an offender operates. Thus, an illegal use of the mails or of other instruments of commerce may subject the user to prosecution in the district where he sent the goods, or in the district of their arrival, or in any intervening district. Plainly enough, such leeway not only opens the door to needless hardship to an accused by prosecution remote from home and from appropriate facilities for defense. It also leads to the appearance of abuses, if not to abuses, in the selection of what may be deemed a tribunal favorable to the prosecution.

"These are matters that touch closely the fair administration of criminal justice and public confidence in it, on which it ultimately rests. These are important factors in any consideration of the effective enforcement of the criminal law. They have been adverted to, from time to time, by eminent judges; and Congress has not been unmindful of them. Questions of venue in criminal cases, therefore, are not merely matters of formal legal procedure. They raise deep issues of public policy in the light of which legislation must be construed. If an enactment of Congress equally permits the underlying spirit of the constitutional concern for trial in the vicinage to be respected rather than to be disrespected, construction should go in the direction of constitutional policy even though not commanded by it." United States v. Johnson, 323 U.S. 273, 275–76 (1944).

Although proper venue is a constitutional right, and is a fact to be proved, it does not have to be proved beyond a reasonable doubt like other elements of an offense. Proof by a preponderance of the evidence is sufficient. Furthermore, the test of waiver of a right to proper venue is more relaxed than the test for waiver of other constitutional rights. And a failure to instruct on venue is not, like a failure to instruct on other essential elements of an offense, invariably plain error requiring reversal. United States v. Miller, 111 F.3d 747 (10th Cir.1997) (failure to instruct on venue was reversible error, because not clear beyond a reasonable doubt that guilty verdict incorporated finding of proper venue).

FEDERAL RULES OF CRIMINAL PROCEDURE

Rule 18.

PLACE OF PROSECUTION AND TRIAL

Except as otherwise permitted by statute or by these rules, the prosecution shall be had in a district in which the offense was committed. The court shall fix the place of trial within the district with due regard to the convenience of the defendant and the witnesses and the prompt administration of justice.

Rule 20.

TRANSFER FROM THE DISTRICT FOR PLEA AND SENTENCE

(a) Indictment or Information Pending. A defendant arrested, held, or present in a district other than that in which an indictment or information is pending against that defendant may state in writing a wish to plead guilty or nolo contendere, to waive trial in the district in which the indictment or information is pending, and to consent to disposition of the case in the district in which that defendant was arrested, held, or present, subject to the approval of the United States attorney for each district. Upon receipt of the defendant's statement and of the written approval of the United States attorneys, the clerk of the court in which the indictment or information is pending shall transmit the papers in the proceeding or certified copies thereof to the clerk of the court for the district in which the defendant is arrested, held, or present, and the prosecution shall continue in that district.

(b) Indictment or Information Not Pending. A defendant arrested, held, or present, in a district other than the district in which a complaint is pending against the defendant may state in writing a wish to plead guilty or nolo contendere, to waive venue and trial in the district in which the warrant was issued, and to consent to disposition of the case in the district in which the defendant was arrested, held, or present, subject to the approval of the United States attorney for each district. Upon filing the written waiver of venue in the district in which the defendant is present, the prosecution may proceed as if venue were in such district.

(c) Effect of Not Guilty Plea. If after the proceeding has been transferred pursuant to subdivision (a) or (b) of this rule the defendant pleads not guilty, the clerk shall return the papers to the court in which the prosecution was commenced, and the proceeding shall be restored to the docket of that court. The defendant's statement that the defendant wishes to plead guilty or nolo contendere shall not be used against the defendant.

(d) Juveniles. A juvenile (as defined in 18 U.S.C. § 5031) who is arrested, held, or present in a district other than that in which the juvenile is alleged to have committed an act in violation of a law of the United States not punishable by death or life imprisonment may, after having been advised by counsel and with the approval of the court and the United States attorney for each district, consent to be proceeded against as a juvenile delinquent in the district in which the juvenile is arrested, held, or present. The consent shall be given in writing before the court but only after the court has apprised the juvenile of the juvenile's rights, including the right to be returned to the district in which the juvenile is alleged to have committed the act, and of the consequences of such consent.

Rule 21.

TRANSFER FROM THE DISTRICT FOR TRIAL

(a) For Prejudice in the District. The court upon motion of the defendant shall transfer the proceeding as to that defendant to another district whether or not such district is specified in the defendant's motion if the court is satisfied that there exists in the district where the prosecution is pending so great a prejudice against the defendant that the defendant cannot obtain a fair and impartial trial at any place fixed by law for holding court in that district.

(b) Transfer in Other Cases. For the convenience of parties and witnesses, and in the interest of justice, the court upon motion of the defendant may transfer the proceeding as to that defendant or any one or more of the counts thereof to another district.

(c) Proceedings on Transfer. When a transfer is ordered the clerk shall transmit to the clerk of the court to which the proceeding is transferred all papers in the proceeding or duplicates thereof and any bail taken, and the prosecution shall continue in that district.

Rule 22.

TIME OF MOTION TO TRANSFER

A motion to transfer under these rules may be made at or before arraignment or at such other time as the court or these rules may prescribe.

---

394. "[T]he *locus delicti* must be determined from the nature of the crime alleged and the location of the act or acts constituting it." United States v. Anderson, 328 U.S. 699, 703 (1946). For example, if the crime consists of failure to perform an act which the defendant has a duty to perform, the place where the act should have been performed is the *locus delicti*. Id. See, e.g., United States v. DiJames, 731 F.2d 758 (11th Cir.1984) (prosecution for failure to file required report; venue only in place prescribed by statute for filing, even though agency would have accepted report elsewhere); United States v. Bagnell, 679 F.2d 826 (11th Cir.1982) (interstate obscenity prosecution). See generally Travis v. United States, 364 U.S. 631, 634–35 (1961).

395. "[V]enue is an essential element to be proved by the Government. However, venue need not be proved by direct evidence. It may be established, as any other facts, by the evidence as a whole or by circumstantial evidence." United States v. Budge, 359 F.2d 732, 734 (7th Cir.1966). "The general rule governing proof of venue is that there need be no positive testimony that the violation occurred at a specific place, but that it is sufficient if it can be concluded from the evidence as a whole that the act was committed at the place alleged in the indictment." United States v. Karavias, 170 F.2d 968, 970 (7th Cir.1948). See United States v. Miller, 111 F.3d 747 (10th Cir.1997).

396. 18 U.S.C. § 3237. "Offenses begun in one district and completed in another.

"(a) Except as otherwise expressly provided by enactment of Congress, any offense against the United States begun in one district and completed in another, or committed in more than one district, may be inquired of and

AO 94 (Rev. 8/97) Commitment to Another District

UNITED STATES DISTRICT COURT

District of

| UNITED STATES OF AMERICA | COMMITMENT TO ANOTHER |
| v. | DISTRICT |

DOCKET NUMBER		MAGISTRATE JUDGE CASE NUMBER	
District of Arrest	District of Offense	District of Arrest	District of Offense

CHARGES AGAINST THE DEFENDANT ARE BASED UPON AN

☐Indictment   ☐Information   ☐Complaint   ☐Other (specify)

charging a violation of   U.S.C. §

DISTRICT OF OFFENSE

DESCRIPTION OF CHARGES:

CURRENT BOND STATUS:

☐Bail Fixed at   and conditions were not met
☐Government moved for detention and defendant detained after hearing in District of Arrest
☐Government moved for detention and defendant detained pending detention hearing in District of Offense
☐Other (specify)

Representation: ☐Retained Own Counsel   ☐ Federal Defender Organization   ☐CJA Attorney   ☐None

Interpreter Required?   ☐No   ☐Yes   Language:

DISTRICT OF

TO: THE UNITED STATES MARSHAL

You are hereby commanded to take custody of the above named defendant and to transport that defendant with a certified copy of this commitment forthwith to the district of offense as specified above and there deliver the defendant to the United States Marshal for that District or to some other officer authorized to receive the defendant.

| Date | United States Judge or Magistrate Judge |

RETURN

This commitment was received and executed as follows:

DATE COMMITMENT ORDER RECEIVED	PLACE OF COMMITMENT	DATE DEFENDANT COMMITTED

DATE:	UNITED STATES MARSHAL	(BY) DEPUTY MARSHAL

prosecuted in any district in which such offense was begun, continued, or completed.

"Any offense involving the use of the mails, transportation in interstate or foreign commerce, or the importation of an object or person into the United States is a continuing offense and, except as otherwise expressly provided by enactment of Congress, may be inquired of and prosecuted in any district from, through, or into which such commerce, mail matter, or imported object or person moves."

————

United States v. Busic

549 F.2d 252 (2d Cir.1977).

■ IRVING R. KAUFMAN, CHIEF JUDGE:

Prominent among the injuries inflicted upon the American colonists by King George III, according to the signers of the Declaration of Independence, was the despised practice of "transporting us beyond Seas to be tried for pretended offences."[3] This revulsion for adjudication of criminal charges in a remote region, before a jury drawn from a hostile or insouciant citizenry, was responsible for the codification of both Article III, section 2 and the Sixth Amendment to the Constitution. Today, when our vast country can be traversed in a matter of hours, these provisions stand as bulwarks against prosecutorial overreaching in forcing the defendant to answer accusations in a spatially distant and unfriendly environment. But two centuries have wrought changes in our society that have increased both the range of crimes that federal courts confront and the factors underlying the selection of the proper situs of trial. The instant case presents to us five alleged "skyjackers," a variety of malefactor of which the Founders never would have dreamed, and requires us to determine whether it is impermissible to try them in the Eastern District of New York, which embraces the busy airport at which they boarded the airplane they are charged with hijacking and is part of the major metropolitan area in which they reside and effected significant steps toward the ultimate commission of their crime. We believe that trial in that District is proper under the Air Piracy Act, and accords with the relevant constitutional policy. Accordingly, we reverse the order of the district court that dismissed on the basis of improper venue the substantive counts of the indictment, and remand the case for trial.

3. H. Commager, Documents of American History 101 (8 ed. 1968).

I. FACTS

. . .

Zvonko and Julienne Busic, Petar Matanic, Frane Pesut and Mark Vlasic were indicted for the September 10, 1976 hijacking of TWA Flight 355, which was scheduled to fly from LaGuardia Airport in New York City to Chicago. During the preceding several days, pursuant to a carefully devised plan, appellee Zvonko Busic had supplied false names when purchasing five tickets for the flight at various locations in New York City, including LaGuardia Airport. Prior to embarkation he placed a powerful explosive device in a Grand Central Station locker and discarded the key in the Hudson River. The appellees boarded the aircraft with a previously prepared typewritten hijack note and several cast iron pots, which escaped confiscation by security personnel because of an ingenious ruse. By wrapping them with gift paper and ribbons, the appellees convinced the operators of the airport's metal detection devices that the pots were presents for acquaintances. In addition, prior to boarding the appellees had prepared several imitation dynamite sticks by wrapping a quantity of putty in black tape commonly used by electricians. They also had filled their luggage with political pamphlets which they intended to scatter widely by throwing them out of the aircraft as it flew over several European cities.

These were the largely unknown background facts as they existed when the flight crew closed the doors of TWA Flight 355. Shortly thereafter, but before the airplane left the ground, a passenger attempted to use a lavatory in the rear of the cabin. Prior to reaching his destination, however, he confronted Vlasic, who was blocking the aisle. Drawing the passenger's attention to a large leather bag at his feet, Vlasic uttered the following command: "Stop, do not use the lavatory, there are three bombs in this bag. This is a hijack, return to your seat." The passenger complied.

The import of Vlasic's statement was clear and correct. Scant moments later, at an undetermined point beyond the boundaries of the Eastern District of New York, Zvonko Busic handed a note to a flight attendant for transmittal to the pilot. It read:

1. This airplane is hijacked.

2. We are in possession of five gelignite bombs, four of which are set up in cast iron pans, giving them the same kind of force as a giant grenade.

3. In addition, we have left the same kind of bomb in a locker across from the Commodore Hotel on 42nd Street. To find the locker, take the subway entrance by the Bowery Savings Bank. After passing through the token booth, there are three windows belonging to the bank. To the left of these windows are the lockers. The number of the locker is 5713.

4. Further instructions are contained in a letter inside this locker. The bomb can only be activated by pressing the switch to which it is attached, but caution is suggested.

5. The appropriate authorities should be notified from the plane immediately.

6. The plane will ultimately be heading in the direction of London, England.

Two to six minutes later, when the aircraft was in the vicinity of Buffalo, New York, the pilot received the message. By this time Busic, who had transformed the iron pots into imitation bombs in the lavatory, appeared in the cockpit and opened his jacket to reveal a "dynamite vest," which he threatened to detonate if his demands were not met. The pilot, pursuant to the hijacker's orders, flew the airplane first to Montreal and then to Gander, Newfoundland where 33 hostages were released prior to a transatlantic voyage. The hijackers eventually surrendered in Paris.

Authorities in New York, meanwhile, descended upon the locker in Grand Central Station referred to in the hijacking message and which contained the authentic explosive device planted by Busic as well as a list of demands. Following the instructions concerning publication set forth in the note, the New York Times, Washington Post, Chicago Tribune, Los Angeles Times and International Herald Tribune proceeded to afford prominent coverage in their morning editions to a Croatian "Appeal to the American People." Tragically, New York City police officer Brian Murray was killed while attempting to defuse the Grand Central bomb. Upon his return to New York, Zvonko Busic is alleged to have said: "We are proud of what we did. Don't be surprised if you hear about other attacks in the future. We are defending a just cause, yet we are with handcuffs on our wrists."

II. PROCEEDINGS BELOW

The grand jury charged the two Busics, Matanic, Pesut and Vlasic with two counts of air piracy, which are identical except that the first also alleges that the commission of the offense resulted in the death of officer Murray, 49 U.S.C. § 1472(i)(2), and conspiracy, 18 U.S.C. § 371. The appellees moved to dismiss the substantive counts of the indictment[4] because, they argued, venue was improper in the Eastern District. Judge Bartels granted the motion on November 22, 1976 and the Government appealed.

Judge Bartels was aware, as he stated in his opinion, that "none of the defendants and none of the witnesses will have anything more than a fortuitous connection with any district over which the plan flew other than the Eastern District of New York and its surrounding metropolitan area." Moreover, he realized that "the most logical place for air piracy cases to be tried would be in the district where defendants boarded the aircraft." He stressed that the appellees "conspired, prepared to commit the offense, had the intent to commit the crime and boarded the plane in this district." Nevertheless, he said they had not seized and exercised actual control over the aircraft before it had entered the airspace of the Western District of New York. And he reasoned that although 49 U.S.C. § 1473(a) authorized the laying of venue in, *inter alia*, any district where the offense of air piracy

---

4. It is conceded that venue for the conspiracy count is proper in the Eastern District of New York, where several overt acts occurred. . . .

had "begun," the acts here had not reached that stage "where the preparations have progressed to the first steps toward the commission of the crime, such as the first contact with the aircraft personnel notifying them of the intention to hijack" prior to the airplane's passing the boundaries of the Eastern District. Thus he concluded that under the relevant statutory provision venue clearly was improper in Brooklyn. We disagree and believe that the appellees plainly are triable in the place where the crime had "begun," the Eastern District of New York.

III. DISCUSSION

The Constitution and 49 U.S.C. § 1473(a) establish the parameters for our consideration of the instant appeal. Article III, section 2 provides that trials "shall be held in the State where the said Crimes shall have been committed; but when not committed within any State, the Trial shall be at such Place or Places as the Congress may by Law have directed." The Sixth Amendment, adopted after the Judiciary Act of 1789 divided the states into federal judicial districts, speaks similarly: "In all criminal prosecutions, the accused shall enjoy the right to a speedy and public trial, by an impartial jury of the State and district wherein the crime shall have been committed, which district shall have been previously ascertained by law. . . ." In cases of air piracy, Congress by special statute has determined that

> Whenever the offense is begun in one jurisdiction and completed in another, or committed in more than one jurisdiction, it may be dealt with, inquired of, tried, determined, and punished in any jurisdiction in which such offense was begun, continued, or completed, in the same manner as if the offense had been actually or wholly committed therein. 49 U.S.C. § 1473(a).

The appellees contend that the facts presented here make § 1473(a) susceptible to only one narrow constitutional reading, which would advance the moment of beginning so near the point of consummation of the crime that the words might as well be read as synonymous and without any significant statutory difference. They argue that the essence of the crime of air piracy, according to the language in the Act, is the intentional and forcible "seizure or exercise of control" of an aircraft. Thus the offense charged here cannot be committed until there is a transfer of control from pilot to hijacker. This, they say, did not occur until the airplane was flying over Buffalo. Moreover, they claim that the requisite transfer of control had not "begun" until Busic gave his threatening note to a member of the flight crew who then transmitted it to the captain. This event transpired, they argue, after the aircraft left the Eastern District and thus, the appellees are not triable there since all of their conduct prior to the precise moment when the hijack note was passed constituted "mere preparation" rather than a "beginning" of the crime.

We do not think that this tortured and hyperconstricted reading of the statute is warranted. Congress responded to a national epidemic of hijackings by making air piracy a federal crime. A major benefit of this action, according to the Report of the House Committee on Interstate and Foreign

Commerce, was the expected alleviation of the insuperable difficulties that law enforcement officials encountered in determining the exact state and county in which the seizure of an aircraft occurred. Recent airborne crimes had dramatically underscored gaps in existing laws that provided suspects with a haven from prosecution. . . . Any rational construction of § 1473(a) must account for Congress's special concern to permit a just and convenient locus for prosecution of this most unique crime which can begin and continue to be committed over several states in this high speed jet travel age in a matter of minutes. Accordingly, it appears—and the appellees do not seriously dispute—that Congress intended the Government to enjoy the broadest possible choice of venue within constitutional bounds.

The facts of this case bear eloquent testimony to the fact that the crime of hijacking had begun in the Eastern District of New York. Essential to the success of the appellees' scheme was their ability to board the aircraft with the cast iron pots and imitation dynamite sticks. Their goal was accomplished through an ingeniously conceived stratagem designed to circumvent the suspicion of airport security personnel. Busic purchased tickets for the flight at LaGuardia and elsewhere through the use of fictitious names. He planted a bomb in a locker at Grand Central Terminal with a list of demands. The appellees also filled their luggage with Croatian freedom pamphlets for ultimate distribution in European cities. Once aboard the airplane, and before it left the ground, Vlasic obstructed access to the lavatory (into which Busic went to construct his imitation explosive devices) and announced, "This is a hijack." In short, every one of the appellees' acts prior to the actual transmittal of the typewritten note was unambiguously corroborative of their unequivocal intention to hijack Flight 355. Under these circumstances it is obvious to us that 49 U.S.C. § 1473(a) serves its purpose well and intelligently by permitting prosecution in the Eastern District of New York.

It is equally clear to us that this result does not violate any constitutional rights of the appellees. Although Article III, section 2 concerns venue (place of trial) and the Sixth Amendment vicinage (residence of petit jurors), both can be traced to the ancient historical fact that at one time jurors decided cases on the basis of personal knowledge . . . and were drawn from the vicinity of the crime. . . . An even more significant source of these constitutional standards, however, can be discerned in the vigorous reaction of the American colonists evoked by Parliament's provision that trials of individuals accused of treason in Massachusetts be conducted in England. The Virginia Resolves responded to that edict by declaring: "thereby the inestimable Privilege of being tried by a Jury from the Vicinage, as well as the Liberty of summoning and producing Witnesses on such Trial, will be taken away from the Party accused." Journals of the House of Burgesses of Virginia, 1766–1769, at 214 (Kennedy ed. 1906).

The Framers' mandate for trial in the vicinity of the crime was meant to be a safeguard against the injustice and hardship involved when the accused was prosecuted in a place remote from his home and acquaintances. Indeed, the appellees in this case urge us to enforce this privilege, and cite to us Justice Frankfurter's oft-repeated language in United States v. Johnson . . . [p. 800 above].

Of course, the appellees would have us hold that the "vicinage" contemplated by the Founders and Justice Frankfurter forbade the Government, in this instance, from proceeding in the Eastern District and mandated that it prosecute in Buffalo, a city whose only contact with this case is the mere fortuity of being five miles below the speeding jet airplane that the appellees had just hijacked. We cannot perceive any justification in the Constitution for such a result.

We do not believe that the appellees' blind insistence that the dictionary meaning of the term "seizure" mechanically govern our interpretation of "begun" is warranted. Congress did not direct its statute to an abstract world of Platonic forms, but to the real world of action. We are compelled, therefore, to reject the appellees' attempt, by their crabbed construction of the term "begun," to fasten upon the federal Air Piracy Act the precise over-technicality that Congress explicitly wished to avoid. The many purposeful and unambiguous acts of the appellees in the Eastern District clearly support our determination that the crime of hijacking had begun there within the intent of Congress. It is incomprehensible to us that courts must conduct a potentially fruitless search to determine exactly where a crime is committed when the alleged perpetrators are traveling at 600 m.p.h. In the case before us the note was passed in New Jersey or Pennsylvania, but Busic first confronted the pilot in western New York State. If the steward had tripped, Busic may not have reached his destination until the aircraft passed over Ohio, or was speeding over the middle of Lake Erie. And since the appellees concede that the Government could indict and try them at any point over which the jet flew after leaving the Buffalo airspace, we are hard pressed to accept the validity of the argument that constitutional restrictions on prosecutorial discretion preclude trying this case in the Eastern District of New York, which Judge Bartels correctly recognized as the sensible one, but instead permit prosecution in other districts over which the aircraft chanced to fly after seizure, no matter how fortuitous the contact.

Finally, we believe that the extensive case law under 18 U.S.C. § 3237(a), the venue provision for so-called continuous crimes after which 49 U.S.C. § 1473(a) was modeled, supports, to the extent that it is relevant, the result we have reached. Generally applicable to mobile offenses other than air piracy, section 3237 requires an initial judicial inquiry into whether a particular crime involves a single act or movement. If the court determines, after considering the nature of the offense and the legislative and constitutional policies . . . that it requires only a single act, then the prosecution must proceed in the district where the crime was committed in toto; if the crime, however, involves a continuous course of conduct, the offense may be tried wherever it was "begun, continued or completed." Since the appellees concede, as they must, that hijacking is by its very nature a continuous crime, the many cases that limit prosecution to the solitary district in which the offense was "committed," and adjure conducting the trial where mere preparatory acts took place, are clearly distinguishable. . . .

The proper focus of our inquiry, rather, is upon cases such as United States v. Cashin, 281 F.2d 669 (2d Cir.1960) in which this court realized that the crime of use of the mails to facilitate a fraudulent scheme in violation of the Securities Act was begun in Alabama where "most of the acts necessary to [the] execution" of the crime occurred, although the alleged mailing took place in New York. Id. at 674. . . . The principle that is gleaned from these cases is that when the nature of the offense defies the notion that it was committed in a single district Congress may, within constitutional norms, fix venue wherever sufficient purposeful acts occurred. . . . In the case before us involving hijacking, a crime which Congress considered sufficiently unique to require its own special venue provision, we conclude that the appellees' alleged acts in the Eastern District of New York easily surpassed this behavioral threshold.

. . .

---

397. "[M]ere inconvenience, interference with one's routine occupational and personal activities, and other incidental burdens which normally follow when one is called upon to resist a serious charge do not ipso facto make the necessary showing that a transfer is required in the interest of justice. As a general rule a criminal prosecution should be retained in the original district. To warrant a transfer from the district where an indictment was properly returned it should appear that a trial there would be so unduly burdensome that fairness requires the transfer to another district of proper venue where a trial would be less burdensome; and, necessarily, any such determination must take into account any countervailing considerations which may militate against removal." United States v. United States Steel Corporation, 233 F.Supp. 154, 157 (S.D.N.Y.1964).

In United States v. Jessup, 38 F.R.D. 42 (M.D.Tenn.1965), a prosecution for mail fraud (18 U.S.C. §§ 1341–42), the court concluded on the basis of "such practical factors as the place of residence of the defendant, the expense and trouble to be caused by a trial in a far removed district, the expense involved in the transportation of witnesses, the volume of records and the difficulty of moving them, the economic loss to be suffered by an extended period away from one's place of work, [and] the advantage of being able to provide the jury with views of immovable exhibits, if permitted by the court," that the case should be transferred from Tennessee to Mississippi to avoid "substantial hardship" to the defendants. Id. at 45, 48. The court said that "apparently the only factor on the Government's side disfavoring a transfer is the fact that the indictments were obtained in this district and the United States Attorney here is familiar with this complex case, and has, doubtless engaged in some preliminary preparation"; this, the court said, "is of little moment since all of the factors militating in favor of a transfer were, or should have been known to the Government when it chose to prosecute in this district rather than in Mississippi or in one of the many other districts wherein it alleges these charges could have been brought." Id. at 48. Compare United States v. Stratton, 649 F.2d 1066 (5th Cir.1981) (grant of motion to transfer by some defendants resulted in improper venue for nonconsenting codefendants). See generally Jones v. Gasch, 404 F.2d 1231 (D.C.Cir.1967).

398. A motion for transfer is "addressed to the sound discretion of the trial court," whose decision "should not be overturned where there is no clear showing of abuse." Estes v. United States, 335 F.2d 609, 613–14 (5th Cir.1964).

Speedy Trial

"In all criminal prosecutions, the accused shall enjoy the right to a speedy and public trial. . . ." U.S. Constitution amend. VI.

"The right of a speedy trial is necessarily relative. It is consistent with delays and depends upon circumstances. It secures rights to a defendant. It does not preclude the rights of public justice." Beavers v. Haubert, 198 U.S. 77, 87 (1905). See Pollard v. United States, 352 U.S. 354 (1957). "[T]he Sixth Amendment's guarantee of a speedy trial . . . is an important safeguard to prevent undue and oppressive incarceration prior to trial, to minimize anxiety and concern accompanying public accusation and to limit the possibilities that long delay will impair the ability of an accused to defend himself. However, in large measure because of the many procedural safeguards provided an accused, the ordinary procedures for criminal prosecution are designed to move at a deliberate pace. A requirement of unreasonable speed would have a deleterious effect both upon the rights of the accused and upon the ability of society to protect itself." United States v. Ewell, 383 U.S. 116, 120 (1966).

399. "The right to a speedy trial is not a theoretical or abstract right but one rooted in hard reality on the need to have charges promptly exposed. If the case for the prosecution calls on the accused to meet charges rather than rest on the infirmities of the prosecution's case, as is the defendant's right, the time to meet them is when the case is fresh. Stale claims have never been favored by the law, and far less so in criminal cases. Although a great many accused persons seek to put off the confrontation as long as possible, the right to a prompt inquiry into criminal charges is fundamental and the duty of the charging authority is to provide a prompt trial. This is brought sharply into focus when, as here, the accused presses for an early confrontation with his accusers and with the State. Crowded dockets, the lack of judges or lawyers, and other factors no doubt make some delays inevitable. Here, however, no valid reason for the delay existed; it was exclusively for the convenience of the State. On this record the delay with its consequent prejudice is intolerable as a matter of fact and impermissible as a matter of law." Dickey v. Florida, 398 U.S. 30, 37–38 (1970).

In Smith v. Hooey, 393 U.S. 374 (1969), the Court elaborated the reasons for affording a speedy trial and said that they were fully applicable to a person already in prison for another offense.

"At first blush it might appear that a man already in prison under a lawful sentence is hardly in a position to suffer from 'undue and oppressive incarceration prior to trial.' But the fact is that delay in bringing such a person to trial on a pending charge may ultimately result in as much oppression as is suffered by one who is jailed without bail upon an untried charge. First, the possibility that the defendant already in prison might receive a sentence at least partially concurrent with the one he is serving may be forever lost if trial of the pending charge is postponed. Secondly, under procedures now widely practiced, the duration of his present imprisonment may be increased, and the conditions under which he must serve his sentence greatly worsened, by the pendency of another criminal charge outstanding against him.

"And while it might be argued that a person already in prison would be less likely than others to be affected by 'anxiety and concern accompanying public accusation,' there is reason to believe that an outstanding untried charge (of which even a convict may, of course, be innocent) can have fully as depressive an effect upon a prisoner as upon a person who is at large. . . .

"Finally, it is self-evident that 'the possibilities that long delay will impair the ability of an accused to defend himself' are markedly increased when the accused is incarcerated in another jurisdiction. Confined in a prison, perhaps far from the place where the offense covered by the outstanding charge allegedly took place, his ability to confer with potential defense witnesses, or even to keep track of their whereabouts, is obviously impaired. And, while 'evidence and witnesses disappear, memories fade, and events lose their perspective' [Note, 77 Yale L.J. 767, 769 (1968)], a man isolated in prison is powerless to exert his own investigative efforts to mitigate these erosive effects of the passage of time." Id. at 378–80. The Court held that a state could not disregard a defendant's right to a speedy trial on the sole ground that he was imprisoned in another jurisdiction.

400. In Klopfer v. North Carolina, 386 U.S. 213, 226 (1967), the Court declared that the right to a speedy trial was "one of the most basic rights preserved by our Constitution," and held that it was an element of due process constitutionally required of the states in state criminal proceedings.

Klopfer was a professor at Duke University who participated in a civil rights sit-in at a restaurant. He was indicted and prosecuted for criminal trespass, a misdemeanor. After one trial at which the jury failed to reach a verdict, the prosecutor obtained a *"nolle prosequi* with leave," over Klopfer's objection.

"Under North Carolina criminal procedure, when the prosecuting attorney of a county, denominated the solicitor, determines that he does not desire to proceed further with a prosecution, he may take a *nolle prosequi,* thereby declaring 'that he will not, at that time, prosecute the suit further. Its effect is to put the defendant without day, that is, he is discharged and permitted to go whithersoever he will, without entering into a recognizance to appear at any other time.' Wilkinson v. Wilkinson, 159 N.C. 265, 266–267, 74 S.E. 740, 741 (1912). But the taking of the *nolle prosequi* does not permanently terminate proceedings on the indictment. On the contrary, 'When a *nolle prosequi* is entered, the case may be restored to the trial docket when ordered by the judge upon the solicitor's application.' State v. Klopfer, 266 N.C. 349, 350, 145 S.E.2d 909, 910 (1966). And if the solicitor petitions the court to *nolle prosequi* the case 'with leave,' the consent required to reinstate the prosecution at a future date is implied in the order 'and the solicitor (without further order) may have the case restored for trial.' Ibid. Since the indictment is not discharged by either a *nolle prosequi* or a *nolle prosequi* with leave, the statute of limitations remains tolled. . . .

. . .

"The consequence of this extraordinary criminal procedure is made apparent by the case before the Court. A defendant indicted for a misdemeanor may be denied an opportunity to exonerate himself in the discretion of the solicitor and held subject to trial, over his objection, throughout the unlimited period in which the solicitor may restore the case to the calendar. During that period, there is no means by which he can obtain a dismissal or have the case restored to the calendar for trial. In spite of this result, both the Supreme Court and the Attorney General state as a fact, and rely upon it for affirmance in this case, that this procedure as applied to the petitioner placed no limitations upon him, and was in no way violative of his rights. With this we cannot agree.

. . .

". . . The petitioner is not relieved of the limitations placed upon his liberty by this prosecution merely because its suspension permits him to go 'whithersoever he will.' The pendency of the indictment may subject him to public scorn and deprive him of employment, and almost certainly will force curtailment of his speech, associations and participation in unpopular causes. By indefinitely prolonging this oppression, as well as the 'anxiety and concern accompanying public accusation,"[5] the criminal procedure condoned in this case by the Supreme Court of North Carolina clearly denies the petitioner the right to a speedy trial which we hold is guaranteed to him by the Sixth Amendment of the Constitution of the United States." 386 U.S. at 214, 216, 221–22.

401. Median time intervals from filing to disposition of criminal defendants disposed of by United States District Courts, Oct. 1, 1996–Sept. 30, 1997[6]:

	Total	Dismissed	Plea of Guilty	Court Trial	Jury Trial
Number	63,148	6,607	51,918	899	3,724
Median (months)	5.8	5.0	5.7	1.1	10.5

————

Barker v. Wingo

407 U.S. 514, 92 S.Ct. 2182, 33 L.Ed.2d 101 (1972).

■ MR. JUSTICE POWELL delivered the opinion of the Court.

. . .

I

On July 20, 1958, in Christian County, Kentucky, an elderly couple was beaten to death by intruders wielding an iron tire tool. Two suspects, Silas Manning and Willie Barker, the petitioner, were arrested shortly thereafter. The grand jury indicted them on September 15. Counsel was appointed on September 17, and Barker's trial was set for October 21. The

---

5. United States v. Ewell, 383 U.S. 116, 120 (1966).

6. From Table D–6, Annual Report of the Director of the Administrative Office of the United States Courts, 1997. "Filing" means the return of an indictment or the filing of an information. "Disposition" means dismissal of the case, return of a verdict of not guilty, or the imposition of sentence following a guilty plea or verdict of guilty. The very low median time for disposition of court trials is misleading. It includes a disproportionately large number of misdemeanors committed on U.S. military installations tried by U.S. magistrates in the District Courts for the Middle District of Georgia and the Eastern District of Virginia. Were those cases excluded, the median time would be between four and five months.

Commonwealth had a stronger case against Manning, and it believed that Barker could not be convicted unless Manning testified against him. Manning was naturally unwilling to incriminate himself. Accordingly, on October 23, the day Silas Manning was brought to trial, the Commonwealth sought and obtained the first of what was to be a series of 16 continuances of Barker's trial.[7] Barker made no objection. By first convicting Manning, the Commonwealth would remove possible problems of self-incrimination and would be able to assure his testimony against Barker.

The Commonwealth encountered more than a few difficulties in its prosecution of Manning. The first trial ended in a hung jury. A second trial resulted in a conviction, but the Kentucky Court of Appeals reversed because of the admission of evidence obtained by an illegal search. . . . At his third trial, Manning was again convicted, and the Court of Appeals again reversed because the trial court had not granted a change of venue. . . . A fourth trial resulted in a hung jury. Finally, after five trials, Manning was convicted, in March 1962, of murdering one victim, and after a sixth trial, in December 1962, he was convicted of murdering the other.

The Christian County Circuit Court holds three terms each year—in February, June, and September. Barker's initial trial was to take place in the September term of 1958. The first continuance postponed it until the February 1959 term. The second continuance was granted for one month only. Every term thereafter for as long as the Manning prosecutions were in process, the Commonwealth routinely moved to continue Barker's case to the next term. When the case was continued from the June 1959 term until the following September, Barker, having spent 10 months in jail, obtained his release by posting a $5,000 bond. He thereafter remained free in the community until his trial. Barker made no objection, through his counsel, to the first 11 continuances.

When on February 12, 1962, the Commonwealth moved for the twelfth time to continue the case until the following term, Barker's counsel filed a motion to dismiss the indictment. The motion to dismiss was denied two weeks later, and the Commonwealth's motion for a continuance was granted. The Commonwealth was granted further continuances in June 1962 and September 1962, to which Barker did not object.

In February 1963, the first term of court following Manning's final conviction, the Commonwealth moved to set Barker's trial for March 19. But on the day scheduled for trial, it again moved for a continuance until the June term. It gave as its reason the illness of the ex-sheriff who was the chief investigating officer in the case. To this continuance, Barker objected unsuccessfully.

The witness was still unable to testify in June, and the trial, which had been set for June 19, was continued again until the September term over Barker's objection. This time the court announced that the case would be

7. There is no explanation in the record why although Barker's initial trial was set for October 21, no continuance was sought until October 23, two days after the trial should have begun.

dismissed for lack of prosecution if it were not tried during the next term. The final trial date was set for October 9, 1963. On that date, Barker again moved to dismiss the indictment, and this time specified that his right to a speedy trial had been violated. The motion was denied; the trial commenced with Manning as the chief prosecution witness; Barker was convicted and given a life sentence.

Barker appealed his conviction to the Kentucky Court of Appeals, relying in part on his speedy trial claim. The court affirmed. . . .

II

The right to a speedy trial is generically different from any of the other rights enshrined in the Constitution for the protection of the accused. In addition to the general concern that all accused persons be treated according to decent and fair procedures, there is a societal interest in providing a speedy trial which exists separate from, and at times in opposition to, the interests of the accused. The inability of courts to provide a prompt trial has contributed to a large backlog of cases in urban courts which, among other things, enables defendants to negotiate more effectively for pleas of guilty to lesser offenses and otherwise manipulate the system. In addition, persons released on bond for lengthy periods awaiting trial have an opportunity to commit other crimes. It must be of little comfort to the residents of Christian County, Kentucky, to know that Barker was at large on bail for over four years while accused of a vicious and brutal murder of which he was ultimately convicted. Moreover, the longer an accused is free awaiting trial, the more tempting becomes his opportunity to jump bail and escape. Finally, delay between arrest and punishment may have a detrimental effect on rehabilitation.

If an accused cannot make bail, he is generally confined, as was Barker for 10 months, in a local jail. This contributes to the overcrowding and generally deplorable state of those institutions. Lengthy exposure to these conditions "has a destructive effect on human character and makes the rehabilitation of the individual offender much more difficult."[8] At times the result may even be violent rioting. Finally, lengthy pretrial detention is costly. The cost of maintaining a prisoner in jail varies from $3 to $9 per day, and this amounts to millions across the Nation. In addition, society loses wages which might have been earned, and it must often support families of incarcerated breadwinners.

A second difference between the right to speedy trial and the accused's other constitutional rights is that deprivation of the right may work to the accused's advantage. Delay is not an uncommon defense tactic. As the time between the commission of the crime and trial lengthens, witnesses may become unavailable or their memories may fade. If the witnesses support

---

8. Testimony of James V. Bennett, Director, Bureau of Prisons, Hearings on Federal Bail Procedures before the Subcommittee on Constitutional Rights and the Subcommittee on Improvements in Judicial Machinery of the Senate Committee on the Judiciary, 88th Cong., 2d Sess., 46 (1964).

the prosecution, its case will be weakened, sometimes seriously so. And it is the prosecution which carries the burden of proof. Thus, unlike the right to counsel or the right to be free from compelled self-incrimination, deprivation of the right to speedy trial does not *per se* prejudice the accused's ability to defend himself.

Finally, and perhaps most importantly, the right to speedy trial is a more vague concept than other procedural rights. It is, for example, impossible to determine with precision when the right has been denied. We cannot definitely say how long is too long in a system where justice is supposed to be swift but deliberate. As a consequence, there is no fixed point in the criminal process when the State can put the defendant to the choice of either exercising or waiving the right to a speedy trial. If, for example, the State moves for a 60-day continuance, granting that continuance is not a violation of the right to speedy trial unless the circumstances of the case are such that further delay would endanger the values the right protects. It is impossible to do more than generalize about when those circumstances exist. There is nothing comparable to the point in the process when a defendant exercises or waives his right to counsel or his right to a jury trial. Thus, . . . any inquiry into a speedy trial claim necessitates a functional analysis of the right in the particular context of the case. . . .

The amorphous quality of the right also leads to the unsatisfactorily severe remedy of dismissal of the indictment when the right has been deprived. This is indeed a serious consequence because it means that a defendant who may be guilty of a serious crime will go free, without having been tried. Such a remedy is more serious than an exclusionary rule or a reversal for a new trial, but it is the only possible remedy.

III

Perhaps because the speedy trial right is so slippery, two rigid approaches are urged upon us as ways of eliminating some of the uncertainty which courts experience in protecting the right. The first suggestion is that we hold that the Constitution requires a criminal defendant to be offered a trial within a specified time period. The result of such a ruling would have the virtue of clarifying when the right is infringed and of simplifying courts' application of it. Recognizing this, some legislatures have enacted laws, and some courts have adopted procedural rules which more narrowly define the right. The United States Court of Appeals for the Second Circuit has promulgated rules for the district courts in that Circuit establishing that the government must be ready for trial within six months of the date of arrest, except in unusual circumstances, or the charge will be dismissed. This type of rule is also recommended by the American Bar Association.

But such a result would require this Court to engage in legislative or rulemaking activity, rather than in the adjudicative process to which we should confine our efforts. We do not establish procedural rules for the States, except when mandated by the Constitution. We find no constitutional basis for holding that the speedy trial right can be quantified into a specified number of days or months. The States, of course, are free to prescribe a reasonable period consistent with constitutional standards, but our approach must be less precise.

The second suggested alternative would restrict consideration of the right to those cases in which the accused has demanded a speedy trial. Most States have recognized what is loosely referred to as the "demand rule," although eight States reject it. It is not clear, however, precisely what is meant by that term. Although every federal court of appeals that has considered the question has endorsed some kind of demand rule, some have regarded the rule within the concept of waiver, whereas others have viewed it as a factor to be weighed in assessing whether there has been a deprivation of the speedy trial right. We shall refer to the former approach as the demand-waiver doctrine. The demand-waiver doctrine provides that a defendant waives any consideration of his right to speedy trial for any period prior to which he has not demanded a trial. Under this rigid approach, a prior demand is a necessary condition to the consideration of the speedy trial right. This essentially was the approach the Sixth Circuit took below.

Such an approach, by presuming waiver of a fundamental right from inaction, is inconsistent with this Court's pronouncements on waiver of constitutional rights. The Court has defined waiver as "an intentional relinquishment or abandonment of a known right or privilege." Johnson v. Zerbst, 304 U.S. 458, 464 (1938). Courts should "indulge every reasonable presumption against waiver," Aetna Ins. Co. v. Kennedy, 301 U.S. 389, 393 (1937), and they should "not presume acquiescence in the loss of fundamental rights," Ohio Bell Tel. Co. v. Public Utilities Comm'n, 301 U.S. 292, 307 (1937). . . . The Court has ruled similarly with respect to waiver of other rights designed to protect the accused. . . .

In excepting the right to speedy trial from the rule of waiver we have applied to other fundamental rights, courts that have applied the demand-waiver rule have relied on the assumption that delay usually works for the benefit of the accused and on the absence of any readily ascertainable time in the criminal process for a defendant to be given the choice of exercising or waiving his right. But it is not necessarily true that delay benefits the defendant. There are cases in which delay appreciably harms the defendant's ability to defend himself. Moreover, a defendant confined to jail prior to trial is obviously disadvantaged by delay as is a defendant released on bail but unable to lead a normal life because of community suspicion and his own anxiety.

The nature of the speedy trial right does make it impossible to pinpoint a precise time in the process when the right must be asserted or waived, but that fact does not argue for placing the burden of protecting the right solely on defendants. A defendant has no duty to bring himself to trial; the State has that duty as well as the duty of insuring that the trial is consistent with due process. Moreover, for the reasons earlier expressed, society has a particular interest in bringing swift prosecutions, and society's representatives are the ones who should protect that interest.

It is also noteworthy that such a rigid view of the demand-waiver rule places defense counsel in an awkward position. Unless he demands a trial early and often, he is in danger of frustrating his client's right. If counsel is willing to tolerate some delay because he finds it reasonable and helpful in preparing his own case, he may be unable to obtain a speedy trial for his client at the end of that time. Since under the demand-waiver rule no time runs until the demand is made, the government will have whatever time is otherwise reasonable to bring the defendant to trial after a demand has been made. Thus, if the first demand is made three months after arrest in a jurisdiction which prescribes a six-month rule, the prosecution will have a total of nine months—which may be wholly unreasonable under the circumstances. The result in practice is likely to be either an automatic, *pro forma* demand made immediately after appointment of counsel or delays which, but for the demand-waiver rule, would not be tolerated. Such a result is not consistent with the interests of defendants, society, or the Constitution.

We reject, therefore, the rule that a defendant who fails to demand a speedy trial forever waives his right. This does not mean, however, that the defendant has no responsibility to assert his right. We think the better rule is that the defendant's assertion of or failure to assert his right to a speedy trial is one of the factors to be considered in an inquiry into the deprivation of the right. Such a formulation avoids the rigidities of the demand-waiver rule and the resulting possible unfairness in its application. It allows the trial court to exercise a judicial discretion based on the circumstances, including due consideration of any applicable formal procedural rule. It would permit, for example, a court to attach a different weight to a situation in which the defendant knowingly fails to object from a situation in which his attorney acquiesces in long delay without adequately informing his client, or from a situation in which no counsel is appointed. It would also allow a court to weigh the frequency and force of the objections as opposed to attaching significant weight to a purely *pro forma* objection.

In ruling that a defendant has some responsibility to assert a speedy trial claim, we do not depart from our holdings in other cases concerning the waiver of fundamental rights, in which we have placed the entire responsibility on the prosecution to show that the claimed waiver was knowingly and voluntarily made. Such cases have involved rights which must be exercised or waived at a specific time or under clearly identifiable circumstances, such as the rights to plead not guilty, to demand a jury trial, to exercise the privilege against self incrimination, and to have the assistance of counsel. We have shown above that the right to a speedy trial is unique in its uncertainty as to when and under what circumstances it must be asserted or may be deemed waived. But the rule we announce today, which comports with constitutional principles, places the primary burden on the courts and the prosecutors to assure that cases are brought to trial. We hardly need add that if delay is attributable to the defendant, then his waiver may be given effect under standard waiver doctrine, the demand rule aside.

We, therefore, reject both of the inflexible approaches—the fixed-time period because it goes further than the Constitution requires; the demand-waiver rule because it is insensitive to a right which we have deemed fundamental. The approach we accept is a balancing test, in which the conduct of both the prosecution and the defendant are weighed.[9]

IV

A balancing test necessarily compels courts to approach speedy trial cases on an *ad hoc* basis. We can do little more than identify some of the factors which courts should assess in determining whether a particular defendant has been deprived of his right. Though some might express them in different ways, we identify four such factors: Length of delay, the reason for the delay, the defendant's assertion of his right, and prejudice to the defendant.

The length of the delay is to some extent a triggering mechanism. Until there is some delay which is presumptively prejudicial, there is no necessity for inquiry into the other factors that go into the balance. Nevertheless, because of the imprecision of the right to speedy trial, the length of delay that will provoke such an inquiry is necessarily dependent upon the peculiar circumstances of the case. To take but one example, the delay that can be tolerated for an ordinary street crime is considerably less than for a serious, complex conspiracy charge.

Closely related to length of delay is the reason the government assigns to justify the delay. Here, too, different weights should be assigned to different reasons. A deliberate attempt to delay the trial in order to hamper the defense should be weighed heavily against the government. A more neutral reason such as negligence or overcrowded courts should be weighed less heavily but nevertheless should be considered since the ultimate responsibility for such circumstances must rest with the government rather than with the defendant. Finally, a valid reason, such as a missing witness, should serve to justify appropriate delay.

We have already discussed the third factor, the defendant's responsibility to assert his right. Whether and how a defendant asserts his right is closely related to the other factors we have mentioned. The strength of his efforts will be affected by the length of the delay, to some extent by the reason for the delay, and most particularly by the personal prejudice, which is not always readily identifiable, that he experiences. The more serious the deprivation, the more likely a defendant is to complain. The defendant's assertion of his speedy trial right, then, is entitled to strong evidentiary weight in determining whether the defendant is being deprived of the right. We emphasize that failure to assert the right will make it difficult for a defendant to prove that he was denied a speedy trial.

---

9. Nothing we have said should be interpreted as disapproving a presumptive rule adopted by a court in the exercise of its supervisory powers which establishes a fixed time period within which cases must normally be brought. . . .

A fourth factor is prejudice to the defendant. Prejudice, of course, should be assessed in the light of the interests of defendants which the speedy trial right was designed to protect. This Court has identified three such interests: (i) to prevent oppressive pretrial incarceration; (ii) to minimize anxiety and concern of the accused; and (iii) to limit the possibility that the defense will be impaired. Of these, the most serious is the last, because the inability of a defendant adequately to prepare his case skews the fairness of the entire system. If witnesses die or disappear during a delay, the prejudice is obvious. There is also prejudice if defense witnesses are unable to recall accurately events of the distant past. Loss of memory, however, is not always reflected in the record because what has been forgotten can rarely be shown.

We have discussed previously the societal disadvantages of lengthy pretrial incarceration, but obviously the disadvantages for the accused who cannot obtain his release are even more serious. The time spent in jail awaiting trial has a detrimental impact on the individual. It often means loss of a job; it disrupts family life; and it enforces idleness. Most jails offer little or no recreational or rehabilitative programs. The time spent in jail is simply dead time. Moreover, if a defendant is locked up, he is hindered in his ability to gather evidence, contact witnesses, or otherwise prepare his defense. Imposing those consequences on anyone who has not yet been convicted is serious. It is especially unfortunate to impose them on those persons who are ultimately found to be innocent. Finally, even if an accused is not incarcerated prior to trial, he is still disadvantaged by restraints on his liberty and by living under a cloud of anxiety, suspicion, and often hostility. . . .

We regard none of the four factors identified above as either a necessary or sufficient condition to the finding of a deprivation of the right of speedy trial. Rather, they are related factors and must be considered together with such other circumstances as may be relevant. In sum, these factors have no talismanic qualities; courts must still engage in a difficult and sensitive balancing process. But, because we are dealing with a fundamental right of the accused, this process must be carried out with full recognition that the accused's interest in a speedy trial is specifically affirmed in the Constitution.

V

The difficulty of the task of balancing these factors is illustrated by this case, which we consider to be close. It is clear that the length of delay between arrest and trial—well over five years—was extraordinary. Only seven months of that period can be attributed to a strong excuse, the illness of the ex-sheriff who was in charge of the investigation. Perhaps some delay would have been permissible under ordinary circumstances, so that Manning could be utilized as a witness in Barker's trial, but more than four years was too long a period, particularly since a good part of that period was attributable to the Commonwealth's failure or inability to try Manning under circumstances that comported with due process.

Two counterbalancing factors, however, outweigh these deficiencies. The first is that prejudice was minimal. Of course, Barker was prejudiced to some extent by living for over four years under a cloud of suspicion and anxiety. Moreover, although he was released on bond for most of the period, he did spend 10 months in jail before trial. But there is no claim that any of Barker's witnesses died or otherwise became unavailable owing to the delay. The trial transcript indicates only two very minor lapses of memory—one on the part of a prosecution witness—which were in no way significant to the outcome.

More important than the absence of serious prejudice, is the fact that Barker did not want a speedy trial. Counsel was appointed for Barker immediately after his indictment and represented him throughout the period. No question is raised as to the competency of such counsel. Despite the fact that counsel had notice of the motions for continuances, the record shows no action whatever taken between October 21, 1958, and February 12, 1962, that could be construed as the assertion of the speedy trial right. On the latter date, in response to another motion for continuance, Barker moved to dismiss the indictment. The record does not show on what ground this motion was based, although it is clear that no alternative motion was made for an immediate trial. Instead the record strongly suggests that while he hoped to take advantage of the delay in which he had acquiesced, and thereby obtain a dismissal of the charges, he definitely did not want to be tried. . . . The probable reason for Barker's attitude was that he was gambling on Manning's acquittal. The evidence was not very strong against Manning, as the reversals and hung juries suggest, and Barker undoubtedly thought that if Manning were acquitted, he would never be tried. . . .

That Barker was gambling on Manning's acquittal is also suggested by his failure, following the pro forma motion to dismiss filed in February 1962, to object to the Commonwealth's next two motions for continuances. Indeed, it was not until March 1963, after Manning's convictions were final, that Barker, having lost his gamble, began to object to further continuances. At that time, the Commonwealth's excuse was the illness of the ex-sheriff, which Barker has conceded justified the further delay.

We do not hold that there may never be a situation in which an indictment may be dismissed on speedy trial grounds where the defendant has failed to object to continuances. There may be a situation in which the defendant was represented by incompetent counsel, was severely prejudiced, or even cases in which the continuances were granted ex parte. But barring extraordinary circumstances, we would be reluctant indeed to rule that a defendant was denied this constitutional right on a record that strongly indicates, as does this one, that the defendant did not want a speedy trial. We hold, therefore, that Barker was not deprived of his due process right to a speedy trial.

. . .[10]

---

[10] Justice White wrote a concurring opinion, which Justice Brennan joined.

402. The Court emphasized that once the defendant is arrested, the constitutional right to a speedy trial comes into play, whether or not he has been formally charged by indictment or information, in Dillingham v. United States, 423 U.S. 64 (1975).

Delay attributable to the government's interlocutory appeal while the defendant is under indictment or subject to restraint is governed by *Barker.* United States v. Loud Hawk, 474 U.S. 302 (1986) (5–4).

The right to a speedy trial applies to the period between conviction and sentence. See Pollard v. United States, 352 U.S. 354, 361 (1957) ("arguendo"); Perez v. Sullivan, 793 F.2d 249 (10th Cir.1986) (additional cases cited). In *Perez*, the court concluded that a 15-month delay between conviction pursuant to a guilty plea and sentence, during which period the defendant was in jail, did not violate the right to a speedy trial. See Burkett v. Cunningham, 826 F.2d 1208 (3d Cir.1987) (5½-year delay in sentencing; conviction vacated). See also United States v. Mohawk, 20 F.3d 1480 (9th Cir.1994) (10-year delay between defendant's conviction and decision of his timely appeal, although "appalling" and "unconscionable," does not prohibit retrial following reversal of his conviction).

In Moore v. Arizona, 414 U.S. 25, 26 (1973), the Court observed that in Barker v. Wingo, it had "expressly rejected the notion that an affirmative demonstration of prejudice was necessary to prove a denial of the constitutional right to a speedy trial. . . . In addition to possible prejudice, any court must thus carefully weigh the reasons for the delay in bringing an incarcerated defendant to trial." On the element of prejudice, see Cain v. Smith, 686 F.2d 374 (6th Cir.1982), which the court described as a "paradigm example" of the prejudice suffered by a defendant who is detained before trial. See also United States v. Calloway, 505 F.2d 311 (D.C.Cir.1974) (discussing the harmful personal effects of pretrial detention; indictment dismissed).

The Court held that an 8½-year delay between the defendant's indictment and trial violated his right to a speedy trial, in Doggett v. United States, 505 U.S. 647 (1992) (5–4). The Court observed that the right to a speedy trial protects a defendant's interest in fair adjudication, which excessive delay may affect in unidentifiable ways. In this case, the delay presumptively prejudiced the defendant, despite his failure to cite specific demonstrable prejudice. The other *Barker* factors also weighing in the defendant's favor, his right to a speedy trial was denied.

For a very restrictive application of the *Barker* test, see Flowers v. Warden, Connecticut Correctional Institution, Somers, 853 F.2d 131 (2d Cir.1988) (other cases cited), reversing 677 F.Supp. 1275 (D.Conn.1988).

Courts have held that the Due Process Clause confers a right to the decision of a criminal appeal without unreasonable delay; and, although *Barker* was based on the Sixth Amendment's right to a speedy trial, they have applied the *Barker* tests to determine whether the appeal right was violated. E.g., United States v. Smith, 94 F.3d 204 (6th Cir.1996).

403. The Court confirmed the statement in Barker v. Wingo, p. 814 above, that "the only possible remedy" for denial of the right to a speedy trial is dismissal of the charges, [id. at 817, in Strunk v. United States, 412 U.S. 434 (1973).

The denial of a pretrial motion to dismiss an indictment because of alleged denial of the right to a speedy trial is *not* an order that is subject to interlocutory appellate review. United States v. MacDonald, 435 U.S. 850 (1978). The Court contrasted denial of a pretrial motion to dismiss on the ground of double jeopardy, see Abney v. United States, 431 U.S. 651 (1977). The basis for the speedy trial claim, the Court said, is often not clear before the trial, because it may not be possible to measure prejudice from the delay. Furthermore, the right to a speedy trial is denied by the delay before trial, not by the trial itself—unlike the protection of the Double Jeopardy Clause, which is a right not to be tried a second time. Also, allowance of an interlocutory appeal would furnish an easy means of delaying trial. The Court observed that denial of a motion to dismiss before trial does not mean that another motion made after trial, when prejudice would be apparent, would also be denied.

United States v. Marion

404 U.S. 307, 92 S.Ct. 455, 30 L.Ed.2d 468 (1971).

■ MR. JUSTICE WHITE delivered the opinion of the Court.

This appeal requires us to decide whether dismissal of a federal indictment was constitutionally required by reason of a period of three years between the occurrence of the alleged criminal acts and the filing of the indictment.

On April 21, 1970, the two appellees were indicted and charged in 19 counts with operating a business known as Allied Enterprises, Inc., which was engaged in the business of selling and installing home improvements such as intercom sets, fire control devices, and burglary detection systems. Allegedly, the business was fraudulently conducted and involved misrepresentations, alterations of documents, and deliberate nonperformance of contracts. The period covered by the indictment was March 15, 1965, to February 6, 1967; the earliest specific act alleged occurred on September 3, 1965, the latest on January 19, 1966.

On May 5, 1970, appellees filed a motion to dismiss the indictment "for failure to commence prosecution of the alleged offenses charged therein within such time as to afford [them their] rights to due process of law and to a speedy trial under the Fifth and Sixth Amendments to the Constitution of the United States." No evidence was submitted, but from the motion itself and the arguments of counsel at the hearing on the motion, it appears that Allied Enterprises had been subject to a Federal Trade Commission cease-and-desist order on February 6, 1967, and that a series of articles appeared in the Washington Post in October 1967, reporting the results of that newspaper's investigation of practices employed by home improvement firms such as Allied. The articles also contained purported statements of the then United States Attorney for the District of Columbia describing his office's investigation of these firms and predicting that indictments would soon be forthcoming. Although the statements attributed to the United States Attorney did not mention Allied specifically, that company was mentioned in the course of the newspaper stories. In the summer of 1968, at the request of the United States Attorney's office, Allied delivered certain of its records to that office, and in an interview there appellee Marion discussed his conduct as an officer of Allied Enterprises. The grand jury that indicted appellees was not impaneled until September 1969, appellees were not informed of the grand jury's concern with them until March 1970, and the indictment was finally handed down in April.

Appellees moved to dismiss because the indictment was returned "an unreasonably oppressive and unjustifiable time after the alleged offenses." They argued that the indictment required memory of many specific acts and conversations occurring several years before, and they contended that the delay was due to the negligence or indifference of the United States Attorney in investigating the case and presenting it to a grand jury. No specific prejudice was claimed or demonstrated. The District Court judge dismissed the indictment for "lack of speedy prosecution" at the conclusion of the hearing and remarked that since the Government must have become aware of the relevant facts in 1967, the defense of the case "is bound to have been seriously prejudiced by the delay of at least some three years in bringing the prosecution that should have been brought in 1967, or at the very latest early 1968."

[W]e reverse the judgment of the District Court.

. . .

II

Appellees do not claim that the Sixth Amendment was violated by the two-month delay between the return of the indictment and its dismissal. Instead, they claim that their rights to a speedy trial were violated by the period of approximately three years between the end of the criminal scheme charged and the return of the indictment; it is argued that this delay is so substantial and inherently prejudicial that the Sixth Amendment required the dismissal of the indictment. In our view, however, the Sixth Amendment speedy trial provision has no application until the putative defendant in some way becomes an "accused," an event that occurred in this case only when the appellees were indicted on April 21, 1970.

. . . On its face, the protection of the Amendment is activated only when a criminal prosecution has begun and extends only to those persons who have been "accused" in the course of that prosecution. These provisions would seem to afford no protection to those not yet accused, nor would they seem to require the Government to discover, investigate, and accuse any person within any particular period of time. The Amendment would appear to guarantee to a criminal defendant that the Government will move with the dispatch that is appropriate to assure him an early and proper disposition of the charges against him. "[T]he essential ingredient is orderly expedition and not mere speed." Smith v. United States, 360 U.S. 1, 10 (1959).

Our attention is called to nothing in the circumstances surrounding the adoption of the Amendment indicating that it does not mean what it appears to say, nor is there more than marginal support for the proposition that, at the time of the adoption of the Amendment, the prevailing rule was that prosecutions would not be permitted if there had been long delay in presenting a charge. The framers could hardly have selected less appropriate language if they had intended the speedy trial provision to protect against pre-accusation delay. No opinions of this Court intimate support for appellees' thesis, and the courts of appeals that have considered the question in constitutional terms have never reversed a conviction or dismissed an indictment solely on the basis of the Sixth Amendment's speedy trial provision where only pre-indictment delay was involved.

Legislative efforts to implement federal and state speedy trial provisions also plainly reveal the view that these guarantees are applicable only after a person has been accused of a crime. . . .

. . .

Appellees' position is, therefore, at odds with long-standing legislative and judicial constructions of the speedy trial provisions in both national and state constitutions.

III

It is apparent also that very little support for appellees' position emerges from a consideration of the purposes of the Sixth Amendment's speedy trial provision, a guarantee that this Court has termed "an important safeguard to prevent undue and oppressive incarceration prior to trial, to minimize anxiety and concern accompanying public accusation and to limit the possibilities that long delay will impair the ability of an accused to defend himself." United States v. Ewell, 383 U.S. 116, 120 (1966). . . . Inordinate delay between arrest, indictment, and trial may impair a defendant's ability to present an effective defense. But the major evils protected against by the speedy trial guarantee exist quite apart from actual or possible prejudice to an accused's defense. To legally arrest and detain, the Government must assert probable cause to believe the arrestee has committed a crime. Arrest is a public act that may seriously interfere with the defendant's liberty, whether he is free on bail or not, and that may disrupt his employment, drain his financial resources, curtail his associations, subject him to public obloquy, and create anxiety in him, his family and his friends. . . . So viewed, it is readily understandable that it is either a formal indictment or information or else the actual restraints imposed by arrest and holding to answer a criminal charge that engage the particular protections of the speedy trial provision of the Sixth Amendment.

Invocation of the speedy trial provision thus need not await indictment, information, or other formal charge. But we decline to extend the reach of the amendment to the period prior to arrest. Until this event occurs, a citizen suffers no restraints on his liberty and is not the subject of public accusation; his situation does not compare with that of a defendant who has been arrested and held to answer. Passage of time, whether before or after arrest, may impair memories, cause evidence to be lost, deprive the defendant of witnesses, and otherwise interfere with his ability to defend himself. But this possibility of prejudice at trial is not itself sufficient reason to wrench the Sixth Amendment from its proper context. Possible prejudice is inherent in any delay, however short; it may also weaken the Government's case.

The law has provided other mechanisms to guard against possible as distinguished from actual prejudice resulting from the passage of time between crime and arrest or charge. As we said in United States v. Ewell, supra, at 122, "the applicable statute of limitations . . . is . . . the primary guarantee against bringing overly stale criminal charges." Such statutes represent legislative assessments of relative interests of the State and the defendant in administering and receiving justice; they "are made for the repose of society and the protection of those who may [during the limitation] . . . have lost their means of defence." Public Schools v. Walker, 9 Wall. 282, 288 (1870). These statutes provide predictability by specifying a limit beyond which there is an irrebuttable presumption that a defendant's right to a fair trial would be prejudiced. As this Court observed in Toussie v. United States, 397 U.S. 112, 114–115 (1970):

> "The purpose of a statute of limitations is to limit exposure to criminal prosecution to a certain fixed period of time following the occurrence of those acts the legislature has decided to punish by criminal sanctions. Such a limitation is designed to protect individuals from having to defend themselves against charges when the basic facts may have become obscured by the passage of time and to minimize the danger of official punishment because of acts in the far-distant past. Such a time limit may also have the salutary effect of encouraging law enforcement officials promptly to investigate suspected criminal activity."

There is thus no need to press the Sixth Amendment into service to guard against the mere possibility that pre-accusation delays will prejudice the defense in a criminal case since statutes of limitation already perform that function.

Since appellees rely only on potential prejudice and the passage of time between the alleged crime and the indictment, see Part IV, infra, we perhaps need go no further to dispose of this case, for the indictment was the first official act designating appellees as accused individuals and that event occurred within the statute of limitations. Nevertheless, since a criminal trial is the likely consequence of our judgment and since appellees may claim actual prejudice to their defense, it is appropriate to note here that the statute of limitations does not fully define the appellees' rights with respect to the events occurring prior to indictment. Thus, the Government concedes that the Due Process Clause of the Fifth Amendment would require dismissal of the indictment if it were shown at trial that the pre-indictment delay in this case caused substantial prejudice to appellees' rights to a fair trial and that the delay was an intentional device to gain tactical advantage over the accused. . . . However, we need not, and could not now, determine when and in what circumstances actual prejudice resulting from preaccusation delays requires the dismissal of the prosecution. Actual prejudice to the defense of a criminal case may result from the shortest and most necessary delay; and no one suggests that every delay-caused detriment to a defendant's case should abort a criminal prosecution. To accommodate the sound administration of justice to the rights of the defendant to a fair trial will necessarily involve a delicate judgment based on the circumstances of each case. It would be unwise at this juncture to attempt to forecast our decision in such cases.

IV

In the case before us, neither appellee was arrested, charged, or otherwise subjected to formal restraint prior to indictment. It was this event, therefore, that transformed the appellees into "accused" defendants who are subject to the speedy trial protections of the Sixth Amendment.

The 38-month delay between the end of the scheme charged in the indictment and the date the defendants were indicted did not extend beyond the period of the applicable statute of limitations here. Appellees have not, of course, been able to claim undue delay pending trial, since the indictment was brought on April 21, 1970, and dismissed on June 8, 1970. Nor have appellees adequately demonstrated that the pre-indictment delay by the Government violated the Due Process Clause. No actual prejudice to the conduct of the defense is alleged or proved, and there is no showing that the Government intentionally delayed to gain some tactical advantage over appellees or to harass them. Appellees rely solely on the real possibility of prejudice inherent in any extended delay: that memories will dim, witnesses become inaccessible, and evidence be lost. In light of the applicable statute of limitations, however, these possibilities are not in themselves enough to demonstrate that appellees cannot receive a fair trial and to therefore justify the dismissal of the indictment. Events of the trial may demonstrate actual prejudice, but at the present time appellees' due process claims are speculative and premature.

. . . [11]

---

[11] Justice Douglas wrote an opinion concurring in the result, which Justice Brennan and Justice Marshall joined, in which he urged that the right to a speedy trial was applicable to the period before indictment but, unless actual prejudice could be shown, had not been violated in this case.

404. *Marion* was applied in United States v. MacDonald, 456 U.S. 1 (1982) (6–3). In that case, the defendant, an army officer, was charged with murder by the military authorities. The charges were subsequently dismissed. More than four years later, he was indicted for the murders by a grand jury. The Court declared that during the interim period, the defendant was in the same position as a person under investigation but not charged with any crime. The Court indicated that its reasoning would apply in ordinary situations in which a defendant is charged, the charges are dismissed, and the defendant is subsequently charged a second time.

In United States v. Loud Hawk, 474 U.S. 302 (1986) (5–4), the indictment of the defendants was dismissed with prejudice under Rule 48(b), Fed.R.Crim.P., p. 831 below, and the government appealed under 18 U.S.C. § 3731 (see p. 896 below). Almost four years later, the court of appeals reversed the dismissal. The defendants were not detained during the intervening period. They were subsequently indicted again. After further proceedings, the indictments were dismissed on the basis that the defendants' right to a speedy trial had been violated. The Court held that the period after dismissal of the first indictment, when the defendants were not subject to any restriction of their liberty, was covered by *MacDonald* and should not be considered in weighing a claim that the right to a speedy trial has been denied.

See United States v. Lai Ming Tanu, 589 F.2d 82 (2d Cir.1978), in which the defendant was arrested by state police and thereafter indicted by the state. Federal officials had cooperated in the investigation leading to the arrest. Later, the state court dismissed the prosecution on speedy trial grounds. Long afterwards she was prosecuted by federal officials for the same offense. Without concluding that the right to a speedy trial or due process could never be invoked in such a case, the court held that dismissal of the federal indictment was not required. See also United States v. Ashford, 924 F.2d 1416 (7th Cir.1991) (5½-year delay between arrest and trial not violative of due process).

405. In United States v. Lovasco, 431 U.S. 783, 790 (1977) (8–1) the Court reaffirmed its conclusion in *Marion*, above, "that proof of prejudice is generally a necessary but not sufficient element of a due process claim, and that the due process inquiry must consider the reasons for the delay as well as the prejudice to the accused."

"It requires no extended argument to establish that prosecutors do not deviate from 'fundamental conceptions of justice' when they defer seeking indictments until they have probable cause to believe an accused is guilty; indeed it is unprofessional conduct for a prosecutor to recommend an indictment on less than probable cause. It should be equally obvious that prosecutors are under no duty to file charges as soon as probable cause exists but before they are satisfied they will be able to establish the suspect's guilt beyond a reasonable doubt. To impose such a duty 'would have a deleterious effect both upon the rights of the accused and upon the ability of society to protect itself,' United States v. Ewell, 383 U.S. [116 (1966)] at 120. From the perspective of potential defendants, requiring prosecutions to commence when probable cause is established is undesirable because it would increase the likelihood of unwarranted charges being filed, and would add to the time during which defendants stand accused but untried. These costs are by no means insubstantial since, as we recognized in *Marion*, a formal accusation may 'interfere with the defendant's liberty . . . disrupt his employment, drain his financial resources, curtail his associations, subject him to public obloquy, and create anxiety in him, his family and his friends.' 404 U.S., at 320. From the perspective of law enforcement officials, a requirement of immediate prosecution upon probable cause is equally unacceptable because it could make obtaining proof of guilt beyond a reasonable doubt impossible by causing potentially fruitful sources of information to evaporate before they are fully exploited. And from the standpoint of the courts, such a requirement is unwise because it would cause scarce resources to be consumed on cases that prove to be insubstantial, or that involve only some of the responsible parties or some of the criminal acts. Thus, no one's interests would be well served by compelling prosecutors to initiate prosecutions as soon as they are legally entitled to do so.

"It might be argued that once the Government has assembled sufficient evidence to prove guilt beyond a reasonable doubt, it should be constitutionally required to file charges promptly, even if its investigation of the entire criminal transaction is not complete. Adopting such a rule, however, would have many of the same consequences as adopting a rule requiring immediate prosecution upon probable cause.

"First, compelling a prosecutor to file public charges as soon as the requisite proof has been developed against one participant on one charge would cause numerous problems in those cases in which a criminal transaction involves more than one person or more than one illegal act. In some instances, an immediate arrest or indictment would impair the prosecutor's ability to continue his investigation, thereby preventing society from bringing lawbreakers to justice. In other cases, the prosecutor would be able to obtain additional indictments despite an early prosecution, but the necessary result would be multiple trials involving a single set of facts. Such trials place needless burdens on defendants, law enforcement officials, and courts.

"Second, insisting on immediate prosecution once sufficient evidence is developed to obtain a conviction would pressure prosecutors into resolving doubtful cases in favor of early—and possibly unwarranted—prosecutions. The determination of when the evidence available to the prosecution is sufficient to obtain a conviction is seldom clear-cut, and reasonable persons often will reach conflicting conclusions. . . . The decision whether to prosecute, therefore, required a necessarily subjective evaluation of the strength of the circumstantial evidence available and the credibility of respondent's denial. Even if a prosecutor concluded that the case was weak and further investigation appropriate, he would have no assurance that a reviewing court would agree. To avoid the risk that a subsequent indictment would be dismissed for preindictment delay, the prosecutor might feel constrained to file premature charges, with all the disadvantages that entails.

"Finally, requiring the Government to make charging decisions immediately upon assembling evidence sufficient to establish guilt would preclude the Government from giving full consideration to the desirability of not prosecuting in particular cases. The decision to file criminal charges, with the awesome consequences it entails, requires consideration of a wide range of factors in addition to the strength of the Government's case, in order to determine whether prosecution would be in the public interest. Prosecutors often need more information than proof of a suspect's guilt, therefore, before deciding whether to seek an indictment. . . . Requiring prosecution once the evidence of guilt is clear, however, could prevent a prosecutor from awaiting the information necessary for such a decision.

"We would be most reluctant to adopt a rule which would have these consequences absent a clear constitutional command to do so. We can find no such command in the Due Process Clause of the Fifth Amendment." 431 U.S. at 790–95.

In United States v. Crouch, 84 F.3d 1497, 1523 (5th Cir.1996) (en banc), the court held that a dismissal for pre-indictment delay requires a showing that the delay "was intentionally brought about by the government for the purpose of gaining some tactical advantage over the accused in the contemplated prosecution or for some other bad faith purpose" and that "the delay caused actual, substantial prejudice to his defense. The requisite delay may not be presumed, rebuttably or otherwise, merely from the length of the delay. See Bennett v. Lockhart, 39 F.3d 848 (8th Cir.1994) (nine-year delay); United States v. Bartlett, 794 F.2d 1285 (8th Cir.1986) (five-year delay); Stoner v. Graddick, 751 F.2d 1535 (11th Cir.1985) (19-year delay).

On the problem of delay before an arrest in order to protect the "cover" of an undercover police officer who makes a large number of narcotics purchases before "surfacing," see United States v. Jones, 524 F.2d 834 (D.C.Cir.1975); Ross v. United States, 349 F.2d 210 (D.C.Cir.1965).

FEDERAL RULES OF CRIMINAL PROCEDURE

Rule 48.

DISMISSAL

. . .

(b) By Court. If there is unnecessary delay in presenting the charge to a grand jury or in filing an information against a defendant who has been held to answer to the district court, or if there is unnecessary delay in bringing a defendant to trial, the court may dismiss the indictment, information or complaint.

SPEEDY TRIAL ACT OF 1974
18 U.S.C. §§ 3161–3174.

§ 3161. Time limits and exclusions

(a) In any case involving a defendant charged with an offense, the appropriate judicial officer, at the earliest practicable time, shall, after consultation with the counsel for the defendant and the attorney for the Government, set the case for trial on a day certain, or list it for trial on a weekly or other short-term trial calendar at a place within the judicial district, so as to assure a speedy trial.

(b) Any information or indictment charging an individual with the commission of an offense shall be filed within thirty days from the date on which such individual was arrested or served with a summons in connection with such charges. If an individual has been charged with a felony in a district in which no grand jury has been in session during such thirty-day period, the period of time for filing of the indictment shall be extended an additional thirty days.

(c)(1) In any case in which a plea of not guilty is entered, the trial of a defendant charged in an information or indictment with the commission of an offense shall commence within seventy days from the filing date (and making public) of the information or indictment, or from the date the defendant has appeared before a judicial officer of the court in which such charge is pending, whichever date last occurs. If a defendant consents in writing to be tried before a magistrate on a complaint, the trial shall commence within seventy days from the date of such consent.

(2) Unless the defendant consents in writing to the contrary, the trial shall not commence less than thirty days from the date on which the defendant first appears through counsel or expressly waives counsel and elects to proceed pro se.

(d)(1) If any indictment or information is dismissed upon motion of the defendant, or any charge contained in a complaint filed against an individual is dismissed or otherwise dropped, and thereafter a complaint is filed against such defendant or individual charging him with the same offense or an offense based on the same conduct or arising from the same criminal episode, or an information or indictment is filed charging such defendant with the same offense or an offense based on the same conduct or arising from the same criminal episode, the provisions of subsections (b) and (c) of this section shall be applicable with respect to such subsequent complaint, indictment, or information, as the case may be.

(2) If the defendant is to be tried upon an indictment or information dismissed by a trial court and reinstated following an appeal, the trial shall commence within seventy days from the date the action occasioning the trial becomes final, except that the court retrying the case may extend the period for trial not to exceed one hundred and eighty days from the date the action occasioning the trial becomes final if the unavailability of witnesses or other factors resulting from the passage of time shall make trial within seventy days impractical. The periods of delay enumerated in section 3161(h) are excluded in computing the time limitations specified in this section. The sanctions of section 3162 apply to this subsection.

(e) If the defendant is to be tried again following a declaration by the trial judge of a mistrial or following an order of such judge for a new trial, the trial shall commence within seventy days from the date the action occasioning the retrial becomes final. If the defendant is to be tried again following an appeal or a collateral attack, the trial shall commence within seventy days from the date the action occasioning the retrial becomes final, except that the court retrying the case may extend the period for retrial not to exceed one hundred and eighty days from the date the action occasioning the retrial becomes final if unavailability of witnesses or other factors resulting from passage of time shall make trial within seventy days impractical. The periods of delay enumerated in section 3161(h) are excluded in computing the time limitations specified in this section. The sanctions of section 3162 apply to this subsection.

. . .

(h) The following periods of delay shall be excluded in computing the time within which an information or an indictment must be filed, or in computing the time within which the trial of any such offense must commence:

(1) Any period of delay resulting from other proceedings concerning the defendant, including but not limited to—

(A) delay resulting from any proceeding, including any examinations, to determine the mental competency or physical capacity of the defendant;

(B) delay resulting from any proceeding, including any examination of the defendant, pursuant to section 2902 of title 28, United States Code;[12]

(C) delay resulting from deferral of prosecution pursuant to section 2902 of title 28, United States Code;

12. 28 U.S.C. § 2902 provides for examination of persons charged with an offense to determine whether they are addicted to narcotics and "likely to be rehabilitated through treatment," and, if so, for their civil commitment for treatment.

(D) delay resulting from trial with respect to other charges against the defendant;

(E) delay resulting from any interlocutory appeal;

(F) delay resulting from any pretrial motion, from the filing of the motion through the conclusion of the hearing on, or other prompt disposition of, such motion;

(G) delay resulting from any proceeding relating to the transfer of a case or the removal of any defendant from another district under the Federal Rules of Criminal Procedure;

(H) delay resulting from transportation of any defendant from another district, or to and from places of examination or hospitalization, except that any time consumed in excess of ten days from the date an order of removal or an order directing such transportation, and the defendant's arrival at the destination shall be presumed to be unreasonable;

(I) delay resulting from consideration by the court of a proposed plea agreement to be entered into by the defendant and the attorney for the Government; and

(J) delay reasonably attributable to any period, not to exceed thirty days, during which any proceeding concerning the defendant is actually under advisement by the court.

(2) Any period of delay during which prosecution is deferred by the attorney for the Government pursuant to written agreement with the defendant, with the approval of the court, for the purpose of allowing the defendant to demonstrate his good conduct.

(3)(A) Any period of delay resulting from the absence or unavailability of the defendant or an essential witness.

(B) For purposes of subparagraph (A) of this paragraph, a defendant or an essential witness shall be considered absent when his whereabouts are unknown and, in addition, he is attempting to avoid apprehension or prosecution or his whereabouts cannot be determined by due diligence. For purposes of such subparagraph, a defendant or an essential witness shall be considered unavailable whenever his whereabouts are known but his presence for trial cannot be obtained by due diligence or he resists appearing at or being returned for trial.

(4) Any period of delay resulting from the fact that the defendant is mentally incompetent or physically unable to stand trial.

(5) Any period of delay resulting from the treatment of the defendant pursuant to section 2902 of title 28, United States Code.

(6) If the information or indictment is dismissed upon motion of the attorney for the Government and thereafter a charge is filed against the defendant for the same offense, or any offense required to be joined with that offense, any period of delay from the date the charge was dis-

missed to the date the time limitation would commence to run as to the subsequent charge had there been no previous charge.

(7) A reasonable period of delay when the defendant is joined for trial with a codefendant as to whom the time for trial has not run and no motion for severance has been granted.

(8)(A) Any period of delay resulting from a continuance granted by any judge on his own motion or at the request of the defendant or his counsel or at the request of the attorney for the Government, if the judge granted such continuance on the basis of his findings that the ends of justice served by taking such action outweigh the best interest of the public and the defendant in a speedy trial. No such period of delay resulting from a continuance granted by the court in accordance with this paragraph shall be excludable under this subsection unless the court sets forth, in the record of the case, either orally or in writing, its reasons for finding that the ends of justice served by the granting of such continuance outweigh the best interests of the public and the defendant in a speedy trial.

(B) The factors, among others, which a judge shall consider in determining whether to grant a continuance under subparagraph (A) of this paragraph in any case are as follows:

(i) Whether the failure to grant such a continuance in the proceeding would be likely to make a continuation of such proceeding impossible, or result in a miscarriage of justice.

(ii) Whether the case is so unusual or so complex, due to the number of defendants, the nature of the prosecution, or the existence of novel questions of fact or law, that it is unreasonable to expect adequate preparation for pretrial proceedings or for the trial itself within the time limits established by this section.

(iii) Whether, in a case in which arrest precedes indictment, delay in the filing of the indictment is caused because the arrest occurs at a time such that it is unreasonable to expect return and filing of the indictment within the period specified in section 3161(b), or because the facts upon which the grand jury must base its determination are unusual or complex.

(iv) Whether the failure to grant such a continuance in a case which, taken as a whole, is not so unusual or so complex as to fall within clause (ii), would deny the defendant reasonable time to obtain counsel, would unreasonably deny the defendant or the Government continuity of counsel, or would deny counsel for the defendant or the attorney for the Government the reasonable time necessary for effective preparation, taking into account the exercise of due diligence.

(C) No continuance under subparagraph (A) of this paragraph shall be granted because of general congestion of the court's calendar, or lack of diligent preparation or failure to obtain available witnesses on the part of the attorney for the Government.

(9) Any period of delay, not to exceed one year, ordered by a district court upon an application of a party and a finding by a preponderance of the evidence that an official request, as defined in section 3292 of this title, has been made for evidence of any such offense and that it reasonably appears, or reasonably appeared at the time the request was made, that such evidence is, or was, in such foreign country.

(i) If trial did not commence within the time limitation specified in section 3161 because the defendant had entered a plea of guilty or nolo contendere subsequently withdrawn to any or all charges in an indictment or information, the defendant shall be deemed indicted with respect to all charges therein contained within the meaning of section 3161, on the day the order permitting withdrawal of the plea becomes final.

(j)(1) If the attorney for the Government knows that a person charged with an offense is serving a term of imprisonment in any penal institution, he shall promptly—

(A) undertake to obtain the presence of the prisoner for trial; or

(B) cause a detainer to be filed with the person having custody of the prisoner and request him to so advise the prisoner and to advise the prisoner of his right to demand trial.

(2) If the person having custody of such prisoner receives a detainer, he shall promptly advise the prisoner of the charge and of the prisoner's right to demand trial. If at any time thereafter the prisoner informs the person having custody that he does demand trial, such person shall cause notice to that effect to be sent promptly to the attorney for the Government who caused the detainer to be filed.

(3) Upon receipt of such notice, the attorney for the Government shall promptly seek to obtain the presence of the prisoner for trial.

(4) When the person having custody of the prisoner receives from the attorney for the Government a properly supported request for temporary custody of such prisoner for trial, the prisoner shall be made available to that attorney for the Government (subject, in cases of interjurisdictional transfer, to any right of the prisoner to contest the legality of his delivery).

(k)(1) If the defendant is absent (as defined by subsection (h)(3)) on the day set for trial, and the defendant's subsequent appearance before the court on a bench warrant or other process or surrender to the court occurs more than 21 days after the day set for trial, the defendant shall be deemed to have first appeared before a judicial officer of the court in which the information or indictment is pending within the meaning of subsection (c) on the date of the defendant's subsequent appearance before the court.

(2) If the defendant is absent (as defined by subsection (h)(3)) on the day set for trial, and the defendant's subsequent appearance before the court on a bench warrant or other process or surrender to the court occurs not more than 21 days after the day set for trial, the time limit required by subsection (c), as extended by subsection (h), shall be further extended by 21 days.

§ 3162. Sanctions

(a)(1) If, in the case of any individual against whom a complaint is filed charging such individual with an offense, no indictment or information is filed within the time limit required by section 3161(b) as extended by section 3161(h) of this chapter, such charge against that individual contained in such complaint shall be dismissed or otherwise dropped. In determining whether to dismiss the case with or without prejudice, the court shall consider, among others, each of the following factors: the seriousness of the offense; the facts and circumstances of the case which led to the dismissal; and the impact of a reprosecution on the administration of this chapter and on the administration of justice.

(2) If a defendant is not brought to trial within the time limit required by section 3161(c) as extended by section 3161(h), the information or indictment shall be dismissed on motion of the defendant. The defendant shall have the burden of proof of supporting such motion but the Government shall have the burden of going forward with the evidence in connection with any exclusion of time under subparagraph 3161(h)(3). In determining whether to dismiss the case with or without prejudice, the court shall consider, among others, each of the following factors: the seriousness of the offense; the facts and circumstances of the case which led to the dismissal; and the impact of a reprosecution on the administration of this chapter and on the administration of justice. Failure of the defendant to move for dismissal prior to trial or entry of a plea of guilty or nolo contendere shall constitute a waiver of the right to dismissal under this section.

(b) In any case in which counsel for the defendant or the attorney for the Government (1) knowingly allows the case to be set for trial without disclosing the fact that a necessary witness would be unavailable for trial; (2) files a motion solely for the purpose of delay which he knows is totally frivolous and without merit; (3) makes a statement for the purpose of obtaining a continuance which he knows to be false and which is material to the granting of a continuance; or (4) otherwise willfully fails to proceed to trial without justification consistent with section 3161 of this chapter, the court may punish any such counsel or attorney, as follows:

(A) in the case of an appointed defense counsel, by reducing the amount of compensation that otherwise would have been paid to such counsel pursuant to section 3006A of this title in an amount not to exceed 25 per centum thereof;

(B) in the case of a counsel retained in connection with the defense of a defendant, by imposing on such counsel a fine of not to exceed 25 per centum of the compensation to which he is entitled in connection with his defense of such defendant;

(C) by imposing on any attorney for the Government a fine of not to exceed $250;

(D) by denying any such counsel or attorney for the Government the right to practice before the court considering such case for a period of not to exceed ninety days; or

(E) by filing a report with an appropriate disciplinary committee.

The authority to punish provided for by this subsection shall be in addition to any other authority or power available to such court.

(c) The court shall follow procedures established in the Federal Rules of Criminal Procedure in punishing any counsel or attorney for the Government pursuant to this section.

. . .

§ 3164. Persons detained or designated as being of high risk

(a) The trial or other disposition of cases involving—

(1) a detained person who is being held in detention solely because he is awaiting trial, and

(2) a released person who is awaiting trial and has been designated by the attorney for the Government as being of high risk,

shall be accorded priority.

(b) The trial of any person described in subsection (a)(1) or (a)(2) of this section shall commence not later than ninety days following the beginning of such continuous detention or designation of high risk by the attorney for the Government. The periods of delay enumerated in section 3161(h) are excluded in computing the time limitation specified in this section.

(c) Failure to commence trial of a detainee as specified in subsection (b), through no fault of the accused or his counsel, or failure to commence trial of a designated releasee as specified in subsection (b), through no fault of the attorney for the Government, shall result in the automatic review by the court of the conditions of release. No detainee, as defined in subsection (a), shall be held in custody pending trial after the expiration of such ninety-day period required for the commencement of his trial. A designated releasee, as defined in subsection (a), who is found by the court to have intentionally delayed the trial of his case shall be subject to an order of the court modifying his nonfinancial conditions of release under this title to insure that he shall appear at trial as required.

. . .

§ 3173. Sixth amendment rights

No provision of this chapter shall be interpreted as a bar to any claim of denial of speedy trial as required by amendment VI of the Constitution.

. . . [13]

---

[13] Other provisions of the Speedy Trial Act, omitted here, provide for each district court to adopt a plan for implementation of the Act and for periodic reports to Congress.

406. Section 3161(c)(1) of the Speedy Trial Act provides that a trial must begin within 70 days of the filing of an indictment or information. A trial begins for purposes of the Act with the voir dire of the jury. In United States v. Fox, 788 F.2d 905 (2d Cir.1986), the voir dire was conducted and a jury was selected just before the statutory period would have expired. The trial was then adjourned by the court; the jury was not sworn and the trial did not begin until more than five months later. The trial judge gave no reason for the delay. The court of appeals said that "nothing in the Act justifies this kind of delay," id. at 909, and dismissed the indictment. It remanded for a determination whether the dismissal should be with or without prejudice. See, following *Fox*, United States v. Stayton, 791 F.2d 17 (2d Cir.1986) (23-month delay between voir dire and trial; dismissal with prejudice).

The provision in § 3161(c)(2) that a trial shall not commence "less than thirty days from the date on which the defendant first appears through counsel" does not require that a new 30-day period begin when a superseding indictment is filed. United States v. Rojas-Contreras, 474 U.S. 231 (1985).

On the provisions of § 3161(h) for exclusion of certain delays from the period within which the trial must begin, especially subsection (8) dealing with continuances, see United States v. Carrasquillo, 667 F.2d 382 (3d Cir.1981).

The excludable delay covered by § 3161(h)(1)(F) of the Speedy Trial Act for a hearing on a motion is not limited to delay that is "reasonably necessary." Excluded from the Act's 70-day limitation is "all time between the filing of a motion and the conclusion of the hearing on that motion, whether or not a delay in holding that hearing is 'reasonably necessary.'" Henderson v. United States, 476 U.S. 321, 330 (1986) (5–4). The Court held that delay after the conclusion of a hearing on a motion while a court is awaiting the submission of additional papers is also excluded. In United States v. Moran, 998 F.2d 1368 (6th Cir.1993), however, the court held that the period of a continuance for filing suppression motions and the period after all papers are submitted while the motion is pending, in excess of the 30 days allowed by the Rule, are not excludable; nor could a retroactive "ends of justice" ruling authorize the exclusion after the fact.

On the provision of § 3162(a)(1) for dismissal with or without prejudice, see United States v. Giambrone, 920 F.2d 176 (2d Cir.1990) (dismissal with prejudice justified by government's "extremely lax" attitude to speedy trial); United States v. Brown, 770 F.2d 241 (1st Cir.1985) (dismissal without prejudice upheld).

In United States v. Taylor, 487 U.S. 326, 343 (1988) (6–3), the Court concluded that, in light of all the circumstances, including the district court's failure to give sufficient explicit consideration to the factors set forth in § 3162(a)(2) of the Speedy Trial Act, the district court's decision to dismiss with, rather than without, prejudice, "in order to send a strong message to the Government that unexcused delays will not be tolerated," was an abuse of discretion.

**UNITED STATES DISTRICT COURT
DISTRICT OF MASSACHUSETTS**

UNITED STATES OF AMERICA   MAG. JUDGE NO. _____

V.   CRIMINAL NO._____

_____

ORDER OF EXCLUDABLE DELAY

In accordance with the Speedy Trial Act of 1974, as amended, this Court

hereby orders excludable delay from _____ to _____

for the reason checked below.

_____   _____
Date   **U.S. District Judge**
          U.S. Magistrate Judge

REFER TO DOCUMENT(S) #_____

[ ]	XA	Proceedings including examinations to determine mental competency or physical capacity	18U.S.C.§3161(h)(1)(A)
[ ]	XD	Interlocutory Appeal	18U.S.C.§3161(h)(1)(E)
[ ]	XE	Pretrial motions from filing date to hearing or disposition	18U.S.C.§3161(h)(1)(F)
[ ]	XG	Proceedings under advisement	18U.S.C.§3161(h)(1)(J)
[ ]	XH	Miscellaneous proceedings concerning defendant	18 U.S.C.§3161(h)(1)
[ ]	XM	Absence or unavailability of defendant or essential government witness	18 U.S.C.§3161(h)(3)
[ ]	XN	Period of mental or physical incompetency or physical inability to stand trial	18 U.S.C.§3161(h)(4)
[ ]	XT	Continuance granted in the interest of justice	18 U.S.C.§3161(h)(8)

(XDELAY1.frm - 01/93)   [koexcl.]

Denial of a motion to dismiss under the Speedy Trial Act is *not* an order subject to interlocutory appellate review. United States v. Bilsky, 664 F.2d 613 (6th Cir.1981) (following *MacDonald*, p. 824 above).

Continuance

407. "The matter of continuance is traditionally within the discretion of the trial judge, and it is not every denial of a request for more time that violates due process even if the party fails to offer evidence or is compelled to defend without counsel. . . . Contrariwise, a myopic insistence upon expeditiousness in the face of a justifiable request for delay can render the right to defend with counsel an empty formality. . . . There are no mechanical tests for deciding when a denial of a continuance is so arbitrary as to violate due process. The answer must be found in the circumstances present in every case, particularly in the reasons presented to the trial judge at the time the request is denied." Ungar v. Sarafite, 376 U.S. 575, 589 (1964). See Morris v. Slappy, 461 U.S. 1 (1983).

"A motion for a continuance is addressed to the sound discretion of the trial court, and its ruling will not be disturbed on appeal unless there is a showing that there has been an abuse of that discretion. . . . This issue must be decided on a case by case basis in light of the circumstances presented, particularly the reasons for continuance presented to the trial court at the time the request is denied. . . .

. . .

"[T]he cases are so numerous and involve such varying factual contexts and bases for decision that merely cataloging them is a task of significant proportion. We have deemed the following factors highly relevant in assessing claims of inadequate preparation time: the quantum of time available for preparation, the likelihood of prejudice from denial, the accused's role in shortening the effective preparation time, the degree of complexity of the case, and the availability of discovery from the prosecution. We have also explicitly considered the adequacy of the defense actually provided at trial, the skill and experience of the attorney, any pre-appointment or pre-retention experience of the attorney with the accused or the alleged crime, and any representation of the defendant by other attorneys that accrues to his benefit.

"Within this general category of cases, a particularly common claim is that a continuance was necessary to interview and subpoena potential witnesses. The panels of this court that have ruled on such claims have considered the diligence of the defense in interviewing witnesses and procuring their presence, the probability of procuring their testimony within a reasonable time, the specificity with which the defense is able to describe their expected knowledge or testimony, the degree to which such testimony is expected to be favorable to the accused, and the unique or cumulative nature of the testimony. A general rule recently has emerged: 'A movant must show that due diligence has been exercised to obtain the attendance of the witness, that substantial favorable testimony would be tendered by the witness, that the witness is available and willing to testify, and that the denial of a continuance would materially prejudice the defendant.' United States v. Miller, 513 F.2d 791, 793 (5 Cir.1975). . . .

. . .

"Several lessons to defense lawyers should emerge. . . . The first is that, in cases where there is a substantial basis for a continuance, the attorney should present the claim as early as possible. Second, the attorney should exercise all reasonable diligence to prepare for trial despite the time constraints confronting him. Finally, such claims should be advanced with all the specificity and detail that is feasible under the circumstances. While some of these 'lessons' are rules of law under *Miller* with respect to continuances to interview and subpoena witnesses, they are counsels of wisdom in any continuance situation. Only with detailed information as to counsel's efforts and the legitimate justifications for extra time can the court conclude that the motion is made for reasons other than delay. Only then can it be expected to subordinate the very legitimate needs of both the criminal justice system and the defendant for speedy and economical justice.

"Finally . . . we must reiterate that a scheduled trial date should never become such an overarching end that it results in the erosion of the defendant's right to a fair trial. If forcing a defendant to an early trial date substantially impairs his ability to effectively present evidence to rebut the prosecution's case or to establish defenses, then pursuit of the goal of expeditiousness is far more detrimental to our common purposes in the criminal justice system than the delay of a few days or weeks that may be sought. The district courts to whom these difficult and inexact judgments are committed have, in the majority of cases, made them with a proper consideration of the rights of defendants to due process of law as well as the demands of judicial economy. Where . . . it is possible to see how a denial of continuance resulted from a reasonable resolution of the various factors confronting a court, we will uphold its action, even if it may seem somewhat harsh." United States v. Uptain, 531 F.2d 1281, 1285–87, 1290–91 (5th Cir.1976).

United States Ex Rel. Carey v. Rundle

409 F.2d 1210 (3d Cir.1969).

■ ALDISERT, CIRCUIT JUDGE.

In this case we come to grips with a familiar phrase: "every defendant in a criminal proceeding is entitled to have counsel of his own choice". This is a lay expression, albeit often articulated by those trained in the law as a paraphrase of the Sixth Amendment: "In all criminal prosecutions, the accused shall . . . have the Assistance of Counsel for his defense."

We must decide whether the Sixth and Fourteenth Amendments command an absolute right to a particular counsel for a particular trial at a particular time.

The relator was arrested on June 2, 1966, and appeared at a preliminary hearing on June 4, at which time he was represented by private counsel. After he was indicted by the grand jury, his case came on for trial on August 29, at which time the Commonwealth appeared with its witnesses and was prepared to go to trial. The defendant, however, reported that he could not proceed because he did not have counsel.

Upon ascertaining that the defendant had been represented by Attorney A. Charles Peruto at the preliminary hearing, the court summoned Mr. Peruto to the courtroom. The attorney reported that although he had represented the defendant at the preliminary hearing, he had entered no appearance as counsel for the defendant in the court proceedings. He stated unequivocally that he did not represent the defendant and that he had no intention of doing so. Because of the defendant's insistence that he desired private counsel, the court postponed the trial until September 28 to afford him an additional thirty days to obtain counsel of his choice. At the same time the court ordered the Voluntary Defender to file an appearance for the defendant and to be ready to proceed on the September date in the event the defendant was not successful in his attempt to retain private counsel.

The appointed day came and the case was called for trial. The Commonwealth again was ready to proceed. Still without private counsel but represented by the Voluntary Defender, the defendant requested a continuance of one day to obtain notes of the testimony adduced at the preliminary hearing. Two days passed. On September 30, the case was again called, at which time the Commonwealth was ready to proceed for the third time. Speaking through the Voluntary Defender, the defendant again requested a continuance, stating that he did not desire representation by the Voluntary Defender and insisted upon retaining private counsel. The motion was denied; the court ordered the Voluntary Defender to sit with the defendant at counsel table and the trial began. Thereupon, the defendant elected to proceed nonjury.

At the noon recess, Attorney Milton Leidner appeared in the courtroom and informed the court: "The mother of Harry Carey was at my office and as a result of conversation I told her I would enter my appearance and represent him. I subsequently went on trial and in my absence she did bring a check into the office and it is a good check." He said that he had not filed his appearance, but he was prepared to do so: "If the case is continued, yes. I cannot try it now. I am already on trial." The court then announced that "this case is continued until Monday morning at 10 A.M." Mr. Leidner interjected that he had another case listed for the same day. The court refused to continue the trial any later than Monday. Mr. Leidner then said, "I will withdraw my appearance and refund the retainer which I didn't receive but only placed it in my drawer." The trial then proceeded to a conclusion; the defendant was found guilty.

After exhausting state remedies, Carey filed a petition for federal habeas corpus relief alleging a denial of due process. The writ was granted and the Commonwealth has appealed.

We begin with the premise that the right to counsel is a vital ingredient in the scheme of due process. . . .

. . .

Concurrently a doctrine has evolved which guarantees the defendant sufficient time and opportunity to obtain counsel of his own choice.

Desirable as it is that a defendant obtain private counsel of his own choice, that goal must be weighed and balanced against an equally desirable public need for the efficient and effective administration of criminal justice. The calendar control of modern criminal court dockets, especially in metropolitan communities, is a sophisticated operation constantly buffeted by conflicting forces. The accused's rights—such as those relating to a speedy trial, to an adequate opportunity to prepare the defense, and to confront witnesses—are constantly in potential or real conflict with the prosecution's legitimate demands for some stability in the scheduling of cases. The availability of prosecution witnesses is often critically dependent on the predictability of the trial list. That delays and postponements only increase the reluctance of witnesses to appear in court, especially in criminal matters, is a phenomenon which scarcely needs elucidation.

Moreover, it is not only the prosecution which may suffer from unscheduled changes in the calendar. To permit a continuance to accommodate one defendant may in itself prejudice the rights of another defendant whose trial is delayed because of the continuance. Played to an extreme conclusion, this indiscriminate game of judicial musical chairs could collapse any semblance of sound administration, and work to the ultimate prejudice of many defendants awaiting trial in criminal courts.

This is not to say that there should be an arbitrary and inelastic calendaring of cases without due regard, for example, to the existence of conflicting demands for the service of a particular counsel by different courts or by the schedules within a multi-judge court. In judicial administration, too, there should be no absolutes. It is the trial judge who must balance the conflicting demands of court administration with the rights of the accused, conscious, however, that when he considers the rights of those accused of crime, he must consider not only those involved in the case immediately before him but also those of other defendants awaiting trial whose rights may be affected by the consequences of trial delay.

. . .

Due process demands that the defendant be afforded a fair opportunity to obtain the assistance of counsel of his choice to prepare and conduct his defense. The constitutional mandate is satisfied so long as the accused is afforded a fair or reasonable opportunity to obtain particular counsel, and so long as there is no arbitrary action prohibiting the effective use of such counsel. The conclusion becomes inescapable, therefore, that although the right to counsel is absolute, there is no absolute right to a particular counsel.

In the case at bar the defendant was afforded due process. Putting aside the two and a half month period from June 4, when he was represented by private counsel at the preliminary hearing, until August 28, when he was advised in open court that this lawyer was not representing him at the trial, the defendant was specifically informed that the court was affording him one additional month to obtain private counsel to prepare his defense and that his trial was postponed for one month to a day certain. One month is not a constitutionally inadequate time period in which to obtain counsel and prepare a defense, where, as here, the lines of communication were at all times open and defendant can show no good reason why he could not have contacted and retained an attorney within this time period.

To offset any further delay or complications, counsel was appointed for him in the person of the Voluntary Defender, who, in the intervening month, made several attempts to prepare his defense. The defendant steadfastly refused this assistance. When the appointed day came, he was still without private counsel. Nevertheless, a second continuance of two days was granted to enable counsel to gather certain specific information. On the Friday when the trial began, he was given the opportunity of counsel which he rejected, preferring to go to trial *in propria persona*. The court ordered appointed counsel to sit at his side and to be available for expert advice and counsel. It was only when the trial was already in progress that private counsel did in fact appear in the courtroom.

When the trial judge expressed a willingness to adjourn the hearing and begin anew the following Monday, he was extending a courtesy not required, under these circumstances, by the constitutional demands of due process. On three different occasions, the case had been called for trial. On three different occasions the Commonwealth had assembled its witnesses and announced its readiness to proceed.

In accommodating the conflicting considerations of either extending additional time for the defendant to obtain counsel of his choice or moving forward with the orderly process of judicial administration, the trial judge was called upon to exercise his discretion. We cannot say that the discretion he exercised impinged upon the constitutional rights of the defendant before him.

Accordingly, we will reverse the judgment of the district court.

---

408. The difficulty of reconciling a reluctant defendant's right to counsel with the need for orderly, expeditious proceedings has troubled the courts. In Bostick v. United States, 400 F.2d 449 (5th Cir.1968), for example, the trial judge stated: "This Court undertook for a period of seven months to bring this case to trial. During this interval the defendants Bostick and Lainhart, though incarcerated and unable to make bond, used every device and machination known to the law, and then perhaps invented a few of their own, to defeat the orderly disposition of the case. The transcript of these preliminary proceedings, which I have just re-read to refresh my recollection, is so fantastic as to be almost beyond belief. It presents the question as to whether ever, under any circumstances, a district court in the orderly administration of its functions can bring a criminal case to trial over the objection of the defendant.

. . .

"I am convinced beyond the shadow of a doubt that the various artifices practiced by these two defendants prior to trial in continually gaining continuances, and in claiming that while entirely able financially to do so they were still unsuccessful in securing counsel of their own choice were deliberate, were not in good faith, and—with the knowledge that they had no hopes of success in the trial court—was for the express purpose of preserving this question for appeal and, thereafter habeas corpus." Id. at 453–54. The court of appeals agreed: "The defendants used their right to counsel as a means of frustrating the orderly processes of justice." Id. at 451.

See, e.g., United States v. Poston, 902 F.2d 90 (D.C.Cir.1990); Sampley v. Attorney General of North Carolina, 786 F.2d 610 (4th Cir.1986). Cf. United States v. Kennard, 799 F.2d 556 (9th Cir.1986) (denial of continuance to obtain counsel for second trial after defendant had waived counsel at first trial was error).

The denial of a continuance was held to be an abuse of discretion in United States v. Gallo, 763 F.2d 1504, 1524 (6th Cir.1985): "When defense counsel makes reasonable requests for a continuance in a highly complex case, and is afforded only ten days following arraignment to prepare for trial, the trial judge's denial of the motion constitutes an abuse of discretion and violates the defendant's sixth amendment right to counsel." See also United States v. Goldberg, 67 F.3d 1092 (3d Cir.1995) (defendant's conduct did not forfeit right to counsel); United States v. Rankin, 779 F.2d 956 (3d Cir.1986) (denial of continuance while defense counsel was occupied in another trial); Gandy v. Alabama, 569 F.2d 1318 (5th Cir.1978) (same). *Gandy* was distinguished in United States v. Barrentine, 591 F.2d 1069 (5th Cir.1979).

409. When defense counsel is retained by an unknown defendant who is not obviously a "good risk" and who is reasonably likely to be convicted and sentenced to prison, it is common for defense counsel not to proceed with the case until he has received at least some part of his fee. If defense counsel appears before the magistrate and requests a continuance of the preliminary hearing or before the calendar judge and requests a continuance of the trial without good reason except that the defendant has not paid a fee as agreed, should the magistrate or judge grant the continuance (the defendant presumably having consented)? If not, should counsel be permitted to withdraw from the case (making a continuance inevitable)? Why (not)? See generally United States v. Uptain, 531 F.2d 1281, 1290 (5th Cir.1976).[14]

410. Consider the situation of a defendant in a "big" case, who is indicted only after the prosecutor has completed an intensive investigation of the facts of the alleged crime and the possibility of proving the crime in court. The prosecutor is generally limited only by the statute of limitations, which usually allows him all the time he needs to develop his case, track down leads, evaluate potential witnesses, and the like. He may, and in the case of the federal government at least, ordinarily will have available whatever resources are reasonably necessary for investigation and trial preparation. This will include not only the superior laboratory and other resources of the Federal Bureau of Investigation, such as experience in preparing charts and diagrams and other trial exhibits; it will include also the means for the prosecutor himself to travel and do what else is necessary for him to prepare for the trial. A prosecutor assigned to a big, complex case may have no other assignment to distract his attention. Within broad limits, he is not obliged to weigh the cost in time and his own or his client's money of an investigation or a particular piece of trial preparation. When he wishes to interview potential witnesses, he has the authority of the government behind him, and can take advantage of the ordinary citizen's habit of supporting the law. He can, for example, summon witnesses to his office or arrange to visit them in their places of work or at their homes, by using an "official" document or an "official" tone of voice, which has no more force behind it than a request.

---

14. "Misunderstandings about fees are a vexatious and unnecessary irritant in the lawyer-client relationship. . . . Counsel is cautioned to advise the client that failure to pay the full fee before trial will result in counsel's withdrawal from the case: Experience indicates that criminal fees are hard to collect after trial, no matter what its outcome." 1 A. Amsterdam, Trial Manual 5 for the Defense of Criminal Cases 119 (5th ed. 1988). See Cross v. United States, 392 F.2d 360, 364–68 (8th Cir.1968) (trial counsel assertedly followed "principle he had learned in some twenty years of practice—that of not representing a criminal defendant unless paid in advance").

The defendant may be aroused to action only after the prosecution has made its case. Witnesses may already have been lined up, and those who have not may be unwilling to discuss the matter further with anyone. Investigative leads may be cold or too uncertain to be pursued easily or, given limitations of resources, at all.

The questions posed by differences in resources are by no means answered by the judicious granting and withholding of continuances. Nevertheless, continuances are relevant to the disparity between prosecution and defense with respect to the resource of time, which exists because the prosecution is the initiator of a criminal case and, within very broad limits, can wait until he is ready. The significance of the disparity depends to a large extent on the availability of other resources for quick, effective action. See generally United States v. Cronic, 466 U.S. 648 (1984), p. 1054 below.

Most defense counsel will be quick to point out that so long as a defendant is not in prison, he is well off. The passage of time may make prosecution witnesses unavailable or uncertain or unconvincing. A big case developed by a prosecutor is to some extent "his" or "her" case—which cannot easily be prosecuted by someone else should the prosecutor become unavailable. On the other hand, justice delayed *is* to some extent justice denied, even if, as in criminal cases, criminal justice is not intended to and does not "right" a wrong. The relevance of punishment to a crime is diminished by too long delay; society's response loses some of its character as punishment and to that extent loses its justification.

How far should we honor the request for a continuance based on alleged difficulties and delays in investigation and trial preparation? A timely request for a continuance of a few days or weeks ordinarily would and certainly should be granted. What of cases in which the indictment follows a year or more of investigation and the defense requests a continuance of several months (and then perhaps a second continuance of several months more)?

Discovery

FEDERAL RULES OF CRIMINAL PROCEDURE

Rule 16.

DISCOVERY AND INSPECTION

(a) Governmental Disclosure of Evidence.

(1) Information Subject to Disclosure.

(A) Statement of Defendant. Upon request of a defendant the government must disclose to the defendant and make available for inspection, copying, or photographing: any relevant written or recorded statements made by the defendant, or copies thereof, within the possession, custody, or control of the government, the existence of which is known, or by the exercise of due diligence may become known, to the attorney for the government; that portion of any written record containing the substance of any relevant oral statement made by the defendant whether before or after arrest in response to interrogation by any person then known to the defendant to be a government agent; and recorded testimony of the defendant before a grand jury which relates to the offense charged. The government must also disclose to the defendant the substance of any other relevant oral statement made by the defendant whether before or after arrest in response to interrogation by any person then known by the defendant to be a government agent if the government intends to use that statement at trial. Upon request of a defendant which is an organization such as a corporation, partnership, association or labor union, the government must disclose to the defendant any of the foregoing statements made by a person who the government contends (1) was, at the time of making the statement, so situated as a director, officer, employee, or agent as to have been able legally to bind the defendant in respect to the subject of the statement, or (2) was, at the time of the offense, personally involved in the alleged conduct constituting the offense and so situated as a director, officer, employee, or agent as to have been able legally to bind the defendant in respect to that alleged conduct in which the person was involved.

(B) Defendant's Prior Record. Upon request of the defendant, the government shall furnish to the defendant such copy of the defendant's prior criminal record, if any, as is within the possession, custody, or control of the government, the existence of which is known, or by the exercise of due diligence may become known, to the attorney for the government.

(C) Documents and Tangible Objects. Upon request of the defendant the government shall permit the defendant to inspect and copy or photograph books, papers, documents, photographs, tangible objects, buildings or places, or copies or portions thereof, which are within the possession, custody or control of the government, and which are material to the preparation of the defendant's defense or are intended for use by the government as evidence in chief at the trial, or were obtained from or belong to the defendant.

(D) Reports of Examinations and Tests. Upon request of a defendant the government shall permit the defendant to inspect and copy or photograph any results or reports of physical or mental examinations, and of scientific tests or experiments, or copies thereof, which are within the possession, custody, or control of the government, the existence of which is known, or by the exercise of due diligence may become known, to the attorney for the government, and which are material to the preparation of the defense or are intended for use by the government as evidence in chief at the trial.

(E) Expert Witnesses. At the defendant's request, the government shall disclose to the defendant a written summary of testimony that the government intends to use under Rules 702, 703, or 705 of the Federal Rules of Evidence during its case-in-chief at trial. If the government requests discovery under subdivision (b)(1)(C)(ii) of this rule and the defendant complies, the government shall, at the defendant's request, disclose to the defendant a written summary of testimony the government intends to use under Rules 702, 703, or 705 as evidence at trial on the issue of the defendant's mental condition. The summary provided under this subdivision shall describe the witnesses' opinions, the bases and the reasons for those opinions, and the witnesses' qualifications.

(2) Information Not Subject to Disclosure. Except as provided in paragraphs (A), (B), (D), and (E) of subdivision (a)(1), this rule does not authorize the discovery or inspection of reports, memoranda, or other internal government documents made by the attorney for the government or any other government agent investigating or prosecuting the case. Nor does the rule authorize the discovery or inspection of statements made by government witnesses or prospective government witnesses except as provided in 18 U.S.C. § 3500.[15]

(3) Grand Jury Transcripts. Except as provided in Rules 6, 12(i) and 26.2, and subdivision (a)(1)(A) of this rule, these rules do not relate to discovery or inspection of recorded proceedings of a grand jury.

(b) The Defendant's Disclosure of Evidence.

(1) Information Subject to Disclosure.

(A) Documents and Tangible Objects. If the defendant requests disclosure under subdivision (a)(1)(C) or (D) of this rule, upon compliance with such request by the government, the defendant, on request of the government, shall permit the government to inspect and copy or photograph books, papers, documents, photographs, tangible objects, or copies or portions thereof, which are within the possession, custody, or control of the defendant and which the defendant intends to introduce as evidence in chief at the trial.

(B) Reports of Examinations and Tests. If the defendant requests disclosure under subdivision (a)(1)(C) or (D) of this rule, upon compliance with such request by the government, the defendant, on request of the government, shall permit the government to inspect and copy or photograph any results or reports of physical or mental examinations and of scientific tests or experiments made in connection with the particular case, or copies thereof, within the possession or control of the defendant, which the defendant intends to introduce as evidence in chief at the trial or which were prepared by a witness whom the defendant intends to call at the trial when the results or reports relate to that witness' testimony.

(C) Expert Witnesses. Under the following circumstances, the defendant shall, at the government's request, disclose to the government a written summary of testimony that the defendant intends to use under Rules 702, 703, or 705 of the Federal Rules of Evidence as evidence at trial: (i) if

[15] See p. 1026 below.

the defendant requests disclosure under subdivision (a)(1)(E) of this rule and the government complies, or (ii) if the defendant has given notice under Rule 12.2(b) of an intent to present expert testimony on the defendant's mental condition. This summary shall describe the witnesses' opinions, the bases and reasons for those opinions, and the witnesses' qualifications.

(2) Information Not Subject to Disclosure. Except as to scientific or medical reports, this subdivision does not authorize the discovery or inspection of reports, memoranda, or other internal defense documents made by the defendant, or the defendant's attorneys or agents in connection with the investigation or defense of the case, or of statements made by the defendant, or by government or defense witnesses, or by prospective government or defense witnesses, to the defendant, the defendant's agents or attorneys.

(c) Continuing Duty to Disclose. If, prior to or during trial, a party discovers additional evidence or material previously requested or ordered, which is subject to discovery or inspection under this rule, such party shall promptly notify the other party or that other party's attorney or the court of the existence of the additional evidence or material.

(d) Regulation of Discovery.

(1) Protective and Modifying Orders. Upon a sufficient showing the court may at any time order that the discovery or inspection be denied, restricted, or deferred, or make such other order as is appropriate. Upon motion by a party, the court may permit the party to make such showing, in whole or in part, in the form of a written statement to be inspected by the judge alone. If the court enters an order granting relief following such an ex parte showing, the entire text of the party's statement shall be sealed and preserved in the records of the court to be made available to the appellate court in the event of an appeal.

(2) Failure to Comply with a Request. If at any time during the course of the proceedings it is brought to the attention of the court that a party has failed to comply with this rule, the court may order such party to permit the discovery or inspection, grant a continuance, or prohibit the party from introducing evidence not disclosed, or it may enter such other order as it deems just under the circumstances. The court may specify the time, place and manner of making the discovery and inspection and may prescribe such terms and conditions as are just.

(e) Alibi Witnesses. Discovery of alibi witnesses is governed by Rule 12.1.

----

411. There is extensive authority for the proposition that the federal courts have "inherent" authority to order discovery in criminal cases independently of and beyond that for which provision is made in the federal rules. "Prior to the promulgation of the Rules, federal criminal procedure grew out of the inherent power of the courts to develop their own procedure. Sometimes this residual power was exercised by the enactment of local rules of court and sometimes by the process of adjudication. I doubt that the Rules, although a comprehensive regulation of federal criminal procedure, entirely supplant the residual power of the court. I doubt the advisability of reading an imaginative implication into Rule 16 that would deprive the court of its inherent power, shut off the development of discovery by adjudication and thus freeze its limits along the lines determined by cases which had been decided when the Rules were formulated. In my view, to the extent that Rule 16 does not express a policy prohibiting discovery not explicitly authorized by the Rules, the court is free, either by local rule or by adjudication, to permit discovery on the basis of its inherent power. The question as to when the court should permit this discovery is essentially one of policy, not of power." United States v. Taylor, 25 F.R.D. 225, 228 (E.D.N.Y.1960). See generally United States v. Nolte, 39 F.R.D. 359 (N.D.Cal.1965). Cf. United States v. Nobles, 422 U.S. 225, 231 (1975), referring to "the federal judiciary's inherent power to require the prosecution to produce the previously recorded statements of its witnesses so that the defense may get the full benefit of cross-examination and the truth-finding process may be enhanced."

Defendant's statements

----

412. In Cicenia v. LaGay, 357 U.S. 504 (1958), the Court adhered to the view expressed in Leland v. Oregon, 343 U.S. 790, 801–802 (1952), that although it might be "better practice" to make a defendant's statements available to the defense before trial, "in the absence of a showing of prejudice to the defendant it was not a violation of due process for a State to deny counsel an opportunity before trial to inspect his client's confession," 357 U.S. at 511. Compare the statement in Clewis v. Texas, 386 U.S. 707, 712 n.8 (1967), that "in some circumstances it may be a denial of due process for a defendant to be refused any discovery of his statements to the police."

413. See United States v. Bailleaux, 685 F.2d 1105, 1114 (9th Cir.1982), discussing Rule 16(a)(1)(A) generally, in which the court said: "[T]he government should disclose any statement made by the defendant that may be relevant to any possible defense or contention that the defendant might assert. Ordinarily, a statement made by the defendant during the course of the investigation of the crime charged should be presumed to be subject to disclosure, unless it is clear that the statement cannot be relevant. Where the Government is in doubt, the written or recorded statement should be disclosed, if a proper request is made."

In United States v. McElroy, 697 F.2d 459, 464 (2d Cir.1982), the court observed: "Rule 16(a)(1)(A) requires the government to disclose the substance not only of the incriminating post-arrest oral statements which it intends to use at trial, but also the substance of the defendant's responses to any *Miranda* warnings which preceded the statements. Disclosure, to be meaningful, must be made of the defendant's responses both to the warnings which immediately preceded his admissions and to any other set(s) of warnings given the defendant from arrest onwards. Requiring the government to make such disclosure will bring to light *Miranda* violations that might otherwise remain hidden because the defendant misunderstands his rights, fails fully to inform defense counsel, or is unable to remember."

Rule 16(a)(1)(A) does not cover written notes that record oral statements previously made to persons other than known government agents. In re United States, 834 F.2d 283 (2d Cir.1987). The court also reaffirmed that Rule 16(a)(1)(A) does not apply to statements of coconspirators. The district court had ordered the government to disclose statements of coconspirators that the government intended to offer in evidence as containing an admission of the defendant. Accord United States v. Roberts, 811 F.2d 257 (4th Cir.1987).

United States v. Gladney, 563 F.2d 491 (1st Cir.1977), discusses the government's obligation to furnish items "the existence of which is known, or by the exercise of due diligence may become known, to the attorney for the government."

See United States v. Lanoue, 71 F.3d 966 (1st Cir.1995) (failure to comply with Rule 16(d)(1)(A); conviction vacated).

414. "The presumption that defendants in criminal cases are commonly disposed to take the witness stand and lie has played a major role in decisions denying discovery of the type sought here. Give him his confession or grand jury testimony, the argument runs, and a defendant is likely to tailor his falsehoods on the stand to avoid inconsistencies with the presumably truthful (and self-incriminating) things he said when, without counsel, he confessed or testified before the grand jury. . . . As it has been put here, the argument is stated argumentatively and perhaps less favorably than it is phrased by its proponents. But its net worth is not much greater than the adverse formulation is meant to imply.

"To begin with, given the drift of contemporary law on the right to counsel and the privilege against self-incrimination, there is *prima facie* a suspect quality in the theory that the Government should be free to extract from an uncounseled potential defendant, and then withhold from both him and his lawyer, 'voluntary' admissions which, when he has counsel, he will want to avoid by committing perjury. Passing that, the point is built one-sidedly of untested folklore. It has been dismissed as an 'old hobgoblin' by Mr. Justice Brennan (see 33 F.R.D. at 62). . . . It may be, of course, that the 'hobgoblin,' like other things that alarm us in the night, is simply the heightened after-image of genuine experience which cannot be altogether denied or discounted. But nobody knows the degree of the probability of perjury; certainly, nobody has even a hunch sufficient to override the solid claims of all defendants because some may use a legitimate means of trial preparation (the way some always do) as a device for the subversion of justice.

"There are more things wrong with the perjury theory. It overlooks, *inter alia*, that it is a lawyer who ordinarily moves for discovery, representing that he has a proper purpose for what is on its face a responsible professional request. One must, of course, avoid the appearance of naiveté at all costs. But this has not yet been thought to require abandonment of the presumption—without which we are all lost—that the members of our bar behave regularly and refrain from suborning perjury.

"When we allow ourselves to indulge that presumption, other excesses in the fear of perjury begin to appear. The defense lawyer, in addition to the obstacles he presents for the prosecutor's progress toward conviction, performs a familiar and important role in the stipulation of indisputable facts and the counseling of guilty pleas where such steps are warranted in the potential interests of his client as well as the community. His service along such lines, no less than others, is likely to be more effective and intelligent when he can know, along with the prosecutor, what things the defendant has confessed or said in the past along with the (possibly different) things the defendant is currently claiming.

"If we can (as we can) imagine the case of a truthful defendant, he is entitled to check whether the written or transcribed statement or the grand jury transcript contains errors, or possible errors. Nobody who has read transcripts (or watched the witness say whether he was asked those questions and gave those answers) preserves illusions about even the best of reporters or typists. Apart from this relatively small problem, the witness bent on telling the truth, but knowing the trickery and imperfection of memory, may well be unnerved, or at least disquieted, when he is forbidden to see what he said months or years earlier under trying circumstances. For these and other good reasons, no lawyer or judge could feel comfortable testifying a second time when he was barred from access to an existing transcript of his testimony about the same subjects on an earlier occasion.

"The perjury theory is not only partial because it is incomplete; it is also one-sided. The Government's witnesses, knowing they face cross-examination, are regularly and understandably refreshed in their recollection before taking the stand by reading their prior grand jury testimony, reports or statements. This is accepted practice even though the experience underlying our curbstone judgments includes occasions when prosecution witnesses have placed some values above the search for truth. We tell juries of the interest of witnesses, defendants as well as others. But we also tell them that they may not discount or enhance testimony in advance because of the status or proponent of the witness. Can we in good conscience treat a guess about the likelihood of perjury as justification for ignoring such principles and placing the defense at so stark a disadvantage as that for which the Government argues?

"Finally, the worry about perjury, whatever its basis, reflects an exaggerated attribution to defendants of a sinister power to 'beat the system.' The defendant who plays games with his prior inconsistent statements is not in an enviable plight. Unless we have told ourselves myths about the 'great engine' of cross-examination, it serves as a powerful antidote to the recent fabrication, however artfully contrived. Every lawyer knows this. We all know, too, that some will manage by foul measures to conceal the truth and defeat justice. But that is an everyday risk of according to both sides the opportunity to pervert rules of fundamental fairness. It is not a justification for scrapping the rules or weighting them on the side of the prosecution." United States v. Projansky, 44 F.R.D. 550, 555–57 (S.D.N.Y.1968) (Frankel, J.).

415. "It is difficult to understand why a defendant should be denied pretrial inspection of his own statement in the absence of circumstances affirmatively indicating disservice to the public interest.

"If a suspect refused to give a statement unless assured a copy, it would be an injudicious prosecutor who would not agree. And if the suspect were then represented by competent counsel, that stipulation would be required. Why, then, should the State refuse a copy to the suspect who was unrepresented and uninformed?

"We must be mindful of the role of a confession. It frequently becomes the core of the State's case. It is not uncommon for the judicial proceeding to become more of a review of what transpired at headquarters than a trial of the basic criminal event itself. No one would deny a defendant's right thoroughly to investigate the facts of the crime to prepare for trial of that event. When a confession is given and issues surrounding it tend to displace the criminal event as the focus of the trial, there should be like opportunity to get at the facts of the substituted issue. Simple justice requires that a defendant be permitted to prepare to meet what thus looms as the critical element of the case against him.

"The need for an opportunity to prepare to deal with a defendant's statement must be evident. If voluntariness is in issue, the content of the confession may be revealing. Counsel would need time to explore thoroughly the truth of the factual assertions therein, to inquire whether it contains anything more than the State knew at the time when defendant was apprehended, and to consider whether the content itself supports or negates the defendant's claim of involuntariness. Pretrial inspection may be equally necessary even though defendant concedes he freely gave the statement.

This is so because the impact of the statement upon guilt may turn upon how the facts are stated, or upon the absence of exculpatory facts which a defendant may claim were revealed to the interrogator or would have been revealed if the inquiry had been complete. In murder cases in which guilt is not disputed, the manner of expression or the omission of palliative circumstances may have additional significance because of their influence upon the jury's determination as to punishment. Or the confession may contain prejudicial material which should be exscinded and as to which counsel should not be required to make a hurried decision in the courtroom. The possible situations may be multiplied. The virtue of the adversary approach to a trial lies precisely in the opportunity for a full and fair presentation, and hence where the State has had a unilateral examination of a defendant, he should be enabled, as far as feasible, to prepare to explore the completeness and fairness of a policeman's or prosecutor's development of the story in the confession.

"In the foregoing, we speak of what *may* be the significance of pretrial inspection. The fact is that counsel for a defendant does not know or cannot be sure whether he needs the inspection until he has had it. It is no answer to say that a defendant 'must remember' what he said. If the defendant actually does remember, it cannot harm the State to furnish a copy. But as every trial lawyer knows, witnesses do not recall their statements with precision or detail. And when one considers the emotional sway which likely attends a wholly voluntary confession of crime . . . it is idle to assert that a defendant 'must remember.'" State v. Johnson, 145 A.2d 313, 315–16 (N.J.1958).

416. "The government requests that if the motion [by defendant Ross for an order permitting him to inspect and copy his statement to government officials] be granted the order be so restricted as to bar counsel for Ross from permitting examination of the statement by counsel for his co-defendants. While the court is empowered . . . to so limit the order, I do not believe that the showing made by the government is sufficient to justify the requested restriction. The government argues that Rule 16(a)(1) is available only to the author of a statement or confession. This is true, but the purpose of Rule 16(a)(1) is not simply to permit a confessing defendant to refresh his recollection. A statement produced under the rule serves not only to inform a defendant of the contents of the statement, so that he may explain his admissions, but provides his counsel with information which might lead to the discovery of other evidence important to the defense. Persons mentioned in the statement as accomplices are certainly sources of information, and counsel should be permitted to interview them. Such interviews, even if ethically permissible, are not likely to be fruitful unless counsel for the co-defendants consent, and it is improbable that consent would be given without pre-knowledge of the contents of the statement. To grant the government's request would rob Rule 16(a)(1) of much of its vitality." United States v. Bailey, 262 F.Supp. 331, 332–33 (D.Kan.1967).

Documents, Tangible Objects, Reports of Examinations and Tests

———

United States v. Gatto

763 F.2d 1040 (9th Cir.1985).

■ WALLACE, CIRCUIT JUDGE:

The federal government appeals the district court's order excluding evidence seized by Utah state officials in a trash search operation about which the federal government failed to notify the defense until a few weeks before trial was to begin, even though the state had obtained the evidence two years earlier. It also appeals the district court's subsequent dismissal of the action with prejudice for failing to proceed to trial before the appeal of the exclusion order was resolved. . . . We reverse and remand.

I

Early in 1982, the Sacramento field office of the Federal Bureau of Investigation (FBI) began investigating operations at the Los Gatos, California, office of Sunburst Industries, a company with offices there and in Salt Lake City, Utah. On July 7, 1982, as a result of the Sacramento investigation, a grand jury returned an indictment charging the defendants with 47 counts of mail fraud, wire fraud, interstate transportation of forged or altered securities, and conspiracy. The district court ordered the federal government to provide discovery "in accordance with FRCrimP 16." Over the next eighteen months, there were numerous pretrial motions dealing with discovery and admissibility of evidence. Finally, a jury trial was set for April 24, 1984.

On March 28, 1984, however, the federal prosecutors notified defense counsel that they had just discovered, and intended to introduce into evidence during their case-in-chief, numerous documents obtained by the State of Utah's Organized Crime and Criminal Identification Bureau (Utah Bureau) in a trash search operation conducted at the Salt Lake City office of Sunburst Industries between November 30, 1981 and May 19, 1982. They claimed that a conversation between Sacramento-based FBI agents and a Utah state official on March 21, 1984 had made them aware of the documents for the first time. The district court granted a defense motion for an evidentiary hearing on why the existence of this evidence had not been disclosed earlier in the discovery process.

After holding a six-day evidentiary hearing, the district judge issued an order excluding any evidence the federal government obtained from the Utah authorities which the Utah authorities had seized pursuant to the trash search operation, as well as such evidence obtained as a result of the trash search. He also ordered the government to identify any evidence it possessed and intended to introduce during trial that could be directly traced to the trash search operation. The trial date was continued to May 1, 1984.

The district judge based his ruling on the authority of rule 16(d)(2), Fed.R.Crim.P., and his inherent supervisory powers. He explicitly did not base it on the fourth amendment. He observed that rule 16(a)(1)(C) required the government to make available to the defense any documents within the government's possession, custody, or control that are material to the defense or intended for use in the government's case-in-chief. He further stated that rule 16(d)(2) gives federal courts the discretionary authority to grant a continuance, exclude evidence, or enter any other order deemed just in the circumstances if any party fails to comply with a discovery order. The district judge also reasoned that he had inherent supervisory power to punish discovery misconduct. . . .

The district judge concluded that the facts of this case allowed him to exercise both his rule 16(d)(2) and his supervisory powers against the government because the federal prosecutors and the Sacramento FBI agents helping them were either negligent or reckless in not discovering and disclosing the existence of the trash search evidence in a more timely manner. The record shows that neither the Sacramento-based officials nor the Salt Lake City FBI agent who served as a liaison between the Sacramento investigators and the federal investigation of Sunburst's Utah activities actually possessed, had custody of, or controlled the trash search evidence before March 27, 1984. Moreover, the district judge never made any finding to the contrary. He merely found that the federal officials were negligent or reckless in not learning about, asserting control over, and disclosing the existence of the documents earlier. He found that a number of federal officials unconnected with the Sacramento investigation had at least heard about the trash search operation as early as December 1981. He also found that the Salt Lake City FBI agent had heard about the operation and had passed on one document which could be traced to the trash search operation long before the Sacramento-based officials alleged that they learned about the operation. The district judge said he found it inconceivable that the experienced Salt Lake City FBI agent would not have reported the existence of the trash search material to his fellow investigators in Sacramento. He made no finding, however, that the federal prosecutors had any advance knowledge of the trash search or that the Salt Lake City FBI agent realized the extent or importance of the documents in the state's possession. Moreover, he stopped short of finding that the Sacramento-based FBI agents were lying about their asserted ignorance. The district judge concluded, however, that the behavior of the Sacramento-based FBI agents amounted either to negligence or recklessness because not even bureaucratic difficulties could excuse their failure to learn about the trash search.

The district judge reasoned that these facts neither required him to dismiss the case nor allowed him merely to order a continuance, which he admitted was the normal remedy. He stated that dismissal was unacceptable because there was no proof that the government had intentionally or willfully concealed the evidence, the problem occurred before trial began, the evidence was not exculpatory, and any tainted evidence left over could be dealt with at trial on a piece-by-piece basis. He maintained that a continuance was insufficient, however, because it failed to satisfy either the demands of due process or notions of fair play and substantial justice, because the time, effort, and money that would be lost would be prejudicial, unfair, and unjust to the defendants. He observed that the indictment had been filed nearly two years before, and thus the sword had hung over the defendants long enough, that they had spent sufficient money on their defense, and that the court had expended sufficient judicial resources in managing the case. Moreover, the trial was set to begin in four days, and postponing it would inconvenience both the court and the defense attorneys in reclearing their calendars. Finally, a related state trial would be delayed if a continuance were ordered.

The government appealed this exclusionary order pursuant to 18 U.S.C. § 3731 before trial began. While its appeal was pending, the government unsuccessfully attempted either to stay the commencement of trial or to convince the district court that it had lost jurisdiction over the case while the appeal was pending. On the day trial was to begin, the government refused to proceed on the ground that it was entitled first to exercise its statutory right to appeal the exclusionary order under 18 U.S.C. § 3731. It argued that to proceed would take the meaning out of its right to appeal the exclusionary order because the evidence excluded was substantial proof of material facts. The district judge advised the government of his planned action and then dismissed the case pursuant to rule 48(b), Fed.R.Crim.P., with prejudice. He reasoned that the government was willing to proceed before discovering the trash search evidence, apparently concluding that it had sufficient evidence to convict the defendants. He cited several cases to build the proposition that rule 48(b) gave him the discretionary authority to dismiss a case for unnecessary delay either with or without prejudice, whether or not there are constitutional rights at stake. He justified his dismissal of the case with prejudice on grounds that the government's refusal to proceed was a "flagrant refusal to abide by this Court's previous orders," an "unnecessary delay," and the "rankest abuse of prosecutorial discretion." The government also appealed this dismissal, and we granted its motion to consolidate its two appeals.

II

. . .

The delay in disclosure in this case did not violate any constitutional provision, federal statute, specific discovery order, or any other recognized right except perhaps rule 16, Fed.R.Crim.P. . . . Moreover, the fact that rule 16 contains specific remedies for its violation eliminates any justification for an exercise of supervisory power to create any other remedy for it. We hold, therefore, that the separation-of-powers principle barred the district court from exercising any supervisory power to exclude the evidence in this case.

III

The government also argues that the district court erred in excluding the evidence pursuant to rule 16(d)(2), Fed.R.Crim.P., because rule 16 applies only to documents that are within the federal government's actual possession, custody, or control, because the prosecution's failure to learn about the trash search documents and to make its disclosure earlier was not negligent or reckless, because a continuance was the appropriate remedy if it did violate rule 16, and because the exclusionary order was overbroad. We agree with the government's first reason, and therefore need not reach the remaining issues.

Rule 16(d)(2) states that a district court has discretionary authority to "order [a] party to permit the discovery or inspection, grant a continuance, or prohibit the party from introducing evidence not disclosed, or it may enter such other order as it deems just under the circumstances" to remedy a failure by the government to permit inspection and copying of tangible evidence described by rule 16(a)(1)(C), which is evidence "within the possession, custody or control of the government, and which [is] material to the preparation of [the] defense or [is] intended for use by the government as evidence in chief at the trial." The government intended to use the trash search evidence in its case-in-chief. Thus, the only question is whether the evidence was "within the possession, custody or control" of the federal government.

The record shows that neither the Sacramento-based officials nor the Salt Lake City FBI agent actually possessed, had custody of, or controlled the trash search evidence before March 27, 1984. Moreover, the district judge never made any finding to the contrary. Thus, the precise issue we face is whether rule 16(a)(1)(C) ever requires the federal government to disclose and produce documents that are in the actual possession, custody or control of state officials, the relevance of which the federal government negligently or recklessly fails to appreciate. . . .

Our first question is whether, pursuant to rule 16(a)(1)(C), the "government" includes any persons other than the prosecutors. We have not faced this question before. The district court appears to have taken the position that the "government" included the Sacramento-based FBI agents assisting the federal prosecutor in this case as well as the FBI agent in Salt Lake City who was coordinating information.

. . . We need not resolve whether the district court correctly included the identified FBI agents for purposes of rule 16(a)(1)(C). Even if we assume the district judge was correct, the critical issue pertains to possession of the records.

The important question, therefore, is whether the documents must be in the actual possession or control of the FBI agents or whether constructive possession or control is sufficient. Under rule 16(a)(1)(A), which deals with statements of a defendant, we have recognized that the prosecutor's actual possession is not necessary in all cases. . . .

The cases discussing a prosecutor's due diligence obligation under rule 16(a)(1)(A) are not relevant to our case under rule 16(a)(1)(C). We have already assumed for purposes of this appeal that the government included the designated FBI agents. Rule 16(a)(1)(A) only requires the government to disclose any of the defendant's statements that are "within the possession, custody or control of the government, the existence of which is known, or by the exercise of due diligence may become known, to the attorney for the government." Thus, the due diligence requirement establishing constructive possession relates solely to the prosecutor and whether he should have been aware of a statement in the possession of another *federal* agency. As no such language is found in rule 16(a)(1)(C), a literal reading of the entire rule requires us to conclude that Congress intended no such constructive possession extension. Moreover, even if such language were found in rule 16(a)(1)(C), it would only create a due diligence requirement over documents in the possession, custody, or control of some federal agency. We would still be required to find some special reason to justify extending the requirement to documents in the possession, custody, or control of state authorities.

Because we find no due diligence language in rule 16(a)(1)(C) at all, nor any special reason to deviate from its plain language, we conclude that it triggers the government's disclosure obligation only with respect to documents within the federal government's actual possession, custody, or control. . . .

. . .

Therefore, we conclude that the triggering requirement under rule 16(a)(1)(C) is that the papers, documents, and tangible objects be in the actual possession, custody or control of the government. Here, they were not. The fashioning of a due diligence constructive possession or control addition to the rule by the district judge was erroneous and, therefore, his suppression of the trash cover evidence based upon rule 16 must be reversed.

The defendants may have been put into a difficult position because the government announced, four weeks before trial, that it had 382 tangible items it planned to introduce into evidence. Although the district court could not suppress the evidence pursuant to any supervisory powers or rule 16, and the parties have cited to us no other authority for such an order, the district judge could have considered more searchingly whether a continuance was appropriate under the circumstances simply as a matter of proper case management. The record is barren as to how much time longer than four weeks, if any, the defendants would have needed to prepare to meet this new evidence—indeed, the defendants did not even request a continuance. Thus, we cannot review whether a continuance would have been appropriate here.

. . .

SCHROEDER, CIRCUIT JUDGE, dissenting.

I respectfully dissent. Fed.R.Crim.P. 16(a)(1)(C) requires the prosecution to produce relevant documents anywhere within the government's "possession, custody or control." The rule is not limited to documents physically resting in federal agency file folders and should reach at least far enough to encompass these documents, which were at the prosecutors' fingertips.

The documents in question were the product of a joint investigation by Utah and Federal Authorities. The Utah trash search was linked to this Sacramento prosecution by an extensive network of state and federal authorities, including an FBI agent in Utah who acted as liaison between the Utah investigators and the Sacramento prosecutors. The trash search was also linked to this prosecution by a federally funded computer network designed to make evidence readily available to all participating state and federal agencies. No reasonable explanation appears in this record for the prosecutors' twin failures to obtain and disclose these documents long before the eve of trial. The district court found the prosecution negligent to the point of recklessness and came just short of finding an intentional withholding of documents.

In my view, these documents were within the government's "control" pursuant to the meaning of rule 16. The majority's contrary holding rewards prosecutors who wait until the last minute to examine available evidence. It encourages gamesmanship and delay rather than forthrightness and efficiency.

That these documents were material, indeed key, to the prosecution is demonstrated by the government's refusal to go forward with its case upon their suppression. Prejudice to the defendants, had the district court refused to order suppression, is similarly clear. As the district court observed, the government created a dilemma for defendants by forcing them to go to trial unprepared or to expend more time and money in further preparation of an already very costly case. Therefore, I would hold that in the circumstances of this case, the district court did not abuse its discretion when it dismissed the indictment with prejudice after the government refused to proceed. . . .

———

417. In United States v. Armstrong, 517 U.S. 456 (1996) (8–1), another aspect of which is considered in note 312 p. 649 above, the court held that the reference in Rule 16(a)(1)(C) to documents, tangible objects, and so forth that are "material to the preparation of the defendant's defense" includes only items that are material to "the defendant's response to the Government's case in chief." Id. at 462. In particular, it did not cover items that might have a bearing on the defendant's claim of discriminatory prosecution.

418. The government's obligation of discovery under Rule 16(a)(1)(C) is not limited to documents within the judicial district, in the actual possession of the prosecutor. Its obligation turns on "the extent to which the prosecutor has knowledge of and access to the documents sought by the defendant in each case. . . . The prosecutor will be deemed to have knowledge of and access to anything in the possession, custody or control of any federal agency participating in the same investigation of the defendant." United States v. Bryan, 868 F.2d 1032, 1036 (9th Cir.1989). In United States v. Santiago, 46 F.3d 885 (9th Cir.1995), the court emphasized that a government agency's involvement in the investigation of the defendant is a sufficient, but not necessary, factor to show the prosecutor's knowledge of and access to documents.

419. The defendant, Barnard, was convicted of murder in the Louisiana courts and attacked the conviction by a federal petition for habeas corpus.

"Prior to the trial he moved for permission of the Court to allow inspection of the murder weapon and bullet by a ballistics expert of his own choosing. That this was not a frivolous request is evident since one of the most damaging pieces of evidence against Barnard was the identification of the murder bullet as having been fired by a .22 Luger pistol traced to his possession. Seventy-five percent of this slug was destroyed and the identification was made on the remaining 25%. This fact alone raises the possibility that had Barnard been assisted by a ballistics expert of his own he may have been able to shake the identification testimony of the State's experts. Barnard's motion was denied.

"Under Louisiana procedure pre-trial discovery of evidence in the hands of the prosecution is limited to the defendant's confessions and to narcotics. . . . In affirming Barnard's conviction the Supreme Court of Louisiana said that, although . . . production of evidence is required where the evidence is favorable to the accused, there had been no showing that an examination of the murder weapon and bullet would be favorable to Barnard. . . . [D]ue process cannot be sidestepped by such a facile distinction.

"The question is not one of discovery but rather the defendant's right to the means necessary to conduct his defense. . . . Fundamental fairness is violated when a criminal defendant on trial for his liberty is denied the opportunity to have an expert of his choosing, bound by appropriate safeguards imposed by the Court, examine a piece of critical evidence whose nature is subject to varying expert opinion.

"Neither are we persuaded by the State's contention that Barnard waived his right to complain of the denial of this request to examine the weapon by failing to move for a continuance when the pistol was placed into evidence.

. . .

". . . In view of the earlier unsuccessful effort to obtain inspection upon which to base countervailing expert opinion the asserted practice of allowing a continuance—more accurately, an interruption of a trial then in progress—has built-in hazards so prejudicial to the accused in the eyes of the jury that it does not under the circumstances of this case present a viable alternative to pretrial discovery going to the very heart of the case and fundamental due process fairness." Barnard v. Henderson, 514 F.2d 744, 746–47 (5th Cir.1975) (conviction vacated).

Barnard was discussed and applied in White v. Maggio, 556 F.2d 1352 (5th Cir.1977) (failure to grant pretrial discovery of bullets used to show that fatal bullet came from defendant's gun). The court said that "under *Barnard* a writ of habeas corpus should issue only if the state prevented inspection by defense experts of tangible evidence that is both 'critical' to the conviction and subject to varying expert opinion." Id. at 1356.

420. Does the court have authority, on motion of the defendant or otherwise, to require the complaining witness or another witness for the prosecution to submit to a mental or physical examination? If so, on what basis? See, for example, United States v. Dildy, 39 F.R.D. 340 (D.D.C.1966), in which the defendant, who was charged with rape, moved that the court require the complainant to submit to a psychiatric examination and blood tests of herself and her infant child. See generally United States v. Benn, 476 F.2d 1127, 1130–31 (D.C.Cir.1972).

FEDERAL RULES OF CRIMINAL PROCEDURE

Rule 17.

SUBPOENA

. . .

(c) For Production of Documentary Evidence and of Objects. A subpoena may also command the person to whom it is directed to produce the books, papers, documents or other objects designated therein. The court on motion made promptly may quash or modify the subpoena if compliance would be unreasonable or oppressive. The court may direct that books, papers, documents or objects designated in the subpoena be produced before the court at a time prior to the trial or prior to the time when they are to be offered in evidence and may upon their production permit the books, papers, documents or objects or portions thereof to be inspected by the parties and their attorneys.

421. "It was intended by the rules to give some measure of discovery. Rule 16 was adopted for that purpose. It gave discovery as to documents and other materials otherwise beyond the reach of the defendant which . . . might be numerous and difficult to identify. The rule was to apply not only to documents and other materials belonging to the defendant, but also to those belonging to others which had been obtained by seizure or process. This was a departure from what had theretofore been allowed in criminal cases.

"Rule 16 deals with documents and other materials that are in the possession of the Government and provides how they may be made available to the defendant for his information. In the interest of orderly procedure in the handling of books, papers, documents and objects in the custody of the Government accumulated in the course of an investigation and subpoenaed for use before the grand jury and on the trial, it was provided by Rule 16 that the court could order such materials made available to the defendant for inspection and copying or photographing. In that way, the control and possession of the Government is not disturbed. Rule 16 provides the only way the defendant can reach such materials so as to inform himself.

"But if such materials or any part of them are not put in evidence by the Government, the defendant may subpoena them under Rule 17(c) and use them himself. It would be strange indeed if the defendant discovered some evidence by the use of Rule 16 which the Government was not going to introduce and yet could not require its production by Rule 17(c). There may be documents and other materials in the possession of the Government not subject to Rule 16. No good reason appears to us why they may not be reached by subpoena under Rule 17(c) as long as they are evidentiary. That is not to say that the materials thus subpoenaed must actually be used in evidence. It is only required that a good-faith effort be made to obtain evidence. The court may control the use of Rule 17(c) to that end by its power to rule on motions to quash or modify.

"It was not intended by Rule 16 to give a limited right of discovery, and then by Rule 17 to give a right of discovery in the broadest terms. Rule 17 provided for the usual subpoena *ad testificandum* and *duces tecum*, which may be issued by the clerk, with the provision that the court may direct the materials designated in the subpoena *duces tecum* to be produced at a specified time and place for inspection by the defendant. Rule 17(c) was not intended to provide an additional means of discovery. Its chief innovation was to expedite the trial by providing a time and place *before* trial for the inspection of the subpoenaed materials. . . . However, the plain words of the Rule are not to be ignored. They must be given their ordinary meaning to carry out the purpose of establishing a more liberal policy for the production, inspection and use of materials at the trial. There was no intention to exclude from the reach of process of the defendant any material that had been used before the grand jury or could be used at the trial. In short, any document or other materials, admissible as evidence, obtained by the Government by solicitation or voluntarily from third persons is subject to subpoena." Bowman Dairy Co. v. United States, 341 U.S. 214, 218–21 (1951).

Witnesses

18 U.S.C. § 3432

Indictment and list of jurors and witnesses for prisoner in capital cases

A person charged with treason or other capital offense shall at least three entire days before commencement of trial be furnished with a copy of the indictment and a list of the veniremen, and of the witnesses to be produced on the trial for proving the indictment, stating the place of abode of each venireman and witness, except that such list of the veniremen and witnesses need not be furnished if the court finds by a preponderance of the evidence that providing the list may jeopardize the life or safety of any person.

The amendments to Rule 16 transmitted to Congress in 1974 included a subsection (a)(1)(E) as follows:

"Government witnesses. Upon request of the defendant the government shall furnish to the defendant a written list of the names and addresses of all government witnesses which the attorney for the government intends to call in the presentation of the case in chief together with any record of prior felony convictions of any such witness which is within the knowledge of the attorney for the government. When a request for discovery of the names and addresses of witnesses has been made by a defendant, the government shall be allowed to perpetuate the testimony of such witnesses in accordance with the provisions of Rule 15."

The Advisory Committee's Note accompanying this provision observed that many states had provisions for pretrial disclosure of witnesses for the prosecution and that the ABA Standards also provided for such disclosure. Disclosure of the criminal record of prosecution witnesses, the Committee said, "places the defense in the same position as the government, which normally has knowledge of the defendant's record and the record of anticipated defense witnesses. In addition, the defendant often lacks means of procuring this information on his own." With respect to the danger that witnesses would be intimidated not to testify or to change their testimony, the Committee said that the government could move for a protective order or for an order to perpetuate a witness's testimony by deposition for use at trial if the witness became unavailable or changed his testimony.

After considerable debate, Congress deleted that provision from the amended rule. The Conference Report stated only: "A majority of the Conferees believe it is not in the interest of the effective administration of criminal justice to require that the government or the defendant be forced to reveal the names and addresses of its witnesses before trial. Discouragement of witnesses and improper contacts directed at influencing their testimony were deemed paramount concerns in the formulation of this policy." H.R.Rep. No. 94–414 (to accompany H.R. 6799), 94th Cong., 1st Sess. 12 (1975).

Rule 12.1, p. 874 below, however, provides for reciprocal discovery of witnesses whose testimony will be offered to sustain or contradict a defense of alibi.

UNITED STATES ATTORNEYS' MANUAL

9–6.200 Pretrial Disclosure of Witness Identity

[I]t is the Department's position that pretrial disclosure of a witness' identity should not be made if there is, in the judgment of the prosecutor, any reason to believe that such disclosure would endanger the safety of the witness or any other person, or lead to efforts to obstruct justice. Factors relevant to the possibility of witness intimidation or obstruction of justice include, but are not limited to, the types of charges pending against the defendant, any record or information about the propensity of the defendant or the defendant's confederates to engage in witness intimidation or obstruction of justice, and any threats directed by the defendant or others against the witness. In addition, pretrial disclosure of a witness' identity should not ordinarily be made against the known wishes of any witness.

However, pretrial disclosure of the identity of a government witness may often promote the prompt and just resolution of the case. Such disclosure may enhance the prospects that the defendant will plead guilty or lead to the initiation of plea negotiations; in the event the defendant goes to trial, such disclosure may expedite the conduct of the trial by eliminating the need for a continuance.

Accordingly, with respect to prosecutions in federal court, a prosecutor should give careful consideration, as to each prospective witness, whether— absent any indication of potential adverse consequences of the kind mentioned above—reason exists to disclose such witness' identity prior to trial. It should be borne in mind that a decision by the prosecutor to disclose pretrial the identity of potential government witnesses may be conditioned upon the defendant's making reciprocal disclosure as to the identity of potential defense witnesses. Similarly, where appropriate in light of the facts and circumstances of the case, a prosecutor may determine to disclose only the identity, but not the current address or whereabouts, of a witness.

In sum, whether or not to disclose the identity of a witness prior to trial is committed to the discretion of the federal prosecutor, and that discretion should be exercised on a case-by-case, and witness-by-witness basis. Considerations of witness safety and willingness to cooperate, and the integrity of the judicial process, are paramount.

Gregory v. United States

369 F.2d 185 (D.C.Cir.1966).

[The defendant was convicted of murder, robbery, and assault.]

■ J. SKELLY WRIGHT, CIRCUIT JUDGE:

. . .

The prosecutor embarrassed and confounded the accused in the preparation of his defense by advising the witnesses to the robberies and murder not to speak to anyone unless he were present. Six days before the trial began, defense counsel and the prosecutor, Mr. Weitzel, appeared before a motions judge. Defense counsel asked for the judge's assistance because two eye witnesses to the murder and robbery had declined "to talk to me unless Mr. Weitzel is present or unless Mr. Weitzel authorizes him to talk to me." Defense counsel asked the judge to direct Mr. Weitzel to allow the witnesses to talk to him. The court ruled: "I can't direct the Government to permit you to talk to a Government witness."

On the day the trial opened, defense counsel asked for the assistance of the trial judge with respect to his difficulty in interviewing the witnesses to the events on trial. Defense counsel stated to the court that the witnesses had refused to talk to him because "the United States Attorney told them not to talk to us." At this point the prosecutor, Mr. Weitzel, stated: "I instructed all the witnesses that they were free to speak to anyone they like. However, it was my advice that they not speak to anyone about the case unless I was present." Mr. Weitzel further advised the trial court that defense counsel's motion had already been denied by a motions judge, whereupon the trial court stated: "Well, I think that disposes of the matter."

After the prosecutor had completed his opening statement, defense counsel called to the court's attention the fact that, according to the opening statement, several witnesses on the list of witnesses provided defense counsel as required by 18 U.S.C. § 3432 would not be called by the Government. Apparently thinking that if the Government had no use for these witnesses he might have, defense counsel again pointed out that he had not been able to interview these witnesses because "they have been told not to talk to us," and asked the court's assistance at least with reference to interviewing the witnesses on the list the Government would not use. The court stated: "There is nothing I can do about it."

The purpose of 18 U.S.C. § 3432 requiring that in capital cases the defendant be furnished a list of the names and addresses of the witnesses to be called by the Government is to assist defense counsel in preparing the defense by interviewing the witnesses. Witnesses, particularly eye witnesses, to a crime are the property of neither the prosecution nor the defense. Both sides have an equal right, and should have an equal opportunity, to interview them. Here the defendant was denied that opportunity which, not only the statute, but elemental fairness and due process required that he have. It is true that the prosecutor stated he did not instruct the witnesses not to talk to defense counsel. He did admit that he advised the witnesses not to talk to anyone unless he, the prosecutor, were present.

We accept the prosecutor's statement as to his advice to the witnesses as true. But we know of nothing in the law which gives the prosecutor the right to interfere with the preparation of the defense by effectively denying defense counsel access to the witnesses except in his presence. Presumably the prosecutor, in interviewing the witnesses, was unencumbered by the presence of defense counsel, and there seems to be no reason why defense counsel should not have an equal opportunity to determine, through interviews with the witnesses, what they know about the case and what they will testify to. In fact, Canon 39 of the Canons of Professional Ethics makes explicit the propriety of such conduct: "A lawyer may properly interview any witness or prospective witness for the opposing side in any civil or criminal action without the consent of opposing counsel or party." Canon 10 of the Code of Trial Conduct of the American College of Trial Lawyers is an almost verbatim provision.

We do not, of course, impugn the motives of the prosecutor in giving his advice to the witnesses. Tampering with witnesses and subornation of perjury are real dangers, especially in a capital case. But there are ways to avert this danger without denying defense counsel access to eye witnesses to the events in suit unless the prosecutor is present to monitor the interview. We cannot indulge the assumption that this tactic on the part of the prosecution is necessary. Defense counsel are officers of the court. And defense counsel are not exempted from prosecution under the statutes denouncing the crimes of obstruction of justice and subornation of perjury. In fact, the Government's motivation in disallowing defense counsel to interview witnesses apparently stems from factors other than fear of tampering. Recent records in this court reveal that the same policy followed in this case is followed even when the witness involved is a member of the police force. . . .

A criminal trial, like its civil counterpart, is a quest for truth. That quest will more often be successful if both sides have an equal opportunity to interview the persons who have the information from which the truth may be determined. The current tendency in the criminal law is in the direction of discovery of the facts before trial and elimination of surprise at trial. A related development in the criminal law is the requirement that the prosecution not frustrate the defense in the preparation of its case. Information favorable to the defense must be made available to the defense. . . . Reversals of convictions for suppression of such evidence, and even for mere failure to disclose, have become commonplace. It is not suggested here that there was any direct suppression of evidence. But there was unquestionably a suppression of the means by which the defense could obtain evidence. The defense could not know what the eye witnesses to the events in suit were to testify to or how firm they were in their testimony unless defense counsel was provided a fair opportunity for interview. In our judgment the prosecutor's advice to these eye witnesses frustrated that effort and denied appellant a fair trial.

. . .

---

422. "[W]e recognize that abuses can easily result when officials elect to inform potential witnesses of their right not to speak with defense counsel. An accused and his counsel have rights of access to potential witnesses that are no less than the accessibility to the potential prosecutors and their investigatory agents. It is imperative that prosecutors and other officials maintain a posture of strict neutrality when advising witnesses of their duties and rights. Their role as public servants and as protectors of the integrity of the judicial process permits nothing less." United States v. Rich, 580 F.2d 929, 934 (9th Cir.1978).

Gregory was distinguished in United States v. Black, 767 F.2d 1334 (9th Cir.1985). The prosecutor sent a letter to prospective witnesses that explained trial and pretrial procedures. The letter said: "At some point prior to trial you may be contacted by an attorney on behalf of the defendant. You may speak to this person if you choose, but have no obligation to do so." The court concluded that the letter stated the law correctly and was not improper. But see United States v. Rogers, 642 F.Supp. 934 (D.Colo.1986), finding that a similar letter was improper and directing that a follow-up letter recommending cooperation with defense counsel be sent. See also People v. Davis, 98 Cal.Rptr. 71 (Ct.App.1971) (disapproving prosecutor's letter to complaining witnesses in statutory rape cases advising them that they did not have to submit to court-ordered psychiatric examination).

When the government finds it necessary to place a prosecution witness in protective custody before trial, "it becomes the duty of the trial court to ensure that counsel for defense has access to the secluded witness under controlled arrangements." United States v. Walton, 602 F.2d 1176, 1180 (4th Cir.1979). The witness may, however, refuse to be interviewed.

423. ABA Standards for Criminal Justice, Prosecution Function and Defense Function (3d ed. 1993): Prosecution Function Standard 3-3.1(d): A prosecutor should not discourage or obstruct communication between prospective witnesses and defense counsel. A prosecutor should not advise any person or cause any person to be advised to decline to give to the defense information which such person has the right to give."

FEDERAL RULES OF CRIMINAL PROCEDURE

Rule 15.

DEPOSITIONS

(a) When Taken. Whenever due to exceptional circumstances of the case it is in the interest of justice that the testimony of a prospective witness of a party be taken and preserved for use at trial, the court may upon motion of such party and notice to the parties order that testimony of such witness be taken by deposition and that any designated book, paper, document, record, recording, or other material not privileged, be produced at the same time and place. If a witness is detained pursuant to section 3144 of title 18, United States Code, [note 488 p. 985 below] the court on written motion of the witness and upon notice to the parties may direct that the witness' deposition be taken. After the deposition has been subscribed the court may discharge the witness.

(b) Notice of Taking. The party at whose instance a deposition is to be taken shall give to every party reasonable written notice of the time and place for taking the deposition. The notice shall state the name and address of each person to be examined. On motion of a party upon whom the notice is served, the court for cause shown may extend or shorten the time or change the place for taking the deposition. The officer having custody of a defendant shall be notified of the time and place set for the examination and shall, unless the defendant waives in writing the right to be present, produce the defendant at the examination and keep the defendant in the presence of the witness during the examination, unless, after being warned by the court that disruptive conduct will cause the defendant's removal from the place of the taking of the deposition, the defendant persists in conduct which is such as to justify exclusion from that place. A defendant not in custody shall have the right to be present at the examination upon request subject to such terms as may be fixed by the court, but a failure, absent good cause shown, to appear after notice and tender of expenses in accordance with subdivision (c) of this rule shall constitute a waiver of that right and of any objection to the taking and use of the deposition based upon that right.

(c) Payment of Expenses. Whenever a deposition is taken at the instance of the government, or whenever a deposition is taken at the instance of a defendant who is unable to bear the expenses of the taking of the deposition, the court may direct that the expense of travel and subsistence of the defendant and the defendant's attorney for attendance at the examination and the cost of the transcript of the deposition shall be paid by the government.

(d) How Taken. Subject to such additional conditions as the court shall provide, a deposition shall be taken and filed in the manner provided in civil actions except as otherwise provided in these rules, provided that (1) in no event shall a deposition be taken of a party defendant without that defendant's consent, and (2) the scope and manner of examination and cross-examination shall be such as would be allowed in the trial itself. The government shall make available to the defendant or the defendant's counsel for examination and use at the taking of the deposition any statement of the witness being deposed which is in the possession of the government and to which the defendant would be entitled at the trial.

(e) Use. At the trial or upon any hearing, a part or all of a deposition, so far as otherwise admissible under the rules of evidence, may be used as substantive evidence if the witness is unavailable, as unavailability is defined in Rule 804(a) of the Federal Rules of Evidence, or the witness gives testimony at the trial or hearing inconsistent with the witness' deposition. Any deposition may also be used by any party for the purpose of contradicting or impeaching the testimony of the deponent as a witness. If only a part of a deposition is offered in evidence by a party, an adverse party may require the offering of all of it which is relevant to the part offered and any party may offer other parts.

(f) Objections to Deposition Testimony. Objections to deposition testimony or evidence or parts thereof and the grounds for the objection shall be stated at the time of the taking of the deposition.

(g) Deposition by Agreement Not Precluded. Nothing in this rule shall preclude the taking of a deposition, orally or upon written questions, or the use of a deposition, by agreement of the parties with the consent of the court.

---

424. In United States v. Mann, 590 F.2d 361 (1st Cir.1978), the government took a deposition of a witness for the prosecution, a 17-year-old Australian, who was then allowed to return to Australia without objection from the government. Over the defendant's objection, the deposition was admitted at trial. The court of appeals held that the government's motion to take a deposition should not have been granted, there not being the "exceptional circumstances" required by Rule 15(a), and that the deposition

AO 90 (Rev. 11/91) Deposition Subpoena in a Criminal Case

United States District Court

_____ DISTRICT OF _____

UNITED STATES OF AMERICA

V.

**DEPOSITION SUBPOENA
IN A CRIMINAL CASE**

CASE NUMBER:

TO:

☐ **YOU ARE COMMANDED** to appear at the place, date, and time specified below to testify at the taking of a deposition in the above case.

PLACE	DATE AND TIME

☐ **YOU ARE ALSO COMMANDED** to bring with you the following document(s) or object(s):

Any organization not a party to this suit that is subpoenaed for the taking of a deposition shall designate one or more officers, directors, or managing agents, or other persons who consent to testify on its behalf, and may set forth, for each person designated, the matters on which the person will testify. Federal Rules of Civil Procedure, 30(b)(6).

U.S. MAGISTRATE JUDGE OR CLERK OF COURT	DATE
(By) Deputy Clerk	

ATTORNEY'S NAME, ADDRESS AND PHONE NUMBER:

should not have been admitted at trial, because the government had not met its burden of showing that the witness was "unavailable." The court indicated that the government should not have acquiesced in the departure of the witness, whose testimony was critical, and that having done so, it should have made stronger efforts to obtain her appearance at trial.

425. The provision in Rule 15(d)(1) that a deposition shall not be taken of a "party defendant" without his consent applies to a codefendant who has pleaded guilty but has not yet been sentenced. United States v. Cassese, 622 F.2d 26 (2d Cir.1979).

Discovery by the government

FEDERAL RULES OF CRIMINAL PROCEDURE

[See Rule 16(b), p. 850 above]

Rule 12.1

NOTICE OF ALIBI

(a) Notice by Defendant. Upon written demand of the attorney for the government stating the time, date, and place at which the alleged offense was committed, the defendant shall serve within ten days, or at such different time as the court may direct, upon the attorney for the government a written notice of the defendant's intention to offer a defense of alibi. Such notice by the defendants hall state the specific place or places at which the defendant claims to have been at the time of the alleged offense and the names and addresses of the witnesses upon whom the defendant intends to rely to establish such alibi.

(b) Disclosure of Information and Witness. Within ten days thereafter, but in no event less than ten days before trial, unless the court otherwise directs, the attorney for the government shall serve upon the defendant or the defendant's attorney a written notice stating the names and addresses of the witnesses upon whom the government intends to rely to establish the defendant's presence at the scene of the alleged offense and any other witnesses to be relied on to rebut testimony of any of the defendant's alibi witnesses.

(c) Continuing Duty to Disclose. If prior to or during trial, a party learns of an additional witness whose identity, if known, should have been included in the information furnished under subdivision (a) or (b), the party shall promptly notify the other party or the other party's attorney of the existence and identity of such additional witness.

(d) Failure to Comply. Upon the failure of either party to comply with the requirements of this rule, the court may exclude the testimony of any undisclosed witness offered by such party as to the defendant's absence from or presence at, the scene of the alleged offense. This rule shall not limit the right of the defendant to testify.

(e) Exceptions. For good cause shown, the court may grant an exception to any of the requirements of subdivisions (a) through (d) of this rule.

(f) Inadmissibility of Withdrawn Alibi. Evidence of an intention to rely upon an alibi defense, later withdrawn, or of statements made in connection with such intention, is not, in any civil or criminal proceeding, admissible against the person who gave notice of the intention.

Rule 12.2

NOTICE OF INSANITY DEFENSE OR EXPERT TESTIMONY OF DEFENDANT'S MENTAL CONDITION

(a) Defense of Insanity. If a defendant intends to rely upon the defense of insanity at the time of the alleged offense, the defendant shall, within the time provided for the filing of pretrial motions or at such later time as the court may direct, notify the attorney for the government in writing of such intention and file a copy of such notice with the clerk. If there is a failure to comply with the requirements of this subdivision, insanity may not be raised as a defense. The court may for cause shown allow late filing of the notice or grant additional time to the parties to prepare for trial or make such other order as may be appropriate.

(b) Expert Testimony of Defendant's Mental Condition. If a defendant intends to introduce expert testimony relating to a mental disease or defect or any other mental condition of the defendant bearing upon the issue of guilt, the defendant shall, within the time provided for the filing of pretrial motions or at such later time as the court may direct, notify the attorney for the government in writing of such intention and file a copy of such notice with the clerk. The court may for cause shown allow late filing of the notice or grant additional time to the parties to prepare for trial or make such other order as may be appropriate.

(c) Mental Examination of Defendant. In an appropriate case the court may, upon motion of the attorney for the government, order the defendant to submit to an examination pursuant to 18 U.S.C. 4241 or 4242. No statement made by the defendant in the course of any examination provided for by this rule, whether the examination be with or without the consent of the defendant, no testimony by the expert based upon such statement, and no other fruits of the statement shall be admitted in evidence against the defendant in any criminal proceeding except on an issue respecting mental condition on which the defendant has introduced testimony.

(d) Failure to Comply. If there is a failure to give notice when required by subdivision (b) of this rule or to submit to an examination when ordered under subdivision (c) of this rule, the court may exclude the testimony of any expert witness offered by the defendant on the issue of the defendant's guilt.

(e) Inadmissibility of Withdrawn Intention. Evidence of an intention as to which notice was given under subdivision (a) or (b), later withdrawn, is not, in any civil or criminal proceeding, admissible against the person who gave notice of the intention.

Rule 12.3

NOTICE OF DEFENSE BASED UPON PUBLIC AUTHORITY

(a) Notice by defendant; government response; disclosure of witnesses.

(1) Defendant's Notice and Government's Response. A defendant intending to claim a defense of actual or believed exercise of public authority on behalf of a law enforcement or Federal intelligence agency at the time of the alleged offense shall, within the time provided for the filing of pretrial motions or at such later time as the court may direct, serve upon the attorney for the Government a written notice of such intention and file a copy of such notice with the clerk. Such notice shall identify the law enforcement or Federal intelligence agency and any member of such agency on behalf of which and the period of time in which the defendant claims the actual or believed exercise of public authority occurred. If the notice identifies a Federal intelligence agency, the copy filed with the clerk shall be under seal. Within ten days after receiving the defendant's notice, but in no event less than twenty days before the trial, the attorney for the Government shall serve upon the defendant or the defendant's attorney a written response which shall admit or deny that the defendant exercised the public authority identified in the defendant's notice.

(2) Disclosure of Witnesses. At the time that the Government serves its response to the notice or thereafter, but in no event less than twenty days before the trial, the attorney for the Government may serve upon the defendant or the defendant's attorney a written demand for the names and addresses of the witnesses, if any, upon whom the defendant intends to rely in establishing the defense identified in the notice. Within seven days after receiving the Government's demand, the defendant shall serve upon the attorney for the Government a written statement of the names and addresses of any such witnesses. Within seven days after receiving the defendant's written statement, the attorney for the Government shall serve upon the defendant or the

defendant's attorney a written statement of the names and addresses of the witnesses, if any, upon whom the Government intends to rely in opposing the defense identified in the notice.

(3) Additional Time. If good cause is shown, the court may allow a party additional time to comply with any obligation imposed by this rule.

(b) Continuing duty to disclose. If, prior to or during trial, a party learns of any additional witness whose identity, if known, should have been included in the written statement furnished under subdivision (a)(2) of this rule, that party shall promptly notify in writing the other party or the other party's attorney of the name and address of any such witness.

(c) Failure to comply. If a party fails to comply with the requirements of this rule, the court may exclude the testimony of any undisclosed witness offered in support of or in opposition to the defense, or enter such other order as it deems just under the circumstances. This rule shall not limit the right of the defendant to testify.

(d) Protective procedures unaffected. This rule shall be in addition to and shall not supersede the authority of the court to issue appropriate protective orders, or the authority of the court to order that any pleading be filed under seal.

(e) Inadmissibility of withdrawn defense based upon public authority. Evidence of an intention as to which notice was given under subdivision (a), later withdrawn, is not, in any civil or criminal proceeding, admissible against the person who gave notice of the intention.

———

Williams v. Florida

399 U.S. 78, 90 S.Ct. 1893, 26 L.Ed.2d 446 (1970).

■ MR. JUSTICE WHITE delivered the opinion of the Court.

Prior to his trial for robbery in the State of Florida, petitioner filed a "Motion for a Protective Order," seeking to be excused from the requirements of Rule 1.200 of the Florida Rules of Criminal Procedure. That rule requires a defendant, on written demand of the prosecuting attorney, to give notice in advance of trial if the defendant intends to claim an alibi, and to furnish the prosecuting attorney with information as to the place where he claims to have been and with the names and addresses of the alibi witnesses he intends to use. In his motion petitioner openly declared his intent to claim an alibi, but objected to the further disclosure requirements on the ground that the rule "compels the Defendant in a criminal case to be a witness against himself" in violation of his Fifth and Fourteenth Amendment rights. The motion was denied. . . . Petitioner was convicted as charged and was sentenced to life imprisonment. The District Court of Appeal affirmed, rejecting petitioner's claims that his Fifth . . . Amendment rights had been violated. We granted certiorari. . . .

I

Florida's notice-of-alibi rule is in essence a requirement that a defendant submit to a limited form of pretrial discovery by the State whenever he intends to rely at trial on the defense of alibi. In exchange for the defendant's disclosure of the witnesses he proposes to use to establish that defense, the State in turn is required to notify the defendant of any witnesses it proposes to offer in rebuttal to that defense. Both sides are under a continuing duty promptly to disclose the names and addresses of additional witnesses bearing on the alibi as they become available. The threatened sanction for failure to comply is the exclusion at trial of the defendant's alibi evidence—except for his own testimony—or, in the case of the State, the exclusion of the State's evidence offered in rebuttal of the alibi.

In this case, following the denial of his Motion for a Protective Order, petitioner complied with the alibi rule and gave the State the name and address of one Mary Scotty. Mrs. Scotty was summoned to the office of the State Attorney on the morning of the trial, where she gave pretrial testimony. At the trial itself, Mrs. Scotty, petitioner, and petitioner's wife all testified that the three of them had been in Mrs. Scotty's apartment during the time of the robbery. On two occasions during cross-examination of Mrs. Scotty, the prosecuting attorney confronted her with her earlier deposition in which she had given dates and times that in some respects did not correspond with the dates and times given at trial. Mrs. Scotty adhered to her trial story, insisting that she had been mistaken in her earlier testimony. The State also offered in rebuttal the testimony of one of the officers investigating the robbery who claimed that Mrs. Scotty had asked him for directions on the afternoon in question during the time when she claimed to have been in her apartment with petitioner and his wife.

We need not linger over the suggestion that the discovery permitted the State against petitioner in this case deprived him of "due process" or a "fair trial." Florida law provides for liberal discovery by the defendant against the State, and the notice-of-alibi rule is itself carefully hedged with reciprocal duties requiring state disclosure to the defendant. Given the ease with which an alibi can be fabricated, the State's interest in protecting itself against an eleventh-hour defense is both obvious and legitimate. Reflecting this interest, notice-of-alibi provisions, dating at least from 1927, are now in existence in a substantial number of States. The adversary system of trial is hardly an end in itself; it is not yet a poker game in which players enjoy an absolute right always to conceal their cards until played. We find ample room in that system, at least as far as "due process" is concerned, for the instant Florida rule, which is designed to enhance the search for truth in the criminal trial by insuring both the defendant and the State ample opportunity to investigate certain facts crucial to the determination of guilt or innocence.

Petitioner's major contention is that he was "compelled . . . to be a witness against himself" contrary to the commands of the Fifth and Fourteenth Amendments because the notice-of-alibi rule required him to give the State the name and address of Mrs. Scotty in advance of trial and thus to furnish the State with information useful in convicting him. No pretrial statement of petitioner was introduced at trial; but armed with Mrs. Scotty's name and address and the knowledge that she was to be petitioner's alibi witness, the State was able to take her deposition in advance of trial and to find rebuttal testimony. Also, requiring him to reveal the elements of his defense is claimed to have interfered with his right to wait until after the State had presented its case to decide how to defend against it. We conclude, however, as has apparently every other court that has considered the issue, that the privilege against self-incrimination is not violated by a requirement that the defendant give notice of an alibi defense and disclose his alibi witnesses.[16]

The defendant in a criminal trial is frequently forced to testify himself and to call other witnesses in an effort to reduce the risk of conviction. When he presents his witnesses, he must reveal their identity and submit them to cross-examination which in itself may prove incriminating or which may furnish the State with leads to incriminating rebuttal evidence. That the defendant faces such a dilemma demanding a choice between complete silence and presenting a defense has never been thought an invasion of the privilege against compelled self-incrimination. The pressures generated by the State's evidence may be severe but they do not vitiate the defendant's choice to present an alibi defense and witnesses to prove it, even though the attempted defense ends in catastrophe for the defendant. However "testimonial" or "incriminating" the alibi defense proves to be, it cannot be considered "compelled" within the meaning of the Fifth and Fourteenth Amendments.

Very similar constraints operate on the defendant when the State requires pretrial notice of alibi and the naming of alibi witnesses. Nothing in such a rule requires the defendant to rely on an alibi or prevents him from abandoning the defense; these matters are left to his unfettered choice. That choice must be made, but the pressures that bear on his pretrial decision are of the same nature as those that would induce him to call alibi witnesses at the trial: the force of historical fact beyond both his and the State's control and the strength of the State's case built on these facts. Response to that kind of pressure by offering evidence or testimony is not compelled self-incrimination transgressing the Fifth and Fourteenth Amendments.

In the case before us, the notice-of-alibi rule by itself in no way affected petitioner's crucial decision to call alibi witnesses or added to the legitimate

---

16. We emphasize that this case does not involve the question of the validity of the threatened sanction, had petitioner chosen not to comply with the notice-of-alibi rule. Whether and to what extent a State can enforce discovery rules against a defendant who fails to comply, by excluding relevant, probative evidence is a question raising Sixth Amendment issues which we have no occasion to explore. . . . It is enough that no such penalty was exacted here.

pressures leading to that course of action. At most, the rule only compelled petitioner to accelerate the timing of his disclosure, forcing him to divulge at an earlier date information that the petitioner from the beginning planned to divulge at trial. Nothing in the Fifth Amendment privilege entitles a defendant as a matter of constitutional right to await the end of the State's case before announcing the nature of his defense, any more than it entitles him to await the jury's verdict on the State's case-in-chief before deciding whether or not to take the stand himself.

Petitioner concedes that absent the notice-of-alibi rule the Constitution would raise no bar to the court's granting the State a continuance at trial on the ground of surprise as soon as the alibi witness is called. Nor would there be self-incrimination problems if, during that continuance, the State was permitted to do precisely what it did here prior to trial: take the deposition of the witness and find rebuttal evidence. But if so utilizing a continuance is permissible under the Fifth and Fourteenth Amendments, then surely the same result may be accomplished through pretrial discovery, as it was here, avoiding the necessity of a disrupted trial. We decline to hold that the privilege against compulsory self-incrimination guarantees the defendant the right to surprise the State with an alibi defense.

. . . [17]

---

426. In Wardius v. Oregon, 412 U.S. 470 (1973), the Court considered a notice-of-alibi rule that contained no provision for reciprocal discovery. The defendant had been barred from presenting evidence to support his alibi because he failed to comply with the rule. The court held that "the Due Process Clause of the Fourteenth Amendment forbids enforcement of alibi rules unless reciprocal discovery rights are given to criminal defendants." Id. at 472.

"[A]lthough the Due Process Clause has little to say regarding the amount of discovery which the parties must be afforded . . . it does speak to the balance of forces between the accused and his accuser. . . . The *Williams* Court was therefore careful to note that 'Florida law provides for liberal discovery by the defendant against the State, and the notice-of-alibi rule is itself carefully hedged with reciprocal duties requiring state disclosure to the defendant.' 399 U.S., at 81 (footnote omitted). The same cannot be said of Oregon law. . . . Oregon grants no discovery rights to criminal defendants,

[17] Chief Justice Burger wrote a concurring opinion. Justice Black wrote an opinion, which Justice Douglas joined, in which he dissented from the Court's opinion on the notice-of-alibi issue. Justice Harlan, Justice Stewart, and Justice Marshall wrote opinions dealing with another aspect of the case.

and, indeed, does not even provide defendants with bills of particulars. More significantly, Oregon, unlike Florida, has no provision which requires the State to reveal the names and addresses of witnesses it plans to use to refute an alibi defense.

"We do not suggest that the Due Process Clause of its own force requires Oregon to adopt such provisions. . . . But we do hold that in the absence of a strong showing of state interests to the contrary, discovery must be a two-way street. The State may not insist that trials be run as a 'search for truth' so far as defense witnesses are concerned, while maintaining 'poker game' secrecy for its own witnesses. It is fundamentally unfair to require a defendant to divulge the details of his own case while at the same time subjecting him to the hazard of surprise concerning refutation of the very pieces of evidence which he disclosed to the State." 412 U.S. at 474–76.

See Mauricio v. Duckworth, 840 F.2d 454 (7th Cir.1988) (prosecution's failure to disclose alibi rebuttal witness although defense disclosed all its witnesses violated due process).

Taylor v. Illinois

484 U.S. 400, 108 S.Ct. 646, 98 L.Ed.2d 798 (1988).

■ JUSTICE STEVENS delivered the opinion of the Court.

As a sanction for failing to identify a defense witness in response to a pretrial discovery request, an Illinois trial judge refused to allow the undisclosed witness to testify. The question presented is whether that refusal violated the petitioner's constitutional right to obtain the testimony of favorable witnesses. We hold that such a sanction is not absolutely prohibited by the Compulsory Process Clause of the Sixth Amendment and find no constitutional error on the specific facts of this case.

I

A jury convicted petitioner in 1984 of attempting to murder Jack Bridges in a street fight on the south side of Chicago on August 6, 1981. The conviction was supported by the testimony of Bridges, his brother, and three other witnesses. They described a twenty-minute argument between Bridges and a young man named Derrick Travis, and a violent encounter that occurred over an hour later between several friends of Travis, including the petitioner, on the one hand, and Bridges, belatedly aided by his brother, on the other. The incident was witnessed by twenty or thirty bystanders. It is undisputed that at least three members of the group which included Travis and petitioner were carrying pipes and clubs that they used to beat Bridges. Prosecution witnesses also testified that petitioner had a gun, that he shot Bridges in the back as he attempted to flee, and that, after Bridges fell, petitioner pointed the gun at Bridges' head but the weapon misfired.

Two sisters, who are friends of petitioner, testified on his behalf. In many respects their version of the incident was consistent with the prosecution's case, but they testified that it was Bridges' brother, rather than petitioner, who possessed a firearm and that he had fired into the group hitting his brother by mistake. No other witnesses testified for the defense.

Well in advance of trial, the prosecutor filed a discovery motion requesting a list of defense witnesses. In his original response, petitioner's attorney identified the two sisters who later testified and two men who did not testify. On the first day of trial, defense counsel was allowed to amend his answer by adding the names of Derrick Travis and a Chicago Police Officer; neither of them actually testified.

On the second day of trial, after the prosecution's two principal witnesses had completed their testimony, defense counsel made an oral motion to amend his "Answer to Discovery" to include two more witnesses, Alfred Wormley and Pam Berkhalter. In support of the motion, counsel represented that he had just been informed about them and that they had probably seen the "entire incident."

In response to the court's inquiry about the defendant's failure to tell him about the two witnesses earlier, counsel acknowledged that defendant had done so, but then represented that he had been unable to locate Wormley. After noting that the witnesses' names could have been supplied even if their addresses were unknown, the trial judge directed counsel to bring them in the next day, at which time he would decide whether they could testify. The judge indicated that he was concerned about the possibility "that witnesses are being found that really weren't there."

The next morning Wormley appeared in court with defense counsel. After further colloquy about the consequences of a violation of discovery rules, counsel was permitted to make an offer of proof in the form of Wormley's testimony outside the presence of the jury. It developed that Wormley had not been a witness to the incident itself. He testified that prior to the incident he saw Jack Bridges and his brother with two guns in a blanket, that he heard them say "they were after Ray [petitioner] and the other people," and that on his way home he "happened to run into Ray and them" and warned them "to watch out because they got weapons." On cross-examination, Wormley acknowledged that he had first met the defendant "about four months ago" (i.e., over two years after the incident). He also acknowledged that defense counsel had visited him at his home on the Wednesday of the week before the trial began. Thus, his testimony rather dramatically contradicted defense counsel's representations to the trial court.

After hearing Wormley testify, the trial judge concluded that the appropriate sanction for the discovery violation was to exclude his testimony. The judge explained:

"THE COURT: All right, I am going to deny Wormley an opportunity to testify here. He is not going to testify. I find this a blatant violation of the discovery rules, willful violation of the rules. I also feel that defense attorneys have been violating discovery in this courtroom in the last three or four cases blatantly and I am going to put a stop to it and this is one way to do so.

"Further, for whatever value it is, because this is a jury trial, I have a great deal of doubt in my mind as to the veracity of this young man that testified as to whether he was an eyewitness on the scene, sees guns that are wrapped up. He doesn't know Ray but he stops Ray.

"At any rate, Mr. Wormley is not going to testify, be a witness in this courtroom." App. 28.

. . .

In this Court petitioner makes two arguments. He first contends that the Sixth Amendment bars a court from ever ordering the preclusion of defense evidence as a sanction for violating a discovery rule. Alternatively, he contends that even if the right to present witnesses is not absolute, on the facts of this case the preclusion of Wormley's testimony was constitutional error. Before addressing these contentions, we consider the State's argument that the Compulsory Process Clause of the Sixth Amendment is merely a guarantee that the accused shall have the power to subpoena witnesses and simply does not apply to rulings on the admissibility of evidence.

II

In the State's view, no Compulsory Process Clause concerns are even raised by authorizing preclusion as a discovery sanction, or by the application of the Illinois rule in this case. . . .

As we noted just last Term, "[o]ur cases establish, at a minimum, that criminal defendants have the right to the government's assistance in compelling the attendance of favorable witnesses at trial and the right to put before a jury evidence that might influence the determination of guilt." Pennsylvania v. Ritchie, 480 U.S. 39, 56 (1987). Few rights are more fundamental than that of an accused to present witnesses in his own defense . . . . Indeed, this right is an essential attribute of the adversary system itself. . . . The right to compel a witness' presence in the courtroom could not protect the integrity of the adversary process if it did not embrace the right to have the witness' testimony heard by the trier of fact. The right to offer testimony is thus grounded in the Sixth Amendment even though it is not expressly described in so many words . . . . We cannot accept the State's argument that this constitutional right may never be offended by the imposition of a discovery sanction that entirely excludes the testimony of a material defense witness.

III

Petitioner's claim that the Sixth Amendment creates an absolute bar to the preclusion of the testimony of a surprise witness is just as extreme and just as unacceptable as the State's position that the Amendment is simply irrelevant. The accused does not have an unfettered right to offer testimony that is incompetent, privileged, or otherwise inadmissible under standard rules of evidence. The Compulsory Process Clause provides him with an effective weapon, but it is a weapon that cannot be used irresponsibly.

There is a significant difference between the Compulsory Process Clause weapon and other rights that are protected by the Sixth Amendment—its availability is dependent entirely on the defendant's initiative. Most other Sixth Amendment rights arise automatically on the initiation of the adversarial process and no action by the defendant is necessary to make them active in his or her case. While those rights shield the defendant from potential prosecutorial abuses, the right to compel the presence and present the testimony of witnesses provides the defendant with a sword that may be employed to rebut the prosecution's case. The decision whether to employ it in a particular case rests solely with the defendant. The very nature of the right requires that its effective use be preceded by deliberate planning and affirmative conduct.

The principle that undergirds the defendant's right to present exculpatory evidence is also the source of essential limitations on the right. The adversary process could not function effectively without adherence to rules of procedure that govern the orderly presentation of facts and arguments to provide each party with a fair opportunity to assemble and submit evidence to contradict or explain the opponent's case. The trial process would be a shambles if either party had an absolute right to control the time and content of his witnesses' testimony. Neither may insist on the right to interrupt the opposing party's case and obviously there is no absolute right to interrupt the deliberations of the jury to present newly discovered evidence. The State's interest in the orderly conduct of a criminal trial is sufficient to justify the imposition and enforcement of firm, though not always inflexible, rules relating to the identification and presentation of evidence.

The defendant's right to compulsory process is itself designed to vindicate the principle that the "ends of criminal justice would be defeated if judgments were to be founded on a partial or speculative presentation of the facts." United States v. Nixon, 418 U.S. [683 (1974)], at 709. Rules that provide for pretrial discovery of an opponent's witnesses serve the same high purpose. Discovery, like cross-examination, minimizes the risk that a judgment will be predicated on incomplete, misleading, or even deliberately fabricated testimony. The "State's interest in protecting itself against an eleventh-hour defense"[18] is merely one component of the broader public interest in a full and truthful disclosure of critical facts.

To vindicate that interest we have held that even the defendant may not testify without being subjected to cross-examination. . . . Moreover, in United States v. Nobles, 422 U.S. 225 (1975), we upheld an order excluding

---

18. . . . *Williams* v. *Florida*, 399 U.S. 78, 81–82 (1970). . . .

the testimony of an expert witness tendered by the defendant because he had refused to permit discovery of a "highly relevant" report. . . .

Petitioner does not question the legitimacy of a rule requiring pretrial disclosure of defense witnesses, but he argues that the sanction of preclusion of the testimony of a previously undisclosed witness is so drastic that it should never be imposed. He argues, correctly, that a less drastic sanction is always available. Prejudice to the prosecution could be minimized by granting a continuance or a mistrial to provide time for further investigation; moreover, further violations can be deterred by disciplinary sanctions against the defendant or defense counsel.

It may well be true that alternative sanctions are adequate and appropriate in most cases, but it is equally clear that they would be less effective than the preclusion sanction and that there are instances in which they would perpetuate rather than limit the prejudice to the State and the harm to the adversary process. One of the purposes of the discovery rule itself is to minimize the risk that fabricated testimony will be believed. Defendants who are willing to fabricate a defense may also be willing to fabricate excuses for failing to comply with a discovery requirement. The risk of a contempt violation may seem trivial to a defendant facing the threat of imprisonment for a term of years. A dishonest client can mislead an honest attorney, and there are occasions when an attorney assumes that the duty of loyalty to the client outweighs elementary obligations to the court.

We presume that evidence that is not discovered until after the trial is over would not have affected the outcome. It is equally reasonable to presume that there is something suspect about a defense witness who is not identified until after the eleventh hour has passed. If a pattern of discovery violations is explicable only on the assumption that the violations were designed to conceal a plan to present fabricated testimony, it would be entirely appropriate to exclude the tainted evidence regardless of whether other sanctions would also be merited.

In order to reject petitioner's argument that preclusion is *never* a permissible sanction for a discovery violation it is neither necessary nor appropriate for us to attempt to draft a comprehensive set of standards to guide the exercise of discretion in every possible case. It is elementary, of course, that a trial court may not ignore the fundamental character of the defendant's right to offer the testimony of witnesses in his favor. But the mere invocation of that right cannot automatically and invariably outweigh countervailing public interests. The integrity of the adversary process, which depends both on the presentation of reliable evidence and the rejection of unreliable evidence; the interest in the fair and efficient administration of justice; and the potential prejudice to the truth-determining function of the trial process must also weigh in the balance.

A trial judge may certainly insist on an explanation for a party's failure to comply with a request to identify his or her witnesses in advance of trial. If that explanation reveals that the omission was willful and motivated by a desire to obtain a tactical advantage that would minimize the effectiveness of cross-examination and the ability to adduce rebuttal evidence, it would be entirely consistent with the purposes of the Confrontation Clause simply to exclude the witness' testimony. . . .

The simplicity of compliance with the discovery rule is also relevant. As we have noted, the Compulsory Process Clause cannot be invoked without the prior planning and affirmative conduct of the defendant. Lawyers are accustomed to meeting deadlines. Routine preparation involves location and interrogation of potential witnesses and the serving of subpoenas on those whose testimony will be offered at trial. The burden of identifying them in advance of trial adds little to these routine demands of trial preparation.

It would demean the high purpose of the Compulsory Process Clause to construe it as encompassing an absolute right to an automatic continuance or mistrial to allow presumptively perjured testimony to be presented to a jury. We reject petitioner's argument that a preclusion sanction is never appropriate no matter how serious the defendant's discovery violation may be.

IV

Petitioner argues that the preclusion sanction was unnecessarily harsh in this case because the *voir dire* examination of Wormley adequately protected the prosecution from any possible prejudice resulting from surprise. Petitioner also contends that it is unfair to visit the sins of the lawyer upon his client. Neither argument has merit.

More is at stake than possible prejudice to the prosecution. We are also concerned with the impact of this kind of conduct on the integrity of the judicial process itself. The trial judge found that the discovery violation in this case was both willful and blatant. In view of the fact that petitioner's counsel had actually interviewed Wormley during the week before the trial began and the further fact that he amended his Answer to Discovery on the first day of trial without identifying Wormley while he did identify two actual eyewitnesses whom he did not place on the stand, the inference that he was deliberately seeking a tactical advantage is inescapable. Regardless of whether prejudice to the prosecution could have been avoided in this particular case, it is plain that the case fits into the category of willful misconduct in which the severest sanction is appropriate. After all, the court, as well as the prosecutor, has a vital interest in protecting the trial process from the pollution of perjured testimony. Evidentiary rules which apply to categories of inadmissible evidence—ranging from hearsay to the fruits of illegal searches—may properly be enforced even though the particular testimony being offered is not prejudicial. The pretrial conduct revealed by the record in this case gives rise to a sufficiently strong inference "that witnesses are being found that really weren't there," to justify the sanction of preclusion.

The argument that the client should not be held responsible for his lawyer's misconduct strikes at the heart of the attorney-client relationship. Although there are basic rights that the attorney cannot waive without the fully informed and publicly acknowledged consent of the client, the lawyer has—and must have—full authority to manage the conduct of the trial. The adversary process could not function effectively if every tactical decision required client approval. Moreover, given the protections afforded by the attorney-client privilege and the fact that extreme cases may involve unscrupulous conduct by both the client and the lawyer, it would be highly impracticable to require an investigation into their relative responsibilities before applying the sanction of preclusion. In responding to discovery, the client has a duty to be candid and forthcoming with the lawyer, and when the lawyer responds, he or she speaks for the client. Putting to one side the exceptional cases in which counsel is ineffective, the client must accept the consequences of the lawyer's decision to forgo cross-examination, to decide not to put certain witnesses on the stand, or to decide not to disclose the identity of certain witnesses in advance of trial. In this case, petitioner has no greater right to disavow his lawyer's decision to conceal Wormley's identity until after the trial had commenced than he has to disavow the decision to refrain from adducing testimony from the eyewitnesses who were identified in the Answer to Discovery. Whenever a lawyer makes use of the sword provided by the Compulsory Process Clause, there is some risk that he may wound his own client.

. . .[19]

———

427. In Michigan v. Lucas, 500 U.S. 145 (1991) (7–2), the Court held that the Sixth Amendment does not flatly prohibit a rule that precludes a defendant in a rape case from introducing evidence concerning the alleged rape victim's past sexual conduct as a sanction for failing to give the required notice of his intention to offer such evidence. The Court said that the notice provision "serves legitimate state interests in protecting against surprise, harassment, and undue delay," which "in some cases justify even the severe sanction" of exclusion of evidence. Id. at 153.

———

[19] Justice Brennan wrote a dissenting opinion, which Justice Marshall and Justice Blackmun joined. Justice Blackmun also wrote a brief dissenting opinion.

United States v. Myers

550 F.2d 1036 (5th Cir.1977).

■ CLARK, CIRCUIT JUDGE:

Larry Allen Myers challenges the validity of his federal bank robbery conviction. He contends that the district court committed reversible error when it (1) refused to strike the testimony of alibi rebuttal witnesses whose identities were not disclosed before the trial. . . . We agree, and therefore we reverse the decision of the district court.

On June 13, 1974, at approximately two o'clock in the afternoon, a branch of the First Federal Savings and Loan Association of Largo, located in Clearwater, Florida, was robbed by a lone gunman. He escaped with an estimated $1500. After changing cars at a nearby motel, the robber disappeared. There is no dispute about how the robbery was committed; the central issue in this case, despite two eye witnesses and hundreds of still photographs taken by an automatic camera, is by whom. The government has proceeded on the theory that it was Myers who entered the bank brandishing a revolver, ordered a teller to place the contents of her cash drawer in a flimsy brown paper bag, and fled. Myers has steadfastly maintained that it was not.

On September 13, 1975, a federal grand jury charged Myers with three counts of violating 18 U.S.C.A. § 2113(a), (b) & (d) (Supp.1976). The government's task in prosecuting Myers on these charges was complicated when a friend of Myers named Dennis Coffie, who bears a remarkable physical resemblance to Myers, pled guilty to having been the lone gunman in the Florida robbery. A superseding indictment consolidating the Florida charges into one count was returned against Myers on August 13, 1975. Since then Myers has been tried twice. The first trial ended with the declaration of a mistrial after the jury announced its inability to reach a verdict. A fortnight later, a second jury found Myers guilty as charged. The district court sentenced him to ten years' imprisonment on February 17, 1976.

Nondisclosure of Alibi Rebuttal Witnesses

Myers' primary argument on this appeal is that the district court committed reversible error when it refused to strike the testimony of the witnesses on whom the government relied to discredit his alibi defense. In order to properly assess the merit of this contention, it is necessary to examine in detail some of the circumstances surrounding the first and second trials.

Prior to the first trial, the government served Myers with a written demand for notice of his intent to assert an alibi defense, pursuant to Rule 12.1 of the Federal Rules of Criminal Procedure. Myers responded on December 23, 1975, indicating that he did intend to offer an alibi defense, and named Ronald Akers, Marlin Downey, and Coffie as his proposed alibi witnesses. The following day the government filed a document styled "Government's Response to Notice of Alibi Defense," in which it listed two tellers from the robbed bank and Janice Johns as the witnesses on whose testimony it planned to rely in attempting to establish Myers' presence at the scene of the robbery. It further stated:

Names and addresses of other witnesses to be relied on to rebut testimony of defendant's alibi witnesses shall be made known to defendant as they are ascertained by the Government under its continuing duty pursuant to the Rule.

Neither Myers nor the government ever supplemented their witness lists.

At the first trial Myers used all three of his proposed witnesses in attempting to establish his alibi defense. Coffie testified that he committed the Florida robbery by himself, and Downey stated that on the afternoon of the robbery he had encountered Myers at Disneyworld, an amusement park located approximately 80 miles from Clearwater. Despite the importance of their testimony, the fate of Myers' alibi defense rested largely on the testimony of Ronald Akers. Akers testified that he and Myers had spent the entire afternoon of June 13, 1974—the day on which the robbery occurred—at Disneyworld, in the company of two girls whom Akers had met the previous evening. Akers explained that he was certain of the date because the girls had to catch a United Airlines flight to Detroit on Saturday, June 15, 1974. He said that he remembered their airline, destination, and date of departure, because he had seen their tickets and because he drove them to the Tampa airport on Saturday morning.

During the week following the first trial, the government investigated Akers' story. On the day before the defense began to present its evidence in the second trial, the United States Attorney prosecuting the case contacted Myers' counsel and suggested that he warn his witnesses against perjuring themselves. He did not mention the possibility that the government might call additional witnesses at the second trial.

The testimony of Coffie, Akers, and Downey at the second trial was substantially the same as it had been at the first. But in reply the government called four witnesses not listed in its response to Myers' notice of his intent to offer an alibi defense, whose statements were designed to discredit Akers' testimony. One of them was Robert Labrenz, an employee of United Airlines. He testified that United had no flight from Tampa to Detroit on June 15, 1974, but that other airlines had such flights. The other three witnesses, Patricia Coogle, Raymond LaBranch, and Roy Pruitt were all employees of a car dealership in Tampa, Florida. Their combined testimony indicated that Akers had been employed at the same car dealership as a mechanic, and had worked 48 hours during the week of June 10, 1974. This was inconsistent with Akers' testimony that he had been unemployed during June of 1974, and tended to conflict with his statement that he had not worked on Thursday and Friday of the week of June 10, 1974.

Before the case was given to the jury, defendant's counsel moved for a mistrial, and, in the alternative, for an order striking the testimony of the four new government witnesses, on the grounds that their names had not been disclosed prior to trial as required by Rule 12.1. The district court denied both motions. It held, first, that the government had not violated the rule, and second, that if it had, good cause existed to grant the government an exemption from the requirements of sections (b) and (c).

. . .

The language of section (b) appears to require disclosure of two types of witnesses: (1) those relied upon "to establish the defendant's presence at the scene of the alleged offense", and (2) "any other witnesses to be relied on to rebut testimony of any of the defendant's alibi witnesses." We think that all four of the undisclosed government witnesses fall within the class delineated by the second phrase. Rebuttal evidence is evidence introduced to refute, contradict, or disprove evidence adduced by an adverse party. Since the testimony of the undisclosed witnesses was concededly introduced for the purpose of showing that Akers' testimony concerning his activities during the week of June 10, 1974, was false, they are alibi rebuttal witnesses within the meaning of Rule 12.1(b). Accordingly, the government had a continuing duty under section (c) to notify the defendant of their existence.

The government's duty to disclose was not discharged by the oblique warning which counsel for the government gave Myers' attorney orally on the eve of the second trial. Section 12.1(b) expressly requires "a written notice stating the names and addresses of the witnesses upon whom the government intends to rely."

. . .

The district court found that in the event the government had violated sections (b) and (c), its noncompliance should be excused. Although the precatory language of section (e) gives the district court the discretionary power to grant exceptions "for good cause shown," there are two reasons why the court below abused its discretion by granting one in this case.

First, the district court failed to describe the circumstances that constituted good cause. Absent such an explanation, granting an exception is improper. We note in passing that none of the after the fact justifications proffered by the Government—that the undisclosed witnesses were merely rebuttal witnesses, that they were not discovered until immediately before trial, and that their testimony was not conclusive—would be sufficient to satisfy the good cause requirement. Second, the government did not apply for an exception to the disclosure requirements at the time the new witnesses were discovered, when compliance with sections (b) and (c) would have been possible if its request had been denied. Rule 12.1 was intended to prevent prejudicial surprise to the parties and to obviate the need for continuances which arise when one side introduces unexpected testimony at trial. . . . These purposes would be frustrated if applications for exceptions could be tendered after undisclosed witnesses had already testified. By then, the harm which the Rule seeks to prevent would have occurred, and the trial judge would be reduced to trying to mitigate the injury to the defendant's case by granting a continuance, retroactively excluding the improper testimony, or in extreme cases, declaring a mistrial.

The district court also abused the discretion conferred upon it by section (d) when he denied the defendant's motions to strike the testimony and documentary evidence furnished by the undisclosed witnesses. . . .

In determining how to exercise its discretionary power to exclude the testimony of undisclosed witnesses under section (d), a district court should consider (1) the amount of prejudice that resulted from the failure to disclose, (2) the reason for nondisclosure, (3) the extent to which the harm caused by nondisclosure was mitigated by subsequent events, (4) the weight of the properly admitted evidence supporting the defendant's guilt, and (5) other relevant factors arising out of the circumstances of the case. . . .

Here the prejudice to the defense was substantial and remained unabated. Myers' counsel was deprived of the opportunity to interview the four undisclosed witnesses, to recheck the stories of Myers, Akers, and Downey in light of the additional evidence, and, most importantly, to reconsider his decision to put Akers and Downey on the stand. The Rule entitles a defendant to evaluate the strategy of advancing an alibi defense in light of the named rebuttal witnesses. In addition, the government's reason for nondisclosure is feeble: it asserts that it did not believe that the witnesses were within the scope of the Rule. While this falls short of bad faith, it thwarts the central purposes of a provision designed to make criminal trials fairer because it tests coverage through confrontation at trial, rather than by submission to the district court in advance. Finally, as counsel for the government conceded at oral argument, the evidence against Myers is weak. Since all four of the factors present in this case weigh in favor of exclusion, the district court abused its discretion when it failed to exclude the testimony of the undisclosed alibi rebuttal witnesses.

. . .

---

428. Criminal discovery and civil discovery. The Food and Drug Administration instituted a civil *in rem* action against products of a corporation of which defendants were officers. The government served interrogatories on the corporation. After the interrogatories were filed, the FDA served notice on the corporation and the defendants that a criminal prosecution was contemplated. The defendants moved to stay the civil proceedings or to extend the time for filing answers to the interrogatories until after the criminal proceedings were terminated. The motion was denied. The FDA decided to recommend prosecution before answers to the interrogatories were received. The Court affirmed the subsequent convictions.

"The respondents urge that . . . the Government's conduct . . . reflected such unfairness and want of consideration for justice as independently to require the reversal of their convictions. On the record before us, we cannot agree that the respondents have made out either a violation of due process or a departure from proper standards in the administration of justice requiring the exercise of our supervisory power. The public interest in protecting consumers throughout the Nation from misbranded drugs requires prompt action by the agency charged with responsibility for administration of the federal food and drug laws. But a rational decision whether to proceed criminally against those responsible for the misbranding may have to await consideration of a fuller record than that before the agency at the time of the civil seizure of the offending products. It would stultify enforcement of federal law to require a governmental agency such as the FDA invariably to choose either to forgo recommendation of a criminal prosecution once it seeks civil relief, or to defer civil proceedings pending the ultimate outcome of a criminal trial.

"We do not deal here with a case where the Government has brought a civil action solely to obtain evidence for its criminal prosecution or has failed to advise the defendant in its civil proceeding that it contemplates his criminal prosecution; nor with a case where the defendant is without counsel or reasonably fears prejudice from adverse pretrial publicity or other unfair injury; nor with any other special circumstances that might suggest the unconstitutionality or even the impropriety of this criminal prosecution.

"Overturning these convictions would be tantamount to the adoption of a rule that the Government's use of interrogatories directed against a corporate defendant in the ordinary course of a civil proceeding would always immunize the corporation's officers from subsequent criminal prosecution. The Court of Appeals was correct in stating that 'the Government may not use evidence against a defendant in a criminal case which has been coerced from him under penalty of either giving the evidence or suffering a forfeiture of his property.'[20] But on this record there was no such violation of the Constitution, and no such departure from the proper administration of criminal justice." United States v. Kordel, 397 U.S. 1, 11–13 (1970).

In United States v. Parrott, 248 F.Supp. 196, 202 (D.D.C.1965), the court said that "the Government may not bring a parallel civil proceeding and avail itself of civil discovery devises to obtain evidence for subsequent criminal prosecution." In Campbell v. Eastland, 307 F.2d 478 (5th Cir.1962), the situations were reversed. Contemplating that they would be indicted for tax fraud, the plaintiffs instituted a civil suit for a tax refund and sought discovery pursuant to Fed.R.Civ.P. 34 of material in the government's files which could not be obtained pursuant to the provisions for criminal discovery. The court of appeals held that the government should not be required to disclose in those circumstances: "[T]axpayers under criminal investigation [should not be able] to subvert the civil rules into a device for obtaining pre-trial discovery against the Government in criminal proceedings," Id. at 488. Compare United States v. Simon, 373 F.2d 649 (2d Cir.), vacated and remanded with instructions to dismiss as moot sub nom. Simon v. Wharton, 389 U.S. 425 (1967) (trustee in bankruptcy would not be enjoined from taking depositions of defendants in related criminal case).

429. In Weatherford v. Bursey, 429 U.S. 545, 559 (1977), the Court observed that "there is no general constitutional right to discovery in a

[20] 407 F.2d at 575–576.

criminal case." Nevertheless, discovery in criminal cases is closely related to the prosecution's constitutional duty to disclose information if nondisclosure would deny the defendant a fair trial. The relation between Rule 16 and the prosecutor's constitutional obligation is discussed, in Giles v. Maryland, 386 U.S. 66 (1967), in the opinions of Justice Fortas, id. at 101–102, and Justice Harlan, id. at 117–18. See United States v. Presser, 844 F.2d 1275 (6th Cir.1988); United States v. Kaplan, 554 F.2d 577 (3d Cir.1977). See generally pp. 951–81 below.

Motions to Suppress Evidence

FEDERAL RULES OF CRIMINAL PROCEDURE

Rule 41.

SEARCH AND SEIZURE

. . .

(f) Motion to Suppress. A motion to suppress evidence may be made in the court of the district of trial as provided in Rule 12.

430. What rules of evidence and standards of proof are applicable in hearings on a motion to suppress? In United States v. Matlock, 415 U.S. 164, 173 (1974), another aspect of which is discussed at p. 181 above, the Court observed that "the same rules of evidence governing criminal jury trials are not generally thought to govern hearings before a judge to determine evidentiary questions." In *Matlock*, the Court concluded that the trial judge had improperly refused to consider reliable hearsay evidence at a suppression hearing; it suggested further that "exclusionary rules, aside from rules of privilege, should not be applicable; and the judge should receive the evidence and give it such weight as his judgment and experience counsel." Id. at 175.

The burden of proof in suppression hearings is discussed in United States v. De La Fuente, 548 F.2d 528, 533–34 (5th Cir.1977): "It is well established that the burdens of production and persuasion generally rest upon the movant in a suppression hearing. . . . Concededly, in some well-defined situations the ultimate burden of persuasion may shift to the government upon an initial showing of certain facts by the defendant. For example, if a defendant produces evidence that he was arrested or subjected to a search without a warrant, the burden shifts to the government to justify the warrantless arrest or search. . . . Or if a defendant shows that a confession was obtained while he was under custodial interrogation, the government then has the burden of proving that the defendant voluntarily waived his privilege against self-incrimination. . . . Similarly, if a defendant seeks to suppress evidence as the fruit of an illegal wiretap and he proves that the tap was in fact unlawful, the burden shifts to the prosecution to prove that the evidence in question was obtained from another source and is not tainted by the illegal surveillance. . . . [E]ven in those situations, the defendant must first discharge his initial burden of producing some evidence on specific factual allegations sufficient to make a prima facie showing of illegality."

431. The Advisory Committee Note to the amendments of Rule 12 proposed in 1974 indicates that not only motions to suppress evidence obtained by an unlawful search and seizure but also motions to suppress other kinds of evidence allegedly unconstitutionally obtained (such as a confession) must be made before trial as required by Rule 12. The Note states "that the same principle should apply whatever the claimed basis for the application of the exclusionary rule of evidence may be." The rule's provision in this respect is generally in conformity with prior law.

432. Rule 12(b)(3) provides that motions to suppress evidence "must be raised prior to trial." Rule 12(f) provides that failure to make such a motion as required "shall constitute waiver thereof, but the court for cause shown may grant relief from the waiver." See p. 773 above.

In Stone v. Powell, 428 U.S. 465, 469 (1976) (6–3), the Court held that federal habeas corpus is not available for consideration of a claim by a state prisoner "that evidence obtained by an unconstitutional search or seizure was introduced at his trial, when he has previously been afforded an opportunity for full and fair litigation of his claim in the state courts." The Court based its holding on the conclusion that "the nature and purpose of the Fourth Amendment exclusionary rule" did not require that it be implemented by a federal collateral hearing in those circumstances. Id. at 481.

"[T]he additional contribution, if any, of the consideration of search-and-seizure claims of state prisoners on collateral review is small in relation to the costs. To be sure, each case in which such claim is considered may add marginally to an awareness of the values protected by the Fourth Amendment. There is no reason to believe, however, that the overall educative effect of the exclusionary rule would be appreciably diminished if search-and-seizure claims could not be raised in federal habeas corpus review of state convictions. Nor is there reason to assume that any specific disincentive already created by the risk of exclusion of evidence at trial or the reversal of convictions on direct review would be enhanced if there were the further risk that a conviction obtained in state court and affirmed on direct review might be overturned in collateral proceedings often occurring years after the incarceration of the defendant. The view that the deterrence of Fourth Amendment violations would be furthered rests on the dubious assumption that law enforcement authorities would fear that federal habeas review might reveal flaws in a search or seizure that went undetected at trial and on appeal. Even if one rationally could assume that some additional incremental deterrent effect would be present in isolated cases, the resulting advance of the legitimate goal of furthering Fourth Amendment rights would be outweighed by the acknowledged costs to other values vital to a rational system of criminal justice." Id. at 493–94. The Court said that except insofar as its supervisory authority over the federal courts might indicate otherwise, a similar rule was applicable to collateral review of claims by a federal prisoner who had failed without cause to comply with Rule 12. See id. at 481 n.16.

In Willett v. Lockhart, 37 F.3d 1265 (8th Cir.1994) (en banc), the court of appeals considered what was meant in Stone v. Powell by "an opportunity for full and fair litigation" of a Fourth Amendment claim. Reviewing cases in other circuits, the court concluded that "a Fourth Amendment claim is *Stone*-barred, and thus unreviewable by a federal habeas court, unless either the state provided no procedure by which the prisoner could raise his Fourth Amendment claim, or the prisoner was foreclosed from using that procedure because of an unconscionable breakdown in the system." 37 F.3d at 1273. It explained: "As *Stone* makes clear, Fourth Amendment claims asserted by state prisoners in federal habeas petitions are to be treated differently from other constitutional claims because of the nature and purpose of the exclusionary rule and the incremental value gained from its implementation in the federal habeas situation compared with the costs it imposes upon the administration of justice. The federal courts on habeas review of such claims are not to consider whether full and fair litigation of the claims *in fact* occurred in the state courts, but only whether the state provided an opportunity for such litigation." Id.

The holding in Stone v. Powell reversed the direction of previous decisions increasing the availability of federal collateral review of state and federal convictions. The cases are reviewed in the Court's opinion and in the dissenting opinion of Justice Brennan. See generally Wainwright v. Sykes, 433 U.S. 72 (1977), p. 1262 below. Stone v. Powell is not applicable to a claim that a conviction was based on statements obtained in violation of Miranda v. Arizona, 384 U.S. 436 (1966), p. 425 above. Withrow v. Williams, 507 U.S. 680 (1993) (5–4). In *Withrow*, the Court observed that unlike the exclusion of evidence on Fourth Amendment grounds, the *Miranda* rules safeguard a fundamental trial right and are related to the fairness of the trial itself and the accuracy of the result. Nor does Stone v. Powell bar consideration of a Sixth Amendment claim of ineffectiveness of counsel based on counsel's alleged failure to assert defendant's claims under the Fourth Amendment. Kimmelman v. Morrison, 477 U.S. 365 (1986). See note 634 p. 1277 below.

———

18 U.S.C. § 3731. Appeal by United States

. . .

An appeal by the United States shall lie to a court of appeals from a decision or order of a district court suppressing or excluding evidence or requiring the return of seized property in a criminal proceeding, not made after the defendant has been put in jeopardy and before the verdict or finding on an indictment or information, if the United States attorney certifies to the district court that the appeal is not taken for purpose of delay and that the evidence is a substantial proof of a fact material in the proceeding.

An appeal by the United States shall lie to a court of appeals from a decision or order, entered by a district court of the United States, granting the release of a person charged with or convicted of an offense, or denying a motion for revocation of, or modification of the conditions of, a decision or order granting release.

The appeal in all such cases shall be taken within thirty days after the decision, judgment or order has been rendered and shall be diligently prosecuted.

The provisions of this section shall be liberally construed to effectuate its purposes.

———

433. In some cases, an order of the district court that is not directly an order "suppressing or excluding evidence," but has the practical effect of exclusion—e.g., a discovery order with which the government has declared it will not comply, the penalty for noncompliance being exclusion of certain evidence—has been held to be within the terms of § 3731. See United States v. Kane, 646 F.2d 4 (1st Cir.1981) (citing cases).

During the pendency of an appeal under § 3731, the district court retains jurisdiction over the case and may in appropriate circumstances grant the defendant's motion to dismiss the indictment with or without prejudice under Rule 48(b). United States v. Gatto, 763 F.2d 1040, 1049–50 (9th Cir.1985).

FEDERAL RULES OF CRIMINAL PROCEDURE

Rule 17.1

PRETRIAL CONFERENCE

At any time after the filing of the indictment or information the court upon motion of any party or upon its own motion may order one or more conferences to consider such matters as will promote a fair and expeditious trial. At the conclusion of a conference the court shall prepare and file a memorandum of the matters agreed upon. No admissions made by the defendant or the defendant's attorney at the conference shall be used against the defendant unless the admissions are reduced to writing and signed by the defendant and the defendant's attorney. This rule shall not be invoked in the case of a defendant who is not represented by counsel.

CHAPTER 13

TRIAL

FEDERAL RULES OF CRIMINAL PROCEDURE

Rule 43.

PRESENCE OF THE DEFENDANT

(a) Presence Required. The defendant shall be present at the arraignment, at the time of the plea, at every stage of the trial including the impaneling of the jury and the return of the verdict, and at the imposition of sentence, except as otherwise provided by this rule.

(b) Continued Presence Not Required. The further progress of the trial to and including the return of the verdict, and the imposition of sentence, will not be prevented and the defendant will be considered to have waived the right to be present whenever a defendant, initially present at trial, or having pleaded guilty or nolo contendere,

   (1) is voluntarily absent after the trial has commenced (whether or not the defendant has been informed by the court of the obligation to remain during the trial),

   (2) in a noncapital case, is voluntarily absent at the imposition of sentence, or

   (3) after being warned by the court that disruptive conduct will cause the removal of the defendant from the courtroom, persists in conduct which is such as to justify exclusion from the courtroom.

(c) Presence Not Required. A defendant need not be present:

   (1) when represented by counsel and the defendant is an organization, as defined in 18 U.S.C. § 18;

   (2) when the offense is punishable by fine or by imprisonment for not more than one year or both, and the court, with the written consent of the defendant, permits arraignment, plea, trial, and imposition of sentence in the defendant's absence;

   (3) when the proceeding involves only a conference or hearing upon a question of law; or

(4) when the proceeding involves a correction of sentence under Rule 35 (b) or (c) or 18 U.S.C. § 3582(c).

––––––––

434. The absence of the defendant and his counsel when the judge received and responded to a request for information from the jury about an appropriate form of verdict was the basis for reversal of a conviction in Rogers v. United States, 422 U.S. 35 (1975). The Court said that under Rule 43, "the jury's message should have been answered in open court and . . . petitioner's counsel should have been given an opportunity to be heard before the trial judge responded." Id. at 39. It added that while a violation of Rule 43 might sometimes be harmless error, it was not in this case, since there was basis for objection by the defense to the judge's response to the jury.

See United States v. Gagnon, 470 U.S. 522 (1985) (6–2) (brief discussion between judge and juror in chambers, in presence of defendant's lawyer; defendant's absence harmless error); Rushen v. Spain, 464 U.S. 114 (1983) (*ex parte* communication between judge and juror; harmless error); Rice v. Wood, 77 F.3d 1138 (9th Cir.1996) (en banc) (defendant's absence at capital sentencing; harmless error); United States v. Fontanez, 878 F.2d 33 (2d Cir.1989) (supplementary instruction; defendant's absence not harmless error); United States v. Toliver, 541 F.2d 958 (2d Cir.1976) (continuation of government testimony during absence of one codefendant because of illness; harmless error).

435. Rule 43 does not permit a defendant to be tried *in absentia* if he absconds before the trial and is absent at its beginning. Crosby v. United States, 506 U.S. 255 (1993). Distinguishing cases in which a trial under way continues after the defendant has absconded, the Court said: "As a general matter, the costs of suspending a proceeding already under way will be greater than the cost of postponing a trial not yet begun. If a clear line is to be drawn marking the point at which the costs of delay are likely to outweigh the interests of the defendant and society in having the defendant present, the commencement of trial is at least a plausible place at which to draw that line." Id. at 261. The Court observed that a defendant who departs during trial is likely to realize that the trial will continue, and that allowing the trial to continue in those circumstances prevents the defendant from aborting a trial if he thinks the verdict will go against him. The Court noted that it did not reach the claim that the Constitution does not permit a trial *in absentia* in the circumstances of this case. For cases considering a defendant's waiver of the right to be present by voluntarily absenting

JS 45 (1/96) (Revised U.S.D.C. MA 8/27/96)

Criminal Case Cover Sheet   U.S. District Court - District of Massachusetts

Place of Offense   Category No. _____   Investigating Agency _____

City _____   Related Case Information:

County _____   Superseding Indictment _____ Docket No. _____
                        Original Defendant _____ New Defendant _____
                        Magistrate Judge Case Number _____
                        Search Warrant Case Number _____
                        R 20/ R 40 from District of _____

Defendant Information:

Defendant Name   _____ Juvenile: _____ Yes _____ No

Alias Name   _____

Address   _____

                   _____

Birthdate _____ SS # _____ Sex _____ Race _____ Nationality_____

Defense Counsel if known: _____

          Address: _____

U.S. Attorney Information: AUSA _____ Phone No. _____

          Address: _____ Bar No. _____

Interpreter: ☐ No   ☐ Yes   List Language and/or dialect: _____

Matter to be SEALED: ☐ No   ☐ Yes

          ☐ Warrant Requested   ☐ Regular Process   ☐ In Custody

Arrest Date _____

☐   In Federal Custody as of _____ in _____

☐   In State Custody at _____ ☐ Serving Sentence ☐ Awaiting Trial

☐   On Pretrial Release

Offenses Charged: ☐ Complaint   ☐ Information   ☐ Indictment

Total # of Counts: ☐ Petty_____   ☐ Misdemeanor_____   ☐ Felony _____

Continue on Page 2 for Entry of U.S.C. Citations

Date: _____ Signature of AUSA: _____

JS 45 (1/96) (Revised U.S.D.C. MA 8/27/96) Page 2 of 2

District Court Case Number (To be filled in by deputy clerk): _____

Name of Defendant _____

U.S.C. CITATIONS

U.S.C. Citations	Description of Offense Charged	Count Numbers
Set 1 _____	_____	_____
Set 2 _____	_____	_____
Set 3 _____	_____	_____
Set 4 _____	_____	_____
Set 5 _____	_____	_____
Set 6 _____	_____	_____
Set 7 _____	_____	_____
Set 8 _____	_____	_____
Set 9 _____	_____	_____
Set 10 _____	_____	_____
Set 11 _____	_____	_____
Set 12 _____	_____	_____
Set 13 _____	_____	_____
Set 14 _____	_____	_____
Set 15 _____	_____	_____
Set 16 _____	_____	_____
Set 17 _____	_____	_____
Set 18 _____	_____	_____
Set 19 _____	_____	_____
Set 20 _____	_____	_____
Set 21 _____	_____	_____
Set 22 _____	_____	_____
Set 23 _____	_____	_____

ADDITIONAL INFORMATION:

_____

_____

_____

_____

(crjs45rv.cov - 9/3/96)

himself from the trial, see Taylor v. United States, 414 U.S. 17 (1973) (voluntary absence constituted waiver); United States v. Houtchens, 926 F.2d 824 (9th Cir.1991) (same); United States v. Crosby, 917 F.2d 362 (8th Cir.1990) (same). In United States v. Latham, 874 F.2d 852 (1st Cir.1989), the court said that the defendant's absence due to hospitalization for an overdose of cocaine was not voluntary and did not constitute a waiver. See also United States v. Benavides, 596 F.2d 137 (5th Cir.1979) (defendant's voluntary absence after selection of jury not a sufficient basis for continuing trial without inquiry into possibility of postponement).

Illinois v. Allen

397 U.S. 337, 90 S.Ct. 1057, 25 L.Ed.2d 353 (1970).

■ MR. JUSTICE BLACK delivered the opinion of the Court.

The Confrontation Clause of the Sixth Amendment to the United States Constitution provides that: "In all criminal prosecutions, the accused shall enjoy the right . . . to be confronted with the witnesses against him. . . ." We have held that the Fourteenth Amendment makes the guarantees of this clause obligatory upon the States. . . . One of the most basic of the rights guaranteed by the Confrontation Clause is the accused's right to be present in the courtroom at every stage of his trial. . . . The question presented in this case is whether an accused can claim the benefit of this constitutional right to remain in the courtroom while at the same time he engages in speech and conduct which is so noisy, disorderly, and disruptive that it is exceedingly difficult or wholly impossible to carry on the trial.

The issue arose in the following way. The respondent, Allen, was convicted by an Illinois jury of armed robbery and was sentenced to serve 10 to 30 years in the Illinois State Penitentiary. The evidence against him showed that on August 12, 1956, he entered a tavern in Illinois and, after ordering a drink, took $200 from the bartender at gunpoint. The Supreme Court of Illinois affirmed his conviction . . . and this Court denied certiorari. . . . Later Allen filed a petition for a writ of habeas corpus in federal court alleging that he had been wrongfully deprived by the Illinois trial judge of his constitutional right to remain present throughout his trial. . . .

The facts surrounding Allen's expulsion from the courtroom are set out in the Court of Appeals' opinion sustaining Allen's contention:

"After his indictment and during the pretrial stage, the petitioner [Allen] refused court-appointed counsel and indicated to the trial court on several occasions that he wished to conduct his own defense. After considerable argument by the petitioner, the trial judge told him, 'I'll let you be your own lawyer, but I'll ask Mr. Kelly [court-appointed counsel] [to] sit in and protect the record for you, insofar as possible.'

"The trial began on September 9, 1957. After the State's Attorney had accepted the first four jurors following their voir dire examination, the petitioner began examining the first juror and continued at great length. Finally, the trial judge interrupted the petitioner, requesting him to confine his questions solely to matters relating to the prospective juror's qualifications. At that point, the petitioner started to argue with the judge in a most abusive and disrespectful manner. At last, and seemingly in desperation, the judge asked appointed counsel to proceed with the examination of the jurors. The petitioner continued to talk, proclaiming that the appointed attorney was not going to act as his lawyer. He terminated his remarks by saying, 'When I go out for lunchtime, you're [the judge] going to be a corpse here.' At that point he tore the file which his attorney had and threw the papers on the floor. The trial judge thereupon stated to the petitioner, 'One more outbreak of that sort and I'll remove you from the courtroom.' This warning had no effect on the petitioner. He continued to talk back to the judge, saying, 'There's not going to be no trial, either. I'm going to sit here and you're going to talk and you can bring your shackles out and straight jacket and put them on me and tape my mouth, but it will do no good because there's not going to be no trial.' After more abusive remarks by the petitioner, the trial judge ordered the trial to proceed in the petitioner's absence. The petitioner was removed from the courtroom. The voir dire examination then continued and the jury was selected in the absence of the petitioner.

"After a noon recess and before the jury was brought into the courtroom, the petitioner, appearing before the judge, complained about the fairness of the trial and his appointed attorney. He also said he wanted to be present in the court during his trial. In reply, the judge said that the petitioner would be permitted to remain in the courtroom if he 'behaved [himself] and [did] not interfere with the introduction of the case.' The jury was brought in and seated. Counsel for the petitioner then moved to exclude the witnesses from the courtroom. The [petitioner] protested this effort on the part of his attorney, saying: 'There is going to be no proceeding. I'm going to start talking and I'm going to keep on talking all through the trial. There's not going to be no trial like this. I want my sister and my friends here in court to testify for me.' The trial judge thereupon ordered the petitioner removed from the courtroom." 413 F.2d, at 233–234.

After this second removal, Allen remained out of the courtroom during the presentation of the State's case-in-chief, except that he was brought in on several occasions for purposes of identification. During one of these latter appearances, Allen responded to one of the judge's questions with vile and abusive language. After the prosecution's case had been presented, the trial judge reiterated his promise to Allen that he could return to the courtroom whenever he agreed to conduct himself properly. Allen gave some assurances of proper conduct and was permitted to be present through the remainder of the trial, principally his defense, which was conducted by his appointed counsel.

The Court of Appeals went on to hold that the Supreme Court of Illinois was wrong in ruling that Allen had by his conduct relinquished his constitutional right to be present . . . .

. . .

The Court of Appeals felt that the defendant's Sixth Amendment right to be present at his own trial was so "absolute" that, no matter how unruly or disruptive the defendant's conduct might be, he could never be held to have lost that right so long as he continued to insist upon it, as Allen clearly did. Therefore the Court of Appeals concluded that a trial judge could never expel a defendant from his own trial and that the judge's ultimate remedy when faced with an obstreperous defendant like Allen who determines to make his trial impossible is to bind and gag him. We cannot agree that the Sixth Amendment, the cases upon which the Court of Appeals relied, or any other cases of this Court so handicap a trial judge in conducting a criminal trial. . . . We accept instead the statement of Mr. Justice Cardozo who, speaking for the Court in Snyder v. Massachusetts, 291 U.S. 97, 106 (1934), said: "No doubt the privilege [of personally confronting witnesses] may be lost by consent or at times even by misconduct." Although mindful that courts must indulge every reasonable presumption against the loss of constitutional rights . . . we explicitly hold today that a defendant can lose his right to be present at trial if, after he has been warned by the judge that he will be removed if he continues his disruptive behavior, he nevertheless insists on conducting himself in a manner so disorderly, disruptive, and disrespectful of the court that his trial cannot be carried on with him in the courtroom. Once lost, the right to be present can, of course, be reclaimed as soon as the defendant is willing to conduct himself consistently with the decorum and respect inherent in the concept of courts and judicial proceedings.

It is essential to the proper administration of criminal justice that dignity, order, and decorum be the hallmarks of all court proceedings in our country. The flagrant disregard in the courtroom of elementary standards of proper conduct should not and cannot be tolerated. We believe trial judges confronted with disruptive contumacious, stubbornly defiant defendants must be given sufficient discretion to meet the circumstances of each case. No one formula for maintaining the appropriate courtroom atmosphere will be best in all situations. We think there are at least three constitutionally permissible ways for a trial judge to handle an obstreperous defendant like Allen: (1) bind and gag him, thereby keeping him present; (2) cite him for contempt; (3) take him out of the courtroom until he promises to conduct himself properly.

I

Trying a defendant for a crime while he sits bound and gagged before the judge and jury would to an extent comply with that part of the Sixth Amendment's purposes that accords the defendant an opportunity to confront the witnesses at the trial. But even to contemplate such a technique, much less see it, arouses a feeling that no person should be tried while shackled and gagged except as a last resort. Not only is it possible that the sight of shackles and gags might have a significant effect on the jury's feelings about the defendant, but the use of this technique is itself something of an affront to the very dignity and decorum of judicial proceedings that the judge is seeking to uphold. Moreover, one of the defendant's primary advantages of being present at the trial, his ability to communicate with his counsel, is greatly reduced when the defendant is in a condition of total physical restraint. It is in part because of these inherent disadvantages and limitations in this method of dealing with disorderly defendants that we decline to hold . . . that a defendant cannot under any possible circumstances be deprived of his right to be present at trial. However, in some situations which we need not attempt to foresee, binding and gagging might possibly be the fairest and most reasonable way to handle a defendant who acts as Allen did here.

II

In a footnote the Court of Appeals suggested the possible availability of contempt of court as a remedy to make Allen behave in his robbery trial, and it is true that citing or threatening to cite a contumacious defendant for criminal contempt might in itself be sufficient to make a defendant stop interrupting a trial. If so, the problem would be solved easily, and the defendant could remain in the courtroom. Of course, if the defendant is determined to prevent *any* trial, then a court in attempting to try the defendant for contempt is still confronted with the identical dilemma that the Illinois court faced in this case. And criminal contempt has obvious limitations as a sanction when the defendant is charged with a crime so serious that a very severe sentence such as death or life imprisonment is likely to be imposed. In such a case the defendant might not be affected by a mere contempt sentence when he ultimately faces a far more serious sanction. Nevertheless, the contempt remedy should be borne in mind by a judge in the circumstances of this case.

Another aspect of the contempt remedy is the judge's power, when exercised consistently with state and federal law, to imprison an unruly defendant such as Allen for civil contempt and discontinue the trial until such time as the defendant promises to behave himself. This procedure is consistent with the defendant's right to be present at trial, and yet it avoids the serious shortcomings of the use of shackles and gags. It must be recognized, however, that a defendant might conceivably, as a matter of calculated strategy, elect to spend a prolonged period in confinement for contempt in the hope that adverse witnesses might be unavailable after a lapse of time. A court must guard against allowing a defendant to profit from his own wrong in this way.

III

The trial court in this case decided under the circumstances to remove the defendant from the courtroom and to continue his trial in his absence until and unless he promised to conduct himself in a manner befitting an American courtroom. As we said earlier, we find nothing unconstitutional about this procedure. Allen's behavior was clearly of such an extreme and aggravated nature as to justify either his removal from the courtroom or his total physical restraint. Prior to his removal he was repeatedly warned by the trial judge that he would be removed from the courtroom if he persisted in his unruly conduct, and, as Judge Hastings observed in his dissenting opinion, the record demonstrates that Allen would not have been at all dissuaded by the trial judge's use of his criminal contempt powers. Allen was constantly informed that he could return to the trial when he would agree to conduct himself in an orderly manner. Under these circumstances we hold that Allen lost his right guaranteed by the Sixth and Fourteenth Amendments to be present throughout his trial.

IV

It is not pleasant to hold that the respondent Allen was properly banished from the court for a part of his own trial. But our courts, palladiums of liberty as they are, cannot be treated disrespectfully with impunity. Nor can the accused be permitted by his disruptive conduct indefinitely to avoid being tried on the charges brought against him. It would degrade our country and our judicial system to permit our courts to be bullied, insulted, and humiliated and their orderly progress thwarted and obstructed by defendants brought before them charged with crimes. As guardians of the public welfare, our state and federal judicial systems strive to administer equal justice to the rich and the poor, the good and the bad, the native and foreign born of every race, nationality, and religion. Being manned by humans, the courts are not perfect and are bound to make some errors. But, if our courts are to remain what the Founders intended, the citadels of justice, their proceedings cannot and must not be infected with the sort of scurrilous, abusive language and conduct paraded before the Illinois trial judge in this case. The record shows that the Illinois judge at all times conducted himself with that dignity, decorum, and patience that befit a judge. Even in holding that the trial judge had erred, the Court of Appeals praised his "commendable patience under severe provocation."

We do not hold that removing this defendant from his own trial was the only way the Illinois judge could have constitutionally solved the problem he had. We do hold, however, that there is nothing whatever in this record to show that the judge did not act completely within his discretion. Deplorable as it is to remove a man from his own trial, even for a short time, we hold that the judge did not commit legal error in doing what he did.

. . .[1]

---

[1] Justice Brennan wrote a concurring opinion. Justice Douglas wrote an opinion stating that the court should not have reached the merits of the case on a stale record.

436. "Because every criminal defendant is entitled under the fourteenth amendment's due process clause to a fair and impartial trial there are four sound reasons underlying the general rule that a defendant should never be shackled during his trial before a jury except in extraordinary circumstances. Without repeating all of them, we note the inherent prejudice to the accused when he is cast in the jury's eyes as a dangerous, untrustworthy and pernicious individual from the very start of the trial. Therefore, only upon a *clear showing* of necessity should shackles ever be employed. One element of such necessity is that less drastic security precautions to prevent escape, even at some additional cost to the state, will not provide the needed protection. In light of the identity of reasons underlying the principle against shackling a defendant during a jury trial, and the principles for dealing with an obstreperous defendant during the trial outlined by the Supreme Court in Illinois v. Allen, 397 U.S. 337 . . . (1970), shackles should only be used as a last resort. Therefore, in our opinion, it is an abuse of discretion precipitously to employ shackles when less drastic security measures will adequately and reasonably suffice." Kennedy v. Cardwell, 487 F.2d 101, 111 (6th Cir.1973). The four reasons to which the court referred are that shackling prejudices the jury, limits the defendant's ability to defend himself by affecting his mental capacities and capacity to testify as a witness, limits his ability to consult with counsel, and detracts from the dignity and decorum of the judicial process.

The use of shackles has been upheld in a number of cases. E.g., United States v. Stewart, 20 F.3d 911 (8th Cir.1994) (defendant was accused of "vicious assault" on a witness in a courtroom and was disruptive); Jones v. Meyer, 899 F.2d 883 (9th Cir.1990) (defendant on trial for murder had previous murder conviction and had made threats); United States v. Fountain, 768 F.2d 790 (7th Cir.1985) (defendants and witnesses were prison inmates previously convicted as murderers); Zygadlo v. Wainwright, 720 F.2d 1221 (11th Cir.1983) (defendant had previously tried to escape). See also Wilson v. McCarthy, 770 F.2d 1482 (9th Cir.1985) (shackling of defense witness upheld).

In Spain v. Rushen, 883 F.2d 712 (9th Cir.1989), however, the court held that the use of shackles denied the defendant due process. Referring to Estelle v. Williams, 425 U.S. 501 (1976), see note 437 below, in Walker v. Butterworth, 599 F.2d 1074, 1076, 1080 (1st Cir.1979), the court of appeals held that the practice of requiring the defendant in certain cases to sit in the prisoner's dock, an enclosure "about four feet square and four feet high, open at the top so that the defendant's head and shoulders can be seen by the jury," was an anachronism and unconstitutional, because it might "dilute the presumption of innocence." The court applied *Walker* in Young v. Callahan, 700 F.2d 32 (1st Cir.1983), but allowed the possibility that the dock might be used in cases where physical restraint of the defendant was necessary.

In Holbrook v. Flynn, 475 U.S. 560 (1986), the Court concluded that the presence in the courtroom of four uniformed, armed law enforcement officers for security reasons during the defendant's trial with five other defendants did not deny him a fair trial. The defendants were detained without bail. The officers were seated in the front row of the spectator section of the courtroom, not far behind the defendants' seats, throughout the trial, which lasted for more than two months. The Court observed that although the presence of security officers in a courtroom might be prejudicial in a particular case, there was no ground for a presumption of prejudice. Their presence, the Court said, is not "the sort of inherently prejudicial practice that, like shackling, should be permitted only where justified by an essential state interest specific to each trial." Id. at 568–69.

Applying Illinois v. Allen, the court upheld the expulsion of the defendant in Foster v. Wainwright, 686 F.2d 1382 (11th Cir.1982). Expulsion was held to have been improper in Badger v. Cardwell, 587 F.2d 968 (9th Cir.1978).

The involuntary administration of antipsychotic medication to a defendant during his trial, without findings by the trial court that such medication was both medically appropriate and, there being no less intrusive means, necessary to the conduct of the trial or to the safety of the defendant or others, violated his right to a fair trial under the Due Process Clause. Riggins v. Nevada, 504 U.S. 127 (1992) (7–2).

437. "[T]he State cannot, consistently with the Fourteenth Amendment, compel an accused to stand trial before a jury while dressed in identifiable prison clothes." Estelle v. Williams, 425 U.S. 501, 512 (1976). Referring to "the possible impairment of the presumption [of innocence] so basic to the adversary system," the Court said that the "constant reminder of the accused's condition implicit in such distinctive, identifiable attire may affect a juror's judgment." Id. at 504–505. The Court noted, however, that some defendants might prefer to be tried in jail clothes. If the defendant failed to make an objection to being tried in them, there was no compulsion and, therefore, no constitutional violation.

The courts have generally condemned a prosecutor's commenting in closing argument about a defendant's behavior in the courtroom and in some cases have reversed convictions. Such comment, it is reasoned, invites the jury to convict on a basis other than the evidence and, further, may indirectly call attention to a defendant's failure to testify. See United States v. Schuler, 813 F.2d 978 (9th Cir.1987).

————

United States v. Carrion

488 F.2d 12 (1st Cir.1973).

PER CURIAM.

Appellant, convicted of knowingly aiding and abetting the distribution of heroin in violation of 21 U.S.C. § 841(a)(1) and 18 U.S.C. § 2, contends that his Fifth and Sixth Amendment rights were abridged during trial because . . . the court refused to appoint an interpreter for him.

. . .

Appellant is a foreign-born national with a limited ability to speak and comprehend English. He claims that, although he admitted to the court some ability to communicate and understand, his counsel's assertion at the start of the trial of the possibility of a "problem of communication" should have prompted the court to hold a special hearing to determine the extent of the problem. As evidence of his difficulty with the language, appellant points to several instances during his own testimony where questions had to be repeated or where his responses were so unclear as to require that he rephrase them. On at least one occasion the court indicated that there was apparently a "language barrier".

The necessity for an interpreter to translate from a defendant's native language into English when the defendant is on the stand, and from English into the defendant's native language when others are testifying, has been elevated to a right when the defendant is indigent and has obvious difficulty with the language. . . . Clearly, the right to confront witnesses would be meaningless if the accused could not understand their testimony, and the effectiveness of cross-examination would be severely hampered. . . . If the defendant takes the stand in his own behalf, but has an imperfect command of English, there exists the additional danger that he will either misunderstand crucial questions or that the jury will misconstrue crucial responses. The right to an interpreter rests most fundamentally, however, on the notion that no defendant should face the Kafkaesque spectre of an incomprehensible ritual which may terminate in punishment.

Yet how high must the language barrier rise before a defendant has a right to an interpreter? It is well settled that there is no right to an interpreter if the foreign-born defendant speaks fluent English and is "completely aware of all the proceedings". Cervantes v. Cox, 350 F.2d 855 (10th Cir.1965). The status of the right becomes less certain, however, where, as in the present case, the defendant has some ability to understand and communicate, but clearly has difficulty.

Because the determination is likely to hinge upon various factors, including the complexity of the issues and testimony presented during trial and the language ability of the defendant's counsel, considerations of judicial economy would dictate that the trial court, coming into direct contact with the defendant, be granted wide discretion in determining whether an interpreter is necessary. . . . It would be a fruitless and frustrating exercise for the appellate court to have to infer language difficulty from every faltering, repetitious bit of testimony in the record. But precisely because the trial court is entrusted with discretion, it should make unmistakably clear to a defendant who may have a language difficulty that he has a right to a court-appointed interpreter if the court determines that one is needed, and, whenever put on notice that there may be some significant language difficulty, the court should make such a determination of need.

Although the trial court in the present case did not hold a formal hearing on the question whether the appellant required a translator, it was obviously sensitive to the appellant's plight in that it did grant pretrial motions made by the appellant's two co-defendants, each asking for an interpreter during the proceedings. Thus, a procedure was available for the appellant to allege and show a language difficulty before trial commenced. Moreover, the court specifically asked counsel whether the appellant was able to communicate and understand English, to which appellant's counsel responded in the affirmative. Finally, the court told the appellant that if, at any point in the proceedings, there was something he did not understand, he need only raise his hand and the testimony would be repeated. We are not prepared to hold that the appellant had a constitutional right to any more than this.

. . .

Voir Dire

FEDERAL RULES OF CRIMINAL PROCEDURE

Rule 23.

TRIAL BY JURY OR BY THE COURT

(a) Trial by Jury. Cases required to be tried by jury shall be so tried unless the defendant waives a jury trial in writing with the approval of the court and the consent of the government.

(b) Jury of Less Than Twelve. Juries shall be of 12 but at any time before verdict the parties may stipulate in writing with the approval of the court that the jury shall consist of any number less than 12 or that a valid verdict may be returned by a jury of less than 12 should the court find it necessary to excuse one or more jurors for any just cause after trial commences. Even absent such stipulation, if the court finds it necessary to excuse a juror for just cause after the jury has retired to consider its verdict, in the discretion of the court a valid verdict may be returned by the remaining 11 jurors.

(c) Trial Without a Jury. In a case tried without a jury the court shall make a general finding and shall in addition, on request made before the general finding, find the facts specially. Such findings may be oral. If an opinion or memorandum of decision is filed, it will be sufficient if the findings of fact appear therein.

———

438. "The trial of all crimes except in cases of impeachment shall be by jury. . . . U.S. Constitution art. 3, § 2.

"In all criminal prosecutions, the accused shall enjoy the right to a speedy and public trial, by an impartial jury of the State and district wherein the crime shall have been committed, which district shall have been previously ascertained by law. . . . U.S. Constitution amend. VI.

"Because we believe that trial by jury in criminal cases is fundamental to the American scheme of justice, we hold that the Fourteenth Amendment guarantees a right of jury trial in all criminal cases which—were they to be tried in a federal court—would come within the Sixth Amendment's guarantee." Duncan v. Louisiana, 391 U.S. 145, 149 (1968).[2]

In *Duncan*, the defendant was tried without a jury and convicted of simple battery, the maximum penalty for which was two years imprisonment and a fine of $300; he was sentenced to 60 days imprisonment and a fine of $150. The state contended that because his sentence was so light he was not entitled to a jury trial. The Court disagreed. "It is doubtless true that there is a category of petty crimes or offenses which is not subject to the Sixth Amendment jury trial provision and should not be subject to the Fourteenth Amendment jury trial requirement here applied to the States. Crimes carrying possible penalties up to six months do not require a jury trial if they otherwise qualify as petty offenses . . . . But the penalty authorized for a particular crime is of major relevance in determining whether it is serious or not and may in itself, if severe enough, subject the trial to the mandates of the Sixth Amendment. District of Columbia v. Clawans, 300 U.S. 617 (1937). The penalty authorized by the law of the locality may be taken 'as a gauge of its social and ethical judgments,' 300 U.S., at 628, of the crime in question. In *Clawans* the defendant was jailed for 60 days, but it was the 90-day authorized punishment on which the Court focused in

———

2. "A criminal process which was fair and equitable but used no juries is easy to imagine. It would make use of alternative guarantees and protections which would serve the purposes that the jury serves in the English and American systems. Yet no American State has undertaken to construct such a system. Instead, every American State . . . uses the jury extensively, and imposes very serious punishments only after a trial at which the defendant has a right to a jury's verdict. In every State . . . the structure and style of the criminal process—the supporting framework and the subsidiary procedures—are of the sort that naturally complement jury trial, and have developed in connection with and in reliance upon jury trial." 391 U.S. at 150 n.14.

UNITED STATES DISTRICT COURT
DISTRICT OF MASSACHUSETTS

UNITED STATES OF AMERICA

      V.   **CRIMINAL NO. _____**

_____

WAIVER OF JURY TRIAL

Now comes the defendant, _____ and waives

his right of trial by jury and elects to be tried before the court.

_____
Defendant

_____
Attorney for the Defendant

_____
Assistant U.S. Attorney

APPROVED:

_____
United States District Judge

_____
Date

(Jurywaiv.frm - 09/92)   [kwvjy.]

determining that the offense was not one for which the Constitution assured trial by jury. In the case before us the Legislature of Louisiana has made simple battery a criminal offense punishable by imprisonment for up to two years and a fine. The question, then, is whether a crime carrying such a penalty is an offense which Louisiana may insist on trying without a jury.

"We think not. So-called petty offenses were tried without juries both in England and in the Colonies and have always been held to be exempt from the otherwise comprehensive language of the Sixth Amendment's jury trial provisions. There is no substantial evidence that the Framers intended to depart from this established common-law practice, and the possible consequences to defendants from convictions for petty offenses have been thought insufficient to outweigh the benefits to efficient law enforcement and simplified judicial administration resulting from the availability of speedy and inexpensive nonjury adjudications. These same considerations compel the same result under the Fourteenth Amendment. Of course the boundaries of the petty offense category have always been ill-defined, if not ambulatory. In the absence of an explicit constitutional provision, the definitional task necessarily falls on the courts, which must either pass upon the validity of legislative attempts to identify those petty offenses which are exempt from jury trial or, where the legislature has not addressed itself to the problem, themselves face the question in the first instance. In either case it is necessary to draw a line in the spectrum of crime, separating petty from serious infractions. This process, although essential, cannot be wholly satisfactory, for it requires attaching different consequences to events which, when they lie near the line, actually differ very little.

"In determining whether the length of the authorized prison term or the seriousness of other punishment is enough in itself to require a jury trial, we are counseled by District of Columbia v. Clawans, supra, to refer to objective criteria, chiefly the existing laws and practices in the Nation. In the federal system, petty offenses are defined as those punishable by no more than six months in prison and a $500 fine. In 49 of the 50 States crimes subject to trial without a jury, which occasionally include simple battery, are punishable by no more than one year in jail. Moreover, in the late 18th century in America crimes triable without a jury were for the most part punishable by no more than a six-month prison term, although there appear to have been exceptions to this rule. We need not, however, settle in this case the exact location of the line between petty offenses and serious crimes. It is sufficient for our purposes to hold that a crime punishable by two years in prison is, based on past and contemporary standards in this country, a serious crime and not a petty offense. Consequently, appellant was entitled to a jury trial and it was error to deny it." 391 U.S. at 159–62.

The Court drew the line between petty offenses and serious crimes in Baldwin v. New York, 399 U.S. 66 (1970). It held that "no offense can be deemed 'petty' for purposes of the right to trial by jury where imprisonment for more than six months is authorized." Id. at 69. The Court relied primarily on the nearly unanimous view that the possibility of imprisonment for six months warranted a right to jury trial: "In the entire Nation, New York City alone denies an accused the right to interpose between himself and a possible prison term of over six months, the commonsense judgment of a jury of his peers.

". . . This near-uniform judgment of the Nation furnishes us with the only objective criterion by which a line could ever be drawn—on the basis of the possible penalty alone—between offenses which are and which are not regarded as 'serious' for purposes of trial by jury." Id. at 71–73.

The category of petty offenses was elaborated further in Blanton v. City of North Las Vegas, 489 U.S. 538 (1989). The Court said that an offense carrying a maximum sentence of six months or less is presumptively, but not necessarily, a petty offense. "A defendant is entitled to jury trial in such circumstances only if he can demonstrate that any additional statutory penalties, viewed in conjunction with the maximum authorized period of incarceration, are so severe that they clearly reflect a legislative determination that the offense in question is a 'serious' one." Id. at 543. In *Blanton*, the crime was driving under the influence of alcohol. The maximum term of imprisonment was six months. The additional penalty of a fine of up to $1000 and the alternative penalty of 48 hours of community service "dressed in distinctive garb" that identifies the person as an offender was not enough to make the crime not a petty offense. *Blanton* was applied in United States v. Nachtigal, 507 U.S. 1 (1993), in which again the defendant was convicted of drunk driving, the maximum penalty for which was six months imprisonment. The Court concluded that a maximum fine of $5000 and an alternative to imprisonment of five years probation did not overcome the presumption of *Blanton* that the crime was a petty offense.

A defendant who is prosecuted in a single trial for multiple petty offenses the aggregate authorized penalties for which exceed six months imprisonment does not have a constitutional right to a jury trial. Lewis v. United States, 518 U.S. 322 (1996) (7–2).

In a companion case to *Baldwin*, Williams v. Florida, 399 U.S. 78 (1970), the Court held that the constitutional right to a trial by jury did not require that the jury be composed of 12 members. "[T]hat particular feature of the jury system appears to have been a historical accident, unrelated to the great purposes which gave rise to the jury in the first place." And, "there is absolutely no indication in 'the intent of the Framers' of an explicit decision to equate the constitutional and common-law characteristics of the jury." Id. at 89–90, 99. Turning to the purpose of the jury trial "to prevent oppression by the Government," the court concluded: "Given this purpose, the essential feature of a jury obviously lies in the interposition between the accused and his accuser of the commonsense judgment of a group of laymen, and in the community participation and shared responsibility that results from that group's determination of guilt or innocence. The performance of this role is not a function of the particular number of the body that makes up the jury. To be sure, the number should probably be large enough to promote group deliberation, free from outside attempts at intimidation, and to provide a fair possibility for obtaining a representative cross-section of the

UNITED STATES DISTRICT COURT
DISTRICT OF MASSACHUSETTS

UNITED STATES OF AMERICA

V.   **CRIMINAL NO.** _____

_____

STIPULATION FOR JURY LESS THAN TWELVE
BUT NOT LESS THAN TEN

On this the _____ day of _____, 19 ____ the

undersigned hereby agree that if, in the opinion of the Court, not more than two

jurors, after being selected to serve, become disqualified, incapacitated or

otherwise unable or unqualified to serve at any stage of the trial, such jurors may

be excused and the trial may continue and a verdict rendered by the remaining

jurors; it being understood that a least ten jurors must be present and participate

in the trial and the verdict.

United States Attorney

By _____
Assistant U.S. Attorney

APPROVED:

_____
Attorney for Defendant

_____   _____
UNITED STATES DISTRICT JUDGE   **Defendant**

(Juryof10.stp - 09/96)   [kstipjury.]

community. But we find little reason to think that these goals are in any meaningful sense less likely to be achieved when the jury numbers six, than when it numbers 12—particularly if the requirement of unanimity is retained. And, certainly the reliability of the jury as a factfinder hardly seems likely to be a function of its size.

"It might be suggested that the 12-man jury gives a defendant a greater advantage since he has more 'chances' of finding a juror who will insist on acquittal and thus prevent conviction. But the advantage might just as easily belong to the State, which also needs only one juror out of twelve insisting on guilt to prevent acquittal. What few experiments have occurred—usually in the civil area—indicate that there is no discernible difference between the results reached by the two different-sized juries. In short, neither currently available evidence nor theory suggests that the 12-man jury is necessarily more advantageous to the defendant than a jury composed of fewer members.

"Similarly, while in theory the number of viewpoints represented on a randomly selected jury ought to increase as the size of the jury increases, in practice the difference between the 12-man and the six-man jury in terms of the cross-section of the community represented seems likely to be negligible. Even the 12-man jury cannot insure representation of every distinct voice in the community, particularly given the use of the peremptory challenge. As long as arbitrary exclusions of a particular class from the jury rolls are forbidden . . . the concern that the cross-section will be significantly diminished if the jury is decreased in size from 12 to six seems an unrealistic one." Id. at 100–102.

A jury of six members, upheld in *Williams*, is, however, the smallest that is constitutionally permissible. Fearing that a jury of less than six would threaten the functions of the jury that made trial by jury a constitutional right, the Court held that a five-member jury was constitutionally inadequate, in Ballew v. Georgia, 435 U.S. 223 (1978). For "much the same reasons," the Court concluded, notwithstanding *Apodaca* and *Johnson*, below, that a person may not be convicted by the verdict of a six-person jury unless the verdict is unanimous. Burch v. Louisiana, 441 U.S. 130 (1979).

The Constitution does not require in *state* criminal prosecutions that the verdict be unanimous. Apodaca v. Oregon, 406 U.S. 404 (1972) (5–4); Johnson v. Louisiana, 406 U.S. 356 (1972) (5–4). In *Apodaca*, four Justices concluded that the Sixth Amendment's right to a jury did not require unanimity. In terms of the jury's function, as described in *Williams*, above, they saw "no difference between juries required to act unanimously and those permitted to convict or acquit by votes of 10 to two or 11 to one. Requiring unanimity would obviously produce hung juries in some situations where nonunanimous juries will convict or acquit. But in either case, the interest of the defendant in having the judgment of his peers interposed between himself and the officers of the State who prosecute and judge him is equally well served." 406 U.S. at 411. Justice Powell agreed that the Sixth Amendment did not require unanimity in state cases, but stated his conclusion that unanimity was required to convict in a *federal* criminal trial. Id. at 366, 371.

In *Johnson*, a majority of the Court concluded that a less than unanimous verdict does not violate the requirement of the Due Process Clause that guilt be proved beyond a reasonable doubt. The defendant was convicted of armed robbery by a 9–3 verdict. The Court said: "[I]t is our view that the fact of three dissenting votes to acquit raises no question of constitutional substance about either the integrity or the accuracy of the majority verdict of guilt. Appellant's contrary argument breaks down into two parts, each of which we shall consider separately: first, that nine individual jurors will be unable to vote conscientiously in favor of guilt beyond a reasonable doubt when three of their colleagues are arguing for acquittal, and second, that guilt cannot be said to have been proved beyond a reasonable doubt when one or more of a jury's members at the conclusion of deliberation still possess such a doubt. Neither argument is persuasive.

"Numerous cases have defined a reasonable doubt as one 'based on reason which arises from the evidence or lack of evidence.' United States v. Johnson, 343 F.2d 5, 6 n.1 (CA2 1965). . . . In considering the first branch of appellant's argument, we can find no basis for holding that the nine jurors who voted for his conviction failed to follow their instructions concerning the need for proof beyond such a doubt or that the vote of any one of the nine failed to reflect an honest belief that guilt had been so proved. Appellant, in effect, asks us to assume that, when minority jurors express sincere doubts about guilt, their fellow jurors will nevertheless ignore them and vote to convict even if deliberation has not been exhausted and minority jurors have grounds for acquittal which, if pursued, might persuade members of the majority to acquit. But the mere fact that three jurors voted to acquit does not in itself demonstrate that, had the nine jurors of the majority attended further to reason and the evidence, all or one of them would have developed a reasonable doubt about guilt. We have no grounds for believing that majority jurors, aware of their responsibility and power over the liberty of the defendant, would simply refuse to listen to arguments presented to them in favor of acquittal, terminate discussion, and render a verdict. On the contrary it is far more likely that a juror presenting reasoned argument in favor of acquittal would either have his arguments answered or would carry enough other jurors with him to prevent conviction. A majority will cease discussion and outvote a minority only after reasoned discussion has ceased to have persuasive effect or to serve any other purpose—when a minority, that is, continues to insist upon acquittal without having persuasive reasons in support of its position. At that juncture there is no basis for denigrating the vote of so large a majority of the jury or for refusing to accept their decision as being, at least in their minds, beyond a reasonable doubt. Indeed, at this point, a 'dissenting juror should consider whether his doubt was a reasonable one . . . [when it made] no impression upon the minds of so many men, equally honest, equally intelligent with himself.' Allen v. United States, 164 U.S. 492, 501 (1896). Appellant offers no evidence that majority jurors simply ignore the reasonable doubts of their colleagues or otherwise act irresponsibly in casting their votes in favor of conviction, and before we alter our own long-standing perceptions about jury behavior and overturn a considered legislative judgment that unanimity is not essential to reasoned jury verdicts, we must have some basis for doing so other than unsupported assumptions.

"We conclude, therefore, that, as to the nine jurors who voted to convict, the State satisfied its burden of proving guilt beyond any reasonable doubt. The remaining question under the Due Process Clause is whether the vote of three jurors for acquittal can be said to impeach the verdict of the other nine and to demonstrate that guilt was not in fact proved beyond such doubt. We hold that it cannot.

"Of course, the State's proof could perhaps be regarded as more certain if it had convinced all 12 jurors instead of only nine; it would have been even more compelling if it had been required to convince and had, in fact, convinced 24 or 36 jurors. But the fact remains that nine jurors—a substantial majority of the jury—were convinced by the evidence. In our view disagreement of three jurors does not alone establish reasonable doubt, particularly when such a heavy majority of the jury, after having considered the dissenters' views, remains convinced of guilt. That rational men disagree is not in itself equivalent to a failure of proof by the State, nor does it indicate infidelity to the reasonable-doubt standard. Jury verdicts finding guilt beyond a reasonable doubt are regularly sustained even though the evidence was such that the jury would have been justified in having a reasonable doubt . . .; even though the trial judge might not have reached the same conclusion as the jury . . . and even though appellate judges are closely divided on the issue whether there was sufficient evidence to support a conviction. . . . That want of jury unanimity is not to be equated with the existence of a reasonable doubt emerges even more clearly from the fact that when a jury in a federal court, which operates under the unanimity rule and is instructed to acquit a defendant if it has a reasonable doubt about his guilt . . . cannot agree unanimously upon a verdict, the defendant is not acquitted, but is merely given a new trial. . . . If the doubt of a minority of jurors indicates the existence of a reasonable doubt, it would appear that a defendant should receive a directed verdict of acquittal rather than a retrial. We conclude, therefore, that verdicts rendered by nine out of 12 jurors are not automatically invalidated by the disagreement of the dissenting three. Appellant was not deprived of due process of law." 406 U.S. at 360–63.

The Court rejected also the claim that the Equal Protection Clause did not allow a state to provide for unanimous verdicts in some cases and not others.

The Court has upheld, against the claim that it denied the right to a jury trial, a "two-tier" court system, by which a person accused of certain crimes is tried first in the lower court, where no jury is available, and then if he is convicted and appeals, is tried *de novo* in the upper court, where a jury is available. Ludwig v. Massachusetts, 427 U.S. 618 (1976) (5–4).

439. In Singer v. United States, 380 U.S. 24, 26 (1965), the Court held that there is not a constitutional right to a nonjury trial and that Rule 23(a) of the Federal Rules of Criminal Procedure "sets forth a reasonable procedure governing attempted waivers of jury trials." "A defendant's only constitutional right concerning the method of trial is to an impartial trial by jury. We find no constitutional impediment to conditioning a waiver of this right on the consent of the prosecuting attorney and the trial judge when, if either refuses to consent, the result is simply that the defendant is subject to an impartial trial by jury—the very thing that the Constitution guarantees him. The Constitution recognizes an adversary system as the proper method of determining guilt, and the Government, as a litigant, has a legitimate interest in seeing that cases in which it believes a conviction is warranted are tried before the tribunal which the Constitution regards as most likely to produce a fair result." Id. at 36.

"Because of this confidence in the integrity of the federal prosecutor, Rule 23(a) does not require that the Government articulate its reasons for demanding a jury trial at the time it refuses to consent to a defendant's proffered waiver. Nor should we assume that federal prosecutors would demand a jury trial for an ignoble purpose." Id. at 37. The Court left open the possibility that there might be circumstances in which a refusal to consent to a nonjury trial would result in the denial of an impartial trial.

440. "An accused is entitled to have charges against him considered by a jury in the selection of which there has been neither inclusion nor exclusion because of race." Cassell v. Texas, 339 U.S. 282, 287 (1950); see Akins v. Texas, 325 U.S. 398 (1945). On the manner in which jury commissioners are required to perform their duty of preparing jury lists, so as to avoid racial discrimination, see *Cassell.* "The statements of the jury commissioners that they chose only whom they knew, and that they knew no eligible Negroes in an area where Negroes made up so large a proportion [15.5%] of the population, prove the intentional exclusion that is discrimination in violation of petitioner's constitutional rights." 339 U.S. at 290.

"[I]n order to show that an equal protection violation has occurred in the context of grand jury selection, the defendant must show that the procedure employed resulted in substantial under-representation of his race or of the identifiable group to which he belongs. The first step is to establish that the group is one that is a recognizable, distinct class, singled out for different treatment under the laws, as written or as applied. . . . Next, the degree of under-representation must be proved, by comparing the proportion of the group in the total population to the proportion called to serve as grand jurors, over a significant period of time. . . . This method of proof, sometimes called the 'rule of exclusion,' has been held to be available as a method of proving discrimination in jury selection against a delineated class. . . . Finally, as noted above, a selection procedure that is susceptible of abuse or is not racially neutral supports the presumption of discrimination raised by the statistical showing. . . . Once the defendant has shown substantial under-representation of his group, he has made out a prima facie case of discriminatory purpose, and the burden then shifts to the State to rebut that case." Castaneda v. Partida, 430 U.S. 482, 494–95 (1977) (5–4). The Court found that where the population of a county was 79.1% Mexican-American and over an 11-year period only 39% of the persons summoned for jury service were Mexican-American, there was substantial under-representation, and a prima facie case of discrimination was made out. It found, furthermore, that the fact that a majority of the elected officials in the county were members of the under-represented group was not enough to rebut the showing of discrimination. See also, e.g., Rose v. Mitchell, 443 U.S. 545 (1979) (7–2) (racial discrimination in selection of foreman of grand jury not shown); Alexander v. Louisiana, 405 U.S. 625 (1972) (racial discrimination in selection of grand jury shown); Alston v. Manson, 791 F.2d 255 (2d Cir.1986) (racial discrimination in selection of petit jury shown); Bowen v. Kemp, 769 F.2d 672 (11th Cir.1985) (sexual discrimination in selection of sentencing jury shown); Bryant v. Wainwright, 686 F.2d 1373 (11th Cir.1982) (racial and sexual discrimination in selection of grand jury panels and foremen not shown); United States ex rel. Barksdale v. Blackburn, 639 F.2d 1115 (5th Cir.1981) (racial discrimination in selection of jury not shown).

Is it proper in any circumstances for the commissioners deliberately to include persons of a particular racial or religious group on the list from which jurors will be selected, or deliberately to seek sources of names of potential jurors which are likely to provide names of those in such a group or groups? Or are the commissioners required, in their effort to avoid discrimination, to develop and pursue a means of preparing jury lists that is blind to race and religion? See Brooks v. Beto, 366 F.2d 1 (5th Cir.1966).

441. A defendant's right to a jury selected from a fair cross-section of the community, as part of the Sixth Amendment right to a jury trial, is violated by a provision excluding or automatically exempting women from jury duty that has the effect that women rarely serve on juries. Taylor v. Louisiana, 419 U.S. 522 (1975). In *Taylor*, the Court rejected its reasoning earlier, in Hoyt v. Florida, 368 U.S. 57 (1961), that a state could give women an automatic exemption from jury service, if they wished, because of the special role of women in society.

"The States are free to grant exemptions from jury service to individuals in case of special hardship or incapacity and to those engaged in particular occupations the uninterrupted performance of which is critical to the community's welfare. . . . It would not appear that such exemptions would pose substantial threats that the remaining pool of jurors would not be representative of the community. A system excluding all women, however, is a wholly different matter. It is untenable to suggest these days that it would be a special hardship for each and every woman to perform jury service or that society cannot spare *any* women from their present duties. This may be the case with many, and it may be burdensome to sort out those who should be exempted from those who should serve. But that task is performed in the case of men, and the administrative convenience in dealing with women as a class is insufficient justification for diluting the quality of community judgment represented by the jury in criminal trials." 419 U.S. at 534–35.

Following *Taylor*, the Court invalidated a statute that exempted women, but not men, from jury service on request. Duren v. Missouri, 439 U.S. 357 (1979) (8–1).

442. The defendant, a white person, challenged the selection of grand jurors and petit jurors on the ground that black persons were systematically excluded. The Supreme Court upheld his standing to make the challenge. Peters v. Kiff, 407 U.S. 493 (1972). Three Justices did so on the ground that such exclusion violated a defendant's right to due process of law. Three Justices concurred on the basis that systematic racial exclusion was a crime, 18 U.S.C. § 243. Three Justices dissented on the basis that no prejudice to the defendant had been shown.

443. Voter lists and voter registration lists have become a preferred method for obtaining names of persons for jury duty. In the federal courts, the use of such lists is prescribed by a provision of the Jury Selection and Service Act of 1968, 28 U.S.C. §§ 1863(b)(2). The statute prescribes that other sources of names in addition to voter lists shall be used "where necessary to foster the policy and protect the rights secured by" the statute: the right to a jury "selected at random from a fair cross section of the community in the district or division wherein the court convenes" and the policy that "all citizens shall have the opportunity to be considered for service on" juries. 28 U.S.C. §1861. In several cases, the courts have rejected a claim that sole reliance on voter lists is impermissible because identifiable groups do not register to vote. In United States v. Lewis, 472 F.2d 252 (3d Cir.1973), for example, the defendant argued that blacks in the community did not register and suggested use of social security rolls, public assistance rolls, and the census. The court said: "[A] group of persons who choose not to vote do not constitute a 'cognizable group.' Further, their non-registration is a result of their own inaction; not a result of affirmative conduct by others to bar their registration. Therefore, while a fair*er* cross section of the community may have been produced by the use of 'other sources of names,' the Plan's sole reliance on voter registration lists was constitutionally permissible." Id. at 256. See generally United States v. Brady, 579 F.2d 1121 (9th Cir.1978).

"A benign and theoretically neutral principle loses its aura of sanctity when it fails to function neutrally." Labat v. Bennett, 365 F.2d 698, 724 (5th Cir.1966). Is an otherwise reasonable basis for excusing prospective jurors from jury duty, such as economic hardship, impermissible if its application will have the effect of eliminating from juries most members of an identifiable racial or religious group? Compare *Labat*, with United States v. Bowe,

360 F.2d 1, 7 n.3 (2d Cir.1966). See also Thiel v. Southern Pacific Co., 328 U.S. 217 (1946). See generally Carmical v. Craven, 457 F.2d 582 (9th Cir.1971) (intelligence test).

---

444. In what circumstances does unrepresentativeness of the jury panel with respect to age invalidate a conviction? Do "young adults" constitute a separately cognizable group. The courts have generally said not. See Johnson v. McCaughtry, 92 F.3d 585 (7th Cir.1996) (additional cases cited).

FEDERAL RULES OF CRIMINAL PROCEDURE

Rule 24.

TRIAL JURORS

(a) Examination. The court may permit the defendant or the defendant's attorney and the attorney for the government to conduct the examination of prospective jurors or may itself conduct the examination. In the latter event the court shall permit the defendant or the defendant's attorney and the attorney for the government to supplement the examination by such further inquiry as it deems proper or shall itself submit to the prospective jurors such additional questions by the parties or their attorneys as it deems proper.

(b) Peremptory Challenges. If the offense charged is punishable by death, each side is entitled to 20 peremptory challenges. If the offense charged is punishable by imprisonment for more than one year, the government is entitled to 6 peremptory challenges and the defendant or defendants jointly to 10 peremptory challenges. If the offense charged is punishable by imprisonment for not more than one year or by fine or both, each side is entitled to 3 peremptory challenges. If there is more than one defendant, the court may allow the defendants additional peremptory challenges and permit them to be exercised separately or jointly.

(c) Alternate Jurors. The court may direct that not more than 6 jurors in addition to the regular jury be called and impanelled to sit as alternate jurors. Alternate jurors in the order in which they are called shall replace jurors who, prior to the time the jury retires to consider its verdict, become or are found to be unable or disqualified to perform their duties. Alternate jurors shall be drawn in the same manner, shall have the same qualifications, shall be subject to the same examination and challenges, shall take the same oath and shall have the same functions, powers, facilities and privileges as the regular jurors. An alternate juror who does not replace a regular juror shall be discharged after the jury retires to consider its verdict. Each side is entitled to 1 peremptory challenge in addition to those otherwise allowed by law if 1 or 2 alternate jurors are to be impanelled, 2 peremptory challenges if 3 or 4 alternate jurors are to be impanelled, and 3 peremptory challenges if 5 or 6 alternate jurors are to be impanelled. The additional peremptory challenges may be used against an alternate juror only, and the other peremptory challenges allowed by these rules may not be used against an alternate juror.

---

445. Rule 24(a) provides that the judge shall decide how the voir dire is conducted. Is it preferable that the judge examine prospective jurors or that defense counsel and the prosecutor do so? Why?

"Appellate courts will not interfere with the manner in which the trial court conducted the voir dire examination unless there has been a clear abuse of discretion. . . .

"It is not an abuse of discretion for the trial judge to insist upon conducting a voir dire examination, but if he does so, he must exercise a sound 'judicial' discretion in the acceptance or rejection of supplemental questions proposed by counsel, to be propounded by the judge, as contemplated by Rule 24(a) of the Fed.R.Crim.Procedure." Silverthorne v. United States, 400 F.2d 627, 638, 640 (9th Cir.1968) (abuse of discretion because judge's examination was "too restrictive in both scope and substance to accord to appellant the right to explore for the impartially fair juror").

446. Rule 24(b) leaves it to the discretion of the trial judge whether joint defendants shall together have more peremptory challenges than each would have if tried alone, and whether their challenges shall be exercised "separately or jointly."

"There is nothing in the Constitution of the United States which requires the Congress to grant peremptory challenges to defendants in criminal cases; trial by an impartial jury is all that is secured. The number of challenges is left to be regulated by the common law or the enactments of Congress. That body has seen fit to treat several defendants, for this purpose, as one party. If the defendants would avail themselves of this privilege they must act accordingly. It may be . . . that all defendants may not wish to exercise the right of peremptory challenge as to the same person or persons, and that some may wish to challenge those who are unobjectionable to others. But this situation arises from the exercise of a privilege granted by the legislative authority and does not invalidate the law. The privilege must be taken with the limitations placed upon the manner of its exercise." Stilson v. United States, 250 U.S. 583, 586–87 (1919).

447. 4 W. Blackstone, Commentaries* 353: "[I]n criminal cases, or at least in capital cases, there is, *in favorem vitae*, allowed to the prisoner an arbitrary and capricious species of challenge to a certain number of jurors, without showing any cause at all; which is called a *peremptory* challenge: a provision full of that tenderness and humanity to prisoners, for which our English laws are justly famous. This is grounded on two reasons. 1. As every one must be sensible what sudden impressions and unaccountable prejudices we are apt to conceive upon the bare looks and gestures of another; and how necessary it is, that a prisoner (when put to defend his life) should have a good opinion of his jury, the want of which might totally disconcert him; the law wills not that he should be tried by any one man against whom he has conceived a prejudice, even without being able to assign a reason for such his dislike. 2. Because, upon challenges for cause shown, if the reasons assigned prove insufficient to set aside the juror, perhaps the bare questioning his indifference may sometimes provoke a resentment; to prevent all ill consequences from which the prisoner is still at liberty, if he pleases, peremptorily to set him aside."

448. The defendant in a capital murder case was required to use a peremptory challenge, one of nine available to the defense, to remove a juror whom the judge erroneously failed to remove for cause. None of the jurors who finally composed the jury was subject to challenge. State law provided that a defendant use peremptory challenges to remove jurors who should have been but were not removed for cause. In these circumstances, the Court concluded, although the defendant had been erroneously deprived of one of his peremptory challenges, there was no violation of his right to an impartial jury or any other constitutional right. Peremptory challenges are within the disposition of the state and are not required by the Constitution. Ross v. Oklahoma, 487 U.S. 81 (1988) (5–4).

Batson v. Kentucky

476 U.S. 79, 106 S.Ct. 1712, 90 L.Ed.2d 69 (1986).

■ JUSTICE POWELL delivered the opinion of the Court.

This case requires us to reexamine that portion of Swain v. Alabama, 380 U.S. 202 (1965), concerning the evidentiary burden placed on a criminal defendant who claims that he has been denied equal protection through the State's use of peremptory challenges to exclude members of his race from the petit jury.

I

Petitioner, a black man, was indicted in Kentucky on charges of second-degree burglary and receipt of stolen goods. On the first day of trial in Jefferson Circuit Court, the judge conducted *voir dire* examination of the venire, excused certain jurors for cause, and permitted the parties to exercise peremptory challenges. The prosecutor used his peremptory challenges to strike all four black persons on the venire, and a jury composed only of white persons was selected. Defense counsel moved to discharge the jury before it was sworn on the ground that the prosecutor's removal of the black veniremen violated petitioner's rights under the Sixth and Fourteenth Amendments to a jury drawn from a cross-section of the community, and under the Fourteenth Amendment to equal protection of the laws. Counsel requested a hearing on his motion. Without expressly ruling on the request for a hearing, the trial judge observed that the parties were entitled to use their peremptory challenges to "strike anybody they want to." The judge then denied petitioner's motion, reasoning that the cross-section requirement applies only to selection of the venire and not to selection of the petit jury itself.

The jury convicted petitioner on both counts. On appeal to the Supreme Court of Kentucky, petitioner pressed, among other claims, the argument concerning the prosecutor's use of peremptory challenges. Conceding that Swain v. Alabama, supra, apparently foreclosed an equal protection claim based solely on the prosecutor's conduct in this case, petitioner urged the court to follow decisions of other states . . . and to hold that such conduct violated his rights under the Sixth Amendment and Section 11 of the Kentucky Constitution to a jury drawn from a cross-section of the community. Petitioner also contended that the facts showed that the prosecutor had engaged in a "pattern" of discriminatory challenges in this case and established an equal protection violation under *Swain*.

The Supreme Court of Kentucky affirmed. In a single paragraph, the court declined petitioner's invitation to adopt the reasoning of [the other state courts]. The court observed that it recently had reaffirmed its reliance on *Swain*, and had held that a defendant alleging lack of a fair cross-section must demonstrate systematic exclusion of a group of jurors from the venire. . . . We granted certiorari . . . and now reverse.

II

In Swain v. Alabama, this Court recognized that a "State's purposeful or deliberate denial to Negroes on account of race of participation as jurors in the administration of justice violates the Equal Protection Clause." 380 U.S., at 203–204. This principle has been "consistently and repeatedly" reaffirmed, id., at 204, in numerous decisions of this Court both preceding and following *Swain*. We reaffirm the principle today.

A

More than a century ago, the Court decided that the State denies a black defendant equal protection of the laws when it puts him on trial before a jury from which members of his race have been purposefully excluded. Strauder v. West Virginia, 100 U.S. 303 (1880). That decision laid the foundation for the Court's unceasing efforts to eradicate racial discrimination in the procedures used to select the venire from which individual jurors are drawn. In *Strauder*, the Court explained that the central concern of the recently ratified Fourteenth Amendment was to put an end to governmental discrimination on account of race. . . . Exclusion of black citizens from service as jurors constitutes a primary example of the evil the Fourteenth Amendment was designed to cure.

In holding that racial discrimination in jury selection offends the Equal Protection Clause, the Court in *Strauder* recognized, however, that a defendant has no right to a "petit jury composed in whole or in part of persons of his own race." Id., at 305. "The number of our races and nationalities stands in the way of evolution of such a conception" of the demand of equal protection. Akins v. Texas, 325 U.S. 398, 403 (1945). But the defendant does have the right to be tried by a jury whose members are selected pursuant to nondiscriminatory criteria. . . . The Equal Protection Clause guarantees the defendant that the State will not exclude members of his race from the jury venire on account of race . . . or on the false assumption that members of his race as a group are not qualified to serve as jurors. . . .

Purposeful racial discrimination in selection of the venire violates a defendant's right to equal protection because it denies him the protection that a trial by jury is intended to secure. "The very idea of a jury is a body . . . composed of the peers or equals of the person whose rights it is selected or summoned to determine; that is, of his neighbors, fellows, associates, persons having the same legal status in society as that which he holds." *Strauder*, supra, at 308. . . . The petit jury has occupied a central position in our system of justice by safeguarding a person accused of crime against the arbitrary exercise of power by prosecutor or judge. . . . Those on the venire must be "indifferently chosen,"[3] to secure the defendant's right under the Fourteenth Amendment to "protection of life and liberty against race or color prejudice." *Strauder*, supra, at 309.

Racial discrimination in selection of jurors harms not only the accused whose life or liberty they are summoned to try. Competence to serve as a juror ultimately depends on an assessment of individual qualifications and ability impartially to consider evidence presented at a trial. . . . A person's race simply "is unrelated to his fitness as a juror." [Thiel v. Southern Pacific Co., 328 U.S. 217 (1946)], at 227 (Frankfurter, J., dissenting). As long ago as *Strauder*, therefore, the Court recognized that by denying a person

---

3. 4 W. Blackstone, Commentaries 350 (Cooley ed. 1899). . . .

participation in jury service on account of his race, the State unconstitutionally discriminated against the excluded juror. . . .

The harm from discriminatory jury selection extends beyond that inflicted on the defendant and the excluded juror to touch the entire community. Selection procedures that purposefully exclude black persons from juries undermine public confidence in the fairness of our system of justice. . . . Discrimination within the judicial system is most pernicious because it is "a stimulant to that race prejudice which is an impediment to securing to [black citizens] that equal justice which the law aims to secure to all others." *Strauder*, supra, at 308.

B

In *Strauder*, the Court invalidated a state statute that provided that only white men could serve as jurors. . . . We can be confident that no state now has such a law. The Constitution requires, however, that we look beyond the fact of the statute defining juror qualifications and also consider challenged selections practices to afford "protection against action of the State through its administrative officers in effecting the prohibited discrimination." Norris v. Alabama, 294 U.S. [587 (1935)], at 589. . . . Thus, the Court has found a denial of equal protection whether the procedures implementing a neutral statute operated to exclude persons from the venire on racial grounds, and has made clear that the Constitution prohibits all forms of purposeful racial discrimination in selection of jurors. While decisions of this Court have been concerned largely with discrimination during selection of the venire, the principles announced there also forbid discrimination on account of race in selection of the petit jury. Since the Fourteenth Amendment protects an accused throughout the proceedings bringing him to justice . . . the State may not draw up its jury lists pursuant to neutral procedures but then resort to discrimination at "other stages in the selection process," Avery v. Georgia, 345 U.S. 559, 562 (1953). . . .

Accordingly, the component of the jury selection process at issue here, the State's privilege to strike individual jurors through peremptory challenges, is subject to the commands of the Equal Protection Clause. Although a prosecutor ordinarily is entitled to exercise permitted peremptory challenges "for any reason at all, as long as that reason is related to his view concerning the outcome" of the case to be tried, United States v. Robinson, 421 F.Supp. 467, 473 (Con.1976), mandamus granted sub nom. United States v. Newman, 549 F.2d 240 (CA2 1977), the Equal Protection Clause forbids the prosecutor to challenge potential jurors solely on account of their race or on the assumption that black jurors as a group will be unable impartially to consider the State's case against a black defendant.

III

The principles announced in *Strauder* never have been questioned in any subsequent decision of this Court. Rather, the Court has been called upon repeatedly to review the application of those principles to particular facts. A recurring question in these cases, as in any case alleging a violation of the Equal Protection Clause, was whether the defendant had met his burden of proving purposeful discrimination on the part of the State. . . . That question also was at the heart of the portion of *Swain v. Alabama* we reexamine today.

A

Swain required the Court to decide, among other issues, whether a black defendant was denied equal protection by the State's exercise of peremptory challenges to exclude members of his race from the petit jury. . . . The record in *Swain* showed that the prosecutor had used the State's peremptory challenges to strike the six black persons included on the petit jury venire. . . . While rejecting the defendant's claim for failure to prove purposeful discrimination, the Court nonetheless indicated that the Equal Protection Clause placed some limits on the State's exercise of peremptory challenges. . . .

The Court sought to accommodate the prosecutor's historical privilege of peremptory challenge free of judicial control . . . and the constitutional prohibition on exclusion of persons from jury service on account of race. . . . While the Constitution does not confer a right to peremptory challenges . . . those challenges traditionally have been viewed as one means of assuring the selection of a qualified and unbiased jury. . . . To preserve the peremptory nature of the prosecutor's challenge, the Court in *Swain* declined to scrutinize his actions in a particular case by relying on a presumption that he properly exercised the State's challenges. . . .

The Court went on to observe, however, that a State may not exercise its challenges in contravention of the Equal Protection Clause. It was impermissible for a prosecutor to use his challenges to exclude blacks from the jury "for reasons wholly unrelated to the outcome of the particular case on trial" or to deny to blacks "the same right and opportunity to participate in the administration of justice enjoyed by the white population." [380 U.S.], at 224. Accordingly, a black defendant could make out a prima facie case of purposeful discrimination on proof that the peremptory challenge system was "being perverted" in that manner. Ibid. For example, an inference of purposeful discrimination would be raised on evidence that a prosecutor, "in case after case, whatever the circumstances, whatever the crime and whoever the defendant or the victim may be, is responsible for the removal of Negroes who have been selected as qualified jurors by the jury commissioners and who have survived challenges for cause, with the result that no Negroes ever serve on petit juries." Id., at 223. Evidence offered by the defendant in *Swain* did not meet that standard. While the defendant showed that prosecutors in the jurisdiction had exercised their strikes to exclude blacks from the jury, he offered no proof of the circumstances under which prosecutors were responsible for striking black jurors beyond the facts of his own case. . . .

A number of lower courts following the teaching of *Swain* reasoned that proof of repeated striking of blacks over a number of cases was necessary to establish a violation of the Equal Protection Clause. Since this interpretation of *Swain* has placed on defendants a crippling burden of proof, prosecutors' peremptory challenges are now largely immune from constitutional scrutiny. For reasons that follow, we reject this evidentiary formulation as inconsistent with standards that have been developed since *Swain* for assessing a prima facie case under the Equal Protection Clause.

. . .

C

The standards for assessing a prima facie case in the context of discriminatory selection of the venire have been fully articulated since *Swain*. . . . These principles support our conclusion that a defendant may establish a prima facie case of purposeful discrimination in selection of the petit jury solely on evidence concerning the prosecutor's exercise of peremptory challenges at the defendant's trial. To establish such a case, the defendant first must show that he is a member of a cognizable racial group . . . and that the prosecutor has exercised peremptory challenges to remove from the venire members of the defendant's race. Second, the defendant is entitled to rely on the fact, as to which there can be no dispute, that peremptory challenges constitute a jury selection practice that permits "those to discriminate who are of a mind to discriminate." Avery v. Georgia, supra, at 562. Finally, the defendant must show that these facts and any other relevant circumstances raise an inference that the prosecutor used that practice to exclude the veniremen from the petit jury on account of their race. This combination of factors in the empanelling of the petit jury, as in the selection of the venire, raises the necessary inference of purposeful discrimination.

In deciding whether the defendant has made the requisite showing, the trial court should consider all relevant circumstances. For example, a "pattern" of strikes against black jurors included in the particular venire might give rise to an inference of discrimination. Similarly, the prosecutor's questions and statements during *voir dire* examination and in exercising his challenges may support or refute an inference of discriminatory purpose. These examples are merely illustrative. We have confidence that trial judges, experienced in supervising *voir dire*, will be able to decide if the circumstances concerning the prosecutor's use of peremptory challenges creates a prima facie case of discrimination against black jurors.

Once the defendant makes a prima facie showing, the burden shifts to the State to come forward with a neutral explanation for challenging black jurors. Though this requirement imposes a limitation in some cases on the full peremptory character of the historic challenge, we emphasize that the prosecutor's explanation need not rise to the level justifying exercise of a challenge for cause. . . . But the prosecutor may not rebut the defendant's prima facie case of discrimination by stating merely that he challenged jurors of the defendant's race on the assumption—or his intuitive judgment—that they would be partial to the defendant because of their shared race. . . . Just as the Equal Protection Clause forbids the States to exclude black persons from the venire on the assumption that blacks as a group are unqualified to serve as jurors . . . so it forbids the States to strike black veniremen on the assumption that they will be biased in a particular case simply because the defendant is black. The core guarantee of equal protection, ensuring citizens that their State will not discriminate on account of race, would be meaningless were we to approve the exclusion of jurors on the basis of such assumptions, which arise solely from the jurors' race. Nor may the prosecutor rebut the defendant's case merely by denying that he had a discriminatory motive or "affirm[ing his] good faith in individual selections." Alexander v. Louisiana, 405 U.S., at 632. If these general assertions were accepted as rebutting a defendant's prima facie case, the Equal Protection Clause "would be but a vain and illusory requirement." Norris v. Alabama, supra, at 598. The prosecutor therefore must articulate a neutral explanation related to the particular case to be tried. The trial court then will have the duty to determine if the defendant has established purposeful discrimination.

IV

The State contends that our holding will eviscerate the fair trial values served by the peremptory challenge. Conceding that the Constitution does not guarantee a right to peremptory challenges and that *Swain* did state that their use ultimately is subject to the strictures of equal protection, the State argues that the privilege of unfettered exercise of the challenge is of vital importance to the criminal justice system.

While we recognize, of course, that the peremptory challenge occupies an important position in our trial procedures, we do not agree that our decision today will undermine the contribution the challenge generally makes to the administration of justice. The reality of practice, amply reflected in many state and federal court opinions, shows that the challenge may be, and unfortunately at times has been, used to discriminate against black jurors. By requiring trial courts to be sensitive to the racially discriminatory use of peremptory challenges, our decision enforces the mandate of equal protection and furthers the ends of justice. In view of the heterogeneous population of our Nation, public respect for our criminal justice system and the rule of law will be strengthened if we ensure that no citizen is disqualified from jury service because of his race.

Nor are we persuaded by the State's suggestion that our holding will create serious administrative difficulties. In those states applying a version of the evidentiary standard we recognize today, courts have not experienced serious administrative burdens, and the peremptory challenge system has survived. We decline, however, to formulate particular procedures to be followed upon a defendant's timely objection to a prosecutor's challenges.

V

In this case, petitioner made a timely objection to the prosecutor's removal of all black persons on the venire. Because the trial court flatly rejected the objection without requiring the prosecutor to give an explanation for his action, we remand this case for further proceedings. If the trial court decides that the facts establish, prima facie, purposeful discrimination and the prosecutor does not come forward with a neutral explanation for his action, our precedents require that petitioner's conviction be reversed. . . .[4]

. . .[5]

---

449. Does *Batson* apply to separately identifiable groups other than African-Americans? Cf. Hernandez v. New York, below. See generally United States v. Di Pasquale, 864 F.2d 271 (3d Cir.1988) (Italian Americans; question not answered). Cases holding that *Batson* does extend to other groups are cited in *Di Pasquale*, 864 F.2d at 276 n.9.

In Murchu v. United States, 926 F.2d 50 (1st Cir.1991), the defendant was prosecuted for offenses involving the illegal exportation of firearms for use by the Irish Republican Army. The prosecutor used peremptory challenges to exclude several jurors with Irish surnames. The defendant also challenged several jurors with Irish surnames, and several persons who served on the jury had "arguably Irish surnames." The defendant argued that the prosecutor's peremptory challenges were invalid on *Batson* grounds. The argument was rejected on the ground that the defendant had not established that persons of Irish ancestry are a cognizable group for *Batson* purposes.

In Holland v. Illinois, 493 U.S. 474 (1990) (5–4), the Court held that a white defendant's right under the Sixth Amendment to be tried by an impartial jury was not violated by a prosecutor's exercise of peremptory challenges to exclude the two black persons on the jury panel, even if the challenges were based on race. The Sixth Amendment requires that the panel be composed of a fair cross section of the community, but not that the jury itself be so composed.

The Equal Protection Clause is, however, applicable in such a case. Powers v. Ohio, 499 U.S. 400 (1991) (7–2). "[T]he Equal Protection Clause prohibits a prosecutor from using the State's peremptory challenges to exclude otherwise qualified and unbiased persons from the petit jury solely by reason of their race, a practice that forecloses a significant opportunity to participate in civic life. An individual juror does not have a right to sit on

---

4. To the extent that anything in Swain v. Alabama, 380 U.S. 202 (1965), is contrary to the principles we articulate today, that decision is overruled.

[5] Justice White, Justice Marshall, and Justice O'Connor wrote concurring opinions. Justice Stevens wrote a concurring opinion, which Justice Brennan joined. Chief Justice Burger wrote a dissenting opinion, which Justice Rehnquist joined. Justice Rehnquist wrote a dissenting opinion, which Chief Justice Burger joined.

any particular petit jury, but he or she does possess the right not to be excluded from one on account of race." Id. at 409. "[A] criminal defendant may object to race-based exclusions of jurors effected through peremptory challenges whether or not the defendant and the excluded juror share the same race." Id. at 402. See Trevino v. Texas, 503 U.S. 562 (1992).

In Hernandez v. New York, 500 U.S. 352 (1991) (6–3), the Court upheld a state trial court's rejection of a *Batson* claim, saying that a trial court's conclusion that the prosecutor's peremptory challenges were not racially based should not be overturned on review unless it is clearly erroneous. The Court said also that "disparate impact should be given appropriate weight in determining whether the prosecutor acted with a forbidden intent," but it was not conclusive on the question whether a peremptory challenge is prima facie racially based. Id. at 362. In *Hernandez*, the defendant was Hispanic. The prosecutor challenged two bilingual Hispanic jurors, on the ground that he questioned their ability to accept the official translator's rendition of testimony in Spanish. The Court said that although in some contexts language proficiency might be a surrogate for race, whether that was so or not depended on the circumstances of the case.

See, e.g., United States v. Uwaezhoke, 995 F.2d 388 (3d Cir.1993) (peremptory challenge of black juror because she was a postal employee and might be involved in a "drug situation" was not facially invalid, and finding that there was no discriminatory intent was not clearly erroneous); United States v. Bishop, 959 F.2d 820 (9th Cir.1992) (peremptory challenge of black juror, based in part on fact that juror lived in predominantly low income, black neighborhood and, the prosecutor thought, was therefore likely to believe that police "pick on black people," was not racially neutral); United States v. Dawn, 897 F.2d 1444 (8th Cir.1990) (use of six of seven peremptory challenges to exclude black jurors did not by itself establish prima facie case of discrimination); United States v. Horsley, 864 F.2d 1543 (11th Cir.1989) (peremptory challenge of single black juror made prima facie case of discrimination).

450. J.E.B. v. Alabama ex rel. T.B. The Court held that the Equal Protection Clause prohibits peremptory challenges based solely on gender, in J.E.B. v. Alabama ex rel. T.B., 511 U.S. 127 (1994) (6–3). *J.E.B.* was a civil case, in which the State, acting on behalf of the mother of a minor child, brought a paternity action and a claim for child support against the petitioner. The State used its peremptory challenges to remove male jurors and the petitioner used his to strike female jurors. The jury was composed entirely of women. Reviewing the history of discrimination against women with respect to jury service, the Court said: "Intentional discrimination on the basis of gender by state actors violates the Equal Protection Clause, particularly where, as here, the discrimination serves to ratify and perpetuate invidious, archaic, and overbroad stereotypes about the relative abilities of men and women." Id. at 130–31. Responding to the State's contention that its challenges to male jurors were reasonably based on the perception that men would be more sympathetic to the petitioner than women, the Court said: "The Equal Protection Clause . . . acknowledges that a shred of truth may be contained in some stereotypes, but requires that state actors look beyond the surface before making judgments about people that are likely to stigmatize as well as to perpetuate historical patterns of discrimination." Id. at 139 n.11.

451. In Georgia v. McCollum, 505 U.S. 42 (1992) (7–2), the Court answered a question left open in *Batson*, 476 U.S. at 89 n.12, and barred racially-based peremptory challenges by the defense. "We hold that the Constitution prohibits a criminal defendant from engaging in purposeful discrimination on the ground of race in the exercise of peremptory challenges. Accordingly, if the State demonstrates a prima facie case of racial discrimination by the defendants, the defendants must articulate a racially neutral explanation for peremptory challenges." 505 U.S. at 59. The case involved charges of assault and battery by white defendants against black victims. The Court said: " '[B]e it at the hands of the State or the defense,' if a court allows jurors to be excluded because of group bias, '[it] is a willing participant in a scheme that could only undermine the very foundation of our system of justice—our citizens' confidence in it.' State v. Alvarado, 221 N.J.Super. 324, 328, 534 A.2d 440, 442 (1987). Just as public confidence in criminal justice is undermined by a conviction in a trial where racial discrimination has occurred in jury selection, so is public confidence undermined where a defendant, assisted by racially discriminatory peremptory strikes, obtains an acquittal." 505 U.S. at 49–50.

The Court found that peremptory challenges by the defense involved state action that implicates the Equal Protection Clause. "In exercising a peremptory challenge, a criminal defendant is wielding the power to choose a quintessential governmental body—indeed, the institution of government on which our judicial system depends." Id. at 54. Also, the State had standing to oppose discriminatory peremptory challenges. "As the representative of all its citizens, the State is the logical and proper party to assert the invasion of the constitutional rights of the excluded jurors in a criminal trial." Id. at 56.

452. "The well-settled rule is that, given a lawfully selected panel, free from any taint of invalid exclusions or procedures in selection and from which all disqualified for cause have been excused, no cause for complaint arises merely from the fact that the jury finally chosen happens itself not to be representative of the panel or indeed of the community." Frazier v. United States, 335 U.S. 497, 507–508 (1948).

453. In Witherspoon v. Illinois, 391 U.S. 510 (1968), the Court held that in a capital case in which the jury had responsibility for fixing the penalty and imposed a sentence of death, a jury from which were excluded "all who expressed conscientious or religious scruples against capital punishment and all who opposed it in principle," id. at 520, "fell woefully short of that impartiality to which the petitioner was entitled under the Sixth and Fourteenth Amendments," id. at 518.

"A man who opposes the death penalty, no less than one who favors it, can make the discretionary judgment entrusted to him by the State and can thus obey the oath he takes as a juror. But a jury from which all such men have been excluded cannot perform the task demanded of it. Guided by neither rule nor standard, 'free to select or reject as it [sees] fit,'[6] a jury that must choose between life imprisonment and capital punishment can do little more—and must do nothing less—than express the conscience of the community on the ultimate question of life or death. Yet, in a nation less than half of whose people believe in the death penalty, a jury composed exclusively of such people cannot speak for the community. Culled of all who harbor doubts about the wisdom of capital punishment—of all who would be reluctant to pronounce the extreme penalty—such a jury can speak only for a distinct and dwindling minority." Id. at 519–20.

The Court said that it would be permissible to exclude persons who stated that their opposition to capital punishment would prevent them from even considering imposition of the death penalty. And with respect to the verdict of guilt the jury was acceptable; the evidence was "too tentative and fragmentary to establish that jurors not opposed to the death penalty tend to favor the prosecution in the determination of guilt." Id. at 517.

Witherspoon was applied in Adams v. Texas, 448 U.S. 38 (1980) (8–1). There the Court held that the exclusion of jurors "whose only fault was to take their responsibilities with special seriousness or to acknowledge honestly that they might or might not be affected," id. at 50–51, by the fact that capital punishment was involved went beyond the inquiry allowed by *Witherspoon* and was constitutionally impermissible. The Constitution does not "permit the exclusion of jurors . . . if they aver that they will honestly find the facts and answer the questions in the affirmative if they are convinced beyond reasonable doubt, but not otherwise, yet who frankly concede that the prospects of the death penalty may affect what their honest judgment of the facts will be or what they may deem to be a reasonable doubt. Such assessments and judgments by jurors are inherent in the jury system, and to exclude all jurors who would be in the slightest way affected by the prospect of the death penalty or by their views about such a penalty would be to deprive the defendant of the impartial jury to which he or she is entitled under the law." Id. at 50. See also Lockett v. Ohio, 438 U.S. 586 (1978), and Davis v. Georgia, 429 U.S. 122 (1976) (6–3).

Adams was reaffirmed in Wainwright v. Witt, 469 U.S. 412 (1985) (7–2). The proper standard for excluding a juror for cause because of the juror's

---

6. People v. Bernette, 30 Ill.2d 359, 370,
197 N.E.2d 436, 443.

views on capital punishment is "whether the juror's views would 'prevent or substantially impair the performance of his duties as a juror in accordance with his instructions and his oath'" (quoting from *Adams*, 448 U.S. at 45). Qualifying *Witherspoon*, the Court emphasized that, to be excludable, a juror need not assert that he would "automatically" vote against capital punishment; nor need a juror's inability to apply the law because of objections to capital punishment be shown with "unmistakable clarity." See Darden v. Wainwright, 477 U.S. 168 (1986) (5–4).

Extending a point made in *Witherspoon*, in Lockhart v. McCree, 476 U.S. 162, 165 (1986) (6–3), the Court held that the Constitution does not prohibit "the removal for cause, prior to the guilt phase of a bifurcated capital trial, of prospective jurors whose opposition to the death penalty is so strong that it would prevent or substantially impair the performance of their duties as jurors at the sentencing phase of the trial." In *Lockhart*, the Court assumed that a "death-qualified" jury was somewhat more likely to convict than one not so qualified. The requirement of a "fair cross-section" of the community, it said, applied to the process of selecting a jury, not its actual composition. And in any case, "groups defined solely in terms of shared attitudes that would prevent or substantially impair members of the group from performing one of their duties as jurors" are not distinctive groups for that purpose. Id. at 174. The Court noted that a state might properly want to have a single jury decide both the guilt and sentencing phases of a capital case. Id. at 175–76. Relying on Lockhart v. McCree, the Court held that the "death qualification" of jurors for the guilt phase of a joint trial at which the codefendant but not the defendant was subject to capital punishment did not violate the defendant's right to an impartial jury. Buchanan v. Kentucky, 483 U.S. 402 (1987) (6–3).

The erroneous exclusion for cause of a juror in a capital case, who is eligible under *Witherspoon*, is reversible constitutional error and may not be treated as harmless error. Gray v. Mississippi, 481 U.S. 648 (1987) (5–4).

In a capital case, in which the jury determines on the basis of aggravating and mitigating factors whether the death penalty should be imposed, the trial court may not refuse to ask potential jurors whether they would automatically impose the death penalty if the defendant were found guilty. Morgan v. Illinois, 504 U.S. 719 (1992) (6–3). "A juror who will automatically vote for the death penalty in every case will fail in good faith to consider the evidence of aggravating and mitigating circumstances as the instructions require him to do. . . . Therefore, based on the requirement of impartiality embodied in the Due Process Clause of the Fourteenth Amendment, a capital defendant may challenge for cause any prospective juror who maintains such views. If even one such juror is empaneled and the death sentence is imposed, the State is disentitled to execute the sentence." Id. at 729.

454. Does a defendant who is prosecuted in the District of Columbia for violation of the federal narcotics laws have the right to challenge for cause prospective jurors who are employees of the federal government? If not, does he have the right to challenge for cause employees of the Department of the Treasury whose work is not connected with the Bureau of Narcotics (administratively within the department)? Assuming that the answer to the first question is, "No," is there a valid objection to a jury composed entirely of government employees as a consequence of the exercise of peremptory challenges by prosecution and defense, without any intention to obtain that result on the part of the prosecution? See Frazier v. United States, 335 U.S. 497 (1948). If the defendant were being tried for willfully failing to comply with a subpoena to appear before the Committee on Un-American Activities of the House of Representatives would he have the right to challenge federal employees for cause? See Dennis v. United States, 339 U.S. 162 (1950). See generally United States v. Segal, 534 F.2d 578 (3d Cir.1976).

455. The defendant was prosecuted for narcotics violations. Shortly before the defendant's trial, some of the persons on the jury panel had been jurors in another case in which a government agent scheduled to testify in the defendant's trial had also testified. The defendant in the prior case had been convicted. Should the defendant's challenges for cause of the persons who had been jurors in the prior case be allowed? See United States v. Garcia, 936 F.2d 648 (2d Cir.1991). If a prospective juror previously sat in a case in which the same prosecutor appeared, should the defendant's challenge of the juror for cause be allowed? See generally United States v. Jefferson, 569 F.2d 260 (5th Cir.1978); United States v. Jones, 486 F.2d 476 (8th Cir.1973).

Less than a week before the defendant's trial for murder, several of the jurors had sat on a jury in a criminal case before another judge; the defendant in that case was tried for embezzlement and was acquitted. After the jury had returned its verdict, the judge criticized it for not convicting the defendant and said that he would have found the defendant guilty in "about two minutes." During the voir dire at the defendant's trial, defense counsel sought to ask prospective jurors who had participated in the earlier case whether the judge's comments would make them more likely to convict the defendant. The judge did not allow the questions. Treating the issue as one involving pretrial publicity (surrounding the verdict in the prior case), see note 456 below, the court of appeals held that the defendant had not been denied a fair trial. Wells v. Murray, 831 F.2d 468 (4th Cir.1987) (additional cases discussed).

456. Pretrial publicity. In Irvin v. Dowd, 366 U.S. 717 (1961), the petitioner was convicted of murder in the Indiana courts and sentenced to death. He sought a writ of habeas corpus based on the claim that he did not receive a fair trial. The Court upheld the claim and vacated the conviction.

"It is not required . . . that the jurors be totally ignorant of the facts and issues involved. In these days of swift, widespread and diverse methods of communication, an important case can be expected to arouse the interest of the public in the vicinity, and scarcely any of those best qualified to serve as jurors will not have formed some impression or opinion as to the merits of the case. This is particularly true in criminal cases. To hold that the mere existence of any preconceived notion as to the guilt or innocence of an accused, without more, is sufficient to rebut the presumption of a prospective juror's impartiality would be to establish an impossible standard. It is sufficient if the juror can lay aside his impression or opinion and render a verdict based on the evidence presented in court. . . .

"The adoption of such a rule, however, 'cannot foreclose inquiry as to whether, in a given case, the application of that rule works a deprivation of the prisoner's life or liberty without due process of law.' Lisenba v. California, 314 U.S. 219, 236. As stated in Reynolds [v. United States, 98 U.S. 145 (1878)] the test is 'whether the nature and strength of the opinion formed are such as in law necessarily . . . raise the presumption of partiality. The question thus presented is one of mixed law and fact. . . .' At p. 156. The affirmative of the issue is upon the challenger. Unless he shows the actual existence of such an opinion in the mind of the juror as will raise the presumption of partiality, the juror need not necessarily be set aside. . . . If a positive and decided opinion had been formed, he would have been incompetent even though it had not been expressed.' At p. 157. . . .

. . .

"Here the build-up of prejudice is clear and convincing. An examination of the then current community pattern of thought as indicated by the popular news media is singularly revealing. For example, petitioner's first motion for a change of venue from Gibson County alleged that the awaited trial of petitioner had become the *cause célèbre* of this small community— so much so that curbstone opinions, not only as to petitioner's guilt but even as to what punishment he should receive, were solicited and recorded on the public streets by a roving reporter, and later were broadcast over the local stations. A reading of the 46 exhibits which petitioner attached to his motion indicates that a barrage of newspaper headlines, articles, cartoons and pictures was unleashed against him during the six or seven months preceding his trial. The motion further alleged that the newspapers in which the stories appeared were delivered regularly to approximately 95% of the dwellings in Gibson County and that, in addition, the Evansville radio and TV stations, which likewise blanketed that county, also carried extensive newscasts covering the same incidents. These stories revealed the details of his background, including a reference to crimes committed when a juvenile, his convictions for arson almost 20 years previously, for burglary and by a court-martial on AWOL charges during the war. He was accused of being a parole violator. The headlines announced his police line-up identification, that he faced a lie detector test, had been placed at the scene of the crime and that the six murders were solved but petitioner refused to confess. Finally, they announced his confession to the six murders and the fact of his indictment for four of them in Indiana. They reported petitioner's offer to plead guilty if promised a 99-year sentence, but also the determination, on the other hand, of the prosecutor to secure the death penalty, and that petitioner had confessed to 24 burglaries (the *modus operandi* of these robberies was compared to that of the murders and the similarity noted). One story dramatically relayed the promise of a sheriff to devote his life to securing petitioner's execution by the State of Kentucky, where petitioner is alleged to have committed one of the six murders, if Indiana failed to do so. Another characterized petitioner as remorseless and without conscience but also as having been found sane by a court-appointed panel of doctors. In many of the stories petitioner was described as the 'confessed slayer of six,' a parole violator and fraudulent-check artist. Petitioner's court-appointed counsel was quoted as having received 'much criticism over being Irvin's counsel' and it was pointed out, by way of excusing the attorney, that he would be subject to disbarment should he refuse to represent Irvin. On the day before the trial the newspapers carried the story that Irvin had orally admitted the murder of Kerr (the victim in this case) as well as 'the robbery-murder of Mrs. Mary Holland; the murder of Mrs. Wilhelmina Sailer in Posey County, and the slaughter of three members of the Duncan family in Henderson County, Ky.'

"It cannot be gainsaid that the force of this continued adverse publicity caused a sustained excitement and fostered a strong prejudice among the people of Gibson County. In fact, on the second day devoted to the selection of the jury, the newspapers reported that 'strong feelings, often bitter and angry, rumbled to the surface,' and that 'the extent to which the multiple murders—three in one family—have aroused feelings throughout the area was emphasized Friday when 27 of the 35 prospective jurors questioned were excused for holding biased pretrial opinions. . . . A few days later the feeling was described as 'a pattern of deep and bitter prejudice against the former pipe-fitter.' Spectator comments, as printed by the newspapers, were 'my mind is made up'; 'I think he is guilty'; and 'he should be hanged.'

"Finally, and with remarkable understatement, the headlines reported that 'impartial jurors are hard to find.' The panel consisted of 430 persons. The court itself excused 268 of those on challenges for cause as having fixed opinions as to the guilt of petitioner; 103 were excused because of conscientious objection to the imposition of the death penalty; 20, the maximum allowed, were peremptorily challenged by petitioner and 10 by the State; 12 persons and two alternates were selected as jurors and the rest were excused on personal grounds, e.g., deafness, doctor's orders, etc. An examination of the 2,783-page *voir dire* record shows that 370 prospective jurors or almost 90% of those examined on the point (10 members of the panel were never asked whether or not they had any opinion) entertained some opinion as to guilt—ranging in intensity from mere suspicion to absolute certainty. A number admitted that, if they were in the accused's place in the dock and he in theirs on the jury with their opinions, they would not want him on a jury.

"Here the 'pattern of deep and bitter prejudice' shown to be present throughout the community . . . was clearly reflected in the sum total of the *voir dire* examination of a majority of the jurors finally placed in the jury box. Eight out of the 12 thought petitioner was guilty. With such an opinion permeating their minds, it would be difficult to say that each could exclude this preconception of guilt from his deliberations. The influence that lurks in an opinion once formed is so persistent that it unconsciously fights detachment from the mental processes of the average man. . . . Where one's life is at stake—and accounting for the frailties of human nature—we can only say that in the light of the circumstances here the finding of impartiality does not meet constitutional standards. Two-thirds of the jurors had an opinion that petitioner was guilty and were familiar with the material facts and circumstances involved, including the fact that other murders were attributed to him, some going so far as to say that it would take evidence to overcome their belief. One said that he 'could not . . . give the defendant the benefit of the doubt that he is innocent.' Another stated that he had a 'somewhat' certain fixed opinion as to petitioner's guilt. No doubt each juror was sincere when he said that he would be fair and impartial to petitioner, but the psychological impact requiring such a declaration before one's fellows is often its father. Where so many, so many times, admitted prejudice, such a statement of impartiality can be given little weight. As one of the jurors put it, 'You can't forget what you hear and see.' With his life at stake, it is not requiring too much that petitioner be tried in an atmosphere undisturbed by so huge a wave of public passion and by a jury other than one in which two-thirds of the members admit, before hearing any testimony, to possessing a belief in his guilt." 366 U.S. at 722–28.

See Patton v. Yount, 467 U.S. 1025 (1984) (6–2) (conviction sustained); Beck v. Washington, 369 U.S. 541 (1962) (same). See also Sheppard v. Maxwell, 384 U.S. 333, 335 (1996) (8–1), in which the Court concluded that "the massive, pervasive and prejudicial publicity that attended his prosecution" deprived the defendant of a fair trial. The Court emphasized both the pretrial publicity and the "carnival atmosphere at trial," id. at 358. The defendant, who was charged with murder, was subsequently retried and acquitted. The New York Times, Nov. 17, 1966, p. 1.

In Mu'Min v. Virginia, 500 U.S. 415 (1991) (5–4), the Court considered the nature and extent of the voir dire required to test the defendant's claim of prejudicial pretrial publicity. The Court held that there was not an absolute requirement that the judge inquire into the specific content of what had been read by a juror who said that he had been exposed to news reports. It said that the trial judge has "wide discretion . . . in conducting *voir dire* in the area of pretrial publicity. . . . [T]his primary reliance on the judgment of the trial court makes good sense. The judge of that court sits in the locale where the publicity is said to have had its effect, and brings to his evaluation of any such claim his own perception of the depth and extent of news stories that might influence a juror. The trial court, of course, does not impute his own perceptions to the jurors who are being examined, but these perceptions should be of assistance to it in deciding how detailed an inquiry to make of the members of the jury venire." Id. at 427.

A state law that categorically denies a change of venue in a trial by jury for a misdemeanor regardless of the extent of local prejudice against the defendant violates the constitutional right to an impartial jury. Groppi

v. Wisconsin, 400 U.S. 505 (1971). See Coleman v. Kemp, 778 F.2d 1487, 1538 (11th Cir.1985), in which the court, after discussing at length the pretrial publicity in a capital murder case, said, "If there were no constitutional right to a change in venue in the instant case, then one can conceive of virtually no case in which a change of venue would be a constitutional necessity."

457. Official witnesses. In a case in which the evidence against the defendant consists largely of the testimony of police officers, should defense counsel be permitted to ask prospective jurors whether they would give greater credence to the testimony of a police officer merely because he is an officer than they would give to the testimony of any other witness? See, e.g., United States v. Lancaster, 96 F.3d 734 (4th Cir.1996) (whether to ask question is within sound discretion of trial judge; no abuse of discretion); United States v. Baldwin, 607 F.2d 1295 (9th Cir.1979) (failure to ask question was error); United States v. Gassaway, 456 F.2d 624 (5th Cir.1972) (failure to ask question was not abuse of discretion).

Ham v. South Carolina

409 U.S. 524, 93 S.Ct. 848, 35 L.Ed.2d 46 (1973).

■ MR. JUSTICE REHNQUIST delivered the opinion of the Court.

Petitioner was convicted in the South Carolina trial court of the possession of marihuana in violation of state law. He was sentenced to 18 months' confinement, and on appeal his conviction was affirmed by a divided South Carolina Supreme Court. . . . We granted certiorari limited to the question of whether the trial judge's refusal to examine jurors on *voir dire* as to possible prejudice against petitioner violated the latter's federal constitutional rights. . . .

Petitioner is a young, bearded Negro who has lived most of his life in Florence County, South Carolina. He appears to have been well known locally for his work in such civil rights activities as the Southern Christian Leadership Conference and the Bi-Racial Committee of the City of Florence. He has never previously been convicted of a crime. His basic defense at the trial was that law enforcement officers were "out to get him" because of his civil rights activities, and that he had been framed on the drug charge.

Prior to the trial judge's *voir dire* examination of prospective jurors, petitioner's counsel requested the judge to ask jurors four questions relating to possible prejudice against petitioner.[7] The first two questions sought to elicit any possible racial prejudice against Negroes; the third question related to possible prejudice against beards; and the fourth dealt with pretrial publicity relating to the drug problem. The trial judge, while putting to the prospective jurors three general questions as to bias, prejudice, or partiality that are specified in the South Carolina statutes,[8] declined to ask any of the four questions posed by petitioner.

The dissenting justices in the Supreme Court of South Carolina thought that this Court's decision in Aldridge v. United States, 283 U.S. 308 (1931), was binding on the State. There a Negro who was being tried for the murder of a white policeman requested that prospective jurors be asked whether they entertained any racial prejudice. This Court reversed the judgment of conviction because of the trial judge's refusal to make such an inquiry. Mr. Chief Justice Hughes, writing for the Court, stated that the "essential demands of fairness" required the trial judge under the circumstances of that case to interrogate the veniremen with respect to racial prejudice upon the request of counsel for a Negro criminal defendant. Id., at 310.

The Court's opinion relied upon a number of state court holdings throughout the country to the same effect, but it was not expressly grounded upon any constitutional requirement. Since one of the purposes of the Due Process Clause of the Fourteenth Amendment is to insure these "essential demands of fairness," e.g., Lisenba v. California, 314 U.S. 219, 236 (1941), and since a principal purpose of the adoption of the Fourteenth Amendment was to prohibit the States from invidiously discriminating on the basis of race . . . we think that the Fourteenth Amendment required the judge in this case to interrogate the jurors upon the subject of racial prejudice. South Carolina law permits challenges for cause, and authorizes the trial judge to conduct *voir dire* examination of potential jurors. The State having created this statutory framework for the selection of juries, the essential fairness required by the Due Process Clause of the Fourteenth

7. The four questions sought to be asked are the following:

"1. Would you fairly try this case on the basis of the evidence and disregarding the defendant's race?

"2. You have no prejudice against negroes? Against black people? You would not be influenced by the use of the term 'black'?

"3. Would you disregard the fact that this defendant wears a beard in deciding this case?

"4. Did you watch the television show about the local drug problem a few days ago when a local policeman appeared for a long time? Have you heard about that show? Have you read or heard about recent newspaper articles to the effect that the local drug problem is bad? Would you try this case solely on the basis of the evidence presented in this courtroom? Would you be influenced by the circumstances that the prosecution's witness, a police officer, has publicly spoken on TV about drugs?"

8. S.C.Code § 38–202 (1962). The three questions asked of all prospective jurors in this case were, in substance, the following:

"1. Have you formed or expressed any opinion as to the guilt or innocence of the defendant, Gene Ham?

"2. Are you conscious of any bias or prejudice for or against him?

"3. Can you give the State and the defendant a fair and impartial trial?"

Amendment requires that under the facts shown by this record the petitioner be permitted to have the jurors interrogated on the issue of racial bias. . . .

We agree with the dissenting justices of the Supreme Court of South Carolina that the trial judge was not required to put the question in any particular form, or to ask any particular number of questions on the subject, simply because requested to do so by petitioner. The Court in *Aldridge* was at pains to point out, in a context where its authority within the federal system of courts allows a good deal closer supervision than does the Fourteenth Amendment, that the trial court "had a broad discretion as to the questions to be asked," 283 U.S., at 310. The discretion as to form and number of questions permitted by the Due Process Clause of the Fourteenth Amendment is at least as broad. In this context, either of the brief, general questions urged by the petitioner would appear sufficient to focus the attention of prospective jurors on any racial prejudice they might entertain.

The third of petitioner's proposed questions was addressed to the fact that he wore a beard. While we cannot say that prejudice against people with beards might not have been harbored by one or more of the potential jurors in this case, this is the beginning and not the end of the inquiry as to whether the Fourteenth Amendment required the trial judge to interrogate the prospective jurors about such possible prejudice. Given the traditionally broad discretion accorded to the trial judge in conducting *voir dire*, Aldridge v. United States, supra, and our inability to constitutionally distinguish possible prejudice against beards from a host of other possible similar prejudices, we do not believe the petitioner's constitutional rights were violated when the trial judge refused to put this question. The inquiry as to racial prejudice derives its constitutional stature from the firmly established precedent of *Aldridge* and the numerous state cases upon which it relied, and from a principal purpose as well as from the language of those who adopted the Fourteenth Amendment. The trial judge's refusal to inquire as to particular bias against beards, after his inquiries as to bias in general, does not reach the level of a constitutional violation.

Petitioner's final question related to allegedly prejudicial pretrial publicity. But the record before us contains neither the newspaper articles nor any description of the television program in question. Because of this lack of material in the record substantiating any pretrial publicity prejudicial to this petitioner, we have no occasion to determine the merits of his request to have this question posed on *voir dire*.

Because of the trial court's refusal to make any inquiry as to racial bias of the prospective jurors after petitioner's timely request therefor, the judgment of the Supreme Court of South Carolina is reversed.[9]

---

[9] Justice Douglas and Justice Marshall wrote opinions concurring in part and dissenting in part.

458. *Ham* was discussed and the circumstances of that case distinguished in Ristaino v. Ross, 424 U.S. 589 (1976) (6–2), involving a black defendant's prosecution for armed robbery and assault on a white security officer. The Court said: "The Constitution does not always entitle a defendant to have questions posed during *voir dire* specifically directed to matters that conceivably might prejudice veniremen against him. . . . [T]he State's obligation to the defendant to impanel an impartial jury generally can be satisfied by less than an inquiry into a specific prejudice feared by the defendant." Id. at 594–95. Unlike the special factors in *Ham*, the mere fact "that the victim of the crimes alleged was a white man and the defendants were Negroes" was not so likely "to distort the trial" that special inquiry was required. Id. at 597.

Ristaino v. Ross was distinguished in Turner v. Murray, 476 U.S. 28 (1986) (7–2), a capital case in which the defendant was black and the victim white. The Court held that "a capital defendant accused of an interracial crime is entitled to have prospective jurors informed of the race of the victim and questioned on the issue of racial bias." Id. at 36–37. That was necessary, the Court said, because there is otherwise "an unacceptable risk of racial prejudice infecting the capital sentence proceeding, in view of the fact that the crime involved interracial violence, the jury's broad discretion in capital sentencing, and the special seriousness of an improper sentence in a capital case." The Court held also (two different Justices dissenting from this portion of the Court's opinion), however, that *Ristaino* controlled with respect to the guilt phase of the trial, since the jury had no special discretion as to that.

Is it proper for the prosecutor or defense counsel to inquire into the religious beliefs of prospective jurors? If so, is it reversible error if the court does not allow defense counsel to ask prospective jurors whether they are affiliated with a church and, if so, what church? See Pope v. United States, 372 F.2d 710, 725–27 (8th Cir.1967), vacated, 392 U.S. 651 (1968). See United States v. Barnes, 604 F.2d 121, 133–43 (2d Cir.1979), for a full discussion of questioning prospective jurors about ethnic background and religion. The trial judge's refusal to ask such questions was upheld.

In United States v. Greer, 968 F.2d 433 (5th Cir.1992), the defendants, members of a white supremacist group, were indicted for conspiring to deprive black, Hispanic, and Jewish persons of their constitutional rights. Defense counsel asked the trial judge to strike for cause all prospective jurors in those groups. The judge refused. Defense counsel also asked the judge to ask prospective jurors whether they were Jewish, which request was also refused. The court of appeals held that the examination of prospective jurors for bias was adequate without that question and, sustaining both the trial judge's rulings, affirmed the convictions by an equally divided court. The dissenting judges concluded that the jurors should have been asked whether they were Jewish.

459. Should defense counsel be allowed to examine a list of the names and addresses (and occupations) of the jury panel before the voir dire?

18 U.S.C. § 3432, p. 866 above, provides that a person charged with a capital offense shall be given a list of the names and addresses of prospective jurors at least three days before trial.

In United States v. Gibbons, 602 F.2d 1044 (2d Cir.1979), counsel was given the names of prospective jurors but not their addresses. The trial judge denied defense counsel's request to ask potential jurors about their residence in New York beyond identifying the borough. On appeal, the defendant claimed that he was denied his right to exercise peremptory challenges. Affirming, the court said: "[T]he right of the peremptory challenge does not command a right to the peremptory question. Whatever the attorney's power to strike a number of venire-persons at will may be, to recognize a correlative right to question at will—without in any way identifying the motivating concern—would strip the judge of his control over the proceedings. Any question could be labelled necessary for some unspoken element in the decision to challenge peremptorily." Id. at 1051.

An anonymous jury was upheld in United States v. Scarfo, 850 F.2d 1015 (3d Cir.1988), in which the defendant was reputedly the head of an organized crime ring. See also United States v. Barnes, 604 F.2d 121, 133–43 (2d Cir.1979), upholding the trial judge's refusal to disclose the names and addresses of jurors because of fear for their personal safety.

If the prosecuting attorney has a report of the FBI summarizing its investigation of the jury panel, for use at the voir dire, should the court direct him to furnish a copy of the report to defense counsel? See Best v. United States, 184 F.2d 131 (1st Cir.1950). See generally United States v. Falange, 426 F.2d 930 (2d Cir.1970).

460. Suppose that during the voir dire a prospective juror inadvertently fails to reveal facts that would have been the basis for a challenge for cause or which defense counsel would probably have regarded as warranting exercise of a peremptory challenge. If the person serves as a juror, the defendant is found guilty, and the undisclosed facts become known thereafter, what should be the result? See, e.g., Rushen v. Spain, 464 U.S. 114 (1983) (juror's knowledge of facts tangentially related to case; conviction sustained); United States v. Perkins, 748 F.2d 1519, 1529–34 (11th Cir.1984) (juror's prior acquaintance with defendant, *inter alia*; conviction reversed); United States v. Vargas, 606 F.2d 341 (1st Cir.1979) (juror's history of mental illness and arrest record; conviction sustained). Cf. Burton v. Johnson, 948 F.2d 1150 (10th Cir.1991) (juror's dishonest response to material question, correct answer to which would have provided basis for challenge for cause, denied defendant a fair trial).

461. "We have long viewed with disfavor the practice prevailing in certain jurisdictions under which a party, ostensibly engaged in exploring the jury's qualifications, is in fact exercising hopefully sophisticated advocacy upon jurors whom it has no real intention of challenging. . . . This not only corrupts the purpose of the voir dire, but places undue emphasis upon those points the party so chooses to make.

"[I]n our opinion the purpose of the voir dire is to ascertain disqualifications, not to afford individual analysis in depth to permit a party to choose a jury that fits into some mold that he believes appropriate for his case." Schlinsky v. United States, 379 F.2d 735, 738 (1st Cir.1967). Compare United States v. Dellinger, 472 F.2d 340, 366–70 (7th Cir.1972) (approving broad questioning).

462. The defendants were prosecuted for violation of the National Motor Vehicle Theft (Dyer) Act, 18 U.S.C. § 2312. Their defense was that they had the consent of the owner, a school principal, to their taking the automobile in question. They claimed that he had invited them to his home and performed a homosexual act on one of them; afterwards he gave them the automobile in return for their agreement not to expose him. If you were defense counsel, would you want to ask prospective jurors whether they would be prejudiced against the defendants if they asserted that the owner of the car had committed a homosexual act? If you were the trial judge, would you allow defense counsel to ask the question? If the trial judge did not allow the question and the defendants were convicted after presenting their defense, would you reverse on appeal? See Maguire v. United States, 358 F.2d 442 (10th Cir.1966).

463. Consider the following checklist for selection of jurors in a case involving the insanity defense:

(1) *Religion.* Least desirable are Roman Catholics, with their "emphasis upon free will, moral responsibility and payment for sins." All "fundamentalist faiths," such as Mormon, Methodist, and Southern Baptist, are "generally non-receptive to the defense." Unitarians, Jews, Congregationalists, and Presbyterians are "most likely to understand the defense."

(2) *Political Affiliation.* Party lines are not so important as "orientation toward liberalism." The "progressive, flexible viewpoint" is to be preferred to the conservative viewpoint. Members of extreme right-wing political groups should be avoided.

(3) *Geographical Region.* The urban north is better than the rural south or the farming midwest. Self-reliant farmers and southern traditionalists should be avoided.

(4) *Nationality.* "For once the sentimental Irish and sympathetic Italian are to be avoided because of their affinity for Catholicism." Scandinavians are more desirable.

(5) *Occupation and Economic Status.* Inadequate education and "limitation of perspective" make members of the lower economic class undesirable. Among the wealthy, however, conservatism is to be feared. Occupations which may indicate a receptive attitude are public relations, teaching, writing, advertising, non-technical research, art, music, show business, and communications. To be avoided are banking, commerce, manufacturing, common labor, clerical, skilled trades, and career military men.

(6) *Race.* Black persons are "generally ill equipped to evaluate psychiatric testimony" because of economic and educational deprivations.

(7) *Intelligence and Education.* A high I.Q. and broad liberal arts education are "an ideal combination" for the defense.

(8) *Age and Sex.* Young persons generally better than extremely old jurors; "women may be slightly more receptive than men." Law and Tactics in Federal Criminal Cases 265–66 (G. Shadoan ed. 1964).

464. The defendant is charged with murder in the first degree and assault with intent to have carnal knowledge. Insanity is the sole defense. The victim is a nine-year-old girl. The defendant is a somewhat retarded boy of 16. It is alleged that after assaulting his victim he drowned her in a bathtub. The penalty for first degree murder, if the jury returns a verdict of guilty without further recommendation, is death.

What questions would you as prosecutor seek to ask or have the judge ask of prospective jurors?

What questions would you as defense counsel seek to ask or have the judge ask of prospective jurors?

Would you as defense counsel ask any additional questions or omit any questions if, so far as you knew, the government's case rested almost entirely on a confession by the defendant the admission of which you expect to challenge on the ground that it was given involuntarily?

What questions which as prosecutor or defense counsel you would want to ask would you as the trial judge not allow?

Does the prosecutor have any (nonconstitutional) obligation *not* to ask questions designed to elicit facts such as age, membership in groups, religion, and occupation, which are irrelevant to the issues which the jury will decide but which, statistically, have a bearing on the way in which a juror will decide the issues? Does it make a difference whether defense counsel opens up such inquiries by asking such questions? Would an appropriate compromise be to forego asking the questions but to use answers to them, if they are asked by defense counsel, as the basis for peremptory challenges?

Opening statement

Leonard v. United States

277 F.2d 834 (9th Cir.1960).

[The defendant was convicted before a jury of transporting a forged instrument in interstate commerce, 18 U.S.C. § 2314. In his opening statement, the prosecutor told the jury that the government's case would include proof of 83 crimes committed by the defendant in addition to the crime charged; this could be done, the prosecutor said, because such proof of other crimes would be admitted under traditional rules of evidence to show intent and to establish the defendant's identity. The other crimes, which the prosecutor catalogued on a blackboard and orally in his statement, involved a series of forged check transactions and attempts; the total number of crimes was reached by adding together each technical "crime" (e.g., each forged check passed gave rise to the distinct crimes of forging and uttering, each of which was counted separately in the total). He said in part: "Thus it is that the Government brings to you, not alone the one crime charged in the indictment, but a great number of other crimes, all of which will be shown to you as having been confessed to by this defendant, although they have not as yet been the subject of indictment or prosecution, conviction, or penalty. These crimes number 84. They are all felonies. Yes, you heard me correctly. I said 84. Incredible, but true. I should say, to be absolutely accurate, 83 other crimes other than the indictment crime." The prosecutor described briefly the method of committing the other crimes and mentioned in passing certain additional crimes (burglary, larceny, breaking and entering) allegedly involved in the series of transactions.

Following the opening statement, which lasted for about 40 minutes, defense counsel moved for a mistrial. The trial judge indicated that he thought the prosecutor had gone "too far afield," but since no objection had been made during the course of the statement, denied the motion for a mistrial. He instructed the jury that it was not to consider the prosecutor's remarks concerning crimes other than the one with which the defendant was charged and that the opening statement was not "evidence" but was "like an argument to the jury."

During the trial, the court ruled that evidence of other crimes was inadmissible. At the request of the prosecutor, the trial judge advised the jury that he had so ruled and that that was the reason why such evidence had not been presented. The blackboard cataloging the crimes remained visible throughout the trial.]

JERTBERG, CIRCUIT JUDGE.

. . .

In our view the record hereinbefore set out is more eloquent and convincing than any words of ours in demonstrating that the appellant was denied his constitutional right to a fair trial. For 40 minutes the trial judge sat silently by while the over-zealous prosecutor recounted crimes alleged to have been committed by the appellant, many of which by no stretch of the imagination were admissible to prove intent or identity. The record is clear that the trial judge was aware of the fact that the fair boundaries of an opening statement to the jury were being flagrantly breached, but expected appointed counsel for appellant to object. The court then denied appellant's motion for a mistrial on the ground that appellant had failed to make timely objection. "Plain errors or defects affecting substantial rights may be noticed although they were not brought to the attention of the court." Rule 52(b), Federal Rules of Criminal Procedure, 18 U.S.C.A. In large measure the statement made by government counsel was an opening statement in name only. An opening statement should be limited to a statement of facts which the government intends or in good faith expects to prove. It should not be argumentative in character, nor should it be designed to destroy the character of the defendant before the introduction of any evidence on the crime charged in the indictment. In our view the prejudice against the appellant which must have been created in the minds of the jurors by government counsel's diatribe was extremely grave. Such prejudice was not removed by subsequent proceedings.

The admonition given by the court to the jury following the motion of appellant for a mistrial was ineffectual. The court simply advised the jury that counsel had the right to make opening statements but that opening statements and arguments of counsel were not to be considered as evidence. The statement clearly implied that the court regarded the opening statement as proper. If at that time the court was of the opinion that the only offense upon which he would admit proof was the one charged in the indictment, he should have admonished the members of the jury to completely erase and put out of their minds all statements made by government counsel concerning other crimes and misconduct attributed to the appellant. . . . If the trial judge was of the view at that time that proof of some of the other alleged crimes would be relevant on the issues of intent and identity he should have so advised the jury, and at the same time should have instructed the jury to completely put out of their minds and disregard all statements by government counsel concerning other alleged crimes and misconduct of the appellant, and that it was their duty to do so. By the admonition to the jury the minds of the jurors were conditioned to expect and look forward to proof of all of the crimes and misconduct mentioned in the opening statement.

By the admonition of the trial court given to the jury at the close of testimony the jury was expressly told that the only reason for the failure of the government to introduce proof of the crimes described in the opening statement was occasioned by "an adverse ruling the government suffered in its efforts to introduce such material." Here again was presented an opportunity to the trial judge to instruct the jury that while opening statements of counsel should not be considered as evidence, the members of the jury must absolutely and completely disregard and put out of their minds all statements of other crimes and misconduct contained in the opening statement.

The prejudice occasioned to the appellant by the opening statement was heightened by the fact that the cataloging of such crimes on the blackboard remained as a constant reminder to the members of the jury throughout the trial.

The record in this case demonstrates that government counsel "overstepped the bounds of that propriety and fairness which should characterize the conduct of such an officer in the prosecution of a criminal offense." Berger v. United States, 295 U.S. 78. . . .

. . .

The judgment is reversed and the cause remanded with instructions to grant appellant a new trial.

———

465. "The only purpose of opening statements is to inform the jury what the case is about and to outline the proof that will be used—on the one hand to establish the commission of the crime and on the other to outline the defense—so that the jurors may more intelligently follow the testimony as it is related by the witnesses." Foster v. United States, 308 F.2d 751, 753 (8th Cir.1962).

466. Reversals on appeal because of improper remarks in the prosecutor's opening statement are rare. Appellate courts are reluctant to require a new trial on the basis of errors committed before the prior trial was well under way, errors, moreover, which in theory amount only to excessive rhetoric, the harm of which is removed by the trial judge's instructions and the jury's good sense. In Frazier v. Cupp, 394 U.S. 731 (1969), for example, the prosecutor referred in the opening statement to testimony of a person who later was called to the stand and refused to testify, asserting his privilege against self-incrimination. Before trial, defense counsel had warned the prosecutor that the witness would refuse to testify and that he should not refer to the expected testimony in the opening statement. The prosecutor had other indications that the witness might testify. The Court observed: "Many things might happen in the course of the trial which would prevent the presentation of all the evidence described in advance. Certainly not every variance between the advance description and the actual presentation constitutes reversible error, when a proper limiting instruction has been given." Id. at 736.

In Cook v. United States, 354 F.2d 529, 532 (9th Cir.1965), the court said it was "difficult to understand" why the prosecutor "chose the dangerous path" of referring in his opening statement to evidence later ruled inadmissible, but concluded that "under all the circumstances" the error was harmless. See also United States v. DeRosa, 548 F.2d 464 (3d Cir.1977) (wiretap evidence ruled inadmissible); United States v. West, 486 F.2d 468 (6th Cir.1973) (expected prosecution witness refused to testify); United States v. Wallace, 453 F.2d 420 (8th Cir.1972). What should defense counsel do to keep references to possibly or probably inadmissible evidence out of the prosecutor's opening statement?

467. "Alluding to the fact that the jury eventually acquitted him on the conspiracy counts, appellant Somers charged that references in the opening statement to his complicity in the conspiracies deprived him of a fair trial. We disagree. We know of no rule of law that requires a mistrial merely because the jury does not believe that a prosecutor's outline (presented in an opening statement) is true beyond a reasonable doubt. Provided that the outline is an objective summary of evidence which the Government reasonably expects to produce, a subsequent failure in proof will not lead to an automatic finding of misconduct. . . . Inasmuch as there is no indication in the record herein that the prosecutor outlined facts concerning Somers that he did not believe he could substantiate, we find no impropriety in the remarks suggesting that Somers played a role in the conspiracies." United States v. Somers, 496 F.2d 723, 738–39 (3d Cir.1974).

468. When does defense counsel make his opening statement? See Karikas v. United States, 296 F.2d 434, 438 (D.C.Cir.1961), in which the court of appeals observed that defense counsel "was within his rights in obtaining permission to withhold his opening statement until the United States had presented its case," and that to do so was "probably a good trial tactic" which enabled him "legitimately [to] frame his defense to meet the evidence adduced by the Government."

See generally United States v. Salovitz, 701 F.2d 17 (2d Cir.1983), holding that there is not a constitutional right to make an opening statement to the jury and that "the making and timing of opening statements" is within the discretion of the trial judge.

469. In United States v. McKeon, 738 F.2d 26 (2d Cir.1984), the court held that an inconsistent opening statement of defense counsel at a prior trial of the defendant on the same charges was admissible against the defendant. In limited circumstances, when there is no other explanation for the inconsistency, the opening statement can be regarded as one by the defendant and can be used to contradict the defendant's case. Since the statement was admissible, the trial judge ruled correctly that the defense counsel who made the statement was disqualified from appearing as counsel in the subsequent trial.

Prosecution and defense

Moore v. Illinois

408 U.S. 786, 92 S.Ct. 2562, 33 L.Ed.2d 706 (1972).

■ MR. JUSTICE BLACKMUN delivered the opinion of the Court.

This state murder case, with the death penalty imposed by a jury, comes here from the Supreme Court of Illinois. . . .

I

Petitioner Lyman A. Moore was convicted in 1964 of the first-degree murder of Bernard Zitek. . . .

II

The homicide was committed on April 25, 1962. The facts are important:

A. The victim, Zitek, operated a bar-restaurant in the village of Lansing, southeast of Chicago. Patricia Hill was a waitress there. Donald O'Brien, Charles A. Mayer, and Henley Powell were customers.

Another bar called the Ponderosa Tap was located in Dolton, also southeast of Chicago. It was owned by Robert Fair. William Joyce was the bartender. One of Fair's customers was Virgle Sanders.

A third bar known as Wanda and Del's was in Chicago. Delbert Jones was the operator. William Leon Thompson was a patron.

The Westmoreland Country Club was in Wilmette, about 50 miles north of Lansing. The manager there was Herbert Anderson.

B. On the evening of April 25 Zitek was tending bar at his place in Lansing. Shortly before 10 p.m. two men, one with a moustache, entered and ordered beer. Zitek admonished the pair several times for using profane language. They continued in their profanity and, shortly, Zitek ejected them. About an hour later a man carrying a shotgun entered. He laid the weapon on the bar and shot and killed Zitek. The gunman ran out, pursued by patrons, and escaped in an automobile.

C. At the trial waitress Hill positively identified Moore as one of the two men ejected from the bar and as the one who returned and killed Zitek. She testified that she had a clear and close view from her working area at the bar and that she observed Zitek's ejection of the two men and the shotgun killing an hour later.

D. A second in-court identification of Moore as the man who killed Zitek was made by the customer Powell. Powell, who at the time was playing pinochle with others, testified that he observed Moore enter the bar with a shotgun and shoot Zitek; that after the shooting he pursued Moore; and that outside the bar Moore stopped momentarily, turned, and shouted, "Don't come any further or I'll shoot you, too."

E. Sanders testified that on April 27, two days after the murder, he was in the Ponderosa Tap and that a customer there, whom Sanders identified as "Slick," remarked to Sanders that it was "open season on bartenders" and that he had shot one in Lansing. At the trial Sanders identified Moore as the man who was in the Ponderosa Tap on April 27. Moore was with another man who had a moustache. The two asked for a ride to Harvey, Illinois. The owner, Fair, agreed to give them the ride.

F. Fair testified that Moore was one of the two men who requested and were given the ride; that during the journey one of them was referred to as "Barbee"; and that one said "something like, 'Well, if we hadn't had that trouble with the bartender in Lansing, we'd have been all right.'"

G. The Ponderosa bartender, Joyce, testified that Sanders and Fair were in that tavern on April 27; that Moore was there at the same time; and that he arranged with Fair for Fair to give Moore and his companion a ride.

It is thus apparent that there were positive in-court identifications of Moore as the slayer by the waitress Hill and by the customer Powell, and that there were in-court identifications of Moore as having been present in the bar in Dolton two days later by Sanders, by Fair, and by Joyce.

H. Six months after the slaying, in the early morning hours of October 31, 1962, a Chicago police officer was shot at from a 1957 Ford automobile. Two men fled the scene. The police "staked out" the car, and several hours later Moore and a moustached man, later identified as Jerry Barbee, were arrested when they approached and entered the vehicle. The automobile proved to be owned by Barbee. A fully loaded sawed-off 16-gauge shotgun was in the car. The shotgun was introduced in evidence at Moore's trial. The State conceded that the gun so introduced was not the murder weapon, and that the State's ballistics technician, if called, would testify that the waddings taken from Zitek's body came, in his opinion, from a 12-gauge shotgun shell.

I. The defense called manager Anderson of the Westmoreland Country Club as a witness. He testified that Moore had been hired as a waiter there on April 24, (the day before the murder); that the club records indicated there was a special party at the club on the evening of April 25; and that Moore was paid for working until sometime between 10 p.m. and midnight. The club's bartender testified to the same effect. Each of these witnesses nevertheless admitted that he could not remember seeing Moore at the club that night, but said that he would have known if he had been absent for any substantial period of time. The club records also indicated that Moore worked at the club the afternoon of April 27, when, according to the testimony of Sanders, Fair, and Joyce, Moore was at the Ponderosa Tap in Dolton.

J. O'Brien, the customer at Zitek's testified for the defense that he observed Zitek eject two men the evening of the 25th, and that Moore was not one of them. Although he was in the restaurant at the time of the homicide, he did not see the person who shot Zitek. A police officer testified that in his opinion O'Brien was drunk at the time.

III

Prior to the trial, the defense moved for disclosure of all written statements taken by the police from any witness. The State agreed to furnish existing statements of prosecution witnesses. At the post-conviction hearing, Moore argued, and the claim is presented here, that he was denied a fair trial because six items of evidence, unknown to him at the time of the trial, were not produced and, in fact, were suppressed by the State:

A. On April 30, 1962, Sanders gave a statement to the police that he had met the man "Slick" for the first time "about six months ago" in Wanda and Del's tavern. Testimony at the post-conviction hearing by Lieutenant Turbin of the Lansing Police Department revealed that at the time of trial the police possessed an FBI report that Moore was in Leavenworth Penitentiary from 1957 to March 4, 1962. That report thus proved that Sanders could not have met Moore at Wanda and Del's in November 1961. The defense was not given a copy of the statement made by Sanders. The prosecuting attorney asserted at the post-conviction hearing that he did not recall having seen the statement before or during the trial.

B. On the day Sanders gave his statement, that is, on April 30, the police raided Wanda and Del's looking for "Slick." "Slick" was not there, but Jones, the tavern's operator, said that he could identify "Slick." After Moore was arrested, Jones was not asked by the police whether Moore was "Slick." The defense was not advised of the raid until after the trial. At the post-conviction hearing Jones testified that Moore was not "Slick." His testimony, however, was stricken on the ground that it pertained to innocence or guilt and was not admissible upon collateral review.

C. After the raid on Wanda and Del's, the police secured from their files a picture of James E. "Slick" Watts and assigned Lieutenant Turbin the task of finding Watts. His search was unsuccessful. Moore asserts that the attempt to find Watts was not made known to the defense until cross-examination of the Lansing police chief at the post-conviction hearing.

D. After Moore was arrested on October 31, he was photographed by the police. The photograph was shown to William Leon Thompson the patron of Wanda and Del's. Thompson testified at the post-conviction hearing that he told Lieutenant Turbin that the picture "didn't, to the best of my knowledge, resemble the man that I knew" as "Slick." He identified a picture of Watts as "the Slick I know." Defense counsel testified that through the course of the trial neither the police nor the prosecutor advised them about Thompson and his disclaimer.

E. At the start of the trial Sanders observed Moore for the first time since the alleged bragging incident at the Ponderosa Tap. Sanders remarked to the prosecuting attorney and to police officers who accompanied him into the courtroom that the person he knew as "Slick" was about 30–40 pounds heavier than Moore and did not wear glasses. One of the officers responded, "Well, you know how the jailhouse beans are." Moore contends that he and defense counsel were not advised of this remark of Sanders until after the trial had concluded.

F. Mayer, one of the card players at Zitek's at the time of the murder, gave the police a written statement. On the back of the statement Officer Koppitz drew a sketch of the seating arrangement at the card table. The diagram shows that the corners of the table pointed north, south, east, and west. Cardplayer Powell was placed on the southwest side. The bar was about 10 feet north of the table. The door was to the southwest. Moore argues that the diagram is exculpatory and contradicts Powell's testimony that he observed the shooting. Defense counsel testified that they were not shown the diagram during the trial.

Moore argues, as to the first five items, that the State did not comply with the general request by the defense for all written statements given by prosecution witnesses; that the State failed to produce the pretrial statement of Sanders and the other evidence contradicting Sanders' identification of Moore as "Slick"; and that the evidence not produced was material and would have been helpful to his defense.

The Illinois court held that the State had not suppressed material evidence favorable to Moore, that the record shows that the prosecution presented its entire file to defense counsel, and that no further request for disclosure was made. . . . Moore submits here the alternative claim that a specific request is not an "indispensable prerequisite" for the disclosure of exonerating evidence by the State and that the defense could not be expected to make a request for specific evidence that it did not know was in existence.

In Brady v. Maryland, 373 U.S. 83 (1963), the petitioner and a companion were found guilty by a jury of first-degree murder and were sentenced to death. In his summation to the jury, Brady's counsel conceded that Brady was guilty, but argued that the jury should return its verdict "without capital punishment." Prior to the trial, counsel had requested that the prosecution allow him to examine the codefendant's extra-judicial statements. Some of these were produced, but another, in which the codefendant admitted the actual homicide, was withheld and did not come to Brady's notice until after his conviction. In a post-conviction proceeding, the Maryland Court of Appeals held that this denied Brady due process of law, and remanded the case for retrial on the issue of punishment. This Court affirmed. It held "that the suppression by the prosecution of evidence favorable to an accused upon request violates due process where the evidence is material either to guilt or to punishment, irrespective of the good faith or bad faith of the prosecution." 373 U.S., at 87.

The heart of the holding in *Brady* is the prosecution's suppression of evidence, in the face of a defense production request, where the evidence is favorable to the accused and is material either to guilt or to punishment. Important, then, are (a) suppression by the prosecution after a request by the defense, (b) the evidence's favorable character for the defense, and (c) the materiality of the evidence. These are the standards by which the prosecution's conduct in Moore's case is to be measured.

Moore's counsel asked several prosecution witnesses if they had given statements to the police. Each witness (Hill, Powell, Fair) who had given a statement admitted doing so and the statement was immediately tendered. The same inquiry was not made of witness Sanders. He was the only state witness who was not asked the question. At the post-conviction hearing the inquiry was made. Sanders admitted making a statement to the police and the statement was tendered.

The record discloses . . . that the prosecutor at the trial submitted his entire file to the defense. The prosecutor, however, has no recollection that Sanders' statement was in the file. The statement, therefore, either was in that file and not noted by the defense or it was not in the possession of the prosecution at the trial.

We know of no constitutional requirement that the prosecution make a complete and detailed accounting to the defense of all police investigatory work on a case. Here, the elusive "Slick" was an early lead the police abandoned when eyewitnesses to the killing and witnesses to Moore's presence at the Ponderosa were found. Unquestionably, as the State now concedes, Sanders was in error when he indicated to the police that he met Moore at Wanda and Del's about six months prior to April 30, 1962. Moore's incarceration at Leavenworth until March shows that conclusion to have been an instance of mistaken identity. But the mistake was as to the identification of Moore as "Slick," not as to the presence of Moore at the Ponderosa Tap on April 27.[10] "Sanders' testimony to the effect that it was Moore he spoke with at the Ponderosa Tap in itself is not significantly, if at all, impeached. Indeed, it is buttressed by the testimony of bartender Joyce and operator Fair, both of whom elaborated the incident by their description of the man, and by Moore's request for a ride to Harvey, Illinois, Fair's providing that ride, and Fair's hearing, on that trip, the reference to one of the men as 'Barbee,'" and a second reference to trouble with a bartender in Lansing.

The other four of the first five items—that Jones told police he could identify "Slick" and subsequently testified that Moore was not "Slick"; that the police had a picture of Watts and assigned the lieutenant, unsuccessfully, to find Watts; that Thompson had been shown a picture of Moore and told the police that Moore was not "Slick"; and that on the day of the trial Sanders remarked that the man he knew as "Slick" looked heavier than Moore—are in exactly the same category. They all relate to "Slick," not Moore, and quite naturally go off on Sanders' initial misidentification of "Slick" with Moore.

---

10. The dissent observes . . . "When confronted with this fact [Moore's imprisonment at Leavenworth], Sanders indicated that it was impossible that petitioner [Moore] was the man with whom he had spoken in the Ponderosa Tavern." This is a misreading of Sanders' testimony. The question and Sanders' answer were:

"Q. And did you tell me and also later on, did you tell the policeman from the State's Attorney's Office that if you had known that this fellow, Lyman Moore, was in the Federal Penitentiary until March 4, 1962, you would definitely not have identified him as being Slick that you knew?

"A. If he's in jail, it would have been impossible to be the same man." Abstract of Record 296.

None of the five items serves to impeach in any way the positive identification by Hill and by Powell of Moore as Zitek's killer, or the testimony of Fair and Joyce that Moore was at the Ponderosa Tap on April 27, or the testimony of Fair that the moustached Barbee was accompanying Moore at that time, and that one of the two men made the additional and undisputed admission on the ride to Harvey. We conclude, in the light of all the evidence, that Sanders' misidentification of Moore as Slick was not material to the issue of guilt.

The remaining claim of suppression relates to the diagram on the back of Mayer's statement to the police.[11] Moore contends that the diagram shows that Powell was seated with his back to the entrance to Zitek's and, thus, necessarily contradicts his testimony that he was looking toward the entrance as he sat at the card table, and that the State knowingly permitted false testimony to remain uncorrected, in violation of Napue v. Illinois, 360 U.S. 264 (1959).

In *Napue* the principal prosecution witness at Napue's murder trial was an accomplice then serving a sentence for the crime. He testified, in response to an inquiry by the prosecutor, that he had received no promise of consideration in return for his testimony. In fact, the prosecutor had promised him consideration, but he did nothing to correct the witness' false testimony. This Court held that the failure of the prosecutor to correct the testimony, which he knew to be false, denied Napue due process of law, and that this was so even though the false testimony went only to the credibility of the witness. . . .

We are not persuaded that the diagram shows that Powell's testimony was false. The officer who drew the diagram testified at the post-conviction hearing that it did not indicate the direction in which Powell was facing or looking at the time of the shooting. Powell testified that his position at the table gave him a view of the bartender; that at the moment he could not bid in the pinochle game and had laid his hand down and was looking toward the door when Moore walked in. There is nothing in the diagram to indicate that Powell was looking in another direction or that it was impossible for him to see the nearby door from his seat at the card table. Furthermore, after the shooting he pursued Moore but stopped when the man warned him that he, too, might be shot.

In summary, the background presence of the elusive "Slick," while somewhat confusing, is at most an insignificant factor. The attempt to identify Moore as "Slick" encountered difficulty, but nothing served to destroy the two-witness identification of Moore as Zitek's assailant, the three-witness identification of Moore as present at the Ponderosa Tap, and two-

---

11. Contrary to the assertion by the dissent that the Mayer statement, with its accompanying diagram, was never made available to the defense, post, at 803 and 809, the trial transcript indicates that during the cross-examination of Officer Koppitz a request was made by the defense for all written statements taken by the officer from persons in Zitek's restaurant at the time of the shooting. The court granted the request and the record recites that statements of Mayer and others were furnished to defense counsel.

witness identification of Moore as one of the men who requested and obtained a ride from the Ponderosa in Dolton to Harvey, Illinois, and Fair's testimony as to the admission made on that ride.

We adhere to the principles of *Brady* and *Napue*, but hold that the present record embraces no violation of those principles.

IV

The 16-gauge shotgun was admitted into evidence at the trial over the objection of the defense that it was not the murder weapon, that it had no connection with the crime charged, and that it was inadmissible under Illinois law. During his closing argument to the jury, the prosecuting attorney stated that the 16-gauge shotgun was not used to kill Zitek, but that Moore and his companion, Barbee, were "the kind of people that use shotguns."[12]

The Supreme Court of Illinois held that the shotgun was properly admitted into evidence as a weapon in Moore's possession at the time of his arrest, and was a weapon "suitable for the commission of the crime charged . . . even though there is no showing that it was the actual weapon used." 42 Ill.2d, at 78, 246 N.E.2d, at 303. Moore claims that the gun's introduction denied him due process.

. . .

[W]e are unable to conclude that the shotgun's introduction deprived Moore of the due process of law guaranteed him by the Fourteenth Amendment. The 16-gauge shotgun, found in the car, was in the constructive possession of both Moore and Barbee when they were arrested after the shooting incident on October 31. There is substantial other evidence in the record that a shotgun was used to kill Zitek, and that he suffered the wounds one would expect from a shotgun fired at close range. The testimony as to the murder itself, with all the details as to the shotgun wounds, is such that we cannot say that the presentation of the shotgun was so irrelevant or so inflammatory that Moore was denied a fair trial. The case is not federally reversible on this ground.

V

[T]he Court today has ruled that the imposition of the death penalty under statutes such as those of Illinois is violative of the Eighth and Fourteenth Amendments, Furman v. Georgia [408 U.S. 238 (1972)]. . . .

The judgment, insofar as it imposes the death sentence, is reversed . . . and the case is remanded for further proceedings.

---

12. Later in his closing argument the prosecuting attorney referred to the 16-gauge shotgun and stated again that a 12-gauge shotgun killed Zitek. He argued that a shotgun is not "the most humane type weapon" and that the death penalty is appropriate in a case in which a shotgun is used to murder a person.

MR. JUSTICE MARSHALL, with whom MR. JUSTICE DOUGLAS, MR. JUSTICE STEWART, and MR. JUSTICE POWELL join, concurring in part and dissenting in part.

. . . I . . . agree that the introduction of the shotgun into evidence at petitioner's trial did not violate the Fourteenth Amendment.[13]

But, I believe that in failing to disclose to petitioner certain evidence that might well have been of substantial assistance to the defense, the State denied him a fair trial.

. . .

Two interrelated defenses were raised against the charge of murder—alibi and misidentification. Petitioner's theory of the case was that he was not at the scene when the murder was committed and that those witnesses who testified that they saw him there were confusing him with someone else.

Only two witnesses affirmatively asserted at trial that they saw the murder and that they could identify petitioner as the assailant. They were Patricia Hill, a waitress in the victim's bar, and Henley Powell, a customer. Aside from their testimony, the only other evidence introduced against petitioner related to statements that he allegedly made two days after the murder.

There is a problem with the eyewitness testimony of Powell that did not become apparent until the post-conviction hearing in the trial court. At trial he testified as follows:

"The defendant (indicating) came into the tavern while I was at the table. I first saw him when he walked in the door with a shotgun. I was sitting at the table along the wall. I was facing where the bartender was standing and I also had a view of the man that walked in the door. I was looking to the west." Abs. 32.

---

13. I find the constitutional question presented by the introduction of this evidence to be much harder than the majority seems to. It was uncontradicted at trial that the weapon introduced against petitioner had no bearing on the crime with which he was charged. It was, in fact, clear that the shotgun admitted into evidence was a 16-gauge gun, whereas the murder weapon was a 12-gauge gun. Despite the fact that the prosecution conceded this in a pretrial bill of particulars, it did everything possible to obfuscate the fact that the weapon admitted into evidence was not the murder weapon. This was highly improper. The record also indicates that the trial judge was confused as to why he thought the weapon should be admitted. At one point he said, "There was testimony here that this was a shotgun killing. And I can see nothing wrong if they say that this defendant, who will be identified by other people, was appre-hended with this gun." Abstract of Record (Abs.), 65. If the trial judge meant to imply that because the crime was committed with a shotgun, it was sufficient to prove that the petitioner possessed *any* shotgun, whether or not is was the murder weapon, he surely erred. But it is impossible to tell from the record in this case precisely what was intended, or whether the judge confused the jury when he admitted the weapon. Although this highly prejudicial and irrelevant evidence was introduced, and although the prosecution did its best to lead the jury to believe that there was a relationship between the murder weapon and the shotgun in evidence, the fact that petitioner's counsel explained to the jury that the two weapons were not identical is, on the very closest balance, enough to warrant our finding that the jury was not improperly misled as to the nature of the evidence before it.

But at the post-conviction hearing it was discovered that police officers who had investigated the murder possessed a statement by one Charles Mayer, who had been sitting with Powell at a table in the bar, which contained a diagram indicating that Powell was seated in a direction opposite that indicated in his trial testimony. This diagram was never made available to defense counsel.

Donald O'Brien, who had also been seated at Powell and Mayer's table, testified at trial and contradicted the testimony of both Powell and Patricia Hill. Although O'Brien admitted that he did not actually see the shooting because his back was to the bar, he was certain that petitioner was not the man who had been ejected from the victim's bar only an hour before the killing. O'Brien's testimony greatly undercut the apparent retaliatory motive that the prosecution attributed to petitioner.[14]

Because of the contradictory testimony of those persons who were present at the scene of the murder, the statements allegedly made by the petitioner after the crime were crucial to the prosecution's case. The key prosecution witness in this regard was Virgle Sanders. He testified that two days after the murder he was in the Ponderosa Tavern, that petitioner (whom he knew as "Slick") was there also, and that petitioner said "[s]omething about it's season or open season on bartenders or something like that." Abs. 44. The bartender also testified that he recognized petitioner as being present at the same time as Sanders. And the owner of the tavern stated that he gave petitioner and petitioner's friend a short ride in his automobile, at the end of which the friend mentioned something about "trouble with the bartender." Abs. 52.

After his trial and conviction petitioner learned that five days after the murder, Sanders gave a statement to the police in which he said that he had met "Slick" for the first time about six months before he spoke to him in the Ponderosa Tavern. As the Court notes, it would have been impossible for Sanders to have met the petitioner at the time specified, because petitioner was in federal prison at that time. At the post-conviction hearing, Sanders said that he was not positive when he first met the man known as "Slick," but that he definitely knew it was before Christmas 1961. Petitioner was not released from federal custody until March 1962. When confronted with this fact, Sanders indicated that it was impossible that petitioner was the man with whom he had spoken in the Ponderosa Tavern. Abs. 296. Sanders' trial identification was further impeached at the post-trial hearing by testimony that on the day of trial he told police officers that petitioner was approximately 30 or 40 pounds lighter than he remembered "Slick" being. Abs. 294.

Sanders' testimony that petitioner and "Slick" were not one and the same was corroborated at the hearing. The reason that Sanders could

---

14. The Court asserts that O'Brien may have been drunk. His testimony at trial made it clear beyond doubt that when the victim ejected the man alleged to be the petitioner from the bar, this witness was perfectly sober. Later, especially after the killing, the witness drank heavily and became intoxicated. No one contradicted this at trial.

remember the first time that he had met "Slick" was that "Slick" had been involved in a scuffle with one William Thompson. Thompson testified at the hearing that he remembered the altercation, that he knew "Slick," that prior to the trial he had told police officers that petitioner was not "Slick," and that he remained certain that petitioner and "Slick" were different people. Finally, Sanders' testimony was corroborated by Delbert Jones, the owner of the tavern where "Slick" and Thompson scuffled. Jones testified that he was certain that petitioner was not the man known as "Slick."

The fact is that Thompson and Jones were both familiar with one James E. Watts, who they knew as "Slick," and who looked very much like the petitioner. The record makes clear that the police suspected Watts as the murderer and assigned a lieutenant to search for him. A raid of Jones' bar was even made in the hope of finding this suspect.

Sanders' testimony at the post-conviction hearing indicates that it was Watts who bragged about the murder, not petitioner. It is true that the bartender and the owner of the Ponderosa Tavern testified at trial that it was petitioner who was in the bar with Sanders, but the bartender had never seen "Slick" before, and the owner was drinking the entire afternoon. Furthermore, the fact remains that petitioner and Watts look very much alike.

Petitioner urges that when the State did not reveal to him Sanders' statement about meeting "Slick" at an earlier time and the corroborative statements of Thompson and Jones, it denied him due process. The Court answers this by saying that the statements were not material. It is evident from the foregoing that the statements were not merely material to the defense, they were absolutely critical. I find myself in complete agreement with Justice Schaeffer's dissent in the Illinois Supreme Court:

> "The defendant's conviction rests entirely upon identification testimony. The facts developed at the post-conviction hearing seriously impeached, if indeed they did not destroy, Sanders's trial testimony. Had those facts, and the identifications of 'Slick' Watts by Thompson and Jones, been available at the trial, the jury may well have been unwilling to act upon the identifications of Patricia Hill and Henley Powell. Far more is involved in this case, in my opinion, than 'the following up of useless leads and discussions with immaterial witnesses.' Certainly if Sanders's identification was material, the . . . testimony of the other witnesses which destroyed that identification [was] also material. Consequently, I believe that the State's nondisclosure denied the defendant the fundamental fairness guaranteed by the constitution. . . ." 42 Ill.2d, at 88–89, 246 N.E.2d, at 308.

Petitioner also urges that the failure of the prosecution to disclose the information concerning where the eyewitness Powell was sitting when he allegedly saw petitioner is another instance of suppression of evidence in violation of the Fourteenth Amendment. Had this been the prosecution's only error, I would join the Court in finding the evidence to be immaterial. But if this evidence is considered together with other evidence that was suppressed, it must be apparent that the failure of the prosecution to disclose it contributed to the denial of due process.

Even if material exculpatory evidence was not made available to petitioner, the State argues that because petitioner did not demand to see the evidence, he cannot now complain about nondisclosure. This argument is disingenuous at best.

Prior to trial, petitioner moved for discovery of all statements given to the prosecutor or the police by any witness possessing information relevant to the case. Abs. 5. In explaining why such a broad motion was made, petitioner's counsel stated that, "We want to circumvent the possibility that a witness gets on the stand and says, 'Yes, I made a written statement,' and then the State's Attorney says, 'But no, we don't have it in our possession,' or they say, 'It's in the possession of Orlando Wilson [Superintendent of Police, Chicago, Ill.],' or 'The Chief of Police of Lansing.'" Abs. 8. In response to the motion, the prosecutor guaranteed defense counsel and the court that he would supply defense counsel with statements made either to the police or to the State's Attorney by witnesses who were called to testify at trial. Ibid. Based on this representation, the motion for discovery was denied. Never was there any implication by the prosecutor that his guarantee was in any way dependent upon petitioner's making repeated and specific requests for such statements after each witness testified at trial. The prosecutor's guarantee certainly covered Sanders' statement. As for the statements of the bartender and owner of the Ponderosa Tavern and the statement and diagram of Charles Mayer, petitioner clearly demanded to see these things before trial. The prosecution took the position that it was bound to reveal only the statements of witnesses who testified. Hence, it is hard to imagine what sort of further demand petitioner might have made. Moreover, the very fact that petitioner made his motion for extensive discovery placed the prosecution on notice that the defense wished to see all statements by any witness that might be exculpatory. The motion served "the valuable office of flagging the importance of the evidence for the defense and thus impos[ing] on the prosecutor a duty to make a careful check of his files." United States v. Keogh, 391 F.2d 138, 147 (CA2 1968).

In my view, both Brady v. Maryland, 373 U.S. 83 (1963), and Napue v. Illinois, 360 U.S. 264 (1959), require that the conviction in this case be reversed. Napue establishes that the Fourteenth Amendment is violated "when the State, although not soliciting false evidence, allows it to go uncorrected." Id., at 269. And Brady holds that suppression of material evidence requires a new trial "irrespective of the good faith or bad faith of the prosecution." Supra, at 87. There can be no doubt that there was suppression of evidence by the State and that the evidence that the State relied on was "false" in the sense that it was incomplete and misleading.

Both before and during the trial the prosecutor met with Sanders and went over the statement that he had given the police five days after the murder. Abs. 301, 315. Thus, it is apparent that the prosecutor not only knew of the statement, but was actively using it to prepare his case. There was also testimony at the post-conviction hearing from the prosecution that it had discussed the location where Powell was sitting when he allegedly saw the murder. While the prosecutor could not remember whether or not he actually had Mayer's statement and diagram in his possession, he had some recollection that before trial he was informed of exactly where everyone at Powell's table was sitting. Abs. 323. No attempt was ever made at trial to communicate this information to the defense.

Moreover, seated at the prosecutor's table throughout the trial was Police Lieutenant Turbin, who had investigated the case and who was assisting the prosecution. At the post-conviction hearing, he testified that throughout the trial he was not only aware of Sanders' statement and Mayer's diagram, but also that he had them in his file. He made no attempt to communicate his information to the prosecutor or to remind him about the evidence.

When the State possesses information that might well exonerate a defendant in a criminal case, it has an affirmative duty to disclose that information. While frivolous information and useless leads can be ignored, if evidence is clearly relevant and helpful to the defense, it must be disclosed.

Obviously some burden is placed on the shoulders of the prosecutor when he is required to be responsible for those persons who are directly assisting him in bringing an accused to justice. But this burden is the essence of due process of law. It is the State that tries a man, and it is the State that must insure that the trial is fair. "A citizen has the right to expect fair dealing from his government, see Vitarelli v. Seaton, 359 U.S. 535, and this entails . . . treating the government as a unit rather than as an amalgam of separate entities." S & E Contractors, Inc. v. United States, 406 U.S. 1, 10 (1972). "The prosecutor's office is an entity and as such it is the spokesman for the Government." Giglio v. United States, 405 U.S. 150, 154 (1972). . . .

My reading of the case leads me to conclude that the prosecutor knew that evidence existed that might help the defense, that the defense had asked to see it, and that it was never disclosed. It makes no difference whatever whether the evidence that was suppressed was found in the file of a police officer who directly aided the prosecution or in the file of the prosecutor himself. When the prosecutor consciously uses police officers as part of the prosecutorial team, those officers may not conceal evidence that the prosecutor himself would have a duty to disclose. It would be unconscionable to permit a prosecutor to adduce evidence demonstrating guilt without also requiring that he bear the responsibility of producing all known and relevant evidence tending to show innocence.

———

470. After the Court handed down its opinion in *Moore*, defense counsel obtained from Virgle Sanders a statement that the majority's construction of his testimony about "Slick" was wrong, and that the man in the Ponderosa Tap was "Slick," not the defendant. At an evidentiary hearing in March 1974, Sanders affirmed that statement and said also that Moore was too short to be "Slick."

On that basis, Moore argued that the Court's conclusion that the information about "Slick" that was withheld from the defense was not material was incorrect, that it clearly was material, and that Sanders' repudiation of his identification of Moore at trial required reversal of his conviction. After considering all the evidence in the case, the Supreme Court of Illinois concluded that Sanders' post-trial statements lacked "that quantum of credibility" that would warrant granting relief. Further, it found that there was enough other evidence to prove Moore's guilt beyond a reasonable doubt. People v. Moore, 327 N.E.2d 324 (Ill.1975). The Court denied certiorari, 423 U.S. 938 (1975). In a separate statement, Justice Stewart noted that the questions raised by Moore would be "fully amenable to reassessment in a federal habeas corpus proceeding." 423 U.S. at 939.

With respect to the non-disclosure of the lead to "Slick" Watts, see Bowen v. Maynard, 799 F.2d 593 (10th Cir.1986); Scurr v. Niccum, 620 F.2d 186 (8th Cir.1980); Grant v. Alldredge, 498 F.2d 376 (2d Cir.1974). In all three cases, the court held that disclosure of the lead to another suspect was required.

———

United States v. Agurs

427 U.S. 97, 96 S.Ct. 2392, 49 L.Ed.2d 342 (1976).

■ MR. JUSTICE STEVENS delivered the opinion of the Court.

After a brief interlude in an inexpensive motel room, respondent repeatedly stabbed James Sewell, causing his death. She was convicted of second-degree murder. The question before us is whether the prosecutor's failure to provide defense counsel with certain background information about Sewell, which would have tended to support the argument that respondent acted in self-defense, deprived her of a fair trial under the rule of Brady v. Maryland, 373 U.S. 83.

The answer to the question depends on (1) a review of the facts, (2) the significance of the failure of defense counsel to request the material, and (3) the standard by which the prosecution's failure to volunteer exculpatory material should be judged.

I

At about 4:30 p.m. on September 24, 1971, respondent, who had been there before, and Sewell, registered in a motel as man and wife. They were assigned a room without a bath. Sewell was wearing a bowie knife in a sheath, and carried another knife in his pocket. Less than two hours earlier, according to the testimony of his estranged wife, he had had $360 in cash on his person.

About 15 minutes later three motel employees heard respondent screaming for help. A forced entry into their room disclosed Sewell on top of respondent struggling for possession of the bowie knife. She was holding the knife; his bleeding hand grasped the blade; according to one witness he was trying to jam the blade into her chest. The employees separated the two and summoned the authorities. Respondent departed without comment before they arrived. Sewell was dead on arrival at the hospital.

Circumstantial evidence indicated that the parties had completed an act of intercourse, that Sewell had then gone to the bathroom down the hall, and that the struggle occurred upon his return. The contents of his pockets were in disarray on the dresser and no money was found; the jury may have inferred that respondent took Sewell's money and that the fight started when Sewell re-entered the room and saw what she was doing.

On the following morning respondent surrendered to the police. She was given a physical examination which revealed no cuts or bruises of any kind, except needle marks on her upper arm. An autopsy of Sewell disclosed that he had several deep stab wounds in his chest and abdomen, and a number of slashes on his arms and hands, characterized by the pathologist as "defensive wounds."

Respondent offered no evidence. Her sole defense was the argument made by her attorney that Sewell had initially attacked her with the knife, and that her actions had all been directed toward saving her own life. The support for this self-defense theory was based on the fact that she had screamed for help. Sewell was on top of her when help arrived, and his possession of two knives indicated that he was a violence-prone person. It took the jury about 25 minutes to elect a foreman and return a verdict.

Three months later defense counsel filed a motion for a new trial asserting that he had discovered (1) that Sewell had a prior criminal record that would have further evidenced his violent character; (2) that the prosecutor had failed to disclose this information to the defense; and (3) that a recent opinion of the United States Court of Appeals for the District of Columbia Circuit made it clear that such evidence was admissible even if not known to the defendant. Sewell's prior record included a plea of guilty to a charge of assault and carrying a deadly weapon in 1963, and another guilty plea to a charge of carrying a deadly weapon in 1971. Apparently both weapons were knives.

The Government opposed the motion, arguing that there was no duty to tender Sewell's prior record to the defense in the absence of an appropriate request; that the evidence was readily discoverable in advance of trial and hence was not the kind of "newly discovered" evidence justifying a new trial; and that, in all events, it was not material.

The District Court denied the motion. It rejected the Government's argument that there was no duty to disclose material evidence unless requested to do so, assumed that the evidence was admissible, but held that it was not sufficiently material. The District Court expressed the opinion that the prior conviction shed no light on Sewell's character that was not already apparent from the uncontradicted evidence, particularly the fact that he carried two knives; the court stressed the inconsistency between the claim of self-defense and the fact that Sewell had been stabbed repeatedly while respondent was unscathed.

The Court of Appeals reversed. The court found no lack of diligence on the part of the defense and no misconduct by the prosecutor in this case. It held, however, that the evidence was material, and that its nondisclosure required a new trial because the jury might have returned a different verdict if the evidence had been received.

The decision of the Court of Appeals represents a significant departure from this Court's prior holding; because we believe that that court has incorrectly interpreted the constitutional requirement of due process, we reverse.

II

The rule of Brady v. Maryland, 373 U.S. 83, arguably applies in three quite different situations. Each involves the discovery, after trial, of information which had been known to the prosecution but unknown to the defense.

In the first situation, typified by Mooney v. Holohan, 294 U.S. 103, the undisclosed evidence demonstrates that the prosecution's case includes perjured testimony and that the prosecution knew, or should have known, of the perjury. In a series of subsequent cases, the Court has consistently held that a conviction obtained by the knowing use of perjured testimony is fundamentally unfair, and must be set aside if there is any reasonable likelihood that the false testimony could have affected the judgment of the jury. It is this line of cases on which the Court of Appeals placed primary reliance. In those cases the Court has applied a strict standard of materiality, not just because they involve prosecutorial misconduct, but more importantly because they involve a corruption of the truth-seeking function of the trial process. Since this case involves no misconduct, and since there is no reason to question the veracity of any of the prosecution witnesses, the test of materiality followed in the *Mooney* line of cases is not necessarily applicable to this case.

The second situation, illustrated by the *Brady* case itself, is characterized by a pretrial request for specific evidence. In that case defense counsel had requested the extrajudicial statements made by Brady's accomplice, one Boblit. This Court held that the suppression of one of Boblit's statements deprived Brady of due process, noting specifically that the statement had been requested and that it was "material." A fair analysis of the holding in *Brady* indicates that implicit in the requirement of materiality is a concern that the suppressed evidence might have affected the outcome of the trial.

Brady was found guilty of murder in the first degree. Since the jury did not add the words "without capital punishment" to the verdict, he was sentenced to death. At his trial Brady did not deny his involvement in the deliberate killing, but testified that it was his accomplice, Boblit, rather than he, who had actually strangled the decedent. This version of the event was corroborated by one of several confessions made by Boblit but not given to Brady's counsel despite an admittedly adequate request.

After his conviction and sentence had been affirmed on appeal, Brady filed a motion to set aside the judgment, and later a post-conviction proceeding, in which he alleged that the State had violated his constitutional rights by suppressing the Boblit confession. The trial judge denied relief largely because he felt that Boblit's confession would have been inadmissible at Brady's trial. The Maryland Court of Appeals disagreed; it ordered a new trial on the issue of punishment. It held that the withholding of material evidence, even "without guile," was a denial of due process and that there were valid theories on which the confession might have been admissible in Brady's defense.

This Court granted certiorari to consider Brady's contention that the violation of his constitutional right to a fair trial vitiated the entire proceeding. The holding that the suppression of exculpatory evidence violated Brady's right to due process was affirmed, as was the separate holding that he should receive a new trial on the issue of punishment but not on the issue of guilt or innocence. The Court interpreted the Maryland Court of Appeals opinion as ruling that the confession was inadmissible on that issue. For that reason, the confession could not have affected the outcome on the issue of guilt but could have affected Brady's punishment. It was material on the latter issue but not the former. And since it was not material on the issue of guilt, the entire trial was not lacking in due process.

The test of materiality in a case like *Brady* in which specific information has been requested by the defense is not necessarily the same as in a case in which no such request has been made. Indeed, this Court has not yet decided whether the prosecutor has any obligation to provide defense counsel with exculpatory information when no request has been made. Before addressing that question, a brief comment on the function of the request is appropriate.

In *Brady* the request was specific. It gave the prosecutor notice of exactly what the defense desired. Although there is, of course, no duty to provide defense counsel with unlimited discovery of everything known by the prosecutor, if the subject matter of such a request is material, or indeed if a substantial basis for claiming materiality exists, it is reasonable to require the prosecutor to respond either by furnishing the information or by submitting the problem to the trial judge. When the prosecutor receives a specific and relevant request, the failure to make any response is seldom, if ever, excusable.

In many cases, however, exculpatory information in the possession of the prosecutor may be unknown to defense counsel. In such a situation he may make no request at all, or possibly ask for "all *Brady* material" or for "anything exculpatory." Such a request really gives the prosecutor no better notice than if no request is made. If there is a duty to respond to a general request of that kind, it must derive from the obviously exculpatory character of certain evidence in the hands of the prosecutor. But if the evidence is so clearly supportive of a claim of innocence that it gives the prosecution notice of a duty to produce, that duty should equally arise even if no request is made. Whether we focus on the desirability of a precise definition of the prosecutor's duty or on the potential harm to the defendant, we conclude that there is no significant difference between cases in which there has been merely a general request for exculpatory matter and cases, like the one we must now decide, in which there has been no request at all. The third situation in which the *Brady* rule arguably applies, typified by this case, therefore embraces the case in which only a general request for "*Brady* material" has been made.

We now consider whether the prosecutor has any constitutional duty to volunteer exculpatory matter to the defense, and if so, what standard of materiality gives rise to that duty.

III

We are not considering the scope of discovery authorized by the Federal Rules of Criminal Procedure, or the wisdom of amending those Rules to enlarge the defendant's discovery rights. We are dealing with the defendant's right to a fair trial mandated by the Due Process Clause of the Fifth Amendment to the Constitution. Our construction of that Clause will apply equally to the comparable clause in the Fourteenth Amendment applicable to trials in state courts.

The problem arises in two principal contexts. First, in advance of trial, and perhaps during the course of a trial as well, the prosecutor must decide what, if anything, he should voluntarily submit to defense counsel. Second, after trial a judge may be required to decide whether a nondisclosure deprived the defendant of his right to due process. Logically the same standard must apply at both times. For unless the omission deprived the defendant of a fair trial, there was no constitutional violation requiring that the verdict be set aside; and absent a constitutional violation, there was no breach of the prosecutor's constitutional duty to disclose.

Nevertheless, there is a significant practical difference between the pretrial decision of the prosecutor and the post-trial decision of the judge. Because we are dealing with an inevitably imprecise standard, and because the significance of an item of evidence can seldom be predicted accurately until the entire record is complete, the prudent prosecutor will resolve doubtful questions in favor of disclosure. But to reiterate a critical point, the prosecutor will not have violated his constitutional duty of disclosure unless his omission is of sufficient significance to result in the denial of the defendant's right to a fair trial.

The Court of Appeals appears to have assumed that the prosecutor has a constitutional obligation to disclose any information that might affect the jury's verdict. That statement of a constitutional standard of materiality approaches the "sporting theory of justice" which the Court expressly rejected in *Brady*. For a jury's appraisal of a case "might" be affected by an improper or trivial consideration as well as by evidence giving rise to a legitimate doubt on the issue of guilt. If everything that might influence a jury must be disclosed, the only way a prosecutor could discharge his constitutional duty would be to allow complete discovery of his files as a matter of routine practice.

Whether or not procedural rules authorizing such broad discovery might be desirable, the Constitution surely does not demand that much. While expressing the opinion that representatives of the State may not "suppress substantial material evidence," former Chief Justice Traynor of the California Supreme Court has pointed out that "they are under no duty to report sua sponte to the defendant all that they learn about the case and about their witnesses." In re Imbler, 60 Cal.2d 554, 569, 387 P.2d 6, 14 (1963). And this Court recently noted that there is "no constitutional requirement that the prosecution to make a complete and detailed accounting to the defense of all police investigatory work on a case." Moore v. Illinois, 408 U.S. 786, 795. The mere possibility that an item of undisclosed information might have helped the defense, or might have affected the outcome of the trial, does not establish "materiality" in the constitutional sense.

Nor do we believe the constitutional obligation is measured by the moral culpability, or the willfulness, of the prosecutor. If evidence highly probative of innocence is in his file, he should be presumed to recognize its significance even if he has actually overlooked it. . . . Conversely, if evidence actually has no probative significance at all, no purpose would be served by requiring a new trial simply because an inept prosecutor incorrectly believed he was suppressing a fact that would be vital to the defense. If the suppression of evidence results in constitutional error, it is because of the character of the evidence, not the character of the prosecutor.

As the District Court recognized in this case, there are situations in which evidence is obviously of such substantial value to the defense that elementary fairness requires it to be disclosed even without a specific request. For though the attorney for the sovereign must prosecute the accused with earnestness and vigor, he must always be faithful to his client's overriding interest that "justice shall be done." He is the "servant of the law, the twofold aim of which is that guilt shall not escape or innocence suffer." Berger v. United States, 295 U.S. 78, 88. This description of the prosecutor's duty illuminates the standard of materiality that governs his obligation to disclose exculpatory evidence.

On the one hand, the fact that such evidence was available to the prosecutor and not submitted to the defense places it in a different category than if it had simply been discovered from a neutral source after trial. For that reason the defendant should not have to satisfy the severe burden of demonstrating that newly discovered evidence probably would have resulted in acquittal. If the standard applied to the usual motion for a new trial based on newly discovered evidence were the same when the evidence was in the State's possession as when it was found in a neutral source, there would be no special significance to the prosecutor's obligation to serve the cause of justice.

On the other hand, since we have rejected the suggestion that the prosecutor has a constitutional duty routinely to deliver his entire file to defense counsel, we cannot consistently treat every nondisclosure as though it were error. It necessarily follows that the judge should not order a new trial every time he is unable to characterize a nondisclosure as harmless under the customary harmless-error standard. Under that standard when error is present in the record, the reviewing judge must set aside the verdict and judgment unless his "conviction is sure that the error did not influence the jury, or had but very slight effect." Kotteakos v. United States, 328 U.S. 750, 764. Unless every nondisclosure is regarded as automatic error, the constitutional standard of materiality must impose a higher burden on the defendant.

The proper standard of materiality must reflect our overriding concern with the justice of the finding of guilt. Such a finding is permissible only if supported by evidence establishing guilt beyond a reasonable doubt. It necessarily follows that if the omitted evidence creates a reasonable doubt that did not otherwise exist, constitutional error has been committed. This means that the omission must be evaluated in the context of the entire record. If there is no reasonable doubt about guilt whether or not the additional evidence is considered, there is no justification for a new trial. On the other hand, if the verdict is already of questionable validity, additional evidence of relatively minor importance might be sufficient to create a reasonable doubt.

This statement of the standard of materiality describes the test which courts appear to have applied in actual cases although the standard has been phrased in different language. It is also the standard which the trial judge applied in this case. He evaluated the significance of Sewell's prior criminal record in the context of the full trial which he recalled in detail. Stressing in particular the incongruity of a claim that Sewell was the aggressor with the evidence of his multiple wounds and respondent's unscathed condition, the trial judge indicated his unqualified opinion that respondent was guilty. He noted that Sewell's prior record did not contradict any evidence offered by the prosecutor, and was largely cumulative of the evidence that Sewell was wearing a bowie knife in a sheath and carrying a second knife in his pocket when he registered at the motel.

Since the arrest record was not requested and did not even arguably give rise to any inference of perjury, since after considering it in the context of the entire record the trial judge remained convinced of respondent's guilt beyond a reasonable doubt, and since we are satisfied that his firsthand appraisal of the record was thorough and entirely reasonable, we hold that the prosecutor's failure to tender Sewell's record to the defense did not deprive respondent of a fair trial as guaranteed by the Due Process Clause of the Fifth Amendment. Accordingly, the judgment of the Court of Appeals is

Reversed.[15]

———

471. In United States v. Bagley, 473 U.S. 667 (1985) (5–3), five members of the Court agreed that the same general test of materiality is applicable whether there is a specific request, a general request, or no request for the evidence. Evidence is material "only if there is a reasonable probability that, had the evidence been disclosed to the defense, the result of the proceeding would have been different. A 'reasonable probability' is a probability sufficient to undermine confidence in the outcome." Id. at 682. See id. at 683 (opinion of White, J.). Writing only for himself and Justice O'Connor among the majority, Justice Blackmun observed that, when a specific request is made, a reviewing court should take into account the possibility that the prosecutor's implied representation that the evidence does not exist affected the preparation or presentation of the defense.

Also in *Bagley*, the Court said that there is no distinction with respect to the requirement of disclosure between impeachment evidence and exculpatory evidence generally. On remand, the court of appeals held that the facts of the case met the test enunciated by the Court and reversed the conviction. Bagley v. Lumpkin, 798 F.2d 1297 (9th Cir.1986).

The *Bagley* test of materiality was applied to *Brady* material—exculpatory evidence in the hands of the prosecution—in the context of a capital case, in Kyles v. Whitley, 514 U.S. 419 (1995) (5–4). The Court said that "once a reviewing court applying *Bagley* has found constitutional error there is no need for further harmless-error review. 514 U.S. at 435. See also United States v. Lloyd, 71 F.3d 408 (D.C.Cir.1995) (*Brady* material withheld by government without wrongdoing and with disclosure to court; *Bagley* applied); Bowen v. Maynard, 799 F.2d 593 (10th Cir.1986) (*Agurs-Bagley* applied; conviction vacated); United States ex rel. Smith v. Fairman, 769 F.2d 386 (7th Cir.1985) (same).

[15] Justice Marshall wrote a dissenting opinion, which Justice Brennan joined.

472. When must the disclosure required by cases like *Brady* and *Agurs* be made? In United States v. Kaplan, 554 F.2d 577, 579–80 (3d Cir.1977), the court said: "Where documentary evidence is exculpatory, it may be within both *Brady* and Rule 16. . . . Thus, on occasion there will be an overlap between the two means a federal defendant uses to obtain information in the possession of the prosecution." When *Brady* applies, the court said, "delayed disclosure by the prosecution is not per se reversible error. . . . If exculpatory evidence can be effectively presented at trial and the defendant is not prevented by lack of time to make needed investigation, there is no reversible prosecutorial conduct in ill-timed presentation." Id. at 580.

Brady-Agurs material for use to challenge government witnesses' credibility on cross-examination need not be turned over before the day on which the witness testifies. "Disclosure at that time will fully allow appellees to effectively use that information to challenge the veracity of the government's witness." United States v. Higgs, 713 F.2d 39 (3d Cir.1983).

473. "More than 30 years ago this Court held that the Fourteenth Amendment cannot tolerate a state criminal conviction obtained by the knowing use of false evidence. Mooney v. Holohan, 294 U.S. 103. There has been no deviation from that established principle." Miller v. Pate, 386 U.S. 1, 7 (1967). In Napue v. Illinois, 360 U.S. 264, 269 (1959), the facts of which are outlined in *Moore*, p. 956 above, the Court said: "The principle that a State may not knowingly use false evidence, including false testimony, to obtain a tainted conviction, implicit in any concept of ordered liberty, does not cease to apply merely because the false testimony goes only to the credibility of the witness. The jury's estimate of the truthfulness and reliability of a given witness may well be determinative of guilt or innocence, and it is upon such subtle factors as the possible interest of the witness in testifying falsely that a defendant's life or liberty may depend." See Giglio v. United States, 405 U.S. 150 (1972), note 475 below; Brown v. Wainwright, 785 F.2d 1457 (11th Cir.1986) (*Giglio* applied).

"We do not believe . . . that the prosecution's duty to disclose false testimony by one of its witnesses is to be narrowly and technically limited to those situations where the prosecutor knows that the witness is guilty of the crime of perjury. Regardless of the lack of intent to lie on the part of the witness, *Giglio* and *Napue* require that the prosecutor apprise the court when he knows that his witness is giving testimony that is substantially misleading. This is not to say that the prosecutor must play the role of defense counsel, and ferret out ambiguities in his witness' responses on cross-examination. However, when it should be obvious to the Government that the witness' answer, although made in good faith, is untrue, the Government's obligation to correct that statement is as compelling as it is in a situation where the Government knows that the witness is intentionally committing perjury." United States v. Harris, 498 F.2d 1164, 1169 (3d Cir.1974).

Prosecutorial (mis)conduct

474. "Formulation of the duty [to disclose evidence to the defense] in terms of wilful or wrongful conduct would seem only to confuse here, and is not necessary under the governing law as we understand it." United States ex rel. Meers v. Wilkins, 326 F.2d 135, 139 (2d Cir.1964). "Where disclosable evidentiary material which came into the possession of the Government has been lost or destroyed, and is unavailable to the defense for that reason, the standards for determining whether sanctions should be imposed on the Government . . . depend on the extent of the Government's culpability for the loss or destruction and the amount of the prejudice to the defense which resulted." United States v. Miranda, 526 F.2d 1319, 1325–26 (2d Cir.1975). Sanctions have not been imposed "where the loss was inadvertent and not deliberate or in bad faith, and there was not such prejudice to the defendant as to deny him a fair trial." Id. at 1327. See, e.g., United States v. Rojas, 502 F.2d 1042 (5th Cir.1974) (accidental damage to tape of conversation); United States v. Sewar, 468 F.2d 236 (9th Cir.1972) (negligent failure to preserve blood sample); United States v. Shafer, 445 F.2d 579 (7th Cir.1971) (evidence taken from defendant destroyed because of dangerousness); Ingram v. Peyton, 367 F.2d 933 (4th Cir.1966) (prosecutor's error in naming principal prosecution witness prevented defense from discovering that witness had been convicted of perjury).

The Due Process Clause does not require law enforcement officials to preserve a sample of the breath of a suspected drunk driver in order to use the results of a breath-analysis test in a criminal prosecution. California v. Trombetta, 467 U.S. 479 (1984). The court noted that the officials had acted in good faith, that the likelihood that the samples would be exculpatory was extremely low, and that there were alternative ways to challenge the accuracy of the results.

475. In Giglio v. United States, 405 U.S. 150 (1972), an assistant United States attorney promised the principal government witness that he would not be prosecuted if he cooperated. The assistant who tried the case was unaware that the promise was made. At trial, the witness denied the existence of a promise. The Court held that *Napue*, note 473 above, was applicable. "[W]hether the nondisclosure was a result of negligence or design, it is the responsibility of the prosecutor. The prosecutor's office is an entity and as such it is the spokesman for the Government. A promise made by one attorney must be attributed, for these purposes, to the Government. . . . To the extent this places a burden on the large prosecution offices, procedures and regulations can be established to carry that burden and to insure communication of all relevant information on each case to every lawyer who deals with it." 405 U.S. at 154. See Davis v. Zant, 36 F.3d 1538 (11th Cir.1994); United States v. Butler, 567 F.2d 885 (9th Cir.1978).

476. The defendant was convicted of assault with intent to murder and unauthorized use of a motor vehicle. The police had in their possession the results of ballistics and fingerprint tests which indicated that the defendant was not involved in the crimes charged. It was not shown that the prosecutor knew of the existence of the reports or that the tests had been made. The court of appeals held that the conviction was invalid.

"[T]he effect of the nondisclosure [is not] neutralized because the prosecuting attorney was not shown to have had knowledge of the exculpatory evidence. Failure of the police to reveal such material evidence in their possession is equally harmful to a defendant whether the information is purposely, or negligently, withheld. And it makes no difference if the withholding is by officials other than the prosecutor. The police are also part of the prosecution, and the taint on the trial is no less if they, rather than the State's Attorney, were guilty of the nondisclosure. If the police allow the State's Attorney to produce evidence pointing to guilt without informing him of other evidence in their possession which contradicts this inference, state officers are practicing deception not only on the State's Attorney but on the court and the defendant. 'The cruelest lies are often told in silence.' If the police silence as to the existence of the reports resulted from negligence rather than guile, the deception is no less damaging.

"The duty to disclose is that of the state, which ordinarily acts through the prosecuting attorney; but if he too is the victim of police suppression of the material information, the state's failure is not on that account excused. We cannot condone the attempt to connect the defendant with the crime by questionable inferences which might be refuted by undisclosed and unproduced documents then in the hands of the police. To borrow a phrase from Chief Judge Biggs, this procedure passes 'beyond the line of tolerable imperfection and falls into the field of fundamental unfairness.'[16]" Barbee v. Warden, Maryland Penitentiary, 331 F.2d 842, 846 (4th Cir.1964). To the same effect, see Smith v. New Mexico Department of Corrections, 50 F.3d 801 (10th Cir.1995) (failure to disclose reports in possession of police but not known to prosecution was *Brady* violation, notwithstanding prosecutor's "open file" policy); United States ex rel. Smith v. Fairman, 769 F.2d 386 (7th Cir.1985) (police witness's failure to disclose exculpatory firearms report).

Citing cases in other circuits, in United States v. Brooks, 966 F.2d 1500 (D.C.Cir.1992), the court held that in responding to a *Brady* request, the government has a duty to search reasonably available files for exculpatory evidence of which it is unaware, if there is a "non-trivial" prospect that the search will yield such evidence. As the difficulty of the search increases, the existence of such a duty depends on the likelihood that evidence will be found increasing accordingly.

In Luna v. Beto, 395 F.2d 35 (5th Cir.1968), the principal witness for the state testified falsely (perhaps unintentionally) that there were no cases

---

16. Curran v. State of Del., 259 F.2d 707, 713 (3rd Cir.1958). . . .

pending against him. In fact, the police had promised to help him with a case pending against him in return for his help in other cases. The prosecutor did not know of the police promise. While the witness was testifying, the police who knew of the promise were excluded from the courtroom as prospective witnesses and did not hear his testimony. Following the defendant's conviction, the defense learned of the promise. Should the conviction be reversed? If so, is reversal constitutionally required? Why (not)?

477. "A public prosecutor or other government lawyer in criminal litigation shall make timely disclosure to counsel for the defendant, or to the defendant if he has no counsel, of the existence of evidence, known to the prosecutor or other government lawyer, that tends to negate the guilt of the accused, mitigate the degree of the offense, or reduce the punishment." American Bar Association Code of Professional Responsibility, Disciplinary Rule 7–103(b). See Rule 3.8(d), ABA Model Rules of Professional Conduct, generally to the same effect.

———

Arizona v. Youngblood

488 U.S. 51, 109 S.Ct. 333, 102 L.Ed.2d 281 (1988).

■ CHIEF JUSTICE REHNQUIST delivered the opinion of the Court.

Respondent Larry Youngblood was convicted by a Pima County, Arizona, jury of child molestation, sexual assault, and kidnaping. The Arizona Court of Appeals reversed his conviction on the ground that the State had failed to preserve semen samples from the victim's body and clothing. 153 Ariz. 50, 734 P.2d 592 (1986). We granted certiorari to consider the extent to which the Due Process Clause of the Federal Constitution requires the State to preserve evidentiary material that might be useful to a criminal defendant.

On October 29, 1983, David L., a 10-year-old boy, attended a church service with his mother. After he left the service at about 9:30 p.m., the boy went to a carnival behind the church, where he was abducted by a middle-aged man of medium height and weight. The assailant drove the boy to a secluded area near a ravine and molested him. He then took the boy to an unidentified, sparsely furnished house where he sodomized the boy four times. Afterwards, the assailant tied the boy up while he went outside to start his car. Once the assailant started the car, albeit with some difficulty, he returned to the house and again sodomized the boy. The assailant then sent the boy to the bathroom to wash up before he returned him to the carnival. He threatened to kill the boy if he told anyone about the attack. The entire ordeal lasted about 1½ hours.

After the boy made his way home, his mother took him to Kino Hospital. At the hospital, a physician treated the boy for rectal injuries. The physician also used a "sexual assault kit" to collect evidence of the attack. The Tucson Police Department provided such kits to all hospitals in Pima County for use in sexual assault cases. Under standard procedure, the victim of a sexual assault was taken to a hospital, where a physician used the kit to collect evidence. The kit included paper to collect saliva samples, a tube for obtaining a blood sample, microscopic slides for making smears, a set of Q-tip like swabs, and a medical examination report. Here, the physician used the swab to collect samples from the boy's rectum and mouth. He then made a microscopic slide of the samples. The doctor also obtained samples of the boy's saliva, blood, and hair. The physician did not examine the samples at any time. The police placed the kit in a secure refrigerator at the police station. At the hospital, the police also collected the boy's underwear and T-shirt. This clothing was not refrigerated or frozen.

Nine days after the attack, on November 7, 1983, the police asked the boy to pick out his assailant from a photographic lineup. The boy identified respondent as the assailant. Respondent was not located by the police until four weeks later; he was arrested on December 9, 1983.

On November 8, 1983, Edward Heller, a police criminologist, examined the sexual assault kit. He testified that he followed standard department procedure, which was to examine the slides and determine whether sexual contact had occurred. After he determined that such contact had occurred, the criminologist did not perform any other tests, although he placed the assault kit back in the refrigerator. He testified that tests to identify blood group substances were not routinely conducted during the initial examination of an assault kit and in only about half of all cases in any event. He did not test the clothing at this time.

Respondent was indicted on charges of child molestation, sexual assault, and kidnaping. The State moved to compel respondent to provide blood and saliva samples for comparison with the material gathered through the use of the sexual assault kit, but the trial court denied the motion on the ground that the State had not obtained a sufficiently large semen sample to make a valid comparison. The prosecutor then asked the State's criminologist to perform an ABO blood group test on the rectal swab sample in an attempt to ascertain the blood type of the boy's assailant. This test failed to detect any blood group substances in the sample.

In January 1985, the police criminologist examined the boy's clothing for the first time. He found one semen stain on the boy's underwear and another on the rear of his T-shirt. The criminologist tried to obtain blood group substances from both stains using the ABO technique, but was unsuccessful. He also performed a P–30 protein molecule test on the stains, which indicated that only a small quantity of semen was present on the clothing; it was inconclusive as to the assailant's identity. The Tucson Police

Department had just begun using this test, which was then used in slightly more than half of the crime laboratories in the country.

Respondent's principal defense at trial was that the boy had erred in identifying him as the perpetrator of the crime. In this connection, both a criminologist for the State and an expert witness for respondent testified as to what might have been shown by tests performed on the samples shortly after they were gathered, or by later tests performed on the samples from the boy's clothing had the clothing been properly refrigerated. The court instructed the jury that if they found the State had destroyed or lost evidence, they might "infer that the true fact is against the State's interest." 10 Tr. 90.

The jury found respondent guilty as charged, but the Arizona Court of Appeals reversed the judgment of conviction. It stated that " 'when identity is an issue at trial and the police permit the destruction of evidence that could eliminate the defendant as the perpetrator, such loss is material to the defense and is a denial of due process.' " 153 Ariz., at 54, 734 P.2d, at 596, quoting State v. Escalante, 153 Ariz. 55, 61, 734 P.2d 597, 603 (App.1986). The Court of Appeals concluded on the basis of the expert testimony at trial that timely performance of tests with properly preserved semen samples could have produced results that might have completely exonerated respondent. The Court of Appeals reached this conclusion even though it did "not imply any bad faith on the part of the State." 153 Ariz., at 54, 734 P.2d, at 596. . . . We now reverse.

Decision of this case requires us to again consider "what might loosely be called the area of constitutionally guaranteed access to evidence." United States v. Valenzuela-Bernal, 458 U.S. 858, 867 (1982). In Brady v. Maryland, 373 U.S. 83 (1963), we held "that the suppression by the prosecution of evidence favorable to the accused upon request violates due process where the evidence is material either to guilt or to punishment, irrespective of the good faith or bad faith of the prosecution." Id., at 87. In United States v. Agurs, 427 U.S. 97 (1976), we held that the prosecution had a duty to disclose some evidence of this description even though no requests were made for it, but at the same time we rejected the notion that a "prosecutor has a constitutional duty routinely to deliver his entire file to defense counsel." Id., at 111. . . .

There is no question but that the State complied with Brady and Agurs here. The State disclosed relevant police reports to respondent, which contained information about the existence of the swab and the clothing, and the boy's examination at the hospital. The State provided respondent's expert with the laboratory reports and notes prepared by the police criminologist, and respondent's expert had access to the swab and to the clothing.

If respondent is to prevail on federal constitutional grounds, then, it must be because of some constitutional duty over and above that imposed by cases such as Brady and Agurs. Our most recent decision in this area of the law, California v. Trombetta, 467 U.S. 479 (1984), arose out of a drunk driving prosecution in which the State had introduced test results indicating the concentration of alcohol in the blood of two motorists. The defendants sought to suppress the test results on the ground that the State had failed to preserve the breath samples used in the test. We rejected this argument for several reasons: first, "the officers here were acting in 'good faith and in accord with their normal practice,'" id., at 488, quoting Killian v. United States, 368 U.S. 231, 242 (1961); second, in the light of the procedures actually used the chances that preserved samples would have exculpated the defendants were slim. . .; and, third, even if the samples might have shown inaccuracy in the tests, the defendants had "alternative means of demonstrating their innocence." Id., at 490. In the present case, the likelihood that the preserved materials would have enabled the defendant to exonerate himself appears to be greater than it was in *Trombetta*, but here, unlike in *Trombetta*, the State did not attempt to make any use of the materials in its own case in chief.

Our decisions in related areas have stressed the importance for constitutional purposes of good or bad faith on the part of the Government when the claim is based on loss of evidence attributable to the Government. . . .

The Due Process Clause of the Fourteenth Amendment, as interpreted in *Brady*, makes the good or bad faith of the State irrelevant when the State fails to disclose to the defendant material exculpatory evidence. But we think the Due Process Clause requires a different result when we deal with the failure of the State to preserve evidentiary material of which no more can be said than that it could have been subjected to tests, the results of which might have exonerated the defendant. Part of the reason for the difference in treatment is found in the observation made by the Court in *Trombetta*, supra, at 486, that "[w]henever potentially exculpatory evidence is permanently lost, courts face the treacherous task of divining the import of materials whose contents are unknown and, very often, disputed." Part of it stems from our unwillingness to read the "fundamental fairness" requirement of the Due Process Clause, see Lisenba v. California, 314 U.S. 219, 236 (1941), as imposing on the police an undifferentiated and absolute duty to retain and to preserve all material that might be of conceivable evidentiary significance in a particular prosecution. We think that requiring a defendant to show bad faith on the part of the police both limits the extent of the police's obligation to preserve evidence to reasonable bounds and confines it to that class of cases where the interests of justice most clearly require it, i.e., those cases in which the police themselves by their conduct indicate that the evidence could form a basis for exonerating the defendant. We therefore hold that unless a criminal defendant can show bad faith on the part of the police, failure to preserve potentially useful evidence does not constitute a denial of due process of law.

In this case, the police collected the rectal swab and clothing on the night of the crime; respondent was not taken into custody until six weeks later. The failure of the police to refrigerate the clothing and to perform tests on the semen samples can at worst be described as negligent. None of this information was concealed from respondent at trial, and the evidence— such as it was—was made available to respondent's expert who declined to perform any tests on the samples. The Arizona Court of Appeals noted in its opinion—and we agree—that there was no suggestion of bad faith on the part of the police. It follows, therefore, from what we have said, that there was no violation of the Due Process Clause.

The Arizona Court of Appeals also referred somewhat obliquely to the State's "inability to quantitatively test" certain semen samples with the newer P–30 test. 153 Ariz., at 54, 734 P.2d, at 596. If the court meant by this statement that the Due Process Clause is violated when the police fail to use a particular investigatory tool, we strongly disagree. The situation here is no different than a prosecution for drunk driving that rests on police observation alone; the defendant is free to argue to the finder of fact that a breathalizer test might have been exculpatory, but the police do not have a constitutional duty to perform any particular tests.

The judgment of the Arizona Court of Appeals is reversed. . . .

. . .[17]

———

478. *Youngblood* is applied in United States v. Cooper, 983 F.2d 928 (9th Cir.1993), in which federal drug agents permitted the destruction before trial of seized laboratory equipment, despite the defendant's claim that it was not adapted to the production of unlawful drugs. The equipment was destroyed because of concern that it might be contaminated.

In United States v. Brimage, 115 F.3d 73 (1st Cir. 1997), the defendants were convicted of firearms offenses, in which they were implicated by a "sting" operation. Part of the sting involved the use of a wired informer, whose conversations with the defendants were overheard by federal agents. The conversations were not recorded. The defendants claimed that the failure to record the conversations was a deliberate effort to avoid the creation or preservation of exculpatory evidence and was, therefore, in bad faith, and they moved for dismissal of the charges. The court upheld the convictions. *Youngblood*, it said, had to do with a failure to preserve evidence already in existence and did not go so far as to require that investigators create evidence for use at trial. It concluded that in some circumstances investigators might have an obligation to record conversations but that there was no evidence of bad faith in this case.

479. Relying on the state constitution, the Supreme Court of Connecticut has held that bad faith is not essential to a finding that the fail-

———

[17] Justice Stevens wrote an opinion concurring in the judgment. Justice Blackmun wrote a dissenting opinion, which Justice Brennan and Justice Marshall joined.

ure of police to preserve potentially exculpatory evidence is a denial of due process. Rather, "a trial court must decide each case depending on its own facts, assess the materiality of the unpreserved evidence and the degree of prejudice to the accused, and formulate a remedy that vindicates his or her rights. . . . The ultimate question for the trial court in such a case is: What remedy best serves the interests of justice?" State v. Morales, 657 A.2d 585 (Conn.1995).

480. How far must the prosecutor go in advising defense counsel of the existence of eye witnesses to an event whom the prosecutor intends not to call as witnesses? Assuming that he has an obligation to disclose the existence of witnesses who would testify affirmatively that the defendant was not the person who committed the crime in question, see, e.g., Jackson v. Wainwright, 390 F.2d 288 (5th Cir.1968), must the prosecutor, in order fairly to call witnesses who will identify the defendant, disclose the existence of witnesses who are unable to testify either way or who would testify that conditions were unsuitable for accurate observation? Can he constitutionally stop short of full disclosure of the names of all eye witnesses known to him? If so, should he do so as a matter of professional ethics? As a matter of good tactics? Who decides who is an eye witness? Does it make any difference whether the prosecutor intends to use any eye witnesses himself? Suppose he concludes that no one—neither those who will nor those who won't identify the defendant—was in a position to observe the event accurately and that he will prove his case entirely by circumstantial evidence. See generally Clarke v. Burke, 440 F.2d 853 (7th Cir.1971); Lee v. United States, 388 F.2d 737 (9th Cir.1968).

481. The practice of a prosecutor communicating with a defendant in the absence of his counsel is discussed at length and sharply criticized, in United States v. Lopez, 765 F.Supp. 1433 (N.D.Cal.1991), vacated, 4 F.3d 1455 (9th Cir.1993) (confirming criticism made by district court). See also United States v. Hammad, 858 F.2d 834 (2d Cir.1988).

Responsibility of the defense

482. "In the end, any allegation of suppression boils down to an assessment of what the State knows at trial in comparison to the knowledge held by the defense." Giles v. Maryland, 386 U.S. 66, 96 (1967) (White, J., concurring in judgment).

In determining whether the prosecutor's failure to disclose information to the defense requires reversal of a conviction, what is the significance of defense counsel's failure to pursue leads that would have led independently to the information?

The defendant was indicted for a violation of the Lindbergh Kidnapping Law, 18 U.S.C. § 1201. The government's case was that the defendant forcibly abducted a girl, drove with her across state lines, and thereafter raped her; he was not charged with rape, which was relevant only to the question whether the girl was returned unharmed (as bearing on the issue of "aggravation" of the kidnapping). The main effort of the defense was to show that the girl was not abducted but went willingly with the defendant. At a preliminary hearing, the girl testified that soon after the defendant's arrest she had been examined by a "Dr. Green." In fact, as federal agents and presumably the prosecutor knew, she had been examined by Dr. Stotlar. The prosecutor did not correct the girl's error or give any information to the defense about the examination. He did not call the doctor to testify or list him on the list of witnesses given to defense counsel, as required by 18 U.S.C. § 3432, p. 866 above. Defense counsel did not locate "Dr. Green" and did not pursue the matter. At trial, he objected to testimony of the girl about the physical examination on the ground of hearsay; he argued to the jury that the government should have produced the doctor to prove that there had been an act of intercourse. After the return of a verdict of guilty, defense counsel learned that the doctor's report indicated that there was no evidence of sexual intercourse. Should the conviction be reversed on appeal? Why (not)? If so, is reversal constitutionally required? See United States v. Poole, 379 F.2d 645 (7th Cir.1967). See also United States v. Benn, 476 F.2d 1127 (D.C.Cir.1972); Levin v. Katzenbach, 363 F.2d 287 (D.C.Cir.1966); United States ex rel. Thompson v. Dye, 221 F.2d 763 (3d Cir.1955).

483. The defendant was prosecuted for rape. A laboratory test for evidence on the defendant's clothing was negative. A police officer told the defendant that the result of the test was negative. There was no other disclosure of the result, and defense counsel did not learn about the test until after the defendant was convicted. Should the conviction be reversed? The Supreme Court of Illinois said no. People v. Raymond, 248 N.E.2d 663 (Ill.1969). The federal court of appeals said yes. United States ex rel. Raymond v. Illinois, 455 F.2d 62 (7th Cir.1971).

484. Expert testimony. Suppose there is doubt about a defendant's sanity at the time of the commission of a crime, and both the prosecutor and defense counsel employ psychiatrists to examine the defendant. If the prosecutor's examining psychiatrist advises him that in his opinion the defendant was not sane at the time the crime was committed or that he has substantial doubt about the defendant's sanity, must the prosecutor advise defense counsel of the psychiatrist's opinion far enough in advance of trial for him to consider and prepare for use of the insanity defense? Suppose several other psychiatrists have examined the defendant for the prosecutor and have concluded that the defendant was clearly sane (and the prosecutor has so advised defense counsel). Does it make a difference whether the insanity defense was raised at the trial? See Ashley v. Texas, 319 F.2d 80 (5th Cir.1963); cf. United States v. Spagnoulo, 960 F.2d 990 (11th Cir.1992).

How far should the prosecutor's duty to disclose *opinion* evidence be extended? Is there any reciprocal obligation of the defense to disclose opinion evidence? Does defense counsel have a professional obligation *not* to disclose opinion evidence?

Witnesses

485. "[T]he Fifth Amendment, in its direct application to the Federal Government, and in its bearing on the States by reason of the Fourteenth Amendment, forbids either comment by the prosecution on the accused's silence or instructions by the court that such silence is evidence of guilt." Griffin v. California, 380 U.S. 609, 615 (1965). *Griffin* was distinguished in United States v. Robinson, 485 U.S. 25 (1988) (5–3). There the Court held that the prosecutor's reference in his closing argument to the defendant's failure to testify, which was in response to defense counsel's statement that the government had not "allowed" the defendant to explain, was not impermissible.

If the defendant so requests, a trial judge is required to instruct the jury not to give evidentiary weight to the defendant's failure to testify. Carter v. Kentucky, 450 U.S. 288 (1981) (8–1). It does not violate the privilege against self-incrimination for the trial judge to give such an instruction over the defendant's objection. Lakeside v. Oregon, 435 U.S. 333 (1978).

FEDERAL RULES OF CRIMINAL PROCEDURE

Rule 17.

SUBPOENA

(a) For Attendance of Witnesses; Form; Issuance. A subpoena shall be issued by the clerk under the seal of the court. It shall state the name of the court and the title, if any, of the proceeding, and shall command each person to whom it is directed to attend and give testimony at the time and place specified therein. The clerk shall issue a subpoena, signed and sealed but otherwise in blank to a party requesting it, who shall fill in the blanks before it is served. A subpoena shall be issued by a United States magistrate judge in a proceeding before the magistrate judge, but it need not be under the seal of the court.

(b) Defendants Unable to Pay. The court shall order at any time that a subpoena be issued for service on a named witness upon an *ex parte* application of a defendant upon a satisfactory showing that the defendant is financially unable to pay the fees of the witness and that the presence of the witness is necessary to an adequate defense. If the court orders the subpoena to be issued the costs incurred by the process and the fees of the witness so subpoenaed shall be paid in the same manner in which similar costs and fees are paid in case of a witness subpoenaed in behalf of the government.

(c) For Production of Documentary Evidence and of Objects. A subpoena may also command the person to whom it is directed to produce the books, papers, documents or other objects designated therein. The court on motion made promptly may quash or modify the subpoena if compliance would be unreasonable or oppressive. The court may direct that books, papers, documents or objects designated in the subpoena be produced before the court at a time prior to the trial or prior to the time when they are to be offered in evidence and may upon their production permit the books, papers, documents or objects or portions thereof to be inspected by the parties and their attorneys.

(d) Service. A subpoena may be served by the marshal, by a deputy marshal or by any other person who is not a party and who is not less than 18 years of age. Service of a subpoena shall be made by delivering a copy thereof to the person named and by tendering to that person the fee for 1 day's attendance and the mileage allowed by law. Fees and mileage need not be tendered to the witness upon service of a subpoena issued in behalf of the United States or an officer or agency thereof.

(e) Place of Service.

(1) In United States. A subpoena requiring the attendance of a witness at a hearing or trial may be served at any place within the United States.

(2) Abroad. A subpoena directed to a witness in a foreign country shall issue under the circumstances and in the manner and be served as provided in Title 28, U.S.C., § 1783.

(f) For Taking Deposition; Place of Examination.

(1) Issuance. An order to take a deposition authorizes the issuance by the clerk of the court for the district in which the deposition is to be taken of subpoenas for the persons named or described therein.

(2) Place. The witness whose deposition is to be taken may be required by subpoena to attend at any place designated by the trial court, taking into account the convenience of the witness and the parties.

(g) Contempt. Failure by any person without adequate excuse to obey a subpoena served upon that person may be deemed a contempt of the court from which the subpoena issued or of the court for the district in which it issued if it was issued by a United States magistrate judge.

(h) Information Not Subject to Subpoena. Statements made by witnesses or prospective witnesses may not be subpoenaed from the government or the defendant under this rule, but shall be subject to production only in accordance with the provisions of Rule 26.2.[18]

---

486. In United States v. Hathcock, 441 F.2d 197 (5th Cir.1971), the defendant sought a subpoena under Rule 17(b) for the production of a witness then in a federal prison in Kansas to testify at a trial in Texas. The cost of transporting the witness was estimated at about $800. The trial judge talked to the witness by telephone, and the witness indicated that he would give material testimony favorable to the defendant. The judge told defense counsel that he would have the witness produced if counsel would assure the court that he would use the witness. Counsel refused to give that assurance because he had not yet been able to interview the witness in private. The witness was not produced. On appeal, the court held that the trial judge had abused his discretion under Rule 17(b).

"Our holding is merely that the appellant in this instance met the burden cast upon him by Rule 17(b) and that the district court abused its discretion in denying the production of the witness. The requirement that defense counsel bind himself in advance to put [the witness] on the stand, regardless of trial developments and the necessity counsel recognized to preserve options as to tactical trial decisions, was doubtless motivated by a desire to save money for the government. It was nonetheless, in our judgment, the imposition of unreasonable conditions upon the right to compulsory process and an almost classic example of abuse of judicial discretion. In stating this we emphasize that our decision in no wise impinges upon the trial judge's necessary discretion in the initial determination of the need for the testimony of the witness, arrived at by weighing numerous factors including materiality, relevancy and competency. Certainly there are frivolous requests for production of witnesses and just as certainly defendants may seek to abuse the right to compulsory process at government expense. In close cases the district court must exercise its sound discretion, bearing in mind that the burden of showing frivolousness or abuse of process is on the government." Id. at 200. See United States v. Greschner, 802 F.2d 373 (10th Cir.1986) (ruling on request for subpoena within discretion of trial

[18] See p. 1024 below.

AO 89 (Rev. 7/95) Subpoena in a Criminal Case

United States District Court

———————————— DISTRICT OF ————————————

V.

SUBPOENA IN A
CRIMINAL CASE

CASE NUMBER:

TO:

☐ YOU ARE COMMANDED to appear in the United States District Court at the place, date and time specified below, or any subsequent place, date and time set by the court, to testify in the above referenced case. This subpoena shall remain in effect until you are granted leave to depart by the court or by an officer acting on behalf of the court.

PLACE	COURTROOM
	DATE AND TIME

☐ YOU ARE ALSO COMMANDED to bring with you the following document(s) or object(s):

U.S. MAGISTRATE JUDGE OR CLERK OF COURT	DATE
(BY) DEPUTY CLERK	

ATTORNEY'S NAME, ADDRESS AND PHONE NUMBER

judge); United States v. Hegwood, 562 F.2d 946 (5th Cir.1977) (subpoena properly refused); Welsh v. United States, 404 F.2d 414 (5th Cir.1968) (refusal to issue subpoena was error).

The purpose of allowing defense counsel to obtain subpoenas *ex parte* under Rule 17(b) is to protect an indigent defendant against advance disclosure of his defense. See *Greschner*, above; United States v. Meriwether, 486 F.2d 498 (5th Cir.1973).

Rule 17(c). See United States v. Messercola, 701 F.Supp. 482 (D.N.J.1988), upholding issuance of a subpoena directing a person to submit to being photographed by the FBI, so the photograph could be used in a photo array to be shown to prosecution witnesses.

487. After failing to respond to a subpoena, Mrs. Carradine was brought into court pursuant to a bench warrant to testify for the state in a prosecution for homicide. After answering preliminary questions, she refused to testify because she feared for her own life and the lives of her six children. The homicide involved members of a slum "youth gang" in Chicago. The state offered to relocate her elsewhere in the city or in the United States, and offered to provide protection for her and her family. She indicated that she did not believe that they could protect her against members of the gang, and said that when she originally gave information about the homicide to a state prosecutor she did so only because he had promised her that she would not have to appear and testify. When she continued to refuse to testify, she was committed to jail. After two weeks in jail, she still refused to testify. She was held in contempt and sentenced to imprisonment for six months. Observing that the circumstances of the case were "particularly distressing," the Supreme Court of Illinois affirmed the sentence. It quoted remarks of the trial court: " '[O]ne of the problems that the court has is that unless we receive the cooperation of the citizens who see certain alleged events take place these events are not going to be rooted out, nor are perpetrators of these acts going to be brought before the bar of justice unless citizens stand up to be counted, and I think this [fear] is not a valid reason for not testifying. If it's a valid reason then we might as well close the doors.' " People v. Carradine, 287 N.E.2d 670, 672 (Ill.1972).

488. 18 U.S.C. § 3144. Release or detention of a material witness.

If it appears from an affidavit filed by a party that the testimony of a person is material in a criminal proceeding, and if it is shown that it may become impracticable to secure the presence of the person by subpoena, a judicial officer may order the arrest of the person and treat the person in accordance with the provisions of section 3142 of this title. No material witness may be detained because of inability to comply with any condition of release if the testimony of such witness can adequately be secured by deposition, and if further detention is not necessary to prevent a failure of justice. Release of a material witness may be delayed for a reasonable period of time until the deposition of the witness can be taken pursuant to the Federal Rules of Criminal Procedure.

See Bacon v. United States, 449 F.2d 933 (9th Cir.1971) (witness in grand jury proceedings).

489. The defendant was prosecuted for murder. At trial, defense counsel offered to stipulate to the identity of the victim and to the fact of death. Over objection, the trial judge allowed the victim's mother to testify to those facts. During her testimony, she broke down and wept. The court upheld the prosecutor's refusal to accept the stipulation. "The weeping of the deceased's mother, a natural reaction to her testimony concerning her son, did not result in reversible prejudice to defendant." People v. Hairston, 294 N.E.2d 748, 753–54 (Ill.1973). See United States v. O'Shea, 724 F.2d 1514 (11th Cir.1984) (offer to stipulate prior conviction of murder); People v. Nicholls, 245 N.E.2d 771, 776–77 (Ill.1969) (offer to stipulate to content of photographs); People v. Hills, 532 N.Y.S.2d 269, 273 (App.Div.1988) (offer to stipulate injuries sustained by victim; whether or not to accept stipulation is "wholly within the prosecutor's discretion"). See generally United States v. Schwartz, 790 F.2d 1059 (3d Cir.1986).

In Old Chief v. United States, 519 U.S. 172, (1997) (5–4), the Court held that the district court abused its discretion when it refused to accept the defendant's offer to stipulate a prior conviction to establish that element of the offense (possession of a firearm by someone with a prior felony conviction, 18 U.S.C. § 922(g)(1)) and instead allowed the prosecutor to present evidence of the prior conviction. The evidence indicated the nature of the offense and raised the possibility that the jury would rely on the prior conviction as evidence of the crime charged. In that circumstance, the Court said, the district court should have accepted the stipulation because its "probative value [was] substantially outweighed by the danger of unfair prejudice," as provided in Federal Rule of Evidence 403.

The Court affirmed "the accepted rule that the prosecution is entitled to prove its case free from any defendant's option to stipulate the evidence away," as a general matter, 117 S.Ct. at 654, but said that it did not apply when all that was at stake was whether or not the defendant had a prior conviction.

490. "The exclusion of witnesses from the courtroom during trial is a time-honored practice designed to prevent the shaping of testimony by hearing what other witnesses say. . . . The decision to sequester or not is within the court's discretionary power and is reviewable only for abuse. . . .

"This court has held that permitting a witness to testify notwithstanding his disregard of the court's order of sequestration is not error, but is within the court's discretion. . . . Such is the general rule following Holder

v. United States, 150 U.S. 91, 92 . . . (1893), where it is stated: 'If a witness disobeys the order of withdrawal, while he may be proceeded against for contempt and his testimony is open to comment to the jury by reason of his conduct, he is not thereby disqualified, and the weight of authority is that he cannot be excluded on that ground merely, although the right to exclude under particular circumstances may be supported as within the sound discretion of the trial court.'

"The Supreme Court there upheld the trial court's admission of testimony from a disobedient witness and had no occasion to spell out the 'particular circumstances' which would support a refusal to permit the witness to testify, nor has it done so in any subsequent case.

"Since the purpose of the order is to gain assurance of credibility and its violation is a legitimate subject of comment in this respect, it seems proper that unless the violation has somehow so discredited the witness as to render his testimony incredible as a matter of law he should not be disqualified from testifying. Since a refusal to permit him to testify penalizes the litigant rather than the disobedient witness himself, it would seem that the 'special circumstances' justifying such refusal should be such as tend to make the litigant a party to and justly subject to sanction for the witness's disobedience." Taylor v. United States, 388 F.2d 786, 788 (9th Cir.1967).

See Barnard v. Henderson, 514 F.2d 744 (5th Cir.1975) (exclusion of witness who inadvertently violated order was error). The trial court's refusal to allow a witness to testify was upheld in United States v. Kiliyan, 456 F.2d 555 (8th Cir.1972) (witness, defendant's wife, remained in court after need for her testimony appeared).

In Geders v. United States, 425 U.S. 80, 87 (1976), the Court affirmed that the trial judge has "broad power to sequester witnesses before, during, and after their testimony," but said that an order directing the defendant not to consult with defense counsel during an overnight recess between the defendant's direct testimony and cross-examination violated his right to counsel under the Sixth Amendment. The Court observed that there were other methods to avoid the danger of improper coaching of the defendant in such circumstances, including arrangement of the trial schedule to avoid prolonged interruptions of testimony.

Geders does not apply to a short recess while the defendant is testifying as a witness. Perry v. Leeke, 488 U.S. 272 (1989) (6–3). The recess in this case was for 15 minutes, between direct and cross examination. The Court reasoned that although a defendant might discuss general trial matters with his counsel overnight, during a short recess of the kind involved here, a defendant was unlikely to discuss anything other than the testimony he was then giving; and a defendant has no right to interrupt his testimony and discuss it with counsel while he is appearing as a witness. See Mudd v. United States, 798 F.2d 1509 (D.C.Cir.1986) (order that counsel not discuss testimony with defendant, then on the witness stand, over weekend was violation of right to counsel that requires reversal without showing of prejudice).

Lee Won Sing v. United States

215 F.2d 680 (D.C.Cir.1954).

■ PER CURIAM.

Appellant was indicted in one count for the illegal purchase and in another for the illegal concealment of narcotics . . . . Lee Poo was jointly charged with appellant in these counts, and separately in three others in the same indictment. He pleaded guilty and testified as the sole witness for appellant, who was convicted as charged. Had the jury believed Lee Poo's testimony the verdict might have been otherwise. His credibility, therefore, was an important factor in the case.

In cross-examining Lee Poo Government counsel asked if it were not a fact that appellant was giving him $20,000 to plead guilty—"to take the plea in this case". No objection was made to the question. Lee Poo answered in the negative and the Government did not offer evidence on the subject. After the judge's charge and before the jury retired defense counsel, pointing out the impact the question must have had on the jury, with its implication that Lee Poo was being paid to perjure himself, requested the court to instruct the jury that the Government, not having brought in evidence to the contrary, was bound by the negative answer given by Lee Poo. The court refused to charge in this manner but did instruct the jury that their verdict must rest upon the testimony of witnesses and other evidence, that questions are not evidence, and that the only thing the jury could properly regard as evidence were answers to questions propounded.

The subject matter of the question of course was highly relevant, having to do with the guilt of appellant and with bribery and perhaps perjury affecting Lee Poo's testimony. But it could not properly be asked unless the prosecution had evidence of or reasonable ground to believe the truth of its implication. . . . Since no effort was made to prove its truth, after Lee Poo's denial, the propriety of the question had to depend upon the existence of reasonable ground. All we have on this is that after the jury retired Government counsel at a bench conference advised the court of an anonymous letter in the hands of the police "from some Chinaman to somebody" to the effect that appellant gave Lee Poo $20,000 to take the blame, and also said there were like rumors. This, without at least some showing of an investigation and its result, is not enough, particularly in view of the highly prejudicial character of the question.

The general instruction given by the court did not remedy the particular problem. The damaging character of the question, considered with the inconclusiveness of the evidence of appellant's guilt, called for a more direct and positive elimination of its influence upon the jury, when request for some instruction to that end was made. For this reason the judgment will be reversed and a new trial awarded.

. . .

491. Criminal record. Whether or not the court gives cautionary instructions, the jury will often regard a defendant's failure to testify as an indication of his guilt. Cf. Griffin v. California, 380 U.S. 609, 617 (1965) (Stewart, J., dissenting). Consequently, there is great pressure on the defendant to testify. The rules of evidence generally permit the record of a witness, including the defendant, to be brought out on cross-examination to show that he is not a person of good character; the more precise inference that the jury is invited to make is that since he is a person who has been convicted of a crime he is likely to lie. It is commonly believed, however, that a jury is unable or unwilling to confine its regard of the defendant's criminal record to its consideration of his veracity as a witness and that it will make the impermissible leap from prior convictions to present guilt.

Rule 609(a) of the Rules of Evidence for United States Courts and Magistrates provides: "General rule. For the purpose of attacking the credibility of a witness, (1) evidence that a witness other than an accused has been convicted of a crime shall be admitted, subject to Rule 403, if the crime was punishable by death or imprisonment in excess of one year under the law under which the witness was convicted, and evidence that an accused has been convicted of such a crime shall be admitted if the court determines that the probative value of admitting this evidence outweighs its prejudicial effect to the accused; and (2) evidence that any witness has been convicted of a crime shall be admitted if it involved dishonesty or false statement, regardless of the punishment." Additional provisions of the rule limit or prohibit the use of such evidence if the conviction is more than ten years old and the person has not been confined pursuant to the conviction for more than ten years, if the conviction has been pardoned or annulled, etc., and if the conviction is a juvenile adjudication. The history of the adoption of the rule and its interpretation are discussed at length in United States v. Smith, 551 F.2d 348, 356–69 (D.C.Cir.1976). For a review of state cases and federal cases before the adoption of Rule 609, see People v. Jackson, 217 N.W.2d 22 (Mich.1974). On the use of prior convictions to impeach the defendant, see generally People v. Barrick, 654 P.2d 1243 (Cal.1982).

In United States v. Toney, 615 F.2d 277 (5th Cir.1980), the court held that under Rule 609(a)(2) of the Federal Rules of Evidence, a trial judge has no authority to prevent a prosecutor from using evidence of a past crime involving "dishonesty or false statement" to impeach the defendant as a witness, despite the possibility that the prejudicial effect of the evidence would outweigh its probative value. See also United States v. Washington, 746 F.2d 104 (2d Cir.1984), upholding a ruling that if the defendant testified, a prior conviction for the same kind of crime for which he was being prosecuted would be admissible on cross-examination.

In order to appeal from a trial judge's ruling *in limine* that a defendant's testimony may be impeached by a prior conviction, the defendant must testify. In the context of the actual testimony, the judge might change the previous ruling; or the prosecutor might conclude not to use the prior conviction for impeachment. Luce v. United States, 469 U.S. 38 (1984).

Luce was distinguished in Biller v. Lopes, 834 F.2d 41 (2d Cir.1987). There, the defendant requested a ruling *in limine* that a previous conviction, then on appeal in the state courts on the ground that it had been obtained in violation of the defendant's privilege against compulsory self-incrimination, would not be admissible on cross-examination, if he took the stand. The trial court declined to make such a ruling, and the defendant did not testify. The previous conviction was later overturned. The court of appeals held that, in those circumstances, failure to make the requested ruling had the effect of extending the constitutional error at the first trial and thereby denying the defendant's privilege against compulsory self-incrimination at the second trial.

Finding *Luce* "neither compelling nor applicable," the Colorado court held that a defendant has a right to a ruling on the admissibility of a prior conviction for impeachment before deciding whether to testify. Apodaca v. People, 712 P.2d 467 (Colo.1985). "A timely judicial ruling on a defendant's motion to suppress prior conviction evidence for the purpose of impeachment serves the vital function of providing the defendant with the meaningful opportunity to make the type of informed decision contemplated by the fundamental nature of the right to testify in one's own defense. The trial court deprived the defendant of that opportunity when it refused to rule on the defendant's motion to prohibit prosecutorial use of prior conviction evidence until such time as the prosecution actually sought to impeach the defendant with such evidence. In effect, the defendant could have testified in this case only by foregoing any opportunity to obtain in advance of actually taking the witness stand a judicial ruling on the most critical factor bearing on his decision whether to testify—that is, the constitutional admissibility of his prior conviction for the purpose of impeachment. We conclude that the trial court's refusal to timely rule on the defendant's motion impermissibly burdened the defendant's exercise of his constitutional right to testify in his own behalf . . . ." Id. at 473.

Similar problems may arise when a defendant's character is put in issue generally and witnesses are asked about their knowledge of specific incidents in the defendant's life. Michelson v. United States, 335 U.S. 469 (1948), discusses at length the evidentiary rules governing character evidence. Concurring in the "general opinion . . . that much of this law is archaic, paradoxical and full of compromises and compensations by which an irrational advantage to one side is offset by a poorly reasoned counterprivilege to the other," id. at 486, the Court nevertheless declined an invitation to adopt new rules. Justice Rutledge, dissenting, argued that to allow a prosecutor to cross-examine character witnesses concerning their knowledge of specific incidents in the defendant's life that have little bearing on his present reputation but "give room for play of the jury's unguarded conjecture and prejudice" was "neither fair play nor *due* process," id. at 495. See Spencer v. Texas, 385 U.S. 554 (1967) (jury may be informed of prior convictions before determination of guilt for sole purpose of sentencing pursuant to habitual criminal statute). See also, discussing *Spencer*, Marshall v. Lonberger, 459 U.S. 422 (1983) (5–4), especially Justice Stevens's dissenting opinion, id. at 447.

In situations of this kind does the prosecutor have an obligation to weigh the probative value of evidence on the issue with respect to which it is admissible against the probable or possible prejudice to the defendant on an issue with respect to which the evidence is not admissible? Can he conscientiously rely on the rules of evidence as having made the relevant decisions for him? Can he rely on the judge's broad authority to control the conduct of a trial (and the judge's willingness to exercise his authority)? Does he have an *obligation* so to rely?

If a prosecutor determines not to use certain rebuttal evidence, such as a defendant's criminal record, because he thinks that it would be improper for him to do so, should he so advise defense counsel in time for him to take advantage of the prosecutor's decision? See United States v. Henderson, 489 F.2d 802, 806 (5th Cir.1973): "[I]t is settled in this circuit that a defendant is not entitled to a prospective ruling on the admissibility of impeachment evidence before he takes the stand. . . . It is the defense counsel's responsibility to evaluate the law and plan his strategy based upon his evaluation; the defendant must take the stand before he is entitled to a ruling on the admissibility of impeachment evidence." Accord United States v. Kennedy, 714 F.2d 968 (9th Cir.1983). What justification can there be for such a rule? Compare United States v. Oakes, 565 F.2d 170 (1st Cir.1977), encouraging the trial court to make an advance ruling.

Does defense counsel have any reciprocal obligations? Suppose the prosecutrix in a rape case was convicted ten years earlier of soliciting prostitution. Suppose further that defense counsel is convinced on the basis of reasonably certain evidence that the conviction was questionable substantively and procedurally defective (say, because obtained without the aid of counsel). Suppose also that defense counsel is convinced on the basis of reasonably certain evidence that the prosecutrix has lived an exemplary life for the past ten years and that he is aware that her husband and two young children, who know nothing about her conviction, will be in the courtroom during the trial. Should defense counsel cross-examine the prosecutrix about her conviction? Cf. Alford v. United States, 282 U.S. 687 (1931).

Suppose the positions are reversed. The woman in question is a witness for the defense. Her testimony will be that she knows the defendant and knows that he has a reputation for good character. Defense counsel, over objection by the prosecutor, has been allowed to show the witness's "credentials," outlined above. Should the prosecutor seek to cross-examine the witness about her conviction?

492. The use of "mug shots" at trial to help a witness make an identification is discussed and additional cases are cited in United States v. Harrington, 490 F.2d 487 (2d Cir.1973). The danger of such use is that it may reveal that a defendant who does not take the stand and whose criminal record would not otherwise be before the jury does in fact have a record. The court concluded that there were three prerequisites for introduction of "mug shots": "1. The government must have a demonstrable need to introduce the photographs; and 2. The photographs themselves, if shown to the jury, must not imply that the defendant has a prior criminal record; and 3. The manner of introduction at trial must be such that it does not draw particular attention to the source or implications of the photographs." Id. at 494. See United States v. Fosher, 568 F.2d 207 (1st Cir.1978) (photographs improperly admitted); with which compare United States v. Cannon, 903 F.2d 849 (1st Cir.1990) (admission of photographs upheld).

493. What obligation does the government have to help a defendant to obtain the testimony of a witness?

In United States v. Domenech, 476 F.2d 1229 (2d Cir.1973), the defendant summoned his brother-in-law, Pereira, to testify. Pereira refused to testify, claiming the privilege against self-incrimination. It appeared that he had pleaded guilty to one count of an indictment and that the remaining count was to be dismissed after he had been sentenced. His claim of privilege was based on the still outstanding count. Should the prosecutor have been required to dismiss that count in order to make Pereira's testimony available to the defendant? The court of appeals said: "Appellant urges that the Government deliberately left count 2 open against Pereira in order to insure that he would not testify for appellant. There is no adequate proof of this charge; leaving the remaining counts open until sentence on the counts to which an accused had pled is the common practice—a reasonable procedure which avoids complexities where the defendant moves before sentence to set aside his guilty plea. In this instance the possible consequence of following the normal usage was to give Pereira a good excuse for refusing to take the stand, and thus of avoiding the dilemma, on the one hand, of a possible perjury charge or a feared impact on his sentence if he testified favorably to Domenech, or, on the other, of giving evidence against his close relative. But we see no escape from holding that Pereira had a constitutional right to act as he did, and, in the absence of any proof of deliberate manipulation or pre-arrangement by the United States Attorney, there is no penalty we can or should impose on the Government because the witness's exercise of his right, for his own purposes, may have redounded to the prosecutor's advantage." Id. at 1231.

The practice of deporting illegal aliens who are material witnesses to an offense for which the defendant is later prosecuted is discussed in United States v. Valenzuela-Bernal, 458 U.S. 858 (1982) (7–2). Relying on Roviaro v. United States, 353 U.S. 53 (1957), p. 1018 below, the Court said that deportation of such persons before the defense counsel has had an opportunity to interview them is not always a violation of the defendant's constitutional rights. Such deportation furthers the federal immigration law and avoids the financial and physical burdens of prolonged detention. In order to establish a violation of his rights under either the Compulsory Process Clause of the Sixth Amendment or the Due Process Clause, the defendant must make a plausible showing that the lost testimony of the deported witnesses would have been material and favorable to the defense, in ways not merely cumulative to the testimony of available witnesses. The Court observed that the lack of an opportunity to interview the witnesses before they were deported would justify relaxing the requirement of specificity of the showing of materiality; but it did not justify dispensing with such a showing altogether.

The United States Attorney has broad authority to seek immunity for a potential witness whose "testimony or other information . . . may be necessary to the public interest" and who has invoked or is likely to invoke the privilege against self-incrimination. 18 U.S.C. § 6003(b). Should she ever be required to do so (subject to dismissal of the prosecution if she refuses) in order to obtain testimony favorable to the defendant? The courts have generally said not. In United States v. Turkish, 623 F.2d 769, 777 (2d Cir.1980), for example, the court said that there is not "in the Due Process Clause a general requirement that defense witness immunity must be ordered whenever it seems fair to grant it." Cf. United States v. Chitty, 760 F.2d 425 (2d Cir.1985). In *Chitty*, observing that "not every unfairness is a violation of due process," the court said: "To raise a constitutional claim, the witness' testimony must have been material, exculpatory, and neither cumulative nor available from any other source." Most courts have rejected the argument that the trial court has inherent authority to grant immunity despite the opposition of the prosecution. E.g., United States v. Thevis, 665 F.2d 616, 639 (5th Cir.1982): "[D]istrict courts may not grant immunity to defense witnesses simply because that witness has essential exculpatory information unavailable from other sources. . . . [T]he two major arguments against granting such judicial use immunity are that the immunity decision would carry the courts into policy assessments which are the traditional domain of the executive branch, and that the immunity would be subject to abuse." See also United States v. Capozzi, 883 F.2d 608 (8th Cir.1989); United States v. Paris, 827 F.2d 395 (9th Cir.1987). But see Government of the Virgin Islands v. Smith, 615 F.2d 964 (3d Cir.1980), holding that the government should be required to seek immunity where necessary to the fact-finding process and that, alternatively, the court has inherent authority to grant use immunity where a fair trial so requires.

Even if the prosecutor is not required to seek immunity for a defense witness, should she sometimes do so? If defense counsel asks her to do so and she declines, should the court at the request of defense counsel give a missing witness instruction?

In Bowles v. United States, 439 F.2d 536 (D.C.Cir.1970), the defendant was prosecuted for murder. Part of his defense was that Raymond Smith was in fact guilty of the crime. Smith indicated out of the hearing of the jury that he would invoke the privilege against self-incrimination. The court declined to give a missing witness instruction or to let the jury know why Smith was not called as a witness. He instructed counsel not to mention Smith's invocation of the privilege. On appeal, the conviction was affirmed.

"We find no error in these rulings. It is well settled that the jury is not entitled to draw any inferences from the decision of a witness to exercise his constitutional privilege whether those inferences be favorable to the prosecution or the defense. . . . The rule is grounded not only in the constitutional notion that guilt may not be inferred from the exercise of the Fifth Amendment privilege but also in the danger that a witness's invoking the Fifth Amendment in the presence of the jury will have a disproportionate impact on their deliberations. The jury may think it high courtroom drama of probative significance when a witness 'takes the Fifth.' In reality the probative value of the event is almost entirely undercut by the absence of any requirement that the witness justify his fear of incrimination and by the fact that it is a form of evidence not subject to cross-examination. . . .

"An obvious corollary to these precepts is the rule that a witness should not be put on the stand for the purpose of having him exercise his privilege before the jury. . . . This would only invite the jury to make an improper inference. For the same reason no valid purpose can be served by informing the jury that a witness has chosen to exercise his constitutional privilege. That fact is not one the jury is entitled to rely on in reaching its verdict.

"The other side of the coin, however, is the rule that the jury is not entitled to draw any inference from a failure to testify that is ascribable to the witness's reliance on his Fifth Amendment privilege. . . . Indeed, this court has held it inappropriate to spark a missing witness inference against the party who would have been called on to produce a witness to incriminate himself. . . .

"In the instant case the District Court properly admonished counsel to make no mention in their closing argument of the lack of testimony from a witness counsel knew would have invoked the Fifth Amendment. Certainly the judge was correct in refusing to charge the jury that an inference could be drawn from the absence of such a witness. . . .

"However, the trial judge could properly have given a neutralizing instruction, one calculated to reduce the danger that the jury will in fact draw an inference from the absence of such a witness. Had either counsel requested the court to instruct the jury that they should draw no inference from Smith's absence because he was not available to either side, it would have been error to refuse this instruction. Appellant's trial counsel did not request such an instruction. There are meaningful tactical reasons why a defense trial counsel might elect not to seek such an instruction. Had such an instruction been sought in this case, the District Court, which noted in colloquy with counsel that Smith 'was not available to either side,' would undoubtedly have granted the request. As it is we see no error in the court's handling of the issues presented when Smith decided to invoke his Fifth Amendment privilege." Id. at 541–42.

Bowles states the general rule. See, e.g., United States v. Lacouture, 495 F.2d 1237 (5th Cir.1974). In Namet v. United States, 373 U.S. 179 (1963), the prosecutor called witnesses who invoked the privilege against self-incrimination; the Court found that there was no error. Compare Robbins v. Small, 371 F.2d 793 (1st Cir.1967) (conviction reversed). See also United States v. Compton, 365 F.2d 1 (6th Cir.1966) (conviction reversed).

494. The defendant was prosecuted for murder. During the voir dire, defense counsel had identified Frank Twitty as a prospective defense witness. After the first day of trial, the prosecutor told Twitty that if the facts were as they appeared, Twitty might himself be liable for several crimes, such as obstruction of justice and being an accessory after the fact of the murder. He advised Twitty to consult an independent lawyer about his own constitutional rights and not to rely on the defendant's lawyer. Was the prosecutor's conduct proper?

After the court was informed of the above, it asked a public defender to advise Twitty. Later, Twitty concluded that he would not testify. The defendant was convicted. Should the conviction be reversed? See United States v. Smith, 478 F.2d 976 (D.C.Cir.1973). See also United States v. Touw, 769 F.2d 571 (9th Cir.1985); United States v. Morrison, 535 F.2d 223 (3d Cir.1976). Compare Peeler v. Wyrick, 734 F.2d 378 (8th Cir.1984) (police officer did not testify as character witness for defendants because police chief threatened him with loss of job; conviction affirmed).

In Webb v. Texas, 409 U.S. 95 (1972), the Court found that the trial judge's threats to prosecute the defendant's only witness for perjury if he lied on the stand "effectively drove that witness off the stand" and denied the defendant due process of law. *Webb* is applied in United States v. Arthur, 949 F.2d 211 (6th Cir.1991), in which the court held that it was an abuse of discretion to induce a defense witness to assert the privilege against self-incrimination. See also Anderson v. Warden, Maryland Penitentiary, 696 F.2d 296, 298 (4th Cir.1982) (judge "openly and successfully" pressed defense witnesses to change testimony). *Webb* is distinguished in United States v. Blackwell, 694 F.2d 1325 (D.C.Cir.1982) (warning about perjury properly given).

495. In Jaffee v. Redmond, 518 U.S. 1, (1996) (8–1), the Court held that under Rule 501 of the Federal Rules of Evidence (providing generally that testimonial privilege shall be governed "by the principles of the common law as they may be interpreted by the courts of the United States in the light of reason and experience") "confidential communications between a licensed psychotherapist and her patients in the course of diagnosis or treatment are protected from compelled disclosure." Id. at 15. The Court held also (7–2) that the privilege extends to confidential communications "made to licensed social workers in the course of psychotherapy." Id. The Court noted that all 50 states and the District of Columbia have enacted some form of psychotherapist privilege.

496. "[W]hen a defendant demonstrates to the trial judge that his sanity at the time of the offense is to be a significant factor at trial, the State must, at a minimum, assure the defendant access to a competent psychiatrist who will conduct an appropriate examination and assist in evaluation, preparation, and presentation of the defense. This is not to say, of course, that the indigent defendant has a constitutional right to choose a psychiatrist of his personal liking or to receive funds to hire his own. Our concern is that the indigent defendant have access to a competent psychiatrist for the purpose we have discussed, and as in the case of the provision of counsel we leave to the States the decision on how to implement this right." Ake v. Oklahoma, 470 U.S. 68, 83 (1985) (8–1).

————

California v. Green

399 U.S. 149, 90 S.Ct. 1930, 26 L.Ed.2d 489 (1970).

■ MR. JUSTICE WHITE delivered the opinion of the Court.

Section 1235 of the California Evidence Code, effective as of January 1, 1967, provides that "[e]vidence of a statement made by a witness is not made inadmissible by the hearsay rule if the statement is inconsistent with his testimony at the hearing and is offered in compliance with Section 770."[19] In People v. Johnson, 68 Cal.2d 646, 441 P.2d 111 (1968) . . . the California Supreme Court held that prior statements of a witness which were not subject to cross-examination when originally made, could not be introduced under this section to prove the charges against a defendant without violating the defendant's right of confrontation guaranteed by the Sixth Amendment and made applicable to the States by the Fourteenth Amendment. In the case now before us the California Supreme Court applied the same ban to a prior statement of a witness made at a preliminary hearing, under oath and subject to full cross-examination by an adequately counseled defendant. We cannot agree with the California court for two reasons, one of which involves rejection of the holding in People v. Johnson.

I

In January 1967, one Melvin Porter, a 16-year-old minor, was arrested for selling marihuana to an undercover police officer. Four days after his arrest, while in the custody of juvenile authorities, Porter named respondent Green as his supplier. As recounted later by one Officer Wade, Porter claimed that Green had called him earlier that month, had asked him to sell some "stuff" or "grass," and had that same afternoon personally delivered a shopping bag containing 29 "baggies" of marihuana. It was from this supply

———

19. Cal.Evid.Code § 1235 (1966). Section 770 merely requires that the witness be given an opportunity to explain or deny the prior statement at some point in the trial. See Cal.Evid.Code § 770 (1966) . . .

that Porter had made his sale to the undercover officer. A week later, Porter testified at respondent's preliminary hearing. He again named respondent as his supplier, although he now claimed that instead of personally delivering the marihuana, Green had showed him where to pick up the shopping bag, hidden in the bushes at Green's parents' house. Porter's story at the preliminary hearing was subjected to extensive cross-examination by respondent's counsel—the same counsel who represented respondent at his subsequent trial. At the conclusion of the hearing, respondent was charged with furnishing marihuana to a minor in violation of California law.

Respondent's trial took place some two months later before a court sitting without a jury. The State's chief witness was again young Porter. But this time Porter, in the words of the California Supreme Court, proved to be "markedly evasive and uncooperative on the stand." People v. Green, 70 Cal.2d 654, 657, 451 P.2d 422, 423 (1969). He testified that respondent had called him in January 1967, and asked him to sell some unidentified "stuff." He admitted obtaining shortly thereafter 29 plastic "baggies" of marihuana, some of which he sold. But when pressed as to whether respondent had been his supplier, Porter claimed that he was uncertain how he obtained the marihuana, primarily because he was at the time on "acid" (LSD), which he had taken 20 minutes before respondent phoned. Porter claimed that he was unable to remember the events which followed the phone call, and that the drugs he had taken prevented his distinguishing fact from fantasy. . . .

At various points during Porter's direct examination, the prosecutor read excerpts from Porter's preliminary hearing testimony. This evidence was admitted under § 1235 for the truth of the matter contained therein. With his memory "refreshed" by his preliminary hearing testimony, Porter "guessed" that he had indeed obtained the marihuana from the backyard of respondent's parents' home, and had given the money from its sale to respondent. On cross-examination, however, Porter indicated that it was his memory of the preliminary testimony which was "mostly" refreshed, rather than his memory of the events themselves, and he was still unsure of the actual episode. . . . Later in the trial, Officer Wade testified, relating Porter's earlier statement that respondent had personally delivered the marihuana. This statement was also admitted as substantive evidence. Porter admitted making the statement . . . and insisted that he had been telling the truth as he then believed it both to Officer Wade and at the preliminary hearing; but he insisted that he was also telling the truth now in claiming inability to remember the actual events.

Respondent was convicted. The District Court of Appeal reversed, holding that the use of Porter's prior statements for the truth of the matter asserted therein, denied respondent his right of confrontation under the California Supreme Court's recent decision in People v. Johnson, supra. The California Supreme Court affirmed, finding itself "impelled" by recent decisions of this Court to hold § 1235 unconstitutional insofar as it permitted the substantive use of prior inconsistent statements of a witness, even though the statements were subject to cross-examination at a prior hearing. We granted the State's petition for certiorari. . . .

II

The California Supreme Court construed the Confrontation Clause of the Sixth Amendment to require the exclusion of Porter's prior testimony offered in evidence to prove the State's case against Green because in the court's view, neither the right to cross-examine Porter at the trial concerning his current and prior testimony, nor the opportunity to cross-examine Porter at the preliminary hearing satisfied the commands of the Confrontation Clause. We think the California court was wrong on both counts.

Positing that this case posed an instance of a witness who gave trial testimony inconsistent with his prior, out-of-court statements, the California court, on the authority of its decision in People v. Johnson, supra, held that belated cross-examination before the trial court, "is not an adequate substitute for the right to cross-examination contemporaneous with the original testimony before a different tribunal." People v. Green, supra, at 659, 451 P.2d at 425. We disagree.

Section 1235 of the California Evidence Code represents a considered choice by the California Legislature between two opposing positions concerning the extent to which a witness' prior statements may be introduced at trial without violating hearsay rules of evidence. The orthodox view, adopted in most jurisdictions, has been that the out-of-court statements are inadmissible for the usual reasons that have led to the exclusion of hearsay statements: the statement may not have been made under oath; the declarant may not have been subjected to cross-examination when he made the statement; and the jury cannot observe the declarant's demeanor at the time he made the statement. Accordingly, under this view, the statement may not be offered to show the truth of the matters asserted therein, but can be introduced under appropriate limiting instructions to impeach the credibility of the witness who has changed his story at trial.

In contrast, the minority view adopted in some jurisdictions and supported by most legal commentators and by recent proposals to codify the law of evidence would permit the substantive use of prior inconsistent statements on the theory that the usual dangers of hearsay are largely nonexistent where the witness testifies at trial. "The whole purpose of the Hearsay rule has been already satisfied [because] the witness is present and subject to cross-examination [and] [t]here is ample opportunity to test him as to the basis for his former statement."[20]

Our task in this case is not to decide which of these positions, purely as a matter of the law of evidence, is the sounder. The issue before us is the considerably narrower one of whether a defendant's constitutional right "to be confronted with the witnesses against him" is necessarily inconsistent with a State's decision to change its hearsay rules to reflect the minority view described above. While it may readily be conceded that hearsay rules

---

20. 3 [J.] Wigmore [Evidence (3rd ed. 1940)] § 1018.

and the Confrontation Clause are generally designed to protect similar values, it is quite a different thing to suggest that the overlap is complete and that the Confrontation Clause is nothing more or less than a codification of the rules of hearsay and their exceptions as they existed historically at common law. Our decisions have never established such a congruence; indeed, we have more than once found a violation of confrontation values even though the statements in issue were admitted under an arguably recognized hearsay exception. . . . The converse is equally true: merely because evidence is admitted in violation of a long-established hearsay rule does not lead to the automatic conclusion that confrontation rights have been denied.

Given the similarity of the values protected, however, the modification of a State's hearsay rules to create new exceptions for the admission of evidence against a defendant, will often raise questions of compatibility with the defendant's constitutional right to confrontation. Such questions require attention to the reasons for, and the basic scope of, the protections offered by the Confrontation Clause.

The origin and development of the hearsay rules and of the Confrontation Clause have been traced by others and need not be recounted in detail here. It is sufficient to note that the particular vice which gave impetus to the confrontation claim was the practice of trying defendants on "evidence" which consisted solely of *ex parte* affidavits or depositions secured by the examining magistrates, thus denying the defendant the opportunity to challenge his accuser in a face-to-face encounter in front of the trier of fact. Prosecuting attorneys "would frequently allege matters which the prisoner denied and called upon them to prove. The proof was usually given by reading depositions, confessions of accomplices, letters, and the like; and this occasioned frequent demands by the prisoner to have his 'accusers,' i.e. the witnesses against him, brought before him face to face. . . ."[21]

But objections occasioned by this practice appear primarily to have been aimed at the failure to call the witness to confront personally the defendant at his trial. So far as appears, in claiming confrontation rights no objection was made against receiving a witness' out-of-court depositions or statements, so long as the witness was present at trial to repeat his story and to explain or repudiate any conflicting prior stories before the trier of fact.

Our own decisions seem to have recognized at an early date that it is this literal right to "confront" the witness at the time of trial that forms the core of the values furthered by the Confrontation Clause. . . . Viewed historically, then, there is good reason to conclude that the Confrontation Clause is not violated by admitting a declarant's out-of-court statements, as long as the declarant is testifying as a witness and subject to full and effective cross-examination.

This conclusion is supported by comparing the purposes of confrontation with the alleged dangers in admitting an out-of-court statement.

21. 1 J. Stephen, A History of the Criminal Law of England 326 (1883). . . .

Confrontation: (1) insures that the witness will give his statements under oath—thus impressing him with the seriousness of the matter and guarding against the lie by the possibility of a penalty for perjury; (2) forces the witness to submit to cross-examination, the "greatest legal engine ever invented for the discovery of truth";[22] (3) permits the jury that is to decide the defendant's fate to observe the demeanor of the witness in making his statement, thus aiding the jury in assessing his credibility.

It is, of course, true that the out-of-court statement may have been made under circumstances subject to none of these protections. But if the declarant is present and testifying at trial, the out-of-court statement for all practical purposes regains most of the lost protections. If the witness admits the prior statement is his, or if there is other evidence to show the statement is his, the danger of faulty reproduction is negligible and the jury can be confident that it has before it two conflicting statements by the same witness. Thus, as far as the oath is concerned, the witness must now affirm, deny, or qualify the truth of the prior statement under the penalty of perjury; indeed, the very fact that the prior statement was not given under a similar circumstance may become the witness' explanation for its inaccuracy—an explanation a jury may be expected to understand and take into account in deciding which, if either, of the statements represents the truth.

Second, the inability to cross-examine the witness at the time he made his prior statement cannot easily be shown to be of crucial significance as long as the defendant is assured of full and effective cross-examination at the time of trial. The most successful cross-examination at the time the prior statement was made could hardly hope to accomplish more than has already been accomplished by the fact that the witness is now telling a different, inconsistent story, and—in this case—one that is favorable to the defendant. We cannot share the California Supreme Court's view that belated cross-examination can never serve as a constitutionally adequate substitute for cross-examination contemporaneous with the original statement. The main danger in substituting subsequent for timely cross-examination seems to lie in the possibility that the witness' "[f]alse testimony is apt to harden and become unyielding to the blows of truth in proportion as the witness has opportunity for reconsideration and influence by the suggestions of others, whose interest may be, and often is, to maintain falsehood rather than truth." State v. Saporen, 205 Minn. 358, 362, 285 N.W. 898, 901 (1939). That danger, however, disappears when the witness has changed his testimony so that, far from "hardening," his prior statement has softened to the point where he now repudiates it.

The defendant's task in cross-examination is, of course, no longer identical to the task that he would have faced if the witness had not changed his story and hence had to be examined as a "hostile" witness giving evidence for the prosecution. This difference, however, far from lessening, may actually enhance the defendant's ability to attack the prior statement. For the witness, favorable to the defendant, should be more than willing to give the

---

22. 5 Wigmore § 1367.

usual suggested explanations for the inaccuracy of his prior statement, such as faulty perception or undue haste in recounting the event. Under such circumstances, the defendant is not likely to be hampered in effectively attacking the prior statement, solely because his attack comes later in time.

Similar reasons lead us to discount as a constitutional matter the fact that the jury at trial is foreclosed from viewing the declarant's demeanor when he first made his out-of-court statement. The witness who now relates a different story about the events in question must necessarily assume a position as to the truth value of his prior statement, thus giving the jury a chance to observe and evaluate his demeanor as he either disavows or qualifies his earlier statement. The jury is alerted by the inconsistency in the stories, and its attention is sharply focused on determining either that one of the stories reflects the truth or that the witness who has apparently lied once, is simply too lacking in credibility to warrant believing either story. The defendant's confrontation rights are not violated, even though some demeanor evidence that would have been relevant in resolving this credibility issue is forever lost.

It may be true that a jury would be in a better position to evaluate the truth of the prior statement if it could somehow be whisked magically back in time to witness a gruelling cross-examination of the declarant as he first gives his statement. But the question as we see it must be not whether one can somehow imagine the jury in "a better position," but whether subsequent cross-examination at the defendant's trial will still afford the trier of fact a satisfactory basis for evaluating the truth of the prior statement. On that issue, neither evidence nor reason convinces us that contemporaneous cross-examination before the ultimate trier of fact is so much more effective than subsequent examination that it must be made the touchstone of the Confrontation Clause.

Finally, we note that none of our decisions interpreting the Confrontation Clause requires excluding the out-of-court statements of a witness who is available and testifying at trial. The concern of most of our cases has been focused on precisely the opposite situation—situations where statements have been admitted in the absence of the declarant and without any chance to cross-examine him at trial. These situations have arisen through application of a number of traditional "exceptions" to the hearsay rule, which permit the introduction of evidence despite the absence of the declarant usually on the theory that the evidence possesses other indicia of "reliability" and is incapable of being admitted, despite good-faith efforts of the State, in any way that will secure confrontation with the declarant. Such exceptions, dispensing altogether with the literal right to "confrontation" and cross-examination, have been subjected on several occasions to careful scrutiny by this Court. In Pointer v. Texas, 380 U.S. 400 (1965), for example, the State introduced at defendant's trial the transcript of a crucial witness' testimony from a prior preliminary hearing. The witness himself, one Phillips, had left the jurisdiction and did not appear at trial. "Because the transcript of Phillips' statement offered against petitioner at his trial had not been taken at a time and under circumstances affording petitioner through counsel an adequate opportunity to cross-examine Phillips," 380 U.S., at 407, we held that its introduction violated the defendant's confrontation rights. Similarly, in Barber v. Page, 390 U.S. 719 (1968), the State introduced the preliminary hearing testimony of an absent witness, incarcerated in a federal prison, under an "unavailability" exception to its hearsay rules. We held that that exception would not justify the denial of confrontation where the State had not made a good-faith effort to obtain the presence of the allegedly "unavailable" witness.

We have no occasion in the present case to map out a theory of the Confrontation Clause that would determine the validity of all such hearsay "exceptions" permitting the introduction of an absent declarant's statements. For where the declarant is not absent, but is present to testify and to submit to cross-examination, our cases, if anything, support the conclusion that the admission of his out-of-court statements does not create a confrontation problem. Thus, in Douglas v. Alabama, 380 U.S. 415 (1965), decided on the same day as *Pointer*, we reversed a conviction in which the prosecution read into the record an alleged confession of the defendant's supposed accomplice, Loyd, who refused to testify on self-incrimination grounds. The confrontation problem arose precisely because Loyd could not be cross-examined as to his prior statement; had such cross-examination taken place, the opinion strongly suggests that the confrontation problem would have been nonexistent. . . .

Again, in Bruton v. United States, 391 U.S. 123 (1968), the Court found a violation of confrontation rights in the admission of a codefendant's confession, implicating Bruton, where the co-defendant did not take the stand. The Court again emphasized that the error arose because the declarant "does not testify and cannot be tested by cross-examination," 391 U.S., at 136, suggesting that no confrontation problem would have existed if Bruton had been able to cross-examine his co-defendant. . . . Indeed, *Bruton's* refusal to regard limiting instructions as capable of curing the error, suggests that there is little difference as far as the Constitution is concerned between permitting prior inconsistent statements to be used only for impeachment purposes, and permitting them to be used for substantive purposes as well.

We find nothing, then, in either the history or the purposes of the Confrontation Clause, or in the prior decisions of this Court, that compels the conclusion reached by the California Supreme Court concerning the validity of California's § 1235. Contrary to the judgment of that court, the Confrontation Clause does not require excluding from evidence the prior statements of a witness who concedes making the statements, and who may be asked to defend or otherwise explain the inconsistency between his prior and his present version of the events in question, thus opening himself to full cross-examination at trial as to both stories.

III

We also think that Porter's preliminary hearing testimony was admissible as far as the Constitution is concerned wholly apart from the question of whether respondent had an effective opportunity for confrontation at the subsequent trial. For Porter's statement at the preliminary hearing had already been given under circumstances closely approximating those that surround the typical trial. Porter was under oath; respondent was represented by counsel—the same counsel in fact who later represented him at the trial; respondent had every opportunity to cross-examine Porter as to his statement; and the proceedings were conducted before a judicial tribunal, equipped to provide a judicial record of the hearings. Under these circumstances, Porter's statement would, we think, have been admissible at trial even in Porter's absence if Porter had been actually unavailable, despite good-faith efforts of the State to produce him. That being the case, we do not think a different result should follow where the witness is actually produced.

This Court long ago held that admitting the prior testimony of an unavailable witness does not violate the Confrontation Clause. Mattox v. United States, 156 U.S. 237 (1895). That case involved testimony given at the defendant's first trial by a witness who had died by the time of the second trial, but we do not find the instant preliminary hearing significantly different from an actual trial to warrant distinguishing the two cases for purposes of the Confrontation Clause. Indeed, we indicated as much in Pointer v. Texas, 380 U.S. 400, 407 (1965), where we noted that "[t]he case before us would be quite a different one had Phillips' statement been taken at a full-fledged hearing at which petitioner had been represented by counsel who had been given a complete and adequate opportunity to cross-examine." And in Barber v. Page, 390 U.S. 719, 725–726 (1968), although noting that the preliminary hearing is ordinarily a less searching exploration into the merits of a case than a trial, we recognized that "there may be some justification for holding that the opportunity for cross-examination of a witness at a preliminary hearing satisfies the demands of the confrontation clause where the witness is shown to be actually unavailable. . . ." In the present case respondent's counsel does not appear to have been significantly limited in any way in the scope or nature of his cross-examination of the witness Porter at the preliminary hearing. If Porter had died or was otherwise unavailable, the Confrontation Clause would not have been violated by admitting his testimony given at the preliminary hearing—the right of cross-examination then afforded provides substantial compliance with the purposes behind the confrontation requirement, as long as the declarant's inability to give live testimony is in no way the fault of the State. . . .

But nothing in Barber v. Page or in other cases in this Court indicates that a different result must follow where the State produces the declarant and swears him as a witness at the trial. It may be that the rules of evidence applicable in state or federal courts would restrict resort to prior sworn testimony where the declarant is present at the trial. But as a constitutional matter, it is untenable to construe the Confrontation Clause to permit the use of prior testimony to prove the State's case where the declarant never appears, but to bar that testimony where the declarant is present at the trial, exposed to the defendant and the trier of fact, and subject to cross-examination. As in the case where the witness is physically unproducible, the State here has made every effort to introduce its evidence through the live testimony of the witness; it produced Porter at trial, swore him as a witness, and tendered him for cross-examination. Whether Porter then testified in a manner consistent or inconsistent with his preliminary hearing testimony, claimed a loss of memory, claimed his privilege against compulsory self-incrimination, or simply refused to answer, nothing in the Confrontation Clause prohibited the State from also relying on his prior testimony to prove its case against Green.

IV

There is a narrow question lurking in this case concerning the admissibility of Porter's statements to Officer Wade. In the typical case to which the California court addressed itself, the witness at trial gives a version of the ultimate events different from that given on a prior occasion. In such a case, as our holding in Part II makes clear, we find little reason to distinguish among prior inconsistent statements on the basis of the circumstances under which the prior statements were given. The subsequent opportunity for cross-examination at trial with respect to both present and past versions of the event, is adequate to make equally admissible, as far as the Confrontation Clause is concerned, both the casual, off-hand remark to a stranger, and the carefully recorded testimony at a prior hearing. Here, however, Porter claimed at trial that he could not remember the events which occurred after respondent telephoned him and hence failed to give any current version of the more important events described in his earlier statement.

Whether Porter's apparent lapse of memory so affected Green's right to cross-examine as to make a critical difference in the application of the Confrontation Clause in this case is an issue which is not ripe for decision at this juncture. . . .

We therefore vacate the judgment of the California Supreme Court and remand the case to that court for further proceedings not inconsistent with this opinion.

. . . [23]

————

497. The Court considered the relationship between the Confrontation Clause and exceptions to the hearsay rule again in Dutton v. Evans, 400 U.S. 74 (1970). There, a prosecution witness was allowed to testify about an out-of-court statement made by one Williams, as a co-conspirator with the

[23] Chief Justice Burger and Justice Harlan wrote concurring opinions. Justice Brennan wrote a dissenting opinion.

defendant. Williams's statement, as reported by the witness, incriminated the defendant. Williams himself was not called as a witness and did not testify. The court concluded, four Justices dissenting, that the witness's testimony was admissible.

The relationship between the Confrontation Clause and the hearsay rule, and California v. Green in particular, are discussed also in Ohio v. Roberts, 448 U.S. 56 (1980) (6–3). The Court summarized its discussion as follows: "[W]hen a hearsay declarant is not present for cross-examination at trial, the Confrontation Clause normally requires a showing that he is unavailable. Even then, his statement is admissible only if it bears adequate 'indicia of reliability.' Reliability can be inferred without more in a case where the evidence falls within a firmly rooted hearsay exception. In other cases, the evidence must be excluded, at least absent a showing of particularized guarantees of trustworthiness." Id. at 66. The Court avoided deciding whether the "mere opportunity" to cross-examine when prior testimony was taken would render such testimony admissible if there was in fact no cross-examination or only "de minimis questioning"; it found that defense counsel's questioning of the witness was the substantial equivalent of cross-examination and satisfied the purposes of the Confrontation Clause even though the witness had not been declared a hostile witness. Id. at 70. The majority and dissenting opinions also discuss at length the requirement of unavailability.

Roberts was applied in Lee v. Illinois, 476 U.S. 530 (1986) (5–4), in which the Court held that the defendant's rights under the Confrontation Clause were violated by admission of the confession of a codefendant who did not take the stand. Although portions of the defendant's own confession corroborated the codefendant's confession, there were insufficient indicia of the latter's reliability. Compare Tennessee v. Street, 471 U.S. 409 (1985). The Court there held that the Confrontation Clause was not implicated in the admission of a codefendant's confession for the nonhearsay purpose of rebutting the defendant's claim that his confession was coerced and derived from the codefendant's confession. The codefendant's confession was admitted only for that limited purpose, according to the judge's instructions to the jury; and, the Court said, there was no viable alternative to its admission for that purpose.

Roberts was distinguished in United States v. Inadi, 475 U.S. 387 (1986) (7–2). Out-of-court statements of unindicted co-conspirators were admitted at the defendant's trial, over his objection. The statements satisfied the rule of evidence governing the admission of co-conspirators' statements made in the course of and in furtherance of a conspiracy. The defendant argued that they should not be admitted nevertheless, because they did not satisfy the requirement of the Confrontation Clause that it be shown that the persons making the statements were unavailable. The Court said that Roberts was not concerned with all aspects of hearsay testimony, but only with prior testimony at a judicial proceeding. The unavailability requirement of Roberts makes sense in that context, because if the witness is available, his present "live" testimony is preferable to his former testimony. A co-conspirator's prior statements, however, are made in a different context from testimony on a witness stand and may provide evidence that live testimony will not reproduce. An unavailability requirement would serve the truth-determining function of a trial little and add considerably to the burden of the prosecution.

The Confrontation Clause does not require a separate inquiry into the reliability of an out-of-court statement admitted under the co-conspirator exception to the hearsay rule. The requirements of the exception itself satisfy the constitutional requirements. Bourjaily v. United States, 483 U.S. 171 (1987) (6–3). Similarly, discussing *Roberts* and *Inadi*, above, the Court held that the Confrontation Clause does not require that the prosecution produce a witness or the witness be declared unavailable in order for the person's testimony to be admitted under the "spontaneous declaration" and "medical examination" exceptions to the hearsay rule. White v. Illinois, 502 U.S. 346 (1992). The Court observed that "where proffered hearsay has sufficient guarantees of reliability to come within a firmly rooted exception to the hearsay rule, the Confrontation Clause is satisfied." Id. at 356.

In United States v. Faison, 679 F.2d 292 (3d Cir.1982), the court of appeals held that it was an abuse of discretion for the trial judge to deny a request for an adjournment so that an important prosecution witness, who was ill, could testify before the jury; instead of the adjournment, the judge allowed the witness's testimony at a prior trial to be introduced.

498. The admission of hearsay statements of a young child, allegedly the victim of sexual abuse, who was found not capable of communicating to a jury, violated the Confrontation Clause, because it did not come within an established hearsay exception and was not supported by particular guarantees of trustworthiness. Idaho v. Wright, 497 U.S. 805 (1990) (5–4).

———

Chambers v. Mississippi

410 U.S. 284, 93 S.Ct. 1038, 35 L.Ed.2d 297 (1973).

■ MR. JUSTICE POWELL delivered the opinion of the Court.

Petitioner, Leon Chambers, was tried by a jury in a Mississippi trial court and convicted of murdering a policeman. The jury assessed punishment at life imprisonment. . . . [T]he petition for certiorari was granted . . . to consider whether petitioner's trial was conducted in accord with principles of due process under the Fourteenth Amendment. We conclude that it was not.

I

The events that led to petitioner's prosecution for murder occurred in the small town of Woodville in southern Mississippi. On Saturday evening, June 14, 1969, two Woodville policemen, James Forman and Aaron "Sonny" Liberty, entered a local bar and pool hall to execute a warrant for the arrest of a youth named C.C. Jackson. Jackson resisted and a hostile crowd of some 50 or 60 persons gathered. The officers' first attempt to handcuff Jackson was frustrated when 20 or 25 men in the crowd intervened and wrestled him free. Forman then radioed for assistance and Liberty removed his riot gun, a 12-gauge sawed-off shotgun, from the car. Three deputy sheriffs arrived shortly thereafter and the officers again attempted to make their arrest. Once more, the officers were attacked by the onlookers and during the commotion five or six pistol shots were fired. Forman was looking in a different direction when the shooting began, but immediately saw that Liberty had been shot several times in the back. Before Liberty died, he turned around and fired both barrels of his riot gun into an alley in the area from which the shots appeared to have come. The first shot was wild and high and scattered the crowd standing at the face of the alley. Liberty appeared, however, to take more deliberate aim before the second shot and hit one of the men in the crowd in the back of the head and neck as he ran down the alley. That man was Leon Chambers.

Officer Forman could not see from his vantage point who shot Liberty or whether Liberty's shots hit anyone. One of the deputy sheriffs testified at trial that he was standing several feet from Liberty and that he saw Chambers shoot him. Another deputy sheriff stated that although he could not see whether Chambers had a gun in his hand, he did see Chambers "break his arm down" shortly before the shots were fired. The officers who saw Chambers fall testified that they thought he was dead but they made no effort at that time either to examine him or to search for the murder weapon. Instead, they attended to Liberty, who was placed in the police car and taken to a hospital where he was declared dead on arrival. A subsequent autopsy showed that he had been hit with four bullets from a .22-caliber revolver.

Shortly after the shooting, three of Chambers' friends discovered that he was not yet dead. James Williams, Berkley Turner, and Gable McDonald loaded him into a car and transported him to the same hospital. Later that night, when the county sheriff discovered that Chambers was still alive, a guard was placed outside his room. Chambers was subsequently charged with Liberty's murder. He pleaded not guilty and has asserted his innocence throughout.

The story of Leon Chambers is intertwined with the story of another man, Gable McDonald. McDonald, a lifelong resident of Woodville, was in the crowd on the evening of Liberty's death. Sometime shortly after that day, he left his wife in Woodville and moved to Louisiana and found a job at a sugar mill. In November of that same year, he returned to Woodville when his wife informed him that an acquaintance of his, known as Reverend Stokes, wanted to see him. Stokes owned a gas station in Natchez,

Mississippi, several miles north of Woodville, and upon his return McDonald went to see him. After talking to Stokes, McDonald agreed to make a statement to Chambers' attorneys, who maintained offices in Natchez. Two days later, he appeared at the attorneys' offices and gave a sworn confession that he shot Officer Liberty. He also stated that he had already told a friend of his, James Williams, that he shot Liberty. He said that he used his own pistol, a nine-shot .22-caliber revolver, which he had discarded shortly after the shooting. In response to questions from Chambers' attorneys, McDonald affirmed that his confession was voluntary and that no one had compelled him to come to them. Once the confession had been transcribed, signed, and witnessed, McDonald was turned over to the local police authorities and was placed in jail.

One month later, at a preliminary hearing, McDonald repudiated his prior sworn confession. He testified that Stokes had persuaded him to confess that he shot Liberty. He claimed that Stokes had promised that he would not go to jail and that he would share in the proceeds of a lawsuit that Chambers would bring against the town of Woodville. On examination by his own attorney and on cross-examination by the State, McDonald swore that he had not been at the scene when Liberty was shot but had been down the street drinking beer in a cafe with a friend, Berkley Turner. When he and Turner heard the shooting, he testified, they walked up the street and found Chambers lying in the alley. He, Turner, and Williams took Chambers to the hospital. McDonald further testified at the preliminary hearing that he did not know what had happened, that there was no discussion about the shooting either going to or coming back from the hospital, and that it was not until the next day that he learned that Chambers had been felled by a blast from Liberty's riot gun. In addition, McDonald stated that while he once owned a .22-caliber pistol he had lost it many months before the shooting and did not own or possess a weapon at that time. The local justice of the peace accepted McDonald's repudiation and released him from custody. The local authorities undertook no further investigation of his possible involvement.

Chambers' case came on for trial in October of the next year. At trial, he endeavored to develop two grounds of defense. He first attempted to show that he did not shoot Liberty. Only one officer testified that he actually saw Chambers fire the shots. Although three officers saw Liberty shoot Chambers and testified that they assumed he was shooting his attacker, none of them examined Chambers to see whether he was still alive or whether he possessed a gun. Indeed, no weapon was ever recovered from the scene and there was no proof that Chambers had ever owned a .22-caliber pistol. One witness testified that he was standing in the street near where Liberty was shot, that he was looking at Chambers when the shooting began, and that he was sure that Chambers did not fire the shots.

Petitioner's second defense was that Gable McDonald had shot Officer Liberty. He was only partially successful, however, in his efforts to bring before the jury the testimony supporting this defense. Sam Hardin, a lifelong friend of McDonald's, testified that he saw McDonald shoot Liberty. A second witness, one of Liberty's cousins, testified that he saw McDonald immediately after the shooting with a pistol in his hand. In addition to the testimony of these two witnesses, Chambers endeavored to show the jury that McDonald had repeatedly confessed to the crime. Chambers attempted to prove that McDonald had admitted responsibility for the murder on four separate occasions once when he gave the sworn statement to Chambers' counsel and three other times prior to that occasion in private conversations with friends.

In large measure, he was thwarted in his attempt to present this portion of his defense by the strict application of certain Mississippi rules of evidence. Chambers asserts in this Court, as he did unsuccessfully in his motion for new trial and on appeal to the State Supreme Court, that the application of these evidentiary rules rendered his trial fundamentally unfair and deprived him of due process of law. It is necessary, therefore, to examine carefully the rulings made during the trial.

II

Chambers filed a pretrial motion requesting the court to order McDonald to appear. Chambers also sought a ruling at that time that, if the State itself chose not to call McDonald, he be allowed to call him as an adverse witness. Attached to the motion were copies of McDonald's sworn confession and of the transcript of his preliminary hearing at which he repudiated that confession. The trial court granted the motion requiring McDonald to appear but reserved ruling on the adverse-witness motion. At trial, after the State failed to put McDonald on the stand, Chambers called McDonald, laid a predicate for the introduction of his sworn out-of-court confession, had it admitted into evidence, and read it to the jury. The State, upon cross-examination, elicited from McDonald the fact that he had rejected his prior confession. McDonald further testified, as he had at the preliminary hearing, that he did not shoot Liberty and that he confessed to the crime only on the promise of Reverend Stokes that he would not go to jail and would share in a sizable tort recovery from the town. He also retold his own story of his actions on the evening of the shooting, including his visit to the cafe down the street, his absence from the scene during the critical period, and his subsequent trip to the hospital with Chambers.

At the conclusion of the State's cross-examination, Chambers renewed his motion to examine McDonald as an adverse witness. The trial court denied the motion, stating: "He may be hostile, but he is not adverse in the sense of the word, so your request will be overruled." On appeal, the State Supreme Court upheld the trial court's ruling, finding that "McDonald's testimony was not adverse to appellant" because "[n]owhere did he point the finger at Chambers." 252 So.2d at 220.

Defeated in his attempt to challenge directly McDonald's renunciation of his prior confession, Chambers sought to introduce the testimony of the three witnesses to whom McDonald had admitted that he shot the officer. The first of these, Sam Hardin, would have testified that, on the night of the shooting, he spent the late evening hours with McDonald at a friend's house after their return from the hospital and that, while driving McDonald home later that night, McDonald stated that he shot Liberty. The State objected to the admission of this testimony on the ground that it was hearsay. The trial court sustained the objection.

Berkley Turner, the friend with whom McDonald said he was drinking beer when the shooting occurred, was then called to testify. In the jury's presence, and without objection, he testified that he had not been in the cafe that Saturday and had not had any beers with McDonald. The jury was then excused. In the absence of the jury, Turner recounted his conversations with McDonald while they were riding with James Williams to take Chambers to the hospital. When asked whether McDonald said anything regarding the shooting of Liberty, Turner testified that McDonald told him that he "shot him." Turner further stated that one week later, when he met McDonald at a friend's house, McDonald reminded him of their prior conversation and urged Turner not to "mess him up." Petitioner argued to the court that, especially where there was other proof in the case that was corroborative of these out-of-court statements, Turner's testimony as to McDonald's self-incriminating remarks should have been admitted as an exception to the hearsay rule. Again, the trial court sustained the State's objection.

The third witness, Albert Carter, was McDonald's neighbor. They had been friends for about 25 years. Although Carter had not been in Woodville on the evening of the shooting, he stated that he learned about it the next morning from McDonald. That same day, he and McDonald walked out to a well near McDonald's house and there McDonald told him that he was the one who shot Officer Liberty. Carter testified that McDonald also told him that he had disposed of the .22-caliber revolver later that night. He further testified that several weeks after the shooting, he accompanied McDonald to Natchez where McDonald purchased another .22 pistol to replace the one he had discarded. The jury was not allowed to hear Carter's testimony. Chambers urged that these statements were admissible, the State objected, and the court sustained the objection. On appeal, the State Supreme Court approved the lower court's exclusion of these witnesses' testimony on hearsay grounds. . . .

In sum, then, this was Chambers' predicament. As a consequence of the combination of Mississippi's "party-witness" or "voucher" rule and its hearsay rule, he was unable either to cross-examine McDonald or to present witnesses in his own behalf who would have discredited McDonald's repudiation and demonstrated his complicity. Chambers had, however, chipped away at the fringes of McDonald's story by introducing admissible testimony from other sources indicating that he had not been seen in the cafe where he said he was when the shooting started, that he had not been having beer with Turner, and that he possessed a .22 pistol at the time of the crime. But all that remained from McDonald's own testimony was a single written confession countered by an arguably acceptable renunciation. Chambers' defense was far less persuasive than it might have been had he been given an opportunity to subject McDonald's statements to cross-examination or had the other confessions been admitted.

III

The right of an accused in a criminal trial to due process is, in essence, the right to a fair opportunity to defend against the State's accusations. The rights to confront and cross-examine witnesses and to call witnesses in one's own behalf have long been recognized as essential to due process. Mr. Justice Black, writing for the Court in In re Oliver, 333 U.S. 257, 273 (1948), identified these rights as among the minimum essentials of a fair trial. . . . Both of these elements of a fair trial are implicated in the present case.

A

Chambers was denied an opportunity to subject McDonald's damning repudiation and alibi to cross-examination. He was not allowed to test the witness' recollection, to probe into the details of his alibi, or to "sift" his conscience so that the jury might judge for itself whether McDonald's testimony was worthy of belief. . . . The right of cross-examination is more than a desirable rule of trial procedure. It is implicit in the constitutional right of confrontation, and helps assure the "accuracy of the truth-determining process." Dutton v. Evans, 400 U.S. 74, 89 (1970). . . . It is, indeed, "an essential and fundamental requirement for the kind of fair trial which is this country's constitutional goal." Pointer v. Texas, 380 U.S. 400, 405 (1965). Of course, the right to confront and to cross-examine is not absolute and may, in appropriate cases, bow to accommodate other legitimate interests in the criminal trial process. . . . But its denial or significant diminution calls into question the ultimate " 'integrity of the fact-finding process' " and requires that the competing interest be closely examined. . . .

In this case, petitioner's request to cross-examine McDonald was denied on the basis of a Mississippi common-law rule that a party may not impeach his own witness. The rule rests on the presumption—without regard to the circumstances of the particular case—that a party who calls a witness "vouches for his credibility." Clark v. Lansford, 191 So.2d 123, 125 (Miss.1966). Although the historical origins of the "voucher" rule are uncertain, it appears to be a remnant of primitive English trial practice in which "oath-takers" or "compurgators" were called to stand behind a particular party's position in any controversy. Their assertions were strictly partisan and, quite unlike witnesses in criminal trials today, their role bore little relation to the impartial ascertainment of the facts.

Whatever validity the "voucher" rule may have once enjoyed, and apart from whatever usefulness it retains today in the civil trial process, it bears little present relationship to the realities of the criminal process. It might have been logical for the early common law to require a party to vouch for the credibility of witnesses he brought before the jury to affirm his veracity. Having selected them especially for that purpose, the party might reasonably be expected to stand firmly behind their testimony. But in modern criminal trials, defendants are rarely able to select their witnesses: they must take them where they find them. Moreover, as applied in this case, the "voucher" rule's impact was doubly harmful to Chambers' efforts to develop his defense. Not only was he precluded from cross-examining McDonald, but, as the State conceded at oral argument, he was also restricted in the scope of his direct examination by the rule's corollary requirement that the party calling the witness is bound by anything he might say. He was, therefore, effectively prevented from exploring the circumstances of McDonald's three prior oral confessions and from challenging the renunciation of the written confession.

In this Court, Mississippi has not sought to defend the rule or explain its underlying rationale. Nor has it contended that its rule should override the accused's right of confrontation. Instead, it argues that there is no incompatibility between the rule and Chambers' rights because no right of confrontation exists unless the testifying witness is "adverse" to the accused. The State's brief asserts that the "right of confrontation applies to witnesses *against* an accused." Relying on the trial court's determination that McDonald was not "adverse," and on the State Supreme Court's holding that McDonald did not "point the finger at Chambers,"[24] the State contends that Chambers' constitutional right was not involved.

The argument that McDonald's testimony was not "adverse" to, or "against," Chambers is not convincing. The State's proof at trial excluded the theory that more than one person participated in the shooting of Liberty. To the extent that McDonald's sworn confession tended to incriminate him, it tended also to exculpate Chambers. And, in the circumstances of this case, McDonald's retraction inculpated Chambers to the same extent that it exculpated McDonald. It can hardly be disputed that McDonald's testimony was in fact seriously adverse to Chambers. The availability of the right to confront and to cross-examine those who give damaging testimony against the accused has never been held to depend on whether the witness was initially put on the stand by the accused or by the State. We reject the notion that a right of such substance in the criminal process may be governed by that technicality or by any narrow and unrealistic definition of the word "against." The "voucher" rule, as applied in this case, plainly interfered with Chambers' right to defend against the State's charges.

B

We need not decide, however, whether this error alone would occasion reversal since Chambers' claimed denial of due process rests on the ultimate impact of that error when viewed in conjunction with the trial court's refusal to permit him to call other witnesses. The trial court refused to allow him to introduce the testimony of Hardin, Turner, and Carter. Each would have testified to the statements purportedly made by McDonald, on three separate occasions shortly after the crime, naming himself as the murderer. The State Supreme Court approved the exclusion of this evidence on the ground that it was hearsay.

The hearsay rule, which has long been recognized and respected by virtually every State, is based on experience and grounded in the notion that

---

24. 252 So.2d, at 220.

untrustworthy evidence should not be presented to the triers of fact. Out-of-court statements are traditionally excluded because they lacked the conventional indicia of reliability: they are usually not made under oath or other circumstances that impress the speaker with the solemnity of his statements; the declarant's word is not subject to cross-examination; and he is not available in order that his demeanor and credibility may be assessed by the jury. . . . A number of exceptions have developed over the years to allow admission of hearsay statements made under circumstances that tend to assure reliability and thereby compensate for the absence of the oath and opportunity for cross-examination. Among the most prevalent of these exceptions is the one applicable to declarations against interest—an exception founded on the assumption that a person is unlikely to fabricate a statement against his own interest at the time it is made. Mississippi recognizes this exception but applies it only to declarations against pecuniary interest. It recognizes no such exception for declarations, like McDonald's in this case, that are against the penal interest of the declarant. . . .

This materialistic limitation on the declaration-against-interest hearsay exception appears to be accepted by most States in their criminal trial processes, although a number of States have discarded it. Declarations against penal interest have also been excluded in federal courts under the authority of Donnelly v. United States, 228 U.S. 243, 272–273 (1913), although exclusion would not be required under the newly proposed Federal Rules of Evidence. Exclusion, where the limitation prevails, is usually premised on the view that admission would lead to the frequent presentation of perjured testimony to the jury. It is believed that confessions of criminal activity are often motivated by extraneous considerations and, therefore, are not as inherently reliable as statements against pecuniary or proprietary interest. While that rationale has been the subject of considerable scholarly criticism, we need not decide in this case whether, under other circumstances, it might serve some valid state purpose by excluding untrustworthy testimony.

The hearsay statements involved in this case were originally made and subsequently offered at trial under circumstances that provided considerable assurance of their reliability. First, each of McDonald's confessions was made spontaneously to a close acquaintance shortly after the murder had occurred. Second, each one was corroborated by some other evidence in the case—McDonald's sworn confession, the testimony of an eyewitness to the shooting, the testimony that McDonald was seen with a gun immediately after the shooting, and proof of his prior ownership of a .22-caliber revolver and subsequent purchase of a new weapon. The sheer number of independent confessions provided additional corroboration for each. Third, whatever may be the parameters of the penal-interest rationale, each confession here was in a very real sense self-incriminatory and unquestionably against interest. . . . McDonald stood to benefit nothing by disclosing his role in the shooting to any of his three friends and he must have been aware of the possibility that disclosure would lead to criminal prosecution. Indeed, after telling Turner of his involvement, he subsequently urged Turner not to "mess him up." Finally, if there was any question about the truthfulness of the extrajudicial statements, McDonald was present in the courtroom and had been under oath. He could have been cross-examined by the State, and his demeanor and responses weighed by the jury. . . . The availability of McDonald significantly distinguishes this case from the prior Mississippi precedent . . . and from the *Donnelly*-type situation, since in both cases the declarant was unavailable at the time of trial.

Few rights are more fundamental than that of an accused to present witnesses in his own defense. . . . In the exercise of this right, the accused, as is required of the State, must comply with established rules of procedure and evidence designed to assure both fairness and reliability in the ascertainment of guilt and innocence. Although perhaps no rule of evidence has been more respected or more frequently applied in jury trials than that applicable to the exclusion of hearsay, exceptions tailored to allow the introduction of evidence which in fact is likely to be trustworthy have long existed. The testimony rejected by the trial court here bore persuasive assurances of trustworthiness and thus was well within the basic rationale of the exception for declarations against interest. That testimony also was critical to Chambers' defense. In these circumstances, where constitutional rights directly affecting the ascertainment of guilt are implicated, the hearsay rule may not be applied mechanistically to defeat the ends of justice.

We conclude that the exclusion of this critical evidence, coupled with the State's refusal to permit Chambers to cross-examine McDonald, denied him a trial in accord with traditional and fundamental standards of due process. In reaching this judgment, we establish no new principles of constitutional law. Nor does our holding signal any diminution in the respect traditionally accorded to the States in the establishment and implementation of their own criminal trial rules and procedures. Rather, we hold quite simply that under the facts and circumstances of this case the rulings of the trial court deprived Chambers of a fair trial.

. . . [25]

---

499. See Green v. Georgia, 442 U.S. 95 (1979) (8–1), a capital case in which, relying on Chambers v. Mississippi, the Court held that the hearsay rule could not be allowed to bar testimony "highly relevant to a critical issue in the punishment phase of the trial," which the state had itself used in the trial of a codefendant.

[25] Justice White wrote a concurring opinion. Justice Rehnquist wrote a dissenting opinion.

Cf. Montana v. Egelhoff, 518 U.S. 37 (1996) (5–4), distinguishing *Chambers* and upholding a state statute providing that voluntary intoxication may not be taken into account in the determination of the existence of a mental state that is an element of a crime. See also United States v. Scheffer, __ U.S. __, 118 S.Ct. 1261 (1998) (8–1), also distinguishing *Chambers*. In *Scheffer*, the Court held that a rule of the Military Rules of Evidence that makes polygraph evidence inadmissible in court-martial proceedings does not unconstitutionally restrict the right of an accused to present a defense.

500. The "voucher" rule at issue in Chambers v. Mississippi, above, is discussed in Lipinski v. New York, 557 F.2d 289, 293–94 (2d Cir.1977), in which the court observed: "The traditional justifications of the rule against impeaching one's own witness are plainly bankrupt. No thoughtful jurist or scholar will today defend the proposition that a party is morally bound by the testimony of his witnesses. And, since it is universally accepted that a party must take his witnesses where he finds them, it is completely unrealistic to imagine him as the guarantor of his witness's veracity in every respect." But, the court added, the rule "appears to be one of those atavisms that no quantity of reasoned criticism seems able to destroy," id. at 293. The rule has been eliminated in federal courts by Rule 607 of the Rules of Evidence for United States Courts and Magistrates, which provides: "The credibility of a witness may be attacked by any party, including the party calling the witness."

In Welcome v. Vincent, 549 F.2d 853 (2d Cir.1977), the court, relying on *Chambers*, held that the trial court should not have restricted defense counsel's effort to question a defense witness about a confession to the same crimes for which the defendants were on trial. On cross-examination by the prosecutor, the witness had denied his involvement in the crime; the defense counsel sought on redirect examination to question him about the confession as a prior inconsistent statement, to impeach his credibility. The trial court refused to permit such questioning on the ground that the witness, having been called by the defense and not having inculpated the defendants, was not a hostile witness. The court held that it is a denial of a fair trial "where another person, present on the witness stand, has previously confessed that he, rather than the defendant on trial, has perpetrated the crime . . . to restrict examination of such a witness, so that his prior confession may not be proven . . . at least when the confession, though retracted, has some semblance of reliability." Id. at 858–59.

Chambers was distinguished and an application of a state voucher rule upheld, in Maness v. Wainwright, 512 F.2d 88 (5th Cir.1975).

501. In Davis v. Alaska, 415 U.S. 308 (1974), a main witness for the prosecution in a burglary and larceny case was a juvenile delinquent, who was on probation by order of a juvenile court. Before he testified, the prosecutor moved that there be no reference to the witness's juvenile record during cross-examination. The motion was in accordance with state law, the purpose of which was to protect a juvenile's anonymity and to further his rehabilitation. Defense counsel agreed not to use the juvenile record to impeach the witness's character but wanted to use the fact that he was on probation to show that he had a motive for cooperating with the police that suggested bias. The motion was granted. In response to defense counsel's questions, the witness testified in a way that intimated that he had not been in trouble with the police; because of the court's order, defense counsel was unable to inquire further.

The Court reversed the defendant's conviction. "The State's policy interest in protecting the confidentiality of a juvenile offender's record cannot require yielding of so vital a constitutional right as the effective cross-examination for bias of an adverse witness. The State could have protected the witness from exposure of his juvenile adjudication in these circumstances by refraining from using him to make out its case; the State cannot, consistent with right of confrontation, require the petitioner to bear the full burden of vindicating the State's interest in the secrecy of juvenile criminal records." Id. at 320.

"[A] criminal defendant states a violation of the Confrontation Clause by showing that he was prohibited from engaging in otherwise appropriate cross-examination designed to show a prototypical form of bias on the part of the witness. . . ." Delaware v. Van Arsdall, 475 U.S. 673, 680 (1986) (7–2). Such a violation may, however, be harmless error. "The correct inquiry is whether, assuming that the damaging potential of the cross-examination were fully realized, a reviewing court might nonetheless say that the error was harmless beyond a reasonable doubt." Id. at 684.

In Crane v. Kentucky, 476 U.S. 683 (1986), having ruled that the defendant's confession to police was voluntary and admissible, the trial judge excluded evidence of the circumstances in which the confession was made, which the defense offered to cast doubt on its credibility. The Court held that the exclusion of potentially exculpatory evidence, without rational justification, denied the defendant a meaningful opportunity to present a defense, protected either by the Due Process Clause or by the Sixth Amendment's Compulsory Process and Confrontation Clauses. See United States v. Lindstrom, 698 F.2d 1154 (11th Cir.1983) (restriction of cross-examination of principal prosecution witness about her history of psychiatric illness and treatment denied right to confront witnesses).

The Confrontation Clause is not violated if an expert witness for the prosecution testifies to a fact and then states on cross-examination that he has forgotten the basis on which he reached his conclusion. Delaware v. Fensterer, 474 U.S. 15 (1985) (per curiam) (7–2). The witness, an FBI agent testified that hair had been removed from the murder victim's head forcibly; on cross-examination he said that he could not recall which of three possible bases for such a conclusion was the one on which he had relied.

Relying on *Fensterer*, the Court held that neither the Confrontation Clause nor the federal hearsay rule bars admission of a witness's out-of-court identification statement if the witness is available at trial but unable, because of loss of memory, to testify about the basis for his statement. The witness testified at the trial that he remembered making the statement and that he was certain at that time that his identification was accurate. United States v. Owens, 484 U.S. 554 (1988) (6–2).

In Pennsylvania v. Ritchie, 480 U.S. 39 (1987) (5–4), a prosecution for child abuse, the Court held that the Confrontation Clause did not require the state to grant pretrial discovery of records of a social service agency containing information pertinent to the case. Under state law, the records were confidential. A plurality of the Court said that the right under the Confrontation Clause is a trial right, and that since defense counsel was permitted to cross-examine all trial witnesses fully, the defendant's right was not denied by nondisclosure of the records. (The Court noted, however, that under *Agurs*, p. 963 above, and *Bagley*, note 471 p. 970 above, the defendant had a right to disclosure of information if there was a reasonable probability that such disclosure would change the outcome of the trial. Id. at 57.) Similarly, in Kentucky v. Stincer, 482 U.S. 730 (1987) (6–3), the Court held that the exclusion of the defendant from a hearing to determine the competency to testify of two child witnesses for the prosecution did not violate his rights under the Confrontation Clause or his right under the Due Process Clause to be present at all stages of a criminal proceeding. The exclusion did not affect the defendant's opportunity for full, effective cross-examination of the witnesses, nor would his presence have helped to ensure a more reliable determination of their competence to testify.

The Confrontation Clause guarantees the right to confront witnesses face to face. The defendant in a child sexual abuse case was denied his right under the clause when the complaining witnesses were permitted to testify behind a screen, which allowed the defendant dimly to see them and to hear their testimony but prevented them from seeing him at all. The case was returned to the state court for consideration whether the violation was harmless error. Coy v. Iowa, 487 U.S. 1012 (1988) (6–2). Returning to the same issue in Maryland v. Craig, 497 U.S. 836 (1990) (5–4), the Court said: "[T]hough we reaffirm the importance of face-to-face confrontation with witnesses appearing at trial, we cannot say that such confrontation is an indispensable element of the Sixth Amendment's guarantee of the right to confront one's accusers." Id. at 849-50. "[W]here necessary to protect a child witness from trauma that would be caused by testifying in the physical presence of the defendant, at least where such trauma would impair the child's ability to communicate, the Confrontation Clause does not prohibit use of a procedure that, despite the absence of face-to-face confrontation, ensures the reliability of the evidence by subjecting it to rigorous adversarial testing and thereby preserves the essence of effective confrontation." Id. at 857. The Court upheld a procedure by which a child witness testifies out of the presence of the defendant, on closed-circuit, one-way television, if the judge finds that testimony in front of the defendant will cause serious emotional distress such that the child cannot reasonably communicate; the defendant is able to watch the testimony on television and to communicate with defense counsel electronically.

502. The exclusion of defendant's hypnotically refreshed testimony because of a flat rule excluding all such testimony violated her right to testify in her own behalf. The trial court's ruling excluding such testimony effectively prevented the defendant from testifying about most of the circumstances of the crime. Although a court might exclude evidence in a particular case if it were not reliable, the wholesale exclusion of the defendant's testimony on the basis of a *per se* rule was not permissible. Rock v. Arkansas, 483 U.S. 44 (1987) (5–4).

503. "[A] defendant is not entitled to an unlimited number of witnesses to testify in his behalf, lest our criminal justice system grind to a complete halt. He is entitled to have compulsory process served only on as many witnesses as will assist him in receiving a fair trial under the circumstances of his case." Ross v. Estelle, 694 F.2d 1008, 1111 (5th Cir.1983). The court held that the defendant was not denied due process by the trial judge's refusal to subpoena more than six out of 14 potential witnesses, whose testimony was "largely cumulative."

Roviaro v. United States

353 U.S. 53, 77 S.Ct. 623, 1 L.Ed.2d 639 (1957).

■ MR. JUSTICE BURTON delivered the opinion of the Court.

This case concerns a conviction for violation of the Narcotic Drugs Import and Export Act, as amended. The principal issue is whether the United States District Court committed reversible error when it allowed the Government to refuse to disclose the identity of an undercover employee who had taken a material part in bringing about the possession of certain drugs by the accused, had been present with the accused at the occurrence of the alleged crime, and might be a material witness as to whether the accused knowingly transported the drugs as charged. For the reasons hereafter stated, we hold that, under the circumstances here present, this was reversible error.

In 1955, in the Northern District of Illinois, petitioner, Albert Roviaro, was indicted on two counts by a federal grand jury. The first count charged that on August 12, 1954, at Chicago, Illinois, he sold heroin to one "John Doe" in violation of 26 U.S.C. § 2554(a). The second charged that on the same date and in the same city he "did then and there fraudulently and knowingly receive, conceal, buy and facilitate the transportation and concealment after importation of . . . heroin, knowing the same to be imported into the United States contrary to law; in violation of Section 174, Title 21, United States Code."

Before trial, petitioner moved for a bill of particulars requesting, among other things, the name, address and occupation of "John Doe." The Government objected on the ground that John Doe was an informer and that his identity was privileged. The motion was denied.

Petitioner, who was represented by counsel, waived a jury and was tried by the District Court. During the trial John Doe's part in the charged transaction was described by government witnesses, and counsel for petitioner, in cross-examining them, sought repeatedly to learn John Doe's identity. The court declined to permit this cross-examination and John Doe was not produced, identified, or otherwise made available. Petitioner was found guilty on both counts . . . . We granted certiorari . . . in order to pass upon the propriety of the nondisclosure of the informer's identity. . . .

At the trial, the Government relied on the testimony of two federal narcotics agents, Durham and Fields, and two Chicago police officers, Bryson and Sims, each of whom knew petitioner by sight. On the night of August 12, 1954, these four officers met at 75th Street and Prairie Avenue in Chicago with an informer described only as John Doe. Doe and his Cadillac car were searched and no narcotics were found. Bryson secreted himself in the trunk of Doe's Cadillac taking with him a device with which to raise the trunk lid from the inside. Doe then drove the Cadillac to 70th Place and St. Lawrence Avenue, followed by Durham in one government car and Field and Sims in another. After an hour's wait, at about 11 o'clock, petitioner arrived in a Pontiac, accompanied by an unidentified man. Petitioner immediately entered Doe's Cadillac, taking a front seat beside Doe. They then proceeded by a circuitous route to 74th Street near Champlain Avenue. Both government cars trailed the Cadillac but only the one driven by Durham managed to follow it to 74th Street. When the Cadillac came to a stop on 74th Street, Durham stepped out of his car onto the sidewalk and saw petitioner alight from the Cadillac about 100 feet away. Durham saw petitioner walk a few feet to a nearby tree, pick up a small package, return to the open right front door of the Cadillac, make a motion as if depositing the package in the car, and then wave to Doe and walk away. Durham went immediately to the Cadillac and recovered a package from the floor. He signaled to Bryson to come out of the trunk and then walked down the street in time to see petitioner re-enter the Pontiac, parked nearby, and ride away.

Meanwhile, Bryson, concealed in the trunk of the Cadillac, had heard a conversation between John Doe and petitioner after the latter had entered the car. He heard petitioner greet John Doe and direct him where to drive. At one point, petitioner admonished him to pull over to the curb, cut the motor, and turn out the lights so as to lose a "tail." He then told him to continue "further down." Petitioner asked about money Doe owed him. He advised Doe that he had brought him "three pieces this time." When Bryson heard Doe being ordered to stop the car, he raised the lid of the trunk slightly. After the car stopped, he saw petitioner walk to a tree, pick up a package, and return toward the car. He heard petitioner say, "Here it is," and "I'll call you in a couple of days." Shortly thereafter he heard Durham's signal to come out and emerged from the trunk to find Durham holding a small package found to contain three glassine envelopes containing a white powder.

A field test of the powder having indicated that it contained an opium derivative, the officers, at about 12:30 a.m., arrested petitioner at his home and took him, along with Doe, to Chicago police headquarters. There petitioner was confronted with Doe, who denied that he knew or had ever seen petitioner. Subsequent chemical analysis revealed that the powder contained heroin.

I

Petitioner contends that the trial court erred in upholding the right of the Government to withhold the identity of John Doe. He argues that Doe was an active participant in the illegal activity charged and that, therefore, the Government could not withhold his identity, his whereabouts, and whether he was alive or dead at the time of trial. The Government does not defend the nondisclosure of Doe's identity with respect to Count 1, which charged a sale of heroin to John Doe, but it attempts to sustain the judgment on the basis of the conviction on Count 2, charging illegal transportation of narcotics. It argues that the conviction on Count 2 may properly be upheld since the identity of the informer, in the circumstances of this case, has no real bearing on that charge and is therefore privileged.

What is usually referred to as the informer's privilege is in reality the Government's privilege to withhold from disclosure the identity of persons who furnish information of violations of law to officers charged with enforcement of that law. . . . The purpose of the privilege is the furtherance and protection of the public interest in effective law enforcement. The privilege recognizes the obligation of citizens to communicate their knowledge of the commission of crimes to law-enforcement officials and, by preserving their anonymity, encourages them to perform that obligation.

The scope of the privilege is limited by its underlying purpose. Thus, where the disclosure of the contents of a communication will not tend to reveal the identity of an informer, the contents are not privileged. Likewise, once the identity of the informer has been disclosed to those who would have cause to resent the communication, the privilege is no longer applicable.

A further limitation on the applicability of the privilege arises from the fundamental requirements of fairness. Where the disclosure of an informer's identity, or of the contents of his communication, is relevant and helpful to the defense of an accused, or is essential to a fair determination of a cause, the privilege must give way. In these situations the trial court may require disclosure and, if the Government withholds the information, dismiss the action. Most of the federal cases involving this limitation on the scope of the informer's privilege have arisen where the legality of a search without a warrant is in issue and the communications of an informer are claimed to establish probable cause. In these cases the Government has been required to disclose the identity of the informant unless there was sufficient evidence apart from his confidential communication.

. . .

We believe that no fixed rule with respect to disclosure is justifiable. The problem is one that calls for balancing the public interest in protecting the flow of information against the individual's right to prepare his defense. Whether a proper balance renders nondisclosure erroneous must depend on the particular circumstances of each case, taking into consideration the crime charged, the possible defenses, the possible significance of the informer's testimony, and other relevant factors.

II

The materiality of John Doe's possible testimony must be determined by reference to the offense charged in Count 2 and the evidence relating to that count. The charge is in the language of the statute. It does not charge mere possession; it charges that petitioner did "fraudulently and knowingly receive, conceal, buy and facilitate the transportation and concealment after importation of . . . heroin, knowing the same to be imported into the United States contrary to law. . . ." While John Doe is not expressly mentioned, this charge, when viewed in connection with the evidence introduced at the trial, is so closely related to John Doe as to make his identity and testimony highly material.

It is true that the last sentence of subdivision (c) of § 2 authorizes a conviction when the Government has proved that the accused possessed narcotics, unless the accused explains or justifies such possession. But this statutory presumption does not reduce the offense to one of mere possession or shift the burden of proof; it merely places on the accused, at a certain point, the burden of going forward with his defense. The fact that petitioner here was faced with the burden of explaining or justifying his alleged possession of the heroin emphasizes his vital need for access to any material witness. Otherwise, the burden of going forward might become unduly heavy.

The circumstances of this case demonstrate that John Doe's possible testimony was highly relevant and might have been helpful to the defense. So far as petitioner knew, he and John Doe were alone and unobserved during the crucial occurrence for which he was indicted. Unless petitioner waived his constitutional right not to take the stand in his own defense, John Doe was his one material witness. Petitioner's opportunity to cross-examine Police Officer Bryson and Federal Narcotics Agent Durham was hardly a substitute for an opportunity to examine the man who had been nearest to him and took part in the transaction. Doe had helped to set up the criminal occurrence and had played a prominent part in it. His testimony might have disclosed an entrapment. He might have thrown doubt upon petitioner's identity or on the identity of the package. He was the only witness who might have testified to petitioner's possible lack of knowledge of the contents of the package that he "transported" from the tree to John Doe's car. The desirability of calling John Doe as a witness, or at least interviewing him in preparation for trial, was a matter for the accused rather than the Government to decide.

Finally, the Government's use against petitioner of his conversation with John Doe while riding in Doe's car particularly emphasizes the unfairness of the nondisclosure in this case. The only person, other than petitioner himself, who could controvert, explain or amplify Bryson's report of this important conversation was John Doe. Contradiction or amplification might have borne upon petitioner's knowledge of the contents of the package or might have tended to show an entrapment.

This is a case where the Government's informer was the sole participant, other than the accused, in the transaction charged. The informer was the only witness in a position to amplify or contradict the testimony of government witnesses. Moreover, a government witness testified that Doe denied knowing petitioner or ever having seen him before. We conclude that, under these circumstances, the trial court committed prejudicial error in permitting the Government to withhold the identity of its undercover employee in the face of repeated demands by the accused for his disclosure. . . .[26]

---

504. "What *Roviaro* . . . makes clear is that this Court was unwilling to impose any absolute rule requiring disclosure of an informer's identity even in formulating evidentiary rules for federal criminal trials." McCray v. Illinois, 386 U.S. 300, 311 (1967).

The courts have generally held that *Roviaro* requires disclosure if the informant was a participant in or witness to the crime charged, but not if he was a mere "tipster" who informed the government about the offense. See, e.g., United States v. Price, 783 F.2d 1132 (4th Cir.1986); Gaines v. Hess, 662 F.2d 1364 (10th Cir.1981); United States v. Silva, 580 F.2d 144 (5th Cir.1978).

505. "[W]here the informant is shown to be a material witness and the government does not plan to use the informant as a witness it owes a duty

---

[26] Justice Clark wrote a dissenting opinion.

to make every reasonable effort to have the informant made available to the defendant to interview or use as a witness, if desired." United States v. Barnes, 486 F.2d 776, 779–80 (8th Cir.1973). See, e.g., Renzi v. Virginia, 794 F.2d 155 (4th Cir.1986) (misleading information supplied to defense by prosecution deprived defense of opportunity to find and produce informer); United States v. Tornabene, 687 F.2d 312 (9th Cir.1982) (government failed to make reasonable efforts to produce informant; new trial ordered); United States v. Tuck, 380 F.2d 857 (2d Cir.1967) (government is not a "guarantor" of informant's appearance but must "accord reasonable cooperation" in securing his appearance).

506. It is a denial of the defendant's constitutional right to confront the witnesses against him to prevent defense counsel from eliciting a witness's true name and address on cross-examination. "[W]hen the credibility of a witness is in issue, the very starting point in 'exposing falsehood and bringing out the truth'[27] through cross-examination must necessarily be to ask the witness who he is and where he lives. The witness' name and address open countless avenues of in-court examination and out-of-court investigation. To forbid this most rudimentary inquiry at the threshold is effectively to emasculate the right of cross-examination itself." Smith v. Illinois, 390 U.S. 129, 131 (1968).

507. In Brooks v. Tennessee, 406 U.S. 605 (1972) (6–3), the Court held that a state statute requiring a defendant to testify, if at all, before other defense witnesses testified was unconstitutional, because it restricted his privilege against self-incrimination, by limiting his ability to choose on the basis of the rest of the evidence whether to speak, and denied him due process, by restricting his ability to prepare his case.

On the defendant's right to testify, see United States v. Panza, 612 F.2d 432 (9th Cir.1979) (defendant's direct testimony stricken after he refused to answer relevant questions on cross-examination). See generally United States ex rel. Wilcox v. Johnson, 555 F.2d 115 (3d Cir.1977), concluding that the federal courts (and some state courts) have appeared to recognize a constitutional right to testify in one's own behalf.

508. On the practice of allowing jurors to participate in the examination of witnesses, by presenting written questions to the judge who then asks the questions of the witnesses, see United States v. George, 986 F.2d 1176 (8th Cir.1993) (practice discussed and upheld); United States v. Sutton, 970 F.2d 1001 (1st Cir.1992). In United States v. Bush, 47 F.3d 511

---

27. See Pointer v. Texas, 380 U.S., at 404.

(2d Cir.1995) the court said that it was within the trial judge's discretion to allow the practice, but discouraged it. *Bush* was followed in United States v. Ajmal, 67 F.3d 12 (2d Cir.1995). The court said that questioning by jurors should be reserved for exceptional circumstances and should not be allowed as "a matter of course." See United States v. Feinberg, 89 F.3d 333 (7th Cir.1996) (questioning of witnesses by jurors is within district judge's discretion); United States v. Thompson, 76 F.3d 442 (2d Cir.1996) (jury improperly allowed to ask questions of witnesses; harmless error).

FEDERAL RULES OF CRIMINAL PROCEDURE

Rule 26.2

PRODUCTION OF WITNESS STATEMENTS

(a) Motion for Production. After a witness other than the defendant has testified on direct examination, the court, on motion of a party who did not call the witness, shall order the attorney for the government or the defendant and the defendant's attorney, as the case may be, to produce, for the examination and use of the moving party, any statement of the witness that is in their possession and that relates to the subject matter concerning which the witness has testified.

(b) Production of Entire Statement. If the entire contents of the statement relate to the subject matter concerning which the witness has testified, the court shall order that the statement be delivered to the moving party.

(c) Production of Excised Statement. If the other party claims that the statement contains privileged information or matter that does not relate to the subject matter concerning which the witness has testified, the court shall order that it be delivered to the court in camera. Upon inspection, the court shall excise the portions of the statement that are privileged or that do not relate to the subject matter concerning which the witness has testified, and shall order that the statement, with such material excised, be delivered to the moving party. Any portion of the statement that is withheld from the defendant over the defendant's objection must be preserved by the attorney for the government, and, if the defendant appeals a conviction, must be made available to the appellate court for the purpose of determining the correctness of the decision to excise the portion of the statement.

(d) Recess for Examination of Statement. Upon delivery of the statement to the moving party, the court, upon application of that party, may recess the proceedings so that counsel may examine the statement and prepare to use it in the proceedings.

(e) Sanction for Failure to Produce Statement. If the other party elects not to comply with an order to deliver a statement to the moving party, the court shall order that the testimony of the witness be stricken from the record and that the trial proceed, or, if it is the attorney for the government who elects not to comply, shall declare a mistrial if required by the interest of justice.

(f) Definition. As used in this rule, a "statement" of a witness means:

(1) a written statement made by the witness that is signed or otherwise adopted or approved by the witness;

(2) a substantially verbatim recital of an oral statement made by the witness that is recorded contemporaneously with the making of the oral statement and that is contained in a stenographic, mechanical, electrical, or other recording or a transcription thereof; or

(3) a statement, however taken or recorded, or a transcription thereof, made by the witness to a grand jury.

(g) Scope of Rule. This rule applies at a suppression hearing conducted under Rule 12, at trial under this rule, and to the extent specified:

(1) in Rule 32(c)(2) at sentencing;

(2) in Rule 32.1(c) at a hearing to revoke or modify probation or supervised release;

(3) in Rule 46(i) at a detention hearing;

(4) in Rule 8 of the Rules Governing Proceedings under 28 U.S.C. § 2255; and

(5) in Rule 5.1 at a preliminary examination.

---

509. In Jencks v. United States, 353 U.S. 657 (1957), the petitioner was convicted of swearing falsely that he was not a member of or affiliated with the communist party (see 18 U.S.C. § 1001). The government's principal witnesses were party members whom the F.B.I. paid to make contemporaneous reports of party activities. They testified at the trial concerning activities in which the petitioner had allegedly participated, and on cross-examination referred to their reports to the F.B.I. Motions for production of the reports for inspection and use in cross-examination were denied. The Court reversed the conviction. It held that the petitioner was entitled to inspect the reports even though a preliminary foundation of inconsistency between them and the witnesses' testimony was not established; "a sufficient foundation was established by the testimony of [the witnesses] that their reports were of the events and activities related in their testimony," id. at 666. "[T]he petitioner was entitled to an order directing the

Government to produce for inspection all reports of . . . [the witnesses] in its possession, written and, when orally made, as recorded by the F.B.I., touching the events and activities as to which they testified at the trial. . . . [F]urther . . . the petitioner is entitled to inspect the reports to decide whether to use them in his defense. Because only the defense is adequately equipped to determine the effective use for purpose of discrediting the Government's witness and thereby furthering the accused's defense, the defense must initially be entitled to see them to determine what use may be made of them. Justice requires no less." Id. at 668–69. The Court held finally that if the government elected not to comply with an order to produce on the ground of privilege, the criminal action must be dismissed.

The "Jencks Act," 18 U.S.C. § 3500, was a congressional response to the Court's holding. It provided for the disclosure of statements of prosecution witnesses, in the manner set forth in Rule 26.2 above. It is clear from the legislative history of the act that it was intended to preserve the core of the Court's holding—that a defendant is entitled to inspect at trial statements of prosecution witnesses which might provide a basis for impeachment—but to eliminate the possibility of general disclosure of the government's files. House Report No. 700, 85th Cong., 1st Sess. 2, for example, stated that the proposed bill "sets standards of interpretation (1) for safeguarding the needless disclosure of confidential information in Government files and at the same time (2) assuring defendants access to the materials in those files which is pertinent to the testimony of Government witnesses."

Although it has generally been assumed that the requirements of the Jencks Act are not constitutionally based, see United States v. Augenblick, 393 U.S. 348, 356 (1969), the substance of the act has been accepted by state courts. See, e.g., State v. Hunt, 138 A.2d 1 (N.J.1958); State v. Foster, 407 P.2d 901 (Or.1965).

Rule 26.2 extends the provisions of the Jencks Act to disclosure of statements of defense witnesses as well. The Court evidently countenanced such an extension in United States v. Nobles, 422 U.S. 225 (1975). In *Nobles*, the trial judge ruled that if the defense called a defense investigator as a witness primarily to impeach the testimony of prosecution witnesses by prior statements made to the investigator, defense counsel would have to turn over to the prosecutor relevant portions of the investigator's report after he had finished testifying. Counsel refused, and the investigator was not allowed to testify about his interviews with the witnesses. The Court held that the ruling at trial was proper.

Judicial construction of the Jencks Act presumably is applicable to construction of Rule 26.2. For construction of the Act, see Simmons v. United States, 390 U.S. 377, 386–89 (1968) (photographs incorporated in statement); Campbell v. United States, 373 U.S. 487 (1963); Clancy v. United States, 365 U.S. 312 (1961); Palermo v. United States, 360 U.S. 343 (1959).

There is no exception from the category of "statements" producible under the Jencks Act for a lawyer's work product; a government lawyer's notes of his interview with a witness are producible if the requirements of the act are otherwise met. Goldberg v. United States, 425 U.S. 94 (1976).

The provisions of Rule 26.2 are not limited to witnesses at the trial itself. Rule 12(i), p. 773 above, provides expressly that Rule 26.2 applies to a hearing on a motion to suppress evidence under Rule 12(b)(3). It provides further that in such a hearing, a law enforcement officer shall be deemed a "witness called by the government." See United States v. Rosa, 891 F.2d 1074 (3d Cir.1989) (Jencks Act material producible by government at sentencing hearing).

What should be the consequence if the government inadvertently loses or destroys statements of a witness? In Killian v. United States, 368 U.S. 231, 242 (1961), the Court said that the destruction of notes "in good faith and in accord with . . . normal practice" would not deprive the defendant of any right. In United States v. Beasley, 576 F.2d 626 (5th Cir.1978), however, the court concluded that a failure in good faith to produce a material statement required reversal of the conviction. Compare United States v. Perry, 471 F.2d 1057 (D.C.Cir.1972). Increasing experience with the requirements of the Act and Rule 26.2 makes it less likely that a court will find good faith if statements that are required to be produced are unavailable. In United States v. Harris, 543 F.2d 1247 (9th Cir.1976), for example, the court declared that the FBI could not consistently with the provisions of the Jencks Act continue its practice of routinely disposing of rough notes of interviews with prospective government witnesses. Preservation of such notes, the court said, "is necessary in order to permit courts to play their proper role in determining what evidence must be produced pursuant to the Jencks Act or other applicable law." Id. at 1253.

The remedy for an untimely production of Jencks Act material is not limited to those in 18 U.S.C. § 3500(d) or, presumably, Rule 26.2(e), if the delay in production was in good faith. In that circumstance, it is not construed as an election "not to comply" for purposes of that provision. Therefore, if the failure to produce is curable, the court can exercise its discretion to provide a remedy other than striking the testimony or declaring a mistrial. United States v. Wables, 731 F.2d 440 (7th Cir.1984).

"[T]he Jencks Act contemplates not only the furnishing of the statement of a witness but a reasonable opportunity to examine it and prepare for its use in the trial." United States v. Holmes, 722 F.2d 37, 40 (4th Cir.1983) (failure to grant continuance; conviction reversed).

———

FEDERAL RULES OF CRIMINAL PROCEDURE

Rule 26.3

MISTRIAL

Before ordering a mistrial, the court shall provide an opportunity for the government, and for each defendant to comment on the propriety of the order, including whether each party consents or objects to a mistrial, and to suggest any alternatives.

_____

Defense

_____

ABA Standards for Criminal Justice,
Prosecution Function and Defense Function (3d ed., 1993).
Defense Function Standards

4-1.2 The Function of Defense Council.

(a) Counsel for the accused is an essential component of the administration of criminal justice. A court properly constituted to hear a criminal case must be viewed as a tripartite entity consisting of the judge (and jury, where appropriate), counsel for the prosecution, and counsel for the accused.

(b) The basic duty defense counsel owes to the administration of justice and as an officer of the court is to serve as the accused's counselor and advocate with courage and devotion and to render effective, quality representation.

. . .

4-1.6 Trial Lawyer's Duty to Administration of Justice.

(a) The bar should encourage through every available means the widest possible participation in the defense of criminal cases by lawyers. Lawyers should be encouraged to qualify themselves for participation in criminal cases both by formal training and through experience as associate counsel.

(b) All such qualified lawyers should stand ready to undertake the defense of an accused regardless of public hostility toward the accused or personal distaste for the offense charged or the person of the defendant.

(c) Such qualified lawyers should not assert or announce a general unwillingness to appear in criminal cases. Law firms should encourage partners and associates to become qualified and to appear in criminal cases.

(d) Such qualified lawyers should not seek to avoid appointment by a tribunal to represent an accused except for good cause, such as: representing the accused is likely to result in violation of applicable ethical codes or other law, representing the accused is likely to result in an unreasonable financial burden on the lawyer, or the client or crime is so repugnant to the lawyer as to be likely to impair the client-lawyer relationship or the lawyer's ability to represent the client.

_____

What limits are there on the obligation of a lawyer who is regularly engaged in the defense of criminal cases to accept as a client anyone who is prepared to pay for his services? On what is the obligation based?

———

ABA Model Code of Professional Responsibility (1981).

Canon 1 A Lawyer Should Assist in Maintaining the Integrity and Competence of the Legal Profession

DR [Disciplinary Rule] 1–102 Misconduct.

(A) A lawyer shall not:

. . .

(4) Engage in conduct involving dishonesty, fraud, deceit or misrepresentation.

(5) Engage in conduct that is prejudicial to the administration of justice.

(6) Engage in any other conduct that adversely reflects on his fitness to practice law.

Canon 4 A Lawyer Should Preserve the Confidences and Secrets of a Client

DR 4–101 Preservation of Confidences and Secrets of a Client.

(A) "Confidence" refers to information protected by the attorney-client privilege under applicable law, and "secret" refers to other information gained in the professional relationship that the client has requested be held inviolate or the disclosure of which would be embarrassing or would be likely to be detrimental to the client.

(B) Except when permitted under DR 4–101(C), a lawyer shall not knowingly:

(1) Reveal a confidence or secret of his client.

(2) Use a confidence or secret of his client to the disadvantage of the client.

. . .

(C) A lawyer may reveal:

. . .

(2) Confidences or secrets when permitted under Disciplinary Rules or required by law or court order.

(3) The intention of his client to commit a crime and the information necessary to prevent the crime.

. . .

Canon 7 A Lawyer Should Represent a Client Zealously Within the Bounds of the Law

EC [Ethical Consideration] 7–5 A lawyer as adviser furthers the interest of his client by giving his professional opinion as to what he believes would likely be the ultimate decision of the courts on the matter at hand and by informing his client of the practical effect of such decision. He may continue in the representation of his client even though his client has elected to pursue a course of conduct contrary to the advice of the lawyer so long as he does not thereby knowingly assist the client to engage in illegal conduct or to take a frivolous legal position. A lawyer should never encourage or aid his client to commit criminal acts or counsel his client on how to violate the law and avoid punishment therefor.

EC 7–27 Because it interferes with the proper administration of justice, a lawyer should not suppress evidence that he or his client has a legal obligation to reveal or produce. In like manner, a lawyer should not advise or cause a person to secrete himself or to leave the jurisdiction of a tribunal for the purpose of making him unavailable as a witness therein.

DR 7–101 Representing a Client Zealously.

. . .

(B) In his representation of a client, a lawyer may:

. . .

(2) Refuse to aid or participate in conduct that he believes to be unlawful, even though there is some support for an argument that the conduct is legal.

DR 7–102 Representing a Client Within the Bounds of the Law.

(A) In his representation of a client, a lawyer shall not:

. . .

(3) Conceal or knowingly fail to disclose that which he is required by law to reveal.

(4) Knowingly use perjured testimony or false evidence.

(5) Knowingly make a false statement of law or fact.

(6) Participate in the creation or preservation of evidence when he knows or it is obvious that the evidence is false.

(7) Counsel or assist his client in conduct that the lawyer knows to be illegal or fraudulent.

(8) Knowingly engage in other illegal conduct or conduct contrary to a Disciplinary Rule.

. . .

Hitch v. Pima County Superior Court

146 Ariz. 588, 708 P.2d 72 (1985).

■ CAMERON, JUSTICE.

This is a special action brought by defendant from an order of the trial court compelling defendant's attorney to deliver potentially inculpatory, physical evidence to the state and requiring that the attorney withdraw from representation. We have jurisdiction pursuant to Ariz. Const. Art. 6, § 5(3) and Rule 7, R.P.Sp.Act., 17A A.R.S.

We must decide three questions:

1. Does a defense attorney have an obligation to turn over to the state potentially inculpatory, physical evidence obtained from a third party?

2. If so, in what manner may this be done?

3. Must he then withdraw as attorney for the defendant?

The essential facts are not in dispute. Defendant was indicted for first degree murder and is currently awaiting trial on that charge. In the course of their investigation, the police interviewed defendant's girlfriend, Diane Heaton, who told them that the victim was in possession of a certain wristwatch shortly before his death. Subsequently, an investigator for the Pima County Public Defender's Office contacted Ms. Heaton and she informed him that she had found a wristwatch in defendant's suit jacket. She also stated that she did not want to turn the evidence over to the police. The investigator contacted defendant's attorney who told him to take possession of the watch and bring it to the attorney's office. The attorney indicated that he did this for two reasons. First, he wanted to examine the watch to determine whether it was the same one that Ms. Heaton had described to the police. Second, he was afraid that she might destroy or conceal the evidence. Shortly thereafter, defendant informed the police that he had taken a watch from the victim. The police were, however, unaware of the location of that watch.

On 11 June 1984, defendant's attorney filed a petition with the Ethics Committee of the Arizona State Bar, requesting an opinion concerning his duties with respect to the wristwatch. The Ethics Committee informed the attorney that he had a legal obligation to turn over the watch to the state and that he also might be compelled to testify as to the original location and source of the evidence. . . .

Defendant's attorney informed the Respondent Judge of the Committee's decision. Judge Veliz ordered that the watch be turned over to the state and that the attorney withdraw from the case. He also stayed the order to allow the filing of this petition for special action. We accepted jurisdiction because this case presents an issue of statewide importance in an area of the law that is unsettled.

I

Must Defendant's Attorney Turn the Evidence Over to the State?

We have previously held that an attorney need not turn over physical evidence obtained from his client if the evidence was such that it could not be obtained from the client against the client's will. . . . We have not, however, ruled as to physical evidence obtained from a third party. As to this question, cases from other jurisdictions are few in number. We do note, however, two cases that have dealt with the issue before us and have found that a defense attorney, as an officer of the court, has an obligation to turn over to the state material evidence obtained from third parties.

The Alaska Supreme Court was confronted with a case in which the defendant's attorney in a kidnapping case had received from a third party written plans for the kidnapping drawn by the client. In reviewing whether counsel violated defendant's right to adequate representation by making the existence of the plans known to the state, the court stated:

> As Morrell notes, authority in this area is surprisingly sparse. The existing authority seems to indicate, however, that a criminal defense attorney has an obligation to turn over to the prosecution physical evidence which comes into his possession, especially where the evidence comes into the attorney's possession through acts of a third party who is neither a client of the attorney nor an agent of a client. After turning over such evidence, an attorney may have either a right or a duty to remain silent as to the circumstances under which he obtained such evidence, but Morrell presents no authority which establishes that a criminal defendant whose attorney chooses to testify regarding to these matters is denied effective assistance of counsel. Morrell v. State, 575 P.2d 1200, 1207 (Alaska 1978).

The California Court of Appeals, in a case in which the defendant's wife had given his attorney a pair of shoes, linked to the murder, which the state seized from defendant's attorney, stated:

> In any event, in the final analysis the controlling question is whether the State's seizure of the evidence violated defendant's rights. It did not. Neither the public defender nor substituted counsel for defendant had the right to withhold the evidence from the State by asserting an attorney-client privilege.

People v. Lee, 3 Cal.App.3d 514, 526, 83 Cal.Rptr. 715, 722 (1970).

Both cases relied on dictum from State v. Olwell, 64 Wash.2d 828, 394 P.2d 681 (1964), in finding that counsel had acted properly. In Olwell, defense counsel was served with a subpoena duces tecum in which he was asked to produce, at a coroner's inquest, all knives in his possession and control relating to the defendant. The attorney refused to indicate whether or not he was in possession of these knives, arguing that to do so would violate the confidential relationship of attorney and client. The Washington Supreme Court found that the subpoena was defective on its face because it required the attorney to reveal information given to him in the course of discussions with his client. The court stated, however:

The attorney should not be a depository for criminal evidence . . . which in itself has little, if any, material value for the purposes of aiding counsel in the preparation of the defense of his client's case. Such evidence given the attorney during legal consultation for information purposes and used by the attorney in preparing the defense of his client's case, whether or not the case ever goes to trial, could clearly be withheld for a reasonable period of time. It follows that the attorney, after a reasonable period, should, as an officer of the court, on his own motion turn the same over to the prosecution.

Id. 394 P.2d at 684–85.

Of course, if the physical evidence is contraband, the attorney may be required to turn over the property even if he obtained that evidence from his client. For example, in a case where the attorney obtained from his client the money taken in a bank robbery and a sawed-off shotgun used in the crime, the attorney was required to turn the property over to the state. In Re Ryder, 381 F.2d 713 (4th Cir.1967). . . .

At issue is the conflict between a defense attorney's obligation to his client and to the court. As the Preamble to the Rules of Professional Conduct notes, a lawyer is both "a representative of [his] clients, an officer of the legal system and a public citizen having special responsibility for the quality of justice." As a representative of his client, a lawyer must act as a zealous advocate, demonstrating loyalty to his client and giving him the best legal advice possible within the bounds of the law. As part of this zealous representation, the lawyer is admonished not to reveal information relating to representation of his client. ER 1.6.

The Comment to ER 1.6 states:

> The principle of confidentiality is given effect in two related bodies of law, the attorney-client privilege (which includes the work product doctrine) in the law of evidence and the rule of confidentiality established in professional ethics. The attorney-client privilege applies in judicial and other proceedings in which a lawyer may be called as a witness or otherwise required to produce evidence concerning a client. The rule of client-lawyer confidentiality applies in situations other than those where evidence is sought from the lawyer through compulsion of law. The confidentiality rule applies not merely to matters communicated in confidence by the client but also to all information relating to the representation, whatever its source. A lawyer may not disclose such information except as authorized or required by the Rules of Professional Conduct or other law.

Because clients are aware that their lawyers will not repeat their communications, they feel that they may make both full and honest disclosure. Trial counsel is thus better able to evaluate the situation and prepare a proper defense. Thus, it has been said that "it is in the interest of public justice that the client be able to make full disclosure." Clark v. State, 159 Tex.Crim.App. 187, 199, 261 S.W.2d 339, 346 . . . (1953).

We note also that the lawyer's role as a zealous advocate is an important one, not only for the client but for the administration of justice. We have chosen an adversary system of justice in which, in theory, the state and the defendant meet as equals—"strength against strength, resource against resource, argument against argument." United States v. Bagley, 473 U.S. 667, 694 n. 2 . . . (1985) (Marshall, J. dissenting). In order to close the gap between theory and practice and thereby ensure that the system is working properly, a defendant must have an attorney who will fight against the powerful resources of the state. It is only when this occurs that we can be assured that the system is functioning properly and only the guilty are convicted.

Balanced against the attorney's obligation to his client is the attorney's obligation as an officer of the court, which requires him "[to aid] in determining truth whenever possible." Note, Ethics, Law and Loyalty: The Attorney's Duty to Turn Over Incriminating Evidence, 32 Stan.L.Rev. 977, 992 (1980). Both sides must have equal access to the relevant information. As the American Bar Association had noted: "[w]here the necessary evaluation and preparation are foreclosed by lack of information, the trial becomes a pursuit of truth and justice only by chance rather than by design, and generates a diminished respect for the criminal justice system, the judiciary and the attorney participants." II ABA Standards for Criminal Justice, comment to Standard 11–1.1(a) (2nd ed.1982) (footnote omitted). . . . Thus, in order to aid the truth determining process an attorney must refrain from impeding the flow of information to the state. The defendant's attorney can neither assist nor obstruct the prosecution in its efforts to discover evidence.

Defendant asks us, in balancing these competing interests, to hold that there is "no affirmative duty on the part of defense counsel to disclose possible inculpatory evidence obtained by counsel during the course of his representation of the client." Defendant maintains that to hold otherwise would cause irreparable harm to the attorney-client relationship.

The National Legal Aid and Defender Association in its amicus brief agrees with defendant that there should be no "absolute affirmative duty rule" requiring defendant's attorney to routinely disclose all physical evidence discovered during investigation of a case. The National Legal Aid and Defender Association suggests that we adopt the "Ethical Standard to Guide [A Lawyer] Who Receives Physical Evidence Implicating His Client in Criminal Conduct," proposed by the Criminal Justice Section's Ethics Committee. This standard reads as follows:

> (a) A lawyer who receives a physical item under circumstances implicating a client in criminal conduct shall disclose the location of or shall deliver that item to law enforcement authorities only: (1) if such is required by law or court order, or (2) as provided in paragraph (d).
>
> (b) Unless required to disclose, the lawyer shall return the item to the source from whom the lawyer receives it, as provided in paragraphs (c) and (d). In returning the item to the source, the lawyer shall advise the source of the legal consequences pertaining to possession or destruction of the item.
>
> (c) A lawyer may receive the item for a period of time during which the lawyer: (1) intends to return it to the owner; (2) reasonably fears that

return of the item to the source will result in destruction of the item; (3) reasonably fears that return of the item to the source will result in physical harm to anyone; (4) intends to test, examine, inspect or use the item in any way as part of the lawyer's representation of the client; or (5) cannot return it to the source. If the lawyer retains the item, the lawyer shall do so in a manner that does not impede the lawful ability of law enforcement to obtain the item.

(d) If the item received is contraband, or if in the lawyer's judgment the lawyer cannot retain the item in a way that does not pose an unreasonable risk of physical harm to anyone, the lawyer shall disclose the location of or shall deliver the item to law enforcement authorities.

(e) If the lawyer discloses the location of or delivers the item to law enforcement authorities under paragraphs (a) or (d), or to a third party under paragraph (c)(1), the lawyer shall do so in the way best designed to protect the client's interest.

29 Cr.L.Rep. 2465–66 (26 August 1981).

We agree with defendant that any requirement that the defendant's attorney turn over to the prosecutor physical evidence which may aid in the conviction of the defendant may harm the attorney-client relationship. We do not believe, however, that this reason, by itself, is sufficient to avoid disclosure. We have stated that "[t]he duty of an attorney to a client *** is subordinate to his responsibility for the due and proper administration of justice. In case of conflict, the former must yield to the latter." State v. Kruchten, 101 Ariz. 186, 191, 417 P.2d 510, 515 (1966). Thus, although we respect the relationship as an important one, we believe it must sometimes be subordinate to the free flow of information, upon which our adversary system is based. Other courts have shared our attitude. As the Kentucky Court of Appeals explained:

It has been said that the reason underlying the attorney-client privilege is to encourage a client to disclose fully the facts and circumstances of his case to his attorney without fear that he or his attorney will be compelled to testify to the communications between them. Since the privilege results in the exclusion of evidence it runs counter to the widely held view that the fullest disclosure of the facts will best lead to the truth and ultimately to the triumph of justice. In reconciling these conflicting principles the courts have pointed out that since the policy of full disclosure is the more fundamental one the privilege is not to be viewed as absolute and is to be strictly limited to the purpose for which it exists.

Hughes v. Meade, 453 S.W.2d 538, 540 (Ky.App.1970). . . . Consistent with this philosophy, we feel that the potential damage to the adversary system is greater, and in need of greater protection, than the attorney-client relationship. We do not wish to create a situation in which counsel is made a repository for physical evidence—a serious and inevitable problem once clients become aware that evidence given to their attorneys, even by friends, may never be turned over to the state.

We, therefore, adopt essentially the ethical standard proposed by the Ethics Committee of the Section on Criminal Justice of the American Bar Association with regards to inculpatory evidence delivered to the attorney by a third party. Our holding is as follows: first, if the attorney reasonably believes that evidence will not be destroyed, he may return it to the source, explaining the laws on concealment and destruction. Second, if the attorney has reasonable grounds to believe that the evidence might be destroyed, or if his client consents, he may turn the physical evidence over to the prosecution. Applying this test to the instant facts, the trial court was correct in ordering the wristwatch to be turned over to the state.

II

How Should the Evidence Be Returned?

Having decided that the evidence must be turned over to the prosecution, we must determine how this can best be done without further prejudice to the defendant. The Ethics Committee's proposed standards provide that when this is done "the lawyer shall do so in [a] way best designed to protect the client's interest." *Standards*, supra.

Amicus National Legal Aid and Defender Association suggests that if the lawyer decides to disclose the item he should do so by delivering the evidence to an agent who would then deliver it to the police without disclosing the source of the item or the case involved. Defendant, however, suggests that the procedure followed in the District of Columbia be considered. According to defendant, inculpatory evidence is delivered to the District of Columbia's bar counsel for subsequent delivery to law enforcement officials. Defendant urges that this Court adopt a system whereby an attorney could anonymously deliver evidence to State Bar counsel, or presidents of local county bar associations, in a sealed package which indicates that it is being delivered due to the affirmative disclosure requirement.

We disagree with both suggestions. Not all items have evidentiary significance in and of themselves. In this case, for instance, the watch is not inculpatory per se; rather, it is the fact that the watch was found in defendant's jacket that makes the watch material evidence. By returning the watch anonymously to the police, this significance is lost. Assuming investigating officials are even able to determine to what case the evidence belongs, they may never be able to reconstruct where it was originally discovered or under what circumstances. . . .

We believe it is simpler and more direct for defendant's attorney to turn the matter over to the state as long as it is understood that the prosecutor may not mention in front of the jury the fact that the evidence came from the defendant or his attorney. . . .

If a defendant is willing to enter a stipulation concerning the chain of possession, location or condition of the evidence, then the evidence may be admitted without the jury becoming aware of the source of the evidence. . . . Under these circumstances, the attorney need not be called as a witness.

III

Must the Attorney Withdraw as Counsel?

Under these procedures, the attorney need not withdraw as counsel. If the attorneys can stipulate as to the chain of possession and no reference is made to the fact that the defendant's attorney turned the matter over to the prosecution, then there is no need for the attorney to withdraw as counsel for the defendant. There may be some cases where the client will believe that his attorney no longer has his best interest in mind. In such a case, it may be wise for the attorney to ask to withdraw. Such request should be liberally granted by the court. Where, however, the client does not object, there is no need for the attorney to withdraw from the case.

DISPOSITION

As to the instant case, we find that defense counsel was forced to take possession of the evidence because of a reasonable fear that to do otherwise would result in its destruction. Because the source was a nonclient, and because he had reason to believe that the witness (source) would conceal or destroy the evidence, the attorney had an obligation to disclose the item and its source to the prosecution.

The order requiring disclosure is affirmed and the order requiring defendant's attorney to withdraw is reversed. The matter is remanded for further proceedings consistent with this opinion.

FELDMAN, JUSTICE, dissenting,

. . .

In my view . . . defense counsel should never be put in the position of helping the government prove its case. Of course, counsel may not mislead, tamper with evidence, lie or promote such acts. To do so would violate his duty as an officer of a court which seeks to ascertain the truth. On the other hand, because defense counsel is neither an assistant to nor an investigator for the prosecutor, his function is neither to gather nor preserve inculpatory evidence for the prosecution. If he engages in such conduct, how can he then put the government to its proof? How can he be a zealous advocate for the defendant when at the same time he is likely to make himself a star witness for the prosecution?

I am led to the inevitable conclusion that defense counsel has no obligation to take possession of inculpatory evidence from third parties. Further, caution and common sense dictate that as a general rule he should never actively seek to obtain such evidence and should refuse possession even if it is offered to him. His guiding principle should be to leave things as they are found. If counsel has reasonable grounds to believe that evidence is in danger of being tampered with or destroyed by a third party, his obligations are satisfied by cautioning that person against such conduct. The majority opinion is ambiguous on this issue, but I believe that we should make it clear to the defense bar that the general rule to be followed in connection with inculpatory evidence is "hands off."

Of course, there are limited exceptions to that general rule. The defense lawyer is justified in obtaining possession of evidence where necessary to test, examine or inspect that evidence in order to determine whether it is exculpatory. Also, the lawyer may expect to use the evidence in the representation of the client. Such limited circumstances are recognized in the standard proposed by the Ethics Committee of the Criminal Justice Section of the American Bar Association . . . .

Although the court purports "essentially" to adopt the standard . . . I believe it misconstrues it. The standard permits defense counsel to give inculpatory evidence to the prosecution only if it is required by court order or rule, if the item received is contraband or if it poses "an unreasonable risk of physical harm to anyone." (See subsec. (a) and (d)). No provision is made for delivery of inculpatory evidence to the prosecution simply because defense counsel fears that it may be destroyed if given back to its source.

In fact, the standard does cover the situation posed by this case. One of the reasons which prompted defense counsel to take the watch from Ms. Heaton was the need to examine it to determine whether it was the watch involved in the burglary. . . . Subsection (c) of the Standard indicates that this is a legitimate purpose for obtaining the evidence. It also indicates that when lawyers have received evidence which proves to be inculpatory it shall be returned to the source "from whom the lawyer receives it" and enjoins the lawyer to "advise the source of the legal consequences pertaining to possession or destruction of the item."

In my view, therefore, the standard clearly contemplates that the defense lawyer shall not obtain or take possession of evidence without good reason; but if he does receive it, when finished with it he must return it to its source and restore everything to the *status quo ante*. It is only if he finds that he is in possession of contraband or an item which may cause serious physical injury to others that the standard permits counsel to deliver inculpatory evidence to the prosecution. Nor does the standard contemplate that the lawyer make himself a repository for the evidence. In fact, the standard indicates that the lawyer may retain evidence only: 1) if he fears that return to the source will result in its destruction; 2) if he believes that on return it may cause serious harm to others; 3) because he intends to test, examine or use the evidence in his representation; or, 4) because he cannot return it to the source. Only under these limited circumstances may the lawyer retain the item "in a manner that does not impede the lawful ability of law enforcement to obtain the item."

Properly interpreted, therefore, the standard would instruct us as follows in the present case: if defense counsel had a legitimate reason to obtain the evidence, such as examination or testing, then it was proper to receive it from the third person who had possession. When so received, it was proper for defense counsel to retain the item while he examined it or had it tested. When he had finished with it and had discovered that he would not need it for trial, it was his duty to return it to the source with instructions as to the consequences of tampering or destruction. If he had a good faith belief that return to the source would result in damage to or destruction of the evidence, then it was his duty to retain the evidence in his possession "in a manner that [did] not impede the lawful ability of law enforcement to obtain the item."

Thus, I believe the majority is incorrect in holding that defense counsel should turn the evidence over to the prosecution. This holding has not only made defense counsel an assistant to the prosecutor's investigator but also an important witness for the prosecution. The future consequences of such a confusion of roles is bound to damage a system which, despite what we are told during periods of hysteria, has survived the test of time.

———

ABA Standards for Criminal Justice,
Prosecution Function and Defense Function (3d ed. 1993).
Defense Function Standards

Part III. Lawyer-Client Relationship

4-3.1 Establishment of Relationship.

(a) Defense counsel should seek to establish a relationship of trust and confidence with the accused and should discuss the objectives of the representation and whether defense counsel will continue to represent the accused if there is an appeal. Defense counsel should explain the necessity of full disclosure of all facts known to the client for an effective defense, and defense counsel should explain the extent to which counsel's obligation of confidentiality makes privileged the accused's disclosures.

. . .

4-3.2 Interviewing the Client.

(a) As soon as practicable, defense counsel should seek to determine all relevant facts known to the accused. In so doing, defense counsel should probe for all legally relevant information without seeking to influence the direction of the client's responses.

(b) Defense counsel should not instruct the client or intimate to the client in any way that the client should not be candid in revealing facts so as to afford defense counsel free rein to take action which would be precluded by counsel's knowing of such facts.

. . .

———

510. In United States v. Morrison, 602 F.2d 529 (3d Cir.1979), an agent of the federal Drug Enforcement Agency visited the defendant and discussed her case with her before the trial in the absence of counsel and without his knowledge. The agent was interested in obtaining her cooperation in an investigation, and suggested that she might be treated leniently if she did so; in that event, he urged, she should replace her lawyer with the public defender. He also questioned the quality of her lawyer's services. Finding that there was "a deliberate attempt to destroy the attorney-client relationship and to subvert the defendant's right to effective assistance of counsel and a fair trial," id. at 533, the court concluded that even without a showing of prejudice, the only remedy was a dismissal of the indictment with prejudice.

The court reversed. Assuming that the defendant's right to counsel had been violated, it concluded nevertheless that, in the absence of any prejudice to the defendant, dismissal of the indictment was inappropriate. 449 U.S. 361 (1981).

See United States v. Walker, 839 F.2d 1483 (11th Cir. 1988) (*Morrison* applied).

511. "On the night of April 3, 1976, Wade (the victim) and Jacqueline Otis, a friend of the defendants, entered a club known as Rich Jimmy's. Defendant Scott remained outside by a shoeshine stand. A few minutes later codefendant Meredith arrived outside the club. He told Scott he planned to rob Wade, and asked Scott to go into the club, find Jacqueline Otis, and ask her to get Wade to go out to Wade's car parked outside the club.

"In the meantime, Wade and Otis had left the club and walked to a liquor store to get some beer. Returning from the store, they left the beer in a bag by Wade's car and reentered the club. Scott then entered the club also and, according to the testimony of Laurie Ann Sam (a friend of Scott's who was already in the club), Scott asked Otis to get Wade to go back out to his car so Meredith could 'knock him in the head.'

"When Wade and Otis did go out to the car, Meredith attacked Wade from behind. After a brief struggle, two shots were fired; Wade fell, and Meredith, witnessed by Scott and Sam, ran from the scene.

"Scott went over to the body and, assuming Wade was dead, picked up the bag containing the beer and hid it behind a fence. Scott later returned, retrieved the bag, and took it home where Otis and Meredith joined him.

". . . James Schenk, Scott's first appointed attorney . . . visited Scott in jail more than a month after the crime occurred and solicited information about the murder, stressing that he had to be fully acquainted with the facts to avoid being 'sandbagged' by the prosecution during the trial. In response, Scott gave Schenk the same information that he had related earlier to the police. In addition, however, Scott told Schenk something

Scott had not revealed to the police: that he had seen a wallet, as well as the paper bag, on the ground near Wade. Scott said that he picked up the wallet, put it in the paper bag, and placed both behind a parking lot fence. He also said that he later retrieved the bag, took it home, found $100 in the wallet and divided it with Meredith, and then tried to burn the wallet in his kitchen sink. He took the partially burned wallet, Scott told Schenk, placed it in a plastic bag, and threw it in a burn barrel behind his house.

"Schenk, without further consulting Scott, retained Investigator Stephen Frick and sent Frick to find the wallet. Frick found it in the location described by Scott and brought it to Schenk." People v. Meredith, 631 P.2d 46, 49 (Cal.1981).

Wade's credit cards were inside the wallet. Scott and Meredith were charged with the robbery and murder of Wade. What should Schenk do?

See also Anderson v. State, 297 So.2d 871 (Fla.Dist.Ct.App.1974). In *Anderson*, the defendant retained a lawyer to defend him against charges of receiving and concealing stolen property. The property in question was subsequently left with the lawyer's receptionist. What should the lawyer do?

Other similar cases are mentioned in the opinion in *Hitch*, p. 1031 above.

512. Investigators of a bank robbery learned immediately after the robbery that one of the suspects had formerly been employed by Genson, a lawyer, and had met with Genson in his office several times shortly after the robbery took place. They learned also that the suspect had given Genson $200 in cash. They told Genson that the cash might be proceeds from the robbery. In re January 1976 Grand Jury, 534 F.2d 719 (7th Cir.1976). What should Genson do? If the money had been given to him as his own (for example, as a fee), was he under an obligation, after the investigators spoke to him, not to dispose of the bills?

513. When, if ever, should defense counsel discuss a case with the complaining witness in an effort to persuade him to drop the case? Should he offer to make restitution to the witness for his loss? May defense counsel properly advise a witness that he has the privilege to refuse to testify on grounds of self-incrimination? May he urge the witness to exercise the privilege? See People v. Wolf, 514 N.E.2d 1218 (Ill.App.Ct. 1987). Compare United States v. Smith, 478 F.2d 976 (D.C.Cir.1973), note 494 p. 595 above.

———

ABA Standards for Criminal Justice,
Prosecution Function and Defense Function (3d ed. 1993).
Defense Function Standards

4-7.6 Examination of Witnesses.

. . .

(b) Defense counsel's belief or knowledge that the witness is telling the truth does not preclude cross-examination.

————

514. The defendant is prosecuted for robbery. You are defense counsel. At trial the complaining witness testifies that she was walking along the street and was mugged by the defendant. She testifies that the person who mugged her, whom she has identified as the defendant, was wearing a grey sweater with a pattern of red and white checks. She describes other clothing of her assailant as well. During a recess the defendant tells you that he doesn't own such a sweater; he was wearing such a sweater on the day of the robbery, but he had borrowed it from a friend. The defendant has throughout denied his guilt.

(a) Should you bring out on cross-examination of the complaining witness the fact that she has bad vision? Or that the street on which the robbery took place was dimly lit?

(b) Should you bring out the fact that the complaining witness has in the past made identifications in court which proved to be incorrect?

(c) If you put the defendant on the stand should you ask him whether he owns a sweater of the kind described?

Suppose the defendant has not denied his guilt, nor has he admitted it. The case against him is very strong. You have advised him to plead guilty, which he has declined to do. Are your answers to questions (a)–(c) different?

515. The defendant is prosecuted for robbery. You are defense counsel. He has not denied his guilt, nor has he admitted it. From what he has told you, it is clear that he did commit the robbery and that it occurred at about 5:00 p.m.

(a) The complaining witness mistakenly testifies that the robbery occurred at 3:00 p.m. On cross-examination she sticks to her account of the robbery and says that she is sure that the time is correct because she looked at her watch just after the robbery. Should you call as a witness a respectable, honest friend of the defendant who will testify that the defendant was watching television with him at 3:00 p.m.?

(b) The complaining witness testifies accurately that the robbery occurred at 5:00 p.m. Should you call as a witness a respectable, honest, but mistaken druggist who will testify that at 5:00 the defendant was in his store across town purchasing medicine for his ill wife? From what the defendant and his wife have told you, it is clear that the defendant was in the drug store much later.

516. If defense counsel believes that one of the prosecution witnesses will be unable to identify the defendant, can he seat another person at the defense table and seat the defendant elsewhere in the courtroom, as a means of testing the witness? If he does something of that sort, are there precautions that he should take? See United States v. Thoreen, 653 F.2d 1332 (9th Cir.1981); People v. Simac, 641 N.E.2d 416 (Ill.1994) (bench trial; conviction of defense counsel for criminal contempt upheld). Consider note 212 p. 388 above.

517. How far may a lawyer go in explaining to a client the significance of his responses to the lawyer's questions? In a homicide case, for example, when the lawyer probes for "all legally relevant information," see ABA Standard 4–3.2, p. 1039 above, ought he, on his own initiative or in response to questions from the client, explain the law relating to mitigating or excusing circumstances, such as provocation or self-defense? How ought a lawyer conduct his conversation with a client in order to be sure that he has missed no "legally relevant information," without at the same time influencing "the direction of the client's responses"?

———

Nix v. Whiteside

475 U.S. 157, 106 S.Ct. 988, 89 L.Ed.2d 123 (1986).

■ CHIEF JUSTICE BURGER delivered the opinion of the Court.

We granted certiorari to decide whether the Sixth Amendment right of a criminal defendant to assistance of counsel is violated when an attorney refuses to cooperate with the defendant in presenting perjured testimony at his trial.

I

A

Whiteside was convicted of second-degree murder by a jury verdict which was affirmed by the Iowa courts. The killing took place on February

8, 1977, in Cedar Rapids, Iowa. Whiteside and two others went to one Calvin Love's apartment late that night, seeking marihuana. Love was in bed when Whiteside and his companions arrived; an argument between Whiteside and Love over the marihuana ensued. At one point, Love directed his girlfriend to get his "piece," and at another point got up, then returned to his bed. According to Whiteside's testimony, Love then started to reach under his pillow and moved toward Whiteside. Whiteside stabbed Love in the chest, inflicting a fatal wound.

Whiteside was charged with murder, and when counsel was appointed he objected to the lawyer initially appointed, claiming that he felt uncomfortable with a lawyer who had formerly been a prosecutor. Gary L. Robinson was then appointed and immediately began investigation. Whiteside gave him a statement that he had stabbed Love as the latter "was pulling a pistol from underneath the pillow on the bed." Upon questioning by Robinson, however, Whiteside indicated that he had not actually seen a gun, but that he was convinced that Love had a gun. No pistol was found on the premises; shortly after the police search following the stabbing, which had revealed no weapon, the victim's family had removed all of the victim's possessions from the apartment. Robinson interviewed Whiteside's companions who were present during the stabbing and none had seen a gun during the incident. Robinson advised Whiteside that the existence of a gun was not necessary to establish the claim of self defense, and that only a reasonable belief that the victim had a gun nearby was necessary even though no gun was actually present.

Until shortly before trial, Whiteside consistently stated to Robinson that he had not actually seen a gun, but that he was convinced that Love had a gun in his hand. About a week before trial, during preparation for direct examination, Whiteside for the first time told Robinson and his associate Donna Paulsen that he had seen something "metallic" in Love's hand. When asked about this, Whiteside responded:

> "[I]n Howard Cook's case there was a gun. If I don't say I saw a gun I'm dead."

Robinson told Whiteside that such testimony would be perjury and repeated that it was not necessary to prove that a gun was available but only that Whiteside reasonably believed that he was in danger. On Whiteside's insisting that he would testify that he saw "something metallic" Robinson told him, according to Robinson's testimony:

> "[W]e could not allow him to [testify falsely] because that would be perjury, and as officers of the court we would be suborning perjury if we allowed him to do it; . . . I advised him that if he did do that it would be my duty to advise the Court of what he was doing and that I felt he was committing perjury; also, that I probably would be allowed to attempt to impeach that particular testimony." App. to Pet. for Cert. A–85.

Robinson also indicated he would seek to withdraw from the representation if Whiteside insisted on committing perjury.

Whiteside testified in his own defense at trial and stated that he "knew" that Love had a gun and that he believed Love was reaching for a gun and he had acted swiftly in self-defense. On cross-examination, he admitted that he had not actually seen a gun in Love's hand. Robinson presented evidence that Love had been seen with a sawed-off shotgun on other occasions, that the police search of the apartment may have been careless, and that the victim's family had removed everything from the apartment shortly after the crime. Robinson presented this evidence to show a basis for Whiteside's asserted fear that Love had a gun.

The jury returned a verdict of second-degree murder, and Whiteside moved for a new trial, claiming that he had been deprived of a fair trial by Robinson's admonitions not to state that he saw a gun or "something metallic." The trial court held a hearing, heard testimony by Whiteside and Robinson, and denied the motion. The trial court made specific findings that the facts were as related by Robinson.

The Supreme Court of Iowa affirmed respondent's conviction. . . . That court held that the right to have counsel present all appropriate defenses does not extend to using perjury, and that an attorney's duty to a client does not extend to assisting a client in committing perjury. Relying on DR 7–102(A)(4) of the Iowa Code of Professional Responsibility for Lawyers, which expressly prohibits an attorney from using perjured testimony, and Iowa Code § 721.2 (now Iowa Code § 720.3 (1985)), which criminalizes subornation of perjury, the Iowa court concluded that not only were Robinson's actions permissible, but were required. The court commended "both Mr. Robinson and Ms. Paulsen for the high ethical manner in which this matter was handled."

B

Whiteside then petitioned for a writ of habeas corpus in the United States District Court for the Southern District of Iowa. In that petition Whiteside alleged that he had been denied effective assistance of counsel and of his right to present a defense by Robinson's refusal to allow him to testify as he had proposed. The District Court denied the writ. Accepting the state trial court's factual finding that Whiteside's intended testimony would have been perjurious, it concluded that there could be no grounds for habeas relief since there is no constitutional right to present a perjured defense.

The United States Court of Appeals for the Eighth Circuit reversed and directed that the writ of habeas corpus be granted. Whiteside v. Scurr, 744 F.2d 1323 (1984). The Court of Appeals accepted the findings of the trial judge, affirmed by the Iowa Supreme Court, that trial counsel believed with good cause that Whiteside would testify falsely and acknowledged that under Harris v. New York, 401 U.S. 222 (1971), a criminal defendant's privilege to testify in his own behalf does not include a right to commit perjury. Nevertheless, the court reasoned that an intent to commit perjury, communicated to counsel, does not alter a defendant's right to effective assistance of counsel and that Robinson's admonition to Whiteside that he would inform the court of Whiteside's perjury constituted a threat to violate the attorney's duty to preserve client confidences. According to the Court of Appeals, this threatened violation of client confidences breached the standards of effective representation set down in Strickland v. Washington, 466 U.S. 668 (1984).[28] The court also concluded that *Strickland*'s prejudice requirement was satisfied by an implication of prejudice from the conflict between Robinson's duty of loyalty to his client and his ethical duties. . . . We . . . reverse.

II

A

The right of an accused to testify in his defense is of relatively recent origin. Until the latter part of the preceding century, criminal defendants in this country, as at common law, were considered to be disqualified from giving sworn testimony at their own trial by reason of their interest as a party to the case. . . . Iowa was among the states that adhered to this rule of disqualification. . . .

By the end of the nineteenth century, however, the disqualification was finally abolished by statute in most states and in the federal courts. . . . Although this Court has never explicitly held that a criminal defendant has a due process right to testify in his own behalf, cases in several Circuits have so held and the right has long been assumed. . . . We have also suggested that such a right exists as a corollary to the Fifth Amendment privilege against compelled testimony. . . .

B

In Strickland v. Washington, we held that to obtain relief by way of federal habeas corpus on a claim of a deprivation of effective assistance of counsel under the Sixth Amendment, the movant must establish both serious attorney error and prejudice. . . .

In *Strickland*, we acknowledged that the Sixth Amendment does not require any particular response by counsel to a problem that may arise. Rather, the Sixth Amendment inquiry is into whether the attorney's conduct was "reasonably effective." To counteract the natural tendency to fault an unsuccessful defense, a court reviewing a claim of ineffective assistance must "indulge a strong presumption that counsel's conduct falls within the wide range of reasonable professional assistance." Id., at 689. . . .

. . .

C

We turn next to the question presented: the definition of the range of "reasonable professional" responses to a criminal defendant client who

---

[28] P. 1063 below.

informs counsel that he will perjure himself on the stand. We must determine whether, in this setting, Robinson's conduct fell within the wide range of professional responses to threatened client perjury acceptable under the Sixth Amendment.

In *Strickland*, we recognized counsel's duty of loyalty and his "overarching duty to advocate the defendant's cause," Ibid. Plainly, that duty is limited to legitimate, lawful conduct compatible with the very nature of a trial as a search for truth. Although counsel must take all reasonable lawful means to attain the objectives of the client, counsel is precluded from taking steps or in any way assisting the client in presenting false evidence or otherwise violating the law. This principle has consistently been recognized in most unequivocal terms by expositors of the norms of professional conduct since the first Canons of Professional Ethics were adopted by the American Bar Association in 1908. . . .

. . . Disciplinary Rule 7–102 of the Model Code of Professional Responsibility (1980), entitled "Representing a Client Within the Bounds of the Law," provides:

"(A) In his representation of a client, a lawyer shall not:

. . .

"(4) Knowingly use perjured testimony or false evidence.

. . .

"(7) Counsel or assist his client in conduct that the lawyer knows to be illegal or fraudulent."

This provision has been adopted by Iowa, and is binding on all lawyers who appear in its courts. . . . The more recent Model Rules of Professional Conduct (1983) similarly admonish attorneys to obey all laws in the course of representing a client . . . . Both the Model Code of Professional Responsibility and the Model Rules of Professional Conduct also adopt the specific exception from the attorney-client privilege for disclosure of perjury that his client intends to commit or has committed. . . . Indeed, both the Model Code and the Model Rules do not merely *authorize* disclosure by counsel of client perjury; they *require* such disclosure. . . .

These standards confirm that the legal profession has accepted that an attorney's ethical duty to advance the interests of his client is limited by an equally solemn duty to comply with the law and standards of professional conduct; it specifically ensures that the client may not use false evidence. This special duty of an attorney to prevent and disclose frauds upon the court derives from the recognition that perjury is as much a crime as tampering with witnesses or jurors by way of promises and threats, and undermines the administration of justice. . . .

. . .

It is universally agreed that at a minimum the attorney's first duty when confronted with a proposal for perjurious testimony is to attempt to dissuade the client from the unlawful course of conduct. . . .

The essence of the brief *amicus* of the American Bar Association reviewing practices long accepted by ethical lawyers, is that under no circumstance may a lawyer either advocate or passively tolerate a client's giving false testimony. This, of course, is consistent with the governance of trial conduct in what we have long called "a search for truth." The suggestion sometimes made that "a lawyer must believe his client not judge him" in no sense means a lawyer can honorably be a party to or in any way give aid to presenting known perjury.

D

Considering Robinson's representation of respondent in light of these accepted norms of professional conduct, we discern no failure to adhere to reasonable professional standards that would in any sense make out a deprivation of the Sixth Amendment right to counsel. Whether Robinson's conduct is seen as a successful attempt to dissuade his client from committing the crime of perjury, or whether seen as a "threat" to withdraw from representation and disclose the illegal scheme, Robinson's representation of Whiteside falls well within accepted standards of professional conduct and the range of reasonable professional conduct acceptable under *Strickland.*

The Court of Appeals assumed for the purpose of the decision that Whiteside would have given false testimony had counsel not intervened . . . .

The Court of Appeals' holding that Robinson's "action deprived [Whiteside] of due process and effective assistance of counsel" [744 F.2d at 1328] is not supported by the record since Robinson's action, at most, deprived Whiteside of his contemplated perjury. Nothing counsel did in any way undermined Whiteside's claim that he believed the victim was reaching for a gun. Similarly, the record gives no support for holding that Robinson's action "also impermissibly compromised [Whiteside's] right to testify in his own defense by conditioning continued representation . . . and confidentiality upon [Whiteside's] *restricted* testimony" [744 F.2d at 1329]. The record in fact shows the contrary: (a) that Whiteside did testify, and (b) he was "restricted" or restrained only from testifying falsely and was aided by Robinson in developing the basis for the fear that Love was reaching for a gun. Robinson divulged no client communications until he was compelled to do so in response to Whiteside's post-trial challenge to the quality of his performance. We see this as a case in which the attorney successfully dissuaded the client from committing the crime of perjury.

Paradoxically, even while accepting the conclusion of the Iowa trial court that Whiteside's proposed testimony would have been a criminal act, the Court of Appeals held that Robinson's efforts to persuade Whiteside not to commit that crime were improper, *first*, as forcing an impermissible choice between the right to counsel and the right to testify; and *second*, as compromising client confidences because of Robinson's threat to disclose the contemplated perjury.

Whatever the scope of a constitutional right to testify, it is elementary that such a right does not extend to testifying *falsely*. . . . [T]here is no right whatever—constitutional or otherwise—for a defendant to use false evidence. . . .

. . .

Robinson's admonitions to his client can in no sense be said to have forced respondent into an *impermissible* choice between his right to counsel and his right to testify as he proposed for there was no *permissible* choice to testify falsely. For defense counsel to take steps to persuade a criminal defendant to testify truthfully, or to withdraw, deprives the defendant of neither his right to counsel nor the right to testify truthfully. . . .

On this record, the accused enjoyed continued representation within the bounds of reasonable professional conduct and did in fact exercise his right to testify; at most he was denied the right to have the assistance of counsel in the presentation of false testimony. Similarly, we can discern no breach of professional duty in Robinson's admonition to respondent that he would disclose respondent's perjury to the court. . . . An attorney's duty of confidentiality, which totally covers the client's admission of guilt, does not extend to a client's announced plans to engage in future criminal conduct. . . . In short, the responsibility of an ethical lawyer, as an officer of the court and a key component of a system of justice, dedicated to a search for truth, is essentially the same whether the client announces an intention to bribe or threaten witnesses or jurors or to commit or procure perjury. No system of justice worthy of the name can tolerate a lesser standard.

. . .

E

We hold that, as a matter of law, counsel's conduct complained of here cannot establish the prejudice required for relief under the second strand of the *Strickland* inquiry. . . .

Whether he was persuaded or compelled to desist from perjury, Whiteside has no valid claim that confidence in the result of his trial has been diminished by his desisting from the contemplated perjury. Even if we were to assume that the jury might have believed his perjury, it does not follow that Whiteside was prejudiced.

. . .

Whiteside's attorney treated Whiteside's proposed perjury in accord with professional standards, and since Whiteside's truthful testimony could not have prejudiced the result of his trial, the Court of Appeals was in error to direct the issuance of a writ of habeas corpus and must be reversed.

. . . [29]

———

ABA Model Rules of Professional Conduct (1996).

Rule 3.3 Candor Toward the Tribunal.

(a) A lawyer shall not knowingly:

. . .

(4) offer evidence that the lawyer knows to be false. . . .

. . .

[29] Justice Brennan and Justice Stevens wrote opinions concurring in the judgment. Justice Blackmun also wrote an opinion concurring in the judgment, which Justice Brennan, Justice Marshall, and Justice Stevens joined. All three opinions expressed the view that it was clear in this case that the defendant had suffered no legally cognizable prejudice, but that the Court should not undertake to prescribe the correct response for an attorney whose client evidently intends to commit perjury at trial.

With respect to the latter issue, Justice Blackmun observed:

"Whether an attorney's response to what he sees as a client's plan to commit perjury violates a defendant's Sixth Amendment rights may depend on many factors: how certain the attorney is that the proposed testimony is false, the stage of the proceedings at which the attorney discovers the plan, or the ways in which the attorney may be able to dissuade his client, to name just three. The complex interaction of factors, which is likely to vary from case to case, makes inappropriate a blanket rule that defense attorneys must reveal, or threaten to reveal, a client's anticipated perjury to the court. Except in the rarest of cases, attorneys who adopt 'the role of the judge or jury to determine the facts,' United States ex rel. Wilcox v. Johnson, 555

F.2d 115, 122 (CA3 1977), pose a danger of depriving their clients of the zealous and loyal advocacy required by the Sixth Amendment." 475 U.S. at 188–89.

Justice Stevens observed:

"[B]eneath the surface of this case there are areas of uncertainty that cannot be resolved today. A lawyer's certainty that a change in his client's recollection is a harbinger of intended perjury—as well as judicial review of such apparent certainty—should be tempered by the realization that, after reflection, the most honest witness may recall (or sincerely believe he recalls) details that he previously overlooked. Similarly, the post-trial review of a lawyer's pretrial threat to expose perjury that had not yet been committed—and, indeed, may have been prevented by the threat—is by no means the same as review of the way in which such a threat may actually have been carried out. Thus, one can be convinced—as I am—that this lawyer's actions were a proper way to provide his client with effective representation without confronting the much more difficult questions of what a lawyer must, should, or may do after his client has given testimony that the lawyer does not believe. The answer to such questions may well be colored by the particular circumstances attending the actual event and its aftermath." 475 U.S. at 190–91.

(c) A lawyer may refuse to offer evidence that the lawyer reasonably believes is false.

. . .

Comment

. . .

Perjury by a Criminal Defendant

Whether an advocate for a criminally accused has the same duty of disclosure [of a client's deception as a lawyer in a civil proceeding] has been intensely debated. While it is agreed that the lawyer should seek to persuade the client to refrain from perjurious testimony, there has been dispute concerning the lawyer's duty when that persuasion fails. If the confrontation with the client occurs before trial, the lawyer ordinarily can withdraw. Withdrawal before trial may not be possible, however, either because trial is imminent, or because the confrontation with the client does not take place until the trial itself, or because no other counsel is available.

The most difficult situation, therefore, arises in a criminal case where the accused insists on testifying when the lawyer knows that the testimony is perjurious. The lawyer's effort to rectify the situation can increase the likelihood of the client's being convicted as well as opening the possibility of a prosecution for perjury. On the other hand, if the lawyer does not exercise control over the proof, the lawyer participates, although in a merely passive way, in deception of the court.

Three resolutions of this dilemma have been proposed. One is to permit the accused to testify by a narrative without guidance through the lawyer's questioning. This compromises both contending principles; it exempts the lawyer from the duty to disclose false evidence but subjects the client to an implicit disclosure of information imparted to counsel. Another suggested resolution, of relatively recent origin, is that the advocate be entirely excused from the duty to reveal perjury if the perjury is that of the client. This is a coherent solution but makes the advocate a knowing instrument of perjury.

The other resolution of the dilemma is that the lawyer must reveal the client's perjury if necessary to rectify the situation. A criminal accused has a right to the assistance of an advocate, a right to testify and a right of confidential communication with counsel. However, an accused should not have a right to assistance of counsel in committing perjury. Furthermore, an advocate has an obligation, not only in professional ethics but under the law as well, to avoid implication in the commission of perjury or other falsification of evidence. . . .

Remedial Measures

If perjured testimony or false evidence has been offered, the advocate's proper course ordinarily is to remonstrate with the client confidentially. If that fails, the advocate should seek to withdraw if that will remedy the situation. If withdrawal will not remedy the situation or is impossible, the advocate should make disclosure to the court. It is for the court then to determine what should be done—making a statement about the matter to the trier of fact, ordering a mistrial or perhaps nothing. If the false testimony was that of the client, the client may controvert the lawyer's version of their communication when the lawyer discloses the situation to the court. If there is an issue whether the client has committed perjury, the lawyer cannot represent the client in resolution of the issue and a mistrial may be unavoidable. An unscrupulous client might in this way attempt to produce a series of mistrials and thus escape prosecution. However, a second such encounter could be construed as a deliberate abuse of the right to counsel and as such a waiver of the right to further representation.

Constitutional Requirements

The general rule—that an advocate must disclose the existence of perjury with respect to a material fact, even that of a client—applies to defense counsel in criminal cases, as well as in other instances. However, the definition of the lawyer's ethical duty in such a situation may be qualified by constitutional provisions for due process and the right to counsel in criminal cases. In some jurisdictions these provisions have been construed to require that counsel present an accused as a witness if the accused wishes to testify, even if counsel knows the testimony will be false. The obligation of the advocate under these Rules is subordinate to such a constitutional requirement.

. . .

518. For other cases presenting the problem of a defendant's false testimony, see United States v. Henkel, 799 F.2d 369 (7th Cir.1986) (Nix v. Whiteside applied); Lowery v. Cardwell, 575 F.2d 727 (9th Cir.1978); United States ex rel. Wilcox v. Johnson, 555 F.2d 115 (3d Cir.1977); McKissick v. United States, 379 F.2d 754 (5th Cir.1967), 398 F.2d 342 (5th Cir. 1968); People v. Johnson, 72 Cal. Rptr. 2d 805 (Dist. Ct. App. 1998); Shockley v. State, 565 A.2d 1373 (Del.1989); People v. Schultheis, 638 P.2d 8 (Colo.1981); Butler v. United States, 414 A.2d 844 (D.C.1980); Thornton v. United States, 357 A.2d 429 (D.C.1976); State v. Henderson, 468 P.2d 136 (Kan.1970).

519. In Hayes v. Kincheloe, 784 F.2d 1434 (9th Cir.1986), the defendant was prosecuted for murder. He pleaded guilty to second-degree murder. In post-conviction proceedings, he claimed that he had not been informed by his lawyer and had not understood that second-degree murder is an intentional killing, and that his plea was, therefore, involuntary. His lawyer stated that he had thought the state could prove a case of first-degree murder and was surprised that he could negotiate a plea to the lesser offense. He stated also that, although he visited the defendant in jail a number of times, he discussed the defendant's account of the events with him minimally. He said: "[T]he reason for that is that if we went to trial, and [Hayes] had stated certain things to me different than what occurred at the trial, it would cause me difficulty in representing him. So my conversations with Mark as to the actual events as he would state them were very very marginal, not much at all." Id. at 1438 n.3. The conviction was vacated.

Consider *Hayes* in connection with Nix v. Whiteside, above.

Cf. ABA Standards for Criminal Justice, Prosecution Function and Defense Function (3d ed. 1993), Defense Function Standard 4-3.2(b): "Defense counsel should not instruct the client or intimate to the client in any way that the client should not be candid in revealing facts so as to afford defense counsel free rein to take action which would be precluded by counsel's knowing of such facts."

520. The defendant has a constitutional right not to appear before a jury in prison clothes. Estelle v. Williams, 425 U.S. 501 (1976). See note 437 p. 908 above.

Suppose the defendant has no presentable clothing of his own? Is it proper for defense counsel to lend the defendant a clean shirt to wear during the trial? Or a jacket? Or a dark blue suit? (Should the prosecutor advise the complaining witness in a rape case to wear modest clothing during the trial? Suppose she suggests this herself. Should the prosecutor advise her not to change her usual appearance?)

Consider DR 7–102(A)(4)–(7) of the ABA Code of Professional Responsibility, p. 1030 above.

521. Defense strategy.

(1) What factors should defense counsel consider when he decides whether or not to put the defendant on the stand?

(2) How can defense counsel prevent the jury from learning from the prosecutor's questions and defense counsel's objections that there is a statement or other evidence in the case to which counsel believes there are valid legal objections? Suppose, for example, the defendant has made a confession at the police station and defense counsel believes that it is inadmissible because the defendant was not advised of his rights.

(3) What should defense counsel do if the prosecution announces in open court that there are several witnesses available to testify whom he intends not to call but whom defense counsel can call if he chooses? See Artis v. Commonwealth, 191 S.E.2d 190 (Va.1972).

(4) How can defense counsel prevent the prosecutor from claiming surprise and using prior statements of witnesses for the prosecution to impeach their testimony favorable to the defendant? Suppose defense counsel has interviewed the witnesses and they tell her before trial that they did give the prosecutor signed statements incriminating the defendant but that

they wish to and will repudiate the statements if called as witnesses at the trial. See Brown v. United States, 411 F.2d 716 (D.C.Cir.1969); Hooks v. United States, 375 F.2d 212 (5th Cir.1967).

(5) How can defense counsel avoid a missing witness instruction with respect to a witness who is crucial to the defense but whom counsel is unable to locate?

(6) Suppose the defendant has two witnesses who will corroborate his alibi but who themselves have long criminal records. How should defense counsel proceed?

522. ABA Standards for Criminal Justice, The Function of the Trial Judge (2d ed. 1978), Standard 2.5: Duty of judge to respect attorney-client relationship. The trial judge should respect the obligation of counsel to refrain from speaking on privileged matters and should avoid putting counsel in a position where counsel's adherence to the obligation, such as by a refusal to answer, may tend to prejudice the client. Unless the privilege is waived, the trial judge should not request counsel to comment on evidence or other matters where counsel's knowledge is likely to be gained from privileged communications."

How should counsel respond if, during the trial, the judge asks a question the answer to which will indicate counsel's belief in the innocence or guilt of his client? See generally United States v. Frazier, 580 F.2d 229 (6th Cir.1978).

Defense counsel

United States v. Cronic

466 U.S. 648, 104 S.Ct. 2039, 80 L.Ed.2d 657 (1984).

■ JUSTICE STEVENS delivered the opinion of the Court.

Respondent and two associates were indicted on mail fraud charges involving the transfer of over $9,400,000 in checks between banks in Tampa, Fla., and Norman, Okla., during a 4-month period in 1975. Shortly before the scheduled trial date, respondent's retained counsel withdrew. The court appointed a young lawyer with a real estate practice to represent respondent, but allowed him only 25 days for pretrial preparation, even though it had taken the Government over four and one-half years to investigate the case and it had reviewed thousands of documents during that investigation. The two codefendants agreed to testify for the Government; respondent was convicted on 11 of the 13 counts in the indictment and received a 25-year sentence.

The Court of Appeals reversed the conviction because it concluded that respondent did not "have the Assistance of Counsel for his defence" that is guaranteed by the Sixth Amendment to the Constitution. This conclusion was not supported by a determination that respondent's trial counsel had made any specified errors, that his actual performance had prejudiced the defense, or that he failed to exercise "the skill, judgment, and diligence of a reasonably competent defense attorney"; instead the conclusion rested on the premise that no such showing is necessary "when circumstances hamper a given lawyer's preparation of a defendant's case."[30] The question presented by the Government's petition for certiorari is whether the Court of Appeals has correctly interpreted the Sixth Amendment.

I

The indictment alleged a "check kiting" scheme. At the direction of respondent, his codefendant Cummings opened a bank account in the name of Skyproof Manufacturing, Inc. (Skyproof), at a bank in Tampa, Fla., and codefendant Merritt opened two accounts, one in his own name and one in the name of Skyproof, at banks in Norman, Okla. Knowing that there were insufficient funds in either account, the defendants allegedly drew a series of checks and wire transfers on the Tampa account aggregating $4,841,073.95, all of which were deposited in Skyproof's Norman bank account during the period between June 23, 1975, and October 16, 1975; during approximately the same period they drew checks on Skyproof's Norman account for deposits in Tampa aggregating $4,600,881.39. The process of clearing the checks involved the use of the mails. By "kiting" insufficient funds checks between the banks in those two cities, defendants allegedly created false or inflated balances in the accounts. After outlining the overall scheme, Count I of the indictment alleged the mailing of two checks each for less than $1,000 early in May. Each of the additional 12 counts realleged the allegations in Count I except its reference to the two specific checks, and then added an allegation identifying other checks issued and mailed at later dates.

At trial the Government proved that Skyproof's checks were issued and deposited at the times and places, and in the amounts, described in the indictment. Having made plea bargains with defendants Cummings and Merritt, who had actually handled the issuance and delivery of the relevant written instruments, the Government proved through their testimony that respondent had conceived and directed the entire scheme, and that he had deliberately concealed his connection with Skyproof because of prior financial and tax problems.

30. 675 F.2d 1126, 1128 (CA10 1982).

After the District Court ruled that a prior conviction could be used to impeach his testimony, respondent decided not to testify. Counsel put on no defense. By cross-examination of Government witnesses, however, he established that Skyproof was not merely a sham, but actually was an operating company with a significant cash flow, though its revenues were not sufficient to justify as large a "float" as the record disclosed. Cross-examination also established the absence of written evidence that respondent had any control over Skyproof, or personally participated in the withdrawals or deposits.

The 4-day jury trial ended on July 17, 1980, and respondent was sentenced on August 28, 1980. His counsel perfected a timely appeal, which was docketed on September 11, 1980. Two months later respondent filed a motion to substitute a new attorney in the Court of Appeals, and also filed a motion in the District Court seeking to vacate his conviction on the ground that he had newly discovered evidence of perjury by officers of the Norman bank, and that the Government knew or should have known of that perjury. In that motion he also challenged the competence of his trial counsel. The District Court refused to entertain the motion while the appeal was pending. The Court of Appeals denied the motion to substitute the attorney designated by respondent, but did appoint still another attorney to handle the appeal. Later it allowed respondent's motion to supplement the record with material critical of trial counsel's performance.

The Court of Appeals reversed the conviction because it inferred that respondent's constitutional right to the effective assistance of counsel had been violated. That inference was based on its use of five criteria: "(1) [T]he time afforded for investigation and preparation; (2) the experience of counsel; (3) the gravity of the charge; (4) the complexity of possible defenses; and (5) the accessibility of witnesses to counsel." 675 F.2d 1126, 1129 (CA10 1982) (quoting United States v. Golub, 638 F.2d 185, 189 (CA10 1980)). Under the test employed by the Court of Appeals, reversal is required even if the lawyer's actual performance was flawless. By utilizing this inferential approach, the Court of Appeals erred.

II

An accused's right to be represented by counsel is a fundamental component of our criminal justice system. Lawyers in criminal cases "are necessities, not luxuries."[31] Their presence is essential because they are the means through which the other rights of the person on trial are secured. Without counsel, the right to a trial itself would be "of little avail,"[32] as this Court has recognized repeatedly. "Of all the rights that an accused person has, the right to be represented by counsel is by far the most pervasive, for it affects his ability to assert any other right he may have."[33]

---

31. . . . Gideon v. Wainwright, 372 U.S. 335, 344 (1963).

32. . . . Powell v. Alabama, 287 U.S. 45 (1932). . . .

33. Schaefer, Federalism and State Criminal Procedure, 70 Harv.L.Rev. 1, 8 (1956).

The special value of the right to the assistance of counsel explains why "[i]t has long been recognized that the right to counsel is the right to the effective assistance of counsel." McMann v. Richardson, 397 U.S. 759, 771, n. 14 (1970). The text of the Sixth Amendment itself suggests as much. The Amendment requires not merely the provision of counsel to the accused, but "Assistance," which is to be "for his defence." Thus, "the core purpose of the counsel guarantee was to assure 'Assistance' at trial, when the accused was confronted with both the intricacies of the law and the advocacy of the public prosecutor." United States v. Ash, 413 U.S. 300, 309 (1973). If no actual "Assistance" "for" the accused's "defence" is provided, then the constitutional guarantee has been violated. To hold otherwise

> "could convert the appointment of counsel into a sham and nothing more than a formal compliance with the Constitution's requirement that an accused be given the assistance of counsel. The Constitution's guarantee of assistance of counsel cannot be satisfied by mere formal appointment." Avery v. Alabama, 308 U.S. 444, 446 (1940) (footnote omitted).

Thus, in *McMann* the Court indicated that the accused is entitled to "a reasonably competent attorney," 397 U.S., at 770, whose advice is "within the range of competence demanded of attorneys in criminal cases." Id., at 771. In Cuyler v. Sullivan, 446 U.S. 335 (1980), we held that the constitution guarantees an accused "adequate legal assistance." Id., at 344. And in Engle v. Isaac, 456 U.S. 107 (1982), the Court referred to the criminal defendant's constitutional guarantee of "a fair trial and a competent attorney." Id., at 134.

The substance of the Constitution's guarantee of the effective assistance of counsel is illuminated by reference to its underlying purpose. "[T]ruth," Lord Eldon said, "is best discovered by powerful statements on both sides of the question."[34] This dictum describes the unique strength of our system of criminal justice. "The very premise of our adversary system of criminal justice is that partisan advocacy on both sides of a case will best promote the ultimate objective that the guilty be convicted and the innocent go free." Herring v. New York, 422 U.S. 853, 862 (1975). It is that "very premise" that underlies and gives meaning to the Sixth Amendment. It "is meant to assure fairness in the adversary criminal process." United States v. Morrison, 449 U.S. 361, 364 (1981). Unless the accused receives the effective assistance of counsel, "a serious risk of injustice infects the trial itself." Cuyler v. Sullivan, 446 U.S., at 343.

Thus, the adversarial process protected by the Sixth Amendment requires that the accused have "counsel acting in the role of an advocate." Anders v. California, 386 U.S. 738, 743 (1967). The right to the effective assistance of counsel is thus the right of the accused to require the prosecution's case to survive the crucible of meaningful adversarial testing. When

---

34. Quoted in Kaufman, Does the Judge Have a Right to Qualified Counsel?, 61 A.B.A.J. 569, 569 (1975).

a true adversarial criminal trial has been conducted—even if defense counsel may have made demonstrable errors—the kind of testing envisioned by the Sixth Amendment has occurred.[35] But if the process loses its character as a confrontation between adversaries, the constitutional guarantee is violated. . . .[36]

III

While the Court of Appeals purported to apply a standard of reasonable competence, it did not indicate that there had been an actual breakdown of the adversarial process during the trial of this case. Instead it concluded that the circumstances surrounding the representation of respondent mandated an inference that counsel was unable to discharge his duties.

In our evaluation of that conclusion, we begin by recognizing that the right to the effective assistance of counsel is recognized not for its own sake, but because of the effect it has on the ability of the accused to receive a fair trial. Absent some effect of challenged conduct on the reliability of the trial process, the Sixth Amendment guarantee is generally not implicated. . . . Moreover, because we presume that the lawyer is competent to provide the guiding hand that the defendant needs . . . the burden rests on the accused to demonstrate a constitutional violation. There are, however, circumstances that are so likely to prejudice the accused that the cost of litigating their effect in a particular case is unjustified.

Most obvious, of course, is the complete denial of counsel. The presumption that counsel's assistance is essential requires us to conclude that a trial is unfair if the accused is denied counsel at a critical stage of his trial. Similarly, if counsel entirely fails to subject the prosecution's case to meaningful adversarial testing, then there has been a denial of Sixth Amendment rights that makes the adversary process itself presumptively unreliable. . . .

Circumstances of that magnitude may be present on some occasions when although counsel is available to assist the accused during trial, the likelihood that any lawyer, even a fully competent one, could provide effective assistance is so small that a presumption of prejudice is appropriate without inquiry into the actual conduct of the trial. . . .

. . .

---

35. Of course, the Sixth Amendment does not require that counsel do what is impossible or unethical. If there is no *bona fide* defense to the charge, counsel cannot create one and may disserve the interests of his client by attempting a useless charade. . . . At the same time, even when no theory of defense is available, if the decision to stand trial has been made, counsel must hold the prosecution to its heavy burden of proof beyond reasonable doubt. And, of course, even when there is a *bona fide* defense, counsel may still advise his client to plead guilty if that advice falls within the range of reasonable competence under the circumstances. . . .

36. Thus, the appropriate inquiry focuses on the adversarial process, not on the accused's relationship with his lawyer as such. If counsel is a reasonably effective advocate, he meets constitutional standards irrespective of his client's evaluation of his performance. . . . It is for this reason that we attach no weight to either respondent's expression of satisfaction with counsel's performance at the time of his trial, or to his later expression of dissatisfaction. . . .

But every refusal to postpone a criminal trial will not give rise to such a presumption. . . . Thus, only when surrounding circumstances justify a presumption of ineffectiveness can a Sixth Amendment claim be sufficient without inquiry into counsel's actual performance at trial.

The Court of Appeals did not find that respondent was denied the presence of counsel at a critical stage of the prosecution. Nor did it find, based on the actual conduct of the trial, that there was a breakdown in the adversarial process that would justify a presumption that respondent's conviction was insufficiently reliable to satisfy the Constitution. The dispositive question in this case therefore is whether the circumstances surrounding respondent's representation—and in particular the five criteria identified by the Court of Appeals—justified such a presumption.

IV

The five factors listed in the Court of Appeals' opinion are relevant to an evaluation of a lawyer's effectiveness in a particular case, but neither separately nor in combination do they provide a basis for concluding that competent counsel was not able to provide this respondent with the guiding hand that the Constitution guarantees.

Respondent places special stress on the disparity between the duration of the Government's investigation and the period the District Court allowed to newly appointed counsel for trial preparation. The lawyer was appointed to represent respondent on June 12, 1980, and on June 19, filed a written motion for a continuance of the trial that was then scheduled to begin on June 30. Although counsel contended that he needed at least 30 days for preparation, the District Court reset the trial for July 14—thus allowing 25 additional days for preparation.

Neither the period of time that the Government spent investigating the case, nor the number of documents that its agents reviewed during that investigation, is necessarily relevant to the question whether a competent lawyer could prepare to defend the case in 25 days. The Government's task of finding and assembling admissible evidence that will carry its burden of proving guilt beyond a reasonable doubt is entirely different from the defendant's task in preparing to deny or rebut a criminal charge. Of course, in some cases the rebuttal may be equally burdensome and time consuming, but there is no necessary correlation between the two. In this case, the time devoted by the Government to the assembly, organization, and summarization of the thousands of written records evidencing the two streams of checks flowing between the banks in Florida and Oklahoma unquestionably simplified the work of defense counsel in identifying and understanding the basic character of the defendants' scheme. When a series of repetitious transactions fit into a single mold, the number of written exhibits that are needed to define the pattern may be unrelated to the time that is needed to understand it.

The significance of counsel's preparation time is further reduced by the nature of the charges against respondent. Most of the Government's case consisted merely of establishing the transactions between the two banks. A competent attorney would have no reason to question the authenticity, accuracy, or relevance of this evidence—there could be no dispute that these transactions actually occurred. As respondent appears to recognize, the only *bona fide* jury issue open to competent defense counsel on these facts was whether respondent acted with intent to defraud. When there is no reason to dispute the underlying historical facts, the period of 25 days to consider the question whether those facts justify an inference of criminal intent is not so short that it even arguably justifies a presumption that no lawyer could provide the respondent with the effective assistance of counsel required by the Constitution.

That conclusion is not undermined by the fact that respondent's lawyer was young, that his principal practice was in real estate, or that this was his first jury trial. Every experienced criminal defense attorney once tried his first criminal case. Moreover, a lawyer's experience with real estate transactions might be more useful in preparing to try a criminal case involving financial transactions than would prior experience in handling, for example, armed robbery prosecutions. The character of a particular lawyer's experience may shed light in an evaluation of his actual performance, but it does not justify a presumption of ineffectiveness in the absence of such an evaluation.

The three other criteria—the gravity of the charge, the complexity of the case, and the accessibility of witnesses—are all matters that may affect what a reasonably competent attorney could be expected to have done under the circumstances, but none identifies circumstances that in themselves make it unlikely that respondent received the effective assistance of counsel.

V

. . . Respondent can therefore make out a claim of ineffective assistance only by pointing to specific errors made by trial counsel. . . .

. . .[37]

---

523. In Holloway v. Arkansas, 435 U.S. 475 (1978) (6–3), the Supreme Court reversed the conviction of three codefendants who had been represented by the same lawyer. Before trial and again during trial, the lawyer, a public defender, had moved for assignment of separate counsel on the ground of a possible conflict of interest. The motion was denied. Each of the defendants testified at trial, their lawyer having again advised the court

---

[37] Justice Marshall concurred in the judgment.

that he could not examine each of them satisfactorily because of the joint defense. The Court declared that while "in some cases multiple defendants can appropriately be represented by one attorney," id. at 482, the failure to appoint separate counsel or to inquire adequately into the need for separate counsel following a timely motion denied the defendants' constitutional right to counsel. Such failure, the Court concluded, required reversal without a showing of specific prejudice.

Holloway was applied in Cuyler v. Sullivan, 446 U.S. 335 (1980). The Court held that ordinarily a defendant must raise the issue of conflict of interest. "Absent special circumstances . . . trial courts may assume either that multiple representation entails no conflict or that the lawyer and his clients knowingly accept such risk of conflict as may exist. . . . Unless the trial court knows or reasonably should know that a particular conflict exists, the court need not initiate an inquiry." Id. at 346–47. The Court held further that the possibility of a conflict of interest from multiple representation is insufficient to show denial of the right to counsel. "In order to establish a violation of the Sixth Amendment, a defendant who raised no objection at trial must demonstrate that an actual conflict of interest adversely affected his lawyer's performance." Id. at 350. See Burger v. Kemp, 483 U.S. 776 (1987) (5–4) (defendants, charged with crimes arising out of joint conduct, represented at separate trials by law partners; *Holloway* claim rejected).

In Walberg v. Israel, 766 F.2d 1071 (7th Cir.1985), *Holloway* was applied in somewhat unusual circumstances. The court concluded that a system whereby appointed counsel for indigents must submit a request for a fee to the appointing judge created a conflict of interest between the defendant and his appointed counsel, whom the judge repeatedly admonished against forcefully urging his client's cause. The consequence, the court said, was that the defendant's right to counsel was denied. See also United States v. Benavidez, 664 F.2d 1255 (5th Cir.1982) (conflict of interest not shown); Camera v. Fogg, 658 F.2d 80 (2d Cir.1981) (representation of three defendants by retained counsel violated right to counsel).

Fed.R.Crim.P. 44(c), p. 557 above, requires that a judge address the question of conflict of interest when two or more defendants are jointly charged or joined for trial and are represented by the same lawyer or lawyers who are associated in practice. The judge must advise each defendant of his right to effective assistance of counsel and "take such measures as may be appropriate" to protect the right.

"[W]here a court justifiably finds an actual conflict of interest, there can be no doubt that it may decline a proffer of waiver [of objection to any conflict of interest of counsel], and insist that defendants be separately represented." Wheat v. United States, 486 U.S. 153, 162 (1988) (5–4). "[A court] must be allowed substantial latitude in refusing waivers of conflicts of interest not only in those rare cases where an actual conflict may be demonstrated before trial, but in the more common cases where a potential for conflict exists which may or may not burgeon into an actual conflict as the trial progresses." Id. at 163.

524. In United States v. Dolan, 570 F.2d 1177 (3d Cir.1978), the court of appeals upheld the trial court's order that an attorney for two codefendants withdraw from the case and represent neither. In view of a clear conflict of interest, the court said, even a defendant's express preference to be represented by that attorney was not sufficient, notwithstanding Faretta v. California, 422 U.S. 806 (1975), p. 1077 below.

525. The defendant, Whitaker, was arrested on a complaint of his wife that he had had sexual intercourse with her daughter by a previous marriage. He admitted the offense. His wife's aunt, Mrs. McElfish, engaged defense counsel, who looked to her for his fee. The wife and the aunt told counsel "that they wanted the case disposed of quickly, quietly and with as little notoriety as possible in order to protect the child involved." The defendant pleaded *nolo contendere* to a charge of statutory rape and was convicted and sentenced to life imprisonment. After he had served more than ten years in prison, he sought his release on habeas corpus, which the district court, although smelling "foul fish," denied. The court of appeals reversed. "[T]he expressed interest of Mrs. Whitaker and Mrs. McElfish in a speedy, unpublicized disposition of the statutory rape charge and in protecting Mrs. Whitaker's daughter may have materially influenced the nature and extent of counsel's efforts to present a defense. . . . All that we need determine is that [defense counsel] was serving an interest or interests which conflicted with that of Whitaker; we need not delineate any specific prejudice to Whitaker flowing from his representation." Whitaker v. Warden, Maryland Penitentiary, 362 F.2d 838, 839–41 (4th Cir.1966).[38]

526. A defendant represented on appeal by a lawyer who, unknown to the defendant, himself is under indictment and has entered into a plea bargain in the same court from which the appeal is taken is denied the effective assistance of counsel. United States v. DeFalco, 644 F.2d 132 (3d Cir.1979).

---

38. ABA Standards for Criminal Justice, Prosecution Function and Defense Function (1993), Defense Function Standard 4-3.5(e): "In accepting payment of fees by one person for the defense of another, defense counsel should be careful to determine that he or she will not be confronted with a conflict of loyalty since defense counsel's entire loyalty is due the accused. Defense counsel should not accept such compensation unless:

(i) the accused consents after disclosure;

(ii) there is no interference with defense counsel's independence of professional judgment or with the client-lawyer relationship; and

(iii) information relating to the representation of the accused is protected from disclosure as required by defense counsel's ethical obligation of confidentiality.

Defense counsel should not permit a person who recommends, employs, or pays defense counsel to render legal services for another to direct or regulate counsel's professional judgment in rendering such legal services."

Strickland v. Washington

466 U.S. 668, 104 S.Ct. 2052, 80 L.Ed.2d 674 (1984).

■ JUSTICE O'CONNOR delivered the opinion of the Court.

This case requires us to consider the proper standards for judging a criminal defendant's contention that the Constitution requires a conviction or death sentence to be set aside because counsel's assistance at the trial or sentencing was ineffective.

I

A

During a 10-day period in September 1976, respondent planned and committed three groups of crimes, which included three brutal stabbing murders, torture, kidnapping, severe assaults, attempted murders, attempted extortion, and theft. After his two accomplices were arrested, respondent surrendered to police and voluntarily gave a lengthy statement confessing to the third of the criminal episodes. The State of Florida indicted respondent for kidnapping and murder and appointed an experienced criminal lawyer to represent him.

Counsel actively pursued pretrial motions and discovery. He cut his efforts short, however, and he experienced a sense of hopelessness about the case, when he learned that, against his specific advice, respondent had also confessed to the first two murders. By the date set for trial, respondent was subject to indictment for three counts of first degree murder and multiple counts of robbery, kidnapping for ransom, breaking and entering and assault, attempted murder, and conspiracy to commit robbery. Respondent waived his right to a jury trial, again acting against counsel's advice, and pleaded guilty to all charges, including the three capital murder charges.

In the plea colloquy, respondent told the trial judge that, although he had committed a string of burglaries, he had no significant prior criminal record and that at the time of his criminal spree he was under extreme stress caused by his inability to support his family. . . . He also stated, however, that he accepted responsibility for the crimes. . . . The trial judge told respondent that he had "a great deal of respect for people who are willing to step forward and admit their responsibility" but that he was making no statement at all about his likely sentencing decision. [App.], at 62.

Counsel advised respondent to invoke his right under Florida law to an advisory jury at his capital sentencing hearing. Respondent rejected the advice and waived the right. He chose instead to be sentenced by the trial judge without a jury recommendation.

In preparing for the sentencing hearing, counsel spoke with respondent about his background. He also spoke on the telephone with respondent's wife and mother, though he did not follow up on the one unsuccessful effort to meet with them. He did not otherwise seek out character witnesses for respondent. . . . Nor did he request a psychiatric examination, since his conversations with his client gave no indication that respondent had psychological problems. . . .

Counsel decided not to present and hence not to look further for evidence concerning respondent's character and emotional state. That decision reflected trial counsel's sense of hopelessness about overcoming the evidentiary effect of respondent's confessions to the gruesome crimes. . . . It also reflected the judgment that it was advisable to rely on the plea colloquy for evidence about respondent's background and about his claim of emotional stress: the plea colloquy communicated sufficient information about these subjects, and by foregoing the opportunity to present new evidence on these subjects, counsel prevented the State from cross-examining respondent on his claim and from putting on psychiatric evidence of its own. . . .

Counsel also excluded from the sentencing hearing other evidence he thought was potentially damaging. He successfully moved to exclude respondent's "rap sheet." . . . Because he judged that a presentence report might prove more detrimental than helpful, as it would have included respondent's criminal history and thereby undermined the claim of no significant history of criminal activity, he did not request that one be prepared. . . .

At the sentencing hearing, counsel's strategy was based primarily on the trial judge's remarks at the plea colloquy as well as on his reputation as a sentencing judge who thought it important for a convicted defendant to own up to his crime. Counsel argued that respondent's remorse and acceptance of responsibility justified sparing him from the death penalty. . . . Counsel also argued that respondent had no history of criminal activity and that respondent committed the crimes under extreme mental or emotional disturbance, thus coming within the statutory list of mitigating circumstances. He further argued that respondent should be spared death because he had surrendered, confessed, and offered to testify against a codefendant and because respondent was fundamentally a good person who had briefly gone badly wrong in extremely stressful circumstances. The State put on evidence and witnesses largely for the purpose of describing the details of the crime. Counsel did not cross-examine the medical experts who testified about the manner of death of respondent's victims.

The trial judge found several aggravating circumstances with respect to each of the three murders. He found that all three murders were especially heinous, atrocious, and cruel, all involving repeated stabbings. All three murders were committed in the course of at least one other dangerous and violent felony, and since all involved robbery, the murders were for pecuniary gain. All three murders were committed to avoid arrest for the accompanying crimes and to hinder law enforcement. In the course of one of the murders, respondent knowingly subjected numerous persons to a grave risk of death by deliberately stabbing and shooting the murder victim's sisters-in-law, who sustained severe—in one case, ultimately fatal—injuries.

With respect to mitigating circumstances, the trial judge made the same findings for all three capital murders. First, although there was no admitted evidence of prior convictions, respondent had stated that he had engaged in a course of stealing. In any case, even if respondent had no significant history of criminal activity, the aggravating circumstances "would still clearly far outweigh" that mitigating factor. Second, the judge found that, during all three crimes, respondent was not suffering from extreme mental or emotional disturbance and could appreciate the criminality of his acts. Third, none of the victims was a participant in, or consented to, respondent's conduct. Fourth, respondent's participation in the crimes was neither minor nor the result of duress or domination by an accomplice. Finally, respondent's age (26) could not be considered a factor in mitigation, especially when viewed in light of respondent's planning of the crimes and disposition of the proceeds of the various accompanying thefts.

In short, the trial judge found numerous aggravating circumstances and no (or a single comparatively insignificant) mitigating circumstance. With respect to each of the three convictions for capital murder, the trial judge concluded: "A careful consideration of all matters presented to the court impels the conclusion that there are insufficient mitigating circumstances . . . to outweigh the aggravating circumstances." See Washington v. State, 362 So.2d 658, 663–664 (Fla.1978) (quoting trial court findings) . . . . He therefore sentenced respondent to death on each of the three counts of murder and to prison terms for the other crimes. The Florida Supreme Court upheld the convictions and sentences on direct appeal.

B

Respondent subsequently sought collateral relief in state court on numerous grounds, among them that counsel had rendered ineffective assistance at the sentencing proceeding. Respondent challenged counsel's assistance in six respects. He asserted that counsel was ineffective because he failed to move for a continuance to prepare for sentencing, to request a psychiatric report, to investigate and present character witnesses, to seek a presentence investigation report, to present meaningful arguments to the sentencing judge, and to investigate the medical examiner's reports or cross-examine the medical experts. In support of the claim, respondent submitted 14 affidavits from friends, neighbors, and relatives stating that they would have testified if asked to do so. He also submitted one psychiatric report and one psychological report stating that respondent, though not under the influence of extreme mental or emotional disturbance, was "chronically frustrated and depressed because of his economic dilemma" at the time of his crimes. App. 7 . . . .

The trial court denied relief without an evidentiary hearing, finding that the record evidence conclusively showed that the ineffectiveness claim was meritless. . . .

. . .

[W]e granted certiorari to consider the standards by which to judge a contention that the Constitution requires that a criminal judgment be overturned because of the actual ineffective assistance of counsel. . . .

II

In a long line of cases . . . this Court has recognized that the Sixth Amendment right to counsel exists, and is needed, in order to protect the fundamental right to a fair trial. . . .

. . .

[T]he Court has recognized that "the right to counsel is the right to the effective assistance of counsel." McMann v. Richardson, 397 U.S. 759, 771, n. 14 (1970). . . .

The Court has not elaborated on the meaning of the constitutional requirement of effective assistance in the . . . class of cases . . . presenting claims of "actual ineffectiveness." In giving meaning to the requirement, however, we must take its purpose—to ensure a fair trial—as the guide. The benchmark for judging any claim of ineffectiveness must be whether counsel's conduct so undermined the proper functioning of the adversarial process that the trial cannot be relied on as having produced a just result.

The same principle applies to a capital sentencing proceeding such as that provided by Florida law. We need not consider the role of counsel in an ordinary sentencing, which may involve informal proceedings and standardless discretion in the sentencer, and hence may require a different approach to the definition of constitutionally effective assistance. A capital sentencing proceeding like the one involved in this case, however, is sufficiently like a trial in its adversarial format and in the existence of standards for decision . . . that counsel's role in the proceeding is comparable to counsel's role at trial—to ensure that the adversarial testing process works to produce a just result under the standards governing decision. For purposes of describing counsel's duties, therefore, Florida's capital sentencing proceeding need not be distinguished from an ordinary trial.

III

A convicted defendant's claim that counsel's assistance was so defective as to require reversal of a conviction or death sentence has two components. First, the defendant must show that counsel's performance was deficient. This requires showing that counsel made errors so serious that counsel was not functioning as the "counsel" guaranteed the defendant by the Sixth Amendment. Second, the defendant must show that the deficient performance prejudiced the defense. This requires showing that counsel's errors were so serious as to deprive the defendant of a fair trial, a trial whose result is reliable. Unless a defendant makes both showings, it cannot be said that the conviction or death sentence resulted from a breakdown in the adversary process that renders the result unreliable.

A

As all the Federal Courts of Appeals have now held, the proper standard for attorney performance is that of reasonably effective assistance. . . . When a convicted defendant complains of the ineffectiveness of counsel's assistance, the defendant must show that counsel's representation fell below an objective standard of reasonableness.

More specific guidelines are not appropriate. The Sixth Amendment refers simply to "counsel," not specifying particular requirements of effective assistance. It relies instead on the legal profession's maintenance of standards sufficient to justify the law's presumption that counsel will fulfill the role in the adversary process that the Amendment envisions. . . . The proper measure of attorney performance remains simply reasonableness under prevailing professional norms.

Representation of a criminal defendant entails certain basic duties. Counsel's function is to assist the defendant, and hence counsel owes the client a duty of loyalty, a duty to avoid conflicts of interest. . . . From counsel's function as assistant to the defendant derive the overarching duty to advocate the defendant's cause and the more particular duties to consult with the defendant on important decisions and to keep the defendant informed of important developments in the course of the prosecution. Counsel also has a duty to bring to bear such skill and knowledge as will render the trial a reliable adversarial testing process. . . .

These basic duties neither exhaustively define the obligations of counsel nor form a checklist for judicial evaluation of attorney performance. In any case presenting an ineffectiveness claim, the performance inquiry must be whether counsel's assistance was reasonable considering all the circumstances. Prevailing norms of practice as reflected in American Bar Association standards and the like . . . are guides to determining what is reasonable, but they are only guides. No particular set of detailed rules for counsel's conduct can satisfactorily take account of the variety of circumstances faced by defense counsel or the range of legitimate decisions regarding how best to represent a criminal defendant. Any such set of rules would interfere with the constitutionally protected independence of counsel and restrict the wide latitude counsel must have in making tactical decisions. . . . Indeed, the existence of detailed guidelines for representation could distract counsel from the overriding mission of vigorous advocacy of the defendant's cause. Moreover, the purpose of the effective assistance guarantee of the Sixth Amendment is not to improve the quality of legal representation, although that is a goal of considerable importance to the legal system. The purpose is simply to ensure that criminal defendants receive a fair trial.

Judicial scrutiny of counsel's performance must be highly deferential. It is all too tempting for a defendant to second-guess counsel's assistance after conviction or adverse sentence, and it is all too easy for a court, examining counsel's defense after it has proved unsuccessful, to conclude that a particular act or omission of counsel was unreasonable. . . . A fair assessment of attorney performance requires that every effort be made to eliminate the distorting effects of hindsight, to reconstruct the circumstances of counsel's challenged conduct, and to evaluate the conduct from counsel's perspective at the time. Because of the difficulties inherent in making the evaluation, a court must indulge a strong presumption that counsel's conduct falls within the wide range of reasonable professional assistance; that is, the defendant must overcome the presumption that, under the circumstances, the challenged action "might be considered sound trial strategy." See Michel v. Louisiana, [350 U.S. 91 (1955)], at 101. There are countless ways to provide effective assistance in any given case. Even the best criminal defense attorneys would not defend a particular client in the same way. . . .

The availability of intrusive post-trial inquiry into attorney performance or of detailed guidelines for its evaluation would encourage the proliferation of ineffectiveness challenges. Criminal trials resolved unfavorably to the defendant would increasingly come to be followed by a second trial, this one of counsel's unsuccessful defense. Counsel's performance and even willingness to serve could be adversely affected. Intensive scrutiny of counsel and rigid requirements for acceptable assistance could dampen the ardor and impair the independence of defense counsel, discourage the acceptance of assigned cases, and undermine the trust between attorney and client.

Thus, a court deciding an actual ineffectiveness claim must judge the reasonableness of counsel's challenged conduct on the facts of the particular case, viewed as of the time of counsel's conduct. A convicted defendant making a claim of ineffective assistance must identify the acts or omissions of counsel that are alleged not to have been the result of reasonable professional judgment. The court must then determine whether, in light of all the circumstances, the identified acts or omissions were outside the wide range of professionally competent assistance. In making that determination, the court should keep in mind that counsel's function, as elaborated in prevailing professional norms, is to make the adversarial testing process work in the particular case. At the same time, the court should recognize that counsel is strongly presumed to have rendered adequate assistance and made all significant decisions in the exercise of reasonable professional judgment.

These standards require no special amplification in order to define counsel's duty to investigate, the duty at issue in this case. As the Court of Appeals concluded, strategic choices made after thorough investigation of law and facts relevant to plausible options are virtually unchallengeable; and strategic choices made after less than complete investigation are reasonable precisely to the extent that reasonable professional judgments support the limitations on investigation. In other words, counsel has a duty to make reasonable investigations or to make a reasonable decision that makes particular investigations unnecessary. In any ineffectiveness case, a particular decision not to investigate must be directly assessed for reasonableness in all the circumstances, applying a heavy measure of deference to counsel's judgments.

The reasonableness of counsel's actions may be determined or substantially influenced by the defendant's own statements or actions. Counsel's actions are usually based, quite properly, on informed strategic choices made by the defendant and on information supplied by the defendant. In particular, what investigation decisions are reasonable depends critically on such information. For example, when the facts that support a certain potential line of defense are generally known to counsel because of what the defendant has said, the need for further investigation may be considerably diminished or eliminated altogether. And when a defendant has given counsel reason to believe that pursuing certain investigations would be fruitless or even harmful, counsel's failure to pursue those investigations may not later be challenged as unreasonable. In short, inquiry into counsel's conversations with the defendant may be critical to a proper assessment of counsel's investigation decisions, just as it may be critical to a proper assessment of counsel's other litigation decisions. . . .

B

An error by counsel, even if professionally unreasonable, does not warrant setting aside the judgment of a criminal proceeding if the error had no effect on the judgment. . . . The purpose of the Sixth Amendment guarantee of counsel is to ensure that a defendant has the assistance necessary to justify reliance on the outcome of the proceeding. Accordingly, any deficiencies in counsel's performance must be prejudicial to the defense in order to constitute ineffective assistance under the Constitution.

In certain Sixth Amendment contexts, prejudice is presumed. Actual or constructive denial of the assistance of counsel altogether is legally presumed to result in prejudice. So are various kinds of state interference with counsel's assistance. . . . Prejudice in these circumstances is so likely that case by case inquiry into prejudice is not worth the cost. . . . Moreover, such circumstances involve impairments of the Sixth Amendment right that are easy to identify and, for that reason and because the prosecution is directly responsible, easy for the government to prevent.

One type of actual ineffectiveness claim warrants a similar, though more limited, presumption of prejudice. In Cuyler v. Sullivan, 446 U.S., at 345–350, the Court held that prejudice is presumed when counsel is burdened by an actual conflict of interest. . . . Even so, the rule is not quite the *per se* rule of prejudice that exists for the Sixth Amendment claims mentioned above. Prejudice is presumed only if the defendant demonstrates that counsel "actively represented conflicting interests" and that "an actual conflict of interest adversely affected his lawyer's performance." Cuyler v. Sullivan, supra, at 350, 348 (footnote omitted).

Conflict of interest claims aside, actual ineffectiveness claims alleging a deficiency in attorney performance are subject to a general requirement that the defendant affirmatively prove prejudice. . . . Even if a defendant shows that particular errors of counsel were unreasonable, therefore, the defendant must show that they actually had an adverse effect on the defense.

It is not enough for the defendant to show that the errors had some conceivable effect on the outcome of the proceeding. Virtually every act or omission of counsel would meet that test . . . and not every error that conceivably could have influenced the outcome undermines the reliability of the result of the proceeding. . . .

On the other hand, we believe that a defendant need not show that counsel's deficient conduct more likely than not altered the outcome in the case. . . .

. . . The result of a proceeding can be rendered unreliable, and hence the proceeding itself unfair, even if the errors of counsel cannot be shown by a preponderance of the evidence to have determined the outcome.

Accordingly, the appropriate test for prejudice finds its roots in the test for materiality of exculpatory information not disclosed to the defense by the prosecution . . . and in the test for materiality of testimony made unavailable to the defense by Government deportation of a witness. . . . The defendant must show that there is a reasonable probability that, but for counsel's unprofessional errors, the result of the proceeding would have been different. A reasonable probability is a probability sufficient to undermine confidence in the outcome.

. . .

The governing legal standard plays a critical role in defining the question to be asked in assessing the prejudice from counsel's errors. When a defendant challenges a conviction, the question is whether there is a reasonable probability that, absent the errors, the factfinder would have had a reasonable doubt respecting guilt. When a defendant challenges a death sentence such as the one at issue in this case, the question is whether there is a reasonable probability that, absent the errors, the sentencer—including an appellate court, to the extent it independently reweighs the evidence— would have concluded that the balance of aggravating and mitigating circumstances did not warrant death.

In making this determination, a court hearing an ineffectiveness claim must consider the totality of the evidence before the judge or jury. Some of the factual findings will have been unaffected by the errors, and factual findings that were affected will have been affected in different ways. Some errors will have had a pervasive effect on the inferences to be drawn from the evidence, altering the entire evidentiary picture, and some will have had an isolated, trivial effect. Moreover, a verdict or conclusion only weakly supported by the record is more likely to have been affected by errors than one with overwhelming record support. Taking the unaffected findings as a given, and taking due account of the effect of the errors on the remaining findings, a court making the prejudice inquiry must ask if the defendant has met the burden of showing that the decision reached would reasonably likely have been different absent the errors.

IV

. . .

Although we have discussed the performance component of an ineffectiveness claim prior to the prejudice component, there is no reason for a court deciding an ineffective assistance claim to approach the inquiry in the same order or even to address both components of the inquiry if the defendant makes an insufficient showing on one. In particular, a court need not determine whether counsel's performance was deficient before examining the prejudice suffered by the defendant as a result of the alleged deficiencies. The object of an ineffectiveness claim is not to grade counsel's performance. If it is easier to dispose of an ineffectiveness claim on the ground of lack of sufficient prejudice, which we expect will often be so, that course should be followed. Courts should strive to ensure that ineffectiveness claims not become so burdensome to defense counsel that the entire criminal justice system suffers as a result.

. . .

V

Having articulated general standards for judging ineffectiveness claims, we think it useful to apply those standards to the facts of this case in order to illustrate the meaning of the general principles. . . .

Application of the governing principles is not difficult in this case. The facts as described above . . . make clear that the conduct of respondent's counsel at and before respondent's sentencing proceeding cannot be found unreasonable. They also make clear that, even assuming the challenged conduct of counsel was unreasonable, respondent suffered insufficient prejudice to warrant setting aside his death sentence.

With respect to the performance component, the record shows that respondent's counsel made a strategic choice to argue for the extreme emotional distress mitigating circumstance and to rely as fully as possible on respondent's acceptance of responsibility for his crimes. Although counsel understandably felt hopeless about respondent's prospects . . . nothing in the record indicates . . . that counsel's sense of hopelessness distorted his professional judgment. Counsel's strategy choice was well within the range of professionally reasonable judgments, and the decision not to seek more character or psychological evidence than was already in hand was likewise reasonable.

The trial judge's views on the importance of owning up to one's crimes were well known to counsel. The aggravating circumstances were utterly overwhelming. Trial counsel could reasonably surmise from his conversations with respondent that character and psychological evidence would be of little help. Respondent had already been able to mention at the plea colloquy the substance of what there was to know about his financial and emotional troubles. Restricting testimony on respondent's character to what had come in at the plea colloquy ensured that contrary character and psychological evidence and respondent's criminal history, which counsel had successfully moved to exclude, would not come in. On these facts there can be little question, even without application of the presumption of adequate performance, that trial counsel's defense, though unsuccessful, was the result of reasonable professional judgment.

With respect to the prejudice component, the lack of merit of respondent's claim is even more stark. The evidence that respondent says his trial counsel should have offered at the sentencing hearing would barely have altered the sentencing profile presented to the sentencing judge. As the state courts and District Court found, at most this evidence shows that numerous people who knew respondent thought he was generally a good person and that a psychiatrist and a psychologist believed he was under considerable emotional stress that did not rise to the level of extreme disturbance. Given the overwhelming aggravating factors, there is no reasonable probability that the omitted evidence would have changed the conclusion that the aggravating circumstances outweighed the mitigating circumstances and, hence, the sentence imposed. Indeed, admission of the evidence respondent now offers might even have been harmful to his case: his "rap sheet" would probably have been admitted into evidence, and the psychological reports would have directly contradicted respondent's claim that the mitigating circumstance of extreme emotional disturbance applied to his case.

. . .

Failure to make the required showing of either deficient performance or sufficient prejudice defeats the ineffectiveness claim. Here there is a double failure. More generally, respondent has made no showing that the justice of his sentence was rendered unreliable by a breakdown in the adversary process caused by deficiencies in counsel's assistance. Respondent's sentencing proceeding was not fundamentally unfair.

. . .[39]

———

527. Should a defendant's conviction be reversed if, without more, he shows that his counsel was a narcotics addict during the period when he represented the defendant? Does it matter whether or not the defendant knew of his counsel's condition? See United States v. Butler, 167 F.Supp. 102 (E.D.Va.1957). See also Tippins v. Walker, 77 F.3d 682 (2d Cir.1996) (defense counsel asleep during substantial portions of trial; ineffective assistance of counsel per se); Vance v. Lehman, 64 F.3d 119 (3d Cir.1995) (shortly after defendant's trial, defense counsel's license to practice law was revoked because of unrelated unprofessional conduct occurring before trial; not ineffective assistance per se); Scarpa v. Dubois, 38 F.3d 1 (1st Cir.1994) (substandard performance of counsel does not warrant conclusive presumption of prejudice); Bellamy v. Cogdell, 974 F.2d 302 (2d Cir.1992) (counsel with mental and physical ailments; not ineffective assistance per se).

Has a defendant who is convicted of possession of heroin been denied the effective assistance of counsel if defense counsel fails to make a sound

[39] Justice Brennan wrote an opinion concurring in part and dissenting in part. Justice Marshall wrote a dissenting opinion.

motion to suppress the heroin seized from the defendant because he does not know the "common-place" state rule "that defendant could challenge the legality of the search and seizure even though he denied that the heroin was taken from him and asserted no proprietary interest in the premises that were entered," People v. Ibarra, 386 P.2d 487, 491 (Cal.1963)? See generally People v. Pope, 590 P.2d 859 (Cal.1979) (en banc) (*Ibarra* rejected).

Should a defendant's conviction be reversed if it is shown that "in order to avoid the appearance of impropriety," defense counsel followed a general policy of not attempting to interview before trial witnesses whose testimony is (apparently) favorable to the prosecution? See Thomas v. Wyrick, 535 F.2d 407 (8th Cir.1976).

528. To what extent must defense counsel who has made a clearly supportable tactical decision about the introduction of evidence or a challenge to the evidence of the prosecution discuss the decision with his client? If he fails to do so when he should have, in what circumstances ought his failure be a basis for reversal? See United States v. Moore, 554 F.2d 1086 (D.C.Cir.1976).

529. Should it make any difference to a claim of ineffective assistance of counsel whether defense counsel was retained or appointed? In Cuyler v. Sullivan, 446 U.S. 335 (1980), the Court said not. "A proper respect for the Sixth Amendment disarms petitioner's contention that defendants who retain their own lawyers are entitled to less protection than defendants for whom the State appoints counsel. We may assume with confidence that most counsel, whether retained or appointed, will protect the rights of an accused. But experience teaches that, in some cases, retained counsel will not provide adequate representation. The vital guarantee of the Sixth Amendment would stand for little if the often uninformed decision to retain a particular lawyer could reduce or forfeit the defendant's entitlement to constitutional protection. Since the State's conduct of a criminal trial itself implicates the State in the defendant's conviction, we see no basis for drawing a distinction between retained and appointed counsel that would deny equal justice to defendants who must choose their own lawyers." Id. at 344-45.

530. In Wilson v. Mintzes, 761 F.2d 275 (6th Cir.1985), the court held that the standards applicable to a claim for relief for ineffective assistance of counsel that were elaborated in Strickland v. Washington, above, are not applicable to a request for substitution of retained counsel during the course of a trial. In *Wilson*, the defendant expressed dissatisfaction with his counsel during the trial and asked for a continuance to obtain different counsel. The court distinguished the right to effective assistance of counsel from the right to choose one's counsel. It said: "[I]t is clear that when an accused is financially able to retain an attorney, the choice of counsel to assist him rests ultimately in his hands and not in the hands of the State." Id. at 280. Conceding that the right to a continuance in order to change counsel requires a balance of competing interests, the court said that neither ineffective assistance of counsel nor prejudice need be shown, since the right to counsel of one's choice "is premised on respect for the individual," id. at 286, and not on the fairness of the proceeding or the consequence of the choice. In the circumstances of the case, the court said, a continuance should have been granted.

531. In Lockhart v. Fretwell, 506 U.S. 364 (1993) (7–2), the Court held that defense counsel's failure to make an objection in a state sentencing proceeding, which objection was supported by a decision that was subsequently overruled, is not "prejudice" within the meaning of Strickland v. Washington. To hold otherwise, the Court said, would give criminal defendants "a windfall to which they are not entitled." Id. at 366. "Unreliability or unfairness does not result if the ineffectiveness of counsel does not deprive the defendant of any substantive or procedural right to which the law entitles him." Id. at 372.

See also Wainwright v. Torna, 455 U.S. 586 (1982) (7–1–1). In that case, the defendant had been convicted of felonies in state court. The convictions were affirmed on appeal. The state supreme court dismissed an application for certiorari on the ground that it had not been filed in time. The defendant sought federal habeas corpus, claiming that he had been denied the effective assistance of counsel because of his retained counsel's failure to file the application in time. The Court held that the district court had correctly denied the petition for habeas corpus. Relying on Ross v. Moffitt, 417 U.S. 600 (1974), it observed that there was not a constitutional right to counsel to pursue discretionary state appeals. Accordingly, it said, the defendant "could not be deprived of the effective assistance of counsel" by his retained counsel's failure. 455 U.S. at 588.

Johns v. Smyth

176 F.Supp. 949 (E.D.Va.1959).

[The defendant was convicted of murder and sentenced to life imprisonment. The killing occurred while the defendant and the deceased were inmates at the state penitentiary. The defendant made a statement on the day following the killing to the effect that he killed his victim after the latter took hold of him and suggested an unnatural sexual act; the prison authorities' investigation suggested other motives for the killing. The defendant sought his release by a petition for habeas corpus in the federal district court.]

■ WALTER E. HOFFMAN, DISTRICT JUDGE.

. . .

Little need be said of the trial. The accused did not testify. No proposed instructions were submitted to the trial judge in behalf of the defendant, although under the law of Virginia it was possible for the defendant to have been convicted of involuntary manslaughter and received a sentence of only five years. The defense attorney agreed with the prosecutor that the case would be submitted to the jury without argument of counsel. The instructions given by the court were generally acceptable in covering the categories of first and second degree murder, but failed to mention the possibility of a manslaughter verdict.

Standing alone these complaints would have no merit as they may properly be considered as trial tactics. However, when we look at the motivating force which prompted these decisions of trial counsel, it is apparent that "tactics" gave way to "conscience". In explanation of the agreement not to argue the case before the jury, the court-appointed attorney said:

"I think an argument to the jury would have made me appear ridiculous in the light of evidence that was offered.

. . .

"I had enough confidence in the judgment of the jury to know that they could have drawn an inference, and I would have been a hypocrite and falsifier if I had gone before the jury and argued in the light of what Johns told me that that statement was accurate.

. . .

"Well, sir, I did not and I wouldn't be dishonest enough to do it in the light of Mr. Johns' statement to me. You can say what the law is and what the record discloses, but if I asked a client, an accused on defense, to explain some such statement as this and he gives me the explanation that Johns gave me, I consider it dishonest. You can talk about legal duty to client all you wish, but I consider it dishonest for me to get up before a jury and try to argue that the statement that came out from the Commonwealth was true when Johns had told me that it wasn't. The explanation that he gave me was very vague." Immediately thereafter, the following occurred:

"Q. That you could not conscientiously argue to the jury that he should be acquitted? A. I definitely could not.

"Q. Regardless of what the law is or what your duty to a client is? A. You can talk about law and you can talk about my duty to clients, I felt it was my—that I couldn't conscientiously stand up there and argue that point in the light of what Johns had told me." The attorney was then asked whether he ever considered requesting permission to withdraw from the case. He replied in the negative.

No attorney should "frame" a factual defense in any case, civil or criminal, and it is not intimated by this opinion that the attorney should plant the seeds of falsehood in the mind of his client. In the instant case, however, the evidence adduced by the prosecution suggested some provocation for the act through the summary of the statement given by the defendant on the day following the killing. When the defendant was interviewed by his court-appointed attorney, the attorney stated that he had reason to doubt the accuracy of the defendant's statement. It was at this time that the attorney's conscience actuated his future conduct which continued throughout the trial. If this was the evidence presented by the prosecution, the defendant was entitled to the faithful and devoted services of his attorney uninhibited by the dictating conscience. The defendant could not be compelled to testify against himself, and if the prosecution saw fit to use the defendant's statement in aid of the prosecution, the attorney was duty bound to exert his best efforts in aid of his client. The failure to argue the case before the jury, while ordinarily only a trial tactic not subject to review, manifestly enters the field of incompetency when the reason assigned is the attorney's conscience. It is as improper as though the attorney had told the jury that his client had uttered a falsehood in making the statement. The right to an attorney embraces effective representation throughout all stages of the trial, and where the representation is of such low caliber as to amount to no representation, the guarantee of due process has been violated. . . .

The entire trial in the state court had the earmarks of an *ex parte* proceeding. If petitioner had been without the services of an attorney, but had remained mute, it is unlikely that he would have been worse off. The state argues that the defendant may have received a death sentence. Admitting this to be true, it affords no excuse for lack of effective representation.

. . .

[I]t would be a dark day in the history of our judicial system if a conviction is permitted to stand where an attorney, furnished to an indigent defendant, candidly admits that his conscience prevented him from effectively representing his client according to the customary standards prescribed by attorneys and the courts.

Counsel for petitioner will prepare an appropriate order granting the writ of habeas corpus. . . .

————

532. The right to counsel does not guarantee a "meaningful relationship" between an accused and his counsel. Morris v. Slappy, 461 U.S. 1 (1983).

With *Johns*, compare Willis v. United States, 489 F.2d 707 (9th Cir.1973). Counsel was appointed to represent the petitioner in a collateral attack on his conviction. After investigating the petitioner's claims, counsel concluded that they were without legal basis and asked leave of the court to withdraw from the case. The court of appeals observed that counsel had "misconceived his role." Effective representation "requires more than an independent investigation that leads counsel to conclude the client's claim has no legal basis. It is for the court to pass on the legal basis of the claim after its presentation by counsel in as favorable a manner as it permits." 489 F.2d at 708.

The result in *Johns* was questioned in United States ex rel. Wilkins v. Banmiller, 205 F.Supp. 123, 128 n.5 (E.D.Pa.1962).

533. The trial of the defendant is scheduled to begin on Monday morning. After having repeatedly advised the defendant that he would not represent him without having been paid in advance for his services, defense counsel receives a check on the preceding Wednesday. On Friday morning, defense counsel learns that the check has bounced. What should he do? See United States v. Marx, 553 F.2d 874 (4th Cir.1977).

ABA Standards for Criminal Justice, Prosecution Function and Defense Function (3d ed. 1993), Defense Function Standard 4-3.3: Fees

"(a) Defense counsel should not enter into an agreement for, charge, or collect an illegal or unreasonable fee.

(b) In determining the amount of the fee in a criminal case, it is proper to consider the time and effort required, the responsibility assumed by counsel, the novelty and difficulty of the questions involved, the skill requisite to proper representation, the likelihood that other employment will be precluded, the fee customarily charged in the locality for similar services, the gravity of the charge, the experience, reputation and ability of defense counsel and the capacity of the client to pay the fee."

See Winkler v. Keane, 7 F.3d 304 (2d Cir.1993) (agreement that counsel would receive higher fee if defendant were acquitted created conflict of interest; but no effect adverse to defendant was shown).

———

Faretta v. California

422 U.S. 806, 95 S.Ct. 2525, 45 L.Ed.2d 562 (1975).

■ MR. JUSTICE STEWART delivered the opinion of the Court.

The Sixth and Fourteenth Amendments of our Constitution guarantee that a person brought to trial in any state or federal court must be afforded the right to the assistance of counsel before he can be validly convicted and punished by imprisonment. This clear constitutional rule has emerged from a series of cases decided here over the last 50 years. The question before us now is whether a defendant in a state criminal trial has a constitutional right to proceed *without* counsel when he voluntarily and intelligently elects to do so. Stated another way, the question is whether a State may constitutionally hale a person into its criminal courts and there force a lawyer upon him, even when he insists that he wants to conduct his own defense. It is not an easy question, but we have concluded that a State may not constitutionally do so.

I

Anthony Faretta was charged with grand theft in an information filed in the Superior Court of Los Angeles County, Cal. At the arraignment, the Superior Court Judge assigned to preside at the trial appointed the public defender to represent Faretta. Well before the date of trial, however, Faretta requested that he be permitted to represent himself. Questioning by the judge revealed that Farretta had once represented himself in a criminal prosecution, that he had a high school education, and that he did not want to be represented by the public defender because he believed that that office was "very loaded down with . . . a heavy case load." The judge responded that he believed Faretta was "making a mistake" and emphasized that in further proceedings Faretta would receive no special favors. Nevertheless, after establishing that Faretta wanted to represent himself and did not want a lawyer, the judge, in a "preliminary ruling," accepted Faretta's waiver of the assistance of counsel. The judge indicated, however, that he might reverse this ruling if it later appeared that Faretta was unable adequately to represent himself.

Several weeks thereafter, but still prior to trial, the judge *sua sponte* held a hearing to inquire into Faretta's ability to conduct his own defense, and questioned him specifically about both the hearsay rule and the state law governing the challenge of potential jurors. After consideration of Faretta's answers, and observation of his demeanor, the judge ruled that Faretta had not made an intelligent and knowing waiver of his right to the assistance of counsel, and also ruled that Faretta had no constitutional right to conduct his own defense. The judge, accordingly, reversed his earlier ruling permitting self-representation and again appointed the public defender to represent Faretta. Faretta's subsequent request for leave to act as cocounsel was rejected, as were his efforts to make certain motions on his own behalf. Throughout the subsequent trial, the judge required that Faretta's defense be conducted only through the appointed lawyer from the public defender's office. At the conclusion of the trial, the jury found Faretta guilty as charged, and the judge sentenced him to prison.

. . .

II

In the federal courts, the right of self-representation has been protected by statute since the beginnings of our Nation. Section 35 of the Judiciary

Act of 1789, 1 Stat. 73, 92, enacted by the First Congress and signed by President Washington one day before the Sixth Amendment was proposed, provided that "in all the courts of the United States, the parties may plead and manage their own causes personally or by the assistance of . . . counsel. . . ." The right is currently codified in 28 U.S.C. § 1654.

With few exceptions, each of the several States also accords a defendant the right to represent himself in any criminal case. The Constitutions of 36 States explicitly confer that right. Moreover, many state courts have expressed the view that the right is also supported by the Constitution of the United States.

This Court has more than once indicated the same view. In Adams v. United States ex rel. McCann, 317 U.S. 269, 279, the Court recognized that the Sixth Amendment right to the assistance of counsel implicitly embodies a "correlative right to dispense with a lawyer's help." . . .

The *Adams* case does not, of course, necessarily resolve the issue before us. It held only that "the Constitution does not force a lawyer upon a defendant." Id., at 279. Whether the Constitution forbids a State from forcing a lawyer upon a defendant is a different question. But the Court in *Adams* did recognize, albeit in dictum, an affirmative right of self-representation:

"The right to assistance of counsel and the *correlative right to dispense with a lawyer's help* are not legal formalisms. They rest on considerations that go to the substance of an accused's position before the law. . . .

". . . What were contrived as protections for the accused should not be turned into fetters. . . . To deny an accused a choice of procedure in circumstances in which he, though a layman, is as capable as any lawyer of making an intelligent choice, is to impair the worth of great Constitutional safeguards by treating them as empty verbalisms.

". . . When the administration of the criminal law . . . is hedged about as it is by the Constitutional safeguards for the protection of an accused, to deny him in the exercise of his free choice the right to dispense with some of these safeguards . . . is to imprison a man in his privileges and call it the Constitution." Id. at 279–280 (emphasis added).

In other settings as well, the Court has indicated that a defendant has a constitutionally protected right to represent himself in a criminal trial. . . .

The United States Courts of Appeals have repeatedly held that the right of self-representation is protected by the Bill of Rights. . . .

This Court's past recognition of the right of self-representation, the federal-court authority holding the right to be of constitutional dimension, and the state constitutions pointing to the right's fundamental nature form a consensus not easily ignored. . . . We confront here a nearly universal conviction, on the part of our people as well as our courts, that forcing a lawyer upon an unwilling defendant is contrary to his basic right to defend himself if he truly wants to do so.

III

This consensus is soundly premised. The right of self-representation finds support in the structure of the Sixth Amendment, as well as in the English and colonial jurisprudence from which the Amendment emerged.

A

. . .

The Sixth Amendment does not provide merely that a defense shall be made for the accused; it grants to the accused personally the right to make his defense. It is the accused, not counsel, who must be "informed of the nature and cause of the accusation," who must be "confronted with the witnesses against him," and who must be accorded "compulsory process for obtaining witnesses in his favor." Although not stated in the Amendment in so many words, the right to self-representation—to make one's own defense personally—is thus necessarily implied by the structure of the Amendment. The right to defend is given directly to the accused; for it is he who suffers the consequences if the defense fails.

The counsel provision supplements this design. It speaks of the "assistance" of counsel, and an assistant, however expert, is still an assistant. The language and spirit of the Sixth Amendment contemplate that counsel, like the other defense tools guaranteed by the Amendment, shall be an aid to a willing defendant—not an organ of the State interposed between an unwilling defendant and his right to defend himself personally. To thrust counsel upon the accused, against his considered wish, thus violates the logic of the Amendment. In such a case, counsel is not an assistant, but a master; and the right to make a defense is stripped of the personal character upon which the Amendment insists. It is true that when a defendant chooses to have a lawyer manage and present his case, law and tradition may allocate to the counsel the power to make binding decisions of trial strategy in many areas. . . . This allocation can only be justified, however, by the defendant's consent, at the outset, to accept counsel as his representative. An unwanted counsel "represents" the defendant only through a tenuous and unacceptable legal fiction. Unless the accused has acquiesced in such representation, the defense presented is not the defense guaranteed him by the Constitution, for, in a very real sense, it is not *his* defense.

B

The Sixth Amendment, when naturally read, thus implies a right of self-representation. This reading is reinforced by the Amendment's roots in English legal history.

. . .

C

In the American Colonies the insistence upon a right of self-representation was, if anything, more fervent than in England.

. . .

In sum, there is no evidence that the colonists and the Framers ever doubted the right of self-representation, or imagined that this right might be considered inferior to the right of assistance of counsel. To the contrary, the colonists and the Framers, as well as their English ancestors, always conceived of the right to counsel as an "assistance" for the accused, to be used at his option, in defending himself. The Framers selected in the Sixth Amendment a form of words that necessarily implies the right of self-representation. That conclusion is supported by centuries of consistent history.

IV

There can be no blinking the fact that the right of an accused to conduct his own defense seems to cut against the grain of this Court's decisions holding that the Constitution requires that no accused can be convicted and imprisoned unless he has been accorded the right to the assistance of counsel. . . . For it is surely true that the basic thesis of those decisions is that the help of a lawyer is essential to assure the defendant a fair trial. And a strong argument can surely be made that the whole thrust of those decisions must inevitably lead to the conclusion that a State may constitutionally impose a lawyer upon even an unwilling defendant.

But it is one thing to hold that every defendant, rich or poor, has the right to the assistance of counsel, and quite another to say that a State may compel a defendant to accept a lawyer he does not want. . . .

It is undeniable that in most criminal prosecutions defendants could better defend with counsel's guidance than by their own unskilled efforts. But where the defendant will not voluntarily accept representation by counsel, the potential advantage of a lawyer's training and experience can be realized, if at all, only imperfectly. To force a lawyer on a defendant can only lead him to believe that the law contrives against him. Moreover, it is not inconceivable that in some rare instances, the defendant might in fact present his case more effectively by conducting his own defense. Personal liberties are not rooted in the law of averages. The right to defend is personal. The defendant, and not his lawyer or the State, will bear the personal consequences of a conviction. It is the defendant, therefore, who must be free personally to decide whether in his particular case counsel is to his advantage. And although he may conduct his own defense ultimately to his own detriment, his choice must be honored out of "that respect for the individual which is the lifeblood of the law." Illinois v. Allen, 397 U.S. 337, 350–351 (Brennan, J., concurring).

V

When an accused manages his own defense, he relinquishes, as a purely factual matter, many of the traditional benefits associated with the right to counsel. For this reason, in order to represent himself, the accused must "knowingly and intelligently" forgo those relinquished benefits. Johnson v. Zerbst, 304 U.S., at 464–465. . . . Although a defendant need not himself have the skill and experience of a lawyer in order competently and intelligently to choose self-representation, he should be made aware of the dangers and disadvantages of self-representation, so that the record will establish that "he knows what he is doing and his choice is made with eyes open." Adams v. United States ex rel. McCann, 317 U.S., at 279.

Here, weeks before trial, Faretta clearly and unequivocally declared to the trial judge that he wanted to represent himself and did not want counsel. The record affirmatively shows that Faretta was literate, competent, and understanding, and that he was voluntarily exercising his informed free will. The trial judge had warned Faretta that he thought it was a mistake not to accept the assistance of counsel, and that Faretta would be required to follow all the "ground rules" of trial procedure. We need make no assessment of how well or poorly Faretta had mastered the intricacies of the hearsay rule and the California code provisions that govern challenges of potential jurors on voir dire. For his technical legal knowledge, as such, was not relevant to an assessment of his knowing exercise of the right to defend himself.

In forcing Faretta, under these circumstances, to accept against his will a state-appointed public defender, the California courts deprived him of his constitutional right to conduct his own defense. . . .

. . .

MR. CHIEF JUSTICE BURGER, with whom MR. JUSTICE BLACKMUN and MR. JUSTICE REHNQUIST join, dissenting.

[T]here is nothing desirable or useful in permitting every accused person, even the most uneducated and inexperienced, to insist upon conducting his own defense to criminal charges. Moreover, there is no constitutional basis for the Court's holding, and it can only add to the problems of an already malfunctioning criminal justice system. . . .

I

. . .

As the Court seems to recognize . . . the conclusion that the rights guaranteed by the Sixth Amendment are "personal" to an accused reflects nothing more than the obvious fact that it is he who is on trial and therefore has need of a defense. But neither that nearly trivial proposition nor the language of the Amendment, which speaks in uniformly mandatory terms, leads to the further conclusion that the right to counsel is merely supplementary and may be dispensed with at the whim of the accused. Rather, this Court's decisions have consistently included the right to counsel as an integral part of the bundle making up the larger "right to a defense as we know it." . . .

The reason for this hardly requires explanation. The fact of the matter is that in all but an extraordinarily small number of cases an accused will lose whatever defense he may have if he undertakes to conduct the trial himself. . . .

Obviously, these considerations do not vary depending upon whether the accused actively desires to be represented by counsel or wishes to proceed pro se. Nor is it accurate to suggest, as the Court seems to later in its opinion, that the quality of his representation at trial is a matter with which only the accused is legitimately concerned. . . . Although we have adopted an adversary system of criminal justice . . . the prosecution is more than an ordinary litigant, and the trial judge is not simply an automaton who insures that technical rules are adhered to. Both are charged with the duty of insuring that justice, in the broadest sense of that term, is achieved in every criminal trial. . . . That goal is ill-served, and the integrity of and public confidence in the system are undermined, when an easy conviction is obtained due to the defendant's ill-advised decision to waive counsel. The damage thus inflicted is not mitigated by the lame explanation that the defendant simply availed himself of the "freedom" "to go to jail under his own banner. . . ." United States ex rel. Maldonado v. Denno, 348 F.2d 12, 15 (CA2 1965). The system of criminal justice should not be available as an instrument of self-destruction.

In short, both the "spirit and the logic" of the Sixth Amendment are that every person accused of crime shall receive the fullest possible defense; in the vast majority of cases this command can be honored only by means of the expressly guaranteed right to counsel, and the trial judge is in the best position to determine whether the accused is capable of conducting his defense. True freedom of choice and society's interest in seeing that justice is achieved can be vindicated only if the trial court retains discretion to reject any attempted waiver of counsel and insist that the accused be tried according to the Constitution. This discretion is as critical an element of basic fairness as a trial judge's discretion to decline to accept a plea of guilty. . . .

. . .[40]

---

534. *Faretta* does not confer a right to be represented by a lay person who is not qualified to appear as a lawyer. United States v. Wilhelm, 570 F.2d 461 (3d Cir.1978).

See Savage v. Estelle, 924 F.2d 1459 (9th Cir.1990) (defendant with severe speech impediment, who was unable to communicate with jury, did not have right to defend himself).

On waiver of the right to self-representation, see Brown v. Wainwright, 665 F.2d 607 (5th Cir.1982). See also United States v. Flewitt, 874 F.2d 669 (9th Cir.1989) (defendant's pretrial actions did not justify denial of right to self-representation).

[40] Justice Blackmun also wrote a dissenting opinion, which Chief Justice Burger and Justice Rehnquist joined.

UNITED STATES DISTRICT COURT
DISTRICT OF MASSACHUSETTS

UNITED STATES OF AMERICA

V.

CRIMINAL NO._____

_____

WAIVER OF COUNSEL BY DEFENDANT

I, the above named defendant, hereby acknowledge that the Court has informed and advised me of my rights under the Constitution of the United States to have the assistance of counsel for my defense.

I hereby waive this constitutional right and elect to proceed without the assistance of counsel.

_____
Defendant

_____
Witness

Date:_____

535. In McKaskle v. Wiggins, 465 U.S. 168 (1984) (6–3), the Court discussed the role of standby counsel when the defendant elects to defend himself.

"First, the *pro se* defendant is entitled to preserve actual control over the case he chooses to present to the jury. This is the core of the *Faretta* right. If standby counsel's participation over the defendant's objection effectively allows counsel to make or substantially interfere with any significant tactical decisions, or to control the questioning of witnesses, or to speak *instead* of the defendant on any matter of importance, the *Faretta* right is eroded.

"Second, participation by standby counsel without the defendant's consent should not be allowed to destroy the jury's perception that the defendant is representing himself. The defendant's appearance in the status of one conducting his own defense is important in a criminal trial, since the right to appear *pro se* exists to affirm the accused's individual dignity and autonomy. . . .

. . .

". . . *Faretta* rights are adequately vindicated in proceedings outside the presence of the jury if the *pro se* defendant is allowed to address the court freely on his own behalf and if disagreements between counsel and the *pro se* defendant are resolved in the defendant's favor whenever the matter is one that would normally be left to the discretion of counsel.

. . .

"Participation by standby counsel in the presence of the jury is more problematic. It is here that the defendant may legitimately claim that excessive involvement by counsel will destroy the appearance that the defendant is acting *pro se*. This, in turn, may erode the dignitary values that the right to self-representation is intended to promote and may undercut the defendant's presentation to the jury of his own most effective defense. Nonetheless, we believe that a categorical bar on participation by standby counsel in the presence of the jury is unnecessary.

. . .

"*Faretta* does not require a trial judge to permit 'hybrid' representation . . . . But if a defendant is given the opportunity and elects to have counsel appear before the court or jury, his complaints concerning counsel's subsequent unsolicited participation lose much of their force. A defendant does not have a constitutional right to choreograph special appearances by counsel. Once a *pro se* defendant invites or agrees to any substantial participation by counsel, subsequent appearances by counsel must be presumed to be with the defendant's acquiescence, at least until the defendant expressly and unambiguously renews his request that standby counsel be silenced.

. . .

"*Faretta* rights are also not infringed when standby counsel assists the *pro se* defendant in overcoming routine procedural or evidentiary obstacles to the completion of some specific task, such as introducing evidence or objecting to testimony, that the defendant has clearly shown he wishes to complete. Nor are they infringed when counsel merely helps to ensure the defendant's compliance with basic rules of courtroom protocol and procedure. In neither case is there any significant interference with the defendant's actual control over the presentation of his defense. . . . A defendant does not have a constitutional right to receive personal instruction from the trial judge on courtroom procedure. Nor does the Constitution require judges to take over chores for a *pro se* defendant that would normally be attended to by trained counsel as a matter of course. . . .

"Accordingly, we make explicit today what is already implicit in *Faretta*: A defendant's Sixth Amendment rights are not violated when a trial judge appoints standby counsel—even over the defendant's objection—to relieve the judge of the need to explain and enforce basic rules of courtroom protocol or to assist the defendant in overcoming routine obstacles that stand in the way of the defendant's achievement of his own clearly indicated goals. Participation by counsel to steer a defendant through the basic procedures of trial is permissible even in the unlikely event that it somewhat undermines the *pro se* defendant's appearance of control over his own defense." Id. at 178–84.

See United States v. Torres, 793 F.2d 436 (1st Cir.1986) (*McKaskle* applied).

---

536. Public trial. "[T]he right to attend criminal trials is implicit in the guarantees of the First Amendment; without the freedom to attend such trials, which people have exercised for centuries, important aspects of freedom of speech and 'of the press could be eviscerated.' Branzburg [v. Hayes], 408 U.S. [665 (1972)], at 681." Richmond Newspapers, Inc. v. Virginia, 448 U.S. 555, 580 (1980).[41] The trial judge in a murder case had granted the defendant's motion, without objection by the prosecution, that the trial be closed to the public. The reasons for closure were to avoid the possibility that the jury would read newspaper reports and to avoid possible distractions during the trial. The Court noted that although the Sixth Amendment gives a defendant the right to a public trial, he has no right to a private trial. It observed that the trial judge had made no findings to support his order; in particular, there had been no inquiry whether other methods

---

41. In Gannett Co. v. DePasquale, 443 U.S. 368 (1979), the Court had held that the public does not have a right to attend a trial under the Sixth Amendment, which guarantees a public trial for the benefit of the defendant alone. Although there is a "strong societal interest in public trials," such interest "is a far cry . . . from the creation of a constitutional right on the part of the public." Id. at 383.

would not have sufficed to ensure a fair trial. It concluded: "Absent an overriding interest articulated in findings, the trial of a criminal case must be open to the public." Id. at 581.

A state statute requiring the exclusion of the press and public during the testimony of a minor victim in a sex-offense trial violates the First Amendment. In individual cases, exclusion might be permissible; but a statute requiring exclusion without a particular determination of the need in each case is invalid. Globe Newspaper Co. v. Superior Court, 457 U.S. 596 (1982) (6–3).

During a trial for rape, the judge excluded the press from the voir dire of individual jurors. The press was permitted to attend only the general voir dire. All but about three days of the voir dire, which lasted for six weeks, was held in closed session. The Court held that the right to a public trial was violated. Press-Enterprise Co. v. Superior Court, 464 U.S. 501 (1984). It observed that it was not "crucial" whether the right belongs to the defendant or the public, or is inherent in the system and benefits both. "The presumption of openness may be overcome only by an overriding interest based on findings that closure is essential to preserve higher values and is narrowly tailored to serve that interest. The interest is to be articulated along with findings specific enough that a reviewing court can determine whether the closure order was properly entered." Id. at 508, 510. The Court noted that in some cases, a potential juror's compelling interest in privacy might warrant closing the proceedings.

Applying the cases above, the Court concluded that the right of the public to attend criminal trials was violated by an order denying release of the transcript of an extended closed preliminary hearing, which, under state law, is an elaborate proceeding and often the most important stage of the criminal process. Press-Enterprise Co. v. Superior Court, 478 U.S. 1 (1986) (7–2). Denial of public access is permissible, the court said, only if closure is essential to preserve more important values and tailored to that end. "If the interest asserted is the right of the accused to a fair trial, the preliminary hearing shall be closed only if specific findings are made demonstrating that, first, there is a substantial probability that the defendant's right to a fair trial will be prejudiced by publicity that closure would prevent and, second, reasonable alternatives to closure cannot adequately protect the defendant's fair trial rights." Id. at 14.

In Waller v. Georgia, 467 U.S. 39, 46 (1984), the Court said that "there can be little doubt that the explicit Sixth Amendment right of the accused is no less protective of a public trial than the implicit First Amendment right of the press and public." It said that although the right to an open trial "may give way in certain cases to other rights or interests, such as the defendant's right to a fair trial or the government's interest in inhibiting disclosure of sensitive information," such circumstances are rare, and "the balance of interests must be struck with special care." Id. at 45. The Court held that closure of a pretrial hearing on a motion to suppress evidence, in order to avoid disclosure of wiretap material about other persons, was improper.

The court considered the circumstances in which a criminal trial may be closed to the public, in Ayala v. Speckard, 131 F.3d 62 (2d Cir.1997) (en banc). The case involved several drug prosecutions, in each of which an undercover police officer had purchased narcotics from the defendant. The officer testified that he expected to return to work as an undercover agent in the same area in which he had worked previously and that if his identity were known, his life would be in danger. In those circumstances, the court said, closure during the witness's testimony was permissible. "We believe the sensible course is for the trial judge to recognize that open trials are strongly favored, to require persuasive evidence of serious risk to an important interest in ordering any closure, and to realize that the more extensive is the closure requested, the greater must be the gravity of the required interest and the likelihood of risk to that interest." Id. at 70.

537. In Nebraska Press Ass'n v. Stuart, 427 U.S. 539 (1976), the Court held that it was improper for a trial judge to issue an order restraining news media from reporting specified categories of highly incriminating evidence in a sensational murder case until after a jury was impaneled. The trial took place in a small Nebraska town. Relying on the First Amendment's protection of freedom of the press, a majority of the Court did not absolutely bar the "extraordinary remedy" of a prior restraint on publication in order to protect the defendant's right to a fair trial, but indicated that it could rarely, if ever, be used. Justice Brennan, Justice Stewart, and Justice Marshall would have imposed an absolute bar to prior restraints; Justice White and Justice Stevens indicated that if they were obliged to address the question they might reach the same conclusion.

538. The Constitution does not absolutely prohibit radio, television, or photographic coverage of a criminal trial over the objection of a defendant. The defendant is entitled to an opportunity to show that in a particular case such coverage was inconsistent with a fair trial, but there is no *per se* prohibition. Chandler v. Florida, 449 U.S. 560 (1981).

For cases in which the defendant's conviction was reversed because of undue publicity of the trial, see Sheppard v. Maxwell, 384 U.S. 333 (1966) ("carnival atmosphere at trial"), p. 939 above; Estes v. Texas, 381 U.S. 532 (1965).

Motion for Judgment of Acquittal

FEDERAL RULES OF CRIMINAL PROCEDURE

Rule 29.

MOTION FOR JUDGMENT OF ACQUITTAL

(a) Motion Before Submission to Jury. Motions for directed verdict are abolished and motions for judgment of acquittal shall be used in their place. The court on motion of a defendant or of its own motion shall order the entry of judgment of acquittal of one or more offenses charged in the indictment or information after the evidence on either side is closed if the evidence is insufficient to sustain a conviction of such offense or offenses. If a defendant's motion for judgment of acquittal at the close of the evidence offered by the government is not granted, the defendant may offer evidence without having reserved the right.

(b) Reservation of Decision on Motion. The court may reserve decision on a motion for judgment of acquittal, proceed with the trial (where the motion is made before the close of all the evidence), submit the case to the jury and decide the motion either before the jury returns a verdict or after it returns a verdict of guilty or is discharged without having returned a verdict. If the court reserves decision, it must decide the motion on the basis of the evidence at the time the ruling was reserved.

(c) Motion After Discharge of Jury. If the jury returns a verdict of guilty or is discharged without having returned a verdict, a motion for judgment of acquittal may be made or renewed within 7 days after the jury is discharged or within such further time as the court may fix during the 7-day period. If a verdict of guilty is returned the court may on such motion set aside the verdict and enter judgment of acquittal. If no verdict is returned the court may enter judgment of acquittal. It shall not be necessary to the making of such a motion that a similar motion has been made prior to the submission of the case to the jury.

United States v. Taylor

464 F.2d 240 (2d Cir.1972).

■ FRIENDLY, CHIEF JUDGE.

The sole question meriting discussion in this opinion is the sufficiency of the evidence to warrant submission to the jury of the question whether

Taylor "with intent to defraud" kept in possession and concealed a quantity of counterfeit Federal Reserve notes found in a car which Taylor, accompanied by one MacDonald, was driving from Canada into the United States.

I

Counsel for appellant asks us, as many others have done, to overrule the so-called "Second Circuit rule," first enunciated by Judge Learned Hand in United States v. Feinberg, 140 F.2d 592, 594 (2 Cir.) . . . (1944), and later challenged, at great length but without success, by Judge Jerome Frank in United States v. Masiello, 235 F.2d 279, 285 (2 Cir.) . . . (1956) (concurring opinion). The "rule" in this circuit has been that "the standard of evidence necessary [for the judge] to send a case to the jury is the same in both civil and criminal cases," even though the jury must apply a higher standard before rendering a verdict in favor of the proponent in the latter. United States v. Feinberg, supra, 140 F.2d at 594. Despite our reverence for Judge Hand, perhaps in part because of our desire to remove one of his rare ill-advised opinions from public debate, we agree that the time for overruling the *Feinberg* "single test" standard has arrived.

It is, of course, a fundamental of the jury trial guaranteed by the Constitution that the jury acts, not at large, but under the supervision of a judge. . . . Before submitting the case to the jury, the judge must determine whether the proponent has adduced evidence sufficient to warrant a verdict in his favor. Dean Wigmore considered, 9 Evidence § 2494 at 299 (3d ed. 1940), the best statement of the test to be that of Mr. Justice Brett in Bridges v. Railway Co. [1874] L.R. 7 H.L. 213, 233:

> [A]re there facts in evidence which if unanswered would justify men of ordinary reason and fairness in affirming the question which the Plaintiff is bound to maintain?

It would seem at first blush—and we think also at second—that more "facts in evidence" are needed for the judge to allow men, and now women, "of ordinary reason and fairness" to affirm the question the proponent "is bound to maintain" when the proponent is required to establish this not merely by a preponderance of the evidence but, as all agree to be true in a criminal case, beyond a reasonable doubt. Indeed, the latter standard has recently been held to be constitutionally required in criminal cases. In re Winship, 397 U.S. 358, 361–364 . . . (1970). We do not find a satisfying explanation in the *Feinberg* opinion why the judge should not place this higher burden on the prosecution in criminal proceedings before sending the case to the jury.

After acknowledging "that in their actual judgments the added gravity of the consequences [in criminal cases] makes them [the judges] more exacting," 140 F.2d at 594, Judge Hand based the refusal to require a higher standard of sufficiency in criminal cases on authority and a belief that "[w]hile at times it may be practicable" to "distinguish between the evidence which should satisfy reasonable men, and the evidence which should satisfy reasonable men beyond a reasonable doubt[,] . . . in the long run the line between them is too thin for day to day use." Id.

However the argument from authority may have stood in 1944, that battle has now been irretrievably lost. . . . Almost all the circuits have adopted something like Judge Prettyman's formulation in Curley v. United States, 81 U.S.App.D.C. 389, 160 F.2d 229, 232–233 . . . (1947). This, along with its rationale, reads as follows:

> The functions of the jury include the determination of the credibility of witnesses, the weighing of the evidence, and the drawing of justifiable inferences of fact from proven facts. It is the function of the judge to deny the jury any opportunity to operate beyond its province. The jury may not be permitted to conjecture merely, or to conclude upon pure speculation or from passion, prejudice or sympathy. The critical point in this boundary is the existence or non-existence of reasonable doubt as to guilt. If the evidence is such that reasonable jurymen must necessarily have such a doubt, the judge must require acquittal, because no other result is permissible within the fixed bounds of jury consideration. But if a reasonable mind might fairly have a reasonable doubt or might fairly not have one, the case is for the jury, and the decision is for the jurors to make. The law recognizes that the scope of a reasonable mind is broad. Its conclusion is not always a point certain, but, upon given evidence, may be one of a number of conclusions. Both innocence and guilt beyond a reasonable doubt may lie fairly within the limits of reasonable conclusion from given facts. The judge's function is exhausted when he determines that the evidence does or does not permit the conclusion of guilt beyond a reasonable doubt within the fair operation of a reasonable mind.
>
> The true rule, therefore, is that a trial judge, in passing upon a motion for directed verdict of acquittal, must determine whether upon the evidence, giving full play to the right of the jury to determine credibility, weigh the evidence, and draw justifiable inferences of fact, a reasonable mind might fairly conclude guilt beyond a reasonable doubt. If he concludes that upon the evidence there must be such a doubt in a reasonable mind, he must grant the motion; or, to state it another way, if there is no evidence upon which a reasonable mind might fairly conclude guilt beyond a reasonable doubt, the motion must be granted. If he concludes that either of the two results, a reasonable doubt or no reasonable doubt, is fairly possible, he must let the jury decide the matter. (footnotes omitted)

On Judge Hand's second point, while we agree there will be few cases where application of Judge Prettyman's test would produce a different result, we cannot say these are non-existent, as indeed he conceded. The Supreme Court has recognized the feasibility of a standard intermediate between preponderance and proof beyond a reasonable doubt, to wit, clear and convincing evidence. . . . Implicit in the Court's recognition of varying burdens of proof is a concomitant duty on the judge to consider the applicable burden when deciding whether to send a case to the jury.

. . .

539. Rule 29(c). Reversing the trial judge's order granting a motion for judgment of acquittal following a verdict of guilty, the court in United States v. Hemphill, 544 F.2d 341, 344 (8th Cir.1976), said: "In passing upon the defendant's post-trial motion for judgment of acquittal notwithstanding the jury's verdict, it was not the prerogative of the district court to resolve conflicts in the testimony, or to pass upon the credibility of witnesses or the weight to be given their testimony; those were jury functions; and the district court was not at liberty to set aside the verdict of the jury simply because the trial judge may have thought that the jury reached the wrong result. The district court was required, and we are required, to view the evidence in the light most favorable to the government, and to give to the government the benefit of all favorable inferences reasonably to be drawn from the evidence. And if the verdict of the jury was sustained by substantial evidence, it should not have been set aside by the district court on factual grounds."

A district court does not have authority to consider a motion for judgment of acquittal made after the jury has returned a verdict, if the motion is made outside the time limit prescribed by Rule 29(c). Carlisle v. United States, 517 U.S. 416 (1996) (7–2). The Court noted that Rule 45(b) expressly prohibits enlargement of the times specified in Rule 29. It held also that the courts' inherent supervisory authority does not include a deviation from the requirements of the Federal Rules.

Closing Argument

FEDERAL RULES OF CRIMINAL PROCEDURE

Rule 29.1

CLOSING ARGUMENT

After the closing of evidence the prosecution shall open the argument. The defense shall be permitted to reply. The prosecution shall then be permitted to reply in rebuttal.

Herring v. New York

422 U.S. 853, 95 S.Ct. 2550, 45 L.Ed.2d 593 (1975).

■ Mr. Justice Stewart delivered the opinion of the Court.

A New York law confers upon every judge in a nonjury criminal trial the power to deny counsel any opportunity to make a summation of the evidence before the rendition of judgment. N.Y.Crim.Proc.Law § 320.20(3)(c) (1971). In the case before us we are called upon to assess the constitutional validity of that law.

I

The appellant was brought to trial in the Supreme Court of Richmond County, N.Y., upon charges of attempted robbery in the first and third degrees and possession of a dangerous instrument. He waived a jury.

The trial began on a Thursday, and, after certain preliminaries, the balance of that day and most of Friday were spent on the case for the prosecution. The complaining witness, Allen Braxton, testified that the appellant had approached him outside his home in a Staten Island housing project at about six o'clock on the evening of September 15, 1971, and asked for money. He said that when he refused this demand, the appellant had swung a knife at him. On cross-examination, the appellant's lawyer attempted to impeach the credibility of this evidence by demonstrating inconsistencies between Braxton's testimony and other sworn statements that Braxton had previously made. The only other witness for the prosecution was the police officer who had arrested the appellant upon the complaint of Braxton. The officer testified that Braxton had reported the alleged incident to him, and that the appellant, when confronted by the officer later in the evening, had denied Braxton's story and said that he had been working for a Mr. Taylor at the time of the alleged offense. The officer testified that he had then arrested the appellant and found a small knife in his pocket.

At the close of the case for the prosecution, the court granted a defense motion to dismiss the charge of possession of a dangerous instrument on the ground that the knife in evidence was too small to qualify as a dangerous instrument under state law. The trial was then adjourned for the two-day weekend.

Proceedings did not actually resume until the following Monday afternoon. The first witness for the defense was Donald Taylor, who was the appellant's employer. He testified that he recalled seeing the appellant on the job premises at about 5:30 p.m. on the day of the alleged offense. The appellant then took the stand and denied Braxton's story. He said that he had been working on a refrigerator at his place of employment during the time of the alleged offense, and further testified that Braxton, a former neighbor, had threatened on several occasions to "fix" him for refusing to give Braxton money for wine and drugs.

At the conclusion of the case for the defense, counsel made a motion to dismiss the robbery charges. This motion was denied. The appellant's lawyer then requested to "be heard somewhat on the facts." The trial judge replied: "Under the new statute, summation is discretionary, and I choose not to hear summations." The judge thereupon found the appellant guilty of attempted robbery in the third degree, and subsequently sentenced him to serve an indeterminate term of imprisonment with a maximum of four years. . . .

II

. . .

[T]he right to the assistance of counsel has been understood to mean that there can be no restrictions upon the function of counsel in defending a criminal prosecution in accord with the traditions of the adversary factfinding process that has been constitutionalized in the Sixth and Fourteenth Amendments. . . . The right to the assistance of counsel has thus been given a meaning that ensures to the defense in a criminal trial the opportunity to participate fully and fairly in the adversary factfinding process.

There can be no doubt that closing argument for the defense is a basic element of the adversary factfinding process in a criminal trial. Accordingly, it has universally been held that counsel for the defense has a right to make a closing summation to the jury, no matter how strong the case for the prosecution may appear to the presiding judge. The issue has been considered less often in the context of a so-called bench trial. But the overwhelming weight of authority, in both federal and state courts, holds that a total denial of the opportunity for final argument in a nonjury criminal trial is a denial of the basic right of the accused to make his defense.

. . .

The widespread recognition of the right of the defense to make a closing summary of the evidence to the trier of the facts, whether judge or jury, finds solid support in history. In the 16th and 17th centuries, when notions of compulsory process, confrontation, and counsel were in their infancy, the essence of the English criminal trial was argument between the defendant and counsel for the Crown. Whatever other procedural protections may have been lacking, there was no absence of debate on the factual and legal issues raised in a criminal case. As the rights to compulsory process, to confrontation, and to counsel developed, the adversary system's commitment to argument was neither discarded nor diluted. Rather, the reform in procedure had the effect of shifting the primary function of argument to summation of the evidence at the close of trial, in contrast to the "fragmented" factual argument that had been typical of the earlier common law.

It can hardly be questioned that closing argument serves to sharpen and clarify the issues for resolution by the trier of fact in a criminal case. For it is only after all the evidence is in that counsel for the parties are in a position to present their respective versions of the case as a whole. Only then can they argue the inferences to be drawn from all the testimony, and point out the weaknesses of their adversaries' positions. And for the defense, closing argument is the last clear chance to persuade the trier of fact that there may be reasonable doubt of the defendant's guilt. . . .

The very premise of our adversary system of criminal justice is that partisan advocacy on both sides of a case will best promote the ultimate objective that the guilty be convicted and the innocent go free. In a criminal trial, which is in the end basically a factfinding process, no aspect of such advocacy could be more important than the opportunity finally to marshal the evidence for each side before submission of the case to judgment.

This is not to say that closing arguments in a criminal case must be uncontrolled or even unrestrained. The presiding judge must be and is given great latitude in controlling the duration and limiting the scope of closing summations. He may limit counsel to a reasonable time and may terminate argument when continuation would be repetitive or redundant. He may ensure that argument does not stray unduly from the mark, or otherwise impede the fair and orderly conduct of the trial. In all these respects he must have broad discretion. . . .

But there can be no justification for a statute that empowers a trial judge to deny absolutely the opportunity for any closing summation at all. The only conceivable interest served by such a statute is expediency. Yet the difference in any case between total denial of final argument and a concise but persuasive summation could spell the difference, for the defendant, between liberty and unjust imprisonment.

Some cases may appear to the trial judge to be simple—open and shut—at the close of the evidence. And surely in many such cases a closing argument will, in the words of Mr. Justice Jackson, be "likely to leave [a] judge just where it found him."[42] But just as surely, there will be cases where closing argument may correct a premature misjudgment and avoid an otherwise erroneous verdict. And there is no certain way for a trial judge to identify accurately which cases these will be, until the judge has heard the closing summation of counsel.

The present case is illustrative. This three-day trial was interrupted by an interval of more than two days—a period during which the judge's memory may well have dimmed, however conscientious a note-taker he may have been. At the conclusion of the evidence on the trial's final day, the appellant's lawyer might usefully have pointed to the direct conflict in the trial testimony of the only two prosecution witnesses concerning how and when the appellant was found on the evening of the alleged offense. He might also have stressed the many inconsistencies, elicited on cross-examination, between the trial testimony of the complaining witness and his earlier sworn statements. He might reasonably have argued that the testimony of the appellant's employer was entitled to greater credibility than that of the complaining witness, who, according to the appellant, had threatened to "fix" him because of personal differences in the past. There is no way to

---

42. R. Jackson, The Struggle for Judicial Supremacy 301 (1941).

know whether these or any other appropriate arguments in summation might have affected the ultimate judgment in this case. The credibility assessment was solely for the trier of fact. But before that determination was made, the appellant, through counsel, had a right to be heard in summation of the evidence from the point of view most favorable to him.

In denying the appellant this right under the authority of its statute, New York denied him the assistance of counsel that the Constitution guarantees. . . .

. . .[43]

Harris v. United States

402 F.2d 656 (D.C.Cir.1968).

■ BURGER, CIRCUIT JUDGE:

Appellant was convicted in the District Court of the unauthorized use of a motor vehicle under 22 D.C.Code § 2204 (1967). His appeal raises only one issue: the propriety of certain remarks made by the prosecutor in his closing argument to the jury.

This claim is raised for the first time on appeal as "plain error" under Rule 52(b) Fed.R.Crim.P. At trial there was no objection—either during the argument or thereafter, at the bench—and no request for a corrective instruction, or motion for a mistrial. In short, Appellant invoked none of several possible methods for bringing these remarks to the attention of the trial judge who was best able to assess their effect on the jury and to undertake corrective measures. The problem of raising objections to improper argument of either counsel presents obvious practical difficulties. Counsel may, of course, object during the argument, but unless the departure from the proprieties is egregious neither the court nor the jury is likely to look favorably upon such an interruption at that stage. The more usual treatment is for counsel to approach the bench at the conclusion of the summing up and request an immediate instruction to correct the impact of objectionable material. In the gravest situation it may be his duty to raise the issue of a mistrial. However, since none of these avenues was pursued here, we find no basis for reversal. . . . The trial judge may also properly stop a lawyer whose summation exceeds permissible grounds; the judge's interruption does not involve the risk that counsel takes when he objects in the midst of a closing argument and such action by the court, while limited to serious transgressions, may avoid declaring a mistrial or reversible error.

---

[43] Justice Rehnquist wrote a dissenting opinion, which Chief Justice Burger and Justice Blackmun joined.

It is nevertheless clear that the prosecutor's remarks in the present case were of a kind that ought not be made. The defense was based upon Appellant's testimony that he had not stolen the car in question but that someone he presumed to be its owner, and who was unknown to Appellant, had lent him the car. His claim was that when he could not find this person later in the evening in order to return the car he decided to keep it overnight and return it the next morning to the parking lot where he had borrowed it. Before morning, however, he was arrested. The complainant testified that at approximately 10:00 p.m. he had parked his car by the stage door of the theater in whose parking lot Appellant testified the loan was made, and that when he returned the car had been removed. The Appellant testified that the accommodating stranger gave him the car at about 8:30 p.m. Thus complainant's testimony was that he did not arrive at the theater with his car until nearly two hours *after* Appellant said the "Good Samaritan" lender had turned it over to him. It is, of course, not surprising that the jury declined to believe this excessively implausible tale.

But our concern is not with the merits of the case, since the evidence against Appellant—including his own bizarre story—is overwhelming. The prosecutor attacked Appellant's version as an incredible tale. This was, of course, a permissible argument. But he went beyond this and made comments on Appellant's testimony that we consider of questionable propriety. He stated: "I ask you to reject it in toto the defense of John Harris because it reeks of fabrication, it lacks merit, it is not reasonable." He went on: "He would urge upon you that his defense is that he took this car in innocence [sic] but mistaken belief that he had the consent of the owner. If you really believe that, then he is pulling the wool over your eyes." And further: "Reasonably, there is a total fabrication. I would submit, ladies and gentlemen, it is a lie."

We address ourselves to these remarks not because we view them as having had significant impact on this case but because of the frequent nonobservance of the prohibition against expressions of personal opinions on the ultimate issue by counsel. The challenged statements are in essence an opinion of counsel as to the veracity of witnesses in circumstances where veracity may determine the ultimate issue of guilt or innocence. Appellant's testimony is a "lie" or "fabrication" only if the jury accepts all of the complainant's testimony and rejects the hypothesis that the claimed third person did intervene and Appellant merely forgot the precise time at which the events in question occurred. Appellant's testimony permitted the prosecutor to ask the jury to consider whether it was implausible, unbelievable, highly suspect, even ridiculous. Many strong adjectives could be used but it was for the jury, and not the prosecutor, to say which witnesses were telling the truth. Neither counsel should assert to the jury what in essence is his opinion on guilt or innocence. Yet this is the effect of remarks such as those of the prosecutor here when the accused gives testimony directly conflicting with that of the government's witnesses.

The precise words here challenged were pointless, if for no other reason, because of the availability of more effective means of characterizing an implausible story.[44] This is more than a matter of semantics; the purpose of the rule forbidding expression of opinion of counsel on the ultimate issue is to keep the focus on the *evidence* and to eliminate the need for opposing counsel to meet "opinions" by urging his own contrary opinion. The impropriety of substituting an attorney's view of the case for the evaluation of the evidentiary facts has been discussed by Drinker in the context of stating one's personal view of his case:

> There are several reasons for the rule, long established, that a lawyer may not properly state his personal belief either to the court or to the jury in soundness of his case. In the first place, his personal belief has no real bearing on the issue; no witness would be permitted so to testify, even under oath, and subject to cross-examination, much less the lawyer without either. Also, if expression of personal belief were permitted, it would give an improper advantage to the older and better known lawyer, whose opinion would carry more weight, and also with the jury at least, an undue advantage to an unscrupulous one. Furthermore, if such were permitted, for counsel to omit to make such a positive assertion might be taken as an admission that he did not believe in his case.

H. Drinker, Legal Ethics 147 (1953) (footnotes omitted).

The First Circuit adopted this reasoning as the basis for a decision that a prosecutor's expression of his "personal opinion of the trustworthiness of the government's evidence and the consequent guilt of the accused" was contrary to Canon 15[45] and merited a reversal. The Court stated:

> To permit counsel to express his personal belief in the testimony (even if not phrased so as to suggest knowledge of additional evidence not known to the jury), would afford him a privilege not even accorded to witnesses under oath and subject to cross-examination. Worse, it creates the false issue of the reliability and credibility of counsel. This is peculiarly unfortunate if one of them has the advantage of official backing.

Greenberg v. United States, 280 F.2d 472, 474–475 (1st Cir. 1960) (footnote omitted).

The challenged statements of the prosecutor here do not fall precisely into the prohibitions of Canon 15 or the observations of Drinker but they come disturbingly close to it since they were another way of saying the

---

44. The prosecutor used the universally accepted and proper form of comment on the contradictions in testimony at one point in his closing statement when he told the jury: ". . . Mr. Harris would urge upon you at the time he got this car it was about 8:00 o'clock, and if you are to believe Mr. Harris, if he got the car at 8:00 o'clock, then you must disbelieve Mr. Gray . . . ."

45. "It is improper for a lawyer to assert in argument his personal belief in his client's innocence or in the justice of his cause." The Code of Professional Responsibility, DR 7–106(C)(4) provides that while appearing before a tribunal a lawyer shall not "assert his personal opinion as to the justness of a cause, as to the credibility of a witness, as to the culpability of a civil litigant, or as to the guilt or innocence of an accused; but he may argue, on his analysis of the evidence, for any position or conclusion with respect to the matters stated herein."

accused was guilty in the prosecutor's opinion. We might add to what others have said on the undesirability of such practices a further comment: lawyers should train themselves to eschew opinions in the course of arguments to juries because this diverts them as well as jurors from their respective functions. By avoiding expressions of personal opinions, the advocates will tend to concentrate on facts, issues and evidence, and make reasoned, even if vigorous, arguments.

The prosecutor is certainly free to strike hard blows at witnesses whose credibility he is challenging. But what he may not do is divert the focus of the jury's consideration of the case from the facts in evidence to the attorney's personal evaluations of the weight of the evidence. The personal evaluations and opinions of trial counsel are at best boring irrelevancies and a distasteful cliche-type argument. At worst, they may be a vague form of unsworn and irrelevant testimony.

. . .

---

540. "[W]e find that two of the statements which the prosecuting attorney made to the jury were highly prejudicial. At one point he stated:

'Again, you are supposed to judge the demeanor and the way a witness conducts himself on the stand; whether you would believe or not, that is your job to determine who you can believe and who you can't believe. And, I think Officer McPherson and Agent Stymus [sic] showed sincerity. I *firmly believe* what they said is the truth. I *know it is the truth*, and I expect you do, too.' (Tr. 122). (emphasis supplied.)

This type of comment has repeatedly been held to amount to reversible error. . . . The Government's proof was not so clear as to render the error harmless. It is somewhat indiscrete for the prosecutor to comment on his own personal assessment of the credibility of the witnesses, even when that assessment derives solely from what the witnesses have said while on the stand. When he makes a statement which could be construed by the jury as implying that he has additional reasons for knowing that what one witness has said is true, which reasons are not known to the jury, such comment is no longer mere indiscretion but constitutes reversible error. Here, the prosecutor said: 'I know it is the truth,' the inference being that he had outside knowledge. Put simply, the prosecutor overstepped the bounds of propriety.

"Additionally, the prosecutor made the following statement to the jury:

'The Government is prosecuting Clyde Lamerson in line with what Mr. Koerner [the defense attorney] says. And, Mr. Lamerson, had [he] not committed a crime, we would not be doing so. It's as simple as that.' (Tr. 128.)

In effect, he stated that the Government prosecutes only the guilty. Even the lesser suggestion that the Government *tries* to prosecute only the guilty has been held reversible error by this Court. In Hall v. United States, 5 Cir.1969, 419 F.2d 582, 587, this Court held:

> 'The statement "we try to prosecute only the guilty" is not defensible. Expressions of individual opinion of guilt are dubious at best. . . . This statement takes guilt as a pre-determined fact. The remark is, at the least, an effort to lead the jury to believe that the whole governmental establishment had already determined appellant to be guilty on evidence not before them. . . . Or, arguably it may be construed to mean that as a pretrial administrative matter the defendant has been found guilty as charged else he would not have been prosecuted, and that the administrative level determination is either binding upon the jury or else highly persuasive to it. Appellant's trial was held and the jury impaneled to pass on his guilt or innocence, and he was clothed in the presumption of innocence. The prosecutor may neither dispense with the presumption of innocence nor denigrate the function of the trial nor sit as a thirteenth juror.' . . ."

United States v. Lamerson, 457 F.2d 371, 372 (5th Cir.1972).

541. "The situation brought before the Court of Appeals was but one example of an all too common occurrence in criminal trials—the defense counsel argues improperly, provoking the prosecutor to respond in kind, and the trial judge takes no corrective action. Clearly two improper arguments—two apparent wrongs—do not make for a right result. Nevertheless, a criminal conviction is not to be lightly overturned on the basis of a prosecutor's comments standing alone, for the statements or conduct must be viewed in context; only by so doing can it be determined whether the prosecutor's conduct affected the fairness of the trial. To help resolve this problem, courts have invoked what is sometimes called the 'invited response' or 'invited reply' rule, which the Court treated in Lawn v. United States, 355 U.S. 339 (1958).

"The petitioners in *Lawn* sought to have the Court overturn their criminal convictions for income tax evasion on a number of grounds, one of which was that the prosecutor's closing argument deprived them of a fair trial. In his closing argument at trial, defense counsel in *Lawn* had attacked the Government for 'persecuting' the defendants. He told the jury that the prosecution was instituted in bad faith at the behest of federal revenue agents and asserted that the Government's key witnesses were perjurers. The prosecutor in response vouched for the credibility of the challenged witnesses, telling the jury that the Government thought those witnesses testified truthfully. In concluding that the prosecutor's remarks, when viewed within the context of the entire trial, did not deprive petitioners of a fair trial, the Court pointed out that defense counsel's 'comments clearly invited the reply.' Id., at 359–360, n. 15.

"This Court's holding in *Lawn* was no more than an application of settled law. Inappropriate prosecutorial comments, standing alone, would not justify a reviewing court to reverse a criminal conviction obtained in an otherwise fair proceeding. Instead, as *Lawn* teaches, the remarks must be examined within the context of the trial to determine whether the prosecutor's behavior amounted to prejudicial error. In other words, the Court must consider the probable effect the prosecutor's response would have on the jury's ability to judge the evidence fairly. In this context, defense counsel's conduct, as well as the nature of the prosecutor's response, is relevant. . . . Indeed most Courts of Appeals, applying these holdings, have refused to reverse convictions where prosecutors have responded reasonably in closing argument to defense counsel's attacks, thus rendering it unlikely that the jury was led astray.

"In retrospect, perhaps the idea of 'invited response' has evolved in a way not contemplated. *Lawn* and the earlier cases cited above should not be read as suggesting judicial approval or—encouragement—[sic] of response-in-kind that inevitably exacerbate the tensions inherent in the adversary process. As *Lawn* itself indicates, the issue is not the prosecutor's license to make otherwise improper arguments, but whether the prosecutor's 'invited response,' taken in context, unfairly prejudiced the defendant.

"In order to make an appropriate assessment, the reviewing court must not only weigh the impact of the prosecutor's remarks, but must also take into account defense counsel's opening salvo. Thus the import of the evaluation has been that if the prosecutor's remarks were 'invited,' and did no more than respond substantially in order to 'right the scale,' such comments would not warrant reversing a conviction.

"Courts have not intended by any means to encourage the practice of zealous counsel's going 'out of bounds' in the manner of defense counsel here, or to encourage prosecutors to respond to the 'invitation.' Reviewing courts ought not to be put in the position of weighing which of two inappropriate arguments was the lesser. 'Invited responses' can be effectively discouraged by prompt action from the bench in the form of corrective instructions to the jury, and when necessary, an admonition to the errant advocate.

"Plainly, the better remedy in this case, at least with the accurate vision of hindsight, would have been for the District Judge to deal with the improper argument of the defense counsel promptly and thus blunt the need for the prosecutor to respond. Arguably defense counsel's misconduct could have warranted the judge to interrupt the argument and admonish him, . . . thereby rendering the prosecutor's response unnecessary. Similarly, the prosecutor at the close of defense summation should have objected to the defense counsel's improper statements with a request that the court give a timely warning and curative instruction to the jury. Defense counsel, even though obviously vulnerable, could well have done likewise if he thought that the prosecutor's remarks were harmful to his client. Here neither counsel made a timely objection to preserve the issue for review. . . . However, interruptions of arguments, either by an opposing counsel or the presiding judge, are matters to be approached cautiously. At the very least, a bench conference might have been convened out of the hearing of the jury once defense counsel closed, and an appropriate instruction given." United States v. Young, 470 U.S. 1, 13–14 (1985) (6–2–1). After reviewing the record, the Court concluded that the prosecutor's improper argument did not constitute "plain error" under Rule 52(b) and reversed the judgment of the court of appeals ordering a new trial.

See Darden v. Wainwright, 477 U.S. 168 (1986) (5–4) (improper closing argument did not deprive defendant of fair trial); United States v. Wilson, 135 F.3d 291 (4th Cir.1998) (improper closing argument; conviction reversed); United States v. Shaw, 701 F.2d 367, 390–92 (5th Cir.1983) (improper closing argument did not deprive defendant of fair trial); United States v. Garza, 608 F.2d 659 (5th Cir.1979) (improper closing argument; conviction reversed).

Instructions

FEDERAL RULES OF CRIMINAL PROCEDURE

Rule 30.

INSTRUCTIONS

At the close of the evidence or at such earlier time during the trial as the court reasonably directs, any party may file written requests that the court instruct the jury on the law as set forth in the requests. At the same time copies of such requests shall be furnished to all parties. The court shall inform counsel of its proposed action upon the requests prior to their arguments to the jury. The court may instruct the jury before or after the arguments are completed or at both times. No party may assign as error any portion of the charge or omission therefrom unless that party objects thereto before the jury retires to consider its verdict, stating distinctly the matter to which that party objects and the grounds of the objection. Opportunity shall be given to make the objection out of the hearing of the jury and, on request of any party, out of the presence of the jury.

542. "Because the court failed to clearly inform counsel of its ruling on his requests, counsel's closing argument was based upon a theory of defense which the court rejected, or at least ignored, in its subsequent instructions. We cannot say that this did not impair the effectiveness of counsel's argument and hence of appellant's defense.

. . .

"The government asserts that the requested instructions were faulty. But that, if true, is of course irrelevant. It was the court's failure to advise counsel of its ruling prior to closing argument, not the soundness of that ruling, which violated Rule 30 and prejudicially affected counsel's summation." Wright v. United States, 339 F.2d 578, 580 (9th Cir.1964) (conviction reversed).

543. "It is of course fundamental that as a general rule the failure to object to an instruction during a criminal prosecution on the ground urged on appeal, forecloses the party from raising the question before the reviewing court. . . . The manifest purpose of . . . [Rule 30] is to avoid whenever possible the necessity of a time-consuming new trial by providing the trial judge with an opportunity to correct any mistakes in the charge." United States v. Provenzano, 334 F.2d 678, 690 (3d Cir.1964). "The very purpose of Rule 30 is to require defendant to make timely objection or forfeit all right to later complain." United States v. Jones, 340 F.2d 599, 601 (4th Cir.1965).

Failure to object to errors in the instructions will not, however, bar reversal under Rule 52(b), p. 1203 below, if there has been "plain error" which must be corrected to avoid the possibility of a "miscarriage of justice." Cross v. United States, 347 F.2d 327, 329–30 (8th Cir.1965). See generally Godfrey v. United States, 353 F.2d 456, 458 (D.C.Cir.1965); United States v. Summerour, 279 F.Supp. 407 (E.D.Mich.1968).

United States v. Stephens

486 F.2d 915 (9th Cir.1973).

■ EUGENE A. WRIGHT, CIRCUIT JUDGE.

Stephens appeals from his conviction after a jury trial for robbery of a national bank [18 U.S.C. § 2113(a) and (d)]. He contends that the trial judge's comments to the jury denied him a fair trial. . . . [W]e reverse.

At the close of Stephens' trial in the district court, the judge said:

"Now my comment. If he went out there and looked at that bank with the idea of whether or not to rob it, he certainly had no compunction about whether or not he should rob it, because that is what he was out there for. So if he had no compunction about whether or not he should rob it, I would conclude from what I have heard here that he must have, or that he did rob it. He certainly went out there to look at it for that purpose, he said so himself. That is the way I would calculate what transpired here, putting that together with the rest of the testimony.

"Now you are the sole and exclusive judges of the facts. You make the determination as to what the facts are. You are not bound to follow anything I say at all, you can totally disregard anything I say, but I am entitled to express my opinion, and you can differ, and totally disregard it, because as I will tell you again, you are the sole and exclusive judges of the facts. But anyone who goes out and looks a bank over for the purpose of robbing it, and then admits that he robs it and then denies that he robbed it, I would conclude that he actually did rob it.

"All right, now again you being the sole and exclusive judges of the fact, it is up to you to make that determination."

We have recently considered jury instructions given in two California state criminal cases in which trial judges stated their opinions that the defendants were guilty beyond a reasonable doubt. Davis v. Craven, 485 F.2d 1138 (9th Cir.1973); Gonsior v. Craven, 449 F.2d 20 (9th Cir.1971). The judge in each case cautioned the jurors that they were the exclusive judges of fact and should exercise independent judgment in weighing the judicial comment. We found no error of constitutional dimension in either case.

In both *Gonsior* and *Davis* we considered United States v. Murdock, 290 U.S. 389 . . . (1933), the only Supreme Court decision brought to our attention that involved a jury instruction comparable to the one with which we are presently concerned. The Court affirmed the reversal of a conviction because of the instruction given, stating that a judge's power to express an opinion as to the guilt of the defendant exists, but that "it should be exercised cautiously and only in exceptional cases." 290 U.S. at 394 . . . . Such an exceptional case exists "where upon the undisputed and admitted facts the defendant's voluntary conduct amounted to the commission of the crime defined by the statute." Id. The Court held in *Murdock* that since the evidence was in conflict as to one element of the crime, the judge's instruction, although tempered with a warning to the jury to act independently, was reversible error.

In *Gonsior*, we emphasized that *Murdock* was an appeal from a federal court conviction and that the Supreme Court did not base its decision on constitutional grounds "but obviously on its power to supervise procedures in the federal courts." 449 F.2d at 22. *Gonsior* and *Davis*, on the other hand, involved petitions for habeas corpus based on state convictions. We held that the jury instructions given in those cases were not errors of constitutional dimension and we refused to impose the *Murdock* rationale on the states.

The present case, as in *Murdock*, is an appeal from a federal conviction. Similarly, this is not that exceptional case where the evidence against defendant is so overwhelming that his guilt is virtually undisputed.

At the time of the bank robbery, defendant was an escapee from the Washington State Penitentiary. There was evidence that he was involved in other criminal activity near the time and place of the robbery. The evidence of his involvement in this bank robbery, however, was far from overwhelming.

Perhaps the strongest evidence against defendant was his confession of the robbery to an FBI agent, a confession which he later repudiated. In addition, a bank employee recognized defendant as one who had been in the bank about the time of the robbery. His description of the clothing worn by defendant matched the description by one of the tellers of the clothing worn by the robber. However, neither the teller who was robbed, nor the one at the adjoining wicket, could identify defendant as the robber. Moreover, neither the handwriting on the demand note nor the fingerprints on the note were those of the defendant.

In light of the absence of overwhelming evidence of guilt, the judge's comments to the jury may well have tipped the scales against defendant, denying him the fair trial to which he was entitled. The instructions to the jurors advising them that they were not bound by his opinion were not sufficient in this case to cure the error.

It is well settled that a judge presiding at a trial in federal court may make comments on the evidence. He must carefully avoid prejudging the defendant, however, concentrating instead on making a fair effort to clear unanswered issues and point out inconsistencies. . . . Judicial comments must be aimed at aiding the jury's fact finding duties, rather than usurping them.

We note that defense counsel took no exception to the instructions given here. A timely instruction could have come only after the instructions and admonitions to the jury. Since it could not have resulted in an additional, curative instruction, it would have served no useful purpose. The absence of such an exception does not foreclose our consideration of the instructions given. . . .

. . .

———

544. "There can be no doubt that a federal judge in a criminal case is more than a mere moderator and may assist the jury in arriving at a just conclusion by explaining and commenting upon the evidence and by expressing his opinion upon the facts, provided he clearly states to the jury that all matters of fact are submitted to their determination. . . . However, since a trial judge's influence upon a jury is necessarily of such great magnitude, a trial judge should exercise care and discretion in expressing an opinion so as not to mislead or, in effect, to destroy the jury's right as the sole arbiters of all fact questions. . . .

"A survey of cases indicates that reviewing courts are hesitant to reverse a judgment due to an allegedly unfair comment within the charge to the jury unless the trial judge clearly became argumentative and assumed the role of an advocate." Franano v. United States, 310 F.2d 533, 537 (8th Cir.1962).

A judge may not direct a verdict of guilt. United Brotherhood of Carpenters & Joiners v. United States, 330 U.S. 395, 408 (1947). In an appropriate case, may a judge instruct the jury that an element of the crime with which the defendant is charged has been established as a matter of law?

"[I]n the criminal prosecution of one charged with the commission of a felony, the defendant has an absolute right to a jury determination upon all essential elements of the offense. This right, emanating from the criminal defendant's constitutional right to trial by jury, is neither depleted nor diminished by what otherwise might be considered the conclusive or compelling nature of the evidence against him. This right is personal to the defendant, and, like his right to a jury trial, is one which he, and he alone, may waive; furthermore, in a situation wherein an understandingly tendered waiver is not forthcoming from the defendant, under no circumstances may the trial court usurp this right by ruling as a matter of law on an essential element of the crime charged." United States v. England, 347 F.2d 425, 430 (7th Cir.1965). But see Guy v. United States, 336 F.2d 595, 597 (4th Cir.1964): "There can be no 'issues of fact' where there is no controversy as to the facts. And there can be no issue as to a fact where credible testimony with respect to it is neither denied or impeached."

545. Reasonable doubt. "[W]e explicitly hold that the Due Process Clause protects the accused against conviction except upon proof beyond a reasonable doubt of every fact necessary to constitute the crime with which he is charged." In re Winship, 397 U.S. 358, 364 (1970).

"The reasonable-doubt standard plays a vital role in the American scheme of criminal procedure. It is a prime instrument for reducing the risk of convictions resting on factual error. The standard provides concrete substance for the presumption of innocence—that bedrock 'axiomatic and elementary' principle whose 'enforcement lies at the foundation of the administration of our criminal law.' Coffin v. United States, [156 U.S. 432 (1895)], at 453. . . .

"The requirement of proof beyond a reasonable doubt has this vital role in our criminal procedure for cogent reasons. The accused during a criminal prosecution has at stake interests of immense importance, both because of the possibility that he may lose his liberty upon conviction and because of the certainty that he would be stigmatized by the conviction. Accordingly, a society that values the good name and freedom of every individual should not condemn a man for commission of a crime when there is reasonable doubt about his guilt. As we said in Speiser v. Randall, [357 U.S. 513 (1958)] at 525–526: 'There is always in litigation a margin of error, representing error in factfinding, which both parties must take into account. Where one party has at stake an interest of transcending value—as a criminal defendant his liberty—this margin of error is reduced as to him by the process of placing on the other party the burden of . . . persuading the factfinder at the conclusion of the trial of his guilt beyond a reasonable doubt. Due process commands that no man shall lose his liberty unless the Government has borne the burden of . . . convincing the factfinder of his guilt.' To this end, the reasonable-doubt standard is indispensable, for it 'impresses on the trier of fact the necessity of reaching a subjective state of certitude of the facts in issue.' Dorsen & Rezneck, In re Gault and the Future of Juvenile Law, 1 Family Law Quarterly, No. 4, pp. 1, 26 (1967).

"Moreover, use of the reasonable-doubt standard is indispensable to command the respect and confidence of the community in applications of the criminal law. It is critical that the moral force of the criminal law not be diluted by a standard of proof that leaves people in doubt whether innocent men are being condemned. It is also important in our free society that every individual going about his ordinary affairs have confidence that his government cannot adjudge him guilty of a criminal offense without convincing a proper factfinder of his guilt with utmost certainty." 397 U.S. at 363–64.

In Victor v. Nebraska, 511 U.S. 1 (1994), the Court considered two capital cases in which the trial judge had explained the standard of reasonable doubt to the jury in terms that, the defendants said, improperly lessened the state's burden of proof. In one case, the judge had referred to proof depending on "moral evidence," "an abiding conviction, to a moral certainty, of the truth of the charge," and "not a mere possible doubt." In the other, the judge had referred to "the strong probabilities of the case" and "a moral certainty," "an actual and substantial doubt." In both cases, the Court concluded that in the context of the instructions as a whole, the questioned phrases were not error. See Sullivan v. Louisiana, 508 U.S. 275 (1993) (deficient reasonable-doubt instruction cannot be harmless error). See generally Smith v. United States, 709 A.2d 78 (D.C. App. 1998) (en banc), approving a specific jury instruction about reasonable doubt.

After examining the historical development of the law of homicide and concluding that "the presence or absence of the heat of passion on sudden provocation . . . has been, almost from the inception of the common law of homicide, the single most important factor in determining the degree of culpability attaching to an unlawful homicide," the Court held that "the Due Process Clause requires the prosecution to prove beyond a reasonable doubt the absence of the heat of passion on sudden provocation when the issue is properly presented in a homicide case." Mullaney v. Wilbur, 421 U.S. 684, 696, 704 (1975). The Court rejected the contention that the rule of *Winship*, above, did not apply because under Maine law murder and manslaughter were not distinct offenses but only "punishment categories of the single offence of felonious homicide," id. at 689; the importance of the distinction to the defendant, the Court said, was no less.

Mullaney v. Wilbur notwithstanding, in Patterson v. New York, 432 U.S. 197 (1977) (5–3), the Court upheld a state statute requiring the defendant to prove by a preponderance of the evidence the affirmative defense of acting under extreme emotional distress in order to reduce the crime of second-degree murder to manslaughter. The Court said that the Due Process Clause does not require a State to "disprove beyond reasonable doubt every fact constituting any and all affirmative defenses related to the culpability of the accused." Id. at 210. The Court noted in particular that it remained constitutional for a State to require a defendant to prove an insanity defense by a preponderance of the evidence. Id. at 206–207. See also the companion case, Hankerson v. North Carolina, 432 U.S. 233 (1977) (self-defense).

The Court relied heavily on *Patterson* in McMillan v. Pennsylvania, 477 U.S. 79 (1986) (5–4), to uphold a state statute providing that a person convicted of specified crimes is subject to a mandatory minimum sentence of five years imprisonment, if the sentencing judge finds by a preponderance of the evidence that the person "visibly possessed a firearm" during commission of the offense. The statute provided that possession of a firearm "shall not be an element of the crime." The Court observed that the sentence required by the statute was within the maximum provided for the offenses and that it served only to reduce the judge's sentencing discretion. It said that although there are "constitutional limits," "in determining what facts must be proved beyond a reasonable doubt the state legislature's definition of the elements of the offense is usually dispositive." Id. at 85. Discussing *Mullaney*, *Patterson*, and *McMillan*, the Court held that a statutory provision authorizing a more severe sentence for an alien who illegally returns to the United States if he was previously deported following conviction of an aggravated felony is a penalty provision and does not define a distinct offense. Almendarez-Torres v. United States, ___ U.S. ___, 118 S.Ct. 1219 (1998) (5–4).

Again relying on *Patterson*, the Court upheld an Ohio statutory provision requiring the defendant to prove an affirmative defense by a preponderance of the evidence, as it was applied to the defense of self-defense in a prosecution for aggravated murder. The latter crime was defined as " 'purposely, and with prior calculation and design caus[ing] the death of another.' " Martin v. Ohio, 480 U.S. 228 (1987) (5–4). The Court noted that the jury was instructed to consider all the evidence, including evidence bearing on self-defense, when it determined whether the prosecution had met its burden of proving the elements of the crime beyond a reasonable doubt.

A presumption that relieves the prosecution of the burden of proving an element of the offense beyond a reasonable doubt is invalid. Sandstrom v. Montana, 442 U.S. 510 (1979). In *Sandstrom*, the trial judge had instructed the jury in a prosecution for deliberate homicide that a person is presumed to intend the ordinary consequences of his voluntary acts. *Sandstrom* was applied in Carella v. California, 491 U.S. 263 (1989); Yates v. Aiken, 484 U.S. 211 (1988); Francis v. Franklin, 471 U.S. 307 (1985) (5–4); Connecticut v. Johnson, 460 U.S. 73 (1983) (5–4). *Sandstrom* is distinguished in Montana v. Egelhoff, 518 U.S. 37 (1996) (5–4), see note 499 p. 515 above. In Rose v. Clark, 478 U.S. 570 (1986) (6–3), the Court held that a violation of *Sandstrom* may be harmless error.

An instruction that witnesses are presumed to speak the truth,[46] in a trial in which the defendant did not testify or call any defense witnesses, was not, when accompanied by full instructions on the government's burden of proof and the presumption of innocence, in conflict with *Winship* and did not deny the defendant due process of law. Cupp v. Naughten, 414 U.S. 141 (1973) (6–3). Such an instruction has, however, been very widely disapproved. See id. at 144 & n.4. An "accomplice instruction" to the effect that the jury should credit the testimony of an accomplice testifying for the defendant only if it believed the testimony beyond a reasonable doubt was impermissible, both because it restricted the defendant's right to present that testimony and because it lowered the government's burden of proof. Cool v. United States, 409 U.S. 100 (1972).

In Taylor v. Kentucky, 436 U.S. 478 (1978) (7–2), the Court held that in the circumstances of the case, the defendant was entitled, on request, to an instruction on the presumption of innocence as well as the requirement of proof beyond a reasonable doubt. In a subsequent case, Kentucky v. Whorton, 441 U.S. 786 (1979) (6–3), the Court said that *Taylor* did not hold that the failure to give a requested instruction on the presumption of innocence is by itself a violation of the Constitution. Such a failure has to be evaluated in light of all the circumstances to determine whether the defendant had a fair trial.

It has been held that an instruction that the defendant has the burden of proving an alibi defense violates due process because it undercuts the government's burden of proving guilt beyond a reasonable doubt. "Evidence of alibi should come into a case like any other evidence and must be submitted to the jury for consideration of whether the evidence as a whole on the issue of presence proves the defendant's guilt beyond a reasonable doubt." Smith v. Smith, 454 F.2d 572, 578 (5th Cir.1971). Accord Stump v. Bennett, 398 F.2d 111 (8th Cir.1968). See Johnson v. Bennett, 393 U.S. 253 (1968).

In Jackson v. Virginia, 443 U.S. 307 (1979), the Court relied on *Winship* for its holding that when a state conviction is attacked by habeas corpus in federal court on the ground of insufficiency of evidence, the court must consider "whether there was sufficient evidence to justify a rational trier of the facts to find guilt beyond a reasonable doubt," id. at 313. The previous

---

46. "Every witness is presumed to speak the truth. This presumption may be overcome by the manner in which the witness testifies, by the nature of his or her testimony, by evidence affecting his or her character, interest, or motives, by contradictory evidence or by a presumption."

standard had been that the conviction should be reversed only if there was "no evidence" to support the conviction. The Court emphasized that the relevant question is whether, viewing the evidence in the light most favorable to the prosecution, "*any* rational trier of fact," id. at 319, could believe the defendant guilty beyond a reasonable doubt, not whether the federal court itself was convinced of his guilt beyond a reasonable doubt. See Moore v. Duckworth, 443 U.S. 713 (1979).

The Constitution does not require that the admissibility of evidence that is challenged on constitutional grounds be established beyond a reasonable doubt. In Lego v. Twomey, 404 U.S. 477 (1972) (4–3), the Court held that it was constitutionally sufficient if the voluntariness of a confession was proved "at least by a preponderance of the evidence." Id. at 489. As for *Winship*, the Court said: "Since the purpose that a voluntariness hearing is designed to serve has nothing whatever to do with improving the reliability of jury verdicts, we cannot accept the charge that judging the admissibility of a confession by a preponderance of the evidence undermines the mandate of In re Winship . . . . Our decision in *Winship* was not concerned with standards for determining the admissibility of evidence or with the prosecution's burden of proof at a suppression hearing when evidence is challenged on constitutional grounds. *Winship* went no further than to confirm the fundamental right that protects 'the accused against conviction except upon proof beyond a reasonable doubt of every fact necessary to constitute the crime with which he is charged.' . . . A high standard of proof is necessary, we said, to ensure against unjust convictions by giving substance to the presumption of innocence. . . . A guilty verdict is not rendered less reliable or less consonant with *Winship* simply because the admissibility of a confession is determined by a less stringent standard. Petitioner does not maintain that either his confession or its voluntariness is an element of the crime with which he was charged. He does not challenge the constitutionality of the standard by which the jury was instructed to decide his guilt or innocence; nor does he question the sufficiency of the evidence that reached the jury to satisfy the proper standard of proof. Petitioner's rights under *Winship* have not been violated." Id. at 486–87.

546. Although a defendant may be required to prove by a preponderance of the evidence that he is not competent to stand trial, Medina v. California, 505 U.S. 437 (1992) (7–2), it is a violation of due process to impose a higher burden of proof ("clear and convincing evidence") that would permit a defendant to be tried "even though it is more likely than not that he is incompetent." Cooper v. Oklahoma, 517 U.S. 348, 350 (1996).

547. Applying the general principle that when a jury has no sentencing function it should be instructed to reach its verdict without regard to what sentence might be imposed if the defendant were found guilty, the Court held that a jury in a federal criminal case ordinarily is not required to be and should not be instructed that if the defendant were found not guilty by reason of insanity he would be involuntarily civilly committed. Shannon v. United States, 512 U.S. 573 (1994) (7–2).

548. Lesser included offense. Fed.R.Crim.P. 31(c): "Conviction of Less Offense. The defendant may be found guilty of an offense necessarily included in the offense charged or of an attempt to commit either the offense charged or an offense necessarily included therein if the attempt is an offense."

An offense is "necessarily included" in another only if "the elements of the lesser offense are a subset of the elements of the charged offense." Schmuck v. United States, 489 U.S. 705, 716 (1989). "Where the lesser offense requires an element not required for the greater offense, no instruction is to be given under Rule 31(c)." Id.

"[A] lesser-offense charge is not proper where, on the evidence presented, the factual issues to be resolved by the jury are the same as to both the lesser and greater offenses. . . . In other words, the lesser offense must be included within but not, on the facts of the case, be completely encompassed by the greater. A lesser-included offense instruction is only proper where the charged greater offense requires the jury to find a disputed factual element which is not required for conviction of the lesser-included offense." Sansone v. United States, 380 U.S. 343, 349–50 (1965). In United States v. Harary, 457 F.2d 471 (2d Cir.1972), the court concluded that even if the lesser and greater offenses were both charged in the indictment, if there was no disputed factual element to distinguish them, the defendant has a right not to have the jury instructed on both.

If a lesser-included offense instruction is appropriate, the defendant is entitled to have it given. Berra v. United States, 351 U.S. 131 (1956). See, e.g., United States v. Carter, 540 F.2d 753 (4th Cir.1976); United States v. Comer, 421 F.2d 1149 (D.C.Cir.1970). In Nichols v. Gagnon, 710 F.2d 1267 (7th Cir.1983), the court held that a state court's erroneous failure to give an instruction on a lesser included offense does not require a federal court to set aside the conviction unless there was a "fundamental miscarriage of justice." The court conjectured about the likely impact of a lesser included offense instruction on the jury's deliberations about the more serious offense. See DeBerry v. Wolff, 513 F.2d 1336 (8th Cir.1975). See also Beck v. Alabama, 447 U.S. 625 (1980) (7–2), p. 1189 below.

In United States v. Tsanas, 572 F.2d 340 (2d Cir.1978), the court discussed the instructions to be given the jury about its consideration of a lesser offense. The court held that the defendant should have his choice whether the jury should be instructed: (1) that it may consider the lesser offense only after reaching a unanimous verdict of not guilty on the greater, or (2) that it may consider the lesser offense if it cannot agree about the greater. If the defendant expresses no preference, the court can give either instruction.

549. The "Allen charge." In Commonwealth v. Tuey, 62 Mass. (8 Cush.) 1, 2–3 (1851), after the jury had deliberated for several hours without reaching agreement, the court instructed them in substance:

"The only mode, provided by our constitution and laws for deciding questions of fact in criminal cases, is by the verdict of a jury. In a large proportion of cases, and perhaps, strictly speaking, in all cases, absolute certainty cannot be attained or expected. Although the verdict to which a juror agrees must of course be his own verdict, the result of his own convictions, and not a mere acquiescence in the conclusion of his fellows, yet, in order to bring twelve minds to a unanimous result, you must examine the questions submitted to you with candor, and with a proper regard and deference to the opinions of each other. You should consider that the case must at some time be decided; that you are selected in the same manner, and from the same source, from which any future jury must be; and there is no reason to suppose that the case will ever be submitted to twelve men more intelligent, more impartial, or more competent to decide it, or that more or clearer evidence will be produced on the one side or the other. And with this view, it is your duty to decide the case, if you can conscientiously do so. In order to make a decision more practicable, the law imposes the burden of proof on one party or the other, in all cases. In the present case, the burden of proof is upon the commonwealth to establish every part of it, beyond a reasonable doubt; and if, in any part of it, you are left in doubt, the defendant is entitled to the benefit of the doubt, and must be acquitted. But, in conferring together, you ought to pay proper respect to each other's opinions, and listen, with a disposition to be convinced, to each other's arguments. And, on the one hand, if much the larger number of your panel are for a conviction, a dissenting juror should consider whether a doubt in his own mind is a reasonable one, which makes no impression upon the minds of so many men, equally honest, equally intelligent with himself, and who have heard the same evidence, with the same attention, with an equal desire to arrive at the truth, and under the sanction of the same oath. And, on the other hand, if a majority are for acquittal, the minority ought seriously to ask themselves, whether they may not reasonably, and ought not to doubt the correctness of a judgment, which is not concurred in by most of those with whom they are associated; and distrust the weight or sufficiency of that evidence which fails to carry conviction to the minds of their fellows."

The jury returned a verdict of guilty. The conviction was affirmed.

In Allen v. United States, 164 U.S. 492, 501–502 (1896), the Court upheld the giving of a similar charge, saying: "While, undoubtedly, the verdict of the jury should represent the opinion of each individual juror, it by no means follows that opinions may not be changed by conference in the jury-room. The very object of the jury system is to secure unanimity by a comparison of views, and by arguments among the jurors themselves. It certainly cannot be the law that each juror should not listen with deference to the arguments and with a distrust of his own judgment, if he finds a large majority of the jury taking a different view of the case from what he does himself. It cannot be that each juror should go to the jury-room with a blind determination that the verdict shall represent his opinion of the case at that moment; or, that he should close his ears to the arguments of men who are equally honest and intelligent as himself."

The so-called "Allen charge" has been used regularly since; but it has been criticized with increasing frequency and intensity and has been rejected altogether by some courts. See, e.g., United States v. Thomas, 449 F.2d 1177 (D.C.Cir.1971) (Allen charge rejected). See also United States v. Paniagua-Ramos, 135 F.3d 193 (1st Cir.1998) (improper Allen charge); Potter v. United States, 691 F.2d 1275 (8th Cir.1982) (same). Cases are collected and the Allen charge is discussed generally in United States v. Seawell, 550 F.2d 1159 (9th Cir.1977), in which the court concluded that the coercive impact of the charge is such that it should never be repeated a second time in response to a report of further deadlock, unless the jury requests its repetition. But see United States v. Robinson, 560 F.2d 507 (2d Cir.1977) (second Allen-type charge is not error *per se*). Even when the Allen charge itself is rejected, supplemental instructions to a jury which is unable to reach a verdict are allowed; the rejected language is that which encourages a dissenting juror to change his mind.

In connection with the giving of Allen-type instructions, trial judges have sometimes asked the jury foreman the numerical division among the jurors, a practice that is forbidden in the federal courts. Brasfield v. United States, 272 U.S. 448 (1926). The issue is discussed in Ellis v. Reed, 596 F.2d 1195 (4th Cir.1979).

An Allen-type charge accompanied by a poll of the jurors whether further deliberation would be helpful, during the sentencing phase of a capital case, was found not to be coercive and not to deny the defendant's constitutional rights, in Lowenfield v. Phelps, 484 U.S. 231 (1988) (6–3).

Verdict

FEDERAL RULES OF CRIMINAL PROCEDURE

Rule 31.

VERDICT

(a) Return. The verdict shall be unanimous. It shall be returned by the jury to the judge in open court.

(b) Several Defendants. If there are two or more defendants, the jury at any time during its deliberations may return a verdict or verdicts with respect to a defendant or defendants as to whom it has agreed; if the jury cannot agree with respect to all, the defendant or defendants as to whom it does not agree may be tried again.

(c) Conviction of Less Offense. The defendant may be found guilty of an offense necessarily included in the offense charged or of an attempt to commit either the offense charged or an offense necessarily included therein if the attempt is an offense.

(d) Poll of Jury. After a verdict is returned but before the jury is discharged, the court shall, on a party's request, or may on its own motion, poll the jurors individually. If the poll reveals a lack of unanimity, the court may direct the jury to deliberate further or may declare a mistrial and discharge the jury.

(e) Criminal Forfeiture. If the indictment or the information alleges that an interest or property is subject to criminal forfeiture, a special verdict shall be returned as to the extent of the interest or property subject to forfeiture, if any.

---

550. The (apocryphal) request of the foreman of the jury for 11 dinners and a bale of hay is well known. How long and in what circumstances can a jury be required to continue its deliberations after it has become deadlocked? "It is well established that the determination of how long a disagreeing jury will be kept together and required to continue their deliberation is a matter of sound judicial discretion which, in the absence of abuse, will not be disturbed." People v. Presley, 254 N.Y.S.2d 400 (App.Div.1964), aff'd, 209 N.E.2d 729 (N.Y.1965). See, e.g., De Grandis v. Fay, 335 F.2d 173 (2d Cir.1964); Commonwealth v. Moore, 157 A.2d 65 (Pa.1959).

551. "[T]he courts have consistently held that the right to a unanimous verdict is so important that it is one of the few rights of a criminal defendant that cannot, under any circumstances, be waived." United States v. Smedes, 760 F.2d 109, 113 (6th Cir.1985). When the jury has not reached a unanimous verdict and the defendant agrees to accept the verdict of 11 jurors, courts have had to distinguish between the unanimous verdict of 11 jurors and the non-unanimous (11–1) verdict of 12 jurors. See *Smedes*, and cases cited.

Distinguishing cases in other circuits, the Court of Appeals for the Eleventh Circuit has held that a defendant can waive the right to a unanimous jury provided by Rule 31(a). Such waiver should be allowed, the court said, if the following conditions are met: ". . . (1) the waiver should be initiated by the defendant, not the judge or prosecutor; (2) the jury must have had a reasonable time to deliberate and should have told the court only that it could not reach a decision, but not how it stood numerically; (3) the judge should carefully explain to the defendant the right to a unanimous verdict and the consequences of a waiver of that right; and (4) the judge should question the defendant directly to determine whether the waiver is being made knowingly and voluntarily." Sanchez v. United States, 782 F.2d 928, 934 (11th Cir.1986).

552. In Griffin v. United States, 502 U.S. 46 (1991), the Court upheld the validity of a general verdict of guilty even though the case was submitted to the jury on alternative theories, with respect to one of which there was insufficient evidence to sustain a guilty verdict. The defendant had been prosecuted, along with other defendants, for conspiracy; the evidence implicated her in one alleged conspiratorial objective but not the other. The Court distinguished cases in which a guilty verdict is returned following submission to the jury of theories one of which is constitutionally defective or legally inadequate. The Court also noted that when there is insufficient evidence to sustain one of several theories of the prosecution's case, the preferable practice is for the court to give an instruction removing the theory from the jury's consideration.

The defendant in Schad v. Arizona, 501 U.S. 624 (1991) (5–4), was convicted of first-degree murder on instructions that permitted the jury to convict if it was unanimous for guilt either on a theory of "willfull, deliberate, or premeditated" murder or on a theory of felony murder, without requiring unanimity on one theory or the other. The Court said that a general verdict that did not specify one of several alleged means of committing a crime was permissible. The problem presented, then, was to describe "the point at which differences between means become so important that they may not reasonably be viewed as alternatives to a common end, but must be treated as differentiating what the Constitution requires to be treated as separate offenses." Id. at 633. In order to decide whether a verdict based on alternative theories satisfies the due process requirement of fundamental fairness, a court should "look both to history and wide practice as guides to fundamental values, as well as to narrower analytical methods of testing the moral and practical equivalence" of the theories in question. The Court said also that there is a "threshold presumption of legislative competence" to determine whether there are different but equivalent ways to satisfy an element of a crime. Id. at 637-38. Noting that historically and generally in current law, deliberate murder and felony murder have both been regarded as sufficient to establish the *mens rea* requirement of first-degree murder, the Court affirmed the conviction.

AO 156 (Rev. 5/85)   Verdict

United States District Court

_____ DISTRICT OF _____

V.

VERDICT

CASE NUMBER:

WE, THE JURY, FIND:

_____   _____
FOREPERSON'S SIGNATURE   DATE

553. After the jury had deliberated for about four hours spread over two days and reached a verdict that the trial judge refused to accept because he believed it was inconsistent with his instructions, one juror became unable to continue. The judge recalled an alternate juror over defense counsel's objection, and the jury reached a verdict. The court held that this was a clear violation of the Rule 24(c) requirement that alternate jurors be discharged after the jury retires and that the alternate juror could not be seated over the defendant's objection. United States v. Lamb, 529 F.2d 1153 (9th Cir.1975). *Lamb* was distinguished in United States v. Foster, 711 F.2d 871 (9th Cir.1983), in which the court upheld the seating of an alternate juror pursuant to defense counsel's advance waiver of the requirement of Rule 24(c).

———

Remmer v. United States

347 U.S. 227, 74 S.Ct. 450, 98 L.Ed. 654 (1954).

■ MR. JUSTICE MINTON delivered the opinion of the Court.

The petitioner was convicted by a jury on several counts charging willful evasion of the payment of federal income taxes. A matter admitted by the Government to have been handled by the trial court in a manner that may have been prejudicial to the petitioner, and therefore confessed as error, is presented at the threshold and must be disposed of first.

After the jury had returned its verdict, the petitioner learned for the first time that during the trial a person unnamed had communicated with a certain juror, who afterwards became the jury foreman, and remarked to him that he could profit by bringing in a verdict favorable to the petitioner. The juror reported the incident to the judge, who informed the prosecuting attorneys and advised with them. As a result, the Federal Bureau of Investigation was requested to make an investigation and report, which was accordingly done. The F.B.I. report was considered by the judge and prosecutors alone, and they apparently concluded that the statement to the juror was made in jest, and nothing further was done or said about the matter. Neither the judge nor the prosecutors informed the petitioner of the incident, and he and his counsel first learned of the matter by reading of it in the newspapers after the verdict.

The above-stated facts were alleged in a motion for a new trial, together with an allegation that the petitioner was substantially prejudiced, thereby depriving him of a fair trial, and a request for a hearing to determine the circumstances surrounding the incident and its effect on the jury. A supporting affidavit of the petitioner's attorneys recited the alleged occurrences and stated that if they had known of the incident they would have moved for a mistrial and requested that the juror in question be replaced by an alternate juror. Two newspaper articles reporting the incident were attached to the affidavit. The Government did not file answering affidavits. The District Court, without holding the requested hearing, denied the motion for a new trial. . . .

In a criminal case, any private communication, contact, or tampering, directly or indirectly, with a juror during a trial about the matter pending before the jury is, for obvious reasons, deemed presumptively prejudicial, if not made in pursuance of known rules of the court and the instructions and directions of the court made during the trial, with full knowledge of the parties. The presumption is not conclusive, but the burden rests heavily upon the Government to establish, after notice to and hearing of the defendant, that such contact with the juror was harmless to the defendant. . . .

We do not know from this record, nor does the petitioner know, what actually transpired, or whether the incidents that may have occurred were harmful or harmless. The sending of an F.B.I. agent in the midst of a trial to investigate a juror as to his conduct is bound to impress the juror and is very apt to do so unduly. A juror must feel free to exercise his functions without the F.B.I. or anyone else looking over his shoulder. The integrity of jury proceedings must not be jeopardized by unauthorized invasions. The trial court should not decide and take final action *ex parte* on information such as was received in this case, but should determine the circumstances, the impact thereof upon the juror, and whether or not it was prejudicial, in a hearing with all interested parties permitted to participate.

We therefore vacate the judgment of the Court of Appeals and remand the case to the District Court with directions to hold a hearing to determine whether the incident complained of was harmful to the petitioner, and if after hearing it is found to have been harmful, to grant a new trial.

. . .

---

554. Relying on *Remmer*, the Court reversed a decision in a federal habeas corpus proceeding that a defendant's conviction should be vacated because one of the jurors was actively seeking a job as an investigator in the district attorney's office while the defendant's trial was in progress. The prosecutor was aware of the facts during the trial and withheld them from the judge and defense counsel until after the trial was complete. In a post-conviction proceeding in the state court, the trial judge had conducted a hearing and denied the motion to vacate the conviction. Such a hearing, the Court concluded, at which the judge found that the verdict had not been affected, was adequate to protect the defendant's rights. Smith v. Phillips, 455 U.S. 209 (1982) (6–3).

See Parker v. Gladden, 385 U.S. 363 (1966) (8–1) (bailiff in charge of jury expressed opinion that defendant was guilty to jurors; conviction reversed); Turner v. Louisiana, 379 U.S. 466 (1965) (8–1) (sequestered jury in constant association with deputy sheriffs, who were principal witnesses for prosecution; conviction reversed).

555. "[T]he testimony of jurors should not be received to show matters which essentially inhere in the verdict itself and necessarily depend upon the testimony of the jurors and can receive no corroboration." Hyde v. United States, 225 U.S. 347, 384 (1912). " '[O]n a motion for a new trial on the ground of bias on the part of one of the jurors, the evidence of jurors as to the motives and influences which affected their deliberations is inadmissible either to impeach or to support the verdict. But a juryman may testify to any facts bearing upon the question of the existence of any extraneous influence, although not as to how far that influence operated upon his mind. So a juryman may testify in denial or explanation of acts or declarations outside of the jury room, where evidence of such acts has been given as ground for a new trial.'" Mattox v. United States, 146 U.S. 140, 149 (1892) (quoting Woodward v. Leavitt, 107 Mass. 453 (1871)). "While this rule can be criticized as forbidding inquiry into the subject most truly pertinent, it represents a pragmatic judgment how best to attempt reconciliation of the irreconcilable. . . . Where an extraneous influence is shown, the court must apply an objective test, assessing for itself the likelihood that the influence would affect a typical juror." Miller v. United States, 403 F.2d 77, 83 n.11 (2d Cir.1968).

Following the defendant's conviction and before he was sentenced, defense counsel made a motion to examine trial jurors to determine whether any juror had consumed alcoholic beverages during the lunch breaks in the course of the trial. The motion was based on unsolicited information from one juror that some jurors had done so. There was also an indication that some jurors had ingested drugs during the trial. Relying on Federal Rule of Evidence 606(b), the Court held that alcohol or drug use was analogous to a juror's physical or mental condition and, as such, a matter "internal" to the jury's deliberations, not subject to inquiry after the verdict. Even if an inquiry might be proper if there were evidence of extreme abuse showing strong evidence of incompetence, the allegations in this case were far less than that. Tanner v. United States, 483 U.S. 107 (1987) (5–4). See United States v. Dioguardi, 492 F.2d 70 (2d Cir.1974) (juror's letter to defendant after trial raised doubt of her competence; conviction affirmed).

556. "[W]e see no basis for doubting the authority of the trial judge to direct that any interrogation of jurors after a conviction shall be under his supervision. To determine how far such questioning shall be permitted and in what manner it shall be done requires a weighing of two conflicting desiderata. One is the protection of the defendant's right to a fair trial before 'an impartial jury.' The other is avoidance of the dangers presented by inquiries that go beyond objective facts: inhibition of jury-room deliberations, harassment of jurors, and increased incidence of jury tampering. . . .

. . .

"Appellant's assertion that a defendant must be as free to interrogate jurors after a conviction as he is to interrogate prospective witnesses before trial does not require extended answer. Inquiry of jurors after a verdict seeks to impugn the validity of judicial action on the ground of misconduct of a member of the tribunal. The court has a vital interest in seeing that jurors are not harassed or placed in doubt about what their duty is and that false issues are not created. The argument that interviews by a private investigator involve less harassment than such methods as we have outlined is unconvincing. A juror so interviewed often does not know what he is supposed to do or supposed not to do. Moreover, except when the interview yields nothing, it is only the beginning. In any event such considerations go to the exercise of the power, not to its existence." Miller v. United States, 403 F.2d 77, 81–82 (2d Cir.1968).

557. On the basis of affidavits that defense counsel obtained from two jurors and testimony of another juror in a hearing on the defendant's petition for habeas corpus, the district judge found: "In substance, the jurors or some of them were told by other jurors during the trial and the deliberations: that the defendant had been in trouble all his life; that he had been suspended from the police force in connection with the unauthorized use of a prowl car; that he had been involved in a fight in a tavern; that one of the jurors' husband was an investigator and that he knew all about plaintiff's background and character, which was bad; and that petitioner's father was always getting him out of trouble." The district judge set aside the convictions, and the state appealed. The court of appeals affirmed. United States ex rel. Owen v. McMann, 435 F.2d 813 (2d Cir.1970).

"Both parties recognize Parker v. Gladden, 385 U.S. 363 . . . (1966), to be the starting point for discussion. That case makes it plain that if a bailiff testified he had entered the jury room and had made statements such as the district court found were here made by jurors about Owen, the confrontation clause of the Sixth Amendment and the due process clause of the Fourteenth would require a judgment of conviction to be set aside. We think the result would be the same if a non-juror, who was neither a court officer nor a witness, admitted to having made such statements to the jury here. . . .

"If our analysis is correct up to this point, we must affirm unless (1) it makes a legally significant difference that the remarks here were by jurors rather than the hypothetical non-juror or (2) New York may lawfully rule out jurors' testimony as a source of proof of the facts here alleged or (3) petitioner has waived his rights.

. . .

"While Parker v. Gladden, supra, consistently with the precedents it cites, demonstrates the Court's continuing concern with protecting a criminal defendant from the possibility of a verdict based on a consideration of facts not properly before the jury, it is thus not automatically determinative when the extra-record remarks are by jurors themselves. The invocation of the confrontation clause in *Parker* was entirely appropriate to shield the defendant from comments to the jury by one whose statements, if admissible at all, could have properly been received only from the witness stand, subject to the procedural safeguards which the Sixth Amendment requires. But, so far as we know, the Court has never suggested that jurors, whose duty it is to consider and discuss the factual material properly before them, become 'unsworn witnesses' within the scope of the confrontation clause simply because they have considered any factual matters going beyond those of record. To resort to the metaphor that the moment a juror passes a fraction of an inch beyond the record evidence, he becomes 'an unsworn witness' is to ignore centuries of history and assume an answer rather than to provide the basis for one.

"Although accurate knowledge of what goes on in the jury room is unhappily limited . . . we suspect there are many cases where jurors make statements concerning the general credibility or incredibility of the police, the need of backing them up even when there is reasonable doubt of guilt or putting brakes upon them even when there is none, the desirability of overcoming reasonable doubt because of the repugnance of particular crimes or of yielding to less than reasonable doubt because of their insignificance, and concerning other matters that would invalidate a judgment if uttered by a judge. . . . Yet this is the very stuff of the jury system, and we have recognized . . . that the standards for judges and juries are not the same. . . . The touchstone of decision in a case such as we have here is thus not the mere fact of infiltration of some molecules of extra-record matter, with the supposed consequences that the infiltrator becomes a 'witness' and the confrontation clause automatically applies, but the nature of what has been infiltrated and the probability of prejudice. . . .

"[A] good definition of the right line has recently been drawn by Judge Goldberg in United States v. McKinney, 429 F.2d 1019, 1022–1023 (5 Cir.1970): 'All must recognize, of course, that a complete sanitizing of the jury room is impossible. We cannot expunge from jury deliberations the subjective opinions of jurors, their additudinal expositions, or their philosophies. These involve the very human elements that constitute one of the strengths of our jury system, and we cannot and should not excommunicate them from jury deliberations. Nevertheless, while the jury may leaven its deliberations with its wisdom and experience, in doing so it must not bring extra *facts* into the jury room. In every criminal case we must endeavor to see that jurors do not [consider] in the confines of the jury room . . . specific facts about the specific defendant then on trial. . . . To the greatest extent possible all factual [material] must pass through the judicial sieve, where the fundamental guarantees of procedural law protect the rights of those accused of crime.' Owen's case falls on the impermissible side of this by no means bright line, although perhaps not by much. On the basis of the judge's findings, the jurors' statements went beyond Owen's being something of a ne'er-do-well; they included allegations of at least two specific incidents which had not been and probably could not have been received in evidence, and which Owen had had no opportunity to refute.

"We thus reach the second asserted basis of distinction from the statements by a hypothetical non-juror with which we began, namely, that the evidence came from the jurors themselves. . . . [T]he State argues that we should be mindful of the compelling public policy considerations, emphasized by the Supreme Court, which underlie the general rule against jurors' impeachment of their own duly rendered verdict: '[L]et it once be established that verdicts solemnly made and publicly returned into court can be attacked and set aside on the testimony of those who took part in their publication and all verdicts could be, and many would be, followed by an inquiry in the hope of discovering something which might invalidate the finding. Jurors would be harassed . . . in an effort to secure from them evidence of facts which might establish misconduct sufficient to set aside a verdict. If evidence thus secured could be thus used, the result would be to make what was intended to be a private deliberation, the constant subject of public investigation; to the destruction of all frankness and freedom of discussion and conference.' McDonald v. Pless, 238 U.S. 264, 267–268 . . . (1915). Since the sole proof of prejudice in the instant case comes from the post-trial interrogation of the jurors with respect to what transpired during their deliberations, and since New York evidence law . . . has allegedly embraced this policy by clamping a tight seal on jurors' revealing what they heard in the jury room . . . we are urged to refrain from carving an exception to a rule which, it is argued, represents a firmly imbedded policy of both New York State and federal courts.

"While we have taken note of this policy . . . we have also recognized . . . that the prohibition is not an absolute. . . . [I]f we were to take the inscrutable silence of the state courts to mean what the Attorney General says it does, we would be obliged to disregard a state evidentiary rule preventing what in this case is the only method of proving that the defendant had been denied due process by the jury's consideration of prejudicial extra-record facts. . . ." 435 F.2d at 815–20.

See United States v. Howard, 506 F.2d 865 (5th Cir.1975) (*Owen* followed).

558. When a jury is polled pursuant to Rule 31(d), each juror is required to state whether the verdict announced by the foreman is in fact his or her verdict. The rule provides that if there is not unanimous concurrence, the jury may be sent back to deliberate further. If a juror indicates doubt about a guilty verdict during a poll, the judge must be careful not to influence the juror to vote for the announced verdict in an effort to resolve any confusion that the juror may have. His best course, unless the juror's doubt is manifestly not about the substance of the verdict, is to send the jury back to deliberate further, without comment. See, e.g., United States v. Sexton, 456 F.2d 961 (5th Cir.1972), in which a variety of cases are described.

559. Inconsistent verdicts. In Dunn v. United States, 284 U.S. 390 (1932), the Court held that inconsistent verdicts of guilty and not guilty on different counts of a single indictment are permissible. Writing for the Court, Justice Holmes relied mistakenly on the proposition that where a defendant is charged with different crimes in separate indictments and tried on each indictment separately, "the same evidence being offered in support of each, an acquittal on one could not be pleaded as *res judicata* of the other," id. at 393. The rule is to the contrary. "[R]es judicata may be a defense in a second prosecution. That doctrine applies to criminal as well as civil proceedings . . . and operates to conclude those matters in issue which the verdict determined though the offenses be different." Sealfon v. United States, 332 U.S. 575, 578 (1948).

Holmes's error notwithstanding, *Dunn* was reaffirmed and applied in United States v. Powell, 469 U.S. 57 (1984):

"We believe that the *Dunn* rule rests on a sound rationale that is independent of its theories of res judicata, and that it therefore survives an attack based upon its presently erroneous reliance on such theories. As the *Dunn* Court noted, where truly inconsistent verdicts have been reached, '[t]he most that can be said . . . is that the verdict shows that either in the acquittal or the conviction the jury did not speak their real conclusions, but that does not show that they were not convinced of the defendant's guilt.' *Dunn*, [284 U.S.], at 393. The rule that the defendant may not upset such a verdict embodies a prudent acknowledgement of a number of factors. First, as the above quote suggests, inconsistent verdicts—even verdicts that acquit on a predicate offense while convicting on the compound offense—should not necessarily be interpreted as a windfall to the Government at the defendant's expense. It is equally possible that the jury, convinced of guilt, properly reached its conclusion on the compound offense, and then through mistake, compromise, or lenity, arrived at an inconsistent conclusion on the lesser offense. But in such situations the Government has no recourse if it wishes to correct the jury's error; the Government is precluded from appealing or otherwise upsetting such an acquittal by the Constitution's Double Jeopardy Clause. . . .

"Inconsistent verdicts therefore present a situation where 'error,' in the sense that the jury has not followed the court's instructions, most certainly has occurred, but it is unclear whose ox has been gored. Given this uncertainty, and the fact that the Government is precluded from challenging the acquittal, it is hardly satisfactory to allow the defendant to receive a new trial on the conviction as a matter of course. . . . [N]othing in the Constitution would require such a protection, and we therefore address the problem only under our supervisory powers over the federal criminal process. For us, the possibility that the inconsistent verdicts may favor the criminal defendant as well as the Government militates against review of such convictions at the defendant's behest. This possibility is a premise of *Dunn's* alternative rationale—that such inconsistencies often are a product of jury lenity. Thus, *Dunn* has been explained by both courts and commentators as a recognition of the jury's historic function, in criminal trials, as a check against arbitrary or oppressive exercises of power by the Executive Branch. . . .

"The burden of the exercise of lenity falls only on the Government, and it has been suggested that such an alternative should be available for the difficult cases where the jury wishes to avoid an all-or-nothing verdict. . . . Such an act is, as the *Dunn* Court recognized, an 'assumption of a power which [the jury has] no right to exercise,' but the illegality alone does not mean that such a collective judgment should be subject to review. The fact that the inconsistency may be the result of lenity, coupled with the Government's inability to invoke review, suggests that inconsistent verdicts should not be reviewable.

"We also reject, as imprudent and unworkable, a rule that would allow criminal defendants to challenge inconsistent verdicts on the ground that in their case the verdict was not the product of lenity, but of some error that worked against them. Such an individualized assessment of the reason for the inconsistency would be based either on pure speculation, or would require inquiries into the jury's deliberations that courts generally will not undertake. Jurors, of course, take an oath to follow the law as charged, and they are expected to follow it. . . . To this end trials generally begin with *voir dire*, by judge or counsel, seeking to identify those jurors who for whatever reason may be unwilling or unable to follow the law and render an impartial verdict on the facts and the evidence. But with few exceptions . . . once the jury has heard the evidence and the case has been submitted, the litigants must accept the jury's collective judgment. Courts have always resisted inquiring into a jury's thought processes . . .; through this deference the jury brings to the criminal process, in addition to the collective judgment of the community, an element of needed finality.

"Finally, we note that a criminal defendant already is afforded protection against jury irrationality or error by the independent review of the sufficiency of the evidence undertaken by the trial and appellate courts. This review should not be confused with the problems caused by inconsistent verdicts. Sufficiency of the evidence review involves assessment by the courts of whether the evidence adduced at trial could support any rational determination of guilt beyond a reasonable doubt. . . . This review should be independent of the jury's determination that evidence on another count was insufficient. The Government must convince the jury with its proof, and must also satisfy the courts that given this proof the jury could rationally have reached a verdict of guilt beyond a reasonable doubt. We do not believe that further safeguards against jury irrationality are necessary." 469 U.S. at 64–67.

560. On the jury's power to exercise lenity despite the instruction that it is to follow the law, see generally United States v. Dougherty, 473 F.2d 1113 (D.C.Cir.1972). The defendants in *Dougherty* were prosecuted for unlawful entry into Dow Chemical Company offices and destruction of property, as a protest against the Vietnam war. They requested an instruction that the jury was authorized to "nullify" the judge's instructions and return a verdict of not guilty notwithstanding the law. The court agreed that a jury has such power and that its exercise has been desirable in some instances; but it concluded that the requested instruction should not be given.

561. The defendant was prosecuted for tax evasion. After being charged that it was the court's duty to determine punishment if the jury found the defendant guilty, the jury returned a verdict of guilty, subscribed to which was a notation that the "[j]ury, however, respectfully request that this court give to J. Sydney Cook, Jr., every degree of leniency possible." On being polled, ten jurors indicated that their verdict of guilty was "based on the note" or "as noted" at the bottom of the verdict. The trial court denied defense counsel's request that the jurors be asked whether their verdict was "qualified" by the request for leniency or whether they would have voted to convict if advised that the request for leniency went beyond their province. Acknowledging that the general rule is that a recommendation of clemency should be treated as surplusage, the court held that the extreme circumstances of the case left a doubt whether the verdict was unqualified, and reversed the conviction. Cook v. United States, 379 F.2d 966 (5th Cir.1967).

See Rogers v. United States, 422 U.S. 35, 38 (1975), in which, citing *Cook* and noting the exception made in that case, the Court said: "Generally, a recommendation of leniency made by a jury without statutory authorization does not affect the validity of the verdict and may be disregarded by the sentencing judge."

562. The defendant moved for a judgment of acquittal under Rule 29 after the close of the government's case and again at the close of the entire case. The trial judge denied both motions. The jury returned a verdict of guilty. Thereafter, the judge imposed sentence (probation and a fine) and signed a judgment of conviction. He then ordered that the indictment be dismissed. As he explained, he did so because although he believed that the government's evidence was legally sufficient to warrant a conviction, for which reason he had denied the motions under Rule 29, he himself believed that the testimony of the main government witness was incredible

AO 245A (Rev. 7/87) Judgment of Acquittal

United States District Court

———————— DISTRICT OF ————————

UNITED STATES OF AMERICA

JUDGMENT OF ACQUITTAL

V.

CASE NUMBER:

The Defendant was found not guilty. IT IS ORDERED that the Defendant is acquitted, discharged and any bond exonerated.

_____

Signature of Judicial Officer

_____

Name and Title of Judicial Officer

_____

Date

and that there was danger of a miscarriage of justice. He observed that to have granted a new trial "in the interest of justice" under Rule 33 would have served no purpose. He took the peculiar course he did because he was uncertain of a trial judge's authority to terminate a criminal proceeding in favor of an accused despite the absence of a specific error warranting him to do so.

The court of appeals held that the trial judge had no such authority: "It is plain that no Rule of Federal Criminal Procedure confers any such power. We have already discussed Rule 29 and shown its inapplicability. The other pertinent provision is Rule 33 relating to the grant of a new trial. We have no doubt that, on [the defendant's] timely motion, the judge had power to grant a new trial if he thought, in the language of the Rule, that this was 'required in the interest of justice' even though, in his phrase, 'no specific error' warranted this. But admittedly no Rule gives the judge an overriding power to terminate a criminal prosecution in which the Government's evidence has passed the test of legal sufficiency simply because he thinks that course would be most consonant with the interests of justice.

"We believe the failure of the Rules to bestow such a power precludes its exercise. . . .

"Apart from what we regard as the preclusive effect of the silence of the Rules, we have not been pointed to any precedent for such an inherent power." United States v. Weinstein, 452 F.2d 704, 715 (2d Cir.1971).

CHAPTER 14

NEW TRIAL

FEDERAL RULES OF CRIMINAL PROCEDURE

Rule 33.

NEW TRIAL

On a defendant's motion, the court may grant a new trial to that defendant if the interests of justice so require. If trial was by the court without a jury, the court may—on defendant's motion for new trial—vacate the judgment, take additional testimony, and direct the entry of a new judgment. A motion for new trial based on newly discovered evidence may be made only within three years after the verdict or finding of guilty. But if an appeal is pending, the court may grant the motion only on remand of the case. A motion for a new trial based on any other grounds may be made only within 7 days after the verdict or finding of guilty or within such further time as the court may fix during the 7-day period.

United States v. Puco

338 F.Supp. 1252 (S.D.N.Y.), aff'd, 461 F.2d 846 (2d Cir.1972).

■ LASKER, DISTRICT JUDGE. Following conviction in a non-jury trial for selling narcotics and conspiring to do so, defendant has moved (a) pursuant to Rule 33, F.R.Crim.P., to vacate the verdict, authorize the taking of new evidence, and direct "entry of a not guilty verdict on the ground of newly discovered evidence," . . . .

(a) The Rule 33 Motion

The critical question at trial was whether or not the defendant attended a meeting on January 11, 1970, with the government's chief witness, Michael Fiore, at which the defendant agreed to procure narcotics.

Puco's sole defense was an alibi. He claimed that on the night of January 11, 1970, he was in Baltimore, Maryland, at Louise's Restaurant, and he produced a number of witnesses who testified in support of that claim, although not all of them were able specifically to state that he was at Louise's actually on the evening of January 11th. The present motion offers further testimony to corroborate the alibi. The excuse for not producing these witnesses at trial is that defendant did not know until the first day of the trial that the government would claim that Puco attended a conspiratorial meeting on January 11th and the defendant could not marshal his witnesses in anticipation of such evidence.

The criteria for determination of a motion for a new trial have been ably stated in United States v. Fassoulis, 203 F.Supp. 114, 117 (S.D.N.Y.1962). A motion for a new trial may not be granted unless the court is "satisfied that the evidence (1) is in fact newly discovered, i.e., discovered since the trial; (2) could not with due diligence have been discovered earlier; (3) is not merely cumulative or impeaching; (4) is material to the issues, and finally, (5) is such, and of such nature, that upon a retrial it will probably produce an acquittal."

. . .

In the instant case, defendant proposes to produce four witnesses to further establish his defense that he was not in New York on the evening of a conspiratorial meeting to arrange the cocaine sale for which he was convicted, but was in Baltimore, Maryland.

Defendant offers first that Clem Florio, a turf analyst and boxing editor for the Baltimore News American, would testify that he was with defendant during the afternoon of January 11th, but has no knowledge of his whereabouts on the evening of the 11th. Defendant's case included testimony that he was present in Baltimore during the day of January 11th, and thus this offer of proof would be merely cumulative and irrelevant, or, at most, of marginal relevance to fixing where defendant was on the night in question.

Next, defendant offers to call Elizabeth Worthington, a former waitress at Louise's Restaurant, where defendant claims he had dinner on the evening involved. In an affidavit she states: "On Monday Jan 11 I worked from 5–12 at the restaurant. I remember Mr. Puco being in the Restaurant that evening and him saying he was leaving in the morning, so I went over and gave him a farewell kiss." (Affidavit of Elizabeth Paule Worthington, sworn to August 11, 1971). This statement, and the balance of the affidavit from which it is taken, are in substance the same as made by defendant's witness Gloria Hicks, a cook at Louise's Restaurant, who testified that she remembered defendant being in the restaurant "all day and all night" on January 11th. Although this evidence is cumulative, it would carry some weight if considered alone in a situation where inconsistent testimony and credibility are at issue. January 11 is the key date here, and this witness does appear to offer valuable testimony, however repetitive it may be of that already in the record. Nonetheless, there is no showing that this testimony could not have been discovered and adduced earlier in the exercise of due diligence. No recess to permit defendant to locate and bring this witness to the trial was requested, and since her affidavit indicates that she spent a fair amount of time with defendant during his stay in Baltimore prior to the evening in question, it seems unlikely that he would have forgotten her presence and the utility of her testimony to his defense.

Defendant's third offer of new evidence is the testimony of Ralph De Felice, a Philadelphia resident and friend of Joe Di Natale. His affidavit states: "I had dinner with Mr. Puco at Louise's on Sunday Jan 10th and Monday evening Jan 11th," (signed and affirmed August 11, 1971). This evidence suffers from the same deficiency as that of Elizabeth Worthington; it could have been discovered prior to—or during—trial, and as to the alibi it is cumulative. Moreover, the affidavit conflicts with trial testimony of defendant's witness Joe Di Natale, who testified that while De Felice was at dinner at the restaurant on the 10th he was not present on the 11th.

Finally, defendant offers the testimony of Rebecca Fine, a waitress at Louise's Restaurant. Her affidavit (signed and affirmed August 11, 1971) states: "I waited on Mr. Puco and served him meals for a four or five day period during the time Mr. De Natale's horses ran and for several days after. All this was during the second week in January 1971." This, like the offer of evidence of Florio, is cumulative, could have been discovered with due diligence, and is irrelevant or of marginal relevance to determination of where the defendant was on the evening of January 11th.

"It is well settled that motions for new trials are not favored and should be granted only with great caution." United States v. Costello, 255 F.2d 876, 879 (2d Cir.1958). Defendant has contended that he was in Baltimore during the evening of January 11th, and yet at trial called none of the witnesses he now proposes to present. Even if the affidavits of the proposed witnesses are to be believed, the defendant must have known at the time of trial of their presence with him in Maryland on the critical "alibi night" of January 11th. There is no showing that they were unavailable to defendant before or during the trial. "Yet the defense never sought to subpoena [them] or to have the government produce [them], or to have the case adjourned until [they] could be located." United States v. Lanza, 329 F.2d 422, 423 (2d Cir.1964). The fact that some of these "new" witnesses state that they did not know their information was of value to defendant until after his trial is immaterial, for it is not what the witness knows, but what defendant knows about the witnesses which determines whether material evidence could have been discovered with due diligence before or during trial.

Moreover, even if the offers of proof were uniformly material, undiscoverable before trial and not merely cumulative, defendant would fail by the key test, which requires that the evidence "is such, and of such nature, that upon a retrial it will probably produce an acquittal." United States v. Fassoulis, supra. Only the affidavits of De Felice and Worthington could be considered to add anything to the weight of defendant's evidence were they to be admitted. However, the proposed testimony of De Felice has already been contradicted by the testimony of defendant's own witness, Di Natale, to the effect that De Felice was not present at Louise's Restaurant on January 11th. Worthington's testimony might be more important, but, as indicated above, is basically cumulative of that of Gloria Hicks.

But the proposed testimony must be weighed in the total setting of the trial, which includes the astonishing fact that, although all the defense witnesses stated that defendant's son, Steve Puco, Jr., was with him and them at Louise's Restaurant on January 11th, and although Puco Jr. was present in the courtroom throughout the trial (and identified from the witness stand as the defendant's son by Maurice Jacobs in the first instance and other defense witnesses thereafter), he was never called to testify as an alibi witness in support of his own father. It is a reasonable inference that if he had been called he would not have corroborated the story of the other defense witnesses.

The burden of satisfying the requirements of Rule 33 is on the defendant, and he has failed to meet that burden. There is no reason to believe that in this judge-tried case the holding of a hearing could clarify or alter this conclusion. Even taking the facts as here alleged, a new trial would not be warranted. . . . Accordingly, defendant's motion under Rule 33 is denied.

. . .

————

Jones v. United States

279 F.2d 433 (4th Cir.1960).

■ HAYNSWORTH, CIRCUIT JUDGE.

This is an appeal from the denial of a motion for a new trial based upon after-discovered evidence, the confession of another that he and an accomplice, not the defendants, were the bank robbers.

On a Sunday evening in January 1958, a branch bank in Marlow Heights, Maryland, was robbed. Two armed bandits, wearing "Frankenstein" masks, forced their way into the apartment of the manager of the branch, a Mr. Cranford. They forced Mr. Cranford to accompany one of them to the bank, and, there, to open the night depository. The other, armed with a sawed-off shotgun, remained in the Cranford apartment to guard Mrs. Cranford until receipt of a telephone call from the accomplice to inform him that the accomplice had gained possession of the money.

In May 1958, Jones and Princeler were tried and convicted of the crime. The question was one of identification. The Cranfords had picked the defendants out of lineups and identified them as the bandits, despite the fact that when the crime was committed most of the features of the bandits were concealed by the masks. This identification was strongly supported by circumstantial evidence which connected the defendants with two masks, a sawed-off shotgun and a pair of shoes, identified by the Cranfords as having been used by the bandits, and with a severed piece of a barrel of a shotgun which experts testified had been cut from the sawed-off shotgun. The defendants sought, unsuccessfully, to establish alibis.

Jones and Princeler appealed to this Court. We affirmed their convictions. . . .

From January until June 1958, Jones and Princeler were held in the Baltimore City Jail. From February 14, 1958 until April 24, 1958 one McNicholas was also incarcerated in the Baltimore City Jail upon a charge of robbery of a bank in Sparrows Point, Maryland, on February 12, 1958. There was testimony that Jones, Princeler and McNicholas talked together during exercise periods. One of their fellow prisoners testified he overheard Jones and McNicholas discussing plans for McNicholas to take the blame for the crime with which Jones and Princeler were charged. By the testimony of yet another prisoner, the defendants sought to impeach this testimony upon the ground that the witness sought favor in the hope of parole.

In June 1958, McNicholas, then confined in Lewisburg Penitentiary, sought an interview with FBI agents, to whom on June 16, he gave a written statement in which he said he and an unidentified friend robbed the Marlow Heights bank and that Jones and Princeler were innocent. Some of what little detail there is in this statement was retracted by McNicholas in subsequent statements and testimony.

McNicholas, in August 1958, and Jones, in October, were transferred to the Atlanta Penitentiary. Together there, they discussed their affairs, including the McNicholas confession. They collaborated in the preparation of a written statement, dated December 12, 1958, which McNicholas subsequently signed before a notary. This is the statement which was used to support the motions for new trial.

. . .

At the full hearing held in October [1959], McNicholas testified at length as did Jones, Princeler and a number of other witnesses. McNicholas continued to insist that he and another, whom he still refused to identify, had committed the crime. He testified that the masks and the sawed-off shotgun, introduced as exhibits in the Jones-Princeler trial and identified by the Cranfords, were not those used by him and his accomplice. His testimony contains some detail which counsel contend would support a finding that he was present in the Cranford apartment. It also contains some discrepancies and is contradicted in part by other testimony and his own prior statements. What knowledge of the Cranfords and of their apartment he displayed could have been acquired from Jones and Princeler and from his reading of portions of the transcript of the testimony at the Jones-Princeler trial.

A psychiatrist, who had examined McNicholas in 1958, testified he was a neurotic of above-average intelligence who sought punishment for antisocial conduct. He expressed the opinion that confession of a crime he had not committed would be consistent with his behavior pattern.

At the conclusion of the hearing, the District Judge reviewed the testimony, noted that the attitude of McNicholas was "unappetizing and unpersuasive," and found that his story was inherently improbable and unworthy of belief. He denied the motions.

. . .

The principal contention on appeal is that the District Judge, in acting upon the motion, had no right to consider the credibility of the proffered evidence. Essentially, the position is that the inquiry of the trial judge, in considering after-discovered evidence, is limited to the diligence of the movant, the admissibility of the evidence and its materiality if it should be accepted as true. Since the McNicholas testimony would have been admissible if it had been offered at the trial and would have produced a different result if it had been accepted as true by the jury, it is said that however unlikely it may be that a jury would believe such testimony, it was beyond the discretionary power of the trial judge to deny the motion.

Doubtless, it is true that where the after-discovered evidence consists of admitted fact, a court should hesitate to choose between permissible ultimate inferences without regard for the traditional function of the jury. If . . . the fact discovered by the defense after the trial was known to the prosecution and suppressed by it so as to impair to some extent, the fairness of the trial, the area in which the trial judge may exercise his discretion to deny the motion may be further circumscribed.

Where there is a grave question of the credibility of the after-discovered evidence, however, the role of the trial judge is that of the fact-finder, so much so that the Supreme Court has said an appeal from his resolution of the facts should be dismissed as frivolous.[1] The rule has been applied where, as here, a third party confession is the after-discovered evidence upon which the motion for new trial is founded.

This remedial procedure, a motion for new trial based upon after-discovered evidence, is designed to serve the ends of justice. It is made available as a means of relief from manifest injustice. That purpose would hardly be served if the law required the trial judge, who heard all of the evidence and saw all of the witnesses, to assume that a jury would believe testimonial evidence however improbable and unworthy of belief he finds it to be. If the purpose of the remedy is to be served, without subjecting it to undue abuse, the trial judge who approaches the question of the probable effect of the new evidence upon the result, in the event of a new trial, should be vested with a broad discretion in considering matters of credibility as well as of materiality. Stringent or artificial limitations upon the exercise of the discretionary power of the trial judge to grant new trials could only subvert the purpose of the remedy.

The contention is also made that the McNicholas testimony is so persuasive that the District Court could not reasonably conclude that a jury

---

1. United States v. Johnson, 327 U.S. 106, 66 S.Ct. 464, 90 L.Ed. 562.

which heard it, with all of the other testimony, would probably convict Jones and Princeler. In an oral opinion, delivered at the conclusion of the hearing on the motion, the District Court reviewed the facts and noted the infirmities in the McNicholas story and its lack of corroboration. In the light of the evidence that Jones and Princeler were the culprits, we think the analysis of the facts by the District Court was entirely reasonable and his conclusion within the range of his discretionary power.

. . .

563. The defendant was convicted of entering a store in which he had been employed and stealing $1,125.66. On the night after the crime, he disappeared. Three years later he told a sheriff elsewhere that he was wanted for the theft of $1,175 from the store. At his trial he testified that he had seen the store open on the night of the theft and had become frightened and fled; he had learned of the details of the theft the next day by reading a newspaper story which gave $1,175 as the amount of the theft. The prosecutor ridiculed this testimony; he argued that it was unlikely that such a story would appear in an out-of-town newspaper and that if there had been such a story the amount of the theft would have been reported accurately. Six days after the defendant was convicted, his counsel made a motion for a new trial and offered to show that there had been a newspaper story on the day in question that had reported a theft of $1,175. The crime and the trial occurred in Washington, D.C. Defense counsel had discovered the story in Washington newspapers, which were available in the town where the defendant said he had been on the day following the theft, on file in the Library of Congress. Should the motion for a new trial be granted? See Delbridge v. United States, 262 F.2d 710 (D.C.Cir.1958).

564. The appellant was tried before a judge without a jury and convicted of assault and larceny. "A government witness working in a filling station testified he saw two men approach an automobile; one of them seized a coat from the car of the complaining witness Carpenter and both men ran when a chase ensued. Carpenter, owner of the coat, followed them into an alley and apprehended one Martin, who was holding the stolen coat. The second man fled.

"The day Martin entered a guilty plea in court, appellant came into the courtroom and sat beside Carpenter, who was in court in connection with the case. Carpenter concluded that appellant was Martin's companion at the time of the coat theft and he so informed a detective then present.

Appellant explained his presence in court as being there to observe the case of a friend whose case was on the calendar that day. A check showed that the case he described was in fact on the calendar. Later he was arrested and charged.

"Appellant's defense was the testimony of his mother, his wife and a neighbor who testified he was in his home 7 or 8 miles from the scene of the crime at the hour of its commission. Appellant denied knowing Martin, his alleged accomplice, and denied being present at the time of the crime. Carpenter made a positive identification of appellant. He testified that when he caught up with the two men in the alley, appellant brandished a knife but fled when Carpenter grappled with Martin.

"On the second day following his conviction, appellant moved for a new trial on the grounds of newly discovered evidence, submitting an affidavit of Martin in which the latter absolved appellant of any part in the crimes. Martin also appeared as a witness at the hearing on the motion and testified he had met appellant when the latter was sent to jail and that he, Martin, volunteered this explanation because he did not want a guiltless man to suffer. Martin named one Tatum as his companion on the day of the offense but absolved Tatum of guilt in the theft saying that he, Martin, had seized the coat on a sudden impulse and that Tatum was not aware that the act was to occur.

"Appellant's attorney gave his own affidavit at the hearing in which he recited that he had interviewed Tatum who told him that he, not appellant, was present with Martin on the day in question but had not known Martin was to seize the coat; Tatum was quoted as saying he had run in fright and because Martin ran. Tatum was in the courtroom during the hearing on the new trial motion and presumably heard appellant's attorney read the affidavit identifying him as Martin's companion on the day of the crime. Tatum's presence in court was made known when he was asked by one of the attorneys to stand to compare his height and build with that of appellant. The trial judge noted that there was a substantial difference in height. Carpenter, confronted with both men, again identified appellant as Martin's companion. He said it was 7 p.m. on the day in question (March 28, 1960) and dusk but that he 'could see all right.'" Brodie v. United States, 295 F.2d 157, 158–59 (D.C.Cir.1961).

Should the motion for a new trial be granted? Suppose it had not been made until after the seven-day period prescribed by Rule 33 for motions on grounds other than newly discovered evidence?

565. "Appellant was convicted by a jury of taking indecent liberties with a child under the age of sixteen years, in violation of § 22–3501(a), D.C.Code (1940, Supp. VII). He resided in an apartment near that of the child and her mother, though under separate roofs. It is not disputed that at the time in question the child, a girl twelve years of age, was in appellant's apartment and did a dance there when only he and she were present.

She said he then took the liberties complained of, with his hand upon parts of her person. He denies that this occurred. There is also disagreement in their testimony as to the reason for her coming to his apartment. She says he called to her from his window when she was below on the street. He denies this, saying she came to the apartment inquiring for his daughter, whom she knew and with whom she testified she was on friendly terms. Each claims the other was the instigator of the dance. After she had told her mother, the latter called the child's married sister who asked a neighbor across the hall what she should do about it. The police were then called.

"Thus it is seen that the testimony upon which the conviction rests came from the child and was denied by the accused. The Government at the close of its case tendered the mother to the defendant if he wished to call her. A short recess was taken, after which the evidence was concluded by the testimony of the defendant and others he called. The mother and married sister were not called. Four days after the verdict a motion for a new trial was made, resting primarily upon an affidavit of the mother. In it she states she was present when the child came home on the evening in question. The child had testified that when she came home she was crying. The affidavit of the mother says her daughter first came in through the living room and there was nothing unusual about her appearance until she came out of the bathroom, went into the kitchen, and, crying bitterly, told the mother of the alleged accident. The affidavit also states, 'When I asked Gertrude why she went to Mr. Benton's apartment, she said that she was looking for Barbara Jean, the daughter of Mr. Benton. At the time, Gertrude had been angry for a time with this little girl, Barbara Jean, and had not been on speaking terms with her. . . .' This is at variance in two respects with the testimony of Gertrude on the trial. As we have shown, she testified that she was called by appellant to come, and that she was friendly with his daughter, Barbara Jean. The mother's affidavit concludes, '. . . and in my opinion, my conscience does not allow me to believe that anything happened to my girl on that night, I heard what Mr. Benton said, and I heard what my daughter said.' " Benton v. United States, 188 F.2d 625, 626–27 (D.C.Cir.1951).

Should the motion for a new trial be granted? Suppose it had not been made until after the seven-day period prescribed by Rule 33 for motions on grounds other than newly discovered evidence?

566. The defendant was convicted of a narcotics offense largely on the testimony of Challenger, an informer. Two days after the jury returned its verdict and before the defendant was sentenced, Challenger made an affidavit in which he recanted his testimony and expressed his belief that the defendant was innocent. Defense counsel made a motion for a new trial. Soon afterwards, defense counsel sought to withdraw his motion, because Challenger had asked for his affidavit back and had reaffirmed his testimony at trial. Challenger claimed that the affidavit was given under pressure from the defendant's family. Following a hearing, the trial judge concluded that Challenger was "completely irresponsible," and that there was "no reason to believe that on one occasion more than another he was telling the truth." Should the motion for a new trial be granted? See United States v. Troche, 213 F.2d 401 (2d Cir.1954). On the problem of the recanting witness, see United States v. Mackin, 561 F.2d 958 (D.C.Cir.1977); Lindsey v. United States, 368 F.2d 633 (9th Cir.1966). See generally Sanders v. Sullivan, 863 F.2d 218 (2d Cir.1988).

In United States v. Sanchez, 969 F.2d 1409, 1414 (2d Cir.1992), the court said that a trial judge should ordinarily defer to the jury's assessment of the credibility of witnesses and should grant a new trial on the basis of a conclusion that a witness committed perjury only if she believes that the jury would probably have acquitted without that testimony and "only with great caution and in the most extraordinary circumstances."

567. The defendant was convicted of a drug offense. More than seven days after the final judgment, two codefendants, who had pleaded guilty on the first day of his trial, filed affidavits stating that he was innocent. They had told the court at the defendant's trial that they would not testify but would assert the privilege against self-incrimination, because they had not yet been sentenced. In those circumstances, the court held that the codefendants' affidavits might qualify as newly discovered evidence even though they were known to the defense at the time of the trial, because they were then unavailable to the defense. United States v. Montilla-Rivera, 115 F.3d 1060 (1st Cir.1997). See also Newsom v. United States, 311 F.2d 74 (5th Cir.1962).

568. Referring to the grant of a new trial "when required in the interest of justice," in a case involving highly unusual circumstances, the court said: "If the complete record, testimonial and physical, leaves a strong doubt as to the defendant's guilt, even though not so strong a doubt as to require a judgment of acquittal, the district judge may be obliged to grant a new trial." United States v. Morales, 910 F.2d 467, 468 (7th Cir.1990).

CHAPTER 15

SENTENCE AND JUDGMENT

---

569. "[T]he sentencing process, as well as the trial itself, must satisfy the requirements of the Due Process Clause. Even though the defendant has no substantive right to a particular sentence within the range authorized by statute, the sentencing is a critical stage of the criminal proceeding at which he is entitled to the effective assistance of counsel. . . . The defendant has a legitimate interest in the character of the procedure which leads to the imposition of sentence even if he may have no right to object to a particular result of the sentencing process." Gardner v. Florida, 430 U.S. 349, 358 (1977).

The Sentencing Reform Act of 1984, 28 U.S.C. §§ 991–998, provided for a United States Sentencing Commission to promulgate binding Sentencing Guidelines for federal offenses. The principal goals of the guidelines were to eliminate the great variation among sentences for persons similarly situated and convicted of the same offense and to eliminate the uncertainty about the length of time a person would actually spend in prison. In addition, the guidelines were intended to promote sentences the formal terms of which reflected the actual sentences and to promote sentences for different crimes that reflected their relative seriousness.

Sentencing Guidelines were promulgated in 1987. They establish categories of criminal conduct, specific offense characteristics, and "adjustments," which are applied according to a formula to determine the sentence. Parole was eliminated. The guidelines were upheld against a constitutional challenge that they delegated excessive legislative authority to the Commission and violated the principle of separation of powers. Mistretta v. United States, 488 U.S. 361 (1989) (8–1).

The Court has held that the Sentencing Commission's commentary to the guidelines is authoritative and binding on the federal courts, unless it violates the Constitution or a federal statute or is a plainly erroneous reading of or plainly inconsistent with the guideline it interprets. Stinson v. United States, 508 U.S. 36 (1993).

For an extensive review of a sentencing court's authority under the Guidelines to depart from the sentences prescribed therein, see Koon v. United States, 518 U.S. 81 (1996).

18 U.S.C. § 3553(e) empowers a district court to sentence a defendant below the statutory minimum "upon motion of the Government," based on the defendant's "substantial assistance" in the investigation or prosecution of another person. The Sentencing Guidelines contain a similar provision. In Wade v. United States, 504 U.S. 181 (1992), the Court held that a federal district court has authority to review a prosecutor's refusal to file such a motion for an "unconstitutional motive," such as the defendant's race or religion but not simply on the alleged ground that there was a basis for such a motion. See United States v. Paramo, 998 F.2d 1212 (3d Cir.1993) (prosecutor's refusal to file motion for downward sentencing departure, allegedly to penalize defendant for exercising right to trial, is subject to review).

There have been a very large number of opinions of the federal courts of appeals and district courts construing and applying the Sentencing Guidelines. The front pages of advance sheets of the Federal Reporter System have citations to cases applying the guidelines arranged according to the provision in issue.

The problem of plea-bargaining in the context of the Sentencing Guidelines is discussed in United States v. Bethancurt, 692 F.Supp. 1427 (D.D.C.1988). Judge Greene concludes: "[I]f the elimination of sentencing disparity was the goal the Congress had in mind when it enacted the new law, it achieved that objective only in the context of judicial sentencing: prosecutorial decisions are likely to result in as much unwarranted sentencing disparity as existed before, if not more so, and they will do so under conditions of decreased fairness." Id. at 1435–36.

FEDERAL RULES OF CRIMINAL PROCEDURE

Rule 32.

SENTENCE AND JUDGMENT

(a) In General; Time for Sentencing. When a presentence investigation and report are made under subdivision (b)(1), sentence should be imposed without unnecessary delay following completion of the process prescribed by subdivision (b)(6). The time limits prescribed in subdivision (b)(6) may be either shortened or lengthened for good cause.

(b) Presentence Investigation and Report.

(1) When Made. The probation officer must make a presentence investigation and submit a report to the court before the sentence is imposed, unless:

(A) the court finds that the information in the record enables it to exercise its sentencing authority meaningfully under 18 U.S.C. § 3553; and

(B) the court explains this finding on the record.

Notwithstanding the preceding sentence, a presentence investigation and report, or other report containing information sufficient for the court to enter an order of restitution, as the court may direct, shall be required in any case in which restitution is required to be ordered.

(2) Presence of Counsel. On request, the defendant's counsel is entitled to notice and a reasonable opportunity to attend any interview of the defendant by a probation officer in the course of a presentence investigation.

(3) Nondisclosure. The report must not be submitted to the court or its contents disclosed to anyone unless the defendant has consented in writing, has pleaded guilty or nolo contendere, or has been found guilty.

(4) Contents of the Presentence Report. The presentence report must contain—

(A) information about the defendant's history and characteristics, including any prior criminal record, financial condition, and any circumstances that, because they affect the defendant's behavior, may be helpful in imposing sentence or in correctional treatment;

(B) the classification of the offense and of the defendant under the categories established by the Sentencing Commission under 28 U.S.C. § 994(a), as the probation officer believes to be applicable to the defendant's case; the kinds of sentence and the sentencing range suggested for such a category of offense committed by such a category of defendant as set forth in the guidelines issued by the Sentencing Commission under 28 U.S.C. § 994(a)(1); and the probation officer's explanation of any factors that may suggest a different sentence—within or without the applicable guideline—that would be more appropriate, given all the circumstances;

(C) a reference to any pertinent policy statement issued by the Sentencing Commission under 28 U.S.C. §994(a)(2);

(D) verified information, stated in a nonargumentative style, containing an assessment of the financial, social, psychological, and medical impact on any individual against whom the offense has been committed;

(E) in appropriate cases, information about the nature and extent of nonprison programs and resources available for the defendant;

(F) in appropriate cases, information sufficient for the court to enter an order of restitution;

(G) any report and recommendation resulting from a study ordered by the court under 18 U.S.C. § 3552(b); and

(H) any other information required by the court.

(5) Exclusions. The presentence report must exclude:

(A) any diagnostic opinions that, if disclosed, might seriously disrupt a program of rehabilitation;

(B) sources of information obtained upon a promise of confidentiality; or

(C) any other information that, if disclosed, might result in harm, physical or otherwise, to the defendant or other persons.

(6) Disclosure and Objections.

(A) Not less than 35 days before the sentencing hearing—unless the defendant waives this minimum period—the probation officer must furnish the presentence report to the defendant, the defendant's counsel, and the attorney for the Government. The court may, by local rule or in individual cases, direct that the probation officer not disclose the probation officer's recommendation, if any, on the sentence.

(B) Within 14 days after receiving the presentence report, the parties shall communicate in writing to the probation officer, and to each other, any objections to any material information, sentencing classifications, sentencing guideline ranges, and policy statements contained in or omitted from the presentence report. After receiving objections, the probation officer may meet with the defendant, the defendant's counsel, and the attorney for the Government to discuss those objections. The probation officer may also conduct a further investigation and revise the presentence report as appropriate.

(C) Not later than 7 days before the sentencing hearing, the probation officer must submit the presentence report to the court, together with an addendum setting forth any unresolved objections, the grounds for those objections, and the probation officer's comments on the objections. At the same time, the probation officer must furnish the revisions of the presentence report and the addendum to the defendant, the defendant's counsel, and the attorney for the Government.

(D) Except for any unresolved objection under subdivision (b)(6)(B), the court may, at the hearing, accept the presentence report as its findings of fact. For good cause shown, the court may allow a new objection to be raised at any time before imposing sentence.

(c) Sentence.

(1) Sentencing Hearing. At the sentencing hearing, the court must afford counsel for the defendant and for the Government an opportunity to comment on the probation officer's determinations and on other matters relating to the appropriate sentence, and must rule on any unresolved objections to the presentence report. The court may, in its

discretion, permit the parties to introduce testimony or other evidence on the objections. For each matter controverted, the court must make either a finding on the allegation or a determination that no finding is necessary because the controverted matter will not be taken into account in, or will not affect, sentencing. A written record of these findings and determinations must be appended to any copy of the presentence report made available to the Bureau of Prisons.

(2) Production of Statements at Sentencing Hearing. Rule 26.2 (a)-(d) and (f) applies at a sentencing hearing under this rule. If a party elects not to comply with an order under Rule 26.2(a) to deliver a statement to the movant, the court may not consider the affidavit or testimony of the witness whose statement is withheld.

(3) Imposition of Sentence. Before imposing sentence, the court must:

(A) verify that the defendant and defendant's counsel have read and discussed the presentence report made available under subdivision (b)(6)(A). If the court has received information excluded from the presentence report under subdivision (b)(5) the court—in lieu of making that information available—must summarize it in writing, if the information will be relied on in determining sentence. The court must also give the defendant and the defendant's counsel a reasonable opportunity to comment on that information;

(B) afford defendant's counsel an opportunity to speak on behalf of the defendant;

(C) address the defendant personally and determine whether the defendant wishes to make a statement and to present any information in mitigation of the sentence; and

(D) afford the attorney for the Government an opportunity equivalent to that of the defendant's counsel to speak to the court; and

(E) if sentence is to be imposed for a crime of violence or sexual abuse, address the victim personally if the victim is present at the sentencing hearing and determine if the victim wishes to make a statment or present any information in relation to the sentence.

(4) In Camera Proceedings. The court's summary of information under subdivision (c)(3)(A) may be in camera. Upon joint motion by the defendant and by the attorney for the Government, the court may hear in camera the statements—made under subdivision (c)(3)(B), (C), (D) and (E)—by the defendant, the defendant's counsel, or the attorney for the Government.

(5) Notification of Right to Appeal. After imposing sentence in a case which has gone to trial on a plea of not guilty, the court must advise the defendant of the right to appeal. After imposing sentence in any case, the court must advise the defendant of any right to appeal the sentence, and of the right of a person who is unable to pay the cost of

an appeal to apply for leave to appeal in forma pauperis. If the defendant so requests, the clerk of the court must immediately prepare and file a notice of appeal on behalf of the defendant.

(d) Judgment.

(1) In General. A judgment of conviction must set forth the plea, the verdict or findings, the adjudication, and the sentence. If the defendant is found not guilty or for another reason is entitled to be discharged, judgment must be entered accordingly. The judgment must be signed by the judge and entered by the clerk.

(2) Criminal Forfeiture. If a verdict contains a finding that property is subject to a criminal forfeiture, or if a defendant enters a guilty plea subjecting property to such forfeiture, the court may enter a preliminary order of forfeiture after providing notice to the defendant and a reasonable opportunity to be heard on the timing and form of the order. The order of forfeiture shall authorize the Attorney General to seize the property subject to forfeiture, to conduct any discovery that the court considers proper to help identify, locate, or dispose of the property, and to begin proceedings consistent with any statutory requirements pertaining to ancillary hearings and the rights of third parties. At sentencing, a final order of forfeiture shall be made part of the sentence and included in the judgment. The court may include in the final order such conditions as may be reasonably necessary to preserve the value of the property pending any appeal.

(e) Plea Withdrawal. If a motion to withdraw a plea of guilty or nolo contendere is made before sentence is imposed, the court may permit the plea to be withdrawn if the defendant shows any fair and just reason. At any later time, a plea may be set aside only on direct appeal or by motion under 28 U.S.C. § 2255.

(f) Definitions. For purposes of this rule—

(1) "victim" means any individual against whom an offense has been committed for which a sentence is to be imposed, but the right of allocution under subdivision (c)(3)(E) may be exercised instead by—

(A) a parent or legal guardian if the victim is below the age of eighteen years or incompetent; or

(B) one or more family members or relatives designated by the court if the victim is deceased or incapacitated;

if such person or persons are present at the sentencing hearing, regardless of whether the victim is present; and

(2) "crime of violence or sexual abuse" means a crime that involved the use or attempted or threatened use of physical force against the person or property of another, or a crime under chapter 109A of title 18, United States Code.

570. "[I]t is improper for the prosecutor to convey information or to discuss any matter relating to the merits of the case or sentence with the judge in the absence of counsel." Haller v. Robbins, 409 F.2d 857, 859 (1st Cir.1969).

571. Allocution. "The design of Rule 32(a) did not begin with its promulgation; its legal provenance was the common-law right of allocution. As early as 1689, it was recognized that the court's failure to ask the defendant if he had anything to say before sentence was imposed required reversal. . . . Taken in the context of its history, there can be little doubt that the drafters of Rule 32(a) intended that the defendant be personally afforded the opportunity to speak before imposition of sentence. We are not unmindful of the relevant major changes that have evolved in criminal procedure since the seventeenth century—the sharp decrease in the number of crimes which were punishable by death, the right of the defendant to testify on his own behalf, and the right to counsel. But we see no reason why a procedural rule should be limited to the circumstances under which it arose if reasons for the right it protects remain. None of these modern innovations lessens the need for the defendant, personally, to have the opportunity to present to the court his plea in mitigation. The most persuasive counsel may not be able to speak for a defendant as the defendant might, with halting eloquence, speak for himself. We are buttressed in this conclusion by the fact that the Rule explicitly affords the defendant two rights: 'to make a statement in his own behalf,' and 'to present any information in mitigation of punishment.' We therefore reject the Government's contention that merely affording defendant's counsel the opportunity to speak fulfills the dual role of Rule 32(a).

". . . Trial judges before sentencing should, as a matter of good judicial administration, unambiguously address themselves to the defendant. Hereafter trial judges should leave no room for doubt that the defendant has been issued a personal invitation to speak prior to sentencing." Green v. United States, 365 U.S. 301, 304–305 (1961).

In Hill v. United States, 368 U.S. 424, 428 (1962), however, the Court said that in the absence of any aggravating circumstances failure to ask a defendant whether he wished to say anything before imposition of sentence "is not a fundamental defect which inherently results in a complete miscarriage of justice, nor an omission inconsistent with the rudimentary demands of fair procedure," and is not a basis for collateral attack of a conviction. Compare United States v. Behrens, 375 U.S. 162 (1963).

"While it is not error, in some circumstances, for a defendant to be absent during *trial* . . . a defendant *must* be present at sentencing. Only in the most extraordinary circumstances, and where it would otherwise work an injustice, should a court sentence a defendant *in absentia*, and then only under appropriate safeguards, as where the defendant has expressly waived his right to be present either by sworn affidavit or in open court for the record." United States v. Brown, 456 F.2d 1112, 1114 (5th Cir.1972).

572. Rule 32(a)(1) also gives the attorney for the government an opportunity to speak at sentencing. In United States v. Doe, 655 F.2d 920 (9th Cir.1980), the court held that the *defendant* is entitled to have the court give the prosecutor an opportunity to speak.

Failure to give the attorney for the government an opportunity to speak at sentencing constitutes an illegal imposition of sentence, which can be corrected, on motion by the government, under Rule 35(a). Imposition of a greater sentence in these circumstances is not violative of the Double Jeopardy Clause. United States v. Crawford, 769 F.2d 253 (5th Cir.1985). (But cf. United States v. Lopez, 26 F.3d 512 (5th Cir.1994)).

573. Before a sentencing court can make an upward departure from the Sentencing Guidelines "on a ground not identified as a ground for upward departure either in the presentence report or in a prehearing submission by the Government, Rule 32 requires that the district court give the parties reasonable notice that it is contemplating such a ruling. This notice must specifically identify the ground on which the district court is contemplating an upward departure." Burns v. United States, 501 U.S. 129, 138–39 (1991) (5–4).

———

FEDERAL RULES OF CRIMINAL PROCEDURE

Rule 32.1

REVOCATION OR MODIFICATION OF PROBATION OR SUPERVISED RELEASE

(a) Revocation of Probation or Supervised Release.

(1) Preliminary Hearing. Whenever a person is held in custody on the ground that the person has violated a condition of probation or supervised release, the person shall be afforded a prompt hearing before any judge, or a United States magistrate [*sic*—magistrate judge] who has been given authority pursuant to 28 U.S.C. § 636 to conduct such hearings, in order to determine whether there is probably [*sic*] cause to hold the person for a revocation hearing. The person shall be given

(A) notice of the preliminary hearing and its purpose and of the alleged violation;

(B) an opportunity to appear at the hearing and present evidence in the person's own behalf;

(C) upon request, the opportunity to question witnesses against the person unless, for good cause, the federal magistrate [*sic*—magistrate judge] decides that justice does not require the appearance of the witness; and

(D) notice of the person's right to be represented by counsel.

The proceedings shall be recorded stenographically or by an electronic recording device. If probable cause is found to exist, the person shall be held for a revocation hearing. The person may be released pursuant to Rule 46(c) pending the revocation hearing. If probable cause is not found to exist, the proceeding shall be dismissed.

(2) Revocation Hearing. The revocation hearing, unless waived by the person, shall be held within a reasonable time in the district of jurisdiction. The person shall be given

(A) written notice of the alleged violation;

(B) disclosure of the evidence against the person;

(C) an opportunity to appear and to present evidence in the person's own behalf;

(D) the opportunity to question adverse witnesses; and

(E) notice of the person's right to be represented by counsel.

(b) Modification of Probation or Supervised Release. A hearing and assistance of counsel are required before the terms or conditions of probation or supervised release can be modified, unless the relief to be granted to the person on probation or supervised release upon the person's request or the court's own motion is favorable to the person, and the attorney for the government, after having been given notice of the proposed relief and a reasonable opportunity to object, has not objected. An extension of the term of probation or supervised release is not favorable to the person for the purposes of this rule.

(c) Production of Statements.

(1) In General. Rule 26.2(a)–(d) and (f) applies at any hearing under this rule.

(2) Sanctions for Failure to Produce Statement. If a party elects not to comply with an order under Rule 26.2(a) to deliver a statement to the moving party, the court may not consider the testimony of a witness whose statement is withheld.

Rule 34.

ARREST OF JUDGMENT

The court on motion of a defendant shall arrest judgment if the indictment or information does not charge an offense or if the court was without jurisdiction of the offense charged. The motion in arrest of judgment shall be made within 7 days after verdict or finding of guilty, or after plea of guilty or *nolo contendere*, or within such further time as the court may fix during the 7–day period.

Rule 35.

CORRECTION OR REDUCTION OF SENTENCE

(a) Correction of a Sentence on Remand. The court shall correct a sentence that is determined on appeal under 18 U.S.C. 3742 to have been imposed in violation of law, to have been imposed as a result of an incorrect application of the sentencing guidelines, or to be unreasonable, upon remand of the case to the court—

(1) for imposition of a sentence in accord with the findings of the court of appeals; or

(2) for further sentencing proceedings if, after such proceedings, the court determines that the original sentence was incorrect.

(b) Reduction of Sentence For Substantial Assistance. If the Government so moves within one year after the sentence is imposed, the court may reduce a sentence to reflect a defendant's subsequent substantial assistance in investigating or prosecuting another person, in accordance with the guidelines and policy statements issued by the Sentencing Commission under 28 U.S.C. § 994. The court may consider a government motion to reduce a sentence made one year or more after the sentence is imposed if the defendant's substantial assistance involves information or evidence not known by the defendant until one year or more after sentence is imposed. In evaluating whether substantial assistance has been rendered, the court may consider the defendant's pre-sentence assistance. In applying this subdivision, the court may reduce the sentence to a level below that established by statute as a minimum sentence.

(c) Correction of Sentence by Sentencing Court. The court, acting within 7 days after the imposition of sentence, may correct a sentence that was imposed as a result of arithmetical, technical, or other clear error.

---

574. "[T]he narrow function of Rule 35 is to permit correction at any time of an illegal *sentence*, not to re-examine errors occurring at the trial or other proceedings prior to the imposition of sentence." Hill v. United States, 368 U.S. 424, 430 (1962).

Williams v. New York

337 U.S. 241, 69 S.Ct. 1079, 93 L.Ed. 1337 (1949).

■ MR. JUSTICE BLACK delivered the opinion of the Court.

A jury in a New York state court found appellant guilty of murder in the first degree. The jury recommended life imprisonment, but the trial judge imposed sentence of death. In giving his reasons for imposing the death sentence the judge discussed in open court the evidence upon which the jury had convicted stating that this evidence had been considered in the light of additional information obtained through the court's "Probation Department, and through other sources." Consideration of this additional information was pursuant to § 482 of New York Criminal Code which provides:

> ". . . Before rendering judgment or pronouncing sentence the court shall cause the defendant's previous criminal record to be submitted to it, including any reports that may have been made as a result of a mental, psychiatric or physical examination of such person, and may seek any information that will aid the court in determining the proper treatment of such defendant."

The Court of Appeals of New York affirmed the conviction and sentence over the contention that as construed and applied the controlling penal statutes are in violation of the due process clause of the Fourteenth Amendment of the Constitution of the United States "in that the sentence of death was based upon information supplied by witnesses with whom the accused had not been confronted and as to whom he had no opportunity for cross-examination or rebuttal. . . ." 298 N.Y. 803, 804, 83 N.E.2d 698, 699. Because the statutes were sustained over this constitutional challenge the case is here on appeal under 28 U.S.C. § 1257(2).

The narrow contention here makes it unnecessary to set out the facts at length. The record shows a carefully conducted trial lasting more than two weeks in which appellant was represented by three appointed lawyers who conducted his defense with fidelity and zeal. The evidence proved a wholly indefensible murder committed by a person engaged in a burglary. The judge instructed the jury that if it returned a verdict of guilty as charged, without recommendation for life sentence, "The Court must impose the death penalty," but if such recommendation was made, "the Court may impose a life sentence." The judge went on to emphasize that "the Court is not bound to accept your recommendation."

About five weeks after the verdict of guilty with recommendation of life imprisonment, and after a statutory pre-sentence investigation report to the judge, the defendant was brought to court to be sentenced. Asked what he had to say, appellant protested his innocence. After each of his three lawyers had appealed to the court to accept the jury's recommendation of a life sentence, the judge gave reasons why he felt that the death sentence should be imposed. He narrated the shocking details of the crime as shown by the trial evidence, expressing his own complete belief in appellant's guilt. He stated that the pre-sentence investigation revealed many material facts concerning appellant's background which though relevant to the question of punishment could not properly have been brought to the attention of the jury in its consideration of the question of guilt. He referred to the experience appellant "had had on thirty other burglaries in and about the same vicinity" where the murder had been committed. The appellant had not been convicted of these burglaries although the judge had information that he had confessed to some and had been identified as the perpetrator of some of the others. The judge also referred to certain activities of appellant as shown by the probation report that indicated appellant possessed "a morbid sexuality" and classified him as a "menace to society." The accuracy of the statements made by the judge as to appellant's background and past practices was not challenged by appellant or his counsel, nor was the judge asked to disregard any of them or to afford appellant a chance to refute or discredit any of them by cross-examination or otherwise.

The case presents a serious and difficult question. The question relates to the rules of evidence applicable to the manner in which a judge may obtain information to guide him in the imposition of sentence upon an already convicted defendant. Within limits fixed by statutes, New York judges are given a broad discretion to decide the type and extent of punishment for convicted defendants. Here, for example, the judge's discretion was to sentence to life imprisonment or death. To aid a judge in exercising this discretion intelligently the New York procedural policy encourages him to consider information about the convicted person's past life, health, habits, conduct, and mental and moral propensities. The sentencing judge may consider such information even though obtained outside the courtroom from persons whom a defendant has not been permitted to confront or cross-examine. It is the consideration of information obtained by a sentencing judge in this manner that is the basis for appellant's broad constitutional challenge to the New York statutory policy.

Appellant urges that the New York statutory policy is in irreconcilable conflict with the underlying philosophy of a second procedural policy grounded in the due process of law clause of the Fourteenth Amendment. That policy as stated in In re Oliver, 333 U.S. 257, 273, is in part that no person shall be tried and convicted of an offense unless he is given reasonable notice of the charges against him and is afforded an opportunity to examine adverse witnesses. That the due process clause does provide these salutary and time-tested protections where the question for consideration is the guilt of a defendant seems entirely clear from the genesis and historical evolution of the clause. . . .

Tribunals passing on the guilt of a defendant always have been hedged in by strict evidentiary procedural limitations. But both before and since the American colonies became a nation, courts in this country and in England practiced a policy under which a sentencing judge could exercise a wide discretion in the sources and types of evidence used to assist him in determining the kind and extent of punishment to be imposed within limits fixed by law. Out-of-court affidavits have been used frequently, and of course in the smaller communities sentencing judges naturally have in mind their knowledge of the personalities and backgrounds of convicted offenders. A recent manifestation of the historical latitude allowed sentencing judges appears in Rule 32 of the Federal Rules of Criminal Procedure. That rule provides for consideration by federal judges of reports made by probation officers containing information about a convicted defendant, including such information "as may be helpful in imposing sentence or in granting probation or in the correctional treatment of the defendant. . . ."

In addition to the historical basis for different evidentiary rules governing trial and sentencing procedures there are sound practical reasons for the distinction. In a trial before verdict the issue is whether a defendant is guilty of having engaged in certain criminal conduct of which he has been specifically accused. Rules of evidence have been fashioned for criminal trials which narrowly confine the trial contest to evidence that is strictly relevant to the particular offense charged. These rules rest in part on a necessity to prevent a time-consuming and confusing trial of collateral issues. They were also designed to prevent tribunals concerned solely with the issue of guilt of a particular offense from being influenced to convict for that offense by evidence that the defendant had habitually engaged in other misconduct. A sentencing judge, however, is not confined to the narrow issue of guilt. His task within fixed statutory or constitutional limits is to determine the type and extent of punishment after the issue of guilt has been determined. Highly relevant—if not essential—to his selection of an appropriate sentence is the possession of the fullest information possible concerning the defendant's life and characteristics. And modern concepts individualizing punishment have made it all the more necessary that a sentencing judge not be denied an opportunity to obtain pertinent information by a requirement of rigid adherence to restrictive rules of evidence properly applicable to the trial.

Undoubtedly the New York statutes emphasize a prevalent modern philosophy of penology that the punishment should fit the offender and not merely the crime. . . . The belief no longer prevails that every offense in a like legal category calls for an identical punishment without regard to the past life and habits of a particular offender. This whole country has traveled far from the period in which the death sentence was an automatic and commonplace result of convictions—even for offenses today deemed trivial. Today's philosophy of individualizing sentences makes sharp distinctions for example between first and repeated offenders. Indeterminate sentences the ultimate termination of which are sometimes decided by non-judicial agencies have to a large extent taken the place of the old rigidly fixed punishments. The practice of probation which relies heavily on nonjudicial implementation has been accepted as a wise policy. Execution of the United States parole system rests on the discretion of an administrative parole board. . . . Retribution is no longer the dominant objective of the criminal law. Reformation and rehabilitation of offenders have become important goals of criminal jurisprudence.

Modern changes in the treatment of offenders make it more necessary now than a century ago for observance of the distinctions in the evidential procedure in the trial and sentencing processes. For indeterminate sentences and probation have resulted in an increase in the discretionary powers exercised in fixing punishments. In general, these modern changes have not resulted in making the lot of offenders harder. On the contrary a strong motivating force for the changes has been the belief that by careful study of the lives and personalities of convicted offenders many could be less severely punished and restored sooner to complete freedom and useful citizenship. This belief to a large extent has been justified.

Under the practice of individualizing punishments, investigational techniques have been given an important role. Probation workers making reports of their investigations have not been trained to prosecute but to aid offenders. Their reports have been given a high value by conscientious judges who want to sentence persons on the best available information rather than on guesswork and inadequate information. To deprive sentencing judges of this kind of information would undermine modern penological procedural policies that have been cautiously adopted throughout the nation after careful consideration and experimentation. We must recognize that most of the information now relied upon by judges to guide them in the intelligent imposition of sentences would be unavailable if information were restricted to that given in open court by witnesses subject to cross-examination. And the modern probation report draws on information concerning every aspect of a defendant's life. The type and extent of this information make totally impractical if not impossible open court testimony with cross-examination. Such a procedure could endlessly delay criminal administration in a retrial of collateral issues.

The considerations we have set out admonish us against treating the due process clause as a uniform command that courts throughout the Nation abandon their age-old practice of seeking information from out-of-court sources to guide their judgment toward a more enlightened and just sentence. New York criminal statutes set wide limits for maximum and minimum sentences. Under New York statutes a state judge cannot escape his grave responsibility of fixing sentence. In determining whether a defendant shall receive a one-year minimum or a twenty-year maximum sentence, we do not think the Federal Constitution restricts the view of the sentencing judge to the information received in open court. The due process clause should not be treated as a device for freezing the evidential procedure of sentencing in the mold of trial procedure. So to treat the due process clause would hinder if not preclude all courts—state and federal—from making progressive efforts to improve the administration of criminal justice.

It is urged, however, that we should draw a constitutional distinction as to the procedure for obtaining information where the death sentence is imposed. We cannot accept the contention. Leaving a sentencing judge free to avail himself of out-of-court information in making such a fateful choice of sentences does secure to him a broad discretionary power, one susceptible of abuse. But in considering whether a rigid constitutional barrier should be created, it must be remembered that there is possibility of abuse wherever a judge must choose between life imprisonment and death. And it is conceded that no federal constitutional objection would have been possible if the judge here had sentenced appellant to death because appellant's trial manner impressed the judge that appellant was a bad risk for society, or if the judge had sentenced him to death giving no reason at all. We cannot say that the due process clause renders a sentence void merely because a judge gets additional out-of-court information to assist him in the exercise of this awesome power of imposing the death sentence.

Appellant was found guilty after a fairly conducted trial. His sentence followed a hearing conducted by the judge. Upon the judge's inquiry as to why sentence should not be imposed, the defendant made statements. His counsel made extended arguments. The case went to the highest court in the state, and that court had power to reverse for abuse of discretion or legal error in the imposition of the sentence. That court affirmed. We hold that appellant was not denied due process of law.[1]

. . .[2]

---

575. Look again at Rule 32, p. 1139 above. How much do its provisions reflect the policies enunciated in *Williams*? In what respects is the rule in its present form inconsistent with *Williams*? See also United States v. Burch, 873 F.2d 765 (5th Cir.1989), in which the court said that when Congress approved the Sentencing Guidelines, see p. 1138 above, it abandoned the philosophy of *Williams* that "the punishment should fit the offender and not merely the crime," p. 1150 above. The court said that the sentencing judge should not have considered the defendant's high level of education and socio-economic status as aggravating sentencing factors.

A majority of the Court of Appeals for the Eighth Circuit held, over a dissent, that adoption of the Sentencing Guidelines did not have the effect of making the Confrontation Clause applicable to sentencing proceedings. United States v. Wise, 976 F.2d 393 (8th Cir.1992). Although the Guidelines restricted the sentencing judge's discretion, it "has not so transformed the sentencing phase that it constitutes a separate criminal proceeding." Id. at 401. The dissenting opinion observed that both the philosophy and practice of sentencing had so changed since the decision in *Williams* that the conclusion to the contrary in that case was "obsolete." Id. at 409. The conclu-

---

1. What we have said is not to be accepted as a holding that the sentencing procedure is immune from scrutiny under the due process clause. See Townsend v. Burke, 334 U.S. 736.

[2] Justice Murphy wrote a dissenting opinion. Justice Rutledge noted his dissent.

sion in *Wise* was upheld in United States v. Silverman, 976 F.2d 1502 (6th Cir.1992) (en banc).

576. "Submission of the report to the court before [the defendant has pleaded guilty or been convicted] constitutes error of the clearest kind. . . . To permit the *ex parte* introduction of this sort of material to the judge who will pronounce the defendant's guilt or innocence or who will preside over a jury trial would seriously contravene the rule's purpose of preventing possible prejudice from premature submission of the presentence report." Gregg v. United States, 394 U.S. 489, 492 (1969).

577. 18 U.S.C. § 3661: "No limitation shall be placed on the information concerning the background, character, and conduct of a person convicted of an offense which a court of the United States may receive and consider for the purpose of imposing an appropriate sentence."

"[O]nce the guilt of the accused has been properly established, the sentencing judge, in determining the kind and extent of punishment to be imposed, is not restricted to evidence derived from the examination and cross-examination of witnesses in open court but may, consistently with the Due Process Clause of the Fourteenth Amendment, consider responsible unsworn or 'out-of-court' information relative to the circumstances of the crime and to the convicted person's life and characteristics." Williams v. Oklahoma, 358 U.S. 576, 584 (1959).

A sentencing court is not precluded under the federal Sentencing Guidelines from considering conduct of the defendant underlying charges of which he has been acquitted. United States v. Watts, 519 U.S. 148, (1997) (per curiam) (7–2). The Court noted that an acquittal of the criminal charge does not establish that the defendant did not engage in the conduct in question.

578. In Gardner v. Florida, 430 U.S. 349 (1977) (8–1), the court held that a sentence of death imposed in part on the basis of information in a presentence report that the defendant had no opportunity to contest was unconstitutional. Distinguishing its holding in Williams v. New York, p. 1148 above, the Court said that the death penalty had now been recognized by a majority of the Court as "a different kind of punishment than any other which may be imposed in this country." Id. at 357. Furthermore, the Court said, the application of requirements of due process to the sentencing procedure had been made clearer since *Williams* was decided. Id. at 358.

———

Specht v. Patterson

386 U.S. 605, 87 S.Ct. 1209, 18 L.Ed.2d 326 (1967).

■ MR. JUSTICE DOUGLAS delivered the opinion of the Court.

We held in Williams v. New York, 337 U.S. 241, that the Due Process Clause of the Fourteenth Amendment did not require a judge to have hearings and to give a convicted person an opportunity to participate in those hearings when he came to determine the sentence to be imposed. . . .

That was a case where at the end of the trial and in the same proceeding the fixing of the penalty for first degree murder was involved—whether life imprisonment or death.

The question is whether the rule of the *Williams* case applies to this Colorado case where petitioner, having been convicted for indecent liberties under one Colorado statute that carries a maximum sentence of 10 years (Colo.Rev.Stat.Ann. § 40–2–32 (1963)) but not sentenced under it, may be sentenced under the Sex Offenders Act, Colo.Rev.Stat.Ann. §§ 39–19–1 to 10 (1963), for an indeterminate term of from one day to life without notice and full hearing. . . .

The Sex Offenders Act may be brought into play if the trial court "is of the opinion that any . . . person [convicted of specified sex offenses], if at large, constitutes a threat of bodily harm to members of the public, or is an habitual offender and mentally ill." § 1. He then becomes punishable for an indeterminate term of from one day to life on the following conditions as specified in § 2:

"(2) A complete psychiatric examination shall have been made of him by the psychiatrists of the Colorado psychopathic hospital or by psychiatrists designated by the district court; and

"(3) A complete written report thereof submitted to the district court. Such report shall contain all facts and findings, together with recommendations as to whether or not the person is treatable under the provisions of this article; whether or not the person should be committed to the Colorado state hospital or to the state home and training schools as mentally ill or mentally deficient. Such report shall also contain the psychiatrist's opinion as to whether or not the person could be adequately supervised on probation."

This procedure was followed in petitioner's case; he was examined as required and a psychiatric report prepared and given to the trial judge prior to the sentencing. But there was no hearing in the normal sense, no right of confrontation and so on.

Petitioner insists that this procedure does not satisfy due process because it allows the critical finding to be made under § 1 of the Sex Offenders Act (1) without a hearing at which the person so convicted may confront and cross-examine adverse witnesses and present evidence of his own by use of compulsory process, if necessary; and (2) on the basis of hearsay evidence to which the person involved is not allowed access.

We adhere to Williams v. New York, supra; but we decline the invitation to extend it to this radically different situation. These commitment proceedings whether denominated civil or criminal are subject both to the Equal Protection Clause of the Fourteenth Amendment . . . and to the Due Process Clause. We hold that the requirements of due process were not satisfied here.

The Sex Offenders Act does not make the commission of a specified crime the basis for sentencing. It makes one conviction the basis for commencing another proceeding under another Act to determine whether a person constitutes a threat of bodily harm to the public, or is an habitual offender and mentally ill. That is a new finding of fact . . . that was not an ingredient of the offense charged. The punishment under the second Act is criminal punishment even though it is designed not so much as retribution as it is to keep individuals from inflicting future harm. . . .

. . .

. . . Under Colorado's criminal procedure, here challenged, the invocation of the Sex Offenders Act means the making of a new charge leading to criminal punishment. The case is not unlike those under recidivist statutes where an habitual criminal issue is "a distinct issue" (Graham v. West Virginia, 224 U.S. 616, 625) on which a defendant "must receive reasonable notice and an opportunity to be heard." Oyler v. Boles, 368 U.S. 448, 452 . . . . Due process, in other words, requires that he be present with counsel, have an opportunity to be heard, be confronted with witnesses against him, have the right to cross-examine, and to offer evidence of his own. And there must be findings adequate to make meaningful any appeal that is allowed. . . . None of these procedural safeguards we have mentioned is present under Colorado's Sex Offenders Act. We therefore hold that it is deficient in due process as measured by the requirements of the Fourteenth Amendment. . . .

. . . [3]

---

579. Specht v. Patterson was distinguished in McMillan v. Pennsylvania, 477 U.S. 79 (1986) (5–4), in which the Court upheld a state statute providing that a person convicted of specified felonies is subject to a mandatory minimum sentence of five years imprisonment, if the sentencing judge finds by a preponderance of the evidence that he "visibly possessed a firearm" while committing the crime. The statute " 'ups the ante' " for the

[3] Justice Harlan noted his agreement with the Court's conclusions, on different premises.

defendant, the Court said, but does not radically alter the sentencing procedure, as did the Colorado procedure at issue in *Specht.* Id. at 89. (The Court concluded also that possession of a firearm was not an element of the offense, requiring proof beyond a reasonable doubt, under *In re Winship,* note 545 p. 1106 above.)

580. Townsend v. Burke, 334 U.S. 736 (1948), which the Court cited in Williams v. New York, p. 1148 above, 337 U.S. at 252 n.18, held that the uncounseled defendant's sentence, based on "assumptions concerning his criminal record which were materially untrue" denied him due process of law. "[I]t is the careless or designed pronouncement of sentence on a foundation so extensively and materially false, which the prisoner had no opportunity to correct by the services which counsel would provide, that renders the proceedings lacking in due process." Id. at 741.

"[A] defendant must be permitted to state his version of the facts to the court; where the possibility of reliance on misinformation is shown, this right must be extended to permit that presentation by the defendant which will enable the sentencing judge to grasp the relevant facts correctly. . . . In appropriate circumstances, this may mean that a defendant will be permitted to submit affidavits or documents, supply oral statements, or even participate in an evidentiary hearing; alternatively, further corroboration of sentencing data may be required. And while in such cases the procedure to be followed lies within the sound discretion of the sentencing judge, a court's failure to take appropriate steps to ensure the fairness and accuracy of the sentencing process must be held to be plain error and an abuse of that discretion.

"Presentence reports, prepared by probation officers for use at sentencing, often call for an exercise of the Court's discretion in this regard. The contents of the reports are not subject to the rules of evidence, and experience has shown that they are heavily relied upon by sentencing judges. Accuracy is therefore of prime concern. Reflecting this concern, defendants have been given increasingly greater access to presentence reports in order to point out inaccuracies. Rule 32(c)(3)(A) [now Rule 32(b)(6)(A)] mandates disclosure of the report—save for any sentence recommendation—upon request of the defendant; disclosure may be withheld only if rehabilitation of the defendant will be thereby jeopardized, or harm is likely to result to the defendant or others.

"To enable a defendant to effectively present his version of the facts to the court by pointing out inaccuracies in the presentence report, we have held that a defendant must be given adequate time to prepare and present a rebuttal to information which he contests. . . ." United States v. Robin, 545 F.2d 775, 779–80 (2d Cir.1976). To the same effect, see, e.g., United States v. Espinoza, 481 F.2d 553 (5th Cir.1973). See generally United States v. Woody, 567 F.2d 1353, 1357–64 (5th Cir.1978).

The requirement of Rule 32(c)(1), formerly Rule 32(c)(3)(D), that the trial judge indicate in writing his resolution of controverted material in the presentence report is discussed in United States v. Fernandez-Angulo, 897 F.2d 1514 (9th Cir.1990). Noting that there was a split in the circuits on the issue, the court held: "[W]hen the defendant challenges the factual accuracy of any matters contained in the presentence report, the district court must, at the time of sentencing, make the findings or determinations required by Rule 32. If the district court fails to make the required findings or determinations, the sentence must be vacated and the defendant resentenced." Id. at 1516. Failure to append to the presentence report a statement of the findings or determinations, as the rule requires, is only a "technical error," the court said, which does not require resentencing. Id. at 1517.

581. Other criminal conduct. Rule 32(b)(4)(A) provides that the presentence report shall contain the defendant's criminal record. The report commonly includes not only a record of convictions but also information about arrests, pending charges, and criminal activity generally. In United States v. Weston, 448 F.2d 626, 634 (9th Cir.1971), the court held that the sentencing judge had improperly relied on information from the government sources about the defendant's deep involvement in narcotics traffic, which the defendant denied and which had too little indication of dependability. "A rational penal system must have some concern for the probable accuracy of the informational inputs in the sentencing process." Id. at 634.

The court held that pending indictments recited in a presentence report and mentioned by the sentencing judge could be considered, in United States v. Metz, 470 F.2d 1140 (3d Cir.1972). "The fact that the other criminal activity has not been passed on by a court should not be controlling, for 'of necessity, much of the information garnered by the probation officer will be hearsay and will doubtless be discounted accordingly, *but the very object of the process is scope.*' United States v. Doyle, 348 F.2d [715 (2d Cir.1965)] at 721. (Emphasis added). In fact, the kind of evidence here objected to is more reliable than the hearsay evidence which the sentencing judge can clearly consider, for unlike hearsay, the indictments are based on testimony given under oath and required the existence of probable cause to believe that [the defendant] had committed the other offenses.

"We believe that the probable trustworthiness of information concerning other criminal charges is far more significant than the procedural stages of the other charges. United States v. Sweig, 454 F.2d 181 (2d Cir.1972), held that the sentencing judge could properly consider evidence with respect to crimes of which the defendant had been *acquitted. Sweig* turns on the reliability of the evidence considered, for the evidence 'was given under oath and was subject to cross-examination and the judge had the opportunity for personal observation of the witnesses.' 454 F.2d at 184. . . .

". . . We hold that indictments for other criminal activity are of sufficient reliability to warrant their consideration by a sentencing judge." 470 F.2d at 1142.

A convicted defendant's refusal without adequate explanation to cooperate with officials investigating a criminal conspiracy in which he was an admitted participant may properly be considered as a factor in the determination of his sentence. Roberts v. United States, 445 U.S. 552 (1980) (8–1).

A sentence may not, however, be based on prior convictions that are constitutionally invalid because of the denial of counsel. United States v. Tucker, 404 U.S. 443 (1972). A conviction for a misdemeanor without the assistance of counsel that was valid when entered, because no sentence of imprisonment was imposed (see Scott v. Illinois, 440 U.S. 367 (1979), note 292 p. 558 above) may, however, be the basis for sentence enhancement following a subsequent conviction. Nichols v. United States, 511 U.S. 738 (1994) (6–3).

In Curtis v. United States, 511 U.S. 485 (1994) (6–3), the Court held that a defendant sentenced in federal court does not have a constitutional right to attack collaterally the validity of a prior state conviction used as the ground for enhancement of the federal sentence, unless the attack is based on the alleged denial of his right to counsel. *Curtis* involved the sentence-enhancement provision of the Armed Career Criminal Act of 1984, 18 U.S.C. § 924(e). The Court concluded that, unlike some of the other sentence-enhancement provisions that authorize collateral attack on a conviction used for enhancement, the ACCA provision does not, and that the Constitution requires that such attack be allowed only with respect to the right to counsel.

582. In United States v. Grayson, 438 U.S. 41 (1978) (6–3), the Court held that it is permissible for the trial judge, when imposing sentence, to take into account the defendant's observed false testimony at trial. "A defendant's truthfulness or mendacity while testifying on his own behalf, almost without exception, has been deemed probative of his attitudes toward society and prospects for rehabilitation and hence relevant to sentencing." Id. at 50. Responding to the argument that such a rule might inhibit a defendant from testifying truthfully, the Court said that it was not imposing a rigid rule that sentences of defendants who testify falsely be enhanced. "Rather, we are reaffirming the authority of a sentencing judge to evaluate carefully a defendant's testimony on the stand, determine—with a consciousness of the frailty of human judgment—whether that testimony contained willful and material falsehoods, and, if so, assess in light of all the other knowledge gained about the defendant the meaning of that conduct with respect to his prospects for rehabilitation and restoration to a useful place in society." Id. at 55.

Federal Sentencing Guideline § 3C1.1 provides for enhancement of the sentence of a defendant who, by committing perjury, obstructs the administration of justice. In United States v. Dunnigan, 507 U.S. 87 (1993), the Court upheld the provision against the challenge that it undermines a defendant's right to testify. The Court said that "if a defendant objects to a sentence enhancement resulting from her trial testimony, a district court must review the evidence and make independent findings necessary to establish a wilful impediment to or obstruction of justice, or an attempt to do the same." Id. at 95.

583. Courts have generally held that evidence inadmissible at trial because of a violation of the defendant's Fourth Amendment rights may nevertheless be considered by the trial judge at sentencing. E.g., United States v. Lynch, 934 F.2d 1226 (11th Cir.1991); United States v. Lee, 540 F.2d 1205 (4th Cir.1976); United States v. Schipani, 435 F.2d 26 (2d Cir.1970). "Both the sentencing court and the post-sentencing administrative agencies are entitled to know all of the facts, including prior alleged offenses that did not result in a conviction. They are, of course, limited to a consideration of information that is accurate, but they are not precluded from considering prior charges that were dismissed or alleged offenses for which charges were not filed because of illegally obtained evidence." United States v. Graves, 785 F.2d 870, 876 (10th Cir.1986) (additional cases cited). Cf. United States v. Hernandez Camacho, 779 F.2d 227 (5th Cir.1985) (sentencing judge may consider defendant's testimony at hearing on motion to suppress evidence). But cf. Verdugo v. United States, 402 F.2d 599 (9th Cir.1968), holding that illegally obtained evidence could not be used at sentencing, where the purpose of the search was to obtain evidence that would increase the defendant's sentence: "[W]here . . . the use of illegally seized evidence at sentencing would provide a substantial incentive for unconstitutional searches and seizures, that evidence should be disregarded by the sentencing judge." Id. at 613. *Verdugo* is discussed and qualified in United States v. Kim, 25 F.3d 1426 (9th Cir.1994).

UNITED STATES DISTRICT COURT FOR THE DISTRICT OF COLUMBIA PRESENTENCE REPORT[4]

I OFFENSE:

On January 29, 1968, at the conclusion of an eight day jury trial, before the Honorable Frank Solomon, defendant Reddish and codefendants Scott A. Scarlet, Albert Maroon, Jr. and Roy Ruby were found guilty of counts one to twelve, inclusive. Count one charges the four defendants with

---

4. This presentence report is based on an actual case; it was prepared for use at an Executive Meeting of the Judicial Council for the District of Columbia Circuit in November 1968. Names have been changed.

Unauthorized Use of an Automobile, on or about November 15, 1966, which belonged to Richard A. Thomas. Count two charges, on November 22, 1966, the entry of the Brookland Branch of The National Bank of Washington, FDIC insured, with intent to commit a robbery. Counts three, five, seven, nine, and eleven, cite the Federal charge of actual Bank Robbery of monies in the possession of said bank, in the aggregate total of $15,308.32; counts four, six, eight, ten, and twelve cite the D.C. Criminal Code charge of Robbery. Defendant Reddish was named in the thirteenth count of the indictment, charged with Carrying a Dangerous Weapon, pistol, however, this charge was dismissed during trial on the oral motion of the Government.

Official Version:

Your Honor undoubtedly remains familiar with the facts and testimony offered during the jury trial of this case. A brief review, however, is offered. Approximately only minutes to 9:55 a.m., November 22, 1966, three Negro male subjects, wearing masks over their faces, also armed with pistols, entered the Brookland Branch of The National Bank of Washington, D.C., 3006—12th Street, N.E. and announced a bank robbery: "All right folks, this is it, get on the floor!" Two of the subjects hurdled the counter in front of the teller cages and started grabbing all available monies from the respective teller cages. The aggregate sum of $15,308.02 was seized by subjects and placed in bank money bags. When an automobile horn sounded outside, more or less as a signal, the three original subjects then fled the bank and entered an awaiting 1965 Ford Mustang car, last seen to speed away on Perry Street, N.E. The bank manager and a teller pushed the alarm button; also, they and a private citizen outside of the bank managed to note the license number of the fleeing Mustang, which was later conveyed to responding police officers. The official time of the robbery was established as at 9:55 a.m.

Within minutes of the reported robbery, cruising police officers spotted the aforementioned, aforedescribed Mustang car parked in the 1300 block of Perry Street, N.E., only a few blocks away from the scene of the bank robbery. A black, automatic loaded pistol, plus rolls of coins and paper money, were found and recovered from the aforementioned car. A quick canvass of nearby houses resulted in one witness telling the police officers that a small U-Haul truck had been parked in front of her residence at 1324 Perry Street since about 9:30 a.m.; also, the witness stated that she heard the same truck suddenly speed away at a high rate of speed, at about 10 a.m. A lookout was immediately broadcast for the U-Haul truck; several minutes later, the same truck was observed and stopped by police officers in the 1000 block of Kenilworth Avenue, N.E. After the police officers stopped the aforementioned truck, the driver, later identified as defendant Ernest Reddish, alighted from the driver's side of the truck. As he and the police officers approached one another, the latter observed a pistol handle protruding from subject's pants pocket; also, the officers glimpsed two subjects quickly looking out of the rear window of the truck and suddenly duck down. Defendant Reddish was immediately placed under arrest and a .38 caliber loaded pistol was seized from his pocket. Upon looking into the truck and observing three Negro subjects lying on the floor, the police officers immediately radioed for assistance, at the same time, ordered the three subjects not to move. Upon the arrival of police assistance, the three subjects were ordered from the truck and were immediately placed under arrest. A search of the truck resulted in the recovery of two cloth bank bags containing $14,911.00 in money, also, a (third) pistol, which one of the subjects had dropped as he emerged from the truck; further, a pair of sunglasses, silk handkerchiefs (used to cover their faces as masks) and four pairs of gloves were recovered, all or most of which had been used in the robbery. A personal search of codefendant Ruby's person resulted in the recovery of $320 in bills, which was identified as "bait" money taken during the robbery. A total of $15,297.00 in money was recovered, respectively, from the 1965 Mustang, the truck and from codefendant Ruby; $11.32 apparently was not recovered. After being arrested at 10:19 a.m. and charged with the instant bank robbery-holdup, the four defendants were transported to the Robbery Squad Office, where all four subjects denied the offense. In a subsequent lineup, the bank manager and other witnesses from inside the bank apparently could not be sure of any identification. On the other hand, a private citizen witness, who observed the robbery taking place as she entered the bank but managed to walk outside whereupon she observed the awaiting 1965 Mustang, parked in front of the bank and was able to look at the Negro driver behind the wheel, viewed the same lineup, and identified codefendant, Scott A. Scarlet, as the one she saw behind the wheel and who drove the other subjects away from the hold-up scene.

Intense investigation by both local police and FBI Agents resulted in the uncovering of the fact that the instant truck had been rented by one Alex Alexander, an uncle of defendant Reddish. He informed interrogating officers that he had rented the truck at the request of defendant Reddish and had turned same over to him; the latter had given him $25.00 with which to do so. Mr. Alexander also stated that the license tags found on the instant Mustang had come from a Dodge vehicle which had been given to Reddish and himself to repair and personally use. Alexander denied any knowledge of the intended use of the truck, or about the bank robbery. In subsequent contact with FBI Agents, he identified codefendant Maroon and defendant Reddish as close, long-term friends. As to the pieces of clothing recovered from the floor of the truck—a green raincoat, (2) black kerchiefs, (3) pillow cases, (4) multi-colored scarfs—most were identified by bank tellers—witnesses, as having been worn by the hold-up subjects.

Your Honor is apprised of subsequent aggravating, additional information, that on February 11, 1967, while on bond in CC # 000–67, the defendant was arrested in a new case charging assault on two police officers and Carrying a Dangerous Weapon, gun. The new case is represented in CC # 500–67, which is scheduled for trial during the week of February 12, 1968. Also, while on bond in CC # 000–67, and CC # 500–67 the defendant was arrested on November 18, 1967 charged with two counts of Assault with a Dangerous Weapon, gun, now represented in # 00–68, for which no trial date has been scheduled. Subject secured his release on bond ($10,000) in CC # 00–68, on December 5, 1967.

II DEFENDANT'S VERSION OF OFFENSE:

In the writer's presentence interview with this defendant, he advised that he did not take the witness stand during his trial. He denied any knowledge of the bank robbery. He immediately elaborated that he was planning to move from his residence and was looking for a place to rent, also, a garage to rent to store excess furniture. He stated that he had been searching in the area of Rhode Island Avenue and Monroe Street, N.E., and eventually turned into an alley paralleling 13th and 12th Streets, N.E., off Newton Street, N.E. Here, he says he saw a mattress waiting to be picked up by the trash people. It looked relatively in good condition, and he thought he would examine same closely. He says he left his parked truck, and, after looking at the mattress, picked it up and carried it back to the truck. When he threw the mattress in the back of the truck, he then claimed finding National Bank of Washington bank bags, containing a very large sum of money. After examining the money, also, noting that no one was around, he said he got "hungry" and took off, "asking no questions".

He then indicated coming upon codefendant Maroon, who was standing on a corner with Ruby and Scarlet. He stopped the truck and Maroon and the other two subjects entered the truck. He indicated only that this was on Kenilworth Avenue near the Benning Road viaduct. After pulling away from the curb, the police came up from behind him and pulled him over. "Only I knew what was up front (meaning the money bags)", . . . "I decided not to say anything to the police". He concluded his version by denying, again, having any knowledge of the bank robbery, or anything else as to how the money bags from the robbery got into his truck.

The defendant offered the foregoing in a very explicit matter-of-fact manner, without any overt concern for his predicament, or remorse for the case itself. What concern was expressed, and perhaps in a manner to entice some sympathy in his behalf, centered around frequent references made to his wife and children and their welfare. He impressed the writer as very sophisticated, also adept at concealing inner feelings of hostility, particularly centered around the police.

III PRIOR RECORD:

| 3–11–58 | Unauthorized Use of Vehicle | Probation, indefinite. |

The defendant was apprehended while riding, with three other juveniles, in a stolen car. On March 21, 1958, Judge Wise of D.C. Juvenile Court placed him on indefinite probation supervision.

| 4–26–58 | Unauthorized Use of Vehicle | Sentenced to National Training School for Boys. |

Within five weeks after being placed on juvenile probation supervision in the above case, the defendant was arrested as the driver of a stolen car which had been rented by a doctor. Facts indicate he led the police on a high speed chase, which ended in a collision and more than $1,000 damages inflicted on the stolen automobile. On April 29, 1958, he was found involved in D.C. Juvenile Court, who immediately ordered him committed to the National Training School for Boys under a minority commitment. . . . The defendant made a satisfactory adjustment while at the National Training School and gained his release on parole on June 20, 1959.

| 11–7–59(17) | Assault with Dangerous Weapon (Shod foot) | No disposition indicated. |

The defendant was arrested with several other youths and charged with assaulting two young victims, one of whom the defendant kicked while lying on the ground. As a result of the arrest and circumstances surrounding same, the Youth Division of the U.S. Board of Parole issued a parole violation warrant, ordering his return to the National Training School.

| 11–30–59 | Parole Violation Warrant | Returned to National Training School for Boys, effective 1–20. |

| 4–8–60 | Escape from National Training School | |

Adult:

| 2–2–61 | Affray | Consolidated records, Dept. of Prisons, Raleigh, N.C. | 30 days jail |

| 9–15–61 | Assault with Dangerous Weapon | " " " " " " | Two years |

Circumstances surrounding this arrest and two year sentence presently remain unknown. The FBI Report, however, indicated the defendant escaped on October 11, 1961, only to be recaptured on the following day, October 12, 1961.

| 10–25–62 | Escape | Consolidated Records, Dept. of Prisons, Raleigh, N.C. | Three months added to the two year sentence. |

| 5–23–66 Washington, D.C. | Carrying a Dangerous Weapon, Pistol | | ISS, probation— one year |

The arrest facts indicate a man entered a High's Dairy Store in northeast Washington, and announced a robbery by stating, "Give me all the money in your pocket", whereupon he displayed a pistol in his pants pocket. When a second female clerk suddenly emerged from the rear of the store, the man hastily said, "I'm only kidding, I'm not going to shoot you"; he then walked out of the store. The police responded to the scene, obtained a description of the suspect, and shortly afterward, came upon three young adults, including this defendant, one who matched the description of the suspect. All three suspects were searched. Police seized a loaded .38 caliber Empire State revolver, containing five rounds, from the person of defendant Reddish. A .38 caliber revolver was seized from a second subject—Lew E. Wood, who was identified as the suspect who had entered the High's Store and announced the robbery attempt. The third suspect—Pat A. Kidd, was identified as a strong suspect in a different robbery holdup violation. . . . After a presentence investigation the defendant was placed on probation, on August 18, 1967. The writer has reviewed the probation department file in D.C. Court of General Sessions; no indication was reflected in the file as to the issuance of a probation violation warrant in their case, based on the defendant's arrest and/or conviction in CC # 000–67.

11–22–66	Bank Robbery (Holdup)	Instant Case CC # 000–67
2–11–67	Assault on Police Officers (2) Carrying Dangerous Weapon, Gun	Indicted in CC # 500–67

As previously mentioned, while on bond in the instant case, on February 11, 1967, about 4:20 p.m., police officers observed the defendant in a 1966 Chevelle automobile with four other subjects. When the police officer (Moore) approached and asked the defendant for his operator's license, the police officer also observed one subject to push a paper bag under the car seat, but not before the officer had observed a pistol barrel protruding from the bag. When Officer Moore sought to obtain possession of the gun, defendant Reddish is said to have instigated an assault on the officer. When the officer's partner (Flynn) responded, a second occupant of the car, James Jamison, 21, intercepted and yoked Officer Flynn into unconsciousness. When Jamison continued to assault the unconscious officer, Officer Moore shot Jamison, necessitating his removal to a hospital. A third off-duty police officer assisted Officer Moore to subdue and maintain Reddish's arrest. Also, codefendant Maroon, who had been an original occupant of the car, stepped from the gathered crowd and began assaulting both police officers in an attempt to free this defendant Reddish. However, Maroon was subdued and his arrest also effected. Additional facts indicate that four guns (one an automatic pistol), two ski masks, gloves and clotheslines were seized as evidence from the aforementioned car. Reddish, Jamison and codefendant Maroon have been named in a three count indictment in CC # 500–67, which is scheduled for trial during the week of February 21, 1968.

11–18–67	Assault with Dangerous Weapon, Gun	Indicted in CC # 00–68.

Arrest facts indicate the police responded to a report that Joseph and Jane Johnson, husband and wife, were shot in front of their home at 1000 Curry Avenue, S.E., by means of a gun held in the hands of this defendant. The defendant has now been indicted, however, a trial date has not been scheduled.

IV FAMILY HISTORY:

This defendant was born in Whiteville, Columbus County, North Carolina on August 9, 1942, and was brought to Washington, D.C. by his mother when approximately three or four years of age. He is the oldest of two boys of his natural parents, Ernest and Chellin, nee Redd, Reddish, who are respectively said to be about 50 and 45 years of age. The defendant has advised us he never knew his real father. However, after the birth of his younger brother, James, now 23, and serving in the Army in Vietnam, his mother "took to living in a common-law type marriage" with a Manuel Reddish, 52, whom he calls his stepfather, a chef cook, whom he understands to be his father's natural uncle. Subsequently, four children, two half-brothers and two half-sisters of the defendant, 18 to 13 years of age, resulted from the illicit relationship of the stepfather and mother. About five years ago, the defendant said his stepfather finally separated from his mother, due to the mother's problems with alcoholism. The stepfather now has custody of the four children. The defendant indicated the stepfather's address is known only as a corner house at 8th and W Streets, S.W., his mother is said to be "living with another man", somewhere in the vicinity of 3rd and F Streets, N.E.

The defendant described his early home life, aside from material needs and food being plentiful, as a poor and an unhappy one. He indicated the family frequently moved from one place to another, hardly ever remained in one house for more than one year, and primarily due to his mother's alcoholism problem, wherein she mismanaged financial affairs to cater to her problem. The defendant also indicated his parents argued frequently and became embroiled in actual altercations. The defendant says his relationship with his mother was "only fair" whereas he denied having a satisfactory relationship with the stepfather. From this point, the defendant went on to discuss his past social-legal difficulties and ascribed same as due to the lack of a decent home, the lack of interest and failure to provide proper supervision by his parents, thus, the desire to escape from the "unpleasantness of it all."

Past social, institutional records substantiate a very poor social-familial background, that the parents were seemingly concerned primarily with their own personal pursuits and were inadequate as stable, suitable parental figures. Several of the children have been known to local social-legal agencies; the defendant's half-brother, John Toney, 14, is presently a ward of the local welfare department's child-welfare division, confined at the Cedar Knoll Institution at the D.C. Children's Center.

The defendant has, more or less, been on his own since his initial commitment to the National Training School for Boys at fifteen years of age. While he appeared deliberately guarded about saying anything about leaving the District for North Carolina, or about his confinement period in North Carolina State Penal Institutions, he did claim he entered marriage in 1963 upon his return to the District, and has subsequently sought to live a relatively stable life.

V MARITAL HISTORY:

The defendant married Yvette May Oates, now 22, on September 28, 1963, in a religious ceremony in a private house in the District (verified). The defendant says he met his wife during the period after escaping from the National Training School and before "lighting out for North Carolina", by which time he had caused his future wife to conceive their first child. The two parties now have four children: Chalmers (DOB: 1–22–61); Wanda Pansy (DOB: 6–3–64); Ernest IV (DOB: 3–25–66) and Doretta (DOB:

5–13–67). The defendant professed having great interest in his wife and children and claims his prime concern is the life now centered around providing for his family as to a decent home, something which he missed in his own early background. His wife was interviewed, however, she was not able to talk freely, due to a dental infection. She did, however, profess love for the defendant, claims he is a good father and a good husband. The wife is not employed, nor expects to be. She says she will turn to public assistance should her husband be committed to jail in the instant case. Otherwise, during the writer's discussion of the offense with the defendant, the wife remained silent.

VI HOME AND NEIGHBORHOOD:

Since October 1967, the defendant and his wife and family have been living in a National Capitol Housing Authority row house, which contains three bedrooms, for which they are paying $52 per month rent. From January to October 1967, the family lived in a rented, small crowded one bedroom apartment on Dorchester Lane, S.E.; from December 5, 1964 to January 1967, the family occupied a basement apartment at 3192 Anacostia Avenue, S.E., from which they were evicted when the owner claimed he wanted the entire house for his own family. Prior thereto, it would appear the defendant and his family frequently moved about the southeast and northeast sections of the District, in unstable, crowded living situations, predominantly in lower class neighborhoods noted for high crime rates.

VII EDUCATION:

The defendant last attended Eliot Junior High School, where he was repeating the ninth grade before being committed to the National Training School for Boys. His public school record reflects poor grades, mostly D's and/or failing marks. It is interesting that at the National Training School, the defendant seemingly attended to his academic studies sufficient to have completed eleventh grade level courses. Intelligence examinations at the training school reflected an I.Q. of 83, considered low-average academic intelligence; one psychologist viewed the defendant as having the potential for above-average intellectual performance ability. At the National Training School, the defendant also received some vocational training in auto mechanics, in which field he was described as having favorable potentials. This defendant has impressed the writer as functioning on or about a tenth or eleventh grade social-intellectual level, yet to be highly sophisticated in criminal activities.

VIII RELIGION:

The defendant professes the Baptist faith, but admits he rarely attends church. His conscious concern towards religious values, as a way of life, appears very nil.

IX INTERESTS AND LEISURE TIME ACTIVITIES:

The defendant says his primary leisure time activities and interests center around boxing, swimming and auto drag racing.

X HEALTH:

This defendant stands 5'9", and says he weighs 200 pounds. He appears very dark brown skinned in complexion and evidences an old vertical scar on his left temple. He claims good physical health; he says he suffered a dislocated right hip while at the National Training School, which resulted in six months hospitalization, however, he denies any subsequent after effects. He describes himself as a social drinker, denies alcohol to be a problem.

During the presentence interview, the defendant was viewed as free from any signs of disturbing personality problems. He evidenced himself to be very fluent and tried to be very persuasive in relating his version of the offense. However, the greater impression is that of a young adult, who, though overtly appearing docile, is quite sophisticated in talking with people in authority. Past impressions of other professional workers and trained specialists describe this defendant as having an extensive suppressed feeling of hostility, particularly towards people in positions of authority. He has also been described as quick to react in antisocial, aggressive behavior. His amenability to personal counselling is questioned by this writer; his response to same would undoubtedly be superficial, without a sincere desire to emotionally integrate counselling.

XI EMPLOYMENT:

October 1967 to December 1967, three months: The defendant says he has been employed as a laborer for the General Construction Company, 1200 Congress Street, S.E. Verification was not made; it is interesting to note that the defendant was confined in the D.C. Jail from November 18, 1967 until December 5, 1967, as a consequence of his arrest in CC # 00–68, on the foregoing date. Subsequent employment has been intermittent due to weather conditions.

May 1967 to October 1967, five months: The defendant worked at the Terry Auto Body Shop in the rear of 1450 R. Street, N.W. under a work and training program funded through the D.C. Department of Public Welfare.

March 1964 to November 22, 1966, 32 months: The defendant worked as a truck-driver air-compressor operator for the Bell Air Compressor Rental Company. This company rented out air compressor trucks to construction contractors. His employment earnings varied between $75 to $100 per week, dependent upon the demand for such rental service.

September 1963 to December 1963, four months: Scott General Contractors employed the defendant as a laborer during the foregoing period until the job expired.

Verification of past employment was established at the three latter employers. The writer was advised that the defendant has the ability to be a satisfactory worker, though occasional absenteeism was noted. This writer is impressed with a fairly satisfactory employment record on the part of the defendant. The defendant also indicated he has augmented regular daytime employment, particularly wintertime employment when working conditions are limited, by working part-time and evening jobs, primarily those requiring a delivery truck-driver.

XII MILITARY SERVICE:

The defendant does not have active military service. He has registered with the Selective Service Board No. 24 in Whiteville, Columbus County, North Carolina (SS # 00 00 00 000). He says his draft classification is 4–F, due to his criminal record.

XIII FINANCIAL CONDITION:

The defendant denies any assets. He says he possesses a 1965 Pontiac automobile, which he has a time payment contract on, with $1,000 outstanding. The instant car, according to the defendant, was to be surrendered during the week of February 5, 1968. The defendant denied any other outstanding obligations.

XIV EVALUATIVE SUMMARY:

This 25 year old married defendant stands convicted of multiple charges involving a holdup bank robbery, for which he faces sentencing along with three codefendants. Remorse for his actions and/or concern for his present predicament appears lacking. He has established a substantial criminal record, before and subsequent to the instant offense. Such a record portrays an individual who is completely defiant of the law and order and the well-being of others in society. In addition to the instant offense, he still faces trial on multiple charges of assaulting police officers and carrying dangerous weapons (guns); also, a second trial remains pending, which involves an assault with a dangerous weapon, again, a gun.

The defendant is the unfortunate product of parents who were ill-equipped and, least of all, personally-socially adequate for handling the responsibilities of such a role; whose home situation was deprived and least conducive to providing happiness, the proper preparations and motivations for eventually developing into a decent, meaningful member of society. The converse has been the reaction; negative inner feelings of hostility and anti-social, aggressive behavior have developed and long smoldered, finally erupting, within the past year, particularly into acts revealing the severe potential for violence.

The Court is dealing with a defendant who, overtly, appears docile and passive, yet who is now manifesting a manner of sophistication which was concealed or masked, a type of individual society needs least. His amenability for responding to corrective treatment techniques would seemingly offer a poor prognosis. If treatment is to have any potential, corrective measures would certainly have to be employed over a substantial duration in a controlled environmental situation.

Respectfully submitted,

Chief U.S. Probation Officer

By:

U.S. Probation Officer

584. Disclosure of the contents of a presentence report to third persons is discussed in United States v. Charmer Indus., Inc., 711 F.2d 1164 (2d Cir.1983). The defendant, a corporation, was convicted in the federal district court in New York of antitrust violations. A presentence report was prepared to assist the court in determining the amount of the fine. The report was later used by an Arizona state agency in connection with a licensing proceeding involving the defendant's subsidiary. Observing that a presentence report has "many of the characteristics—and frailties—of material presented to a grand jury," the court concluded "that the district court should not authorize disclosure of a presentence report to a third person in the absence of a compelling demonstration that disclosure of the report is required to meet the ends of justice." Id. at 1175. Other cases are cited. But see United States v. Schlette, 842 F.2d 1574 (9th Cir.1988) (disclosure of dead defendant's presentence report to newspaper and to estate of person whom defendant had killed was justified).

585. Sentence following retrial. In North Carolina v. Pearce, 395 U.S. 711 (1969), the Court held that a defendant whose conviction is set aside and who is subsequently retried and convicted must be given credit for the portion of the first sentence already served, but that there is no constitutional bar to the imposition of a new sentence more severe than that originally imposed, on the basis of "events subsequent to the first trial."[5]

"To say that there exists no absolute constitutional bar to the imposition of a more severe sentence upon retrial is not, however, to end the inquiry. There remains for consideration the impact of the Due Process Clause of the Fourteenth Amendment.

5. The requirement that the defendant be given credit for the portion of the original sentence already served was based on the Double Jeopardy Clause. See note 609 p. 1224 below. With respect to the imposition of a more severe sentence following retrial, the Court rejected arguments based on the Double Jeopardy Clause and the Equal Protection Clause of the Fourteenth Amendment: "The [equal protection] theory advanced is that, since convicts who do not seek new trials cannot have their sentences increased, it creates an invidious classification to impose that risk only upon those who succeed in getting their original convictions set aside. The argument, while not lacking in ingenuity, cannot withstand close examination. In the first place, we deal here not with increases in existing sentences, but with the imposition of wholly new sentences after wholly new trials. Putting that conceptual nicety to one side, however, the problem before us simply cannot be rationally dealt with in terms of 'classifications.' A man who is retried after his first conviction has been set aside may be acquitted. If convicted, he may receive a shorter sentence, he may receive the same sentence, or he may receive a longer sentence than the one originally imposed. The result may depend upon a particular combination of infinite variables peculiar to each individual trial. It simply cannot be said that a State has invidiously 'classified' those who successfully seek new trials, any more than that the State has invidiously 'classified' those prisoners whose convictions are *not* set aside by denying the members of that group the opportunity to be acquitted. To fit the problem of this case into an equal protection framework is a task too Procrustean to be rationally accomplished." 395 U.S. at 722–23.

(Rev. 6/90)

**UNITED STATES DISTRICT COURT
DISTRICT OF MASSACHUSETTS**

UNITED STATES OF AMERICA

        V.

CRIMINAL NO._____

_____

        Defendant

**MEMORANDUM OF SENTENCING HEARING
AND
REPORT OF STATEMENT OF REASONS**

_____**D.J.**

       Counsel and the defendant were present for sentencing hearing on_____. The matters set forth were reviewed and considered. The reasons for sentence pursuant to Title 18 U.S.C. 3553(c), as set forth herein, were stated in open court.

1.   Was the presentence investigation report (PSI) reviewed by counsel and defendant including any additional materials received concerning sentencing?   ___Yes ___No

2.(a)   Was information withheld pursuant to FRCrP 32(c)(3)(A)?   ___Yes ___No

  (b)   If yes to (a), has summary been provided by the court pursuant to FRCrP 32(c)(3)(B)?   ___Yes ___No

3.(a)   Were all factual statements contained in the PSI adopted without objection?   ___Yes ___No

  (b)   If no to (a) the PSI was adopted in part with the exception of the following factual issues in dispute:

  (c)   Disputed issues have been resolved as follows after ___evidentiary hearing, ___further submissions and/or ___arguments:

[kmemsen.]

4.(a)   Are any legal issues in dispute?   ___Yes ___No

            If yes, describe disputed issues and their resolution:

5.(a)   Is there any dispute as to guideline applications (such as
            offense level, criminal history category, fine or restitution)
            as stated in the PSI?   ___Yes ___No

            If yes, describe disputed areas and their resolution:

(b)   Tentative findings as to applicable guidelines are:

            Total Offense Level:_____

            Criminal History Category:_____

            _____to _____ months imprisonment

            _____to_____ months supervised release

            $_____to $_____fine (plus $_____ cost of
                                                 imprisonment/supervision)

            $_____ restitution

            $_____ special assessment ($_____ on each of
                               counts   )

6.(a)   Are there any legal objections to tentative findings?   ___Yes ___No

(b)   If no, findings are adopted by the Court.

(c)   If yes, describe objections and how they were addressed:

            OR sentence hearing is continued to _____
            to allow for preparation of oral argument or filing of written
            submissions by _____.

7.(a)   Remarks by counsel for defendant.[1]   ___Yes ___No

  (b)   Defendant speaks on own behalf.   ___Yes ___No

  (c)   Remarks by counsel for government.   ___Yes ___No

8.(a)   The sentence will be imposed in accordance with the prescribed forms in the
        Bench Book Sec. 5.02 as follows:

        _____months imprisonment

        _____months/intermittent community confinement

        _____months probation

        _____months supervised release

        $_____fine (including cost of imprisonment/supervision)

        $_____restitution

        $_____special assessment ($_____on each of
                                            counts _____)

        Other provisions of sentence: (community service, forfeiture, etc.)

  (b)___   After imposing sentence, the Court has advised the defendant of the defendant's right to
           appeal within 10 days of the entry of judgment in accordance with FRCrP 32(a)(2).

_____

[1] The order of argument and/or recommendations and allocution may be altered to accord with the
Court's practice.

3

9.   **Statement of reasons for imposing sentence.**
        Check appropriate space.

(a)___   Sentence is within the guideline range and that range does not exceed 24 months and the Court finds no reason to depart from the sentence called for by application of the guidelines.

OR___   Sentence is within the guideline range and that range exceeds 24 months and the reasons for imposing the selected sentence are:

(b)___   Sentence departs from the guideline range as a result of

        ___ substantial cooperation upon motion of the government

        OR

        ___ a finding that the following (aggravating or mitigating) circumstance exists that is of a kind or degree not adequately taken into consideration by the Sentencing Commission in formulating the guidelines and that this circumstance should result in a sentence different from that described by the guidelines for the following reasons:

(c)___   Is restitution applicable in this case?   ___Yes ___No

        Is full restitution imposed?   ___Yes ___No

        If no, less than full restitution is imposed for the following reasons:

(d)___   Is a fine applicable in this case?   ___Yes ___No

Is the fine within the guidelines imposed?   ___Yes ___No

If no, the fine is not within guidelines or no fine is imposed for the following reasons:

_____ Defendant is not able, and even with the use of a reasonable installment schedule is not
likely to become able, to pay all or part of the required fine; or

_____ Imposition of a fine would unduly burden the defendant's dependants; or

_____ Other reasons as follows:

10.   Was a plea agreement submitted in this case?   ___Yes ___No

Check appropriate space:

_____ The Court has accepted a Rule 11(e)(1)(A) charge agreement because it is satisfied that
the agreement adequately reflects seriousness of the actual offense behavior and
accepting the plea agreement will not undermine the statutory purposes of sentencing.

_____ The Court has accepted either a Rule 11(e)(1)(B) sentence recommendation or a Rule
11(e)(1)(C) sentence agreement that is within the applicable guideline range.

_____ The Court has accepted either a Rule 11(e)(1)(B) sentence recommendation or a Rule
11(e)(1)(C) sentence agreement that departs from the applicable guideline range because
the Court is satisfied that such a departure is authorized by 18 U.S.C. 3553(b).

11.   Suggestions for guideline revisions resulting from this case are
submitted by an attachment to this report.   ___Yes ___No

12.   The PSI is adopted as part of the record, either in whole or in part as discussed above and is
to be maintained by the U.S. Probation Department under seal unless required for appeal.

13.   Judgment will be prepared by the clerk in accordance with above.

14.   The clerk will provide this Memorandum of Sentencing Hearing And Report of Statement of
Reasons to the U.S. Probation Department for forwarding to the Sentencing Commission, and
if the above sentence includes a term of imprisonment, to the Bureau of Prisons.

_____   _____
DATE   UNITED STATES DISTRICT JUDGE

(stofreas.frm - 09/96)   [kmemsen.]

5

"It can hardly be doubted that it would be a flagrant violation of the Fourteenth Amendment for a state trial court to follow an announced practice of imposing a heavier sentence upon every reconvicted defendant for the explicit purpose of punishing the defendant for his having succeeded in getting his original conviction set aside. Where . . . the original conviction has been set aside because of a constitutional error, the imposition of such a punishment, 'penalizing those who choose to exercise' constitutional rights, 'would be patently unconstitutional.' United States v. Jackson, 390 U.S. 570, 581. And the very threat inherent in the existence of such a punitive policy would, with respect to those still in prison, serve to 'chill the exercise of basic constitutional rights.' Id., at 582. . . . But even if the first conviction has been set aside for nonconstitutional error, the imposition of a penalty upon the defendant for having successfully pursued a statutory right of appeal or collateral remedy would be no less a violation of due process of law. . . . This Court has never held that the States are required to establish avenues of appellate review, but it is now fundamental that, once established, these avenues must be kept free of unreasoned distinctions that can only impede open and equal access to the courts. . . .' . . .

"Due process of law, then, requires that vindictiveness against a defendant for having successfully attacked his first conviction must play no part in the sentence he receives after a new trial. And since the fear of such vindictiveness may unconstitutionally deter a defendant's exercise of the right to appeal or collaterally attack his first conviction, due process also requires that a defendant be freed of apprehension of such a retaliatory motivation on the part of the sentencing judge.

"In order to assure the absence of such a motivation, we have concluded that whenever a judge imposes a more severe sentence upon a defendant after a new trial, the reasons for his doing so must affirmatively appear. Those reasons must be based upon objective information concerning identifiable conduct on the part of the defendant occurring after the time of the original sentencing proceeding. And the factual data upon which the increased sentence is based must be made part of the record, so that the constitutional legitimacy of the increased sentence may be fully reviewed on appeal." Id. at 723–26.

Discussing *Pearce*, the Court said: "If it was not clear from the Court's holding in *Pearce*, it is clear from our subsequent cases applying *Pearce* that due process does not in any sense forbid enhanced sentences or charges, but only enhancement motivated by *actual vindictiveness* toward the defendant for having exercised guaranteed rights. . . . [W]here the presumption applies, the sentencing authority or the prosecutor must rebut the presumption that an increased sentence or charge resulted from vindictiveness; where the presumption does not apply, the defendant must affirmatively prove actual vindictiveness." Wasman v. United States, 468 U.S. 559, 568–69 (1984). In *Wasman*, the defendant was given an increased sentence on retrial. The sentencing judge explained the sentence as based on an intervening conviction for a crime committed before the first sentence was imposed. The Court held that the presumption of vindictiveness raised by *Pearce* had been rebutted.

There is no presumption of vindictiveness if the first sentence was imposed following conviction on a plea of guilty and, the defendant having successfully appealed from that conviction, the second sentence is imposed following a trial. Alabama v. Smith, 490 U.S. 794 (1989) (8–1). In those circumstances, the Court reasoned, the trial may reveal additional facts about the crime or about the defendant, and the element of plea-bargaining is not present. "[T]here are enough justifications for a heavier second sentence that it cannot be said to be more likely than not that a judge who imposes one is motivated by vindictiveness." Id. at 802.

The reasoning of *Pearce* was held to preclude the state from charging a defendant with a felony based on the same act for which he had been convicted of a misdemeanor, after he had exercised his right to appeal from the latter conviction and have a trial *de novo*. Blackledge v. Perry, 417 U.S. 21 (1974). See Thigpen v. Roberts, 468 U.S. 27 (1984) (6–3) (Blackledge v. Perry applied). See also United States v. Jamison, 505 F.2d 407 (D.C.Cir.1974) (indictment for first-degree murder barred following mistrial on indictment for second-degree murder, absent justification in intervening circumstances).

Pearce does not preclude imposition of a more severe sentence following a trial *de novo*, pursuant to a procedure whereby less serious cases may be tried once in an inferior court and the defendant if convicted may freely elect to have an entirely independent trial thereafter in a court of general jurisdiction, at which the issues of guilt and penalty are determined without regard to the proceedings in the inferior court. Colten v. Kentucky, 407 U.S. 104 (1972). Nor does *Pearce* preclude a more severe sentence on retrial if sentencing at the second trial is entrusted to the jury, "so long as the jury is not informed of the prior sentence and the second sentence is not otherwise shown to be a product of vindictiveness." Chaffin v. Stynchcombe, 412 U.S. 17, 35 (1973). See also Texas v. McCullough, 475 U.S. 134 (1986), in which at the first trial, sentence was imposed by the jury, the trial judge then granted the defendant's motion for a new trial (on the basis of prosecutorial misconduct), and, at the second trial, the judge imposed sentence at the request of the defendant. The judge entered findings of fact to support the longer sentence. The Court held that in those circumstances, there was no presumption of vindictiveness. It held further that even if such a presumption were applied, the trial judge's findings were sufficient to overcome it.

Nature of the penalty

586. "Whatever views may be entertained regarding severity of punishment, whether one believes in its efficacy or its futility . . . these are peculiarly questions of legislative policy." Gore v. United States, 357 U.S.

386, 393 (1958). "[T]he Due Process Clause of the Fourteenth Amendment does not, nor does anything in the Constitution, require a State to fix or impose any particular penalty for any crime it may define or to impose the same or 'proportionate' sentences for separate and independent crimes." Williams v. Oklahoma, 358 U.S. 576, 586 (1959). "Save as limited by constitutional provisions safeguarding individual rights, a State may choose means to protect itself and its people against criminal violation of its laws. The comparative gravity of criminal offenses and whether their consequences are more or less injurious are matters for its determination. . . . It may inflict a deserved penalty merely to vindicate the law or to deter or to reform the offender or for all of these purposes. For the determination of sentences, justice generally requires consideration of more than the particular acts by which the crime was committed and that there be taken into account the circumstances of the offense together with the character and propensities of the offender. His past may be taken to indicate his present purposes and tendencies and significantly to suggest the period of restraint and the kind of discipline that ought to be imposed upon him." Pennsylvania ex rel. Sullivan v. Ashe, 302 U.S. 51, 55 (1937). See Howard v. Fleming, 191 U.S. 126 (1903).

587. "[C]ruel and unusual punishments [shall not be] inflicted." U.S. Constitution amend. VIII.

"Difficulty would attend the effort to define with exactness the extent of the constitutional provision which provides that cruel and unusual punishments shall not be inflicted; but it is safe to affirm that punishments of torture . . . and all others in the same line of unnecessary cruelty, are forbidden by that amendment to the Constitution." Wilkerson v. Utah, 99 U.S. 130, 135–36 (1878) (sentence of death by being publicly shot is not a cruel and unusual punishment for crime of murder). "Punishments are cruel when they involve torture or a lingering death; but the punishment of death is not cruel, within the meaning of that word as used in the Constitution. It implies there something inhuman and barbarous, something more than the mere extinguishment of life." In re Kemmler, 136 U.S. 436, 447 (1890).

The Cruel and Unusual Punishments Clause is discussed at length in Rummel v. Estelle, 445 U.S. 263 (1980) (5–4), in which the Court held that it was not a violation of the Clause for a third felony offender to be sentenced under a recidivist statute to life imprisonment, with eligibility for parole after 12 years. The defendant had argued that the three felonies for which he had been convicted (fraudulent use of a credit card, passing a forged check, and false pretenses) were relatively minor and that the sentence of life imprisonment was therefore excessive. Relying on Rummel v. Estelle, the Court reversed a ruling below that a 40-year sentence for possession and distribution of less than nine ounces of marijuana was so "grossly disproportionate" to the crime that it violated the Cruel and Unusual Punishments Clause. Hutto v. Davis, 454 U.S. 370 (1982) (6–3).

In Solem v. Helm, 463 U.S. 277, 290 (1983) (5–4), however, the Court held that under the Eighth Amendment, "a criminal sentence must be proportionate to the crime for which the defendant has been convicted." It said: "Reviewing courts, of course, should grant substantial deference to the broad authority that legislatures necessarily possess in determining the types and limits of punishments for crimes as well as to the discretion that trial courts possess in sentencing convicted criminals. But no penalty is *per se* constitutional. . . . [A] single day in prison may be unconstitutional in some circumstances." Ibid. Among the factors that should be considered are "(i) the gravity of the offense and the harshness of the penalty; (ii) the sentences imposed on other criminals in the same jurisdiction; and (iii) the sentences imposed for commission of the same crime in other jurisdictions." Id. at 292. The defendant in Solem v. Helm had been sentenced as a recidivist to life imprisonment without possibility of parole for passing a bad check, his seventh conviction for a nonviolent felony. The Court concluded that the sentence was prohibited by the Eighth Amendment. *Rummel* and *Hutto* were distinguished.

In Harmelin v. Michigan, 501 U.S. 957 (1991) (5–4), the Court again considered the issue of sentence proportionality. Three Justices (opinion by Justice Kennedy, which Justice O'Connor and Justice Souter joined) adhered to the view that "the Cruel and Unusual Punishments Clause encompasses a narrow proportionality principle," which forbids only "extreme sentences" that are "'grossly disproportionate.'" Id. at 997, 1001. Two Justices (opinion by Justice Scalia, which Chief Justice Rehnquist joined) concluded that the Clause does not include any principle of proportionality. On those bases, the Court upheld a mandatory sentence of life imprisonment without possibility of parole for possession of more than 650 grams of cocaine. The four dissenting Justices concluded that under Solem v. Helm, the sentence was unconstitutional.

In Weems v. United States, 217 U.S. 349 (1910), the Court held that a statute that prescribed a penalty of not less than 12 years imprisonment, along with "accessory" penalties and disabilities including wearing a chain, hard labor, and perpetual disabilities after his release, for the crime of falsifying public records violated the constitutional prohibition against cruel and unusual punishments.

Four Justices concluded that expatriation of a native-born American who was convicted by courtmartial of deserting during wartime was a cruel and unusual punishment, in Trop v. Dulles, 356 U.S. 86 (1958): "We believe . . . that use of denationalization as a punishment is barred by the Eighth Amendment. There may be involved no physical mistreatment, no primitive torture. There is instead the total destruction of the individual's status in organized society. It is a form of punishment more primitive than torture, for it destroys for the individual the political existence that was centuries in the development. The punishment strips the citizen of his status in the national and international political community. His very existence is at the sufferance of the country in which he happens to find himself. While any one country may accord him some rights, and presumably as long as he

AO 245B (Rev. 8/96) Judgment in a Criminal Case
　　　　Sheet 1

UNITED STATES DISTRICT COURT

District of ————————————

UNITED STATES OF AMERICA	**JUDGMENT IN A CRIMINAL CASE**
V.	(For Offenses Committed On or After November 1, 1987)
	CASE NUMBER:

THE DEFENDANT:

Defendant's Attorney _____

☐　pleaded guilty to count(s) _____

☐　pleaded nolo contendere to count(s) _____
　　which was accepted by the court.

☐　was found guilty on count(s) _____
　　after a plea of not guilty.

Title & Section	**Nature of Offense**	**Date Offense Concluded**	**Count Number(s)**

　　The defendant is sentenced as provided in pages 2 through _____ of this judgment. The sentence is imposed pursuant to the Sentencing Reform Act of 1984.

☐　The defendant has been found not guilty on count(s) _____

☐　Count(s) _____ (is)(are) dismissed on the motion of the United States.

　　IT IS FURTHER ORDERED that the defendant shall notify the United States Attorney for this district within 30 days of any change of name, residence, or mailing address until all fines, restitution, costs, and special assessments imposed by this judgment are fully paid.

Defendant's Soc. Sec. No.:_____

Defendant's Date of Birth.: _____

Defendant's USM No.: _____

Defendant's Residence Address:

_____

_____

_____

_____

Defendant's Mailing Address:

_____

_____

_____

_____

Date of Imposition of Judgment
_____

Signature of Judicial Officer
_____

Name and Title of Judicial Officer
_____

Date
_____

AO 245B (Rev. 8/96) Judgment in a Criminal Case:
     Sheet 2 — Imprisonment

Judgment — Page _____ of _____

DEFENDANT:
CASE NUMBER:

IMPRISONMENT

The defendant is hereby committed to the custody of the United States Bureau of Prisons to be imprisoned for a total term of _____ .

☐ The court makes the following recommendations to the Bureau of Prisons:

☐ The defendant is remanded to the custody of the United States Marshal.

☐ The defendant shall surrender to the United States Marshal for this district:

    ☐ at _____ a.m./p.m. on _____ .

    ☐ as notified by the United States Marshal.

☐ The defendant shall surrender for service of sentence at the institution designated by the Bureau of Prisons:

    ☐ before 2 p.m. on _____ .

    ☐ as notified by the United States Marshal.

    ☐ as notified by the Probation or Pretrial Services Office.

RETURN

I have executed this judgment as follows:

_____

_____

_____

Defendant delivered on _____ to _____

at _____ with a certified copy of this judgment.

_____

UNITED STATES MARSHAL

By _____

    Deputy U.S. Marshal

AO 245B (Rev. 8/96) Judgment in a Criminal Case
    Sheet 2 Reverse — Imprisonment

Judgement — Page _____ of _____

DEFENDANT:
CASE NUMBER:

ADDITIONAL IMPRISONMENT TERMS

remained in this country he would enjoy the limited rights of an alien, no country need do so because he is stateless. Furthermore, his enjoyment of even the limited rights of an alien might be subject to termination at any time by reason of deportation. In short, the expatriate has lost the right to have rights.

"This punishment is offensive to cardinal principles for which the Constitution stands. It subjects the individual to a fate of ever-increasing fear and distress. He knows not what discriminations may be established against him, what proscriptions may be directed against him, and when and for what cause his existence in his native land may be terminated. He may be subject to banishment, a fate universally decried by civilized people. He is stateless, a condition deplored in the international community of democracies. It is no answer to suggest that all the disastrous consequences of this fate may not be brought to bear on a stateless person. The threat makes the punishment obnoxious.

"The civilized nations of the world are in virtual unanimity that statelessness is not to be imposed as punishment for crime. It is true that several countries prescribe expatriation in the event that their nationals engage in conduct in derogation of native allegiance. Even statutes of this sort are generally applicable primarily to naturalized citizens. But use of denationalization as punishment for crime is an entirely different matter. The United Nations' survey of the nationality laws of 84 nations of the world reveals that only two countries, the Philippines and Turkey, impose denationalization as a penalty for desertion. In this country the Eighth Amendment forbids this to be done." Id. at 101–103.

The Court has held that a state statute which made "the 'status' of narcotic addiction a criminal offense" even if the addict "has never touched any narcotic drug within the State or been guilty of any irregular behavior" imposed a cruel and unusual punishment. Robinson v. California, 370 U.S. 660, 666, 667 (1962).

"It is unlikely that any State at this moment in history would attempt to make it a criminal offense for a person to be mentally ill, or a leper, or to be afflicted with a venereal disease. A State might determine that the general health and welfare require that the victims of these and other human afflictions be dealt with by compulsory treatment, involving quarantine, confinement, or sequestration. But, in the light of contemporary human knowledge, a law which made a criminal offense of such a disease would doubtless be universally thought to be an infliction of cruel and unusual punishment in violation of the Eighth and Fourteenth Amendments. . . .

"We cannot but consider the statute before us as of the same category. . . . To be sure, imprisonment for ninety days [the statutory minimum sentence, received by the defendant] is not, in the abstract, a punishment which is either cruel or unusual. But the question cannot be considered in the abstract. Even one day in prison would be a cruel and unusual punishment for the 'crime' of having a common cold." Id. at 666–67. The Court said that the state might establish programs of compulsory treatment and "might impose criminal sanctions, for example, against the unauthorized manufacture, prescription, sale, purchase, or possession of narcotics within its borders." Id. at 664.

A majority of the Court declined to apply the reasoning of *Robinson* to the case of a chronic alcoholic convicted of being drunk in a public place. Powell v. Texas, 392 U.S. 514 (1968). Four Justices said that the "primary purpose" of the cruel and unusual punishment clause "has always been considered, and properly so, to be directed at the method or kind of punishment imposed for the violation of criminal statutes; the nature of the conduct made criminal is ordinarily relevant only to the fitness of the punishment imposed." Id. at 531–32. As for *Robinson*: "The entire thrust of *Robinson's* interpretation of the Cruel and Unusual Punishments Clause is that criminal penalties may be inflicted only if the accused has committed some act, has engaged in some behavior, which society has an interest in preventing, or perhaps in historical common law terms, has committed some *actus reus*. It thus does not deal with the question of whether certain conduct cannot constitutionally be punished because it is, in some sense, 'involuntary' or 'occasioned by a compulsion.' " Id. at 533.[6]

588. Excessive Fines. The Eighth Amendment's prohibition against "excessive fines" applies to a civil in rem forfeiture, under 21 U.S.C. § 881(a)(4), (7), of property used to facilitate a drug offense, because the forfeiture functions at least partially as punishment. Austin v. United States, 509 U.S. 602 (1993). The Court did not consider what makes a fine excessive. See generally United States v. Bajakajian, 118 S.Ct. 2028, ___ U.S. ___ (1998) (5–4) (disproportional punitive forfeiture violates Excessive Fines Clause).

6. Justice White, concurring in the result, said: "If it cannot be a crime to have an irresistible compulsion to use narcotics, Robinson v. California . . . I do not see how it can constitutionally be a crime to yield to such a compulsion. Punishing an addict for using drugs convicts for addiction under a different name. Distinguishing between the two crimes is like forbidding criminal conviction for being sick with flu or epilepsy but permitting punishment for running a fever or having a convulsion. Unless *Robinson* is to be abandoned, the use of narcotics by an addict must be beyond the reach of the criminal law. Similarly, the chronic alcoholic with an irresistible urge to consume alcohol should not be punishable for drinking or for being drunk." 392 U.S. at 548–49. He concurred on the ground that it was not shown that the defendant, albeit compelled to drink, was likewise compelled to be drunk in public, the crime for which he was convicted.

Four Justices dissented. "It is settled that the Federal Constitution places some substantive limitation upon the power of state legislatures to define crimes for which the imposition of punishment is ordered. . . .

. . .

"*Robinson* stands upon a principle which, despite its subtlety, must be simply stated and respectfully applied because it is the foundation of individual liberty and the cornerstone of the relations between a civilized state and its citizens: Criminal penalties may not be inflicted upon a person for being in a condition he is powerless to change. . . .

. . .

"[The facts of this case] call into play the principle that a person may not be punished if the condition essential to constitute the defined crime is part of the pattern of his disease and is occasioned by a compulsion symptomatic of the disease. This principle, narrow in scope and applicability, is implemented by the Eighth Amendment's prohibition of 'cruel and unusual punishment,' as we construed that command in *Robinson*." Id. at 566–67, 569.

589. Restitution. Federal law provides that as part of a sentence the court may "order, in addition to or, in the case of a misdemeanor, in lieu of any other penalty authorized by law, that the defendant make restitution to any victim of such offense, or if the victim is deceased, to the victim's estate." 18 U.S.C. § 3663(a)(1)(A). In the case of an offense resulting in bodily injury to the victim, restitution may include an amount to cover medical and related expenses, lost income, and funeral and related expenses. § 3663(b)(2). The statute provides: "To the extent that the court determines that the complication and prolongation of the sentencing process resulting from the fashioning of an order of restitution under this section outweighs the need to provide restitution to any victims, the court may decline to make such an order." § 3663(a)(1)(B)(ii). The procedure for issuing an order of restitution is set forth in 18 U.S.C. § 3664. When it determines whether to order restitution, the court is directed to consider "the amount of the loss sustained by each victim as a result of the offense," and "the financial resources of the defendant, the financial needs and earning ability of the defendant and the defendant's dependents, and such other factors as the court deems appropriate." §3663(a)(1)(B)(i)–(ii). If the defendant is convicted of a crime of violence, an offense against property, an offense relating to tampering with consumer products, or in which an identifiable person or persons suffered a physical injury or pecuniary loss, the court is, generally, directed to order restitution. 18 U.S.C. § 3663A.

In United States v. Fountain, 768 F.2d 790 (7th Cir.1985), the defendants, prison inmates, were convicted in one case of the murder of a prison guard and in the other of the murder of one guard and other crimes including assault on guards, who were injured and one of whom was permanently disabled. The trial judge ordered restitution to the estates of the murdered victims, to the disabled victim, and to the Department of Labor for payments it incurred to the guards or their estates. In one case, the total restitution ordered was nearly $490,000, and in the other it was $70,000. Discussing the restitution order, the court of appeals said:

"The defendants argue that the statute is unconstitutional, because it allows a victim of crime to obtain from the sentencing judge what amounts to a judgment for tort damages, thus thwarting the defendant's Seventh Amendment right to trial by jury in any federal suit at law in which the stakes exceed $20. The argument is unpersuasive when pushed to the extreme of saying that *any* order that a criminal defendant pay a victim money for which the victim could get a judgment in a suit at law is a judgment at law for purposes of the Seventh Amendment. If by 'restitution' in criminal law (a distinct concept from civil restitution) we mean simply an order in a criminal case that the criminal restore to his victim what he has taken from him, we are speaking of a form of criminal remedy that predates the Seventh Amendment. Restitution indeed is the earliest criminal remedy. Before there is organized government, criminal misconduct is punished by forcing the criminal to compensate the victim or the victim's family . . . . Even after the rise of the state we find restitution used as a criminal remedy, as in an English statute of 1529 . . . .

"The question is, what does restitution as a criminal remedy comprehend? As the word implies and history confirms, the original conception is that of forcing the criminal to yield up to his victim the fruits of the crime. The crime is thereby made worthless to the criminal. This form of criminal restitution is sanctioned not only by history but also by its close relationship to the retributive and deterrent purposes of criminal punishment. The fact that tort law may also have deterrent purposes . . . does not make every payment to the victim of crime a tort sanction; it just shows that tort and criminal law overlap. In fact their differentiation is a relatively modern development. . . .

"An order to make restitution of medical and funeral expenses and lost earnings has a weaker connection with the traditional purposes of criminal law. But since medical expenses are restorative, making the criminal reimburse them can be analogized to forcing him to return stolen goods; so can making him restore any earnings that the victim lost as a result of the crime. The analogy is particularly close where, as in the present cases, the criminal wanted to injure his victim, as distinct from injuring him as merely a byproduct of an acquisitive crime. And with regard to all three types of loss—medical, funeral, and earnings—making the criminal bear them serves a useful purpose in the administration of the criminal law. It brings home to him the enormity of his conduct, by forcing him to pay expenses directly related to his victim's suffering.

"That forms of criminal restitution other than ordering stolen goods restored to the owner do not have so clear a historical pedigree does not matter. What matters is that criminal restitution is not some newfangled effort to get around the Seventh Amendment but a traditional criminal remedy; its precise contours can change through time without violating the Seventh Amendment. If Congress creates a new cause of action and does not specify the mode of trial, we must look to the nearest historical analogy to decide whether there is a right of trial by jury. . . . Here Congress has made clear that the judge rather than the jury is to determine the facts; and its judgment is entitled to our consideration. Moreover, there is a close historical analogy to restitution in a criminal proceeding of the victim's medical and funeral expenses and lost earnings: restitution of stolen goods, an established criminal remedy when the Seventh Amendment was adopted. Restitution is frequently an equitable remedy, meaning, of course, that there is no right of jury trial. . . . We therefore join those courts that have upheld under the Act orders for restitution of medical bills, lost wages, and the value of personal property destroyed by the criminal. . . .

"Restitution as a criminal remedy becomes problematic only where it goes beyond the fruits of the crime or the out-of-pocket expenses of the victim or his lost earnings and includes compensation for earnings . . . that would have been received in the future. Compensation for the loss of future earnings is quintessentially civil. The reason is not merely historical, or conceptual; there is, indeed, no difference of principle between past and future earnings, so far as the purposes of criminal punishment are concerned. To disable a person from working, temporarily or permanently, is to deprive him of his human capital; it is a detail whether the consequence is to deprive him of earnings he would have had in the past or earnings he would have had in the future. The reason for treating past and future earnings differently is practical: the calculation of lost future earnings involves the difficult problem of translating an uncertain future stream of earnings into a present value. . . . It is not a problem meet for solution in a summary proceeding ancillary to sentencing for a criminal offense.

. . .

". . . Obeying the statutory directive that 'the imposition of such order . . . not unduly complicate or prolong the sentencing process,' 18 U.S.C. § 3579(d), [see 18 U.S.C. § 3663(a)(1)(B)(ii)], we hold that an order requiring a calculation of lost future earnings unduly complicates the sentencing process and hence is not authorized by the Victim and Witness Protection Act—unless, to repeat a vital qualification, the amount is uncontested, so that no calculation is required.

"For reasons already stated, we have no difficulty with the portion of the restitution order that relates solely to the medical and funeral expenses of the victims or the past wages of which they were deprived by the defendants' crimes. Nor do we doubt that the Department of Labor is a 'person' within the meaning of the third-party payment provision of the statute. . . . [W]e can think of no reason why a federal agency, alone among third-party payors, natural and institutional, should not be reimbursed if it compensates a victim of crime. . . .

"The defendants complain, finally, that the judge disregarded their poverty in ordering them to pay amounts which, even as reduced to eliminate the substantial payments for lost future earnings, will far exceed the realistic earning capacity of indigent prisoners unlikely ever to be released from prison. But the statute does not say that indigency is a defense, only that it is a factor the judge is required to take into account . . . and he did that. The judge was worried that such accomplished and audacious murderers might have a story to sell to a publisher or broadcaster, and he wanted to make sure they would never reap any gain from their crimes. This is a proper ground for ordering restitution beyond the defendants' present or foreseeable ability to pay. The prospect that these multiple murderers might someday be cashing royalty checks for the stories of their crimes while their victims remain uncompensated for the losses that the murderers inflicted is an insult to the victims and an affront to the society's moral beliefs. It might be too late then for the victims or their survivors to bring wrongful-death actions; the statute of limitations might have run. They could if they want sue now and get a judgment that they could renew till the day (if it ever arrives) when the defendants have money to pay it, but we do not think they should be put to this expense, so likely to be futile.

". . . Everyone knows that [the defendants] cannot *now* make restitution. The point of the order is to make sure that should they ever be able to do so out of earnings from the press or the media, they shall do so. This is a reasonable measure which requires no findings of fact." 768 F.2d at 800–803.

The provision for restitution "to any victim of such offense" authorizes "an award of restitution only for the loss caused by the specific conduct that is the basis of the offense of conviction"; it does not authorize an award of restitution for losses related to other alleged offenses for which the defendant is charged but not convicted. Hughey v. United States, 495 U.S. 411 (1990).

New York's "Son of Sam" law, which provided that proceeds from crime stories written by the criminal be used to compensate the victim of the crime was struck down by the Court as a violation of the First Amendment, in Simon & Schuster, Inc. v. Members of New York State Crime Victims Board, 502 U.S. 105 (1991). The Court concluded that the statute was a content-based, financial disincentive to speech, which was not justified by a compelling interest of the state. The Court said that a state has a compelling interest in compensating victims from the fruits of a crime, but that the statute was not narrowly tailored to serve that interest.

590. Capital punishment. In three cases involving two defendants who were sentenced to death for rape and one who was sentenced to death for murder, the Court held that "the imposition and carrying out of the death penalty in these cases constitutes cruel and unusual punishment in violation of the Eighth and Fourteenth Amendments." Furman v. Georgia, 408 U.S. 238 (1972). All nine Justices wrote opinions. Justice Brennan and Justice Marshall concluded flatly that capital punishment violated the Eighth Amendment's prohibition against cruel and unusual punishments. Justice Douglas, Justice Stewart, and Justice White concurred on the ground that the death penalty was arbitrarily applied and for that reason was unconstitutional. The other four Justices wrote dissenting opinions. The requirement that the death penalty not be imposed in an "arbitrary and capricious" manner was applied in Woodson v. North Carolina, 428 U.S. 280 (1976) (5–4), and Roberts v. Louisiana, 428 U.S. 325 (1976) (5–4).

A majority of the Court has upheld the death penalty in certain circumstances. In lengthy opinions, the Court upheld capital punishment for murder, imposed under statutory schemes in Georgia, Florida, and Texas, which focused attention on the circumstances of the crime and provided for consideration of aggravating or mitigating factors and which included measures to prevent arbitrary imposition of the penalty. Gregg v. Georgia, 428 U.S. 153 (1976); Proffitt v. Florida, 428 U.S. 242 (1976); Jurek v. Texas, 428 U.S. 262 (1976). Justice Brennan and Justice Marshall dissented, adhering to their views in *Furman*.

A sentence of death for the crime of rape is "grossly disproportionate and excessive punishment" and is therefore prohibited by the Eighth Amendment. Coker v. Georgia, 433 U.S. 584 (1977). The Court noted that Georgia was the only jurisdiction in the United States that currently authorized capital punishment for rape of an adult woman, and only two others authorized capital punishment if the victim was a child. It noted that in most cases, Georgia juries had not sentenced rapists to death. These facts, four Justices said, confirmed their view that capital punishment for rape was excessive. (Opinion of Justice White, which Justice Stewart, Justice Blackmun, and Justice Stevens joined.) In brief concurring opinions, Justice Brennan and Justice Marshall adhered to their views in *Furman*. Justice Powell, concurring in part and dissenting in part, indicated that he would not foreclose the possibility that capital punishment in cases of aggravated rape might be permissible. Chief Justice Burger and Justice Rehnquist dissented. The Court has held also that imposition of the death penalty for felony murder is inconsistent with the Cruel and Unusual Punishments Clause if the person sentenced did not himself "kill, attempt to kill, or intend that a killing take place or that lethal force . . . be employed," Enmund v. Florida, 458 U.S. 782, 797 (1982) (5–4). Distinguishing *Enmund*, the Court held that the Eighth Amendment does not prohibit capital punishment for a defendant convicted of felony murder, who does not himself kill or intend to kill but whose participation in the felony "is major and whose mental state is one of reckless indifference to the value of human life." Tison v. Arizona, 481 U.S. 137, 152 (1987) (5–4). *Enmund*, the majority said, barred capital punishment for someone like Enmund himself: "[T]he minor actor in an armed robbery, not on the scene, who neither intended to kill nor was found to have had any culpable mental state." Id. at 149.

In Godfrey v. Georgia, 446 U.S. 420 (1980) (6–3), the Court invalidated a sentence of death imposed pursuant to a statute allowing capital punishment for a murder that "was outrageously or wantonly vile, horrible or inhuman in that it involved torture, depravity of mind, or an aggravated battery to the victim." Four Justices (in addition to Justice Brennan and Justice Marshall) concluded that application of the statute to the facts of the case required so broad and vague a construction that it violated the Eighth and Fourteenth Amendments. *Godfrey* was applied in Maynard v. Cartwright, 486 U.S. 356 (1988). But see Lewis v. Jeffers, 497 U.S. 764 (1990) (5–4) (death sentence under similar statute upheld). In Arave v. Creech, 507 U.S. 463 (1993) (7–2), the Court said that an Idaho statute specifying that for purposes of capital punishment sentencing, it is an aggravating circumstance that "[b]y the murder, or circumstances surrounding its commission, the defendant exhibited utter disregard for human life," as construed by the state court, provided adequate guidance for exercise of discretion. The state court had said that the phrase " 'is meant to be reflective of acts or circumstances surrounding the crime which exhibit the highest, the utmost, callous disregard for human life, i.e., the cold-blooded, pitiless slayer.' " Id. at 468. See Tuilaepa v. California, 512 U.S. 967 (1994) (8–1) (sentencing factors having a "common-sense core of meaning" not unconstitutionally vague).

The sentencing authority must be permitted to consider all mitigating factors in the individual case. Lockett v. Ohio, 438 U.S. 586 (1978). Even for a narrowly restricted category of homicide, a mandatory death sentence is not permissible. See Sumner v. Shuman, 483 U.S. 66 (1987) (6–3) (person convicted of murder who is serving sentence of life imprisonment); Roberts v. Louisiana, 431 U.S. 633 (1977) (5–4) (first-degree murder of police officer engaged in performance of his duties).

The Court has considered a wide variety of questions about which aggravating and mitigating factors may or must be considered and the manner in which they are considered. See, Buchanan v. Angelone, ___ U.S. ___, 118 S.Ct. 757 (1998) (6–3); Tuggle v. Netherland, 516 U.S. 10 (1995); Johnson v. Texas, 509 U.S. 350 (1993) (5–4) (defendant's youth at time of crime); Sochor v. Florida, 504 U.S. 527 (1992); Walton v. Arizona, 497 U.S. 639 (1990) (5–4); Clemons v. Mississippi, 494 U.S. 738 (1990); McKoy v. North Carolina, 494 U.S. 433 (1990) (6–3); Boyde v. California, 494 U.S. 370 (1990) (5–4); Blystone v. Pennsylvania, 494 U.S. 299 (1990) (5–4); Penry v. Lynaugh, 492 U.S. 302 (1989); Franklin v. Lynaugh, 487 U.S. 164 (1988) (6–3); Johnson v. Mississippi, 486 U.S. 578 (1988); Mills v. Maryland, 486 U.S. 367 (1988) (5–4); Lowenfield v. Phelps, 484 U.S. 231 (1988) (7–2); Hitchcock v. Dugger, 481 U.S. 393 (1987); Skipper v. South Carolina, 476 U.S. 1 (1986); Barclay v. Florida, 463 U.S. 939 (1983) (6–3); Zant v. Stephens, 462 U.S. 862 (1983) (7–2); Eddings v. Oklahoma, 455 U.S. 104 (1982) (5–4).

The Constitution does not require that a sentence of death be imposed by a jury. "In light of the facts that the Sixth Amendment does not require jury sentencing, that the demands of fairness and reliability in capital cases do not require it, and that neither the nature of, nor the purpose behind, the death penalty requires jury sentencing, we cannot conclude that placing responsibility on the trial judge to impose the sentence in a capital case is unconstitutional." Spaziano v. Florida, 468 U.S. 447, 464 (1984) (6–3). Accordingly, it is permissible for a state to authorize a judge to override a jury recommendation against capital punishment. The Court noted that 30 out of 37 states that have a capital punishment statute give the decision to the jury; and only three of the remaining seven allow a judge to override a jury's recommendation of life imprisonment. Id. at 463. A capital sentencing statute that requires the sentencing judge to consider a jury's sentencing recommendation but does not specify the weight that the judge is to give the recommendation is constitutional. Harris v. Alabama, 513 U.S. 504 (1995) (8–1).

In Beck v. Alabama, 447 U.S. 625 (1980) (7–2), the Court held that a death sentence was invalid because the jury was not permitted to consider a verdict of guilty of a lesser included, noncapital offense even though the evidence would have supported such a verdict. See Hopper v. Evans, 456 U.S. 605 (1982). Failure to give an instruction on an available lesser-included offense does not require reversal if an instruction on another lesser included offense supported by the evidence was given. Schad v. Arizona, 501 U.S. 624 (1991) (5–4). Nor does Beck require that instructions be given on lesser included offenses for which the defendant cannot be convicted because of the statute of limitations. The defendant may choose to waive the statute of limitations in order to have the benefit of the instruction; but if he does not, the jury should not be led to believe that the defendant can be convicted of crimes for which he cannot be convicted. To trick the jury in that way would undermine the public's confidence in criminal justice and disserve the goal of rationality. Spaziano, above.

In Caldwell v. Mississippi, 472 U.S. 320 (1985) (5–3), the Court held that the prosecutor's argument to a capital sentencing jury suggesting that responsibility for determining the appropriateness of a death sentence rested not with the jury but with the appellate court on review violated the Eighth Amendment's special requirement of reliability of the judgment that a sentence of death is appropriate in the specific case. Construing *Caldwell*, the Court held that informing a sentencing jury that the defendant was already under sentence of death for another crime did not unconstitutionally undermine the jury's sense of responsibility for determining the appropriateness of capital punishment. Romano v. Oklahoma, 512 U.S. 1 (1994) (5–4). The prior sentence was disclosed as part of the state's proof that the defendant had previously been convicted of a violent felony and would constitute a continuing threat to society, which were aggravating factors bearing on the sentence.

In a capital sentencing proceeding, if the defendant's future dangerousness is in issue and the only alternative to the death penalty is imprisonment without possibility of parole, due process requires that the jury be informed that the defendant, if imprisoned, would not be eligible for parole. Simmons v. South Carolina, 512 U.S. 154 (1994) (7–2). See California v. Ramos, 463 U.S. 992 (1983) (5–4) (state court's instruction to jury at penalty hearing that Governor might commute life sentence without parole, without instruction that Governor might also commute death sentence, was not unconstitutional).

A claim that the Constitution prohibits psychiatric testimony about the defendant's future dangerousness at the sentencing hearing was rejected in Barefoot v. Estelle, 463 U.S. 880 (1983) (6–3). Also, a capital sentencing jury is not constitutionally barred from hearing a "victim impact" statement, which provides information about the impact of the crime on the victim and the victim's family. Payne v. Tennessee, 501 U.S. 808 (1991) (6–3). Nor is it impermissible to instruct the jury that it "must not be swayed by mere sentiment, conjecture, sympathy, passion, prejudice, public opinion or public feeling" during the penalty phase of a capital case. California v. Brown, 479 U.S. 538, 539 (1987) (5–4). In *Brown*, the defendant had contended that the instruction might lead the jury not to give proper attention and weight to mitigating factors bearing on the sentence.

In Dawson v. Delaware, 503 U.S. 159 (1992) (8–1), the Court held that the defendant's First Amendment right of association was violated by the admission at a capital sentencing hearing of evidence that he belonged to a white racist prison organization called the Aryan Brotherhood. The Court said that the First Amendment does not absolutely prohibit evidence about a person's associations and beliefs, but that in this case the evidence was altogether irrelevant.

The Eighth Amendment does not require "a state appellate court, before it affirms a death sentence, to compare the sentence in the case before it with the penalties imposed in similar cases if requested to do so by the prisoner." Pulley v. Harris, 465 U.S. 37, 44 (1984) (7–2).

"The Eighth Amendment prohibits the State from inflicting the penalty of death upon a prisoner who is insane." Ford v. Wainwright, 477 U.S. 399, 410 (1986) (7–2). Accordingly, if the sanity of a condemned prisoner is in issue, the state must provide a procedure to determine the issue "with the high regard for truth that befits a decision affecting the life or death of a human being." Id. at 411. Without specifying in detail what constitutes an adequate procedure, the Court said that "the adversary presentation of relevant information [should] be as unrestricted as possible," and "the manner of selecting and using the experts responsible for producing that 'evidence' [should] be conducive to the formation of neutral, sound, and professional judgments as to the prisoner's ability to comprehend the nature of the penalty." Id. at 417. The Eighth Amendment does not, however, prohibit imposition of the death penalty on a person who is mentally retarded and has the reasoning capacity of a seven-year-old (he having been found competent to stand trial and his insanity defense having been rejected). Penry v. Lynaugh, 492 U.S. 302 (1989) (5–4).

Four Justices have concluded that the Eighth Amendment prohibits the execution of a person who was less than 16 years old at the time of the commission of the offense. Thompson v. Oklahoma, 487 U.S. 815 (1988) (5–4) (Stevens, Brennan, Marshall, Blackmun). Justice O'Connor concurred in the judgment vacating the sentence of death, on the ground that the Oklahoma legislature had not specifically addressed the question whether a person could be executed for a crime committed when he was less than 16; the statute in this case specified no minimum age. She declined to decide the more general question.

The Eighth Amendment does not prohibit imposition of capital punishment for a crime committed at the age of 17 or 16. Stanford v. Kentucky, 492 U.S. 361 (1989) (5–4).

In McCleskey v. Kemp, 481 U.S. 279 (1987) (5–4), the Court rejected a claim that the imposition of capital punishment was constitutionally invalid because racial considerations had entered into the decision whether it would be imposed. The defendant was black and was convicted of killing a white person during the course of a robbery. Under Georgia law, a jury recommended that he be sentenced to death following a sentencing hearing, and the judge accepted the jury's recommendation. The claim of racial discrimination was supported by extensive statistical studies of Georgia murder cases, which showed, inter alia, that black defendants who kill white victims have the greatest likelihood of being sentenced to death. According to one statistical model, defendants charged with killing white victims were 4.3 times as likely to be sentenced to death than defendants charged with killing black victims. The Court emphasized that there was no evidence other than the statistical studies that racial discrimination was a factor in this case. It observed that discretion is intended to and does play a large role in capital sentencing proceedings and that were the statistical evidence accepted as proof of racial discrimination in this case, comparable proof of statistical disparities related to any impermissible factor might likewise invalidate a death sentence. "At most," the Court said, "the [statistical] study indicates a discrepancy that appears to correlate with race," but it "does not demonstrate a constitutionally significant risk of racial bias affecting the Georgia capital-sentencing process." 481 U.S. at 312, 313.

In Lankford v. Idaho, 500 U.S. 110 (1991) (5–4), the Court held that imposition of the death penalty violated due process, because the defendant did not have adequate notice at the time of the sentencing hearing that the judge was considering a death sentence.

In Herrera v. Collins, 506 U.S. 390 (1993) (6–3), the Court rejected, in the circumstances of the case, the argument that "the Eighth and Fourteenth Amendments . . . prohibit the execution of a person who is innocent of the crime for which he was convicted." Id. at 398. The petitioner had been convicted of capital murder and sentenced to death. Petitions for state and federal habeas corpus were denied. Ten years later, he filed another petition for federal habeas corpus, in which he alleged that he was innocent of the crimes. The petition was accompanied by four affidavits to the effect that the petitioner was innocent.

The Court said that a claim of innocence based on newly discovered evidence was not and never had been a ground for federal habeas relief, unless it was accompanied by an independent claim of a constitutional error in the underlying state criminal proceeding. The function of habeas, it said, is not to correct errors of fact. The petition here, it said, was in the manner of a motion for a new trial on the basis of newly discovered evidence, which is confined within a two-year time limit by Federal Rule 33. Executive clemency is the "fail safe" for situations outside the rule. Id. at 415.

The Court added: "We may assume, for the sake of argument in deciding this case, that in a capital case a truly persuasive demonstration of 'actual innocence' made after trial would render the execution of a defendant unconstitutional, and warrant federal habeas relief if there were no state avenue open to process such a claim. But because of the very disruptive effect that entertaining claims of actual innocence would have on the need for finality in capital cases, and the enormous burden that having to retry cases based on often stale evidence would place on the States, the threshold showing for such an assumed right would necessarily be extraordinarily high." Id. at 417. The Court concluded that the petitioner's showing fell "far short" of that threshold. In a concurring opinion, Justice O'Connor said, "I cannot disagree with the fundamental legal principle that executing the innocent is inconsistent with the Constitution." Id. at 419. However, she said, the petitioner "is not innocent, in any sense of the word." Id. She emphasized the overwhelming evidence of his guilt and the weakness of the affidavits accompanying the petition.

Herrera was distinguished in Schlup v. Delo, 513 U.S. 298 (1995) (5–4), in which the defendant coupled his claim of innocence with a claim of constitutional error at trial. The Court said that whereas in Herrera's case, "the evidence of innocence would have had to be strong enough to make his execution 'constitutionally intolerable' *even if* his conviction was the product of a fair trial," the petitioner in this case had only to "establish sufficient doubt about his guilt to justify the conclusion that his execution would be a miscarriage of justice *unless* his conviction was the product of a fair trial." Id. at 853. The test, the Court said, is whether "it is more likely than not that no reasonable juror would have convicted him in the light of the new evidence." Id. at 867.

A defendant who seeks federal habeas corpus to set aside a conviction and capital sentence and who is financially unable to obtain counsel and other necessary services has a statutory right to the appointment of counsel and the furnishing of such services. 21 U.S.C. § 848(q)(4)(B). The right includes a right to assistance in the preparation of the habeas corpus application, which can be claimed by filing a motion requesting the appointment of counsel for the habeas corpus proceeding. McFarland v. Scott, 512 U.S. 849 (1994) (6–3). A district court has jurisdiction to enter a stay of execution where necessary to give effect to the right. Id. (5–4).

"In a capital case the grant of a stay of execution directed to a State by a federal court imposes on that court the concomitant duty to take all steps necessary to ensure a prompt resolution of the matter, consistent with its duty to give full and fair consideration to all of the issues presented in the case." In re Blodgett, 502 U.S. 236 (1992). See generally Barefoot v. Estelle, 463 U.S. 880 (1983) (6–3).

The imposition of capital punishment under the Uniform Code of Military Justice was upheld in Loving v. United States, 517 U.S. 748 (1996).

591. Application of the Cruel and Unusual Punishments Clause to the conditions of imprisonment is discussed in Rhodes v. Chapman, 452 U.S. 337 (1981) (8–1), in which the Court reversed a ruling below that the housing of two inmates in a single cell, in all the circumstances of the case, was unconstitutional. The Court observed that "the Constitution does not mandate comfortable prisons" and that prisons "which house persons convicted of serious crimes, cannot be free of discomfort." Id. at 349. In discharging their responsibility, "courts cannot assume that state legislatures and prison officials are insensitive to the requirements of the Constitution or to the perplexing sociological problems of how best to achieve the goals of the penal function in the criminal justice system: to punish justly, to deter future crime, and to return imprisoned persons to society with an improved chance of being useful, law-abiding citizens." Id. at 353.

In Wilson v. Seiter, 501 U.S. 294 (1991) (5–4), referring to some earlier cases, the Court said that conditions of imprisonment that are not intended as punishment do not violate the Cruel and Unusual Punishment Clause unless they are accompanied by a culpable state of mind of the responsible prison officials. (*Rhodes*, the Court said, had been concerned only with the "objective component" of an Eighth Amendment claim—"Was the deprivation sufficiently serious?"—and did not eliminate the "subjective component"—"Did the officials act with a sufficiently culpable state of mind?" Id. at 298.) The requisite culpable state of mind is at least deliberate indifference to the conditions in question. The Court observed: "*Some* conditions of confinement may establish an Eighth Amendment violation 'in combination' when each would not do so alone, but only when they have a mutually enforcing effect that produces the deprivation of a single identifiable human need such as food, warmth, or exercise—for example, a low cell temperature at night combined with a failure to issue blankets. . . . To say that some prison conditions may interact in this fashion is a far cry from saying that all prison conditions are a seamless web for Eighth Amendment purposes. Nothing so amorphous as 'overall conditions' can rise to the level of cruel and unusual punishment when no specific deprivation of a single human need exists." Id. at 304–305.

In a civil suit by a federal prisoner against prison officials, explaining the meaning of "deliberate indifference," the Court said: "[A] prison official cannot be found liable under the Eighth Amendment for denying an inmate humane conditions of confinement unless the official knows of and disregards an excessive risk to inmate health or safety; the official must both be aware of facts from which the inference could be drawn that a substantial risk of serious harm exists, and he must also draw the inference." Farmer v. Brennan, 511 U.S. 825 (1994). The Court rejected the inmate's argument that an objective standard rather than an official's subjective state of mind should control.

See generally the concurring and dissenting opinion of Judge Posner in Johnson v. Phelan, 69 F.3d 144, 151 (7th Cir.1995).

Rhodes v. Chapman and a generally less favorable attitude toward judicial oversight of the performance of administrative functions substantially reduced, if it did not quite halt, a flow of cases in which the courts had reviewed the administration of prisons and, frequently, required improved conditions on constitutional grounds. See the opinion of Justice Brennan, concurring in the judgment, in Rhodes v. Chapman, in which he states that "individual prisons or entire prison systems in at least 24 States have been declared unconstitutional under the Eighth and Fourteenth Amendments, with litigation underway in many others." Id. at 353–54. The cases to which Justice Brennan referred are cited id. at 353–54 n.1.

592. The Equal Protection Clause prohibits a state from imprisoning an indigent beyond the maximum term of imprisonment fixed by statute because of nonpayment of a fine that he is financially unable to pay. "A statute permitting a sentence of both imprisonment and fine cannot be parlayed into a longer term of imprisonment than is fixed by the statute since to do so would be to accomplish indirectly as to an indigent that which cannot be done directly." Williams v. Illinois, 399 U.S. 235, 243 (1970). The court noted that it was not dealing with "a judgment of confinement for nonpayment of a fine in the familiar pattern of alternative sentence of '$30 or 30 days.'" Id.

Williams was applied in Tate v. Short, 401 U.S. 395 (1971), to the imprisonment of an indigent who was sentenced to be imprisoned because he could not pay accumulated fines for traffic offenses; the court had no other jurisdiction to impose imprisonment. *Williams* and *Tate* were applied in Bearden v. Georgia, 461 U.S. 660 (1983), holding that a state court cannot revoke probation of an indigent convict because of failure to pay a fine and make restitution, unless (1) he wilfully refused to pay or failed to make adequate bona fide efforts to acquire the funds with which to pay, or (2) no alternative sentence will meet the state's interest in punishment and deterrence.

Distinguishing *Williams*, *Tate*, and *Bearden*, the court of appeals held that the defendant was not denied equal protection or due process by the sentencing judge's refusal to credit him for time while he was detained before trial because he was unable to make bail; he was detained for 284 days. Vasquez v. Cooper, 862 F.2d 250 (10th Cir.1988).

593. Consecutive sentences. To what extent can a court extend punishment by imposing consecutive sentences for distinct crimes arising out of the same "transaction"? In Bell v. United States, 349 U.S. 81, 82–84 (1955), the Court said that while "the punishment appropriate for the diverse federal offenses is a matter for the discretion of Congress, subject only to constitutional limitations, more particularly the Eighth Amendment," doubt about congressional intent "should be resolved in favor of lenity" and "against turning a single transaction into multiple offenses." In Gore v. United States, 357 U.S. 386 (1958), the Court held that no rule of lenity was applicable where the defendant was convicted of three different narcotics offenses all based on a single sale of heroin and given consecutive sentences: "The fact that an offender violates by a single transaction several regulatory controls devised by Congress as means for dealing with a social evil as deleterious as it is difficult to combat does not make the several different regulatory controls single and identic. . . . It is one thing for a single transaction to include several units relating to proscribed conduct under a single provision of a statute.[7] It is a wholly different thing to evolve a rule of lenity for three violations of three separate offenses created by Congress at three different times, all to the end of dealing more and more strictly with, and seeking to throttle more and more by different legal devices, the traffic in narcotics." Id. at 389, 391. Cumulative punishments for a single offense violates the Double Jeopardy Clause. See note 603 p. 1214 below.

594. Review. "The question of appellate review of sentencing has recently received much advocacy as a needed reform to prevent unjustifiable disparities in the sentences meted to co-defendants. The arguments pro and con for such a review have almost universally been left to the

---

7. In *Bell*, the Court had held that the transportation of two women across state lines on a single trip in violation of the Mann Act, 18 U.S.C. § 2421, was but a single violation of the act.

legislative branch of government. Appellate courts have generally refused to disturb the trial court's discretion in this matter unless the punishment is so disproportionate to the offense committed and to the sentences received by co-defendants 'as to be completely arbitrary and shocking to the sense of justice and thus to constitute cruel and unusual punishment in violation of the Eighth Amendment. . . .'" Rodriquez v. United States, 394 F.2d 825, 826 (5th Cir.1968). For cases in which the appellate court found exceptional circumstances not involving cruel and unusual punishment that called for reconsideration of sentence, see, e.g., Thomas v. United States, 368 F.2d 941 (5th Cir.1966); Coleman v. United States, 357 F.2d 563 (D.C.Cir.1965); cf. Leach v. United States, 334 F.2d 945 (D.C.Cir.1964).

A state procedure that allows a sentence review panel to increase as well as decrease the sentence of a defendant who applied for review was upheld in Robinson v. Warden, 455 F.2d 1172 (4th Cir.1972). Accord Walsh v. Picard, 446 F.2d 1209 (1st Cir.1971). In *Walsh*, the court rejected the argument that the reviewing agency was constitutionally required at least to state its reasons for increasing a sentence.

Enactment of the Sentencing Guidelines, see p. 1138 above, greatly increased the number of appeals from a sentence, both by the defendant and by the government, pursuant to 18 U.S.C. § 3742, below.

————

18 U.S.C. § 3742

Review of a sentence

(a) Appeal by a defendant. A defendant may file a notice of appeal in the district court for review of an otherwise final sentence if the sentence—

(1) was imposed in violation of law;

(2) was imposed as a result of an incorrect application of the sentencing guidelines; or

(3) is greater than the sentence specified in the applicable guideline range to the extent that the sentence includes a greater fine or term of imprisonment, probation, or supervised release than the maximum established in the guideline range, or includes a more limiting condition of probation or supervised release under section 3563(b)(6) or (b)(11) than the maximum established in the guideline range; or

(4) was imposed for an offense for which there is no sentencing guideline and is plainly unreasonable.

(b) Appeal by the Government. The Government may file a notice of appeal in the district court for review of an otherwise final sentence if the sentence—

(1) was imposed in violation of law;

(2) was imposed as a result of an incorrect application of the sentencing guidelines;

(3) is less than the sentence specified in the applicable guideline range to the extent that the sentence includes a lesser fine or term of imprisonment, probation, or supervised release than the minimum established in the guideline range, or includes a less limiting condition of probation or supervised release under section 3563(b)(6) or (b)(11) than the minimum established in the guideline range; or

(4) was imposed for an offense for which there is no sentencing guideline and is plainly unreasonable.

The Government may not further prosecute such appeal without the personal approval of the Attorney General, the Solicitor General, or a deputy solicitor general designated by the Solicitor General.

(c) Plea agreements. In the case of a plea agreement that includes a specific sentence under rule 11(e)(1)(C) of the Federal Rules of Criminal Procedure—

(1) a defendant may not file a notice of appeal under paragraph (3) or (4) of subsection (a) unless the sentence imposed is greater than the sentence set forth in such agreement; and

(2) the Government may not file a notice of appeal under paragraph (3) or (4) of subsection (b) unless the sentence imposed is less than the sentence set forth in such agreement.

(d) Record on review. If a notice of appeal is filed in the district court pursuant to subsection (a) or (b), the clerk shall certify to the court of appeals—

(1) that portion of the record in the case that is designated as pertinent by either of the parties;

(2) the presentence report; and

(3) the information submitted during the sentencing proceeding.

(e) Consideration. Upon review of the record, the court of appeals shall determine whether the sentence—

(1) was imposed in violation of law;

(2) was imposed as a result of an incorrect application of the sentencing guidelines;

(3) is outside of the applicable guideline range, and is unreasonable, having regard for—

(A) the factors to be considered in imposing a sentence, as set forth in chapter 227 of this title; and

(B) the reasons for the imposition of the particular sentence, as stated by the district court pursuant to the provisions of section 3553(c); or

(4) was imposed for an offense for which there is no applicable sentencing guideline and is plainly unreasonable.

The court of appeals shall give due regard to the opportunity of the district court to judge the credibility of the witnesses, and shall accept the findings of fact of the district court unless they are clearly erroneous and shall give due deference to the district court's application of the guidelines to the facts.

(f) Decision and disposition. If the court of appeals determines that the sentence—

(1) was imposed in violation of law or imposed as a result of an incorrect application of the sentencing guidelines, the court shall remand the case for further sentencing proceedings with such instructions as the court considers appropriate;

(2) is outside the applicable guideline range and is unreasonable or was imposed for an offense for which there is no applicable sentencing guideline and is plainly unreasonable, it shall state specific reasons for its conclusions and—

(A) if it determines that the sentence is too high and the appeal has been filed under subsection (a), it shall set aside the sentence and remand the case for further sentencing proceedings with such instructions as the court considers appropriate;

(B) if it determines that the sentence is too low and the appeal has been filed under subsection (b), it shall set aside the sentence and remand the case for further sentencing proceedings with such instructions as the court considers appropriate;

(3) is not described in paragraph (1) or (2), it shall affirm the sentence.

(g) Application to a sentence by a magistrate [sic—magistrate judge]. An appeal of an otherwise final sentence imposed by a United States magistrate [sic—magistrate judge] may be taken to a judge of the district court, and this section shall apply (except for the requirement of approval by the Attorney General or the Solicitor General in the case of a Government appeal) as though the appeal were to a court of appeals from a sentence imposed by a district court.

(h) Guideline not expressed as a range. For the purpose of this section, the term "guideline range" includes a guideline range having the same upper and lower limits.

CHAPTER 16

APPEAL

———

"While bringing this appeal had about the same hope of success as running a three-legged filly in the Kentucky Derby, we commend appellant's attorney for doing his best with what he had." Platts v. United States, 378 F.2d 396, 397 (9th Cir.1967).

———

595. "[I]t is well settled that there is no constitutional right to an appeal. . . . Indeed, for a century after this Court was established, no appeal as of right existed in criminal cases, and, as a result, appellate review of criminal convictions was rarely allowed. . . . The right of appeal, as we presently know it in criminal cases, is purely a creature of statute; in order to exercise that statutory right one must come within the terms of the applicable statute. . . ." Abney v. United States, 431 U.S. 651, 656 (1977).[1]

A defendant has a right to counsel on his first appeal as of right. Douglas v. California, 372 U.S. 353 (1963). The Due Process Clause guarantees the defendant in a state criminal prosecution the effective assistance of counsel on such an appeal. Evitts v. Lucey, 469 U.S. 387 (1985) (7–2).

An indigent defendant does not have a constitutional right to have appointed counsel on appeal argue every nonfrivolous issue that the defendant wants to have argued. Counsel's professional judgment may prevail over the defendant's wishes. Jones v. Barnes, 463 U.S. 745 (1983) (7–2). See McCoy v. Court of Appeals of Wisconsin, District 1, 486 U.S. 429 (1988) (5–3), upholding, against the claim that it denied effective assistance of counsel, a state rule providing that a court-appointed counsel who wants to withdraw from an appeal on the ground that it is frivolous must explain why potential

---

[1]. The general statutory basis for appeals from judgments of the federal district courts is 28 U.S.C. § 1291.

UNITED STATES DISTRICT COURT
DISTRICT OF MASSACHUSETTS

_____

V.   **CASE NO.** _____

_____

NOTICE OF APPEAL

Notice is hereby given that _____ above named,

hereby appeals from the _____ entered in the above

entitled action on _____ .

By the Court,

_____   _____
,Date   **Deputy Clerk**

(notofapp.frm - 09/92)   [app., kdapp., kgapp., kcustapp.]

issues on appeal lack merit. See also Miller v. Smith, 115 F.3d 1136 (4th Cir.1997) (en banc), holding that a state can limit provision of a free trial transcript for indigents to defendants who are represented on appeal by the public defender's office; it is not required to provide a transcript to an indigent who had secured the services *pro bono* of a private attorney.

FEDERAL RULES OF APPELLATE PROCEDURE

Rule 4.

APPEAL AS OF RIGHT—WHEN TAKEN

. . .

(b) Appeal in a Criminal Case.—In a criminal case, a defendant shall file the notice of appeal in the district court within 10 days after the entry either of the judgment or order appealed from, or of a notice of appeal by the Government. A notice of appeal filed after the announcement of a decision, sentence, or order—but before entry of the judgment or order—is treated as filed on the date of and after the entry. If a defendant makes a timely motion specified immediately below, in accordance with the Federal Rules of Criminal Procedure, an appeal from a judgment of conviction must be taken within 10 days after the entry of the order disposing of the last such motion outstanding, or within 10 days after the entry of the judgment of conviction, whichever is later. This provision applies to a timely motion:

(1) for judgment of acquittal;

(2) for arrest of judgment;

(3) for a new trial on any other ground than newly discovered evidence; or

(4) for a new trial based on the ground of newly discovered evidence if the motion is made before or within 10 days after entry of the judgment.

A notice of appeal filed after the court announces a decision, sentence, or order but before it disposes of any of the above motions, is ineffective until the date of the entry of the order disposing of the last such motion outstanding, or until the date of the entry of the judgment of conviction, whichever is later. Notwithstanding the provisions of Rule 3(c), a valid notice of appeal is effective without amendment to appeal from an order disposing of any of the above motions. When an appeal by the government is authorized by statute, the notice of appeal must be filed in the district court within 30 days after (i) the entry of the judgment or order appealed from or (ii) the filing of a notice of appeal by any defendant.

A judgment or order is entered within the meaning of this subdivision when it is entered on the criminal docket. Upon a showing of excusable neglect, the district court may—before or after the time has expired, with or without motion and notice—extend the time for filing a notice of appeal for a period not to exceed 30 days from the expiration of the time otherwise prescribed by this subdivision.

The filing of a notice of appeal under this Rule 4(b) does not divest a district court of jurisdiction to correct a sentence under Fed.R.Crim.P. 35(c), nor does the filing of a motion under Fed.R.Crim.P. 35(c) affect the validity of a notice of appeal filed before entry of the order disposing of the motion.

––––––

596. On the meaning of "excusable neglect," see Buckley v. United States, 382 F.2d 611 (10th Cir.1967), in which the court said that the defendant was charged with the inexcusable neglect of his counsel and that "a District Court's ruling as to the presence or absence of excusable neglect should be overturned only if there has been a clear abuse of discretion." Id. at 614. See also Romero v. Peterson, 930 F.2d 1502 (10th Cir.1991) (excusable neglect has "the 'common sense meaning of the two simple words applied to the facts which are developed'").

597. The defendant Worcester was convicted of filing false income tax returns with intent to evade taxes. "[T]he district court, in offering to suspend sentence and place Worcester on probation, stated that if he did not 'welcome this offer [of probation, but preferred] to run the risk of the 18 months sentence which I originally said I would impose, and to seek by appeal or otherwise a complete vindication . . .' he was free to do so. 190 F.Supp. at 553. We can only construe this to mean that if Worcester replied that he was not content to accept probation without appealing, but chose the alternative of appealing, he ran the risk that the sentence he would have to appeal from would be a jail sentence. That Worcester's counsel so understood is clear from his reply, which is part of the record, to the court's offer in which he states that Worcester '. . . agrees to be bound by the conditions contained therein, including the waiver of his right of appeal.' The court did not respond that this was an erroneous understanding.

"The court was without right to bargain thus with the defendant, or to put a price on an appeal. A defendant's exercise of a right of appeal must be free and unfettered. Just as it is unfair to handicap him because of his poverty . . . it is unfair to use the great power given to the court to determine sentence to place a defendant in the dilemma of making an unfree choice. . . . It is no answer to say that the defendant need not accept the court's 'offer.' The vice is that vis-a-vis the court he is in an unequal position.

"Were the rule otherwise, we can only too readily envisage the possibilities of abuse. A judge who fears he has committed reversible error during the trial, and does not like the thought of being reversed, informs the defendant that he is considering a substantial sentence, but that if the defendant will demonstrate his repentance, or his good citizenship, by waiving appeal, he will suspend it." Worcester v. Commissioner, 370 F.2d 713, 718 (1st Cir.1966). See North Carolina v. Pearce, 395 U.S. 711 (1969), note 585 p. 1169 above.

FEDERAL RULES OF CRIMINAL PROCEDURE

Rule 52.

HARMLESS ERROR AND PLAIN ERROR

(a) Harmless Error. Any error, defect, irregularity or variance which does not affect substantial rights shall be disregarded.

(b) Plain Error. Plain errors or defects affecting substantial rights may be noticed although they were not brought to the attention of the court.

---

598. Harmless error. "If, when all is said and done, the conviction is sure that the error did not influence the jury, or had but very slight effect, the verdict and the judgment should stand, except perhaps where the departure is from a constitutional norm or a specific command of Congress. . . . But if one cannot say, with fair assurance, after pondering all that happened without stripping the erroneous action from the whole, that the judgment was not substantially swayed by the error, it is impossible to conclude that substantial rights were not affected. The inquiry cannot be merely whether there was enough to support the result, apart from the phase affected by the error. It is rather, even so, whether the error itself had substantial influence. If so, or if one is left in grave doubt, the conviction cannot stand." Kotteakos v. United States, 328 U.S. 750, 764–65 (1946).

---

599. Plain error. "The language of the rule implies, and the cases hold, only that while orderly administration of justice requires general adherence to the rule that errors be asserted in the trial court, exceptions must be recognized in unusual circumstances involving seriously prejudicial deficiencies in the trial process." Reisman v. United States, 409 F.2d 789, 791 (9th Cir.1969). "We are not here concerned with technical error or with prejudicial error, or even with our view of what we may deem to be the obvious guilt or innocence of the individual appellants. In the words of Fed.R.Crim.P. 52(b) we are concerned only with any errors 'affecting substantial rights'. As the Supreme Court stated in United States v. Atkinson, 297 U.S. 157, 160 . . . (1936) we may—and we must—notice errors which 'seriously affect the fairness . . . of judicial proceedings.' The circumstances must be 'exceptional' and the error must be such as to prejudice 'in a substantial manner appellant's right to a fair trial.' Polansky v. United States, 332 F.2d 233, 235 (1st Cir.1964)." McMillen v. United States, 386 F.2d 29, 35 (1st Cir.1967). See United States v. Santana-Camacho, 833 F.2d 371 (1st Cir.1987) (prosecutor's misrepresentation of evidence in closing statement constituted plain error).

In Olano v. United States, 507 U.S. 725 (1993) (6–3), the trial judge suggested to the two defendants and their counsel that two alternative jurors might sit in the jury room during the jury's deliberations. One of the counsel approved of the suggestion, and the judge apparently concluded that he was speaking for the other counsel, who made no objection, as well. Rule 24(c), p. 922 above, states that alternative jurors "shall be discharged after the jury retires to consider its verdict."

Affirming the statement in *Atkinson*, above, the Court said that reversal of a conviction under Rule 52(e) is authorized only if the error is "plain" and "affect[s] substantial rights," and that it is within the discretion of the court of appeals. 507 U.S. at 734. Rule 52(b) "normally requires the same kind of inquiry" to determine whether an error was prejudicial that is required under Rule 52(a), "with one important difference. It is the defendant rather than the Government who bears the burden with respect to prejudice." Id. Concluding that the defendants had not shown specific prejudice, the Court held that the defendants' convictions should be affirmed. See United States v. Perez, 116 F.3d 840 (9th Cir.1997) (en banc), applying *Olano* and distinguishing between waiver of a right as "invited error" and forfeiture of a right.

In Johnson v. United States, 520 U.S. 461 (1997), applying *Olano*, the Court held that an action of the trial court that was correct at the time of the trial but is plainly erroneous at the time of the appeal, because of a change in the applicable law, satisfies the plain error requirement of Rule 52(b). The error in question was a failure to charge the jury on an element of the offense, which had previously been regarded as a matter of law for the judge. The court nevertheless did not reverse the conviction, because it concluded that the error did not affect the fairness or integrity of the proceedings.

Chapman v. California

386 U.S. 18, 87 S.Ct. 824, 17 L.Ed.2d 705 (1967).

■ MR. JUSTICE BLACK delivered the opinion of the Court.

Petitioners, Ruth Elizabeth Chapman and Thomas LeRoy Teale, were convicted in a California state court upon a charge that they robbed, kidnaped, and murdered a bartender. She was sentenced to life imprisonment and he to death. At the time of the trial, Art. I, § 13, of the State's Constitution provided that "in any criminal case, whether the defendant testifies or not, his failure to explain or to deny by his testimony any evidence or facts in the case against him may be commented upon by the court and by counsel, and may be considered by the court or the jury." Both petitioners in this case chose not to testify at their trial, and the State's attorney prosecuting them took full advantage of his right under the State Constitution to comment upon their failure to testify, filling his argument to the jury from beginning to end with numerous references to their silence and inferences of their guilt resulting therefrom. The trial court also charged the jury that it could draw adverse inferences from petitioners' failure to testify. Shortly after the trial, but before petitioners' cases had been considered on appeal by the California Supreme Court, this Court decided Griffin v. California, 380 U.S. 609, in which we held California's constitutional provision and practice invalid on the ground that they put a penalty on the exercise of a person's right not to be compelled to be a witness against himself, guaranteed by the Fifth Amendment to the United States Constitution and made applicable to California and the other States by the Fourteenth Amendment. . . . On appeal, the State Supreme Court . . . admitting that petitioners had been denied a federal constitutional right by the comments on their silence, nevertheless affirmed, applying the State Constitution's harmless-error provision, which forbids reversal unless "the court shall be of the opinion that the error complained of has resulted in a miscarriage of justice." We granted certiorari limited to these questions:

"Where there is a violation of the rule of Griffin v. California, 380 U.S. 609, (1) can the error be held to be harmless, and (2) if so, was the error harmless in this case?" 383 U.S. 956–957.

In this Court petitioners contend that both these questions are federal ones to be decided under federal law; that under federal law, we should hold that denial of a federal constitutional right, no matter how unimportant, should automatically result in reversal of a conviction, without regard to whether the error is considered harmless; and that, if wrong in this, the various comments on petitioners' silence cannot, applying a federal standard, be considered harmless here.

I

Before deciding the two questions here—whether there can ever be harmless constitutional error and whether the error here was harmless—we must first decide whether state or federal law governs. . . .

[The Court concluded that federal law governs.]

II

We are urged by petitioners to hold that all federal constitutional errors, regardless of the facts and circumstances, must always be deemed harmful. Such a holding, as petitioners correctly point out, would require an automatic reversal of their convictions and make further discussion unnecessary. We decline to adopt any such rule. All 50 States have harmless-error statutes or rules, and the United States long ago through its Congress established for its courts the rule that judgments shall not be reversed for "errors or defects which do not affect the substantial rights of the parties." 28 U.S.C. § 2111. None of these rules on its face distinguishes between federal constitutional errors and errors of state law or federal statutes and rules. All of these rules, state or federal, serve a very useful purpose insofar as they block setting aside convictions for small errors or defects that have little, if any, likelihood of having changed the result of the trial. We conclude that there may be some constitutional errors which in the setting of a particular case are so unimportant and insignificant that they may, consistent with the Federal Constitution, be deemed harmless, not requiring the automatic reversal of the conviction.

III

In fashioning a harmless-constitutional-error rule, we must recognize that harmless-error rules can work very unfair and mischievous results when, for example, highly important and persuasive evidence, or argument, though legally forbidden, finds its way into a trial in which the question of guilt or innocence is a close one. What harmless-error rules all aim at is a rule that will save the good in harmless-error practices while avoiding the bad, so far as possible.

The federal rule emphasizes "substantial rights" as do most others. The California constitutional rule emphasizes "a miscarriage of justice," but the California courts have neutralized this to some extent by emphasis, and perhaps overemphasis, upon the court's view of "overwhelming evidence." We prefer the approach of this Court in deciding what was harmless error in our recent case of Fahy v. Connecticut, 375 U.S. 85. There we said: "The question is whether there is a reasonable possibility that the evidence complained of might have contributed to the conviction." Id., at 86–87. Although our prior cases have indicated that there are some constitutional rights so basic to a fair trial that their infraction can never be treated as harmless error,[2] this statement in *Fahy* itself belies any belief that all trial errors which violate the Constitution automatically call for reversal. At the same time, however, like the federal harmless-error statute, it emphasizes an intention not to treat as harmless those constitutional errors that "affect substantial rights" of a party. An error in admitting plainly relevant evidence which possibly influenced the jury adversely to a litigant cannot, under *Fahy*, be conceived

---

2. See, e.g., Payne v. Arkansas, 356 U.S. 560 (coerced confession); Gideon v. Wainwright, 372 U.S. 335 (right to counsel); Tumey v. Ohio, 273 U.S. 510 (impartial judge).

of as harmless. Certainly error, constitutional error, in illegally admitting highly prejudicial evidence or comments, casts on someone other than the person prejudiced by it a burden to show that it was harmless. It is for that reason that the original common-law harmless-error rule put the burden on the beneficiary of the error either to prove that there was no injury or to suffer a reversal of his erroneously obtained judgment. There is little, if any, difference between our statement in Fahy v. Connecticut about "whether there is a reasonable possibility that the evidence complained of might have contributed to the conviction" and requiring the beneficiary of a constitutional error to prove beyond a reasonable doubt that the error complained of did not contribute to the verdict obtained. We, therefore, do no more than adhere to the meaning of our *Fahy* case when we hold, as we now do, that before a federal constitutional error can be held harmless, the court must be able to declare a belief that it was harmless beyond a reasonable doubt. While appellate courts do not ordinarily have the original task of applying such a test, it is a familiar standard to all courts, and we believe its adoption will provide a more workable standard, although achieving the same result as that aimed at in our *Fahy* case.

. . .

[The Court concluded that the error in this case had not been harmless.]

. . .[3]

———

600. Reversing what had previously been understood to be the rule, see *Chapman*, p. 1206 above, the Court held that the erroneous admission of a coerced confession may be harmless error, in Arizona v. Fulminante, 499 U.S. 279 (1991) (5–4). The Court said:

"It is evident from a comparison of the constitutional violations which we have held subject to harmless error, and those which we have held not, that involuntary statements or confessions belong in the former category. The admission of an involuntary confession is a 'trial error,' similar in both degree and kind to the erroneous admission of other types of evidence. The evidentiary impact of an involuntary confession, and its effect upon the composition of the record, is indistinguishable from that of a confession obtained in violation of the Sixth Amendment—of evidence seized in violation of the Fourth Amendment—or of a prosecutor's improper comment on a defendant's silence at trial in violation of the Fifth Amendment. When

[3] Justice Stewart wrote an opinion concurring in the result. Justice Harlan wrote a dissenting opinion.

reviewing the erroneous admission of an involuntary confession, the appellate court, as it does with the admission of other forms of improperly admitted evidence, simply reviews the remainder of the evidence against the defendant to determine whether the admission of the confession was harmless beyond a reasonable doubt.

"Nor can it be said that the admission of an involuntary confession is the type of error which 'transcends the criminal process.' This Court has applied harmless-error analysis to the violation of other constitutional rights similar in magnitude and importance and involving the same level of police misconduct. For instance, we have previously held that the admission of a defendant's statements obtained in violation of the Sixth Amendment is subject to harmless-error analysis. . . . We have also held that the admission of an out-of-court statement by a nontestifying codefendant is subject to harmless-error analysis. . . . The inconsistent treatment of statements elicited in violation of the Sixth and Fourteenth Amendments, respectively, can be supported neither by evidentiary or deterrence concerns nor by a belief that there is something more 'fundamental' about involuntary confessions. This is especially true in a case such as this one where there are no allegations of physical violence on behalf of the police. A confession obtained in violation of the Sixth Amendment has the same evidentiary impact as does a confession obtained in violation of a defendant's due process rights. Government misconduct that results in violations of the Fourth and Sixth Amendments may be at least as reprehensible as conduct that results in an involuntary confession. . . . Indeed, experience shows that law enforcement violations of these constitutional guarantees can involve conduct as egregious as police conduct used to elicit statements in violation of the Fourteenth Amendment. It is thus impossible to create a meaningful distinction between confessions elicited in violation of the Sixth Amendment and those in violation of the Fourteenth Amendment." Id. at 310–12. A majority of the Court held, however, that the admission of the confession in *Fulminante* was not harmless error.

Discussing which constitutional errors may be harmless error and which are never harmless error, the Court held that constitutionally inadequate instructions about the prosecution's burden of proof beyond a reasonable doubt are in the latter category. Sullivan v. Louisiana, 508 U.S. 275 (1993). Without adequate instructions on the burden of proof, the Court said, there has effectively been no jury verdict of guilt; so it is meaningless to ask whether a jury would have returned the same verdict had there been no error. The error in this case, it said, was a "structural error," to which harmless-error analysis does not apply.

In determining whether a jury instruction stating a presumption that unconstitutionally shifts the burden of proof to the defendant is harmless error (see Rose v. Clark, 478 U.S. 570 (1986) (6–3)), a reviewing court should first "ask what evidence the jury actually considered in reaching its verdict" and "then weigh the probative force of that evidence as against the probative force of the presumption standing alone." Yates v. Evatt, 500 U.S. 391, 405 (1991) (7–2). In order to find that the erroneous instruction was harmless error, the court must conclude that "the force of the evidence presumably considered by the jury in accordance with the instructions is so overwhelming as to leave it beyond a reasonable doubt that the verdict resting on that evidence would have been the same in the absence of the presumption." Id. at 405.

See Connecticut v. Johnson, 460 U.S. 73 (1983) (5–4), in which the Court said that an instruction (referring to a "conclusive presumption") that may have removed an issue of fact from the jury's consideration is never harmless error, except perhaps in "rare situations," such as when the issue is conceded by the defendant or is not relevant to the charge on which he is convicted.

See also Delaware v. Van Arsdall, 475 U.S. 673 (1986), p. 1016 above; Rushen v. Spain, 464 U.S. 114 (1983) (*ex parte* communication between judge and juror; harmless error); Milton v. Wainwright, 407 U.S. 371 (1972) (5–4) (admission of confession, if error, was harmless); Harrington v. California, 395 U.S. 250 (1969) (6–3) (violation of *Bruton*, note 390 p. 791 above; harmless error).

601. In United States v. Hasting, 461 U.S. 499 (1983), the court of appeals had reversed the convictions of five defendants for kidnapping and other crimes arising out of the brutal abduction and rape of three women, on the ground that in his closing argument the prosecutor had violated defendants' right under Griffin v. California, 380 U.S. 609 (1965), p. 981 above. Assuming that the court of appeals's action had been an exercise of its supervisory power, intended to enforce its admonitions to prosecutors not to make impermissible comments at trial, the Court said that the harmless-error rule of *Chapman* cannot be evaded by an assertion of supervisory power. "Supervisory power to reverse a conviction is not needed as a remedy when the error to which it is addressed is harmless since, by definition, the conviction would have been obtained notwithstanding the asserted error. Further, in this context, the integrity of the process carries less weight, for it is the essence of the harmless-error doctrine that a judgment may stand only when there is no 'reasonable possibility that the [practice] complained of might have contributed to the conviction.' Fahy v. Connecticut, 375 U.S. 85, 86–87 (1963). Finally, deterrence is an inappropriate basis for reversal where, as here, the prosecutor's remark is at most an attenuated violation of *Griffin* and where means more narrowly tailored to deter objectionable prosecutorial conduct are available.

"To the extent that the values protected by supervisory authority are at issue here, these powers may not be exercised in a vacuum. Rather, reversals of convictions under the court's supervisory power must be approached 'with some caution,' [United States v.] *Payner*, 447 U.S. [727 (1980)], at 734, and with a view toward balancing the interests involved, id., at 735–736, and n.8 . . . . [T]he Court of Appeals failed in this case to give appropriate—if, indeed, any—weight to these relevant interests. It did not consider the trauma the victims of these particularly heinous crimes would experience in a new trial, forcing them to relive harrowing experiences now long past, or the practical problems of retrying these sensitive issues more than four years after the events. . . . The conclusion is inescapable that the Court of Appeals focused exclusively on its concern that the prosecutors within its jurisdiction were indifferent to the frequent admonitions of the court. The court appears to have decided to deter future similar comments by the drastic step of reversal of these convictions. But the interests preserved by the doctrine of harmless error cannot be so lightly and casually ignored in order to chastise what the court viewed as prosecutorial overreaching.

. . .

". . . In holding that the harmless-error rule governs even constitutional violations under some circumstances, the Court recognized that, given the myriad safeguards provided to assure a fair trial, and taking into account the reality of the human fallibility of the participants, there can be no such thing as an error-free, perfect trial, and that the Constitution does not guarantee such a trial. . . . *Chapman* [v. California, 386 U.S. 18 (1967)] reflected the concern, later noted by Chief Justice Roger Traynor of the Supreme Court of California, that when courts fashion rules whose violations mandate automatic reversals, they 'retrea[t] from their responsibility, becoming instead "impregnable citadels of technicality."' R. Traynor, The Riddle of Harmless Error 14 (1970) (quoting Kavanagh, Improvement of Administration of Criminal Justice by Exercise of Judicial Power, 11 A.B.A.J. 217, 222 (1925)).

"Since *Chapman*, the Court has consistently made clear that it is the duty of a reviewing court to consider the trial record as a whole and to ignore errors that are harmless, including most constitutional violations. . . . The goal, as Chief Justice Traynor has noted, is 'to conserve judicial resources by enabling appellate courts to cleanse the judicial process of prejudicial error without becoming mired in harmless error.' Traynor, supra, at 81.

"Here, the Court of Appeals, while making passing reference to the harmless-error doctrine, did not apply it. Its analysis failed to strike the balance between disciplining the prosecutor on the one hand, and the interest in the prompt administration of justice and the interests of the victims on the other." 461 U.S. at 506–509. Examining the record, the Court concluded that the prosecutor's comment was harmless error and reversed the judgment below ordering a new trial. See, to the same effect, Bank of Nova Scotia v. United States, 487 U.S. 250 (1988) (8–1).

In Rose v. Clark, 478 U.S. 570 (1986) (6–3), the Court said that circumstances in which the doctrine of harmless error does not apply are exceptional. "Harmless-error analysis . . . presupposes a trial at which the defendant, represented by counsel, may present evidence and argument before an impartial judge and jury." Id. at 578. Beyond that, "if the defendant had counsel and was tried by an impartial adjudicator, there is a strong presumption that any other errors that may have occurred are subject to harmless-error analysis. The thrust of the many constitutional rules governing the conduct of criminal trials is to ensure that those trials lead to fair and correct judgments. Where a reviewing court can find that the record developed at trial establishes guilt beyond a reasonable doubt, the interest in fairness has been satisfied and the judgment should be affirmed." Id. at 579.

———

FEDERAL RULES OF CRIMINAL PROCEDURE

Rule 38.

STAY OF EXECUTION

(a) Death. A sentence of death shall be stayed if an appeal is taken from the conviction or sentence.

(b) Imprisonment. A sentence of imprisonment shall be stayed if an appeal is taken from the conviction or sentence and the defendant is released pending disposition of appeal pursuant to Rule 9(b) of the Federal Rules of Appellate Procedure. If not stayed, the court may recommend to the Attorney General that the defendant be retained at, or transferred to, a place of confinement near the place of trial or the place where an appeal is to be heard, for a period reasonably necessary to permit the defendant to assist in the preparation of an appeal to the court of appeals.

(c) Fine. A sentence to pay a fine or a fine and costs, if an appeal is taken, may be stayed by the district court or by the court of appeals upon such terms as the court deems proper. The court may require the defendant pending appeal to deposit the whole or any part of the fine and costs in the registry of the district court, or to give bond for the payment thereof, or to submit to an examination of assets, and it may make any appropriate order to restrain the defendant from dissipating such defendant's assets.

(d) Probation. A sentence of probation may be stayed if an appeal from the conviction or sentence is taken. If the sentence is stayed, the court shall fix the terms of the stay.

(e) Criminal Forfeiture, Notice to Victims, and Restitution. A sanction imposed as part of the sentence pursuant to 18 U.S.C. 3554, 3555, or 3556 may, if an appeal of the conviction or sentence is taken, be stayed by the district court or by the court of appeals upon such terms as the court finds appropriate. The court may issue such orders as may be reasonably necessary to ensure compliance with the sanction upon disposition of the appeal, including the entering of a restraining order or an injunction or requiring a deposit in whole or in part of the monetary amount involved into the registry of the district court or execution of a performance bond.

(f) Disabilities. A civil or employment disability arising under a Federal statute by reason of the defendant's conviction or sentence, may, if an appeal is taken, be stayed by the district court or by the court of appeals under such terms as the court finds appropriate. The court may enter a restraining order or an injunction, or take any other action that may be reasonably necessary to protect the interest represented by the disability pending disposition of the appeal.

———

FEDERAL RULES OF APPELLATE PROCEDURE

Rule 9.

RELEASE IN A CRIMINAL CASE

(a) Appeal from an Order Regarding Release Before Judgment of Conviction. The district court must state in writing, or orally on the record, the reasons for an order regarding release or detention of a defendant in a criminal case. A party appealing from the order, as soon as practicable after filing a notice of appeal with the district court, must file with the court of appeals a copy of the district court's order and its statement of reasons. An appellant who questions the factual basis for the district court's order must file a transcript of any release proceedings in the district court or an explanation of why a transcript has not been obtained. The appeal must be determined promptly. It must be heard, after reasonable notice to the appellee, upon such papers, affidavits, and portions of the record as the parties present or the court may require. Briefs need not be filed unless the court so orders. The court of appeals or a judge thereof may order the release of the defendant pending decision of the appeal.

(b) Review of an Order Regarding Release After Judgment of Conviction. A party entitled to do so may obtain review of a district court's order regarding release that is made after a judgment of conviction by filing a notice of appeal from that order with the district court, or by filing a motion with the court of appeals if the party has already filed a notice of appeal from the judgment of conviction. Both the order and the review are subject to Rule 9(a). In addition, the papers filed by the applicant for review must include a copy of the judgment of conviction.

(c) Criteria for Release. The decision regarding release must be made in accordance with applicable provisions of 18 U.S.C. §§ 3142, 3143, and 3145(c).

CHAPTER 17

DOUBLE JEOPARDY

"[N]or shall any person be subject for the same offense to be twice put in jeopardy of life or limb. . . ." U.S. Constitution amend. V.

---

602. "[W]e today find that the double jeopardy prohibition of the Fifth Amendment represents a fundamental ideal in our constitutional heritage, and that it should apply to the States through the Fourteenth Amendment. . . .

. . .

"The fundamental nature of the guarantee against double jeopardy can hardly be doubted. Its origins can be traced to Greek and Roman times, and it became established in the common law of England long before this Nation's independence. . . . As with many other elements of the common law, it was carried into the jurisprudence of this Country through the medium of Blackstone, who codified the doctrine in his Commentaries. '[T]he plea of *autrefoits acquit*, or a former acquittal,' he wrote, 'is grounded on this universal maxim of the common law of England, that no man is to be brought into jeopardy of his life more than once for the same offence.' Today, every State incorporates some form of the prohibition in its constitution or common law." Benton v. Maryland, 395 U.S. 784, 794–95 (1969).

In Crist v. Bretz, 437 U.S. 28 (1978) (6–3), the Court held explicitly that the federal rule that jeopardy attaches when the jury is empaneled and sworn is an integral part of the guarantee against double jeopardy and is binding on the states.

603. "[T]he Fifth Amendment guarantee against double jeopardy . . . has been said to consist of three separate constitutional protections. It protects against a second prosecution for the same offense after acquittal. It protects against a second prosecution for the same offense after conviction. And it protects against multiple punishments for the same offense." North Carolina v. Pearce, 395 U.S. 711, 717 (1969).

See Sanabria v. United States, 437 U.S. 54 (1978) (7–2), applying, in unusual circumstances, the rule that there can be no retrial after an acquittal. See also Smalis v. Pennsylvania, 476 U.S. 140 (1986) (grant of demurrer challenging sufficiency of the evidence at close of prosecution's case was an acquittal under the Double Jeopardy Clause, appeal from which is barred).

The Double Jeopardy Clause bars a government appeal from a judgment of acquittal under Rule 29(c), p. 1089 above, entered after the jury, having failed to reach a verdict, has been discharged. United States v. Martin Linen Supply Co., 430 U.S. 564 (1977).

In Serfass v. United States, 420 U.S. 377 (1975) (8–1), the Court held that the Double Jeopardy Clause did *not* bar an appeal by the government from pretrial dismissal of an indictment based on a legal ruling that the trial judge made after examining records and an affidavit containing evidence to be presented at trial. Notwithstanding the trial judge's reliance on such material, jeopardy had not attached, since the defendant had not been put to trial before the trier of the facts. See United States v. Sanford, 429 U.S. 14 (1976).

In United States v. Wilson, 420 U.S. 332 (1975) (7–2), after the jury returned a verdict of guilty at the defendant's trial, the trial judge reconsidered his pretrial motion to dismiss the indictment for undue delay before indictment and granted it; the delay, the judge concluded, had prejudiced his right to a fair trial. The government appealed. The court of appeals dismissed the appeal on the ground that since the trial court had relied on facts brought out at trial for its conclusion that the defendant had been prejudiced, the dismissal was equivalent to an acquittal; the appeal, therefore, violated the Double Jeopardy Clause.

The Court held that the appeal was proper. It said that "where there is no threat of either multiple punishment or successive prosecutions, the Double Jeopardy Clause is not offended. . . . Although review of any ruling of law discharging a defendant obviously enhances the likelihood of conviction and subjects him to continuing expense and anxiety, a defendant has no legitimate claim to benefit from an error of law when that error could be corrected without subjecting him to a second trial before a second trier of fact." Id. at 344–45. Since reversal on appeal of the order of dismissal would simply reinstate the jury's verdict, an appeal was permissible.

Reversing a ruling it had made only three terms before (United States v. Jenkins, 420 U.S. 358 (1975)), the Court held that if the defendant successfully moves to have the trial terminated before submission of the question of his guilt to judge or jury, the government is not barred from an appeal and, if it is successful on the appeal, a retrial. United States v. Scott, 437 U.S. 82 (1978) (5–4). The defendant's motion for a dismissal because of pretrial delay had been granted at the close of the evidence. The Court said: "We think that in a case such as this the defendant, by deliberately choosing to seek termination of the proceedings against him on a basis unrelated to factual guilt or innocence of the offense of which he is accused, suffers no injury cognizable under the Double Jeopardy Clause if the Government is permitted to appeal from such a ruling of the trial court in favor of the defendant. We do not thereby adopt the doctrine of 'waiver' of double jeopardy rejected in *Green* [v. United States, 355 U.S. 184 (1957), p. 1219 below]. Rather, we conclude that the Double Jeopardy Clause, which guards against Government oppression, does not relieve a defendant from the consequences of his voluntary choice. In *Green* the question of defendant's factual guilt or innocence of murder in the first degree was actually submitted to the jury as a trier of fact; in the present case, respondent successfully avoided such a submission of the first count of the indictment by persuading the trial court to dismiss it on a basis which did not depend on guilt or innocence. He was thus neither acquitted nor convicted, because he himself successfully undertook to persuade the trial court not to submit the issue of guilt or innocence to the jury which had been empaneled to try him." 437 U.S. at 98–99.

604. A defendant may not be prosecuted for an offense after having been tried and convicted of a lesser included offense. It "is invariably true of a greater and lesser included offense [that] the lesser offense . . . requires no proof beyond that which is required for conviction of the greater. . . . The greater offense is therefore by definition the 'same' for purposes of double jeopardy as any lesser offense included in it." Brown v. Ohio, 432 U.S. 161, 168 (1977) (6–3). "[W]hatever the sequence may be, the Fifth Amendment forbids successive prosecution and cumulative punishment for a greater and lesser included offense." Id. at 169. Accord Harris v. Oklahoma, 433 U.S. 682 (1977) (prosecution for underlying felony after conviction for felony murder). See Illinois v. Vitale, 447 U.S. 410 (1980) (5–4) (*Brown* applied). In *Brown*, the Court noted that "an exception may exist where the State is unable to proceed on the more serious charge at the outset because the additional facts necessary to sustain that charge have not occurred or have not been discovered despite the exercise of due diligence." 432 U.S. at 169 n.7.

Brown was distinguished in Montana v. Hall, 481 U.S. 400 (1987) (6–2), in which the defendant was indicted for sexual assault on his stepdaughter. He moved to dismiss on the ground that under state law the offense was incest, not sexual assault. The motion was granted. He was then convicted of incest. He appealed successfully, on the ground that the incest statute at the time of the offense did not apply to sexual assault on a stepchild. The Court held that a retrial was not barred. The case, it said, "falls squarely within the rule that retrial is permissible after a conviction is reversed on appeal." Id. at 404. *Brown* was distinguished also in Garrett v. United States, 471 U.S. 773 (1985) (5–3), holding that the Double Jeopardy Clause does not prohibit a prosecution for a "continuing criminal enterprise" (21 U.S.C. § 848) after the defendant has been convicted of one of the underlying predicate offenses. See also Jeffers v. United States, 432 U.S. 137 (1977) (defendant, having objected to trial together of greater and lesser charges, convicted of lesser charge at first trial).

In Ohio v. Johnson, 467 U.S. 493 (1984) (7–2), the defendant was charged in a single indictment with involuntary manslaughter, grand theft, murder, and aggravated robbery, all four counts arising out of the same events involving a killing and theft. He pleaded guilty to the first two counts over the state's objection, and was sentenced. The trial court then granted his motion to dismiss the latter two counts on the ground that the conviction of the lesser included offenses precluded further prosecution of the more serious offenses arising out of the same acts. The Court reversed. The joinder of the greater and lesser charges in a single prosecution is permissible. Here, the state never sought to try the charges separately. Nor were the guilty pleas an implied acquittal of the more serious offenses. The defendant's guilty pleas do not bar the state from one full opportunity to prove the crimes charged in the indictment. *Johnson* was applied in Gilmore v. Zimmerman, 793 F.2d 564 (3d Cir.1986), in which, at the sentencing hearing, the trial judge on his own motion struck a guilty plea that he had previously accepted. The plea to the lesser offense had been worked out by the prosecutor and defense counsel and was acceptable to both sides. The judge's reason for rejecting it was that there was an insufficient factual basis.

See Whalen v. United States, 445 U.S. 684 (1980) (7–2). The defendant was convicted of rape and of killing the same victim in the perpetration of rape. Construing federal statutory law, the Court concluded that the imposition of consecutive sentences for the two offenses was impermissible. *Whalen* was distinguished in Missouri v. Hunter, 459 U.S. 359 (1983) (7–2), in which the Court, finding a clear legislative intent to permit the imposition of cumulative sentences under two statutes proscribing the same conduct, held that the Double Jeopardy Clause does not prohibit the imposition of consecutive sentences under the statutes in a single trial. The Court observed that the Clause's protection against multiple prosecutions was not involved because the charges were joined in a single trial.

After the defendant had been convicted of the lesser offense of aggravated robbery, he was charged with aggravated murder and convicted following a jury verdict. On appeal, concluding that the charge of aggravated murder violated the Double Jeopardy Clause, the state court substituted a conviction for murder and reduced the defendant's sentence accordingly. It concluded that the jury's verdict necessarily supported the conviction for murder, all the elements of the lesser offense being excluded. On habeas corpus, the federal court of appeals held that the substituted conviction was invalid; it said that the defendant had only to show a "reasonable possibility" that he was prejudiced by the barred charge. The Court reversed. It held that "when a jeopardy-barred conviction is reduced to a conviction for a lesser included offense which is not jeopardy-barred, the burden shifts to the defendant to demonstrate a reasonable probability that he would not have been convicted of the non-jeopardy-barred offense absent the presence of the jeopardy-barred offense." Morris v. Mathews, 475 U.S. 237, 246–47 (1986) (7–2). The Court stated that the case was not one for application of the harmless error standard. Rather, it was a case in which there was error that was not harmless. The question, it said, was whether substitution of the lesser conviction was an adequate remedy. Cf. Jones v. Thomas, 491 U.S. 376 (1989) (5–4) (defendant improperly sentenced cumulatively in single trial for felony murder and underlying felony could be made to serve balance of longer sentence for murder after shorter sentence for felony, already fully served, was vacated.)

605. The defendant in Witte v. United States, 515 U.S. 389 (1995), was convicted on a plea of guilty to drug offenses. The presentence report described additional drug offenses during the same period, which were not included among those to which he pleaded guilty. Over the objection of the defendant and the government, the court considered the latter offenses as "relevant conduct" for sentencing purposes, which resulted in an increase in his sentence under the Sentencing Guidelines. On the basis of a downward departure from the prescribed sentence, the final sentence was much less than the minimum prescribed standard sentence. Thereafter, the defendant was indicted for uncharged offenses that had been considered at the prior sentencing. He moved to dismiss the indictment on the ground that punishment for those offenses was prohibited by the Double Jeopardy Clause as multiple punishments for the same offense. The Court rejected his claim. Referring to prior cases, it said that "use of evidence of related criminal conduct to enhance a defendant's sentence for a separate crime within the authorized statutory limits does not constitute punishment for that conduct within the meaning of the Double Jeopardy Clause." Id. at 399.

606. Reviewing a wavering line of prior decisions, the Court held that a civil forfeiture is not a punishment for purposes of the Double Jeopardy Clause and, therefore, that punishing a defendant for an offense and, in a separate civil proceeding, declaring the forfeiture of his property for the same offense is not prohibited. United States v. Ursery, 518 U.S. 267 (1996) (8–1).

The Court returned to the general issue of when a penalty imposed in a noncriminal proceeding bars a subsequent prosecution, in Hudson v. United States, ___ U.S. ___, 118 S.Ct. 488 (1997). The petitioners were bankers who were assessed money penalties for violations of banking laws and regulations and barred from banking activities, in proceedings of the Office of the Comptroller of the Currency. They were subsequently indicted for the same conduct that was involved in the prior proceedings. The Court held that the Double Jeopardy Clause did not prohibit their prosecution, because the prior penalties were noncriminal. It said that whether "a particular punishment is criminal or civil is, at least initially, a matter of statutory construction." Id. at 493. Even if the legislature intended the punishment as civil, however, if it had too many indicia of criminality it might be treated as criminal for purposes of the Double Jeopardy Clause. Quoting from Kennedy v. Mendozo-Martinez, 372 U.S. 144, 168–69 (1963) the Court said that among such indicia were: "(1) '[w]hether the sanction involves an affirmative disability or restraint'; (2) 'whether it has historically been regarded as a punishment'; (3) 'whether it comes into play only on a finding of *scienter*'; (4) 'whether its operation will promote the traditional aims of punishment-retribution and deterrence'; (5) 'whether the behavior to which it applies is already a crime'; (6) 'whether an alternative purpose to which it may rationally be connected is assignable for it'; and (7) 'whether it appears excessive in relation to the alternative purpose assigned.'" A conclusion that a statutory civil sanction is in effect criminal is permissible only if there is " 'the clearest proof'," United States v. Ward, 448 U.S. 242, 249 (1980), that it is criminal in nature. 118 S.Ct. at 493.

See Kansas v. Hendricks, ___ U.S. ___, 117 S.Ct. 2072 (1997) (5–4), in which the Court held that the Double Jeopardy Clause was not violated by provisions of the Kansas Sexually Violent Predator Act establishing procedures for the civil commitment of persons who are likely to engage in "predatory acts of sexual violence" because of a "mental abnormality" or a "personality disorder." After serving nearly ten years of a sentence for a sexual offense against two boys, the petitioner was scheduled for release. The state filed civil commitment proceedings under the statute. Following a jury trial at which he was found beyond a reasonable doubt to be a sexually violent predator, he was civilly committed. Applying tests like those stated in *Mendoza-Martinez*, above, the court concluded that the commitment was noncriminal.

607. Denial of a motion to dismiss an indictment on the ground of double jeopardy is a "final decision" under 28 U.S.C. § 1291 and is, therefore, immediately appealable. Abney v. United States, 431 U.S. 651 (1977). Such a ruling, the Court said, constitutes "a final rejection of a criminal defendant's double jeopardy claim." Furthermore, the claim "is collateral to, and separable from the principal issue at the accused's impending criminal trial," and postponement of the appeal would undermine the right not to be put to trial twice for the same offense. Id. at 659. See Richardson v. United States, 468 U.S. 317 (1984) (8–1), applying *Abney* to an appeal from the denial of a motion for a judgment of acquittal on the ground of insufficient evidence, which motion if granted would have barred retrial because of the Double Jeopardy Clause.

———

Green v. United States

355 U.S. 184, 78 S.Ct. 221, 2 L.Ed.2d 199 (1957).

■ Opinion of the Court by MR. JUSTICE BLACK, announced by MR. JUSTICE DOUGLAS.

This case presents a serious question concerning the meaning and application of that provision of the Fifth Amendment to the Constitution which declares that no person shall ". . . be subject for the same offence to be twice put in jeopardy of life or limb. . . ."

The petitioner, Everett Green, was indicted by a District of Columbia grand jury in two counts. The first charged that he had committed arson by maliciously setting fire to a house. The second accused him of causing the death of a woman by this alleged arson which if true amounted to murder in the first degree punishable by death. Green entered a plea of not guilty to both counts and the case was tried by a jury. After each side had presented its evidence the trial judge instructed the jury that it could find Green guilty of arson under the first count and of either (1) first degree murder or (2) second degree murder under the second count. The trial judge treated second degree murder, which is defined by the District Code as the killing of another with malice aforethought and is punishable by imprisonment for a term of years or for life, as an offense included within the language charging first degree murder in the second count of the indictment.

The jury found Green guilty of arson and of second degree murder but did not find him guilty on the charge of murder in the first degree. Its verdict was silent on that charge. The trial judge accepted the verdict, entered the proper judgments and dismissed the jury. Green was sentenced to one to three years' imprisonment for arson and five to twenty years' imprisonment for murder in the second degree. He appealed the conviction of second degree murder. The Court of Appeals reversed that conviction because it was not supported by evidence and remanded the case for a new trial. . . .

On remand Green was tried again for first degree murder under the original indictment. At the outset of this second trial he raised the defense of former jeopardy but the court overruled his plea. This time a new jury found him guilty of first degree murder and he was given the mandatory death sentence. Again he appealed. Sitting *en banc*, the Court of Appeals rejected his defense of former jeopardy . . . and affirmed the conviction. . . . We granted certiorari . . . .

The constitutional prohibition against "double jeopardy" was designed to protect an individual from being subjected to the hazards of trial and possible conviction more than once for an alleged offense. In his Commentaries, which greatly influenced the generation that adopted the Constitution, Blackstone recorded: ". . . the plea of *autrefois acquit*, or a former acquittal, is grounded on this universal maxim of the common law of England, that no man is to be brought into jeopardy of his life more than once for the same offence." Substantially the same view was taken by this Court in Ex parte Lange, 18 Wall. 163, at 169: "The common law not only prohibited a second punishment for the same offence, but it went further and forbid a second trial for the same offence, whether the accused had suffered punishment or not, and whether in the former trial he had been acquitted or convicted." The underlying idea, one that is deeply ingrained in at least the Anglo-American system of jurisprudence, is that the State with all its resources and power should not be allowed to make repeated attempts to convict an individual for an alleged offense, thereby subjecting him to embarrassment, expense and ordeal and compelling him to live in a continuing state of anxiety and insecurity, as well as enhancing the possibility that even though innocent he may be found guilty."

In accordance with this philosophy it has long been settled under the Fifth Amendment that a verdict of acquittal is final, ending a defendant's jeopardy, and even when "not followed by any judgment, is a bar to a subsequent prosecution for the same offence." United States v. Ball, 153 U.S. 662, 671. Thus it is one of the elemental principles of our criminal law that the Government cannot secure a new trial by means of an appeal even though an acquittal may appear to be erroneous. . . .

Moreover it is not even essential that a verdict of guilt or innocence be returned for a defendant to have once been placed in jeopardy so as to bar a second trial on the same charge. This Court, as well as most others, has taken the position that a defendant is placed in jeopardy once he is put to trial before a jury so that if the jury is discharged without his consent he cannot be tried again. . . . This prevents a prosecutor or judge from subjecting a defendant to a second prosecution by discontinuing the trial when it appears that the jury might not convict. At the same time jeopardy is not regarded as having come to an end so as to bar a second trial in those cases where "unforeseeable circumstances . . . arise during [the first] trial making its completion impossible, such as the failure of a jury to agree on a verdict." Wade v. Hunter, 336 U.S. 684, 688–689.

At common law a convicted person could not obtain a new trial by appeal except in certain narrow instances. As this harsh rule was discarded courts and legislatures provided that if a defendant obtained the reversal of a conviction by his own appeal he could be tried again for the same offense. Most courts regarded the new trial as a second jeopardy but justified this on the ground that the appellant had "waived" his plea of former jeopardy by asking that the conviction be set aside. Other courts viewed the second trial as continuing the same jeopardy which had attached at the first trial by reasoning that jeopardy did not come to an end until the accused was acquitted or his conviction became final. But whatever the rationalization, this Court has also held that a defendant can be tried a second time for an offense when his prior conviction for that same offense had been set aside on appeal. . . .

In this case, however, we have a much different question. At Green's first trial the jury was authorized to find him guilty of either first degree murder (killing while perpetrating a felony) or, alternatively, of second degree murder (killing with malice aforethought). The jury found him guilty of second degree murder, but on his appeal that conviction was reversed and the case remanded for a new trial. At this new trial Green was tried again, not for second degree murder, but for first degree murder, even though the original jury had refused to find him guilty on that charge and it was in no way involved in his appeal. For the reasons stated hereafter, we conclude that this second trial for first degree murder placed Green in jeopardy twice for the same offense in violation of the Constitution.

Green was in direct peril of being convicted and punished for first degree murder at his first trial. He was forced to run the gantlet once on that charge and the jury refused to convict him. When given the choice between finding him guilty of either first or second degree murder it chose the latter. In this situation the great majority of cases in this country have regarded the jury's verdict as an implicit acquittal on the charge of first degree murder. But the result in this case need not rest alone on the assumption, which we believe legitimate, that the jury for one reason or another acquitted Green of murder in the first degree. For here, the jury was dismissed without returning any express verdict on that charge and without Green's consent. Yet it was given a full opportunity to return a verdict and no extraordinary circumstances appeared which prevented it from doing so. Therefore it seems clear, under established principles of former jeopardy, that Green's jeopardy for first degree murder came to an end when the jury was discharged so that he could not be retried for that offense. . . . In brief, we believe this case can be treated no differently, for purposes of former jeopardy, than if the jury had returned a verdict which expressly read: "We find the defendant not guilty of murder in the first degree but guilty of murder in the second degree."

After the original trial, but prior to his appeal, it is indisputable that Green could not have been tried again for first degree murder for the death resulting from the fire. A plea of former jeopardy would have absolutely barred a new prosecution even though it might have been convincingly demonstrated that the jury erred in failing to convict him of that offense. And even after appealing the conviction of second degree murder he still could not have been tried a second time for first degree murder had his appeal been unsuccessful.

Nevertheless the Government contends that Green "waived" his constitutional defense of former jeopardy to a second prosecution on the first degree murder charge by making a *successful* appeal of his improper conviction of second degree murder. We cannot accept this paradoxical contention. "Waiver" is a vague term used for a great variety of purposes, good and bad, in the law. In any normal sense, however, it connotes some kind of voluntary knowing relinquishment of a right. . . . When a man has been convicted of second degree murder and given a long term of imprisonment it is wholly fictional to say that he "chooses" to forego his constitutional defense of former jeopardy on a charge of murder in the first degree in order to secure a reversal of an erroneous conviction of the lesser offense. In short, he has no meaningful choice. And as Mr. Justice Holmes observed, with regard to this same matter in Kepner v. United States, 195 U.S. 100, at 135: "Usually no such waiver is expressed or thought of. Moreover, it cannot be imagined that the law would deny to a prisoner the correction of a fatal error, unless he should waive other rights so important as to be saved by an express clause in the Constitution of the United States."

It is true that in *Kepner*, a case arising in the Philippine Islands under a statutory prohibition against double jeopardy, Mr. Justice Holmes dissented from the Court's holding that the Government could not appeal an acquittal in a criminal prosecution. He argued that there was only one continuing jeopardy until the "case" had finally been settled, appeal and all, without regard to how many times the defendant was tried, but that view was rejected by the Court. The position taken by the majority in *Kepner* is completely in accord with the deeply entrenched principle of our criminal law that once a person has been acquitted of an offense he cannot be prosecuted again on the same charge. This Court has uniformly adhered to that basic premise. For example, in United States v. Ball, 163 U.S. 662, 671, a unanimous Court held: "The verdict of acquittal was final, and could not be reviewed, on error or otherwise, without putting [the defendant] twice in jeopardy, and thereby violating the Constitution." . . .

Using reasoning which purports to be analogous to that expressed by Mr. Justice Holmes in *Kepner*, the Government alternatively argues that Green, by appealing, prolonged his original jeopardy so that when his conviction for second degree murder was reversed and the case remanded he could be tried again for first degree murder without placing him in new jeopardy. We believe this argument is also untenable. Whatever may be said for the notion of continuing jeopardy with regard to an offense when a defendant has been convicted of that offense and has secured reversal of the conviction by appeal, here Green was not convicted of first degree murder and that offense was not involved in his appeal. If Green had only appealed his conviction of arson and that conviction had been set aside surely no one would claim that he could have been tried a second time for first degree murder by reasoning that his initial jeopardy on that charge continued until every offense alleged in the indictment had been finally adjudicated.

Reduced to plain terms, the Government contends that in order to secure the reversal of an erroneous conviction of one offense, a defendant must surrender his valid defense of former jeopardy not only on that offense but also on a different offense for which he was not convicted and which was not involved in his appeal. Or stated in the terms of this case, he must be willing to barter his constitutional protection against a second prosecution for an offense punishable by death as the price of a successful appeal from an erroneous conviction of another offense for which he has been sentenced to five to twenty years' imprisonment. As the Court of Appeals said in its first opinion in this case, a defendant faced with such a "choice" takes a "desperate chance" in securing the reversal of the erroneous conviction. The law should not, and in our judgment does not, place the defendant in such an incredible dilemma. Conditioning an appeal of one offense on a coerced surrender of a valid plea of former jeopardy on another offense exacts a forfeiture in plain conflict with the constitutional bar against double jeopardy.

. . .

. . . The right not to be placed in jeopardy more than once for the same offense is a vital safeguard in our society, one that was dearly won and one that should continue to be highly valued. If such great constitutional protections are given a narrow, grudging application they are deprived of much of their significance. We [conclude] that the second trial of Green for first degree murder was contrary to both the letter and spirit of the Fifth Amendment.

. . .[1]

---

608. *Green* was applied to a case in which after reversal of his conviction for the lesser offense, the defendant was again prosecuted for the more serious offense and again convicted of the *lesser* offense, in Price v. Georgia, 398 U.S. 323 (1970).

In Cichos v. Indiana, 385 U.S. 76 (1966), the defendant was charged with reckless homicide and involuntary manslaughter. He was convicted of reckless homicide on a jury verdict reciting only that he was guilty of that crime. He appealed successfully and was retried on both counts. He was again convicted of reckless homicide and sentenced. Under Indiana law, involuntary manslaughter was punishable more severely than reckless homicide, but the elements of the two crimes were the same, so that proof of reckless homicide necessarily established "an unlawful killing that amounts to involuntary manslaughter." Id. at 78. The Supreme Court accepted the conclusions of the Indiana Supreme Court that the effect of charging the two crimes was to give the jury discretion on the issue of sentencing and that its verdict did not constitute an acquittal of the more serious offense. On that basis, the Court concluded that the issue presented in *Green* was not present in the case.

Compare Pacelli v. United States, 588 F.2d 360 (2d Cir.1978), in which the defendant was convicted of a conspiracy charge and related substantive charges. The conspiracy charge was later found to have been barred by the Double Jeopardy clause. The court upheld the convictions of the substantive counts, on the basis that the defendant's trial on the substantive counts had not been prejudiced by the joinder.

The defendant in United States ex rel. Jackson v. Follette, 462 F.2d 1041 (2d Cir.1972), was convicted of first-degree murder for the killing of a police officer after an armed robbery. At trial, the jury was instructed with respect to premeditated murder and felony murder, both constituting mur-

---

[1] Justice Frankfurter wrote a dissenting opinion, which Justice Burton, Justice Clark, and Justice Harlan joined.

der in the first degree, and told that if it found the defendant guilty of one, it should say nothing about the other. The conviction was for premeditated murder. The conviction was reversed on collateral attack. The defendant was tried again on both theories of murder. This time he was convicted for felony murder. After discussing *Green*, *Price*, and *Cichos* and observing that the case was *sui generis*, the court concluded that there had been no "substantial unfairness" to the defendant, since he would have been subject to retrial for premeditated murder in any event and the same evidence would have been admissible, and that "fairness to the public" demanded that the conviction be affirmed. Id. at 1050. In analogous circumstances, the court found that *Green* was applicable and that the defendant could not be put to trial a second time on the count on which the jury had not returned a verdict. Terry v. Potter, 111 F.3d 454 (6th Cir.1997).

609. The Double Jeopardy Clause requires that a person who has been convicted and sentenced, whose conviction is subsequently set aside, and who is convicted and sentenced a second time be given credit toward the second sentence for any portion of the first sentence that he served.

"We think it is clear that this basic constitutional guarantee is violated when punishment already exacted for an offense is not fully 'credited' in imposing sentence upon a new conviction for the same offense. The constitutional violation is flagrantly apparent in a case involving the imposition of a maximum sentence after reconviction. Suppose, for example, in a jurisdiction where the maximum allowable sentence for larceny is 10 years imprisonment, a man succeeds in getting his larceny conviction set aside after serving three years in prison. If, upon reconviction, he is given a 10-year sentence, then, quite clearly, he will have received multiple punishments for the same offense. For he will have been compelled to serve separate prison terms of three years and 10 years, although the maximum single punishment for the offense is 10 years imprisonment. Though not so dramatically evident, the same principle obviously holds true whenever punishment already endured is not fully subtracted from any new sentence imposed.

"We hold that the constitutional guarantee against multiple punishments for the same offense absolutely requires that punishment already exacted must be fully 'credited' in imposing sentence upon a new conviction for the same offense. If, upon a new trial, the defendant is acquitted, there is no way the years he spent in prison can be returned to him. But if he is reconvicted, those years can and must be returned—by subtracting them from whatever new sentence is imposed." North Carolina v. Pearce, 395 U.S. 711, 718–19 (1969).

The Double Jeopardy Clause does not, however, bar imposition of a more severe sentence following the second conviction than that originally imposed if the second sentence is based on "events subsequent to the first trial." Id. at 723. "Long-established constitutional doctrine makes clear that, beyond the requirement [of "credit"] already discussed, the guarantee against double jeopardy imposes no restrictions upon the length of a sentence imposed upon reconviction. . . .

"Although the rationale for this 'well-established part of our constitutional jurisprudence' has been variously verbalized, it rests ultimately upon the premise that the original conviction has, at the defendant's behest, been wholly nullified and the slate wiped clean. As to whatever punishment has actually been suffered under the first conviction, that premise is, of course, an unmitigated fiction. . . . But, so far as the conviction itself goes, and that part of the sentence that has not yet been served, it is no more than a simple statement of fact to say that the slate *has* been wiped clean. The conviction *has* been set aside, and the unexpired portion of the original sentence will never be served. A new trial may result in an acquittal. But if it does result in a conviction, we cannot say that the constitutional guarantee against double jeopardy of its own weight restricts the imposition of an otherwise lawful single punishment for the offense in question. To hold to the contrary would be to cast doubt upon the whole validity of the basic principle . . . and upon the unbroken line of decisions that have followed that principle for almost 75 years. We think those decisions are entirely sound, and we decline to depart from the concept they reflect." Id. at 719–21. See note 585 p. 1169 above.

610. Is the holding of *Green*, p. 1219 above, consistent with the holding of North Carolina v. Pearce, note 609 above, that a defendant may be given a more severe sentence on a second conviction than was imposed on a prior conviction of the same offense? In Stroud v. United States, 251 U.S. 15 (1919), on which the Court relied in *Pearce*, the defendant, having been convicted of first-degree murder on a jury verdict specifying "without capital punishment," was subsequently retried and convicted of first-degree murder without a recommendation dispensing with capital punishment and was sentenced to death. The Court affirmed the judgment. The opinion for the Court in *Green* stated that *Stroud* is "clearly distinguishable," the defendant in *Stroud* having been retried for first-degree murder "after he had successfully asked an appellate court to set aside a prior conviction for that same offense." 355 U.S. at 195 n.15. The dissenting opinion in *Green* stated that *Stroud* is "of special relevance." Id. at 213. "As a practical matter, and on any basis of human values, it is scarcely possible to distinguish a case in which the defendant is convicted of a greater offense from one in which he is convicted of an offense that has the same name as that of which he was previously convicted but carries a significantly different punishment, namely death rather than imprisonment." Id.[1] The majority in *Pearce* appears to concede that conceptually the problems of the two cases are closely related.

---

1. *Stroud* is not mentioned in the Court's opinion in Cichos v. Indiana, 385 U.S. 76 (1966), note 608 p. 1223 above.

Justice Harlan, in *Pearce*, concluded that *Green* had discarded *Stroud* and should control the solution to the problem of resentencing: "Every consideration enunciated by the Court in support of the decision in *Green* applies with equal force to the situation at bar. In each instance, the defendant was once subjected to the risk of receiving a maximum punishment, but it was determined by legal process that he should receive only a specified punishment less than the maximum. . . . And the concept or fiction of an 'implied acquittal' of the greater offense . . . applies equally to the greater sentence: in each case it was determined at the former trial that the defendant or his offense was of a certain limited degree of 'badness' or gravity only, and therefore merited only a certain limited punishment. . . .

"If, as a matter of policy and practicality, the imposition of an increased sentence on retrial has the same consequences whether effected in the guise of an increase in the degree of offense or an augmentation of punishment, what other factors render one route forbidden and the other permissible under the Double Jeopardy Clause? It cannot be that the provision does not comprehend 'sentences'—as distinguished from 'offenses'—for it has long been established that once a prisoner commences service of sentence, the Clause prevents a court from vacating the sentence and then imposing a greater one. . . .

"The Court does not suggest otherwise, but in its view, apparently, when the conviction itself and not merely the consequent sentence has been set aside, or when either has been set aside at the defendant's behest, the 'slate has been wiped clean,' and the Double Jeopardy Clause presents no bar to the imposition of a sentence greater than that originally imposed. . . .

. . .

"[United States v.] *Ball*, [163 U.S. 662 (1896)] held, simply, that a defendant who succeeds in getting his first conviction set aside may thereafter be retried for the same offense of which he was formerly convicted. This is, indeed, a fundamental doctrine in our criminal jurisprudence, and I would be the last to undermine it. But *Ball* does not speak to the question of what *punishment* may be imposed on retrial. I entirely fail to understand the Court's suggestion, unless it assumes that *Ball* must stand or fall on the question-begging notion that, to quote the majority today, 'the original conviction has, at the defendant's behest, been wholly nullified and the slate wiped clean.' . . .

"In relying on this conceptual fiction, the majority forgets that Green v. United States, prohibits the imposition of an increased punishment on retrial precisely *because* convictions are usually set aside only at the defendant's behest, and not in spite of that fact . . . the defendant's choice to appeal an erroneous conviction is protected by the rule that he may not again be placed in jeopardy of suffering the greater punishment not imposed at the first trial. Moreover, in its exaltation of form over substance and policy, the Court misconceives, I think, the essential principle of *Ball* itself:

" 'While different theories have been advanced to support the permissibility of retrial, of greater importance than the conceptual abstractions employed to explain the *Ball* principle are the implications of that principle for the sound administration of justice. Corresponding to the right of an accused to be given a fair trial is the societal interest in punishing one whose guilt is clear after he has obtained such a trial. It would be a high price indeed for society to pay were every accused granted immunity from punishment because of any defect sufficient to constitute reversible error in the proceedings leading to conviction.' United States v. Tateo, 377 U.S. 463, 466 (1964).

"To be sure, this societal interest is compromised to a degree if the second judge is forbidden to impose a greater punishment on retrial than was meted out at the first trial. For example, new facts may develop between the first and second trial which would, as an initial matter, be considered in aggravation of sentence. By the same token, however, the prosecutor who was able to prove only second degree murder at the former trial might improve his case in the interim and acquire sufficient evidence to prove murder in the first degree. In either instance, if one views the second trial in a vacuum, the defendant has received less punishment than is his due. But in both cases, the compromise is designed to protect other societal interests, and it is, after *Green*, a compromise compelled by the Double Jeopardy Clause." 395 U.S. at 746–50 (concurring and dissenting opinion).

Justice Harlan's argument in *Pearce* was rejected again in United States v. DiFrancesco, 449 U.S. 117 (1980) (5–4). The Court there concluded that the Double Jeopardy Clause does not prohibit an appeal from a sentence by the government, on the ground that the sentence is too lenient. *DiFrancesco* was applied in Pennsylvania v. Goldhammer, 474 U.S. 28 (1985) (5–4).

In Bullington v. Missouri, 451 U.S. 430 (1981) (5–4), however, a majority of the Court distinguished *Stroud*. The defendant was convicted of murder. At a separate sentencing hearing, at which the two possible sentences were death and life imprisonment, the jury chose the latter penalty. The defendant's conviction was reversed and he was retried and again found guilty. The Court concluded that the first jury's sentencing decision precluded a sentence of death after the second trial. Acknowledging that the Court generally had not interpreted the Double Jeopardy Clause to bar imposition of a harsher sentence at retrial after an original conviction has been set aside, the majority concluded that the procedures followed in this case were more like those followed at a trial to determine guilt or innocence than those followed at a typical sentencing proceeding. The opinion noted particularly that the jury was given only two choices of sentence, that the prosecutor sought to establish facts to justify the death sentence, that the jury was required to find such facts beyond a reasonable doubt, and that it was required to reach a decision to impose the death sentence unanimously. See Arizona v. Rumsey, 467 U.S. 203 (1984) (7–2) (*Bullington* applied). *Bullington* does not apply to noncapital sentencing proceedings. Monge v. California, ___ S.Ct. ___, ___ U.S. ___ (5–4) (retrial of sentence enhancement provision).

Bullington was distinguished in Poland v. Arizona, 476 U.S. 147 (1986) (6–3). In *Poland*, the defendants were sentenced to death on the basis of an "aggravating circumstance" the evidence for which the reviewing court found to be insufficient. The defendants were convicted a second time and again sentenced to death, on the basis of aggravating circumstances not considered at the first sentencing hearing. Failure to consider the latter circumstances, the Court said, was not an "acquittal" for purposes of the Double Jeopardy Clause. See Schiro v. Farley, 510 U.S. 222 (1994) (7–2), in which the Court held that it did not violate the prohibition against successive prosecutions for the state to present evidence that a killing was intentional as an aggravating factor at the sentencing hearing, after a jury had returned a verdict of guilty on a count of felony murder without reaching a verdict on a count of "knowingly" killing the victim.

In Ricketts v. Adamson, 483 U.S. 1 (1987) (5–4), the defendant was charged with first-degree murder. As part of the plea agreement, he agreed to testify against two other persons allegedly involved in the murder. The agreement provided that if he did not testify, the entire agreement would be void and the original charge would be reinstated. He testified as agreed. While the other defendants' convictions were on appeal, he was sentenced and began service of the sentence. The other defendants' convictions were reversed. The defendant agreed to testify at their retrial only if certain conditions, including his release from custody afterwards, were met. Upon his refusal to testify, the original charge was reinstated, and he was convicted of first-degree murder. In those circumstances, the Court said, in view of the explicit terms of the plea agreement, the Double Jeopardy Clause was not violated. The Court concluded that it was immaterial that there was a disagreement about the construction of the plea agreement (concerning the defendant's obligation to testify at the second trial), which was resolved by a court or that, following the adverse resolution of that issue, the defendant offered to testify and, the original charge having been reinstated, the state rejected the offer.

In United States v. Whitley, 734 F.2d 994 (4th Cir.1984), the defendant pleaded guilty to one count of a four-count indictment and was sentenced. The other three counts were dismissed. Thereafter, the defendant filed a motion to vacate the conviction and sentence. The motion was granted, and the case was remanded for trial. The defendant was retried on the original indictment and convicted on all four counts. He was sentenced to a substantially longer term of imprisonment than that of the first sentence. The court held that the increased sentence was prohibited by Pearce, since "absent a reasoned explanation to justify increased punishment, to uphold the sentence would create a reasonable apprehension of vindictiveness which would have a chilling effect on defendants' exercise of their rights to appeal." Id. at 997. The original sentence was for a lesser included offense of the original charges, and the sentencing judge was aware of the facts of the crime. Had the original sentence been for one of several distinct charges, rather than for crimes arising out of a single transaction, and the second sentence for distinct crimes not covered by the first sentence, the result would have been different.

611. The defendant was charged in a three-count indictment with (1) bank robbery by force and violence, (2) larceny, and (3) armed bank robbery. The maximum penalty for each count was, respectively, imprisonment for (1) 20 years, (2) ten years, and (3) 25 years. At trial the jury, following an erroneous instruction that if it found the defendant guilty of one count it need not consider the other counts, returned a verdict, "Guilty as charged," without specifying which count it had in mind. A sentence of 20 years imprisonment was imposed. The conviction was reversed because of the error in the instructions. On what counts can the defendant be retried? See United States v. Schmidt, 376 F.2d 751 (4th Cir.1967).

612. "It is elementary in our law that a person can be tried a second time for an offense when his prior conviction for that same offense has been set aside by his appeal." Forman v. United States, 361 U.S. 416, 425 (1960). See United States v. Tateo, 377 U.S. 463 (1964). "From the standpoint of a defendant, it is at least doubtful that appellate courts would be as zealous as they now are in protecting against improprieties at the trial or pretrial stage if they knew that reversal of a conviction would put the accused irrevocably beyond the reach of further prosecution." Id. at 466.

Overruling a previous decision, the Court held in Burks v. United States, 437 U.S. 1 (1978), that the prohibition against double jeopardy does *not* permit retrial of a defendant who successfully appeals from denial of a motion for judgment of acquittal on the ground that the evidence is insufficient to sustain the verdict. Distinguishing a reversal for trial error from a reversal for insufficient evidence, the Court said that in the latter case, the "appellate reversal means that the Government's case was so lacking that it should not have even been *submitted* to the jury. Since we necessarily afford absolute finality to a jury's *verdict* of acquittal—no matter how erroneous its decision—it is difficult to conceive how society has any greater interest in retrying a defendant when, on review, it is decided as a matter of law that the jury could not properly have returned a verdict of guilty." Id. at 16. See Hudson v. Louisiana, 450 U.S. 40 (1981) (*Burks* applied).

Burks was distinguished in Tibbs v. Florida, 457 U.S. 31 (1982) (5–4). There, the Court contrasted reversal of a conviction on a finding that the verdict was against the weight of the evidence with a holding that the evidence was not legally sufficient to support the verdict, and held that in the former situation retrial was permissible. The distinction between *Burks* and *Tibbs* was explored in Carter v. Estelle, 691 F.2d 777 (5th Cir.1982) (*Burks* applied).

Burks was distinguished also in Justices of the Municipal Court v. Lydon, 466 U.S. 294 (1984), in which the defendant was convicted at a bench trial and was entitled thereafter to a *de novo* jury trial. He had claimed at the bench trial that he should be acquitted because insufficient evidence of guilt had been introduced. In this case, the Court said, unlike *Burks*, there had been no judicial determination that the evidence was insufficient to convict. *Burks* does not entitle the defendant to a ruling on his claim before he can be retried under the two-tier system.

Burks does not require that after a mistrial has been declared because of a hung jury, an appellate court review the denial of the defendant's motion for a judgment of acquittal on the ground that the government had failed to introduce sufficient evidence to sustain a verdict of guilty. Richardson v. United States, 468 U.S. 317 (1984) (7–2). The Court said that *Burks* does not "extend beyond the procedural setting in which it arose," that is, "once a defendant obtained an unreversed appellate ruling that the Government had failed to introduce sufficient evidence to convict him at trial, a second trial was barred by the Double Jeopardy Clause." Id. at 323. There having been no such ruling, retrial was not barred. Nor is *Burks* applicable when a conviction is set aside on appeal because of the erroneous admission of evidence. The Double Jeopardy Clause does not prohibit a retrial, provided that all the evidence admitted at the first trial, including that which was erroneously admitted, was sufficient to sustain a conviction. Lockhart v. Nelson, 488 U.S. 33 (1988) (6–3).

Mistrial

See Rule 26.3, p. 1027 above.

United States v. Jorn

400 U.S. 470, 91 S.Ct. 547, 27 L.Ed.2d 543 (1971).

■ MR. JUSTICE HARLAN delivered the judgment of the Court in an opinion joined by The CHIEF JUSTICE, MR. JUSTICE DOUGLAS, and MR. JUSTICE MARSHALL.

The Government directly appeals the order of the United States District Court for the District of Utah dismissing, on the ground of former jeopardy, an information charging the defendant-appellee with willfully assisting in the preparation of fraudulent income tax returns, in violation of 26 U.S.C. § 7206(2).

Appellee was originally charged in February 1968 with 25 counts of violating § 7206(2). He was brought to trial before Chief Judge Ritter on August 27, 1968. After the jury was chosen and sworn, 14 of the counts were dismissed on the Government's motion. The trial then commenced, the Government calling as its first witness an Internal Revenue Service agent in order to put in evidence the remaining 11 allegedly fraudulent income tax returns the defendant was charged with helping to prepare. At the trial judge's suggestion, these exhibits were stipulated to and introduced in evidence without objection. The Government's five remaining witnesses were taxpayers whom the defendant allegedly had aided in preparation of these returns.

After the first of these witnesses was called, but prior to the commencement of direct examination, defense counsel suggested that these witnesses be warned of their constitutional rights. The trial court agreed, and proceeded, in careful detail, to spell out the witness' right not to say anything that might be used in a subsequent criminal prosecution against him and his right, in the event of such a prosecution, to be represented by an attorney. The first witness expressed a willingness to testify and stated that he had been warned of his constitutional rights when the Internal Revenue Service first contacted him. The trial judge indicated, however, that he did not believe the witness had been given any warning at the time he was first contacted by the IRS, and refused to permit him to testify until he had consulted an attorney.

The trial judge then asked the prosecuting attorney if his remaining four witnesses were similarly situated. The prosecutor responded that they had been warned of their rights by the IRS upon initial contact. The judge, expressing the view that any warnings that might have been given were probably inadequate, proceeded to discharge the jury; he then called all the taxpayers into court, and informed them of their constitutional rights and of the considerable dangers of unwittingly making damaging admissions in these factual circumstances. Finally, he aborted the trial so the witnesses could consult with attorneys.

The case was set for retrial before another jury, but on pretrial motion by the defendant, Judge Ritter dismissed the information on the ground of former jeopardy. The Government filed a direct appeal to this Court, and we noted probable jurisdiction. . . .

. . .

II

The Fifth Amendment's prohibition against placing a defendant "twice in jeopardy" represents a constitutional policy of finality for the defendant's benefit in federal criminal proceedings. A power in government to subject the individual to repeated prosecutions for the same offense would cut deeply into the framework of procedural protections which the Constitution establishes for the conduct of a criminal trial. And society's awareness of the heavy personal strain which a criminal trial represents for the individual defendant is manifested in the willingness to limit the Government to a single criminal proceeding to vindicate its very vital interest in enforcement of criminal laws. Both of these considerations are expressed in Green v. United States, 355 U.S. 184, 187–188 (1957), where the Court noted that the policy underlying this provision "is that the State with all its resources and power should not be allowed to make repeated attempts to convict an individual for an alleged offense, thereby subjecting him to embarrassment, expense and ordeal and compelling him to live in a continuing state of anxiety and insecurity, as well as enhancing the possibility that even though innocent he may be found guilty." These considerations have led this Court to conclude that a defendant is placed in jeopardy in a criminal proceeding once the defendant is put to trial before the trier of the facts, whether the trier be a jury or a judge. . . .

But it is also true that a criminal trial is, even in the best of circumstances, a complicated affair to manage. The proceedings are dependent in the first instance on the most elementary sort of considerations, e.g., the health of the various witnesses, parties, attorneys, jurors, etc., all of whom must be prepared to arrive at the courthouse at set times. And when one adds the scheduling problems arising from case overloads, and the Sixth Amendment's requirement that the single trial to which the double jeopardy provision restricts the Government be conducted speedily, it becomes readily apparent that a mechanical rule prohibiting retrial whenever circumstances compel the discharge of a jury without the defendant's consent would be too high a price to pay for the added assurance of personal security and freedom from governmental harassment which such a mechanical rule would provide. As the Court noted in Wade v. Hunter, 336 U.S. 684, 689 (1949), "a defendant's valued right to have his trial completed by a particular tribunal must in some circumstances be subordinated to the public's interest in fair trials designed to end in just judgments."

Thus the conclusion that "jeopardy attaches" when the trial commences expresses a judgment that the constitutional policies underpinning the Fifth Amendment's guarantee are implicated at that point in the proceedings. The question remains, however, in what circumstances retrial is to be precluded when the initial proceedings are aborted prior to verdict without the defendant's consent.

In dealing with that question, this Court has, for the most part, explicitly declined the invitation of litigants to formulate rules based on categories of circumstances which will permit or preclude retrial. Thus, in United States v. Perez, 9 Wheat. 579 (1824), this Court held that a defendant in a capital case might be retried after the trial judge had, without the defendant's consent, discharged a jury that reported itself unable to agree. Mr. Justice Story's opinion for the Court in Perez expressed the following thoughts on the problem of reprosecution after a mistrial had been declared without the consent of the defendant:

> "We think, that in all cases of this nature, the law has invested Courts of justice with the authority to discharge a jury from giving any verdict, whenever, in their opinion, taking all the circumstances into consideration, there is a manifest necessity for the act, or the ends of public justice would otherwise be defeated. They are to exercise a sound discretion on the subject; and it is impossible to define all the circumstances, which would render it proper to interfere. To be sure, the power ought to be used with the greatest caution, under urgent circumstances, and for very plain and obvious causes; and, in capital cases especially, Courts should be extremely careful how they interfere with

any of the chances of life, in favour of the prisoner. But, after all, they have the right to order the discharge; and the security which the public have for the faithful, sound, and conscientious exercise of this discretion, rests, in this, as in other cases, upon the responsibility of the Judges, under their oaths of office." Id., at 580.

The *Perez* case has since been applied by this Court as a standard of appellate review for testing the trial judge's exercise of his discretion in declaring a mistrial without the defendant's consent. . . .

But a more recent case—Gori v. United States, 367 U.S. 364 (1961)— while adhering in the main to the *Perez* theme of a "manifest necessity" standard of appellate review—does suggest the possibility of a variation on that theme according to a determination by the appellate court as to which party to the case was the beneficiary of the mistrial ruling. In *Gori*, the Court was called upon to review the action of a trial judge in discharging the jury when it appeared to the judge that the prosecution's questioning of a witness might lead to the introduction of evidence of prior crimes. We upheld reprosecution after the mistrial in an opinion which, while applying the principle of *Perez*, appears to tie the judgment that there was no abuse of discretion in these circumstances to the fact that the judge was acting "in the sole interest of the defendant." 367 U.S., at 369. . . .

In the instant case, the Government, relying principally on *Gori*, contends that even if we conclude the trial judge here abused his discretion, reprosecution should be permitted because the judge's ruling "benefited" the defendant and also clearly was not compelled by bad-faith prosecutorial conduct aimed at triggering a mistrial in order to get another day in court. If the judgment as to who was "benefited" by the mistrial ruling turns on the appellate court's conclusion concerning which party the trial judge was, in point of personal motivation, trying to protect from prejudice, it seems reasonably clear from the trial record here that the judge's insistence on stopping the trial until the witnesses were properly warned was motivated by the desire to protect the witnesses rather than the defendant. But the Government appears to view the question of "benefit" as turning on an appellate court's *post hoc* assessment as to which party would in fact have been aided in the hypothetical event that the witnesses had been called to the stand after consulting with their own attorneys on the course of conduct that would best serve to insulate them personally from criminal and civil liability for the fraudulent tax returns. That conception of benefit, however, involves nothing more than an exercise in pure speculation. In sum, we are unable to conclude on this record that this is a case of a mistrial made "in the sole interest of the defendant." . . .

Further, we think that a limitation on the abuse-of-discretion principle based on an appellate court's assessment of which side benefited from the mistrial ruling does not adequately satisfy the policies underpinning the double jeopardy provision. Reprosecution after a mistrial has unnecessarily been declared by the trial court obviously subjects the defendant to the same personal strain and insecurity regardless of the motivation underlying the trial judge's action. The Government contends, however, that the policies evinced by the double jeopardy provision do not reach this sort of injury; rather the unnecessarily inflicted second trial must, in the Government's view, appear to be the result of a mistrial declaration which "unfairly aids the prosecution or harasses the defense." Govt. Brief 8.

Certainly it is clear beyond question that the Double Jeopardy Clause does not guarantee a defendant that the Government will be prepared, in all circumstances, to vindicate the social interest in law enforcement through the vehicle of a single proceeding for a given offense. Thus, for example, reprosecution for the same offense is permitted where the defendant wins a reversal on appeal of a conviction. . . . The determination to allow reprosecution in these circumstances reflects the judgment that the defendant's double jeopardy interests, however defined, do not go so far as to compel society to so mobilize its decisionmaking resources that it will be prepared to assure the defendant a single proceeding free from harmful governmental or judicial error. But it is also clear that recognition that the defendant can be reprosecuted for the same offense after successful appeal does not compel the conclusion that double jeopardy policies are confined to prevention of prosecutorial or judicial overreaching. For the crucial difference between reprosecution after appeal by the defendant and reprosecution after a *sua sponte* judicial mistrial declaration is that in the first situation the defendant has not been deprived of his option to go to the first jury and, perhaps, end the dispute then and there with an acquittal. On the other hand, where the judge, acting without the defendant's consent, aborts the proceeding, the defendant has been deprived of his "valued right to have his trial completed by a particular tribunal." See Wade v. Hunter, 336 U.S. 684, 689 (1949).

If that right to go to a particular tribunal is valued, it is because, independent of the threat of bad-faith conduct by judge or prosecutor, the defendant has a significant interest in the decision whether or not to take the case from the jury when circumstances occur which might be thought to warrant a declaration of mistrial. Thus, where circumstances develop not attributable to prosecutorial or judicial overreaching, a motion by the defendant for mistrial is ordinarily assumed to remove any barrier to reprosecution, even if the defendant's motion is necessitated by prosecutorial or judicial error. In the absence of such a motion, the *Perez* doctrine of manifest necessity stands as a command to trial judges not to foreclose the defendant's option until a scrupulous exercise of judicial discretion leads to the conclusion that the ends of public justice would not be served by a continuation of the proceedings. . . .

The conscious refusal of this Court to channel the exercise of that discretion according to rules based on categories of circumstances . . . reflects the elusive nature of the problem presented by judicial action foreclosing the defendant from going to his jury. But that discretion must still be exercised; unquestionably an important factor to be considered is the need to hold litigants on both sides to standards of responsible professional conduct in the clash of an adversary criminal process. Yet we cannot evolve rules based on the source of the particular problem giving rise to a question whether a mistrial should or should not be declared, because, even in circumstances where the problem reflects error on the part of one counsel or the other, the trial judge must still take care to assure himself that the situation warrants action on his part foreclosing the defendant from a potentially favorable judgment by the tribunal.

In sum, counsel for both sides perform in an imperfect world; in this area, bright-line rules based on either the source of the problem or the intended beneficiary of the ruling would only disserve the vital competing interests of the Government and the defendant. The trial judge must recognize that lack of preparedness by the Government to continue the trial directly implicates policies underpinning both the double jeopardy provision and the speedy trial guarantee. . . . Alternatively, the judge must bear in mind the potential risks of abuse by the defendant of society's unwillingness to unnecessarily subject him to repeated prosecutions. Yet, in the final analysis, the judge must always temper the decision whether or not to abort the trial by considering the importance to the defendant of being able, once and for all, to conclude his confrontation with society through the verdict of a tribunal he might believe to be favorably disposed to his fate.

III

Applying these considerations to the record in this case, we must conclude that the trial judge here abused his discretion in discharging the jury. Despite assurances by both the first witness and the prosecuting attorney that the five taxpayers involved in the litigation had all been warned of their constitutional rights, the judge refused to permit them to testify, first expressing his disbelief that they were warned at all, and then expressing his views that any warnings that might have been given would be inadequate. . . . In probing the assumed inadequacy of the warnings that might have been given, the prosecutor was asked if he really intended to try a case for willfully aiding in the preparation of fraudulent returns on a theory that would not incriminate the taxpayers. When the prosecutor started to answer that he intended to do just that, the judge cut him off in midstream and immediately discharged the jury. . . . It is apparent from the record that no consideration was given to the possibility of a trial continuance; indeed, the trial judge acted so abruptly in discharging the jury that, had the prosecutor been disposed to suggest a continuance, or the defendant to object to the discharge of the jury, there would have been no opportunity to do so. When one examines the circumstances surrounding the discharge of this jury, it seems abundantly apparent that the trial judge made no effort to exercise a sound discretion to assure that, taking all the circumstances into account, there was a manifest necessity for the sua sponte declaration of this mistrial. . . . Therefore, we must conclude that in the circumstances of this case, appellee's reprosecution would violate the double jeopardy provision of the Fifth Amendment.

. . .[2]

---

[2] Chief Justice Burger wrote a brief concurring opinion. Justice Black and Justice Brennan filed a statement that they believed that the court lacked jurisdiction over the case, but that they joined the judgment of the court. Justice Stewart wrote a dissenting opinion which Justice White and Justice Blackmun joined.

Illinois v. Somerville

410 U.S. 458, 93 S.Ct. 1066, 35 L.Ed.2d 425 (1973).

■ MR. JUSTICE REHNQUIST delivered the opinion of the Court.

We must here decide whether declaration of a mistrial over the defendant's objection, because the trial court concluded that the indictment was insufficient to charge a crime, necessarily prevents a State from subsequently trying the defendant under a valid indictment. We hold that the mistrial met the "manifest necessity" requirement of our cases, since the trial court could reasonably have concluded that the "ends of public justice" would be defeated by having allowed the trial to continue. Therefore, the Double Jeopardy Clause of the Fifth Amendment, made applicable to the States through the Due Process Clause of the Fourteenth Amendment, Benton v. Maryland, 395 U.S. 784 (1969), did not bar retrial under a valid indictment.

I

On March 19, 1964, respondent was indicted by an Illinois grand jury for the crime of theft. The case was called for trial and a jury impaneled and sworn on November 1, 1965. The following day, before any evidence had been presented, the prosecuting attorney realized that the indictment was fatally deficient under Illinois law because it did not allege that respondent intended to permanently deprive the owner of his property. Under the applicable Illinois criminal statute, such intent is a necessary element of the crime of theft, and failure to allege intent renders the indictment insufficient to charge a crime. But under the Illinois Constitution, an indictment is the sole means by which a criminal proceeding such as this may be commenced against a defendant. Illinois further provides that only formal defects, of which this was not one, may be cured by amendment. The combined operation of these rules of Illinois procedure and substantive law meant that the defect in the indictment was "jurisdictional"; it could not be waived by the defendant's failure to object, and could be asserted on appeal or in a post-conviction proceeding to overturn a final judgment of conviction.

Faced with this situation, the Illinois trial court concluded that further proceedings under this defective indictment would be useless and granted the State's motion for a mistrial. On November 3, the grand jury handed down a second indictment alleging the requisite intent. Respondent was arraigned two weeks after the first trial was aborted, raised a claim of double jeopardy which was overruled, and the second trial commenced shortly thereafter. The jury returned a verdict of guilty, sentence was imposed, and the Illinois courts upheld the conviction. Respondent then sought federal habeas corpus, alleging that the conviction constituted double jeopardy contrary to the prohibition of the Fifth and Fourteenth Amendments. . . . [T]he Seventh Circuit held that respondent's petition for habeas corpus should have been granted because, although he had not been tried and *acquitted* . . . jeopardy had attached when the jury was impaneled and sworn, and a declaration of mistrial over respondent's objection precluded a retrial under a valid indictment. For the reasons stated below, we reverse that judgment.

II

The fountainhead decision construing the Double Jeopardy Clause in the context of a declaration of a mistrial over a defendant's objection is United States v. Perez, 9 Wheat. 579 (1824). . . . [The opinion quotes the passage from *Perez* quoted in United States v. Jorn, 400 U.S. 470 (1971), p. 1232 above.]

This formulation, consistently adhered to by this Court in subsequent decisions, abjures the application of any mechanical formula by which to judge the propriety of declaring a mistrial in the varying and often unique situations arising during the course of a criminal trial. The broad discretion reserved to the trial judge in such circumstances has been consistently reiterated in decisions of this Court. . . .

In reviewing the propriety of the trial judge's exercise of his discretion, this Court, following the counsel of Mr. Justice Story, has scrutinized the action to determine whether, in the context of that particular trial, the declaration of a mistrial was dictated by "manifest necessity" or the "ends of public justice." The interests of the public in seeing that a criminal prosecution proceed to verdict, either of acquittal or conviction, need not be forsaken by the formulation or application of rigid rules that necessarily preclude the vindication of that interest. This consideration, whether termed the "ends of public justice," United States v. Perez, supra, at 580, or, more precisely, "the public's interest in fair trials designed to end in just judgments," Wade v. Hunter, [336 U.S. 684 (1949)] at 689, has not been disregarded by this Court.

. . .

While virtually all of the cases turn on the particular facts and thus escape meaningful categorization, . . . it is possible to distill from them a general approach, premised on the "public justice" policy enunciated in United States v. Perez, to situations such as that presented by this case. A trial judge properly exercises his discretion to declare a mistrial if an impartial verdict cannot be reached, or if a verdict of conviction could be reached but would have to be reversed on appeal due to an obvious procedural error in the trial. If an error would make reversal on appeal a certainty, it would not serve "the ends of public justice" to require that the Government proceed with its proof when, if it succeeded before the jury, it would automatically be stripped of that success by an appellate court. . . . While the declaration of a mistrial on the basis of a rule or a defective procedure that would lend itself to prosecutorial manipulation would involve an entirely different question . . . such was not the situation in the above cases or in the instant case.

. . .

III

. . .

We believe that in light of the State's established rules of criminal procedure, the trial judge's declaration of a mistrial was not an abuse of discretion. Since this Court's decision in Benton v. Maryland, supra, federal courts will be confronted with such claims that arise in large measure from the often diverse procedural rules existing in the 50 States. Federal courts should not be quick to conclude that simply because a state procedure does not conform to the corresponding federal statute or rule, it does not serve a legitimate state policy. . . .

In the instant case, the trial judge terminated the proceeding because a defect was found to exist in the indictment that was, as a matter of Illinois law, not curable by amendment. The Illinois courts have held that even after a judgment of conviction has become final, the defendant may be released on habeas corpus, because the defect in the indictment deprives the trial court of "jurisdiction." The rule prohibiting the amendment of all but formal defects in indictments is designed to implement the State's policy of preserving the right of each defendant to insist that a criminal prosecution against him be commenced by the action of a grand jury. The trial judge was faced with a situation . . . in which a procedural defect might or would preclude the public from either obtaining an impartial verdict or keeping a verdict of conviction if its evidence persuaded the jury. If a mistrial were constitutionally unavailable in situations such as this, the State's policy could only be implemented by conducting a second trial after verdict and reversal on appeal, thus wasting time, energy, and money for all concerned. Here, the trial judge's action was a rational determination designed to implement a legitimate state policy, with no suggestion that the implementation of that policy in this manner could be manipulated so as to prejudice the defendant. . . . Here, the delay was minimal, and the mistrial was, under Illinois law, the only way in which a defect in the indictment could be corrected. Given the established standard of discretion set forth in *Perez*, *Gori* [v. United States, 367 U.S. 364 (1961)], and *Hunter*, we cannot say that the declaration of a mistrial was not required by "manifest necessity" and the "ends of public justice."

Our decision in *Jorn*, relied upon by the court below and respondent, does not support the opposite conclusion. While it is possible to excise various portions of the plurality opinion to support the result reached below, divorcing the language from the facts of the case serves only to distort its holdings. That opinion dealt with action by a trial judge that can fairly be described as erratic. The Court held that the lack of apparent harm to the defendant from the declaration of a mistrial did not itself justify the mistrial, and concluded that there was no "manifest necessity" for the mistrial, as opposed to less drastic alternatives. The Court emphasized that the absence of any manifest need for the mistrial had deprived the defendant of his right to proceed before the first jury, but it did not hold that that right may never be forced to yield, as in this case, to "the public's interest in fair trials designed to end in just judgments." The Court's opinion in *Jorn* is replete with approving references to Wade v. Hunter, supra, which latter case stated:

> "The double-jeopardy provision of the Fifth Amendment, however, does not mean that every time a defendant is put to trial before a competent tribunal he is entitled to go free if the trial fails to end in a final judgment. Such a rule would create an insuperable obstacle to the administration of justice in many cases in which there is no semblance of the type of oppressive practices at which the double-jeopardy prohibition is aimed. There may be unforeseeable circumstances that arise during a trial making its completion impossible, such as the failure of a jury to agree on a verdict. In such event the purpose of law to protect society from those guilty of crimes frequently would be frustrated by denying courts power to put the defendant to trial again. And there have been instances where a trial judge has discovered facts during a trial which indicated that one or more members of the jury might be biased against the Government or the defendant. It is settled that the duty of the judge in this event is to discharge the jury and direct a retrial. *What has been said is enough to show that a defendant's valued right to have his trial completed by a particular tribunal must in some instances be subordinated to the public's interest in fair trials designed to end in just judgments.*" Wade v. Hunter, 336 U.S., at 688–689 (footnote omitted; emphasis added).

The determination by the trial court to abort a criminal proceeding where jeopardy has attached is not one to be lightly undertaken, since the interest of the defendant in having his fate determined by the jury first impaneled is itself a weighty one. . . . Nor will the lack of demonstrable additional prejudice preclude the defendant's invocation of the double jeopardy bar in the absence of some important countervailing interest of proper judicial administration. . . . But where the declaration of a mistrial implements a reasonable state policy and aborts a proceeding that at best would have produced a verdict that could have been upset at will by one of the parties, the defendant's interest in proceeding to verdict is outweighed by the competing and equally legitimate demand for public justice. . . .

. . . [3]

---

613. In Wade v. Hunter, 336 U.S. 684 (1949), on which the Court relied in *Somerville*, above, the defendant was an American soldier who was tried

---

[3] Justice White wrote a dissenting opinion, which Justice Douglas and Justice Brennan joined. Justice Marshall also wrote a dissenting opinion.

for rape before a general court-martial in Germany during World War II. Before the first trial ended the charges were withdrawn; they were transmitted to another command which convened a new court-martial at which the defendant was convicted. The Court found that "the tactical situation brought about by a rapidly advancing army was responsible for withdrawal of the charges from the first court-martial," id. at 691, and rejected the petitioner's claim that he had been subjected to double jeopardy. See also Armstrong v. United States, 367 F.2d 821 (7th Cir.1966) (assassination of President Kennedy during trial).

614. Gori v. United States, 367 U.S. 364 (1961). The defendant was brought to trial before a jury on a charge of receiving stolen goods. On the first day of trial, during presentation of the government's case, the trial judge on his own motion declared a mistrial; the defendant's counsel neither approved nor objected to the action, the apparent reason for which was that the trial judge believed that the prosecutor's questions "presaged inquiry calculated to inform the jury of other crimes by the accused, and [the judge] took action to forestall it," id. at 366. The court of appeals affirmed the petitioner's conviction at a subsequent trial, although it thought the mistrial was not required by the prosecutor's conduct; it found, and the Court agreed, "that the order was the product of the trial judge's extreme solicitude . . . in favor of the accused," id. at 367. The Court affirmed, saying: "Judicial wisdom counsels against anticipating hypothetical situations in which the discretion of the trial judge may be abused and so call for the safeguard of the Fifth Amendment—cases in which the defendant would be harassed by successive, oppressive prosecutions, or in which a judge exercises his authority to help the prosecution, at a trial in which its case is going badly, by affording it another, more favorable opportunity to convict the accused. Suffice that we are unwilling, where it clearly appears that a mistrial has been granted in the sole interest of the defendant, to hold that its necessary consequence is to bar all retrial. It would hark back to the formalistic artificialities of seventeenth century criminal procedure so to confine our federal trial courts by compelling them to navigate a narrow compass between Scylla and Charybdis. We would not thus make them unduly hesitant conscientiously to exercise their most sensitive judgment—according to their own lights in the immediate exigencies of trial—for the more effective protection of the criminal accused." Id. at 369–70.

In Arizona v. Washington, 434 U.S. 497 (1978) (6–3), the defendant had been convicted of murder and a new trial ordered because the prosecutor withheld exculpatory evidence. At the second trial, defense counsel in his opening statement referred to the previous trial and the suppression of evidence. The prosecutor moved for a mistrial, on the basis that the reasons for the order of a new trial were inadmissible and defense counsel's remarks were incurably prejudicial to the prosecution, so that a mistrial was a "manifest necessity." Over the defendant's objection, the judge granted the motion for a mistrial, without expressly considering alternatives or expressly finding that there was manifest necessity.

The Court concluded that the defendant's subsequent retrial did not violate the Double Jeopardy Clause. The standard of manifest necessity, it said, required a "high degree" of need. Id. at 506. When a mistrial is granted because the prosecutor wants to improve his case or for the purpose of harassment or a tactical advantage, "the strictest scrutiny" of the need for a new trial is warranted. Id. at 508. At the other extreme are cases in which a mistrial follows a jury deadlock; there, the trial judge's judgment that a mistrial is appropriate is "accorded great deference." The Court concluded that on the facts of this case also, the trial judge's ruling was "entitled to special respect." Id. at 510. Otherwise, a trial judge's effort to protect an orderly, impartial procedure might be impaired by fear that if he declared a mistrial erroneously, a retrial would be barred. Accordingly, in this case the public interest in a fair trial prevailed over the defendant's right to have a trial concluded by the first jury impaneled. The Court added that the failure to make the finding of manifest necessity explicit was immaterial.

For additional cases applying the test of manifest necessity, see, e.g., Gilliam v. Foster, 75 F.3d 881 (4th Cir.1996) (en banc) (jury saw unadmitted but relevant, nonprejudicial photographs; no manifest necessity); United States v. Sloan, 36 F.3d 386 (4th Cir.1994) (defendant failed to testify after counsel had stated that defendant would testify; no manifest necessity); United States v. Huang, 960 F.2d 1128 (2d Cir.1992) (uncertified interpreter; no manifest necessity); United States v. Bates, 917 F.2d 388 (9th Cir.1990) (corrigible error in prosecutor's presentation of evidence; no manifest necessity); United States v. Crotwell, 896 F.2d 437 (10th Cir.1990) (mistrial as to one codefendant; no manifest necessity as to other codefendant as a matter of "judicial economy"); Taylor v. Dawson, 888 F.2d 1124 (6th Cir.1989) (testimony believed by trial judge to be inadmissible; no manifest necessity); United States v. Ruggiero, 846 F.2d 117 (2d Cir.1988) (possibility of jury tampering; manifest necessity); United States ex rel. Clauser v. McCevers, 731 F.2d 423 (7th Cir.1984) (indictment invalid; manifest necessity); United States v. Sartori, 730 F.2d 973 (4th Cir.1984) (judge recused himself; no manifest necessity); United States v. Mastrangelo, 662 F.2d 946 (2d Cir.1981) (trial judge believed that defendant was responsible for murder of key prosecution witness; manifest necessity); Harris v. Young, 607 F.2d 1081 (4th Cir.1979) (prosecutor failed to comply fully with discovery order; no manifest necessity); United States ex rel. Stewart v. Hewitt, 517 F.2d 993 (3d Cir.1975) (court official responsible for care of jury was defendant's father-in-law; manifest necessity).

615. Downum v. United States, 372 U.S. 734 (1963). The defendant was brought to trial for mail theft and forging and uttering stolen checks. Both sides had announced that they were ready to proceed and a jury was selected and sworn. After a noon recess the prosecution asked that the jury be discharged because a key witness on some counts was not present. Despite the defendant's objection the jury was discharged. Two days later the case proceeded to trial over the defendant's plea of former jeopardy, a new jury was sworn, and the defendant was convicted. Noting that the prosecutor proceeded to trial without ensuring that the witness would be present and elected not to dismiss the counts for which the witness was essential and try the remaining counts, the Court accepted the defendant's claim of double jeopardy and reversed the conviction. Compare Brock v. North Carolina, 344 U.S. 424 (1953) (mistrial on state's motion to secure testimony of witness not a violation of Due Process Clause).

616. In United States v. Dinitz, 424 U.S. 600 (1976) (6–2), the trial judge excluded one of the defendant's lawyers after the lawyer had repeatedly violated the judge's instructions about his opening statement. The defendant moved for a mistrial, which was granted. Before his second trial, he moved to dismiss the indictment on the ground that the Double Jeopardy Clause barred a retrial. The Court held that in the absence of bad faith, the judge's action even if erroneous did not bar another trial following a mistrial on the defendant's motion. See Lee v. United States, 432 U.S. 23 (1977) (8–1), in which, relying on *Dinitz*, the Court said that retrial was permissible after the trial court, having already heard the evidence, granted the defendant's motion to dismiss the information because it failed to allege an essential element of the offense; the dismissal, the Court concluded, was functionally the same as a mistrial. See also United States v. DiPietro, 936 F.2d 6 (1st Cir.1991) (defense counsel's failure to object to mistrial, due to prosecutor's statements in closing argument, bars claim of double jeopardy).

617. "Prosecutorial conduct that might be viewed as harassment or overreaching, even if sufficient to justify a mistrial on defendant's motion . . . does not bar retrial absent intent on the part of the prosecutor to subvert the protections afforded by the Double Jeopardy Clause. . . . Only where the governmental conduct in question is intended to 'goad' the defendant into moving for a mistrial may a defendant raise the bar of Double Jeopardy to a second trial after having succeeded in aborting the first on his own motion." Oregon v. Kennedy, 456 U.S. 667, 675–76 (1982). See United States v. Catton, 130 F.3d 805 (7th Cir.1997) (discussing application of *Kennedy* to error leading to reversal of conviction; insufficient proof that prosecutor committed error deliberately to avoid likely acquittal); United States v. Doyle, 121 F.3d 1078 (7th Cir.1997) (same; insufficient proof that prosecutor intended to abort trial).

618. The defendants were indicted for second-degree murder. At trial, defense counsel obtained a mistrial on grounds not involving prosecutorial or judicial misconduct. Defendants were then indicted and convicted of first-degree murder. The court held that *Pearce* and later cases, see note 585 p. 1169 above, barred an indictment for the more serious offense without justification in the intervening circumstances. United States v. Jamison, 505 F.2d 407 (D.C.Cir.1974).

619. It is clear that a defendant can be brought to trial a second time after a mistrial because the jury is unable to reach a verdict. United States v. Perez, 22 U.S. (9 Wheat.) 579 (1824). If the jury is unable to reach a verdict at the second trial, can the defendant be tried a third time? Or a fourth? Cases are reviewed in State v. Witt, 572 S.W.2d 913 (Tenn.1978), in which the court concluded that although no constitutional provision precluded a fourth trial after a third hung jury, "trial judges have the inherent authority to terminate a prosecution in the exercise of a sound judicial discretion, where, as here, repeated trials, free of prejudicial error, have resulted in genuinely deadlocked juries and where it appears that at future trials substantially the same evidence will be presented and that the probability of continued hung juries is great." Id. at 917.

To the same effect, see State v. Abbati, 493 A.2d 513 (N.J.1985). The court said: "We hold that a trial court may dismiss an indictment with prejudice after successive juries have failed to agree on a verdict when it determines that the chance of the State's obtaining a conviction upon further retrial is highly unlikely. The trial court must carefully and expressly consider the following factors, which shall govern its ultimate decision whether to dismiss the indictment: (1) the number of prior mistrials and the outcome of the juries' deliberations, so far as is known; (2) the character of prior trials in terms of length, complexity, and similarity of evidence presented; (3) the likelihood of any substantial difference in a subsequent trial, if allowed; (4) the trial court's own evaluation of the relative strength of each party's case; and (5) the professional conduct and diligence of respective counsel, particularly of the prosecuting attorney. The court must also give due weight to the prosecutor's decision to reprosecute, assessing the reasons for that decision, such as the gravity of the criminal charges and the public's concern in the effective and definitive conclusion of criminal prosecutions. Conversely, the court should accord careful consideration to the status of the individual defendant and the impact of a retrial upon the defendant in terms of untoward hardship and unfairness." Id. at 521–22.

On the problem of repetitive trials, see generally Robinson v. Wade, 686 F.2d 298 (5th Cir.1982), in which, after the defendant had been convicted and sentenced to death three times and the convictions reversed on appeal, the court held that a fourth trial was not barred.

Collateral Estoppel

———

Ashe v. Swenson

397 U.S. 436, 90 S.Ct. 1189, 25 L.Ed.2d 469 (1970).

■ MR. JUSTICE STEWART delivered the opinion of the Court.

. . .

Sometime in the early hours of the morning of January 10, 1960, six men were engaged in a poker game in the basement of the home of John Gladson at Lee's Summit, Missouri. Suddenly three or four masked men, armed with a shotgun and pistols, broke into the basement and robbed each of the poker players of money and various articles of personal property. The robbers—and it has never been clear whether there were three or four of them—then fled in a car belonging to one of the victims of the robbery. Shortly thereafter the stolen car was discovered in a field, and later that morning three men were arrested by a state trooper while they were walking on a highway not far from where the abandoned car had been found. The petitioner was arrested by another officer some distance away.

The four were subsequently charged with seven separate offenses—the armed robbery of each of the six poker players and the theft of the car. In May 1960 the petitioner went to trial on the charge of robbing Donald Knight, one of the participants in the poker game. At the trial the State called Knight and three of his fellow poker players as prosecution witnesses. Each of them described the circumstances of the holdup and itemized his own individual losses. The proof that an armed robbery had occurred and that personal property had been taken from Knight as well as from each of the others was unassailable. The testimony of the four victims in this regard was consistent both internally and with that of the others. But the State's evidence that the petitioner had been one of the robbers was weak. Two of the witnesses thought that there had been only three robbers altogether, and could not identify the petitioner as one of them. Another of the victims, who was the petitioner's uncle by marriage, said that at the "patrol station" he had positively identified each of the other three men accused of the holdup, but could say only that the petitioner's voice "sounded very much like" that of one of the robbers. The fourth participant in the poker game did identify the petitioner, but only by his "size and height, and his actions."

The cross-examination of these witnesses was brief, and it was aimed primarily at exposing the weakness of their identification testimony. Defense counsel made no attempt to question their testimony regarding the holdup itself or their claims as to their losses. Knight testified without contradiction that the robbers had stolen from him his watch, $250 in cash, and about $500 in checks. His billfold, which had been found by the police in the possession of one of the three other men accused of the robbery, was admitted in evidence. The defense offered no testimony and waived final argument.

The trial judge instructed the jury that if it found that the petitioner was one of the participants in the armed robbery, the theft of "any money" from Knight would sustain a conviction. He also instructed the jury that if the petitioner was one of the robbers, he was guilty under the law even if he had not personally robbed Knight. The jury—though not instructed to elaborate upon its verdict—found the petitioner "not guilty due to insufficient evidence."

Six weeks later the petitioner was brought to trial again, this time for the robbery of another participant in the poker game, a man named Roberts. The petitioner filed a motion to dismiss, based on his previous acquittal. The motion was overruled, and the second trial began. The witnesses were for the most part the same, though this time their testimony was substantially stronger on the issue of the petitioner's identity. For example, two witnesses who at the first trial had been wholly unable to identify the petitioner as one of the robbers, now testified that his features, size, and mannerisms matched those of one of their assailants. Another witness who before had identified the petitioner only by his size and actions now also remembered him by the unusual sound of his voice. The State further refined its case at the second trial by declining to call one of the participants in the poker game whose identification testimony at the first trial had been conspicuously negative. The case went to the jury on instructions virtually identical to those given at the first trial. This time the jury found the petitioner guilty, and he was sentenced to a 35-year term in the state penitentiary.

. . . The petitioner then brought the present habeas corpus proceeding in the United States District Court for the Western District of Missouri, claiming that the second prosecution had violated his right not to be twice put in jeopardy. Considering itself bound by this court's decision in Hoag v. New Jersey, 356 U.S. 464, the District Court denied the writ . . . .

[T]he operative facts here are virtually identical to those of Hoag v. New Jersey, supra. In that case the defendant was tried for the armed robbery of three men who, along with others, had been held up in a tavern. The proof of the robbery was clear, but the evidence identifying the defendant as one of the robbers was weak, and the defendant interposed an alibi defense. The jury brought in a verdict of not guilty. The defendant was then brought to trial again, on an indictment charging the robbery of a fourth victim of the tavern holdup. This time the jury found him guilty. After appeals in the state courts proved unsuccessful, Hoag brought his case here.

Viewing the question presented solely in terms of Fourteenth Amendment due process—whether the course that New Jersey had pursued had "led to fundamental unfairness," 356 U.S., at 467—this Court declined to reverse the judgment of conviction, because "in the circumstances shown by this record, we cannot say that petitioner's later prosecution and conviction violated due process." 356 U.S., at 466. The Court found it unnecessary to decide whether "collateral estoppel"—the principle that bars relitigation between the same parties of issues actually determined at a previous trial—is a due process requirement in a state criminal trial, since it accepted New

Jersey's determination that the petitioner's previous acquittal did not in any event give rise to such an estoppel. . . . And in the view the Court took of the issues presented, it did not, of course, even approach consideration of whether collateral estoppel is an ingredient of the Fifth Amendment guarantee against double jeopardy.

The doctrine of Benton v. Maryland, 395 U.S. 784, puts the issues in the present case in a perspective quite different from that in which the issues were perceived in Hoag v. New Jersey, supra. The question is no longer whether collateral estoppel is a requirement of due process, but whether it is a part of the Fifth Amendment's guarantee against double jeopardy. And if collateral estoppel is embodied in that guarantee, then its applicability in a particular case is no longer a matter to be left for state court determination within the broad bounds of "fundamental fairness," but a matter of constitutional fact we must decide through an examination of the entire record. . . .

"Collateral estoppel" is an awkward phrase, but it stands for an extremely important principle in our adversary system of justice. It means simply that when an issue of ultimate fact has once been determined by a valid and final judgment, that issue cannot again be litigated between the same parties in any future lawsuit. Although first developed in civil litigation, collateral estoppel has been an established rule of federal criminal law at least since this court's decision more than 50 years ago in United States v. Oppenheimer, 242 U.S. 85. As Mr. Justice Holmes put the matter in that case, "It cannot be that the safeguards of the person, so often and so rightly mentioned with solemn reverence, are less than those that protect from a liability in debt." 242 U.S., at 87. As a rule of federal law, therefore, "[i]t is much too late to suggest that this principle is not fully applicable to a former judgment in a criminal case, either because of lack of 'mutuality' or because the judgment may reflect only a belief that the Government had not met the higher burden of proof exacted in such cases for the Government's evidence as a whole although not necessarily as to every link in the chain." United States v. Kramer, 289 F.2d 909, 913.

The federal decisions have made clear that the rule of collateral estoppel in criminal cases is not to be applied with the hypertechnical and archaic approach of a 19th century pleading book, but with realism and rationality. Where a previous judgment of acquittal was based upon a general verdict, as is usually the case, this approach requires a court to "examine the record of a prior proceeding, taking into account the pleadings, evidence, charge, and other relevant matter, and conclude whether a rational jury could have grounded its verdict upon an issue other than that which the defendant seeks to foreclose from consideration."[4] The inquiry "must be set in a practical frame and viewed with an eye to all the circumstances of the proceedings." Sealfon v. United States, 332 U.S. 575, 579. Any test more technically restrictive would, of course, simply amount to a rejection of the rule of collateral estoppel in criminal proceedings, at least in every case where the first judgment was based upon a general verdict of acquittal.

---

4. Mayers & Yarbrough, *Bis Vexari:* New Trials and Successive Prosecutions, 74   Harv.L.Rev. 1, 38–39. . . .

Straightforward application of the federal rule to the present case can lead to but one conclusion. For the record is utterly devoid of any indication that the first jury could rationally have found that an armed robbery had not occurred, or that Knight had not been a victim of that robbery. The single rationally conceivable issue in dispute before the jury was whether the petitioner had been one of the robbers. And the jury by its verdict found that he had not. The federal rule of law, therefore, would make a second prosecution for the robbery of Roberts wholly impermissible.

The ultimate question to be determined, then, in the light of Benton v. Maryland, supra, is whether this established rule of federal law is embodied in the Fifth Amendment guarantee against double jeopardy. We do not hesitate to hold that it is. For whatever else that constitutional guarantee may embrace . . . it surely protects a man who has been acquitted from having to "run the gantlet" a second time. Green v. United States, 355 U.S. 184, 190.

The question is not whether Missouri could validly charge the petitioner with six separate offenses for the robbery of the six poker players. It is not whether he could have received a total of six punishments if he had been convicted in a single trial of robbing the six victims. It is simply whether, after a jury determined by its verdict that the petitioner was not one of the robbers, the State could constitutionally hale him before a new jury to litigate that issue again.

After the first jury had acquitted the petitioner of robbing Knight, Missouri could certainly not have brought him to trial again upon that charge. Once a jury had determined upon conflicting testimony that there was at least a reasonable doubt that the petitioner was one of the robbers, the State could not present the same or different identification evidence in a second prosecution for the robbery of Knight in the hope that a different jury might find that evidence more convincing. The situation is constitutionally no different here, even though the second trial related to another victim of the same robbery. For the name of the victim, in the circumstances of this case, had no bearing whatever upon the issue of whether the petitioner was one of the robbers.

In this case the State in its brief has frankly conceded that following the petitioner's acquittal, it treated the first trial as no more than a dry run for the second prosecution: "No doubt the prosecutor felt the state had a provable case on the first charge and, when he lost, he did what every good attorney would do—he refined his presentation in light of the turn of events at the first trial." But this is precisely what the constitutional guarantee forbids.

. . . [5]

---

[5] Justice Black and Justice Harlan wrote brief concurring opinions. Justice Brennan wrote a concurring opinion, which Justice Douglas and Justice Marshall joined, in which he argued that "the Double Jeopardy Clause requires the prosecution, except in most limited circumstances, to join at one trial all the charges against a defendant that grow out of a single criminal act, occurrence, episode, or transaction." 397 U.S. at 453–54. Chief Justice Burger wrote a dissenting opinion.

620. *Ashe* was applied to other sets of facts in Harris v. Washington, 404 U.S. 55 (1971), and Turner v. Arkansas, 407 U.S. 366 (1972), both involving collateral estoppel on the issue of the identity of the person who committed the crimes charged in successive prosecutions.

In United States v. Nash, 447 F.2d 1382 (4th Cir.1971), the defendant testified at her trial for mail theft, was acquitted, and was subsequently prosecuted for perjury at the first trial. The court held that collateral estoppel barred reconsideration of the truthfulness of her testimony at the first trial since, on the facts of the case, "it is inconceivable that there would have been an acquittal if the jury had not accorded truth to her testimony." Id. at 1385. Accord United States v. Hernandez, 572 F.2d 218 (9th Cir.1978). Cf. United States v. Bailey, 34 F.3d 683 (8th Cir.1994) (dismissal of prior indictment alleging facts contained in subsequent indictment; *Hernandez* distinguished). In Cardillo v. Zyla, 486 F.2d 473 (1st Cir.1973), a convicted defendant sought damages against witnesses at his trial who, he alleged, had committed perjury. The court said that his claim for damages was "inseparable from the issues at the heart of the criminal prosecution" and that "to litigate them would inevitably be to relitigate to greater or lesser degree the nine-day criminal trial," id. at 475, and held that collateral estoppel applied.

In United States v. Gugliaro, 501 F.2d 68 (2d Cir.1974), however, the defendant testified at his trial for conspiracy, mail fraud, and other offenses and ultimately (after a second trial on the conspiracy count) was acquitted on all counts. He was then prosecuted for perjury at the first trial and convicted. The court of appeals reviewed the application of collateral estoppel in such circumstances and, concluding that the jury in the prior trials had not necessarily concluded that the facts stated in the defendant's testimony were true when it acquitted him, affirmed the conviction. Accord United States v. Dipp, 581 F.2d 1323 (9th Cir.1978).

See Nichols v. Scott, 69 F.3d 1255 (5th Cir.1995), discussing generally whether the government is estopped to assert a set of facts different from those it had asserted at the prior trial of a codefendant. The defendant and the codefendant were indicted for the murder of the victim of a robbery that they had committed together. The medical evidence was that the victim had died from a single gunshot wound. At the sentencing hearing of the codefendant, who had pleaded guilty, the prosecutor urged that he had fired the fatal shot. Subsequently, at the defendant's trial, the same prosecutor argued that the defendant had fired the fatal shot but that even if the codefendant had fired the shot, the defendant also was guilty of capital murder. At the sentencing hearing also, the prosecutor argued that the defendant had fired the fatal shot, but did not emphasize that aspect of the case. The court held that collateral estoppel was not applicable because the defendant was not a party in the prior proceedings; nor was there an affirmative finding by the jury in the prior proceedings that the codefendant had fired the fatal shot. Nor would the court invoke the doctrine of "judicial estoppel," which would bar the state from taking a position inconsistent with that it had taken previously. The court said that the doctrine was not constitutionally based and that it had "apparently never been applied against the government in a criminal case." Id. at 1272.

621. Neither the Double Jeopardy Clause nor the Due Process Clause bars the prosecution from introducing otherwise admissible evidence of criminal conduct having to do with a crime of which the defendant has been acquitted. The acquittal establishes only that the defendant was not guilty beyond a reasonable doubt. The admission of the evidence at a subsequent trial is not subject to so high a standard. Dowling v. United States, 493 U.S. 342 (1990) (6–3). In *Dowling*, the defendant had been acquitted of burglary and robbery charges. At a subsequent trial for a bank robbery, the victim of the earlier crimes testified that he was the person who had entered the house and committed them. Her testimony was admitted to strengthen his identification as the bank robber and to link him with another person who was involved in both crimes. The jury was told that the defendant had been acquitted of the earlier crimes. Aside from the different quanta of proof, the Court said, the jury at the first trial might have acquitted the defendant on some basis other than his identification as the person involved in the earlier incident. *Dowling* is applied in United States v. Felix, 503 U.S. 378 (1992).

622. Ciucci v. Illinois, 356 U.S. 571 (1958). The defendant was charged in separate indictments with murdering his wife and three children. In successive trials, he was convicted of the murder of his wife and two of the children. Penalties of imprisonment were imposed at the first two trials and the death penalty at the third. To the claim that the prosecutor had "announced a determined purpose to prosecute petitioner until a death sentence was obtained," the Supreme Court responded: "The State was constitutionally entitled to prosecute these individual offenses singly at separate trials and to utilize therein all relevant evidence [in this case, evidence of all four deaths], in the absence of proof establishing that such a course of action entailed fundamental unfairness." Id. at 573.[6]

Ciucci was decided on the authority of Hoag v. New Jersey, 356 U.S. 464 (1958), which was overruled by *Ashe*, above. The difference between *Ciucci* and *Ashe* is that the defendant in the former case was *convicted* at each of the successive trials. Unless a theory similar to Justice Brennan's "single

---

6. Following the decision in *Ciucci*, in 1961, the Illinois legislature enacted as part of the criminal code a requirement that, when the defendant may be prosecuted for more than one offense arising out of the same conduct, the offenses must be prosecuted in a single prosecution if the prosecutor knows of the offenses at the beginning of the prosecution and the offenses are within the jurisdiction of a single court, unless justice requires otherwise. 720 Ill.Comp.Stat.Ann. §5/3–3(b). This requirement was applied, e.g., in People v. Golson, 207 N.E.2d 68 (Ill.1965). A similar rule has been adopted by some courts. See, e.g., State v. Gregory, 333 A.2d 257 (N.J.1975) (additional cases and comment cited).

transaction" theory, see p. 1247 n.5 above, is adopted, *Ciucci* is not disturbed by *Ashe*. The issue is discussed in Moton v. Swenson, 488 F.2d 1060 (8th Cir.1973).

623. Does the Double Jeopardy Clause or the Due Process Clause require that collateral estoppel be applied to a pretrial ruling that evidence be suppressed?

"A hypothetical case may help in the consideration of this problem. Defendant X is the subject of two indictments in two counties, one for bank robbery, the other for having stolen an automobile to be used as the getaway car. He pleads not guilty to both charges and notifies the state that he proposes to prove an alibi, which will exonerate him of both offenses, and for which he has strong support. The state's reliance will be on weak identification evidence and a confession to both crimes. The bank robbery charge is to be tried first. X moves to suppress the confession on a number of grounds—use of physical violence; deprivation of food, water, and rest; promises of immunity, etc. Both sides recognize that determination of the motion will very likely decide the case. After a hearing of several days, a judge suppresses the confession. The state elects not to exercise a right to appeal, drops the bank robbery indictment, and indicates its intention to press the stolen car indictment. X moves again to suppress the confession. The state insists on a hearing, saying it has new evidence to rebut X's claims. Does due process permit it to be given one?" United States ex rel. DiGiangiemo v. Regan, 528 F.2d 1262, 1265 (2d Cir.1975). The court concluded that the state should not be given a second hearing on the motion to suppress.

Cf. United States ex rel. Hubbard v. Hatrak, 588 F.2d 414 (3d Cir.1978), in which the defendant claimed the benefit of collateral estoppel with respect to a finding at the prior separate trial of a cofelon for the same crimes. The court concluded that a nonparty collateral estoppel rule is not required by due process.

624. For the purpose of deciding when there is a sufficient "identity of offenses" to support a claim of double jeopardy, how is it determined whether successive prosecutions are for a single offense or for multiple offenses?

" 'A conviction or acquittal upon one indictment is no bar to a subsequent conviction and sentence upon another, unless the evidence required to support a conviction upon one of them would have been sufficient to warrant a conviction upon the other. The test is not whether the defendant has already been tried for the same act, but whether he has been put in jeopardy for the same offense. A single act may be an offense against two statutes; and if each statute requires proof of an additional fact which the other does not, an acquittal or conviction under either statute does not exempt the defendant from prosecution and punishment under the other.'" Gavieres v. United States, 220 U.S. 338, 342 (1911) (quoting Morey v. Commonwealth, 108 Mass. 433, 434 (1871)). Blockburger v. United States, 284 U.S. 299 (1932), is the case most frequently cited. See Garrett v. United States, 471 U.S. 773 (1985) (5–3) (distinct statutory offenses); Albernaz v. United States, 450 U.S. 333 (1981) (same). See also Ball v. United States, 470 U.S. 856 (1985) (simultaneous prosecution under overlapping statutes is permissible, but not conviction and punishment under different statutes for the same conduct).

The *Blockburger* test, as it is called, was expanded in Grady v. Corbin, 495 U.S. 508 (1990) (5–4). The defendant was convicted of traffic offenses. Thereafter, he was indicted for homicide, arising out of the death of a person injured in the accident caused by the traffic offenses. The prosecution filed a bill of particulars specifying the traffic offenses as the basis of the homicide charges. The Court held that the homicide prosecution was barred. "[T]he Double Jeopardy Clause bars any subsequent prosecution in which the government, to establish an essential element of an offense charged in that prosecution, will prove conduct that constitutes an offense for which the defendant has already been prosecuted." Id. at 521. Distinguishing *Dowling*, note 621 p. 1249 above, the Court said: "The critical inquiry is what conduct the State will prove, not the evidence the State will use to prove that conduct. . . . [T]he presentation of specific evidence in one trial does not forever prevent the government from introducing that same evidence in a subsequent proceeding." Id. at 521–22. (The Court noted also that the person injured in the accident had died before the defendant was convicted of the traffic offenses, avoiding the problem suggested in Brown v. Ohio, 432 U.S. 161, 169 n.7 (1977) (6–3), discussed in note 604 p. 1215 above. 495 U.S. at 516 n.7.) Cf. United States v. Felix, 503 U.S. 378 (1992) (*Grady* not followed). Three years later, Grady v. Corbin was overruled, and the *Blockburger* test was restored. United States v. Dixon, 509 U.S. 688 (1993) (5–4).

In Rutledge v. United States, 517 U.S. 292 (1996), the Court held that under the *Blockburger* test, a conspiracy to distribute a controlled substance (21 U.S.C. § 846) was a lesser included offense of conducting a continuing criminal enterprise (21 U.S.C. § 848), because the "in concert" element of the latter offense was based on the § 846 conspiracy. The petitioner had been sentenced to a concurrent life sentence and was assessed $50 (under 18 U.S.C. § 3013) for each offense. Without ruling on other aspects of the case, the Court concluded that at least the double assessment amounted to cumulative punishment and was barred by the Double Jeopardy Clause.

625. The Department of Justice has announced as a general policy "'that several offenses arising out of a single transaction should be alleged and tried together and should not be made the basis of multiple prosecutions, a policy dictated by considerations both of fairness to defendants and of efficient and orderly law enforcement.'" Petite v. United States, 361 U.S. 529, 530 (1960). See Thompson v. United States, 444 U.S. 248 (1980); Rinaldi v. United States, 434 U.S. 22 (1977).

626. The prosecution of a defendant as an adult after an adjudicatory hearing in the Juvenile Court and a determination that he had violated a criminal statute and a subsequent finding that he was unfit for treatment as a juvenile violates the Double Jeopardy Clause. Breed v. Jones, 421 U.S. 519 (1975). The Court observed that its holding would not interfere with the flexibility of juvenile proceedings; the decision whether to transfer a juvenile for proceedings as an adult could be made prior to an adjudicatory hearing on the merits.

Breed v. Jones was distinguished in Swisher v. Brady, 438 U.S. 204 (1978) (6–3). In that case, the Court upheld a Maryland procedure by which the state can file exceptions in the juvenile court to a master's proposed finding of nondelinquency and the court can accept, reject, or modify the finding, but only on the basis of the record before the master or additional evidence to which the parties do not object. The Court concluded that the entire procedure was a unitary one and that the juvenile court's review of the master's finding did not place a juvenile in jeopardy a second time.

627. Successive prosecutions by the federal government and a state or by different states for crimes arising out of the same transaction and proved by the same evidence are not constitutionally impermissible double jeopardy. "In applying the dual sovereignty doctrine . . . the crucial determination is whether the two entities that seek successively to prosecute a defendant for the same course of conduct can be termed separate sovereigns. This determination turns on whether the two entities draw their authority to punish the offender from distinct sources of power." Heath v. Alabama, 474 U.S. 82, 88 (1985) (7–2). In *Heath*, the defendant was convicted of murder in Georgia and sentenced to life imprisonment. He was then convicted of murder for the same act in Alabama and sentenced to death. See also Abbate v. United States, 359 U.S. 187 (1959) (state-federal); Bartkus v. Illinois, 359 U.S. 121 (1959) (federal-state). Successive prosecutions by a municipality and the same state violate the Double Jeopardy Clause. Waller v. Florida, 397 U.S. 387 (1970).

The Department of Justice has a policy against duplicating a state prosecution. *Petite*, note 625 above, 361 U.S. at 531. See United States v. Fritz, 580 F.2d 370 (10th Cir.1978) (*Petite* policy is an internal rule of government that does not confer a right on the defendant).

CHAPTER 18

COLLATERAL ATTACK

———

Sunal v. Large

332 U.S. 174, 67 S.Ct. 1588, 91 L.Ed. 1982 (1947).

■ MR. JUSTICE DOUGLAS delivered the opinion of the Court.

Sunal and Kulick registered under the Selective Training and Service Act of 1940, 54 Stat. 885, 57 Stat. 597, 50 U.S.C.App. § 301, et seq. Each is a Jehovah's Witness and each claimed the exemption granted by Congress to regular or duly ordained ministers of religion. § 5(d). The local boards, after proceedings unnecessary to relate here, denied the claimed exemptions and classified these registrants as I–A. They exhausted their administrative remedies but were unable to effect a change in their classifications. Thereafter they were ordered to report for induction—Sunal on October 25, 1944, Kulick on November 9, 1944. Each reported but refused to submit to induction. Each was thereupon indicted, tried and convicted under § 11 of the Act for refusing to submit to induction. Sunal was sentenced on March 22, 1945, Kulick on May 7, 1945, each to imprisonment for a term of years. Neither appealed.

At the trial each offered evidence to show that his selective service classification was invalid. The trial courts held, however, that such evidence was inadmissible, that the classification was final and not open to attack in the criminal trial. On February 4, 1946, we decided Estep v. United States and Smith v. United States, 327 U.S. 114. These cases held on comparable facts that a registrant, who had exhausted his administrative remedies and thus obviated the rule of Falbo v. United States, 320 U.S. 549, was entitled, when tried under § 11, to defend on the ground that his local board exceeded its jurisdiction in making the classification—for example, that it had no basis in fact. 327 U.S. pp. 122–123.

It is plain, therefore, that the trial courts erred in denying Sunal and Kulick the defense which they tendered. Shortly after the Estep and Smith cases were decided, petitions for writs of habeas corpus were filed on behalf of Sunal and Kulick. In each case it was held that habeas corpus was an available remedy. In Sunal's case the Circuit Court of Appeals for the Fourth Circuit held that there was a basis in fact for the classification and affirmed a judgment discharging the writ. . . . In Kulick's case the Circuit Court of Appeals for the Second Circuit reversed a District Court holding that there was evidence to support the classification . . . and ruled, without examining the evidence, that since Kulick had been deprived of the defense he should be discharged from custody without prejudice to further prosecution. . . . The cases are here on petitions for writs of certiorari, which we granted because of the importance of the questions presented.

The normal and customary method of correcting errors of the trial is by appeal. Appeals could have been taken in these cases, but they were not. It cannot be said that absence of counsel made the appeals unavailable as a practical matter. . . . Defendants had counsel. Nor was there any other barrier to the perfection of their appeals. . . . Moreover, this is not a situation where the facts relied on were dehors the record and therefore not open to consideration and review on appeal. . . . The error was of record in each case. It is said, however, that the failure to appeal was excusable, since under the decisions as they then stood—March 22, 1945, and May 7, 1945—the lower courts had consistently ruled that the selective service classification could not be attacked in a prosecution under § 11. . . . It is also pointed out that on April 30, 1945, we had denied certiorari in a case which sought to raise the same point, and that Estep v. United States, supra, and Smith v. United States, supra, were brought here and decided after Sunal's and Kulick's time for appeal had passed. The argument is that since the state of the law made the appeals seem futile, it would be unfair to those registrants to conclude them by their failure to appeal.

We put to one side comparable problems respecting the use of *habeas corpus* in the federal courts to challenge convictions obtained in the state courts. . . . So far as convictions obtained in the federal courts are concerned, the general rule is that the writ of *habeas corpus* will not be allowed to do service for an appeal. . . . There have been, however, some exceptions. That is to say, the writ has at times been entertained either without consideration of the adequacy of relief by the appellate route or where an appeal would have afforded an adequate remedy. Illustrative are those instances where the conviction was under a federal statute alleged to be unconstitutional, where there was a conviction by a federal court whose jurisdiction over the person or the offense was challenged, where the trial or sentence by a federal court violated specific constitutional guaranties. It is plain, however, that the writ is not designed for collateral review of errors of law committed by the trial court—the existence of any evidence to support the conviction, irregularities in the grand jury procedure, departure from a statutory grant of time in which to prepare for trial, and other errors in trial procedure which do not cross the jurisdictional line. . . .

Yet the latter rule is not an absolute one; and the situations in which *habeas corpus* has done service for an appeal are the exceptions. Thus where the jurisdiction of the federal court which tried the case is challenged or where the constitutionality of the federal statute under which conviction was had is attacked, *habeas corpus* is increasingly denied in case an appellate procedure was available for correction of the error. Yet, on the other hand, where the error was flagrant and there was no other remedy available for its correction, relief by *habeas corpus* has sometimes been granted. As stated by Chief Justice Hughes in Bowen v. Johnston, 306 U.S. 19, 27, the rule which requires resort to appellate procedure for the correction of errors "is not one defining power but one which relates to the appropriate exercise of power." That rule is, therefore, "not so inflexible that it may not yield to exceptional circumstances where the need for the remedy afforded by the writ of *habeas corpus* is apparent." Id. p. 27. That case was deemed to involve "exceptional circumstances" by reason of the fact that it indicated "a conflict between state and federal authorities on a question of law involving concerns of large importance affecting their respective jurisdictions." Id. p. 27. The Court accordingly entertained the writ to examine into the jurisdiction of the court to render the judgment of conviction.

The same course was followed in Ex parte Hudgings, 249 U.S. 378, where petitioner was adjudged guilty of contempt for committing perjury. The Court did not require the petitioner to pursue any appellate route but issued an original writ and discharged him, holding that perjury without more was not punishable as a contempt. That situation was deemed exceptional in view of "the nature of the case, of the relation which the question which it involves bears generally to the power and duty of courts in the performance of their functions, of the dangerous effect on the liberty of the citizen when called upon as a witness in a court which might result if the erroneous doctrine upon which the order under review was based were not promptly corrected. . . ." Id. p. 384. . . .

The Circuit Courts of Appeals thought that the facts of the present cases likewise presented exceptional circumstances which justified resort to *habeas corpus* though no appeals were taken. In their view the failure to appeal was excusable, since relief by that route seemed quite futile.

But denial of certiorari by this Court in the earlier case imported no expression of opinion on the merits. . . . The same chief counsel represented the defendants in the present cases and those in the *Estep* and *Smith* cases. At the time these defendants were convicted the *Estep* and *Smith* cases were pending before the appellate courts. The petition in the *Smith* case was, indeed, filed here about two weeks before Kulick's conviction and about a month after Sunal's conviction. The same road was open to Sunal and Kulick as the one Smith and Estep took. Why the legal strategy counseled taking appeals in the *Smith* and *Estep* cases and not in these we do not know. Perhaps it was based on the facts of these two cases. For the question of law had not been decided by the Court; and counsel was pressing for a decision here. The case, therefore, is not one where the law was changed after the time for appeal had expired. . . . It is rather a situation where at the time of the convictions the definitive ruling on the question of law had not crystallized. Of course, if Sunal and Kulick had pursued the appellate course and failed, their cases would be quite different. But since they chose not to pursue the remedy which they had, we do not think they should now be allowed to justify their failure by saying they deemed any appeal futile.

We are dealing here with a problem which has radiations far beyond the present cases. The courts which tried the defendants had jurisdiction over their persons and over the offense. They committed an error of law in excluding the defense which was tendered. That error did not go to the jurisdiction of the trial court. Congress, moreover, has provided a regular, orderly method for correction of all such errors by granting an appeal to the Circuit Court of Appeals and by vesting us with certiorari jurisdiction. It is not uncommon after a trial is ended and the time for appeal has passed to discover that a shift in the law or the impact of a new decision has given increased relevance to a point made at the trial but not pursued on appeal. . . . If in such circumstances, *habeas corpus* could be used to correct the error, the writ would become a delayed motion for a new trial, renewed from time to time as the legal climate changed. Error which was not deemed sufficiently adequate to warrant an appeal would acquire new implications. Every error is potentially reversible error; and many rulings of the trial court spell the difference between conviction and acquittal. If defendants who accept the judgment of conviction and do not appeal can later renew their attack on the judgment by *habeas corpus*, litigation in these criminal cases will be interminable. Wise judicial administration of the federal courts counsels against such course, at least where the error does not trench on any constitutional rights of defendants nor involve the jurisdiction of the trial court.

An endeavor is made to magnify the error in these trials to constitutional proportions by asserting that the refusal of the proffered evidence robbed the trial of vitality by depriving defendants of their only real defense. But as much might be said of many rulings during a criminal trial. Defendants received throughout an opportunity to be heard and enjoyed all procedural guaranties granted by the Constitution. Error in ruling on the question of law did not infect the trial with lack of procedural due process. As stated by Mr. Justice Cardozo in Escoe v. Zerbst, 295 U.S. 490, 494, "When a hearing is allowed but there is error in conducting it or in limiting its scope, the remedy is by appeal. When an opportunity to be heard is denied altogether, the ensuing mandate of the court is void, and the prisoner confined thereunder may have recourse to *habeas corpus* to put an end to the restraint."

. . .

MR. JUSTICE RUTLEDGE, dissenting.

. . .

The writ should be available whenever there clearly has been a fundamental miscarriage of justice for which no other adequate remedy is presently available. Beside executing its great object, which is the preservation of personal liberty and assurance against its wrongful deprivation, considerations of economy of judicial time and procedures, important as they undoubtedly are, become comparatively insignificant. This applies to situations involving the past existence of a remedy presently foreclosed, as well as to others where no such remedy has ever been afforded.

In the prevailing state of our criminal law, federal and state, there are few errors, either fundamental or of lesser gravity, which cannot be corrected by appeal timely taken, unless the facts disclosing or constituting them arise after the time has expired. If the existence of a remedy by appeal at some stage of the criminal proceedings is to be taken for the criterion, then in very few instances, far less than the number comprehended by our decisions, will the writ be available. Taken literally, the formula so often repeated, that the writ is not a substitute for appeal, is thus in conflict with every case where the ground upon which the writ has been allowed either was or might have been asserted on appeal. The formula has obvious validity in the sense that the writ is not readily to be used for overturning determinations made on appeal or for securing review where no specification has been made or no appeal has been taken of matters not going to make the conviction a gross miscarriage of justice.

But any effort to shut off the writ's functioning merely because appeal has not been taken in a situation where, but for that fact alone, the writ would issue, seems to me to prescribe a system of forfeitures in the last area where such a system should prevail. Certainly a basic miscarriage of justice is no less great or harmful, either to the individual or to the general cause of personal liberty, merely because appeal has not been taken, than where appeal is taken but relief is wrongfully denied.

These considerations apply with special force, though not exclusively, where good reason existed, as I think did here, for failure to note the appeal in the brief time allowed. Whether or not the inferior federal courts were justified in taking the *Falbo* [v. United States, 320 U.S. 549 (1944)] decision for more than its specific ruling, the fact remains that their broadly prevailing view was that that case had cut off all right to make such defenses as Sunal and Kulick tendered.

In that prevailing climate of opinion in those courts, there was hardly any chance that appeal to the federal circuit courts of appeals would bring relief by their action. The chances for reversal therefore hung almost exclusively upon the doubtful, not to say slender,[1] chance that this Court in the exercise of its discretionary power would grant certiorari.

The deprivation here was of the right to make any substantial defense. I do not think a trial which forecloses the basic right to defend, upon the only valid ground available for that purpose, is any less unfair or conclusive as against the office of *habeas corpus* than one which takes place when the court is without jurisdiction to try the offense, as when the charge is made under an unconstitutional statute or for other reason sets forth no lawfully prescribed offense, or when the court loses jurisdiction by depriving the accused of his constitutional right to counsel. That right is no more and no

---

1. Although denial of certiorari is not to be taken as expression of opinion in any case, it would be idle to claim that it has no actual or reasonable influence upon the practical judgment of lawyers whether appeal should be noted and taken upon the chance that in a case substantially identical this Court's discretion would be exercised, in the absence of conflict, in a contrary manner at the stage of application for certiorari.

less than an important segment of the right to have any valid defense advanced and considered. It becomes almost meaningless if the larger right to defend is itself cut off.

. . .[2]

---

628. "The writ of habeas corpus is the fundamental instrument for safeguarding individual freedom against arbitrary and lawless state action. Its pre-eminent role is recognized by the admonition in the Constitution that: 'The Privilege of the Writ of Habeas Corpus shall not be suspended. . . . U.S. Const., Art. I, § 9, cl. 2. The scope and flexibility of the writ—its capacity to reach all manner of illegal detention—its ability to cut through barriers of form and procedural mazes—have always been emphasized and jealously guarded by courts and lawmakers. The very nature of the writ demands that it be administered with the initiative and flexibility essential to insure that miscarriages of justice within its reach are surfaced and corrected." Harris v. Nelson, 394 U.S. 286, 290–91 (1969). "[T]he basic purpose of the writ is to enable those unlawfully incarcerated to obtain their freedom." Johnson v. Avery, 393 U.S. 483, 485 (1969).

For important steps in the expansion of habeas corpus from a remedy narrowly available to test the jurisdiction of the sentencing court to a means for asserting the denial of a constitutional right at trial, see Frank v. Mangum, 237 U.S. 309 (1915); Moore v. Dempsey, 261 U.S. 86 (1923); Mooney v. Holohan, 294 U.S. 103 (1935); and Brown v. Allen, 344 U.S. 443 (1953). The development of the writ is traced in Fay v. Noia, 372 U.S. 391, 399–426 (1963) (6–3), and, with different significance, in Wainwright v. Sykes, 433 U.S. 72, 77–85 (1977). (That portion of the opinion is partially omitted below, p. 1264.) See also Justice Harlan's dissenting opinion in Fay v. Noia, 372 U.S. at 449–63.

629. Collateral attack in the federal courts on state and federal convictions is covered generally by 28 U.S.C. §§ 2241–2255. Applications for writs of habeas corpus by state prisoners in particular are covered by § 2254; motions under § 2255 replace applications for habeas corpus by federal prisoners. The background of § 2255 is discussed in United States v. Hayman, 342 U.S. 205 (1952). The statute does not limit the remedy of habeas cor-

---

[2] Justice Burton concurred in the result. Justice Frankfurter wrote a dissenting opinion. Justice Murphy noted that he joined Justice Rutledge's dissenting opinion and added a further note.

pus; it "was intended simply to provide in the sentencing court a remedy exactly commensurate with that which had previously been available by habeas corpus in the court of the district where the prisoner was confined." Hill v. United States, 368 U.S. 424, 427 (1962). See Davis v. United States, 417 U.S. 333 (1974).

The availability of relief under §§ 2254 and 2255 was narrowed in 1996 by the Antiterrorism and Effective Death Penalty Act of 1996, 110 Stat. 1214. Among the important provisions are that a state prisoner cannot obtain habeas relief solely because a state court misapplied constitutional principles to the facts, but only if the state court's determination was not only erroneous but "unreasonable," and a one-year statute of limitations, applicable to federal and state prisoners, which ordinarily begins to run on the date on which the conviction becomes final. Special, largely technical, provisions are applicable to capital cases. See Felker v. Turpin, 518 U.S. 651 (1996). See also Stewart v. Martinez-Villareal, ___ U.S. ___, 118 S.Ct. 1618 (1998) (7–2); Calderon v. Thompson, ___ U.S. ___, 118 S.Ct. 1489 (1998) (5–4).

The Court has promulgated rules governing cases under both sections and model forms to be used in an application to the district court for relief under them. In addition, the Federal Rules of Civil Procedure are generally applicable to cases under § 2254, see Fed.R.Civ.P 81(a)(2). The Federal Rules of Civil Procedure or Criminal Procedure may be applied to motions under § 2255, see Rule 12 of the Rules Governing Section 2255 Proceedings.

The requirement that state remedies be exhausted before a petition for habeas corpus is brought in federal court for relief from a state conviction is discussed at length in Rose v. Lundy, 455 U.S. 509 (1982) (8–1). A majority of the Court held that a petition containing some claims the state remedies for which have been exhausted and some claims the state remedies for which have not must be dismissed in its entirety; a minority thought that the federal court should consider the former claims. On the exhaustion requirement, see generally Anderson v. Harless, 459 U.S. 4 (1982) (6–3); Daye v. Attorney General of State of New York, 696 F.2d 186 (2d Cir.1982).

On federal habeas corpus review, a state conviction is reversible for constitutional error of the "trial type" (errors occurring in the presentation of evidence to the jury) only if the error "had substantial and injurious effect or influence in determining the jury's verdict," Kotteakos v. United States, 328 U.S. 750, 776 (1946). Such error is not subject on collateral review to the standard of Chapman v. California, 386 U.S. 18, 24 (1967), requiring reversal unless the error "was harmless beyond a reasonable doubt." Brecht v. Abrahamson, 507 U.S. 619 (1993) (6–3). In *Brecht*, the error was the prosecution's references to the defendant's post-*Miranda* silence, in violation of Doyle v. Ohio, 426 U.S. 610 (1976), note 265 p. 488 above. *Brecht* was applied in California v. Roy, 519 U.S. 2 (1996) (per curiam).

"When a federal judge in a habeas proceeding is in grave doubt about whether a trial error of federal law had 'substantial and injurious effect or influence in determining the jury's verdict,' that error is not harmless. And the petitioner must win." O'Neal v. McAninch, 513 U.S. 432, 436 (1995) (6–3). The Court observed that treating the error in such circumstances as not harmless will "at least often" avoid holding someone in custody in violation of the Constitution, whereas treating the error as harmless "would virtually guarantee that many, *in fact*, will be held in unlawful custody." Id. at 442.

The Court has held that the rule of Stone v. Powell, 428 U.S. 465 (1976), see note 432 p. 894 above, is *not* applicable to a claim that the conviction was based on statements obtained in violation of Miranda v. Arizona, 384 U.S. 436 (1966). Withrow v. Williams, 507 U.S. 680 (1993) (5–4). The Court observed that, unlike the exclusion of evidence that was involved in Stone v. Powell, the *Miranda* rules safeguard a fundamental trial right and are related to the fairness of the trial itself and the accuracy of the result.

On the standard for federal collateral review of state determinations of fact, see Marshall v. Lonberger, 459 U.S. 422 (1983) (5–4). See also Maggio v. Fulford, 462 U.S. 111 (1983) (6–3).

The voluntariness of a confession is not an issue of fact with respect to which a state court's finding is presumed to be correct, under 28 U.S.C. § 2254(d), in a federal habeas corpus proceeding. It is an issue of law about which the federal court must make an independent determination. State court findings of subsidiary issues of fact bearing on the ultimate determination of voluntariness are binding, unless there are other reasons for independent federal review. Miller v. Fenton, 474 U.S. 104 (1985) (8–1).

630. The defendants in United States v. Chambers, 291 U.S. 217 (1934), were indicted for violations of the federal prohibition law. Before their trial the Twenty-First Amendment to the Constitution, which repealed the Eighteenth Amendment, was ratified. The district court dismissed the indictment; and the government appealed. The Court affirmed, saying: "The National Prohibition Act, to the extent that its provisions rested upon the grant of authority to the Congress by the Eighteenth Amendment, immediately fell with the withdrawal by the people of the essential constitutional support. The continuance of the prosecution of the defendants after the repeal of the Eighteenth Amendment, for a violation of the National Prohibition Act alleged to have been committed in North Carolina, would involve an attempt to continue the application of the statutory provisions after they had been deprived of force. This consequence is not altered by the fact that the crimes in question were alleged to have been committed while the National Prohibition Act was in effect. The continued prosecution necessarily depended upon the continued life of the statute which the prosecution seeks to apply. In case a statute is repealed or rendered inoperative, no further proceedings can be had to enforce it in pending prosecutions unless competent authority has kept the statute alive for that purpose." Id. at 222–23. See also Massey v. United States, 291 U.S. 608 (1934) (conviction of violation of prohibition law affirmed on appeal but no final judgment rendered before ratification of Twenty-First Amendment; conviction vacated).

If a judgment of conviction has become final before repeal of the statute on which the conviction is based, however, the repeal does not preclude execution of sentence. E.g., United States ex rel. Randall v. United States Marshal, 143 F.2d 830 (2d Cir.1944). See generally Bell v. Maryland, 378 U.S. 226 (1964).

631. The Court has struggled with the problem of when and how far to give retroactive effect to changes favorable to the defendant in the constitutional requirements of criminal procedure. For steps along the way, see, e.g., Linkletter v. Walker, 381 U.S. 618 (1965) (7–2), and Solem v. Stumes, 465 U.S. 638 (1984) (6–3). In Teague v. Lane, 489 U.S. 288 (1989) (7–2), four members of the Court expressed the view that "unless they fall within an exception to the general rule, new constitutional rules of criminal procedure will not be applicable to those cases which have become final before the new rules are announced." Id. at 310. "In general . . . a case announces a rule when it breaks new ground or imposes a new obligation on the States or the Federal Government. . . . To put it differently, a case announces a new rule if the result was not *dictated* by precedent existing at the time the defendant's conviction became final." Id. at 301. There are exceptions to the general rule against retroactivity if the newly announced constitutional rule places "'certain kinds of primary, private individual conduct beyond the power of the criminal law-making authority to proscribe'" (quoting Mackey v. United States, 401 U.S. 667, 692 (1971) (opinion of Harlan, J.)) or if it is one of those "watershed rules of criminal procedure," those "new procedures without which the likelihood of an accurate conviction is seriously diminished." The opinion adds that "we believe it unlikely that many such components of basic due process have yet to emerge." Id. at 311, 313.

The analysis of *Teague* has been adopted by the Court and was applied in O'Dell v. Netherland, __ U.S. __, 117 S.Ct. 1969 (1997) (5–4) (capital sentencing proceeding; new rule principle applied); Lambrix v. Singletary, 520 U.S. 518 (1997) (5–4) (same); Gray v. Netherland, 518 U.S. 152 (1996) (5–4) (evidentiary notice requirement; new rule principle applied); Caspari v. Bohlen, 510 U.S. 383 (1994) (8–1) (*Bullington*, p. 1227 above, extended to noncapital sentencing proceeding; new rule principle applied); Graham v. Collins, 506 U.S. 461 (1993) (5–4) (capital sentencing proceeding; new rule principle applied); Stringer v. Black, 503 U.S. 222 (1992) (6–3) (new rule principle not applicable); Butler v. McKellar, 494 U.S. 407 (1990) (5–4); Saffle v. Parks, 494 U.S. 484 (1990) (5–4); and Penry v. Lynaugh, 492 U.S. 302 (1989) (new rule principle not applicable). In Butler v. McKellar, the Court said that the "'new rule' principle validates reasonable good-faith interpretations of existing precedents made by state courts even though they are shown to be contrary to later decisions." 494 U.S. at 414. It indicated that an interpretation is reasonable if the correct interpretation was "susceptible to debate among reasonable minds." Id. at 415. The Court held that *Teague* is not applicable to a ruling that modified the scope of a federal criminal statute; the ruling was made after the defendant had pleaded guilty on the basis of the prior statutory construction. Bousley v. United States, ___ U.S. ___, 118 S.Ct. 1604 (1998) (7–2).

———

Wainwright v. Sykes

433 U.S. 72, 97 S.Ct. 2497, 53 L.Ed.2d 594 (1977).

■ MR. JUSTICE REHNQUIST delivered the opinion of the Court.

We granted certiorari to consider the availability of federal habeas corpus to review a state convict's claim that testimony was admitted at his trial in violation of his rights under Miranda v. Arizona, 384 U.S. 436 (1966), a claim which the Florida courts have previously refused to consider on the merits because of noncompliance with a state contemporaneous-objection rule. Petitioner Wainwright, on behalf of the State of Florida, here challenges a decision of the Court of Appeals for the Fifth Circuit ordering a hearing in state court on the merits of respondent's contention.

Respondent Sykes was convicted of third-degree murder after a jury trial in the Circuit Court of DeSoto County. He testified at trial that on the evening of January 8, 1972, he told his wife to summon the police because he had just shot Willie Gilbert. Other evidence indicated that when the police arrived at respondent's trailer home, they found Gilbert dead of a shotgun wound, lying a few feet from the front porch. Shortly after their arrival, respondent came from across the road and volunteered that he had shot Gilbert, and a few minutes later respondent's wife approached the police and told them the same thing. Sykes was immediately arrested and taken to the police station.

Once there, it is conceded that he was read his *Miranda* rights, and that he declined to seek the aid of counsel and indicated a desire to talk. He then made a statement, which was admitted into evidence at trial through the testimony of the two officers who heard it, to the effect that he had shot Gilbert from the front porch of his trailer home. There were several references during the trial to respondent's consumption of alcohol during the preceding day and to his apparent state of intoxication, facts which were acknowledged by the officers who arrived at the scene. At no time during the trial, however, was the admissibility of any of respondent's statements challenged by his counsel on the ground that respondent had not understood the *Miranda* warnings. Nor did the trial judge question their admissibility on his own motion or hold a factfinding hearing bearing on that issue.

Respondent appealed his conviction, but apparently did not challenge the admissibility of the inculpatory statements. He later filed in the trial court a motion to vacate the conviction and, in the State District Court of Appeals and

Supreme Court, petitions for habeas corpus. These filings, apparently for the first time, challenged the statements made to police on grounds of involuntariness. In all of these efforts respondent was unsuccessful.

Having failed in the Florida courts, respondent initiated the present action under 28 U.S.C. § 2254, asserting the inadmissibility of his statements by reason of his lack of understanding of the *Miranda* warnings. The United States District Court for the Middle District of Florida ruled that Jackson v. Denno, 378 U.S. 368 (1964), requires a hearing in a state criminal trial prior to the admission of an inculpatory out-of-court statement by the defendant. It held further that respondent had not lost his right to assert such a claim by failing to object at trial or on direct appeal, since only "exceptional circumstances" of "strategic decisions at trial" can create such a bar to raising federal constitutional claims in a federal habeas action. The court stayed issuance of the writ to allow the state court to hold a hearing on the "voluntariness" of the statements.

Petitioner warden appealed this decision to the United States Court of Appeals for the Fifth Circuit. That court first considered the nature of the right to exclusion of statements made without a knowing waiver of the right to counsel and the right not to incriminate oneself. It noted that Jackson v. Denno, supra, guarantees a right to a hearing on whether a defendant has knowingly waived his rights as described to him in the *Miranda* warnings, and stated that under Florida law "[t]he burden is on the State to secure [a] prima facie determination of voluntariness, not upon the defendant to demand it." 528 F.2d 522, 525 (1976).

The court then directed its attention to the effect on respondent's right of Florida Rule Crim.Proc. 3.190(i), which it described as "a contemporaneous objection rule" applying to motions to suppress a defendant's inculpatory statements. It focused on this Court's decisions in Henry v. Mississippi, 379 U.S. 443 (1965); Davis v. United States, 411 U.S. 233 (1973); and Fay v. Noia, 372 U.S. 391 (1963), and concluded that the failure to comply with the rule requiring objection at the trial would only bar review of the suppression claim where the right to object was deliberately bypassed for reasons relating to trial tactics. . . . Concluding that "[t]he failure to object in this case cannot be dismissed as a trial tactic, and thus a deliberate by-pass," the court affirmed the District Court order that the State hold a hearing on whether respondent knowingly waived his *Miranda* rights at the time he made the statements.

The simple legal question before the Court calls for a construction of the language of 28 U.S.C. § 2254(a), which provides that the federal courts shall entertain an application for a writ of habeas corpus "in behalf of a person in custody pursuant to the judgment of a state court only on the ground that he is in custody in violation of the Constitution or laws or treaties of the United States." But, to put it mildly, we do not write on a clean slate in construing this statutory provision. . . . For more than a century . . . this Court has grappled with the relationship between the classical common-law writ of habeas corpus and the remedy provided in 28 U.S.C. § 2254. Sharp division within the Court has been manifested on more than one aspect of the perplexing problems which have been litigated in this connection. Where the habeas petitioner challenges a final judgment of conviction rendered by a state court, this Court has been called upon to decide no fewer than four different questions, all to a degree interrelated with one another: (1) What types of federal claims may a federal habeas court properly consider? (2) Where a federal claim is cognizable by a federal habeas court, to what extent must that court defer to a resolution of the claim in prior state proceedings? (3) To what extent must the petitioner who seeks federal habeas exhaust state remedies before resorting to the federal court? (4) In what instances will an adequate and independent state ground bar consideration of otherwise cognizable federal issues on federal habeas review?

Each of these four issues has spawned its share of litigation. . . .

. . .

. . . Only the fourth area—the adequacy of state grounds to bar federal habeas review—is presented in this case. The foregoing discussion of the other three is pertinent here only as it illustrates this Court's historic willingness to overturn or modify its earlier views of the scope of the writ, even where the statutory language authorizing judicial action has remained unchanged.

As to the role of adequate and independent state grounds, it is a well-established principle of federalism that a state decision resting on an adequate foundation of state substantive law is immune from review in the federal courts. . . . The application of this principle in the context of a federal habeas proceeding has therefore excluded from consideration any questions of state *substantive* law, and thus effectively barred federal habeas review where questions of that sort are either the only ones raised by a petitioner or are in themselves dispositive of his case. The area of controversy which has developed has concerned the reviewability of federal claims which the state court has declined to pass on because not presented in the manner prescribed by its *procedural* rules. The adequacy of such an independent state procedural ground to prevent federal habeas review of the underlying federal issue has been treated very differently than where the state-law ground is substantive. . . .

In *Brown* [v. Allen, 344 U.S. 443 (1953)], petitioner Daniels' lawyer had failed to mail the appeal papers to the State Supreme Court on the last day provided by law for filing, and hand delivered them one day after that date. Citing the state rule requiring timely filing, the Supreme Court of North Carolina refused to hear the appeal. This Court . . . held that federal habeas was not available to review a constitutional claim which could not have been reviewed on direct appeal here because it rested on an independent and adequate state procedural ground. 344 U.S., at 486–487.

In Fay v. Noia, supra, respondent Noia sought federal habeas to review a claim that his state-court conviction had resulted from the introduction of a coerced confession in violation of the Fifth Amendment to the United States Constitution. While the convictions of his two codefendants were reversed on that ground in collateral proceedings following their appeals,

Noia did not appeal and the New York courts ruled that his subsequent *coram nobis* action was barred on account of that failure. This Court held that petitioner was nonetheless entitled to raise the claim in federal habeas, and thereby overruled its decision 10 years earlier in Brown v. Allen, supra:

> "[T]he doctrine under which state procedural defaults are held to constitute an adequate and independent state law ground barring direct Supreme Court review is not to be extended to limit the power granted the federal courts under the federal habeas statute." 372 U.S., at 399.

As a matter of comity but not of federal power, the Court acknowledged "a limited discretion in the federal judge to deny relief . . . to an applicant who had deliberately by-passed the orderly procedure of the state courts and in so doing has forfeited his state court remedies." Id., at 438. In so stating, the Court made clear that the waiver must be knowing and actual— "'an intentional relinquishment or abandonment of a known right or privilege.'" Id., at 439, quoting Johnson v. Zerbst, 304 U.S., at 464. Noting petitioner's "grisly choice" between acceptance of his life sentence and pursuit of an appeal which might culminate in a sentence of death, the Court concluded that there had been no deliberate bypass of the right to have the federal issues reviewed through a state appeal.

A decade later we decided Davis v. United States, supra, in which a federal prisoner's application under 28 U.S.C. § 2255 sought for the first time to challenge the makeup of the grand jury which indicted him. The Government contended that he was barred by the requirement of Fed.Rule Crim.Proc. 12(b)(2) providing that such challenges must be raised "by motion before trial." The Rule further provides that failure to so object constitutes a waiver of the objection, but that "the court for cause shown may grant relief from the waiver." We noted that the Rule "promulgated by this Court and, pursuant to 18 U.S.C. § 3771, 'adopted' by Congress, governs by its terms the manner in which the claims of defects in the institution of criminal proceedings may be waived," 411 U.S., at 241, and held that this standard contained in the Rule, rather than the Fay v. Noia concept of waiver, should pertain in federal habeas as on direct review. Referring to previous constructions of Rule 12(b)(2), we concluded that review of the claim should be barred on habeas, as on direct appeal, absent a showing of cause for the noncompliance and some showing of actual prejudice resulting from the alleged constitutional violation.

Last Term, in Francis v. Henderson, 425 U.S. 536 (1976), the rule of *Davis* was applied to the parallel case of a state procedural requirement that challenges to grand jury composition be raised before trial. The Court noted that there was power in the federal courts to entertain an application in such a case, but rested its holding on "considerations of comity and concerns for the orderly administration of criminal justice. . . ." 425 U.S., at 538–539. While there was no counterpart provision of the state rule which allowed an exception upon some showing of cause, the Court concluded that the standard derived from the federal rule should nonetheless be applied in that context since "'[t]here is no reason to . . . give greater preclusive effect to procedural defaults by federal defendants than to similar defaults by state defendants.'" Id., at 542, quoting Kaufman v. United States, 394 U.S. 217, 228 (1969). As applied to the federal petitions of state convicts, the *Davis* cause-and-prejudice standard was thus incorporated directly into the body of law governing the availability of federal habeas corpus review.

To the extent that the dicta of Fay v. Noia may be thought to have laid down an all-inclusive rule rendering state timely objection rules ineffective to bar review of underlying federal claims in federal habeas proceedings— absent a "knowing waiver" or a "deliberate bypass" of the right to so object— its effect was limited by *Francis*, which applied a different rule and barred a habeas challenge to the makeup of a grand jury. Petitioner Wainwright in this case urges that we further confine its effect by applying the principle enunciated in *Francis* to a claimed error in the admission of a defendant's confession.

. . .

We . . . conclude that Florida procedure did, consistently with the United States Constitution, require that respondent's confession be challenged at trial or not at all, and thus his failure to timely object to its admission amounted to an independent and adequate state procedural ground which would have prevented direct review here. . . . We thus come to the crux of this case. Shall the rule of Francis v. Henderson supra, barring federal habeas review absent a showing of "cause" and "prejudice" attendant to a state procedural waiver, be applied to a waived objection to the admission of a confession at trial? We answer that question in the affirmative.

As earlier noted in the opinion, since Brown v. Allen, 344 U.S. 443 (1953), it has been the rule that the federal habeas petitioner who claims he is detained pursuant to a final judgment of a state court in violation of the United States Constitution is entitled to have the federal habeas court make its own independent determination of his federal claim, without being bound by the determination on the merits of that claim reached in the state proceedings. This rule of Brown v. Allen is in no way changed by our holding today. Rather, we deal only with contentions of federal law which were *not* resolved on the merits in the state proceeding due to respondent's failure to raise them there as required by state procedure. We leave open for resolution in future decisions the precise definition of the "cause"-and- "prejudice" standard, and note here only that it is narrower than the standard set forth in dicta in Fay v. Noia, 372 U.S. 391 (1963), which would make federal habeas review generally available to state convicts absent a knowing and deliberate waiver of the federal constitutional contention. It is the sweeping language of Fay v. Noia going far beyond the facts of the case eliciting it, which we today reject.

The reasons for our rejection of it are several. The contemporaneous- objection rule itself is by no means peculiar to Florida, and deserves greater respect than *Fay* gives it, both for the fact that it is employed by a coordinate jurisdiction within the federal system and for the many interests which it serves in its own right. A contemporaneous objection enables the record to be made with respect to the constitutional claim when the recollections of witnesses are freshest, not years later in a federal habeas proceeding. It enables the judge who observed the demeanor of those witnesses to make the factual determinations necessary for properly deciding the federal constitutional question. While the 1966 amendment to § 2254 requires deference to be given to such determinations made by state courts, the determinations themselves are less apt to be made in the first instance if there is no contemporaneous objection to the admission of the evidence on federal constitutional grounds.

A contemporaneous-objection rule may lead to the exclusion of the evidence objected to, thereby making a major contribution to finality in criminal litigation. Without the evidence claimed to be vulnerable on federal constitutional grounds, the jury may acquit the defendant, and that will be the end of the case; or it may nonetheless convict the defendant, and he will have one less federal constitutional claim to assert in his federal habeas petition. If the state trial judge admits the evidence in question after a full hearing, the federal habeas court pursuant to the 1966 amendment to § 2254 will gain significant guidance from the state ruling in this regard. Subtler considerations as well militate in favor of honoring a state contemporaneous-objection rule. An objection on the spot may force the prosecution to take a hard look at its hole card, and even if the prosecutor thinks that the state trial judge will admit the evidence he must contemplate the possibility of reversal by the state appellate courts or the ultimate issuance of a federal writ of habeas corpus based on the impropriety of the state court's rejection of the federal constitutional claim.

We think that the rule of Fay v. Noia, broadly stated, may encourage "sandbagging" on the part of defense lawyers, who may take their chances on a verdict of not guilty in a state trial court with the intent to raise their constitutional claims in a federal habeas court if their initial gamble does not pay off. The refusal of federal habeas courts to honor contemporaneous-objection rules may also make state courts themselves less stringent in their enforcement. Under the rule of Fay v. Noia, state appellate courts know that a federal constitutional issue raised for the first time in the proceeding before them may well be decided in any event by a federal *habeas* tribunal. Thus, their choice is between addressing the issue notwithstanding the petitioner's failure to timely object, or else face the prospect that the federal habeas court will decide the question without the benefit of their views.

The failure of the federal habeas courts generally to require compliance with a contemporaneous-objection rule tends to detract from the perception of the trial of a criminal case in state court as a decisive and portentous event. A defendant has been accused of a serious crime, and this is the time and place set for him to be tried by a jury of his peers and found either guilty or not guilty by that jury. To the greatest extent possible all issues which bear on this charge should be determined in this proceeding: the accused is in the courtroom, the jury is in the box, the judge is on the bench, and the witnesses, having been subpoenaed and duly sworn, await their turn to testify. Society's resources have been concentrated at that time and place in order to decide, within the limits of human fallibility, the question of guilt or innocence of one of its citizens. Any procedural rule which encourages the result that those proceedings be as free of error as possible is thoroughly desirable, and the contemporaneous-objection rule surely falls within this classification.

We believe the adoption of the *Francis* rule in this situation will have the salutary effect of making the state trial on the merits the "main event," so to speak, rather than a "tryout on the road" for what will later be the determinative federal habeas hearing. There is nothing in the Constitution or in the language of § 2254 which requires that the state trial on the issue of guilt or innocence be devoted largely to the testimony of fact witnesses directed to the elements of the state crime, while only later will there occur in a federal habeas hearing a full airing of the federal constitutional claims which were not raised in the state proceedings. If a criminal defendant thinks that an action of the state trial court is about to deprive him of a federal constitutional right there is every reason for his following state procedure in making known his objection.

The "cause"-and-"prejudice" exception of the *Francis* rule will afford an adequate guarantee, we think, that the rule will not prevent a federal habeas court from adjudicating for the first time the federal constitutional claim of a defendant who in the absence of such an adjudication will be the victim of a miscarriage of justice. Whatever precise content may be given those terms by later cases, we feel confident in holding without further elaboration that they do not exist here. Respondent has advanced no explanation whatever for his failure to object at trial,[3] and, as the proceeding unfolded, the trial judge is certainly not to be faulted for failing to question the admission of the confession himself. The other evidence of guilt presented at trial, moreover, was substantial to a degree that would negate any possibility of actual prejudice resulting to the respondent from the admission of his inculpatory statement.

We accordingly conclude that the judgment of the Court of Appeals for the Fifth Circuit must be reversed, and the cause remanded to the United States District Court for the Middle District of Florida with instructions to dismiss respondent's petition for a writ of habeas corpus.

It is so ordered.

3. In Henry v. Mississippi, 379 U.S., at 451, the Court noted that decisions of counsel relating to trial strategy, even when made without the consultation of the defendant, would bar direct federal review of claims thereby foregone, except where "the circumstances are exceptional."

Last Term in Estelle v. Williams [425 U.S. 501 (1976)], the Court reiterated the burden on a defendant to be bound by the trial judgments of his lawyer.

"Under our adversary system, once a defendant has the assistance of counsel the vast array of trial decisions, strategic and tactical, which must be made before and during trial rests with the accused and his attorney." 425 U.S., at 512.

MR. CHIEF JUSTICE BURGER, concurring.

I concur fully in the judgment and in the Court's opinion. I write separately to emphasize one point which, to me, seems of critical importance to this case. In my view, the "deliberate bypass" standard enunciated in Fay v. Noia, 372 U.S. 391 (1963), was never designed for, and is inapplicable to, errors—even of constitutional dimension—alleged to have been committed during trial.

In Fay v. Noia, the Court applied the "deliberate bypass" standard to a case where the critical procedural decision—whether to take a criminal appeal—was entrusted to a convicted defendant. Although Noia, the habeas petitioner, was represented by counsel, he himself had to make the decision whether to appeal or not; the role of the attorney was limited to giving advice and counsel. In giving content to the new deliberate-bypass standard, *Fay* looked to the Court's decision in Johnson v. Zerbst, 304 U.S. 458 (1938), a case where the defendant had been called upon to make the decision whether to request representation by counsel in his federal criminal trial. Because in both *Fay* and *Zerbst*, important rights hung in the balance of the *defendant's own decision*, the Court required that a waiver impairing such rights be a knowing and intelligent decision by the defendant himself. As *Fay* put it:

> "If a habeas applicant, after consultation with competent counsel or otherwise, understandingly and knowingly forewent the privilege of seeking to vindicate his federal claims in the state courts . . . then it is open to the federal court on habeas to deny him all relief. . . ." 372 U.S., at 439.

The touchstone of *Fay* and *Zerbst*, then, is the exercise of volition by the defendant himself with respect to his own federal constitutional rights. In contrast, the claim in the case before us relates to events during the trial itself. Typically, habeas petitioners claim that unlawfully secured evidence was admitted . . . or that improper testimony was adduced, or that an improper jury charge was given . . . or that a particular line of examination or argument by the prosecutor was improper or prejudicial. But unlike *Fay* and *Zerbst*, preservation of this type of claim under state procedural rules does not generally involve an assertion by the defendant himself; rather, the decision to assert or not to assert constitutional rights or constitutionally based objections at trial is necessarily entrusted to the defendant's attorney, who must make on-the-spot decisions at virtually all stages of a criminal trial. As a practical matter, a criminal defendant is rarely, if ever, in a position to decide, for example, whether certain testimony is hearsay and, if so, whether it implicates interests protected by the Confrontation Clause; indeed, it is because "'[e]ven the intelligent and educated layman has small and sometimes no skill in the science of law'" that we held it constitutionally required that every defendant who faces the possibility of incarceration be afforded counsel. Argersinger v. Hamlin, 407 U.S. 25 (1972); Gideon v. Wainwright, 372 U.S. 335, 345 (1963).

Once counsel is appointed, the day-to-day conduct of the defense rests with the attorney. He, not the client, has the immediate—and ultimate—responsibility of deciding if and when to object, which witnesses, if any, to call, and what defenses to develop. Not only do these decisions rest with the attorney, but such decisions must, as a practical matter, be made without consulting the client. The trial process simply does not permit the type of frequent and protracted interruptions which would be necessary if it were required that clients give knowing and intelligent approval to each of the myriad tactical decisions as a trial proceeds.

Since trial decisions are of necessity entrusted to the accused's attorney, the *Fay-Zerbst* standard of "knowing and intelligent waiver" is simply inapplicable. The dissent in this case, written by the author of Fay v. Noia, implicitly recognizes as much. According to the dissent, *Fay* imposes the knowing-and-intelligent-waiver standard "where possible" during the course of the trial. In an extraordinary modification of *Fay*, Mr. Justice Brennan would now require "that the lawyer actually exercis[e] his expertise and judgment in his client's service, and with his client's knowing and intelligent participation *where possible*"; he does not intimate what guidelines would be used to decide when or under what circumstances this would actually be "possible." Post, at 116. (Emphasis supplied.) What had always been thought the standard governing the *accused's* waiver of his own constitutional rights the dissent would change, in the trial setting, into a standard of conduct imposed upon the defendant's *attorney*. This vague "standard" would be unmanageable to the point of impossibility.

. . .

MR. JUSTICE BRENNAN, with whom MR. JUSTICE MARSHALL joins, dissenting.

. . .

I

I begin with the threshold question: What is the meaning and import of a procedural default? If it could be assumed that a procedural default more often than not is the product of a defendant's conscious refusal to abide by the duly constituted, legitimate processes of the state courts, then I might agree that a regime of collateral review weighted in favor of a State's procedural rules would be warranted. *Fay*, however, recognized that such rarely is the case; and therein lies *Fay*'s basic unwillingness to embrace a view of habeas jurisdiction that results in "an airtight system of [procedural] forfeitures." 372 U.S., at 432.

. . .

[A]ny realistic system of federal habeas corpus jurisdiction must be premised on the reality that the ordinary procedural default is born of the inadvertence, negligence, inexperience, or incompetence of trial counsel. . . . The case under consideration today is typical. . . . [A]ny realistic reading of the record demonstrates that we are faced here with a lawyer's simple error.

Fay's answer thus is plain: the bypass test simply refuses to credit what is essentially a lawyer's mistake as a forfeiture of constitutional rights. . . .

II

What are the interests that Sykes can assert in preserving the availability of federal collateral relief in the face of his inadvertent state procedural default? Two are paramount.

As is true with any federal habeas applicant, Sykes seeks access to the federal court for the determination of the validity of his federal constitutional claim. . . .

. . .

[U]ndue deference to local procedure can only serve to undermine the ready access to a federal court to which a state defendant otherwise is entitled. But federal review is not the full measure of Sykes' interest, for there is another of even greater immediacy: assuring that his constitutional claims can be addressed to *some* court. For the obvious consequence of barring Sykes from the federal courthouse is to insulate Florida's alleged constitutional violation from any and all judicial review because of a lawyer's mistake. From the standpoint of the habeas petitioner, it is a harsh rule indeed that denies him "any review at all where the state has granted none," Brown v. Allen, 344 U.S. [443 (1953)], at 552 (Black, J., dissenting)—particularly when he would have enjoyed both state and federal consideration had his attorney not erred.

. . .

. . . I believe that *Fay's* commitment to enforcing intentional but not inadvertent procedural defaults offers a realistic measure of protection for the habeas corpus petitioner seeking federal review of federal claims that were not litigated before the State. The threatened creation of a more "airtight system of forfeitures" would effectively deprive habeas petitioners of the opportunity for litigating their constitutional claims before any forum and would disparage the paramount importance of constitutional rights in our system of government. Such a restriction of habeas corpus jurisdiction should be countenanced, I submit, only if it fairly can be concluded that *Fay's* focus on knowing and voluntary forfeitures unduly interferes with the legitimate interests of state courts or institutions. The majority offers no suggestion that actual experience has shown that *Fay's* bypass test can be criticized on this score. And, as I now hope to demonstrate, any such criticism would be unfounded.

III

A regime of federal habeas corpus jurisdiction that permits the reopening of state procedural defaults does not invalidate any state procedural rule as such; Florida's courts remain entirely free to enforce their own rules as they choose, and to deny any and all state rights and remedies to a defendant who fails to comply with applicable state procedure. The relevant inquiry is whether more is required—specifically, whether the fulfillment of important interests of the State necessitates that federal courts be called upon to impose additional sanctions for inadvertent noncompliance with state procedural requirements such as the contemporaneous-objection rule involved here.

Florida, of course, can point to a variety of legitimate interests in seeking allegiance to its reasonable procedural requirements, the contemporaneous-objection rule included. . . . As *Fay* recognized, a trial, like any organized activity, must conform to coherent process, and "there must be sanctions for the flouting of such procedure." 372 U.S., at 431. The strict enforcement of procedural defaults, therefore, may be seen as a means of deterring any tendency on the part of the defense to slight the state forum, to deny state judges their due opportunity for playing a meaningful role in the evolving task of constitutional adjudication, or to mock the needed finality of criminal trials. All of these interests are referred to by the Court in various forms.

The question remains, however, whether any of these policies or interests are efficiently and fairly served by enforcing both intentional and inadvertent defaults pursuant to the identical stringent standard. I remain convinced that when one pierces the surface justifications for a harsher rule posited by the Court, no standard stricter than *Fay*'s deliberate-bypass test is realistically defensible.

Punishing a lawyer's unintentional errors by closing the federal courthouse door to his client is both a senseless and misdirected method of deterring the slighting of state rules. It is senseless because unplanned and unintentional action of any kind generally is not subject to deterrence; and, to the extent that it is hoped that a threatened sanction addressed to the defense will induce greater care and caution on the part of trial lawyers, thereby forestalling negligent conduct or error, the potential loss of all valuable state remedies would be sufficient to this end. And it is a misdirected sanction because even if the penalization of incompetence or carelessness will encourage more thorough legal training and trial preparation, the habeas applicant, as opposed to his lawyer, hardly is the proper recipient of such a penalty. Especially with fundamental constitutional rights at stake, no fictional relationship of principal-agent or the like can justify holding the criminal defendant accountable for the naked errors of his attorney. This is especially true when so many indigent defendants are without any realistic choice in selecting who ultimately represents them at trial. Indeed, if responsibility for error must be apportioned between the parties, it is the State, through its attorney's admissions and certification policies, that is more fairly held to blame for the fact that practicing lawyers too often are ill-prepared or ill-equipped to act carefully and knowledgeably when faced with decisions governed by state procedural requirements.

Hence, while I can well agree that the proper functioning of our system of criminal justice, both federal and state, necessarily places heavy reliance on the professionalism and judgment of trial attorneys, I cannot accept a system that ascribes the absolute forfeiture of an individual's constitutional claims to situations where his lawyer manifestly exercises *no* professional judgment at all—where carelessness, mistake, or ignorance is the explanation for a procedural default. Of course, it is regrettable that certain errors that might have been cured earlier had trial counsel acted expeditiously must be corrected collaterally and belatedly. I can understand the Court's wistfully wishing for the day when the trial was the sole, binding and final "event" of the adversarial process—although I hesitate to agree that in the eyes of the criminal defendant it has ever ceased being the "main" one. . . . But it should be plain that in the real world, the interest in finality is repeatedly compromised in numerous ways that arise with far greater frequency than do procedural defaults. . . . Indeed, the very existence of the well-established right collaterally to reopen issues previously litigated before the state courts . . . represents a congressional policy choice that is inconsistent with notions of strict finality—and probably more so than authorizing the litigation of issues that, due to inadvertence, were never addressed to any court. Ultimately, all of these limitations on the finality of criminal convictions emerge from the tension between justice and efficiency in a judicial system that hopes to remain true to its principles and ideals. Reasonable people may disagree on how best to resolve these tensions. But the solution that today's decision risks embracing seems to me the most unfair of all: the denial of any judicial consideration of the constitutional claims of a criminal defendant because of errors made by his attorney which lie outside the power of the habeas petitioner to prevent or deter and for which, under no view of morality or ethics, can he be held responsible.

In short, I believe that the demands of our criminal justice system warrant visiting the mistakes of a trial attorney on the head of a habeas corpus applicant only when we are convinced that the lawyer actually exercised his expertise and judgment in his client's service, and with his client's knowing and intelligent participation where possible. This, of course, is the precise system of habeas review established by Fay v. Noia.

IV

. . .

One final consideration deserves mention. Although the standards recently have been relaxed in various jurisdictions, it is accurate to assert that most courts, this one included, traditionally have resisted any realistic inquiry into the competency of trial counsel. There is nothing unreasonable, however, in adhering to the proposition that it is the responsibility of a trial lawyer who takes on the defense of another to be aware of his client's basic legal rights and of the legitimate rules of the forum in which he practices his profession. If he should unreasonably permit such rules to bar the assertion of the colorable constitutional claims of his client, then his conduct may well fall below the level of competence that can fairly be expected of him. For almost 40 years it has been established that inadequacy of counsel undercuts the very competence and jurisdiction of the trial court and is always open to collateral review. Johnson v. Zerbst, 304 U.S. 458 (1938). Obviously, as a practical matter, a trial counsel cannot procedurally waive his own inadequacy. If the scope of habeas jurisdiction previously governed by Fay v. Noia is to be redefined so as to enforce the errors and neglect of lawyers with unnecessary and unjust rigor, the time may come when conscientious and fairminded federal and state courts, in adhering to the teaching of Johnson v. Zerbst, will have to reconsider whether they can continue to indulge the comfortable fiction that all lawyers are skilled or even competent craftsmen in representing the fundamental rights of their clients.[4]

---

632. In Engle v. Isaac, 456 U.S. 107 (1982) (7–2), several respondents who had been convicted in the Ohio state courts of homicide or assault sought habeas corpus in the federal district court. Each claimed that the trial judge had erroneously instructed the jury that the defendant had the burden of proving self defense by a preponderance of the evidence. State law required contemporaneous objection to jury instructions. Defense counsel had made no objection.

The defendant's constitutional claim was that under prior cases, notably Mullaney v. Wilbur, 421 U.S. 684 (1975), p. 1107 above, absence of self defense was an element of the crimes charged against them, which the Due Process Clause required the state to prove beyond a reasonable doubt. This claim, the Court said, was "colorable." Neither "futility" of pressing a claim in the state court (because Ohio courts had long ruled to the contrary) nor "novelty" of the claim constituted cause for the failure to press the claim in the state courts. While *Sykes* did not necessarily require defense counsel "to exercise extraordinary vision or to object to every aspect of the proceedings in the hope that some aspect might mask a latent constitutional claim," the respondents' claims in these cases "were far from unknown at the time of their trials," and they did not lack "the tools to construct their constitutional claim." 456 U.S. at 130–32. "Where the basis of a constitutional claim is available, and other defense counsel have perceived and litigated that claim, the demands of comity and finality counsel against labeling alleged unawareness of the objection as cause for a procedural default." Id. at 134.

Two years after the decision in Engle v. Isaac, the Court decided Reed v. Ross, 468 U.S. 1 (1984) (5–4). In that case also, the defendant's claim was that the jury had been instructed, contrary to *Mullaney*, that the defendant had the burden of proof on an element of the offense. As in the earlier case, defense counsel did not raise the issue at trial. Nor did he raise the issue on appeal. A state rule of procedure barred relief on the latter ground. The Court held that Ross's claim was cognizable by habeas corpus in federal court.

The difference between the two cases, the court said, was that Ross's trial and appeal occurred in 1969 and the trial of the defendants in Engle v.

---

[4] Justice Stevens wrote a concurring opinion. Justice White wrote an opinion con-   curring in the judgment.

Isaac in 1975. In the intervening years, the Court's decision in In re
Winship, 397 U.S. 358 (1978), and other federal court decisions had laid the
basis for the *Mullaney* argument (*Mullaney* itself having been decided in
1975, after the trial of two of the defendants and before the trial of the
third). Therefore, defense counsel in Engle v. Isaac had had more reason to
object to the jury instructions than had defense counsel in *Ross*. The novelty of the claim in Ross's case satisfied the requirement of "cause" for the
procedural default.

"Because of the broad range of potential reasons for an attorney's failure to comply with a procedural rule, and the virtually limitless array of
contexts in which a procedural default can occur, this Court has not given
the term 'cause' precise content. . . . Nor do we attempt to do so here.
Underlying the concept of cause, however, is at least the dual notion that,
absent exceptional circumstances, a defendant is bound by the tactical decisions of competent counsel . . . and that defense counsel may not flout state
procedures and then turn around and seek refuge in federal court from the
consequences of such conduct. . . . A defense attorney, therefore, may not
ignore a State's procedural rules in the expectation that his client's constitutional claims can be raised at a later date in federal court. . . . Similarly,
he may not use the prospect of federal habeas corpus relief as a hedge
against the strategic risks he takes in his client's defense in state court. . . .
In general, therefore, defense counsel may not make a tactical decision to
forgo a procedural opportunity—for instance, an opportunity to object at
trial or to raise an issue on appeal—and then, when he discovers that the
tactic has been unsuccessful, pursue an alternative strategy in federal
court. The encouragement of such conduct by a federal court on habeas corpus review would not only offend generally accepted principles of comity,
but would also undermine the accuracy and efficiency of the state judicial
systems to the detriment of all concerned. Procedural defaults of this nature
are, therefore, 'inexcusable,' Estelle v. Williams, 425 U.S. 501, 513 (1976)
(Powell, J., concurring), and cannot qualify as 'cause' for purposes of federal
habeas corpus review.

"On the other hand, the cause requirement may be satisfied under certain circumstances when a procedural failure is not attributable to an
intentional decision by counsel made in pursuit of his client's interests. And
the failure of counsel to raise a constitutional issue reasonably unknown to
him is one situation in which the requirement is met. If counsel has no reasonable basis upon which to formulate a constitutional question . . . it is safe
to assume that he is sufficiently unaware of the question's latent existence
that we cannot attribute to him strategic motives of any sort.

. . .

"Accordingly, we hold that where a constitutional claim is so novel that
its legal basis is not reasonably available to counsel, a defendant has cause
for his failure to raise the claim in accordance with applicable state procedures." 468 U.S. at 13–16. Confining its discussion to the facts of the particular case and distinguishing Engle v. Isaac on the basis noted above, the

Court concluded that "Ross' claim was sufficiently novel in 1969 to excuse his attorney's failure to raise the *Mullaney* issue at that time." Id. at 20.

Four Justices dissented. The dissenting opinion called the majority's basis for distinguishing Engle v. Isaac a "bizarre line of reasoning," 468 U.S. at 25. It said further: "[T]his equating of novelty with cause pushes the Court into a conundrum which it refuses to recognize. The more 'novel' a claimed constitutional right, the more unlikely a violation of that claimed right undercuts the fundamental fairness of the trial. To untie this knot in logic, the Court proposes a definition of novelty that makes a claim novel if the legal basis for asserting the claim is not reasonably available. . . . This standard, of course, has no meaningful content independent of the factual setting in which it is applied. The Court's attempt to give content to this novelty standard, however, is simply too facile; under its application, virtually any new constitutional claim can be deemed 'novel.'" Id. at 22.

The standard of cause for a procedural default is elaborated further in Murray v. Carrier, 477 U.S. 478 (1986) (7–2). The Court said that an inadvertent failure of competent counsel to raise a substantive claim of error on appeal does not constitute cause that permits federal collateral attack on a state conviction. "[T]he existence of cause for a procedural default must ordinarily turn on whether the prisoner can show that some objective factor external to the defense impeded counsel's efforts to comply with the State's procedural rule." Examples of such "objective impediments," the Court said, are "a showing that the factual or legal basis for a claim was not reasonably available to counsel" (citing Reed v. Ross) or that "'some interference by officials' . . . made compliance impracticable." Id. at 488. See Amadeo v. Zant, 486 U.S. 214 (1988) (cause for procedural default established by officials' concealment of factual basis for challenge to jury composition that was subject of default).

In Murray v. Carrier, the Court noted that the cause-and-prejudice test applied to procedural defaults on appeal as well as at trial. A procedural default on appeal is found not to satisfy the cause standard, in Smith v. Murray, 477 U.S. 527 (1986) (5–4). Defense counsel had deliberately not raised an objection to the admission of certain evidence at the sentencing hearing, because he concluded that the objection would probably fail; it later appeared that the objection had merit. Concluding that the legal issue did not meet the novelty standard of Reed v. Ross, the Court said that a deliberate procedural default "is the very antithesis of the kind of circumstance that would warrant excusing a defendant's failure to adhere to a State's legitimate rules for the fair and orderly disposition of its criminal cases." Id. at 534.

See generally United States v. Frady, 456 U.S. 152 (1982) (6–1), declaring that the cause-and-prejudice standard and not the plain error standard is applicable on collateral attack of a federal conviction. "[T]o obtain collateral relief a prisoner must clear a significantly higher hurdle than would exist on direct appeal." Id. at 166. Engle v. Isaac, above, similarly rejects the plain error standard for federal collateral attack of a state conviction.

633. Wainwright v. Sykes and succeeding cases applying the cause-and-prejudice standard effectively replaced Fay v. Noia's "deliberate bypass" test, see pp. 1264–65 above, without rejecting it altogether. (*Sykes* had left open the question whether *Fay* remained applicable to its own facts, the failure to take any appeal at all. 433 U.S. at 88 n.12. See, to the same effect, Murray v. Carrier, note 632 p. 1276 above, 477 U.S. at 492.) In Coleman v. Thompson, 501 U.S. 722 (1991) (6–3), the Court interred the *Fay* rule for all purposes: "We now make it explicit: In all cases in which a state prisoner has defaulted his federal claims in state court pursuant to an independent and adequate state procedural rule, federal habeas review of the claims is barred unless the prisoner can demonstrate cause for the default and actual prejudice as a result of the alleged violation of federal law, or demonstrate that failure to consider the claims will result in a fundamental miscarriage of justice. *Fay* was based on a conception of federal/state relations that undervalued the importance of state procedural rules. The several cases after *Fay* that applied the cause and prejudice standard to a variety of state procedural defaults represent a different view. We now recognize the important interest in finality served by state procedural rules, and the significant harm to the States that results from the failure of federal courts to respect them." Id. at 750. The *Coleman* opinion reviews the cases after *Sykes* leading up to this result.

634. As Justice Brennan observed in his dissenting opinion in Wainwright v. Sykes, see p. 1273 above, the requirement of cause for a procedural default can have no application when the constitutional claim is ineffective assistance of counsel. The Court made that explicit in Murray v. Carrier, 477 U.S. 478, 488 (1986) (7–2): "[I]f the procedural default is the result of ineffective assistance of counsel, the Sixth Amendment itself requires that responsibility for the default be imputed to the State. . . . Ineffective assistance of counsel, then, is cause for a procedural default." The Court added, however, that the doctrine of exhaustion of state remedies, see p. 1259 above, "generally requires that a claim of ineffective assistance be presented to the state courts as an independent claim before it may be used to establish cause for a procedural default. The question whether there is cause for a procedural default does not pose any occasion for applying the exhaustion doctrine when the federal habeas court can adjudicate the question of cause—a question of federal law—without deciding an independent and unexhausted constitutional claim on the merits. But if a petitioner could raise his ineffective assistance claim for the first time on federal habeas in order to show cause for a procedural default, the federal habeas court would find itself in the anomalous position of adjudicating an unexhausted constitutional claim for which state court review might still be available." Id. at 489. See generally Kimmelman v. Morrison, 477 U.S. 365 (1986). The test of ineffective assistance of counsel is that elaborated in Strickland v. Washington, p. 1063 above. See, e.g., Frey v. Fulcomer, 974 F.2d 348 (3d Cir.1992) (capital sentencing proceeding).

In Coleman v. Thompson, 501 U.S. 722 (1991) (6–3), the Court noted that a claim of ineffective assistance of counsel is a constitutional claim only if the defendant has a Sixth Amendment right to counsel in the first place. Accordingly, ineffective assistance of counsel in state collateral proceedings, in which the state has no constitutional obligation to provide counsel, is not cause for a procedural default. "[W]here the State has no responsibility to ensure that the petitioner was represented by competent counsel . . . the petitioner bears the risk in federal habeas for all attorney errors made in the course of representation." Id. at 754.

635. The Court has established a number of rules to assist federal courts in determining whether a state court's decision rests on a federal ground or a state procedural ground. "[W]hen . . . a state court decision fairly appears to rest primarily on federal law, or to be interwoven with federal law, and when the adequacy and independence of any possible state law ground is not clear from the face of the opinion, we will accept as the most reasonable explanation that the state court decided the case the way it did because it believed that federal law required it to do so. . . . If the state court decision indicates clearly and expressly that it is alternatively based on bona fide separate, adequate, and independent grounds, we, of course, will not undertake to review the decision." Michigan v. Long, 463 U.S. 1032, 1040–41 (1983) (6–3) (direct review). See Harris v. Reed, 489 U.S. 255 (1989) (8–1) (habeas corpus); Caldwell v. Mississippi, 472 U.S. 320 (1985) (5–3). Even though federal issues were presented to the state court, the presumption stated in *Long* does not apply unless its factual premise—that the state decision "appears to rest primarily on federal law, or to be interwoven with federal law"—is met. Coleman v. Thompson, 501 U.S. 722 (1991) (6–3). If the state court's opinion denying relief is unexplained, the presumption is that "where there has been one reasoned state judgment rejecting a federal claim, later unexplained orders upholding that judgment or rejecting the same claim rest upon the same ground. . . . [W]here . . . the last reasoned opinion on the claim explicitly imposes a procedural default [it is presumed] that a later decision rejecting the claim did not silently disregard that bar and consider the merits." Ylst v. Nunnemaker, 501 U.S. 797, 803 (1991) (6–3).

636. In James v. Kentucky, 466 U.S. 341 (1984) (7–1), the trial judge did not give the instruction to the jury required by Carter v. Kentucky, note 485 p. 981 above. On appeal, the state court held that the failure to give the instruction was not reversible error because the defendant had called it an "admonition" rather than an "instruction" in his request. The Court reversed, holding that there was not a procedural fault providing an adequate and independent state ground for denying the constitutional claim. The "distinction between admonitions and instructions," it said, "is not the sort of firmly established and regularly followed state practice that can prevent implementation of federal constitutional rights." Id. at 348–49.

637. In Engle v. Isaac, 456 U.S. 107, 135 (1982) (7–2), the Court said that the cause-and-prejudice test was adequate to correct miscarriages of justice. "The terms 'cause' and 'actual prejudice' are not rigid concepts; they take their meaning from the principles of comity and finality. . . . In appropriate cases those principles must yield to the imperative of correcting a fundamentally unjust incarceration." In Murray v. Carrier, 477 U.S. 478, 495–96 (1986) (7–2), quoting Engle v. Isaac, 456 U.S. at 135, it reiterated its confidence "that, for the most part, 'victims of a fundamental miscarriage of justice will meet the cause-and-prejudice standard.'" It went on to say: "But we do not pretend that this will always be true. Accordingly, we think that in an extraordinary case, where a constitutional violation has probably resulted in the conviction of one who is actually innocent, a federal habeas court may grant the writ even in the absence of a showing of cause for the procedural default." Id. at 496. The case was remanded for a determination whether that standard had been met. See also Bousley v. United States, ___ U.S. ___, 118 S.Ct. 1604 (1998) (7–2) (remand for determination of actual innocence); Kuhlmann v. Wilson, 477 U.S. 436, 454 (1986) (6–3) (no miscarriage of justice); Smith v. Murray, 477 U.S. 527, 537–38 (5–4) (same).

In Sawyer v. Whitley, 505 U.S. 333 (1992), the defendant challenged the exclusion of certain evidence at a sentencing hearing, at which he was sentenced to death. The cause-and-prejudice test was not met. In the context of capital punishment, the Court said, the "actual innocence" test means that a petitioner "must show by clear and convincing evidence that but for a constitutional error, no reasonable juror would have found him eligible for the death penalty" under the applicable state law. Id. at 350. The Court concluded that that test had not been met in this case. *Sawyer* was distinguished in Schlup v. Delo, 513 U.S. 298 (1995) (5–4), in which the defendant's claim of innocence was accompanied by a claim of constitutional error at trial.

638. The tests developed for a federal habeas petitioner's procedural default in state court are also the tests for abuse of the writ on a second or successive habeas petition. McCleskey v. Zant, 499 U.S. 467 (1991) (6–3). "When a prisoner files a second or subsequent application, the government bears the burden of pleading abuse of the writ. The government satisfies this burden if, with clarity and particularity, it notes petitioner's prior writ history, identifies the claims that appear for the first time, and alleges that petitioner has abused the writ. The burden to disprove abuse then becomes petitioner's. To excuse his failure to raise the claim earlier, he must show cause for failing to raise it and prejudice therefrom as those concepts have been defined in our procedural default decisions. The petitioner's opportunity to meet the burden of cause and prejudice will not include an evidentiary hearing if the district court determines as a matter of law that petitioner cannot satisfy the standard. If petitioner cannot show cause, the failure to raise the claim in an earlier petition may nonetheless be excused if he or she can show that a fundamental miscarriage of justice would result from a failure to entertain the claim." Id. at 494-95. See Kuhlmann v. Wilson, 477 U.S. 436, 444–55 (1986).

The tests apply also to a federal habeas petitioner's effort to obtain an evidentiary hearing on a claim with respect to which he failed to develop the factual basis in state court. Unless one of the tests is met, an evidentiary hearing in federal court is unavailable. Keeney v. Tamayo-Reyes, 504 U.S. 1 (1992) (5–4).

639. The defendant, represented by competent counsel, pleaded guilty to four counts of an indictment charging that he committed four burglaries on a day when, it later appeared, he was in jail. Should the conviction be set aside on collateral attack? Does it matter (1) that the pleas in question were accompanied by a plea to another count charging a burglary which the defendant could have and presumably did commit; (2) that he received consecutive sentences of five years imprisonment on each count; (3) that the prosecuting attorney asserts that the date specified in the indictment was incorrect because of a typographical error? See Quarles v. Dutton, 379 F.2d 934 (5th Cir.1967).

640. Custody. In the federal courts, the writ of habeas corpus is available only to a person in "custody." 28 U.S.C. § 2241.[5] At one time, under the traditional principle that the writ tested the legality of detention, if a favorable answer to the questions the petitioner sought to raise would not require his release, the writ was not available. A prisoner could not attack a judgment pursuant to which he was not currently in custody. McNally v. Hill, 293 U.S. 131 (1934). In Peyton v. Rowe, 391 U.S. 54 (1968), *McNally* was overruled. The Court concluded that a prisoner serving consecutive sentences could use habeas corpus to attack not only the sentence he was then serving but also any sentence he was to serve thereafter. The Court observed that postponement of a hearing would make the determination of factual issues more difficult. It noted also that the statute, while requiring that the prisoner be in custody, did not limit relief to release from custody but authorized the courts to dispose of the case "as law and justice require,"

---

5. A federal court may in exceptional cases grant relief in the nature of *coram nobis* to a person who is not in custody, under the "all-writs provision," 28 U.S.C. § 1651(a): "The Supreme Court and all courts established by Act of Congress may issue all writs necessary or appropriate in aid of their respective jurisdictions and agreeable to the usages and principles of law." United States v. Morgan, 346 U.S. 502 (1954). See Mathis v. United States, 369 F.2d 43 (4th Cir.1966).

UNITED STATES DISTRICT COURT
DISTRICT OF MASSACHUSETTS

WRIT OF HABEAS CORPUS

TO THE MARSHAL FOR THE DISTRICT OF MASSACHUSETTS, or any of her

deputies, and to:

YOU ARE COMMANDED to have the body of _____ now in

your custody, before the United States District Court for the District of Massachusetts, United States

Post Office and Courthouse Building, Courtroom No._____, on the _____ floor, Boston,

Massachusetts on _____, at _____ M.

for the purpose of _____

in the case of UNITED STATES OF AMERICA V. _____

CR Number _____

     And you are to retain the body of said _____ while before said

Court upon said day and upon such other days thereafter as his attendance before said Court shall be

necessary, and as soon as may be thereafter to return said _____ to the

institution from which he was taken, under safe and secure conduct, to be there imprisoned as if he

had not been brought therefrom for the purpose aforesaid. And have you then and there this Writ with

your doings herein.

Dated this _____ day of_____, 19_____ .

_____
UNITED STATES DISTRICT JUDGE
UNITED STATES MAGISTRATE JUDGE

                      TONY ANASTAS, CLERK

                      By:_____
        SEAL   **Deputy Clerk**

(Habcorp.wrt - 10/96)   [kwhcap.] or
                                     [kwhcat.]

28 U.S.C. § 2243. See Garlotte v. Fordice, 515 U.S. 39 (1995) (7–2) (*Peyton* applied; prisoner is in custody for purpose of attacking conviction already served, if conviction affects eligibility for parole under sentence currently being served); Maleng v. Cook, 490 U.S. 488 (1989) (*Peyton* applied to state sentence consecutive to federal sentence presently being served). Parole is sufficient "custody" to make the writ available, Jones v. Cunningham, 371 U.S. 236 (1963) (writ available to test restraints on a "petitioner's liberty to do those things which in this country free men are entitled to do," 371 U.S. at 243). It has been held that probation is sufficient custody, e.g., Olson v. Hart, 965 F.2d 940 (10th Cir.1992), as also is a requirement of community service, Barry v. Bergen County Probation Dept, 128 F.3d 152 (3d Cir.1997).

In Hensley v. Municipal Court, 411 U.S. 345 (1973), the Court held that a defendant who had been convicted and sentenced to imprisonment and was at large on his own recognizance pending execution of his sentence was in custody for purposes of habeas corpus. The holding presumably applies to all defendants who are released on any form of bail; but the Court indicated that the doctrine of exhaustion of state remedies would preclude federal habeas corpus for defendants before trial or a final appeal. See Justices of Municipal Court v. Lydon, 466 U.S. 294 (1984) (*Hensley* applied). See also Lillios v. State of New Hampshire, 788 F.2d 60 (1st Cir.1986) (fine and suspension of driver's license not custody); Harts v. Indiana, 732 F.2d 95 (7th Cir.1984) (one-year suspension of driver's license; same).

The custody requirement for federal habeas corpus is not met when the only punishment imposed is a fine, even though the conviction may be attended by "the ordinary collateral consequences or civil disabilities flowing from a fine-only conviction." Hanson v. Circuit Court of First Judicial Circuit, 591 F.2d 404, 407 (7th Cir.1979). Cases to the same effect in other circuits are cited id. at 405 n.1.

The petitioner in Parker v. Ellis, 362 U.S. 574 (1960), completed service of his sentence and was released from state prison after his petition had been dismissed by the district court, the court of appeals had affirmed, and the Court had granted certiorari, but before it heard the case. The Court dismissed the writ of certiorari on the ground that the case had become moot: "[I]t is a condition upon this Court's jurisdiction to adjudicate an application for habeas corpus that the petitioner be in custody when that jurisdiction can become effective," id. at 576. *Parker* was overruled in Carafas v. LaVallee, 391 U.S. 234 (1968) (petition for certiorari filed and granted after petitioner released from custody): "[U]nder the statutory scheme, once the federal jurisdiction has attached in the District Court, it is not defeated by the release of the petitioner prior to completion of proceedings on such application," id. at 238. The Court added: "Petitioner is entitled to consideration of his application for relief on its merits. He is suffering, and will continue to suffer, serious disabilities because of the law's complexities and not because of his fault, if his claim that he has been illegally convicted is meritorious." Id. at 239. Among the consequences of his conviction mentioned by the Court were that "he cannot engage in certain businesses; he cannot serve as an official of a labor union for a specified period of time; he cannot vote in any election held in New York State; he cannot serve as a juror." Id. at 237. In Maleng v. Cook, above, the Court observed that its decision in *Carafas* depended not on the collateral consequences of the conviction but on "the fact that the petitioner had been in physical custody under the challenged conviction at the time the petition was filed." 490 U.S. at 492. "The negative implication of this holding," it said, "is . . . that once the sentence for a conviction has completely expired, the collateral consequences of that conviction are not themselves sufficient to render an individual 'in custody' for the purposes of a habeas attack on it." Id. See Spencer v. Kemna, ___ U.S. ___, 118 S.Ct. 978 (1998) (8–1).

Are any or all of the consequences mentioned by the Court in *Carafas* sufficient to warrant collateral proceedings to determine the validity of a conviction if the proceedings are not commenced until after the prisoner has been released from custody? See Cappetta v. Wainwright, 406 F.2d 1238 (5th Cir.1969) (invalidation of conviction and sentence fully served would effect reduction of sentence presently being served).

641. Does a State have any constitutional obligation to afford an avenue for collateral attack on a conviction on federal constitutional grounds? If so, why? In Young v. Ragen, 337 U.S. 235 (1949), the Supreme Court referred to "the requirement that prisoners be given some clearly defined method by which they may raise claims of denial of federal rights." Id. at 239.[6] The question was raised in Case v. Nebraska, 381 U.S. 336 (1965), but the subsequent enactment of adequate state legislation made a decision of the question unnecessary. Compare Testa v. Katt, 330 U.S. 386 (1947).

---

6. The Court may have had in mind only the narrower question whether the requirement of exhaustion of state remedies could be invoked when the existence of any such remedy was problematic.

INDEX

References are to pages.